International Economics

Twelfth Edition

Thomas A. Pugel
New York University

 Irwin

Boston   Burr Ridge, IL   Dubuque, IA   Madison, WI   New York   San Francisco   St. Louis
Bangkok   Bogotá   Caracas   Kuala Lumpur   Lisbon   London   Madrid   Mexico City
Milan   Montreal   New Delhi   Santiago   Seoul   Singapore   Sydney   Taipei   Toronto

The **McGraw·Hill** Companies

 Irwin

INTERNATIONAL ECONOMICS

Published by McGraw-Hill/Irwin, a business unit of The McGraw-Hill Companies, Inc., 1221 Avenue of the Americas, New York, NY, 10020. Copyright © 2004, 2000, 1996, 1991, 1986, 1982, 1978, 1973, 1968, 1963, 1958, 1953 by The McGraw-Hill Companies, Inc. All rights reserved. No part of this publication may be reproduced or distributed in any form or by any means, or stored in a database or retrieval system, without the prior written consent of The McGraw-Hill Companies, Inc., including, but not limited to, in any network or other electronic storage or transmission, or broadcast for distance learning.

Some ancillaries, including electronic and print components, may not be available to customers outside the United States.

This book is printed on acid-free paper.

domestic   1 2 3 4 5 6 7 8 9 0 DOC/DOC 0 9 8 7 6 5 4 3
international 1 2 3 4 5 6 7 8 9 0 DOC/DOC 0 9 8 7 6 5 4 3

ISBN 0-07-248748-8

Publisher: *Gary Burke*
Executive sponsoring editor: *Paul Shensa*
Editorial assistant: *Karen Minnich*
Marketing manager: *Martin D. Quinn*
Senior producer, Media technology: *Melissa Kansa*
Project manager: *Jim Labeots*
Production supervisor: *Gina Hangos*
Director of design BR: *Keith J. McPherson*
Photo research coordinator: *Kathy Shive*
Photo researcher: *David A. Tietz*
Supplement producer: *Matthew Perry*
Senior digital content specialist: *Brian Nacik*
Cover designer: *JoAnne Schopler*
Cover image: *National Museum of American Art, Washington DC/Art Resource, NY. Noland, Kenneth Split. 1959.*
Typeface: *10.75/12 Times*
Compositor: *Precision Graphics*
Printer: *R. R. Donnelley*

Library of Congress Cataloging-in-Publication Data
Pugel, Thomas A.
    International economics / Thomas A. Pugel.-- 12th ed.
      p. cm.
    Lindert's name appeared first on earlier ed.
    Lindert was co-author for the 7th-10th eds.
    Includes index.
    ISBN 0-07-248748-8 (alk. paper) -- ISBN 0-07-119875-X (int. : alk. paper)
    1. International economic relations. 2. Commercial policy. 3. Foreign exchange. I. Title.
  HF1411.L536 2004
  337--dc21

                    2002044914

INTERNATIONAL EDITION ISBN 0-07-119875-X
Copyright © 2004. Exclusive rights by The McGraw-Hill Companies, Inc. for manufacture and export.
This book cannot be re-exported from the country to which it is sold by McGraw-Hill.
The International Edition is not available in North America.

http://www.mhhe.com

Preface

With this twelfth edition I am honored to take over the stewardship of the book. I joined Peter Lindert as co-author for the tenth edition, and he has now passed the book to my care, just as Charles Kindleberger, the original author of the book, did when Peter succeeded him as the book's author. We are all very happy that the book reaches its golden anniversary with this edition. I also enjoy the mirth of a literary improbability—I am the author of a book that was first published in the year I was born.

I maintain the characteristics and objectives of the book that have guided all its editions. The book

- combines rigorous economic analysis with attention to the issues of economic policy that are alive and important today

- is written to be concise and readable

- uses economic terminology when it enhances the economic logic of the analysis, but avoids jargon for jargon's sake.

I follow these principles when I teach international economics to undergraduates and masters students. I believe that the book benefits as I incorporate what I learn from the classroom into it.

The world is now deeply into the second great wave of globalization, in which product, capital, and labor markets are becoming more and more integrated across countries. This second wave, which began in about 1950, has now lasted about as long as the first, which began in about 1870 and ended with World War I (or perhaps with the onset of the Depression in 1930). As indicators of the current process of globalization, we see that international trade, foreign direct investments, cross-border lending, and international portfolio investments are growing faster than world production. Information and data now spread around the world instantly through the Internet and other global electronic media. As the world becomes more integrated, countries become more interdependent. Increasingly, events and policy changes in one country affect many other countries. Also increasingly, companies make decisions about production and product development based on global markets.

CURRENT EVENTS AND NEW EXAMPLES

The global economy is an exciting place. It is a joy and a challenge for me to incorporate the events and policy changes that continue to transform it, and to find the new examples that show the effects of globalization (both its upside and its downside). Here are some of the current and recent events that are included in this edition to provide new examples that show the practical use of our economic analysis:

- President Bush imposed new tariffs on steel imports into the United States in March 2002

- the euro completely replaced the separate national currencies of twelve member countries of the European Union in early 2002

- the rise of electronic brokering is changing how the foreign exchange markets work

- China and Taiwan joined the World Trade Organization in 2001

- the members of the World Trade Organization launched a new round of multilateral trade negotiations (the Doha round) in 2001

- the long recession in Argentina turned into a financial and economic meltdown in early 2002, with the Argentinean peso plummeting after the country's government abandoned the fixed exchange rate of one peso equal to one U.S. dollar

- Cemex, a multinational enterprise based in Mexico, has risen rapidly to become the third largest cement producer in the world

- the European Union is preparing to expand by adding up to a dozen countries as new members, perhaps as early as 2004

- Ecuador adopted the U.S. dollar as its own currency, in place of its sucre, in 2000

- the Japanese government has repeatedly intervened in the foreign exchange market to prevent the yen from appreciating against the U.S. dollar

- The International Monetary Fund provided a huge loan to Turkey in 2000, to try to prevent Turkey's financial crisis from deepening

IMPROVING THE BOOK: ORGANIZATION AND TOPICS

In this edition I introduce a number of improvements to the pedagogical structure of the book.

- The shaded boxes that contain material separate from the text are now labeled by type: *Focus on Labor*, *Case Study*, and *Extension*. This will make it easier for instructors and students to see what kind of material is in the box, and how it relates to what is presented in the text of the chapter. In addition, I have added many new boxes, especially case studies.

- The order of Chapter 5 and 6 has been reversed from the eleventh edition. With this change all of the essentials of trade theories (productivity differences, factor endowments and factor proportions, product differentiation and monopolistic competition, oligopoly, and agglomeration based on external economies) are presented in consecutive chapters. The new Chapter 6 then can use these concepts and tools to examine issues of sectoral changes, trade, innovation, and growth.

- Several key strengths of Part II (trade policy) are further enhanced. The discussion of nontariff barriers to trade in Chapter 8 has been sharpened. Chapter 10 now focuses completely on allegedly unfair trade (dumping and subsidies) and administered protection through antidumping and countervailing actions. A new box presents the examples of chicken, supercomputers and steel. In Chapter 12 the environmental effects of the Uruguay Round agreements are examined, adding strength to the book's unique and powerful treatment of trade and the environment.

- The discussion of the political economy of import barriers is now included in Chapter 9 as the capstone of the discussion of arguments for and against protection. A new box presents a case study of sugar as an example of the interplay between politics and economics.

- The twelfth edition has a single chapter that examines international resource movements, focusing on multinational enterprises and labor migration. This is now in Part II of the book, because of its link to government policy issues, rather than at the end of the book as it was in the previous edition.

- The book weaves discussion of labor issues into a number of chapters in Parts I and II. This topic is of great interest to students (and almost everybody else). The tour begins in Chapter 1, with a discussion of labor standards and conditions, issues prominent in the Seattle protests against the WTO and the ongoing protests against globalization. It continues through boxes that Focus on Labor in Chapters 3, 4, 6, and 9. Labor issues are also prominent in the discussion of the winners and losers from free trade in Chapters 4 and 5, trade adjustment assistance in Chapter 9, and labor migration in Chapter 14.

- The discussion of the determinants of exchange rates is now collected into a single chapter. Chapter 18 begins with an analysis of exchange rates in the short run, drawing on concepts like uncovered interest parity that were just presented in Chapter 17. Chapter 18 then examines exchange rates in the long run (purchasing power parity and the monetary approach). It concludes with a discussion of overshooting as a rather odd way that we may get from the short run to the long run.

- The chapter on international financial crises, which had been at the end of the book, is now included in Part III. This placement emphasizes the links of these crises to international financial flows and exchange rate policies.

- A new appendix presents the aggregate demand-aggregate supply framework as an approach to open-economy macroeconomics. This provides flexibility for instructors who would like to include this approach in their course.

FORMAT AND STYLE

I have been careful to retain the goals of clarity and honesty that have made *International Economics* an extraordinary success in classrooms and courses around the world. There are plenty of quick road signs at the start of and within chapters. The summaries at the end of the chapters offer an integration of what has been discussed. Students get the signs, "Here's where we are going, here's where we have just been." I have added more bullet-point and numbered lists, to add to the visual appeal of the text and to emphasize sets of determinants or effects.

I am candid about ranking some tools or facts ahead of others. The undeniable power of some of the economist's tools is applied repeatedly to events and issues without apology. Theories and concepts that fail to improve on common sense are not oversold.

The format of the book is fine-tuned for better learning. Most exam-worthy **terms** appear in boldface in the text, with their definitions usually contiguous. Words and phrases that deserve *special emphasis* are in italics.

Each chapter (except for the short introductory chapter) has at least ten questions and problems. The answers to all odd-numbered questions and problems are included in the material at the end of the book. As a reminder, these odd-numbered questions are marked with a ✦.

Box

Shaded boxes appear in different type with a different right-edge format and two columns per page, in contrast to the style of main text. As noted above, the boxes provide discussions of labor issues, case studies, and extensions of the concepts presented in the text.

SUPPLEMENTS

Power Point Slides

New to this edition, the PowerPoint Slides will be available on the Instructor's CD-ROM and via the course website. These presentations include slides with figures and graphs to make teaching and learning more accessible.

Test Bank

For the first time ever, the twelfth edition of *International Economics* has an accompanying test bank. Prepared by Andrew Hill and Scott Klokis of the University of Delaware, the 500-question bank offers a plethora of testing options for the instructor, and will include such types of questions as multiple-choice, fill-in-the-blank, matching, true/false, and short-answer.

Instructor's Manual

Written by the author, the Instructor's Manual contains chapter overviews, teaching tips, and suggested answers to the even-numbered questions and problems that are contained in the textbook.

Study Guide

Written by Kerry Odell of Scripps College, the same author as the previous editions, the Study Guide is similar in format and quality to 11e. Each chapter is broken down into six sections—Objectives of the Chapter, Key Terms, Warm-Up Questions, Multiple-Choice Questions, Problems, and Discussion Topics—and is available to enhance student performance at minimal cost.

Instructor's CD-ROM

New to this edition, electronic versions of all instructor supplements (including the PowerPoint presentation, Instructor's Manual, and 500-question Test Bank) may be conveniently accessed on an Instructor's CD. This makes it easy for instructors to use the various supplements designed to enhance the professor's teaching experience.

COURSE WEBSITE

The website to accompany Pugel's twelfth edition provides the most complete content for any international text of its kind. Organized into separate sections for the instructor and the student, this much enhanced website provides a wide variety of learning devices geared specifically for either group.

For the student:

- interactive graphing exercises
- free study guide samples
- downloadable PowerPoints
- learning tips for students
- book-level glossary
- an outline
- a list of chapter-specific key terms
- a set of testing components including multiple choice, essay, fill-in-the-blank, true/false and matching questions

For the instructor:

- downloadable Instructor Manual
- downloadable PowerPoints
- group learning exercises
- online resource links for additional economic information
- links to professional resources

Acknowledgments

I offer my deepest thanks to the many people whose advice helped me to improve *International Economics* in its twelfth edition. My first thanks are to Peter H. Lindert, my co-author on the previous several editions. I was most happy to join Peter as co-author, and I have learned much from him about the art of writing for the community of students who want to deepen their knowledge and understanding of the global economy.

I love teaching international economics, and I am grateful to my students for the many suggestions and insights that I have received from them. I especially thank my colleagues Richard Levich, Jianping Mei, Roy Smith, Paul Wachtel, and Harvey Poniachek for information and suggestions. I thank Professor Rachel McCulloch of Brandeis University and Professor Michel-Henry Bouchet of CERAM Sophia Antipolis (France) for comments on the previous edition. I am indebted to Professor Stephen S. Golub of Swarthmore College for providing an update of his results on productivity and wages (used in the box "Absolute Advantage Does Matter" in Chapter 3). I am grateful to Professor Li Kening of Beijing Materials College, who both translated the eleventh edition into Chinese, and pointed out passages in the book that could be improved or corrected. I also thank my brother, Michael Pugel, who shared with me his knowledge of technology issues from his perspective as an electrical engineer. In addition, I thank Gloria Asuncion and Janine Alberti, who provided help with the preparation of the manuscript.

I express my gratitude to the reviewers whose detailed and thoughtful comments and critiques provided guidance as I wrote the twelfth edition:

Trisha Bezmen
Old Dominion University

Frank Biggs
Principia College

James Butkiewicz
University of Delaware

Debasish Chakraborty
Central Michigan University

Jamshid Damooei
California Lutheran University

Manjira Datta
Arizona State University

Eric Drabkin
Hawaii Pacific University

Amy Glass
Texas A&M University

Stefan Norrbin
Florida State University

Rose Marie Payan
California Polytechnic University

Kamal Saggi
Southern Methodist University

John Stiver
University of Connecticut

Andreas Savvides
Oklahoma State University

Jiawen Yang
George Washington University

My final acknowledgment and thanks are to Charles P. Kindleberger, who was one of my teachers during my graduate studies. He started this book 50 years ago, and I strive to meet the standards of excellence and relevance that he set for the book.

Thomas A. Pugel

Brief Contents

Contents

Chapter Eleven
Trade Blocs and Trade Blocks   247

Chapter Twelve
Trade and the Environment   273

Chapter Thirteen
Trade Policies for Developing and Transition Countries   309

Chapter Fourteen
Multinationals and Migration: International Factor Movements   339

About the Author

Thomas A. Pugel

Thomas A. Pugel is Professor of Economics and International Business at the Stern School of Business, New York University and a Fellow of the Teaching Excellence Program at the Stern School. His research and publications focus on international industrial competition and government policies toward international trade and industry. Professor Pugel has been Visiting Professor at Aoyama Gakuin University in Japan and a member of the U.S. faculty at the National Center for Industrial Science and Technology Management Development in China. He received the university-wide Distinguished Teaching Award at New York University in 1991, and twice he was voted Professor of the Year by the graduate students at the Stern School of Business. He studied economics as an undergraduate at Michigan State University and earned a Ph.D. in economics from Harvard University.

Chapter One

International Economics Is Different

Nations are not like regions or families. They are sovereign, meaning that no central court can enforce its will on them with a global police force. Being sovereign, nations can put all sorts of barriers between their residents and the outside world. A region or family must deal with the political reality that others within the same nation can outvote it and can therefore coerce it or tax it. A family or region has to compromise with others who have political voice. A nation feels less pressure to compromise and often ignores the interests of foreigners. A nation uses policy tools that are seldom available to a region and never available to a family. A nation can have its own currency, its own barriers to trading with foreigners, its own government taxing and spending, and its own laws of citizenship and residence.

As long as countries exist, international economics will be a body of analysis distinct from the rest of economics. The special nature of international economics makes it fascinating and sometimes difficult. Let's look at four recent events that frame the scope of this book.

FOUR EVENTS

Steel

In March 2002, President George W. Bush imposed taxes of up to 30 percent on many kinds of steel imported into the United States. Informed observers viewed this action as the most dramatic protectionist step taken by a U.S. president in many decades. Why would a Republican president who strongly advocates free trade put up such blocks to trade? What are the consequences?

International economics is different because we must follow at least two parallel strands of the story to answer these questions. One strand of the story is what's happening within the country—in this case the United States. The other strand is what's happening between countries that have an interest in the event.

Let's look first at the story within the United States. The large integrated producers in the American steel industry have been in decline since the early 1960s. In 1998, following the Asian economic crisis, low-priced steel imports grew rapidly as foreign producers that had been selling to the crisis countries shifted their sales to the U.S. market. The Republican Bush won the 2000 election in part by making charges against the incumbent Democratic administration that it had ignored the pleas for help from steelworkers and steel firms.

In June 2001 President Bush took the unusual step of asking the U.S. International Trade Commission to investigate whether imports were causing serious injury to the American steel industry and, if so, what could be done about it. In December 2001 the commission reported that imports were hurting the industry and suggested that the government place either higher taxes on imports (such taxes are called *tariffs*) or new limits on the quantities of imports (called *quotas*). It was up to President Bush to decide what to do.

If we focus on the large integrated firms in the American steel industry, then we can see a case for compassion. Most of these firms had declared bankruptcy but continued to operate once relieved of servicing some of their debts. Employment in the industry was shrinking (though much of this decline was the result of technological innovation and rising productivity). The industry wanted tariffs of at least 40 percent on all steel imports, to give the firms time to improve their competitive position. A few days before President Bush announced his decision, thousands of steelworkers rallied in Washington in support of protection.

However, President Bush found himself in a dilemma of his own making. Steel producers and steelworkers were not the only groups in the United States that would be affected by his decision. Many U.S. firms buy and use steel to make their own products.

The administration and the steel producers tried to put a happy face on the tariffs that President Bush did impose. The administration hoped to reduce imports without hurting domestic steel users. U.S. trade representative Robert Zoelick said, "It's our belief that this will give the U.S. steel industry the opportunity to get back on its feet but without having any detrimental effect on the U.S. economy." Thomas Usher, chief executive of U.S. Steel Corporation, said that the tariffs "will only result in modest and reasonable price increases." If Zoelick and Usher had read this book, they would know better.

The firms that use steel—including producers of autos, appliances, heavy machinery, machine tools, and large buildings—knew better. They had formed groups like the Consuming Industries Trade Action Coalition and the Emergency Committee for American Trade to fight the impending tariffs. They argued that the tariffs would hurt hundreds of companies that employ far more than the 200,000 workers in the American steel industry.

When the tariffs were announced, the head of the Emergency Committee predicted, "A 30 percent tariff won't solve the integrated steel industry's problems, but it will force other American manufacturers to move steel-intensive production overseas, close U.S. plants, and outsource U.S. parts and components in order to compete."

And so it came to pass. In the months after the tariffs were imposed, prices of many kinds of steel rose by 20 to 30 percent. Even user companies that thought they were safe because they had long-term contracts with set prices were in for surprises. American steel firms broke these contracts and demanded higher prices. Steel imports declined by 30 percent. The country was paying a price to maintain the American steel industry. Gary Hufbauer, of the Institute for International Economics, estimated that the cost to U.S. consumers of maintaining one steelworker's job was over $300,000 per year. It would be much cheaper to pay the worker to be idle.

Thus, one strand of the story is about domestic political battles that use international trade as the battleground. Most observers believe that President Bush made a calculated domestic political decision to help the steel firms and steelworkers. He hoped to gain votes in West Virginia, Pennsylvania, and Ohio for Republican candidates in the 2002 congressional elections. He hoped that voters elsewhere would not notice the price they were paying to provide this help. In Chapters 7–9 we will carefully examine the effects of tariffs and other forms of protection on different groups in a country. In addition, as we will see in Chapter 10, the Bush tariffs are not the only protection for American steel. Since the late 1960s the American steel industry has also been adept at gaining protection by using other laws that attack allegedly unfair practices by foreign exporters.

The other strand of the story brings in the other countries affected by the new U.S. tariffs. About one-third of the imports hit by the new tariffs were exports from the countries of the European Union (EU). The tariffs also hit exports from Japan, South Korea, China, and Taiwan. (The U.S. tariffs specifically exempted exports from Canada and Mexico, partners in the North American Free Trade Agreement, and many developing countries that were not major sources of steel.)

Foreign countries had two reactions. First, they acted to prevent "deflection" of exports that would have gone the United States. Second, they complained to the World Trade Organization (WTO) that the U.S. action violated the international rules to which the United States had agreed as a member of the WTO.

When the U.S. government imposed the new tariffs on steel imports, foreign producers that had been planning to export to the United States had to look elsewhere. Indeed, some deflection was literal, consisting of ships on the ocean that changed destination. A number of countries—including the EU, China, Mexico, Venezuela, and Malaysia—quickly raised import barriers of their own, to prevent a flood of steel imports into their markets. (The EU is not really a "country" but rather a regional entity created by agreement among its member countries. However, in matters of trade policy the EU functions like a country. We discuss the EU and other trade blocs in Chapter 11.) These countries did not want to risk harm to their steel producers, even if their consumers would benefit from the cheap steel imports. The danger is that all of this raising of import barriers could get out of hand, leading to a general trade war like the devastating one the world experienced in the early 1930s.

If the whole world were one country—a global nation—the rising barriers to the trade of steel would have been prevented or controlled quickly. If the laws of this global nation resembled those of the United States, the whole issue would have been left to the marketplace. Within a nation, it is usually illegal for one region to put a special tax on products produced in other regions of the country. So the United States could not have imposed the new tariff, and the other countries would not have responded with tariffs of their own.

The world has tried to set up a system of rules about international trade. The World Trade Organization oversees these rules and serves as a forum for settling trade disputes. After the U.S. government imposed the new steel tariffs, the second thing that foreign governments did was to complain to the WTO that the U.S. action violated the international rules. The U.S. government claimed that it imposed the new tariffs as a "safeguard," a form of temporary protection against imports permitted under WTO rules when a surge of imports causes serious harm to an industry in the country. The U.S. government said that the tariffs would be temporary, ending in three years.

A number of other countries—including the European Union, Japan, South Korea, China, Brazil, Taiwan, Switzerland, Norway, and Thailand—complained to the WTO that the U.S. actions violated other aspects of the rules covering safeguards. These governments claimed that there was no recent sharp increase in steel imports into the United States. Any import surge had ended in 1998, and since then steel imports into the United States had declined by one-quarter. They also claimed that factors other than imports were the main cause of the decline of the big integrated steel producers in the United States. Production by U.S. minimills costs less than production by the big U.S. integrated firms. Minimills had been steadily gaining market share. The U.S. government disputed these complaints, stating that the import surge had not really reversed itself and that imports were a serious cause of injury.

If the WTO process runs its normal course, it will take perhaps two years for the organization to rule on whether the U.S. steel tariffs meet the WTO rules. Even if the U.S. tariffs are judged to be in violation of the rules, the dispute may not be resolved. If the U.S. government refuses to change its action or offer other compensation, the WTO can authorize retaliation by the injured countries. For instance, the European Union is claiming damage of about $2 billion per year. The WTO could authorize the EU to impose 100 percent tariffs on this amount of imports from the United States.

This kind of fight between regions would not rage in the political arena for so long if the whole world were one country. The global nation's supreme court would rule one way or the other, and the court's ruling would be definitive. But actual nations are sovereign; they have their separate jurisdictions and separate policies. The WTO has only as much impact as the individual nations allow it to have. Tariffs and other trade barriers are part of what makes international economics so different.

Poor Workers in Poor Countries

Many of the world's people are very poor. These people work in the informal sector, scratching out an existence. Even those who have employment for pay often receive wages that are very low in comparison to wages in the United States, Western Europe, and Japan—while working in conditions that are much worse. One way in which international economics is different is that it forces us to think about some very large differences between countries.

We all would like to have a world in which people are well off in their incomes and work conditions. During the past decade, some groups in the developed countries have staged protests and taken actions to try to help poor workers in poor countries. These groups, often called *nongovernmental organizations*, include nonprofit organizations like the Council on Economic Priorities and student groups at many of the leading universities in the United States.

One result of these protests and pressures was an agreement in the International Labor Organization that all countries should respect four core labor standards: freedom of association and the right to collective bargaining, no forced labor, no child labor, and no discrimination in respect of employment or occupation. Many countries are still far from achieving these four core standards. The International Labor Organization itself has no way to enforce these standards outside of disseminating information to bring pressure on countries that are major violators.

Many of us believe in these core standards as a matter of morals—these are human rights. This does not mean that international economics is not relevant or useful. Even for those who believe that improving the lot of poor workers in poor countries is essential, there is still the question of how to make it happen.

Let's focus on the issue of child labor (the other standards and issues have many similar features). It is estimated that, globally, about 125 million children under 15 years of age work full-time, and about the same number work part-time. In the poorest countries nearly half of children ages 5 to 14 work. How can we successfully reduce these numbers? Using economics, here are some things that we know or suspect.

Many activists blame globalization for widespread child labor, terrible working conditions, and mass poverty in the poor countries.[1] One claim is that rising international competition drives firms to pressure their governments for weaker regulations—a "race to the bottom." While this is theoretically possible, there is little evidence that it is happening. More broadly, affiliates of foreign multinational firms and local firms that produce for export in developing countries generally pay better wages and have better working conditions than local firms producing for local sale in these countries. Workers in these countries generally seek jobs in these "globalized" firms. Also, multinational firms do little of their investing in countries with very poor respect for core labor standards (with the notable exception of coastal China). Poverty is most dire in Africa, rural India, and rural China. It is not a coincidence that these are the places in the world that globalization has almost not touched.

---

[1] Globalization is the process of intensifying the connections between national economies, through international trade, foreign direct investments by multinational firms, and international financial investments.

In Seattle in 1999, the site of one of the largest protests about issues related to globalization, then-President Bill Clinton said the United States would support allowing countries to impose trade sanctions against countries that violate child labor and other core standards. Trade sanctions may make us feel better, but they probably won't accomplish our goal of helping children. If countries do not change their practices, and we reduce imports of products produced by child labor, we are likely to drive down the wages of child workers, making them poorer. Even if countries adopt laws against child labor, the laws probably will just drive these children into working in the informal part of the economy, with wages and working conditions worse than those they already endure.

Activist groups have put pressure on companies in the developed countries whose products are produced in poor countries using child labor. The pressure has been strongest in clothing, targeting companies like Levi Strauss, Nike, and Wal-Mart, as well as universities that sell items emblazoned with their logos. Again, boycotts and other such actions may make us feel better, but their effect is limited. Only about 5 percent of children work in production for export. Even if we reduce this number, the children are most likely to shift to other employment in which wages and conditions are worse.

We actually know the long-run solution to eliminating child labor: economic growth and rising incomes. When families are very poor, a child's income can be crucial to family survival. When average incomes per person rise to about $5,000, child labor nearly disappears as an issue. Even U.S. history attests to this dynamic. Substantial child labor existed in the United States into the early 20th century. Indeed, U.S. respect for core labor standards is less than 100 years old. Better working conditions are a normal good. When we are very poor, we worry most about material survival. When our incomes rise, we use some of the rising income to "buy" better working conditions. Looked at this way, international trade is part of the solution. We know that countries that are more open to trade tend to grow faster.

However, we don't want just to wait for the long run to get here. What can be done now that has a good chance to speed up the process? If children are not working, what do we want them to do? The answer is clear—go to school. Poor families whose children are working know that their families would be better off in the future if their children received more education now, but they cannot invest for the future because their survival is at stake. Here is a problem that we could do something about. We need programs that pay very poor families to send their children to school. These programs exist and are successful. In Mexico and Brazil, poor families are paid to keep their children in school. In Bangladesh and Pakistan, children are shifted from work to school, the families are paid a monthly stipend, and adult family members are moved into work positions previously held by their children. The number of children who attend school through these programs is small, only a few tens of thousands, but it is a start. As we will see in Chapter 9, this policy approach is an application of what we will call the *specificity rule*.

The Euro

In early 2002, the national moneys of 12 European countries disappeared. They were replaced by one new money, the *euro*. The idea of a common currency had seemed like a dream only 15 years earlier but has now become a reality. The countries using the euro as their "national" currency are 12 of the 15 members of the European Union. The exceptions as of mid-2002 are Britain, Denmark, and Sweden.

Adopting a single currency may seem like a natural choice. If the nations of the EU want to have a large unified economy like the United States, why shouldn't they have a unified currency like the United States? There are certainly advantages to having nations share a common currency. It's convenient—you don't have to change your money every time you cross a national border, any more than you need to change your money when you drive from Kansas to Missouri. It's less risky—you don't have to worry about the changing value of one local money relative to the local money in neighboring countries. There is evidence that having the same currency stimulates trade between countries, though there is debate about how large the trade increase is. So the basic question of this chapter is clearly raised by the euro: Why should international economics be any different from economic life within a country?

There are reasons why countries, including the three holdouts in the EU, are deeply reluctant to abandon their own national moneys in favor of an international money. Having your country's central bank control the national money supply gives it the ability to influence national prices, production, and jobs. Do you want your country to give up control of money to some international institution beyond your country's control? For most countries, the answer is no. They feel that it is important to maintain their national monetary sovereignty, basically because they feel they can manage their own economy better than an outside institution can.

In some countries the answer is actually "Yes, we do want to cede control over our money supply to some outside institution." The 12 countries now using the euro made that decision. The European Central Bank now sets monetary policy for the "euro area." For these 12 countries, adopting the euro is part of a much broader effort to create a true union of countries that have common policies for the economy and for other areas such as defense and foreign affairs. The decision to adopt the euro was largely political, but it will have major economic effects on these countries.

The idea of giving up monetary sovereignty is also popular in countries where disastrous national policies have ruined their own currencies by oversupplying them until price inflation made each unit of the national currency nearly worthless. As a last resort, a few countries have decided to shut down their own central banks and to replace their national currencies with some stable foreign currency. This process is called *dollarization,* although the U.S. dollar is not the only foreign currency that has been used. In 2000 Ecuador was in economic turmoil. By dollarizing, Ecuador's economy became noticeably more stable. Other countries have tried to gain this stability by tightly fixing the value of their currency to the dollar or to some other foreign currency. Argentina's experience with this approach is discussed in the next section of this chapter. We examine the basis for government policy toward the exchange rate in Chapter 24.

Use of the euro will probably grow during the next decade for two reasons. First, the three current holdout countries are likely to adopt the euro as the advantages of joining the monetary union become increasingly attractive. Second, the EU is likely to expand by adding new member countries. As of mid-2002 there were a dozen countries (Estonia, Latvia, Lithuania, Poland, Czech Republic, Slovakia, Hungary, Slovenia, Romania, Bulgaria, Malta, and Cyprus) actively negotiating to join. There are tough issues that must be resolved before membership can be granted. A change in governance procedures for EU decision making is probably needed if the number of member countries goes to 25 or more. Financial aspects of membership, including the ability of new members to draw on the expensive and protectionist common agricultural policy, must be hashed out. Still, by 2010 it is likely that at least 25 countries will be members of the EU and will be using the euro as their "national" currency.

Argentina: From Darling to Delinquent

In the late 1980s Argentina was in deep trouble. Its economy was a mess, with hyperinflation of over 2,000 percent per year for both 1989 and 1990. The international value of its currency was in free fall. Its government seemed capable of nothing but mismanagement.

Amazingly, a few years later Argentina had become one of the most attractive of the "emerging economies." It was a model of sensible economic policies, and its economy had become one the best performing in the world. Then, in 1998 things started to go wrong. By late 2001 Argentina's economy was unraveling fast. Its political situation was in the throes of upheaval, too.

How did all this happen in such a short time? The answer is a tale with a hero who later became a villain, a story of how national government policies interact with global forces and foreign investors.

Argentina's hyperinflation in the late 1980s is not difficult to understand. The government was running a large budget deficit, and the central bank was running the printing presses overtime to shovel money to the government for its spending. With way too much money chasing the limited products available, product prices soared. Inflation exploded.

Enter Domingo Cavallo, an economist with a doctorate from Harvard. As Argentina's economy minister, he developed a plan, based on strict convertibility between the Argentinean peso and the U.S. dollar. He put in place a fixed exchange rate of 1 peso to $1. This completely tied the hands of the central bank, which became merely a *currency board,* a government agency that stood ready to exchange pesos for dollars at the fixed rate. No more running of the peso printing press, unless people were willing to buy each peso by turning in a dollar. It took a few years for this shock treatment to have its full effect, but by 1994 inflation was down to 4 percent. To Argentineans weary of extraordinary inflation, Cavallo was the national hero.

Argentina's government adopted other policy changes to solidify its role as the darling of foreign investors. The government removed rules limiting international investment into and out of Argentina. It privatized a number of government-owned companies, with foreign investors buying large stakes in some of them. It accomplished some reduction in the fiscal budget deficit. Foreign investors saw all this and they liked it. Foreign capital flowed into Argentina. As a result of the near-zero inflation and the investment flowing in, Argentina's interest rates fell to surprisingly low levels. The economy took off. During 1991–1998 Argentina's production of goods and services (its real gross domestic product) grew at an average rate of nearly 6 percent per year. It began to look possible that Argentina would grow to regain the economic status that it had before World War II, when its income per person was equal to that of Canada, France, and Germany.

However, storm clouds began to appear, coming from over the national border. In 1997 the Asian crisis hit the global economy, with the "Asian miracle" countries—Thailand, Indonesia, South Korea, Malaysia, and the Philippines—becoming the pariahs of global finance. The Russian crisis followed in 1998. Foreign investors became nervous about emerging economies in general. They began to question whether countries with large foreign debts could continue to service the debts by paying interest and paying down the principal.

With the international liberalizations of the early 1990s, Argentina's businesses and people increasingly were buying more goods and services from foreigners than they were selling to them. This deficit on goods and services could be financed as long as foreigners continued to lend to Argentina. The fixed exchange rate actually encouraged Argentineans to import and discouraged exports. In the early years of the fixed exchange rate, the high Argentinean inflation made it harder to export and attractive to import. Beginning in 1997, the Argentinean peso rode along with the U.S. dollar as the dollar rose in value against other currencies, especially the Brazilian currency. The results of these changes was a decline in the competitiveness of Argentina's products in comparison with the prices of products produced in other countries.

Beginning in 1997, a series of bad foreign shocks hit Argentina's economy. These shocks interacted with rigidities that remained in the Argentinean economy, the result of excessive regulation and government bureaucracy. In 1998, Argentina's economy went into a recession. As the economy slowed, the government budget deficit increased. Foreign investors began to seriously consider the possibilities of a devaluation of the peso and a default on government debt. Investment inflows dried up by 2001. Interest rates in Argentina rose, which only made the recession worse. Without borrowing from foreigners, Argentina could no longer buy more goods and services from foreigners than it was selling to them. Imports plummeted as incomes in Argentina declined with the recession.

In late 2000 it looked like foreigners were coming to the rescue. In December the government announced that it had established a $40 billion rescue package, including commitments of $14 billion from the International Monetary Fund (IMF).

When things did not improve much, the government called on Domingo Cavallo to return as Argentina's economy minister. Unfortunately, Cavallo did not have another miracle up his sleeve. He did enact some policies to boost international competitiveness, including a broad scheme of subsidies to exports and taxes on imports. He had some success in reducing the fiscal budget deficit, but not enough. The Argentinean people began to fear for the soundness of the banking system. Depositors ran to the banks to get their money out. In December the IMF stopped making new loans to the Argentinean government under the rescue package because the government had not met the conditions set by the fund for improvements in government policies. In a final effort to save the system, including the fixed exchange rate, Cavallo ordered severe limits on the withdrawals from bank accounts. Angry protests spawned looting and rioting, with 23 deaths. Vilified by the people, Cavallo left the government. A few days later the country's president resigned. Argentina then had four new presidents in two weeks.

After all this the crisis became really serious. The government ended the fixed exchange rate in early 2002. The peso's value was then set by the market, and by May a peso was worth less than 30 U.S. cents. The government defaulted on its $150 billion debt, including almost $100 billion owed to foreigners. The terms of the debt were altered, and in the process investors took large losses. This was the largest default ever, anywhere.

The economy was in a shambles. The banking system was nearly nonfunctional. During 2002, production of goods and services declined by over 10 percent, the inflation rate rose to over 20 percent, and unemployment soared to over 25 percent.

What a series of events. What a complex set of relationships. Argentina's story shows how different international finance can be. In 1991 Argentina's government used international economic tools—the currency board and the fixed exchange rate—to conquer the national economic menace of high inflation. Argentina then thrived using funding from foreign investors. But shocks from abroad pushed the economy into a long-lasting recession. The views of the same foreign investors turned quite negative. A huge decline in the exchange-rate value of the peso accompanied a financial crisis. Foreign investors incurred huge losses, and the economy was in depression.

We will examine many of these issues in Parts III and IV of this book. For example, in Chapter 17 we explore foreign financial investment. In Chapters 19 and 24 we look at why a government would or would not choose a fixed exchange rate. We analyze the effects of international trade and investment on national production, unemployment, and inflation pressures in Chapters 21–23. And in Chapter 20 we take a close look at international financial crises.

Why is international finance so different from domestic finance? Why do financial firms keep studying something called country risk? International finance is different because, again, nations are independent sovereign states. The opportunities for profitable investments can be attractive when a sovereign government shifts toward market-friendly policies. But the risks can also be great, since a country can also get into trouble through its own bad policies or through bad luck that brings negative shocks from outside the country. The government of a country in trouble is often unwilling to pay off foreign creditors when its own people are hurting. When the debtor is a sovereign government, the foreign creditors cannot just take the delinquent borrower to court and seize some of its assets.

ECONOMICS AND THE NATION-STATE

It should be clear from the four events described above that international economics is a special field of study because nations are sovereign. Each nation has its own government policies. For each nation, these policies are almost always designed to serve some group(s) inside that nation. Countries almost never care as much about the interests of foreigners as they do about national interests. Think of any recent debate about restricting cheap imports from other countries—say Asian imports into the United States. How loudly have Americans spoken out to defend the Asian jobs and incomes that would be lost if U.S. jobs and incomes are protected? Conversely, in China, where imports are also often blocked, how much outcry does one hear about how these import barriers are limiting jobs and incomes in the United States or Thailand?

The fact that nations have their sovereignty and their separate policies and their separate self-interests means that *nobody is in charge of the whole world economy*. The global economy has no global government, benevolent or otherwise. It is true that there are international organizations that try to manage aspects of the global economy, particularly the World Trade Organization, the International Monetary Fund, the United Nations, and the World Bank. But each country has the option to ignore or defy these global institutions if it really wants to.

Among the most important policies that each country can manipulate separately are monetary policy, fiscal policy, and policies toward the international movement of productive resources (people and financial capital).

Different Moneys

To many economists, and especially regular people, the principal difference between domestic and international trade and investment is that international transactions often involve the use of different moneys. That is very different from transactions within a country. You cannot issue your own money, nor can your family, nor can the state of Ohio.

The existence of separate moneys means that the value of one money relative to another can change. We could imagine otherwise. If a U.S. dollar were worth exactly 10 Swedish kronor for 10 centuries, people would certainly come to think of a krona and a dime as the same money. But this does not happen. Since the 1970s the price ratios between the major currencies have been fluctuating by the minute. We must treat the dollar and the krona, for example as different moneys.

Most countries have their own national money, but, as we saw with the euro, some countries share the same money. The supply of each kind of money is controlled by the monetary authority or central bank in charge of that money. Monetary policy affects not only the country using that money but also other countries, even if they use different moneys. Monetary policies affect the relative value of different moneys. Parts III and IV explore the special relationships between national moneys.

Different Fiscal Policies

For each sovereign country, its separate government has its own public spending, power to tax, and power to regulate. As a rule, differences in the spending, tax, and regulatory policies of different countries are more pronounced than differences between the policies of states, provinces, or prefectures in one country. In the international arena, differences in tax policies can cause large flows of funds and products that would not have existed without the tax discrepancies. Banks set up shop in the Bahamas, where their capital gains are less taxed and their books less scrutinized. Shipping firms register in Liberia or Panama, where registration costs little and where they are free from other countries' requirements to use higher-cost national maritime workers. Each country's array of import tariffs and export subsidies and duties are part of its separate fiscal policy. We examine the microeconomic effects of policies toward international trade in Part II, and the macroeconomic effects of different fiscal policies in Part IV.

Factor Mobility

In differentiating international from domestic economics, classical economists stressed the behavior of the factors of production. Labor, land, and capital were seen as mobile within a country, in the sense that these resources could be put to different productive uses within the country. For example, a country's land could be used to grow wheat or to raise dairy cattle or as the site for a factory. But, the classical economists believed, these resources were not mobile across national borders. Outside of war land does not move from one country to another. They also downplayed the ability of workers or capital to move from one country to another.

If true, this difference between intranational factor mobility and international factor immobility would have implications for many features of the global economy. For instance, the wages of French workers of a given training and skill would be more or less the same, regardless of which industry the workers happened to be part of. But this French wage level could be very different from the wage for comparable workers in Germany, Italy, Canada, or Australia. The same equality of return within a country, but differences internationally, was believed to be true for land and capital.

This distinction of the classical economists is partly valid today. Land is the least mobile factor internationally. Workers and capital do move internationally, in response to opportunities for economic gain. Still, there appear to be differences of degree in mobility interregionally and internationally. People usually migrate within their own country more readily than they will emigrate abroad. This is true partly because identity of language, customs, and tradition is more likely to exist within a country than between countries. In addition, national governments impose greater limitations on international migration than they do on relocation within the country. Capital is also more mobile within than between countries. Even financial capital, which in many ways is free to move internationally, is subject to a "home bias" in which people prefer to invest within their own country. We examine international resource mobility in Chapter 14, and examine aspects of international financial investments in Part III.

THE SCHEME OF THIS BOOK

We begin our exploration of international economics with international trade theory and policy. In Part I we look at why countries trade goods and services. In Part II we examine what government policies toward trade would bring benefits and to whom. These first two parts of the book might be called international microeconomics. The focus of Parts III and IV shifts to finance and macroeconomics. In Part III we enter the world of different moneys, exchange rates, foreign exchange markets, balance of payments, and international investors. Part IV surveys the effects of a national government's choice of exchange rate policy on the country's macroeconomic performance, especially unemployment and inflation. In a few places this organization creates some momentary inconvenience, as when we look at the exchange rate link between cutting imports and reducing exports in Part I before we have discussed exchange rates in depth. Yet there are gains in logic in proceeding from micro to macro, as in the way that the demand and supply analysis of trade in individual products sets the stage for the use of the same tools at a more aggregate level in the study of international finance.

Part **One**

The Theory
of International Trade

Chapter **Two**

The Basic Theory Using Demand and Supply

For centuries people have been fighting over whether governments should allow trade between countries. There have been, and probably always will be, two sides to the argument. Some argue that just letting everybody trade freely is best for both the country and the world. Others argue that trade with other countries makes it harder for some people to make a good living. Both sides are at least partly right.

International trade matters a lot. Its effects on the economic life of people in a country are enormous. Imagine a world in which your country did not trade at all with other countries. It isn't hard to do. Imagine what kind of job you would be likely to get, and think of what products you could buy (or not buy) in such a world. For the United States, for example, start by imagining that it lived without its $100 billion a year in imported oil. Americans would have to cut back on energy use because the remaining domestic oil (and natural gas and other energy sources) would be more expensive. Americans who produce oil and other energy sources might be pleased with such a scenario. Those who work in the auto industry and those who need to heat their homes would not. Similar impacts would be felt by producers and consumers in other parts of the economy suddenly stripped of imports like DVD players and clothing. On the export side, suppose that Boeing could sell airplanes and American farmers could sell their crops only within the United States, and that U.S. universities could admit only domestic students. In each case there are people who gain and people who lose from cutting off international trade. Every one of these differences between less trade and more trade has strong effects on what career you choose. Little wonder, then, that people are always debating the issue of having less or more trade.

Each side of the trade debate needs a convincing story of just how trade matters and to whom. Yet that story, so useful in the arena of policy debate, requires an even more basic understanding of why people trade as they do when allowed to trade, exporting some products and importing others. If we do not know how people decide what goods and services to trade, it is hard to say what the effects of trade are or whether trade should be restricted by governments.

FOUR QUESTIONS ABOUT TRADE

This chapter and the rest of Part I tackle the issue of how trade works by comparing two worlds. In one world no trade is allowed. In the other, governments just stand aside and let individual businesses and households trade freely across national borders. We seek answers to four key questions:

1. Why do countries trade? More precisely, what determines which products a country exports and which products it imports?

2. How does trade affect production and consumption in each country?

3. How does trade affect the economic well-being of each country? In what sense can we say that a country gains or loses from trade?

4. How does trade affect the distribution of economic well-being or income among various groups within the country? Can we identify specific groups that gain from trade and other groups that lose because of trade?

A LOOK AHEAD

The chapters in Part I explore these four questions about trade. Our basic theory of trade says that trade usually results from the interaction of competitive demand and supply. This chapter goes straight to the basic picture of demand and supply. It suggests how to measure the gains that trade brings to some people and the losses it brings to others. Chapter 3 launches an exploration of what lies behind the demand and supply curves and discovers the concept of comparative advantage. Countries have different comparative advantages for the fundamental reason that people, and therefore countries, differ from each other in the productive resources they own. Chapter 4 looks at the strong impacts of trade on people who own those productive resources—the human labor and skills, the capital, the land, and other resources. Some ways of making a living are definitely helped by trade, while others are hurt. Chapter 5 examines how actual trade may reflect forces calling for theories that go beyond our basic ideas of demand and supply and of comparative advantage. Chapter 6 shows some key links between trade and economic growth.

Part I explores a diverse set of leading theories. Fortunately, the basic theory of competitive supply and demand serves many purposes fairly well. But the basic theory includes some special cases and some extensions. It also has been challenged by new views, about which economists are still debating.

Part II uses the theories of Part I to explore a broad range of government policy issues. Chapters 7 through 9 set out on a journey to map the border between good trade barriers and bad ones. This journey turns out to be intellectually challenging, calling for careful reasoning. Chapter 10 explores how firms and governments often push for more trade rather than less, promoting exports more than a competitive marketplace would. Chapter 11 switches to the economics of trade blocs like the European Union and the North American Free Trade Area. Chapter 12 faces the growing debate over how environmental concerns should affect trade policy. Chapter 13 looks at Third World trade and what developing countries can do about it. Chapter 14 examines the economics of emigration and immigration and the roles of global companies in the transfer of resources, including technology, between countries.

DEMAND AND SUPPLY

Let's review the economics of demand and supply before we apply these tools to examine international trade. The product that we use as an example is motorbikes. We assume that the market for motorbikes is competitive. Although the analysis appears to be only about a single product (here, motorbikes), it actually is broader than this. Demanders make decisions about buying this product instead of other products. Suppliers use resources to produce this product, and the resources used in producing motorbikes are not available to produce other products. What we are studying is actually one product relative to all other goods and services in the economy.

Demand

What determines how much of a product is demanded? A consumer's problem is to get as much happiness or well-being (in economists' jargon, *utility*) as possible by spending the limited income that the consumer has available. A basic determinant of how much a consumer buys of a product is the person's taste, preferences, or opinions of the product. Given the person's tastes, the price of the product (relative to the price of other products) also has a major influence on how much of the product is purchased. At a higher price for this product, the consumer usually economizes and reduces the quantity purchased. Another major influence is the consumer's income. If the consumer's income increases, the consumer buys more of many products, probably including more of this product. (The consumer buys more if this product is a "normal good." This is not the only possibility— quantity purchased is unchanged if demand is independent of income, and quantity goes down if the product is an "inferior good." In this text we almost always examine only normal goods, as we consider these to be the usual case.)

How much the consumer demands of the product thus depends on a number of influences: tastes, the price of this product, the prices of other products, and income. We would like to be able to picture demand. We do this by focusing on

FIGURE 2.1

Demand and
Supply for
Motorbikes

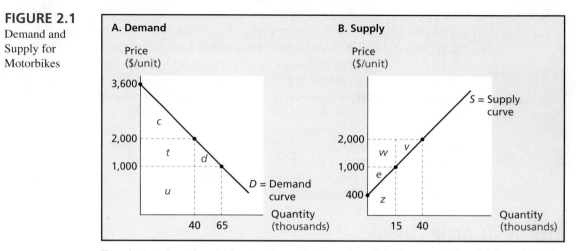

The market demand curve for motorbikes slopes downward. A lower price results in a larger quantity demanded. The market supply curve for motorbikes slopes upward. A higher price results in a larger quantity supplied.

one major determinant, the product's price. After we add up all consumers of the product, we use a market demand curve like the demand curve for motorbikes shown as D in Figure 2.1A.[1] We have a strong presumption that the demand curve slopes downward. An increase in the product's price (say, from $1,000 per motorbike to $2,000) results in a decrease in quantity demanded (from 65,000 to 40,000 motorbikes purchased per year). This is a movement along the demand curve because of a change in the product's price. The increase in price results in a lower quantity demanded as people (somewhat reluctantly) switch to substitute products (e.g., bicycles) or make do with less of the more expensive product (forgo buying a second motorbike with different features or of a different color).

How responsive is quantity demanded to a change in price? One way to measure responsiveness is by the slope of the demand curve (actually, by the inverse of the slope, because price is on the vertical axis). A steep slope indicates low responsiveness of quantity to a change in price (quantity does not change that much). A flatter slope indicates more responsiveness. The slope is a measure of responsiveness, but it can also be misleading. By altering the units used on the axes, the demand curve can be made to look flat or steep.

A measure of responsiveness that is "unit-free" is **elasticity,** the *percent* change in one variable resulting from a 1 *percent* change in another variable. The **price elasticity of demand** is the percent change in quantity demanded resulting from a 1 percent increase in price. Quantity falls when price increases (if the demand curve slopes downward), so the price elasticity of demand is a negative number (though we often drop the *negative* when we talk about it). If the price

---

[1] The equation for this demand curve is $Q_D = 90{,}000 - 25P$ (or $P = 3{,}600 - 0.04Q_D$).

elasticity is a large (negative) number (above 1), then quantity demanded is substantially responsive to a price change—demand is *elastic.* If the price elasticity is a small (negative) number (less than 1), then quantity demanded is not that responsive—demand is *inelastic.*

In drawing the demand curve, we assume that other things that can influence demand—income, other prices, and tastes—are constant. If any of the other influences changes, then the entire demand curve shifts.

Consumer Surplus

The demand curve shows the value that consumers place on units of the product, because it indicates the highest price that some consumer is willing to pay for each unit. Yet, in a competitive market, consumers pay only the going market price for these units. Consumers who are willing to pay more benefit from buying at the market price. Their well-being is increased, and we can measure how much it increases.

To see this, consider first the value that consumers place on the total quantity of the product that they actually purchase. We can measure the value unit by unit. For the first motorbike demanded, the demand curve in Figure 2.1A tells us that somebody would be willing to pay a very high price (about $3,600)—the price just below where the demand curve hits the price axis. The demand curve tells us that somebody is willing to pay a slightly lower price for the second motorbike, and so on down the demand curve for each additional unit.

By adding up all of the demand curve heights for each unit that is demanded, we see that the whole area under the demand curve (up to the total consumption quantity) measures the total value to consumers from buying this quantity of motorbikes. For instance, for 40,000 motorbikes the total value to consumers is $112 million, equal to area $c + t + u$. This amount can be calculated as the sum of two areas that are easier to work with: the area of the rectangle $t + u$ formed by price and quantity, equal to $2,000 \times 40,000$, plus the area of triangle c above this rectangle, equal to $(1/2) \times (\$3,600 - \$2,000) \times 40,000$. (Recall that the area of a triangle like c is equal to one-half of the product of its height and base.) This total value can be measured as a money amount, but it ultimately represents the *willingness* of consumers, if necessary, to forgo consuming other goods and services to buy this product.

The marketplace does not give away motorbikes for free, of course. The buyers must pay the market price (a money amount, but ultimately the value of other goods and services that the buyers must give up to buy this product). For instance, at a price of $2,000 per motorbike, consumers buy 40,000 motorbikes and pay $80 million in total (price times quantity, equal to area $t + u$).

Because many consumers value the product more highly than $2,000 per motorbike, paying the going market price still leaves consumers with a *net gain* in economic well-being. The net gain is the difference between the value that consumers place on the product and the payment that they must make to buy the product. This net gain is called **consumer surplus,** the increase in the economic well-being of consumers who are able to buy the product at a market price lower than the highest price that they are willing and able to pay for the product. For a market price of $2,000 in Figure 2.1A, the consumer surplus is the difference between the total value to consumers (area $c + t + u$) and the total payments to buy the product (area $t + u$). Consumer surplus thus is equal to area c, the area below the demand curve and above the price line. This contribution to the economic well-being of consumers through the use of this market is $32 million, equal to $(1/2) \times (\$3,600 - \$2,000) \times 40,000$.

A major use of consumer surplus is to measure the impact on consumers of a change in market price. For instance, what is the effect in our example if the market price of motorbikes is $1,000 instead of $2,000? Consumers are better off— they pay a lower price and decide to buy more. How much better off? Consumer surplus increases from a smaller triangle (extending down to the $2,000 price line) to a larger triangle (extending down to the $1,000 price line). The increase in consumer surplus is area $t + d$. This increase can be calculated as the area of rectangle t, equal to $(\$2,000 - \$1,000) \times 40,000$, plus the area of triangle d, equal to $(1/2) \times (\$2,000 - \$1,000) \times (65,000 - 40,000)$. The increase in consumer surplus is $52.5 million. The lower market price results in both an increase in economic well-being for consumers who would have bought anyway at the higher price (area t) and an increase in economic well-being for those consumers who are drawn into purchasing by the lower price (area d).

Supply

What determines how much of a product is supplied by a business firm (or other producer) into a market? A firm supplies the product because it is trying to earn a profit on its production and sales activities. One influence on how much a firm supplies is the price that the firm receives for its sales. The other major influence is the cost of producing and selling the product.

For a competitive firm, if the price at which the firm can sell another unit of its product exceeds the extra (or marginal) cost of producing it, then the firm should supply that unit because it makes a profit on it. The firm then will supply units up to the point at which the price received just about equals the extra cost of another unit. The cost of producing another unit depends on two things: the resources or inputs (such as labor, capital, land, and materials) needed to produce the extra unit, and the prices that have to be paid for these inputs.

We would like to be able to picture supply, and we do so by focusing on how the price of the product affects quantity supplied. After we add up all producers of the product, we use a market supply curve like the supply curve S for motorbikes in Figure 2.1B.[2] We usually presume that the supply curve slopes upward. An increase in the product's price (say, from $1,000 per motorbike to $2,000) results in an increase in quantity supplied (from 15,000 to 40,000 motorbikes produced and sold per year). This is a movement along the supply curve. In a

---

[2] The equation for this supply curve is $Q_S = -10,000 + 25P$ (or $P = 400 + 0.04Q_S$).

competitive industry, an additional motorbike is supplied if the price received covers the extra cost of producing and selling this additional unit. If additional units can be produced only at a rising extra or marginal cost, then a higher price is necessary to draw out additional quantity supplied. The supply curve turns out to be the same as the curve showing the marginal cost of producing each unit.

How responsive is quantity supplied to a change in the market price? One way to measure responsiveness is by the slope of the supply curve. Quantity supplied is more responsive if the slope is flatter. A "unit-free" measure is the **price elasticity of supply**—the percent increase in quantity supplied resulting from a 1 percent increase in market price. Quantity supplied is not that responsive to price—supply is inelastic—if the price elasticity is less than 1. Quantity supplied is substantially responsive—supply is elastic—if the price elasticity is greater than 1.

In drawing the supply curve, we assume that other things influencing supply are constant. These other things include the conditions of availability of inputs and the technology that determines what inputs are needed to produce extra units of the product. If any of these other influences changes, then the entire supply curve shifts.

Producer Surplus

The supply curve shows the lowest possible price at which some producer would be willing to supply each unit. Producers actually receive the going market price for these units. Producers who would have been willing to supply at a lower price benefit from selling at the market price. Indeed, we can measure how much their well-being increases.

To see this, consider first the total (variable) costs of producing and selling the total quantity that is actually supplied. We can measure this cost unit by unit. For the first motorbike supplied into the market, the supply curve in Figure 2.1B tells us that some producer would be willing to supply this for about $400, the price just above where the supply curve hits the axis. This amount just covers the extra cost of producing and selling this first unit. The supply curve tells us that some producer is willing to supply the second motorbike for a slightly higher price, because the extra cost of the second unit is a little higher, and so on.

By adding up all of the supply curve heights for each unit supplied, we find that the whole area under the supply curve (up to the total quantity supplied) is the total cost of producing and selling this quantity of motorbikes. For instance, the total cost of producing 15,000 motorbikes is equal to area z in Figure 2.1B. This total cost can be measured as a money amount, but for the whole economy it ultimately represents an **opportunity cost**—the value of other goods and services that are not produced because resources are instead used to produce this product (motorbikes).

The total revenue received by producers is the product of the market price and the quantity sold. For instance, at a price of $1,000 per motorbike, producers sell 15,000 motorbikes, so they receive $15 million in total revenue (equal to area $e + z$).

Because producers would have been willing to supply some motorbikes at a price below $1,000, receiving the going market price for all units results in a *net gain* in their economic well-being. The net gain is the difference between the revenues received and the costs incurred. This net gain is called **producer surplus,** the increase in the economic well-being of producers who are able to sell the product at a market price higher than the lowest price that would have drawn out their supply. For a market price of $1,000 in Figure 2.1B, the producer surplus is the difference between total revenues (area $e + z$) and total costs (area z). Producer surplus is thus equal to area e, the area above the supply curve and below the price line. Producer surplus in this case is $4.5 million, equal to $(1/2) \times (\$1,000 - \$400) \times 15,000$.

A major use of producer surplus is to measure the impact on producers of a change in market price. For instance, what is the effect if the market price is $2,000 instead of $1,000? Producers are better off—they receive a higher price and decide to produce and sell more. Producer surplus increases from a smaller triangle (extending up to the $1,000 price line) to a larger triangle (extending up to the $2,000 price line). The increase in producer surplus is equal to area $w + v$, or $(\$2,000 - \$1,000) \times 15,000$ plus $(1/2) \times (\$2,000 - \$1,000) \times (40,000 - 15,000)$, which equals $27.5 million. The higher market price results in both an increase in economic well-being for producers who would have supplied anyway at the lower price (area w) and an increase in well-being for producers of the additional units supplied (area v).

A National Market with No Trade

If D in Figure 2.1A represents the *national* demand for the product and S in Figure 2.1B represents the *national* supply, we can combine these into the single picture for the national market for this product, as shown in Figure 2.2. If there is no international trade, then equilibrium occurs at the price at which the market clears domestically, with national quantity demanded equal to national quantity supplied. In Figure 2.2 this no-trade equilibrium occurs at point A, with a price of $2,000 per motorbike, and total quantity supplied and demanded of 40,000 motorbikes. Both consumers and producers benefit from having this market, as consumer surplus is area c and producer surplus is area h (the same as area $e + w + v$ in Figure 2.1B). In this example, both gain the same amount of surplus, $32 million each. In general, these two areas do not have to be equal, though both will be positive amounts. For instance, consumer surplus will be larger than producer surplus if the demand curve is steeper (more inelastic) or the supply curve is flatter (more elastic) than those shown in Figure 2.2.

TWO NATIONAL MARKETS AND THE OPENING OF TRADE

To discuss international trade in motorbikes, we need at least two countries. We will call the country whose national market was shown in Figure 2.2 the United States. This U.S. national market is also shown in the left-hand graph of Figure

FIGURE 2.2

The Market for
Motorbikes:
Demand and
Supply

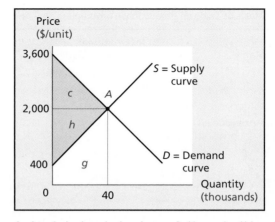

The market for motorbikes can be pictured using demand and supply curves. In this example, which may be a national market with no international trade, the market reaches equilibrium at a price of $2,000 per motorbike, with 40,000 motorbikes produced and purchased during the time period (e.g., a year). Under these conditions, consumers get consumer surplus equal to area c and producers get producer surplus equal to area h.

2.3; we add the subscript US to make this clear. We will call the other country the "rest of the world." The "national" market for the rest of the world is shown in the right-hand graph of Figure 2.3. Demand for motorbikes within the rest of the world is D_f, and supply is S_f. With no trade, the market equilibrium in the rest of the world occurs at point H, with a price of $700 per motorbike. To focus on the basic aspects of the situation, we will assume that prices in the two countries are stated in the same monetary units.

Starting from this initial situation of no trade in motorbikes between the two countries, can an observant person profit by initiating some trade? Using the principle of "buy low, sell high," the person could profit by buying motorbikes for $700 per motorbike in the rest of the world and selling them for $2,000 per motorbike in the United States, earning profit (before any other expenses) of $1,300 per motorbike. This is called **arbitrage**—buying something in one market and reselling the same thing in another market to profit from a price difference.

Free-Trade Equilibrium

As international trade in motorbikes develops between these two countries, it affects market prices in the countries:

- The additional supply into the United States, created by imports, reduces the market price in the United States.

- The additional demand met by exports increases the market price in the rest of the world.

In fact, if there are no transport costs or other frictions, free trade results in the two countries having the same price for motorbikes. We will call this free-trade equilibrium price the **international price** or **world price**.

FIGURE 2.3   The Effects of Trade on Production, Consumption, and Price, Shown with Demand and Supply Curves

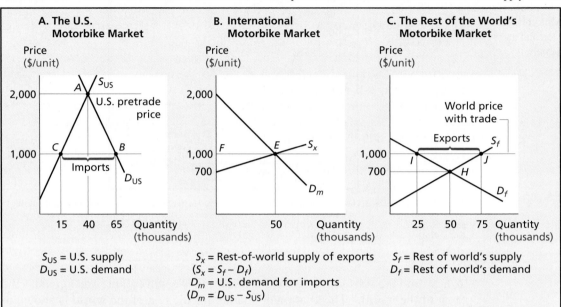

In the international market for motorbikes, the desire to trade is the (horizontal) difference between national demand and supply. The difference between U.S. demand and supply, on the left, is graphed in the center diagram as the U.S. demand for imports (the D_m curve). The difference between foreign supply and demand, on the right, is graphed in the center diagram as the foreign supply of exports (the S_x curve). The interactions of demand and supply in both countries determine the world price of motorbikes and the quantities produced, traded, and consumed.

Effects of Trade	Price	Quantity Supplied	Quantity Demanded
United States	Down	Down	Up
Rest of the world	Up	Up	Down

What will this free-trade equilibrium price be? We can picture the price by constructing the market for international trade in motorbikes. The U.S. **demand for imports** can be determined for each possible price at which the United States might import. This demand for imports is the excess demand (quantity demanded minus quantity supplied) for motorbikes within the U.S. national market. For instance, at a price of $2,000 per motorbike, the U.S. national market clears by itself, and there is no excess demand and no demand for imports. If the price in the U.S. market is $1,000 per motorbike, then there is excess demand of distance *CB,* equal to 50,000 units, creating a demand for imports of 50,000 motorbikes at this price. If excess demands at other prices below $2,000 per motorbike are measured, the curve D_m, representing U.S. demand for imports, can be drawn, as shown in the middle graph of Figure 2.3.

The export supply from the rest of the world can be determined in a similar way. The **supply of exports** is the excess supply (quantity supplied minus quantity demanded) of motorbikes in the rest-of-the-world market. For instance, at a price of $700 per unit, this market clears by itself, and there is no excess supply and no export supply. If the price in this market is $1,000 per motorbike, then excess supply is distance *IJ,* equal to 50,000 units, creating a supply of exports of 50,000 motorbikes at this price. If excess supplies for other prices above $700 per motorbike are measured, the curve S_x, representing export supply from the rest of the world, can be drawn, as shown in the middle graph of Figure 2.3.

Free-trade equilibrium occurs at the price that clears the international market. In Figure 2.3 this is at point *E,* where quantity demanded of imports equals quantity supplied of exports. The volume of trade (*FE*) is 50,000 motorbikes and the free-trade equilibrium price is $1,000 per motorbike.

This equilibrium can also be viewed as equating total world demand and supply. The international price is the price in each national market with free trade. At the price of $1,000 per motorbike, total world quantity demanded is 90,000 units (65,000 in the United States and 25,000 in the rest of the world), and total world quantity supplied is also 90,000 units (15,000 plus 75,000). The excess demand within the U.S. market (*CB*) of 50,000 motorbikes is met by the excess supply from the rest-of-the-world market (*IJ*).

What would happen if the world price for some reason was (temporarily) different from $1,000 per motorbike? At a slightly higher price (say, $1,100 per motorbike):

- The U.S. excess (or import) demand would be less than 50,000 motorbikes.

- The rest of the world's excess (or export) supply would be above 50,000 units.

Because export quantity supplied exceeds import quantity demanded, the imbalance creates pressure for the price to fall back to the equilibrium value of $1,000 per motorbike. Conversely, a price below $1,000 would not last because U.S. import quantity demanded would be above the foreign export quantity supplied.

Effects in the Importing Country

Opening trade in motorbikes has effects on economic well-being (in economists' jargon, *welfare*) in both the United States and the rest of the world. We will first examine changes in the importing country, the United States. Figure 2.4 reproduces Figure 2.3 and adds labels for the areas relevant to consumer and producer surplus.

Effects on Consumers and Producers
For the United States (the importing country), the shift from no trade to free trade lowers the market price. U.S. consumers of the product benefit from this change and increase their quantity consumed. The concept of consumer surplus allows us to quantify what the lower price is worth to consumers. With free trade, consumer surplus is the area below the demand curve and above the international

FIGURE 2.4   The Effects of Trade on Well-Being of Producers, Consumers, and the Nation as a Whole

		Welfare Effects of Free Trade			
	United States			**Rest of the World**	
Group	**Surplus with Free Trade**	**Surplus with No Trade**	**Net Effect of Trade**	**Group**	**Net Effect of Trade**
Consumers	$a + b + c + d$	c	$a + b + d$	Consumers	$-(j + k)$ [a loss]
Producers	e	$a + e$	$-a$ [a loss]	Producers	$j + k + n$
U.S. as a whole				Rest of the world	
(consumers plus				as a whole	
producers)	$a + b + c + d + e$	$c + a + e$	$b + d$		n

price line of $1,000 per motorbike, equal to area $a + b + c + d$ (the same as area $t + c + d$ in Figure 2.1A). Thus, in comparison with the no-trade consumer surplus of area c, the opening of trade brings consumers of this product a gain of area $a + b + d$ (equal to $52.5 million, area $t + d$ in Figure 2.1A). This gain is spread over many people who consume this product (including some who are also producers of the product).

U.S. producers of this product (in their role as producers) are hurt by the shift from no trade to free trade. They receive a lower price for their product and shrink production. Producer surplus decreases from area $e + a$ with no trade (the same as area $e + w + v$ in Figure 2.1B) to only area e. The loss in producer surplus is area a (equal to $27.5 million). Area a is a loss of producer surplus both on the 15,000 motorbikes still produced in the United States and on the 25,000 that are no longer produced in the United States as imports capture this part of the market.[3]

Net National Gains

If U.S. consumers gain area *a* + *b* + *d* from the opening of trade and U.S. producers lose area *a,* what can we say about the net effect of trade on the United States? There is no escaping the basic point that *we cannot compare the welfare effects on different groups without imposing our subjective weights to the economic stakes of each group.* Our analysis allows us to quantify the separate effects on different groups, but it does not tell us how important each group is to us. In our example, how much of the consumer gain does the producer loss of $27.5 million offset in our minds? No theorem or observation of economic behavior can tell us. The result depends on our value judgments.

Economists have tended to resolve the matter by imposing the value judgment that we shall call the **one-dollar, one-vote metric** here and throughout this book. The one-dollar, one-vote metric says that the analyst will value any dollar of gain or loss equally, regardless of who experiences it. The metric implies a willingness to judge trade issues on the basis of their effects on aggregate well-being, without regard to their effects on the distribution of well-being. This does not signify a lack of interest in the issue of distribution. It only means that one considers the distribution of well-being to be a matter better handled by compensating those hurt by a change or by using some other direct means of redistributing well-being toward those groups (for example, the poor) whose dollars of well-being seem to matter more to us. If any desirable adjustment of the distribution of well-being is handled directly, then trade can be judged in terms of simple aggregate gains and losses.

You need not accept this value judgment. You may feel that the stake of, say, motorbike producers matters much more to you, dollar for dollar, than the stake of motorbike consumers. You might feel this way, for example, if you knew that the

---

[3] Figure 2.4 does not enable us to identify the "producers" experiencing these losses of producer surplus. If one views the supply curve as the marginal cost curve facing competitive entrepreneurs who face fixed prices for both outputs and inputs, then the change in producer surplus is the change in these entrepreneurs' profits. Taking this approach implicitly assumes that workers and suppliers of capital are completely unaffected by the fortunes of the industry because they can just take their labor and capital elsewhere and earn exactly the same returns. Yet this narrow focus is not justified, either by the real world or by the larger model that underlies the demand and supply curves.

Though the present diagrams cannot show the entire model of international trade at once, they are based on a general equilibrium model that shows how trade affects the rates of pay of productive inputs as well as commodity prices and quantities. As we shall see in Chapter 4, anything that changes the relative price of a product also changes the distribution of income within the nation. The issue of how trade affects the distribution of income will be taken up later. Now the key point is simply that as the price of motorbikes drops and the economy moves from point *A* to point *C,* the producer surplus being lost probably is a loss to workers and other input suppliers to the industry, not just a loss to the industry's entrepreneurs. To know how the change in producer surplus is divided among these groups, one would have to consult the full model that will be complete by the end of Chapter 4.

producers are poor unskilled laborers whereas the consumers are rich. And you might also feel that there is no politically feasible way to compensate the poor workers for their income losses from the opening of trade. If so, you may wish to say that each dollar lost by producers means five or six times as much to you as each dollar gained by consumers. Taking this stand leads you to conclude that opening trade violates your conception of the national interest. Even in this case, however, you could still find the demand–supply analysis useful. It is a way of quantifying the separate stakes of groups whose interests you weight unequally.

If the one-dollar, one-vote metric is accepted, then the **net national gains from trade** equal the difference between what one group gains and what the other group loses. If motorbike consumers gain area $a + b + d$ and motorbike producers lose area a, the net national gain from trade is area $b + d$, or a triangular area worth \$25 million per year [$= (1/2) \times (65{,}000 - 15{,}000$ motorbikes$) \times (\$2{,}000 - \$1{,}000)$ per motorbike]. It turns out that very little information is needed to measure the net national gain. All that is needed is an estimate of the amount of trade and an estimate of the change in price brought about by trade.

Effects in the Exporting Country

For the rest of the world (the exporting country), the analysis follows a similar path. Here the shift from no trade to free trade increases the market price. The increase in price benefits motorbike producers in the rest of the world, whose producer surplus increases by area $j + k + n$ in Figure 2.4. The increase in price hurts motorbike consumers, whose consumer surplus decreases by area $j + k$. In the exporting country, producers of the product gain and consumers lose. Using the one-dollar, one-vote metric, we can say that the rest of the world gains from trade, and that its net gain from trade equals area n.

Which Country Gains More?

This analysis shows that each country gains from international trade, so it is clear that the whole world gains from trade. Trade is a positive-sum activity. At the same time, the gains to the countries generally are not equal—area $b + d$ is generally not equal to area n. These two triangles can be compared rather easily. They both have the same base (equal to 50,000 units, the volume of trade). The height of each triangle is the change in price in the shift from no trade to free trade for each country. Thus, the country that experiences the larger price change has a larger value of the net gains from trade.

The gains from opening trade are divided in direct proportion to the price changes that trade brings to the two sides. If a nation's price ratio changes x percent (as a percentage of the free-trade price) and the price in the rest of the world changes y percent, then

$$\frac{\text{Nation's gain}}{\text{Rest of world's gains}} = \frac{x}{y}$$

The side with the less elastic (steeper) trade curve (import demand curve or export supply curve) gains more.

In Figure 2.4, the United States gains more. Its gains from trade in this product are $25 million. Its price changes from $2,000 to $1,000, equal to 100 percent of the free-trade price $1,000. The gains from trade for the rest of the world are $7.5 million. Its price changes from $700 to $1,000, equal to 30 percent of the free-trade price.

Summary: Early Answers to the Four Trade Questions

Extending the familiar demand–supply framework to international trade has given us useful preliminary answers to the four basic questions about international trade. The contrast between no trade and free trade offers these conclusions:

1. Why do countries trade? Demand and supply conditions differ between countries, so prices differ between countries if there is no international trade. Trade begins as someone conducts **arbitrage** to earn profits from the price difference between previously separated markets. A product will be exported from countries where its price was lower without trade to countries where its price was higher.

2. How does trade affect production and consumption in each country? The move from no trade to a free-trade equilibrium changes the product price from its no-trade value to the free-trade equilibrium **international price** or **world price.** The price change in each country results in changes in quantities consumed and produced. In the country importing the product, trade raises the quantity consumed and lowers the quantity produced of that product. In the exporting country, trade raises the quantity produced and lowers the quantity consumed of the product.

3. Which country gains from trade? If we use the **one-dollar, one vote metric,** then both do. Each country's **net national gains from trade** are proportional to the change in its price that occurs in the shift from no trade to free trade. The country whose prices are disrupted more by trade gains more.

4. Within each country, who are the gainers and losers from opening trade? The gainers are the consumers of imported products and the producers of exportable products. Those who lose are the producers of import-competing products and the consumers of exportable products.

Suggested Reading

Suranovic (2000) discusses seven types of fairness and applies them to international trade. He calls our one-dollar, one-vote metric "maximum benefit fairness."

Questions and Problems

✦ 1. What is consumer surplus? Using real-world data, what information would you need to measure consumer surplus for a product?

2. What is producer surplus? Using real-world data, what information would you need to measure producer surplus for a product?

✦ 3. How can a country's supply and demand curves for a product be used to determine the country's supply-of-exports curve? What does the supply-of-exports curve mean?

4. How can a country's supply and demand curves for a product be used to determine the country's demand-for-imports curve? What does the demand-for-imports curve mean?

✦ 5. A tropical country can produce winter coats, but there is no domestic demand for these coats. Explain how this country can gain from free trade in winter coats.

6. The United States exports a substantial amount of scrap iron and steel to Japan and other countries. Why do some U.S. users of scrap iron and steel support a prohibition on these exports?

✦ 7. Explain what is wrong with the following statement: "Trade is self-eliminating. Opening up trade opportunities drives prices and costs into equality between countries. But once prices and costs are equalized, there is no longer any reason to trade the product from one country to another, and trade stops."

8. In 2000, the United States imported about 3.6 billion barrels of oil. Perhaps it would be better for the United States if it could end the billions of dollars of payments to foreigners by not importing this oil. After all, the United States can produce its own oil (or other energy products that substitute for oil). If the United States stopped all oil imports suddenly, it would be very disruptive. But perhaps the United States could gain if it gradually restricted and then ended oil imports in an orderly transition. If we allow time for adjustments by U.S. consumers and producers of oil, and we perhaps are a bit optimistic about how much adjustment is possible, then the following two equations show domestic demand and supply conditions in the United States:

$$\text{Demand: } P = 92 - 10Q_D$$
$$\text{Supply: } P = 0.5 + 8.5Q_S$$

where quantity Q is in billions of barrels per year and price P is in dollars per barrel.

a. With free trade and an international price of $26 per barrel, how much oil does the United States produce domestically? How much does it consume? Show the demand and supply curves on a graph and label these points. Indicate on the graph the quantity of U.S. imports of oil.

b. If the United States stopped all imports of oil (in a way that allowed enough time for orderly adjustments as shown by the equations), how much oil would be produced in the United States? How much would be consumed? What would be the price of oil in the United States with no oil imports? Show all of this on your graph.

c. If the United States stopped all oil imports, which group(s) in the United States would gain? Which group(s) would lose? As appropriate, refer to your graph in your answer.

◆ 9. Consider Figure 2.3 which shows free trade in motorbikes. Assume that consumers in the United States shift their tastes in favor of motorbikes. What is the effect on the U.S. domestic demand and/or supply curve(s)? What is the effect on the U.S. demand-for-imports curve? What is the effect on the equilibrium international price?

10. Consider again Figure 2.3, which shows free trade in motorbikes. Assume that U.S. productivity in producing motorcycles increases. What is the effect on the U.S. domestic demand and/or supply curve(s)? What is the effect on the U.S. demand-for-imports curve? What is the effect on the equilibrium international price?

◆ 11. The equation for the demand curve for writing paper in Belgium is

$$Q_D = 350 - (P/2) \text{ (or } P = 700 - 2Q_D)$$

The equation for the supply curve for writing paper in Belgium is

$$Q_S = -200 + 5P \text{ [or } P = 40 + (Q_S/5)]$$

a. What are the equilibrium price and quantity if there is no international trade?

b. What are the equilibrium quantities for Belgium if the nation can trade freely with the rest of the world at a price of 120?

c. What is the effect of the shift from no trade to free trade on Belgian consumer surplus? On Belgian producer surplus? What is the net national gain or loss for Belgium?

12. Country I has the usual demand and supply curves for Murky Way candy bars. Country II has a typical demand curve too, but it cannot produce Murky Way candy bars.

a. Use supply and demand curves for the domestic markets and for the international market. Show in a set of graphs the free-trade equilibrium for Murky Way candy bars. Indicate the equilibrium world price. How does this world price compare to the no-trade price in Country I? Indicate how many Murky Ways are traded during each time period with free international trade.

b. Show graphically and explain the effects of the shift from no trade to free trade on surpluses in each country. Indicate the net national gain or loss from free trade for each country.

Chapter **Three**

Why Everybody Trades: Comparative Advantage and Factor Proportions

Chapter 2 examined international trade focusing on a single product. That analysis helped answer some major questions about international trade, but only indirectly addressed some others. For an industry with expanding production, where do the additional resources come from? For a shrinking industry, what happens to the resources no longer needed? If consumers increase or decrease the quantity demanded of one product, what effect does this have on demand for other products?

Full analysis of international trade requires consideration of the entire economy. Yet the entire economy is very complex—it consists of thousands of products and the various resources needed to produce them. Fortunately, we can gain major insights by considering an economy composed of just two products. For international trade, one product can be exported and the other imported. This two-product economy captures an essential feature of international trade: A country tends to be a net exporter of some products and a net importer of others.

This chapter analyzes the general equilibrium of a two-product economy to address the first of our four basic trade questions: Why do countries trade? In fact, why does everybody—every country as well as every person—find it worthwhile to produce and export (sell) some things and to import (buy) other things? We proceed in three steps:

1. David Ricardo's principle of comparative advantage allows us to explain trade better than most people's intuition and better than Adam Smith's original explanation of trade patterns.

2. Next, a pair of tools—production-possibility curves and community indifference curves—allows us to perform a number of tasks. They can express Ricardo's principle of comparative advantage and some of Chapter 2's points about the effects of trade, and they set the stage for improvements that others made to Ricardo's theory.

3. The Heckscher–Ohlin theory of trade explores some deeper reasons why people trade. This theory emphasizes international differences in the abundance of the "factors of production" (land, labor, skills, capital, and natural resources). Differences in factor abundance are a source of comparative advantage because there are also differences in the use of each factor in the production of different products.

This is one of the longest chapters in this book. You may want to read it a few sections at a time. The journey through the chapter is worth it. The chapter as a whole illustrates the flow of how our understanding of comparative advantage has developed.

ADAM SMITH'S THEORY OF ABSOLUTE ADVANTAGE

In the late 18th and early 19th centuries, first Adam Smith and then David Ricardo explored the basis for international trade as part of their efforts to make a case for free trade. Their writings were responses to the doctrine of mercantilism prevailing at the time. (See accompanying box.) Their classic theories swayed policymakers for a whole century, even though today we view them as only special cases of a more basic, and more powerful, theory of trade.

In his *Wealth of Nations,* Adam Smith promoted free trade by comparing nations to households. Every household finds it worthwhile to produce only some of the products it consumes, and to buy other products using the proceeds from what the household can sell to others. The same should apply to nations:

> It is the maxim of every prudent master of a family, never to attempt to make at home what it will cost . . . more to make than to buy. The tailor does not attempt to make his own shoes, but buys them from the shoemaker. . .
>
> What is prudence in the conduct of every private family, can scarce be folly in that of a great kingdom. If a foreign country can supply us with a commodity cheaper than we ourselves can make it, better buy it of them with some part of the product of our own industry, employed in a way in which we have some advantage.

An example can show Smith's reasoning. The two "countries" in the example are the United States and the rest of the world. The two products are wheat and cloth (perhaps broadly representing agricultural products and manufactured products). Each product is produced using one resource called labor. (Smith focused on labor because he thought that all "value" was determined by and measured in hours of labor. In this respect he was imitated by David Ricardo and Karl Marx, who also believed that labor was the basis for all value. We don't have to take this literally— we can consider "labor" to be a bundle of resources used to produce products.)

Case Study   Mercantilism: Older than Smith—and Alive Today

Mercantilism was the philosophy that guided European thinking about international trade in the several centuries before Adam Smith published his *Wealth of Nations* in 1776. Mercantilists viewed international trade as a source of major benefits to a nation. Merchants engaged in trade, especially those selling exports, were good—hence the name *mercantilism*. But mercantilists also maintained that government regulation of trade was necessary to provide the largest national benefits. Trade merchants would serve their own interests and not the national interest, in the absence of government guidance.

A central belief of mercantilism was that national well-being or wealth was based on national holdings of gold and silver (specie or bullion). Given this view of national wealth, exports were viewed as good and imports (except for raw materials not produced at home) were seen as bad. If a country sells (exports) more to foreign buyers than the foreigners sell to the country (the country's imports), then the foreigners have to pay for the excess of their purchases by shipping gold and silver to the country. The gain in gold and silver increases the country's well-being, according to the mercantilist belief. Imports are undesirable because they reduce the country's ability to accumulate these precious metals. Imports were also feared because they might not be available to the country in time of war. In addition, gold and silver accruing to the national rulers could be especially valuable in helping to maintain a large military for the country. Based on mercantilist thinking, governments (1) imposed an array of taxes and prohibitions designed to limit imports and (2) subsidized and encouraged exports.

Because of its peculiar emphasis on gold and silver, mercantilism viewed trade as a zero-sum activity—one country's gains come at the expense of some other countries, since a surplus in international trade for one country must be a deficit for some

other(s). The focus on promoting exports and limiting imports also provided major benefits for domestic producer interests (in both exporting and import-competing industries).

Adam Smith and economists after him pointed out that the mercantilists' push for more exports and fewer imports turns social priorities upside down. National well-being is based on the ability to consume products (and other "goods" such as leisure time and a clean environment) now and in the future. The importance of national production and exports is only indirect: They provide the income to buy products to consume. Imports are part of the expanding national consumption that a nation seeks, not an evil to be suppressed. Exports are not desirable on their own; rather, exports are useful because they pay for the imports. As the text shows, trade freely transacted between countries can lead to gains for all countries—trade is a positive-sum activity. Indeed, even the goal of acquiring gold and silver can be self-defeating if this acquisition expands the domestic money supply and leads to domestic inflation of product prices—an argument first expounded by David Hume even before Smith did his writing.

Although the propositions of the mercantilists have been refuted, and countries no longer focus on piling up gold and silver, mercantilist thinking is still very much alive today. It now has a sharp focus on employment. Neo-mercantilists believe that exports are good because they create jobs in the country. Imports are bad because they take jobs from the country and give them to foreigners. Once again, trade is depicted as a zero-sum activity. There is no recognition that trade can bring gains to all countries (including mutual gains in employment as prosperity rises throughout the world). Although it does not always win the policy debates, mercantilist thinking pervades discussions of international trade in countries all over the world.

Suppose that the United States is better than the rest of the world at producing wheat, and the rest of the world is better than the United States at producing cloth. It is probably not a surprise that international trade can create benefits, because the United States can focus on producing what it does best (wheat) and export it, and the rest of the world can focus on producing what it does best (cloth) and export it. Let's look at this more closely.

What do we mean by "better at producing?" We can indicate each country's ability to produce each product in one of two equivalent ways. First, we can measure **labor productivity**—the number of units of output that a worker can produce in one hour. Second, we can look at the number of hours that it takes a worker to produce one unit of output—this is just the reciprocal of labor productivity. Here are some numbers for our example:

	In the United States		In the Rest of the World
Productivity:			
Yard of cloth per labor hour	0.25	<	1.0
Bushels of wheat per labor hour	0.5	>	0.4
Labor hours to make:			
1 yard of cloth	4.0	>	1.0
1 bushel of wheat	2.0	<	2.5

In this numerical example, the United States has an **absolute advantage** in producing wheat, because the U.S. labor productivity in wheat is higher than the rest of the world's labor productivity in wheat. Similarly, the rest of the world has an absolute advantage in producing cloth.

If there is no trade, then each country will have to produce both products to satisfy its demand for the products. If the countries then open to free trade, each can shift its labor resources toward producing the good in which it has the absolute advantage. In the United States, shifting 1 hour of labor results in a decrease of 0.25 yards of cloth and in increase of 0.5 bushels of wheat. In the rest of the world, shifting 1 hour of labor results in a decrease of 0.4 bushels of wheat and an increase of 1 yard of cloth. Total world production increases. For each product, production using labor that has high productivity replaces production using labor that has low productivity.

International trade makes these shifts in production possible even if consumers in each country want to buy something different from what is produced in the country. For instance, in the United States the apparent shortage of (or apparent excess demand for) clothing (as clothing production decreases) is met by imports of clothing from the rest of the world. The United States pays for these imports of clothing by exporting some of the extra wheat produced.

Thus, Adam Smith showed the benefits of free trade by showing that global production efficiency is enhanced because trade allows each country to exploit its absolute advantage in producing some product(s). At least one country is better off with trade, and this country's gain is not at the expense of the other country. In many cases both countries will gain from trade by splitting the benefits of the enhanced global production.

Smith's reasoning was fundamentally correct, and it helped to persuade some governments to dismantle inefficient barriers to international trade over the 100 years after he wrote *Wealth of Nations.* Yet his argument failed to put to rest a fear that others had already expressed even before he wrote. What if our country has no absolute advantage? What if the foreigners are better at producing everything than we are? Will they want to trade? If they do, should we want to? That fear existed in the minds of many of Smith's English contemporaries, who worried that the Dutch were more productive than they at making anything. It persists into the 21st century too. In the wake of World War II, many nations thought they could not possibly compete with the highly productive Americans at anything and wondered how they could gain from free trade. Today some Americans have the same fear in reverse: Aren't foreigners getting better at making everything that enters international trade, and won't the United States be hurt by free trade? We turn next to the theory that first answered these fears and established a fundamental principle of international trade.

RICARDO'S THEORY OF COMPARATIVE ADVANTAGE

David Ricardo's main contribution to our understanding of international trade was to show that there is a basis for beneficial trade whether or not countries have any absolute advantage. His contribution is based on a careful examination of opportunity cost. The **opportunity cost** of producing more of a product in a country is the amount of production of the other product that is given up. The opportunity cost exists because production resources must be shifted from the other product to this product. (We already used this idea in the discussion of absolute advantage, when we shifted labor from producing one product to producing the other product.)

Ricardo's writings in the early 19th century demonstrated the **principle of comparative advantage:** A country will export the goods and services that it can produce at a low opportunity cost and import the goods and services that it would otherwise produce at a high opportunity cost.

The key word here is *comparative,* meaning "relative" and "not necessarily absolute." Even if one country is absolutely more productive at producing everything and the other country is absolutely less productive, they both can gain by trading with each other as long as their relative (dis)advantages in making different goods are different. Each of these countries can benefit from trade by exporting products in which it has the greatest relative advantage (or least relative disadvantage), and importing products in which it has the least relative advantage (or the greatest relative disadvantage). Ricardo's approach is actually a double comparison—between countries and between products.

Ricardo drove home the point with a simple numerical example of gains from trading two products (cloth and wine) between two countries (England and Portugal). Here is a similar illustration, using wheat and cloth in the United States and the rest of the world:

	In the United States		In the Rest of the World
Productivity:			
Yard of cloth per labor hour	0.25	<	1.0
Bushels of wheat per labor hour	0.5	<	0.67
Labor hours to make:			
1 yard of cloth	4.0	>	1.0
1 bushel of wheat	2.0	>	1.5

Here, one country has inferior productivity in both goods. The United States has absolute disadvantages in both goods—lower productivity or larger numbers of hours to produce one unit of each good. What products (if any) will the United States export or import? Can trade bring net national gains to both countries?

As in the absolute-advantage case, we can begin by imagining the two countries separately with no trade between them. Each country will have to produce both products to meet local demands for the two products. What will the product prices be in each country? With no trade, the prices of the two products within each country will be determined by conditions within each country. To keep our focus on real values and activities, we are going to try to ignore money for as long as we can. Rather than looking at money prices (dollars per bushel or dollars per yard), we will use the **relative price**—the ratio of one product price to another product price. It's as if we are in a world without money, a world of barter between real products like wheat and cloth.[1]

Ricardo, like Smith, believed that, in competitive markets, product prices reflect the costs of the labor needed to produce the products. With no trade, 4 hours of labor in the United States could produce either 2 bushels of wheat or 1 yard of cloth. The price of 1 yard of cloth is then 2 bushels of wheat in the United States. (Two bushels of wheat is also the opportunity cost of producing cloth in the United States—product prices reflect costs.) In the rest of the world, 1 hour of labor could produce 1 yard of cloth or 2/3 bushel of wheat. The price (and the opportunity cost) of a yard of cloth is 0.67 bushels of wheat in the rest of the

---

[1] We keep money hiding in the wings throughout most of Parts I and II, allowing it to take center stage only in the more macroeconomic Parts III and IV. Money appears briefly in the box later in this chapter titled "What If Trade Doesn't Balance?" and again in Chapter 4, both times to help us think about how exchange rates relate to real prices like the bushel/yard prices used here. Part II switches to what look like ordinary money prices, such as dollars per bicycle in Chapter 7. Even there, however, the prices do not have much to do with money. As in Chapter 2, the dollars are really units of all products other than the one being pictured (e.g., motorbikes).

world. Thus, within the two isolated economies, national prices would follow the relative labor costs of cloth and wheat:

	In the United States	In the Rest of the World
With no international trade:		
Price of cloth	2.0 bushels/yard	0.67 bushel/yard
Price of wheat	0.5 yard/bushel	1.5 yards/bushel

There is really only one ratio in each country because the price of wheat is just the reciprocal of the price of cloth.

Now let trade be possible between the United States and the rest of the world. Somebody will notice the difference between the national prices for each good and will try to profit from that difference. The principle is simple and universal: As long as prices differ in two places (by more than any cost of transporting between the places), there is a way to profit through **arbitrage**—buying at the low price in one place and selling at the high price in the other place.

Perhaps the first alert person will think of sending cloth to the United States in exchange for U.S. wheat. Consider the arbitrage profit that the person could make. She acquires cloth in the rest of the world, giving up 0.67 bushels of wheat for each yard. She then ships this cloth to the United States and sells it there for 2.0 bushels per yard. To keep things simple, we will usually assume that the cost of transporting products between the countries is zero.[2] Therefore, by buying low (at 0.67) and selling high (at 2.0), she can make an arbitrage profit of 1.33 bushels of wheat for each yard of cloth that she exports from the rest of the world (and imports into the United States). Somebody else could profit by acquiring wheat in the United States at the low price of 0.5 yard per bushel, shipping the wheat to the rest of the world, and selling it for the higher price of 1.5 yard per bushel.

The opening of profitable international trade will start pushing the two separate national price ratios toward a new worldwide equilibrium. As people remove cloth from the rest of the world by exporting it, cloth becomes more expensive relative to wheat in the rest of the world. Meanwhile, cloth becomes cheaper in the United States, thanks to the additional supply of cloth imported from the rest

---

[2] The assumption of zero transport costs is relatively harmless. If transport costs are positive but not too large, they reduce the gains from trading but do not reverse any of our major conclusions. In addition, in a world with many products, high transport costs for some products could prevent any trade in those products. For instance, many services are nontraded products because the cost of getting the seller and buyer together are too high. (No Canadian or American would travel to China just to get a cheap haircut.) Yet other services can be and are traded at low cost, especially if the service is "transported" electronically. For instance, the author of this book recently completed consulting research for the European Union in which all communication, including the delivery of completed work, was conducted by e-mail and telephone.

of the world. So, cloth tends to get more expensive where it was cheap at first, and cheaper where it was more expensive. (A similar process occurs for wheat.) The tendencies continue until the two national relative prices become one world equilibrium relative price. Normal trade on an ongoing basis will be conducted at this equilibrium relative price.

What will the equilibrium international price be? We cannot say for sure without knowing how strongly the two countries demand each of the two products. We do know something—the equilibrium international price ratio must fall within the range of the two price ratios that prevailed in each country before trade began:

$$2.0 \geq \text{International price of cloth} \geq 0.67 \text{ (bushel/yard)}$$

or, equivalently,

$$0.5 \leq \text{International price of wheat} \leq 1.5 \text{ (yards/bushel)}$$

Why? Consider what would happen if this were not true. For instance, consider an international price of only 0.4 bushel per yard. At this low price of cloth, the rest of the world would want to import cloth and export wheat because the price of cloth on the international market is now below the cost of producing cloth at home (0.67 bushel/yard). No deal could be made, though. At this low cloth price the United States would also want to import cloth and export wheat. No equilibrium is possible, and the cloth price would be pushed up as a result of the excess demand for cloth. (Similar reasoning applies to show the lack of an equilibrium if the cloth price is above 2 bushels/yard.) The only way for the two sides to agree on trading is to have the cloth price somewhere in the range 0.67 to 2.0 bushels/yard.

Suppose that the strengths of demand for the products, which we will examine more closely later in this chapter, lead to an equilibrium international cloth price that has the convenient value of 1 bushel/yard. Then both countries gain from international trade. The United States gains:

- It produces a bushel of wheat by giving up only 0.5 yard of cloth.

- It can export this bushel and receive 1 yard of cloth.

The rest of the world gains:

- It produces a yard of cloth by giving up only 0.67 bushel of wheat.

- It can export this yard and receive 1 bushel of wheat.

How do absolute advantage and comparative advantage relate to each other? Smith's example of each country having an absolute advantage in one product is also a case of comparative advantage. Our detailed analysis of comparative advantage could be applied to the numerical example of absolute advantage in the previous section. But, comparative advantage is more general and powerful. What matters is that the two countries have different price ratios if there is no trade. It does not matter why prices differ. A country will have a comparative advantage even if it has no absolute advantage. The basis for trade and the gains from trade arise from differences between the countries in opportunity costs of the goods. In our numerical example of comparative advantage, the opportunity cost of a bushel of wheat within the United States (0.5 yard/bushel) was lower than this opportunity cost in the rest of the world (1.5 yards/bushel). The United States will export wheat, even though it has an absolute disadvantage in producing both wheat and cloth.[3]

RICARDO'S CONSTANT COSTS AND THE PRODUCTION-POSSIBILITY CURVE

Ricardo's numerical illustration succeeded in proving the principle of comparative advantage. We can also show Ricardo's comparative advantage using diagrams indicating what each country can produce and consume.

Figure 3.1 pictures production, consumption, and trade for the United States and the rest of the world. Let's examine national production first. Each country can use its resources (labor) to produce various amounts of the two products, wheat and cloth. To show what a nation is capable of producing requires a curve (or line) that shows all of these possibilities. For example, consider that the United States has 100 billion hours of labor available during the year, and that labor productivities are as shown in the Ricardian numerical example (0.5 bushels of wheat per hour and 0.25 yards of cloth per hour). Then, the United States can make 50 billion bushels of wheat per year if it only produces wheat— or it can make 25 billion yards of cloth per year if it makes only cloth. The United States can also produce a mix of wheat and cloth, say, 20 billion bushels of wheat and 15 billion yards of cloth. If we graph all of these points, we have the country's **production-possibility curve (ppc),** which shows all combinations of amounts of different products that an economy can produce with full employment of its resources and maximum feasible productivity of these resources.

The solid lines in Figure 3.1 are the ppc's for the United States and the rest of the world (assuming that the rest of the world also has 100 billion hours of labor available annually). Note that each is a straight line with a constant slope (steepness). This slope indicates the cost of extra cloth, the number of bushels of wheat each country would have to give up to make each extra yard of cloth. In this case, the cost is always 50/25 = 2 bushels per yard for the United States, the same opportunity cost of cloth as in the numerical example. With no trade and competitive markets, this cost is also the relative price of cloth in the United States. For the rest of the world the cost of extra cloth is 67/100 = 2/3. This is also the relative price of cloth in the rest of the world with competitive markets and no trade.

---

[3] While absolute advantage does not determine the trade pattern in cases like this, it does determine living standards. Having an absolute advantage in all products means that the country is more productive than other countries are. High-productivity countries have high real wages and are rich countries. Low-productivity countries have low real wages and are poor countries. See the box titled "Absolute Advantage Does Matter."

If free trade is so good, why are so many people against it? As we discussed in Chapter 1, activists and protesters have recently been complaining loudly that trade has bad effects on

- Workers in developing countries.

- Workers in the industrialized countries.

- The natural environment.

Analysis of absolute advantage and comparative advantage focuses on a resource called labor, so let's focus on trade and workers. (Most of our examination of issues related to the natural environment is concentrated in Chapter 12.)

Can the classical analysis pioneered by Smith and Ricardo really tell us anything about current controversies? The most interesting case is the one presented in the text, in which one country (now call it the North) has an absolute advantage in the production of all products, and the other country (now call it the South) has an absolute disadvantage. Three prominent questions can be examined within this framework:

1. If labor in the North is so productive, will workers in the South be overwhelmed so that free trade makes the South poorer?

2. If wages in the South are so low, will workers in the North be overwhelmed so that free trade makes the North poorer?

3. Does trade lead to harm to and exploitation of workers in the South, as indicated by the low wages (and/or poor working conditions)?

The text has already answered the first question. The South will have a comparative advantage in some set of products, and production of these products will thrive in that country. The opening of trade will lead to reductions of jobs producing the products that are imported from the North, but these workers can shift to the expanding export-oriented industries. While there may be some transition costs borne by the workers who must shift from one industry to another, the South still gets the gains from trade—generally, it is richer, not poorer.

How is it that some products produced by (absolutely) low-productivity workers in the South can compete successfully? The answer must be that workers in the South have low wages. The cost of producing a unit of a product is the ratio between the wage rate paid to a worker and the productivity of the worker. Production cost can be low if wages are low, or if productivity is high, and what really matters is the relationship between the two.

For the South's comparative-advantage products (the ones for which the productivity disadvantage is smallest), the lower wages lead to low production costs and the ability to export successfully. For the comparative-disadvantage products, the large productivity disadvantage is not offset by the lower wages, and these products are imported from the North.

But if wages in the South are low, how can products produced by high-wage workers in the North compete? The answer to this second question is the other side of the answer to the first. The North has comparative advantage in a set of products because in these products its (absolute) productivity advantage is the largest. Even with high wages, the cost of producing these products is low because the workers are highly productive. The North can successfully export these products, because high productivity leads to low production costs. By using its comparative advantage (maximizing its absolute productivity advantage), the North gets the gains from trade—generally it is also richer, not poorer.

But is this fair? Why should the workers in the North have high wages and the workers in the South have low wages? Does this show that the workers in the South are being exploited by trade? Amazingly, a big part of the answer to these questions is that *absolute advantage does matter.* But it matters not for determining the trade pattern but rather *for determining national wage levels and national living standards.* Workers can receive high wages and enjoy high living standards if they are highly productive. Workers with low productivity are paid low wages. (See the accompanying figure for recent evidence for a number of countries that shows how true this is.) The low wages in the South are the result of the low labor productivity, and wages in the South are going to be low with or without trade. Trade does not exploit these workers. In fact, because of the gains from trade, workers in the South can earn somewhat higher wages and somewhat better living standards. Still, as long as productivity remains low in the South, workers in the South will remain relatively poor, even with free trade.

Is there anything we can do if we still think that it is unfair that workers in the South earn such low wages? Trade by itself is not the solution (though it also is not the culprit). Some kind of government mandate to pay higher wages in the South is also not the solution. Forcing higher wages would raise production costs, and this would just shrink some of the export-oriented industries that have productivity levels not much below the productivity levels in the North. The true solution must be to find ways to increase the productivity of workers in the South. While Ricardo's approach does not indicate what determines labor productivity, we know some changes that would be desirable: increasing worker quality by enhancing education and health, upgrading production technologies and management practices, and reforming or liberalizing restrictive and distortionary government policies. In short, absolute advantage matters—to raise wages and living standards, we have to raise productivity.

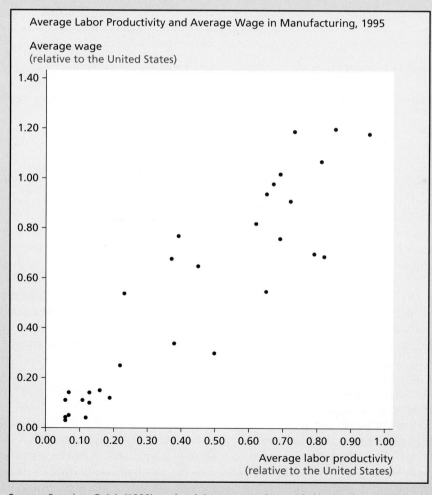

Average Labor Productivity and Average Wage in Manufacturing, 1995

Average wage
(relative to the United States)

Average labor productivity
(relative to the United States)

For each country's manufacturing sector, the average labor productivity and average wage are measured relative to the United States, for 1995. The figure shows that there is a strong tendency for the average wage to be higher in countries with higher average labor productivity. Here are the countries that are included in the sample:

- Bottom left (relative productivity less than 0.20): Ghana, Hungary, India, Indonesia, Malawi, Malaysia, Mauritius, Mexico, Senegal, Thailand, Zimbabwe.

- Middle (relative productivity between 0.20 and 0.50): Brazil, Chile, Hong Kong, Israel, Singapore, South Africa, Spain.

- Top right (relative productivity greater than 0.60): Australia, Belgium, Canada, Denmark, France, Germany, Italy, Japan, South Korea, Netherlands, Norway, Sweden, United Kingdom.

Source: Based on Golub (1999); updated data generously provided by Stephen Golub.

FIGURE 3.1

The Gains from
Trade, Shown
for Ricardo's
Constant-Cost
Case

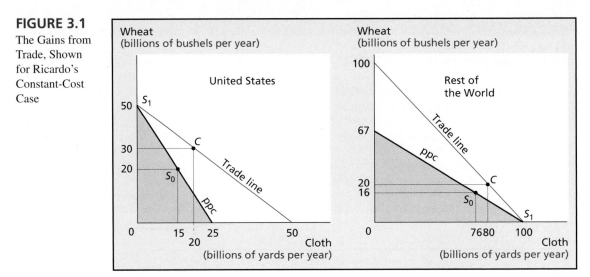

The solid lines are the production-possibility curves (ppc's), showing what each nation can produce. With no trade, each country's consumption is limited by its ability to produce so that consumption occurs at a point like S_0 in each country. With free trade, each country specializes in producing only one good, at S_1. Each country can reach its desirable levels of consumption (consuming at a point like C) by trading along the colored trade line.

Result: Both countries gain from trade. For each country, specializing and trading make it possible to consume more of both goods at C, relative to a no-trade point like S_0 on the ppc.

The ppc's in Figure 3.1 are drawn as straight lines to reflect Ricardo's belief that each labor-productivity value is constant. Constant productivities imply that the trade-off in production—the marginal or opportunity cost of each good—is constant in each country.

To set the stage for the more modern portrayals of the basis for trade, let us use Figure 3.1 to restate Ricardo's conclusions about the basis for trade and the gains from trade. If neither country traded, each could only consume and enjoy combinations of wheat and cloth that are on (or below) its ppc, combinations like those shown as S_0 in Figure 3.1. When trade is opened, each nation can trade at a price between 2/3 and 2 bushels per yard. Again, let us suppose that demand conditions make the free-trade price equal 1 bushel per yard. Each country then specializes in producing only the good in which it has a comparative advantage, at point S_1. To show how each nation gains from trade at this price, we need to consider how trade should be drawn on the diagram. When a nation sells its exports to get imports, it ends up consuming a different set of goods. How different? In a diagram such as Figure 3.1, the line connecting where a nation produces and where it consumes is a line along which wheat trades for cloth at the world price ratio, 1 bushel per yard. Two trade (or price) lines are shown in Figure 3.1.

If the United States specializes in making only wheat, at S_1, it can export wheat for cloth imports at the world price ratio, moving along the trade line. Giving up wheat and gaining cloth imports means moving southeast along the trade line.

Extension What If Trade Doesn't Balance?

You may be struck by a contradiction between the spirit of the trade theory and recent headlines about international trade.

The theory assumes that trade balances. In diagrams like Figure 3.1, the theory assumes equality between the market value of exports and the market value of imports (both values calculated using the international price ratio). The balance seems guaranteed by the absence of money from the diagram, as noted in this chapter's footnote 1. As long as countries are just bartering wheat for cloth, they must think U.S. wheat exports have exactly the same market value as U.S. cloth imports. Trade must balance.

Yet the news media have been announcing huge U.S. trade deficits every year since 1975. Imports of goods and services keep exceeding exports. (Conversely, Japan, Germany, and France have been running merchandise trade surpluses in most years since that time.) What's going on? How can the basic theory of trade be so silent about the most newsworthy aspect of international trade flows? Isn't the theory wrong in its statements about the reasons for trade or the gains from trade? Maybe Ricardo was too optimistic about every country's having enough comparative advantage to balance its overall trade.

These are valid questions, and they deserve a better answer than simply, "Well, the model assumes balanced trade." In later chapters, we will add details about how trade deficits and surpluses relate to exchange rates, money, and finance. But the real answer is more fundamental: The model is not really wrong in assuming balanced trade, even for a country that currently has a huge trade deficit or trade surplus!

Take the case of the U.S. trade deficit. It looks as though exports are always less than imports. Well, yes and no. Yes, the trade balance (more precisely the "current-account" balance in Chapter 15) has stayed negative for many years. But a country with a current-account deficit pays for it by either piling up debts or giving up assets to foreigners. Such a country is *exporting* paper IOUs, such as bonds, that are a present claim on future goods. The value of these net exports of paper IOUs matches the value of the ordinary current-account deficit.

There is no need to add paper bonds to our wheat-and-cloth examples because the bonds are a claim on future wheat and cloth. Today, the United States may be importing more cloth than it is exporting wheat, but this deficit is matched by the expected value of its net exports of extra wheat someday when it pays off the debt. Trade is expected to balance over the very long run. That expectation could prove wrong in the future: Maybe the United States will default on some of its foreign debts, or maybe price inflation (deflation) will make it give up less (more) wheat than expected. Still, today's transactions are based on the *expectation* that trade will balance in the long run.

The United States could consume anywhere along this colored line. Clearly, this is a better set of consumption options than if the United States did not trade. For each point like S_0, where the nation consumes what it produces, there are better consumption points like C, where it can end up consuming more of everything by specializing and trading. The United States gains from trade. It is equally clear that the rest of the world also gains from specializing in cloth production (at S_1) and trading some of that cloth for wheat, moving northwest along its trade line to consume at some point like C. Thus, Figure 3.1 is a different way to view the workings of comparative advantage with Ricardian constant costs.

Later writers challenged Ricardo's simple assumption of constant marginal costs. First, they noted empirically that many industries seem to be characterized by rising, rather than constant, marginal costs. More and more of other goods have to be given up to produce each succeeding extra unit of one good. Second, they thought of some good reasons for expecting that marginal costs would rise when one industry expands at the expense of others. Even if every industry has constant returns to scale, the shift from one industry to another may involve increasing marginal costs for the whole country because of subtle effects stemming from the fact that different goods use resource inputs in different proportions.

Perhaps the most damaging objection to the assumption of constant marginal costs is that it implies something that fails to fit the facts of international trade and production patterns. The constancy of marginal costs in Figure 3.1 leads us to conclude that each country would maximize its gain by specializing its production completely in its comparative-advantage good.[4]

The real world fails to show total specialization. In Ricardo's day, it may have been reasonable for him to assume that England grew no wine grapes and relied on foreign grapes and wines. However, even with cloth imports from England, the other country in his example, Portugal, made most of its own cloth. Complete specialization is no more common today. The United States and Canada continue to produce some of their domestic consumption of products that they partially import—textiles, cars, and furniture, for example.

INCREASING MARGINAL COSTS

In the modern theory of international trade, economists replace the constant-cost assumption used in the Ricardian approach with a more realistic assumption about marginal costs. They assume **increasing marginal costs:** As one industry expands at the expense of others, increasing amounts of the other products must be given up to get each extra unit of the expanding industry's product.

What does the ppc look like with increasing marginal costs? It is "bowed out," as shown in the top half of Figure 3.2. To see why a bowed-out ppc shows increasing marginal costs, consider what happens to the marginal cost of producing an extra yard of cloth as we shift more and more resources from wheat production to cloth production. When the economy is producing only 20 billion yards of cloth, the slope of the production-possibility curve at point S_1 tells us that one extra yard could be made each year by giving up 1 bushel of wheat. When 40 billion yards

[4] With constant costs one of the two trading countries can fail to specialize completely only in the special case in which the international price ratio settles at the same price ratio prevailing in that country with no trade. In this case the country whose price ratio does not change is a "large" country and the other country is a "small" country. The large country continues to produce both goods with free trade because the small country cannot export enough to satisfy all demand for this product in the large country. Figure 3.1 assumes that the countries are of sufficiently similar "size" that both completely specialize in production.

FIGURE 3.2

Production
Possibilities
Under
Increasing
Costs

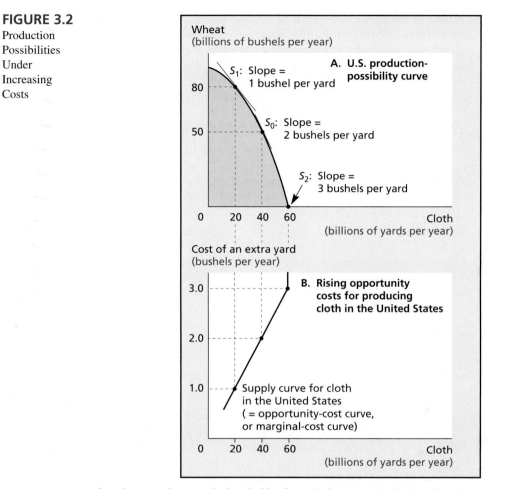

Increasing opportunity costs can be shown in either of two equivalent ways: as changing slopes along a bowed-out production-possibility curve or as an upward-sloping supply (or marginal-cost) curve.

Note: For the analysis of the production-possibility curve, we ignore the fact that the slopes of the tangent lines are negative.

are being made each year, getting the resources to make another yard a year means giving up 2 bushels of wheat, as shown by the steeper slope at point S_0. To push cloth production up to 60 billion yards per year requires giving up wheat in amounts that rise to 3 bushels for the last yard of cloth.

The increasing costs of extra cloth are also increasing costs of producing extra wheat. When one starts from a cloth-only economy at point S_2 and shifts increasing amounts of resources into growing wheat, the cost of an extra bushel rises (from 1/3 yard at S_2 to 1/2 yard at S_0, 1 yard at S_1, and so forth).

The increasing marginal costs reappear in a familiar form in the lower half of Figure 3.2. Here the vertical axis shows the marginal costs of extra cloth, which are the slopes in the upper half of the figure. The resulting curve is a supply curve for cloth (such as we used in Chapter 2). The set of competitive U.S. cloth producers would use the marginal costs of producing extra cloth to decide how much cloth to supply at each possible market price of cloth. The two ways of picturing increasing marginal costs in Figure 3.2 show the link between the two-product analysis of this chapter and the one-product focus of Chapter 2.

What's Behind the Bowed-Out Production-Possibility Curve?

What information do we need to derive the production-possibility curve of each country? Why are increasing-cost curves (bowed-out in shape) more realistic than the constant-cost (straight-line) ppc's?

A country's production-possibility curve is derived from information on both total factor (resource) supplies and the production functions that indicate how factor inputs can be used to produce outputs in various industries. In Appendix B we show how the production-possibility curves are derived under several common assumptions about production functions in individual industries.

We can sketch the explanation for the realism of increasing costs (and the bowed-out shape) even without a rigorous demonstration. The starting points are that

- There are several kinds of factor inputs (land, skilled labor, unskilled labor, capital, and so forth).

- Different products use factor inputs in different proportions.

To stay with our wheat-and-cloth example, wheat uses relatively more land and less labor than cloth, whether the yarn for the cloth comes from synthetic fibers or from natural fibers such as cotton or silk. This basic variation in input proportions can set up an increasing-cost (bowed-out) production-possibility curve even if constant returns to scale exist in each industry. When resources are released from cloth production and are shifted into wheat production, they will be released in proportions different from those initially prevailing in wheat production. The cloth industry will release a lot of labor and not much land. But wheat production generally requires a lot of land and not much labor. To employ these factors, the wheat industry must shift toward using more labor-intensive techniques. The effect is close to that of the law of diminishing returns (which, strictly speaking, refers to the case of adding more of one factor to fixed amounts of the others): Adding so much labor to slowly changing amounts of land causes the gains in wheat production to decline as more and more resources, mainly labor, are released from cloth production. Thus, fewer and fewer extra bushels of wheat production are gained by each extra yard of lost cloth production.

What Production Combination Is Actually Chosen?

Out of all the possible production points along the production-possibility curve, which one point does the nation select? That depends on the price ratio that competitive firms face. Suppose that the market price of cloth in terms of wheat is two bushels per yard. If you are a competitive firm vying with other firms around you, you will see one of these three conditions at any production point:

- If the opportunity cost of producing another yard of cloth is *less* than the 2 bushels per yard that you can sell it for, then try to make more cloth (and take resources away from wheat). Firms would react this way at a point like S_1 in Figure 3.2, where the opportunity cost is less (the slope of the ppc is flatter) than 2 bushels per yard.

- If the opportunity cost of producing another yard of cloth is *more* than the 2 bushels you can sell it for, then try to make less cloth (and shift resources into growing wheat). Firms would react this way at a point like S_2, where the opportunity cost is greater (the slope of the ppc is steeper) than 2 bushels per yard.

- If the opportunity cost of producing another yard of cloth is *equal* to the 2 bushels you can sell it for, then you are producing the right amount. There is no reason to shift any production between cloth and wheat. Firms would react this way at point S_0.

By choosing to produce at S_0 (40 billion yards of cloth and 50 billion bushels of wheat) when the price is 2 bushels per yard, firms end up maximizing the value of national production. The price is represented by a price line whose slope is 2 bushels per yard. The price line with this slope is tangent to the ppc at S_0.[5] The tangent point is important. For the price shown by the slope of the price line, you cannot increase the value of national production, measured in either yards or bushels, by moving to any other point on the production-possibility curve.[6]

What happens if the relative price of cloth declines to 1 bushel per yard? With a lower price of cloth, we expect that cloth production will decrease. The resources released as cloth production decreases are shifted into wheat production, and wheat output increases. After a period of transition, during which resources are shifted from the cloth industry to the wheat industry, the production point chosen by the country will shift to point S_1. The tangent line at S_1 has a slope of 1 bushel per yard and represents a new price line. The production combination chosen has less cloth (20) and more wheat (80).

---

[5] To make our descriptions less cluttered, we will consistently use positive values for the slopes of price lines (and similar lines like tangents to a ppc), even though the slopes are actually negative.

[6] This can be seen by extending the two-bushels-per-yard price line from point S_0 to touch either axis in Figure 3.2. The point where the extended line hits the horizontal axis is the value of the whole national production of wheat plus cloth, expressed as the amount of cloth that it could be traded for. Similarly, the point where the extended line hits the vertical axis is the value of the same national production, expressed in bushels of wheat. You can see that this value is greater when the nation produces at S_0 than when it produces at any other point on the ppc, as long as the price (and the slope of a price line through this other point) is 2 bushels per yard.

COMMUNITY INDIFFERENCE CURVES

The production-possibility curve pictures the production side of a country's economy. To complete the picture of the economy, we need a way to depict the determinants of demand for two products simultaneously.

For an individual, economists typically begin with the notion that each individual derives well-being (or happiness or utility) from consuming various goods and services. Figure 3.3 shows the usual way of relating an individual's well-being to amounts of two goods, again wheat and cloth, that the individual consumes. Instead of drawing the level of well-being in a third dimension rising out of the printed page, economists draw contours called indifference curves. An **indifference curve** shows the various combinations of consumption quantities (here wheat and cloth) that lead to the same level of well-being or happiness. For example, the indifference curve I_0 shows that the individual is *indifferent* between points A, B, and C, each of which gives the same level of well-being. That is, the individual would be equally happy consuming 80 bushels of wheat and 20 yards of cloth, *or* 40 of both, *or* 20 of wheat and 80 of cloth.

Any consumption point below and to the left of I_0 is worse than A or B or C in the eyes of this individual. Points above and to the right of I_0 are better. For example, point D, on the better indifference curve I_1, yields a higher level of happiness than A or B or C. Point E, on I_2, is even more preferred.

Each indifference curve is typically presumed to have a bowed shape as shown in the figure. The individual has an infinite number (a complete map) of indifference curves, representing infinitesimally small differences in well-being,

FIGURE 3.3

Indifference Curves Relating an Individual's Utility Levels to Consumption of Two Goods

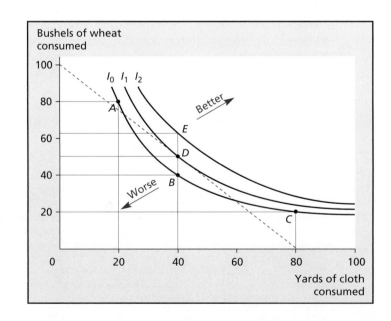

and showing the person's preferences regarding various combinations of the products. Our diagrams typically show only a small number of indifference curves from this complete map.

The actual consumption point chosen by the individual depends on the budget constraint facing the person—the income that the individual has available to spend on these products and the prices of the products. The budget constraint is $Y = P_W \cdot Q_W + P_C \cdot Q_C$, assuming that the individual spends all his income Y on the two products wheat (W) and cloth (C). For given income and prices, the equation is a straight line showing combinations of cloth and wheat that the individual is able to purchase with this income: $Q_W = (Y/P_W) - (P_C/P_W) \cdot Q_C$. The slope of this budget constraint is the (negative of the) price ratio P_C/P_W, the relative price of cloth, so we usually refer to this budget constraint as a price line.

Given the budget constraint or price line, the individual chooses consumption to be as well off as possible—to reach the highest feasible indifference curve. This is the indifference curve that is just tangent to the price line. In Figure 3.3, the dashed colored line shows the budget constraint for an individual who could purchase 100 bushels of wheat if he spent all of his income on wheat ($Y/P_W = 100$) and who faces the relative price of cloth equal to 1.25 in the markets ($P_C/P_W = 1.25$). Given this budget constraint, the individual should choose to consume 50 bushels of wheat and 40 yards of cloth (at point D). The consumer reaches the level of well-being shown by I_1.

When exploring trade issues, we want to portray how the entire nation, not just one individual, decides on consumption quantities and what this decision implies for the economic well-being of the nation as a whole. Can we portray a large group of people (like a country) as having a set of indifference curves? Although there are problems with this portrayal, a single set of indifference curves for a group of people is remarkably useful as a tool for our analysis. We will utilize **community indifference curves,** which purport to show how the economic well-being of a whole group depends on the whole group's consumption of products. In what follows, we look at sets of indifference curves like those in Figure 3.3 as if they were community indifference curves for thousands or millions of people. We will use community indifference curves, along with the price line representing the national budget (or income) constraint, as the basis for the choice of national quantities demanded and consumed of wheat and cloth.

Nonetheless, we must keep in mind that economic theory raises difficult questions about community indifference curves. First, the shapes of individual indifference curves differ from person to person. There is no completely clear way to "add up" individuals' indifference curves to obtain community indifference curves. Second, the concept of national well-being or welfare is not well defined. How can we say whether the community is better off with an average of 40 bushels less and 40 yards more? Some members of the community gain, while others lose. Who can say that the increase in satisfaction of the one is greater than the decrease in satisfaction of the other? Levels of satisfaction or well-being cannot be compared from one person to another.

These are real difficulties. We will use community indifference curves because they are convenient and neat. They are reasonable for depicting the basis for national demand patterns for two products simultaneously. Under certain assumptions they provide information on national well-being or welfare, but some caution is needed in using them in this way. Higher national well-being, as shown by a higher community indifference curve, does not mean that each person is actually better off.

PRODUCTION AND CONSUMPTION TOGETHER

Figure 3.4 summarizes information on the U.S. economy. The production capabilities of the United States are shown by the bowed-out (increasing-cost) production-possibility curve, and U.S. consumption preferences are shown by a map of community indifference curves, of which three are shown.

Without Trade

With no trade the United States must be self-sufficient and must find the combination of domestically produced wheat and cloth that will maximize community well-being. In this case, I_1 is the best (highest) indifference curve that the United States can achieve. To reach I_1, the United States must produce at S_0 on its production-possibility curve. At this tangent point, the United States produces and consumes 40 billion yards of cloth and 50 billion bushels of wheat. The relative price of cloth in the United States with no trade is 2 bushels/yard.

Point S_0 is the no-trade equilibrium for the United States. If, instead, the United States found itself at any other point on the U.S. production-possibility curve, consumers or producers would want to shift toward S_0. To see this, consider the example in which the economy begins at S_1, with a price ratio set by the slope of the ppc (a relative price of 1 bushel/yard). Consumers would find that this makes cloth look so cheap that they would rather buy more cloth than 20 billion yards and less wheat than 80 billion bushels. Producers will follow this change in demand and shift resources into cloth production and out of wheat. The tendency to alter production will persist until the economy produces and consumes, at S_0, the no-trade (or autarky) equilibrium.

With Trade

To show the effects of opening the world to international trade, we examine the economies of both countries. The left side of Figure 3.5A shows the U.S. economy (the same as in Figure 3.4). The right side shows the economy of the rest of the world. The no-trade equilibrium in each country is at point S_0. With no trade the U.S. relative price of cloth would be 2 bushels per yard, while the relative price in the rest of the world would be 0.67 bushel per yard.

As in previous examples, the difference in price ratios with no trade provides the immediate basis for trade. With free trade the United States imports cloth from the rest of the world and exports wheat to the rest of the world. This trade

FIGURE 3.4

Indifference
Curves and
Production
Possibilities
Without Trade

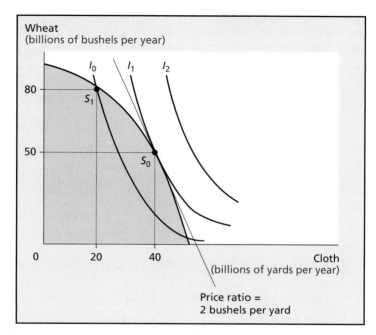

Without trade, the best an efficient economy can do is to move to the production point that touches the highest community indifference curve. This best no-trade point is S_0, where the nation both produces and consumes, reaching indifference curve I_1.

tends to decrease the relative price of cloth in the United States and increase the relative price of cloth in the rest of the world. With free trade (and assuming no transport costs), trade results in an equilibrium international price ratio in the range of 0.67 to 2 bushels per yard. The price ratio for this free-trade equilibrium is the price that results in the quantity of wheat exported by the United States being equal to the quantity of wheat imported by the rest of the world, and the quantity of cloth exported by the rest of the world being equal to the quantity of cloth imported by the United States.

For the conditions in each country shown by their production-possibility curves and community indifference curves, the free-trade equilibrium occurs at a price ratio of 1 bushel per yard. In the shift from no trade to free trade, producers in the United States respond to the lower relative price of cloth (and thus higher relative price of wheat) by reducing production of cloth and increasing production of wheat, shifting production from point S_0 to S_1. With production at S_1, the United States can trade wheat for cloth with the rest of the world at the price of 1 bushel per yard. Consumption can be at any point along the price line that is tangent to the ppc at point S_1 (a line indicating a price ratio of 1 bushel per yard). Along this price line, the United States will consume at point C_1, the tangent point with the highest achievable community indifference curve I_2.

In the rest of the world, the shift from no trade to free trade increases the relative price of cloth. Producers respond by increasing production of cloth and

FIGURE 3.5
Two Views of
Free Trade and
Its Effects

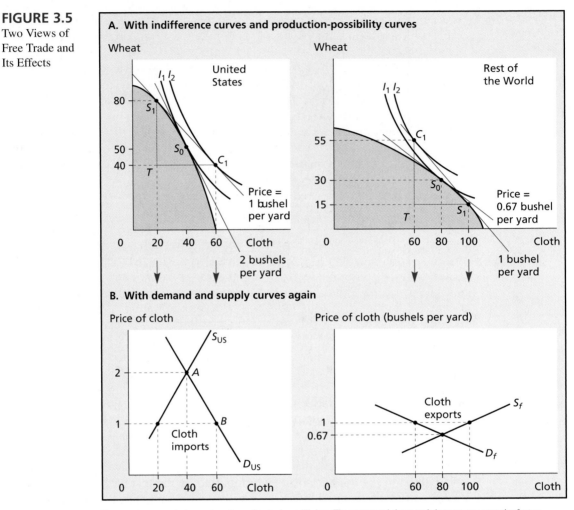

A. With indifference curves and production-possibility curves

Wheat — United States

Wheat — Rest of the World

B. With demand and supply curves again

Price of cloth

Price of cloth (bushels per yard)

There are two convenient ways to portray a free-trade equilibrium. The upper panel shows trade between two countries for two products, with each country producing at point S_1 and consuming at its point C_1. The lower panel shows the same thing using supply and demand curves that focus on one product (cloth), the approach discussed in Chapter 2.

decreasing production of wheat from point S_0 to S_1. The rest of the world can trade away from their production point at the international equilibrium price ratio. Consumption can be at any point along the price line tangent to the ppc at S_1. Given this price line, the rest of the world will consume at point C_1.

At the international price ratio of 1 bushel per yard, the United States is willing to export 40 billion bushels of wheat, the difference between the 80 produced domestically at point S_1 and the 40 consumed domestically at point C_1. The rest of the world wants to import 40 billion bushels of wheat, equal to the difference between the 55 consumed domestically and the 15 produced domestically. At this price ratio, the United States wants to import 40 billion yards of cloth (60 consumed minus 20 produced domestically). The rest of the world is willing to export 40 billion yards (100 produced minus 60 consumed domestically). Thus, the international trade markets for both products are in equilibrium, confirming that the price ratio of 1 bushel per yard is the international equilibrium price ratio.

The export–import quantities in each country can be summarized by the "trade triangles" that show these quantities. The trade triangle for the United States is shown by the right triangle S_1TC_1, and that for the rest of the world C_1TS_1. International equilibrium is achieved when these two trade triangles are the same size so that both sides agree on the amounts traded.

We will generally assume that there is only one free-trade equilibrium international price ratio for a given set of supply and demand conditions in each country. To see why a price ratio other than 1 bushel per yard generally will not be an international equilibrium, consider a price line flatter (making cloth even cheaper) than the price of 1 bushel per yard. The United States would respond to such a price by producing above and to the left of point S_1 and trading large volumes of wheat for cloth to consume out beyond C_1. The catch, however, is that the rest of the world would not want to trade so much at a price ratio that makes its cloth cheaper than 1 bushel per yard. This can be seen by finding the tangency of the new flat price line to the rest of the world's production-possibility and indifference curves on the right side of Figure 3.5A. The result of a price ratio making cloth cheaper than 1 bushel per yard is closer to S_0, the no-trade point. With the rest of the world willing to export only a small amount of cloth at such a price, the large demand for imported cloth by the United States would increase the relative price of cloth. The price would return to the equilibrium unitary price shown in Figure 3.5.

Demand and Supply Curves Again

The community indifference curves also can be combined with the production-possibility curves to plot out demand curves for cloth or wheat. A demand curve for cloth shows how the quantity of cloth demanded responds to its price. To derive the U.S. demand curve for cloth, start in Figure 3.5A with a price ratio and find how much cloth the United States would be willing and able to consume at that price. At 2 bushels per yard, the United States is willing and able to consume 40 billion yards a year (at S_0). At 1 bushel per yard, the United States would consume 60 billion yards (at C_1). These demand points could be replotted in Figure 3.5B, with the prices on the vertical axis. Point S_0 above becomes point A below; point C_1 above becomes point B below; and so forth. The same could be done for the rest of the world. (The demand-curve derivation is like that found in ordinary price-theory textbooks, except that the nation's income constraint slides along a production-possibility surface instead of rotating on a fixed-income point.) In this way the handy demand–supply framework can be derived from community indifference curves and production-possibility curves. The international equilibrium

Case Study   The Opening of Trade and China's Shift Out of Agriculture

The real world does in fact reveal the behavior portrayed in the diagrams and discussion of this chapter. Countries do react to the opening of trade in the ways predicted by diagrams like those in Figure 3.5.

A good example still in progress is China's response to becoming a major trading nation after the near-total isolation and self-sufficiency that Chairman Mao imposed between 1958 (at the start of the Great Leap Forward) and 1976 (the year of Mao's death and the end of the Great Proletarian Cultural Revolution). Though China covers a huge geographic area, it is not a land-abundant country. Rather, it is labor-abundant and land-scarce. True to the ancient Chinese saying "Many people, little land," the country has over 20 percent of the world's population but only about 8 percent of its farmable land. For such a labor-abundant country, this chapter's theories would predict the following responses to the chance to trade with the rest of the world:

- China should export labor-intensive products like clothing and import land-intensive products like wheat.

- China should shift resources out of producing land-intensive products like wheat and into producing labor-intensive products like clothing.

- China's production specialization should be incomplete. The country should go on producing some land-intensive products, though these should be a lower-share of production than before.

- China should be a more prosperous country with trade than without trade. The theory even allows for the possibility that China could consume more of all goods, including both wheat and clothing.

All these predictions have been coming true in China since 1976. The trade pattern is what we would expect: China has become a strong exporter of all sorts of manufactured products, including clothing, that take advantage of the country's abundant labor supply. China has also turned to imports for a rising share of its consumption of land-abundant products, including wheat.

All over China, people have noticed the shift of production out of agriculture and into export-oriented

focusing on a single product (the approach discussed in Chapter 2 and shown in Figure 3.5B) is therefore consistent with the general equilibrium approach using two products.[7]

THE GAINS FROM TRADE

There are two ways to use a figure like Figure 3.5A to show that each nation gains from international trade. First, trade allows each country to consume at a point (C_1) that lies beyond its own ability to produce (its production-possibility

[7] The theoretical literature on international trade often uses the indifference curves and production-possibility curve to derive an *offer curve*. An offer curve is a way of showing how a nation's offer of exports for imports from the rest of the world depends on the international price ratio. A nation's offer curve shows the same information as its export supply or import demand curve from Chapter 2. Appendix C discusses how an offer curve can be derived and used.

industry. For example, in the crowded countryside of Shandong province, villages that once struggled with poor soil to grow wheat and corn for cities like Tianjin or Beijing have abandoned farming and now make furniture and pharmaceuticals. Even the relatively fertile villages of Jiangsu province, near the mouth of the Yangtse River, make textiles, steel, and other industrial goods. Similarly, in the south, Guangdong province used to send its rice north to Beijing. Now Guangdong, a leader in China's rapid industrialization, consumes more rice than it produces, supplementing local crops with rice imports from Thailand.

Both public opinion and the available statistics agree that the great majority of China's population have gained purchasing power. Some Chinese do fear becoming dependent on imports of food. The fears seem to be greater in the government than in the population at large. The government in the 1990s decided to channel a larger share of taxpayers' money into promoting agricultural production, to retard the shift away from being self-sufficient in food. Yet many are less worried. Wu Xiedong, leader of one of those Jiangsu villages that switched from growing grain to making textiles and steel, is optimistic about the shift.

As he put it in 1995, "As long as the present policy that allows farmers to go into industry doesn't change, we will continue to grow very fast." As for relying on imported food, Wu says, "America has lots of grain, right? If America buys my steel, I'll buy America's grain. Then we can all get rich."* So far, so good. China's food consumption per capita has risen faster than China's food production per capita (which has also risen, thanks to reforms that have raised the country's productivity on all fronts).

China's experience mirrors what happened earlier to Japan, Korea, Taiwan, and Hong Kong. All of these labor-abundant and land-scarce areas reacted to the opening of trade by shifting into labor-intensive industry and out of land-intensive agriculture, and all of them prospered.

*Note the "if" part of this statement. If U.S. policy blocked imports of industrial products from China, using tools like those we discuss in Part II, the Chinese would also reduce imports from the United States. The gains from trade then would be reduced.

Source: Reprinted by permission of *The Wall Street Journal*, © 1995. Dow Jones & Company, Inc. All Rights Reserved Worldwide.

curve). This is a gain from trade as long as we view more consumption as desirable. It is the same demonstration of the gains from trade that we used for the Ricardian approach earlier in the chapter. Second, trade allows each country to achieve a higher community indifference curve (I_2 rather than I_1 with no trade). However, the use of community indifference curves to show national gains from trade may hide the fact that opening trade actually hurts some groups while bringing gains to others. We take up this issue of the distribution of gains and losses in the next chapter.

How much each country gains from trade depends on the international price ratio in the ongoing international trade equilibrium. As individuals we benefit from receiving high prices for the things that we sell (such as our labor services) and paying low prices for the things that we buy. A similar principle applies to countries.

A country gains more from trade if it receives a higher price for its exports relative to the price that it pays for its imports. For each country, the gains from trade depend on the country's international **terms of trade,** which are the price the country receives from foreign buyers for its export product(s), relative to the price that the country pays foreign sellers for its import product(s).

In our example, the rest of the world exports cloth and imports wheat, so the terms of trade for the rest of the world are the relative price of cloth. In Figure 3.5A we can show that the rest of the world would gain more from trade if its terms of trade were better—if the international relative price of cloth were higher. Then the international price line would be steeper than the line through S_1 and C_1, and the rest of the world could reach a community indifference curve higher than I_2. For the United States, its terms of trade are the relative price of wheat, its export good. The United States would gain more from trade if the relative price of wheat were higher, resulting in a flatter international price line than the line through S_1 and C_1. Then the United States could reach a community indifference curve higher than I_2.

TRADE AFFECTS PRODUCTION AND CONSUMPTION

Figure 3.5A shows that there are substantial effects on production quantities when trade is opened. The opening has two types of implications for production. First, *within each country* output expands for the product in which the country has a comparative advantage—more wheat in the United States and more cloth in the rest of the world. In each country, the growing industry expands by acquiring factor resources from the other industry in the economy. The import-competing industry reduces its domestic production—cloth in the United States and wheat in the rest of the world. Although production shifts in each country, the countries do not (necessarily) specialize completely in producing their export product if the production-possibility curve is bowed-out because of increasing costs.

Second, the shift from no trade to free trade results in more efficient *world* production as each country expands output of the product in which it is initially the lower-cost producer. In the particular case shown in Figure 3.5A, the efficiency gains show up as an increase in world production of wheat (from 50 + 30 = 80 with no trade to 80 + 15 = 95 with trade), while world cloth production is unchanged at 120.

In each country, opening to trade also alters the quantities consumed of each product, as the consumption point shifts from S_0 with no trade to C_1 with free trade. Consumer theory indicates that the quantity consumed of the importable product in each country will increase. The relative price of the importable product declines in each country so consumers in the country buy more of it (a positive substitution effect). Meanwhile, real income rises in each country (as a result of the gains from trade) so consumers buy even more (a positive income effect). The quantity consumed of the exportable product in each country could increase, stay the same, or decrease because of opposing pressures from a negative substitution effect (resulting from the higher relative price of the exportable good) and a positive income effect (as real income rises). In the particular case shown in Figure 3.5A, the quantities consumed of the exportable product actually decrease (50 to 40 for wheat in the United States and 80 to 60 for cloth in the rest of world), but other outcomes for these two consumption quantities are possible.

WHAT DETERMINES THE TRADE PATTERN?

Our general view of national economies engaged in international trade is shown in Figure 3.5A. The immediate basis for the pattern of international trade that we see here is that relative product prices would differ between the two countries if there was no trade. But why would product prices differ with no trade? They can differ because

- Production conditions differ—the relative shapes of the production-possibility curves differ between the countries.

- Consumption conditions differ—the relative shapes and positions of the community indifference curves differ between the countries.

- Some combination of these two differences.

In our example the basis for the United States to import cloth could be that the United States has a high demand for cloth, perhaps due to a harsh climate or fashion consciousness. Although this kind of explanation may apply to a few products, most analysis focuses on production-side differences as the basis for no-trade price differences, assuming that demand patterns are similar for the countries.

Production-side differences can be a basis for the international trade pattern when the relative shapes of the production-possibility curves differ. For instance, in Figure 3.5A, the ppc for the United States is skewed toward production of wheat, and the ppc for the rest of the world is skewed toward production of cloth. Why do we see these production-side differences? There are two basic reasons.

First, the production technologies or resource productivities may differ between countries. For instance, the United States may have superior technology to produce wheat and somehow keep its secret from the rest of the world. The better technology results in relatively high resource productivity in U.S. wheat production. This will skew the U.S. production-possibility curve toward producing larger amounts of wheat, resulting in a comparative advantage for the United States to produce and export wheat. This type of comparative advantage was the basis for trade in the Ricardian approach.

Although technology or productivity differences can be a production-side basis for comparative advantage, for the remainder of this chapter and in Chapter 4 we assume that they are not. Instead, we assume that both countries have access to the same technologies for production and are capable of achieving similar levels of resource productivity. This assumption is plausible if technology spreads internationally because it is difficult for a country to keep its technology secret. (Issues related to technology will be taken up in Chapters 5 and 6.)

The second reason that the relative shapes of the production-possibility curves can differ is more subtle but has become the basis for the orthodox modern theory of comparative advantage. It is the Heckscher–Ohlin theory based on (1) differences across countries in the availability of factor resources and (2) differences across products in the use of these factors in producing the products.

THE HECKSCHER–OHLIN (H–O) THEORY: FACTOR PROPORTIONS ARE KEY

The leading theory of what determines nations' trade patterns emerged in Sweden. Eli Heckscher, the noted Swedish economic historian, developed the core idea in a brief article in 1919. A clear overall explanation was developed and publicized in the 1930s by Heckscher's student Bertil Ohlin. Ohlin, like Keynes, managed to combine a distinguished academic career—professor at Stockholm and later a Nobel laureate—with political office (Riksdag member, party leader, and government official during World War II). Ohlin's persuasive narrative of the theory and the evidence that seemed to support it were later reinforced by another Nobel laureate, Paul Samuelson, who derived mathematical conditions under which the Heckscher–Ohlin (H–O) prediction was strictly correct.[8]

The Heckscher–Ohlin theory of trade patterns says, in Ohlin's own words,

> Commodities requiring for their production much of [abundant factors of production] and little of [scarce factors] are exported in exchange for goods that call for factors in the opposite proportions. Thus indirectly, factors in abundant supply are exported and factors in scanty supply are imported. (Ohlin, 1933, p. 92)

Or, more succinctly, the **Heckscher–Ohlin theory** predicts that a country exports the product(s) that use its abundant factor(s) intensively and imports the product(s) using its scarce factor(s) intensively.

To judge this plausible and testable argument more easily, we need definitions of factor abundance and factor-use intensity. Consider labor:

- A country is relatively **labor-abundant** if it has a higher ratio of labor to other factors than does the rest of the world.

- A product is relatively **labor-intensive** if labor costs are a greater share of its value than they are of the value of other products.

The H–O explanation of trade patterns begins with a specific hunch as to why product prices might differ between countries before they open trade. Heckscher and Ohlin predicted that the key to comparative costs lies in factor proportions used in production. If cloth costs 2 bushels a yard in the United States and less than a bushel a yard elsewhere, it must be primarily because the United States

---

[8] Ohlin backed the H–O theory with real-world observation and appeals to intuition. Samuelson took the mathematical road, adding assumptions that allowed a strict proof of the theory's main prediction. Samuelson assumed (1) that there are two countries, two goods, and two factors (the frequent "$2 \times 2 \times 2$" simplification); (2) that factor supplies are fixed for each country, fully employed, and mobile between sectors within each country, but immobile between countries; (3) that the consumption patterns of the two countries are identical; and (4) that both countries share the same constant-returns-to-scale production technologies. The H–O predictions follow logically in Samuelson's narrow case and seem broadly accurate in the real world. Our analysis in the text is based on Samuelson's depiction of the theory.

has relatively less of the factors that cloth uses intensively, and relatively more of the factors that wheat uses intensively, than does the rest of the world.

Let *land* be the factor that wheat uses more intensively and *labor* be the factor that cloth uses more intensively. Let all costs be decomposable into land and labor costs (e.g., it takes certain amounts of land and labor to make fertilizer for growing wheat and certain other amounts of land and labor to make cotton inputs for cloth making). Therefore, the H–O theory predicts that the United States exports wheat and imports cloth because wheat is land-intensive and cloth is labor-intensive and

$$\frac{\text{(U.S. land supply)}}{\text{(U.S. labor supply)}} > \frac{\text{(Rest of world's land supply)}}{\text{(Rest of world's labor supply)}}$$

Under these conditions[9] with no international trade, land should rent more cheaply in the United States than elsewhere, and labor should command a higher wage rate in the United States than elsewhere. The cheapness of land cuts costs more in wheat farming than in cloth making. Conversely, the scarcity of labor should make cloth relatively expensive in the United States. This, according to H–O, is why product prices differ in the direction they do before trade begins. And, the theory predicts, it is the difference in relative factor endowments and the pattern of factor intensities that make the United States export wheat instead of cloth (and import cloth instead of wheat) when trade opens up.

Summary   International trade occurs because product prices would differ if there was no trade. This chapter focuses on theories emphasizing production-side differences between countries as the reason for product prices to differ without trade. Three variants emphasizing the supply side are Adam Smith's theory of **absolute advantage,** David Ricardo's **principle of comparative advantage,** and the **Heckscher–Ohlin (H–O) theory** stressing factor proportions.

The principle of comparative advantage is based on the importance of **opportunity cost**—the amount of other products that must be foregone to produce more of a particular product. The principle states that a country will export products that it can produce at low opportunity cost in return for imports of products that it would otherwise produce at high opportunity cost. Ricardo focused on differences in **labor productivities.** He showed that beneficial trade occurs even if a country is worse (less productive) at producing everything (relative to the rest of the world).

---

[9] Take care not to misread the relative factor endowment inequality. It does not say the United States has absolutely more land than the rest of the world. Nor does it say that the United States has less labor. In fact, the United States really has less of both. Nor does it say the United States has more land than it has labor—a meaningless statement in any case. (How many acres or hectares are "more than" how many hours of labor?)

Rather it is an inequality between *relative* endowments. Here are two correct ways of stating it: (1) There is more land per laborer in the United States than in the rest of the world and (2) the U.S. share of the world's land is greater than its share of the world's labor.

Ricardo's approach assumed constant marginal costs. Dropping his constant-cost assumption to allow for **increasing marginal costs** makes it easier to explain why countries do not specialize completely in producing only one product.

International differences in the shapes of the bowed-out (increasing cost) **production-possibility curves (ppc's)** can occur because (1) different products use the factors of production in different proportions and (2) countries differ in their relative factor endowments. Hecksher and Ohlin used these ideas to build a modern theory of comparative advantage. The H–O theory of trade patterns predicts that nations export products that use their relatively abundant factors more intensively in exchange for imports of goods that use their scarce factors more intensively.

All three of these approaches conclude that trade is not a zero-sum game in which one country gains only what the other country loses. The whole world gains from trade, and each country is at least as well off with free trade as with no trade. The gains from trade for each country can be demonstrated in two ways. First, trade allows the country to consume beyond its own ability to produce—it allows consumption outside of its production-possibility curve. Second, trade allows the country to reach a higher **community indifference curve,** indicating that the country reaches a higher level of national economic well-being or welfare.

Suggested Reading

Irwin (1996) provides a good survey of thoughts about the advantages and disadvantages of free trade, starting with the ancient Greeks and continuing through mercantilists, Smith, Ricardo, and recent economic analysis. The technical literature on free trade is vast and cannot be cited at length here. For advanced technical surveys, see Chapters 1–3, 7, and 8 of Jones and Kenen, Vol. I (1984).

Roy Ruffin (1988) has improved the Ricardian model of comparative advantage so that it generates the predictions of the Heckscher–Ohlin model. He does so by interpreting productivity differences in the one-factor Ricardian approach as differences in relative factor endowments.

Questions and Problems

✦ 1. "According to Ricardo's analysis, a country exports any good whose production requires fewer labor hours per unit than the labor hours per unit needed to produce the good in the foreign country. That is, the country exports any good in which its labor productivity is higher than the labor productivity for this good in the foreign country." Do you agree or disagree? Why?

2. "For my country, imports are the good thing about international trade, whereas exports are more like the necessary evil." Do you agree or disagree? Why?

✦ 3. The country of Pugelovia has an endowment (total supply) of 20 units of labor and 3 units of land, whereas the rest of the world has 80 units of labor and 7 units of land. Is Pugelovia labor-abundant? Is Pugelovia land-abundant? If wheat is land-intensive and cloth is labor-intensive, what is the Heckscher–Ohlin prediction for the pattern of trade between Pugelovia and the rest of the world?

4. Explain how a supply curve can be obtained or derived from an increasing-cost production-possibility curve. Use Figure 3.4 to derive the supply curve for cloth. For a bit more challenge, use Figure 3.4 to derive the supply curve for wheat.

✦ 5. In your answer to this question, use a diagram like Figure 3.4, making it large enough so that you can see the curves and quantities clearly. The no-trade point is as shown in Figure 3.4, a price ratio of 2 (bushels per yard) and 40 units of cloth demanded. Sketch the derivation of the portion of the country's cloth demand curve for cloth prices of 2 and below. (To do this, examine a price of about 1.5, then 1.0, and then 0.5. In your analysis you will need to show additional community indifference curves—ones that exist but are not shown explicitly in Figure 3.4.)

6. Return to your answer for question 5. For prices below 2, which good does the country export? Which good does it import? How does the quantity (demanded or needed) of imports change as the price changes? What is happening to the country's terms of trade as the price declines? What is happening to the country's well-being or welfare as the price declines?

✦ 7. You are given the information shown in the table about production relationships in Lindertania and the rest of the world.

	Inputs per Bushel of Rice Output	Inputs per Yard of Cloth Output
Lindertania	75	100
Rest of the world	50	50

You make several Ricardian assumptions: These are the only two commodities, there are constant ratios of input to output whatever the level of output of rice and cloth, and competition prevails in all markets.

a. Does Lindertania have an absolute advantage in producing rice? Cloth?

b. Does Lindertania have a comparative advantage in producing rice? Cloth?

c. If no international trade is allowed, what price ratio would prevail between rice and cloth within Lindertania?

d. If free international trade is opened up, what are the limits for the equilibrium international price ratio? What product will Lindertania export? Import?

8. Consider another Ricardian example, using standard Ricardian assumptions:

	Labor Hours per Bottle of Wine	Labor Hours per Kilogram of Cheese
Vintland	15	10
Moonited Republic	10	4

Vintland has 30 million hours of labor in total per year. Moonited Republic has 20 million hours of labor per year.

a. Which country has an absolute advantage in wine? In cheese?

b. Which country has a comparative advantage in wine? In cheese?

c. Graph each country's production-possibility curve. Using community indifference curves, show the no-trade equilibrium for each country (assuming that with no trade, Vintland consumes 1.5 million kilos of cheese and Moonited Republic consumes 3 million kilos of cheese).

d. When trade is opened, which country exports which good? If the equilibrium international price ratio is ½ bottle of wine per kilo of cheese, what happens to production in each country?

e. In this free-trade equilibrium, 2 million kilos of cheese and 1 million bottles of wine are traded. What is the consumption point in each country with free trade? Show this graphically using community indifference curves.

f. Does each country gain from trade? Explain, referring to your graphs as is appropriate.

◆ 9. The real wage is the purchasing power of 1 hour of labor. That is, for each product it is the number of units of the product that a worker can buy with his earnings from 1 hour of work. In a Ricardian model, for any product actually produced by the worker, the worker is simply paid according to her productivity (units of output per hour). This is then her real wage in terms of this product. In your answer to this question, use the numerical example from the section on Ricardo's theory of comparative advantage.

a. With no trade, what is the real wage of labor with respect to each good in the United States? In the rest of the world? Which country's labor has the higher "average" real wage?

b. With free trade and an equilibrium price ratio of 1 bushel per yard, each country completely specializes. What is the real wage with respect to wheat in the United States? By using international trade to obtain cloth, what is the new value of the real wage with respect to cloth in the United States? What does this tell us about gains from trade for the United States? What is the real wage with respect to cloth in the rest of the world? By using international trade to obtain wheat, what is the new value of the real wage with respect to wheat in the rest of the world? What does this tell us about the gains from trade for the rest of the world?

c. With free trade, which country's labor has the higher "average" real wage? In what sense does absolute advantage matter?

10. In your answer to this question, use the numerical example from the section on Ricardo's theory of comparative advantage. What is the effect on the pattern of trade predicted by the Ricardian analysis if the number of labor hours required to make a unit of wheat in the United States is reduced by half (that is, if its productivity doubles)? Now return to the initial numbers. What is the

effect on the pattern of trade if instead the number of hours required to make a unit of cloth in the United States is reduced by half (productivity doubles)?

◆ 11. Extending what you know about production-possibility curves, try to draw the production-possibility curve (ppc) for a nation consisting of four individuals who work separately. The four individuals have these different abilities:

Person A   can make 1 unit of cloth or 2 units of wheat or any combination in between (e.g., can make 0.5 cloth and 1 wheat by spending half time on each).

Person B   can make 2 cloth or 1 wheat or any combination in between.

Person C   can make 1 cloth or 1 wheat or any combination in between.

Person D   can make 2 cloth or 3 wheat or any combination in between.

What is the best they can all produce? That is, draw the ppc for the four of them. Try it in these stages:

a. What is the most wheat they could grow if they spent all of their time growing wheat only? Plot that point on a cloth–wheat graph.

b. What is the most cloth they could make? Plot that point.

c. Now here's the tricky part. Find the best combinations they could produce when producing some of both, where *best* means they could make that combination but could not make more of one good without giving up some of the other.

12. In your answer to this question, use a diagram like Figure 3.4 and start from a no-trade point like S_0 with a no-trade price ratio of 2 bushels per yard. Now trade is opened and the country can trade whatever it wants at an international price ratio of 1 bushel per yard. (In your answers, you will need to picture additional community indifference curves that exist but are not shown explicitly in Figure 3.4.)

a. Show that the country can gain from trade even if the country does not change its production point. (Production stays at point S_0.) (*Hint:* The price line with slope of 1 will go through point S_0 but will not be tangent to the production-possibility curve.)

b. Show that the country can gain even more from trade if it also adjusts the production point to its optimal position (given the price ratio of 1).

c. What happens to the volume of trade as the country's position shifts from that shown in part *a* to that shown in part *b*?

Chapter **Four**

Who Gains and Who Loses from Trade?

If countries gain from opening trade, why do free-trade policies have so many opponents year in and year out? The answer does not lie mainly in public ignorance about the effects of trade. Trade *does* typically hurt some groups within any country. Many opponents of freer trade probably perceive this point correctly. A full analysis of trade requires that we identify the winners and losers from freer trade. Chapter 2 provided one look at these groups by focusing on producers and consumers of a product. But this distinction is not completely valid. People who are consumers also own and provide factor resources that are used in production. Is there another useful way to examine the winners and losers?

A virtue of the Heckscher–Ohlin (H–O) theory of trade patterns is that it offers realistic predictions of how trade affects the income of groups representing different factors of production (e.g., landlords, workers). In each country international trade divides society into gainers from trade and losers from trade because changes in relative product prices are likely to raise the rewards to some factors and lower the rewards to others. A key purpose of this chapter is to show the implications of the Heckscher–Ohlin theory for the income received by the different factors of production.

The Heckscher–Ohlin theory claims to provide powerful insights into the basis for trade and the effects of trade, including the gains and losses for different production factors. How well does it actually fit the world's trade? A second key purpose of the chapter is to examine the empirical evidence on Heckscher–Ohlin. Does Heckscher–Ohlin explain actual trade patterns? Does it identity the factors that gain and lose from trade?

WHO GAINS AND WHO LOSES WITHIN A COUNTRY

According to the Heckscher–Ohlin approach, trade arises from differences in the availability of factor inputs in different countries and differences in the proportions in which these factors are used in producing different products. Opening to trade alters domestic production (for instance, from S_0 to S_1 in Figure 3.5A in the previous chapter). There is expansion in the export-oriented sector (the one using the country's abundant factor intensively in production). There is contraction in the import-competing sector (the one using the country's scarce factor intensively). The changes in production have one set of effects on incomes in the short run, but another in the long run.

Short-Run Effects of Opening Trade

In the **short run** laborers, plots of land, and other inputs are tied to their current lines of production. The demand for these factors, and therefore the incomes or returns they earn, depend on the sector in which they are employed. Some people will enjoy higher demand for the factors they have to offer, because their factors are employed in the sector that is attempting to expand its production. With the opening to free trade, the expanding industries in our example are wheat in the United States and cloth in the rest of the world. In the United States landlords in wheat-growing areas can charge higher rents because their land is in strong demand. U.S. farmworkers in wheat-growing areas are likely to get (temporarily) higher wages. Foreign clothworkers can also demand and get higher wage rates. Foreign landlords in the areas raising cotton and wool for clothmaking can also get higher rents.

Meanwhile, the sellers of factors to the declining industries—U.S. clothworkers, U.S. landlords in areas supplying the cloth-making industry, foreign wheat-area landlords and farmhands—lose income through reduced demand and therefore reduced prices for their services.

For the short run, then, gains and losses divide by output sector: All groups tied to rising sectors gain, and all groups tied to declining sectors lose. One would expect employers, landlords, and workers in the declining sectors to unite in protest.

The Long-Run Factor-Price Response

In the **long run,** factors can move between sectors in response to differences in returns. Sellers of the same factor will eventually respond to the income gaps that have been opened up in the short run. Some U.S. clothworkers will find better-paying jobs in the wheat sector. As the supply of labor into the wheat sector increases, wages in the wheat sector decline. As the remaining supply of labor to the cloth sector shrinks, wages in the cloth sector increase. Some U.S. cotton- and wool-raising land will also get better rents by converting to wheat-related production, bringing rents in different areas back in line. Similarly, foreign farmhands and landlords will find the pay better in the cloth-related sector. As the supplies of the factors to the two sectors changes in the long run, wages and rents in the cloth sector decrease, and wages and rents in the wheat sector increase. The full process of the effects of opening trade on factor prices in the long run is summarized in Figure 4.1.

When the factors respond by moving to the better-paying sectors, will all wages and rents be bid back to their pretrade levels? No, they will not. In the long

FIGURE 4.1

How Free Trade Affects Income Distribution in the Long Run: The Whole Chain of Infuence

	In the United States	In the Rest of the World
Initial prices:	Wheat cheap, cloth expensive	Wheat expensive, cloth cheap
	Trade opens: — wheat → ← cloth —	
Prices respond to trade.	P_{wheat} up, P_{cloth} down	P_{wheat} down, P_{cloth} up
Production responds to prices.*	Produce more wheat. Produce less cloth.	Produce less wheat. Produce more cloth.
Crucial step— National factor markets change.	For each yard of cloth sacrificed, many workers and few acres laid off; extra wheat demands few workers and much land.	For each bushel of wheat sacrificed, much land and few workers laid off; extra cloth demands many workers and little land.
National factor prices respond.	Wage rates fall and rents rise (in both sectors).	Wage rates rise and rents fall (in both sectors).
Long-run results:	Product prices equalized between countries. Net gains for both countries but different effects on different groups. Winners: U.S. landowners, foreign workers. Losers: U.S. workers, foreign landowners.	

*At this point, the short-run effects come into play, but the economy continues to move toward the longer-run effects shown in the rest of this figure.

run, wage rates end up lower for *all* U.S. workers and higher for *all* foreign workers. All land rents end up higher in the United States and lower in the rest of the world (each relative to its level with no trade).

What drives this crucial result is the imbalance in the changes in factor supply and demand. Wheat growing is more land-intensive and less labor-intensive than cloth making. Therefore, the amounts of each factor being hired in the expanding sector will fail to match the amounts being released in the other sector. The imbalances create pressures for factor prices to adjust.

In the United States, for example, expanding wheat production creates demand for a lot of land and very few workers, whereas cutting cloth production releases a lot of workers and not so much land.[1] Something has to give. The only

[1] This passage uses convenient shorthand that is quantitatively vague: "a lot of" land, "very few" workers, and so on. These should give the right impressions with a minimum of verbiage. For more precision about the implied inequalities, see the numerical example in the box "A Factor-Ratio Paradox."

FIGURE 4.2
Winners and
Losers: Short
Run Versus
Long Run

Effects of Free Trade in the Short Run

(After product prices change and production attempts to respond, but before factors move between sectors)

	In the United States		In the Rest of the World	
	On Landowners	**On Laborers**	**On Landowners**	**On Laborers**
In wheat	Gain	Gain	Lose	Lose
In cloth	Lose	Lose	Gain	Gain

Effects of Free Trade in the Long Run

(After factors move between sectors in response to changes in factor demands, as shown in Figure 4.1)

	In the United States		In the Rest of the World	
	On Landowners	**On Laborers**	**On Landowners**	**On Laborers**
In wheat	Gain	Lose	Lose	Gain
In cloth	Gain	Lose	Lose	Gain

Reminder: The gains and losses to the different groups do not cancel out leaving zero net gain. In the long run, both countries get net gains. In the short run, net national gains or losses depend partly on the severity of any temporary unemployment of displaced factors.

way the employment of labor and land can adjust to the available national supplies is for factor prices to change. The production shift toward land-intensive, labor-sparing wheat raises rents and cut wages *throughout* the United States in the long run. The rise in rents and the fall in wages both continue until producers come up with more land-saving and labor-using ways of making wheat and cloth. Once they do, rents and wages stabilize—but U.S. rents still end up higher and wages lower than before trade opened up. The same kind of reasoning makes the opposite results hold for the rest of the world.

Trade, then, makes some people absolutely better off and others absolutely worse off in each of the trading countries. The gainers and losers in the short run are somewhat different from those in the long run, because more adjustment can occur in the long run. Figure 4.2 summarizes the discussion of winners and losers in the short and long runs.

THREE IMPLICATIONS OF THE H–O THEORY

The Heckscher–Ohlin model has three major implications for factor incomes. These implications follow from the sort of analysis done in the previous section.

Extension   A Factor-Ratio Paradox

The effects of trade on factor use have their paradoxical side. By assumption, the same fixed amounts of factor supplies get reemployed in the long run. But everything else about factor use changes. To deepen understanding of several subtleties that help explain how trade makes gainers and losers, this box poses a paradox:

> In one country, trade makes the land/labor ratio fall in both industries—but this ratio stays the same for the country as a whole. In the rest of the world, the same kind of paradox holds in the other direction: Trade makes the land/labor ratio rise in both industries—but this ratio again stays the same overall.

How, in the United States, could something that falls in both industries stay the same for the two industries together? How, in the rest of the world, could it rise in both yet stay the same for the two together?

The explanation hinges on a tug-of-war that is only hinted at in the main text of this chapter. Here is what the tug-of-war looks like for the United States in our ongoing example. Trade shifts both land and labor toward the land-intensive wheat sector, yet rising rents and falling wages induce both sectors to come up with more labor-intensive ways of producing. The two effects just offset each other and remain consistent with the same fixed total factor supplies.

Let's look at a set of numbers illustrating how our wheat–cloth trade might plausibly change factor-use ratios in the United States and the rest of the world:

| Sector | United States Before (with No Trade) | | | | Rest of the World Before (with No Trade) | | | |
	Output	Land Use	Labor Use	Land/Labor Ratio	Output	Land Use	Labor Use	Land/Labor Ratio
Wheat	50	35	35	1.000	30	16	32	0.500
Cloth	40	18	65	0.277	80	18	160	0.113
Whole economy		53	100	0.530		34	192	0.177

| Sector | After (with Free Trade) | | | | After (with Free Trade) | | | |
	Output	Land Use	Labor Use	Land/Labor Ratio	Output	Land Use	Labor Use	Land/Labor Ratio
Wheat	80	48	64	0.750 (down)	15	9	12	0.750 (up)
Cloth	20	5	36	0.139 (down)	100	25	180	0.139 (up)
Whole economy		53	100	0.530 (same)		34	192	0.177 (same)

Here we have both the factor-ratio paradox and its explanation. In the United States the change in factor prices has induced both wheat producers and cloth producers to come up with production methods having lower land/labor ratios (more labor-intensive techniques). Yet the same fixed factor supplies are employed.

One can see that the key is the shift of U.S. output toward land-intensive wheat. If it had been the only change, the national land/labor ratio would have risen. This is what induced the rise in rents and the fall in wages. The increase in the cost of land and the decrease in the cost of labor in turn induce firms to shift to more labor-intensive (less land-intensive) production techniques in both industries. (The same points apply in mirror image for the rest of the world.)

The Stolper–Samuelson Theorem

The conclusion that opening to trade splits a country into specific gainers and losers in the long run is an application of a general relationship called the **Stolper–Samuelson theorem.**[2] This theorem states that, given certain conditions and assumptions, including full adjustment to a new long-run equilibrium, an event that changes product prices in a country unambiguously has two effects:

- It raises the real return to the factor used intensively in the rising-price industry.

- It lowers the real return to the factor used intensively in the falling price industry.

A shift from no trade to free trade is an event that changes product prices. For instance, in our example, the opening of trade increases the relative price of wheat in the United States. The Stolper–Samuelson theorem then predicts a rise in the real income of the owners of land (the factor used intensively in producing wheat) and a decline in the real income of the providers of labor (the factor used intensively in producing cloth). In the rest of the world, the real income of labor increases and the real income of landowners decreases.

Stolper and Samuelson showed that this result does not depend at all on how much of each product is consumed by the households of landowners and laborers. The result clashed with an intuition many economists had shared. It seemed, for instance, that if U.S. laborers spent a very large share of their incomes on cloth, they might possibly gain from free trade by having cheaper cloth. Not so, according to the theorem. Opening trade must enable one of the two factors to buy more of either good. It will make the other factor poorer in its ability to buy either good.

Let's use an example to see why. Under competition, the price of each product must equal its marginal cost. In our wheat–cloth economy, price must equal the marginal land and labor costs in each sector:

$$P_{\text{wheat}} = \text{Marginal cost of wheat} = ar + bw$$

and

$$P_{\text{cloth}} = \text{Marginal cost of cloth} = cr + dw$$

where the product prices are measured in the same units (e.g., units of a commodity, or dollars), r is the rental rate earned on land, and w is the wage rate paid to labor. The coefficients a, b, c, and d are physical input/output ratios. These indicate how much land (a and c) or labor (b and d) is required to produce 1 unit

---

[2] Four important conditions and assumptions are needed for the Stolper–Samuelson theorem: (1) The country produces positive amounts of two goods (e.g., wheat and cloth) with two factors of production (e.g., land and labor) used in producing each good. One good (wheat) is relatively land-intensive; the other (cloth) is relatively labor-intensive. (2) Factors are mobile between sectors and fully employed overall in the economy. In addition, it is often assumed that total factor supplies (factor endowment sizes) are fixed, though this can be relaxed somewhat. (3) Competition prevails in all markets. (4) Production technology involves constant returns to scale (e.g., if all factors used in producing a product double, then output of the product doubles).

of each good. The easiest case to consider is one where these input/output coefficients are constant.

Suppose that the price of wheat rises 10 percent and the price of cloth stays the same. The higher price of wheat (and the resulting expansion of wheat production) will bid up the return to at least one factor. In fact, it is likely to raise the rental rate for land, since growing wheat uses land intensively. So r rises. Now look at the equation for the cloth sector. If r rises and the price of cloth stays the same, then the wage rate w must fall absolutely. The contraction of cloth production drives down the wage rate. Next take the fall of w back to the equation for the wheat sector. If w is falling and P_{wheat} is rising 10 percent, then r must be rising *more* than 10 percent to keep the equation valid. So if wheat is the land-intensive sector,

$$P_{wheat} \uparrow \text{ by 10\% and } P_{cloth} \text{ steady means } r \uparrow \text{ more than 10\% and } w \downarrow.$$

Thus a shift in relative product prices brings an even more magnified response in factor prices. The factor used intensively in production in the rising-price sector has its market reward (e.g., r in our example) rise even faster than the product price rises. Therefore, its real return (its purchasing power with respect to either product) rises. A factor used intensively in the other sector has its real purchasing power cut. In our example, the lower wage rate means workers lose purchasing power with respect to both the higher-priced wheat and the stable-priced cloth. The real wage rate decreases.

The same principle emerges no matter how we change the example (e.g., even if we let the price of wheat stay the same and increase the price of cloth instead, so that the real wage rate rises and the real rental rate declines, or even if we let producers change the input/output coefficients a, b, c, and d in response to changes in r and w).[3] The principle really just follows from the fact that price must equal marginal cost under competition, both before and after trade (or some other event) has changed the price ratio between wheat and cloth.

The Specialized-Factor Pattern

The Stolper–Samuelson theorem uses only two factors and two products. Its results are part of a broader pattern, one that tends to hold for any number of factors and products.

• The more a factor is specialized, or concentrated, in the production of a product whose relative price is rising, the more this factor stands to gain from the change in the product price.

---

[3] For a numerical example, let both prices start at 100, let r and w both start at 1, and let $a = 40$, $b = 60$, $c = 25$, and $d = 75$. Let the price of wheat rise by 10 percent to 110. Your task is to deduce what values of r and w could satisfy the new wheat equation $110 = 40 r + 60 w$, while still satisfying the cloth equation $100 = 25 r + 75 w$. You should get that r rises to 1.5 and w falls to 5/6.

The text says that the result still holds even if a, b, c, and d change. To be more precise, the result still holds if a or c falls when r rises, or if b or d falls when w rises. These are the economically plausible directions of response, so the result holds in all plausible cases.

- The more a factor is concentrated into the production of a product whose relative price is falling, the more it stands to lose from the change in product price.

This pattern should seem plausible. You may wonder whether it is meant as a pattern for the short run, when factors are immobile, or for the long run. The answer is both. Consider the issue of opening to free trade. The longer a factor continues to be associated with producing exportables, the greater its stake in freer trade. The longer it is associated with production threatened by imports, the more it gains from limits on trade. In the extreme case, a factor that can be used only in one sector has a lifelong or permanent stake in the price of that sector's product. A good example of such an immobile factor is farmland, which is hard to convert to other uses. There is little difference between the short run and the long run when it comes to farmland. If the land is of a type that will always be good only for growing import-competing crops, there is nothing subtle about the landowner's stake in policies that keep out imports of those crops.

The Factor-Price Equalization Theorem

The same Heckscher–Ohlin trade model that leads to the Stolper–Samuelson result also leads to an even more surprising prediction about the effects of trade on factor prices in different countries. Beginning with a proof by Paul Samuelson in the late 1940s, the **factor-price equalization theorem** was established about the effect of trade on international differences in factor prices.[4] This theorem states that, given certain conditions and assumptions, free trade equalizes not only product prices but also the prices of individual factors between the two countries. To see what this means, consider our standard example of free trade in cloth and wheat. The theorem predicts that, even if factors cannot migrate between countries directly, with free trade

- Laborers (of the same skill level) earn the same wage rate in both countries, and

- Units of land (of comparable quality) earn the same rental return in both countries.

This is a remarkable conclusion. It follows from the effects of opening trade on factor prices in each country. With no trade, workers in the United States, the labor-scarce country, earn a high wage rate, and workers in the rest of the world (labor-abundant) earn a low wage rate. The opening of trade results in a lowering

---

[4] The important conditions and assumptions needed for the factor-price equalization theorem include all four of those for the Stolper–Samuelson theorem (see footnote 2) and the following additional ones: (5) Both countries produce positive amounts of both goods with free trade. (Both are incompletely specialized in production.) (6) Trade is free of government restrictions or barriers to trade (like tariffs). (7) There are no transport costs. (8) The technologies available (or the production functions) are the same for both countries. (9) There are no factor-intensity reversals. (If wheat is the relatively land-intensive good in one country, then it is also the relatively land-intensive good in the other country.)

of the wage rate in the United States and a rise of the wage rate in the rest of the world (recall Figure 4.1). If product prices are the same in the two countries with free trade, if production technologies are the same, and if both countries produce both products (among other necessary conditions), then the wage rate is also the same for the two countries with free trade. (You might try to develop similar reasoning for land rents.)

The factor-price equalization theorem implies that laborers will end up earning the same wage rate in all countries, even if labor migration between countries is not allowed. Trade makes this possible, within the assumptions of the model, because the factors that cannot migrate between countries end up being implicitly shipped between countries in commodity form. Trade makes the United States export wheat and import cloth. Since wheat is land-intensive and cloth is labor-intensive, trade is in effect sending a land-rich commodity to the rest of the world in exchange for labor-rich cloth. It is as though each factor were migrating toward the country in which it was scarcer before trade.

DOES HECKSCHER–OHLIN EXPLAIN ACTUAL TRADE PATTERNS?

The Heckscher–Ohlin approach to trade provides important insights, in theory, about the gains from trade, the effects of trade on production and consumption, and the effects of trade on the incomes of production factors. These insights are based on the hunch by Heckscher and Ohlin about the basis for trade—why countries export some products and import others. To know if the Heckscher–Ohlin theory actually is useful, we must consider whether this hunch is right. Does it help to explain real-world trade patterns?

The first formal efforts to test the H–O theory used the simple model of two factors of production and U.S. trade data. These tests failed to confirm the H–O theory. (See the box "The Leontief Paradox" on page 78.) More recent tests recognize that more than two types of production factors are relevant to the H–O explanation of trade patterns.

Economists have tested the H–O theory in several ways. Complete tests require information on the factor endowments of different countries, international trade for various products, and the factor proportions used in producing these products. The upshot of these tests can be seen through a look at factor endowments and trade patterns.

Factor Endowments

Figure 4.3 shows the shares of several countries in the "world" endowments of certain factors of production. To recognize the patterns of relative abundance and scarcity here, a country's share of the world endowment of one factor should be compared to that country's shares of the world endowments of other factors. Physical (or nonhuman) capital is relatively abundant in the industrialized countries, including the United States and the five other countries shown specifically in the figure.

Case Study   The Leontief Paradox

What we now know about the mixtures of productive factors that make up the exports and imports of leading nations has been learned largely because Wassily Leontief was puzzled in the 1950s. Leontief, a Nobel Prize winner in economics, set off a generation of fruitful debate by following the soundest of scientific instincts: testing whether the predictions of a theory really fit the facts.

Leontief decided to test the Heckscher–Ohlin theory that countries will export products whose production requires more of the country's abundant factors and import products whose production relies more on the country's scarce factors. He assumed that the U.S. economy at that time was capital-abundant (and labor-scarce) relative to the rest of the world.

LEONTIEF'S *K/L* TEST

Leontief computed the ratios of capital stocks to numbers of workers in the U.S. export and import-competing industries in 1947. This computation required figuring out not only how much capital and labor were used directly in each of these several dozen industries but also how much capital and labor were used in producing the materials purchased from other industries. As the main pioneer in input-output analysis, he had the advantage of knowing just how to multiply the input-output matrix of the U.S. economy by vectors of capital and labor inputs, export values, and import values to derive the desired estimates of capital/labor ratios in exports and import-competing pro-

duction. So the test of the H–O theory was set. If the United States was relatively capital-abundant, then the U.S. export bundle should embody a higher capital/labor ratio (K_x/L_x), than the capital/labor ratio embodied in the U.S. production that competed with imports (K_m/L_m).

Leontief's results posed a paradox that puzzled him and others: In 1947, the United States was exporting labor-intensive goods to the rest of the world in exchange for relatively capital-intensive imports! The key ratio (K_x/L_x)/(K_m/L_m) was only 0.77 when H–O said it should be well above unity. Other studies confirmed the bothersome Leontief paradox for the United States between World War II and 1970.

BROADER AND BETTER TESTS

The most fruitful response to the paradox was to introduce other factors of production besides just capital and labor. Perhaps, reasoned many economists (including Leontief himself), we should make use of the fact that there are different kinds of labor, different kinds of natural resources, different kinds of capital, and so forth. Broader calculations of factor content have paid off in extra insights into the basis for U.S. trade. True, the United States was somewhat capital-abundant, yet it failed to export more capital services than it imported. But the post-Leontief studies showed that the United States was also abundant in farmland and highly skilled labor. And the United States is indeed a net exporter of products that use these factors intensively, as H–O predicts.

Highly skilled labor, represented here by professional and technical workers, is also abundant in the industrialized countries. This category includes scientists and engineers, a key input into the research and development (R&D) that influences international competition in high technology goods. Indeed, most scientists and engineers engaged in R&D in the world work in the United States, Japan, Germany, France, and the United Kingdom.

Unskilled labor, represented here by the lowest-skilled stratum (illiterate labor), is relatively scarce in the developed countries. The developing countries

FIGURE 4.3   Shares of the World's Factor Endowments, Late 1990s

	Physical Capital	Highly Skilled Labor[a]	Medium-Skilled Labor[b]	Unskilled Labor[c]	Arable Land	Forestland
United States	22.2%	11.3%	6.8%	0.5%	17.6%	9.1%
Canada	1.9	2.0	0.7	0.1	4.5	9.8
Japan	25.2	3.7	3.5	0.1	0.5	1.0
Germany	8.8	5.5	1.6	0.1	1.2	0.4
France	5.3	3.7	1.0	0.1	1.8	0.6
United Kingdom	3.3	2.6	1.4	0.1	0.6	0.1
Other industrialized countries	15.2	10.1	4.0	0.3	9.2	10.4
Developing countries	18.2	61.1	80.9	98.6	64.6	68.6

Notes: All figures are approximations. The "world" refers to 91 countries (21 industrialized countries and 70 developing countries) for which reasonable data are available. Physical capital and the land categories are for 1998, the labor categories are for 1999.

[a] Workers in professional and technical occupations. For some countries, estimates based on prior year or on neighboring countries.

[b] Literate workers who do not belong to the professional and technical category.

[c] Illiterate workers.

Sources: Physical capital estimated from information on gross fixed capital formation from World Bank, *World Development Indicators,* 2001. Data on labor from World Bank, *World Development Indicators,* 2001, and International Labor Office, *Yearbook of Labor Statistics,* various years. Data on land from World Bank, *World Development Indicators,* 2001.

show the opposite pattern of abundance and scarcity for physical capital, highly skilled labor, and unskilled labor. For medium-skilled labor (the non-scientific skilled and semiskilled workers), the international contrasts are not nearly so sharp. Countries have them in shares that tend to be in the middle of the abundance–scarcity spectrum.

Figure 4.3 confirms what we know about the distribution of the world's arable (farmable) land and forestland. These types of land are relatively concentrated in North America and certain other developed and developing countries (e.g., Australia, Argentina). Europe and Japan are poorly endowed with arable land and forestland. Unfortunately, we do not have good data on the endowments of other natural resources (for instance, minerals and metal ores) in the ground. Still, we can surmise the world pattern. Canada is relatively abundantly endowed, though the United States is not. Other leading resource-abundant countries are the oil producers and the metal ore producers (Australia, Bolivia, Chile, Jamaica, Zambia).

International Trade

If Heckscher and Ohlin have given us the right prediction, the unequal distribution of factors should be mirrored in the patterns of trade, with each country exporting those goods and services that use its abundant factors relatively intensively.

International trade patterns broadly confirm the H–O prediction that nations tend to export the products using their abundant factors intensively. Consider first the United States. U.S. exports and imports for selected goods are shown in

FIGURE 4.4
U.S.
International
Trade in
Selected
Products, 2001

A. Products Whose Trade Is Consistent with H–O Theory

	U.S. Exports ($billions)	U.S. Imports ($billions)	Net Exports as a Percentage of Total Trade*
Wheat (041)	3.38	0.28	+85
Corn (044)	4.76	0.14	+94
Coffee (071)	0.37	1.68	−64
Soybeans (2222)	5.45	0.03	+99
Coal (321)	1.83	0.67	+46
Petroleum and petroleum products (33)	8.54	84.99	−82
Primary plastic materials (57)	13.51	6.31	+36
Aircraft (792)	44.69	21.09	+36
Clothing and accessories (84)	7.01	63.79	−80
Shoes and other footwear (85)	0.81	15.25	−90
Medical instruments (872)	8.09	5.47	+19
Toys (8942)	0.68	8.74	−86

B. Products Whose Trade Appears to Be Inconsistent with H–O Theory

	U.S. Exports ($ billions)	U.S. Imports ($ billions)	Net Exports as a Percentage of Total Trade*
Pharmaceuticals (54)	15.42	18.65	−9
Iron and steel (67)	5.97	13.74	−39
Engines for motor vehicles (7132)	6.86	6.66	+1
Computers (752)	27.39	47.65	−27
Automobiles (781)	18.36	109.97	−71

Note: Commodity numbers from the Standard International Trade Classification, revision 3, are shown in parentheses.
*Net exports as a percentage of total trade equals exports of this product minus imports of this product, divided by exports plus imports of this product. This percentage is an indicator of "revealed comparative advantage" in the product.

Source: Organization for Economic Cooperation and Development, *International Trade by Commodity Statistics,* SITC Revision 3, 2001.

Figure 4.4. The United States is relatively abundant in arable land, and tends to be a net exporter (exports exceed imports) of temperate-zone agricultural products, such as wheat, corn, and soybeans. The United States is an importer of tropical-zone agricultural products like coffee. The United States has abundant endowments of some natural resources, such as coal, and tends to be a net exporter of these resource products. It is a net importer (imports exceed exports) of many other natural resource products, such as petroleum, which are found more abundantly in some other countries.

The United States is relatively abundant in skilled labor, including scientists and engineers employed in R&D, and tends to be a net exporter of products that are skilled-labor–intensive or technology-intensive, including primary plastic materials, aircraft, and medical instruments. Less-skilled labor is relatively scarce in the United States, so the country is a net importer of less-skilled-labor–intensive products like clothing, shoes, and toys. (The United States is also a major net exporter of business services—for instance, marketing, management, accounting, and consulting—reflecting the abundance of skilled labor that is important in producing these services.)

The pattern of U.S. trade in some other goods appears to be inconsistent with H–O. Five of these are shown in Figure 4.4. The United States is a net importer of steel and motor vehicles (automobiles). The United States both exports and imports large amounts of pharmaceuticals, computers and vehicle engines. Factor proportions do not seem to be able to explain U.S. trade patterns for these products. In Chapter 5 we will examine other theories that may explain them.

The trade pattern of Japan is also broadly consistent with H–O. Arable land and natural resources are scarce in Japan, which is crucially dependent on imports of agricultural, fishing, forestry, and mineral products. Without trade, Japan would be a far poorer country. Japan has relatively abundant skilled labor (including scientists and engineers), and tends to export skilled-labor–intensive manufactured products. Although Japan several decades ago was a net exporter of less-skilled-labor–intensive products, the country now is a net importer of these products, a pattern consistent with its current relative scarcity in less-skilled labor.

Canada is relatively abundant in natural resources and tends to export primary products. Even its exports of manufactures tend to be intensive in natural resources used as important inputs into the manufacturing process. Examples include petrochemicals, metals, wood products, and paper. Ohlin was not surprised by the Canadian trade pattern, and neither are we.

The comparative-advantage patterns for Western European countries are more muted. They have comparative advantages rather like those of Japan, but their trade patterns are not so extreme, with more balance in export–import ratios for various products.

In general, trade patterns fit the H–O theory reasonably well but certainly not perfectly.[5]

---

[5] A comprehensive test by Bowen, Leamer, and Sveikauskas (1987) measured the ability of factor endowments and U.S. input–output patterns to predict the net factor flows through trade in 1967. Out of 324 cases, defined by 12 factors and 27 countries, H–O correctly predicted the sign of net exports in 61 percent of the cases. This share was better than a coin flip, but only modestly so. The results of more recent testing by Trefler (1995) indicate that all three of the bases for trade noted in Chapter 3 may be important for explaining actual trade—namely, factor endowment differences, technology differences, and a bias toward consuming domestically produced products. The magnitudes of the technology differences that Trefler finds are similar to the differences in labor productivity shown on the horizontal axis of the figure in Chapter 3's box on absolute advantage (p. 45).

WHAT ARE THE EXPORT-ORIENTED AND IMPORT-COMPETING FACTORS?

The link of factor endowments to international trade patterns emphasized in the H–O theory also suggests, through the logic of the Stolper–Samuelson theorem, the effects of trade on factor groups' incomes and purchasing power. National policymakers need to know which factor groups are likely to gain and lose from liberalizing trade. The policymakers can then anticipate different groups' views on trade or plan ahead for ways to compensate groups that are harmed, if society wishes to do so.

The U.S. Pattern

Figure 4.5 shows the factor content of U.S. exports and of U.S. imports competing with domestic production. Overall, labor incomes account for a greater share of the value of U.S. exports than of the value of U.S. imports. This reflects two facts. First the number of jobs associated with U.S. exports is about the same as the number associated with an equal value of imports. (See the box "U.S. Jobs and Foreign Trade.") Second, the average skill and pay levels are higher on the export side. In fact, it seems wise to divide labor into at least two types—skilled and unskilled—as in Figure 4.5. Skilled labor in the United States is an export-oriented factor, while

FIGURE 4.5

A Schematic View of the Factor Content of U.S. Exports and Competing Imports

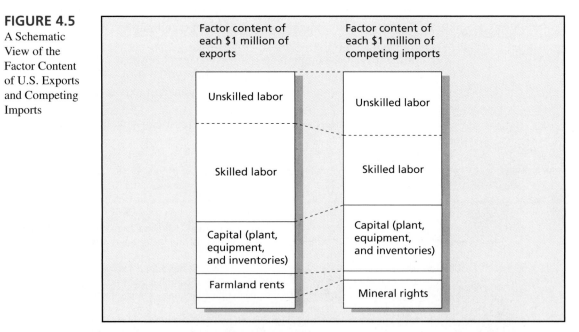

Note: Vertical distances are meant to give rough impressions of factor-content proportions in U.S. exports and the set of outputs that would replace the U.S. imports that compete with domestic products.

Focus on Labor   U.S. Jobs and Foreign Trade

The U.S. Congress has sometimes come close to passing comprehensive bills to slash U.S. imports through tariffs or other barriers. These attempts have been defended as necessary to protect U.S. jobs. Does more trade mean fewer U.S. jobs? Does less trade mean more U.S. jobs? Economists have developed a relatively clear and surprising answer.

Consider general restrictions that reduce U.S. imports across the board. Such restrictions are likely to result in no increase in U.S. jobs at given wage rates! This is because (1) reducing U.S. imports also tends to reduce U.S. exports and (2) the average jobs content of U.S. exports is about equal to that of U.S. imports.

There are four reasons to think that reducing imports reduces exports. First, exports use importable inputs. If these imports are not so readily available, U.S. exports become less competitive. Second, foreigners who lose sales to us cannot buy so much from us. As foreigners lose income from exports to us, they buy less of many things, including less of our exports. Third, foreign governments may retaliate by increasing their own protection against imports. U.S. exports decline as they face additional foreign barriers.

Fourth, cutting our imports may create pressures for changes in exchange rates. We will discuss exchange rates further in Parts III and IV. Here we depart briefly from barter trade to recognize that most trade is paid for with national currencies. Reducing demand for imports also reduces demand for foreign currencies used to pay for the imports. If the foreign currencies then lose value—thus increasing the exchange-rate value of the U.S. dollar—the higher dollar value tends to make U.S. goods more expensive to foreign buyers. In response they buy less of our exports.

The combination of these four effects results in roughly a dollar-for-dollar cut in exports if imports are cut. If both exports and imports are cut, the effect on U.S. jobs then depends on whether more jobs are created in the expanding import-competing industries than are lost in the declining-export industries. Estimates from different studies vary somewhat.

Overall, the studies indicate that the net change in total jobs would probably be small if U.S. imports and U.S. exports decreased by the same amount. (In addition, the average wage rate tends to be higher in export industries.)

If a sweeping cut in imports would probably not increase jobs much, why would labor groups favor such import cuts? The largest lobbyist for protection against imports is the American Federation of Labor–Congress of Industrial Organizations (AFL–CIO). The goods-sector membership of this organization is concentrated in industries that are more affected by import competition than is the economy (or labor) as a whole. It is practical for the AFL–CIO to lobby for protectionist bills that would defend the jobs of AFL–CIO members and their wages even if these bills would cost many jobs and wages outside of this labor group. To understand who is pushing for protection, it is important to know whose incomes are most tied to competition against imports.

This discussion refers to a general restriction against U.S. imports. Selective barriers against specific imports would alter the net effect on U.S. jobs. For instance, studies of existing U.S. barriers, which are selective, show that they are most restrictive on goods having a higher-than-average jobs content, especially in less-skilled jobs categories. Thus, existing U.S. import barriers bring some increase in U.S. jobs, even though raising new barriers against all imports probably would not increase U.S. jobs.

We conclude by noting that the validity of focusing on jobs gained and lost through trade is itself debatable. Jobs gained or lost through changes in international trade are themselves a small part of overall changes in jobs in the economy. Many different sources of pressure for change, including shifts in demand and changes in technologies, result in changes in the number and types of jobs in the country. A well-functioning economy is dynamic—employment shifts between sectors to reallocate workers (and other resources) to their highest-value uses. While there are disruptions in the short run, the reallocations are crucial to economic growth.

unskilled labor is an import-competing factor. Farmland is another export-oriented factor. Physical capital (as suggested by the Leontief paradox) and mineral rights generally are import-competing factors.

The Canadian Pattern

Canada, by contrast, implicitly exports and imports the factor mixtures sketched in Figure 4.6. One clear similarity to the U.S. pattern is that both countries are net exporters of the services of farmland through their positions as major grain exporters. Another similarity is that Canada is a net exporter of skilled labor and a net importer of unskilled labor. In contrast to the United States, Canada is a net importer of labor overall and a slight net exporter of nonhuman capital (some of it owned, however, by U.S. firms' subsidiaries in Canada). Finally, Canada is a heavy net exporter of mineral-rights services through its exports of both the minerals extracted from the ground and manufactured products made with these minerals.

Patterns in Other Countries

The patterns of factor content have also been roughly measured for other countries. Two such results deserve quick mention here.

The factor content of *oil-exporting countries* is not surprising. They explicitly export mineral rights in large amounts, of course. The less populous oil exporters, particularly the oil nations of the Arabian peninsula, also export capital services through the foreign investment of much of their financial wealth. The

FIGURE 4.6

The Factor Content of Canada's Exports and Competing Imports

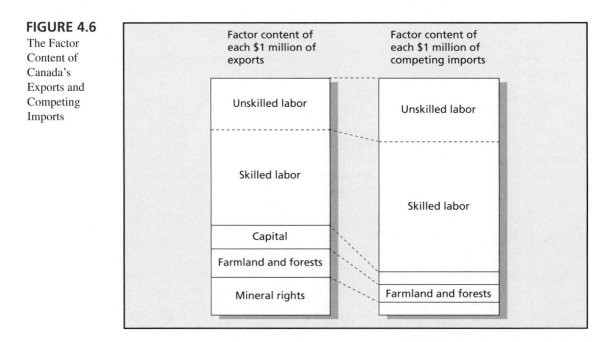

same countries implicitly import just about every other factor: all human factors and farmland.

The *oil-importing developing countries* implicitly import capital and human skills as well as oil. They export unskilled labor, the services of agricultural land, and minerals other than oil. This pattern has important implications for the distributional effects of trade. For many developing countries, lower-income groups selling unskilled labor or working small farm plots have the greatest positive stake in foreign trade since their products are the exportable ones. Restrictions on international trade often widen the income gaps between rich and poor in developing countries. We examine trade issues for developing countries in depth in Chapter 13.

DO FACTOR PRICES EQUALIZE INTERNATIONALLY?

Perhaps the most remarkable conclusion of the Heckscher–Ohlin theory is that trade can equalize the price of each factor of production across countries. The factor-price equalization theorem is more than just remarkable. It is also clearly wrong in the strong form in which it is stated. Even the most casual glance at the real world shows that factor prices are not fully equalized across countries. For example, the same labor skill does not earn the same real pay in all countries. Machine operators do not earn the same pay in Mexico or India as in the United States or Canada. Neither do hair stylists. Given the large number of assumptions—some of them not realistic—that are necessary to prove the strong form of the factor-price equalization theorem, it is not surprising that the real world is not fully consistent with the theorem. For instance, in the real world governments do impose barriers to free trade, and technologies (or production functions) are not exactly the same in all countries.

Does a weaker form of the theorem work? That is, does trade tend to make factor prices more similar across countries than they would be with no trade? In our ongoing example, with no trade the return to land (the abundant factor) in the United States would be low, and the return to land (the scarce factor) in the rest of the world would be high. Opening to trade increases the return to land in the United States and reduces the return to land in the rest of the world—an example of a *tendency* toward international factor-price equalization.

That is exactly what happened before World War I: As Europe expanded its trade with land-rich America and Australia, the high land rents in Europe tended to stagnate while the low land rents of America and Australia shot up, reducing the global inequality of land rent. Another real-world example of the tendency toward equalization is the rise in real wage rates in the industrializing countries of Asia (such as Singapore, and South Korea) as these countries have strongly integrated themselves into world trade. Wage rates in these countries are approaching wage rates in the Western industrialized countries for comparable types (skills) of workers. Although we still do not see full factor-price equalization in the real world, there appear to be tendencies toward equalization.

Summary: Fuller Answers to the Four Trade Questions

This chapter examines the effects of trade on income distribution. Combining these insights with the basic view of trade offered in Chapters 2 and 3, we can summarize by answering the four basic questions about trade introduced at the start of Chapter 2.

1. Why do countries trade? Supply and demand conditions differ between countries because production conditions and consumer tastes differ. The main theories emphasize differences in production conditions rather than in tastes. Ricardo argued that trade is profitable because countries have different comparative advantages in producing different goods. His examples stressed differences in resource productivities. The Heckscher–Ohlin theory agrees that comparative advantages in production are the basis for trade, but H–O explains comparative advantage in terms of underlying differences in factor endowments. Each country tends to export those goods that intensively use its relatively abundant factors of production. The evidence is that the Heckscher–Ohlin theory explains a good part of the world's actual trade patterns reasonably well, but that some important aspects of trade patterns do not square easily with H–O.

2. How does trade affect production and consumption in each country? In the country importing a good, it will raise consumption and lower production of that good. In the exporting country, it will raise production of that good, but in the general case we cannot say for sure what happens to the quantity consumed of that good. With the exception of the latter conclusion, these answers are unchanged since Chapter 2.

3. Which country gains from trade? Both countries gain. Trade makes every nation better off in the net national sense defined in Chapter 2. Each country's net national gains are proportional to the change in its price from its no-trade value, so the country whose prices are disrupted more by trade gains more. (Later chapters will show how an already-trading nation can be made worse off by trading more, but some trade is better than no trade at all.)

4. Within each country, who are the gainers and losers from opening trade? This chapter has concentrated on this fourth question. Its answers go well beyond those summarized at the end of Chapter 2.

In the **short run,** with factors unable to move much between sectors, the gainers and losers are defined by the product sector, not by what factors of production the people are selling. The gainers are those who consume imported goods and produce exportable goods. Those who lose are the producers of import-competing goods and consumers of exportable goods. So far, the answer remains close to the answer given at the end of Chapter 2.

In the **long run,** when factors can move between sectors and the economy achieves full employment, the division between gainers and losers looks different. The **Stolper–Samuelson theorem** shows that

- If you make your living selling a factor that is more abundant in your country than it is in other countries, you gain from trade (by receiving a higher real income), regardless of what sector you work in or what goods you consume.

Examples are scientists and grain-area landowners in the United States, and less-skilled laborers in China.

- If you make your living selling a factor that is relatively scarce in your country, you lose from trade (by receiving a lower real income), regardless of what sector you work in or what goods you consume. Examples are less-skilled laborers in the United States, and scientists and grain-area landowners in China.

A corollary of these long-run effects on different groups' fortunes is that trade can reduce international differences in how well a given factor of production is paid. A factor of production (for instance, less-skilled labor) tends to lose its high reward in countries where it was scarce before trade and to gain in countries where it was abundant before trade. Under certain conditions the **factor-price equalization theorem** holds: Free trade will equalize a factor's rate of pay in all countries, even if the factor itself is not free to move between countries. Those conditions for perfect equalization are not often met in the real world, but there is real-world evidence that opening trade tends to make factor prices less unequal between countries.

Suggested Reading

The contrast between factors' short-run and long-run fortunes from expanded trade was explicitly derived by Mussa (1974).

For excellent surveys of empirical tests of trade theories, see Deardorff (1984), and Leamer and Levinsohn (1995). Tough tests of the Heckscher–Ohlin theory appear in Leamer (1984); Bowen, Leamer, and Sveikauskas (1987); and Trefler (1993, 1995). For a sampling from the vast literature on the factor content of U.S. foreign trade, see Leamer (1980), Stern and Maskus (1981), Brecher and Choudhri (1982), and Maskus (1985). On Canada's foreign trade, see Postner (1975).

Questions and Problems

✦ 1. As a result of the North American Free Trade Agreement (NAFTA), the United States and Canada are shifting toward free trade with Mexico. According to the Stolper–Samuelson theorem, how will this shift affect the real wage of unskilled labor in Mexico? In the United States or Canada? How will it affect the real wage of skilled labor in Mexico? In the United States or Canada?

2. "The factor-price equalization theorem indicates that with free trade the real wage earned by labor becomes equal to the real rental rate earned by landowners." Is this correct or not? Why?

✦ 3. "Opening up free trade does hurt people in import-competing industries in the short run. But in the long run, when people and resources can move between industries, everybody ends up gaining from free trade." Do you agree or disagree? Explain.

4. One of your relatives suggests to you that our country should stop trading with other countries because imports take away jobs and lower our national well-being. How would you try to convince him that this is probably not the right way to look at international trade and its effects on the country?

◆ 5. The empirical results that Leontief found in his tests are viewed as a paradox. Why?

6. Consider our standard model of the economy, with two goods (wheat and cloth) and two factors (land and labor). A decrease now occurs in the relative price of wheat. What are the short-run and long-run effects on the earnings of each of the following: Labor employed in the wheat industry? Labor in the cloth industry? Land used in the wheat industry? Land in the cloth industry?

◆ 7. In the long run in a perfectly competitive industry, price equals marginal cost and firms earn no economic profits. The following two equations describe this long-run situation for prices and costs, where the numbers indicate the amounts of each input (labor and land) needed to produce a unit of each product (wheat and cloth):

$$P_{wheat} = 60w + 40r$$
$$P_{cloth} = 75w + 25r$$

a. If the price of wheat is initially 100 and the price of cloth is initially 100, what are the values for the wage rate w and the rental rate r? What is the labor cost per unit of wheat output? Per unit of cloth? What is rental cost per unit of wheat? Per unit of cloth?

b. The price of cloth now increases to 120. What are the new values for w and r (after adjustment to the new long-run situation)?

c. What is the change in the real wage (purchasing power of labor income) with respect to each good? Is the real wage higher or lower "on average"? What is the change in the real rental rate (purchasing power of land income) with respect to each good? Is the real rental rate higher or lower "on average"?

d. Relate your conclusions in part c to the Stolper–Samuelson theorem.

8. You are given the following input cost shares in the wheat and cloth industries for the country of Pugelovia:

	For Each Dollar of		
	Wheat Output	Cloth Output	Overall National Income
Total labor input	$0.60	$0.59	$0.60
Total land input	0.15	0.06	0.10
Total capital input	0.25	0.35	0.30
	$1.00	$1.00	$1.00

Suppose that a change in demand conditions in the rest of the world raises the price of wheat relative to cloth, so producers in Pugelovia try to expand production of wheat in order to export more wheat.

a. If all factors are *immobile* between the wheat and cloth sectors, who gains from this change? Who loses?

b. If all factors are freely *mobile* between the wheat and cloth sectors, who gains from this change? Who loses?

✦ 9. From the following information calculate the total input shares of labor and capital in each dollar of cloth output:

	For Each Dollar of		
	Cloth Output	Synthetic Fiber Output	Cotton Fiber Output
Direct labor input	$0.50	$0.30	$0.60
Direct capital input	0.20	0.70	0.40
Synthetic fiber input	0.10	0.00	0.00
Cotton fiber input	0.20	0.00	0.00
All inputs	$1.00	$1.00	$1.00

Cloth is the only product that this country exports. The total input share of labor in producing $1.00 of import substitutes in this country is $0.55, and the total input share of capital is $0.45. Is this trade pattern consistent with the fact that this country is relatively labor-abundant and capital-scarce?

10. Consider the following data on some of Japan's exports and imports in 2000, measured in billions of U.S. dollars:

Product	Japanese Exports	Japanese Imports
Food (0)	1.8	41.1
Metal ores (28)	0.9	8.7
Petroleum and petroleum products (33)	1.3	53.8
Pharmaceuticals (54)	2.7	4.8
Iron and steel (67)	14.8	3.7
Computers (752)	14.8	17.5
Automobiles (781)	56.9	7.0
Aircraft (792)	1.5	3.0
Clothing and accessories (84)	0.5	19.7
Shoes and other footwear (85)	0.1	3.0
Medical instruments (872)	1.5	2.6

Note: Commodity numbers from the Standard International Trade Classification are shown in parentheses.

For which of these products do Japan's exports and imports appear to be consistent with the predictions of the Heckscher–Ohlin theory? Which appear to be inconsistent?

Chapter **Five**

Alternative Theories of Trade

When the facts change, theories often need to change with them. The facts of international trade seem to be moving in directions that force us to expand on the standard theory of Chapters 2 through 4. Here we explore facts about world trade and the leading theories that try to explain the aspects that are not consistent with the standard theory.

One key fact is the importance of two-way trade by a country in very similar products—both exporting and importing products in the same industry. Another key fact is the dominance of a few large firms in some world industries. These facts point us toward considering theories based on types of market structure different from the perfectly competitive markets of standard trade theory. We will examine three major alternatives:

- Monopolistic competition (with its emphasis on product differentiation).

- Global oligopoly.

- Industries that concentrate in a few places because of scale economies that arise from interactions among the firms located within each area.

TRADE FACTS IN SEARCH OF BETTER THEORY

According to trade theory based on comparative advantage, nations should trade with each other to exploit their production-side differences. We would expect that industrialized countries (like the United States, Japan, and Germany) would trade with the developing countries. This part of the trade pattern is generally well explained by comparative-advantage theory.

According to comparative-advantage theory, nations that are similar in their production-side capabilities (and in their general demand patterns) should trade little with each other. Industrialized countries are similar in many aspects of their factor endowments (physical capital, skilled labor, and unskilled labor) and also in their technologies and technological capabilities. Comparative-advantage theory predicts that these countries should trade rather little with each other, except for some trade based in primary products (for instance, food products and minerals) resulting from differences in endowments of arable land and natural resources.

In fact, industrialized countries trade extensively with each other. Trade between industrialized countries is about half of all world trade. Over 70 percent of the exports of industrialized countries go to other industrialized countries, and about four-fifths of these exports are nonfood manufactured products. These facts appear to be inconsistent with comparative-advantage theory.

The Rise of Intra-Industry Trade

Perhaps there is still some comparative-advantage basis for production specialization across industries among the industrialized countries. That is, perhaps each industrialized country specializes in and exports products in a particular range of industries, exploiting some subtle production-side comparative advantage. A close look at the data suggests that this is not true. Much trade in manufactured goods between industrialized countries is **intra-industry trade**—two-way trade in which the country both exports and imports the same or very similar products (products in the same industry). Economists coined this term in the 1970s to describe such trade as Hondas for Volkswagens, French wine for Italian wine, or Boeing airplanes for Airbus airplanes.

To describe the phenomenon more carefully, specialists divide a country's trade in an industry's products into the part that is net trade (or interindustry trade) and the part that is intra-industry trade. **Net trade** is the value of the difference between exports and imports for the product. Net trade is positive (net exports) if the country's exports of the product are larger; it is negative (net imports) if imports of the product are larger. We use theories of comparative advantage to try to explain a country's net trade in different products (as we did for some U.S. trade toward the end of Chapter 4).

Intra-industry trade is the part of total trade that is not net trade—the part that is matched exports and imports. For instance, in Figure 4.4 we noted that the United States exported $27.39 billion of computers and imported $47.65 billion of computers in 2001. The magnitude of net, or interindustry, trade in computers was $20.26 billion. Intra-industry trade was $54.78 billion ($27.39 billion of exports matched by the same amount of imports). Intra-industry trade in computers was most (73 percent) of total U.S. trade in computers ($75.04 billion). (Note that in calculating the amount of intra-industry trade, we care only about the magnitude of any net trade, not whether the net trade is positive or negative.)

The importance of intra-industry trade in a country's overall trade (in total or for a broad class of industries such as manufacturing) can be calculated as an index using information on the exports (X) and imports (M) of each constituent industry:

$$\text{Intra-industry trade (IIT) share} = 1 - \left(\frac{\text{Sum of } |X - M|}{\text{Sum of } X + M} \right)$$

FIGURE 5.1

Intra-Industry
Trade (IIT) as
a Percentage
of Trade in
Nonfood
Manufactured
Goods with
Other
Industrialized
Countries

Country	1970	1987
United States	45.3	51.0
Canada	44.8	55.7
Japan	23.6	22.2
West Germany	58.9	65.5
France	65.5	72.3
United Kingdom	57.8	68.8

For trade in nonfood manufactured goods (SITC 5 through 8) with other industrialized countries, intra-industry trade has been increasing and is more than half of overall trade for most industrialized countries. The estimates are based on nearly 1,000 different individual industries (the five-digit level of the SITC) and refer to trade among 14 industrialized countries (the 6 shown and 8 other European countries).

Source: Vona (1990).

The absolute values of $(X - M)$ are the magnitudes of net trade for each constituent industry. The IIT share is a number between 0 and 1 (or 100 percent). If all trade is between industries, like the trade of wheat for cloth in Chapters 3 and 4, then for each industry either exports (X) or imports (M) is 0. In this extreme case, all trade is interindustry, and the IIT share is 0. At the other extreme, if all trade involves matched exports and imports $(X = M)$ for each industry, the IIT share is 1 (or 100 percent). If some trade is net trade and some trade is intra-industry trade, the IIT share will have a value between 0 and 1, with its size indicating the importance of the part that is intra-industry trade.

Figure 5.1 reports information on the importance of intra-industry trade in the trade of nonfood manufactured products among industrialized countries. The estimates are based on dividing this sector into almost 1,000 different industries so that they presumably are not biased by a failure to disaggregate the sector's products into meaningful, narrowly defined industries.[1] For five of the six countries shown, by 1987 IIT was more than half of the country's overall trade in these products with other industrialized countries. Japan is the exception. (Some have blamed Japanese government policies for making Japan different in its dearth of intra-industry trade, but this has not been proved or disproved decisively.) In addition, the importance of intra-industry trade has tended to rise over time. This is true of all the countries shown in Figure 5.1 except Japan.

We also know from other studies that IIT is more prevalent where trade barriers and transport costs are low, such as within free-trade areas like the European Union.

---

[1] In the analysis of intra-industry trade, a well-defined industry would consist of products viewed as close substitutes by consumers and produced using very similar factor intensities. The latter is needed to conform to the definition of an industry stressed in the factor-proportions theory. Although we cannot prove that each of these nearly 1,000 industries meets this definition, it seems unlikely that the industries are too aggregated. If the industry definition is too aggregated, estimates of the IIT share tend to be biased upward because some interindustry trade (measured at the correct level of individual industries) can appear to be intra-industry trade when several industries are incorrectly added up into a single too-broad "industry."

In Figure 5.1 the IIT shares are particularly high for the three European countries. Furthermore, IIT is more characteristic of the (high-income) industrialized countries, and IIT shares tend to be lower for the (low-income) developing countries.

Intra-industry trade seems to call for a different kind of analysis from the standard trade models of Chapters 3 and 4. While there are several reasons that we might observe or measure intra-industry trade, the major explanation focuses on the role of **product differentiation**—consumers view the products of an industry as close but not perfect substitutes for each other. If IIT is based on two-way trade in varieties of the same basic product, then growth in IIT over time and higher IIT for higher-income countries can be understood partly from the demand side. Income growth shifts demand toward luxuries, and product variety is a luxury. The higher the incomes of consumers, the more consumers can seek variety in the products that they buy. Thus, affluent people vary their choices of wines, beers, automobiles, music, clothing, travel experiences, and so on. Some varieties will be imported, while the varieties produced in the country can be exported to affluent consumers in other countries. IIT results.

Yet, demand effects cannot be the whole story. Why are products produced in only a limited number of varieties, rather than in the nearly infinite number of varieties that would be appropriate to match precisely the tastes of each individual consumer in the world? That is, why are differentiated products generally not produced to be fully customized to the specific demand of each individual? Something on the supply side limits the actual number of varieties offered on the market. Full customization (with each variety produced at a small individual scale) would be too costly. Scale economies in some aspect of production (or distribution) encourage larger production for each variety. Thus, scale economies limit the number of different varieties offered into the market.

Global Industries Dominated by a Few Large Firms

One major set of facts about actual trade that may require theory beyond comparative advantage is the substantial trade among industrialized countries, much of which involves exchanges of very similar products (intra-industry trade). The second major set of facts about actual trade that challenges the standard theory involves a departure from the assumption of highly competitive international markets.

Some important industries in the world are dominated by a few large firms. Production of commercial aircraft is dominated by two firms: Boeing and Airbus. Production of microprocessors is dominated by Intel and Motorola. In such industries as steel, five firms account for half or more of world sales.

Analysis of these industries using our standard model may not be appropriate. The assumption of perfect competition may not be suitable; rather, these industries are global oligopolies. In the latter part of this chapter we will discuss some aspects of international competition in this type of industry. One key departure from the standard theory is the importance of scale economies in the production activities of the firm. Exploiting substantial scale economies is an explanation of why a few firms come to dominate some industries.

ECONOMIES OF SCALE

Our standard theory of international trade assumed constant returns to scale. With **constant returns to scale,** average cost (or unit cost) does not change when the quantity of output changes, assuming both long-run adjustments of all factor inputs and constant factor input prices. (The latter assumption is important. In the H–O approach, each industry actually experiences rising unit costs as it expands. This occurs because industry expansion actually drives up the price of the factor used intensively by the industry, as we discussed in Chapter 4.)

The major alternative theories of international trade use the existence of economies of scale as a major departure. The discussion of the basis for intra-industry trade and the discussion of global oligopolies both suggested a key role for scale economies. **Economies of scale,** or increasing returns to scale, exist if increasing expenditures on all inputs (with input prices constant) increases the output quantity by a larger percentage. Therefore, the *average cost* of producing each unit of output *declines,* as output increases. For instance, economies of scale exist if doubling all input amounts (labor, capital, and so forth) more than doubles output. Economies of scale are often not easy to measure precisely, but they appear to be of some importance in many industries.

In discussing scale economies, several distinctions are important. First, scale economies can be internal to each firm, or they can be external to the individual firm. Scale economies are **internal** if the expansion of the size of the firm itself is the basis for the decline in its average cost. Larger firms may be able to reduce average cost through greater use of specialization by their workers, use of more specialized machines, or the spreading of up-front fixed costs, such as research and development or production setup costs, over more units of output.

Scale economies **external** to the individual firm relate to the size of the entire industry within a specific geographic area. The average cost of the typical firm declines as the output of the industry within this area is larger. External scale economies can arise if concentrating the industry geographically gives rise to better input markets. For instance, the concentration of an industry's firms in a specific geographic area may attract greater local supplies of specialized services for the industry or larger pools of specialized kinds of labor required by the industry. External economies can also result as new knowledge about product and production technology diffuses quickly among firms in the area, through direct contacts among the firms or as skilled labor transfers from firm to firm. External scale economies appear to explain the clustering of some industries—high-technology semiconductor, computer, and related producers in Silicon Valley; banking and finance in New York City; filmmaking in Hollywood (and in Bombay, India, known as Bollywood); stylish clothing, shoes, and accessories in Italy; and watches in Switzerland. We will discuss the relationship of external scale economies to international trade in the last section of this chapter.

A second major distinction is the size or extent of scale economies, especially for economies that are internal to the firm. How much does average cost decline as output expands? How large must a firm be to exploit all (or most) economies of scale? The answers to these questions matter a lot for the type of structure that arises on the seller side of the market.

If scale economies are modest or moderate, then there is room in the industry for a large number of firms. If, in addition, products are differentiated, then we have a mild form of imperfect competition called **monopolistic competition,** a type of market structure in which a large number of firms compete vigorously with each other in producing and selling varieties of the basic product. Because each firm's product is somewhat different, each firm has some control over the price that it charges for its product. This contrasts with the perfectly competitive market structure used in standard trade theory. With perfect competition, each of the industry's many small firms takes the market price as given and believes that it has no direct control or influence on this market price.

If scale economies are substantial over a large range of output, then it is likely that a few firms will grow to be large in order to reap the scale economies. If a few large firms dominate the global industry, perhaps because of substantial scale economies, then we have an **oligopoly.** The large firms in an oligopoly know that they can control or influence prices. A key issue in an oligopoly is how actively these large firms compete with each other. If they do not compete too aggressively, then it is possible for the firms to earn economic (or pure) profit, profit greater than the normal return to invested capital. In the extreme, the industry could be a global **monopoly,** in which one firm dominates the world industry.

MONOPOLISTIC COMPETITION AND TRADE

International trade with product differentiation and monopolistic competition has been analyzed in the past quarter century by Paul Krugman, Elhanan Helpman, and others. To set the stage for this type of analysis, we turn first to monopolistic competition within a closed national economy, using a model pioneered by Edward Chamberlin in the 1930s. As the hybrid name suggests, monopolistic competition is somewhat like monopoly and somewhat like competition. It is like monopoly in that the individual firm has some control over the price it charges, because it produces a unique good that consumers consider to be somewhat different from the varieties offered by other firms in the industry. The firm faces a downward-sloping demand curve for its product. It is like competition in that the entry and exit of firms eventually push each firm toward zero pure profit. Some scale economies exist that are internal to the firm, but they are moderate. Entry is fairly easy, so a large number of firms compete in the overall market. The firm's product competes so closely with the other varieties that the firm cannot extract pure profits above all costs, at least not for very long.

Figure 5.2 imagines a firm, say, Honda, facing monopolistic competition in Japan's national market for compact cars. Let's first review how Honda would use its monopoly power to maximize its profit. We assume that Honda uses only pricing to influence buyer decisions, and that it must set one price and offer this price to all potential buyers. To maximize its pure profits, Honda should produce

FIGURE 5.2

A Monopolistic-
Competitive
Firm in a
Market Before
Trade Opens

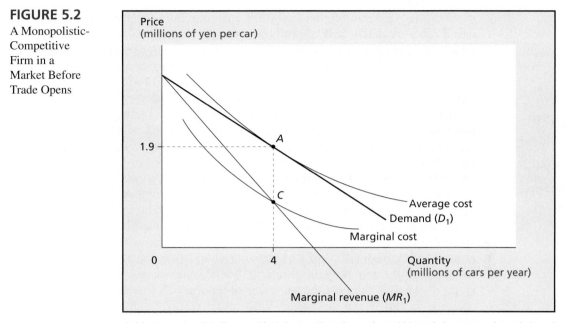

A typical firm in a monopolistically competitive industry produces the quantity at which marginal revenue equals marginal cost. In the long run the firm earns no economic profit because price equals average cost at that quantity.

and sell all units for which the extra (or marginal) revenue from selling the unit exceeds the extra (or marginal) cost of producing the unit. Honda's best quantity, therefore, is the quantity for which marginal revenue just about equals marginal cost (and the marginal cost of units beyond this best quantity would exceed the marginal revenue of these additional units).

What do we know about Honda's revenue and costs? Revenues depend on demand. Because Honda faces a downward sloping demand curve (like D_1 in Figure 5.2), Honda must lower its price (for all units) if it plans to sell an additional unit. The extra revenue that Honda receives from this extra unit is less than the price of the unit itself because Honda loses some revenue on the other units it is selling by lowering the price to all buyers. In the figure, the marginal revenue curve MR_1 is below the demand curve (and marginal revenue can be negative).

Costs depend on production technology and input prices. If there are some economies of scale, then (long-run) average cost decreases as planned output expands, at least for some range of output. This is the downward-sloping portion of the average cost curve shown in Figure 5.2. If average cost is declining as output expands, then marginal cost is less than average cost. (The low cost of the extra or marginal unit is pulling the average cost down.) The marginal cost curve could have various possible shapes. One reasonable shape is shown in the figure.

We can now use Figure 5.2 to see how Honda maximizes its profits. Honda should plan to produce and sell units up to 4 million cars because the extra revenue of each of these units exceeds the extra cost. Honda should not produce and sell any units above 4 million. For each of these units, extra revenue is less than extra cost. Profits are maximized at 4 million units, where marginal revenue equals marginal cost at point *C*. To sell this many cars, Honda charges "what the traffic will bear," the price of 1.9 million yen per car dictated by the demand curve at point *A*.

We have just shown how Honda tries to act like a monopoly. Honda could indeed be a pure monopoly for a while. When Honda first enters the market, its product may be very different from any other model. During this time Honda could make substantial economic profits. Strong demand would allow Honda to set price well above its average cost. After a while, though, there will be increasing competition from rivals' car models even if they are not identical to Honda's compact car. Honda may continue to find its maximum profits at optimal points like *C*, but eventually the entry of new firms into the compact auto industry will drive Honda's pure profits down to zero. Figure 5.2 shows an equilibrium in which entry, or even just the threat of entry, by new competing firms has pushed Honda's demand curve down so that it just touches the average cost curve. At point *A*, with output at 4 million cars per year, price just equals average cost, leaving the firm with no pure profits.[2] Point *A*'s equilibrium is on the downward slope of the average cost curve, because auto production benefits from some economies scale.

Opening to Trade

If this closed national market for automobiles is now opened to trade, two things will happen:

- First, Honda (and other Japanese producers) can now export to consumers in foreign markets that prefer the Japanese car models.

- Second, Honda (and other Japanese producers) will face some additional competition from imports of car models produced by foreign firms like Volkswagen.

In the short run after trade is opened, Honda may earn some pure profits if foreign demand for its model is large, or it may suffer some economic losses if the import competition is severe. Honda and other firms in the world industry must make adjustments. Some firms in the industry may exit, or new firms may enter.

When the transition to a new long-run equilibrium is complete, Honda (assuming it does not exit) will again find its price just equal to its average cost level, but the situation has probably changed somewhat. Figure 5.3 shows the initial equilibrium before trade was opened at point *A* (the same point *A* as in Figure 5.2). It also shows the new equilibrium at point *B*, after trade is opened and further competitive adjustments occur. The new demand curve facing

---

[2] One might wonder how we know that the equilibrium at point *A* (price = average cost) occurs at exactly the same output as the optimization at point *C* (marginal revenue = marginal cost), as drawn in Figure 5.2. One can use differential calculus to prove that both outputs must be the same. At point *A* we know not only that price equals average cost but also that the demand curve and the average cost curve are tangent to each other. These two pieces of information are enough to prove that marginal cost must equal marginal revenue at that same output.

FIGURE 5.3

The Same
Monopolistic
Competitor in
an Automobile
Market After
Opening Trade

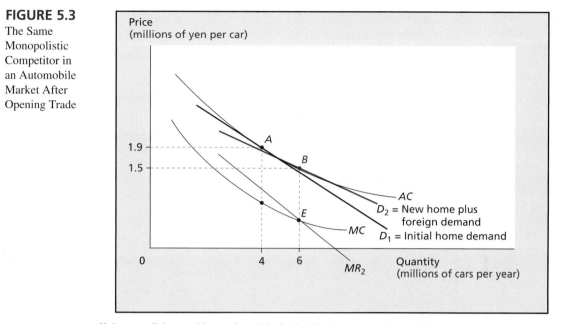

Under monopolistic competition, opening trade leads a firm like this one to expand its production and lower its price.

Honda (home plus foreign demand) is D_2. We presume that demand in this large world market, with more competitors offering more different models, is more elastic than the initial home-only demand, resulting in a flatter D_2 demand curve. The new marginal revenue curve is MR_2. Now marginal revenue equals marginal cost at point E, with 6 million Honda cars produced and sold at a price of 1.5 million yen per car. The net result of the opening of trade is that Honda's output is greater and its price is lower.

So far we have focused on a single firm (Honda) selling in the market. We can also picture the entire market. Figure 5.4 shows what is happening for the overall market. It resembles a supply-and-demand diagram, but the interpretation is a bit different.

The price curve P shows the relationship between the number of varieties (or different models) available in the market and the price that a firm can charge for its variety. As the number of varieties increases, the price decreases, because the demand for each variety becomes more elastic (the demand curve facing each firm becomes flatter).

The unit cost curve UC shows the relationship between the unit (or average) cost level for each variety and the number of varieties produced. Given the size of the market, unit cost increases as the number of varieties increases, because the production level for each variety declines as more varieties crowd into the market. (The market UC curve is different from the individual firm's AC curve. The UC curve keeps track of the entire market by focusing on the number of varieties, and using this to infer the cost level achieved by each individual firm.)

FIGURE 5.4

The Automobile
Market, with No
Trade and with
Free Trade

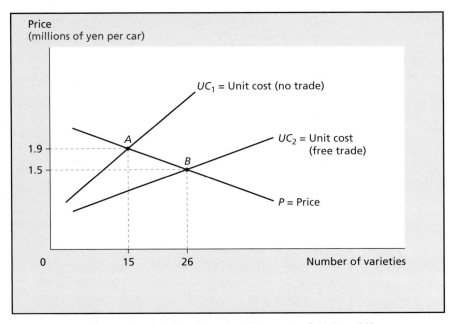

Under monopolistic competition, opening trade leads to a lower price and larger number of varieties available to consumers.

The equilibrium for the overall market is at the intersection of the two curves. We can see this by considering what happens if the number of varieties is different from that shown by the intersection. If the number of varieties is less, then price would be above average cost. Firms earn supernormal profits, so new firms enter the market offering new varieties. If the number of varieties instead is greater, then firms earn losses and some varieties disappear (exit) from the market.

With no trade, the size of the market is limited to the domestic market, and the unit cost curve is UC_1. The market equilibrium is at point *A,* with 15 different models (Honda Civic, Toyota Corolla, and so forth) produced and offered for sale in the national market, each at a price of 1.9 million yen. When international trade in this type of product becomes possible, the size of the market increases (to the entire world market). As the size of the market increases, the unit cost curve shifts down to UC_2. With a larger market, more varieties can be produced with no cost penalty. (The price curve does not shift, because it does not depend on the size of the market.) With free trade, the equilibrium shifts to point *B.* The price of a compact is competed down to 1.5 million yen, and 26 different models will be offered for sale to consumers. For a single country some of these 26 models will be produced domestically, and some will be imported. Also, some of the country's production will be exported to foreign consumers.

Basis for Trade

What is the basis for Honda (and other Japanese producers) to export automobiles? At first glance, it appears to be scale economies. But the downward-sloping average cost (*AC*) curve presumably is not special to Honda. Internal scale economies stem from engineering realities common to all auto producers. Other firms, including non-Japanese producers, have similar downward-sloping average cost curves, so there may be no comparative advantage.

Rather, the basis for exporting is the production of a unique model demanded by some consumers in foreign markets. Product differentiation is also the basis for some amount of auto imports into Japan. The result is intraindustry trade. The role of scale economies is that firms in each country produce only a limited number of models (or varieties) of the basic product. These models can be exported, but the country also imports other models (or varieties) from foreign producers. Economies of scale encourage production specialization for different varieties within the same industry. Intra-industry trade in differentiated products can be large, even between countries that are similar in their general production capabilities.

In addition to intra-industry trade, this industry may also have some net trade—that is, Japan may be either a net exporter or a net importer of automobiles. The basis for the net trade can be comparative advantage. For instance, if autos are capital-intensive and Japan is capital-abundant, then Japan will tend to be a net exporter of autos. The Heckscher–Ohlin theory can explain the part of trade that is net trade, even though there is also substantial intraindustry trade.

Once we recognize product differentiation and the competitive marketing activities that go with it (for instance, styling, advertising, and service), net trade in an industry's products can also reflect other differences between countries and their firms. Net trade in a product can be the result of differences in international marketing capabilities. Or, it can reflect shifting consumer tastes given the history of choices of which specific varieties are produced by each country. For instance, Japanese firms focused on smaller car models, and they benefited from a consumer shift toward smaller cars in the United States following the oil price shocks of the 1970s. Japanese auto producers also marketed their cars skillfully and developed a reputation for high quality at reasonable prices. Japan developed large net exports in automobile trade with the United States during the 1970s and 1980s. Some of this was the result of comparative cost advantages, but another part was the result of focusing on smaller cars at the right time and skillful marketing.

Gains from Trade

Product differentiation, monopolistic competition, and intra-industry trade add major insights into the national gains from trade and the effects of trade on the well-being or welfare of different groups in the country. A major additional source of national gains from trade is the *increase in the number of varieties* of products that become available to consumers through imports, when the country opens to trade. For instance, the economic well-being of consumers increases when they can choose to purchase an automobile not only from the domestic models such as Honda but also from imported foreign models such as Volkswagen, because some may prefer the Volkswagen. Another source of gains from trade arises from the international competition that can *lower the prices of domestic varieties*, as shown in Figure 5.4, bringing additional gains to home consumers.

These national gains from trade accrue to consumers generally. They can be added to trade's other effects on the well-being of different groups within the country. Two major insights result.

First, the opening (or expansion) of trade has little impact on the domestic distribution of factor income if the (additional) trade is intra-industry. Because extra exports occur as imports take part of the domestic market, the total output of the domestic industry is not changed much. There is little of the interindustry shifts in production that put pressures on factor prices. In this case, all groups can gain from the (additional) trade because of gains from additional product variety.

Second, gains from greater variety can offset any losses in factor income resulting from interindustry shifts in production that do occur. Groups that appear to lose real income as a result of Stolper–Samuelson effects will not lose as much; and they could actually believe that their well-being is enhanced overall if they value the access to greater product variety that trade brings. For instance, many people would be willing to give up a few dollars of annual income to continue to have numerous models of imported automobiles available for purchase.

A good example of these types of effects is the expansion of trade in manufactured goods within Western Europe during the past four decades, much of it intra-industry trade. This expansion of trade has led to few political complaints. There has been little pressure for redistribution of factor income domestically as this trade has expanded. Europeans generally have gained from access to a greater variety of products.

OLIGOPOLY AND INTERNATIONAL TRADE

Oligopoly exists when a few firms supply much of the market. Global oligopoly could occur, for instance, if substantial scale economies internal to each firm give large firms a cost advantage over any smaller rival firms.

Each large firm in an oligopoly knows that it is competing with a few other large firms. It knows that any action that it takes (such as lowering its price, increasing its advertising, or introducing a new product) is likely to provoke reactions from its rivals. We can model this interdependence among oligopoly firms as a game. Consider a simple example: Picture competition between two dominant large firms as a choice of competition strategy by each. Each firm can choose either to compete aggressively (for instance, setting low prices or using a lot of advertising) or to restrain its competition (setting high prices or using advertising moderately).

The outcome of the game depends on which strategy each firm chooses. The best outcome for both firms together is usually for both to restrain their competition, in which case they both earn substantial economic profits. However, if they cannot cooperate with each other, then the play of the game may result in both competing aggressively. If one firm decides to restrain its competition, then the other often can earn even higher profits by competing aggressively to gain a large market share. In this case the first firm may well suffer losses rather than earn profits. Both know that the other is likely to act in this way, so neither is willing to restrain its competition—both compete aggressively and earn low profits. They are caught in what is called a *prisoners' dilemma.*

The firms can attempt to find a way out of the dilemma by cooperating to restrain their competition. If they can, then they both earn substantial profits (rather than both earning low profits). The cooperation may be by formal agreement (although this is illegal in the United States and many other countries). The cooperation may be tacit or implicit, based on recognition of mutual interests and patterns of behavior established over time. However, even if the firms can somehow agree to cooperate, the cooperation is always in danger of breaking down. Each firm has an incentive to try to gain even more profit by "cheating" on the agreement.

Unfortunately, there is no one "best" way for firms to play more complex, dynamic oligopoly games that are more realistic than this simple two-firm game. The application of game theory to oligopoly has its limits. Nonetheless, game theory does highlight that cooperating with rivals is possible (though not assured) in an oligopoly. Firms in an oligopoly can earn economic profits, and these can be substantial if competition is restrained.

We offer several observations in lieu of a full theory of oligopoly and trade. Consider the pattern of trade for a product produced by a global oligopoly. If substantial scale economies exist, production tends to be concentrated in a few countries in order to take advantage of the scale economies. These countries will then tend to be net exporters of the product, while other countries are importers.

How does this trade pattern get established? History matters. Firms initially chose these production locations for a number of reasons. One prominent reason presumably was that comparative advantage indicated low-cost production with access to required factor inputs at these locations. However, even if the location initially was consistent with comparative advantage, this can change over time. Once the production locations are chosen and high-volume production achieves scale economies in these locations, the pattern of production and trade can persist even if other countries could potentially produce the good more cheaply.

Production may not develop at a potentially lower-cost location because production volume there must be high enough to achieve the available scale economies. A smaller scale of production would result in higher average cost that can cancel out any other cost advantages to the location. Achieving high production volume in the new location means that the new producer must gain a large share of the market. This may not be possible without an extended period of losses for the entrant because (1) the increase in supply lowers prices or (2) established firms in other locations may fight the entrant using other competitive reactions. Thus, production in this lower-cost location may fail to develop. This problem for the potential entrant firm and country is an example of an infant-industry situation, which we will discuss further in Chapter 9.

Does it matter in which countries the production is located (or, perhaps more precisely, which countries own the oligopoly firms)? The answer is that it can matter to national well-being, especially if the oligopoly firms earn economic (or pure) profit on their export sales. (This same point applies to the national location or ownership of a global monopoly.) These pure profits arise from the ability to charge high export prices to foreign buyers, thus enhancing the country's terms of trade. (The pure profits can also be seen simply as an addition to national income that comes from foreign buyers.)

Putting all of this together, we see that the current pattern of national locations for a global oligopoly is somewhat arbitrary, and the small number of countries that have the industry's production obtain additional gains from trade if the firms earn pure profits on their exports. The national gain from having high-profit oligopoly firms in a country is the basis for a national government to use various policies to influence the location decisions (or the global market shares) of the oligopoly firms in favor of domestic production. These issues are taken up further in the discussion of strategic trade policy in Chapter 10.

EXTERNAL SCALE ECONOMIES AND TRADE

A final case worth examining is an industry that benefits from substantial external scale economies. External economies exist when the expansion of the entire industry's production within a geographic area lowers the average cost in the long run for each firm in the industry in the area. These types of scale economies are also called agglomeration economies, indicating the advantages to firms that locate close to each other. If there are no or only modest internal scale economies, then a large number of small firms can exist in the industry. We then have a case in which substantial external scale economies coexist with a highly competitive industry.

If an expansion of an industry lowers costs for each firm, then new export opportunities (or any other source of demand growth) can have a dramatic effect. Figure 5.5 imagines that a national semiconductor industry is competitive, but characterized by external economies of scale. There is an initial equilibrium at point *A,* with many firms competing to sell 40 million units at $19 a unit. Here the usual short-run supply and demand curves (S_1 and D_1) intersect in the usual way. What is new in the diagram is the coexistence of the upward-sloping supply curve S_1 with the downward-sloping long-run average cost curve. The upward-sloping supply curve is the sum of small individual firms' views of the market. Each firm operates at given levels of industry production, which it cannot affect very much. It reacts to a change in price according to its own upward-sloping supply curve, and the sum of these supply curves is shown as S_1.

The industry's downward-sloping average cost curve comes into play when demand shifts. To bring out points about international trade, let us imagine that opening up a new export market shifts demand from D_1 to D_2. Each firm would respond to the stronger demand by raising output. If each firm acted alone and affected only itself, the extra demand would push the market up the supply curve S_1 to a point like *C.* Yet the new export business raises the whole industry's output

FIGURE 5.5

External
Economies
Magnify an
Expansion in a
Competitive
Industry

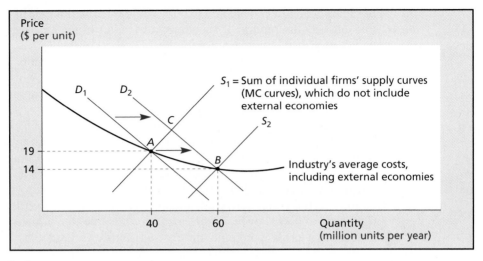

Results:

- In industries that can reap external economies (e.g., knowledge spillovers from firm to firm), a rise in demand triggers a great expansion of supply and lowers costs and price.
- Therefore, increasing trade brings gains to all consumers (home-country and foreign alike) as well as to the exporting producers.
- Corollary: Among nations having the same initial factor endowments, cost curves, and demand curves, whichever nation moved first to capture its export market would gain a cost advantage in this product.

and employment, bringing additional external economies. For instance, there could be more development and exchange of useful information, which raises productivity and cuts costs throughout the industry. This means, in effect, a sustained rightward movement of the industry supply curve. To portray the cost-cutting more conveniently than with multiple shifts of the supply curve, Figure 5.5 shows the average cost curve, including external economies. The external economies lead to a decline in average cost as industry output expands. As Figure 5.5 is drawn, we imagine that demand and supply expansion catch up with each other at point *B,* a new equilibrium.

What are the welfare effects of the opening of trade for an industry with external economies? Producers of the product in an exporting country tend to gain producer surplus as a result of the expansion of industry output, although the decline in price will mitigate the gain. Producers in importing countries lose producer surplus. Consumers in the importing countries gain consumer surplus as price declines and their consumption increases. Consumers in the exporting country also gain consumer surplus as price declines and consumption quantity increases. Here is a definite contrast to the standard case (e.g., Figure 2.4), where local buyers suffer from price increases on goods that become exportable with the opening of trade.

What explains the pattern of trade that emerges in industries subject to external scale economies? Many of the issues are similar to those raised with respect to substantial internal scale economies. Production tends to be concentrated in a small number of locations. If trade is opened, some locations, such as that shown in Figure 5.5, will expand and export, while other nations shrink or cease production and rely on imports. It is not easy to predict which locations will expand and which will shrink or cease production. The size of the domestic market with no trade may be important if the larger domestic market permits domestic firms to be low-cost producers when trade is opened. Historical luck or a push from government policy may be important if the first countries to capture export markets become the low-cost producers.

The outcome is analogous to the production of pearls. Which oysters produce pearls depends on luck or outside human intervention. An oyster gets its pearl from the accidental deposit of a grain of sand or from a human's introducing a grain of sand. The external economies case is one in which a lasting production advantage is acquired by luck or policy even if there are no differences in nations' initial comparative advantages. The production locations and pattern of trade tend to persist even if other locations are potentially lower-cost. Other locations cannot easily overcome the scale advantages of established locations. These other locations may view this as an infant-industry problem.

Summary: How Does Trade Really Work?

This chapter examined several theories that have broadened our answers to the four major questions about trade. The alternative theories focus on

- **Product differentiation** and monopolistic competition.
- Substantial **internal scale economies** and global oligopoly.
- **External scale economies.**

According to the standard trade theory emphasizing comparative advantage, the similarity of industrialized countries in factor endowments and technological capabilities suggests little reason for trade among them. Yet we observe the opposite. Trade among industrialized countries represents about half of world trade. Furthermore, an increasing fraction of world trade consists of **intra-industry trade (IIT),** in which a country both exports and imports items in the same product category. A challenge for trade theory is to explain why we have so much IIT and whether the standard model's conclusions about the gains from trade and the effects of trade still hold.

Much IIT involves trade in differentiated products—exports and imports of different varieties of the same basic product. Part of the reason that we have rising intra-industry trade is that product variety is a luxury in a prospering world. Rising per capita incomes cause an even faster rise in demand for luxuries. Yet, by itself, increasing demand does not explain intra-industry trade. To put intra-industry trade in proper perspective, we need to consider features on the producers' side of the same expanding markets.

Moderate internal economies of scale and **monopolistic competition** are important to understanding intra-industry trade. Firms competing using differentiated products are able to export to some consumers in foreign markets even as they face competition from imports of varieties produced by foreign firms. Net trade in these differentiated products may still be based on comparative advantage.

Another major fact is that some industries are dominated by a few large firms. Global **oligopoly** can arise when there are substantial scale economies internal to each firm. These large firms choose production locations to maximize their profits, and comparative advantages are likely to be prominent in such location decisions. Over time, conditions may change, but the production locations and the trade pattern do not necessarily change, because of the scale advantages of the established locations.

Some other industries, while competitively populated by a large number of firms, also tend to concentrate in a few production locations because of scale economies that are external to the individual firm. External scale economies depend on the size of the entire industry in the location. It can be difficult to predict or explain which production locations prosper. Home market size, history, luck, and government policy may affect which country locations capitalize on the external economies.

Thinking about imperfect competition and economies of scale also adds to our understanding of the gains from trade and the effects of trade on different groups. It does not contradict the main conclusions of the standard competitive-market analysis of Chapters 2 through 4. Rather, it broadens the set of conditions under which we see gains from trade, with some changes in how any gains or losses are distributed among the groups. Figure 5.6 summarizes gains and losses for three kinds of trade: the standard competitive trade of Chapters 2 through 4 plus two of the three kinds of trade analyzed in this chapter. Oligopoly is not included because we do not have a single generally accepted model.

Relative to standard competitive trade, both trade based on monopolistic competition and trade based on external economies provide additional benefits to consumers, especially consumers of exportable products. In the case of monopolistic competition, the additional gains come from (1) access to greater product variety and (2) a tendency for additional competition to lower product prices. In

FIGURE 5.6
Summary of Gains and Losses from Opening Up Trade in Three Cases

	Kind of Trade		
Group	**Standard Competition (Chapters 2–4)**	**Monopolistic Competition (IIT)* (This Chapter)**	**External Economies (This Chapter)**
Exporting country	Gain	Gain	Gain
Export producers	Gain	*	Gain
Export consumers	Lose	Gain	Gain
Importing country	Gain	Gain	Gain
Import-competing producers	Lose	*	Lose
Import consumers	Gain	Gain	Gain
Whole world	Gain	Gain	Gain

* In monopolistic competition that results in intra-industry trade (IIT), producers are both exporters and import-competing at the same time. If trade is mostly or completely IIT, then the effects on producers as a group tend to be small.

Note: The gains and losses to producers in all cases refer to changes in producer surplus in the short run. In the long run, these gains and losses shift to the factors most closely tied to the export or import-competing industries (according to the Stolper–Samuelson theorem).

the case of external economies, gains to consumers in the exporting country arise from the decline in the price for the good as the local industry expands and achieves greater external economies. Relative to standard competitive trade, trade based on monopolistic competition has less of an impact on producing firms and factor incomes, because firms under pressure from import competition also have the opportunity to export into foreign markets.

Although not portrayed fully in Figure 5.6, global oligopoly (or monopoly) also has implications for well-being. Trade allows firms to concentrate production in a few locations, achieving scale economies that lower costs and can reduce prices charged to consumers. Furthermore, a global oligopoly (or monopoly) firm can earn pure profits on its export sales. In comparison with standard competitive trade, these pure profits on exports add to both the gains to export producers and the national gains from trade for the exporting country.

Where does the theory of trade patterns stand?

The standard model of Chapters 2 through 4, complete with both demand and supply sides, has the virtue of breadth. We can use it to explain most trade patterns as long as we equip it with a long list of explanatory variables. Its weakness lies in that same breadth, that same ability to expand to explain any case: The problem is that we *need* to equip it with a long list of explanatory variables to explain all the real-world trade patterns. That gets cumbersome. For example, to explain why Toyota Corporation developed an advantage in exporting automobiles to the whole world, we have to start with the personal entrepreneurial vision of Eishi Toyoda and call it a "factor endowment" of Toyota Corporation and of Japan. This is a valid way to use our standard model in explaining Toyota's success, but it does not give us any predictive power, any ability to forecast.

The Heckscher–Ohlin variant of the standard model makes the stronger assertion that the way to explain who exports what to whom is to look at factor proportions alone, concentrating on a few main factors of production. That has the scientific virtue of giving more testable and falsifiable predictions than the broadest standard model (of which it is a special case). But, as we saw in Chapter 4, the tests of the Heckscher–Ohlin model give it only a middling grade. It predicts the correct direction of trade better than a coin flip, but only modestly better.

Our ability to predict (explain) trade patterns is improved if we add technology differences and models based on scale economies and imperfect competition. Technology differences can be a basis for comparative advantage. We will explore in depth the relationship between technological progress and trade in the next chapter.

The monopolistic competition model suggests that product differentiation can be a basis for successful exporting, although it does not predict which specific varieties of a differentiated product will be produced by which countries. The models based on substantial scale economies (internal or external) indicate that production tends to be concentrated at a small number of locations, but they do not precisely identify which specific countries will be the production locations. History, luck, and perhaps early government policy can have a major impact on the actual production locations.

Suggested Reading

Intra-industry trade is measured and interpreted in Grubel and Lloyd (1975), Greenaway and Milner (1988), and Vona (1990 and 1991).

A readable summary of early work on imperfect-competition models of international trade is found in Krugman (1983); a more technical survey appears in Helpman (1990). Technical presentations of both monopolistic competition and global oligopoly models of trade are in Helpman and Krugman (1985). Ottaviano and Puga (1998) survey recent analyses of external scale economies and the "new economic geography." Porter (1990) examines the role of clusters of firms in international competition. Helpman (1999) surveys empirical testing of traditional and alternative trade theories.

Questions and Problems

◆ 1. "According to the Heckscher–Ohlin theory, countries should engage in a lot of intra-industry trade." Do you agree or disagree? Why?

2. Economies of scale are important in markets that are not perfectly competitive. What is the key role of economies of scale in the analysis of markets that are monopolistically competitive? What is the key role in oligopoly?

◆ 3. "Once we recognize that product differentiation is the basis for much international trade, there are likely to be more winners and fewer losers in a country when the country shifts from no trade to free trade." There may be several reasons why this statement is true. What are the reasons? Explain each briefly.

4. A country is the only production site in the world for hyperhoney infinite pasta, a wonderful product produced using a delicate, highly perishable extract obtainable from some trees that grow only in this country. Furthermore, there is no domestic demand for this product in the country, so all production will be exported. The country's government has the choice of forming the pasta-producing industry either as a monopoly or as a large number of small pasta producers that will act as perfect competitors. What is your advice to the country's government about which market structure to choose for the pasta industry?

◆ 5. Production of a good is characterized by external economies of scale. Currently there is no trade in the product, and the product is produced in two countries. If trade is opened in this product, all production will be driven to occur in only one country.

   a. With free trade, why would production only occur in one country?
   b. Does opening trade bring gains to both countries? Explain.

6. The world market for large passenger jet airplanes is an oligopoly dominated by two firms: Boeing in the United States and Airbus in Europe.

   a. Explain why the market equilibrium might involve either a low price for airplanes or a high price for airplanes.
   b. From the perspective of the well-being of the United States (or Europe), why might a high-price equilibrium be desirable?
   c. What price outcome is desirable for Japan or Brazil? Why?
   d. If the outcome is the high-price equilibrium, does Japan or Brazil still gain from importing airplanes? Explain.

◆ 7. A monopolistically competitive industry exists in both Pugelovia and the rest of the world, but there has been no trade in this type of product. Trade in this type of product is now opened.

  a. Explain how opening trade affects domestic consumers of this type of product in Pugelovia.

  b. Explain how opening trade affects domestic producers of this type of product in Pugelovia.

 8. Measurement of intra-industry trade can be understood more firmly with a numerical example. In your answer to this question, use the data on U.S. and Japanese exports and imports shown in Figure 4.4 and question 10 from Chapter 4. Use only the data on the eight manufactured products shown there for both countries (pharmaceuticals, iron and steel, computers, automobiles, aircraft, clothing, shoes, and medical instruments).

  a. What is the intra-industry trade share for these eight products for the United States?

  b. What is the intra-industry trade share for these eight products for Japan?

  c. For these eight products, which country engages in relatively more intra-industry trade?

◆ 9. For major product categories, North–South trade between the industrial countries and the rest of the world in 1999 looked something like this (in billions of dollars):

Product Category	Exports (*X*) by the Industrial Countries to the Rest of the World	Imports (*M*) into the Industrial Countries from the Rest of the World
Food, beverages, and tobacco	$ 65	$ 76
Petroleum and other fuels	21	127
Chemicals	114	34
Machinery and transport equipment	481	341
Clothing	15	101

  a. Calculate the intra-industry trade share for each individual product category. Calculate the net trade for each product category as a percentage of total trade ($X + M$) in the category.

  b. Which product categories have the highest intra-industry trade share. Why might this be?

  c. What might explain the pattern of net trade (net exports or net imports) across the categories that show substantial net trade as a percentage of total trade?

 10. You are an adviser to the Indian government. Until now, government policy in India has been to severely limit imports into India, resulting also in a low level of Indian exports. The government is considering a policy shift to much freer trade.

  a. What are the three strongest arguments that you can offer to the Indian government about why the policy shift to freer trade is desirable for India?

  b. Which groups in India will be the supporters of the policy shift toward freer trade? Which groups will be the opponents?

Chapter Six

Growth and Trade

The world keeps changing, and trade responds. Real investments expand countries' stocks of physical capital. Population growth adds new members to the labor force. Education and training expand labor skills. Discoveries of resource deposits change our estimates of countries' endowments of natural resources. Land reclamation and other shifts in land use can alter the amount of land available for production. New technologies improve capabilities to produce goods and services. New products enter the market. Consumer tastes change, altering demands for various products. Each of these forces affects trade patterns.

The Heckscher–Ohlin theory, introduced in Chapter 3, is a snapshot of the international economy during a period of time. We can also use the H–O model to show the effects of changes over time. In a way we have already done this in previous chapters—the shift from no trade to free trade is an example of one kind of change that can occur over time.

This chapter focuses on changes in productive capabilities that can occur in the economy over time. These production-side changes are usually called **economic growth** (although we can also consider cases of decline). There are two fundamental sources of long-run economic growth:

- Increases in countries' endowments of production factors (e.g., physical capital, labor, and land).

- Improvements in production technologies (and other intangible influences on resource productivity).

In this chapter we will analyze the implications of economic growth, especially the implications for international trade flows and national economic well-being or welfare. Our analysis focuses on "before" and "after" pictures, with the after picture showing the economy after it fully adjusts (in the long run) to the growth that we are analyzing.

Some of the growth effects explored here will agree with common intuition, but some will not. In particular, we will discover two odd effects of growth. First, an increase in a country's endowment of only one of its production factors actually causes national production of some products to decline. This result is the basis for concerns that discovering and extracting new deposits of natural resources such as oil can retard the country's industrial development. Second, it is possible that expanding a country's ability to make the products that it exports can actually make the country worse off. This perverse outcome could be of concern to a country that is a large exporter of a primary commodity such as coffee beans or copper ore.

These surprising results are part of this chapter's tour of the variety of ways in which economic growth can affect trade and national well-being. The chapter also examines links between technology and trade, including technology differences as a basis for comparative advantage, the cycle of innovation of new technologies and diffusion of these technologies internationally, and the impact that openness to international trade can have on economic growth.

BALANCED VERSUS BIASED GROWTH

Growth in a country's production capabilities, whether from endowment increases or technology improvements, shifts the country's production-possibility curve outward. As the ppc shifts out, we are interested in knowing the effects on

- The general shape of the production possibility curve.

- The specific production quantities for the different products, if product prices remain the same (as their pregrowth values).

The three panels in Figure 6.1 represent different possibilities for types of growth experienced by the United States. The first case, Figure 6.1A, is **balanced growth,** in which the ppc shifts out proportionately so that its relative shape is the same. In this case, growth would result in the same proportionate increase in production of all products if product prices remain the same. For instance, before the growth, production is at point S_1, 80 wheat and 20 cloth, and the relative price of cloth is 1 bushel per yard. As a result of growth the ppc shifts out. At the same relative price (implying another price line parallel to the one through S_1), the country would produce at point S_2, 112 wheat and 28 cloth. Balanced growth could be the result of increases in the country's endowments of all factors by the same proportion. Or it could be the result of technology improvements of a similar magnitude in both industries.

Growth can also be biased toward producing more of one of the products. In this case the shift in the production-possibility curve will be skewed toward the faster-growing product. Figure 6.1B shows growth that is biased toward producing more cloth. If the relative product price remains unchanged, production quantities do not change proportionately. For instance, with production initially at point S_1, growth biased toward cloth shifts production to a point like S_3 if the relative price remains at 1 bushel per yard. Cloth production increases from 20 to 40 units. Wheat production in this case remains unchanged at 80. Other examples of this type of **biased growth** could have wheat production either growing somewhat (but by less than the percent increase in cloth production) or decreasing below 80.

Figure 6.1C shows growth that is biased toward wheat production. The ppc shift is skewed toward wheat. At the relative price of 1 bushel per yard, the pro-

FIGURE 6.1 Balanced and Biased Growth

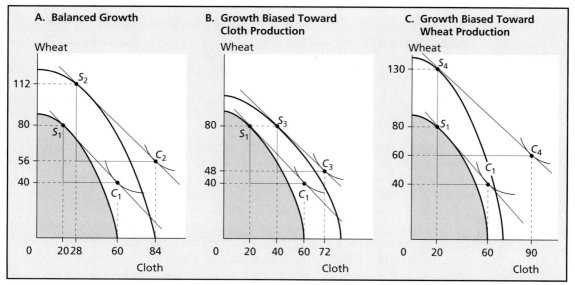

Before growth, the United States produces at point S_1 and consumes at point C_1. Balanced growth expands the ppc in a uniform or neutral way. Biased growth expands the ppc in a way skewed toward one good or the other. If the price ratio remains unchanged, then production growth (to point S_2, S_3, S_4) increases national income and increases consumption of both goods (points C_2, C_3, C_4). By altering production and consumption, growth may change the country's willingness to trade (the size of its trade triangle). For balanced growth and for growth biased toward wheat, the case of increased willingness to trade is shown. For growth biased toward cloth, the case of less willingness to trade is shown.

duction point would shift from S_1 to a point like S_4. In this example, wheat production increases from 80 to 130 and cloth production remains unchanged. In other specific examples of growth biased toward wheat, cloth production might either increase by a lesser percentage than wheat production increases or decrease.

Biased growth arises when the country's endowments of different factors grow at different rates, or when improvements in production technologies are larger in one of the industries than in the other. A specific example of unbalanced growth in factor endowments is the situation in which one factor grows but the other factor is unchanged. A specific example of different rates of technology improvement is the situation in which technology in one industry is improving but technology in the other industry is not changing.[1]

---

[1] The case in which technology in one industry is improving but no other production-side growth is occurring actually looks a little different from the graphs in Figures 6.1B and 6.1C. For instance, growth biased toward cloth could occur if only cloth production technology is improving. In this case the ppc shifts out in a manner that is skewed toward cloth, *and the ppc intercept with the wheat axis does not change.* This wheat intercept shows no production of cloth, so the better cloth technology does not expand the production capability. The rest of the ppc shifts out, as any cloth production benefits from the improved cloth technology. A similar reasoning applies to an improvement only in wheat technology. In this case the ppc intercept with the cloth axis does not change, but the rest of the ppc shifts out.

GROWTH IN ONLY ONE FACTOR

The case in which only one factor is growing has important implications, summarized in the **Rybczynski theorem:** In a two-good world, and assuming that product prices are constant, growth in the country's endowment of one factor of production, with the other factor unchanged, has two results:

- An increase in the output of the good that uses the growing factor intensively.

- A decrease in the output of the other good.[2]

To see the logic behind this theorem, consider the case in which only labor is growing. The most obvious place in which to put the extra labor to work is in the labor-intensive industry—cloth in our ongoing example. Thus, it is not surprising that cloth production increases.

With the production techniques in use, increasing cloth production requires not only extra labor but also some amount of extra land. But the amount of land available in the country (the country's land endowment) did not grow. The cloth sector must obtain this extra land from the wheat sector. Wheat production decreases as the amount of land used to produce wheat declines. (In addition, as wheat production declines, it releases both land and labor, all of which must be reemployed into cloth production. Therefore, the proportionate expansion of cloth production will actually be larger than the proportion by which the overall labor endowment grows.)

Figure 6.2 shows the effects of this growth in the labor endowment. As a result of the growth, the ppc shifts out at all points. Even if the country produced wheat only, the extra labor presumably could be employed in wheat production to generate some extra wheat output. However, the outward shift in the ppc is biased toward more cloth production, the industry in which labor is the more important production factor. If the relative price is initially 1 bushel per yard and remains unchanged, then growth shifts production from point S_1 to a point like S_5 on the new ppc. Cloth production increases from 20 to 35, and wheat production decreases from 80 to 74.

The Rybczynski theorem suggests that development of a new natural resource, such as oil or gas in Canada or Britain, may retard development of other lines of production, such as manufactures. (See the box "The Dutch Disease and Deindustrialization.") Conversely, rapid accumulation of new capital and worker skills can cause a decline in domestic production of natural resource products and

---

[2] The other important conditions and assumptions include (1) the country produces positive amounts of both goods before and after growth, with both factors used in producing each good; (2) factors are mobile between sectors and fully employed; and (3) the technology of production is unchanged. Rybczynski (1955) also explored the changes in the terms of trade that are likely to accompany factor growth, as we will do subsequently in this chapter. (You may abbreviate his name as "Ryb" when answering exam questions.)

FIGURE 6.2

Single-Factor
Growth: The
Rybczynski
Theorem

Growth in one production factor, with the other factor not growing, results in strongly biased growth. If only labor grows, the ppc shifts out in a way that is biased toward more cloth production. If the price ratio remains the same, the actual production point shifts from S_1 to S_5. The Rybczynski theorem indicates that cloth production increases and wheat production decreases.

make the country more reliant on imported materials. This happened to the United States in the 1800s. The United States shifted from being a net exporter to a net importer of minerals as it grew relative to the rest of the world. One of the causes of this shift was the rapid growth of production of manufactured goods as the United States accumulated skills and capital.

CHANGES IN THE COUNTRY'S WILLINGNESS TO TRADE

Growth alters a country's capabilities in supplying products. Growth also alters the country's demand for products, for instance, by changing the income that people in the country have to spend. As production and consumption change with growth, a country's willingness or interest in engaging in international trade can change. That is, even if the relative price between two products stays constant, the country could either

- increase its willingness to trade (it could want to export and import more) or

- decrease its willingness to trade (it could want to export and import less).

To analyze this further, we assume as usual that both goods are normal goods so that an increase in income (with product prices unchanged) increases the quantities demanded of each of the goods.[3]

---

[3] An alternative assumption is that one of the two goods is inferior so that quantity demanded of this inferior good would decrease as income increases. While this case is possible, it would complicate the discussion without adding major insights.

Case Study   The Dutch Disease and Deindustrialization

Developing a new exportable natural resource can cause problems. One, discussed later in this chapter, is the problem of "immiserizing growth": If you are already exporting and your export expansion lowers the world price of your exports, you could end up worse off. A second is the apparent problem called the **Dutch disease,** in which new production of a natural resource results in a decline in production of manufactured products (deindustrialization).

For the Netherlands, the origin of the disease was the development of new natural gas fields under the North Sea. It seemed that the more the Netherlands developed its natural gas production, the more depressed its manufacturers of traded goods became. Even the windfall price increases that the two oil shocks offered the Netherlands (all fuel prices skyrocketed, including that for natural gas) seemed to add to industry's slump. The Dutch disease has been thought to have spread to Britain, Norway, Australia, and other countries that have newly developed natural resources.

The main premise of this fear is correct: Under many realistic conditions, the windfall of a new natural resource does indeed erode profits and production in the manufactured goods sector. Deindustrialization occurs for the same reason that underlies the Rybczynski theorem introduced in this chapter: The new sector draws resources away from the manufacturing sector. Specifically, to develop production of the natural resource, the sector must hire labor away from the manufacturing sector, and it must obtain capital that otherwise would have been invested in the manufacturing sector. Thus, the manufacturing sector contracts.

Journalistic coverage of the link between natural resource development and deindustrialization tends to discover the basic Rybczynski effect in a different way. The press tends to notice that the development of the exportable natural resource causes the nation's currency to rise in value on foreign exchange markets because of the increased demand for the country's currency as foreign buyers pay for their purchases. A higher value of the nation's currency makes it harder for its firms to compete against foreign products whose price is now relatively lower. To the manufacturing sector this feels like a drop in demand, and the sector contracts. The foreign exchange market, in gravitating back toward the original balance of trade, is simply producing the same result we would get from a barter trade model: If you export more of a good, you'll end up either exporting less of another good or importing more. Something has to give so that trade will return to the same balance as before.

Even though the Dutch disease does lead to some deindustrialization, it is not clear that this is really a national problem. Merely shifting resources away from the manufacturing sector into the production of natural resources is not necessarily bad, despite a rich folklore assuming that industrial expansion is somehow key to prosperity. The country usually gains from developing production of its natural resources, as long as this growth does tip into the realm of the immiserizing.

We can examine changes in the country's willingness to trade in each of the three cases of growth shown in Figure 6.1. In each graph the change in willingness can be shown by the change in the size of the trade triangle. The trade triangle is a handy way to summarize willingness to trade because it shows how much the country wants to export and import. Before the growth occurs we presume that the country was at a free-trade equilibrium with production at S_1 and consumption at C_1. The trade triangle connecting S_1 and C_1 shows exports of 40 wheat and imports of 40 cloth.

Consider first the case of balanced supply-side growth, Figure 6.1A. As we showed previously, production shifts to S_2 with growth. Proportionate expansion of production means that wheat production increases by 32 and cloth by 8. With the relative price constant, the price line shifts out. The country has more income and expands its consumption quantities for both products. However, this by itself is not enough to indicate the change in the country's willingness to trade. Here are the two major possibilities:

- If the consumption of wheat increases by less than 32, then the quantity of wheat available for export will increase. The size of the trade triangle and the country's willingness to trade will increase.

- If the consumption of wheat expands by more than 32, then the quantity of wheat available for export will decrease. The size of the trade triangle and the country's willingness to trade will decrease.[4]

The changes in the consumption quantities depend on the tastes of the consumers in the country. Tastes are summarized by the shapes of the community indifference curves and the specific community indifference curve that is tangent to the postgrowth price line. The case actually shown in Figure 6.1A has the new community indifference curve tangent to the new price line at point C_2, so that the quantities consumed expand proportionately to 56 wheat and 84 cloth. In this case, the increase in wheat consumption (16) is less than the increase in wheat production (32), so the trade triangle and the country's willingness to trade expand.

Suppose next that growth is biased toward cloth, as shown in Figure 6.1B. Production shifts to S_3 with growth, raising cloth production with no change in wheat production. More wheat is consumed (as the consumption point shifts to a point like C_3), so there is less wheat available for export. In this case, the trade triangle and the country's willingness to trade shrink. A similar analysis applies to the growth shown in Figure 6.2, growth even more biased toward cloth production.[5]

When growth is biased toward wheat, as shown in Figure 6.1C, our demand for cloth increases as consumption shifts to a point like C_4, so we want to import more. The strong growth of wheat production also increases the amount available for export. The trade triangle expands, showing the country's greater willingness to trade.

---

[4] We could also reach the same conclusions by focusing on changes in the quantities of cloth produced and consumed. In the order presented in the text, consumption of cloth would increase by more than production increases so that desired imports increase; or consumption would rise by less so that desired imports would decline. Of course, it is also possible that the quantities produced and consumed of cloth would increase by equal amounts (as would those for wheat), in which case the trade triangle and the country's willingness to trade would not change.

[5] If the growth is sufficiently biased toward producing more of the good that is initially imported, the country's pattern of trade could reverse itself, making the country an exporter of cloth and an importer of wheat. For example, as noted at the end of the previous section, the United States shifted from exporting to importing minerals since the late 1800s. There is nothing immutable about the trade pattern—comparative advantage and disadvantage can reverse over time.

EFFECTS ON THE COUNTRY'S TERMS OF TRADE

Changes in a country's willingness to trade can alter the country's terms of trade if the country is large enough for its trade to have an impact on the international equilibrium. In turn, any change in the country's terms of trade affects the extent to which the country benefits from its growth.

In this section we first examine the case of a **small country,** one whose trade does not affect the international price ratio. We then examine the case of the **large country,** one whose trade can have an impact on the relative international price ratio (that is, an effect on the price the country receives for its exports, the price it pays for its imports, or both). Note that the definitions of *small country* and *large country* are based on the ability of the country to have a noticeable effect on one or more international prices. Even a country that we think of as having a small economy can be a large country. For instance, Ghana is a major exporter of cocoa. Changes in its export supply would affect world cocoa prices.

Small Country

If a country is small (that is, a price-taker in world markets), then its trade has no impact on the international price ratio (the country's terms of trade). The graphs shown in Figure 6.1 represent the full analysis of growth by the small country. In each of these cases the country gains from its growth in the sense that it reaches a higher community indifference curve (at point C_2, C_3, or C_4, depending on the type of growth).

Large Country

If a country is large, a change in its willingness to trade affects the equilibrium international price ratio. Consider first the case in which growth reduces the country's willingness to trade at any given price, as shown in Figure 6.3 (which reproduces the ppc shift of Figure 6.1B). The reduction in the country's demand for imports reduces the relative price of the import good (or the reduction in the country's supply of exports increases the relative price of the export good). This change in the equilibrium international price is an improvement in the country's terms of trade. In this case, the country gets two benefits from growth:

- The production benefit from growth as the ppc shifts out.

- The benefit from improved terms of trade as it receives a better price for its exports relative to the price that it has to pay for its imports.

In Figure 6.3 the improved terms of trade are shown in a flatter price line (a lower relative price of cloth, the import good). In response, the country shifts its production point to S_6 on the new ppc and decides to consume at a point C_6. With this ppc growth and no change in the terms of trade, the country would reach the level of well-being associated with the community indifference curve through C_3 (48 wheat and 72 cloth) in Figure 6.1B. The improvement in the

FIGURE 6.3
Growth Biased
Toward
Replacing
Imports in a
Large Country

A large country can gain in two ways from an expanding ability to produce the import-competing good—here, cloth. In addition to the gains from being able to produce more (already shown in Figure 6.1B), it can improve its terms of trade. By demanding fewer imports (a decreased willingness to trade), it makes cloth cheaper on world markets. After growth, the relative price of cloth declines to 2/3 bushel per yard in the example shown. The country's remaining imports cost less. Thus, the country gains more from growth, as consumption shifts from C_1 to C_6, because the price line becomes flatter.

terms of trade permits the country to reach the higher level of well-being associated with the community indifference curve through C_6 (54 wheat and 82 cloth) in Figure 6.3.

Consider next the case in which growth increases the country's willingness to trade. The increase in the country's demand for imports increases the relative price of the import good (or the increase in the country's supply of exports reduces the relative price of the export good). This change in the equilibrium international price ratio is a deterioration in the country's terms of trade. In this case the overall effect on the country's well-being is not clear. Growth brings a production benefit, but the country is hurt by the subsequent decline in its terms of trade. (It receives a lower price for its export products relative to the price that it pays for its import products.)

If the terms of trade do not decline by too much, then the country gains overall from growth, but not by as much as it would if the terms of trade did not change. However, if the adverse movement is large, a surprising consequence is possible.

Immiserizing Growth

What happens if the terms of trade decline a great deal in response to growth in the country's ability to produce its export good? If the terms of trade decline substantially, the country's well-being could fall. (Or, in the in-between case, the country's well-being could be unchanged.) The possibility of a decline in well-being is shown in Figure 6.4, in which a large improvement in wheat-production

FIGURE 6.4

Immiserizing
Growth in a
Large Country

A large country actually could be made worse off by an improvement in its ability to produce the products it exports. Such a perverse case of immiserizing growth is shown here. By expanding its ability to produce wheat, its export good, the large country increases its supply of exports (expands its willingness to trade).This drives down the relative price of wheat in world markets. Looked at the other way, this causes an increase (here a tripling) of the relative price that it must pay for its imports of cloth. The decline in the country's terms of trade is so bad, in this case, that it outweighs the benefits of the extra ability to produce. Consumer enjoyment is lower at C_7 than at the initial consumption point C_1.

technology results in a shift in the ppc that is strongly skewed toward expanding wheat production. For a relatively steep price line (showing a large decline in the country's terms of trade), the country's production is at point S_7 on the new ppc and its consumption at point C_7. The level of well-being for C_7 is less than that for point C_1 before growth.

This possibility is a remarkable result, first analyzed carefully by Jagdish Bhagwati. It is called the possibility of **immiserizing growth:** Growth that expands the country's willingness to trade can result in such a large decline in the country's terms of trade that the country is worse off.

Three conditions seem crucial for immiserizing growth to occur:

1. The country's growth must be strongly biased toward expanding the country's supply of exports (increasing its willingness to trade), and the increase in export supply must be large enough to have a noticeable impact on world prices.

2. The foreign demand for the country's exports must be price inelastic so that an expansion in the country's export supply leads to a large drop in the international price of the export product.

3. Before the growth, the country must be heavily engaged in trade so that the welfare loss from the decline in the terms of trade is great enough to offset the gains from being able to produce more.

Countries that export a diversified selection of export products do not seem to be at much risk of experiencing immiserizing growth. A developing country that relies on one or a few primary products (agricultural or mineral products) is more at risk. For example, consider a country like Zambia that relies on a mineral ore (e.g., copper) for nearly all its export revenues. A discovery that leads to the opening of several new large mines would increase its ore exports and greatly reduce the international price of this ore. As a result of the decline in the price, the country could be worse off. For instance, the money value of Zambia's exports of copper ore could decline (if the price falls more than the export quantity increases), and Zambia then could not afford to import as much as before the growth.

It may seem foolish for a nation to undergo an expansion that makes itself worse off. But remember that the expansion would be undertaken, both in the model and in the real world, by individual competitive firms, each of which might profit individually from its own expansion. Individual rationality can sometimes add up to collective irrationality.

The possibility of immiserizing growth offers large countries a policy lesson that transcends the cases in which it actually occurs. By itself, the case of immiserizing growth is probably just a curious rarity. Even for large countries the necessary conditions listed above are not likely to be met very often. Yet a larger point emerges from Figures 6.3 and 6.4. Notice that *any* effect of growth in the national economy on the terms of trade affects the national gains from encouraging that growth. Suppose that the government is debating which industries to favor with tax breaks or subsidies, and has to choose between encouraging import-replacing industries and encouraging export-expanding ones. In Figure 6.3 we found that the country reaped greater benefits if its expansion of import-competing capabilities causes a drop in the price of imports. By contrast, in Figure 6.4, expanding export industries is less beneficial because it lowers the relative price of exports. This is true whether or not the bad terms-of-trade effect is big enough to outweigh the gains from being more productive. So a large country has reason to favor import-replacing industries over export industries: *If* other things are truly equal, why not favor industries that turn world prices in your favor rather than against you?[6] We return to this point when discussing trade policy for developing countries in Chapter 13.

TECHNOLOGY AND TRADE

This chapter's discussion of biased growth can be linked to the general discussion of the basis for comparative advantage presented in Chapter 3. As we noted there, comparative advantage skews countries' capabilities for producing various

---

[6] Remember, however, that the whole reason for favoring import replacement here relates to turning international prices in this nation's favor. For the world as a whole, there can be no such gain and no immiserizing growth. One country's gains (losses) from changes in the terms of trade equal another country's losses (gains).

products. In presenting the Heckscher–Ohlin theory, we spent much time discussing differences in factor endowments as the basis for comparative advantage.

Another basis for comparative advantage is differences in production technologies available in the various countries. Technology differences tend to skew production in each country toward producing the product(s) in which the country has the relatively better technology (that is, the technology of greatest advantage or least disadvantage).

Technology-based comparative advantage can arise over time as technological change occurs at different rates in different sectors and countries. For instance, in our ongoing example from Chapters 3 and 4, improvements in the production technology used in the wheat industry in the United States over time would skew U.S. production capabilities toward producing larger amounts of wheat. The U.S. ppc would shift out in a way biased toward wheat production (as in Figure 6.1C). These technology improvements could include improved farming practices or better seed varieties. If the technology for wheat production is not improving in a comparable manner in the rest of the world, then the United States can develop a comparative advantage in wheat based on its relative technology advantage in wheat.

In some ways this technology-based explanation is an alternative that competes with the H–O theory. Technology differences can become an important cause (sometimes the dominant cause) of the pattern of trade in specific products. For instance, the fact that the United States has become a net importer of steel products can be explained in part by the adoption of newer production technologies for steel in Japan and other countries.

In other ways technology differences can be consistent with an H–O view of the world, at least one using an extended and dynamic H–O approach. To see this, we must consider the question of where the technological improvements come from.

Some technological improvement happens by chance or through the unusual efforts of individuals. However, most industrially useful new technology now comes from organized efforts that we call **research and development (R&D).** This R&D is done largely by businesses and focuses on improvements in production technologies for existing products and on new production technologies for new or improved products. Products or industries in which R&D is relatively important—such as aircraft, semiconductors, and pharmaceuticals—are usually called *high technology.* Ongoing (and costly) R&D within these high-tech industries can create an ongoing stream of new and improved technology over time.

The most obvious link to the H–O theory is the national location of R&D itself. R&D is a production activity that is intensive in highly skilled labor—scientists and engineers in particular. Most of the world's R&D is done in the few advanced countries with an abundance of this type of labor, especially the United States, Germany, Japan, France, and the United Kingdom. Another factor of importance is capital willing to take the substantial risks involved in financing R&D investments. The relative abundance of *venture capital* (outsiders' purchase of ownership in new businesses) in the United States is the basis for a U.S.

advantage, while other countries like Japan depend more on internal funding of R&D within its large corporations.

The national location of production using the new technology, which is what is shown explicitly in our ppc graph, is not so clear-cut. It seems reasonable that the first use in production could be in the same country in which the R&D was done. However, technology can spread internationally. This international spread or "trade" in technology is called **diffusion.** New technology is difficult to keep secret, and other countries have an incentive to obtain the technology improvements. Indeed, the creator of the new technology has the incentive to apply it in production in the national location(s) in which the new technology is most suitable (and therefore most profitable). H–O theory suggests that the suitable location matches the factor proportions of production using the new technology to the factor endowments of the national location.

Individual Products and the Product Cycle

One effort to find a pattern in these technology activities is the **product cycle hypothesis,** first advanced by Raymond Vernon. When a product is first invented (born), it still must be perfected. Additional R&D is needed, and production is often in small amounts by skilled workers. In addition, the major demand is mostly in the high-income countries since most new products are luxuries in the economist's sense. Close communication is needed between the R&D, production, and marketing people in the producing firm. All this suggests that both R&D and initial production are likely to be in an advanced developed country.

Over time, the product and its production technology become more standardized and familiar (mature). Factor intensity tends to shift away from skilled labor and toward less-skilled labor. The technology diffuses and production locations shift into other countries, eventually into developing countries that are abundant in less-skilled labor.

Trade patterns change in a manner consistent with shifting production locations. The innovating country is initially the exporter of the new product, but it eventually becomes an importer. Although it is dynamic and emphasizes additional considerations like demand and communication, many aspects of this product cycle hypothesis are consistent with H–O theory.

The product cycle hypothesis does fit the experience of products in many industries in the past century. Pocket (or handheld) calculators are an example. These were pioneered by Texas Instruments and Hewlett-Packard in the United States in the early 1970s. Soon Sharp and other Japanese consumer electronics firms began to dominate a product whose characteristics had begun to stabilize. More recently, assembly production shifted into the developing countries.

Nonetheless, the usefulness of the product cycle hypothesis is limited for several reasons. These have to do with the unpredictable lengths or progression of the phases of the cycle. In many industries—especially high-tech industries—product and production technologies are continually evolving because of ongoing R&D. Rejuvenation or replenished youthfulness is important. In addition, international diffusion often occurs within multinational (or "global") corporations. In this case, the cycle can essentially disappear. New technology developed by a multinational corporation in one of its research facilities in a leading developed country can be transferred within the corporation for its first production use in affiliates in other countries, including those in developing countries.

Openness to Trade Affects Growth

So far, most of the discussion in this chapter has looked at how growth in production capabilities can affect international trade. Clearly, growth can have a major impact on international trade. There is also likely to be an impact in the other direction, from trade to growth. Openness to international trade can have an impact on how fast a country's economy can grow—how fast its production capabilities are growing over time.

We can gain major insights into this relationship by considering how openness to trade can affect the technologies that the country can use. As we noted previously, in the discussion of the product life cycle, there are two sources of new technology for a country: technology developed domestically and technology imported from foreign countries. If a country closes itself to international trade, it probably also cuts itself off from this second source of new technology. By failing to absorb and use new technologies developed in other countries, this closed country is likely to grow more slowly. Looked at in the other way, countries that are open to international trade (and international exchanges more generally) tend to grow faster. Let's consider more closely the reasons for this relationship. (We might also note that the relationship is actually complex, so that none of these reasons is completely straightforward. We will focus on generally positive effects, without providing the caveats that may apply.)

Trade provides access to new and improved products. For our production-side analysis, capital goods are an important type of input into production that can be imported. Trade allows a country to import new and improved capital goods, which thus "embody" better technology that can be used in production to raise productivity. The foreign exporters can also enhance the process, for instance, by advising the importing firms on the best ways to use the new capital goods. Paul Romer, one of the pioneers of "new growth theory," has estimated that the gains from being able to import unique foreign imports that embody new technology can be much larger than the traditional gains from trade highlighted in Chapters 2 and 3.

More generally, openness to international activities leads the firms and people of the country to have more contact with technology developed in other countries. This greater awareness makes it more likely that the country will gain the use of the new technology, through purchase of capital goods or through licensing or imitation of the technology.

Openness to international trade can also have an impact on the incentive to innovate. Trade can provide additional competitive pressure on the country's firms. The pressure drives the firms to seek better technology to raise their productivity in order to build their international competitiveness. Trade also provides a

Focus on Labor   Trade, Technology, and U.S. Wages

Americans have reason to worry about trends in real wages since the early 1970s. One major trend has been a rising gap between the wages of relatively skilled workers and the wages of less-skilled workers. For instance, from the mid-1970s to the late-1990s, the ratio of the average wage of college graduates to that of high school graduates increased by about 20 percent. Many less-skilled workers have seen their wages decline in real (purchasing power) terms.

Meanwhile, the importance of international trade increased dramatically for the United States. The ratio of the sum of exports and imports to total national production (GDP) approximately doubled from about 12 percent in the early 1970s to about 24 percent in the late-1990s. Do we see here the effects on U.S. wages of a "race to the bottom" driven by rising imports? More precisely, is this the Stolper–Samuelson theorem at work, as rising trade alters the returns to scarce and abundant factors in the United States?

Given the political implications of the trend toward greater wage inequality, economists have studied it carefully. While increasing trade presumably has had some effect on wage rates through the Stolper–Samuelson effect, economists have generally concluded that trade has not been the main culprit.

For the Stolper–Samuelson theorem to be the main culprit—the predominant effect—at least two other things should be true. First, the changes in factor prices should result from changes in product prices. Specifically, a decline in the relative price of less-skilled-labor–intensive goods should be behind the decline in the relative wages of less-skilled workers. Second, and more subtly, the change in the relative wage should induce industries to become more intensive in their use of the now cheaper less-skilled labor. (See the box "A Factor-Ratio Paradox" in Chapter 4, page 73.)

Slaughter (2000) surveys a number of recent economic studies of product prices, factor intensities, and wages. He concludes that research shows that neither of these two things appears to have occurred. Research on U.S. manufacturing industries indicates that during the 1980s and 1990s, there is no clear trend in the relative international price of manufactured goods that use less-skilled labor intensively. The data also show that most manufacturing industries became more intensive in their use of skilled labor and less intensive in less-skilled labor.

The lack of change in the relative prices of traded goods and the rising skill intensity of production are not consistent with the Stolper–Samuelson theorem. The implication is that changes in international trade prices are not the predominant cause of the rising wage inequality. Other economists have concluded similarly that changes in the trade flows themselves (imports and exports) are not the predominant cause.

If not trade, then what? Most researchers have concluded that the major driving force changing demands for skilled and unskilled labor has been technological change. In fact, technological change may be pressuring relative wages in two ways.

First, technological progress has been faster in industries that are more intensive in skilled labor. As the cost and prices of some skill-intensive products decline, and the quality of these products is improved, demand for the products increases. As demand shifts toward skill-intensive products and their production increases, the demand for skilled labor expands, increasing the relative wage of skilled labor.

Second, the technological progress that has occurred within individual industries appears to be biased in favor of using more skilled labor. This bias increases demand for skilled labor even more, reinforcing the pressure for an increase in wage inequality. We see this bias in the shift toward greater use of computers generally and in the shift toward computer-controlled flexible manufacturing systems in manufacturing specifically.

The United Kingdom has also experienced rising wage inequality between skilled and unskilled workers, though the change is not as large as in the United States. In most other countries in Western Europe and in Canada, these pressures seem to have played themselves out somewhat differently. Labor market institutions like high minimum wages have prevented wage rates for less-skilled workers from declining so much. Instead, unemployment has increased since the early 1970s and has remained high. While inequality of earnings has not increased so much in Canada and Western Europe, unemployment, especially among the less skilled, has become a serious problem.

larger market in which to earn returns to innovation. If sales into foreign markets provide additional returns, then the incentive to innovate increases, and firms devote more resources to R&D activities.

Openness to international trade thus can enhance the technology that a country can use, both by facilitating the diffusion of foreign-developed technology into the country and by accelerating the domestic development of technology. Furthermore, these increases in the current technology base can be used to develop additional innovations in the future. This is a key insight of the new growth theory mentioned above, which posits that economic policies and activities influence the growth rate. The current technology base provides a source of increasing returns over time to ongoing innovation activities. The growth rate for the country's economy (and for the whole world) increases in the long run.

In conclusion, openness to trade can accelerate long-run economic growth. This indicates an additional source of gains from international trade (or from openness to international activities more generally). Empirically, there is a strong positive correlation between the growth rate of a country and its international openness. This is not proof of causation, but it is consistent with the theoretical analysis that suggests why openness can raise growth. We take up this issue again in Chapter 13, when we discuss developing countries.

Summary

Economic growth (expansion of a country's production capabilities) results from increases in the country's endowments of factors of production or from technological improvements. **Balanced growth** shifts the country's production-possibility curve outward in a proportionate manner. If the product price ratio is unchanged, production of each product increases proportionately. Consumption of both products also increases. This alters the country's trade triangle and its willingness to trade unless the increases in quantities produced and consumed are equal. For instance, if the growth in production quantity of the exportable product exceeds the growth in its consumption quantity, then the trade triangle and the willingness to trade increase.

Biased growth shifts the ppc outward in a manner that is skewed toward one product. If the product price ratio is unchanged, production of this product expands, but production of the other product increases by a lesser proportion, stays the same, or declines. The **Rybczynski theorem** states that a kind of very biased growth, in which the endowment of only one factor is growing, results in a decrease in production by the sector that is not intensive in the growing factor. The **Dutch disease** is a real-world example. In the Dutch case the endowment growth was the discovery of natural gas deposits. Shifting labor and capital to the extraction of this gas led to a decline in the country's manufacturing sector.

If growth is biased toward producing more of the import-competing product, the country's trade triangle and its willingness to trade tend to shrink. If growth is biased toward producing more of the exportable product, the country's trade triangle and its willingness to trade tend to expand.

The trade of a **small country** has no impact on international prices. The analysis of growth in a small country is straightforward because its growth does not alter its terms of trade.

The trade of a **large country** does have an impact on international prices. If growth results in a large country becoming less willing to trade, then the relative price of the country's export product increases. In this case, growth benefits the country both by expanding its production capabilities and by improving its terms of trade.

If growth results in a large country becoming more willing to trade, then the relative price of its export product decreases. This deterioration in the terms of trade reduces the benefits to the country of growing productive capabilities. Indeed, it is possible that, if the terms of trade decline substantially, the country could be worse off after growing—a possibility called **immiserizing growth.**

The relationship of technology to the shape of the ppc indicates that differences in technology between countries can be a basis for trade. In some ways, this technology explanation competes with the Heckscher–Ohlin theory. The technology explanation of trade is that countries export products in which they have relative technology advantages. In other ways, technology differences can be linked to H–O. For instance, the **research and development** that leads to new technologies tends to be located in countries that are well endowed with the highly skilled labor (e.g., scientists and engineers) that is needed to conduct the R&D. The **product cycle hypothesis** is an attempt to offer a dynamic theory of technology and trade by emphasizing that the location of production of a product is likely to shift from the leading developed countries to developing countries as the product moves from its introduction to maturity and standardization.

Openness to international trade can also influence the rate of economic growth by affecting the rate at which the country's production technology is improving. With international openness, **diffusion** of new foreign technology into the country increases, because of imports of capital goods that embody the foreign technology, or licensing or imitation of the foreign technology. Innovation by domestic firms increases, because of competitive pressure and the greater returns available through foreign sales. Empirically, there is a significant positive relationship between the international openness of a country and the economic growth rate of that country.

Suggested Reading   A classic theoretical study of the effects of technological progress on a country's economy and trade (using techniques similar to those presented in Appendix B) is Findlay and Grubert (1959). The product cycle hypothesis of trade is put forth in Vernon (1966), but doubts are voiced by Vernon himself (1979). Slaughter (1999, 2000), Cline (1997), and Lawrence (1996) each survey the effects of trade and other influences on rising wage inequality. Anderson and Smith (2000) and Robertson (2000) examine the effects of trade on wages in Canada and Mexico, respectively.

Grossman and Helpman (1995) provide a technical survey of economic theories of the relationships between technology and trade. Romer (1994) and Rivera-Batiz and Romer (1991) present technical discussions of the effects of trade openness on growth.

When you feel that you are nearing mastery of the theoretical material in Chapters 2 through 6, give yourself a test by looking at the first 10 paradoxes in Magee (1979). First look at Magee's listing of the paradoxes on his pages 92–93; then try to prove or explain them before looking at the answers.

Questions and Problems

◆1. Pugelovia's growth has been oriented toward expansion of its export industries. How do you think Pugelovia's terms of trade have been changing during this time period?

2. "According to the Rybczynski theorem, an increase in the country's labor force will result in an increase in the quantity produced of the labor-intensive good, with no change in the quantity produced of the other good." Do you agree or disagree? Why?

◆3. A number of Latin American countries export coffee and import other goods. A long-term drought now reduces coffee production in the countries of this region. Assume that they remain exporters of coffee. Explain why the long-term drought in the region might lead to an increase in the region's well-being or welfare. What would make this gain in well-being more likely?

4. "A country whose trade has almost no impact on world prices is at great risk of immiserizing growth." Do you agree or disagree? Why?

◆5. Why does the Heckscher–Ohlin theory predict that most research and development (R&D) activity is done in the industrialized countries?

6. If every new product goes through a product cycle, will the technological initiator (e.g., the United States or Japan) eventually develop chronic overall "trade deficits"?

◆7. Explain the effect of each of these on the shape and position of the country's production-possibility curve:

   a. A proportionate increase in the total supplies (endowments) of all factors of production.

   b. New management practices that can be used in all industries to improve productivity by about the same amount in all industries.

   c. New production technology that improves productivity in the wheat industry, with no effect on productivity in the cloth industry.

8. Which of the following can lead to a *reversal* of the country's trade pattern (that is, a shift in which a previously exported good becomes an imported good, or a previously imported good becomes an export good)? Consider each separately. Explain each.

   a. Growth in the country's total supply (endowment) of the factor that is initially scarce in the country.

   b. International diffusion of technology.

   c. Shifting tastes of the country's consumers.

◆ 9. A free-trade equilibrium exists in which the United States exports machinery and imports clothing from the rest of the world. The goods are produced with two factors: capital and labor. The trade pattern is the one predicted by the H–O theory. An increase now occurs in the U.S. endowment of capital, its abundant factor.

    a. What is the effect on the shape and position of the U.S. production-possibility curve?

    b. What is the effect on the actual production quantities in the United States if the product price ratio is unchanged? Explain.

    c. What is the effect on the U.S. willingness to trade?

    d. Assuming that the U.S. growth does affect the international equilibrium price ratio, what is the direction of the change in this price ratio?

    e. Is it possible that U.S. national well-being declines as a result of the endowment growth and the resulting change in the international price ratio? Explain.

10. A free-trade equilibrium exists in a two-region, two-product world. The United States exports food and imports clothing. A long-term drought now occurs in East Asia.

    a. What is the effect on East Asia's willingness to trade?

    b. Assuming that each region is large enough to influence international prices, how does East Asia's drought affect the equilibrium international price ratio?

    c. Show on a graph and explain the effect of all this on the following *in the United States:* (1) Quantities produced of food and clothing. (2) Quantities consumed of food and clothing. (3) U.S. well-being.

    d. Which group in the United States is likely to gain real income in the long run as a result of all this? Which group in the United States is likely to lose real income?

◆ 11. A free-trade equilibrium exists in which the United States exports food and imports clothing. U.S. engineers now invent a new process for producing clothing at a lower cost. This process cannot be used in the rest of the world.

    a. What is the effect on the U.S. production-possibility curve?

    b. What is the effect on the U.S. willingness to trade? (Assume that the United States remains an importer of clothing.)

    c. Assuming that the change in the United States is large enough to affect international prices, will the equilibrium international price of clothing rise or will it fall?

12. Continue with the scenario of question 11—the new process in the United States and the resulting change in the international equilibrium price ratio. Focus now on effects in the rest of the world.

    a. Show graphically and explain the effect on quantities produced, quantities consumed, and well-being in the rest of the world.

    b. Explain as precisely as possible why well-being changes in the rest of the world.

Part **Two**

Trade Policy

Chapter Seven

Analysis of a Tariff

Most economists favor letting nations trade freely, with few tariffs or other barriers to trade. Indeed, economists have tended to be even more critical of trade barriers than have other groups in society, even though economists have taken great care to list the exceptional cases in which they feel trade barriers can be justified. Such agreement among economists is rare. Why should they agree on this one issue?

The striking consensus in favor of free trade is based primarily on a body of economic analysis demonstrating that there are usually net gains from freer trade, both for nations and for the world. Chapter 2 showed, with demand and supply curves, that free trade brings greater aggregate well-being than no trade. The main task of this chapter and the following chapters of Part II is to compare free-trade policies with a wide range of trade barriers, barriers that do not necessarily shut out all international trade. It is mainly on this more detailed analysis of trade policies that economists have based their view that free trade is generally better than partial restrictions on trade, with a list of exceptions. This analysis makes it easier to understand what divides the majority of economists from groups calling for restrictions on trade.

To see what is lost or gained by putting up barriers to international trade, let us take a close look at the effects of the classic kind of trade barrier, a tariff on an imported product. This chapter spells out who is likely to gain and who is likely to lose from a tariff, and explains conditions under which a nation could end up better off from a tariff. Chapters 8 through 10 will extend the basic story told here.

A **tariff,** as the term is used in international trade, is a tax on importing a good or service into a country, usually collected by customs officials at the place of entry. Tariffs come in two main types. A **specific tariff** is stipulated as a money amount per physical unit of import, such as dollars per ton of steel bars, or dollars per eight-cylinder two-door sports car. An **ad valorem** (on the value) tariff is a percentage of the estimated market value of the goods when they reach the importing country. We will not pay much attention to this distinction, because it makes almost no difference to our conclusions.

For the industrialized countries, tariff rates on most products have decreased to relatively low levels in the process of liberalization that began in the 1930s. In

2000, tariff rates averaged 4 to 7 percent on imports into the United States, Canada, the European Union, and Japan. But tariffs on some products are much higher, up to 99 percent in the United States, 49 percent in Canada, 198 percent in the European Union, and 126 percent in Japan. Average tariff rates are higher in most developing countries. For instance, the average tariff rate on imports into Mexico was about 13 percent in 2000, with tariffs ranging up to 254 percent.

A PREVIEW OF CONCLUSIONS

Our exploration of the pros and cons of a tariff will be detailed enough to warrant listing its main conclusions here at the outset. This chapter and Chapters 8 and 9 will discuss how

- A tariff almost always lowers world well-being.

- A tariff usually lowers the well-being of each nation, including the nation imposing the tariff.

- As a general rule, whatever a tariff can do for the nation, something else can do better.

- There are exceptions to the case for free trade:

  a. The first exception is the "nationally optimal" tariff discussed near the end of this chapter. When a nation can affect the prices at which it trades with foreigners, it can gain from its own tariff. (The world as a whole loses, however.)

  b. Chapter 9 presents some "second-best" arguments for a tariff: In cases where other incurable distortions exist in the economy, imposing a tariff may be better than doing nothing.

  c. In a narrow range of cases with distortions that are specific to international trade itself, a tariff can be better than any other policy, and not just better than doing nothing.

- A tariff absolutely helps those groups tied closely to the production of import substitutes, even when the tariff is bad for the nation as a whole.

You may wish to review these overall conclusions after we have completed the analysis of import barriers in this and the next two chapters.

THE EFFECT OF A TARIFF ON PRODUCERS

Intuition suggests that domestic producers which compete against imports will benefit from a tariff. If the government places a tax on imports of the product, the domestic price of the imported product will rise. Domestic producers can then expand their own production and sales, or raise the price they charge, or both.

The tariff, by taxing imports to make imports less competitive in the domestic market, should make domestic producers better off.

The demand and supply analysis of a tariff agrees with our intuition. It goes beyond intuition, though, by allowing us to calculate just how much a tariff benefits producers.

We begin with a demand–supply view of the U.S. market for bicycles without any tariff. For most of this chapter, we deal with the simple case in which our nation is a competitive "price-taker" in the world markets for the products we trade. This is the same "small country" that we defined in Chapter 6. For a small country, the price that the country must pay the foreign sellers is not affected by how much the small country imports of the product.

In the free-trade situation shown in Figure 7.1, bicycles are imported freely at the given world price of $300, an equilibrium price determined by competition between foreign bikes and comparable domestic bikes. At this price consumers buy S_0 bikes a year from domestic suppliers and import M_0 bikes a year, buying a total of $D_0 = S_0 + M_0$ bikes. To use illustrative numbers, let's say that consumers buy $D_0 = 1.6$ (million bikes a year), domestic producers make $S_0 = 0.6$, and the remaining $M_0 = 1.0$ are imported.

Recall from Chapter 2 that producer surplus is the amount that producers gain from being able to sell bikes at the going market price. Graphically, producer surplus is the area above the supply curve and below the market price line. Let's review why this is producer surplus.

The supply curve tells us, for each possible quantity supplied, the lowest price that will draw out another bike produced and supplied. This is true because the

FIGURE 7.1

The U.S. Market for Bicycles with Free Trade

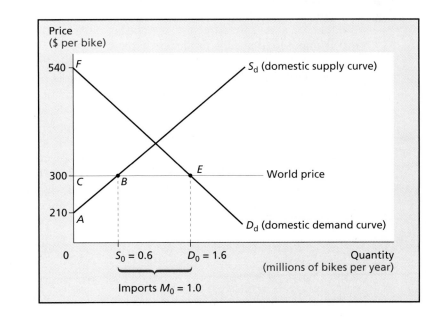

supply curve indicates the marginal cost of each additional unit. A competitive producer will supply an additional unit as long as the price (the extra revenue) covers the marginal (or extra) cost. Thus, according to the supply curve S_d in Figure 7.1, some firm is willing to supply the very first bike for $210 (at point A). This firm receives the market price of $300, bringing a net gain (producer surplus) of $90 on this first unit. Similarly, as we go up the supply curve from point A toward point B, we find that the vertical distance between the supply curve and the price of $300 shows the gains that producers are getting on each additional unit.

By summing the gain on each unit supplied, we see that producers receive the area of triangle *CBA* as producer surplus—the amount by which the price exceeds the incremental costs, unit by unit. We might immediately think that this is a measure of profit, and much or all of it could be profit. But it is possible that other resources used in production may also share in the producer surplus. For instance, the expansion of quantity produced could drive up wage rates for the type of labor used in the industry, because the industry increases its demand for this labor.

Now imagine a tariff of 10 percent on imported bikes.[1] Because this is a small country, foreign exporters insist on continuing to receive $300 for each bike they export. So the 10 percent tariff is $30 per bike, *and* this amount is passed on to consumers. The domestic price of imported bikes rises to $330.

When the tariff is imposed, domestic producers can also raise the price that they charge for their bikes. If domestic and imported bikes are perfect (or very close) substitutes, then domestic producers raise their price to $330. When the tariff drives the domestic market price to $330, domestic firms respond by raising their output and sales, as long as the higher price exceeds the marginal cost of supplying the extra units.

Figure 7.2 shows the same bicycle market introduced in Figure 7.1. When the tariff is imposed, domestic producers expand output by 200,000 units, from S_0 to S_1. Each of these units from S_0 to S_1 is now profitable for some domestic firm to produce. The marginal cost of each of these units is between $300 and $330, which is less than the new, tariff-inclusive price of $330.

With the tariff in place, domestic producer surplus is area $g + a$, the area below the new $330 price line and the above domestic supply curve. As a result of the tariff, domestic producer surplus increases by area a, which equals $21 million per year. We can think of this as composed of two pieces. First, the rectangular part of area a covering the first 0.6 million bikes reflects the higher price received on units that are supplied even if there is no tariff. Second, the triangle at the right-hand end of area a reflects the additional producer surplus earned on the extra 0.2 million bikes supplied.

---

[1] The U.S. bicycle example is realistic in some ways. The Bicycle Manufacturers Association at times lobbied Congress for higher bicycle tariffs to stem import competition, but to no avail. Imports have now claimed over 90 percent of the U.S. market for bicycles.

FIGURE 7.2

The Effect
of a Tariff
on Producers

Shaded area a = Producer's gain from tariff = $21 million

The $30 tariff on imports allows domestic producers to expand their production from S_0 to S_1. The $30 bike tariff gives domestic producers extra surplus on all the bikes they would have produced even without the tariff (an extra $30 \times S_0$) plus smaller net gains on additional sales [gain equaling $1/2 \times \$30 \times (S_1 - S_0)$].

THE EFFECT OF A TARIFF ON CONSUMERS

Intuition also suggests that buyers of a good imported from abroad will be hurt by a tariff. Consumers end up paying a higher price, or buying less of the product, or both. Again, we can use demand and supply analysis to calculate the consumer loss.

First, let's return to the free-trade situation (before the tariff is imposed) shown in Figure 7.1. With free trade domestic consumers buy D_0 bikes at the world price of $300. Recall from Chapter 2 that consumer surplus is the amount that consumers gain from being able to buy bikes at the going market price. Graphically, consumer surplus is the area below the demand curve and above market price line. To see this, recall that the demand curve tells us the highest price that some consumer is willing to pay for each additional bike. Thus, according to the demand curve in Figure 7.1, some consumer is willing to pay $540 for the first bike (at point F). This consumer can buy the bike at the market price of $300, so the consumer receives a net gain (consumer surplus) of $240 on that first unit. As we go down the demand curve from point F to point E, we find that the vertical distances between the demand curve and the world price of $300 show us the bargains that these consumers are getting. These consumers pay less for bikes than the maximum amount they would have been willing to pay. By summing the net gain on

FIGURE 7.3

The Effect
of a Tariff
on Consumers

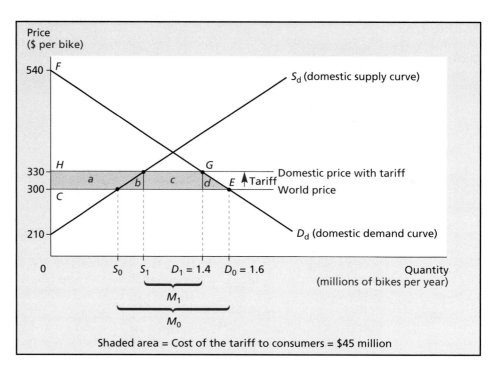

An import tariff of $30 raises the price consumers must pay for either imported or domestic bikes. Quantity demanded falls from D_0 to D_1. The tariff costs consumers both the full $30 on every bike they continue to buy (a loss of $30 \times D_1$) and the net enjoyment on bikes they would have bought at the lower tariff-free price but do not buy at the higher price including the tariff [an additional loss of $1/2 \times \$30 \times (D_0 - D_1)$].

each unit purchased, we see that the entire area (*FEC*) between the demand curve and the $300 price line tells us the total amount of consumer surplus.

Now the government imposes a tariff of 10 percent on imported bikes. Figure 7.3 shows the consumers' view of the bicycle market with the tariff. The tariff raises the price that consumers must pay for bikes (both imported and domestically produced) to $330.

By raising the price to $330, the tariff forces consumers who were buying the 1.6 million bikes to make a decision:

- Some will continue to buy bikes, paying $30 more per bike.

- Some will decide that a bike is not worth $330 to them, so they will not buy at the higher price.

In Figure 7.3, quantity demanded falls from D_0 to D_1, a decrease of 0.2 million bikes. The net loss to consumers is the shaded area $a + b + c + d$, because consumer surplus declines from triangle *FEC* to triangle *FGH*. Area $a + b + c$ is the loss of $30 per bike of consumer surplus for those who continue to buy bikes at the higher price. Area d is the loss of consumer surplus for those who stop buying bikes. In our example, the consumer surplus loss is $45 million per year.

What domestic consumers lose from the tariff (here $45 million) is larger than what domestic producers gain ($21 million). The reason is straightforward: Producers gain the price markup on only the domestic output, while consumers are forced to pay the same price markup on both domestic output and imports. Figures 7.2 and 7.3 bring this out clearly for the bicycle example. The tariff brought bicycle producers only area *a* in gains, but it cost consumers this same area *a* plus areas *b* + *c* + *d*. As far as the effects on bicycle consumers and bicycle producers alone are concerned, the tariff is definitely a net loss.

THE TARIFF AS GOVERNMENT REVENUE

The effects of a tariff on the well-being of consumers and producers do not exhaust its effects on the importing country. As long as the tariff is not so high as to prohibit all imports, it also brings revenue to the country's government. This revenue equals the unit amount of the tariff times the volume of imports with the tariff. In Figure 7.3 the total government revenue from collecting the tariff is area *c*, equal to $18 million per year (the tariff of $30 times the imports of $M_1 = 0.6$ million).

The country's government could do any of several things with the tariff revenue. The revenue could be used to pay for extra government spending on socially worthwhile projects. It could be matched by an equal cut in some other tax, such as the income tax. Or it could just become extra income for greedy government officials. Although what form the tariff takes can certainly matter, the central point is that this revenue accrues to somebody within the country. It counts as an element of national gain to be weighed in with the consumer losses and producer gains from the tariff.[2]

THE NET NATIONAL LOSS FROM A TARIFF

By combining the effects of the tariff on consumers, producers, and the government, we can determine the net effect of the tariff on the importing nation as a whole.

The first key step is to impose a social value judgment. How much do you really care about each group's gains or losses? If one group gains and another loses, how big must the gain be to outweigh the other group's loss? To make any overall judgment, you must first decide how to weigh each dollar of effect on each group. That is unavoidable. Anybody who expresses an opinion on whether a tariff is good or bad necessarily does so on the basis of a personal value judgment about how important each group is.

The basic analysis starts out by using the **one-dollar, one-vote metric:** *Every dollar of gain or loss is just as important as every other dollar of gain or*

---

[2] We note a possible exception. Part of the tariff may be used up as real resource costs of administering and enforcing the tariff; thus this amount does not represent a national gain.

loss, regardless of who the gainers or losers are. Let's use this measure of well-being here just as we did in Chapter 2. Later we discuss what difference it would make if we choose to weigh one group's dollar stakes more heavily than those of other groups.

If the one-dollar, one-vote metric is applied, then a tariff like the one graphed in Figures 7.2 and 7.3 brings a clear net loss to the importing nation and to the world as a whole. Figure 7.4 shows the same bicycle example. We have seen that the dollar value of the consumer losses exceeds the dollar value of the producer gains from the tariff. We have also seen that the government collects some tariff revenue, an element of national gain. The left side of Figure 7.4 makes it clear that the dollar value of what the consumers lose (area $a + b + c + d$), exceeds even the sum of the producer gains (area a), and the government tariff revenues (area c).

FIGURE 7.4 The Net National Loss from a Tariff in Two Equivalent Diagrams

Consumers lose	Area $a + b + c + d$		= $45 million (loss)
Producers gain	Area a		= $21 million
Government collects	Area c	in tariff revenue	= $18 million
Net national loss from the tariff = Area	b	$+ d$	= $6 million

For a small importing country, a tariff brings a net national loss. What it costs consumers is greater than what it brings producers plus the government's tariff revenue. The two reasons for the net loss are summarized in areas b and d. Area b (the production effect) represents the loss from making at higher marginal cost what could have been bought for less from foreign exporters. Area d (the consumption effect) represents the loss from discouraging import consumption that is worth more than what the nation would pay the foreign exporters.

The same net national loss can be shown in another way. The right side of Figure 7.4 shows the market for imports of bicycles. As we saw in Chapter 2, we can derive our demand curve for imports of bicycles by subtracting the domestic supply curve from the domestic demand curve for bicycles at each price (horizontally). That is, for each possible price, the quantity demanded of imported bicycles equals the domestic quantity demanded minus the domestic quantity supplied at that price.

We can use the right side of Figure 7.4 to show some of the same information that is shown on the left side. With free trade, the price of imports is $300. The country imports M_0 bikes. With the imposition of the tariff, the domestic price of imported bikes rises to $330. The country then imports only M_1 bikes. The government collects tariff revenue equal to area c.

The net national loss from the tariff is shown on the right side as the area of triangle $b + d$. To see that this triangle has the same area as the sum of the areas of the two triangles b and d on the left side, consider the heights and bases of the triangles. All of the triangles have the same height (the tariff per unit). The base of triangle b is the reduction in imports that are replaced by domestic production. The base of triangle d is the import reduction that results from the lower domestic consumption. The two bases add up to the total reduction in imports, the base of triangle $(b + d)$. With the same height and combined bases, the sum of the areas of triangles b and d equals the area of triangle $b + d$.

The net national loss from the tariff shown in Figure 7.4 is not hard to estimate empirically. The key information we need consists only of the amount of the tariff per unit and the estimated volume by which the tariff reduces imports, ΔM. The usual way of arriving at this information is to find out the percent price markup the tariff represents, the initial dollar value of imports, and the percent elasticity, or responsiveness, of import quantities to price changes. It is handy, and perhaps surprising, that the net national loss from the tariff can be estimated just using information on imports, as on the right side of Figure 7.4, without even knowing the domestic demand and supply curves. In our bicycle example, the net loss $b + d$ equals $6 million.

Why is there a net loss? What economic logic lies behind the geometric finding that the net national loss equals areas $b + d$? With a little reflection, we can see that these areas represent gains from international trade and specialization that are lost because of the tariff. **Area *d*,** sometimes called the **consumption effect** of the tariff, shows the loss to consumers in the importing nation based on the reduction in their total consumption of bicycles. They would have been willing to pay prices up to $330 to get the extra foreign bicycles. The extra bicycles would have cost the nation only $300 a bike in payments to foreign sellers. Yet the tariff discourages them from buying these bicycles. What the consumers lose in area d, nobody else gains. Area d is a "deadweight" loss, the inefficiency for those consumers squeezed out of buying bicycles because the tariff artificially raises the domestic price.

Area *b* is a welfare loss based on the fact that some consumer demand is shifted from imports to more expensive domestic production. The tariff raises

Extension   The Effective Rate of Protection

To gain more understanding of how much protection is given to domestic producers by a country's tariffs, we need to take a closer look at how products are produced. We are interested in how tariffs affect domestic "value added" in an industry. Value added is the amount that is available to make payments to the primary production factors in the industry. That is, value added is the sum of wages paid to labor, the rents paid to landowners, and the profits and other returns to the owners and providers of capital.

In addition to these primary factors, firms also use various kinds of components and material inputs in production. This is more important than it sounds. It means that many tariffs matter to the industry, not just the tariff on the product it produces. Specifically, firms in a given industry are affected by tariffs on their purchased inputs as well as by the tariff on the product they sell. Firms producing bicycles, for example, would be hurt by tariffs on steel or rubber. This complicates the task of measuring the effect of the whole set of tariffs on an individual industry's firms.

To give these points their due requires a detailed portrayal of supply–demand interactions in many markets at once. To cut down on the elaborate details, economists have developed a simpler measure that does part of the job. The measure quantifies the effects of the whole tariff structure on one industry's value added per unit of output without trying to estimate how much its output, or other outputs and prices, would change. The **effective rate**

of protection of an individual industry is defined as the percentage by which the entire set of a nation's trade barriers raises the industry's value added per unit of output.

The effective rate of protection for the industry can be quite different from the percent tariff paid by consumers on its output (the "nominal" rate of protection). This difference is brought out clearly by the example on the facing page.

What are the effects of a 10 percent tariff on bicycle imports and a 5 percent tariff on imports of steel, rubber, and all other material inputs into the bicycle industry? The 10 percent tariff on bicycles by itself raises their price and the value added by the bicycle industry by $30 per bike, as before. The 5 percent tariff on bicycle inputs costs the bicycle industry $11 per bike by raising the prices of inputs. The two sets of tariffs together would raise the industry's unit value added by only $19 per bike. But this extra $19 represents a protection of value added (incomes) in the bicycle industry of 23.8 percent of value added, not just 10 percent or less, as one might have thought from a casual look at the nominal tariff rates themselves.

This example illustrates two of the basic points brought out by the concept of effective rate of protection:

- A given industry's incomes, or value added, will be affected by trade barriers on its inputs as well as trade barriers on its output.

domestic production from 0.6 to 0.8 million bikes at the expense of imports. The domestic supply curve (which also shows the marginal cost of domestic production) is assumed to be upward sloping. Each extra bicycle costs more and more to produce, rising from a resource cost of $300 up to a cost of $330. The domestic resource cost of producing these bicycles is more than the $300 price at which the bicycles are available abroad. This extra cost of shifting to more expensive home production, called the **production effect** of the tariff, is represented by area *b*. Like area *d*, it is a deadweight loss. It is part of what consumers pay, but neither the government nor bicycle producers gain it. It is the amount by which the cost of drawing domestic resources away from other uses exceeds the savings

- The effective rate of protection will be greater than the nominal rate when the industry's output is protected by a higher duty than the tariff duties on its inputs.

We add three other insights. First, if the tariff rates on the inputs are the same as the tariff rate on the output, then this rate is also the effective rate of protection. (Try this by modifying our example by using a 5 percent tariff on bicycles.) Second, the effective rate of protection can be negative. The tariff structure can penalize value added in the industry. (Try this using a 2 percent tariff on bicycles.) Third, export producers are penalized with something like negative effective protection if their costs are increased by tariffs on the inputs they use in production. (Try this by changing our example to one in which the country's bicycle producers try to sell to foreign buyers at the world price of $300 per bike.)

Illustrative calculation of an effective rate of protection

$$\text{Effective rate of protection for bicycle industry} = \frac{v' - v}{v} = \frac{\$99 - \$80}{\$80} = 23.8\%$$

To see who is getting protected by trade barriers, it helps (1) to distinguish an industry and its suppliers and (2) to look at the effects of the whole set of barriers, not just the one directly protecting the industry. In this case, the tariff on bicycles helps the domestic bike industry, but the tariffs on the inputs the bicycle industry buys hurt it. The net result in this case is an "effective rate of protection" of 23.8 percent.

from not paying foreigners to sell us the 200,000 extra units. Thus, the gains from trade lost by the tariff come in two forms: the consumption effect of area *d* plus the production effect of area *b*.

The basic analysis of a tariff identifies areas *b* and *d* as the net national loss from a tariff only if certain assumptions are granted. One key assumption is that the one-dollar, one-vote metric is an appropriate measure of different groups' interest. Use of this measure implies that consumers' losses of areas *a* and *c* were exactly offset, dollar for dollar, by producers' gain of area *a* and the government's collection of area *c*. That is what produced (*b* + *d*) as the net loss for the nation. Suppose that you personally reject this metric. Suppose, for example, that you think that each dollar of gain for the bicycle producers is somehow more important to you than each dollar of consumer loss, perhaps because you see the bicycle consumers as a group society has pampered too much. If that is your view, you will not accept areas *b* and *d* as the net national loss from the tariff. The same basic analysis of the tariff is still useful to you, however. You can stipulate how much more weight you put on each dollar of effect on bicycle producers than on each dollar for consumers. Then you can apply your own differential weights to each group's dollar stake to see whether the net effect of the tariff is still negative.

THE TERMS-OF-TRADE EFFECT AND A NATIONALLY OPTIMAL TARIFF

It is time to relax a key assumption we have been making. So far, this chapter has used the small-country assumption: We have assumed that the importing nation, here the United States, cannot affect the world price of the imported good. In particular, the tariff on bicycle imports did not affect the world price of bicycles, which stood fixed at $300, tariff or no tariff.

The small-country assumption is often valid. Many individual nations as importers have small shares of world markets for individual commodities. Any feasible change in a small-country's demand for imports is so small that it has (almost) no effect on the big world market. For instance, if Costa Rica reduced its demand for imported bicycles by imposing a tariff, the effect on the world market would be imperceptible. Costa Rican importers would still have to pay foreign suppliers the same world price if they wanted to buy any of their bicycles. Similarly, Singapore could not expect to force foreign sellers of rice to supply it more cheaply. Any attempt to do so would simply prove that Singapore was a price-taker on the world market by causing rice exporters to avoid Singapore altogether, with little effect on the world rice price.

Yet in some cases a nation has a large enough share of the world market for one of its imports that the country's buying can affect the world price unilaterally. A nation collectively can have this **monopsony power** even in cases in which no individual buyer within the nation has it. For example, the United States looms large in the world auto market. If the U.S. government imposes a tariff on imported autos, the reduction in U.S. demand for foreign autos would have a noticeable adverse affects on foreign exporters. In the face of lower U.S. demand, those exporters would fight to maintain sales by reducing their export prices. The United States probably has the same monopsony power to some extent in the world markets for many other goods.

A nation with such power over foreign selling prices could exploit this advantage with a tariff on imports. Let's look at a case in which a **large country** can affect the world price of a good it imports, just by imposing a tariff. In this case, the tariff has a **terms-of-trade effect.** Recall that in Part I we defined the terms of trade as the ratio of the international prices of our exports to the international prices of our imports.

Suppose that the United States (now a large country) imposes a small tariff on bicycles. Imposing the tariff makes the price paid by U.S. consumers exceed the price paid to foreign suppliers. Now, however, the tariff is likely to lower the foreign price a bit as well as raise the domestic price a bit. As long as foreign exporters can produce and sell to the United States smaller amounts at a lower marginal cost, they are likely to prefer to cut their price to the United States a bit to limit the drop in their sales to the United States. Why? Because before the tariff, under free trade, they were selling an amount of bicycles to the United States that just brought their marginal cost up to the world price, say $300, which was also the price in the United States. If the U.S. government imposes a tariff on each bike, the foreign bicycle exporters might try to insist that they be paid the same old $300 on each bicycle. But if they did, the price to U.S. buyers would now equal $300 plus the tariff, and U.S. customers would buy fewer bikes. For each competing foreign exporter, that means losing some sales at their $300 price. But the marginal cost is now less than $300 at the lower rate of production and sales. Each of them would be better off shaving the world price a bit below $300 as long as the price that they charge is still above the now-lower marginal cost. The United States succeeds in paying a lower price to foreigners on every imported bike, even though the tariff-inclusive price to U.S. consumers is higher than $300.

This is what makes it possible for the United States to gain as a nation from its own tariff. To be sure, there is still a loss in economic efficiency both for the United States and for the world. By discouraging some imports that would have been worth more to buyers than the price being paid to cover the foreign seller's costs—and by shifting some production to higher-cost domestic producers—the tariff still has its costs. But as long as the tariff is small, those costs are outweighed for the United States by the gains from continuing most of the previous imports at a lower price paid to foreign exporters. So, for tariff rates that are not too high, the United States as a nation is better off than with free trade.

Figure 7.5 shows the effects of a rather small tariff, in this case $6 per bicycle. As in Figure 7.4, the right side of Figure 7.5 shows the market for bicycles in the United States, and the left side shows the market for bicycle imports into the United States. Because the United States is a large country relative to foreign export capacity, the foreign supply-of-exports curve slopes upward (instead of being flat at a given world price, as in Figure 7.4B).

With free trade, the market for bicycle imports clears at the price of $300, and the United States imports 1 million bikes. If the U.S. government then imposes a tariff of $6 per bike, the tariff drives a wedge of $6 between the price that exporters receive and the price that importers pay. Even with this tariff wedge, the market still must clear. The quantity of exports (from the supply-of-exports curve) must equal the quantity of imports (from the demand-for-imports curve), given the $6 difference in price.

In Figure 7.5A, the $6 tariff drives up the domestic price of imports to $303 and lowers the price charged by foreign exporters to $297. The quantity traded declines by a small amount, to 0.96 million bikes. We can use these conclusions to show what is happening in the U.S. market for bikes. If the domestic price

FIGURE 7.5   A Large Country Imposes a Small Tariff

If the foreign export supply curve slopes up, an importing country collectively has some power over the price that it pays foreigners for its imports, even if individual importers have no such power. The importing country can exploit this monopsony power. Here, the United States imposes a relatively small tariff of $6 per bike imported. The United States has net gain in well-being of area *e* minus areas *b* and *d*.

rises to $303, the domestic quantity produced rises to 0.62 million bikes and the domestic quantity demanded declines to 1.58 million bikes.

What is the effect of the tariff on the national well-being of the United States? Consumer surplus decreases by area *a + b + c + d*, and producer surplus increases by area *a*. The government collects tariff revenue equal to area *c + e* (the tariff of $6 per unit times 0.96 million units imported). Who *really* pays the tariff? For a large country, domestic consumers still pay part of the tariff, area *c*. The new wrinkle *for a large importing country* is that *foreign exporters also pay part of the tariff* (area *e*), because they lower their export price when the tariff is imposed. If foreigners pay part of our taxes, then this is a gain to the importing country (though not to the world as a whole).

What is the overall effect on the importing country if it imposes a small tariff? The importing country still loses areas *b* and *d*, the triangles of inefficiency that we also saw for the small-country case. This small loss is easily outweighed by the gain of area *e*, the part of the tariff that is absorbed by foreign exporters when they lower their export price. *For a suitably small tariff imposed by a large importing country, the importing country gains national well-being*, because area *e* is larger than areas *b* and *d*. For tariff rates that are not too high, the United States is better off than with free trade. In the case of a $6 tariff, the net gain to the United States is $2.82 million, which is the gain of area *e* ($2.88 million) minus the loss of area *b* + *d* ($0.06 million).

If a small tariff works for the nation with power over prices, higher tariffs work even better—but only up to a point. To see the limits to a nation's monopsony power, we can start by noting that *a prohibitive tariff cannot be optimal.* Suppose that the United States were to put a tariff on bicycle imports that was so high as to make all imports unprofitable. A tariff of over $150 a bike in Figure 7.5 would drive the price received by foreign suppliers below $225. Foreign suppliers would decide not to sell any bicycles to the United States at all. Lacking any revenues earned partly at the expense of foreign suppliers, the United States would find itself saddled with nothing but the loss of all gains from international trade in bicycles.

Is there a "best" tariff rate for the large importing country to impose, if it is purely driven by its own national well-being? The answer is yes, assuming that the rest of the world does not retaliate. This best tariff is called the **nationally optimal tariff,** the tariff that creates the largest net gain for the country imposing it. For a large country, this optimal tariff lies between no tariff and a prohibitively high one.

The optimal tariff can be derived in the same way as the optimal price reduction for any monopsonist, any buyer with market power. Appendix D derives the formula for the optimal tariff rate. It turns out that the optimal tariff rate, as a fraction of the price paid to foreigners, equals the reciprocal of the price elasticity of foreign supply of our imports.

It makes sense that the lower the foreign supply elasticity, the higher our optimal tariff rate. The more inelastically foreigners keep to supplying a nearly fixed amount to us, the more we can get away with exploiting them. Conversely, if their supply is infinitely elastic (the small-country case), facing us with a fixed world price, then we cannot get them to accept lower prices. If their supply elasticity is infinite, our own tariff hurts only us, and the optimal tariff is zero.

Figure 7.6 shows an optimal tariff for a large country. The nation gains the price reduction on foreign bicycle imports, represented by area *e*. This considerably exceeds what the nation loses by reducing its imports of bicycles (area *b* + *d*). The national gain, *e* − *b* − *d,* is greater than the national gain at any other tariff rate.[3]

For the world as a whole, however, the nationally optimal tariff is still unambiguously bad. What the nation gains is less than what foreigners lose from our tariff. Figure 7.6 shows this. The United States gains area *e* only at the expense of foreign suppliers, dollar for dollar, leaving no net effect on the world from this redistribution of income through the price change. But foreign suppliers suffer

---

[3] As Figure 7.6 is drawn, the tariff rate does fit the optimal-tariff formula. The rate equals $50/$275 or about 18.2 percent. The elasticity of foreign supply works out to be 5.5 at this point on the foreign supply curve, so the tariff rate of about 18.2 percent is the reciprocal of 5.5. This would not be true for any other tariff rate.

FIGURE 7.6

The Nationally
Optimal Tariff

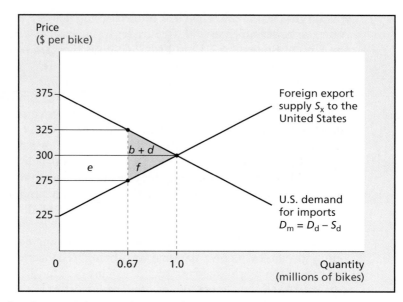

The large importing country in theory can gain the most by imposing an optimal tariff. Here the nationally optimal tariff is $50 per bike, and the importing country gains area e – area $b + d$. The foreign country is harmed, losing area f, and it may retaliate. Even without retaliation, the world is worse off because of the nationally optimal tariff. The global inefficiency equals area $b + d$ and area f.

more than that. They also lose area f in additional surplus on the exports discouraged by the tariff. Therefore, the world loses areas $b + d$ and f. This large triangle (the shaded area in Figure 7.6) is a loss of part of the global gains from trade. U.S. consumers value foreign bicycles more highly above the level of imports of 0.67 million a year than it costs foreign suppliers to make and sell them. The tariff may be nationally optimal, but it still means a net loss to the world.

Even for large nations, it might be unwise to levy what looks like an optimal tariff. Even if individual foreign suppliers cannot fight back, their governments can. Foreign governments may retaliate by putting up new tariff barriers against our exports. Knowing this, even large countries like the United States restrain the use of their power in individual import markets.

Summary

A **tariff** is a tax on imports. It redistributes well-being from domestic consumers of the product to domestic producers and the government, which collects the tariff revenue. For a **small country** (one that cannot affect world prices), a tariff on imports lowers national well-being. It costs consumers more than it benefits producers and the government.

To reinforce your understanding of these basic effects of a tariff on well-being, imagine how you might describe each of them to legislators who are considering a tariff law. Remember what this performance in the policy arena requires. You have to speak in language that is clear to a wide audience. You can't use any diagram or equation—no legislator will be impressed by such abstractions. You can, however, use the following concise verbal descriptions to explain each of the key effects shown by lettered areas in Figures 7.2 through 7.4:

1. "By raising the price on strictly domestic sales, a tariff redistributes incomes from consumers to producers. The amount redistributed is the price increase times the average quantity of domestic sales." (This describes area *a*.)

2. "A tariff shifts some purchases from foreign goods to home goods. This costs more resources to make at home than to buy abroad." (This describes **area *b*,** the **production effect.**)

3. "A tariff makes consumers pay tax revenue directly to the government." (This describes area *c*.)

4. "A tariff discourages some purchases that were worth more than they cost the nation." (This describes **area *d*,** the **consumption effect.**)

5. "Both by shifting some purchases toward costly home goods and by discouraging some purchases worth more than they cost the nation, the tariff costs the nation as a whole. The cost equals one-half the tariff amount times the drop in our imports." (This describes area *b* + *d*, the net national loss.)

The effects of tariffs on producer interests are further clarified by the concept of the **effective rate of protection,** which measures the percent effect of the entire tariff structure on the value added per unit of output in each industry. This concept incorporates the point that incomes in any one industry are affected by the tariffs on many products.

When a country as a whole can affect the price at which foreigners supply imports, the country has **monopsony power.** For such a large country, a positive tariff can increase national well-being because the tariff has a beneficial **terms-of-trade effect.** The **nationally optimal tariff** yields the largest possible gain. However, this tariff is only optimal if foreign governments do not retaliate with tariffs on our exports. With or without retaliation, the nationally optimal tariff is still bad for the world as a whole.

Suggested Reading   For a good example of practical estimates of the welfare effects of trade barriers, see the estimates for 21 imported products in Hufbauer and Elliott (1994).

Questions and Problems

◆ 1. What is the minimum quantitative information you would need to calculate the net national loss from a tariff in a small price-taking country?

2. "A tariff on imports of a product hurts domestic consumers of this product more than it benefits domestic producers of the product." Do you agree or disagree? Why?

◆ 3. What is the production effect of a tariff? How would you describe it in words, without reference to any diagram or numbers? How would you show it on a diagram, and how would you compute its value?

4. What is the consumption effect of a tariff? How would you describe it in words, without reference to any diagram or numbers? How would you show it on a diagram, and how would you compute its value?

♦ 5. You have been asked to quantify the effects of a country's tariff on sugar. The hard part of the work is already done: Somebody has estimated how many pounds of sugar would be produced, consumed, and imported by the country if there were no sugar duty. You are given the information shown in the table.

	Situation with Import Tariff	Estimated Situation without Tariff
World price	$0.10 per pound	$0.10 per pound
Tariff	$0.02 per pound	0
Domestic price	$0.12 per pound	$0.10 per pound
Domestic consumption (billions of pounds per year)	20	22
Domestic production (billions of pounds per year)	8	6
Imports (billions of pounds per year)	12	16

Calculate the following measures:

a. The domestic consumers' gain from removing the tariff.

b. The domestic producers' loss from removing the tariff.

c. The government tariff revenue loss.

d. The net effect on national well-being.

6. Suppose that Canada produces 1.4 million bicycles a year and imports another 1 million; there is no tariff or other import barrier. Bicycles sell for $400 each. Parliament is considering a $40 tariff on bicycles like the one portrayed in Figures 7.2 through 7.4. What is the maximum net national loss that this could cause Canada? What is the minimum national loss if Canada is a small country that cannot affect the world price? (*Hint:* Draw a diagram like Figure 7.4 and put the numbers given here on it. Next, imagine the possible positions and slopes of the relevant curves.)

♦ 7. As in question 5, you have been asked to quantify the effects of removing an import duty; somebody has already estimated the effects on the country's production, consumption, and imports. This time the facts are different. The import duty in question is a 5 percent tariff on imported motorcycles. You are given the information shown in the table.

	Current Situation with 5 Percent Tariff	Estimated Situation Without Tariff
World price of motorcycles	$2,000 per cycle	$2,050 per cycle
Tariff at 5 percent	$100 per cycle	0
Domestic price	$2,100 per cycle	$2,050 per cycle
Number of cycles purchased domestically per year	100,000	105,000
Number of cycles produced domestically per year	40,000	35,000
Number of cycles imported per year	60,000	70,000

Calculate the following:

a. The consumer gain from removing the duty.

b. The producer loss from removing the duty.

c. The government tariff revenue loss.

d. The net effect on the country's well-being.

Why does the net effect on the country as a whole differ from the result in question 5?

8. For the international trade market for bicycles shown in Figure 7.5, demonstrate that a rather large tariff, for instance, a tariff which resulted in imports of 0.33 million bicycles, would not be an optimal tariff for the importing country.

✦ 9. This problem concerns the effective rate of protection. With free trade, each dollar of value added in the domestic cloth-making industry is divided as follows: 40 cents value added, 30 cents for cotton yarn, and 30 cents for other fibers. Suppose that a 25 percent ad valorem tariff is placed on cloth imports and a 1/6 tariff (16.7 percent) goes on cotton yarn imports. (There is no tariff on imports of other fibers.) Work out the division of the tariff-ridden unit value of $1.25 (the free-trade unit cloth value of $1 plus the cloth tariff) into value added, payments for cotton, and payments for other fibers. Then calculate the effective rate of protection.

10. What is the formula for the nationally optimal tariff? What is the optimal tariff if the foreign supply of our imports is infinitely elastic?

Chapter **Eight**

Nontariff Barriers to Imports

Protecting domestic producers against import competition

- Clearly helps those producers.

- Harms domestic consumers of the products.

- Probably hurts the importing nation as a whole.

- Almost surely hurts the world as a whole.

So it is with a typical tariff barrier, as suggested in Chapter 7, and so it is with other kinds of barriers against imports that we will analyze in this chapter. Knowing this, you might expect that protectionist interests will have most sway at the national or even local level, while the interests of consumers and the world as a whole will be better defended at the global level. That is in fact the case.

This chapter has three major purposes:

- To examine various kinds of nontariff barriers to imports and their effects.

- To survey evidence on how large the deadweight losses from protectionism actually are.

- To discuss the role of the World Trade Organization (and the General Agreement on Tariffs and Trade, which came before it) as the locus of global agreements to liberalize trade.

Those agreements have succeeded in cutting tariffs. But as tariffs have declined, the use of nontariff import barriers to provide protection has increased. Global trade agreements have only recently tried to reduce these nontariff barriers, and they have not made nearly so much progress against them as they have against tariffs.

TYPES OF NONTARIFF BARRIERS TO IMPORTS

A **nontariff barrier (NTB)** to imports is any policy used by the government to reduce imports, other than a simple tariff on imports. Nontariff barriers can take many forms, including import quotas, discriminatory product standards, buy-at-home rules for government purchases, and administrative red tape to harass importers of foreign products.

An NTB reduces imports by operating through one or more of the following channels:

• Limiting the quantity of imports.

• Increasing the cost of getting imports into the market.

• Creating uncertainty about the conditions under which imports will be permitted.

Figure 8.1 provides a listing of major types of NTBs and indicates the main way that each affects imports. Although antidumping duties and countervailing duties are not listed in the figure, they are also often considered NTBs. Because governments claim that they impose these kinds of duties in response to unfair practices by foreign exporters, we defer an in-depth discussion of antidumping and countervailing duties to Chapter 10. Here we will examine carefully several types of NTBs listed in Figure 8.1.

THE IMPORT QUOTA

The best-known nontariff barrier is the **import quota** (or just **quota**), a limit on the total quantity of imports of a product allowed into the country during a period of time (for instance, a year). One way or another, the government gives out a limited number of licenses to import the quota quantity legally and prohibits importing without a license. As long as the quota quantity is less than the quantity that people would want to import without the quota, the quota has an impact on the market for this product.

There are several reasons why protectionists and government officials may favor using a quota instead of a tariff. For instance,

• A quota ensures that the quantity of imports is strictly limited; a tariff would allow import quantity to increase if foreign producers cut their prices or if our domestic demand increases.

• A quota gives government officials greater power. As we will see below, these officials often have administrative authority over who gets the import licenses under a quota system, and they can use this power to their advantage (for instance, by taking bribes).

Note that these are not arguments showing that an import quota is in the national interest.

FIGURE 8.1   Major Types of NTBs

Type	What It Is	Channel of Effects
Import quota	Quantitative limit on imports	Quantity
Voluntary export restraint (VER)	Quantitative limit on exports (based on threat of import restriction)	Quantity
Tariff-quota	Allows imports to enter the country at a low or zero tariff up to a specified quantity; imposes a higher tariff on imports above this quantity	Quantity (if the tariff for potential imports above the specified quantity is so high that it is prohibitive, so that there are no imports above the specified quantity)
Government procurement	Laws and government rules that favor local products when the government is the buyer	Quantity (for instance, an outright prohibition) Cost of importing (for instance, special procedures for imports)
Local content and mixing requirements	Require specified use of local labor, materials, or other products	Quantity
Technical and product standards	Discriminate against imports by writing or enforcing standards in a way that adversely affects imports more than domestic products	Cost (to conform to standards or demonstrate compliance) Uncertainty (if approval procedures are unclear)
Advance deposit	Requires some of the value of intended imports to be deposited with the government, and allows the government to pay low- or zero-interest on these deposits	Cost (foregone interest)
Import licensing	Requires importers to apply for and receive approval for intended imports	Cost (of application procedure) Uncertainty (if basis for approval is unclear)
Other customs procedures (classification of product, valuation of product, procedures for clearing)	Affect the amount of tariff duties owed or the quota limit applied; procedures can be slow or costly	Cost Uncertainty

Let's compare the quota to a tariff as a way of impeding imports. As we saw in Chapter 7, a tariff increases the domestic price of the imported product and reduces the quantity imported. A quota reduces the quantity imported. Does a quota also increase the domestic price of the imported product? We will see that the answer is yes. In fact, we will see that, in most ways, the effects of a quota are the same as the effects of a tariff that leads to the same quantity of imports as the quota, if markets are perfectly competitive.

As we did with the analysis of the tariff, we begin our analysis of the quota with the small-country case and then proceed to the large-country case. Our analysis in the text assumes that all relevant markets are highly competitive. (The box "A Domestic Monopoly Prefers a Quota" examines an alternative case.)

Quota versus Tariff for a Small Country

The effects of a quota on bicycles are portrayed in Figure 8.2 for a small importing country facing a given world price of $300 per bicycle. Recall that a country is "small" if its decisions about how much to import of a product have no effect on the going world price of the product. That is, the foreign supply of exports to this small country is infinitely elastic at this price. In our example in Figure 8.2, the country would import 1.0 million bikes per year with free trade. The government then imposes a quota that limits imports to a smaller quantity, say, 0.6 million bikes per year.

The quota alters the available supply of bicycles within the importing country. For all domestic prices above the world price, the total (domestic plus import) supply within the country equals the domestic supply curve plus the fixed quota quantity (Q_Q) of imports. At the world price of $300 there would be excess demand for bicycles in the importing country. The market in the importing country will clear only at the higher price of $330, as shown by the intersection of the total available supply curve ($S_d + Q_Q$) and the domestic demand curve (D_d) on the left side of Figure 8.2. At the domestic price of $330, the domestic quantity supplied is 0.8 million, the quantity imported is the quota quantity of 0.6 million, and

FIGURE 8.2   The Effects of an Import Quota under Competitive Conditions, Small Importing Country

A quota cuts off the supply of imports by placing an absolute limit (Q_Q) on what can be bought from abroad. Under the competitive conditions shown here, the effects of an import quota are the same as those of a tariff that cuts imports just as much (with the possible exception of who gets shaded area *c*). To see this, compare the prices, quantities, and areas *a, b, c,* and *d* shown here with those shown in Figure 7.4.

the domestic quantity demanded is 1.4 million. (We can see the same effect on domestic price by using the country's demand-for-imports curve shown in the left side of the figure. If the quota limits imports to 0.6 million, then the demand for imports indicates a price of $330.)

These effects on domestic price and quantities should sound familiar. They are the same as the effects of the 10 percent tariff shown in Figures 7.2 through 7.4. For a competitive market, the effects of a quota on price, quantities, and well-being are the same as those of an equivalent tariff, with one possible exception. Here are the effects that are the same. In comparison with free trade:

- The quota results in a higher price and larger production quantity, so domestic producers gain surplus equal to area *a*.

- With the higher price and smaller consumption quantity, domestic consumers lose surplus equal to area *a* + *b* + *c* + *d*.

- Area *b* is a loss to the country. The quota induces domestic producers to increase production from 0.6 to 0.8 million. The marginal costs of producing these additional bicycles at home rise up to $330 (along S_d), when these additional bicycles instead could be purchased from foreign exporters for only $300.

- Area *d* is also a loss to the country. The quota reduces quantity consumed from 1.6 million to 1.4 million. The consumer surplus lost on these bicycles is not a gain to anyone else.

Therefore, the quota creates the same two deadweight losses (*b* + *d*), as does the tariff.

This leaves rectangular area *c,* the "possible exception" to the equivalence. With a tariff, area *c* is government tariff revenue. With a quota, what is it? Who gets it?

Ways to Allocate Import Licenses

The quota license to import is a license to buy the product from foreign suppliers at the world price of $300 and resell these units at the domestic price of $330. The quota results in a price markup (or economic rent) of $30 per unit imported. For all units imported with the quota, the markup totals to rectangular area *c*.

Who gets this rectangle of price markup? That depends on how the licenses to import the quota quantity are distributed. Here are the main ways to allocate import licenses:

- The government allocates the licenses for free to importers using a rule or process that involves (almost) no resource costs.

- The government auctions off the licenses to the highest bidders.

- The government allocates the licenses through application and selection procedures that require the use of substantial resources.

Extension   A Domestic Monopoly Prefers a Quota

The analysis of an import quota presented in the text presumes that the domestic industry in the importing country is highly competitive. With perfect competition we saw that the effect of the quota on domestic producer surplus is the same as the effect of a tariff that results in the same quantity of imports. In this case the domestic industry would not have a strong preference between the quota and the equivalent tariff.

Domestic industries are often highly competitive, but not always. Especially for a small country, in some industries no more than one or two domestic firms can achieve scale economies in production if they are selling only to local consumers. This would be true for industries like automobiles or steel.

If the domestic industry is a monopoly, would the monopoly have a preference between a tariff and a quota? The answer is yes. The monopoly prefers the quota (even if the monopoly does not get any of the price markup on the imports themselves). Let's look at this more closely. (We assume that the importing country is a small country, but the same idea holds for the large-country case.)

The domestic monopoly would like to use its market power to set the domestic price to maximize its profits. But with free trade the world price becomes the domestic price. Imports entering the country at the world price prevent the domestic monopoly from charging a higher price than the world price. If it did try to charge a higher price, most consumers would just buy imports. Free trade is a good substitute for national antitrust or antimonopoly policy.

If the country's government imposes a tariff, the domestic price rises to be the world price plus the tariff. The pricing power of the monopoly is still severely limited. If the monopoly tries to charge more than this tariff-inclusive price, again most consumers would just buy imports. Domestic consumers can buy as much of the imported product as they wish, as long as they are willing to pay the tariff-inclusive price. They will not pay more for the locally produced product.

If instead the country's government imposes a quota, the whole game changes. No matter how high the monopoly raises its domestic price, imports cannot exceed the quota quantity. Domestic consumers cannot just shift to imports, because there is a strict limit on how much they can import. The marginal source of more of the product is now the domestic monopoly. After allowing for the quota quantity of imports, the domestic monopoly can set the domestic price to maximize its profits. In comparison to a tariff that results in the same quantity of imports, the domestic monopoly prefers an import

Tariff, domestic monopoly

quota, because the monopoly can set a higher price and garner larger profits. However, these higher profits come at a cost to the importing country as a whole. If the domestic industry is a monopoly, the quota causes a larger net national loss.

A pair of graphs for the domestic monopoly can highlight the differences between the tariff and the quota. The figure on the previous page shows the case of the tariff. With free trade at the world price P_0, the monopolist cannot charge a price higher than P_0, so the monopoly produces all units for which its marginal costs are less than this free-trade price. The tariff raises the domestic price to P_1, but the monopolist cannot charge a higher price than this tariff-inclusive price. The monopolist increases production from S_0 to S_1 and increases its profits by area a. Imports with the tariff are M_1. The net loss in national well-being because of the tariff equals area $b + d$.

The figure below shows what happens if this same M_1 quantity of imports is instead set as a quota. With the fixed quota quantity of imports, the monopoly views its market as domestic demand less this quota quantity (for all prices above the world price P_0). That is, the monopoly faces the downward-sloping net demand curve (the domestic demand curve minus the quota quantity). Using the net demand curve, the monopoly can determine the marginal revenue from lowering price to sell additional units. The monopoly

maximizes profit when marginal revenue equals marginal cost, producing and selling quantity S_2 and charging price P_2.

In comparison with the tariff, the monopoly uses the quota to increase the product price ($P_2 > P_1$), to reduce the quantity that it produces and sells ($S_2 < S_1$), and to increase its profit. The monopoly prefers the quota, but the monopoly's gain comes with some additional social cost. In comparison with the tariff, the economic inefficiency of the quota is larger. The nation as a whole loses not only area $b + d$ but also the shaded area. The shaded area is the additional social loss from unleashing the monopoly's power to restrict production and raise prices. Additional consumers are squeezed out of the market, and they suffer an additional loss of consumer surplus that is not a gain for any other group.

We can combine this conclusion with the conclusions reached in the text. For the nation as a whole, at best the quota is no worse than an equivalent tariff as a way of impeding imports. The import quota is worse than the tariff in two cases:

- If quota licenses are allocated through resource-using application and selection procedures.

- If a dominant domestic firm can use the quota to assert its monopoly pricing power.

Import quota, domestic monopoly

Let's look at each of these, examining who gets area c and whether this affects our view of the inefficiency of the quota.

Fixed Favoritism

Import licenses adding up to the total quota can be allocated for free on the basis of **fixed favoritism,** in which the government simply assigns the licenses to firms (and/or individuals) without competition, applications, or negotiation. In this case the importers lucky enough to receive the import licenses will get area c. Each of them should be able to buy from some foreign exporter(s) at the world price (playing different foreign exporters off against each other if any one of them tries to charge a higher price). They can resell the imports at the higher domestic price. The price difference is pure profit ($30 per bike in our example). Area c is then a redistribution of well-being from domestic consumers in the importing country to the favored importers with the quota licenses. Using the one-dollar, one-vote metric, this method of allocating the quota licenses does not create any additional inefficiency (as long as no resources are used up in allocating the quota rights).

One common way of fixing the license recipients and amounts is to give the licenses to firms that were doing the importing before the quota was imposed, in the same proportion to the amounts that they had previously been importing. This is how the U.S. government ran its oil import quotas between 1959 and 1973. Licenses to import were simply given to companies on the basis of the amount of oil they had imported before 1959. There is a political reason for allocating import licenses in this way. The importers generally will be hurt by the imposition of a quota, and they would then be a group opposing the quota. However, if they receive the valuable quota licenses, they are much less likely to oppose the quota. Although they will have a lower volume of import business, the importing that they do will be very profitable.

Auction

The government can run an **import-license auction,** selling import licenses on a competitive basis to the highest bidders. Would someone be willing to pay something to buy a quota license? Yes, because the right to acquire imports at the low world price and sell these imports at the higher domestic price is valuable. How much would some individuals be willing to pay in a competitive auction? An amount very close to the price difference—in our example, an amount very close to $30 per bike. If the winning bids in the auction are very close to this price difference, who gets area c? The government gets (almost all of) it, in the form of auction revenues. In this case, the auction revenues to the government will be (almost) equal to the revenues that the government would instead collect with the equivalent tariff.

Public auctions of import-license auctions are rare. They were used in Australia, New Zealand, and Colombia in the 1980s. In New Zealand, once or twice a year the government auctioned the rights to import over 400 different goods. For a sample of these auctions for which data are available, the bidders paid, on average, about 20 percent of the world price to acquire the quota licenses. The quotas for these products were equivalent to an average tariff of about 20 percent.

There is an informal variant of a quota auction that is probably more prevalent. Corrupt government officials can do a thriving business by selling import licenses "under the table" to whoever pays them the highest bribes. As with other forms of corruption, this variant of the auction entails some social costs that go beyond economic market inefficiency. Persistent corruption can cause talented persons to become bribe-harvesting officials instead of pursuing productive careers. Public awareness of corruption also raises social tensions over injustice in high places.

Resource-Using Procedures

Instead of holding an auction, the government can insist that firms (and/or individuals) that want to acquire licenses must compete for them in some way other than simple bidding or bribing. **Resource-using application procedures** include allocating quota licenses on a first-come, first-served basis; on the basis of demonstrating need or worthiness; or on the basis of negotiations. With first-come, first-served allocation, those seeking the licenses use resources to try to get to and stay at the front of the line. An example of allocation by worthiness is awarding quota licenses for materials or components based on how much production capacity firms have for producing the products that use these inputs. This approach encourages resource wastage because it causes firms to overinvest in production capacity in the hope of obtaining more quota licenses. An example of resource wastage from negotiation is the time and money spent on lobbying with government officials to press each firm's case for receiving quota licenses.

What amount of resources would be used by firms seeking quota licenses? It would be rational for the firms to use resources up to the value of the licenses themselves—that is, up to the value of area c. Using resources in this way is privately sensible for each individual firm seeking to get the economic rents created by the licenses. But, from the point of view of the entire country, these resources used up in the rent-seeking activities are being wasted (compared to the other two ways of allocating quota licenses, or compared to having no quota at all).

With resource-using procedures, some or all of area c is turned into a loss to society by wasting productive resources. The inefficiency of the quota is greater than area $b + d$, because it also includes some of area c. In this case the quota is worse than the equivalent tariff in its effects on net national well-being.

Quota versus Tariff for a Large Country

Figure 8.3 shows the effects of a quota for a country whose import demand for this product is large enough to affect world prices. A large country faces an upward-sloping foreign supply-of-exports curve. With free trade, the country would import 1.0 million bicycles per year and the world price would be $300 per bicycle. The government then imposes an import quota that reduces the import quantity to 0.8 million bicycles. By looking at the left-hand side of Figure 8.3, we see the effects of the quota on prices. Domestic import buyers will pay $315 per bicycle if the import quantity is limited to 0.8 million. Foreign exporters will compete among themselves to make this limited amount of export sales, and they will bid the export price down to $285.

FIGURE 8.3   The Effects of an Import Quota Under Competitive Conditions, Large Importing Country

Under the competitive conditions shown here, the effects of an import quota are the same as those of a tariff that cuts imports just as much (with the possible exception of who gets shaded area $c + e$). To see this, compare the prices, quantities, and areas a, b, c, d, e, and f shown here with those shown in Figure 7.5.

We can use these prices and the right-hand side of Figure 8.3 to see what is happening in the domestic market for the country that is importing bicycles. When the domestic price increases to $315, domestic quantity supplied increases to 0.7 million and domestic quantity consumed decreases to 1.5 million.

We can compare a quota to its equivalent tariff for the large country case, by comparing Figure 8.3 to Figure 7.5. We reach the same general conclusion for the large-country case that we reached for the small-country case. With the same exception of who gets the price markup from the quota (area $c + e$ in the large-country case), the effects of the quota are the same as those of the equivalent tariff. If the quota licenses can be distributed with minimal resource costs, then the effect on net national well-being of the import quota is the gain of area e less the loss of area $b + d$. If the exporters are passive, then a large country can gain net national well-being by imposing an import quota, and there is an optimal quota that maximizes the gain in national well-being. Using the tariff-quota equivalence, Figure 7.6, which shows the nationally optimal tariff, also tells us that the nationally optimal quota here is 0.67 million bicycles per year. The cautions for the use of an optimal quota are the same as those for the optimal tariff. The quota hurts the foreign country, and the foreign country may choose to retaliate. Even if the foreign country does not retaliate, the quota causes worldwide inefficiency. In comparison with free trade, the loss in world well-being is area $b + d$ plus area f in the left-hand side of Figure 8.3.

VOLUNTARY EXPORT RESTRAINTS (VERs)

A **voluntary export restraint (VER)** is an odd-looking trade barrier in which the importing country government coerces the foreign exporting country to agree "voluntarily" to restrict its exports to this country. The export restraint usually requires that foreign exporting firms act like a cartel, restricting sales and raising prices. Yes, that's right—through the VER the importing country actually gives foreigners monopoly power, forces them to take it, and calls their compliance voluntary!

VERs are used by large countries as a rear-guard action to protect their industries that are having trouble competing against a rising tide of imports. For instance, since the early 1960s the United States, the European Union, and some other industrialized countries have forced most developing countries to impose export quotas on most kinds of textiles and clothing. This set of VERs is called the Multi-Fiber Arrangement. The export quotas were initially imposed as "temporary" restraints in response to protectionist pleas from import-competing firms that they needed time to adjust to the rising foreign competition. The quotas have lasted for decades and spread over time to more products and more exporting countries. It is estimated that they raise U.S. clothing prices by about 20 percent on average. The industrialized countries have agreed to phase out these quotas by 2005, but they will probably be replaced (at least for some products) by other forms of protection.

Since the late 1960s a series of domestic industries, including steel and automobiles, has lobbied the U.S. government for import limits as they faced rising import competition. The U.S. government has wanted to avoid the embarrassment of imposing import quotas or raising tariffs. These actions would violate the international rules of the World Trade Organization and would contradict general U.S. support for freer trade. For a number of products, the U.S. government instead pressured foreign suppliers to limit the quantity of their exports to the U.S. market. (The box "Auto VER: Protection with Integrity?" provides information on the background and effects of Japan's export limits for cars.)

In addition to the United States, the European Union and Canada have used VERs as a major form of import restriction. The countries most often forced to restrict their exports have been Japan, Korea, and the transition countries of Central and Eastern Europe. In addition to textiles and clothing, the products most often restricted are agricultural products, steel, footwear, electronics, and machine tools. As part of the Uruguay Round agreement, the industrialized countries have committed to phasing out the use of VERs.

The graphical analysis of a VER is very similar to that of an import quota. For instance, we can use Figure 8.2 to show the effects of a VER for a small importing

Case Study   Auto VER: Protection with Integrity?

Before the mid-1970s import totals of automobiles into the United States were minuscule. Then, in the late 1970s sales of Japanese-made automobiles accelerated in the United States. American buyers were looking for smaller cars in the wake of substantial increases in the price of oil. Japanese manufacturers offered good-quality smaller cars at attractive prices. Japanese cars were capturing a rapidly growing share of the U.S. auto market, U.S. production of cars was declining, American autoworkers were losing their jobs, and the U.S. auto companies were running low on profits.

In early 1981 the protectionist-pressure tachometer was in the red zone. Japanese auto exports were caught in the headlights, with Congress ready to impose strict import quotas if necessary. Ronald Reagan, the new U.S. president, had a problem. In March 1981, his cabinet was having a key discussion about auto quotas. Reagan's autobiography later explained his thinking at that moment:

As I listened to the debate, I wondered if there might be a way in which we could maintain the integrity of our position in favor of free trade while at the same time doing something to help Detroit and ease the plight of thousands of laid-off assembly workers.

The Japanese weren't playing fair in the trade game. But I knew what quotas might lead to: I didn't want to start an all-out trade war, so I asked if anyone had any suggestions for striking a balance between the two positions. [Then–Vice President] George Bush spoke up: "We're *all* for free enterprise, but would any of us find fault if Japan announced without any request from us that they were going to *voluntarily* reduce their exports of autos to America?"

I knew the Japanese read our newspapers and must know about the sentiment building up in Congress for quotas on their cars; I also knew there must be some apprehension in Tokyo that, once Congress imposed quotas on automobiles, there was a good possibility it might try to limit imports of other Japanese products.

I liked George's idea and told the cabinet I'd heard enough and would make a decision, but didn't tell them what it was. After the meeting, I

country. The amount Q_Q is now the export quota imposed by the VER. (Similarly, the graphs showing the effects of the VER for a large importing country would be nearly identical to Figure 8.3.)

Consider the small importing country shown in Figure 8.2. The two key differences between a VER (or any other form of export quota) and an import quota are the *effect on the export price* and *who gets area c*, the price markup or economic rent created by the quantitative limit on trade. Recall that with an import quota the quota rights to import are given to importers. If foreign export supply is competitive, these importers should be able to buy at the world price ($300 in our bicycle example) and sell these imports domestically at the higher price ($330). The price markup (area *c*) stays within the importing country.

With the VER, the exporting country's government usually distributes licenses to export specified quantities to its producers. The export producers should realize that there is much less incentive to compete among themselves for export sales. Instead, they should act like a cartel that has agreed to limit total sales and to divide up the market. Faced with limited export quantity (0.6 million bikes in [arranged an extra meeting during the already-scheduled visit of Japanese Foreign Minister Masayoshi Ito to Washington] . . .

Foreign Minister Ito . . . was brought into the Oval Office for a brief meeting . . . I told him that our Republican administration firmly opposed import quotas but that strong sentiment was building in Congress among Democrats to impose them.

"I don't know whether I'll be able to stop them," I said, "But I think if you *voluntarily* set a limit on your automobile exports to the country, it would probably head off the bills pending in Congress and there wouldn't be any mandatory quotas."*

The Japanese government got the message and "voluntarily" agreed to make sure that Japanese firms put the brakes on their exports to the United States. Maximum Japanese exports to the United States for each of the years 1981 through 1983 were set at a quantity of 1.8 million vehicles per year, about 8 percent less than what they had exported in 1980. As total automobile sales in the United States increased substantially after the 1981–1982 recession, the export limit was raised in 1984 to 2 million and in 1985 to 2.3 million. The export restraint continued to exist until 1994, but from 1987 on actual Japanese exports to the United States were less than the quota quantity. By 1987 Japanese firms were producing large numbers of cars in factories that they had recently built in the United States. (We examine this kind of foreign direct investment in Chapter 14.)

As a result of the VER, the profits of U.S. auto companies increased, as did production and employment in U.S. auto factories. What did the VER cost the United States? One recent careful study estimated that the VER cost U.S. consumers about $13 billion in lost consumer surplus, and that it imposed a net loss to the United States of about $3 billion. Other estimates of these costs are even higher. "Protection with integrity" does not come cheap.

* Ronald Reagan (1990), pp. 253–55, as quoted in Low (1993), pp. 114–15. Emphasis in the original.

Figure 8.2), the exporters should charge the highest price that the market will bear. *The export price rises to $330,* the highest price that import demanders will pay for this quantity. Therefore, *the foreign exporters now get area c* as additional revenue on the VER-limited quantity of exports.[1]

How does the cost *to the importing country* of a VER compare to either an import quota or free trade? *In comparison to the import quota* (which uses minimal resources to administer), the VER causes a loss of area *c*. This is the amount paid to the foreign exporters rather than kept within the importing country. We

[1] I learned of an interesting variation on this effect from one of my students a number of years ago. I noticed that each time I saw him outside of class he was driving a different expensive car. I complimented him on this, and he said that his family in India was doing very well. When I asked what they did, he said that they owned some of the VER rights to export clothing from India to countries like the United States. He said that his family actually did not bother to make clothing; instead they simply rented the export rights to local clothing manufacturers. Thus, his family did very well by getting some of area *c* created by the clothing VERs.

can also view it as a national loss due to a deterioration in the importing country's terms of trade (the higher price paid to foreign exporters) because of the VER.[2] *In comparison to free trade,* the net loss to the importing country because of the VER is area $b + c + d$. The VER may be a politically attractive way of offering protection to an import-competing industry, but it is also economically expensive for the importing country. (In addition, note that *for the world as whole* the net loss in comparison to free trade is only area $b + d$. Area c is a transfer from consumers in the importing country to producers in the exporting country, so it is not a loss to the whole world.)

There is another important effect of the VER. For many products foreign producers can adjust the mix of varieties or models of the product that they export, while remaining within the overall quantitative limit. Usually, the profit margin on higher-quality varieties is larger, so the exporters shift toward exporting these varieties (a process called "quality upgrading"). As the Japanese firms implemented the VER on their auto exports to the United States, one part of their strategy was to the shift the mix of models exported, away from basic subcompact cars (like the Honda Civic) and toward larger, fancier models (like the Honda Accord and eventually the Acura line). (In this auto case, there was one more notable effect. To avoid the sales limits created by the VER, Japanese automobile firms set up assembly operations in the United States. More generally, any import protection can serve as an incentive for direct investment into the importing country by the thwarted foreign exporters. We examine foreign direct investment in Chapter 14.)

OTHER NONTARIFF BARRIERS

In addition to quotas and VERs, there are many other kinds of nontariff import barriers. Indeed, we should be impressed with governments' creativity in coming up with new ways to discriminate against imports. Let's look more closely at three other NTBs from the vast toolkit used against imports. (The box "Carrots Are Fruit, Snails Are Fish, and Cows Need Passports" provides more examples of creativity.)

---

[2] In the long run, a VER arrangement tends to wear down in a way that an import quota might not. A VER is, in effect, a cartel among the exporting firms. Like any cartel, success in getting a higher profit markup attracts other suppliers. Take the VERs for textiles and clothing, for example. When they were implemented, they did not include potential suppliers who could later become competitive. In particular they initially left out the People's Republic of China, which had isolated itself in the 1960s. Later, China began to export aggressively. If China had simply competed openly outside of the VER arrangement, the price markup would have eroded. To prevent this, the U.S. government had to bring China within the VER arrangement and shift some of the total VER allotments from other suppliers to China. As more and more new suppliers arrive on the scene, looking for a share of the U.S. market, prices tend to decline toward free-trade prices, unless the VER can be expanded to include the new suppliers and tightened to limit the expansion of the total quantity imported.

Case Study   Carrots Are Fruit, Snails Are Fish, and Cows Need Passports

Governments have shown perhaps their greatest trade-policy creativity when deciding in what categories different imported goods belong. Their decisions are by no means academic. The stakes are high because an import that falls into one category can be allowed into the country duty-free, whereas the same import defined as falling into a related category is subject to a high tariff or banned altogether.

You can bet that if definitions matter so much to trade policy, there will be intense lobbying over each commodity's official definition. Protectionists will insist that an imported product be defined as belonging to the category with the high import barrier, but importing firms will demand that it be put in the duty-free category. When such strong pressures are brought on government, don't always expect logic in the official definitions.

Some of the resulting rules are bizarre. While examples can be found in any country's trade classifications, health codes, and the like, a particularly striking array of regulations was passed by the European Union (EU) in 1994:

- Carrots are a fruit. This definition allows Portugal to sell its carrot jam throughout Western Europe without high duties.

- The land snail, famously served in French restaurants, is a fish. Therefore, European snail farmers can collect fish farm subsidies.

- Cattle must have individual passports to prevent their being taken from one EU country to another, in search of better subsidies or easier health-code enforcement. The numbers on the passports are not the same as the 14-digit numbers stamped on their ear tags.

The United States has similarly bent the rules, modifying the definition of a car versus a passenger van versus a truck, to reflect different pressures in protectionist debates. In the early 1990s Carla Hills, then the U.S. trade representative, was compelled to call the same car both American and "not American." She told the Japanese government that car exports from U.S. factories owned by Japanese firms to Japan were Japanese, not American. They did not count when the U.S. government examined the size of American car exports to Japan. At the same time, she told European governments that the cars exported to Europe from these same Japanese-owned factories in the United States were American, so they were not subject to European quotas on Japanese car imports.

With even greater ingenuity private firms have changed the look and the names of their products to try to get around each set of official definitions. For instance, a VER on down-filled ski *parkas* led to the innovation of two new products that were not subject to VERs. One product was a down-filled ski *vest* that had one side of a zipper on each armhole. The other product was a *matched pair of sleeves,* with one side of a zipper at the top of each sleeve. Once the two products were imported "separately," the distributor knew what to do.

Such games have been played with great frequency over the definitions of products. As long as definitions mean money gained or lost, products will be defined in funny ways.

Source: Scripps Howard News Service, December 20, 1994.

Product Standards

If you are looking for rich variety and imagination in import barriers, try the panoply of laws and regulations pertaining to product quality, including those enforced in the names of health, sanitation, safety, and the environment. Such standards can be noble efforts to enhance society's well-being, by addressing market failures that lead to unsafe conditions and environmental degradation.

Standards that accomplish these goals need not discriminate against imports. But, if a government is determined to protect local producers, it can always write rules that can be met more easily by local products than by imported products. For instance, the standards can be tailored to fit local products, but to require costly modifications to foreign products. Or, the standards can be higher for imported products or enforced more strictly. Or, the testing and certification procedures can be more costly, slower, or more uncertain for foreign products. Here are some examples to illustrate the ingenuity of the standard-setters.

In an obvious effort to protect domestic ranchers, the U.S. government in the past has found hidden health hazards in the way beef cattle are raised in Argentina. Similarly, the European Union (EU) has banned imports of beef from cattle that have received growth hormones, claiming that it is responding to public concerns about health dangers. The United States asserts that this is actually protection of European beef producers, because the scientific evidence indicates that beef from cattle that receive growth hormones is safe and poses no risk to human health.

The EU requires that foreign facilities producing dairy products and many other animal products be approved as meeting EU public health standards. But it has not devoted many resources to the approval process, leading to waits of months for simple approvals. Health regulations set by the Mexican government require inspection and approval of factories making herbal and nutritional products that are sold in Mexico. However, the Mexican authorities refuse to inspect factories in other countries.

The U.S. government has complained that Japan's procedures for approving pharmaceuticals and medical devices is slow. For instance, the Japanese government often requires clinical trials on Japanese patients, even though such trials simply duplicate those completed successfully in other countries. The U.S. government also battled with the Japanese government over aluminum baseball bats! For several years around 1980, U.S.-made aluminum bats were refused certification as acceptable, even though the American bats were the basis for the Japanese safety standards. And, when the U.S. bats became eligible for certification, the Japanese government for several years insisted on inspecting each imported bat one by one, a time-consuming and costly process.

Product standards usually do not raise tariff or tax revenues for the importing country's government. On the contrary, enforcing these rules uses up government resources (and businesses must use resources to meet the standards). The standards can bring a net gain in overall well-being to the extent that they truly protect health, safety, and the environment. Yet it is easy for governments to disguise costly protectionism in virtuous clothing.

Domestic Content Requirements

A **domestic content requirement** mandates that a product produced and sold in a country must have a specified minimum amount of domestic production value, in the form of wages paid to local workers or materials and components produced within the country. Domestic content requirements can create import protection at two levels. They can be a barrier to imports of the products that do not meet the content rules. And they can limit the import of materials and components that otherwise would have been used in domestic production of the products. For instance, local content requirements for automobiles, used by Malaysia and other countries, force local auto manufacturers to use more domestically produced automobile components and parts (for instance, sheet metal or seat covers). If the domestic content requirement is set high enough, it can force domestic production of such expensive parts as engines or transmissions.

A closely related NTB, sometimes called a **mixing requirement,** stipulates that an importer or import distributor must buy a certain percentage of the product locally. For instance, the Philippines government requires that certain retail stores in the country must source at least 30 percent of their inventory in the Philippines. Such mixing requirements have also been used to restrict imports of foreign entertainment. Canada has often imposed "Canada time" requirements on radio and TV stations, forcing them to devote a certain share of their air time to songs and shows recorded in Canada. Similarly, as we will see in Chapter 11, the EU, led by France, has waged a sustained war against American entertainment, partly by stipulating that minimum percentages of various forms of entertainment must be from domestic studios.

Like product standards, domestic content and mixing requirements do not generate tariff or tax revenue for the government. The gains on the price markups are captured by the protected home-country sellers of the protected products. These requirements create the usual deadweight losses because the protected local products are less desired or more costly to produce.

Government Procurement

Governments are major purchasers of goods and services. One estimate is that government purchases of products that could be traded internationally amounts to close to one-tenth of all product sales in the industrialized countries. Government procurement practices can be a nontariff barrier to imports, if the purchasing processes are biased against foreign products, as they often are. In many countries the governments buy relatively few imported products and instead buy mostly locally produced products.

In the United States, the Buy America Act of 1933 is the basic law that mandates that government-funded purchases favor domestic products. For different types of purchases the bias takes different forms, including prohibitions on buying imports, local content requirements, and mandating that domestic products be purchased unless imported products are priced much lower (for instance, at least one-third lower). More than half of the states and many cities and towns also have "Buy American" or "buy local" rules for purchases by their governments.

Many other countries have similar rules and practices. For instance, in Japan the U.S. government has complained that the Japanese government has limited foreign sales of telecommunications products and services to the government and government-owned companies by using both standards that are biased toward local products and short time periods for bidding. In Greece the specifications for the goods and services that the government plans to buy are often vague and tend to favor local suppliers. It also appears that the Greek government informally favors Greek and other EU firms when making purchasing decisions. Furthermore, in some countries (Italy is often cited as an example) the informal bias is reinforced by widespread corruption in the process of awarding government contracts.

HOW BIG ARE THE COSTS OF PROTECTION?

We have examined the effects of tariffs and nontariff barriers to imports. How important are these effects? Are the costs large or small? Large or small relative to what? We'll look at their importance first for the whole national economy, and then for specific products that receive high levels of protection.

As a Percentage of GDP

One popular way of weighing the importance of any economic cost or benefit is to see whether it is a big part of the national economy, which we usually measure by the value of domestic production (gross domestic product, or GDP). Surprisingly, our basic theory indicates that the costs of protection for a typical industrialized country are small, even if we ignore any favorable changes in the country's terms of trade (the small-country assumption).

Consider a diagram like Figure 7.4B. For a small country that imposes a tariff, area $b + d$, the net national loss from the tariff, equals one-half the tariff rate times the reduction in the import quantity. Using this equality and some mathematical manipulation, we can write the expression for the net national loss as a percentage of GDP:[3]

$$\frac{\text{Net national loss from the tariff}}{\text{GDP}} = \frac{1}{2} \times \text{Tariff rate} \times \frac{\text{Percent reduction in import quantity}}{} \times \frac{\text{Import value}}{\text{GDP}}$$

[3] Here is how we get this formula. Our analysis of tariffs in Chapter 7 indicates that the net national loss (a money amount) is the area of the triangle $b + d$ (or the sum of the two triangles b and d). Recalling that the area of a triangle is equal to one-half of the product of the base (the change in imports as the result of the tariff) and height (the tariff money amount per unit, which is equal to the percentage tariff rate times the import price):

Net national loss from the tariff = $\frac{1}{2}$ · (Reduction of import quantity) · (Tariff rate · Import price)

Then, divide the first term in parentheses on the right side of the equation by the import quantity (so it becomes reduction in import quantity divided by import quantity, which is the percent reduction in import quantity, stated in decimal form) and multiply the second term by the import quantity (so we obtain import price times import quantity, which is import value, as part of the expression). We then have:

Net national loss from the tariff = $\frac{1}{2}$ · (Percent reduction of import quantity) · (Tariff rate · Import value)

Now divide both sides of the equation by the money value of GDP, and rearrange terms to obtain the expression in the text.

A similar expression applies to a product affected by an import quota or some other nontariff barrier. (The percentage increase in domestic price that results from the NTB replaces the tariff rate.) Furthermore, we can use this expression to examine the effect of all tariffs and nontariff barriers imposed by the country. (Roughly, we get this expression if we add up all the losses for all products protected against imports.)

How large is the loss? Suppose, for example, that a nation's import tariffs are all 10 percent and that they cause a 20 percent reduction in import quantities. Suppose that total imports affected by these tariffs are 20 percent of GDP. In this realistic case, the net national loss from all tariffs on imports equals $1/2 \times 0.10 \times 0.20 \times 0.20$, or only 0.2 percent of GDP! The net national loss from import protection is not likely to be large, for a country that has rather low tariff levels and that is not that dependent on imports. The cost of protection is now relatively small for industrialized countries because the governments of these countries have cooperated to lower their trade barriers so much during the past half-century. (We also note that that 0.2 percent of U.S. GDP is about $20 billion, an amount that most of us would not think to be absolutely small.)

However, we also know that estimates based on this simple calculation can underestimate the costs of protection as a share of GDP. Here are five ways in which the true cost is probably bigger than the calculation above shows:

- *Foreign retaliation.* If our country has introduced barriers, other governments may retaliate by putting new barriers against our exports. The true costs would be higher than any shown in the diagram or the calculation above. The costs would be much higher in the event of a trade war, in which each side counter-retaliates with still higher import barriers.

- *Enforcement costs.* Any trade barrier has to be enforced by government officials. That is costly because the people enforcing the trade barrier could have been productively employed elsewhere. Part of the revenues collected by the government (area *c* in our diagram) are the waste of society's resources used to enforce the barrier. This is a loss to the country, not just a pure redistribution from consumers to the government.

- *Rent-seeking costs.* Local firms seeking protection may use techniques such as lobbying that also use resources. If this is the case, then part of the producer surplus created by protection (area *a* in our diagram) is also a loss due to wasted resources, rather than a pure redistribution from consumers to producers. In addition, firms and individuals may use resources to try to claim the tariff revenues or the price markup on the quota quantity of imports, another reason that some of area *c* could be a national loss due to wasted resources.

- *Rents to foreign producers.* VERs encourage foreign exporters to raise their export prices. This is a third reason that some or all of area *c* could be a loss to the importing country.

- *Innovation.* Protection can mute the incentive to innovate new technology, because there is less competitive pressure. In addition, protection can cause a loss to national well-being because it reduces the number of varieties of products available in the domestic market. (Recall the discussion in Chapter 5.)

For any or all of these reasons the cost of protection could be noticeably larger than the estimates from the simple calculations above, but it is not easy to say how much larger.

Furthermore, a subtle implication of the simple equation is that increasing existing barriers brings rapidly rising national costs. The percent reduction in imports equals the tariff rate, which is the percentage increase in import price, times the price elasticity of demand for imports. The net loss formula can be rewritten as follows:[4]

$$\frac{\text{Net national loss from the tariff}}{\text{GDP}} = \frac{1}{2} \times \text{Tariff rate} \times \left(\text{Tariff rate} \times \frac{\text{Price elasticity}}{\text{of import demand}} \right) \times \frac{\text{Import value}}{\text{GDP}}$$

The tariff rate (or the price markup from a quota) has a squared effect on the net national loss. This means that doubling today's tariffs (or NTBs) would quadruple their cost, and tripling them would increase their cost by nine times. There is still a lot at stake in debates about increasing barriers to imports.

For Specific Products with High Protection

Almost all countries have some products that are highly protected—products that have high tariff rates, restrictive quotas, or other restrictive NTBs. The political reason for import barriers is often to enhance the incomes of a threatened domestic industry. These high barriers add large amounts of income to the protected industry. The high barriers also create costs that can be large. How much does it cost society for each dollar of protected income? If it cost the rest of society only $1.03, it is not expensive to provide assistance to the threatened industry. If it costs $2.00 for every dollar of income protected, that would strike most observers as expensive.

To get a quick idea of how much it might cost society to create a dollar of protected income, let's return to the calculation that led to our conclusion that import barriers cost only 0.2 percent of GDP. In this case, the tariffs gave domestic producers a 10 percent hike in the price of their products. If the threatened industries were 20 percent of GDP, then their gains in producer surplus, as a percentage of GDP, would be close to 10 percent times 20 percent, or 2.0 percent of GDP. Every dollar transferred to provide income for the protected industries also costs society an additional 10 cents (equal to 0.2 divided by 2.0) in deadweight losses.

---

[4] The only difference between the previous equation in the text to this one is the middle expression on the right side of the new expression. The tariff rate is also the percentage change in import price, because it shows the percent by which the tariff-inclusive domestic price exceeds the world price. The price elasticity of import demand measures the percentage change in import quantity per 1 percent change in import price. Putting these together, we see that

Percent reduction in import quantity = Tariff rate · Price elasticity of import demand

Thus, every dollar of protected income costs the rest of society $1.10 (the $1.00 transferred plus the extra loss of $0.10), even in this example in which the level of protection is moderate.

For highly protected industries, the costs are often much larger than this. Figure 8.4 shows us the various losses and gains for 21 products that are highly protected in the United States. In this analysis, the United States is a large country, so the calculations are based on diagrams like Figures 7.5 and 8.3. The upper panel shows that billions of dollars are at stake for these highly protected industries.

In the lower panel, we see the costs to other groups of a dollar of protected income. For each dollar of protected producer income, consumers lose more than $2 on average for the 21 cases. The United States as a whole loses $0.49 for each dollar of protected income. That is, other Americans lose $1.49 for each $1.00 gained by the protected U.S. industries. This is a rather large cost to other Americans, to protect incomes in these industries.

The world as a whole loses $0.35 for each dollar of protected U.S. producer income. Per dollar of protected income, this is $0.26 of deadweight losses in the United States plus $0.09 of deadweight losses to foreigners based on their loss of exports to the United States.

As we would expect from our analyses presented in Chapter 7 and earlier in this chapter, there is an interesting contrast between industries protected by tariffs or quotas and those protected by VERs. For tariffs and quotas, the United States, as a large country, experiences gains from terms of trade improvements. Foreign producers cut their export prices when U.S. demand decreases due to the tariff or quota. In fact, the tariffs actually bring net gains to the United States, because the terms of trade gains are larger than the deadweight losses. For VERs, the United States experiences losses from terms-of-trade declines. Foreign producers increase their export prices when told to limit their exports.

Messerlin (2001) uses a similar method to generate estimates for highly protected sectors in the European Union. He finds, for instance, that it costs EU consumers about $4 per dollar of protected EU producers' gain. Per dollar of income maintained in highly protected industries, protection in the EU is noticeably more costly than it is in the United States.

WTO: TARIFF SUCCESS AND NEW CHALLENGES

During the past 60 years, governments of the industrialized countries reached a series of global agreements that have largely reduced their tariff rates on industrial goods to low levels. Import quotas on these goods have also mostly ceased as well. However, as we saw in this chapter, national governments have sometimes substituted other nontariff barriers to imports for the tariffs and quotas that are disappearing. It has proved more difficult to find global agreements that limit these other nontariff barriers. In addition, national governments only recently began to take up the challenges of freeing international trade in agricultural products and in services.

FIGURE 8.4   Losses and Gains from U.S. Protection, Selected Products, 1990

	Protected U.S. Producers Gain (Area a)[a]	U.S. Consumers Loss (Area a + b + c + d)	U.S. Terms-of-Trade Gain (Area e)[b]	U.S. Deadweight Loss (Area b + d)[b]	U.S. Net National Gain (Area e – b – d)[b]	Foreign Deadweight Loss (Area f)	Net World Loss (Area b + d + f)
In Millions of Dollars							
Tariffs in 14 sectors[c]	679	1,956	465	70	395	32	102
Import quotas in 2 sectors[d]	1,791	2,564	72	600	–528	18	618
VERs and similar export quantity limits in 5 sectors[e]	12,312	25,857	–6,870	2,603	–9,473	711	3,314
All 21 sectors	14,782	30,375	–6,333	3,273	–9,739	761	4,034
In Dollars per Dollar of Protected U.S. Producers' Gain							
Tariffs in 14 sectors[c]		2.88	0.68	0.10	0.58	0.05	0.15
Import quotas in 2 sectors[d]		1.43	0.04	0.34	–0.29	0.01	0.35
VERs and similar export quantity limits in 5 sectors[e]		2.10	–0.56	0.21	–0.77	0.06	0.27
All 21 sectors		2.05	–0.43	0.22	–0.66	0.05	0.27

[a] Areas refers to areas indicated in Figures 7.5 and 8.3.

[b] Except for VERs and similar export quotas, for which this is area *e*, the markup lost, relative to free trade, instead of area *e*.

[c] The 14 tariff-protected sectors are ball bearings, benzenoid chemicals, canned tuna, ceramic articles, ceramic tiles, costume jewelry, frozen concentrated orange juice, glassware, luggage, polyethylene resins, rubber footwear, softwood lumber, women's nonathletic footwear, and women's handbags.

[d] The 2 sectors protected by import quotas are dairy products and coastal shipping.

[e] Of the 5 sectors protected by VERs and similar export quantity limits, apparel, textiles, and machine tools were protected by VERs, and peanuts and sugar were protected by export quotas assigned to foreign countries by the U.S. government.

Source: Hufbauer and Elliott (1994).

Since 1995, the **World Trade Organization (WTO)** has overseen the global rules of government policy toward international trade and provided the forum for negotiating global agreements to improve these rules. The WTO subsumed and expanded on the **General Agreement and Tariffs and Trade (GATT),** a "provisional agreement" signed by 23 countries in 1947. The WTO (like the GATT before it) espouses three major principles: (1) liberalization of trade; (2) nondiscrimination, or the most-favored nation (MFN) principle; and (3) no unfair encouragement for exports.

Among other improvements, the WTO has a much stronger dispute settlement procedure than the GATT had. If a member country complains to the WTO about government policy in another member country, and if this dispute cannot be resolved by discussion, a panel of experts examines the case and reaches a decision. A country can appeal the decision by this panel, but it cannot block it just by objecting. If a complaint is upheld, retaliation is authorized if the offending country does not correct its policy. Since its inception in 1995, the WTO has received more than 260 complaints for resolution.

As of early 2002, the WTO had 144 member countries that agreed to its rules. In addition, nearly 30 countries, including Russia and Saudi Arabia, have been negotiating to become members. (The box "China Joins the WTO" indicates what a country must do to become a WTO member.) The WTO's headquarters is in Geneva, Switzerland.

Under the GATT, member countries pursued eight rounds of negotiations to lower governmental barriers to trade: Geneva 1947, Annecy 1949, Torquay 1950–1951, Geneva 1956, Dillon 1960–1962, Kennedy 1964–1967, Tokyo 1973–1979, and Uruguay 1986–1993. These multilateral trade negotiations have been very successful in reducing tariffs.

It hasn't been easy. From the start, the agreements had to excuse some of the least reformable sectors to focus on sectors where agreements were possible. Agricultural protection and subsidies received little attention until the Uruguay Round. Developing countries usually were under less pressure to liberalize, though some have unilaterally liberalized their trade in the past 25 years. Still, the average tariffs of industrialized countries (excluding agricultural products) have fallen from about 40 percent in the 1940s to about 3 percent with full implementation of the Uruguay Round tariff agreements. Part of the credit for this liberalization goes to the negotiating procedures set up under the GATT. Each nation's government is able to defend its tariff-cutting "concessions" against the protests of domestic protectionists as the price the country must pay to give its exporters better access to other markets. This mercantilist logic is bad economics—we know that imports are something the country gains and exports are something the country gives up—but it seems to be useful politics.

The negotiations have had less success, however, in attacking nontariff barriers. The protective effects of nontariff barriers are harder to measure than those of a tariff. As a result, it is harder to get international agreement on what constitutes an exchange of "comparable" NTB reductions. Perhaps because these barriers are harder to measure and compare, protectionism has increasingly used NTBs since the early 1970s.

Case Study   China joins the WTO

After 15 years of negotiations, China became a member of the WTO in late 2001. To become a member, China had to obtain acceptance from all WTO members. Negotiations between China and several other countries, including the United States and the European Union, were complex and sometimes difficult.

Here are some of the major commitments that the Chinese government made to gain membership in the WTO:

- *Tariff reductions:* For industrial products, the average tariff will fall from 25 percent to 9 percent (with dramatic reductions for some products—for instance, the tariff on auto imports will fall from 80–100 percent to 25 percent).

- *Services:* Limits on foreign direct investment in banking, financial securities, fund management, insurance, law, and telecommunication services will be liberalized.

- *Transport and product distribution:* Limits on foreign firms performing transport and distribution services will be removed.

- *Agriculture:* The average tariff will fall from 32 percent to 15 percent, no export subsidies will be granted, and domestic subsidies will be limited.

These liberalizations will be phased in during various time periods up to 2007.

These are big commitments—in some ways they go well beyond what members who joined the WTO years ago have agreed to. Making these changes is likely to be very disruptive within the Chinese economy, although there is some foreign concern that the Chinese government (or the prefectural and local governments in China) will find subtle barriers to minimize the liberalizations. In any case, many state enterprises will probably go belly up or be acquired by foreign firms. Large numbers of Chinese workers will become unemployed if their enterprises fail. Why would China make these commitments?

One part of the answer is that China gains the general benefits of WTO membership, including MFN treatment, access to the dispute settlement procedures, and participation in multilateral trade negotiations. Of special importance to China, other countries must end the quota system for textiles and apparel by 2005 (as previously agreed in the Uruguay Round). One estimate indicates the Chinese exports of clothing will increase by 300 percent when the quotas are lifted.

Another part of the answer is domestic politics in China. Reformers within the Chinese government leadership can use the WTO commitments to solidify and expand economic reforms. The reformers want to attract more foreign direct investment and pursue the long-run economic gains of better resource allocation.

A final note: Shortly after China joined, Taiwan also joined the WTO, not as a separate country, but as a separate customs area (the same status that Hong Kong and Macao have as separate members of the WTO). China had blocked the membership of Taiwan until after China joined.

The Tokyo Round was the first to take up the issue of NTBs. Agreements were reached on technical standards, government procurement, import licensing procedures, and customs valuation. The agreements have had only modest effects.

The Uruguay Round was the most comprehensive multilateral trade negotiation ever (and, not unrelated, also the longest ever). In addition to lowering tariff rates on industrial products and establishing the WTO, national governments agreed to phase out the global web of VERs on textiles and clothing (the Multi-Fiber Arrangement) by 2005, and to end the use of most other VERs. National governments also agreed to reduce their use of domestic content requirements. It will be harder for a national government to require that firms in a country can sell only those products that have most of their value produced by people in the country.

The Uruguay Round agreement covers three areas that had received almost no attention in previous rounds. First, the treatment of agricultural goods was shifted to be similar to that of industrial goods. Tariffs have replaced many agricultural quotas and other NTBs. The new tariffs were usually set high enough that there is no increase in trade. The gain is indirect: Tariffs may prove easier to liberalize in future international negotiations. In addition, governments agreed to reduce their domestic subsidies to agricultural production, their export subsidies for agricultural products, and the volume of exported products that receive these subsidies.

Second, the agreement created global rules requiring protection of intellectual property (patents, copyrights, and trademarks). It attacks the practice in many countries of copying ("pirating") innovating firms' products without getting, and paying for, a license to use these innovations.

Third, the Uruguay Round established a new set of rules, the General Agreement on Trade in Services. Many countries block international trade in services with outright bans on foreign suppliers and with legal red tape. The agreement contains little in the way of liberalization. As with agricultural products, it instead provides a framework for future negotiations to liberalize services trade. Indeed, in 1997, 69 countries agreed to open up national markets for basic telecommunications services. Also in 1997, 70 countries agreed to remove restrictions in banking, securities, and insurance.

The ninth round of multilateral trade negotiations began in late 2001. It was tough getting to this start, with a miss in Seattle in 1999 amid intense antiglobalization protests and stubborn disagreements among delegates from different countries about what should be negotiated in the new round. The Doha Round has an agenda that is almost as ambitious as that of the Uruguay Round. It is expected to take years to complete. (For more information on this new round, see the box "The Rocky Road to Doha.")

AMERICA'S "SECTION 301": UNILATERAL PRESSURE

The U.S. government has not been content to pursue better access to foreign market for U.S. exports only through the WTO. **Section 301** of the Trade Act of 1974 gives the president the power to negotiate to eliminate "unfair trade practices" of foreign governments that limit imports from the United States or other countries. As part of the process, the U.S. government threatens to enact new barriers to imports from the allegedly offending country if it does not change its policies. (U.S. law also has "Super 301," which mandates an annual review of foreign practices to set priorities for U.S. efforts to lower foreign trade barriers, and "Special 301," which mandates an annual report on countries that do not provide adequate protection to intellectual property.)

What are the effects of unilateral actions by the U.S. government to open foreign markets with a threat of retaliation? That depends on whether the threatened

Case Study   The Rocky Road to Doha

In the late 1990s discussions began about a new round of multilateral trade negotiations. It turned out to be quite hard to get to the new round. A major effort to begin the new round occurred at the WTO ministerial conference in Seattle in late 1999, but it was not to be. Two problems prevented the start, one outside the meeting place and the other within.

Outside the meeting place a huge antiglobalization protest swirled, sometimes violently. An unusual coalition of groups came together for the protest—environmentalists, human-rights activists, consumer advocates, organized labor (unions), anti-immigration groups, animal-rights activists, and anarchists. With such disparate groups involved, it is not easy to summarize their positions. Prominent complaints and demands, some of them contradictory with others, included:

- That the WTO is too powerful, that it usurps the sovereignty of national governments, and that it is undemocratic and secretive.

- That the WTO should use its substantial powers to achieve goals other than free trade, especially such goals as strict global environmental protection and better wages and working conditions in developing countries. (See Chapter 1 for discussion of the controversies about labor standards.)

- That the WTO is the tool of big business, and that freer trade benefits corporations and capitalists while hurting the global environment, local cultures, and workers in all countries.

The protests also disrupted and delayed the beginning of the conference.

Inside the meeting place the delegates could not find common ground on the agenda that would be addressed in the new round of negotiations. The agenda is important because it foreshadows the actual results that will be achieved in the round. The United States favored a narrow agenda, and the European Union a broad one. In addition, the developing countries were intent on having a major role in molding the

agenda to fit their interests. Decisions in the WTO are based on a consensus among the national government members. Because the national ministers could not agree on an agenda, the effort failed. (There was also disagreement about the name of the expected round. U.S. negotiators favored the "Clinton Round," and the French favored anything but this. The futuristic "Millennium Round" and the mundane "Seattle Round" were the other leading candidates.)

After a hiatus the drive toward a new round gained speed in 2001. The effort to find consensus on an agenda resumed in November 2001 at the ministerial meeting in Doha, Qatar, a location apparently chosen because it was essentially inaccessible to protesters. After much wrangling and after the meeting was extended, the ministers finally agreed on the agenda for the ninth round of multilateral trade negotiations. Each of the three major groups (the United States, the European Union, and the developing countries, led by India), compromised to reach the consensus. In addition to the staple of lowering tariffs on industrial products, here are other important items on the agenda:

- *NTBs such as government procurement and customs procedures:* Renew negotiations on rules to liberalize.

- *Agricultural products:* Phase out all export subsidies, reduce domestic subsidies further, and reduce tariff and other barriers to imports.

- *Services:* Expand liberalization efforts to more sectors.

- *Antidumping and antisubsidy laws:* Clarify and improve the rules to reduce the usage of these procedures. (Antidumping and antisubsidy laws are discussed at length in Chapter 10.)

- *Patented drugs:* Developing countries have the right to override the intellectual property rules to gain access to low-priced medicines to protect public health.

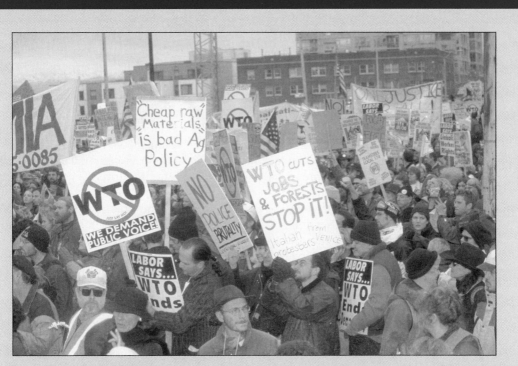

© Paul Conklin/PhotoEdit, Inc.

- *Environment:* Clarify the consistency of WTO rules with multilateral environmental treaties and agreements. (Trade and the environment is discussed in depth in Chapter 12.)

- *Dispute settlement:* Improve the dispute settlement procedure so that it is easier for developing countries to use it.

In addition, the ministers agreed that negotiations in two new areas—rules about government policies toward foreign direct investment, and principles for the use of antitrust policy (also called competition policy)—would begin in the year 2007.

In reaching this consensus the United States dropped its opposition to including drug patents and antidumping laws in the agenda, the European Union dropped its opposition to targeting substantial liberal-ization for agricultural goods, and the developing countries dropped their opposition to including foreign direct investment and antitrust policy. The United States succeeded in getting agriculture and services in the agenda. The European Union succeeded in getting foreign direct investment, antitrust, and the environment in the agenda (although the EU wanted a broader mandate for this part of the agenda). The developing countries succeeded in getting patented drugs, agricultural products, and antidumping laws in the agenda. The developing countries also succeeded in blocking inclusion of labor standards.

The agenda for the Doha Round is more ambitious than many observers expected. It will probably take years for the completion of the round. This will certainly be true if the road to completion is anywhere near as rocky as the road to the agenda.

country gives in and removes the practices that the United States says are unfair. Let's look at a case in which the other country gave in to U.S. demands to change its unfair trade practices; then we will consider what happens if it does not.

One case in which the U.S. complaint had some success occurred in 1995. Chinese producers of computer software, pharmaceuticals, agricultural and chemical products, books and periodicals, and audiovisual products such as compact discs and movies were making and selling copies of American products without paying license fees to the American owners of the patents, copyrights, and trademarks. Using Section 301, the U.S. government threatened to slap high tariffs on Chinese goods if China did not start honoring U.S. intellectual property rights within a few weeks. In this case, the threat seemed to work. The Chinese government agreed to start enforcing foreign patents, copyrights, and trademarks, imposing penalties on Chinese firms found to be in violation. The U.S. government did achieve some of its objectives, although enforcement of intellectual property rights in China remains weak.

What if the other country refuses to change the practices the United States objects to? Under Section 301 the U.S. government can then retaliate by imposing high tariffs on an arbitrary set of products imported from the other country. These products may have nothing to do with the foreign industries benefiting from the unfair practices in the foreign country. For example, in the case of the EU ban on imports of beef from cattle treated with growth hormones, the U.S. government pursued a Section 301 case, alleging that the ban was unjustified and unfair. After negotiations between the governments failed to resolve the dispute, the United States retaliated by imposing high tariffs on imports from the EU of various products, including beef, hams, tomatoes, certain beverages, and pet food. Carrying out the retaliation against the other country's goods is likely to reduce the well-being of both sides.

There is a real danger that using Section 301 will backfire in this way. Of the 100 or so Section 301 cases since 1974, nearly a quarter of them ended in retaliation by the U.S. government. Still, in about half of the cases the United States succeeded at least partially in achieving its objectives (improved market access, reduced foreign subsidies, or improved protection of intellectual property). Even for the successes, however, increases in U.S. exports usually were small (with the exception of large increases in U.S. exports of cigarettes, beef, and semiconductors to Japan, following negotiated resolutions of Section 301 complaints).

Not surprisingly, other countries resent U.S. government use of this law. They have been irked by the self-righteous tone with which the United States has written and used 301. They detect protectionist hypocrisy by the Americans. They also rightly point out that 301 allows the United States to conduct its own unilateral "trade crimes" trials, deciding by itself what is "unfair."

There has been a drop-off in Section 301 cases since the early 1990s. The WTO has a binding dispute settlement process, a major improvement over the weak process available under the GATT. U.S. complaints are now much more likely to be sent to and resolved using the WTO. For instance, Kodak's complaint about barriers protecting the Japanese film market began as a Section 301 case in

1995. Kodak complained that its low share in the Japanese market (about 10 percent) was due to Japanese government support of Fuji's domination of distribution channels in Japan. In 1996, the U.S. government shifted the complaint to the WTO dispute settlement process. In 1998, the WTO ruled against the complaint, citing insufficient evidence of unacceptable protectionist actions by the Japanese government. In this case the decision was against the U.S. complaint, but most WTO rulings on other U.S. complaints have been in favor of the United States. The United States is likely to continue to rely mostly on the WTO dispute settlement process rather than using Section 301. In addition, the establishment of the WTO also limits the U.S. ability to retaliate unilaterally using Section 301. Foreign countries can complain about the retaliation using the WTO dispute settlement process. It would be very difficult for the U.S. government to defend its unilateral action in front of a decidedly multilateral organization.

Summary

Nontariff barriers (NTBs) reduce imports by limiting quantities, increasing costs, or creating uncertainties. Government officials in a country have many reasons for imposing NTBs, but economic efficiency apparently is not a valid reason for this choice. The basic analysis of the main nontariff barrier to trade, an **import quota,** indicates that it is at least as bad as a tariff. It is more costly than the tariff if it creates domestic monopoly power or if resources are used up in the private pursuit of licenses to import items legally.

A form of protection that became important in the 1980s, especially in the United States and the EU, is the **voluntary export restraint (VER)** arrangement. Here the importing country threatens foreign exporters with stiff barriers if they do not agree to restrict exports by themselves. Under a negotiated VER arrangement, the main foreign exporters form a cartel among themselves, agreeing to cut export quantities. At the same time, they are allowed to charge the full markup on their limited sales to the importing country, where the product has become more expensive. A curious result is that the importing country, which insisted on the VER in the first place, loses even more than if it had collected a tariff or quota markup itself.

Other important nontariff barriers include **domestic content requirements, mixing requirements,** government procurement favoring domestic products, and a host of quality and safety standards that have protectionist effects.

The net costs of import barriers, both tariff and nontariff, look small from some perspectives but large from others. They look small as a share of GDP when calculated in terms of the ordinary deadweight loss triangles. Yet this analysis overlooks foreign retaliation, enforcement costs, rent-seeking, and other considerations that can make import barriers more expensive. In relation to the protection provided to incomes in protected sectors, the net costs of import barriers are often rather large.

In 1995, the **World Trade Organization (WTO)** was born as the forum for global rules toward international trade. Member countries of the WTO, and the **General Agreement on Tariffs and Trade (GATT)** before it, conduct multilateral trade negotiations to lower trade barriers. Quotas on industrial products have largely been eliminated, and tariffs have been gradually reduced to low levels through the negotiated agreements, but the use of other NTBs has been rising. The Tokyo Round and the Uruguay Round included some efforts to reduce the use of NTBs. The new Doha Round will continue the global negotiations to liberalize tariff and nontariff barriers.

Under **Section 301** of the U.S. trade law, the U.S. government can unilaterally use the threat of imposing new import barriers, in an effort to force foreign-country governments to remove allegedly unfair policies that limit the access of U.S. exports to these countries. With the advent of the much-improved dispute settlement procedure in the WTO, the U.S. has reduced its use of Section 301.

Suggested Reading

Deardorff and Stern (1998) provide a broad survey of nontariff barriers to imports. Trionfetti (2000) examines government procurement as an NTB. Jones (1994) examines the rise of VERs. Berry, Levinsohn, and Pakes (1999) provide a technical analysis of the VER on Japanese auto exports to the United States. Findlay and Warren (2000) present evidence on barriers to trade in services, and Hoekman (2000) looks at gains from liberalizing services trade. Footer and Graber (2000) examine barriers to trade in cultural goods and services (films, music recordings, and so forth).

The costs of U.S. protectionism are quantified by Hufbauer and Elliott (1994). The meaning of such costs, with extra treatment of the effects on foreign exporters, is interpreted by Feenstra (1992). Messerlin (2001) reports the costs of protectionism for the European Union. Hufbauer (1996) provides a survey of similar studies for other countries. Feenstra (1995) provides a technical survey of work estimating the effects of protection.

U.S. policy and its conflicts with the WTO are neatly summarized by Destler (1995). Schott (1994) and Whalley and Hamilton (1996) survey the accomplishments and shortcomings of the Uruguay Round. Hoekman and Kostecki (2001) examine the WTO's rules and activities. Bütler and Hauser (2000) analyze the WTO dispute settlement system. Sampson (2000) presents an overview of issues facing the WTO.

Bayard and Elliott (1994) provide an in-depth analysis of Section 301, and Elliott and Richardson (1997) update some of this analysis. Kherallah and Beghin (1998) examine the outcomes of Section 301 cases.

Questions and Problems

♦ 1. What are import quotas? Why do some governments use them instead of just using tariffs to restrict imports by the same amounts? Is it because quotas bring a bigger national gain than tariffs?

2. What are voluntary export restraint (VER) agreements? Why do some governments force foreign exporters into them instead of just using quotas or tariffs to restrict imports by the same amounts? Is it because VERs bring the importing country a bigger national gain than quotas or tariffs?

◆3. Under what conditions could an import quota and a tariff have exactly the same effect on price, and bring the same gains and losses (given a tariff level that restricts imports just as much as the quota would)?

4. Define each of the following import policies, and describe its likely effects on the well-being of the importing country as a whole: (a) product standards and (b) domestic content requirements.

◆5. To protect Kodak jobs, the United States might decide to cut its imports of photographic film by 60 percent. It could do so by either (a) imposing a tariff high enough to cut film imports by 60 percent or (b) persuading Fuji and other foreign filmmakers to set up a VER arrangement to cut their exports of film to the United States by 60 percent. Which of these two policies would be less damaging to the United States? Which would be less damaging to the world as a whole? Explain.

6. The United States is considering adopting a regulation that foreign apples can be imported only if they are grown and harvested using the same techniques that are used in the United States. These methods are used in the United States to meet various government standards about worker safety and product quality.

   a. As a representative of the U.S. government, you are asked to defend the new import regulation before the WTO. What will you say?
   b. As a representative of foreign apple growers, you are asked to present the case that this regulation is an unfair restriction on trade. What will you say?

◆7. A small country imports sugar. With free trade at the world price of $0.10 per pound, the country's national market is:

Domestic production	120 million pounds per year
Domestic consumption	440 million pounds per year
Imports	320 million pounds per year

The country's government now decides to impose a quota that limits sugar imports to 240 million pounds per year. With the import quota in effect, the domestic price rises to $0.12 per pound, and domestic production increases to 160 million pounds per year. The government auctions the rights to import the 240 million pounds.

   a. Calculate how much domestic producers gain or lose from the quota.
   b. Calculate how much domestic consumers gain or lose from the quota.
   c. Calculate how much the government receives in payment when it auctions the quota rights to import.
   d. Calculate the net national gain or loss from the quota. Explain the *economic* reason(s) for this net gain or loss.

8. A small country's protectionism can be summarized: The typical tariff rate is 50 percent, the (absolute value of the) price elasticity of demand for imports is 1, imports would be 20 percent of the country's GDP with free trade, and the protected industries represent 15 percent of GDP. Using our triangle analysis, what is the approximate magnitude of the economic costs of the tariff protection, as a percentage of the country's GDP? As a percentage of the gain of producer surplus in the protected sectors?

◆ 9. For a small country, consider a quota and an equivalent tariff that permit the same initial level of imports. The market is competitive, and the government uses fixed favoritism to allocate the quota permits, with no resources expended in the process. There is now an increase in domestic demand (the domestic demand curve D_d shifts to the right). If the tariff rate is unchanged, and if the quota quantity is unchanged, are the two still equivalent? Show this using a graph. Be sure to discuss the effects on domestic price, production quantity, and consumption quantity, on import quantity, and on producer surplus, consumer surplus, deadweight losses, and government revenue or its equivalent for the quota.

10. A Japanese friend asks you to explain and defend American use of Section 301. What will you say?

◆ 11. Suppose that the U.S. government is under heavy pressure from the Rollerblade and K2 companies to put the brakes on imports of Bauer in-line skates from Canada. The protectionists demand that the price of a $200 pair of in-line skates must be raised to $250 if their incomes are to be safe. The U.S. government has three choices: (1) free trade with no protection, (2) a special tariff on in-line skates backed by vague claims that Canada is using unfair trade practices (citing Section 301 of the Trade Act of 1974), and (3) forcing Bauer to agree to a voluntary export restraint. The three choices would lead to these prices and annual quantities:

	With Free Trade	With an $80 Tariff	With a VER
Domestic U.S. price per pair	$200	$250	$250
World price per pair	$200	$170	$170
Imports of in-line skates (millions of pairs)	10	6	6

Note that the $80 tariff restricts imports by 4 million pairs a year, the same restriction that the VER arrangement would enforce.

a. Calculate the U.S. net national gains or losses from the tariff, and the U.S. gains or losses from the VER, relative to free trade. Which of the three choices looks best for the United States as a whole? Which looks worst?

b. Calculate the net national gains or losses for Canada, the exporting country, from the tariff and the VER. Which of the three U.S. choices harms Canada most? Which harms Canada least?

c. Which of the three choices is best for the world as a whole?

Chapter **Nine**

Arguments for and against Protection

Why do most countries have policies that limit imports? Chapters 7 and 8 found only bad barriers, ones that brought net harm to the world economy. Because free trade led to a fully efficient outcome for the world in our analysis, any trade barriers could only be bad. We did find one barrier, the nationally optimal tariff, that could be good for the country that imposed it. However, it too was bad for the world as a whole, and it could end up being bad for the country that tried to impose it if other countries retaliate by raising their own tariffs on products that the first country exports.

A key objective of this chapter is to examine a variety of arguments proposing that import protection is good for the country (and perhaps also for the world) because it allows the country to address some market shortcoming or to achieve some objective other than economic efficiency. We know from the analysis of Chapters 7 and 8 that a tariff or nontariff barrier (NTB) to imports of a product can

- Increase domestic production of the product.

- Increase employment of labor and other resources in this domestic production.

- Decrease domestic consumption of the product.

- Increase government revenue.

- Alter the distribution of income or well-being in the country.

Corresponding to each of these effects, here are five generic arguments in favor of tariffs (or NTBs) that we will examine:

- If there is something extra good about local production of a product, then a tariff can be good for the country, because the tariff leads to more domestic production of the product.

- If there is something extra good about employing people or other resources in producing a product, then a tariff can be good for the country, because the tariff leads to more employment in the sector as local production of the product increases.

- If there is something extra bad about local consumption of a product, then a tariff can be good for the country, because the tariff leads to less domestic consumption of the product.

- If there is something extra good about the government collecting more revenue, then the tariff can be good for the country.

- If it is desirable to enhance the incomes of factors used intensively in the import-competing industry, then a tariff can be good for the country.

In each of these cases, the tariff could also be good for the world as well. (We defer examination of one other generic argument for import protection, that foreign exporters are engaging in unfair trade, until Chapter 10.)

Our analysis here will establish some of the policy conclusions previewed at the start of Chapter 7:

- There are valid "second-best" arguments for protection—situations in which protection could be better than free trade.

- Some other government policies are usually better than import barriers in these situations.

If there are few situations in which import protection is the best policy for a country, why do we see so many import barriers? The second part of the chapter focuses on the politics of protection. We examine how political actions by different self-interested groups in the country can influence political decisions about import barriers. Our political excursion indicates that institutions are important. Import protection is more likely in a representative democracy for products in which import-competing domestic producers organize into effective lobbies but domestic consumers do not.

THE IDEAL WORLD OF FIRST BEST

In Chapters 7 and 8 we assumed an ideal or "first-best" world in which all *private* incentives aligned perfectly with benefits and costs to *society* as a whole. In a first-best world any demand or supply curve can do double duty, representing both private and social benefits or costs. The domestic demand curve represented not only marginal benefits of an extra bicycle to its private buyer but also the extra benefits of another bicycle to society as a whole. The domestic supply curve represented not only the marginal cost to private producers of producing another bicycle at home but also the marginal cost to society as a whole.

The first row of Figure 9.1 summarizes what an economist means by a first-best world. The market price (P) acts as a signal to consumers and producers. Consumers buy the product up to the point where the price they are willing to pay, which equals the extra private benefits (MB) they receive from another unit, just equals the price that they must pay. The extra benefit to society (SMB) is just the extra benefit that the consumer gets. Producers supply the product up to the point where the price they

FIGURE 9.1   Incentive Distortions and Their Effects

Situation	Incentives at the Margin	Effects
First-best world	$P = MB = MC = SMB = SMC$	Exactly the right amount is supplied and demanded.
Distortions		
External costs	$SMC > P (= MB = MC = SMB)$	Too much is supplied because suppliers make and sell extra units for which the social costs exceed the price (which equals *MC* and *MB* and *SMB*). Example: production that pollutes air or water.
External benefits	$SMB > P (= MB = MC = SMC)$	Not enough is demanded because demanders receive only private benefits equal to the price, not the full social benefits. Example: training or education that brings extra gains in attitudes or team skills.
Distorting tax	P with tax $> SMC$	Not enough is supplied because the tax makes the price to buyers exceed the revenue per unit received by suppliers.
Distorting subsidy	P with subsidy $< SMC$	Too much is supplied because the subsidy makes the price to buyers lower than the revenue per unit received by suppliers.
Monopoly power	$P > SMC$	Not enough is demanded because the monopoly sets the price too high.
Monopsony power (a case not developed in this textbook)	$P < SMB$	Not enough is supplied because the monopsony sets its buying price too low. Example: a single firm that dominates a labor market and uses its power to set a low wage.

P = Market price
MB = Private marginal benefit of an activity (to those who demand it)
MC = Private marginal cost of an activity (to those who supply it)
SMB = Social marginal benefit of an activity (to everybody affected)
SMC = Social marginal cost of an activity (to everybody affected)

receive just covers the extra costs (*MC*) of producing the product. The extra costs to society (*SMC*) of producing another unit of this product are just the extra costs that the individual firm incurs. That is, all five marginal values are equal:

Price (*P*) = Buyers' private marginal benefit (*MB*) = Social marginal benefit (*SMB*) = Sellers' private marginal cost (*MC*) = Social marginal cost (*SMC*)

In a first-best world free trade is economically efficient. Free trade allows the "invisible hand" of market competition to reach globally. Private producers, reacting to the signal of the market price, expand production in each country to levels that are as good as possible for the world as whole. Private consumers, also reacting to price signals, expand their purchases of products to levels that make the whole world as well off as possible.

THE REALISTIC WORLD OF SECOND BEST

Our world is not ideal. Distortions exist, and they do not automatically cancel each other out. **Incentive distortions** are gaps between the private and social benefits or costs of an activity. We live in a **"second-best" world,** one that includes incentive distortions. As long as these gaps exist between what private individuals use to make their decisions and the full effects of these decisions on society, *private actions will not lead to the best possible outcomes* for society. Figure 9.1 provides information on six types of distortions.

The first two types of distortions in the figure are **externalities** or **spillover effects** (net effects on parties other than those agreeing to buy or sell in a marketplace). The first example of an externality is the classic case of river pollution, an example we will explore at length in Chapter 12. If the sellers of paper products are not forced to do so, they do not reckon the damage done by the paper mills' river pollution into the cost of their production. So the pollution costs are not incorporated into the price of paper. Similarly, buyers of petroleum fuels do not reckon that the social cost of air pollution from using those fuels is part of the fuel price that they have to pay. If some costs of producing or consuming a product are ignored by the private decision-makers, then too much of the product is produced or consumed.

Our second example of an externality supposes that jobs in a certain import-competing sector generate greater returns for society than are perceived by the people who decide whether or not to take the jobs. These external benefits can happen, for instance, if working in the sector brings gains in knowledge, skills, and attitudes that benefit firms or people other than the workers and employers in the sector. In this example the social marginal benefits (SMB) of working in the sector are higher than the wage rate (or the price, P) that workers receive. If some benefits of the activity are ignored by private decision-makers, then too little of the activity occurs (in the example, too few people are hired into jobs in the sector).

In this chapter we will focus on distortions caused by externalities. In fact, we focus on various kinds of external benefits that are the "extra good" that can accompany local production of a product or employment in producing the product. We only briefly mention here the other four types of distortions shown in Figure 9.1.

In the absence of any other distortion, a tax creates a distortion by artificially raising the price to buyers. Our analysis of a tariff in Chapter 7 is an example of a tax distortion and the inefficiency caused by this distortion.

In the absence of any other distortion, a government subsidy creates a distortion by artificially lowering the price to buyers. Essentially, a subsidy is like a negative tax. We will examine subsidies later in this chapter and also in Chapter 10.

Monopoly power can create a distortion because a powerful seller restricts output to raise price and increase profits. In the box on domestic monopoly in Chapter 8, we saw that free trade could eliminate this distortion by forcing the domestic monopoly to compete with foreign firms. Monopsony power can create a distortion because a powerful buyer sets a price that is too low.

Government Policies toward Externalities

External costs and external benefits pose some of the most intriguing policy problems in economics. How should a society try to fix distortions caused by externalities? There are two basic approaches for government policy. One approach is optimistic about the government's ability to cure these distortions, while the other is pessimistic. The optimistic approach is the *tax-or-subsidy approach* developed by British economist A. C. Pigou. The other approach is the *property-rights approach,* which builds on the ideas of Nobel Prize winner Ronald Coase. This approach suggests that creating new private-property institutions is better than using taxes or subsidies.[1]

In this chapter we use the tax-or-subsidy approach because the trade policy debate is usually over taxes and subsidies (e.g., a tariff is a tax). While we explore how government taxes and subsidies, at their best, *can* cure externality distortions, remember that there is reason to debate whether such government interventions *will* work well in practice.[2] The idea is to explore the best possible cases for government interference with trade. At the same time, we have to keep in mind the real *possibility of government failure* to correctly identify problems and enact solutions.

The tax-or-subsidy approach says that we should spot distortions in people's and firms' private incentives and have a wise government policy correct the incentives with taxes or subsidies. What if social marginal cost exceeds private cost and market price ($SMC > MC = P = MB = SMB$), as in the pollution case? The government should levy a tax of ($SMC - SMB$) to bring everything into equality by raising the price to match the full social marginal cost (including the external costs created by the pollution). If the social marginal benefit exceeds private benefit and the market price ($SMB > MB = P = MC = SMC$), as in the training case, let the government pay a subsidy of ($SMB - SMC$) so that decision makers in the marketplace recognize the full social returns.

Could trade barriers help to cure distortions caused by externalities? Even before we get to the details, we can see that the tax-or-subsidy approach can relate to the debate over trade barriers. If there is a distortion in our economy,

---

[1] For example, the property-rights approach says that, if there is a problem of a paper mill polluting a river, we can make private incentives include all social effects by making the river someone's private property. Either let the downstream river users own it and charge the paper mill for any pollution, or let the paper mill own the river and demand compensation for cleaning it up. Choose between these two property-right assignments by choosing the one that costs less to implement and enforce. The property-rights approach will resurface in Chapter 12's treatment of international environmental issues.

[2] We can see this more broadly and also clear up a possible confusion. In Figure 9.1 a tax and a subsidy are listed as possible sources of distortions. That is, if the market otherwise gets to the first-best solution (because there is no other distortion), then introducing a tax or subsidy causes a distortion. If, instead, a distortion already exists, then the market will not get to the first-best outcome by itself. If a distortion already exists, then an appropriate tax or subsidy can improve the market outcome. But the wrong tax or subsidy could make things even worse.

perhaps cutting imports could help. A quick example is the worker-training case already mentioned. If the social benefit of having workers get training in a certain industry is greater than their current market wage, it is possible that we could reap net social gains by protecting their jobs against foreign competition. This is the kind of issue that we return to repeatedly in this chapter.

The Specificity Rule

Externalities and other incentive distortions complicate the task of judging whether a trade barrier is good or bad for the nation as a whole. Realizing this, some scholars have stressed that there is no cure-all prescription for trade policy in a second-best world. Once you realize that distortions exist, things become complicated. It seems that each situation must be judged on its own merits.

Yet we are not cast totally adrift in this world of distortions. We do not have to shrug and just say "Every case is different. It all depends." There is a useful rule that works well in most cases. The **specificity rule** states that it is usually more efficient to use the government policy tool that acts as directly as possible on the source of the distortion separating private and social benefits or costs. In short, identify the specific source of the problem and intervene directly at this source.

The specificity rule applies to all sorts of policy issues. Let's illustrate it first by using some examples removed from international trade. Suppose that the problem is crime, which creates fear among third parties and direct harm to victims. Since crime is caused by people, we might consider combating crime by reducing the whole population through compulsory sterilization laws or taxes on children. But such actions are obviously inefficient ways of attacking crime since less social friction would be generated (per crime averted) if we fought crime more directly through greater law enforcement and programs to reduce unemployment, a major contributor to crime.

A less extreme example of the specificity rule brings us back to those paper mills polluting rivers. To attack this problem, we could tax all production of paper products or we could subsidize the installation of a particular waste-treatment device. But the specificity rule cautions us to make sure that we are as close as possible to the source of the problem. Taxing all paper products is likely to be too broad an instrument since it discourages the production of all paper without regard to the extent of pollution. The paper manufacturers would get the signal that society wants them to make less paper, but not the signal to look for less polluting ways of making paper. On the other hand, subsidizing the installation of a particular waste treatment device may be too narrow an instrument. Nothing assures us that this specific waste treatment approach is the cheapest way to reduce pollution. Perhaps a change in the internal production processes of the paper mills could cut down on the amount of waste needing any treatment more cheaply than the cost of the waste treatment equipment. The problem arose from the failure to provide the paper manufacturers with incentives for cutting pollution, not from their failure to adopt a particular method. The specificity rule thus directs us to look at incentive policies geared to the act of pollution itself. Taxes or quantitative limits on the amount of pollution discharged (effluent charges and environmental quality standards) are very likely to be better policies to use.

As we will see in the cases we now turn to, the specificity rule tends to cut against import barriers. *Although a barrier against imports can be better than doing nothing in a second-best world, the rule shows us that some other policy instrument is usually more efficient* than a trade barrier in dealing with a domestic distortion.

PROMOTING DOMESTIC PRODUCTION OR EMPLOYMENT

Protectionists often come up with reasons that it is good to maintain high levels of domestic production of a product that is imported or high levels of employment of workers (and perhaps other resources) in this domestic production. They offer reasons that this is good *for the nation as a whole* (and not just for the firms and workers that receive the protection). In fact, most popular second-best arguments for protection can be viewed as variations on the theme of favoring a particular import-competing industry because there are extra social benefits to domestic production or employment in this particular import-competing industry. Here are several versions that we will examine in this chapter:

- Local production of this product produces spillover benefits because other firms and industries benefit from production know-how or management techniques introduced by the firms in this industry.

- Employment in this industry imparts new worker skills and attitudes, and some workers carry these when they switch jobs to work for other firms and industries.

- By producing now at high cost, firms in the industry can find ways to lower their costs over time.

- There are extra costs to workers if they are forced to switch to jobs in other industries.

- The country and its citizens take pride from producing this product locally.

- The product is essential to national defense.

- Employment in the industry is a way to redistribute income to poor or disadvantaged members of society.

In examining these proposed reasons that protection is good for the country, we consider the case of a *small country* (one whose trade has no impact on world prices) so that our analysis is not complicated by any effects of the trade barrier on the country's international terms of trade.

Let us turn first to the pros and cons of a tariff to promote domestic production or employment because this production or employment creates positive externalities (the first two of the reasons shown in the above list). Analysis of these two reasons is important, and we will be able to use the insights from this analysis in examining the other reasons in the list.

Let's look at the case in which a nation might want to encourage domestic production of bicycles because this production creates positive spillovers elsewhere in the country. It could achieve the production objective by putting a $30 tariff on imported bicycles, as shown in the diagram of the national bicycle market in Figure 9.2A. The tariff brings the nation the same elements of net loss that it did back in Chapter 7 (and Figure 7.4A): The nation loses area *b* by producing at greater expense what could be bought for less from abroad, and it loses area *d* by discouraging purchases that would have brought more enjoyment to consumers than the world price of a bicycle. But now something is added: The lower part of the diagram portrays some social side benefits from local production, benefits that are not captured by the domestic bicycle producers. That is, we suppose that the marginal social side benefits of making our own bicycles can be represented by the MSSB curve at the bottom. By raising the domestic price of bicycles, the tariff encourages more production of bicycles. This increase in domestic production, from S_0 to S_1, brings area *g* in extra gains to the nation.

Compared with doing nothing, levying the tariff in Figure 9.2A could be good or bad for the nation, all things considered. The net outcome depends on whether area *g* is larger or smaller than the areas *b* and *d*. To find out, we would have to develop empirical estimates reflecting the realities of the bicycle industry. We would want to estimate the dollar value of the annual side benefits to society and also the slopes of the domestic supply and demand curves. The net national gain $(g - b - d)$ might turn out to be positive or negative. Until we know the specific numbers involved, all we can say, so far, is that the tariff might prove to be better (or worse) than doing nothing.

We should use our institutional imagination, however, and look for other policy tools. The specificity rule prods us to do so. The locus of the problem is really domestic production, not imports. What society wants to encourage is more domestic production of this good, not less consumption or fewer imports of it. Instead of a tariff, why not encourage the domestic production directly by rewarding firms for producing?

Society could directly subsidize the domestic production of bicycles by having the government pay bicycle firms a fixed amount for each bicycle produced and sold. This would encourage them to produce more bicycles. Any increase in production that a given tariff could coax out of domestic firms could also be yielded by a production subsidy. Figure 9.2B shows such a subsidy, namely, a $30 subsidy per bicycle produced domestically. The subsidy increases the revenue per unit sold to $330 ($300 paid by consumers and $30 paid by the government). This subsidy is just as good for domestic bicycle firms as the extra $30 in selling price that the tariff made possible. Either tool gets the firms to raise their annual production from 0.6 to 0.8 million, giving society the same side benefits.

The $30 production subsidy in Figure 9.2B is definitely better than the $30 tariff in Figure 9.2A. Both generate the same social side benefits (area *g*), and both cause domestic firms to produce 0.2 million extra bicycles each year at a higher

FIGURE 9.2   Two Ways to Promote Import-Competing Production

Compare the side effects of two ways of getting the same increase in domestic output (0.2 million = 0.8 – 0.6 million) and in domestic jobs. Both the $30 tariff and the $30 subsidy to domestic production encourage the same change in domestic production. But the tariff also needlessly discourages some consumption of imports (the amount 0.2 million = 1.6 – 1.4 million) that was worth more to the buyers than the $300 each unit of imports would have cost the nation. The production subsidy is better than the tariff because it strikes more directly at the task of raising domestic production of this good.

direct cost than the price at which the nation could buy foreign bicycles. (In both cases this extra cost is area *b*). Yet the subsidy does not discourage the total consumption of bicycles by raising the price above $300. Consumers continue to pay $300 for each bicycle, equal to the world price of obtaining an imported bicycle. They continue to consume 1.6 million bicycles. Consumers do not lose the additional area *d*. This is a clear advantage of the $30 production subsidy over the $30 tariff.

What makes the production subsidy better is its conformity to the specificity rule: Since the locus of the problem is domestic production, it is less costly to attack it in a way that does not also distort the price that consumers pay for the product.

Although this conclusion is broadly valid, a special assumption is needed to make the net advantage of the production subsidy exactly equal area *d*. We are assuming that no other distortions between private and social incentives result when the government comes up with the revenues to pay the production subsidies to the bicycle firms. That is, we are assuming that there is no net social loss from having the government either raise additional taxes or reduce some other spending to pay this subsidy to bicycle producers. This assumption is strictly valid if the extra tax revenues going into the subsidy come from a head tax, a tax on people's existence, which should only redistribute income and not affect production and consumption incentives. Yet head taxes are rare, and the more realistic case of financing the production subsidy by, say, raising income taxes or cutting other government spending programs is somewhat murkier. Raising the income tax distorts people's incentives to earn income through effort. Or if the government spending reallocated to the production subsidy had previously been providing some other public goods worth more than their marginal cost, there is again an extra loss that can attend the production subsidy. Policymakers would have to consider these possible source-of-subsidy distortions. Yet it seems reasonable to presume that such distortions are less important than the distorting of consumption represented by area *d*.

If our concern is with *maintaining or expanding jobs,* rather than output, in the import-competing industry, the same results hold with a slight modification. A production subsidy would still be preferable to the tariff since it still achieves any given expansion in both bicycle production and bicycle jobs at lower social cost. We could come up with even better alternatives, however. If the locus of the problem is really the number of jobs in the bicycle industry, it would be even more efficient to use a policy tool that not only encourages production but also encourages firms to come up with ways of creating more jobs per dollar of bicycle output. A subsidy tied to the number of workers employed is better than a subsidy tied to output.[3] The box "How Much Does It Cost to Protect a Job?" examines the costs of using tariffs and NTBs to prop up jobs in import-competing industries.

So why do governments so often use import barriers instead of direct production or employment subsidies that are less costly to the economy? Once an industry's political lobby is strong enough to get government help, it uses its influence to get a kind of help that is sheltered from political counterattacks. The subsidy favored by our economic analysis provides no such shelter. The subsidy is a highly visible target for fiscal budget cutters. Every year it has to be defended again when the government budget is under review. A tariff or other import barrier, however, gives much better shelter to the industry that seeks continuing government help. Once it is written into the law, it goes on propping up domestic prices without being reviewed. In fact, it generates government revenue (e.g., tariff revenue), giving it more political appeal. We examine the politics of protection in more depth later in this chapter.

---

[3] Alternatively, if the object is to create jobs and cure unemployment *throughout the entire domestic economy,* then it is logical to look first to economywide expansionary policies, such as fiscal policy or monetary policy, and not to policy fixes in any one industry.

THE INFANT INDUSTRY ARGUMENT

The analysis of using a tariff to promote domestic production helps us judge the merits of a number of popular arguments for protection. Of all the protectionist arguments, the one that has always enjoyed the most prestige among both economists and policymakers is the **infant industry argument,** which asserts that a temporary tariff is justified because it cuts down on imports while the infant domestic industry learns how to produce at low enough costs. Eventually the domestic industry will be able to compete without the help of a tariff. The infant industry argument differs from the optimal tariff argument by claiming that in the long run the tariff protection will be good for the world as well as for the nation. It differs from most other tariff arguments in being explicitly dynamic, arguing that the protection is needed only for a while.

The infant industry argument has been popular with aspiring countries at least since Alexander Hamilton used it in his *Report on Manufacturers* in 1791. The United States followed Hamilton's protectionist formula, especially after the Civil War, setting up high tariff walls to encourage production of textiles, ferrous metals, and other goods still struggling to become competitive against Britain. Similarly, Friedrich List reapplied Hamilton's infant industry ideas to the cause of shielding nascent German manufacturing industries against British competition in the early 19th century. The government of Japan has believed strongly in infant industry protection—sometimes, but not always, in the form of import protection. In the 1950s and 1960s in particular, Japan protected its steel, automobile, shipbuilding, and electronics industries before they became tough competitors and the import barriers were removed.

The infant industry argument will continue to deserve attention because there will always be infant industries. As some countries gain the lead in producing new products with new technologies, other countries will have to consider time and again what to do about the development of their own production of these new products.

How It Is Supposed to Work

Figure 9.3 provides a schematic for understanding the infant industry argument, using the example of small farm tractors. Now, as shown in the left side of the figure, no amount of production in this country is cost-competitive by world standards (the current domestic supply curve S_{dn} is everywhere above the world price of $3,000 per tractor). Apparently, no domestic production would occur now with free trade. If the country's government imposes a tariff of 33 percent, the domestic price rises to 4,000 per tractor and domestic firms produce 20,000 tractors. Now (and for as many years as this situation persists) we know that the country incurs inefficiencies of area b and area d because of the tariff.

The payoff to incurring these inefficiencies is that the infant industry grows up. As firms produce tractors, they find ways to lower their costs. At some time in the future the domestic industry's supply curve will shift down to S_{df}. The government

Defenders of protection against imports claim that it is needed to protect domestic jobs. Although it sometimes sounds like any people who lose their jobs to increased imports are unemployed forever, we know that that is not true. Worker loses their jobs for many reasons, and nearly all of them then look for and find other jobs. It may take a while, and the new job may not pay as much (at first) as the previous jobs did, but they will be reemployed.

So the proponents of protection are really saying that restrictions on imports are needed to *maintain jobs in the import-competing industry that is receiving the protection.* We know that import barriers can maintain jobs in an import-competing industry by permitting domestic production at a level higher than it would be with free trade. But we also know from the discussion in the text that the specificity rule shows that an import barrier is not the best government policy to accomplish this objective.

Still, governments do use tariffs and nontariff barriers to prop up domestic production and maintain jobs in import-competing industries. How large are

the costs of doing so? We can examine the costs in two ways. First, how much does it cost domestic consumers of the product per job maintained? That is, what is the consumer surplus loss per job maintained? Second, what is the net cost to the country per job maintained?

We can turn to researchers at the Institute of International Economics to provide some estimates of these costs for highly protected sectors in the United States and the European Union. For the estimates used here (in contrast to those reported in Figure 8.4), we will ignore any effects of tariffs and import quotas on the world prices of the products. Essentially, we are assuming that the importing country is small, our standard assumption for this chapter.*

In Figure 8.4 we used the estimates by Hufbauer and Eliott (1994) of the effects of import barriers for 21 highly protected industries in the United States, as of 1990. Here is what they found out about using import protection to maintain jobs, for all 21 industries and for those in which at least 1,000 jobs were protected:

	Production Worker Jobs Maintained	**Cost per Job Maintained ($ thousands)**	
		To Domestic Consumers	**To the Nation**
All 21 industries	191,764	169	54
Costume jewelry	1,067	97	5
Glassware	1,477	180	6
Rubber footwear	1,701	122	7
Women's footwear	3,702	102	3
Dairy products	2,378	498	44
Sugar	2,261	600	257
Maritime shipping	4,431	415	126
Apparel	152,583	139	51
Textiles	16,203	202	55
Machine tools	1,556	348	247

* If, instead, the importing country is a large country, then including the effects of a change in the world prices would have almost no effect on the estimates of the cost to consumers per job maintained. For each industry both the numerator and the denominator of the calculation used to obtain the estimate would change by about the same proportion. Ignoring the world price change could result in estimates of the net cost to the country per job maintained that are larger than the costs actually are. If the importing country is large enough to drive down a product's world price when it imposes a tariff or quota, then the gains from the improved terms of trade would be set against the standard efficiency losses.

Messerlin (2001) estimated similar effects for 22 highly protected industries in the European Union, for 1990. Here is what he found:

	Production Worker Jobs Maintained	Cost per Job Maintained ($ thousands) To Domestic Consumers	To the Nation
All 22 industries	243,650	191	99
Fertilizers	3,514	164	20
Low-density polyurethane	1,072	252	29
Chemical fibers	1,102	474	64
Integrated circuits	6,027	330	224
Steel	5,152	284	175
Passenger cars	3,694	512	206
Textiles	39,383	162	61
Clothing	33,160	193	100
Cereal grains	46,341	62	18
Meat	40,695	105	29
Sugar	29,129	132	71
Films (France)	6,721	54	42
Telecommunications	19,933	177	125

For the 21 industries in the United States, the jobs maintained by import protection represent about 10 percent of workers in these industries, and less than 0.2 percent of the labor force in the United States. For the European Union, the maintained jobs are about 3 percent of workers in the 22 industries, and also less than 0.2 percent of the labor force.

These estimates show the high cost of maintaining industry jobs through high levels of import protection. For the United States, consumers pay an average of about $169,000 per job maintained, and in Europe about $191,000 per job. Per year, this is over six times the average annual compensation for a manufacturing worker in each country. It would be much cheaper for domestic consumers to simply pay these workers not to work than it is to maintain their jobs using import protection. For some industries the consumer cost per job maintained in the industry is breathtaking:

- For the United States, $600,000 for a sugar job, $498,000 for a dairy products job, and $415,000 for a maritime job.

- For the European Union, $512,000 for an autoworker job, $474,000 for a chemical fiber job, and $330,000 for a semiconductor job.

The net national cost per job is also high in both countries: $54,000 in the United States and $99,000 in the European Union. The net national cost per job is higher than the compensation earned by the typical manufacturing worker. If our goal is to maintain jobs in these industries, the specificity rule says we can do better. Again, just paying the workers to have jobs in which they do nothing would be less costly. Indeed, the cost per person of a high-quality worker adjustment program that offers training and assistance to these workers to find well-paying jobs in other industries would be much less than the net national cost of maintaining these jobs through high import barriers.

It is worth noting that the average net national costs per job are this high because some of the protection is through VERs and similar policies that permit foreign exporters to raise their prices. This cost-increasing effect is substantial for sugar, apparel, textiles, and machine tools in the United States, and for integrated circuits, steel, passenger cars, textiles, clothing, and telecommunications in the European Union. Even if we remove these price markups lost to foreign exporters, the net national cost per job is still rather large—an average $18,000 in the United States and $42,000 in the European Union.

FIGURE 9.3 The Infant Industry Argument

With free trade now, there would be no domestic production. A tariff can induce domestic production now of 20,000 tractors per year. After a number of years of domestic production, the domestic firms will find ways to lower their costs, so the domestic supply curve in the future is lower. The government can remove the tariff in the future, and the future production of 50,000 tractors per year is cost-competitive by world standards.

can then remove the tariff. As shown in the right side of the figure, the country will then have a tractor industry that can produce 50,000 tractors per year at costs that are competitive with world standards. This competitive domestic production creates producer surplus of area v, surplus that would not exist if the country had not protected the industry in its early years. (For simplicity, the example assumes that the world price and the domestic demand curve do not change over time. This is not essential to the story. Also, the domestic industry is shown as still competing with imports in the future. This is not essential to the story either. If the domestic cost curve falls low enough, the industry would become an exporter. The gain for the country in the future is still an area like f.)

How Valid Is It?

Whether the infant industry argument is a valid argument for a (temporary) tariff or other import barrier depends on whether the benefits to the country exceed the costs. The benefits are the stream of future producer surplus amounts (like area v) that accrue to domestic producers once their production becomes cost-competitive by world standards. The costs are the deadweight losses (areas b and d) that the country incurs while the tariff is in place. It is not just that some domestic production in the future becomes cost-competitive. Rather, the cost-competitive future production must create enough surplus to exceed the deadweight losses of the tariff. Because this is an investment problem over time, we should carefully say that it is a valid argument if the present value of the stream of national benefits exceeds the present value of the stream of national costs.

The infant industry argument for protection looks great in theory. Still, there are important questions about how well it works in practice. Here are three questions to ask.

First, *Is any government policy really needed?* The infant industry argument seems to be a story about firms that would make losses when they begin operations but eventually will become profitable. This is not an unusual business problem; in fact, it describes almost any new business. The standard solution is for the firm to obtain private financing, using personal wealth, borrowing from relatives and friends, bank loans, venture capital, and so forth. If private financing is available, there is nothing left for the government to do.

Yet there are at least two reasons why there could be a beneficial role for government assistance. They both follow from distortions of the type that we have been examining in this chapter.

1. *There are imperfections in the financial markets.* Financial institutions like banks and stock markets may be underdeveloped or unwilling to take on certain kinds of risk. If the government cannot act directly to improve financial markets and institutions, then there could be a second-best argument for the government to provide assistance to the infant firms.

2. *The benefits from the early business investments do not accrue to the firms making these early investments.* Infant firms must spend a lot of money to learn about the product and the production process, to train workers, and to master the marketing of the product. They will not be able to earn profits on these early investments if follower firms can enter the industry later and imitate products and production technology, hire away experienced workers, and copy marketing practices. Competition from follower firms then means that the early firms do not earn much in the way of future profits. But if they probably will not earn future profits that can be used to pay back the loans, prudent lenders will not finance their early investments. Essentially, the early firms create positive externalities for the follower firms rather than future profits for themselves. In the face of this distortion, there could be a positive role for the government to provide assistance to the infant industry.

Second, *If the government is going to provide assistance, what government policy is best?* If the goal is to induce early production even when the early firms are not cost-competitive by world standards, we know that *a production subsidy is better than a tariff* or other import barrier. In Figure 9.3A, the national cost of a production subsidy in the early phase is only area *b*, not areas *b* and *d*. Other government policies could be even better if we can identify the exact reason why government intervention is needed. If the problem is imperfections in financial markets and institutions, the government should offer loans to the infant firms. If the problem is that the early firms train workers who then may leave and take their new skills to other firms, the government should offer a subsidy to defray some of the training costs. The specificity rule is very powerful in thinking about the best government policy to use to assist an infant industry. The rule cuts against the tariff.

Third, *Will the infant industry really grow up?* It is cheap to claim to be a firm in an infant industry; it is much harder to become internationally competitive. If the tariff is truly temporary, then firms have a powerful incentive to grow up. But the pressure is much less if the firms expect that they can ask for more time with the tariff because childhood is longer than they planned for. There is a danger that the industry remains high-cost behind the protection of the tariff for a long time. This is probably another reason to favor a subsidy. The subsidy is more likely to be temporary because there is likely to be ongoing political pressure to remove the subsidy.

There are cases of apparently successful infant industry protection, such as computers and semiconductors in Japan. The qualifier *apparently* is used because it is difficult to be sure that the eventual national benefits were more than the initial national costs, and because it is also difficult to show how much of a difference the government assistance actually made in the future success of the national industry. Another apparent success is Airbus in Europe, a case in which the governments provided subsidies and loans, not import protection. There are also many cases of failed infant industry protection. For instance, in the 1980s the Brazilian government shut its market to foreign-made personal computers, hoping to foster local producers. What Brazil got was locally produced PCs that had inferior technology and high prices. With little sign of the growing-up process occurring, Brazil eventually abandoned the effort.

In conclusion, how valid is the infant industry argument? Four conclusions emerge:

1. There can be a case for some sort of government encouragement.

2. A tariff may or may not be good.

3. Some form of government help other than a tariff is a better infant industry policy than a tariff.

4. It is hard for a government to know which industries to support, because it is difficult to predict which industries can reduce their costs enough in the future to create net national benefits.

THE DYING INDUSTRY ARGUMENT AND ADJUSTMENT ASSISTANCE

The same issues and results that arise in the infant industry debate also arise in the debate about saving dying industries from import competition. Once again, protection against imports might or might not be better than doing nothing. And, once again, doing something else is better than blocking imports.

Should the Government Intervene?

With regularity, rising imports of a product threaten the well-being and even the survival of import-competing domestic firms and industries. Time and again society faces a choice: Should the firms be allowed to shrink, perhaps to go out of business, or should they be protected?

If we are in a first-best world, the answer is clear. Since the social value of anything is already included in private incentives, ordinary demand and supply curves are already leading us to the right choice without any government intervention. If rising import competition is driving domestic producers out of business, so be it. Adjustment out of the industry is necessary so that the country can enjoy the net gains from increasing trade. It is true that there will be some losses to workers, managers, investors, and landowners. They must shift their resources into other uses that may not pay quite as well as the original uses did. These losses are already measured in the loss of producer surplus. Consumers gain more, and net national well-being increases.

There are, however, ways in which we could reject the rosy first-best view of the world. One important assumption is that the workers, managers, capital, and land quickly are reemployed in other uses, even if their pay is less. A protectionist would be right to insist that this adjustment does not always work so smoothly. For instance, firms in an import-competing industry are often concentrated in a small geographic area within the country. (For the United States examples include steel firms in the industrial Midwest from Pittsburgh to Chicago and clothing firms in North Carolina.) If large numbers of workers lose their jobs in one of these industries within a short time period, the labor market becomes "congested." Many people are looking for new jobs, and many do not have the skills that match the available jobs. Steelworkers do not easily start new careers as electronics workers next Monday in the same town. Many people will probably suffer through long spells of unemployment.

While these displaced workers and other resources are unemployed, they lose all income, not just the loss of producer surplus that would occur if they could easily shift into the next-best employment. In this case, the amount of their income that imports take away is a loss to society as well as to them. Wouldn't it be better for society to intervene? Wouldn't blocking the rising imports be better than standing by while the domestic industry withers?

The protectionist argument about a dying industry is just as valid as the arguments we examined in the past two sections. And the argument has the same flaws. In fact, it is the same argument, but in a different setting. The argument that workers and other resources will not quickly be reemployed outside the threatened industry can be recast in terms of Figure 9.2. The marginal social side benefit of continuing production, instead of letting it shrink (area g in Figure 9.2), is avoiding the costs of unemployment if resources are forced out of the bicycle industry. Area g's extra benefits from maintaining the level of domestic production exist, in this case, because workers and other resources do not have to bear the lost income and other costs of shifting to employment in other industries. So it may be true that protecting a dying industry against imports is better than doing nothing. It depends, again, on whether area g is greater than areas $b + d$ in Figure 9.2.

However, there is some other policy that works better than putting up import barriers. The specificity rule reminds us to look for the true source of the problem.

The problem is directly about employment or production, not imports. There is, again, no reason to make imports more expensive to consumers as long as we can help producers directly. If the problem is the cost of relocating to other geographic areas, then a subsidy for the costs of moving is better than import protection. If the problem is a mismatch of worker skills and available jobs, then a subsidy for the costs of retraining is better. Or, if the social losses can be avoided only by maintaining current production and employment in the threatened industry, then a subsidy to production (as we showed in Figure 9.2) or to employment in this industry is better.

In fact, governments do sometimes try to help import-threatened industries with something other than import protection. One example was the U.S. government's bailout loans to Chrysler at the end of the 1970s. Chrysler used the loans to make capital improvements that allowed it to survive and repay the loans on time. Of course, not all bailouts work so well. Many just end up being a continual drain on taxpayers, as rounds of new assistance are needed to keep the firms in business.

Trade Adjustment Assistance

Governments in a number of developed countries offer **trade adjustment assistance** to workers and firms in import-threatened industries. For instance, in the United States workers can petition the U.S. Department of Labor for this assistance. If the department accepts that this group of workers is being harmed by increased imports, workers who lose their jobs receive an *extra* 6 to 12 months of unemployment compensation (in addition to the 6 months that is usual in most states), and they are eligible for retraining programs and subsidies for job search and moving expenses.

Trade adjustment assistance sounds like it is reasonably consistent with the specificity rule because it focuses on income losses, retraining, and job mobility. Nonetheless, it is controversial. In the United States it has been attacked from different sides. First, U.S. labor groups that originally backed it have felt betrayed because, in practice, it has provided so little support. The standards for eligibility are rather stringent, and in recent years only about half the petitions for assistance have been accepted. Even for those who qualify for assistance, labor groups believe that it mainly provides temporary compensation (the extended unemployment benefits), and that the retraining has been rather ineffective. The retraining often does not result in new skills and good alternative employment.

From a different side, defenders of the free market question the whole concept of adjustment assistance for import-competing industries. They ask why society should single out this particular group for special aid. Jobs and incomes are affected by many different pressures for change in the economy, including shifts in consumer tastes, technological change, bad management decisions, government rerouting of highways, and bad weather. The government provides general unemployment compensation and some general support for retraining and relocation. Why should the government give more generous assistance to those whose jobs and incomes are affected by rising imports, but not to those affected by the many other reasons that supply and demand shift in a market?

Free-market opponents of trade adjustment assistance also argue that this assistance creates perverse incentives. It encourages people to change their behavior for the worse. First, firms and workers are encouraged to gamble on entering or staying in import-vulnerable industries because they know that extra relief will be given if things work out badly. Second, workers are encouraged to remain unemployed for longer periods of time because they can receive unemployment compensation for a longer time. These perverse incentives (called *moral hazards* in discussions of insurance) do not automatically mean that the assistance program is bad. However, the net benefit of the program is reduced, and it may turn into a net cost, because people change their behavior. (This set of problems affects many other government programs offering assistance. For instance, flood disaster relief helps victims of floods who have incurred large losses, but it also encourages people to settle in flood-prone areas.)

Thus, the economic case for a government to offer trade adjustment assistance is mixed. Still, there may be a good practical and political case for tying extra assistance to import injury. Where foreign trade is involved, free-trade advocacy is weakened because many of its beneficiaries, being foreign, have no votes in the national politics of the importing country. With no votes for foreign workers or firms, there is extra danger that injured workers and firms that lobby aggressively for sweeping protectionist legislation will prevail. More generous adjustment assistance for import-competing groups than for others may be an effective political step to forestall more protectionist policies.

THE DEVELOPING GOVERNMENT (PUBLIC REVENUE) ARGUMENT

Import tariffs can be justified by another second-best argument relating to conditions in less developed countries. In a poor nation, the tariff as a source of revenue may be beneficial and even better than any feasible alternative policy, *both for the nation and for the world as a whole*.

For a developing nation with low living standards, the most serious "domestic distortions" may relate to the government's inability to provide an adequate supply of public goods. A low-income nation like Mauritania would receive large social benefits if it expanded such basic public services as the control of infectious diseases, water control for agriculture, and primary schooling. Yet the administrative resources of many poor nations are not great enough to capture these social gains.

The **developing government argument** states that in poor developing nations the import tariff becomes a crucial source, not of industrial protection but of government revenue. With severe limits on the supply of literate civil servants, Mauritania will find tariffs efficient. Revenue can be raised more cheaply by simply guarding key ports and border crossings with a few customs officials who tax imports than by levying more elaborate kinds of taxes. Production, consumption, income, and property cannot be effectively taxed when they cannot be measured and monitored.

The developing government argument is a valid reason why many low-income countries receive between one-quarter and three-fifths of their government revenue from customs duties, a higher dependence on customs than is found in equally trade-oriented high-income countries such as Canada. (On average for industrialized countries, taxes on international trade are about 2 percent of government revenues.) In principle, a developing-country government can use the tariff revenues to create net social gains, gains that may even benefit the world as a whole. This is not to say that every government that heavily taxes foreign trade is using the money to fund socially worthy investments. Foreign trade has also been heavily taxed by corrupt and wasteful governments, like those ruled by Bokassa (Central African Empire, now a republic); Louis XIV (17th-century France); Marcos (Philippines); Ceausescu (Romania); and Mobuto (Zaire).

OTHER ARGUMENTS FOR PROTECTION: NONECONOMIC OBJECTIVES

The other leading arguments for tariff protection relate to the national pursuit of noneconomic objectives, that is, goals other than achieving economic efficiency. The potential range of such arguments is limitless, but the view that people do not live by imported bread alone usually focuses on three other goals: national pride, national defense, and income distribution. Fortunately, a modified version of the specificity rule applies to a country pursuing a noneconomic objective: *To achieve the noneconomic objective with the least economic cost to the nation, use a policy that acts as directly as possible on the specific objective.*

National Pride

Nations desire symbols as much as individuals do, and knowing that some good is produced within our own country can be as legitimate an object of national pride as having cleaned up a previous urban blight or winning Olympic medals. As long as the pride can be generated only by something collective and nationwide, something not purchased by individuals in the marketplace, there is a case for policy intervention. If the pride is generated by domestic production itself, then the appropriate policy tool is a domestic production subsidy, not an import barrier. Only if the pride comes from self-sufficiency itself is blocking imports the best policy approach.

National Defense

The **national defense argument** says that import barriers would help the nation to have or to be ready to produce products that would be important in a future military emergency. It has a rich history and several interesting twists to its analysis. English mercantilists in the 17th century used the national defense argument to justify restrictions on the use of foreign ships and shipping services: If we force ourselves to buy English ships and shipping, we will foster the growth of a shipbuilding industry and a merchant marine that will be vital in time of war.

Even Adam Smith departed from his otherwise scathing attacks on trade barriers to sanction the restrictive Navigation Acts where shipping and other defense industries were involved. The national defense argument remains a favorite with producers who need a social excuse for protection. In 1984, the president of the Footwear Industry of America, with a straight face, told the Armed Services Committee of Congress,

> In the event of war or other national emergency, it is highly unlikely that the domestic footwear industry could provide sufficient footwear for the military and civilian population . . . We won't be able to wait for ships to deliver shoes from Taiwan, or Korea or Brazil or Eastern Europe . . . [I]mproper footwear can lead to needless casualties and turn sure victory into possible defeat.[4]

The same aroma pervaded the U.S. oil industry's national defense argument used to justify oil import limits from 1959 to 1973.

The importance of having products ready for defense emergencies is clear. Yet a little reflection shows that none of the popular variants of the national defense argument succeeds in making a good case for an import barrier. That is, the popular national defense arguments fail to follow the specificity rule. For instance, if the objective is to maintain domestic production capacity for a product that is crucial to the national defense, then a production subsidy is the policy that has the lower cost to the nation.

The possibilities of storage and depletion also argue against the use of a tariff to create defense capability. If the crucial goods can be stored inexpensively, the cheapest way to prepare for the emergency is to buy them from foreigners at low world prices during peace. Thus, the United States could stockpile low-cost imported footwear instead of producing it domestically at greater cost. And if the crucial goods are depletable mineral resources, such as oil, the case for the tariff is even weaker. Restricting imports of oil when there is no foreign embargo or blockade causes us to use up our own resources faster, cutting the amount we can draw on when an embargo or blockade is imposed. It is better to stockpile imports at relatively low peacetime cost, as the United States has done with its Strategic Petroleum Reserve since the mid-1970s. To believe that restricting imports would increase our untapped reserves, we would have to accept two doubtful propositions: (1) Protecting domestic oil producers makes them discover extra reserves faster than it makes them sell extra oil for peacetime consumption, and (2) there is no more direct way to encourage further oil exploration within the country.

Income Redistribution

A third, less economic objective to which trade policy might be addressed is the distribution of income within the nation. Often one of the most sensitive questions in national politics is either "What does it do to the poor?" or "What effect

---

[4] Quoted in *Far Eastern Economic Review,* October 25, 1984, p. 70.

does it have on different regions or ethnic groups?" A tariff could sometimes be defended on the grounds that it restores equity by favoring some wrongly disadvantaged group, even though it may reduce the overall size of the pie to be distributed among groups. It is certainly important to know the effects of trade policy on the distribution of income within a country, a subject we have already examined in a number of previous chapters.

If the issue is inequity in how income is distributed within our country, why should trade policy be the means of redressing the inequity? Why not attack the problem directly? If, for example, greater income equality is the objective, it is less costly to equalize incomes directly, through tax-and-transfer programs, than to try to equalize incomes indirectly by manipulating the tariff structure. Only if political constraints are somehow so binding that the income distribution can be adjusted only through import policy would import barriers be justified on this ground.

THE POLITICS OF PROTECTION

We have now made much progress in our search for good import barriers. We have found a number of situations in which import protection could be better than free trade, but in nearly all of these some other form of government policy is even better.

If the economic case for import protection is so weak, why do most countries have many import barriers in place? Why are import barriers high for some products and low for others? In each country import barriers are adopted and maintained through a political process of decision making. Understanding the answers to questions about why import barriers exist requires a mixture of political and economic insights. There is a growing literature on the "political economy of trade barriers." It focuses on activities by pressure groups and the self-interested behavior of political representatives who seek to maximize their chances of staying in office.

The Basic Elements of the Political-Economic Analysis

Let's take a look at the political process that leads to a decision about whether or not to impose a tariff on imports of a good, say, socks. As we have seen in previous chapters, imposing the tariff will have different effects on the well-being of different groups in the country, with both winners and losers. In addition, we presume that the tariff would cause some economic inefficiency—a decrease in national well-being because the losers lose more than the winners gain. When will such a tariff be enacted? Why?

There are a number of key elements in our political-economic analysis:

1. *The size of the gains for the winners from protection, and how many individuals are in the group of winners.* Let's call the total gains B_p, and presume that this is the producer surplus gained from securing government protection—the same thing as area *a* in diagrams like Figure 7.4. N_p is the number of individuals benefiting from the protection.

2. *The size of the losses for the losers from protection, and how many individuals are in the group of losers.* In the political fight, they gain by defeating the tariff. Their total gains are B_c, which we presume to be at least as large as areas $a + b + d$ in Figure 7.4. (Consumers may not view the tariff revenue area c as a loss to them if the government uses the revenue to reduce other consumer taxes or spends the revenue on projects valued by the consumers.) N_c is the number of individuals losing from protection (gaining from defeating protection).

3. *Individuals' reasons for taking positions for or against protection.* We presume that direct gains and loses of well-being (B_p and B_c) are reasons for taking positions. There may be other reasons. One is sympathy for groups who are suffering losses. Another is ideology or other closely held core beliefs about politics and economics.

4. *Types of political activities and their costs.* Individuals (and groups of individuals sharing a common interest) can engage in a range of different political activities. Assuming that the country has elections or referendums, individuals can vote. Individuals can themselves engage in lobbying of their government officials, in which the individuals provide information on their position, or they can hire others to lobby for them. Individuals can provide campaign contributions to politicians running for office. Or individuals can provide bribes or other side payments to attempt to gain the support of government officials. The costs of these different types of political activities include both money cost and the opportunity cost of any time or other efforts used in the activity.

5. *Political institutions and the political process.* We will closely examine two types of political processes: first, direct voting on the tariff by all individuals and, second, elected representatives voting on the tariff. These seem most relevant to a democratic system like that used in most industrialized and many developing countries. (Other possibilities include a single decision maker or decision making by an appointed committee of experts.)

When Are Tariffs Unlikely?

Under some circumstances, inefficient trade barriers would be rejected, and we would have a world closer to free trade than we observe. Let's consider two sets of circumstances.

Our first case is direct democracy. Consider what will happen if we have (1) a direct vote by individuals on each tariff (or import barrier), with (2) voting (almost) costless so that (almost) everyone votes, and (3) each person voting based on his or her direct interest as a winner or a loser from protection. Nearly always the number of losers N_c (the number of consumers of the product) is larger than the number of winners N_p (the number of people involved in production of the import-competing product). In the example of socks, nearly everyone buys socks, but only a small number of people work in (or provide substantial amounts of other resources like land or capital to) the sock industry. The sock tariff would be defeated by a large margin. Most trade barriers protect only a minority, and this is probably true even if many trade barriers are combined into a single vote.

The trade barriers that we see in most countries depart from what simple majority-rule democracy would give us. Indeed, countries usually do not use direct votes to set protection. Rather, a group of elected representatives or of some other government officials decides. Winning the political fight is gaining the support of a majority of these representatives or officials.

Are forms of government like representative democracy inherently protectionist? Our second case shows that representative democracy can also lead to little or no protection. Consider what will happen if (1) each group is willing to devote all of its total gain (B_p and B_c) to political activity like lobbying or contributions, and (2) politicians decide which side to support according to the amount of lobbying or contributions they receive. The fact that the tariff causes economic inefficiency means that B_c is larger than B_p. Those opposed to the tariff would be willing to spend up to B_c to prevent the tariff, while the protectionists would not rationally spend more than the smaller stake B_p. The inefficiency of the tariff (equal to $B_c - B_p$) dooms that tariff. Even if the political process does not work exactly like this, it still would tend to reject the more inefficient of protectionist proposals.

When Are Tariffs Likely?

Lobbying and contributions can lead to political decisions enacting protection, if protectionist groups are more effective than other groups in organizing their political activities. In this case we reach a surprising conclusion: The group with the smaller number of individuals can be more effective. We can see two different reasons for this surprising conclusion. Both are based on the fact that each individual in the smaller group tends to have a larger individual gain.

First, consider what happens when there is some fixed cost per individual to being involved in any political activity. This cost could be a minimum amount of time that must be spent, or it could be the per person cost of organizing a group effort to engage in lobbying. If the benefit to the individual is less than the cost to participate, the individual will probably decide not to participate. The average gain per supporter of protection is B_p/N_p, and the average gain per opponent of protection is B_c/N_c. The individual gain tends to be larger as the number of individuals in the group is smaller. In our sock example, the number of sock producers is small, but the gain to each from protection is large (perhaps hundreds or thousands of dollars per year). The number of sock consumers is large, but the loss to each from protection is small (probably a few tens of dollars or less per year). If consumers' benefits from defeating the protectionist measure are small per person, many (or all) of them may decide that it is not worth it to fight protectionism. (That is, they see that B_c/N_c is less than the minimum per person cost of participating.) The protectionist minority is the only active interest group, and it gains the majority of representatives' votes.

Second, consider what happens when some members of the group can decide to "free-ride" on the contributions of others in the group. The **free-rider problem** arises whenever the benefits of a group effort fall on everyone in the group regardless of how much each individual does (or does not) contribute (in time, effort, voting, or money). Each selfishly rational individual tries to get a free ride, letting others advance the common cause. The free-rider problem usually afflicts a large, dispersed group more seriously than it affects a small, well-defined group. Conquering the free-rider problem is what political action groups—special interests—are all about.

Import-competing producers are motivated to participate in the politics of protection. They often overcome the free-rider problem to become a well-organized group with substantial resources to use in political activity. The group lobbies vociferously in favor of protection. The group uses campaign contributions to enhance the chances of electing representatives friendly to their position, to gain access to the representatives for lobbying, to influence the representatives' positions on votes, and to reward those who vote in favor of industry protection. In contrast, each individual in the large, diffuse consumer group has a small incentive to become active and a large incentive to free-ride. But if all or most try to free-ride, the large group of consumers is not organized or has few resources to use for political activity. In our sock example, a trade association may organize and represent the interests of the sock-producing firms, and, if the industry is unionized, the labor unions represent the interest of workers. An organization of sock consumers is unlikely.

The outcome is often that the well-organized protectionist lobby sways a majority of representatives, even though this protection is economically inefficient and hurts a majority of voters. Generally, the politicians in favor of protection trade a small reduction in the individual well-being of many voters, with some loss of votes possible in the next election, for the votes and largess of those protected, including the ability to use their campaign contributions to gain votes in the next election.

The tariffs imposed by the U.S. government on steel imports in 2002, discussed in Chapter 1, provide a stark example of the political economy of protection. The small number of American steel firms are well organized as a political lobbying force. The industry employs only about 200,000 workers, about 0.1 percent of the U.S. workforce, but the United Steelworkers union is also politically active. Users of steel are much more dispersed. They did achieve some organization and mount a campaign to oppose the tariffs, but their effort was not as effective. In addition, steel firms and steelworkers are concentrated in a few states, including West Virginia, Pennsylvania, and Ohio, that were considered crucial for the 2002 and 2004 elections. In March 2002 the protectionists won—President George W. Bush announced new tariffs of up to 30 percent on imports of many types of steel. The box "How Sweet It Is (and Isn't)" presents another example by examining the political-economic forces in play for sugar protection.

In addition to this recognition of the important general role of lobbying and contributions by special interest groups, other specific features of the country's

Case Study   How Sweet It Is (or Isn't)

Do you like to eat things that are sweet? If you do, and if you live in the United States, the European Union, or Japan, then you are a victim of your country's protectionist policies toward sugar. The domestic price of your sugar is more than double the world price. For the United States in mid-2002, the domestic price of raw sugar was $0.21 per pound, and the world price was $0.08 per pound. In the United States, the sugar protection costs consumers about $2 billion per year.

If you live in any of these countries, have you ever sent a letter to your legislative representative asking him or her to oppose sugar protection, a policy that is clearly against your interests? Have you contributed money or time to a group that lobbies the government to end sugar protection? Do you know anyone who has ever done so? Presumably not. Why not? While $2 billion per year sounds like a lot of money, it is only about $8 per person per year. As discussed in the text, the average gain for any one person to oppose this protection is small. It's not worth your effort.

The situation is a little different for sugar producers. For the United States, the increase in domestic producer surplus is more than $1 billion per year. These gains are concentrated in a small number of places and a small number of firms. It is worth it for them to actively seek policies that restrain sugar imports. Two companies in Florida, Flo-Sun and U.S. Sugar, have been particularly active, contributing millions of dollars in recent years to Democratic and Republican congressional candidates and political parties. For Flo-Sun, owned by two brothers, Alfonso and Jose Fanjul, one estimate is that protectionist sugar policies add $65 million per year to their profits. A few million bucks to defend this profit stream is definitely a good investment.

Another group active in lobbying is the American Sugar Alliance, representing major U.S. sugar growers. In addition, the high domestic price for sugar expands demand for corn sweeteners, a close substitute for sugar. Corn farmers in the American Midwest like the sugar protection, and they have a major influence on the positions taken by their states' representatives and senators.

The Coalition for Sugar Reform, which includes food manufacturers that use sugar, consumer groups, taxpayer advocates, and environmental groups, is active in opposing sugar protection. It has some good arguments on its side. As Jeff Nedelman, a spokesperson for the coalition, said, "This is a corporate welfare program for the very rich. The program results in higher prices for consumers, direct payments by U.S. taxpayers to sugar growers, and it's the Achilles heel of U.S. trade policy."* By polluting and disrupting water flows, the protected sugar production in Florida is also a major cause of serious environmental decline in the Everglades. These are good points, but they are no match for the money and organization of the proponents of protection.

Foreign sugar producers, many of them poor farmers in developing countries, are also hurt by protectionist policies in importing countries. Researchers estimate that the world sugar price would rise by 17 percent if the United States removed its sugar policies. But it is not easy for foreign interests to have an effect on the political process. Foreigners don't vote, and political opponents can charge that legislators who openly side with foreigners against U.S. workers and companies are "anti-American."

So the sugar protection policies continue. For the United States, the net cost to the country is close to $1 billion per year. It is not that sugar is so large or important a part of the economy that we have to protect it. In the United States, about 44,000 people work growing sugar, and about 17,000 people work in sugar refining, in total about 0.04 percent of the U.S. labor force. If we shifted to free trade, employment would probably decline by 3,000 (although the decline could be as high as 15,000). The small number of people who lose their jobs could be reemployed with little trouble in other sectors of the economy. Instead, we see the pure political economy of protection, with the producer interests in this case much better organized and effective than the consumers are.

*As quoted in "Sugar Rules Defy Free-Trade Logic," *New York Times,* May 6, 2001.

political institutions affect the political economy of protection. Here are two that are documented for the United States. First, the U.S. Senate gives exactly two senators to each state, regardless of population. States that are mainly rural and agricultural are overrepresented, providing extra support for protection of agricultural industries. Second, for the U.S. House of Representatives, in which there is one representative for each district, it helps to have the production activities of an import-competing industry spread over a substantial number of states or districts so that a large number of representatives are likely to become a core of supporters for protection for the industry.

Applications to Other Trade-Policy Patterns

The simple model of political activity in a representative democracy can also explain other patterns besides the overall favoring of producer interests over consumer interests. Some of these patterns are extensions of the same producer-bias pattern; some are not.

The **tariff escalation** pattern is a general symptom of the importance of group size and concentration to effective lobbying. Economists have found that nominal and effective tariff rates rise with the stage of production. That is, tariff rates are typically higher on final consumer goods than on intermediate goods and raw materials sold to producing firms.[5] The explanation would seem to be that household consumers are a particularly weak lobby, being many people who are not well organized into dues-collecting lobbying associations. Consumer groups fight only weakly against the producers of final products, whose cause is championed by influential large firms and trade associations. When it comes to fights over protecting producers of intermediate goods, the story can be quite different. The buyers of intermediate goods are themselves firms and can organize lobbying efforts as easily as their suppliers can. The outcome of a struggle over tariffs on intermediate goods is thus less likely to favor protection.

The bias in favor of producer interests over consumer interests also shows up in international negotiations to liberalize trade, such as the eight postwar rounds of multilateral trade negotiations. There are curious explicit guidelines as to what constitutes a fair balance of concessions by the different nations at the bargaining table. A concession is any agreement to cut one's own import duties, thereby letting in more imports. Each country is pressured to allow as much import expansion as the export expansion it gets from other countries' import liberalizations. It is odd to see import liberalization treated as a concession by the importing nation. After all, cutting your own import tariffs usually should bring net national gains, not losses. The concession-balancing rule is further evidence of the power of producer groups over consumer groups. The negotiators view their own

---

[5] The tariff escalation pattern does not apply to agricultural products in most industrialized countries, however. Farmers get at least as much effective protection as the processors and wholesalers to whom they sell.

import tariff cuts as sacrifices simply because they have to answer politically to import-competing producer groups but not to masses of poorly organized consumers. In addition, another producer group in the country—producers of exportable products—is also usually active in lobbying to influence the trade negotiations. The balancing "concessions" by other countries to lower foreign import barriers bring benefits to export producers so that they politically support the multilateral trade liberalization.

So far we have presumed that each individual takes a position in favor of or against protection according to his or her own direct self-interest. But, in some cases, it seems that sympathy (or other reasons) determines an individual's position.

Interest groups are often victorious because they gain the sympathy of others, that is, of people who will not directly gain if policy helps the interest group. Political sympathy often surges when a group suffers a big income loss all at once, especially in a general recession. Sympathy creates this **sudden-damage effect.** The sympathy can spring from either of two sources. One is simply compassion for those suffering large income losses. Political sentiments often yield to pleas for protection when a surge of import competition wipes out incomes, just as we provide generous relief for victims of natural disasters. The other source shows up more when a deep recession hits the whole economy. In a recession, an increased number of people are at risk of having their incomes cut. More of them identify with the less fortunate, thinking, "That could be me." One policy response is to help those damaged by import competition, whose pleas are heard above the mild complaints of many consumers who would suffer small individual losses from import barriers. Thus, both a surge in import competition and a general recession raise sympathy for protectionism.

Our discussion began in this section with the general question of why the overall level of trade barriers is higher than the analysis of economic efficiency would justify. But now that we have examined the political economy of trade barriers, we might easily ask the opposite question. Given the power of well-organized import-competing producers favoring protection, as well as the appeal of sympathy for local producers struggling against imports produced by foreign firms, why are our import barriers not so very high? One reason is that there are organized producer groups that are opposed to protection. These include firms that use imported products in their own production, the wholesalers and retailers who distribute imports, and export producers who generally favor free trade. A second reason is that we have used mutual "concessions" during multilateral trade negotiations to lower trade barriers. There is probably also a third reason. Economic ideology probably does have some impact. Politicians who espouse the merits of free enterprise, markets, and competition probably do see that protection is inconsistent with these concepts. This does make them somewhat less likely to support protection.

Summary

There are valid arguments for import barriers, though most are quite different from those usually given. One way or another, all valid defenses of import barriers lean on the existence of relevant distortions (gaps between private and social costs or benefits) or noneconomic objectives.

In a **second-best world** where there are **incentive distortions** in the domestic economy, imposing a tariff may be better than doing nothing. Whether or not it is better will depend on the details of the specific case. Yet, even when imposing the tariff is better than doing nothing, something else is usually better than the tariff. The **specificity rule** is a rough guideline that says: Use the policy tool that is closest to the true source of the distorting gap between private and social incentives. This rule cuts against import barriers, which are usually only indirectly related to the source of the distortion. Thus, many of the main arguments for blocking imports—such as maintaining jobs in an industry, the **infant industry argument,** and the **national defense argument**—are really arguments for government policies other than import barriers.[6] The case for tariffs is most secure in the developing government setting. If a country is poor and its government limited in its administrative ability, then tariffs can be a vital source of government revenue to finance basic public investments and services.

Where, then, are the borders that separate good trade barriers from bad ones? Figure 9.4 maps those borders by summarizing the policy results of the main cases surveyed in this chapter plus Chapter 7's nationally optimal tariff plus two relevant cases coming up in Chapter 10. Note the clear contrast in the answers in the two columns. In the middle column, the answer repeatedly is yes, an import barrier *can* be better than doing nothing, depending on factors discussed in this chapter. In the right column, the answer is generally no, the import barrier is not the best policy tool, except in cases where the exact locus of the distortion is in international trade itself. You may wish to cross-check the results shown in this figure with the detailed discussion of the chapter.

If analysis of economic efficiency indicates that import protection is often a bad policy and seldom the best policy, why do so many countries have so many import barriers? The political economy of trade barriers explains them in terms of the gains for the winners from protection, the losses to those hurt by protection, the costs of engaging in political activities like voting, lobbying, and making campaign contributions, and the way that the political process works.

We can imagine political systems in which protection would be unlikely. If everybody voted directly, the majority would probably vote against a tariff or nontariff barrier because more people would be hurt as consumers than would be helped as producers of the product. Or, if everyone was willing to devote the entire amount that they would gain or lose to political activities like lobbying or

---

[6] At this point you may review Chapter 7's section "A Preview of Conclusions," noting how each case discussed in Chapter 9 fits that preview.

FIGURE 9.4

Can an Import Barrier Be Better Than Doing Nothing, and Is it the Best Policy?

A Summary of Verdicts*

Goal To Be Promoted	Can an Import Barrier Be Better Than Doing Nothing?	Is an Import Barrier the Best Policy Tool?
Domestic production	Yes, it can	No
Domestic jobs	Yes, it can	No
An infant industry	Yes, it can	No
A developing government	Yes, it can	No
National pride	Yes, it can	No, unless only self-sufficiency can make the nation proud
National defense	Yes, it can	No
A fairer income distribution	Yes, it can	No
National monopsony power (a large country)	Yes, it can	For the nation, yes (if no retaliation); for the world, no (Chapter 7's nationally optimal tariff)
Antidumping (Chapter 10)	Usually, no	Usually, no
Counter a foreign export subsidy (Chapter 10)	In some cases	For the nation, no; for the world, yes

Note: Remember that "Yes, it can" does not mean "Yes, it is." To see what separates situations when the import barrier is better than nothing from situations when it is worse, review the text of this chapter.

*In all verdicts except that for national monopsony power, the conclusions refer to a small country so that the conclusions are not confounded by the possibility of optimal-tariff effects on the terms of trade.

campaign contributions, then political representatives would probably oppose protection because the loss to consumers would be larger than the gain to producers.

In reality, some groups are more effective than others at taking political actions to influence the votes of representatives. Producer groups are often more effective than consumer groups, because the benefits of protection are concentrated in a small group of producers. The benefits are large enough to spur actions by individual producers, and the **free-rider problem** is more easily solved in a small group. In addition, support for protection often increases when the losses to the group hurt by rising imports generate sympathy among the rest of the population.

This approach also helps to explain other patterns. The group-size effect can explain the **tariff escalation** pattern. A few large firms buying intermediate goods make a stronger lobby against protection of the products they are buying than do masses of final consumers, each of whom has too small an interest to go to battle over consumer-good import policy. The ability of producer interests to lobby effectively also explains why, in international trade negotiations, each nation treats its own tariff reductions as if they were sacrifices. They are sacrifices for politicians who must answer to well-organized import-competing producer groups. And the concessions offered by other countries to reduce their trade barriers mobilize well-organized groups of export producers to support the multilateral agreement.

Suggested Reading

The theory of trade policy in a second-best world was pioneered by Nobel laureate James Meade (1955). Major contributions were made by Johnson (1965) and Bhagwati (1969). Excellent literature surveys, with varying degrees of technicality, are found in Baldwin (1984), Krueger (1984), and Dixit (1985). Baldwin (1969) forcefully applies the specificity rule to the case of infant industry protection. Tyson (1992) argues, in effect, that Japanese barriers against high technology imports were of great benefit to Japan on infant industry grounds. Kletzer (2001) discusses the experiences of U.S. workers who lost their jobs due to import competition.

Two pioneering theories of political behavior and lobbying biases are Downs (1957) and Olson (1965). Breton (1974) offers similar theories with applications to Canada. Grossman and Helpman (1994) provide an influential technical analysis of the political economy of trade barriers.

Questions and Problems

◆ 1. A single firm's innovations in production technology often benefit the production of other firms, because these other firms learn about the new technology and can use some of the ideas in their own production.
  a. Is there an externality here?
  b. How would an economist rank the following two policies in this situation? Why?
    i. A tariff on imports, to make sure that domestic production using the new technology occurs.
    ii. A subsidy to domestic production, to make sure that domestic production using the new technology occurs.
  c. What third policy (a tax or a subsidy to something) would the economist recommend as even better than these two?

2. What is the specificity rule?

◆ 3. A small price-taking nation imports a good that it could not possibly produce itself at any finite price. Can you describe plausible conditions under which that nation would benefit from an import tariff on the good?

4. What is the infant industry argument for putting up barriers to imports? What are its merits and weaknesses?

◆ 5. Can you describe plausible conditions under which a nation would benefit from subsidizing imports of a good?

6. What is the national defense argument for putting up barriers to imports? Why is import protection probably not the best approach?

◆ 7. Australia has only one firm that makes aircraft. Without assistance from the government, that firm has lost most of its business to imports from the United States and Europe. Which of the following policies would be most costly for the Australian nation as a whole, and which would be least costly?
  Policy A: Paying the lone Australian firm a *production subsidy* per plane, without protecting it against imports.
  Policy B: Imposing a *tariff* equal to the production subsidy in policy A.
  Policy C: Imposing an import *quota* that cuts imports just as much as policy B would.

8. The minister for labor of the small nation of Pembangunan is anxious to encourage domestic production of digital clocks. A small clock industry exists, but only a few producers can survive foreign competition without government help. The minister argues that helping the industry would create jobs and skills that will be carried over into other industries by workers trained in this one. He calls for a 10 percent tariff to take advantage of these benefits. At the same cabinet meeting, the minister for industry argues for a 10 percent subsidy to domestic clock production instead, stating that the same benefits to the nation can be achieved at less social cost.

   a. Show the following diagrammatically:
      i. The effects of the tariff on domestic clock output and consumption.
      ii. The beneficial side effects of the tariff described by the minister for labor.
      iii. The net gains or losses for the nation as a whole.
      iv. All the same effects for the case of the production subsidy.
      v. The differences in the effects of the two alternatives on the government's budget. Which policy would appeal more to a deficit-conscious minister for finance?

   b. Can you describe a policy that captures the alleged benefits of worker training better than either the 10 percent tariff or the 10 percent production subsidy?

✦ 9. Do you favor or oppose the government policy of offering extra adjustment assistance to workers displaced by increasing imports? Why?

10. Assume that the sock-importing countries are determined to expand their domestic production of socks. From the point of view of the sock-*exporting* countries, how would you rate each of these three policies that could be used by the sock importers? Why?

Subsidies to domestic production in the importing countries
Tariffs on sock imports
VERs on sock exports

✦ 11. In Chapter 2 we introduced the one-dollar, one-vote metric. If political decisions in a small country about imposing tariffs were based on this metric, how many tariffs would this country have?

12. What is the free-rider problem, and how does it affect trade policy?

✦ 13. Elected legislative representatives are considering enacting a quota on imports of baseball bats, with the rights to import the quota amount of bats to be given for free to the three companies that currently distribute imported baseball bats. Identify the groups that have a direct interest in whether or not the quota is enacted. How effective do you think each will be in lobbying?

14. What is the tariff escalation pattern? Why does it exist in many countries?

Chapter **Ten**

Pushing Exports

Controversy over export behavior and export policy rivals the perennial fights over import barriers. On the export side, however, the fight takes on a somewhat different form. Here the fight usually centers on the artificial *promotion* of trade rather than on trade barriers. This chapter explores how both businesses and governments may push for more exports than their country would sell under ordinary competition. The underlying policy questions are: Can a country export too much for its own good or for the good of the world? Is that happening today? If so, what should an importing country do about another country's apparently excessive exports?

These questions do not arise in a vacuum. Governments, pressured by business and labor lobbies, have long fought over what producers in importing countries consider artificial and excessive exports from other countries. The heat of debate on this issue intensified during the past two decades. U.S. and European producers charged that Japan, Korea, Brazil, China, and other rapidly growing industrial powers were engaging in "unfair trade" because exports from these countries were priced too low or subsidized by their governments. These countries were repeatedly accused of violating both the rules of ordinary competition and the rules of the World Trade Organization (WTO).

To address the debate over unfair trade, we turn first to dumping, the most important way in which private firms may export more than competitive supply and demand would lead us to expect. Then we explore how governments push exports with outright or subtle subsidies.

DUMPING

Dumping is selling exports at a price that is too low—less than **normal value** (or "fair market value," as it is often called in the United States). There are two meanings of *normal value*:

- The long-standing definition of *normal value* is the price charged to comparable domestic buyers in the home market (or to comparable buyers in other markets). Under this traditional definition, dumping is international price discrimination favoring buyers of exports.

- The second definition of *normal value* arose in the 1970s. It is cost-based—the average cost of producing the product, including overhead costs and profit. Under this second standard, dumping is selling exports at a price that is less than the full average cost of the product.

Why would an exporting firm engage in dumping? Why would it sell exports at a price lower than the price it charges for its product in its home market, or lower than its average cost? There are several reasons. To judge whether dumping is good or bad, it is important to understand the full range of reasons why dumping occurs.

Predatory dumping occurs when a firm temporarily charges a low price in the foreign export market, with the purpose of driving its foreign competitors out of business. Once the rivals are gone, the firm will use its monopoly power to raise prices and earn high profits.

Cyclical dumping occurs during periods of recession. During the part of the cycle when demand is low, a firm tends to lower its price to limit the decline in quantity sold. For instance, in a competitive market initially in long-run equilibrium, price equals full average cost (long-run average cost) for the representative firm. If an industry recession or an economywide recession then causes demand to decline, market price will fall below this full average cost in the short run. A firm continues to produce and sell as long as price exceeds average variable cost. If any of these sales are exports, the firm is dumping.

Seasonal dumping is intended to sell off excess inventories of a product. For instance, toward the end of a fashion season, U.S. clothing manufacturers may decide to sell off any remaining stock of swimsuits at prices that are below full average cost. That is, they have a sale. With production costs sunk, any price above the marginal cost of making the sale is sensible. If some of these low-priced sales are to Canada, the U.S. firm is dumping. Perishable agricultural products are also good candidates for seasonal dumping. A big harvest tends to lower the market price and to provide a larger quantity available for export. Similarly, dumping can be a technique for promoting new products in new markets. This is the equivalent of an introductory sale that an exporting firm could use to establish sales of its product in a new foreign market.

Persistent dumping occurs because a firm with market power uses **price discrimination** between markets to increase its total profit. A firm maximizes profits by charging a lower price to foreign buyers if

- It has less monopoly power (more competition) in the foreign market than it has in its home market, and if

- Buyers in the home country cannot avoid the high home prices by buying the good abroad and importing it cheaply.

When these conditions hold, the firm can make home-country buyers pay a higher price and thus earn a higher total profit. This is not predatory; it is not intended to drive any other firms out of business. And it can persist for a long time—as long as these market differences continue.

FIGURE 10.1   Persistent Dumping

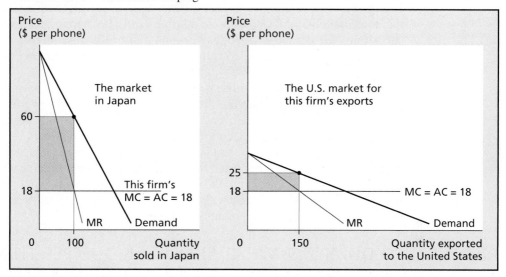

The monopolist uses price discrimination to maximize profits in two markets. The firm charges a higher price in the market where the demand curve is less elastic (steeper). In this case, that is the home market in Japan, perhaps because in its home market the firm is protected from foreign competition. In the more elastic (more competitive) U.S. market, the firm charges a lower price for its exported product. Total profits are the sum of the two shaded rectangles. The price discrimination is viable only if there is no way for consumers in the high-price market to buy the product from the low-price market, and if policymakers in the importing country do not impose antidumping duties.

Figure 10.1 shows such a case of profitable price discrimination under the simplifying assumption that the firm faces a constant marginal cost (and average cost) of production. (In addition, the marginal production cost is the same regardless of whether the product is sold in the home market or exported, because essentially the same product is sold in both places.) The illustration is based on a real case that surfaced in 1989. The U.S. government determined that firms in Japan, Korea, and Taiwan were all guilty of dumping telephones in the U.S. market, causing injury to AT&T (the plaintiff) and other U.S. firms.[1] We illustrate with the case of a single Japanese firm (e.g., Matsushita).

What makes persistent dumping profitable is that the firm faces a less elastic (steeper) demand curve in its home market than in the more competitive foreign market. That is, home-country buyers would not change the quantity they buy very much in response to price, whereas foreign buyers would quickly abandon this firm's product if the firm raised its price much. Sensing this, the firm maximizes profits by equating marginal cost and marginal revenue in each market. In

[1] The actual dumping case involved phone equipment for small businesses, although here we illustrate with the case of personal phones from Japan. The U.S. International Trade Commission estimated dumping margins (home-market price above price on sales to the United States) of 120 to 180 percent for major firms in Japan and Taiwan, but only a trivial difference for Korean firms. The Asian exporters had raised their share of the U.S. phone market for small businesses to 60 percent by 1989.

the U.S. market the profit-maximizing price is $25. With the $25 price U.S. consumers buy 150 telephones a year, at which level marginal revenue just equals the marginal cost of $18. In Japan's home market, where consumers see fewer substitutes for the major Japanese brands, the profit-maximizing price is $60. With the $60 price Japanese consumers buy 100 phones a year, and marginal cost equals marginal revenue at this quantity.

Price discrimination is more profitable for the firm than charging the same price in both markets. Charging the same price would yield lower marginal revenues in Japan than in the United States. As long as transport costs and import barriers in Japan make it uneconomical for Japanese consumers to import low-priced telephones back from the United States, the firm continues to make greater profits by charging a higher price in the Japanese market. Often tariffs or nontariff barriers to import (back into the exporting the country) are what keeps the two markets separate. These barriers also protect the dumper against foreign competition in the higher-priced home market (Japan, in this example).

REACTING TO DUMPING: WHAT SHOULD A DUMPEE THINK?

Domestic firms competing against exports dumped into their market are likely to complain loudly to their government, charging that this is unfair. How should the importing country view dumping? What should be its government policy toward dumping?

In one sense the importing country's view is easy. It should welcome dumping and thank the exporting country. After all, we do not usually argue when someone tries to sell us something at a low price. This instinct seems clearly correct for persistent dumping. Compared to the high price in the exporting country, the importing country gets the gains from additional trade at the low export price. The importing country's terms of trade are better. The benefits to consumers are larger than the losses to the import-competing producers. To see this, consider what will happen to the importing country if it imposes a tariff on the dumped imports, to force the tariff-inclusive price up to about the level in the exporting country. In Figure 10.1, the duty would be 140 percent (= [60 − 25]/25). In this example the tariff of 140 percent is prohibitive. The Japanese firm would cease all exports to the United States. The United States thus would lose all net gains from trade in this product. Although there would be an increase in the surplus of domestic producers when the prohibitive duty was imposed, the loss of domestic consumer surplus would be larger. Through similar logic, the importing country generally should welcome seasonal and introductory-price dumping.

However, the other two types of dumping may not be so simple. There is a sound economic reason for the importing country to view predatory dumping negatively. Although the importing country gains from low-priced imports in the short run, it will lose because of high-priced imports once the exporting firm succeeds in establishing its monopoly power.

A key question is how frequently foreign firms use predatory dumping. Predatory dumping of manufactured goods was widely alleged during the international chaos of the 1920s and 1930s. In truth, there is no clear evidence that widespread predatory dumping has been practiced, despite a rich folklore about it. *Predatory dumping is likely to be rare* in modern markets. An exporting firm considering predatory dumping must weigh the sure losses from low prices in the short run against the possible but uncertain profits in the more distant future. Even if the firm could drive out its current competitors in the importing country, it may expect that, once it raises prices, new firms, including new exporters from other countries, will enter as competitors. The predatory exporter would not be able to raise prices or to keep them high for very long. Recent research suggests that no more than 5 percent of all cases of alleged dumping in the United States, the European Union, Canada, and Mexico show even a moderate possibility for predation (and it is possible that none of these cases involves predation).

Cyclical dumping is the most complicated kind of dumping for the importing country. Most cyclical dumping is probably the normal working of well-functioning, competitive global product markets. When demand declines, the market price falls in the short run. A firm will continue to produce, sell, and even export some amount of the product, as long the revenue earned at least covers variable cost. This is exactly what we want to happen when there is a decline in demand. Production declines somewhat in many countries as the world price falls. There is an efficient global "sharing" of the decline in demand. Once the recession ends, demand, price, and global production will recover. (If instead too much production capacity continues to exist, then eventually there will need to be an efficient global sharing of capacity reduction before price can recover.)

The importing country may not be completely convinced that cyclical dumping is fair just because it is usually globally efficient. When demand declines by, say, 10 percent, which countries absorb how much of global reduction in output? Is it fair that the import-country firms have to reduce their output and suffer losses? In particular, if the decline in demand is a result of a national recession in the exporting country, why is it fair that the exporting country can "export some of its unemployment"?

As usual, it is not easy to answer the question of what is fair. The international sharing of recessions is one of the effects that comes with the general benefits of international trade. We can also recall the key lesson from Chapter 9—use the specificity rule. The real problem here is the concern about producer losses. For instance, if the key concern is about unemployed workers, the country should provide suitable unemployment insurance or adjustment assistance.

ACTUAL ANTIDUMPING POLICIES: WHAT IS UNFAIR?

Our discussion suggests that dumping is often good for the country importing the dumped exports but that two types of dumping could be bad for the importing country. Predatory dumping can be bad if it is successful, but success is probably rare. Cyclical dumping can sometimes unfairly harm the importing country, but much of the time it is probably the normal working of the competitive market. The implication is that the importing-country's government policy toward dumping (its antidumping policy) should examine each case and consider benefits and costs before imposing antidumping duties or other restrictions on dumped imports. In fact, actual government policies are not at all like this.

The WTO rules permit countries to retaliate against dumping, if the dumping injures domestic import-competing producers. Antidumping cases increased rapidly beginning in the 1970s. Prior to the late 1980s, the United States, the European Union, Canada, and Australia were the importing countries that accounted for over 90 percent of antidumping cases, and most countries had no antidumping policies. By 2001, at least 89 countries had antidumping policies in place. Since 1993, importing countries other than the "traditional four" account for more than half of all dumping complaints.

Figure 10.2 shows the importing countries that are the leading users of antidumping policies. The traditional four users (the United States, the European Union, Canada, and Australia) accounted for 84 percent of the world total of 261 new cases in 1989–1990. By 1999–2000, the world total had more than doubled, to 628 new cases, and the traditional four accounted for only 43 percent. India had no antidumping policy in 1990, but by 1999–2000 it was the top initiator of new cases. Similarly, the number of cases in Argentina and South Africa went from 0 to 69 and 37, respectively.

Worldwide, the countries whose exporters are most frequently charged with dumping are the United States, China, Japan, the European Union, Korea, Taiwan, and Brazil. The products most often involved are chemicals, steel and other metals, machinery, textiles and apparel, and electrical products.

Let's look more closely at U.S. antidumping policy. A case usually begins with a complaint from U.S. producers. The U.S. Department of Commerce examines whether dumping has actually occurred, and the U.S. International Trade Commission examines whether U.S. firms have been injured. In addition, negotiations may occur with foreign exporters. If they agree to raise prices or to limit their exports, then the case can be terminated or suspended. (This type of outcome has been common in cases involving steel and chemicals.)

The Department of Commerce usually finds some amount of dumping—the law and the procedures are biased to make showing dumping easy. In more than half of the cases, full average cost is the basis for calculating normal value. In cases that use average cost, obtaining and interpreting data on the costs incurred by foreign exporters are often difficult, so the Commerce Department has leeway in determining what normal value is. The injury standard is not strict, but injury is usually the key to the outcome of a case. If both dumping and injury are found, customs officials are instructed to levy an **antidumping duty**—an extra tariff equal to the discrepancy (the margin) between the actual export price and the normal value. More than half of the cases brought in the United States result in

FIGURE 10.2   Top 10 Initiators of Antidumping Cases

Importing Country	Number of Cases Initiated		Average Antidumping Duty Imposed 1995-1999	Antidumping Orders in Effect, 2001	Average Age (in years) of Orders in Effect, in 2000
	1989-1990	1999-2000			
India	0	106	28*	121	2
European Union	66	96	28	219	4
United States	58	94	48	241	8
Argentina	0	69	85	45	2
Australia	68	39	59	56	5
Canada	28	39	45	89	6
South Africa	0	37	45	109	3
Brazil	3	27	53	52	4
Mexico	18	18	59	66	5
New Zealand	2	14	52	11	6

*For 1990–1994; information for 1995–1999 not available.

Sources: P.K.M. Tharakan, "Is Antidumping Here to Stay?" *World Economy* 22, no. 2 (February 1999), pp. 179–206; Congressional Budget Office "Antidumping Action in the United States and around the World: An Update," CBO Paper, June 2001; World Trade Organization, "Report (2001) of the Committee on Antidumping Practices," G/L/495, October 31, 2001; World Trade Organization, "Antidumping: Antidumping Investigations by Reporting Party," www.wto.org/english/tratop_e/adp_e/adp_e.htm.

antidumping duties or an exporter agreement to restrain their export prices or volumes.

Recent research shows some clear patterns of effects from all this. Shortly after the complaint is filed, the prices of the exporters charged with dumping increase, probably to try to reduce the final dumping margin. Export quantities decrease, because of the higher price and because of the uncertainty about the outcome of the case. If antidumping duties are imposed, the export quantities decrease further, by an average of 70 percent, and often to zero (as we noted for the case shown in Figure 10.1). The exporter also has an incentive to raise its export price. The antidumping duties are reduced or eliminated if a subsequent review by the Department of Commerce finds less or no dumping.

A recent study of the overall effects of imposing antidumping duties concluded that the United States suffers a loss of well-being of nearly $4 billion per year. About half of that amount is deadweight loss (like areas $b + d$ in Figure 7.5 or Figure 8.3). The other half is the transfer to foreign exporters that raise their prices (like area c in Figure 8.3). The net loss to the United States could be lower than this, because the study does not attempt to quantify the value of avoiding any harmful effects from predatory dumping (probably minimal) and cyclical dumping (hard to measure).

Under current antidumping policies in the United States and a growing number of other countries, we get the following results:

1. The procedure is biased toward finding dumping.

2. The injury test considers only harm to import-competing producers. There is no consideration of whether predation or some other source of harm to the country is involved. There is little or no consideration of the benefits to consumers of the low-priced imports.

3. Overall, the process is biased toward imposing antidumping duties, even though this usually lowers the well-being of the importing country. Antidumping duties also generally lower world welfare.

See the box "Antidumping in Action" for specific examples that illustrate these conclusions.

If an exporting country's government believes that an importing country's government violated the WTO's rules in deciding to impose an antidumping duty (or a countervailing duty against a subsidy, which we will discuss later in this chapter), it can complain to the WTO. By mid-2002, eight such complaints, including three about duties imposed by the U.S. government, had proceeded to decisions and efforts to implement them. In all eight cases the dispute resolution panels found errors by the importing countries, including using inappropriate procedures, determining dumping margins (or subsidy rates) in a manner inconsistent with WTO rules, and determining injury using incomplete information or biased analysis. In four cases the importing countries eventually revoked the duties, though sometimes only after further efforts by the importing countries to maintain the duties. In the other four cases the importing countries revised their analyses and maintained the duties, leading to renewed complaints by the affected exporting countries. While the WTO dispute settlement procedure can provide some guard against misuse of antidumping duties, the process is too slow to minimize the effects of such misuse.

Antidumping policy starts out sounding like it is about unfair exports. But a closer examination indicates that something else is going on. Antidumping policy has become a major way for import-competing producers in a growing number of countries to gain new protection against imports, with the usual deadweight costs to the world and to the importing country. As shown in Figure 10.2, the average antidumping duties imposed against foreign exporters are very high, much higher than most regular tariffs, so the deadweight losses can be large. And, as shown in Figure 10.2, the antidumping duties continue for years (the oldest U.S. antidumping duty still in effect in 2000 was 26 years old). There is also the cost of arguing the cases and gathering the data to prove or disprove dumping and injury. In addition, import-competing firms use the threat of a dumping complaint to prod exporters to raise their prices and restrain their competition—the harassment effect—even if no complaint is actually filed.

PROPOSALS FOR REFORM

Although there are exceptions, the current practice of retaliation against dumping is usually bad for the world and for the importing country.[2] Yet this practice is fully consistent with current WTO rules. Reform of the WTO rules is an important item on the agenda for the current Doha Round of multilateral trade negotiations. Three possibilities for reform are discussed in the following paragraphs.

First, *antidumping actions could be limited to situations in which predatory dumping is plausible.* This reform would focus on the type of dumping that is most likely to be bad for the world and for the importing country. It would also align antidumping policy with antitrust policy (as it is called in the United States; it is called competition policy, antimonopoly policy, or similar names in other countries). Pro-competition policies usually forbid any predatory action to gain monopoly power. This reform would try to limit the scope of antidumping policy. However, the procedures in a country could still be biased toward finding both dumping and something potentially predatory about it.

Second, *the injury standard could be expanded to require that weight be given to consumers and users of the product.* This change would shift the discussion toward injury to net national well-being, not just injury to domestic import-competing producers. This reform would also try to limit the scope for antidumping actions in a general way rather than by focusing on one type of dumping.

This reform would also change an odd feature of current antidumping policy, that consumers will be substantially affected by dumping decisions but have no legal standing in the process. In fact, most antidumping actions involve intermediate goods like steel and chemicals. As we noted in Chapter 9, the buyers (like automobile firms) of these products are often well organized politically. They can be effective in opposing import protection on the intermediate products that they buy and use. Current dumping policies give import-competing producers of intermediate products an end run around this political battle. Reforming

---

[2] Here is an example in which retaliation against persistent dumping could bring gains to the whole world. If the "convicted" dumper ceases all price discrimination, continues to serve both markets with a single price that is not too high, and is rewarded by getting the duty removed, the world could end up better off from the temporary punitive use of the duty. The world is better off in the sense that output is redirected to the home-country buyers who valued the good more highly at the margin. One example of this kind of gain is the outcome of the U.S. dumping case against Korean consumer electronics producers, which led to a lowering of the high prices Korean consumers had been paying for these products.

Recall that this is only one of a number of possible outcomes, and the others are usually bad for the world. For instance, the dumpers may move their export-market production to the importing country at some extra expense of world resources. Or they might abandon the controversial foreign market as not worth the bother if it is spoiled by an antidumping duty. The issue of dumping is complex. The text gives the welfare results that seem most likely, however.

Case Study   Antidumping in Action

Dumping laws and antidumping procedures sound technical and boring. The firms that use antidumping complaints to get protection from imports like it that way. Nobody else is much interested in what's going on. Yet the stakes are large. Maybe we should follow the money—now that's more interesting.

Here are three examples of antidumping in real life. One sad moral of these tales is that any exporter that succeeds in building market share is at risk of being accused of dumping, and defense against this charge will be very difficult.

A GAME OF CHICKEN

When it comes to chicken, Americans prefer white meat. South Africans prefer dark meat. Sounds like the basis for mutually beneficial trade. And it would be, if it weren't for those pesky dumping laws.

U.S. chicken producers noticed the differences in demand. They began exporting dark-meat chicken to South Africa. This created extra competition for South African chicken producers, but South African consumers gained more than local producers lost. That's the way trade works. In addition, U.S. chicken producers were happy. The price they received for their dark-meat exports was somewhat higher than the price that could get in the United States. This added to their profitability.

South African chicken producers scratched back. They charged U.S. producers with dumping by exporting dark-meat chicken at a price less than production cost. This is an ideal situation for a biased antidumping authority, because there is no one way to determine this production cost. (What comes first, the dark meat or the white?) In 2000, the South African government determined that the U.S. firm Tyson was dumping by a margin of 200 percent (its export price was only one-third of its estimated production cost) and Gold Kiss was dumping by an incredible 357 percent margin. Something is fowl in South Africa. Good-bye gains from trade.

WHAT'S SO SUPER ABOUT SUPERCOMPUTERS?

In 1996 the Japanese company NEC won the contract to supply a supercomputer to a university consortium funded by the U.S. National Science Foundation, to be used for weather forecasting. This was the first-ever sale of a Japanese supercomputer to an agency of the U.S. government. It seemed to be a major setback for Cray Research, the major U.S. supercomputer maker. But Cray thought it saw unfair trade.

With encouragement from the U.S. Department of Commerce, Cray filed a dumping complaint. NEC guessed that it was not likely to win with the Department of Commerce also acting as the judge, and it refused to participate in the case. Based on information provided by Cray, the U.S. government imposed antidumping duties on NEC supercomputers at the super rate of 454 percent (and at the almost super rate of 173 percent for supercomputers from Fujitsu, the other major Japanese producer). With these antidumping duties in place, no one in the United States would be buying NEC or Fujitsu supercomputers.

Not so super for U.S. users of supercomputers. Or for anyone in the United States who wanted accurate weather forecasts. NEC supercomputers were simply the best in the world for this purpose.

There's one more twist in this wired tale. Hey, maybe it isn't dumping after all. In 2001, Cray was in financial trouble, and its technology was lagging. In exchange for a $25 million investment by NEC and a 10-year contract to be the exclusive distributor of NEC supercomputers in North America, Cray asked the Department of Commerce to end the antidumping duty.

AMERICAN STEEL: THE KING OF ANTIDUMPING

If antidumping were like the Super Bowl, the American steel industry would be the winner. At the end of 2000, nearly half of all antidumping duties in effect in the United States were on steel products. As a comparison, steel accounts for about 5 percent of U.S. imports. How did one industry that employs about 200,000 workers become the king of antidumping?

In the first half of the 20th century, the American steel industry was the world leader in output and productivity. In 1950 the United States produced about half of the world's total steel output. Since then the situation has changed dramatically. Steel producers in other countries increasingly have sourced low-priced raw materials globally (for instance, iron ore from Australia and Brazil). These foreign firms focused on raising productivity and lowering costs. They often had support from their national governments. At the same time, the managers of the large integrated American steel producers made poor decisions, including lagging innovation of technological improvements and payment of uncompetitive high wages and benefits to unionized workers. By 2000, American steel firms accounted for only 12 percent of world production. Nearly half of U.S. production was by minimills, another source of competitive pressure on the large integrated American firms (often called Big Steel).

American steel firms fought back. A large part of their strategy was the use of political lobbying and U.S. trade laws to attack imports. In the 1980s, to head off a large number of steel dumping complaints, the U.S. government forced the European Union and other countries to impose voluntary export restraints (VERs). As these VERs ended, on one day in 1992 American steel firms filed 80 dumping complaints against 20 countries. (Note that American steel producers buy about one-quarter of all steel imported into the United States, in the form of raw steel slabs that they use to make finished steel products. Amazingly, raw steel slab is apparently never dumped into the United States, but all kinds of finished steel products are.)

American steel firms are well organized. Statisticians at steel-producer organizations and at individual steel firms closely examine each month's trade data. When they see an increase of imports in a specific steel product, the American firms are likely to file a dumping complaint. The American firms actually "lose" or withdraw at least half of these complaints. But they don't really lose. For instance, in 1993, American firms filed dumping complaints against exporters of carbon steel rod. In the early months of the investigation, the price of this product in the United States increased by about 25 percent. Eventually, the American firms lost the cases or withdrew the complaints. An executive of a foreign-owned steel firm commented, "But who says they lost? I would say they won. Whatever they spent in legal fees, they probably recouped 50 times in extra revenue. That is the great thing about filing: Even if you lose, you win."*

Another big set of dumping complaints arose in the aftermath of the Asian crisis that began in 1997. Demand collapsed in the crisis countries (especially Korea, Thailand, Indonesia, Malaysia, and the Philippines). A steel firm has substantial fixed costs in the short run. In the face of declining demand and prices it continues to produce and sell steel as long as the price is above average variable cost (which is much lower than full average cost).

*Mr. Nicholas Tolerico, executive vice president of Thyssen, Inc., a U.S. subsidiary of Thyssen AG, a German steel company. Quoted in the *Wall Street Journal,* March 7, 1998.

—Continued on next page

Dumping Cases Involving Steel Products, Filed in the United States, 1998–1999

Product	Date Filed	Number of Countries	Dumping Margins	Injury?
Stainless steel plate-in-coils	3/98	4	7–45%	Yes
Stainless steel round wire	3/98	6	0-36	No
Stainless steel sheet and strip	6/98	8	0-59	Yes
Hot-rolled steel	9/98	3	18–185	Yes
Cut-to-length steel plate	2/99	8	0–72	Yes (6), no (2)
Cold-rolled steel	6/99	12	7–164	No
Seamless pipe	6/99	6	11–108	Yes
Structural beams	8/99	2	25–65	Yes
Tin mill products	10/99	1	32–95	Yes
Circular stainless steel hollow products	10/99	1	62–157	Yes

Steel firms that had been selling to the crisis countries tried to shift sales to other countries. In 1998 imports of finished steel into the United States rose rapidly. Imports went from about 20 percent of U.S. steel consumption in January to about 33 percent late in the year. During this time prices for steel products typically fell by 20 to 25 percent.

The global steel industry is competitive and highly cyclical. A strong case can be made that 1998 was a fairly typical down phase in the global cycle. Normal and competitive or not, American steel firms swung into action. The accompanying figure shows the steel dumping complaints filed in 1998 and 1999. (Half of these cases also charged some of the countries with receiving unfair government subsidies.)

We see several familiar patterns here. First, the Department of Commerce almost always finds dumping, and the margins are often surprisingly large. Second, the International Trade Commission does not always find injury. In the case of cold-rolled steel, the ITC ruled that any injury was mainly due to competition from American minimills and the decline in demand during a strike at General Motors. In addition, just filing the case is usually a win. For instance, in the months after the complaint was filed, imports of hot-rolled steel fell by more than 65 percent, imports of cut-to-length steel plate fell by 33 percent, and imports of cold-rolled steel (a case eventually "lost," as noted above) fell by 20 percent. Also, as a result of the hot-rolled steel case, in 1999 Russia agreed to VERs on a broad range of steel products, and Brazil agreed to a VER on hot-rolled steel.

By 2000, American steel firms had used the U.S. trade laws to roll back the import share of the American market for finished steel to 22 percent. And still the dumping complaints will keep on coming.

antidumping policy to include consumer interests would reopen the battle and probably reduce some of the bad use of antidumping policy.

Third, *antidumping policy could be replaced by more active use of safeguard policy,* another kind of increased import protection allowed by WTO rules. **Safeguard policy** is the use of temporary import protection when a sudden increase in imports causes injury to domestic producers. The intent is to give some time for import-competing firms and their workers to adjust to the increased import competition (recall the discussion of adjustment assistance in Chapter 9).

Defenders of antidumping policy often state that antidumping policy facilitates trade liberalization, because it allows protection for industries that are hurt more than expected by increasing imports. This is really an argument for safeguard policy. Safeguard policy is better because:

- There is no need to show that foreign exporters have done anything unfair.

- The interests of consumers can be considered in the process that leads to the decision of whether or not to impose a safeguard, and what form it will take if imposed.

- The focus is on adjustment by the import-competing producers.

- There is pressure to adjust because the import protection is temporary.

Safeguard actions have not been much used in the United States. One famous case is Harley-Davidson in the 1980s. After a safeguard was imposed, Harley-Davidson came back so strongly and quickly in its battle with Japanese competitors (Suzuki and Honda) that it asked that the safeguard protection be removed earlier than scheduled. More recently, the tariffs on steel imposed by the U.S. government in 2002 (discussed in Chapter 1) were the outcome of the government's investigation of a request by American steel firms for safeguard relief. Clearly, safeguard actions such as these steel tariffs can still be highly controversial, but at least all parties affected have a right to be heard in the debate.

EXPORT SUBSIDIES

Governments promote or subsidize exports more often than they restrict or tax exports.[3] Some government efforts to promote exports are not controversial according to international precepts (although there are questions about how effective they are). Government agencies like the Trade Information Center of the U.S. Department of Commerce provide foreign-market research, information on export procedures and foreign government regulations, and help with contacting buyers. Government agencies sponsor export promotion events like trade fairs and organized trips. Governments establish export processing zones that permit imports of materials and components with easier customs procedures and low or no tariffs.

Governments also provide various forms of financial assistance that benefit their exporters. These **export subsidies** are controversial because they violate international norms about fair trade. Our analysis of export subsidies will conclude that export subsidies are usually bad from a world point of view. However, the international division of gains and losses turns out to be very different from

---

[3] In the United States this is not surprising because the U.S. Constitution prohibits the taxing of exports.

what you would expect just by listening to who favors export subsidies and who complains about them. Export subsidies are bad for the countries that use them, but are good for the countries that complain about them!

Governments subsidize exports in many ways, some of them deliberately subtle to escape detection. They use taxpayers' money to give low-interest loans to exporters or their foreign customers. An example is the U.S. Export-Import Bank, or Eximbank. Founded in the 1930s, it has compromised its name by giving easy credit to U.S. exporters and their foreign customers but not to U.S. importers or their foreign suppliers. Governments also charge low prices on inputs (such as raw materials or domestic transport services) that go into production that will be exported. Income tax rules are also twisted to give tax relief based on the value of goods or services each firm exports.

Export subsidies are small on average, but they loom large in certain products and for certain companies. For instance, most Eximbank loans have been channeled toward a few large U.S. firms and their customers. Boeing, in particular, has been helped to extra foreign aircraft orders by cheap Eximbank credit. More broadly, the biggest export subsidies apply to agricultural products.

What are the effects on the country whose government offers the export subsidy? Let's examine the effects for a *competitive industry,* using our standard supply-and-demand framework. We will reach the following conclusions:

1. An export subsidy expands exports and production of the subsidized product. In fact, the export subsidy can switch the product from being imported to being exported.

2. An export subsidy lowers the price paid by foreign buyers, relative to the price that local consumers pay for the product. In addition, for the export subsidy to work as intended (the government subsidizes only exports, not domestic purchases), something must prevent local buyers from importing the product at the lower foreign price.

3. The export subsidy reduces the net national well-being of the exporting country.

Let's examine three cases to see the validity of these conclusions.

Exportable Product, Small Exporting Country

Figure 10.3 shows a small country, in this case a country whose exports of steel pipes do not affect the world price of $100 per pipe (standard length). With free trade the firms in the country's competitive steel-pipe industry produce 160 million pipes per year and export 90 million (= 160 − 70). The government of this country then decides to offer to its firms an export subsidy of $20 per pipe. The revenue per pipe exported then is $120, equal to the $100 price paid by foreign buyers plus the $20 subsidy. If the pipe firm can get $120 for each pipe exported, it will not sell to any domestic buyer at a price lower than $120. Of course, this is only possible if domestic buyers cannot just buy imported pipes from the world market at $100. Something must keep the export market separate from the domestic market. (This should sound familiar—it sounds like persistent dumping. In

FIGURE 10.3

Export Subsidy,
Small Country,
Exportable
Product

With free trade at the world price of $100, this small country exports 90 million steel pipes. If the country instead offers an export subsidy $20 per unit exported, revenue per unit exported rises to $120, and the exporting firms must receive this amount as the selling price from domestic buyers as well. Domestic production rises from 160 to 190 million, domestic consumption falls from 70 to 50 million, and the country exports 140 million pipes. Domestic producers gain surplus equal to area $e + f + g$, domestic consumers lose surplus equal to area $e + f$, and the cost to the government of paying the export subsidy is area $f + g + h$. The net loss in national well-being because of the export subsidy is area $f + h$.

fact, receiving an export subsidy is another reason why an exporting firm would engage in dumping.)

What are the other effects of the export subsidy in this case? If revenue per unit rises to $120 (for both export and local sales), the quantity produced increases to 190 million. If the domestic price increases to $120, local quantity demanded decreases to 50 million. Quantity exported increases to 140 million (= 190 − 50).

Who are the winners and losers in the exporting country? Producers gain surplus equal to areas $e + f + g$. Consumers lose surplus equal to area $e + f$. The cost to the government of paying the export subsidy is areas $f + g + h$, equal to the export subsidy of $20 per pipe times the 140 million pipes exported with the subsidy.

The export subsidy has increased exports and production of this product, but is it good for the exporting country? Using our one-dollar, one-vote metric, the answer is no. After we cancel out the matching gains and losses, the net loss in national well-being is areas f and h. Area f is the **consumption effect** of the export subsidy, the lost consumer surplus for those consumers squeezed out of the market when the domestic price rises above the world price. Area h is the **production effect** of the export subsidy, the loss due to encouraging domestic production that has a resource cost greater than the world price (the world standard for efficient production). Although these two triangles are on the opposite sides of the graph, because this is an exportable product rather than an importable product, they are the same kinds of effects shown for the import tariff in Figure 7.4. The loss of national well-being for this small exporting country is also a loss for the world.

Exportable Product, Large Exporting Country

We've just seen that a small exporting country harms itself by offering an export subsidy to its competitive exporting industry. Perhaps the results are different if the exporting country is large enough to affect the world price. Not so—in fact, it may be worse.

Figure 10.4 shows this case. With free trade the world price is $100 per pipe. When the exporting-country government offers the export subsidy of $20 per pipe, exporting firms want to export more to get more of the subsidy. To get foreign consumers to buy more of the exported product, the exporting firms must lower the export price. And, just as in the small-country case, domestic buyers in the exporting country must end up paying $20 more than the export price (assuming that they cannot import from the rest of the world at the new world price).

We can see the resulting equilibrium more easily in panel B of Figure 10.4. The export subsidy creates a wedge of $20 between the price that foreign importers pay and the revenue per unit that exporters receive. This $20 wedge "fits" (vertically) at the quantity traded of 110 million pipes. The new world price is $88, the price paid by the importers. The revenue per unit to the exporting firms, and the new price in the exporting country, is $108.

Panel A of Figure 10.4 shows what is happening in the exporting country. At $108 per pipe, production in the exporting country increases from 160 million to 172 million, and domestic consumption decreases from 70 to 62 million. Quantity exported increases from 90 million to 110 million.

FIGURE 10.4   Export Subsidy, Large Country, Exportable Product

With free trade at the world price of 100, this large country exports 90 million steel pipes. If instead the country offers an export subsidy of $20, its extra exports drive the world price down to $88. The revenue per unit received by the exporting firms is $108, and domestic buyers also pay a price of $108. The net loss of well-being for the exporting country is area $f + h + i + j + k + l + m$. The export subsidy both distorts domestic production and consumption and worsens the exporting country's international terms of trade. The inefficiency created for the world is area $f + h + u$.

As in the small-country case, the export subsidy has increased domestic production and exports of pipes. What are the effects on well-being in the exporting country? Producer surplus increases by area $e + f + g$. Consumer surplus falls by area $e + f$. The export subsidy costs the government $20 times the 110 million units exported. This government cost of $2.2 billion is area $f + g + h + i + j + k + l + m$ in Panel A (or area $f + g + h + n + r + t + u$ in Panel B).

The net loss to the exporting country is the shaded area in panel A or B. This net loss has three parts:

- The consumption effect (area f).

- The production effect (area h).

- The loss due to the decline in the exporting country's international terms of trade (area $i + j + k + l + m$ = area $n + r + t + u$).

The export subsidy gives a good bargain to foreign buyers. However, their gain is a loss to the exporting country from selling at a lower world price.

We can also use panel B to see the effect on world well-being. Area $n + r + t$ is increased surplus for the importing country. The net loss to the world is the triangular area $f + h + u$. This is the loss from too much trading of steel pipes.

Switching an Importable Product into an Exportable Product

"If you throw enough money at something, it will happen." This adage applies to export subsidies. They can turn an importable product into one that is exported. Let's see how.

To keep things from getting too complicated, we will examine the small-country case shown in Figure 10.5. With free trade at the world price of $2 per kilogram, the country would import 80 million kilos of butter (= 120 − 40). The government now offers an export subsidy of $2 per kilo, and prevents domestic consumers from importing cheap foreign butter. The revenue per kilo exported now rises to $4, and domestic production increases to 90 million kilos. At the higher domestic price of $4 per kilo, domestic consumers reduce their butter purchases to 60 million kilos. With the export subsidy, the country is now an *exporter* of 30 million kilos.

The export subsidy switches an importable product into an exportable product. Domestic producers gain surplus of area *ACFE*. Domestic consumers lose surplus of area *ABJE*. The cost of the export subsidy to the government is area *BCHG*. The net loss of national well-being looks a bit peculiar, because the triangles of the consumption effect and the production effect overlap each other. The net national loss (and the net loss to the world) is area *BJG plus* area *CHF*.

This example of using export subsidies to create exportables is not farfetched! See the box "Agriculture Is Amazing."

At this point you might want to return to the conclusions stated at the beginning of this section. You should see that these conclusions apply to all three of our cases. If the market is competitive, an export subsidy is bad for the exporting country.

FIGURE 10.5

An Export
Subsidy Turns
an Importable
Product Into
an Export

With free trade and no export subsidy, this small country imports 80 million kilos of butter. If instead the country's government offers an export subsidy of $2 per kilo, the revenue per unit received by producers doubles to $4. The country becomes an exporter of 30 million kilos of butter. The net loss of national well-being is the sum of a production deadweight loss of area *FCH* and a consumption deadweight loss of area *BJG*.

WTO RULES ON SUBSIDIES

As a result of the agreements reached in the Tokyo Round and Uruguay Round of trade negotiations, the WTO now has a clear set of rules for subsidies that may benefit exports.[4] The WTO rules divide subsidies into three types:

- Subsidies linked directly to exporting are *prohibited,* except export subsidies used by the lowest-income developing countries. Example: A firm receives a tax break based on the amount that it exports.

- Subsidies that are not linked directly to exporting but still have an impact on exports are *actionable.* Example: Low-priced electricity is provided to assist production by local firms in an industry, and some of this production is exported.

- Some subsidies are *nonactionable.* These include subsidies for research and development, assistance to disadvantaged regions, and assistance in meeting environmental regulations.

If an importing country's government believes that a foreign country is using a prohibited subsidy or an actionable subsidy that is harming its industry, the importing country can follow one of two procedures:

---

[4] A separate and less stringent set of rules applies to agricultural products. See the box "Agriculture Is Amazing."

- File a complaint with the WTO and use its dispute settlement procedure (used occasionally).

- Use a national procedure similar to that used for dumping (used more often).

If the importing country can show the existence of a prohibited or actionable subsidy and harm to its industry, it is permitted to impose a **countervailing duty,** a tariff used to offset the price or cost advantage created by the export subsidy.

SHOULD THE IMPORTING COUNTRY IMPOSE COUNTERVAILING DUTIES?

How should the *importing country* respond to subsidized exports? Should the country simply enjoy the bargain? Or should the importing-country government heed the complaints from import-competing producers about unfair competition and impose a countervailing duty on the subsidized exports?

If the exporting country is large enough to affect world prices, then the export subsidy lowers the price that the importing country pays for these exports. As we saw in Figure 10.4B, the importing country overall is better off, but the import-competing industry is harmed. By WTO rules, the importing-country government is permitted to impose a countervailing duty. What happens if it does so?

To keep things from getting too complicated, let's use an extreme version of the large-country case examined in Figure 10.4. In this version, all of the export subsidy is passed forward to the buyers of imports in the foreign country. That is, the price charged to importers falls by the full amount of the export subsidy. Still, be warned: Even this simplified case can be confusing. We will focus on two different measures of well-being, one for the importing country and one for the world. We will make comparisons among three different situations: (1) free trade, (2) export subsidy with no countervailing duty, and (3) export subsidy plus countervailing duty.

Figure 10.6 shows the Canadian and international market for cold-rolled steel. With free trade, Canada would import 50 million tons per year from Brazil at the free-trade price of $300 per ton. Then, the Brazilian government offers a subsidy of $50 per ton exported. If all of this is passed on to buyers, the export price declines to $250 per ton. Canadian imports increase to 80 million tons. Canadian production declines to 130 million tons, and Canadian producer surplus declines by area v. Canadian consumption increases to 210 million tons, and Canadian consumer surplus increases by area $v + w + y + z$. The net Canadian gain from the Brazilian export subsidy is area $w + y + z$. Still, Canadian producers are harmed, and they complain about the unfair competition.

For the world, this is too much steel trade. Steel tons that each cost $300 of Brazilian resources to produce are valued at less than $300 per ton by the Canadian buyer (as shown ton-by-ton on the Canadian demand-for-import curve).

What happens if the Canadian government imposes a countervailing duty of $50 per ton of imported steel? The duty-inclusive price of imports rises back to

FIGURE 10.6   A Foreign Export Subsidy and a Countervailing Duty

A. The Domestic Market for Cold-Rolled Steel

Price
($ per ton)

S_d

300
250

v w y z

D_d

0   130   150   200   210   Quantity
(millions of tons)

B. The International Market for Cold-Rolled Steel

Price
($ per ton)

300
250

y $w + z$ x

Canadian
demand
for imports

0   50   80   Quantity
(millions of tons)

The diagram shows the effect of (1) a Brazilian export subsidy on steel to Canada; and (2) a Canadian countervailing duty on imports of subsidized steel exports from Brazil. An odd pattern results: Each policy in turn brings a net loss to the country adopting it, yet for the world as a whole the Canadian countervailing duty undoes the harm done by the Brazilian export subsidy.

$300. In this subsidy-plus-countervailing-duty situation, the world returns to the same price $300 and volume of trade (50 million tons) as with free trade. This makes good sense for *world efficiency,* because the deadweight loss of excessive trade (area x in Figure 10.6B) is eliminated. For the world, the countervailing duty is a successful use of Chapter 9's specificity rule. In this case the world's problem is excessive exports of steel, and the countervailing duty directly affects exactly the problem activity.

Conclusions about the effects of the countervailing duty on *Canada's well-being* depend on what we compare to. *In comparison to the situation with the export subsidy and no countervailing duty,* Canada is worse off for imposing the countervailing duty. That's right—a countervailing duty in this case is bad for the country imposing it, but good for the whole world. We can use figure 10.6A to see the effect on the importing country of imposing the countervailing duty, given that an export subsidy exists. The duty-inclusive price rises to $300. Canadian producers gain area v, Canadian consumers lose area $v + w + y + z$, and the Canadian government collects area y as revenue from the countervailing duty. The net national loss to Canada of imposing the countervailing duty is area $w + z$ (the standard result for imposing a tariff).

Let's look at a second valid comparison, the *comparison between free trade and the combination of the export subsidy and countervailing duty.* In both of these situations, the price in Canada is the same ($300), as are all quantities. The only difference is that the Canadian government is collecting revenue (area y) in the subsidy-and-duty situation. Who is effectively paying the countervailing duty? The Brazilian government! It pays the export subsidy to the Brazilian firms, who pass it on to import buyers in Canada through the lower export price. The Canadian import buyers then send it to the Canadian government when they pay the countervailing duty. The well-being of Canada is higher than it would be with free trade, because the Brazilian government is now effectively paying Canadian taxes.

Because export subsidies are bad for the world as a whole, and retaliating against them is good for the world as whole, WTO rules are wise to allow importing countries to impose countervailing duties. However, it turns out that subsidy complaints and countervailing duties are much less frequent than dumping complaints and antidumping duties. During 1999–2000 only 56 subsidy cases were initiated in the world, and in mid-2001 there were only 87 countervailing actions in effect.

The United States has been the largest user of countervailing duties, with 17 of these new cases and 43 of the countervailing duties in force. The European Union, Canada, and Australia also make some use of countervailing duties. India, Argentina, Taiwan, Indonesia, Thailand, and South Korea are the countries most frequently charged with subsidizing exports. Steel and textiles and clothing are the products most frequently involved. Countervailing duties also tend to be lower than antidumping duties. For instance, for the United States the average countervailing duty is about 10 percent.

While countervailing duties are often good for the world, they can also be misused in the same way that antidumping duties are misused. Import-competing producers have an incentive to complain about possible foreign subsidies to exports, in an effort to gain protection against these exports. Many activities of a government could have some element of subsidy in them. In antisubsidy cases, it is often possible for the complaining firms to establish that some kind of foreign subsidy exists that might benefit exports, perhaps with some help from a government process biased toward helping the import-competing domestic firms. Then, these firms can gain the protection of countervailing duties if they can show that they have been injured by the "subsidized" exports.

The softwood lumber dispute between the United States and Canada is an example of a controversial antisubsidy case. In early 2001 a VER limiting Canadian exports expired. U.S. lumber firms immediately renewed their complaint that Canadian lumber firms benefit from a subsidy because the Canadian government does not charge high enough fees for logging on government lands. The Canadian government contends that its fees are appropriate, so there is no subsidy. The U.S. government found otherwise. The U.S. Commerce Department concluded that the low fee was a subsidy of 19 percent, and concluded that Canadian lumber exporters also were dumping by an additional 8 percent on average. The U.S. International Trade Commission found injury to U.S. firms from the lumber imports that grew rapidly after the VER expired. U.S. lumber producers clearly gain surplus from the combined average duty of 27 percent against Canadian lumber. U.S. consumers lose. Most obviously, the cost of building a typical

Case Study   Agriculture Is Amazing

I don't want to hear about agriculture from
anybody but you . . . Come to think of it,
I don't want to hear about it from you either.
                    —President Kennedy to his top
                        agricultural policy adviser

Agriculture is another world. Sometimes it seems as
if the laws of nature have been repealed. Since the
early 1980s the desert kingdom of Saudi Arabia has
grown more wheat than it can consume, so it has
exported wheat. Wheat is also exported by other
countries with unfavorable soils and climates, including Great Britain and France. And crowded, moun-
tainous Japan has often been a net exporter of rice.

All this happens because governments are more
involved in agriculture than in any other sector of the
private economy. In 2000 government policies in
industrialized countries provided about $245 billion of
support to farmers, equal to about 34 percent of the
farmers' income. Government policies in the European
Union (EU) provided $98 billion (38 percent of farm
income), in the United States $49 billion (22 percent),
and in Japan $60 billion (an amazing 64 percent of the
income of Japanese farmers). The farmers' political
lobbies in these countries are remarkably powerful,
especially relative to the small role of agriculture in the
economy (only about 2 percent of gross domestic
product). Farmers producing rice, milk, and sugar are
the biggest recipients of these subsidies.

About two-thirds of the increased farm income is
provided through price supports. For the typical **price
support,** the government sets a minimum domestic
price for the agricultural product, and the government
buys any amounts that farmers cannot sell into the
market at the minimum (support) price. Domestic
farmers receive at least the minimum price when they

sell, and domestic consumers pay at least the minimum
price when they buy. All of this sounds domestic—
domestic minimum price, domestic farmers, domestic
consumers. Yet something that starts "domestic"
transforms itself on the way to the global markets.

The support price is almost always higher than the
world price for the agricultural product. If the country
would import the product with free trade, the price
support requires that *imports be restricted*. Otherwise, cheap imports would flood into the country and
undermine the price support. If the support price is
not too high (less than or equal to the no-trade price
for the country), then the price support is actually a
form of import protection. The analysis of this type of
price support mirrors that of import barriers presented
in Chapters 7 and 8. Interesting, but not amazing yet.

If the country would export the product with free
trade, but the support price is above the world price,
then the country's farmers produce more than is purchased by domestic consumers. The government
must buy the excess production at the high support
price. The government could just destroy what it buys
or let it rot, but that would be remarkably wasteful.
The government could give it away to needy domestic
families, but there are limits to how much can be
given away before this free stuff starts to undermine
regular domestic demand. The government could
turn to the export market, which sounds like an excellent way to dispose of the excess national production.
Perhaps it is, but the government will take a loss on
each unit exported. This loss, the difference between
the support price that the government pays and the
lower world price that it receives, is an *export subsidy*
from the government. Foreign buyers will not pay the
high domestic support price; they buy only if the government offers a subsidized export price.

In this case, in which an exporting country sets a support price that is above the world price for the product, the price support policy is actually a combination of import protection and export subsidy. The analysis mirrors that accompanying Figures 10.3 and 10.4. We are getting closer to amazing.

Price supports can also *switch agricultural products from being importable to being exported.* Wheat is an example for Britain, France, and other EU members. Butter and other dairy products in the EU are other examples of products that have become exports because of generous price supports. With free trade, wheat, butter, and other dairy products would be imported into the EU because the world prices of these products are lower than the EU's no-trade prices. (More simply, the EU has a comparative disadvantage in these products.) The EU's support prices are so high that EU farmers produce much more than is sold in the EU. The EU uses export subsidies to export some its excess production. The analysis of this case mirrors that for Figure 10.6. Now that's pretty amazing. Domestic price supports morph into a combination of import protection and export subsidies that transform the country from an importer to an exporter of the products.

It takes a lot of government money to create amazement. The EU's Common Agricultural Policy (CAP) covers a broad range of agricultural products (including wheat, butter, and other dairy products). CAP spending represents about *half* of all EU fiscal expenditures. And the amazement brings a large national cost. The inefficiency of the CAP is equal to a loss of about 1 percent of the EU's gross domestic product.

Agriculture has also been another world for WTO rules. In contrast to the rules for industrial products, governments have been permitted to use import quotas and export subsidies. But things are changing. The agricultural provisions of the Uruguay Round trade agreement make agriculture less different, especially for developed countries. Governments are converting all quotas and other nontariff barriers into tariff rates, a process called *tariffication.* Each developed country is reducing its budget outlays for export subsidies by 36 percent and its volume of subsidized exports by 21 percent. Each developed country is supposed to reduce its domestic subsidies to agriculture by 20 percent, with some exceptions. The requirements for developing countries are less stringent.

The effects of these changes are not as large as one might expect. Most developed countries have maintained import protection through artful implementation of the agreement. Generally, highly protected products remain highly protected. The reduction of export subsidies is having some impact, especially in reducing subsidization of exports by the EU. The effects of the general reduction in domestic subsidies are moderate, because major subsidy programs in the United States and the EU were exempt from the cuts.

After the Uruguay Round agreement, agriculture is less different. Tariffication puts import barriers into a form in which they can be compared across countries, and the reduction in subsidies is a step toward less distorted markets. The agreement pulls agricultural products toward the mainstream of international trade rules. It lays the groundwork for future negotiations that may be able to achieve more substantial liberalizations. In this sector that would be amazing.

new home rises by over $1,000. Most new-home buyers can pay this, so they suffer a straight loss of money. The deadweight loss consumption effect occurs for the estimated 300,000 American families that cannot afford the higher house prices. Most of them have modest incomes, and they reluctantly remain in less desirable housing.

If the Canadian logging fee is a subsidy because it is too low, then world well-being is enhanced by the U.S. countervailing duty. However, if the Canadian fee is appropriate and not a subsidy, then the countervailing duty (and perhaps the antidumping duty as well) is simple import protection, with a net loss for the world. It is not an easy call for the referee of world efficiency.

STRATEGIC EXPORT SUBSIDIES COULD BE GOOD

In the previous section we assumed competitive supply and demand, and we reached the conclusion that an export subsidy harmed the exporting country. For some industries this competitive assumption is wrong. Suppose instead that the real-world market in question features the clash of two giant firms, each of which could supply the whole market. The economics of an export subsidy looks very different if international competition in the industry consists of an oligopolistic duel between two giant firms for the global market. (Recall our discussion of oligopoly and trade in Chapter 6.) In this battle of giants, an export subsidy can be either good or bad, both for the exporting country and for the world.

To see the possibility of a good subsidy, let us imagine a simplified case inspired by the continuing real-world competition between Boeing and Europe's Airbus. Suppose that it becomes technologically possible for them to build a new kind of passenger plane, perhaps a superjumbo jet. To keep a clear focus on the key points, let us say that there is no inherent difference between Airbus and Boeing in the cost of making the new plane. Still, aircraft manufacture can benefit from economies of scale—as a firm expands its planned output, the cost of making another unit drops as output rises. Either firm is capable of supplying the whole world market at a low cost. If only one firm captures the whole world market, it will reap some monopoly profits. If both firms produce, they will vie for sales and drive the price down to their low variable costs. In this rivalry case, they make no operating profits.

Figure 10.7 sets the stage by considering what might happen if Airbus and Boeing simultaneously faced a decision about whether to make the new plane. For either of them, it is a tough decision. Let's look at it from Airbus's viewpoint. Should it choose to invest 8 and produce the new planes (left column), or should it not invest and not produce (right column)? Well, that all depends on what Boeing does. If Airbus could be sure Boeing would stay out, it should definitely invest the 8 and produce, making the profits of 100 shown in the lower left box. But what if Boeing does produce? Then the two of them will have a price war and get no operating profits to offset their initial investments of 8.

So choosing to enter the market looks risky for Airbus. It looks similarly risky for Boeing. As you can see by studying the payoffs for the two rows, Boeing

FIGURE 10.7
A Two-Firm
Rivalry Game
With no
Government
Subsidies:
Airbus versus
Boeing

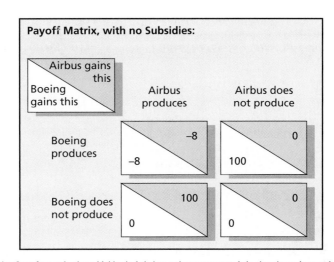

When two competing firms face each other with identical choices and no government help, there is no clear result to the game if both must decide simultaneously. Each would like to be the only producer, but if both decide to produce, both lose. Knowing this, both may decide not to produce.

would want to produce only if it could be sure that Airbus won't produce (upper right box). But in a noncooperative game like this, neither firm can choose the outcome—each can only choose a strategy (column or row). The two firms might react to the threat of competition by producing nothing, leaving the world in the lower right box—with no new planes.

Either government could break through the uncertainty by offering a subsidy to its producer, for instance, a subsidy that covers the producer's initial costs. Again, let's take the European viewpoint. The governments of Britain, France, Germany, and Spain could agree (as they have in the past) to give subsidies to Airbus. If they give Airbus a start-up subsidy of 10, which more than covers its initial costs of 8, we could have the situation shown in panel A in Figure 10.8. Looking down the left column of possibilities, Airbus can see that it should definitely produce. Either it gains only 2 (invest 8, get 10 back in subsidies) in the face of competition from Boeing, or it gains a full 110 if Boeing is frightened off. Airbus gains, and the world's consumers gain (an amount not shown here). Even Europe as a whole gains if Airbus makes the 110 in profits, because after subtracting the subsidy of 10, the net gain to Europe is still 100. So here is a case of a subsidy that is good for the world as a whole, and good for the exporting country (the European Union) as well. This subsidy is a form of **strategic trade policy,** in which government policy helps its own firm's strategy to win the game and claim the prize (here, 100 of economic profit).[5]

---

[5] Another form of strategic trade policy is protection of the home market, if the home market is large and scale economies are important. The domestic firm can then use production to meet demand in its protected home market as the basis for low-cost production that allows it to compete aggressively in the foreign market. Aggressive exporting in this situation is sometimes called strategic dumping.

FIGURE 10.8   A Two-Firm Rivalry Game With Government Subsidies: Airbus versus Boeing

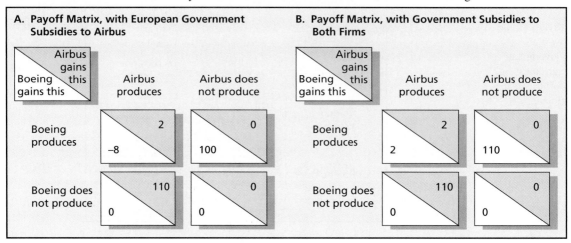

A. If the European government gives Airbus a subsidy of 10, to ensure Airbus a profit of 2 even with full competition, Airbus will choose to produce. Knowing that Airbus will produce, Boeing will choose not to produce. Airbus wins profits of 110. Because the airplane is built, consumers gain some surplus from the new product, and the world as a whole gains well-being. **B.** In this case, with each government offering a subsidy to its firm of 10, both firms will produce the airplane. For each country the cost of the subsidy (10) is greater than the gain to the firm (2). Each country loses by offering its subsidy, unless gains in national consumer surplus (not pictured here) are larger than this net loss of 8.

It's not so easy, though. Suppose that the U.S. government decides to subsidize Boeing's market entry in the same way that the EU subsidizes Airbus. Then we have the problem shown in panel B of Figure 10.8. Each firm sees a green light and decides to produce since each firm makes a positive profit regardless of whether or not the other produces. This is fine for the firms, but each government is spending 10. So *as nations,* the EU and the United States are each losing 8 (for each, this equals the 2 of profits that the firm shows minus the 10 of subsidy cost to the government). The only good news in panel B is hidden from view: The world's consumers gain. But if most of those consumers are outside the EU and the United States, these two nations are still net losers.

These simple examples bring out the two key points about an export subsidy or similar type of subsidy in a global duel between two exporting giants:

1. The subsidy *might* be a good thing for the exporting country, as shown in panel A in Figure 10.8, but

2. The case for giving the subsidy is fragile, depending on too many conditions to be a reliable policy.

In our example, we saw one condition that matters. If another national government also offers its firm strategic policy assistance, it is quite possible that both countries lose well-being. (Notice the similarity of this caveat to Chapter 7's discussion of the nationally optimal tariff and retaliation by the other country.) Another condition that matters is the possibility that there is no prize for the game. For instance, there may not be enough consumer demand for the new product, so economic profits will be negative instead of positive, even if there is only one producer. How would the government separate the false pleas of some of its firms for strategic help from the valid ones? While there is a theoretical case for the national benefit of strategic trade policy, we may be skeptical that a national government could actually use it effectively.

Summary

Dumping is selling exports at less than **normal value**—a price lower than the price in the home market or lower than the full average cost of production. Exporters may engage in dumping to drive foreign competitors out of business (**predatory dumping**), during recessions in industry demand (**cyclical dumping**), to unload excess inventory (**seasonal dumping**), or to increase profits through **price discrimination** (**persistent dumping**). The importing country benefits from the dumped exports because it pays a lower price for its imports. But the importing country could be hurt by predatory dumping (higher prices in the future) or by cyclical dumping (importing unemployment).

The WTO permits the importing country to retaliate with an **antidumping duty,** if dumping is occurring and it is causing injury to the import-competing industry. It appears that the process of imposing antidumping duties has become a major source of new protection for import-competing producers because the process is biased to find dumping and impose duties. The American steel industry is an example of a set of firms that continually complain about dumping to gain relief from import competition. Proposals for reform of antidumping policy include limiting its use to cases where predatory dumping is plausible, incorporating consumer interests in the analysis of injury from dumping, and replacing antidumping policy with more use of **safeguard policy,** in which a government offers temporary protection to assist an industry in adjusting to increasing import competition.

Export subsidies are condemned by the WTO, with the exception of export subsidies to agricultural products. If the market is competitive, an export subsidy brings a loss to the country offering the subsidy and to the world as a whole by causing excessive trade. A **countervailing duty** against subsidized exports brings a loss to the importing country levying it but brings a gain to the world as a whole by offsetting the export subsidy. The combination of an export subsidy and an equal countervailing duty would leave world welfare unchanged, with taxpayers of the export-subsidizing country implicitly making payments to the government of the importing country.

It is at least possible that export subsidies could be good for the exporting nation and for the world as a whole. If export competition takes the form of an oligopoly game between two giant producers, each of which could dominate the market alone (e.g., Boeing versus Airbus), then the government can offer a subsidy to its exporter as a **strategic trade policy.** This firm then may capture the global market and bring gains both to the exporting nation and to the world as a whole. We do not know that such a case has occurred, but it is possible.

Suggested Reading

Niels (2000) provides a survey of a broad range of research on antidumping policy. Stiglitz (1997) provides a critique of U.S. antidumping and antisubsidy policies. Ethier (1982) presents the basic theory of dumping. Finger (1993), Hindley and Messerlin (1996), Prusa (1997), and the articles in Lawrence (1998) discuss actual antidumping policies. Galloway, Blonigen, and Flynn (1999) present estimates of the effects of U.S. antidumping and countervailing duties.

Krueger, Schiff, and Valdes (1992) offer a comparative international perspective on agricultural policies, and Gardner (1988) offers economic analysis of their effects on international trade. Hathaway and Ingco (1996) provide a summary and analysis of the agricultural agreement reached during the Uruguay Round.

Brander (1995) provides a technical survey of strategic trade policy. For a report on the role of government policy in the rise of new exporters in six industries, including steel and aircraft, see Lindert (2000).

Questions and Problems

◆ 1. What are the two official definitions of *dumping?*

2. You have been asked to propose a specific revision of U.S. antidumping policy, to make the policy more likely to contribute to U.S. well-being. What will you propose?

◆ 3. Which of the following three beverage exporters is dumping in the U.S. market? Which is not? How do you know?

	Banzai Brewery (Japan)	Tipper Laurie, Ltd. (UK)	Bigg Redd, Inc. (Canada)
Average unit cost	$10	$10	$10
Price charged at the brewery for domestic sales	10	12	9
Price charged at the brewery for export sales	11	11	9
Price when delivered to the U.S. port	12	13	10

4. What is a countervailing duty?

◆ 5. What would happen to world welfare if the United States paid exporters a subsidy of $5 for every pair of blue jeans they sold to Canada, but Canada charged a $5 countervailing duty on every pair imported into Canada? Would the United States gain from the combination of the export subsidy and import tariff? Would Canada? Explain.

6. Consider the case of an export subsidy for an importing country that has some monopsony power—that is, the case in which the foreign supply-of-exports curve is upward-sloping. Use a graph like that in Figure 10.4.

   a. In comparison with free trade, what is the effect of the export subsidy on the international price and the quantity traded?

   b. The importing country now imposes a countervailing duty that returns the market to the initial free-trade quantity traded. In comparison with the market with just the export subsidy, explain why the countervailing duty is good for the world. Explain why the countervailing duty can also increase the well-being of the importing country.

◆ 7. In the Airbus-versus-Boeing example in Figure 10.7, what strategy should the EU governments follow if the upper left box (*a*) gives Airbus and Boeing each a sure gain of 5 or (*b*) gives Boeing a gain of 5 and Airbus a gain of 0? In each case, should the EU offer a subsidy to Airbus? Explain.

8. Consider the export subsidy shown in Figure 10.3. Assuming that the export subsidy remains $20, what are the effects of a decline in the world price from $100 to $90? Show the effects using a graph and explain them.

◆ 9. You have been hired to write a defense of the idea of having a government plan and subsidize the expansion of an export-oriented industry, taking resources away from the rest of the economy in the short run. Describe how you would defend such an industrial targeting strategy as good for the nation as a whole.

10. You have been hired to discredit the argument you just presented in answering question 9. Present a strong case against getting the government into the export-pushing business.

Chapter **Eleven**

Trade Blocs
and Trade Blocks

Chapters 7 though 9 looked at equal-opportunity import barriers, ones that tax or restrict all imports regardless of country of origin. But some import barriers are meant to discriminate. They tax goods, services, or assets from some countries more than those from other countries. The analysis of Chapters 7 through 9 can now be modified to explain the effects of today's trade discrimination.

We look at two kinds of trade barriers that are designed to discriminate:

1. **Trade blocs.** Each member country can import from other member countries freely, or at least cheaply, while imposing barriers against imports from outside countries. The European Union (EU) has done that, allowing free trade between members while restricting imports from other countries.

2. **Trade embargoes,** or what the chapter title calls "trade blocks." Some countries discriminate completely against certain other countries, usually because of a policy dispute. They deny the outflow of goods, services, or assets to a particular country while allowing export to other countries, or discriminate against imports from the targeted country, or block both exports to and imports from the target.

TYPES OF ECONOMIC BLOCS

Some international groupings discriminate in trade alone, while others discriminate between insiders and outsiders on all fronts, becoming almost like unified nations. To grasp what is happening in Western Europe and North America and may happen elsewhere, we should first distinguish among the main types of economic blocs. Figure 11.1 and the following definitions show the progression of economic blocs toward increasing integration:

FIGURE 11.1
Types of
Economic Blocs

Type of Bloc	Features of Bloc			
	Free Trade Among the Members	Common External Tariffs	Free Movement of Factors of Production	Harmonization* of All Economic Policies (Fiscal, Monetary, Etc.)
Free-trade area	✓			
Customs union	✓	✓		
Common market	✓	✓	✓	
Economic union	✓	✓	✓	✓

*If the policies are not just harmonized by separate governments, but actually decided by a unified government with binding commitments on all members, then the bloc amounts to full economic nationhood. Some authors call this *full economic integration.*

1. A **free-trade area,** in which members remove trade barriers among themselves but keep their separate national barriers against trade with the outside world. One example of a free-trade area, true to its name, is the North American Free Trade Area (NAFTA), which formally began at the start of 1994.

2. A **customs union,** in which members again remove all barriers to trade among themselves and also adopt a common set of external barriers. The European Economic Community (EEC) from 1957 to 1992 included a customs union along with some other agreements. The Southern Common Market (MERCOSUR), formed by Argentina, Brazil, Paraguay, and Uruguay in 1991, is actually a customs union.

3. A **common market,** in which members allow full freedom of factor flows (migration of labor and capital) among themselves in addition to having a customs union. Despite its name, the European Common Market (EEC, which became the European Community, EC, and is now the European Union, EU) was not a common market up through the 1980s because it still had substantial barriers to the international movement of labor and capital. The EU became a true common market, and more, at the end of 1992.

4. Full **economic union,** in which member countries unify all their economic policies, including monetary, fiscal, and welfare policies as well as policies toward trade and factor migration. Most nations are economic unions. Belgium and Luxembourg have had such a union since 1921. The EU is on a path toward full unity.

The first two types of economic blocs are simply trade blocs (i.e., they have removed trade barriers within the bloc but have kept their national barriers to the flow of labor and capital and their national fiscal and monetary autonomy). Trade blocs have proved easier to form than common markets or full unions among sovereign nations, and they are the subject of this chapter. Freedom of factor flows within a bloc is touched on only briefly here—we return to it in Chapter 14. The monetary side of union enters in Part III.

IS TRADE DISCRIMINATION GOOD OR BAD?

By the early 2000s, nearly half of world trade occurred *within* functioning trade blocs, including:

- The 15 countries of the EU.

- The 4 remaining countries of the European Free Trade Area (EFTA).

- The preferential trade agreements that the EU has with 32 other countries (including the 4 EFTA countries).

- The various free-trade agreements among the Central and Eastern Europe countries.

- The 3 countries of NAFTA.

- The trade agreements that Mexico has with the EU, EFTA, Chile, and Israel, in addition to its membership in NAFTA.

- The free-trade areas that the United States has with Israel and Jordan, in addition to its membership in NAFTA.

- The 4 countries of MERCOSUR and its trade agreements with Chile and Bolivia.

- The trade agreements that Turkey has with the EU, EFTA, and 13 other countries.

Indeed, as of 2001 Japan, South Korea, China, Hong Kong, Macau, and Mongolia were the only countries that were not members of some trade bloc.[1] Japan was about to end its holdout—in 2001 it signed a free-trade agreement with Singapore.

How good or how bad is all this trade discrimination? It depends, first, on what you compare it to. Compared to a free-trade policy, putting up new barriers discriminating against imports from some countries is generally bad, like the simple tariff of Chapters 7 through 9. But the issue of trade discrimination usually comes to us from a different angle: Beginning with tariffs and nontariff barriers that apply equally regardless of the source country of the imports, what are the gains and losses from removing barriers only between certain countries? That is, what happens when a trade bloc like the EU or NAFTA gets formed?

Two opposing ideas come to mind. One instinct is that forming a customs union or free-trade area must be good because it is a move toward free trade. If you start from an equally applied set of trade barriers in each nation, having a group of them remove trade barriers among themselves clearly means lower trade barriers in some average sense. Since that idea is closer to free trade, and Chapters 7 through 10 found free trade better with only carefully limited exceptions, it seems reasonable that forming a trade bloc allows more trade and raises

---

[1] Technically, Hong Kong and Macau are separate customs territories, not countries.

world welfare. After all, forming a nation out of smaller regions brings economic gains, doesn't it?

On the other hand, we can think of reasons why forming a free-trading bloc can be bad, even starting from equally applied barriers to all international trade. First, forming the trade bloc may encourage people to buy from higher-cost partner suppliers. The bloc would encourage costly production within the bloc if it kept a high tariff on goods from the cheapest source outside the bloc and no tariff on goods from a more costly source within the bloc. By contrast, a uniform tariff on all imports has the virtue that customers would still do most or all of their buying from the cheapest source. Second, the whole idea of trade discrimination smacks of the bilateralism of the 1930s, when separate deals with individual nations destroyed much of the gains from global trade. The list at the beginning of this section indicates that we again have quite a tangled web of discriminatory agreements. Third, forming blocs may cause international friction simply because letting someone into the bloc will shut others out.

For all these reasons, World Trade Organization (WTO) rules are opposed to trade discrimination in principle. A basic WTO principle is that trade barriers should be lowered equally and without discrimination for all foreign trading partners. That is, the WTO espouses the **most favored nation (MFN) principle.** This principle, dating back to the mid-19th-century wave of free trade led by Britain, stipulates that any concession given to any foreign nation must be given to all nations having MFN status. WTO rules say that all contracting parties are entitled to that status.

However, other parts of WTO rules permit deviations from MFN under specific conditions. One deviation is special treatment for developing countries. Developing countries have the right to exchange preferences among themselves and receive preferential access to markets in the industrialized countries.

Another deviation permits trade blocs involving industrialized countries if the trade bloc removes tariffs and other trade restrictions on most of the trade among its members, and if its trade barriers against nonmembers do not increase on average. In fact, the WTO, and the GATT before it, have applied the rules loosely. No trade bloc has ever been ruled in violation.

THE BASIC THEORY OF TRADE BLOCS: TRADE CREATION AND TRADE DIVERSION

Trade discrimination can indeed be either good or bad. We can give an example of this and, in the process, discover what conditions separate the good from the bad cases.

It may seem paradoxical that the formation of a trade bloc can either raise or lower well-being since removing barriers among member nations looks like a step toward free trade. Yet the analysis of a trade bloc is another example of the not-so-simple theory of the second best, which we discussed in Chapter 9.

The welfare effects of eliminating trade barriers between partners are illustrated in Figure 11.2, which is patterned after Britain's entry into the EC (now the EU).

To simplify the diagram greatly, all export supply curves are assumed to be perfectly flat. We consider two cases. In one, forming the trade bloc is costly because too much trade is diverted from lower-cost to higher-cost suppliers. In the other, forming the trade bloc is beneficial because it creates more low-cost trade.

In Figure 11.2A, the British could buy Japanese cars at £5,000 if there were no tariff. The next cheapest alternative is to buy German cars delivered at £5,500. If there were free trade, at point C, Britain would import only Japanese cars and none from Germany.

Before its entry, however, Britain did not have free trade in automobiles. It had a uniform tariff, imagined here to be £1,000, which marks up the cost of imported Japanese cars from £5,000 to £6,000 in Figure 11.2. No Britons buy the identical German cars because they would cost £6,500 (equal to the £5,500 price charged

FIGURE 11.2   Trade Diversion versus Trade Creation in Joining a Trade Bloc: UK Market for Imported Compact Cars

Starting from a uniform tariff on all compact cars (at point *A*), Britain joins the EU trade bloc, removing tariffs on imports from EU partners like Germany, but not on imports from the cheapest outside source, Japan. With the flat supply curves assumed here, all the original imports of 10,000 cars from the cheapest outside source are replaced with imports from new partner countries (e.g., Germany). In panel A the shift from *A* to *B* creates 5,000 extra imports, bringing national gains for the UK (area *b*). But it also diverts those 10,000 cars from the cheapest foreign supplier to the partner country, imposing extra costs (area *c*). In this case, the loss exceeds the gain, bringing a net loss:

$$\text{Gain area } b = (1/2)(6{,}000 - 5{,}500)(15{,}000 - 10{,}000) = \text{Gain of £1.25 million}$$
$$\text{Loss area } c = (5{,}500 - 5{,}000)(10{,}000) = \text{Loss of £5 million}$$
$$\text{Net loss} = \text{£3.75 million}$$

In panel B, Germany's price is not much greater than that quoted by Japanese suppliers. Removing the tariff on German (and other EU) cars creates 9,000 new imports of cars, yielding the trade-creation gain shown as area *b*. Another 10,000 cars are again diverted from the cheapest supplier (Japan), but this trade diversion costs less than in panel A. So

$$\text{Gain area } b = (1/2)(6{,}000 - 5{,}100)(19{,}000 - 10{,}000) = \text{Gain of £4.05 million}$$
$$\text{Loss area } c = (5{,}100 - 5{,}000)(10{,}000) = \text{Loss of £1.00 million}$$
$$\text{Net gain} = \text{£3.05 million}$$

by the German producers plus the £1,000 tariff). The starting point for our discussion is thus the tariff-ridden point A, with the British government collecting (£1,000 times 10,000 = £10 million) in tariff revenues.

Now let Britain join the EU, as it did in 1973, removing all tariffs on goods from the EU while leaving the same old tariffs on goods from outside the EU. Under the simplifying assumptions made here, German cars now cost only £5,500 in Britain (instead of that plus the £1,000 tariff), while the price of Japanese cars in Britain remains £6,000 because they still incur the tariff. British purchasers of imported cars switch to buying only German cars. In addition, seeing the price of imported cars fall to £5,500 in Britain, they buy more (at point B). Clearly, British car buyers have something to cheer about. They gain the areas *a* and *b* in consumer surplus, thanks to the bargain. But the British government loses all its previous tariff revenue, the area *a* + *c* (£10 million). So, after we cancel out the gain and loss of *a,* Britain ends up with two effects on its well-being:

1. A gain from trade creation (in this case, from the extra 5,000 cars). **Trade creation** is the net volume of new trade created by forming the trade bloc. It causes the national gain shown as area *b* in Figure 11.2. Area *b* represents two kinds of gain in the British economy: gains on extra consumption of the product, and gains on replacement of higher-cost British production by lower-cost partner production.

2. A welfare loss from trade diversion (in this case, from the 10,000 cars). **Trade diversion** is the volume of trade diverted from low-cost outside exporters to higher-cost bloc-partner exporters. It causes the national loss shown as area *c*.

This is the general result: The gains from a trade bloc are tied to trade creation, and the losses are tied to trade diversion.[2]

The net effect on well-being, the trade-creation gain minus the trade-diversion loss, could be positive or negative. In the first case, case A in Figure 11.2, the loss on trade diversion happens to dominate. The gain from trade creation would dominate, however, if the new customs union partners, such as Germany, were almost the lowest-cost suppliers in the world, as assumed in case B of Figure 11.2. If they

---

[2] There is an alternative analysis assuming upward-sloping supply curves for all three countries, with similar but more widely applicable results (e.g., Harry G. Johnson, 1962). One point revealed by the upward-sloping supply analysis is that trade diversion may bring terms-of-trade gains to the bloc partners at the expense of the rest of the world. Diverting demand away from outside suppliers may force them to cut their export prices (i.e., the bloc's import prices). On the export side, diverting bloc sales toward bloc customers and away from outside customers may raise the bloc's export-price index. Thus, the bloc may gain from a higher terms-of-trade ratio (= export price/import price), a possibility assumed away by the flat outside-world supply curve in Figure 11.2.

Another point revealed is that trade diversion brings gains to the partner country that is exporting the product, because its producers charge a higher price on exports to the importing partner and export a larger quantity to this partner. However, the exporting-partner gains are less than the importing-partner losses, so trade diversion still creates a net loss for the trade bloc and for the world. The flat–supply-curve case is used here because its diagram (or its algebra) makes the basic points more clearly.

can supply cars almost as cheaply as the Japanese, then there won't be much cost from diverting Britain's customers away from Japanese compact cars. Case B assumes that the trade-diversion cost is only £100 on each of the diverted 10,000 cars. At the same time, there is a lot of trade creation in case B. Removing the £1,000 tariff on German cars cuts the price of imports from the old £6,000 on Japanese cars with tariff to £5,100 on German cars without tariff, resulting in a substantial gain. In the specific case shown in Figure 11.2, case B, there is a net national (and world) gain from the effects of the customs union on trade in this kind of automobile.[3]

Reflecting the one-good cases in Figure 11.2, you can figure out what conditions dictate whether the gains outweigh the losses. Here are two tendencies that make for greater gains from a customs union:

A. The lower the partner costs relative to the outside-world costs, the greater the gains. Any trade diversion will be less costly.

B. The more elastic the import demand, the greater the gains. The trade creation in response to any domestic price decline will be larger.

So the best trade-creating case is one with costs that are almost as low somewhere within the union as in the outside world and highly elastic demands for imports. Conversely, the worst trade-diverting case is one with inelastic import demands and high costs throughout the new customs union.

OTHER POSSIBLE GAINS FROM A TRADE BLOC

Researchers have identified several other possible sources of gains from forming a trade bloc, although it is usually difficult to quantify how large these are. Several gains arise because *the trade bloc creates a larger market* (bloc-wide rather than only national) in which firms can sell their products with little or no trade barriers. It is easiest to see the possibility for these gains if we think of an extreme case in which the countries that form the bloc all had such high trade barriers before the bloc was formed that they traded little of a product with each other or with the rest of the world. Furthermore, scale economies (as discussed in Chapter 5) are important in producing this product. In this setting, here are three possible sources of additional gains from forming the trade bloc:

- *An increase in competition can reduce prices.* Before the bloc, firms in each country may have monopoly power in their separate national market, so prices are high in each national market. When the national markets are joined in the trade bloc, firms from the partner countries must compete with each other. The

---

[3] To imagine a case of pure trade creation, with no trade diversion at all, just switch the words *Germany* and *Japan* in either half of Figure 11.2. With Germany now the cheapest supplier, nobody in Britain would buy Japanese cars with or without the EU customs union. Forming the union expands trade from point *A* to point *C*, bringing the net gain *ACD*.

extra competition reduces monopoly power and reduces prices. The inefficiency of monopoly pricing is reduced.

- *An increase in competition can lower costs of production.* If firms have monopoly power and substantial protection from foreign competition, there is less pressure on them to minimize costs or implement new technologies. When the national markets are joined in the trade bloc, the extra competition forces firms to pay more attention to reducing costs and improving technology. Studies by the consulting firm McKinsey have repeatedly shown that a key determinant of the differences in the productivity of firms in different countries is the intensity of competition the firms must face.

- *Firms can lower costs by expanding their scale of production.* Before the bloc is formed, the size of a firm was largely limited by the size of its own national market. If scale economies are substantial, the firm may not be large enough to exploit all of the scale economies. When the markets are joined in the trade bloc, each firm now has a larger market to serve. Some firms may expand their size to take advantage of additional scale economies. (Other firms that cannot gain the scale economies fast enough may be driven out of business by these larger firms. This is good for the trade bloc as whole, but some member countries may feel harmed if it is their firms that disappear.)

A final possible source of gains is the possibility that *forming the trade bloc increases opportunities for business investments.* Multinational firms (discussed further in Chapter 14) often seek foreign production locations based on the size of the market that can be served by their affiliates. By expanding the market that can be served with trade barriers, a trade bloc can attract more foreign direct investment into the member countries. Global firms often bring better technologies, management practices, and marketing capabilities. If these "intangibles" diffuse to local firms (positive externalities), then the country gains an extra benefit from the direct investment by foreign firms. More broadly, by increasing the rate of return to business investments as the trade bloc opens new profit opportunities, the formation of the bloc can increase real investment and can therefore expand the overall production capacity of the partner countries.

Not all of these effects occur for every product or member country when a trade bloc is formed, but they do occur for some products and some members. They provide gains from being a member of a trade bloc that are in addition to the gains from trade creation.

THE EU EXPERIENCE

Europe has been the locus of the longest and deepest regional integration. The box "Postwar Trade Integration in Western Europe" provides the highlights of the chronology. In particular, the formation of the EU's customs union was the first major modern trade bloc. Numerous studies have examined its economic effects. Studies in the 1960s and 1970s tended to conclude that the net gains from forming the EU (then the EEC) were small but positive. For example, net gains on trade in manufactured goods calculated by Balassa (1975, p. 115) were a little over one-tenth of 1 percent of members' total GDP. That tiny positive estimate overlooks some losses from the EU, but also overlooks some likely gains. By concentrating on trade in manufactured goods, the literature generally over-looked the significant social losses from the EU's common agricultural policy. This policy protects and subsidizes agriculture so heavily as to bring serious social losses of the sort described in Chapter 10.[4] On the other hand, the studies of the 1960s and 1970s generally confined their measurements to static welfare effects like those in Figure 11.2, omitting possible gains from increased competi-tion, economies of scale, or improved productivity incentives.

Here, unfortunately, is a research frontier still unsettled: We know that economies of scale and better productivity performance are key possible out-comes of economic union, but we still lack good estimates of them. For now, the empirical judgment is threefold: (1) On manufactured goods, the EU has brought enough trade creation to suggest small positive net gains. (2) The static gains on manufactures have probably been smaller than the losses on the common agricul-tural policy. (3) But the net judgment still depends on what we believe about the unmeasured gains from competition, economies of scale, and productivity stimuli.

The formation of a truly common market in 1992 probably brought some addi-tional net gains. The 1992 unification involved removing all sorts of nontariff trade barriers:

- No longer are truckers irked by thousands of trade barriers within the EU, such as frontier checkpoint delays, paperwork, and freight-hauling restrictions.

- The change brought an end to product "quality" codes that were thinly dis-guised devices for protecting higher-cost domestic producers. Examples include German beer purity regulations, Italian pasta protection laws, Belgian chocolate content restrictions, and Greek ice cream specifications.[5] Some stan-dards were harmonized, but in most cases countries mutually recognized the validity of each other's standards.

---

[4] Trade diversion on agricultural products is one reason why empirical studies find that joining the EC in 1973 may have cost Britain dearly. The common agricultural policy meant that British consumers had to lose cheap access to their traditional Commonwealth food suppliers (Australia, Canada, and New Zealand). They had to buy the more expensive EU food products and also had to pay taxes on their remaining imports from the Commonwealth, taxes that were turned over to French, Danish, and Irish farmers as subsidies. This cost Britain an estimated 1.8 percent of GDP in the 1970s, versus a static-analysis gain of less than 0.2 percent of GDP on manufactured goods. The Thatcher government later bargained for a fairer sharing of the burdens of farm subsidies.

[5] The EU has been fashioning controversial new codes regulating the entertainment industry after 1992. In effect, the EU has put a quota on TV and film imports from the United States and other outside suppliers. EU viewers face a world with tighter restrictions on such programs as, in France, "Les Flintstones" and "Deux flics de Miami." The cultural effects are debatable: U.S. shows sometimes have been replaced by imitative EU "original" productions along the lines of the quiz shows "La roue de la fortune" and "Le juste prix."

Case Study   Postwar Trade Integration in Western Europe

1950–1952: Following the Schuman Plan, "the six" (Belgium, France, West Germany, Italy, the Netherlands, and Luxembourg) set up the European Coal and Steel Community. Meanwhile, Benelux is formed by Belgium, the Netherlands, and Luxembourg. Both formations provide instructive early examples of integration.

1957–1958: The six sign the Treaty of Rome setting up the European Economic Community (EEC or "Common Market"). Import duties among them are dismantled and their external barriers are unified in stages between the end of 1958 and mid-1968. Trade preferences are given to a host of developing countries, most of them former colonies of EEC members.

1960: The Stockholm Convention creates the European Free Trade Area (EFTA) among seven nations: Austria, Denmark, Norway, Portugal, Sweden, Switzerland, and the United Kingdom. Barriers among these nations are removed in stages, 1960–1966. Finland joins EFTA as an associate member in 1961. Iceland becomes a member in 1970, Finland becomes a full member in 1986, and Lichtenstein becomes a member in 1991.

1967: The European Community (EC) is formed by the merger of the EEC, the European Atomic Energy Commission, and the European Coal and Steel Community.

1972–1973: Denmark, Ireland, and the United Kingdom join the EC, converting the six into nine. Denmark and the United Kingdom leave EFTA. The United Kingdom agrees to abandon many of its Commonwealth trade preferences. Also, *Ode to Joy* from Beethoven's Ninth Symphony chosen as EC's anthem.

1973–1977: Trade barriers are removed in stages, both among the nine EC members and between them and the remaining EFTA nations. Meanwhile, the EC reaches trade preference agreements with most nonmember Mediterranean countries along the lines of earlier agreements with Greece (1961), Turkey (1964), Spain (1970), and Malta (1970).

1979: European Monetary System begins to operate based on the European Currency Unit. The European Parliament first elected by direct popular vote.

- Capital is now free to flow anywhere in the EU countries.

- Workers from any of the EU countries can now practice their trades and professions anywhere.

How much benefit might such a miscellany of measures bring to the EU? It is hard to say, given the difficulty of measuring such key determinants as increased economies of scale and increasing competition. Recent studies conclude that gains are probably 2 percent or less of GDP.

The EU is on the verge of a major expansion in which up to 12 countries will become members. These new members will add over 25 percent to the EU's total population. But they are relatively poor, so they will add only about 5 percent to the EU's total GDP.

The countries that want to join must meet strict requirements regarding their political, legal, and economic systems. The requirements include a commitment

1981: Greece joins the EC as its 10th full member.

1986: The admission of Portugal and Spain brings to 12 the number of full members in the EC.

1986–1987: Member governments approve and enact the Single European Act, calling for a fully unified market by 1992 and for weighted voting rules that no longer require unanimity in the European Council.

1989–1990: The collapse of the East German government brings a sudden expansion of Germany and therefore of the EC. Unemployment is initially high in the East Germany, but labor and capital start to flow in large volumes between East and West Germany. East Germans are given generous entitlements to the social programs of Germany and the EC.

1991–1995: Ten countries from Central and Eastern Europe establish trade agreements with the EU and begin the process toward EU membership.

End of 1992: The Single European Act takes effect, integrating labor and capital markets throughout the EC.

1993: The Maastricht Treaty is approved, making the EC into the European Union (EU), which calls for unification of foreign policy, for cooperation in fighting crime, and for monetary union.

1995: Following votes with majority approval in each country, Austria, Sweden, and Finland join the EU, bringing the number to 15. As it had done in 1972, Norway rejected membership in its 1994 vote.

1996: The EU forms a customs union with Turkey.

1999: Eleven EU countries establish the euro as a common currency, initially existing along with each country's own currency. Greece becomes the 12th member of the euro area in 2001.

2002: The euro replaces the national currencies of the 12 countries.

to democracy, protection of human rights, quality of government administration, and conformity of national laws to EU standards. These EU standards cover 31 major areas, and documents listing them are 80,000 pages long.

The EU and its current members also confront major questions about such a large expansion. First, there are questions about how a group of 27 countries will govern itself. The process of national voting to approve EU laws, regulations, directives, and procedures will need to be adjusted. Second, eligibility for two expensive EU programs will need to be determined. Most of the countries that will join would be large recipients of money under the current common agricultural policy and the assistance to less developed regions. It appears that payments to the new members will be phased in gradually after they join. Adjustments may also have to be made in the programs, especially the common agricultural policy. Third, there is some controversy about free movement of people. Immigration from the new members would probably go mostly to Germany and Austria, given geography and the economic opportunities. Again, it appears that free labor movement will be phased in gradually.

Ten countries—Cyprus, the Czech Republic, Estonia, Hungary, Latvia, Lithuania, Malta, Poland, Slovenia, and Slovakia—are negotiating to join as early as 2004. Romania and Bulgaria hope to join shortly after this "first wave."[6] Estimates of the economic effects of this enlargement indicate that the new members will enjoy a net gain in well-being of 2–8 percent of their GDP. There will be a small gain for the current EU members and very little impact on the rest of the world.

NORTH AMERICA BECOMES A BLOC

The Canada–U.S. Free-Trade Area

The idea of a free-trade area between Canada and the United States has been debated since the 19th century. As late as 1986, when the two countries had a minor trade war over lumber and corn plus another tiff over Arctic navigational rights, there seemed little chance of forming a trade bloc. But in 1987–1988 the mood swung around and a pact was signed after all. Do the effects show more trade creation than trade diversion? Does Canada or the United States gain more?

Economists tend to expect greater absolute effects on Canada than on the United States. The basic reasoning surfaced back in Chapter 2, where we reasoned that the absolute net national gains should be distributed in proportion to the two nations' price changes caused by the opening of new trade. We expect that Canada's import-demand and export-supply curves are less elastic than the U.S. curves. Therefore, opening new trade should shift Canadian prices more than U.S. prices. If so, the net national gains should be absolutely greater for Canada. So should the relative-price shock to different parts of the economy. Import-competing producers are likely to be hurt more, and consumers and exporters helped more, in Canada than in the United States, even in absolute dollar terms.

Suspecting as much, most studies of the Canada–U.S. free-trade area focused on Canada's stake in it. Some studies concluded that Canada would gain 1 to 2.5 percent of its GDP. A few studies concluded that Canada could gain much more—its GDP could increase by 8 to 10 percent thanks to the free-trade pact, a far larger gain than any EU country has ever gotten from the Common Market so far. In these high estimates more than half of Canada's gain comes from the opening of U.S. markets, rather than from Canada's own removal of trade barriers. Better access to U.S. markets seems especially important in studies that reckon there are economies of scale to be reaped by Canadian industry when faced with a much bigger market.

Studies of the actual effects on Canadian manufacturing industries during the first 10 years of free trade with the United States do show some large positive effects. Increased competition has led to the shutdown of high-cost Canadian

---

[6] Turkey has also been actively seeking to join, but the EU so far has expressed doubts about its ability to meet the governmental and human-rights requirements.

factories and the opening of low-cost ones. Average plant sizes have not gotten much bigger, which seems to question the role of increased economies of scale. But there is some evidence that fewer different products are being produced in these plants, so the economies of scale are probably occurring through longer production runs of the smaller number of products. As a result of all of this, labor productivity in Canadian manufacturing has increased about 5 percent more than it would have without the free-trade area.

Mexico's Liberalization and NAFTA

Starting in 1985, the Mexican government became increasingly determined to break down its own barriers to a freer, more privatized Mexican economy. A series of reforms deregulated business and knocked down barriers to imports of goods and services from other countries. The culmination of this economic liberalization drive was the 1993 signing of an agreement with the United States and Canada to form the **North American Free Trade Area (NAFTA).** NAFTA eliminates tariffs and some nontariff barriers on trade within the area, with some liberalizations phased in over 5- to 15-year periods. It removes barriers to cross-border business investments within the area, and Mexico must phase out performance requirements, including local content requirements and export requirements, that the Mexican government had imposed on foreign businesses operating in Mexico. NAFTA requires open trade and investment in most service industries (including banking and other financial services). Supplemental agreements call for better enforcement of labor and environmental standards, but these have had little effect. NAFTA does not, however, call for free human migration between these countries, nor does it denationalize Pemex, Mexico's huge government oil monopoly.

NAFTA was controversial, especially in Mexico and the United States, from the moment it became a strong political possibility in 1990. Critics in Mexico sounded the alarm that Mexican jobs would be wiped out, widening the already enormous gaps between rich and poor in Mexico. They also warned that the United States would use NAFTA to force Mexico to make many changes in its policies, weakening Mexican sovereignty. On the other side of the border, American labor groups were convinced that they would lose their jobs to Mexicans, whose wage rates were only a tiny fraction of those paid in the United States. This concern was dramatized by H. Ross Perot's famous claim in 1992 that NAFTA would cause a "great sucking sound" as many American jobs were instantly shifted to Mexico. Critics in the United States also decried that NAFTA rewarded and strengthened a corrupt political system in Mexico. In addition, environmentalists in both countries feared that NAFTA would lead to an expansion of the already serious pollution in Mexico, especially in the *maquiladora* industrial towns along the U.S.–Mexican border.

Proponents in Mexico hoped to use NAFTA to have some influence on U.S. trade policies like antidumping, a goal that the Canadians also had for the Canada–U.S. Free Trade Area. They also expected Mexico to attract more investments into Mexico from foreign businesses using Mexico as a base for North

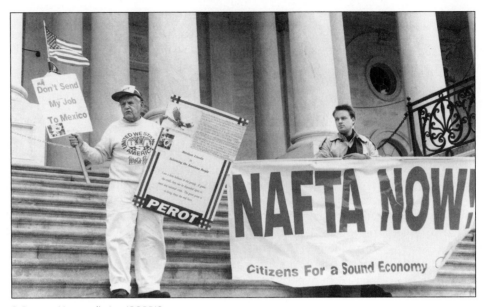

© Reuters Newmedia Inc./CORBIS

American production. Proponents in the United States hoped to solidify the market-oriented reforms in Mexico, making Mexico a more dependable economic and political ally. But proponents of NAFTA were also extravagant in some of their claims, particularly when asserting that defeating NAFTA would send the Mexican economy into a giant depression, forcing an unemployed army to march over the U.S. border in search of jobs.

Concerns over jobs and the environment were so severe within the United States and Canada that they nearly defeated NAFTA. Yet in the end, the proponents prevailed and NAFTA became official at the beginning of 1994.

To get an idea of what is happening as NAFTA frees up trade between Mexico and its neighbors to the north, we can start by looking at actual experience in the years just before NAFTA. Mexico in fact began slashing import barriers as early as 1985 in a bold campaign to bring more competition and efficiency to the Mexican economy. Mexico's tariffs had always been high and were raised even higher after the debt crisis forced Mexico to tighten its belt in 1982. By 1992 they were slashed to an average tariff of only 10 percent on goods from the United States. Meanwhile, U.S. tariffs on goods from Mexico averaged only about 4 percent by 1992. There was more liberalization of trade *before* NAFTA than the hotly debated NAFTA itself could add. During this pre-NAFTA liberalization, incomes and jobs grew both in Mexico and in the United States and Canada, though this basic point went unnoticed by those who foresaw economic doom in NAFTA.

Trying to estimate the effects of NAFTA almost became a new industry in itself. Consulting firms, government economists, and academics produced a variety of forecasts comparing the NAFTA world with a non-NAFTA world. The carefully conducted studies agree in their guarded optimism about the net national effects: The gains from trade creation and other effects are larger than the losses from trade diversion. All three countries will be slight net gainers, and the rest of the world will suffer only negligible damage if any. Figure 11.3 shows a set of estimates that typify the results of the most extensive studies. According to the multisectoral "computable general equilibrium model" of Drusilla Brown, Alan Deardorff, and Robert Stern, Mexico would be the biggest gainer in percent terms, especially in the part of the estimates that adds in the effects of the likely acceleration of foreign investment in Mexico. Canada's predicted gains come in second as a share of the initial levels of national income or wages (though the absolute size of any effect on Canada is probably the smallest of the three countries' absolute effects). The United States is the least affected in percent terms, basically because the U.S. economy is by far the largest of the three, and because most U.S. import barriers removed by NAFTA were already low. Other investigations generally agree with this verdict that NAFTA will raise national incomes and even the demand for labor, though some talk about creating extra jobs instead of about raising wage rates.

Is NAFTA really likely to help everybody? Is there no major group that is hurt by this movement to freer trade? Yes, somebody is hurt. NAFTA corresponds to the kind of result we kept finding in earlier chapters: Freer trade (in this case, NAFTA's discriminatory freeing of trade) absolutely hurts import-competing groups even though the net effect on whole nations or the whole world is positive. Who is hurt in the United States? The main sectors where U.S. incomes and jobs are lost to Mexican competition are apparel (clothing), field crops (e.g., tomatoes), furniture, and autos. On the other hand, Mexico buys more U.S. financial services, chemicals, plastics, and high-tech equipment.

There is a pattern here. The kinds of sectors where U.S. incomes and jobs are affected most by Mexican competition are those that involve less-skilled labor.

FIGURE 11.3
Estimates of the Effects of the North American Free Trade Area on National Incomes and Wage Rates

Percent Changes over a World without NAFTA as Predicted by the Brown–Deardorff–Stern "Computable General Equilibrium Model"

	In Mexico	In United States	In Canada	In the Rest of the World
Effects of Removing Trade Barriers within NAFTA, with No Effects on Capital Flows				
Real national income	1.6	0.1	0.7	–0.0
Real average wage rate	0.7	0.2	0.4	–0.1
Effects of Removing Trade Barriers within NAFTA, with Induced Capital Flows into Mexico				
Real national income	5.0	0.3	0.7	–0.0
Real average wage rate	9.3	0.2	0.5	–0.0

Source: Drusilla K. Brown, Alan V. Deardorff, and Robert M. Stern (1992), as cited in Nora Lustig, Barry Bosworth, and Robert Z. Lawrence (1992), pp. 44–47, 220.

NAFTA allows Mexico's low-skilled apparel workers, for example, the easy access to the U.S. market that they and their Asian competitors have long been denied. Jobs are lost in some U.S. apparel establishments as some of the U.S. clothing firms "outsource" these tasks to Mexico. Foreseeing such a likelihood, the U.S. legislation approving NAFTA called for retraining and other adjustment assistance to import-damaged workers and firms such as those in the apparel sector. For the first six years of NAFTA, about 44,000 workers per year were certified for adjustment assistance. This number rose in 2001 to about 80,000 workers. The magnitudes of job losses seem small in aggregate national perspective. In Mexico too there have been job and wage-rate losses, but they are localized and overshadowed by job and wage-rate gains.

The other group hurt by NAFTA consists of those outside world producers of goods in which Mexico's exports to its northern neighbors displace their exports. NAFTA causes some trade diversion, especially from Asia. Asian makers of cars, clothing, furniture, financial services, and high-tech equipment suffer losses. These losses usually are not large, however, as implied by the low figures in the far-right column in Figure 11.3.

One other seemingly technical feature of NAFTA has received a surprising amount of attention. Because each member of a free-trade area maintains its own barriers against imports from outside the area, a member country must still police its borders, to tax or prohibit imports that might otherwise avoid its higher external barriers by entering through a lower-barrier partner country. Its customs officials must enforce **rules of origin** that determine which products have been produced within the free-trade area, so that they are traded freely within the area, and which products have not been produced within the area. These rules guard against a firm's ruse of doing minimal processing within the area and then claiming that the product is locally produced.

The NAFTA rules of origin are incredibly complex, covering over 200 pages with thousands of different rules for different products. Analysis of these rules has concluded that many of them are protectionist, acting like regional local content requirements. Here is another, more subtle reason for producers from the rest of the world to lose. For instance, the rules of origin for automobiles indicate that autos can trade between NAFTA countries freely only if they have at least 62.5 percent value from North American parts and production. This rule benefits U.S. auto companies and hurts foreign auto companies, even if the latter have assembly facilities in North America. It also reduces world well-being and, probably, North American well-being.

TRADE BLOCS AMONG DEVELOPING COUNTRIES

In several less developed settings in the 1960s and 1970s, a different idea of gains from a trade bloc took shape. The infant industry argument held sway. It was easy to imagine that forming a customs union or free-trade area among developing countries would give the union a market large enough to support a large-scale producer in each modern manufacturing sector without letting in manufacturers from the industrialized countries. The new firms could eventually cut their costs through economies of scale and learning by doing until they could compete internationally, perhaps even without protection.

For all the appeal of the idea, its practice "has been littered with failures," as Pomfret has put it, and the life expectancy of this type of trade bloc was short. The Latin American Free Trade Area (Mexico and all the South American republics) lacked binding commitment to free internal trade even at its creation in 1960, and by 1969 it had effectively split into small groups with minimal bilateral agreements. The Central American Common Market, also created in 1960, scored some small victories for a decade but fell apart in the 1970s. Other short-lived unions with only minimal concessions by their members included a chain of Caribbean unions; the East African Community (Kenya, Tanzania, and Uganda), which disbanded in 1977; and several other African attempts. One centrifugal force was the inherent inequality of benefits from the new import-substituting industries. If economies of scale were to be reaped, the new industrial gains would inevitably be concentrated into one or a few industrial centers. Every member wanted to be the group's new industrial leader, and none wanted to remain more agricultural. No formula for gains-sharing could be worked out. Even the Association of Southeast Asian Nations (ASEAN), with its broader industrial base, was unable to reach stable agreements about freer trade when this was tried in the late 1970s and early 1980s. Mindful of this experience, most experts became skeptical about the chances for great gains from most developing-country trade blocs.

Yet the same institution can succeed later, even after earlier setbacks, especially if economic and political conditions have changed. As we have seen, the idea of a free-trade area between Canada and the United States failed to get launched for about a century before its time arrived.

The key change in the trade policies since the 1970s, as we will examine in more depth in Chapter 13, has been a shift in development philosophy, toward an outward, pro-trade (or at least pro-export) orientation. As in the case of Mexico, many developing countries have pursued economic reforms to liberalize government policies toward trade and business activity more generally. Forming a trade bloc can be part of this thrust to liberalize (although, as we have seen, it is actually liberalizing internal trade while discriminating against external trade).

There is already one major case of Latin American success (so far) despite earlier failures. In 1991, Argentina, Brazil, Paraguay, and Uruguay formed MERCOSUR, which by 1995 had established internal free trade and common external tariffs (averaging 12 percent) for most products, with the rest to be completed by 2006. One highly protected sector is automobiles, with an external tariff of about 34 percent (and an effective rate of protection of over 100 percent). In 1996, Chile became an associate member and established a free-trade area with the MERCOSUR countries, and Bolivia also established an associate agreement. MERCOSUR came under considerable strain with the Brazilian monetary crisis of 1999 and the Argentinean monetary crisis that began in 2001.

Still, trade among MERCOSUR countries has increased rapidly since 1991. One study of the effects of MERCOSUR concluded that it will increase real national incomes by 1 to 2 percent, with much of the gain coming from economies of scale and the benefits of increasing competition among firms from different MERCOSUR countries. However, other observers are more cautious, because trade within MERCOSUR has increased most rapidly in protected capital-intensive products like automobiles, machinery, and electronic goods—products that are not consistent with the member countries' global comparative advantage. It is likely that substantial trade diversion is occurring in these products, and the losses from trade diversion must be set against other gains. MERCOSUR is a success in terms of survival and increasing internal trade, but its net effects on the well-being of its member countries are not yet clear.

TRADE EMBARGOES

Trade discrimination can be more belligerent—a trade block instead of a trade bloc. A nation or group of nations can keep ordinary barriers on its trade with most countries, but insist on making trade with a particular country or countries difficult or impossible. To wage economic warfare, nations have often imposed economic sanctions, embargoes, or boycotts. The term *sanctions* is the most general, referring to either discriminatory restrictions or complete bans on economic exchange. Embargoes and boycotts both refer to complete bans. What is being restricted or banned can be ordinary trade, or it can be trade in services or assets, as in the case of a ban on loans to a particular country.

Waging economic warfare with trade embargoes and other economic sanctions dates back at least to the fifth century BC. In the 1760s the American colonists boycotted English goods as a protest against the infamous Stamp Act and Townshend Acts. In this case, the boycott succeeded—Parliament responded by repealing those acts. The practice of economic sanctions was more frequent in the latter half of the 20th century than in any earlier peacetime era, and the use of sanctions has increased since 1990. The United States practices economic warfare more readily than any other country. In 1998, over 75 foreign countries were the target of some form of economic sanction imposed by a U.S. governmental unit (federal, state, or local). One estimate indicated that up to $20 billion of U.S. exports per year were blocked by sanctions in the mid-1990s, at a net cost to the country of about $1 billion per year.

The effects of banning economic exchanges are easy to imagine. A country's refusal to trade with a "target" country hurts both of them economically, and it creates opportunities for third countries. But who gets hurt the most? The least? Magnitudes matter because they determine whether the damage to the target rewards the initiating country enough to compensate for its own losses on the prohibited trade.

To discover basic determinants of the success or failure of economic sanctions, let us consider a particular kind: a total embargo (prohibition) on exports to

FIGURE 11.4   Effects of an Embargo on Exports to Iraq

Moving from free trade (*F*) to an embargo (*E*) means

Embargoing countries lose	*a*
Iraq loses	*b* + *c*
Other countries gain	*b*
World as a whole loses	$\overline{a + c}$

the target country.[7] Figure 11.4 imagines a total embargo on exports to Iraq. The example portrays one side of the restrictions imposed on Iraq by many countries since 1990, when Iraq first invaded Kuwait. In addition to these restrictions on exports to Iraq, the countries applying sanctions also have refused to import oil or other goods from Iraq or to lend to Iraq. The sanctions were mandated under a United Nations resolution, and most major powers have participated in this action against Iraq. Still, Jordan, Iran, and some other nations have been more sympathetic to Iraq and allowed some trade to continue.

In picturing international trade we will be careful to show export supply to Iraq from both embargoing and nonembargoing countries, even before the embargo. The export supply to Iraq from the nonembargoing countries is shown in Figure 11.4B as S_n, a limited and rather inelastic supply. The export supply from the embargoing countries (before they impose the embargo) is the difference between their domestic supply and domestic demand, which are shown in Figure 11.4A. If we add the two sources of export supply together, we get the total export supply, $S_n + S_e$, available to Iraq before the embargo.

[7] The case of an embargo on imports from the target country is symmetrical to the export case studied here. In standard trade models, the symmetry is exact. As we noted in Part I, the net gains and losses on the export side and those on the import side are the same thing in two guises. As an exercise at the end of this chapter, you are invited to diagram the import embargo case and to identify the gains and losses and what makes them large or small.

Before the embargo, Iraq's import demand (D_m) equals the total export supply at point F on the right side of Figure 11.4. The price is P_0, and Iraq imports Q_0.

When countries decide to put an embargo on exports to Iraq, part of the world export supply to Iraq vanishes. In Figure 11.4B the export supply S_e is removed by the embargo. The remaining export supply to Iraq is only S_n. With their imports thus restricted, Iraqis find importable goods scarcer. The price rises from P_0 to P_1, as the free-trade equilibrium F shifts to the embargo equilibrium E. The new scarcity costs Iraq as a nation the area $b + c$ for reasons already described in Chapter 2 and Chapters 7 through 9. It also has its economic costs for the countries enforcing the embargo, however. They lose area a. The loss a is shown in two equivalent ways: on the left as a difference between producer losses and consumer gains, and on the right as a loss of surplus on exports. Meanwhile, countries not participating in the embargo gain area b on extra sales to Iraq at a higher price. What the world as a whole loses is therefore area $a + c$, the loss from restricting world trade.

Within countries on the two sides of the embargo, different groups will be affected differently. In the embargoing countries (e.g., Canada, the United Kingdom, the United States), the embargo lowers the price below P_0, slightly helping some consumers while hurting producers. Within Iraq, there might be a similar division (not graphed in Figure 11.4), with some import-competing producers benefiting from the removal of foreign competition, while other groups are damaged to a greater extent.

If the embargo brings economic costs to both sides, why do it? Clearly, the countries imposing the embargo have decided to sacrifice area a, the net gains on trade with Iraq, for some other goal, such as preventing Iraq's aggression against its neighbors, forcing Iraq to reveal and destroy germ and other weapons, or forcing the Iraqi government to respect the human rights of minorities. By their actions the embargoing governments imply that putting pressure on Iraq is worth more than area a. The lost area a is presumably not a measure of economic irrationality, but rather a willing sacrifice for a noneconomic goal. As Figure 11.4 is drawn, the hypothetical export embargo is imagined to cause Iraq more economic damage, measured by area $b + c$, than the embargoers' loss represented by area a.[8]

---

[8] In the real-world debate over sanctions, critics consistently argue that the sanctions would harm large numbers of innocent civilians, whose right to a better government is a political outcome that sanctions are supposed to bring about. Thus, in the case of worldwide sanctions against South Africa (1986–1993), critics argued that the sanctions would lower incomes of "nonwhite" South Africans, the very groups the sanctions were supposed to help liberate. It has similarly been argued that sanctions against Iraq have harmed mainly children and minorities. This may be correct in the short run, as all sides of the debate have long known.

To judge whether the sanctions are in the best interests of the oppressed within the target country, the best guide would be their own majority opinion. That opinion is not easily weighed in a context of disenfranchisement, press censorship, and tight police controls. The foreign governments imposing sanctions imply that the policy gains are worth more than their own loss of area a plus the short-run losses that they believe that oppressed parties in the target country are willing to sustain for the cause.

If the targeted regime holds firm to its policy (or its whim), despite the economic losses, then the regime's part of the losses is a lower-bound measure of what it thought the controversial policies are worth to it. If the regime changes the policies as demanded, then the policies were worth less to it than the implied costs.

Embargoes can fail, of course. In a study of sanctions imposed between 1945 and 2000, Gary Hufbauer and Jeffrey Schott concluded that sanctions imposed by the United States failed to affect the policies of the target country in about half the cases before 1970 and about four-fifths of the cases since then. There are two ways in which trade embargoes fail: political failure and economic failure.

Political failure of an embargo occurs when the target country's national decision-makers have so much stake in the policy that provoked the embargoes that they will stick with that policy even if the economic cost to their nation becomes extreme. Such political stubbornness is very likely if the target country is a dictatorship and the dictatorship would be jeopardized by retreating from the policy that provoked the embargo. In such a case, the dictatorship will refuse to budge even as the economic costs mount.

An example of political failure of economically "successful" sanctions was Saddam Hussein's refusal to retreat from Kuwait or, after Iraq was driven from Kuwait, to step down from power. Defenders of the idea of pressuring Saddam Hussein with sanctions were right in asserting that sanctions would bring greater damage to the economy of Iraq than to the embargoing countries. One estimate is that the sanctions have imposed a net cost to Iraq of $10 billion per year. Yet Saddam Hussein's grip on power was so firm in the 1990s that he could be neither removed from power nor forced to make a major change in certain policies, even if a majority of Iraqi citizens suffered great hardship. A counterexample was the UN-based sanctions imposed on South Africa in 1986, which succeeded in hastening the end of apartheid and the minority-rule police state.

The second kind of failure is **economic failure of an embargo,** in which the embargo inflicts little damage on the target country but possibly even great damage on the imposing country. The basic economics of embargoes can contribute to our explanation of why some attempts succeed while others fail. Figure 11.5 leads us to the key points by showing two kinds of (export) embargoes that fail economically. In both cases, elasticities of supply and demand are the key.

In Figure 11.5A, the countries imposing the embargo have a very inelastic export supply curve, implying that their producers really depend on their export business in the target country. Banning such exports and erasing the supply curve S_e from the marketplace costs the embargoing nation(s) a large area a. The target country, by contrast, has a very elastic import demand curve D_m. It cuts its demand greatly when the price goes up even slightly, from P_0 to P_1. Apparently, it can do fairly well with supplies from nonembargoing countries (the S_n curve alone). Accordingly, it loses only the small areas $b + c$. Any nation considering an embargo in such a case must contemplate sustaining the large loss a, in pursuit of only a small damage ($b + c$) to the target country. What works against the embargo in Figure 11.5A is the low elasticity of the embargoing country itself and the high elasticity of either the target country's import demand or its access to competing nonembargo supplies.

Figure 11.5B shows a case in which the embargo "fails" in the milder sense of having little economic effect on either side. Here the embargoing country is fortunate to have an elastic curve of its own (S_e) so that doing without the extra trade costs it only a slight area a. On the other hand, the target country also has the

FIGURE 11.5 Two Kinds of Economically Unsuccessful Embargoes

In panel A the cost to the embargoers, *a,* is much larger than the damage, *b + c,* to the target country. In panel B the costs to both sides are negligible because elasticities are so high.

elastic demand curve D_m and access to the elastic competing supplies S_n. Therefore it sustains only the slight damage *b + c* and presumably can defy the embargo for a long time.

So embargoes and other economic sanctions apply stronger pressure when the embargoing country or countries have high elasticities and the target countries have low ones. When is this likely to be true? Our simple analysis offers suggestions that seem to show up in the real world:

1. Big countries pick on small ones. A country (or group of countries) with a large share of world trade can impose sanctions on a small one without feeling much effect. In economic terms, the big country is likely to have highly elastic trade curves (like S_e in the examples here) because it can deal with much larger markets outside the target country. A small target country, on the other hand, may depend heavily on its trade with the large country or countries. Its economic vulnerability is summarized by low elasticities for trade curves like D_m and S_n. Little wonder that the typical postwar embargo is one imposed by the United States on smaller-trading nations like Cuba, Iran, Nicaragua, and Nigeria.

2. Sanctions have more chance of success if they are extreme and sudden when first imposed. Recall that the damage *b + c* is larger, the lower the target country's trade elasticities. Elasticities are lower in the short run than in the long run, and they are lower when a massive share of national product is involved. The more time the target country has to adjust, the more it can learn to conserve on the embargoed products and develop alternative supplies. Of course, quick and sudden action also raises the damage to the initiating country itself (area *a*), so success may be premised on the embargoing country's having alternatives set up in advance, alternatives that raise its elasticities and shrink area *a*.

3. As suggested by the definition and example of political failure, embargoes have more chance of changing a target government's policies when the citizens hurt by the embargo can apply political pressure on the stubborn head(s) of state, as in a democracy. In a strict dictatorship, the dictator can survive the economic damage to citizens and can hold out longer.

The first of these three points provides insight into why the effectiveness of unilateral sanctions imposed only by the United States has changed over time. In the 1950s, when the United States was predominant, its own sanctions could have some effect on countries like Iran and even Britain and France (in the Suez Canal dispute). With the growth of other countries and their economies, unilateral U.S. sanctions have become much less effective, because S_n (from the rest of the world) has expanded and become more elastic.

One U.S. response has been to push for UN mandates for sanctions that direct all countries to participate. Before 1990, the only UN-mandated sanctions were against South Africa and Rhodesia (now Zimbabwe). Since 1990, the UN has established sanctions against Iraq, Serbia, Somalia, Libya, Liberia, Haiti, Angola, Rwanda, and Sierra Leone.

Another U.S. response has been much more controversial—the use of secondary sanctions to compel other countries to join the U.S. sanctions. For instance, the Helms–Burton Act threatens sanctions to stop foreign firms from making new investments in oil and gas production in Iran and Libya. Foreign countries strongly object to such pressures on their firms. The president has delayed enforcing these laws, but they remain dangerous—they threaten to turn (potential) allies into enemies.

Summary

The **trade bloc** revolution beginning in the late 1980s has raised the importance of trade discrimination. The European Union has developed a true **common market** with uniformity of virtually all regulations and taxes on trade and factor movements, and the EU is progressing toward its stated goal of **economic union,** in which all economic policies are unified. From the Treaty of Rome in 1957 to 1992, the EU had adopted the less binding kind of economic bloc called a **customs union,** in which member countries adopt a uniform external tariff and remove all tariffs and quotas on trade among themselves.

The basic three-country model of a trade bloc shows that its economic benefits for the partner countries and the world depend on its **trade creation,** the amount by which it raises the total volume of world trade. Its costs depend on its **trade diversion,** the volume of trade it diverts from lower-cost outside suppliers to higher-cost partner-country suppliers. Other possible sources of gains to members of a trade bloc include increased competition that lower prices or costs, enhanced ability to achieve scale economies, and attracting more direct investment by foreign companies.

Whether a trade bloc is good or bad overall depends on the difference between its gains from trade creation (and any other positive effects) and its losses from trade diversion. In the case of the EU, for manufactured products, most economists think that its trade creation has slightly outweighed its trade diversion. The 1992 market integration added to the net gains.

Another form of trade bloc is the **free-trade area,** in which member countries remove all tariffs and quotas on trade among themselves but keep their separate barriers on trade with nonmember countries. In this case, member countries must use **rules of origin** and maintain customs administration on the borders between themselves to keep outside products from entering the high-barrier countries cheaply by way of their low-barrier partners. Examples of free-trade areas are the European Free Trade Area created in 1960 and the North American Free Trade Agreement (NAFTA) that came into existence in 1994.

Efforts by developing countries to form trade blocs failed in the 1960s and 1970s, but they have become more successful in the 1990s. Trade among the MERCOSUR countries in South America has expanded rapidly since the bloc was formed in 1991, but some of this expanded intrabloc trade is trade diversion.

Another form of trade discrimination is economic sanctions, such as a trade embargo. Our basic analysis of an export embargo (which has effects symmetrical with those of an import embargo) reveals how the success or failure of such economic warfare depends on trade elasticities. Success is more likely when the embargoing countries have high trade elasticities, meaning that they can easily do without the extra trade. Success is also more likely when the target country has low trade elasticities, meaning that it cannot easily do without trading with the embargoing countries. As the simple theory implies, embargoes are typically imposed by large trading countries on smaller ones, and success is more likely the quicker and more extreme the sanctions.

Suggested Reading

The trade bloc literature is usefully surveyed in Pomfret (1997). Baldwin and Venables (1995) present a technical survey. The World Bank (2000) summarizes its own work on trade blocs. On the economics of the European Union, see Neal and Barbezat (1998) and the Organization for Economic Cooperation and Development (2000). On the 1992 changes, see Cecchini (1988) and Flam (1992).

The predicted effects of the North American Free Trade Area are summarized by Hufbauer and Schott (1993). The larger liberalization of the Mexican economy is analyzed by Lustig (1992). On Canada's stake in trade liberalization, see Wonnacott and Wonnacott (1967, 1982) and Morici (1991). Burfisher, Robinson, and Thierfelder (2001) and Mutti (2001) looks at NAFTA's first years. Flores (1997) provides an analysis of MERCOSUR. Schott (2001) examines the proposed Free Trade Area of the Americas.

The economics and the foreign policy effects of trade embargoes are well analyzed in Hufbauer and Schott (2002). Judgment on sanctions against South Africa was rendered by Hayes (1987).

Questions and Problems

♦ 1. What is the difference between a free-trade area and a customs union?

2. Are trade blocs consistent with the most favored nation principle?

♦ 3. How are trade creation and trade diversion defined, and what roles do they play in the world gains and losses from a trade bloc?

4. Why are rules of origin needed for a free-trade area? How might they be protectionist?

♦ 5. Homeland is about to join Furrinerland in a free-trade area. Before the union, Homeland imports 10 million transistor radios from the outside world market at $100 and adds a tariff of $30 on each radio. It takes $110 to produce each transistor radio in Furrinerland.

  a. Once the free-trade area is formed, what will be the cost to Homeland of the transistor radio trade diverted to Furrinerland?

  b. How much extra imports would have to be generated in Homeland to offset this trade-diversion welfare cost?

6. Which countries are likely to gain, and which are likely to lose, from the North American Free Trade Area? How are the gains and losses likely to be distributed across occupations and sectors of the Mexican economy? The U.S. economy?

♦ 7. Suppose that the United States currently imports 1.0 million pairs of shoes from China at $20 each. With a 50 percent tariff, the consumer price in the United States is $30. The price of shoes in Mexico is $25. Suppose that as a result of NAFTA, the United States imports 1.2 million pairs of shoes from Mexico and none from China. What are the gains and losses to U.S. consumers, U.S. producers, the U.S. government, and the world as a whole?

8. What kinds of countries tend to use economic embargoes? Do embargoes have a greater chance of succeeding if they are applied gradually rather than suddenly?

♦ 9. Which of the following trade policy moves is most certain to bring gains to the world as a whole: (*a*) imposing a countervailing duty against an existing foreign export subsidy, (*b*) forming a customs union in place of a set of tariffs equally applied to imports from all countries, or (*c*) levying an antidumping import tariff? (This question draws on material from Chapter 10 as well as from this chapter.)

10. Draw the diagram corresponding to Figure 11.4 for an embargo on imports from the target country. Identify the losses and gains to the embargoing countries, the target country, and other countries. Describe what values of elasticities are more likely to give power to the embargo effort and what values of elasticities are more likely to weaken it.

Chapter Twelve

Trade and the Environment

Protection. For free traders, this word represents the consummate evil. For environmentalists, it is the ultimate good. Of course, for the trade community, "protection" conjures up images of Smoot and Hawley, while the environmental camp sees clear mountain streams, lush green forests, and piercing blue skies.

Daniel C. Esty, 2001

As nations interact more and more with each other, they have more and more effect on each other's natural environments. Often the international environmental effects are negative, as when activity in one nation pollutes other nations' air and water, or when it uses up natural resources on which other nations depend. These environmental concerns have become irreversibly global and are a growing source of international friction.

Inevitably, international trade has been drawn into the environmental spotlight, both as an alleged culprit in environmental damage and as a hostage to be taken in international environmental disputes. This chapter addresses the rising debate over the proper role of government policies in attacking environmental problems when the problems and policies have international effects.

IS FREE TRADE ANTI-ENVIRONMENT?

One attack on international trade is that it makes environmental problems worse. For instance, perhaps free trade simply promotes production or consumption of products that tend to cause large amounts of pollution. It is difficult to evaluate such a broad claim as this. But it is easy to find cases of the opposite, where government policies that limit or distort trade result in environmental damage. In the early 1980s, the United States forced Japan to limit its exports of autos to the

United States. As a result, U.S. consumers tended to buy U.S. cars that were less fuel-efficient than the Japanese cars they could no longer buy, probably resulting in more pollution. Another well-researched case is the environmental effects of government policies that protect domestic agriculture. The web of import limits and export and production subsidies leads to excessive use of pesticides and fertilizers as protected farmers strive to expand production. Free trade would lead to farming that is more friendly to the environment.

Some kinds of trade can help efforts to protect the environment. Freer trade in capital equipment that incorporates environmentally friendly technologies and freer trade in environmental services can be conduits for improved environmental practices, especially in developing countries.

One fear of environmentalists is that free trade permits production to be shifted to countries that have lax environmental standards. Exports from these "pollution havens" then would serve demand in countries with tighter standards, with the result that total world pollution is higher. However, research on relocation of production in response to differences in environmental standards finds that the effects are small. The costs to firms of meeting environmental protection regulations are usually small (less than 1 or 2 percent of sales revenues), even in the most stringent countries, so the incentive to relocate is usually small. In addition, many companies refrain from setting up high-pollution operations in lax countries because of fears of unexpected liabilities in cases of accidents, general risks to corporate reputations from appearing to cause excessive harm to the environment, and the costs of meeting more stringent regulations that are likely to be adopted in the future in these countries.

Let's turn to look at a concrete example of a recent global shift to freer international trade: the agreements reached during the Uruguay Round of trade negotiations. Does the expansion of trade resulting from these agreements harm or help the environment?

- Our analysis from Chapter 3 indicates that freer trade will alter the *composition* of what is produced and consumed in each country. As the composition of what is produced and consumed changes, the total amounts of pollution will change.

- That analysis also shows that there will be additional gains from trade. These gains could set up two different effects.

  a. The *size* of the economy is larger. The increase in production and consumption probably leads to more pollution, other things being equal.

  b. The higher *income* can lead to more pressure on governments to enact tougher environmental protection policies. For instance, stricter government policies may lead firms to clean up wastes before they are released into the environment or to switch to production methods that create less pollution per unit produced. Demand for a clean environment is a normal good.

Before examining the effects of the Uruguay Round, it's useful to look at how the size and income effects play against each other. How do rising production, consumption, and income in a country actually affect environmental quality?

When income per person (our overall indicator of size and income) rises, does the environment deteriorate or improve? That is, which is larger, the harm from the size effect or the environmental protection from the income effect?

There are likely to be different general patterns for this combined size–income effect, depending on what kind of environmental problem we are examining. Here are the three basic patterns:

1. *Environmental harm declines with rising income per person.* For some issues, the benefits of better environmental quality are so large that the income effect is dominant over (almost) the entire range of income per person. That is, the demand for better environmental quality as income rises is simply larger than any adverse effects from rising production scale.

2. *Environmental harm rises with rising income per person.* For some other issues, the benefits of preventing environmental harm are not considered to be large. The adverse effects from rising size dominate any modest increases in demand for better environmental quality.

3. *The relationship is an inverted U.* For yet other issues, the demand for better environment quality is weak at first, perhaps because the focus when people are poor is on developing production to reduce the grip of material poverty. When income is low, people are willing to accept some environmental harm to increase production and income. This damage rises as economic activity rises. But, at some point at which the dire effects of poverty have been reduced enough, the demand for better environmental quality becomes more forceful. As incomes rise further, more stringent government regulation takes over. The environmental harm declines even though production and consumption are increasing.

Figure 12.1 provides some examples of these patterns for different environmental issues. Some very basic environmental dangers, including airborne heavy particles and lead in water, tend to fall as income rises, as shown in panel A. Some environmental problems rise with greater income, as shown in panel B. These include emissions of carbon dioxide, which we will discuss later in this chapter. The demand to reduce this pollutant is not particularly strong even when incomes are high. The harm from global warming is rather abstract, the costs of reducing these emissions are substantial, and the problem is global, so actions by any one country would have little effect on the problem.

Panel C of Figure 12.1 shows the inverted-U relationship.[1] The pollutants that fit this pattern tend to be those that cause harm within the region or country, so regional or national efforts to abate the pollution provide benefits to the people in that locale. This pattern has been found for such air pollutants as sulfur dioxide (which causes acid rain), airborne particulates, and lead, and such water pollutants as fecal coliform (resulting from inadequate containment or treatment of

---

[1] The inverted-U shape is sometimes called the environmental Kuznets curve, named after the Nobel Prize winner Simon Kuznets. His research on the effects of economic development found an inverted-U relationship between per capita income and income inequality.

FIGURE 12.1   Environmental Problems by Income Level

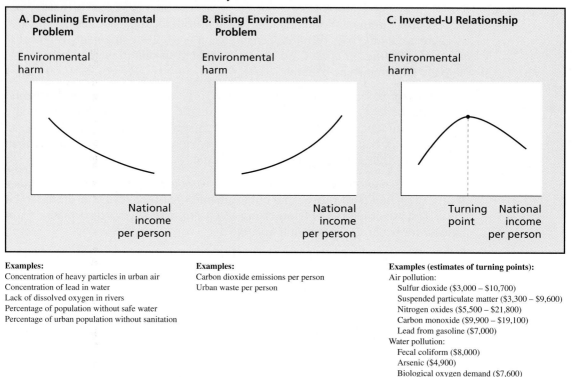

A. Declining Environmental Problem

Environmental harm

National income per person

B. Rising Environmental Problem

Environmental harm

National income per person

C. Inverted-U Relationship

Environmental harm

Turning point   National income per person

Examples:
Concentration of heavy particles in urban air
Concentration of lead in water
Lack of dissolved oxygen in rivers
Percentage of population without safe water
Percentage of urban population without sanitation

Examples:
Carbon dioxide emissions per person
Urban waste per person

Examples (estimates of turning points):
Air pollution:
  Sulfur dioxide ($3,000 – $10,700)
  Suspended particulate matter ($3,300 – $9,600)
  Nitrogen oxides ($5,500 – $21,800)
  Carbon monoxide ($9,900 – $19,100)
  Lead from gasoline ($7,000)
Water pollution:
  Fecal coliform ($8,000)
  Arsenic ($4,900)
  Biological oxygen demand ($7,600)
  Chemical oxygen demand ($7,900)

Source of examples: Edward B. Barbier, "Introduction to the Environmental Kuznets Curve Special Issue," *Environment and Development Economics* 2, no. 4 (December 1997), pp. 369–81.

human and animal wastes) and arsenic. Estimates of *turning points* (beyond which the pollution declines) often are at levels of income per person that are higher than those of most developing countries but lower than those of industrialized countries.

Now we have the tools that we need to examine the environmental effect of the Uruguay Round. Figure 12.2 shows the environmental effects that the trade changes resulting from the Uruguay Round have had on four air pollutants.

The *composition effects* tend to increase levels of all pollutants in the United States, the European Union, and Japan. With the exception of Latin America, the composition effects tend to reduce pollution in the developing countries. The reason for this pattern is Heckscher–Ohlin with a twist. As the world moves toward freer trade, production of capital- and skill-intensive products expands in the industrialized countries and shrinks in the developing countries. These products include most of the products that are environmentally "dirty," including iron and steel, the refining of other metals, chemicals, petroleum refining, and pulp and paper. Production of unskilled-labor–intensive products, like textiles and apparel, shrinks in

FIGURE 12.2   Environmental Effects of the Uruguay Round (Percent Changes in Emissions for Each Type of Pollutant, in Each Place)

	Sulfur Dioxide			Suspended Particulates			Nitrogen Dioxide			Carbon Monoxide		
	Comp[1]	S & I[2]	Total[3]	Comp	S & I	Total	Comp	S & I	Total	Comp	S & I	Total
United States	0.4	−0.7	−0.3	0.2	−0.8	−0.6	0.1	0.0	0.1	0.1	−0.6	−0.5
European Union	0.3	−0.4	−0.1	0.2	−0.3	−0.1	0.1	0.2	0.3	0.2	−0.3	−0.1
Japan	2.0	−0.6	1.4	0.3	−0.5	−0.2	0.3	0.1	0.4	0.3	−1.0	−0.7
Latin America	0.5	0.7	1.2	0.4	0.6	1.0	0.6	0.9	1.5	0.2	0.8	1.0
China	−1.8	2.1	0.3	−0.9	2.0	1.1	−0.3	1.6	1.3	−0.1	1.8	1.7
East Asia	−3.1	1.8	−2.2	−3.0	1.7	−1.3	−0.1	2.0	1.9	−1.9	1.9	0.0
South Asia	−0.6	1.3	0.7	−0.4	1.4	1.0	−0.5	1.0	0.5	−0.5	1.3	0.8
Africa	−0.1	2.8	2.7	0.0	2.7	2.7	0.2	2.0	2.2	0.0	2.4	2.4
World	−0.3	0.2	−0.1	−0.1	0.1	0.0	0.1	0.5	0.6	0.0	0.1	0.1

[1] Composition effect.
[2] Combined size effect and income effect.
[3] Total change = Composition effect + Combined size effect and income effect.

Source: M. A. Cole, A. J. Rayner, and J. M. Bates, "Trade Liberalization and the Environment: The Case of the Uruguay Round," *World Economy* 21, no. 3 (May 1997), pp. 337–47.

the industrialized countries and expands in the developing countries. Most less-skilled-labor–intensive products are environmentally "clean." Thus, as the composition of what is produced changes, pollution-intensive production tends to expand in the high-income industrialized countries and pollution-intensive production tends to decline in the low-income developing countries.

The gains from the Uruguay Round increase size and income. As shown in Figure 12.2, the combined *size and income effects* tend to lower pollution in the industrialized countries for sulfur dioxide, suspended particulates, and carbon monoxide because these countries are beyond the turning points in the inverted-U curves for these three pollutants. The combined size–income effects tend to increase nitrogen dioxide pollution in the European Union and Japan, because the turning point for this pollutant is estimated to be at about the U.S. level of income per person. The combined size–income effects tend to increase pollution in the developing countries because their incomes are lower than the four turning points.

What actually happens to the environment in each place as a result of the Uruguay Round is the sum of the effects. The actual effects (the sums of the composition effects and the combined size and income effects) vary by country and by pollutant. The overall effects for the world are generally small, as are the effects for most countries and pollutants. Even for countries whose pollution increases, the monetary value of the usual gains from freer trade are a large multiple of the monetary cost of any extra pollution. For instance, for the world, the costs of the extra nitrogen dioxide pollution are less than 0.3 percent of the global gains from the freer trade. If we take a slightly different perspective, the world and the individual countries could prevent the extra pollution using only a small part of the gains that they get from the Uruguay Round agreements. In a more limited analysis, the same study that is the source of estimates shown in Figure 12.2 concludes that the Uruguay Round is likely to increase global emissions of carbon dioxide by 3.3 percent. This increase is somewhat larger than that for the other pollutants, but it is still only a small part of the global increase in carbon dioxide that has been occurring.

In summary, free trade is not inherently anti-environment. Relocation of production to avoid stringent environmental standards is small. Shifts toward freer trade cause a variety of changes, but the net effects on overall pollution usually seem to be small.

IS THE WTO ANTI-ENVIRONMENT?

Even if free trade is not itself anti-environment, environmentalists often complain that the global rules of the trading system, the rules of the World Trade Organization (WTO), prevent governments from pursuing strong environmental protection policies. There are some things that are not in doubt. Most important, a government that takes actions to control environmental damage caused by its own firms' production is *not* violating WTO rules. Beyond this, there are questions.

The main preoccupation of the WTO (and the GATT before it) is with liberalizing trade, but the rules also make special mention of environmental concerns. Article XX lists general exceptions to its free-trade approach. While Article XX begins by repeating the signing governments' fear that any exceptions are subject to abuse by protectionists, it does admit exceptional arguments for trade barriers. Two of those arguments are environmental exceptions to the case for free trade:

> Subject to the requirement that such measures are not applied in a manner which would constitute a means of arbitrary or unjustifiable discrimination between countries where the same conditions prevail, or a disguised restriction on international trade, nothing in this Agreement shall be construed to prevent the adoption or enforcement by any contracting party of measures:
>
> . . . (b) necessary to protect human, animal, or plant life or health;
> . . . (g) relating to the conservation of exhaustible natural resources if such measures are made effective in conjunction with restrictions on domestic production or consumption.

There is an obvious tension here. The signing parties conceded that environmental concerns might conceivably justify trade barriers, but they were suspicious that such concerns would be a mere facade, an excuse for protectionists to shut out foreign goods.

There are three important types of policies that may qualify for environmental exceptions. First, *consumption* of products can cause damage. WTO rulings make it clear that a country generally can impose product standards or other limits on consumption to protect the country's health, safety, or the environment, even though such a policy will limit imports. A key is that the policy applies to all consumption, not just to imports. For instance, the WTO ruled that France can prohibit consumption and production of asbestos or asbestos-containing products within its borders, including prohibiting imports of these products. Similarly, the WTO ruled that the United States can impose a gas-guzzler tax on autos that get few miles per gallon, as long as the tax applies to all cars, both domestically produced and foreign.

At the same time, the WTO is vigilant against using environmental standards as disguised protectionism. The WTO ruled that U.S. regulations on average fuel economy of cars sold by each manufacturer violated WTO rules because they treated imports produced by foreign automakers differently from domestic autos. The WTO also ruled that U.S. policies on fuel additives violated the rules because they treated foreign-produced gasoline differently from domestically produced gasoline. The WTO ruled that a ban by Thailand on cigarette imports to promote health violated WTO rules because domestically produced cigarettes continued to be sold. In these three cases the issue was not the environmental health objective itself. Rather, it was the fact that imports were treated differently from domestically produced products without any overarching need to do so.

The WTO does also examine the basis for standards. As a result of the Uruguay Round, product standards to protect health or safety must have a scientific basis. This requirement tries to prevent a government from inventing standards that are written to limit imports. More controversially, it also may prevent a government from responding to public perceptions of risks, such as concern about genetically altered foods, if there is little scientific evidence supporting the public fears.

Second, *production in foreign countries* can cause environmental damage. Can a government limit imports of a foreign product produced using methods that violate the country's own environmental standards? In several recent rulings (discussed in the box "Dolphins, Turtles, and the WTO") the WTO indicated that the environmental exception does not permit a country to limit imports based on production methods used by firms in other countries. Essentially, the WTO is unwilling to let a country use its trade policy to punish another country for having a different environmental policy toward production processes.

Third, there are some environmental problems that are global in scope and that may require global solutions negotiated among many governments. Can a *multilateral environmental agreement* use controls on international trade to implement the agreement, or sanctions on a country's trade to enforce the agreement? Two important multilateral agreements discussed later in this chapter—the Convention on International Trade in Endangered Species and the Montreal Protocol—use trade bans, even for trade with countries that have not signed the agreements. The WTO has not been asked to rule on these agreements. The WTO seems to be comfortable with this multilateral approach to well-defined environmental problems, but it has not actually issued any rulings endorsing them.

Case Study   Dolphins, Turtles, and the WTO

Dolphins have long had a special appeal to humans because of their intelligence and seeming playfulness. The sympathy for dolphins, like the sympathy for all large animals, grows with income. It was inevitable that any threat to dolphins, even though they are not an endangered species, would mobilize a strong defense in the industrialized countries.

Most tuna are caught by methods that do not harm dolphins. But, for unknown reasons, large schools of tuna choose to swim beneath herds of dolphins in the Eastern Tropical Pacific Ocean. Before 1960, this posed no threat to dolphins. Fishing crews used hooks to catch tuna, and dolphins' sonar allowed them to avoid the hooks. However, the 1960s brought a new method for catching tuna, purse-seine fishing, in which speedboats and helicopters effectively herd the dolphins and tuna into limited areas, where vast nets encircle large schools of tuna. As the nets draw tight underwater, the dolphins, being mammals, drown. Six million dolphins have died this way since 1960.

The United States tried to stop this purse-seine netting with the Marine Mammals Protection Act of 1972, but with limited effect. The law can prohibit use of this method in U.S. waters, out to the 200-mile limit, and use of this method by U.S. ships anywhere in the world. Fishing fleets responded to the 1972 law by reflagging as ships registered outside the United States. Between 1978 and 1990, the share of U.S. boats in the Eastern Pacific tuna fleet dropped from 62 percent to less than 10 percent.

The United States still had some economic weapons at its disposal. The government pressured the three main tuna-packing and tuna-retailing firms (StarKist, Bumble Bee, and Chicken of the Sea) to refuse to buy tuna taken with dolphin-unsafe methods. While there have been charges that at least one of the firms packed dolphin-unsafe tuna under its dolphin-safe label, the dolphin-safe scheme does appear to have had some success. Through this and other forms of pressure, the estimated dolphin mortality in tuna fishing dropped from 130,000 in 1986 to 25,000 in 1991.

The United States did not let the matter rest there, however. In 1991, the U.S. government banned tuna imports from Mexico and four other countries. Mexico immediately protested to the GATT, where a dispute resolution panel handed down a preliminary ruling that the U.S. import ban was an unfair trade practice, a protectionist act against Mexico. The GATT panel ruled that the United States cannot restrict imports based on production methods used by firms in other countries. The EU also challenged the U.S. legislation as a violation of the GATT, because it included a "secondary boycott" against tuna imports from any country importing dolphin-unsafe tuna from countries like Mexico that use this fishing method. In 1994, a GATT panel again ruled against the United States.

These rulings show that the WTO (which incorporates the GATT) will not endorse efforts by one country to use trade policy to impose its environmental policies outside of its borders, or to force other countries to change their environmental policies. Environmentalists are furious, because they believe that the WTO places its principles of trade policy ahead of environmental safeguards.

Within these constraints, what can the United States do if it wishes to save more dolphins? One possibility would be a tax or ban on U.S. consumption of dolphin-unsafe tuna. As a domestic measure it might pass WTO scrutiny, although affected foreign producing countries could complain that it was a disguised form of illegitimate import restriction. The major problem probably would be implementing the consumption policy: How does one identify tuna that is caught with dolphin-unsafe methods? A more fruitful possibility is to negotiate with other countries to get them to alter the methods they use to catch tuna, perhaps by offering other benefits in exchange. In 1995, six countries (including Mexico) agreed to adopt dolphin-friendly fishing. However, some fishing fleets could just reflag to yet other countries, so the best solution probably would be a global multilateral agreement on tuna fishing.

Sea turtles, a species threatened with extinction, present a very similar case. Some shrimp are caught with nets that trap and kill sea turtles. A U.S. law passed in 1989 requires shrimpers in U.S. waters to alter their nets with turtle-excluder devices, and it prohibits shrimp imports from countries that fail to

© Dion Ogust, The Image Works

protect sea turtles from deadly entrapment in nets. Four Asian countries filed a complaint with the WTO in 1997, and the WTO issued a ruling against the United States, stating the United States was not permitted to use trade policy to force other countries to adopt environmental polices, even to protect an endangered species. This negative ruling prompted the U.S. government to negotiate and reach agreements with a number of foreign countries. The foreign countries agreed to use nets with turtle-excluder devices, and the United States provided money and training in how to use the modified nets.

Many environmentalists believe that a country should be able to set minimum standards for production methods used by foreign countries, as a condition for exporting to the country. WTO rules oppose the use of trade policy by one country to coerce another country to use certain production methods. The WTO rules are consistent with the principle that an environmental standard appropriate for one country is not necessarily appropriate for another, because economic and environmental conditions differ between countries. In addition, the WTO rules prevent situations in which several countries each require that foreign production meet their standards. A potential exporting country would be unable to export to all of these countries if the various standards were inconsistent with each other.

The WTO generally accepts the legitimacy of protecting the environment and setting minimum environmental standards through negotiations between countries. The appellate body in the sea turtle case said in its report:

> We have not decided that protection and preservation of the environment is of no significance to the members of the WTO. Clearly it is. We have not decided that the sovereign states that are members of the WTO cannot adopt effective measures to protect endangered species, such as sea turtles. Clearly, they can and they should. And we have not decided that sovereign states should not act together bilaterally, plurilaterally, or multilaterally, either within the WTO or in other international fora, to protect endangered species or to otherwise protect the environment. Clearly, they should and do.

THE SPECIFICITY RULE AGAIN

To get a better grip on the links between trade and the environment, we must first revisit some key points of microeconomics. Environmental effects such as pollution call for special policies or institutional changes if, and only if, they are what economists call externalities. Recall from Chapter 9 that externalities are spillovers. An **externality** exists when somebody's activity brings direct costs or benefits to anybody who is not part of the marketplace decision to undertake the activity.[2] If your activity imposes a direct cost on somebody who has no impact on your buying or selling, they bear an external cost. If your activity brings them a direct benefit without their participation, they receive an external benefit.

Also recall that whenever an externality exists, there is a distortion, caused by a gap between private and social costs or benefits. Where there are distortions, a competitive market, in the absence of government policy, results in either too much or too little of the activity, because people see only the private costs and benefits of their actions, not the full social costs and benefits.

Pollution is an externality that imposes an external cost on people who do not have any say over the pollution. That is, the social costs of production or consumption of the product are larger than the private costs that are recognized by the people in the market who make the decisions about producing and consuming. We can see the effects of this distortion using the terminology introduced in Chapter 9. Social marginal cost (SMC, which includes the marginal social side cost of the pollution) exceeds private marginal cost (MC, which does not include the marginal social side cost). In the competitive market, price (P) equals private marginal cost and private marginal benefit (MB). If there are no external benefits, then private marginal benefit is the same as social marginal benefit (SMB). The distortion is that $SMC > MC = P = MB = SMB$. Because some social costs are ignored by market decision-makers, too much of the activity (production and/or consumption) occurs. For the last unit, the social cost of this unit exceeds the social benefit ($SMC > SMB$). This last unit is inefficient, and any other units for which SMC exceeds SMB are also inefficient. By adding more to social cost than they add to social benefit, these last units lower well-being for the society.

Because an externality leads to sub-par performance of a market, there is a role for government policies to enhance the efficiency of the market. As we saw in Chapter 9, the specificity rule is a useful policy guide. The **specificity rule**

---

[2] The definition refers only to "direct" effects on others so as to exclude effects transmitted through prices. If people decide to smoke fewer cigarettes, their not polluting the public air reduces an externality—the external cost to those whose pleasure and health might be hurt by the smoke. But if the switch to nonsmoking drops the price of cigarettes, we will not call the implications of that price drop *externalities*. So externalities do not include the income losses to tobacco companies, the possibly lower wages for tobacco workers, the lower land values in tobacco-raising areas, and so on. Those are just market-price effects, not (direct) externalities. (We stick to this definition even though Alfred Marshall tried to confuse us by calling such market-price effects *pecuniary externalities*.)

says to intervene at the source of the problem. It is usually more efficient to use the policy tool that is specific to the distortion that makes private costs and benefits differ from social costs and benefits.

If, for example, an industry is causing acid rain by discharging sulfurous compounds into the air, the best approach is a policy that restrains the discharge of the sulfur compounds themselves. That is usually better than, say, taxing electrical power, because this latter approach would not send the electric companies the signal that the problem is their emissions of sulfurous compounds. Even worse would be more indirect measures like cutting down on all economic growth or all population growth to reduce the emissions.

There are several ways for a government to attack the externality directly. The two leading strategies to be explored here represent opposing sets of beliefs about the proper role of government in our lives:

- Use of *government taxes and subsidies.* The government could tax private parties to make them recognize the external costs that their actions (e.g., pollution) impose on others. (Correspondingly, it could pay them subsidies to get them to recognize the external benefits their actions give to others.)

- Changing *property rights* so that all relevant resources are somebody's private property. If somebody owns a resource, including even the right to pollute it, then what they decide to do with it depends on what others offer for that resource. If they choose to pollute (or to deplete the resource), it is because they were not offered enough by others to avoid pollution (or depletion). There is a new market for the private property, a market whose absence caused the externality in the first place.

Different as these two approaches are, they are both valid ways to attack an externality. Sometimes one is more practical, sometimes the other. In our discussions, we will often use the tax-and-subsidy approach, but we should keep in mind that the same efficiency-enhancing outcome could sometimes be achieved using the property-rights approach.

A PREVIEW OF POLICY PRESCRIPTIONS

Following the specificity rule, we can develop general guidelines for solutions to international externalities. If we could choose any kind of policy measure whatsoever, the specificity rule would take us on the most direct route: If the externality is pollution in some place, make the pollution itself more expensive; if resource depletion is excessive, make the depletor pay more. Often, though, we cannot hit the exact target, the externality itself. Often the only workable choices are policies toward some economic flow near the target, such as production, consumption, or trade in products related to the externality. What then?

When we have to choose between doing nothing and intervening in product markets *related to* externalities, as a substitute for controlling the externalities directly, we should follow guidelines like those summarized in Figure 12.3.

FIGURE 12.3 Types of Externalities and Product-Market Prescriptions

Source of External Costs (e.g., Pollution) Harming Our Nation	Examples	If the Whole World Had Only One Government, Its Best Product-Market Policy Would Be	Best Product-Market Policy for Our Nation Acting Alone
Just our own production	Chemicals	Tax our production	Tax our production (as in Figure 12.4)
Just foreign production	Acid rain across borders; tuna and dolphins; ivory	Tax foreign production	Tax our imports
World production	CO_2 buildup from fossil fuels; CFCs	Tax world production (or consumption)	Tax our production and imports
Just our own consumption	Fossil fuels, tobacco, narcotics	Tax our consumption	Tax our consumption
Just foreign consumption	Fossil fuels, tobacco, narcotics	Tax foreign consumption	Tax our exports
World consumption	Fossil fuels, tobacco, narcotics	Tax world consumption (or production)	Tax our consumption and exports

Note: *Tax* here means "impose government restrictions." These could be taxes, quantitative quotas, or outright prohibitions.
Remember that only "best product-market policy" interventions are considered here. In many cases, a more direct approach would tax an input or specific technology (e.g., use of high-sulfur coal or fuel-inefficient automobiles) rather than the final product (e.g., electricity from power plants or road transportation). And in other cases, an optimal policy might manipulate more than one product market at once.

The table contains two sets of best-feasible prescriptions: one for the whole world acting as one government, and one for a single nation unable to get cooperation from other governments. These represent the two extremes in international negotiations over issues like pollution or natural-resource depletion: The greater the scope for international cooperation, the more relevant is the column of prescriptions for a world with a single government. The more hopeless it is to gain cooperation, the more we must settle on the single-nation prescriptions in the right column.

If nations cooperate, as if they formed a single world government, there would be essentially no role for international trade policy. In the best of worlds, government would devise a way to tax the activity of pollution itself, to translate its concern about pollution into direct incentives. In the one-world-government column of Figure 12.3, the recommended policies are one step away from taxing pollution itself, taking the form of taxes on production or consumption. They are not taxes on exports or imports.[3] This is because pollution and other externalities seldom arise from trade as such. The specificity rule accordingly calls for taxes

---

[3] It may seem suspicious that Figure 12.3 mentions raising taxes but not lowering them or giving out subsidies. The reason is simply that the cases listed here are all cases of negative externalities, the kind that do harm and must be reduced by taxing the polluting activities. If Figure 12.3 had dealt with the mirror-image cases, in which there are external benefits rather than costs, it would have recommended lower taxes or subsidies.

near the source of the pollution, and taxes on production or consumption are closer to that target than taxes on international trade are.

If one nation must act alone, trade barriers could be an appropriate second-best solution. That would happen if our nation suffered from transborder pollution, either from foreign production (e.g., foreign producers of our steel causing acid rain in our country) or from foreign consumption (e.g., foreign cars burning our exported gasoline upwind from our nation). In this situation, the only way in which our nation can discourage the foreign pollution is by taxing imports of the products made by a polluting process (e.g., foreign steel) or by taxing exports of products that generate pollution when consumed (e.g., gasoline).

The rest of the chapter takes up discussion of each of three types of sources of external costs noted in Figure 12.3. First we look at issues when the external costs are ones we impose on ourselves—domestic pollution and similar national externalities. Then we analyze cases in which the activity of another country imposes an external cost on our country—transborder pollution and similar cross-country externalities. Finally, we examine the challenges of global external costs—global pollution and similar worldwide externalities.

TRADE AND DOMESTIC POLLUTION

Economic activities sometimes produce significant amounts of *domestic pollution* (or similar environmental degradation). That is, the costs of the pollution fall only (or almost completely) on people within the country. *If there are no policies that force market decision-makers to internalize* these external costs, then we reach two surprising conclusions about trade with domestic pollution. First, *free trade can reduce the well-being of the country.* Second, *the country can end up exporting the wrong products;* it exports products that it should import, for instance.

To see this, consider the case of an industry whose production activity creates substantial pollution in the local rivers, lakes, and groundwater. For instance, consider the paper-making industry in a country like Canada. It is very convenient for paper companies to dump their chemical wastes into the local lakes, and the firms view this as a free activity (if the Canadian government has no policy limiting this kind of pollution). The Canadian companies are happy that the lakes are there, and the firms' operations thrive, producing profits, good incomes for their workers, and good products for their customers at reasonable prices.

Other Canadians have a different view, of course. Having the lakes turn brown with chemical waste spoils the scenery, the swimming, the fishing, and other services that they get from their lakes. The dumping of wastes into the lakes imposes an external cost on other users of the lakes.

The top half of Figure 12.4 shows the Canadian market for paper, with the domestic supply curve reflecting the private marginal cost of production and the domestic demand curve reflecting the private marginal benefits of paper consumption (which are also the social marginal benefits if there are no external benefits). The bottom half of Figure 12.4 shows the additional costs imposed on the

FIGURE 12.4   When Domestic Production Causes Domestic Pollution

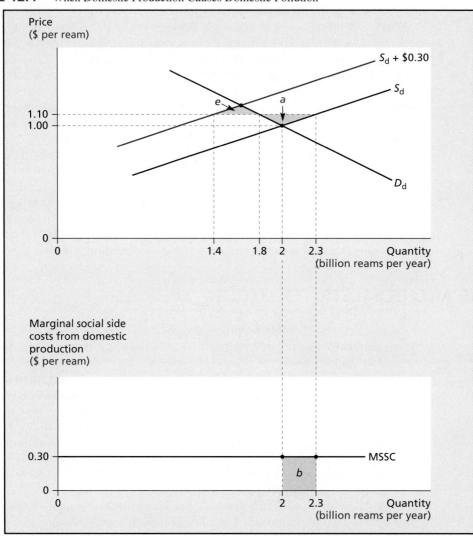

When domestic production causes pollution that imposes an external cost on the country, we find several surprising results about trade. If the government has no policy limiting this pollution, then domestic firms ignore the marginal social side costs (MSSC) of their pollution, and operate along the supply curve S_d. If the world price is $1.10, then the country exports 0.5 billion reams of paper. In comparison with no trade, the country may be worse off, as it is here (gain of the shaded triangle a in the top of the figure, but loss of the shaded rectangle b in the bottom).

The country may also export the wrong products. Here it would be best if the country actually imported 0.4 billion reams. That would happen if a $0.30 tax, equal to the MSSC, made domestic producers operate along the supply curve $S_d + \$0.30$, which reflects all social costs.

country by the pollution that results from production of paper in the country. We keep track of this negative externality using the marginal social side costs (MSSC) of the pollution. (This figure is the analog of Figure 9.2, which showed the case of external benefits.) To keep the analysis simple, we assume that the external cost of the pollution is constant at $0.30 per ream of paper.

With no international trade (and no government policies limiting pollution), the paper market clears at a price of $1 per ream, with 2 billion reams produced and consumed per year. Because there is no recognition in the market of the cost of the pollution, this is overproduction of paper.

Consider the shift to free trade, with an international price of $1.10 per ream (and still no government policies limiting pollution). Domestic production expands to 2.3 billion reams, domestic consumption declines to 1.8 billion, and 0.5 billion reams are exported. For the case shown in Figure 12.4, free trade unfortunately makes the country worse off. The usual gain from trade is shown by the shaded triangle *a* in the upper graph, a gain of $25 million. But the extra production brings pollution that has an extra cost of the shaded area *b* in the lower graph, a social side cost of $90 million ($0.30 per ream on the additional 300 million reams produced). Free trade reduces the well-being of the country by $65 million.

The country's government could avoid this loss by prohibiting exports of paper. But we know from the specificity rule that this is not the best government policy. The best policy attacks pollution directly, for instance by placing a tax on pollution from paper production. If there is no way to reduce pollution per ream produced, then the tax should add $0.30 per ream to the firms' cost of production. The tax forces the firms to recognize the cost of pollution, and it alters their behavior. The domestic supply shifts up by the amount of the tax, to $S_d + \$0.30$. This new supply curve now reflects all social costs, both the private production costs and the external pollution costs.

If this government policy is in place, what happens with free trade? Domestic consumers still buy 1.8 billion reams of paper, but now domestic producers supply only 1.4 billion reams. As shown, it is actually best for the country to import paper, not export it. Because the new supply curve (with the $0.30 tax) includes the social side cost of pollution, we can read the effects of trade on the country from the top half of Figure 12.4, without referring to the bottom half. We find the usual triangle of gains from importing, the shaded triangle *e*.

From this example we see that pollution that imposes costs only on the local economy can still have a major impact on how we think about international trade. *With no government policy limiting pollution,* the country can end up worse off with free trade, and the trade pattern can be wrong. In the case of pollution caused by production that we examined, the country exported a product that it should instead import. (If, instead, the pollution cost is not so high, then the problem is that the country exports too much.)[4]

---

[4] What can happen if pollution is caused by consumption, not production? In this case the country tends to consume too much of the product, so the country could import a product that it should instead export (or, at least, it imports too much of the product).

The country can correct this type of distortion by using a policy that forces polluters to recognize the external cost of their pollution. In our paper example, the government used a pollution tax, but instead it could establish property rights. For instance, people could be given the right to the water. Polluting firms then must pay the owners for the right to pollute. Or a limited number of rights to pollute could be created by the government, so that firms need to buy these rights if they want to pollute.

If domestic firms must pay the pollution tax (or pay for the right to pollute), they probably will not be happy. The pollution tax raises their production costs, and they produce and sell less. In addition, they face competition from imports at the world price of $1.10. Even if they accept the reason for the pollution tax, they may still complain about the imports. If other countries do not impose a similar pollution tax on their producers, then the domestic firms often complain that the imports are unfair. They claim that the lack of foreign pollution controls is a form of implicit subsidy, or that the foreign firms are engaged in "eco-dumping" based on lax foreign government policies.

What are we to make of these complaints? Should the country impose countervailing duties on imports from a country with different pollution policies? From the national perspective of the importing country, the answer is generally no. Foreign production may create pollution in the foreign country, but this has no impact on the importing country if the costs of this foreign pollution affect only foreigners. As with many other complaints about unfair exports, the best policy for the importing country is simply to enjoy the low-price imports. Indeed, under the rules of the World Trade Organization, lax foreign pollution policies are not a legitimate reason for imposing countervailing duties.

From the perspective of the whole world, it depends on why the foreign pollution policies are different from those of the importing country. It may be efficient for the foreign country to have different, and perhaps more lax, pollution policies. The pollution caused by foreign production may not be so costly, because the foreign production itself creates less pollution, because the foreign environment is not so badly affected, or because foreigners place less value on the environment. In our paper example, the production process or the raw materials used in foreign production may create less pollution. Or the foreign country may have larger water resources or rainfall, in which case the pollution is not so damaging because the foreign environment has a larger "assimilative capacity." Or the foreign country may assign a high value to producing income to purchase basic goods because its people are poor and are therefore willing to accept some extra pollution more readily.

On the other hand, the foreign country may simply have policies that are too lax. From the point of view of the foreign country and the world, it would be better if it had tougher pollution policies. As a type of second-best approach, import limits by other countries could improve things. But these limits will not make the importing country better off, even though they might raise world well-being.

TRANSBORDER POLLUTION

In the previous section we considered pollution that had costs only to the country doing the pollution. While we reached some surprising conclusions about free trade in the absence of government policies limiting pollution, we also had a ready solution. The government should implement some form of policy addressing pollution that is occurring in its country. If each country's government addresses its own local pollution problems, then each can enhance its own national well-being. In the process, world well-being is also raised.

However, many types of pollution have transborder effects—effects not just on the country doing the pollution but also on other countries. Examples include air pollution like particulates and sulfur dioxide that drifts across national borders and water pollution when the body of water (river or lake) is in two or more countries. **Transborder pollution** raises major new issues for government policies toward pollution.

Suppose that a German paper company builds a new paper mill on the Danube River, just to the west of where the river flows into Austria. It is very convenient for the paper company to dump its chemical wastes into the river, and it views this as a free activity (if the German government has no policy limiting this kind of pollution). Austrians have a different view. The dumping of wastes into the German Danube imposes an external cost on the Austrians and others (Slovaks, Hungarians, Serbs, Romanians, and Bulgarians) downstream.

The Right Solution

Figure 12.5 shows how we can determine the "right" amount of pollution, the amount that brings the greatest net gain to the world as a whole.[5] The figure focuses directly on pollution, without also showing the supply and demand for paper. It portrays Germany's benefits and Austria's costs from different rates of dumping waste into the Danube by the German paper mill. If left to itself, the German mill dumps as much as it wants into the Danube, ignoring the costs to Austria (and other nations). It will pollute until there is no more that it wants to dump at zero cost. That will be at point *A*, with the paper company dumping 180 million tons of waste per year. Point *A* is a disaster in Austria, where the river damage rises along the marginal cost curve in Figure 12.5.

---

[5] Here, as in other chapters, the interest of the "world as a whole" is the sum of net gains to all parties, with each dollar (or euro) of gain or loss worth the same regardless of whose gain or loss it is. That is, we continue to follow the one-dollar, one-vote metric introduced in Chapter 2. To reject it, we would have to have another set of welfare weights, considering a dollar or euro of gain to the German firm to have a different value from the same value of gain or loss to Austrians.

FIGURE 12.5

A Classic Case of International Pollution With an Ideal Policy Solution

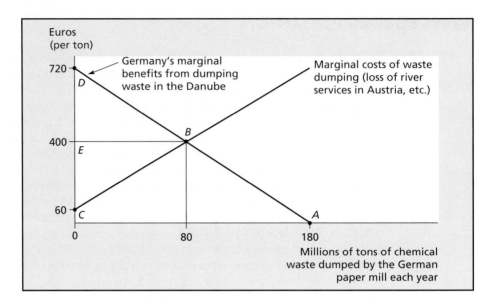

Point *A* is also inefficient from a world perspective. Any pollution beyond 80 million tons is inefficient—it does more damage than it benefits the paper company. In the figure any waste dumping above 80 million tons has marginal costs that are above the marginal benefits. For instance, while the last few tons dumped bring the German firm almost no extra benefits (perhaps because these would be easy to avoid or clean up), these last few tons cost the Austrians about 700 euros per ton.

But, looking at it from the other side, we see that a total ban on dumping into the Danube would also be a mistake in this situation. The total ban, if effectively enforced, would force the paper mill to point *D*. Downstream users would be delighted, of course, to have the river clean. But the complete cleanup costs more than it is worth. That is, allowing the first ton of pollution each year would be worth 720 euros to the paper company (perhaps because it is very costly to capture the last small amounts of waste for alternative disposal). Yet downstream users lose only 60 euros of extra enjoyment and income (at point *C*). The downstream cost of the first ton of pollution is not that high, probably because the river can assimilate this small amount of pollution without much damage. From a world viewpoint, the first ton of pollution should be allowed. In fact, if Figure 12.5 correctly portrays the marginal benefits and costs, pollution up to 80 million tons adds to world well-being because the benefit to Germany from using the Danube for its waste is greater than the costs imposed on Austria. The paper company should be allowed to dump waste up to 80 tons per year, but no more than that. At point *B*, the benefits of using the river as a drain for wastes stop exceeding the costs of doing that. However offensive the idea may be to those who love clean water and don't buy much paper, the economist insists that 80 million tons, not zero tons (or 180 million tons), is the "optimal amount of pollution" in this situation.[6]

To get the right solution, something must be done to make the German paper company recognize the costs of its pollution, and this something cannot be too drastic. The specificity rule indicates that the best government policy is one that acts directly on the problem. A government could use the tax/subsidy approach to guide the use of the Danube to the optimal point *B,* if the government has good estimates of the marginal costs and benefits of the pollution. For instance, the government could tax the paper company 400 euros for every ton it dumps into the river. The company will respond by dumping 80 million tons a year (at point *B*), since up to that 80 millionth ton the company's gain from putting each extra ton of waste in the river exceeds the 400-euro tax. An efficient balance would be struck between the competing uses of the river.

A pollution tax like the one just described might well happen if "the government" were the Austrian government. But here the problem becomes international. Austria has no direct tax power over a paper mill in Germany, except to the extent that the mill happens to do business in Austria. More likely, the tax/subsidy option is in the hands of the German government since the paper mill is on the German side of the border. Germany might not tax the paper mill at all. Dumping 180 tons a year (at point *A* again) brings greater national gains to Germany than the world-efficient pollution tax at point *B*.

The likelihood that one country would decide to go on imposing an external cost on the rest of the world is a setback for the economist seeking global efficiency. To the efficiency-minded economist, it would not matter how we got to point *B* as long as we got there. But the German government has no incentive to tax the German company for its pollution.

We can imagine another way, assigning property rights, to try to get the efficient solution. A World Court could rule that the Danube is the property of the German paper company (or the German government), and Austria must pay the German company to reduce its pollution. Or the World Court could rule that the Danube belongs to Austria, and the German company must buy the right to pollute for each ton it dumps. The Nobel Prize–winning economist Ronald Coase pointed out that *either* court ruling could result in the same amount of pollution, as long as the property rights can be enforced. If the German company owned the river, the Austrian users would be willing to pay 400 euros per ton to reduce pollution to 80 million tons, and the German firm would agree to reduce its pollution to this level. If Austria owned the river, the German firm would be willing to pay 400 euros per ton for the right to dump 80 million tons, and the Austrians would accept this offer. Who gets the money depends on who owns the river, but in either case the same amount of pollution results.

---

[6] At point *B*, allowing 80 million tons of pollution (instead of none) brings the world a net gain of area *BCD*, or $(1/2) \times (720 - 60) \times 80 = 26.4$ billion euros per year.

This private-property approach has a major problem, however, when it comes to international disputes. There is no supreme world court that can enforce a property claim of one country's residents in another country. Austrians have no real legal recourse if the German paper mill insists on discharging all its wastes into the Danube. The Austrian government could threaten to take retaliatory actions against Germany. But it is unlikely that Austria would hold the right kind of power to force Germany to cooperate on the specific issue of the paper mill and the Danube, if the Germans did not want to cooperate. The result is likely to be inefficient.[7]

We therefore get the same striking results for either the tax/subsidy approach or the property-rights approach. The good news is that any of several arrangements *could* give us the efficient compromise solution to the transborder pollution problem (at point *B*). The bad news is that the two sides often would not reach that efficient solution. Instead, negotiations would break down and each side would do as it pleased in its own territory. The result could be costly rampant pollution, as at point *A*, if the polluting firms can do as they please.

A Next-Best Solution

If international negotiations fail, the Austrian government must still consider what it can do on its own. If an international agreement is not possible, what can the government of the country that is being harmed by the other country's pollution do? It cannot tax or restrict the pollution-creating activity in the other country directly. But it may be able to have some influence by adopting policies toward international trade.

In our example, let's say that Austria imports paper from Germany, and that Austrian paper production does not create much pollution (or this pollution is controlled by appropriate Austrian government policies). The Austrian government could attempt to reduce the dumping of waste into the Danube by limiting its imports from Germany (or, if possible, from the specific firm whose factory is responsible for the pollution). The decline in German paper exports reduces German paper production, and this also reduces the amount of waste that is dumped into the Danube. Austria gives up some of the gains from importing paper—that is, Austria suffers the usual deadweight losses from restricting imports. But Austria can still be better off if the gain from reducing the costs of the river pollution

---

[7] As it happens, the German–Austrian case is relatively benign in real life because Germany does care greatly about good relations with Austria, and both are members of the European Union. Yet the question "Whose river is it, anyway?" is destined to arise more and more often. Here are some examples: (1) Turkey has upstream control of the Euphrates, a vital resource for Syria and Iraq. (2) Now that they are separate nations, Russia, Belarus, and the Ukraine will struggle over the headwaters of the Dnieper. (3) If the eight upstream nations use the Nile more intensively, there will be consequences for Egypt. (4) The Zambezi River will be the focus of disputes as Zambia, Angola, Botswana, Zimbabwe, and Mozambique construct dams to support irrigation projects. (5) Several drought-prone nations, most notably Mali and Niger, compete for the waters of the Niger River upstream from Nigeria.

exceeds these usual deadweight costs. If instead Austria exports paper to Germany, then the Austrian government should consider subsidizing paper exports to Germany. The increase in Austrian exports can reduce German import-competing paper production, again leading to less dumping of waste.

There is a major problem with this indirect approach to addressing transborder pollution. The rules of the WTO generally prohibit the Austrian government from increasing its import tariffs or subsidizing its exports. Although, as we have seen, the rules also offer exceptions for measures intended to protect the environment, the WTO interprets this exception narrowly (see again the box "Dolphins, Turtles, and the WTO"). So the WTO probably would not permit Austrian use of trade policy in response to lax German environmental policies.

NAFTA and the Environment

Environmental problems along the Mexico–U.S. border provide a real case of the challenges of transborder pollution. This issue was prominent in the fight over approving the North American Free Trade Agreement (NAFTA), adding to the concerns already discussed in Chapter 11, and it remains important in evaluations of the effects of NAFTA.

Mexico has a strong set of environmental protection laws and regulations on the books, comparable to those of the United States. But Mexican enforcement of these is weak. Weak enforcement is not surprising, and it is not only the result of limited administrative resources. Popular demand for clean air and water is a luxury good. Nations feel they can afford to control many pollutants only when GDP per capita has reached high enough levels. Mexico has sacrificed air and water quality for economic development. Mexico City's smog is as bad as any in the world.

For the United States, a major concern is the pollution emanating from the Mexican side of the Mexico–U.S. border. In the 1960s, the governments of Mexico and the United States encouraged growth of industry just south of the border, where businesses could assemble goods for reentry into the United States without the usual tariffs and quotas. The arid border is not a forgiving place for a large industrial population. The absence of infrastructure for the several thousand *maquiladora* firms producing there, and the millions of people attracted by the jobs available, became all too obvious. U.S. critics can point to unmanaged hazardous wastes, soil erosion, air pollution, raw sewage and other water pollution, lack of organized rubbish disposal, and lack of clean drinking water from Tijuana to the mouth of the Rio Grande. While the pollution is most severe on the Mexican side of the border, major damage also affects the American side. Coal-fired power plants in northern Mexico cause serious air pollution in Texas, and Mexican water pollution is fouling the Rio Grande, a prime source of water for many U.S. towns.

Critics of NAFTA argued that freer trade would yield more environmental damage in the trade-oriented *maquiladora* zone, and they recommended rejecting NAFTA. In response to these criticisms, a side agreement on environmental issues was attached to NAFTA. It established a commission to investigate complaints about failure to enforce national environmental laws. It set up a bank to fund cleanup projects using billions of dollars obtained with governmental backing. Mexico also promised to enforce its environmental standards more effectively. With these additional provisions, environmental lobbying groups were actually divided about the final version of NAFTA. The Sierra Club and Friends of the Earth strongly opposed NAFTA on environmental grounds, while the Audubon Society, the Environmental Defense Fund, the National Wildlife Federation, and the Natural Resources Defense Council gave qualified support to NAFTA with the added environmental provisions.

However, even with these provisions in NAFTA and the general spirit of cooperation it has engendered, progress has been very slow. The commission can investigate, but it has no power to mandate enforcement. It appears to have had little impact on Mexican enforcement of its environmental laws, which remains weak. The bank has lent little, in part because the interest rates it charges are too high for the Mexican local governments. So far the environmental problems along the Mexico–U.S. border show how difficult it can be to address transborder pollution, especially when the two countries do not share the same views about the importance of environmental quality.

GLOBAL ENVIRONMENTAL CHALLENGES

Our discussion of transborder pollution focused on cases in which one country's activities impose external costs on another country. Things become even more controversial when the whole world's economic activities impose external costs on the whole world. Two important global environmental challenges are depletion of the ozone layer and global warming resulting from the buildup of greenhouse gases. Other challenges also have a global dimension, especially those that involve extinction of species or depletion of common resources such as fish stocks. We begin with an overview of important concepts and then examine specific applications.

Global Problems Need Global Solutions

Consider a global environmental problem like the depletion of the ozone layer caused by human release of chemicals. As we will see when we look at this in more detail, many types of activities release these chemicals, and the total of the global release causes the depletion. The harm of ozone depletion has global effects, with some countries more affected than others.

What would each country do if it set its own policy toward this problem? From the purely national viewpoint, each country would recognize that chemical releases have some negative effect on its people, and it might use a policy to limit releases if it thought the national harm was large enough. But, for the whole world, total releases would be much too large. Each country would ignore the harm that its own releases did to other countries, so it would not be sufficiently stringent with its own environmental policy.

To get closer to the best global policy, the countries would need to find some way to cooperate. Each would need to tighten its standards compared to what it would do on its own. If each country does this, the whole world is better off. Many, but perhaps not all, of the countries will also each be better off. Each country incurs some costs in tightening its standards, but each also derives benefits from the reduction of the environmental damage.

Still, it may be very difficult to reach this global agreement. One problem is that there may be disagreement about the costs of the environmental damage or the costs of tightening standards. Science is unlikely to provide a definitive accounting, and countries differ in their willingness to take environmental risks. Even if this problem is not so large, others are likely to arise. Countries that suffer net losses from tightening may be unwilling to take part, unless they receive some other kind of compensation. Even countries that gain from the global agreement have a perverse incentive. A country can gain even more by free-riding. That is, it can gain most of the benefits if other countries abide by the agreement to tighten standards, even if this country does not, and it avoids the costs of tightening its own standards.

Because of the free-rider problem, a global agreement needs some method of enforcement, to get "reluctant" countries to agree in the first place, and to assure that they abide by the agreement after it is established. There is no global organization that can provide these enforcement services. Countries can establish an enforcement mechanism as part of the global agreement, but it is not clear what it should be. It is generally not possible to impose fines directly. One possible penalty is some kind of trade sanctions, to reduce the offending country's gains from trade. As we saw in Chapter 11, such sanctions also have costs for the countries imposing the sanctions, and in any case they often do not work.

This is a sobering analysis. When an environmental problem causes only domestic costs, it is up to the government of the country to address it. When the problem is transborder but regional among a small number of countries, it is more difficult but still may be solvable by negotiations. When the problem is global, a global (or nearly global) multilateral agreement is needed, but negotiating and enforcing this agreement may prove to be very difficult or impossible. To gain more insight, let's turn to four global problems. We begin with a fairly effective global agreement to use trade policy to prevent the extinction of endangered species. Next we depict depletion of ocean fishing stocks and the lack of any effective solutions to this global inefficiency. Then we portray a successful, nearly global agreement to reverse ozone depletion. We conclude with the most daunting of global environmental issues: greenhouse gases and global warming.

Extinction of Species

Extinction of species is a natural process. Still, within the past half century the specific role of human activity in causing extinction has become recognized and controversial. It is reckoned that human activities eliminated only 8 mammal and 24 bird species in the 18th century, then 29 mammals and 61 birds in the 19th century, and 52 mammals and 70 birds from 1900 to 1987. There is a general belief that there is a loss when a species becomes extinct, perhaps because there may be future uses for the species (for instance, as a source of medicinal products). Thus, a global effort to prevent extinction of species can be economically sensible.

Human activities contributing to extinction include destruction of habitat, introduction of predators, and pollution. In addition, excessive hunting and harvesting can also cause extinction. The specificity rule indicates that the best global policy to preserve species would be a policy that promotes the species through such direct means as protected parks and wild areas; ranching, cultivation, and similar management intended to earn profits from the ongoing existence of the species; and zoos and gardens to maintain species in captivity. While there is no global agreement specifically to promote these best solutions, there is a global agreement that attempts to control the pressure of international demand as a source of incentives for excessive hunting and harvesting.

In 1973, over 100 nations signed the Convention on International Trade in Endangered Species of Wild Fauna and Flora (**CITES**). With 158 member countries by 2002, CITES establishes international cooperation to prevent international trade from endangering the survival of species. An international scientific authority decides which species are endangered. Commercial trade is usually banned for species threatened with extinction—about 900 species, including elephants, gray whales, and sea turtles. To export these products for noncommercial purposes, a nation must obtain an export permit from the central authority, and it must have a copy of an import permit from a suitable buyer in a country that signed CITES. Commercial trade is limited for an additional 26,000 species because free trade could lead to the threat of extinction.

No species with a trade ban has become extinct. Some, including the rhino and the tiger, continue to decline, but CITES has probably slowed the declines. Generally, CITES seems to be fairly effective. This is impressive in that most member countries have incomplete national legislation, poor enforcement, and weak penalties for violating the trade bans or controls.

Much of the conflict over endangered species naturally centers on Africa, with its unique biodiversity and its fragile ecosystems. The biggest fight so far has been over the fate of the African elephant, which is hunted for its ivory tusks.

The human slaughter of elephants accelerated at an alarming rate in the 1970s and 1980s. The African elephant population was cut in half within a span of only eight years in the 1980s. The problem was most severe in eastern Africa, north of the Zambezi River. The governments of Kenya, Tanzania, and Zambia, while ostensibly committed to protecting elephants, were not preventing killing by poachers. The threat to elephants was weaker in southern Africa, south of the Zambezi, for three reasons: The governments of Zimbabwe, Botswana, and Namibia enforced conservation more aggressively, agriculture was less of a threat to the wild animal population, and some elephants of Botswana and Zimbabwe had tusks of poor commercial quality.

In 1977, the African elephant was placed on the list of species with controlled trade. Public pressure from affluent countries to save the elephants became intense by the late 1980s. Although the African elephant did not fully meet the official definition, in 1989 it was moved to the list of endangered species. Also in 1989, most of the CITES countries signed a complete ban on exporting or importing ivory. The drastic reduction in demand, especially demand from the affluent countries, caused ivory prices to plummet, from $100 per kilogram to only $3 or $4 per kilogram. Poaching decreased (mostly a movement down the poachers' supply curve) and elephant populations stabilized or even increased.

The bans on trade in African elephants and their ivory appear to be successful. Especially in eastern Africa, it has greatly reduced poaching. However, by itself it may not be a long-run solution. Africa's human population growth will bring more crop cultivation, and cultivation is simply inconsistent with a roaming elephant population. Where crops come, the elephant will go. Even in dry southern Africa, irrigation will eventually bring crops.

Fortunately, there have been further developments. In 1997, Zimbabwe, Botswana, and Namibia (joined later by South Africa and Zambia) asked CITES to end the bans for their elephants. They argued that elephants were not endangered in their countries—in fact, they had too many elephants. They argued that they needed some economic use of elephants to justify the costs of managing the herds. Based on the principle of "sustainable use" that it had previously adopted in 1992, CITES permitted limited hunting of elephants for these three countries. By adopting a role for sustainable use, CITES recognizes that the profit of commercial trade can deter other pressures toward extinction. But CITES now must face the challenge of evaluating claims of sustainable use, rather than simply using its precautionary bans. For many species the ultimate success of CITES probably depends less on its bans and, paradoxically, more on its ability to encourage economic management for commercial uses.

Overfishing

The oceans, along with fish and other marine life, are one of the great global resources. However, major problems can develop because no one actually owns these resources. The world's fish catch peaked in 1988 (ignoring data from China, whose catches seem to be seriously overstated). About a quarter of the earth's 200 main fish stocks are overfished; sustainable catches could be larger if the stocks were better managed. For most fish species, overfishing does not pose a threat of extinction, but it does mean that populations are becoming smaller than they should be. Why are we squandering this resource? What can we do?

We have here an example of the "tragedy of the commons." With open access to fishing and no ownership, the incentive of each fishing firm is to catch as many fish as possible. There is no incentive to conserve. Even if one fishing firm did restrain its catch to maintain the fish stock, others would simply increase their catch. So all fish too much, and the fish stock declines. Rather than limiting their fishing industries, governments often make matters worse by subsidizing them, by up to $54 billion per year. The result is severe overcapacity of fishing boats, perhaps twice as much ship tonnage as would be needed for a sustainable fish catch.

With good management of fishing stocks, the world catch of fish could be 10 to 20 percent larger than it is now. But even single nations have trouble managing their fishing activities. The fishing industry, with its overcapacity, pushes for lesser limits, even if this is helpful only in the short run. Global or multilateral agreements could enhance global fishing. But given the difficulty of negotiating and enforcing such agreements, effective ones are rare. We pay a global cost, in the form of less fish at a higher price.

CFCs and Ozone

The 1940s brought new technologies for using chlorofluorocarbon compounds (CFCs) in several industries. About 30 percent of CFCs came to be used in refrigeration, air conditioning, and heat pumps; about 28 percent in foam blowing; about 27 percent in aerosol propellants; and about 15 percent in dry cleaning and other industrial cleaning and degreasing. By the early 1970s, evidence had accumulated showing that CFCs and the halons used in fire extinguishers, while not directly toxic, were depleting ozone in the upper atmosphere. The chemical process is slow and complex. It takes 7 to 10 years for released CFCs to drift to the stratosphere, where their chlorine compounds interact with different climatic conditions to remove ozone. By 1985, the now-famous ozone holes were clearly detected in the stratosphere near the North and South Poles. Stratospheric ozone is an important absorber of ultraviolet rays from the sun, and its removal raises dangers of skin cancer, reduced farm yields, and climatic change.

In 1987, over 50 nations signed the **Montreal Protocol** on Substances that Deplete the Ozone Layer.[8] The signing parties agreed to ban exports and imports of CFCs and halons. After more scientific evidence accumulated, most signatory nations agreed in 1990 to phase out their own production of these chemicals by 2000, with later deadlines and interim production limits for developing countries.

Note that the protocol called for outright bans and other quantitative limits, not a pollution tax or polluting-product tax like those discussed in Figures 12.3 through 12.5. The reason is that the scientific evidence suggested a steeply rising social-cost curve for CFC emissions into the atmosphere. With the cost curve so vertical, it did not make sense to use tax rates on a trial-and-error basis in the hope of achieving the large cut in pollution. It was better to legislate the bans and limits from the start, without waiting several years to see if some tax schedule had the right effects.

The Montreal Protocol is achieving much of the economic and environmental effect it was supposed to have. By 2002, manufacture of chlorofluorocarbons had almost ended. Concentrations of chlorine-containing compounds in the stratosphere peaked and began to decline in 2000. Yet, because of the slow chemical

---

[8] The signatories were 18 industrial OECD nations, Argentina, Brazil, Mexico, Egypt, Kenya, South Africa, Zambia, Malaysia, Thailand, the (former) Soviet Union, Bulgaria, (former) Czechoslovakia, Hungary, and 25 other developing countries. By 2002, the number of signatories had risen to 183 countries.

process of recovery, the ozone holes will remain for a long time; ozone concentrations in the stratosphere will not return to normal levels until the middle of the 21st century.

Why the success in this case? Why didn't nations try to free-ride by refusing to comply while demanding that others do so, as so often happens? Experts point to several factors that eased the signing and enforcement of the Montreal Protocol:

- The scientific evidence was clearer about CFCs and ozone than it is about other possible human threats to the atmospheric balance.

- A small group of products was involved, for which substitutes appeared to be technologically feasible with limited cost increases.

- Production of CFCs was concentrated in the United States and the EU, and in a few large publicity-conscious firms (mainly DuPont) so that agreement could be easily reached and enforced.

- The same higher-income countries that dominated production and use of these chemicals are also closer to the North and South Pole, so they expected to suffer most of the environmental damage themselves.

Greenhouse Gases and Global Warming

Finally, we turn to the most daunting environmental problem of all. Human activity, especially the burning of fossil fuels, is raising the concentration of carbon dioxide (CO_2) in the earth's atmosphere. Most climate scientists believe that the rise of CO_2 is causing a pronounced warming of the earth's climate through a "greenhouse effect." The warming could bring desertification of vast areas, and could flood major coastal cities and farm areas when it has melted much of the polar ice caps. It is hard to imagine a solution as clean and workable as the Montreal Protocol's phaseout of chlorofluorocarbons. The activities that release carbon dioxide, methane, and other greenhouse gases into the atmosphere are harder to do without than were CFC refrigerants and sprays. In addition, the damage from adverse climatic change would be spread around the globe unpredictably and unevenly.

To see the available options, we should first clear the air, so to speak, by noting some limits on the choices available. Three main points must be made at the outset: (1) The scientific facts are not fully established, (2) three palatable solutions will fall short of arresting the CO_2 buildup, and (3) international trade is not the cause or the cure.

First, the scientific facts about the greenhouse effect are less certain than the facts about CFCs and stratospheric ozone. We do know that atmospheric concentrations of CO_2 have risen by about a third since 1800 and are still rising. Human activity, especially the burning of fossil fuels, is the main source of the buildup, though the magnitudes are still being debated. The effects of the CO_2 buildup cannot be predicted precisely. We do know that there is a greenhouse effect—in fact, it is crucial to keeping the earth's surface and lower atmosphere warm. The earth's average surface temperature has increased about 0.6° C (1° F) in the past half century, mostly since 1980. Most forecasts are that temperatures will rise by anywhere from 1.4° C to 5.8° C during the 21st century, with the median forecast being 2.5° C. Swings in average temperatures are normal in earth's history, but changes of this size in so short a time are not. Even if the earth is getting warmer and CO_2 buildup is the main reason, the climatic changes and economic effects cannot be predicted with any certainty. Some countries would gain from the warming, some would lose, and we are unsure about the magnitudes and about which countries to list in the gaining and losing columns.

This scientific uncertainty argues for a middle policy path that we could call an "insurance" path. Given the risks, it would be foolish to do nothing. It would also be foolish to risk wrecking the world economy with radical changes. Better to start leaning in the direction of cutting greenhouse-gas emissions while knowledge accumulates.

Second, it must be understood that three relatively palatable policy changes will fall far short of stopping the CO_2 buildup:

1. One desirable option is known as the "no-regrets" option. Let's just remove all those unwarranted *subsidies* to energy use that should have been removed anyway. Removing bad energy subsidies would reduce, at most, only 10 to 11 percent of the emissions, and the net global buildup of CO_2 would continue.

2. A second option would be to take CO_2 out of the atmosphere with afforestation, that is, by stopping deforestation and reforesting previously cleared land. Unfortunately, the popular press has overrated and misdirected this solution. The overrating has taken the form of undue emphasis on mature forests, especially in the tropics. Contrary to widespread belief, a mature forest does not absorb CO_2 from the atmosphere. It has achieved an equilibrium in which the absorption of atmospheric CO_2 by plant growth is approximately canceled by the release of CO_2 from decaying plant matter. Only growth of new forests absorbs CO_2 in significant degree. It would take perpetual growth of new forests equal in area to all current U.S. forests to cut the CO_2 buildup by 20 to 25 percent. Forests play much less role in the greenhouse-gas balance than does the burning of fossil fuels.

3. A third option that doesn't work is to wait for depletion of the earth's fossil fuels to push up the price of energy to a point where we stop raising the global CO_2 levels. Finite as planet Earth may be, there is no prospect of exhaustion, or even severe scarcity, of fossil fuels in the next few decades. Even as we have been burning fossil fuels, known reserves have been increasing faster. Earth contains so much oil and other fossil fuels, and our exploration for them has been so incomplete, that our current fuel habits may exhaust our good air long before they exhaust our cheap fuel supplies. To clean up the air, we must artificially raise the price of fuel long before geology will do the job for us.

A third initial point is that international trade policy cannot be the best tool. If we are to attack greenhouse-gas emissions near their source, we must attack either total consumption or total production of fossil fuels, the main human source of greenhouse-gas emissions. International trade in fuels is large, but well below half the total fuel consumption. If we were to tax international trade as such, there would still be too much substitution of one source for another to achieve a large global reduction in emissions. If we relied on taxing international trade in fuels, fuel-importing countries like the United States would substitute home supplies for imports, and fuel-exporting countries like Mexico would divert their fuel from exports to home use.

Thus far, we have limited the search for solutions in three ways. First, sheer scientific uncertainty urges a gradual "insurance" approach, somewhere in between doing nothing and taking radical steps. Second, some hopes—the easy "no-regrets" reforms, afforestation, and naturally rising fuel scarcity—fall short as cures for the CO_2 buildup. Finally, trying to cut emissions by cutting international trade leaves too many options for substituting home fuel use for traded fuel.

We are left to consider the direct approach: tax consumption or production of fossil fuels on a near-global scale. What effects would such a global tax have on world income? Many economists have tried to estimate the effects of greenhouse-gas abatement. Figure 12.6 shows the gist of most studies, drawing on estimates by John Whalley and Randall Wigle. In this case, the tax is levied on each unit of carbon content, to aim as directly as possible at greenhouse-gas emissions. Presuming that we learn that global warming is a serious problem that requires a fairly aggressive approach, the tax is set at a dollar rate that aims to cut emissions in half from 1990 to 2030. The tax of $448 per ton of carbon is a tax of about $54.00 per barrel of crude oil or $1.34 per gallon of gas ($0.34 per liter).

Any variant of the global carbon tax would cut world income (world GDP) by something over 4 percent by the year 2030, according to the first row of numbers in Figure 12.6. That is a significant price to pay for better climate, though it is limited by economies' (estimated) ability to conserve on fossil fuels in response to the tax.

When we look at how the cost is distributed across the major economic regions of the world, we see big differences that would surely spark a heated debate in any world conference over such a tax. In the first column, the tax is levied on fuel producers and the tax revenues are rebated by their governments to the populations of those fuel-producing countries. That brings a 4.5 percent windfall gain to the oil-exporting countries, from a system that taxes the rest of the world heavily.

Alternatively, suppose that the tax is collected on fuel consumption by governments where the fuel is consumed. While that might seem a greater hardship on fuel consumers than the production tax, it is not. On the contrary, if the tax is global and uniform, the share of it that is paid by fuel consumers (as opposed to producers) is the same whether the tax falls directly on consumers or directly on producers. Regardless of who directly pays the tax, the slopes of the demand and supply curves will dictate how the tax burden is split between consumers and producers. Actually, having the tax collected in the consuming countries is a boon to them inasmuch as the revenue is collected and domestically rebated by

FIGURE 12.6   Welfare Effects of Carbon Taxes on Various Regions of the World

	A Tax on the Carbon Content of Fossil Fuel Production, Collected by the Producers' Governments	A Tax on the Carbon Content of Fossil Fuel Consumption, Collected by the Consumers' Governments	A Tax on the Carbon Content of Either Consumption or Production, Rebated on a Global per Capita Basis
Average tax rate ($/ton of carbon)	$448	$448	$448
Welfare Change by 2030 (% of GDP)			
Whole world	−4.4%	−4.4%	−4.2%
European Union	−4.0	−1.0	−3.8
U.S. and Canada	−4.3	−3.6	−9.8
Japan	−3.7	+0.5	−0.9
Other industrial market economies	−2.3	−2.1	−4.4
Oil exporters	+4.5	−18.7	−13.0
Rest of the world	−7.1	−6.8	+1.8

Source: Anderson and Blackhurst (1992), p. 103, citing Whalley and Wigle. For further detailed estimates, see the chapters by Winters and by Piggott, Whalley, and Wigle in Anderson and Blackhurst.

their own governments, as in the middle column of estimates in Figure 12.6. In this case, the industrial countries suffer much less than with the production tax (Japan actually gains on the deal), and the oil-exporting countries take a beating from the loss of world demand.

Finally, if the tax on either fuel production or fuel consumption is distributed around the world so that everybody gets the same tax-revenue rebate per person, the effects would be distributed according to the right-hand column in Figure 12.6. Poor countries, represented by the "rest of the world" category, would receive a net gain because their tax receipts exceed the cost of fuel scarcity. To the extent that the global policy intends to equalize incomes around the world, this approach would have appeal. The larger point, though, is that the differences in how the tax revenues are distributed have such huge consequences for well-being that any world negotiations over the carbon tax would surely be acrimonious.

Actual world negotiations over global warming have indeed been difficult. Industrial countries committed in Rio de Janeiro in 1992 to keep their CO_2 emissions at 1990 levels, but they have not done so. For instance, U.S. emissions were over 12 percent larger in 2000 than in 1990.

A new agreement, the **Kyoto Protocol,** was reached in late 1997. Industrial nations, which account for about half of global greenhouse-gas emissions, agreed to cut their emissions of greenhouse gases to 6 to 8 percent below their 1990 levels by the years 2008–2012 and then to continue reductions. Developing countries refused to make any commitments, however. They argued that they are poor and should not have to slow their economic growth.

The Kyoto Protocol includes some trading among countries of credits for emission reductions. This approach is conceptually attractive—creating a market for the right to emit—and it could be the basis for expanding the agreement in the future. It encourages emission reductions where they can be achieved at lowest cost, so it enhances economic efficiency. (A carbon tax would do this as well, by encouraging reductions to avoid paying the tax.) In addition, the initial allocations of rights could be used to induce developing countries to become part of an expanded agreement in the future, by giving them more than their current share of global emissions.

However, the Kyoto Protocol itself is not likely to meet its objectives. The role of the United States, which is the source of about a fifth of the world's total greenhouse-gas emissions, is a key issue. With no actions by the U.S. government to reduce U.S. emissions, they will be 40 percent above the U.S. target for 2008. In March 2001, President George W. Bush pulled the United States out of the Kyoto process, stating that it was unacceptable because developing countries made no commitments and achieving the emissions target would be too costly for the United States. Nonetheless, the other 178 countries completed the final version of the Kyoto Protocol in late 2001, adding some credits for reforestation and improved agricultural practices that absorb CO_2. As of July 2002 the final version had not yet entered into force, but it will if Russia and one or two other industrialized countries formally ratify it. However, without U.S. participation, the Kyoto Protocol cannot accomplish much. We remain well short of a global approach to global warming.

Summary   International trade is not inherently anti-environment, and the best solution to environmental problems is seldom one that involves trade policy. The rules of the WTO are generally consistent with this application of the specificity rule. They permit countries to impose environmental standards on domestic production activities and on domestic consumption activities (including environment-based product standards). The WTO also offers the possibility of environmental exceptions to its free-trade thrust. But the WTO has usually ruled against a single country that attempts to use trade policy to punish what the country views as environmentally damaging production activities in other countries. The WTO seems to view trade limits that are part of multilateral environmental agreements more favorably.

Because environmental problems like pollution involve an **externality,** government policies are usually needed to get markets to be efficient. In fact, if a country's government fails to implement a policy to limit pollution, free trade may make a country worse off and the country may end up exporting the wrong products.

Transborder pollution is an example of an international externality, in which production (or consumption) activities in one country impose external costs on other countries. As with all external costs, the best solution is one that addresses the pollution directly, by imposing a tax on the pollution, or by establishing property rights (to water or whatever is being polluted, or as limited rights to pollute). However, it is often challenging for the government of the country hurt by the pollution to gain the cooperation of the government of the country doing the pollution. For instance, little progress has been made in reducing environmental problems along the Mexico–U.S. border, even though a side agreement to NAFTA established a commission and a bank for this purpose.

In some cases the environmental problem is global: Global production or consumption is imposing a worldwide external cost. The best approach to a global environmental problem is a global cooperative agreement, but achieving one is usually difficult. Often, there are differences of opinion about the size of the external costs or the appropriate policies to adopt. Countries that suffer little or no harm have little incentive to cooperate and impose costs on themselves. More generally, countries have an incentive to free-ride on the efforts of others. Often an agreement has no real enforcement mechanism. Trade sanctions provide a possible threat against countries that do not abide by an agreement, but, as we saw in Chapter 11, sanctions often do not work.

The chapter concluded with four examples of global environmental problems. Two have been addressed by successful global agreements. An agreement (**CITES**) on using trade limits and trade bans to prevent the extinction of species has been fairly effective. But the ultimate solution may well involve creating economic incentives for "sustainable use" (the propagation and management of the previously endangered species), as the discussion of elephants and ivory suggested. The global agreement on CFCs (the **Montreal Protocol**) has also been effective and should reverse the ozone damage over time. Success here seems to be based on clear scientific evidence, the rather small number of CFC producers, the availability of substitutes at reasonable cost, and the fact that the major producing countries were also those likely to suffer the most damage.

Two problems have not been addressed successfully. Because no one owns the oceans and their resources, overfishing has led to declines in fish stocks. The large number of fishing firms and their political activity to resist limits have prevented effective global agreements. Global warming as a result of the atmospheric buildup of CO_2 and other greenhouse gases is the most daunting global environmental problem. Science does not provide clear guidance on the magnitude of the problem and its likely effects on different countries. All countries contribute to global emissions of greenhouse gases. The **Kyoto Protocol** is an attempt to address the problem, but it probably will have little effect. Most developing countries prefer to pursue growth and rising incomes and are not willing to constrain their development by taking actions to reduce their emissions. More important, the United States has indicated that it will not abide by the Kyoto Protocol.

Suggested Reading

Esty (1994), Uimonen and Whalley (1997), and World Trade Organization (1999) provide excellent surveys of trade and environment issues. Esty (2001), Neumayer (2000), and Irwin (2002) present critical analyses of the controversies. The chapters by Bhagwati and Srinivasan and by Levinson in Bhagwati and Hudec (1996) focus on specific issues. For a series of appraisals of global environmental problems, see World Resources Institute, *World Resources 1992/93* and later years.

Numerous works provide individual case studies. On CFCs, see the chapter by Enders and Porges in Anderson and Blackhurst (1992). On NAFTA and the environment, see Hufbauer et al. (2000). On dolphins and tuna, see Boreman (1992). On elephants and ivory, see Bonner (1993). On greenhouse gases, see Ekins and Barker (2001), Cline (1992), and the special symposium in the Fall 1993 issue of *The Journal of Economic Perspectives*.

Questions and Problems

✦ 1. Does a rise in national production and income per capita tend to worsen or improve air pollution, water pollution, and sanitation? Explain.

2. "One of the benefits of free trade is that it corrects the distortion caused by pollution." Do you agree or disagree? Why?

✦ 3. Which of the following probably violate the rules of the WTO?

   a. A country's government places a tax on domestic production to reduce pollution caused by this production.

   b. A country's government restricts imports of goods produced using production methods that would violate the importing country's environmental protection laws.

   c. A country's government places a tax on domestic consumption of goods (both imported and domestically produced) to reduce pollution caused by this consumption.

   d. A country's government restricts imports of a good, to reduce pollution caused by consumption of this good.

4. Mining of metallic ores often causes harm to the environment in the area around the mines. Some countries impose strict policies to limit the environmental damage caused by this mining, but others do not. The mining companies in the strict countries complain that this is unfair, and ask for limits on imports of ores and metals from the lax countries. As a government official interested in advancing the national interest in a strict country, how would you evaluate the request of your mining companies?

✦ 5. Oil spills from oceangoing tankers are rare but bring huge damages to coastlines when they occur within 200 miles of shore. Unfortunately, most tanker spills do occur on or near coasts. Rank the following alternatives according to how efficient they are in responding to the threat of oil spills. Explain your ranking.

   a. Each nation with an endangered coastline should impose a tax on all imported oil, a tax that raises enough revenue to compensate for any oil-spill damages.

  b. Each coastal nation should impose a tax on all domestically purchased oil, a tax that raises enough revenue to compensate for any oil-spill damages.

  c. Oil-carrying companies should be legally liable for all damages, in the courts of the countries whose national waters are polluted by the spills.

  d. Each coastal nation should intercept all oil tankers in national waters and charge them a fee that will cover the estimated costs of future oil spills.

  e. We might as well save ourselves the expense of trying to prevent spills. They are just accidents beyond the control of the shipping companies; they are part of the cost of having coasts.

6. Consider the example of domestic pollution shown in Figure 12.4. Suppose that the marginal social side cost of the pollution is $0.05 per ream produced (instead of $0.30).

  a. With this different MSSC, does free trade make the country better off or worse off?

  b. To gain the most from trade, should the country export or import paper? How much?

◆ 7. Which of the following would do most to cut the global buildup of carbon dioxide over the next 20 years?

  a. Eliminating all subsidies to energy use.

  b. Restoring the original tropical rain forest.

  c. A tax of $448 per ton of emitted carbon, as described in this chapter.

  d. The trend toward rising fuel scarcity, caused by exhausting the world's reserves of fossil fuels.

8. Assume that the production of cement also produces a substantial amount of air pollution and that a technology is available that can lower the pollution but with somewhat higher production costs for the cement. Because of the availability of raw materials in Lindertania, it produces large amounts of cement, and its exports supply most demand in Pugelovia. But the air pollution from Lindertania's production blows into Pugelovia, causing a noticeable deterioration in Pugelovia's air quality. Although Lindertania suffers some harm itself from this air pollution, it does not now have any policy to reduce the pollution. The Pugelovian government wants to address this air pollution problem.

  a. If the two countries' governments cooperate, what is the best solution to address the problem? Explain.

  b. If Pugelovia must come up with a solution on its own, what should the Pugelovian government do? Explain.

◆ 9. Use your no. 2 pencil to write down your views on this trade-and-environment debate:

  According to the Rainforest Action Network (RAN), a rain-forest wood called jelutong is being logged at a dangerous rate in Indonesia. The reason is that pencil makers recently shifted about 15 percent of their production from the more expensive cedar wood to jelutong, saving $1 on every dozen pencils. The Incense Cedar Institute, which represents three major companies growing cedar in the United States, echoes the concerns of RAN about the threat to tropical rain forests. Speaking for the pencil makers, executives of Dixon Ticonderoga explain that the jelutong wood in Indonesia is not gathered from rain forests, but is planted and harvested on plantations.

What should be done about the use of jelutong wood in making pencils? Should the government of Indonesia block the export of jelutong wood? Should the government of the United States tax or prohibit jelutong imports? Defend your view. If you feel you need more information than is given here, what extra information would be decisive?

10. Why did the Montreal Protocol succeed in limiting global emissions of chlorofluorocarbons (CFCs), whereas the world has found it difficult to limit the emission of CO_2? What differences between the two cases explain the difference in outcome?

Chapter **Thirteen**

Trade Policies for Developing and Transition Countries

Much of the world's attention focuses on the industrialized economies—especially the United States, Japan, and the countries of Western Europe. The attention is not surprising, given that these areas produce about 75 percent of world output and an even greater share of the supply of media services. Yet over 5 billion people (five-sixths of the world's population) live in countries that are considered developing countries. One surprise is how widely the fortunes of these developing countries vary. Some have succeeded in developing, and have experienced high growth rates. Others have experienced serious economic declines.

Figure 13.1 summarizes the best available measures of growth rates in real gross domestic product (GDP) per person for broad regions and for selected individual countries. The first point shown by Figure 13.1 is that the average product per person grew only a little faster in the developing countries than it did in the industrialized countries in the 1990s.[1] With such a small growth advantage, it would take more than three centuries for the developing countries to catch up with the average per capita income in the industrialized countries.

---

[1] Following the global convention, we use the term *developing countries* to refer to countries with low to moderate levels of income per capita.

The choice of terms to describe countries with low income levels has changed constantly over the past century. The general pattern of evolution has been toward increasingly optimistic, or even euphemistic, terminology in official international discourse. In the mid-20th century commentators could still speak of rich and poor countries. Soon, however, neither the high-income nor the low-income countries would abide such a stark contrast. From the mid-1950s to the mid-1960s, it was generally acceptable to speak of *underdeveloped countries* or *less developed countries (LDCs)*. With time, however, even terms like these were viewed as condescending.

From the 1960s through the 1980s, another attractive alternative presented itself. The *Third World* was a handy and relatively judgment-free way to contrast the low- and middle-income countries of the

The most striking pattern shown in Figure 13.1, however, is the wide disparity in growth rates among the developing countries. Some are achieving super-growth, while some have suffered declining income levels during the past decade or more. Incomes have tended to grow fastest in East Asia. The "Four Tigers" (South Korea, Taiwan, Singapore, and Hong Kong) have grown so quickly over the past two decades that they now have relatively high incomes. South Korea's per capita GDP is over $17,000, and those of the other three Tigers are even higher. Several other countries in East Asia also achieved high growth rates, including Malaysia and China. At the rate achieved in 1990–2000, China's per capita income will double in about eight years. The Asian crisis beginning in 1997 set many of these countries back, but the downturns during this crisis did not erase the growth gains of the previous years.

However, in over one-third of the developing countries for which we have data, income per person in fact declined between 1990 and 2000. Most of these were countries in Africa and countries in Central and Eastern Europe and Central Asia that are making a transition from central planning to a market-based econ-omy. The gaps in growth rates are much wider among developing countries than among high-income countries.

Why are the fortunes of developing countries so different, with some growing rapidly while others stay poor? Do differences in their trade policies play a role? Are there lessons about trade policy to be learned by studying what the super-growing *newly industrializing countries (NICs)* did that countries with stagnating or declining incomes did not? And what role do trade policies play in a success-ful transition from central planning to a market economy? This chapter reveals some clear answers and some still-unresolved questions about the trade-policy options for developing and transition countries.

WHICH TRADE POLICY FOR DEVELOPING COUNTRIES?

Trade is important for developing countries. Merchandise exports on average are about 27 percent of gross domestic product in developing countries. (For devel-oped countries exports are about 16 percent of GDP on average.) Over half of exports by developing countries go to industrialized countries, but these are only about 28 percent of industrial-country imports. Developing countries are the

noncommunist world with the high-income market economies (First World) and the communist bloc (Second World). But in 1989–1991 the Second World vanished with the breakup of the communist bloc and the Soviet Union. Without a Second World, what does *Third World* mean? These formerly communist countries became the *transition economies,* and they are now part of the set of developing countries.

Diplomatic practice has retreated to the relatively benign term *developing country.* Few are bothered by two curious implications of this term: (1) that the high-income "developed" countries are no longer developing and (2) that countries whose incomes are dropping are "developing" if and only if their incomes are already low. Another name for developing and transition countries is *emerging economies,* used especially for their emerging financial markets.

FIGURE 13.1   Growth Rates, 1990–2000, and Levels of Income Per Capita, 2000

Region or Nation	Annual Growth Rate in Per Capita GDP, 1990–2000	Per Capita GDP, 2000 (at International Dollar Prices)
23 Industrialized Countries	**1.7**	**27,848**
United States	2.2	34,142
Canada	1.9	27,840
Japan	1.1	26,755
Germany	1.2	25,103
Australia	2.9	25,693
United Kingdom	2.2	23,509
137 Developing and Transition Countries	**2.3**	**4,032**
26 Latin American and Caribbean	1.7	7,234
17 Arab States	0.7	4,793
17 East Asian and Pacific	5.7	4,290
8 South Asian	3.3	2,404
42 Sub-Saharan Africa	−0.3	1,690
25 Transition (Central and Eastern European and Central Asian)	−2.4	6,930
Selected Developing and Transition Countries		
South Korea	4.7	17,380
Slovenia	2.8	17,367
Equatorial Guinea (fastest growing)	18.9	15,073
Hungary	1.9	12,416
Argentina	3.0	12,377
Saudi Arabia	−1.2	11,367
Mauritius	4.0	10,017
Chile	5.2	9,417
South Africa	0.0	9,401
Malaysia	4.4	9,068
Poland	4.5	9,051
Mexico	1.4	9,023
Russia	−4.6	8,377
Brazil	1.5	7,625
China	9.2	3,976
Philippines	1.1	3,971
Ukraine	−8.8	3,816
Indonesia	2.5	3,043
Georgia (worst decline)	−12.4	2,664
India	4.1	2,358
Ghana	1.8	1,964
Pakistan	1.2	1,928
Bangladesh	3.0	1,602
Nigeria	−0.4	896
Sierra Leone (poorest of these 137 countries)	−6.5	490

Note: Measures of gross domestic product per capita adjusted for purchasing power parity (at international dollar prices) are better than the often-cited estimates of average dollar incomes based on exchange-rate conversions. The purchasing power parity estimates reflect the ability to buy a broad range of goods and services at the prices prevailing in each country, whereas using exchange rates to convert other-currency values into U.S. dollars misleads by reflecting only the international prices of goods that are heavily traded between countries. As a rule, comparisons based on exchange-rate conversions overstate the relative poverty of low-income countries by failing to reflect the cheapness of their nontraded services. For more on purchasing power parity, see Chapter 18.

Source: United Nations Development Program, *Human Development Report, 2002* (New York: Oxford University Press, 2002), Table 12.

source of about one-third of all world exports. Still, as we noted in Chapter 5, almost half of world trade is between industrialized countries (one industrialized country exports to another industrialized country).

What role can trade and trade policy play in development? How can trade and trade policy be used to boost incomes and economic growth in poor countries? As we discussed in Chapter 4, many developing countries have comparative advantages based on land (usually with a tropical climate) and in various natural resources "in the ground." Exploiting these comparative advantages would lead to exports of foods, fuels, and other primary products. Developing countries also generally have a comparative advantage based on less-skilled labor. This abundant labor could be used in combination with the land and natural resources in producing primary commodities, or it could be used in the production of less-skilled-labor–intensive manufactures. Developing countries could also seek to develop more advanced manufacturing industries using infant industry policies.

What should the government of, say, Ghana do about imports and exports if it is determined to reverse the economic stagnation that has held down the living standards of its people? To supplement the greater task of reforming its whole economy, Ghana has these basic trade-policy choices:

1. A trade policy that accepts and exploits the country's comparative advantages in *land and natural resources.* For Ghana this means encouraging greater exports of cocoa, coffee, gold, and other *primary products,* but offering no encouragement to industrial development by restricting imports or encouraging exports of manufactured products.

2. A trade policy that attempts to enhance the gains from exporting *primary products* by *raising the world prices* of these products. If the country's exports of a product are large enough, the country could use an *export tax* in a way that is similar to the nationally optimal import tariff of Chapter 7. If the country cannot accomplish much by itself, it could organize or join an *international cartel.* For Ghana, this means taxing exports of cocoa or organizing a cartel of cocoa producers or coffee producers.

3. A policy that taxes and restricts imports to protect and subsidize *new industries* serving the *domestic market.* For Ghana, this might mean forcing Ghanaians to buy more expensive domestic steel, televisions, and airline services. If the strategy nurtures infant industries successfully, firms in these industries eventually can compete at world prices.

4. A trade policy that encourages the development of *new industries* whose products can be readily *exported.* Presumably these new industries would make manufactured products that exploit the country's comparative advantage in *less-skilled labor.* For Ghana, the new exports would probably be textiles, clothing, or the assembly of electrical products.

A developing country today does indeed face this choice alone, for the most part, without much international help other than negotiated trade liberalizations like the Uruguay Round.

In choosing a trade policy, should a developing country just follow the trade-policy guidelines laid out in Chapters 7 through 10? Or are developing countries so different that they need a separate trade policy analysis? The basic answer is that the trade policy conclusions of Chapters 7 through 10 do apply to all countries, whether industrialized or developing. The pros and cons of restricting or subsidizing trade are the same, and the specificity rule still compels us to consider alternatives to trade policy when trade is not the source of the development problem. All that is different in this chapter is the degree of emphasis put on certain points.

Developing countries are different in that they face certain challenges that are less formidable, though still present, in a developed economy. These challenges fall into two categories:

1. *Capital markets work less efficiently in developing countries.* A defining characteristic of a lower-income country is that there are more barriers to the lending of money to the most productive uses. As a result, good projects must overcome a higher cost of capital (interest rate) than the rate at which capital is available to less promising sectors. One underlying reason is that property rights are less clearly defined, holding back the willingness to invest in new assets.

2. Similarly, *labor markets work less efficiently in developing countries.* The wage gaps between expanding and declining sectors are greater than in higher-income countries. The wider wage gaps are an indirect clue that some labor is being kept from moving to its most productive use.

These differences imply some special tasks for the government of a developing country. There is a case for considering which sectors to protect or subsidize or give cheap loans to, if the government cannot quickly eliminate the barriers to efficient capital and labor markets. The government must also decide whether it is realistic to try to change the nation's comparative advantage, for instance, by increasing its investment in education and health care to expand the country's endowment of human skills.

We now explore the alternatives for trade policy for a developing country in the order that we presented them for Ghana: focus on exporting primary products, use export taxes or international cartels to influence the world prices of these primary products, use import protection to develop new manufacturing industries, or encourage the development of export-oriented new manufacturing industries.

ARE THE LONG-RUN PRICE TRENDS AGAINST PRIMARY PRODUCERS?

It seems natural that developing countries export primary products, and these are usually called *traditional exports*. A total of 22 developing countries get more than half of their export revenues from a single primary product, including 14 that rely on petroleum and 3 on coffee. Another 41 developing countries get 20–49 percent of their export income from a single primary product, including 10 that rely on petroleum, 6 on cotton, and 3 each on gold, sugar, timber, diamonds, and bauxite/aluminum. Yet, a recurring idea is that developing countries' growth is held back by relying on exports of primary products (agriculture, forestry, and minerals). Here we explore first whether primary-product exports have a bleak future.

In the 1950s, Raul Prebisch and others argued that developing countries are hurt by a downward trend (and also instability) in primary-product prices. International markets, ran the argument, distribute income unfairly. Since developing countries are net exporters of primary products, they are trapped into declining incomes relative to incomes in the industrialized world.[2]

Does the fear of falling prices sound reasonable? Economic analysis shows that there are at least two major forces depressing, and at least two forces raising, the trend in the prices of primaries relative to manufactures.

The relative price of primary products is depressed by Engel's law and synthetic substitutes.

1. *Engel's law.* In the long run, per capita incomes rise. As they rise, demand shifts toward luxuries—goods for which the income elasticity of demand (percent rise in quantity demanded/percent rise in income causing the change in demand) is greater than 1. At the same time, the world's demand shifts away from staples—goods for which the income elasticity of demand is less than 1. The 19th-century German economist Ernst Engel (not Friedrich Engels) discovered what has become known as Engel's law: The income elasticity of demand for food is less than 1 (i.e., food is a staple). Engel's law is the most durable law in economics that does not follow from definitions or axioms. It means trouble for food producers in a prospering world. If the world's supply expanded at the exact same rate for all products, the relative price of foods would go on dropping because Engel's law says that demand would keep shifting (relatively) away from food toward luxuries.

2. *Synthetic substitutes.* Another force depressing the relative prices of primary products is the development of new human-made substitutes for these natural materials. The more technology advances, the more we are likely to discover ways to replace minerals and other raw materials. The most dramatic case is the development of synthetic rubber around the time of World War I, which ruined the incomes of rubber producers in Brazil, Malaysia, and other countries. Another case is the development of synthetic fibers, which have lowered demand for cotton and wool.

---

[2] Be careful not to assume, as many discussions imply, that there is a tight link between being a developing country and being an exporter of primary products. On average, the developing countries are only slight net exporters of primary products, and import significant amounts of them from North America, Australia, and New Zealand. And their comparative advantage in primary products varies greatly. Some developing countries (e.g., Saudi Arabia) export only primary products, while others (e.g., South Korea) export almost no primary products and are heavily dependent on importing them.

On the other hand, two other basic forces tend to raise the relative prices of primary products:

1. *Nature's limits.* Primary products use land, water, mineral deposits, and other nonrenewable resources. As population and incomes expand, the natural inputs become increasingly scarce, other things being equal. Nature's scarcity eventually raises the relative price of primary products, which use natural resources more intensively than do manufactures.

2. *Relatively slow productivity growth in the primary sector.* For several centuries productivity has advanced more slowly in agriculture, mining, and other primary sectors than in manufacturing. A reason is the tendency for cost-cutting breakthroughs in knowledge to be more important in manufacturing than in primaries (though exceptions to this rule are increasingly frequent in the age of biotechnology). Slow productivity advance translates into a slower relative advance of supply curves in primary-product markets than in manufacturing markets, and therefore a rising relative price of primaries (or a falling relative price of manufactures), other things being equal.

So we have two tendencies that depress the relative price of primary products, and we have two that raise it. How does the tug-of-war work out in the long run? Figure 13.2 summarizes 20th-century experience.

It depends on when you look at the data and how far back into history you look. Studying Figure 13.2A, we can understand why the fear of falling relative primary prices was greatest in the 1950s (when Prebisch's argument achieved popularity) and the 1980s. Those were periods of falling primary prices. On the other hand, little was written about falling primary prices just before World War I, the historical heyday of high prices for farm products and other raw materials. Nor was there much discussion of depressed prices during World War II, the Korean War of 1950–1953, or the boom in primary-product prices in the early 1970s. During such times, many writers revived the Malthusian arguments about the limits to planet Earth.

To stand back from the volatile swings in commodity prices, let's look over as long a period as possible. For Figure 13.2, we can scan the period 1900–2000, though following some price series back to 1870 would tell a similar story. The overall change is clear. By 2000, relative primary-product prices were about half of what they were in 1900. The trend has indeed been downward. Somehow, Engel's law and the technological biases toward replacing primary products have outrun nature's limits and the relative slowness of productivity growth in primary sectors. (Or, in shorthand, Prebisch outran Malthus.) Cutting the relative price in half over 100 years means a downward trend of 0.7 percent a year.

Some commodities have declined in price more seriously than others. The price of rubber snapped downward between 1910 and 1920 and has never really bounced back since. Significant price declines have also been the rule for cocoa, sugar, copper, tin, wheat, and rice. Only wool and coffee showed significantly upward trends between 1900 and 1982, and the price of coffee weakened after

FIGURE 13.2   The Relative Price of Primary Products, 1900–2000

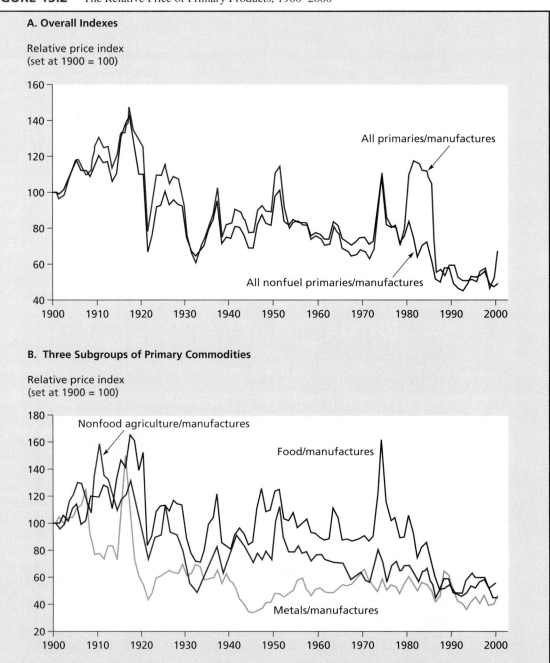

For each commodity group, the relative price index is the ratio of the dollar-price index for the indicated primary products to the dollar-price index for exports of manufactures by industrialized countries.

Sources: Grilli and Yang (1988), updated using information on prices of primary products from International Monetary Fund, *International Financial Statistics Yearbook, 2001* (Washington, D.C.: International Monetary Fund, 2001), and information on the unit values of manufactured-good exports from United Nations Conference on Trade and Development, *Handbook of Statistics, 2001* (New York: United Nations, 2001).

1982. Even fuels like oil and coal lacked a net upward price trend over the 20th century, despite the resounding price flare-ups of 1973–1974 and 1979–1980.

While the net downward trend in primary prices stands as a tentative conclusion, there are two downward-trend biases in the available measures, measures like those presented in Figure 13.2.

1. *The fall in transport costs.* The available data tend to be gathered at markets in the industrial countries. Yet technological improvements in transportation have been great enough to reduce the share of transport costs in those final prices in London, New York, or Tokyo. That has left more and more of the final price back in the hands of the primary-product exporters. Quantifying this known change would tilt the trend in the prices received by producers toward a flatter, less downward trend.

2. *Faster unmeasured quality change in manufactures.* We are using long runs of price data on products that have been getting better over time. Quality improvements (including those in the form of new products) are thought to have been more impressive in manufactures (and services) than in primary products. So what might look like a rise in the relative price of manufactures might be just a rise in their relative quality, with no trend in the relative price for given quality. This data problem is potentially serious, given that many 20th-century data have, for example, followed the prices of machinery exports per ton of exports, as if a ton of today's computers were the same thing as a ton of old electric motors.

When all is said and done, the relative price of primary products may have declined as much as 0.7 percent a year since 1900 (as in Figure 13.2), or there could have been almost no trend. There is a weak case for worrying about being an exporter of agricultural or extractive products on price-trend grounds.

INTERNATIONAL CARTELS TO RAISE PRIMARY-PRODUCT PRICES

Perhaps the developing-country producers of primary products can take actions to turn the price trends in their favor. Perhaps the primary product exporters can become more powerful if they cooperate with each other, using international cartels or other types of concerted action.

The OPEC Victories

History records many attempts at international cartels (international agreements to restrict competition among sellers). The greatest seizure of monopoly power in world history was the price-raising triumph of the Organization of Petroleum Exporting Countries (OPEC)[3] in 1973–1974 and again in 1979–1980.

---

[3]OPEC was created by a treaty among five countries—Iran, Iraq, Kuwait, Saudi Arabia, and Venezuela—in Baghdad in 1960. Since that time, the following countries joined: Qatar (1961), Indonesia and Libya (1962). United Arab Emirates (1967), Algeria (1969), Nigeria (1971), and Ecuador and Gabon (1973).

A chain of events in late 1973 revolutionized the world oil economy. In a few months' time, the 13 members of OPEC effectively quadrupled the dollar price of crude oil, from $2.59 to $11.65 a barrel. Oil-exporting countries became rich almost overnight. The industrial oil-consuming countries sank into their deepest depression since the 1930s. The relative price of oil (what the price of a barrel of oil could buy in terms of manufactured exports from industrial nations) tripled.

The sequel was a plateau of OPEC prosperity, a further jump, and finally growing signs of weakness. From 1974 to 1978, the relative price of oil dipped by about a sixth, but stayed much higher than it had been at any time before 1973. Next came the second wave of OPEC price hikes, the second "oil shock," in 1979–1980. Led by the Iranian Revolution and growing panic among oil buyers, the relative oil price more than doubled. In the mid-1980s, however, OPEC weakened. The relative price of oil dropped suddenly in late 1985, from four to five times the old (pre-1973) real price in 1980–1984 to less than two times the old price for 1986–1989. By 1998, the relative price of oil in world markets had fallen almost to its level back in 1972, but then it nearly doubled from 1998 to 2002.

The tale of oil and OPEC is one of two dramatic cartel victories in the 1970s and a subsequent retreat. The victories and the retreat both need explanation.

First the victories. The oil shocks of 1973–1974 and 1979–1980 were not the result of a failure of supply or exhaustion of earth's available resources. The world's "proved reserves" of known and usable oil have grown even faster than world oil consumption. Nor were the costs of oil extraction rising much.

The 1973–1974 and 1979–1980 oil price jumps were human-made. The key was that world demand was growing far faster than *non-OPEC* supplies. Postwar oil discoveries have been very unevenly distributed among countries. The share of OPEC countries in world crude oil production rose to over 50 percent by 1972. Furthermore, OPEC's share of proved reserves—roughly, its share of future production—was over two-thirds. Ample oil reserves are still being discovered the world over, but they happen to be concentrated increasingly in the Middle East.

By the early 1970s, the United States was for the first time becoming vulnerable to pressure from oil-exporting countries. Largely immune to oil threats in earlier Middle East crises, the United States found itself importing a third of its oil consumption, part of it from Arab countries, by 1973. Today imports are an even higher share, about half, of U.S. oil consumption, and the United States consumes about a quarter of the world's oil. It is still true that the United States, with its huge economy and its cheap-oil consumption policy, plays a leading role in determining the world price of oil.

With their growing importance in world production, and with growing U.S. reliance on oil imports, OPEC countries were able to create a scramble among buyers to pay higher prices for oil in 1973 and again in 1979.

Classic Monopoly as an Extreme Model for Cartels

How big could the cartel opportunity be? That is, if a group of nations or firms were to form a cartel, as OPEC did, what is the greatest amount of gain they could reap at the expense of their buyers and world efficiency? If all of the cartel members could agree on simply maximizing their collective gain, they would behave as though they were a perfectly unified profit-maximizing monopolist. Because a commodity like oil is fungible, they would probably not be able to discriminate by setting different prices to different foreign buyers (except for standard distinctions by quality that we can safely ignore here). The cartel members acting as a monopoly would try to find the price level that would maximize the gap between their total export sales revenues and their total costs of producing exports. When cutting output back to the level of demand yielded by their optimal price, they would take care to shut down their most costly production units (e.g., oil wells) and keep in operation only those with the lowest operating costs.

Figure 13.3 portrays a monopoly or cartel that has managed to extract maximum profits from its buyers. To understand what price and output yield that highest level of profits, and what limits those profits, we must first understand that the optimal price lies above the price that perfect competition would yield, yet below the price that would discourage all sales.

If perfect competition reigned in the world oil market, the marginal-cost curve in Figure 13.3 would also be the supply curve for oil exports. Competitive equilibrium would be at point *C*, where the marginal cost of extra oil exports has risen

FIGURE 13.3

A Cartel
as a Profit-
Maximizing
Monopoly

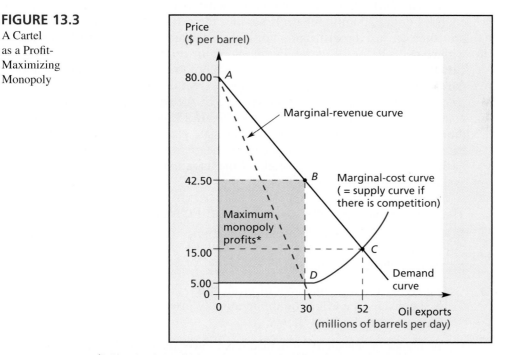

*Before subtracting any fixed costs.
If a cartel were so tightly disciplined as to be a pure monopoly, it would maximize profits according to the familiar monopoly model. It would not keep prices so low and output so high as to behave like a competitive industry, at point *C*. Why not? Because the slightest price increase, starting at point *C*, would give them net gains. Instead the cartel would set price as high, with quantity demanded and output as low, as shown at point *B*. At this level of output (30 million barrels a day), profit is maximized because the marginal revenue gained from a bit more output raising and price cutting just balances the marginal cost of the extra output.

to meet $15, the amount that the extra oil is worth to buyers (as shown by the demand curve).

The cartel members want to set a price higher than the competitive price, but their pricing power is limited by the negative slope of the demand curve for the cartel's product. This point is clear if we just consider the extreme case of a prohibitive price markup. If the cartel were foolish enough to push the price to $80 a barrel in Figure 13.3, it would lose all of its export business, as shown at point *A*. The handsome markup to $80 would be worthless, since nobody would be paying it to the cartel. Thus, the cartel's best price must be well below the prohibitive price.

The cartel members could find their most profitable price by using the model of monopoly: The highest possible profits are those corresponding to the level of sales at which the marginal-revenue curve intersects the marginal-cost curve. These maximum profits would be reaped at point *B* in Figure 13.3, with a price set at $42.50 a barrel, yielding 30 million barrels of export sales a day and monopoly profits of ($42.50 − $5) × 30 million barrels = $1,125 million a day. If the cartel had not been formed, competition would have limited the profits of its members to the area below the $15 price line and above the marginal-cost curve. Given the demand curve and the marginal-cost curve the profit gained by pushing price and quantity to point *B* is the best the cartel can do.

The cartel price that is optimal for its members is not optimal for the world, of course. For the 30 million barrels per day, the extra cartel profits above the $15 price line are just a redistribution of income from buying countries to the cartel, with no net gain for the world. Furthermore, the cartel causes net world losses by curtailing oil exports that would be worth more to buyers around the world than those exports cost the cartel members themselves to produce. The world net loss from the cartel is represented in Figure 13.3 by the area *BCD* (which would equal about $412.5 million a day, as drawn in Figure 13.3). This area shows that what the cartel is costing the world as a whole is the gap between what buyers would have willingly paid for the extra 22 million barrels a day, as shown by the height of the demand curve, and the height of the marginal-cost curve between 30 million barrels and 52 million barrels.

The Limits to and Erosion of Cartel Power

How high is the cartel's profit-maximizing price, if the cartel is functioning at full effectiveness? The theory of cartels provides some rules.[4] The first two rules follow from the monopoly model:

- The higher the marginal cost of production, the higher the price. In Figure 13.3, consider the effect on the monopoly price if the entire marginal-cost curve is higher than that shown.

- The higher the elasticity of demand, the lower the price. If demand is elastic, buyers easily find other ways of spending their money if the product price

---

[4] Appendix D presents the mathematical formula for the optimal cartel price.

rises much. In Figure 13.3, consider the effect on the monopoly price of a different demand curve, one through point *C* and flatter (more elastic) than the curve shown.

However, even a well-functioning cartel usually does not control all of the world's production. If it doesn't, then we have two more rules:

- The larger the share of world production controlled by the cartel, the higher the price. Controlling more of the world production effectively increases the demand for the cartel's production (rather than having this demand lost to outside producers).

- The larger the elasticity of supply of noncartel producers, the lower the price. The elasticity of noncartel supply acts in the same way that the elasticity of demand does. The cartel refrains from raising the price too much because doing so results in too large a loss of sales.

These rules also suggest forces that work increasingly against cartels *over time.* When the cartel is first set up, it may well enjoy low elasticities and a high market share. Yet its very success in raising price is likely to set four anticartel trends in motion: sagging demand, new competing supply, declining market share, and cheating.

Sagging Demand
First, the higher price will make buying countries look for new ways to avoid importing the cartel's product. If the search for substitutes has any success at all, imports of the buying countries will drop over time for any given cartel price. These countries' long-run demand curve for imports of the product is more elastic than their short-run demand curve. This happened to OPEC. As theory predicts, and as some OPEC oil ministers had feared, the oil-importing countries slowly came up with ways to conserve on oil use, such as more fuel-efficient cars.

New Competing Supply
Second, the initial cartel success will accelerate the search for additional supplies in noncartel countries. If the cartel product is an agricultural crop, such as sugar or coffee, the cartel's price hike will cause farmers in other countries to shift increasing amounts of land, labor, and funds from other crops into sugar or coffee. If the cartel product is a depletable mineral resource, such as oil or copper, noncartel countries will respond to the higher price by redoubling their explorations in search of new reserves. If the noncartel countries have any luck at all, their competing supply will become increasingly elastic with time. Again, that happened to OPEC— other countries discovered new oil at a faster rate.

Declining Market Share
Third, the cartel's world market share will fall over time. To raise the product's price without piling up ever-rising unsold inventories, the cartel must cut its output and sales. Since nonmembers will be straining to raise their output and sales,

the cartel's share of the market will drop even if all of its members cooperate solidly. OPEC's share of world oil production fell from over half in the early 1970s to about a third in the later 1990s.

Cheating

Theory and experience add a fourth reason for a decline in cartel power—the incentive for members to cheat on the cartel agreement.

To see why, suppose that you were a member of the successful oil export cartel shown back in Figure 13.3. As a typical cartel member, you have enough oil reserves to pump and sell more than your agreed output (OPEC calls this your production quota) for as long in the future as you need to plan. Raising your output above your production quota might cost you only, say, $6 a barrel at the margin. Buyers are willing to pay close to $42.50 for each barrel you sell, if the other cartel members are faithfully holding down their output. Why not attract some extra buyers to you by shaving your price just a little bit below $42.50, say, to $41? You can do so in the hope that your individual actions will not cause the cartel price to drop much, if at all. Theory says that this incentive to cheat tends to undermine the whole cartel. Perhaps some large members can keep the cartel effective for a while by drastically cutting their own outputs to offset the extra sales from the cheaters. Their aggregate size determines how long they can hold out.

OPEC members cheated on the cartel, even openly, just as theory would predict. Up to the mid-1980s, the largest producer, Saudi Arabia, had to hold the cartel together by cutting its production while others cheated. Then the Saudis themselves shifted to a more competitive stance, and the relative price of oil fell dramatically in late 1985. Since then the oil price has fluctuated in ways that mostly seem consistent with the dynamics of competitive supply and demand.

The usual theory of cartels thus correctly explains why cartel profit margins and profits will erode with time.[5] Yet the theory does not say that cartels are unprofitable or harmless. On the contrary, it underscores the profitability of cartel formation to cartel members. Even a cartel that eventually erodes can bring fortunes to its members.

Other Primary Products

Do theory and OPEC experience hold out hope for developing countries wanting to make large national gains by joining cartels in other primary products besides oil? Not much. There are good reasons for believing that international cartels would collapse faster, with less interim profit, for the non-oil primary products. For agricultural crops in particular, there is the problem of competing supply. Other countries usually can easily expand the acreage they devote to a given crop. Similarly with animal products and forests.

---

[5] These same reasons also imply that a cartel probably would be wise to charge a lower markup, even at the start, than the markup implied by short-run elasticities of demand and noncartel supply. The higher the initial markup, the faster the erosion of the cartel's market share and the lower the optimal markup that the cartel can charge later on.

History agrees with this verdict. Of the 72 commodity cartels set up between the two world wars, only 2 survived past 1945. Of the few dozen set up in the 1970s, only five lived as late as 1985: cocoa, coffee, rubber, sugar, and tin. These five cartels have been so weak that they have had little effect on commodity markets since 1985. For instance, the rubber cartel took its last bounce in 1999, after amassing a large holding of rubber in an effort to boost the market price. (In 2002, Thailand, Indonesia, and Malaysia, which account for more than 70 percent of the world's production of natural rubber, agreed to form a new cartel, the International Tripartite Rubber Organization. The cartel's first action was to attempt a cutback in production of 4 percent and a cutback in exports of 10 percent.)

Given the limits of international cartel power, a developing nation could still tax its own primary-product exports for the sake of economic development. In principle, the strategy could work well. A tax on exports of Nigerian oil, Ghanaian cocoa, or Philippine coconuts could generate revenues for building schools, hospitals, and roads.

Unfortunately, the political economy of some developing countries seems to divert the export-tax revenues away from the most productive uses (as we noted in Chapter 9 when discussing the developing government argument for import tariffs). So it has been with the three examples just imagined. Nigeria's oil revenues are lost in a swollen government bureaucracy. For two decades Ghana's cocoa marketing board used its heavy taxation of cocoa farmers to support luxury imports by officials. The Marcos government distributed the Philippine coconut-tax revenues among a handful of Marcos's friends and relatives.

IMPORT-SUBSTITUTING INDUSTRIALIZATION (ISI)

Exporting primary products is a way for many developing countries to use their comparative advantages based on land and natural resources. But reliance on such traditional exports brings risks, including what appear to be slowly declining relative prices of these products and exposure to the wide swings in world prices. Perhaps shifting the emphasis toward developing new industries, especially in manufacturing, is better for countries that want to grow more rapidly. After all, most high-income countries have industrialized.

To develop, officials from many countries have argued, they must cut their reliance on exporting primary products and must adopt government policies allowing industry to grow at the expense of the agricultural and mining sectors. Can this emphasis on industrialization be justified? If so, should it be carried out by restricting imports of manufactures?

The Great Depression caused many countries to turn toward **import-substituting industrialization (ISI).** In the early 1920s and again in the early 1930s, world prices of most primary products plummeted. Although these price declines did not prove that primary exporters were suffering more than industrial countries, it was common to suspect that this was so. Several primary-product–exporting countries, among them Brazil and Australia, launched industrialization at the expense of industrial imports in the 1930s.

The ISI strategy gained additional prestige among newly independent nations in the 1950s and 1960s. This approach soon prevailed in most developing countries whose barriers against manufactured imports came to match those of the most protectionist prewar industrializers. Though many countries have switched toward more pro-trade and export-oriented policies since the mid-1960s, ISI remains an important policy for developing countries.

ISI at Its Best

To see the state of knowledge about the merits and drawbacks of ISI, let us begin by noting the four main arguments in its favor. If ISI could be fine-tuned to make the most of these arguments, it would be a fine policy indeed.

1. The *infant industry argument* from Chapter 9 returns, with its legitimate emphasis on the economic and social side benefits from industrialization. These side benefits were reviewed in Chapter 9: gains in technological knowledge and worker skills transcending the individual firm, new attitudes more conducive to growth, and national pride. As we saw in Chapter 9, the economist can imagine other tools more suitable to each of these tasks than import barriers. But in an imperfect world these better options may not be at hand, and protection for an infant modern-manufacturing sector could bring gains.

2. The *developing government argument* from Chapter 9 lends further support to ISI. Suppose that the only way that a government can raise revenues for any kind of economic development is to tax imports and exports. Such taxation could bring gains to a nation whose government cannot mobilize resources for health, education, and so on without taxing trade. ISI would be a by-product of such taxation of foreign trade.

3. For a large country, or a large organization of countries, replacing imports can bring better *terms-of-trade effects* than expansion of export industries. Here we return to a theme sounded first in the discussion of "immiserizing growth" in Chapter 6 and again during Chapter 7's discussion of the nationally optimal tariff. Replacing imports with domestic production will, if it has any effect at all on the price of the continuing imports, tend to lower these prices (excluding the tariff or other import charge) and offer the nation a better bargain. If you can affect the prices at which you trade, wouldn't it be better to expand your supply of import-competing industries, forcing foreigners to sell you the remaining imports at a lower price?

4. Replacing imports of manufactures is a way of using *cheap and convenient market information*. A developing country may lack the expertise to judge just which of the thousands of heterogeneous industrial goods it could best market abroad. But government officials (and private industrialists) have an easy way to find which modern manufactures would sell in their own markets. They need only look at the import figures. Here is a handy menu of goods with proven markets.

Experience with ISI

History and recent economic studies offer four kinds of evidence on the merits of ISI. Casual historical evidence suggests a slightly charitable view, while three kinds of detailed tests support a negative verdict.

In support of ISI, it can be said that today's leading industrial countries protected their industry against import competition earlier, when their growth was first accelerating. The United States, for example, practiced ISI from the Civil War until the end of World War II, when most American firms no longer needed protection against imports. Japan, in the 1950s, launched its drive for leadership in steel, automobiles, and electronics with heavy government protection against imports. When these industries were able to compete securely in world markets, Japan removed its redundant protection against imports into Japan.

Such a casual reading of history is at least correct in its premise: The industrialized countries did at times give import protection to industries that became their export strengths. But it is wrong to infer that most cases of industrial protection nurtured sectors that responded with strong productivity gains. On the contrary, even Japan, like the United States and most other industrialized countries, gave its strongest protection to sectors whose decline was long-lasting. In all likelihood, ISI in the earlier history of these countries slowed down their economic growth. Most of the infant industries, in other words, never grew up.

In contrast to the weaknesses of the evidence for ISI, the evidence against it takes three forms that in combination add up to a strong case. The first kind of test casting serious doubt on the merits of ISI is the estimation of its *static effects on national well-being,* using the methods introduced in Chapter 7. A series of detailed country studies quantified the welfare effects of a host of developing-country trade barriers in the 1960s and early 1970s, many of which were designed to promote industrialization. The barriers imposed significant costs on Argentina, Chile, Colombia, Egypt, Ghana, India, Israel, Mexico, Pakistan, the Philippines, South Korea, Taiwan, and Turkey. Only in Malaysia did the import barriers bring a slight gain, here because of a favorable terms-of-trade effect.[6]

By themselves, these standard calculations of welfare costs of trade barriers are vulnerable to the charge of assuming, not proving, that ISI is bad. Such calculations assume that all the relevant effects are captured by measures of consumer and producer surplus, without allowing protection any chance to lower cost curves as it is imagined to do in the infant industry case. It would be fair to demand firmer proof.

A second kind of test looks at what happens when a country *changes its trade-policy orientation* toward manufactures, away from restricting imports (ISI), and toward championing exports. Here there were two dramatic early cases. Until the late 1950s, Taiwan used ISI but then switched to a policy that encouraged exports. It subsequently achieved growth rates of about 10 percent per year.

---

[6]See Bela Balassa (1971), Jagdish Bhagwati and Anne Krueger (1973–1976), and A. Choksi et al. (1991).

South Korea used ISI until policy reforms in the early 1960s increased its incentives for exports and lowered its import barriers. Its growth rate increased to about 10 percent per year. Hong Kong and Singapore also used policies that encouraged exports and achieved high growth rates. Other countries have achieved substantial effects. In the case of Ghana, the ISI strategy was part of a larger heavy hand of government that turned early growth into a 42 percent decline of Ghana's living standards over the decade 1974–1984. The country was saddled with costly industrial white elephants that never became efficient. Only thereafter, after partial reforms that included a partial liberalization of trade policy, did Ghana regain positive economic growth.

A third kind of test *compares growth rates of countries practicing ISI with growth rates of countries using policies that emphasize exporting.* The 1987 *World Development Report* presented the results of the World Bank's study of growth rates in 41 countries, which were placed into four categories according to their trade policy: strongly outward-oriented, moderately outward-oriented, moderately inward-oriented, and strongly inward-oriented. Hong Kong, South Korea, and Singapore followed strongly outward-oriented policies, with low trade barriers and some use of export subsidies (that is, their policies were close to free trade). The strongly inward-oriented countries used high trade barriers. These included Argentina, Bangladesh, Chile (up to 1973), India, and Turkey (to 1973).

In the two time periods that the World Bank examined, 1963–1973 and 1973–1985, the average growth rate of real GDP per person was highest for the three countries with strongly outward-oriented trade policies (6.9 percent and 5.9 percent per year, respectively). The average growth rate in the countries with strongly inward-oriented trade policies was lowest in both periods (1.6 percent and –0.1 percent per year, respectively). An update in the 1994 *World Development Report* found that this pattern also held for the time period 1980–1992 (a 6.2 percent annual growth rate for the strongly outward-oriented countries, and a –0.4 annual growth rate for the strongly inward-oriented countries).

In a 2002 study, the World Bank contrasted the experience of developing countries that have increased their integration into world markets since 1980 with the experience of other countries. The *newly globalizing developing countries,* as the World Bank calls them, are generally countries that

- Had relatively low involvement in international trade and high tariffs in 1980, but then

- Greatly increased their international trade (measured by the increase in the ratio of exports and imports to national GDP) and

- Substantially lowered their tariff rates.

The 24 newly globalizing developing countries have a total population of 3 billion and include Argentina, Bangladesh, Brazil, China, Colombia, India, Nicaragua, Thailand, and Uruguay. The other developing countries have a total population of about 2 billion and include many African countries and countries of the former Soviet Union. Most of these other developing countries concentrate on exporting primary products.

The World Bank found that the newly globalizing developing countries achieved average growth rates of GDP per person of 3.5 percent during the 1980s and 5.0 percent during the 1990s. These average growth rates were above their average annual growth rates in the 1960s (1.4 percent) and 1970s (2.9 percent). Their average growth rates in the 1980s and 1990s were also higher than the average growth rates of other developing countries (0.8 percent and 1.4 percent, respectively) and of the industrialized countries (2.3 percent and 2.2 percent, respectively). The differences between the newly globalizing and other developing countries do not seem to reflect favorable initial economic conditions for the new globalizers. In 1980 the people in the two groups had comparable average levels of education, and the newly globalizing countries on average had somewhat lower incomes per capita.

Such direct comparisons (as in these several World Bank studies) between *countries practicing or adopting freer-trade regimes* and *countries practicing a variant of ISI or resisting further liberalization of their trade policies* have the virtue of simplicity: They look directly at the two variables of interest (trade policies and economic growth). Yet here, as always, correlation cannot prove causation. By itself, this kind of evidence against ISI and restricting trade is subject to the suspicion that maybe some other force caused economic growth to be correlated with freer-trade policies. Or perhaps the causation ran the opposite way—perhaps successful growth itself brings freer-trade policies, even though policies departing from free trade helped promote growth. While it is not possible to answer these concerns fully, economists have conducted more complicated tests of the statistical significance of trade policy. After allowing for the effects of other variables such as investment, initial income, and education, the research tends to confirm that ISI-type trade barriers are a negative influence on economic growth.

If theory suggests that ISI can work well, why does experience make it look like a bad idea? There is no direct contradiction because theory only asserted that ISI *can* be better than free trade under certain conditions. It just so happens that those conditions did not hold since the early 1960s. The theory failed, above all, in the assumption that an informed government tried to maximize national income. Real-world governments are ill-informed, and they lack the power to stop protecting industries that turn out to be inefficient. Worse, many governments have their own self-interest, which conflicts with the goal of maximizing national well-being. Embarking on a policy of ISI has so far not turned any economy into a supergrower like South Korea. More often, the ISI route is the road that turns a South Korea into a North Korea. ISI often results in industries in which domestic firms have high costs and domestic monopoly power, and produce products of low quality.

Outward-oriented policies encourage domestic firms to make use of the country's abundant resources, and the firms can use sales into international markets to achieve scale economies. The efforts to succeed in foreign markets also mean that domestic firms face international competitive pressure, so that they are driven to raise product quality and resource productivity. The country can use its rising exports to pay for its rising imports. At the same time, an outward-oriented policy is not enough by itself to produce high growth rates. It must be part of a set of policies that minimize distortions in the economy, that nurture high rates of investment by establishing clear property rights and an impartial system of business law, and that provide such infrastructure as ports, airports, electricity, and communications.

EXPORTS OF MANUFACTURES TO INDUSTRIAL COUNTRIES

Since 1980, developing countries have turned increasingly toward our fourth trade-policy choice, emphasizing new exports of less-skilled-labor–intensive manufactured goods to the industrialized countries. As Figure 13.4 shows, the switch from primary-product exports to manufactured exports gained momentum in the 1980s and continued through the 1990s. Disillusionment with both primary-product cartels and ISI was probably a factor in the new push.

Is it wise for a developing nation to plan on being able to raise its exports of manufactures to the already industrialized countries? Should Mexico, Ghana, and India follow the example of South Korea, making strategic plans to become major exporters of manufactures? Would the same thing happen without planning, as in the market-directed development of Hong Kong and Taiwan?

For their part, the industrialized countries have not made the task easy. They have, in fact, discriminated against exports of manufactures from developing countries. Nontariff import barriers apply to a greater percentage of goods from developing countries than to goods from other industrial countries. As for tariffs, the rates are in principle nondiscriminatory. Tariff rates differ, however, by type of product. In general, the highest tariff rates among manufactures are those on textiles, apparel, and footwear—the kind of manufactures in which developing countries have their broadest comparative advantage.

Developing countries are thus justified in charging the industrial nations with hypocrisy. The industrial nations have not practiced the policies of free trade and comparative advantage that they have urged on developing countries. Furthermore, the departures of practice from preaching have been greatest on manufactures exported from developing countries. The new Doha Round of multilateral trade negotiations is billed by the World Trade Organization as a "development round" in which a major focus will be improving access for the exports of developing countries into markets in both the industrialized countries and other developing countries. You can watch to see if this vision is being achieved as the negotiations proceed.

Despite some discrimination against their exports, developing countries have been able to break into world markets for their exports of manufactures. One reason is that developing countries have been able to become exporters in standardized manufacturing lines where technological progress has cooled down, such as textiles, tires, and simple electrical appliances. A second reason is that developing countries have become locations for low-cost assembly of more technologically advanced products like computers, with multinational firms from the industrialized countries providing the advanced technology, the components, and the marketing and distribution of the finished products.

FIGURE 13.4
The Changing
Mix of Exports
from Developing
Countries,
1970–1999

	1970	**1975**	**1980**	**1985**	**1990**	**1995**	**1999**
Nonfuel primary products	49.9%	25.8%	18.7%	22.4%	18.7%	17.3%	14.2%
Fuels	32.4	58.6	61.3	42.2	27.5	15.5	14.8
Manufactures	17.4	15.2	18.5	32.4	52.9	65.6	67.9

Note: Columns do not add to 100% because of a small amount of unclassified exports in each year.

Source: United Nations Conference on Trade and Development, *Handbook of International Trade and Development Statistics,* 1987 and 1995 (New York: United Nations, 1988 and 1997), and United Nations Conference on Trade and Development, *Handbook of Statistics, 2001* (New York: United Nations, 2001).

A third reason is that barriers against imports of manufactures from developing countries are not all that solid. Consider barriers based on voluntary export restraints, antidumping duties, or countervailing duties. These barriers can limit increases in exports from countries that have already succeeded in establishing their exports to the industrialized countries. But newcomers can gain market access for new manufactured-product exports because they are not hindered by such country-specific barriers. In this way a developing country can gain valuable new export markets, despite the protectionism of the industrialized countries, although there may eventually be limits on how large these export sales can grow.

All in all, betting on exports of manufactures is part of the most promising strategy for most developing countries. And as Figure 13.4 has made clear, the developing countries are relying more and more on this strategy.

THE SPECIAL CHALLENGES OF TRANSITION

In 1989, a massive transition from central planning to market economies began in the formerly socialist countries of Central and Southeastern Europe. With the breakup of the Soviet Union in 1991, the former Soviet Union countries joined in this transition. This is the most dramatic episode of economic liberalization in history. What role have changing policies toward international trade played in the transition efforts? And what have we learned about trade and transition?

Prior to the transition beginning in 1989–1991, central planning by each national government directed the economies in these countries. National self-sufficiency was a goal of policy. Imports were used to close gaps in the plan, mainly imports of materials and products that were not (yet) available locally, and a state bureaucracy controlled exports and imports. When international trade was necessary, the Soviet Union and its bloc of countries in Central and Southeastern Europe favored trade among themselves and strongly discouraged trade with outside countries. But among themselves these countries had a tough problem—what and how to trade in a balanced way. They tended to use bilateral barter trade, with long lists of exports and imports for each pair of countries. In 1949, six countries set up the Council for Mutual Economic Assistance (CMEA) to promote more efficient and multilateral trade.[7] Still, bilateral trade accounts predominated. The trade pattern that emerged had the Soviet Union specializing in exporting oil and gas (at prices well below world prices) and the other countries exporting industrial and farm products.

As the transition began, these countries had a legacy of poor decision making under central planning, including overdevelopment of heavy industries (like steel and defense), outdated technology, environmental problems, and little established trade with market economies. The countries needed to remove state control of transactions and undertake a major reorientation and reorganization of production. They could expect severe negative effects during the transition, including major decreases in national production. Each country faced daunting problems: Before the turnaround, how bad would it be, and for how long?

Reforms for Transition

Transition involves accomplishing three challenging tasks: (1) shifting to competitive markets and market-determined prices, with a new process of resource allocation; (2) establishing private ownership, with privatization of state businesses; and (3) establishing a legal system, with contract laws and property rights. For success, the transition process must impose *discipline on firms inherited* from the era of central planning, and it must provide *encouragement for new firms* that are not dependent on the government. Opening the economy to international trade and direct investments by foreign firms can be part of both the discipline (through the competition provided by imports) and the encouragement (through access to new export markets and to foreign technology and know-how).

Domestic and international reforms usually advance together in a country, and success requires a consistent combination of reforms. Keeping this in mind, let's focus on the role of trade policy in transition. Figure 13.5 reports a number of indicators of trade, trade policy, and growth in the transition economies. The European Bank for Reconstruction and Development has analyzed each country's progress on trade reform (and other types of reform not reported here). The first two columns of numbers show its estimates of the progress of trade and foreign exchange reforms for 1994 and 2000. The speed and extent of reforms vary across the sets of countries shown in the figure.

With the exceptions of Bosnia and Yugoslavia, both of which were involved in fighting over the future of their region, the Central and Southeastern European countries and the Baltic countries pursued strong, rapid liberalizations. They achieved a rating of 4 (all trade restrictions removed) by 1994. Most of these

---

[7]The six original members of the CMEA were Bulgaria, Czechoslovakia, Hungary, Poland, Romania, and the Soviet Union. Late in 1949, Albania and East Germany joined. In 1962, Albania left and Mongolia joined. Cuba joined in 1972. The CMEA disbanded in 1991. Yugoslavia was never a member of the CMEA, so the countries that have evolved out of communist Yugoslavia (Slovenia, Croatia, Bosnia and Herzegovina, Macedonia, and the current Yugoslavia) had a different history of international trade before transition.

FIGURE 13.5   Trade Reform and Growth in Transition Economies

Country	Progress in Trade and Foreign Exchange Reform, (4+ = Most)		Exports to Industrialized Countries as a Percentage of Total Exports		Percentage Change in Real GDP, 2000 Compared to 1989	Year of Resumption of Real GDP Growth
	1994	2000	1993–1994	1999–2000		
Central and Southeastern European Countries						
Albania	4	4+	87%	95%	2%	1993
Bosnia and Herzegovina	1	3	51	66	NA	NA
Bulgaria	4	4+	54	59	−30	1994
Croatia	4	4+	63	57	−20	1994
Czech Republic	4	4+	59	74	−2	1993
Hungary	4+	4+	69	83	5	1994
Macedonia	4	4	42	59	−23	1996
Poland	4	4+	75	76	27	1992
Romania	4	4	51	70	−23	1993
Slovak Republic	4	4+	35	63	3	1994
Slovenia	4	4+	70	70	14	1993
Yugoslavia	1	1	13	70	−52	1994
Baltic Countries						
Estonia	4	4+	52	72	−18	1995
Latvia	4	4+	38	71	−36	1996
Lithuania	4	4	47	57	−36	1995
CIS Countries						
Armenia	2	4	15	53	−37	1994
Azerbaijan	1	3+	11	61	−48	1996
Belarus	1	2−	17	11	−15	1996
Georgia	1	4+	33	30	−66	1995
Kazakhstan	2	3+	23	30	−32	1996
Kyrgyzstan	3	4	16	43	−34	1996
Moldova	2	4	8	35	−68	2000
Russia	3	2+	55	50	−38	1999
Tajikistan	1	3+	66	42	−53	1997
Turkmenistan	1	1	37	22	−25	1998
Ukraine	1	3	21	24	−61	2000
Uzbekistan	2	1	45	24	−4	1996

NA: Information not available.

Note: "Progress in Trade and Foreign Exchange Reform" is a five category index: (1) widespread controls, (2) some liberalization, (3) removal of almost all restrictions, (4) removal of all restrictions, and (4+) standards and norms of industrialized countries. The "Year of Resumption of Real GDP Growth" is the first year in which the country begins at least two consecutive years of positive real GDP growth.

Sources: European Bank for Reconstruction and Development, *Transition Report 2001;* and International Monetary Fund, *Direction of Trade Statistics Yearbook, 1997* and *2001.*

countries strove to meet the standards for membership in the World Trade Organization (WTO). By 2001, all of these countries except Bosnia, Macedonia, and Yugoslavia were WTO members. In addition, all of these countries except Albania, Bosnia, Croatia, Macedonia, and Yugoslavia established Association Agreements with the European Union (EU) during 1992–1996. They gained free access to the EU market for most manufactures, and are considered to be on a path for full EU membership as early as 2004.

The other FSU countries (the members of the Commonwealth of Independent States, or CIS), have instead followed the path of slow and partial liberalization. As shown in Figure 13.5, none had removed all trade restrictions by 1994, and half had not begun to liberalize (a rating of 1). By 2000, the CIS countries, except Turkmenistan and Uzbekistan, had done some trade liberalization, but only four had removed all restrictions (rating of 4 or 4+). In addition, all except Tajikistan had established Partnership and Cooperation Agreements with the EU, a weaker form of EU relationship, with mutual most-favored-nation tariffs and removal of quotas.

Reform efforts in several countries were set back by the 1998 Russian crisis and its aftermath. To raise government revenues and to increase the prices paid by its trade partners, Russia reimposed taxes on exports of oil, gas, petrochemicals, and metals. To limit the inflows of other products that had become much cheaper after the collapse of the Russian ruble, Kazakhstan banned imports of some products from Russia and imposed high tariffs on imports of these products from Kyrgyzstan and Uzbekistan. In retaliation, Uzbekistan raised some of its tariffs. As shown in Figure 13.5, the trade and foreign exchange regimes in both Russia and Uzbekistan were less liberal in 2000 than they had been in 1994.

Changing Trade Patterns

How do trade patterns evolve as transition occurs? One pressure is clear, toward rapid growth of imports, especially consumer goods, based on pent-up demand. Transition economies must export to pay for their rising imports, and Western Europe and other industrialized countries are crucial as major markets for expanding their exports. However, exporting to demanding customers in the competitive markets of the industrialized countries was not going to be easy. In the late 1980s, before transition began, nearly all trade of each republic in the former Soviet Union was with other Soviet republics and other CMEA countries, and 40 percent or more of the trade of the Central and Southeastern European members of the CMEA was with other CMEA members. Production and trade before transition left the CMEA countries with major deficiencies in their products and businesses, including poor product quality, lack of marketing capabilities, and lack of trade financing.

How successful have the transition countries been in reorienting their trade patterns? The third and fourth columns of numbers in Figure 13.5 provide some answers. By 2000, the countries of Central and Southeastern Europe and the Baltic countries were selling most of their exports to buyers in the industrialized countries. Rapid and deep liberalizations, along with the favorable geographic location closer to the markets of Western Europe, have facilitated the shift by these countries to a desirable export pattern. They increased their exports of light manufactured goods like textiles, clothing, and footwear, even though such exports often face substantial barriers in the industrialized countries, including nontariff barriers in the European Union that continued to limit imports of such "sensitive" products. Another base for success is these countries' low-cost skilled labor, leading to exports of such products as vehicles and machinery.

The information in Figure 13.5 also shows that most of the CIS countries have not reoriented their exports much. In fact, a number of CIS countries send smaller shares of their exports to industrialized countries in 2000 than they did in the early years of transition. Even though Georgia, Kyrgyzstan, and Moldova are now members of the WTO, the CIS countries generally are not noticeably more integrated into world trade than they were in 1990. Many of the CIS countries have resisted trade liberalization and continue to produce manufactured goods of low quality. They can trade these low-quality products with each other, but they cannot export them outside of the region.

Reforms, Recessions, and Renewed Growth

How does all of this combine to determine the success of economic transition? One broad indicator is the growth or decline of domestic production (real GDP). We expect to see a decline in production early in the transition, often called the transition recession, as business practices and economic relationships are disrupted.[8] Only after the reforms begin to take hold can the economy begin to grow back. This process is like that of the shift by a country from no trade to free international trade. As we saw beginning in Chapter 2, the gains from opening to trade are based largely on disrupting previous patterns of production and consumption activities.

The information on real GDP in the last two columns of Table 13.5 paint a fairly clear picture. With the exception of Yugoslavia, which incurred foreign sanctions because of the aggression by the Milosevic regime, the countries of Central and Southeastern Europe suffered through transition recessions that were not that deep and not that long. Four of these countries had grown back to exceed their pretransition GDP by 2000. The recessions in the Baltic countries were somewhat deeper and somewhat longer. The record of the CIS countries is mixed. Most of these countries experienced deep recessions, and some of the recessions lasted for many years. In 2000, the GDP values of these deep-recession countries

---

[8]As officially measured, the declines in output during the transition recession are probably overstated for two reasons. First, the value of output was overstated before transition because many goods were of low quality and little true value, and because political pressures led to falsified reports of high and rising production. Second, the value of output is probably understated during transition because growing private production in the "informal," or underground, economy is not included. Still, the broad patterns in the data are probably meaningful.

remained well below their pretransition levels. However, the recessions in three countries—Belarus, Turkmenistan, and Uzbekistan—were not nearly as deep as those in the other CIS countries.

The key lesson is that the depth and speed of reforms matters for the success of transition. The countries with the shortest recessions and the strongest postrecession growth are countries that quickly enacted a broad, consistent set of reforms, including trade liberalization. The countries that suffered the longest and deepest recessions are the countries caught in the middle, with partial reforms that have been enacted slowly over time and that sometimes are reversed. These partial-reform countries have performed worse than the quick, broad reformers (the countries of Central and Southeastern Europe and the Baltics). They have also performed worse than the three CIS countries that simply resisted enacting any reforms. They seem to be caught in a partial-reform trap, in which special interests that benefit from the partial reforms gain the political and economic power to block or slow any further reform. These special interests include oligarchs and insiders who loot state enterprises and gain control of newly privatized firms, as well as those who earn large profits by arbitraging between controlled and liberalized markets, and those state officials who use their remaining powers for corrupt gains. One advantage of speed in reform is that the reforms are enacted before such special interests have time to coalesce and exert their power.

Looking to the future, many of the transition countries have a solid foundation for economic success based on a well-educated, healthy labor force, with high levels of literacy and numeracy and strength in engineering skills. But the mixture of politics, policy decisions, and geography seems to be driving toward two sets of countries with very different transition results. Most transition countries in Central and Southeastern Europe, as well as the Baltic countries, are positioned for growth and rising living standards. Most other former Soviet Union countries have suffered deep, painful declines and have uncertain futures. This high variance in transition experiences mirrors the high variance in the experiences of developing countries more generally.

Summary

The gaps in living standards are widening among developing countries. Developing countries in East Asia have grown quickly, although they were temporarily set back by the Asian crisis of 1997. For many poor countries in Africa, average incomes have been declining for several decades. And countries in transition from central planning to market economies experienced large declines in output and income during the early years of transition, with most countries of the former Soviet Union experiencing especially large and lingering declines.

Developing countries must decide what trade policies to adopt toward primary-product exports, industrial imports, and industrial exports.

A traditional fear about relying on exports of primary products is that the world market price trends are unfavorable to producers, especially those in developing countries. The evidence shows a downward trend in the relative prices of most primary products, as commonly feared, but the decline has been gradual since 1900. Two factors lowering the relative price of primary products are Engel's law and the development of modern synthetic substitutes for primary materials. Two opposing forces, which would tend to raise primary-product prices, are natural resource limits and the fact that productivity growth is often slower in the primary sectors than in the rest of the economy.

Joining an international cartel could bring gains to a developing country that exports the cartelized product. The greatest cartel success by far is OPEC's pair of price victories in 1973–1974 and 1979–1980. With all international cartels, even OPEC, success breeds decline. Four forces dictate the speed at which a cartel erodes: the rise in product demand elasticity, the rise in the elasticity of competing supplies, the decline in the share of the cartel in the world market, and the rise in cheating by members of the cartel. Because of supply conditions, it is unlikely that cartels in other primary products could achieve anything close to OPEC's success.

One strategy open to developing countries is that of **import-substituting industrialization (ISI).** It could raise national skill levels, bring terms-of-trade gains, and allow planners to economize on market information (since they can just take industrial imports themselves as a measure of demand that could be captured with the help of protection). Studies of ISI and related policies, however, show that income growth is negatively correlated with antitrade policies like ISI, and positively correlated with outward-oriented policies that are closer to free trade. The available evidence supports the fears about ISI raised by the analysis of Chapters 7 through 9.

Another strategy is to concentrate on developing exports of manufactured goods, especially those that are intensive in less-skilled labor. This has been a slowly prevailing trend since the 1960s, though ISI also remains practiced in developing countries. Relying on exports of manufactures has its risks, however. Developing nations have rightly complained about import barriers against their new manufactures erected by the industrialized countries. Such barriers have indeed been higher than the barriers on manufactures traded between industrialized countries. Still, evidence shows that an outward-oriented trade policy encouraging exports of manufactures is part of the most promising strategy for most developing countries.

Changes in international trade policy are an important part of the process of transition from central planning to a market economy. Key issues are the speed and breadth of liberalization of trade policy (and other reforms like shifting from controlled prices to market prices). Countries in Central and Southeastern Europe and the Baltic countries chose broad, rapid liberalizations, and most achieved substantial reorientations of their exports to industrialized-country markets. After declines in national output in the first several years of transition, they have achieved economic growth, and most seem to be positioned for continued growth. Other countries of the former Soviet Union liberalized slowly, and their output declines have been both deep and lingering. As with developing countries generally, we see widening gaps in living standards between these two groups of transition countries, and we see greater success for those countries adopting more open and outward-oriented trade policies.

Suggested Reading

Studies of the ISI and outward-oriented strategies are Krueger (1993), Choksi et al. (1991), Sachs and Warner (1995), Bruton (1998), and World Bank (2002a).

Overviews of the literature on long-run trends in the relative prices of primary products are Scandizzo and Diakosawas (1987) and Grilli and Yang (1988). Gilbert (1996) discusses the failures of cartels in recent decades.

The implications of the pattern of protection in North America and Europe for developing countries seeking to export manufactures are explored at length by Cline (1984). The rationale for, and developing countries' experience with, export-promotion strategies are surveyed in Milner (1990).

The World Bank's *World Development Report 1996* presents a thorough survey of reforms necessary for transition. The European Bank for Reconstruction and Development issues an annual *Transition Report*. Hare (2001) discusses trade policies in transition countries. World Bank (2002b) examines what we have learned from the first decade of transition.

Questions and Problems

◆ 1. List the main pros and cons of taking the import-replacing road to industrialization versus concentrating government aid and private energies on developing new manufacturing exports.

2. Under what conditions would ISI have the greatest chance of being better than any alternative development strategy? What other policies should accompany it?

◆ 3. "The terms of trade move against primary producers in the long run." What is the evidence in support of this proposition? How solid is the evidence?

4. You are an adviser to the government of a country whose exports are mainly a few primary products and whose imports are mainly manufactured products. You are asked to prepare a short report on the forces that are likely to drive the country's terms of trade during the next two decades. What will the main points of your report be?

◆ 5. The United States, China, India, Brazil, and Turkey are forming an international association known as Tobacco's Altruistic Raisers (TAR) to increase the world price of tobacco. TAR's members control 60 percent of world tobacco production. The price elasticity of world demand for tobacco is rather low in the short run but somewhat higher in the long run. The ability of other countries who are not TAR members to increase their production of tobacco is very small for a period of several years; but, with a few years to prepare, other countries could easily expand their tobacco production. You are asked to write a report on the outlook for TAR's success. What will you say in the report?

6. Drawing on material from this chapter and earlier chapters, weigh the pros and cons of restricting and taxing a country's exports of primary products. How could it raise the country's national income? What are the drawbacks of such a policy for a developing country?

✦ 7. Consider Figure 13.3, which shows what a cartel can do if it can act like a monopolist. In Figure 13.3, the cartel supplies the entire world market.

   a. What is the effect on the cartel's profit-maximizing price if a new outside source of supply now develops that can provide 10 million barrels of oil per day at any price above $5.00 per barrel? Show the effect using the graph. (Hint: With this new outside supply, what is the demand that remains for the cartel's oil?)

   b. Instead of the new outside source described in question *a*, consider instead a new outside source of supply that will provide amounts of oil that vary with the world price, according to the following schedule:

   Outside supply (millions of barrels per day) = World price – 5

   (For instance, if the world price is $15, the outside supply is 10 million barrels per day.) Show graphically and explain the effect on the cartel's profit-maximizing price of this new outside supply source.

8. In the 1987 World Bank study, India was categorized as having a strongly inward trade policy. Around 1990, it shifted to an outward-oriented policy. What is your prediction for India's growth rate of income per capita during the 1990s? Do the data reported in Figure 13.1 support your prediction?

✦ 9. One of your friends believes that the challenges of a transition from central planning to a market economy are so large that policies should be changed slowly. If you disagree, what are your major arguments?

10. Ukraine has to decide on a trade-policy strategy to go with other reforms for promoting development. Comment on the merits and drawbacks of the following available choices:

   a. Unilaterally taxing its grain exports.

   b. Joining a grain cartel with North America, Argentina, and Australia, the other main exporters.

   c. Choosing manufactures it could export (e.g., batteries), giving them a profitable home-market base protected by tariffs, and encouraging exports to other countries at competitive world prices.

Chapter **Fourteen**

Multinationals and Migration: International Factor Movements

In the previous chapters of this part, we looked at the economic and political battles over international trade in goods and services. International movements of factors of production are often even more controversial, with the debates even more emotional as well. In this chapter we examine two major forms of international factor movements: those that occur through the foreign activities of multinational enterprises, and those that occur through the international movement of people. In shifting our attention to international factor flows, we are relaxing the assumption that factors do not move internationally, an assumption that we have used through much of the discussion up to this point. That is, we now recognize that factors of production can and do move between countries in amounts that are often large enough to have economic effects and to grab political attention.

The global activities of multinational enterprises raise sensitive issues of whether their objectives conflict with the well-being of individual countries, and whether they have the power to circumvent or overwhelm national-government sovereignty. Developing countries worry both that foreign firms will invest in them and that they won't. They fear exploitation on the one hand and inadequate access to foreign capital, technology, marketing, and management skills on the other. Industrialized countries worry about being both the sources and the recipients of direct investments. As direct investments flow out, don't these reduce exports of products and employment opportunities at home? As direct investments flow in, won't foreigners establish undue influence and control over the local economy?

The first part of this chapter provides a broad survey of what we know about multinationals and foreign direct investment. We explore why direct investments occur. We also examine whether a home country or a host country has good reasons to try to restrict (or encourage) multinational direct investment.

These national issues are important because the policies of national governments remain powerful. All governments prohibit or restrict direct investments into certain lines of activity. Which lines are prohibited vary from one country to another, but the prohibitions are directed toward those activities that are regarded as particularly vulnerable to foreign influence—including natural resources, banking, newspapers and other communications media, and defense industries. Governments also can regulate the local operations of foreign firms in a number of ways. They can require local participation in the ownership or management of the local operations, or they can require training, locally purchased components and parts, local research, or exports. Governments can also use tax policy to influence both the flows of direct investments and the division of the investment returns between the firms and the governments. On the other hand, many governments actively court multinational enterprises by offering various forms of subsidies to attract them to locate in their countries.

Of all the flows that take place between nations, none is more sensitive than the flow of humans. For those who migrate, the dangers are great but the average gain is high. A migrant risks disease or victimization by others, and may fail to find a better income in the country of destination. Many migrants return home unsuccessful and disillusioned. Still, they experience great gains on average, as we might expect from so risky an activity. In some cases political and physical freedom itself is a large gain, as in the case of refugees from repressive regimes. In other cases, the economic gains stand out. Doctors, engineers, and other highly trained personnel from low-income countries such as India and Pakistan have multiplied their incomes several times over by migrating to North America, Australia, Britain, and the Persian Gulf. Mexican craftspeople and campesinos earn enough in Texas or California to retire early (if they wish) in comfortable Mexican homes. Turkish "guest workers" in Germany have also ensured themselves a comfortable living and a quantum jump up the income ranks.

In the countries that receive migrants, ethnic prejudice, general xenophobia, and the direct economic stake of groups that fear competition from immigrants keep the issue especially sensitive. Anti-immigration groups have become more vocal since the early 1990s. In response to rising legal and illegal immigration from Mexico and Central America, the U.S. government enacted a federal law to deny even legal immigrants access to many social programs, though subsequent laws restored some of the benefits. Rising immigration into the European Union, including illegal immigration that is probably larger than that into the United States, has alarmed some Europeans. In Austria, France, and Italy, political parties opposed to immigration have sometimes used virulent rhetoric to try to gain votes. In Germany the government has put up new immigration barriers in response to the growing numbers of refugees from Eastern Europe.

The second part of this chapter examines the economics of international migration. We focus on people who migrate for economic reasons, to understand the effects on labor markets in the sending and receiving countries. As we did for the multinational enterprise, we then examine whether the sending or receiving country has reasons to restrict migration to prevent adverse effects on national well-being.

FOREIGN DIRECT INVESTMENT

The U.S. company IBM pays cash to acquire all of the equity shares of a Taiwanese company that makes computer components. A U.S. investor named Pugel pays cash to buy 10,000 shares (0.1 percent of all outstanding equity shares) of a similar Taiwanese company that also makes computer components. Both of these share purchases are international flows of financial capital from the United States to Taiwan. But only one is foreign *direct* investment. The key difference between the two investments is the degree to which each investor can control or influence the management of the company. In foreign *direct* investment the investor has, or could have, an effective voice in the management of the foreign company. **Foreign direct investment (FDI)** is the flow of funding provided by an investor or lender (usually a firm) to establish or acquire a foreign company or to expand or finance an existing foreign company that the investor owns and controls. IBM's acquisition of the first Taiwanese company is FDI.

In contrast, Pugel does not expect to have any influence on the day-to-day management of the second Taiwanese company. Rather, Pugel is seeking financial returns by adding the 10,000 shares to his investment portfolio. Generally, the term *international portfolio investment* is used for all foreign investments that do not involve management control (that is, all that are not direct investments).

Both foreign direct investment and international portfolio investment are important ways in which financial capital moves between countries. During 1995–2000, the global flows of foreign direct investment averaged $700 billion per year, and the global flows of international portfolio investment averaged $1,200 billion per year. In this chapter we examine the economics of foreign direct investment. As we will see, FDI involves much more than the capital flow, and it is closely related to issues such as international trade and technology that we have been examining in Parts I and II. We defer our analysis of international portfolio investment to Part III of the book, because we need the discussion of foreign exchange rates contained there to analyze the financial returns and risks of international investing.

In many cases, including the acquisition of the Taiwanese company by IBM, we can easily tell whether an investment is (or is not) FDI. In other cases, the investor acquires or owns part of the equity of the foreign company but not all of it. How much ownership is enough to the give the investor the ability to affect the management of the foreign firm? There is no clear-cut answer to this, but it is certainly at most half, and probably less than this. Someone who owns even, say, 20 percent of a firm can have some ability to influence the management of the firm.

The agreed international standard is 10 percent ownership.[1] That is, *foreign direct investment is any flow of lending to, or purchases of ownership in, a foreign firm in which the investor (usually a firm) has (or gains) ownership of 10 percent or more of the foreign firm.* Here are some examples of investments that do and do not fit the official definition of foreign direct investment:

U.S. Foreign Direct Investments	U.S. Portfolio Investments Abroad
Alcoa's purchase of 50 percent of the stock in a new Jamaican bauxite firm	Alcoa's purchase of 5 percent of the stock in a new Jamaican bauxite firm (this 5 percent is the full amount of ownership that Alcoa then has)
A loan from Ford U.S.A. to a Canadian parts-making subsidiary in which Ford holds 55 percent of the equity	A loan from Ford U.S.A. to a Canadian parts-making firm in which Ford U.S.A. holds 8 percent of the equity

Note that direct investment consists of any investment, whether new ownership or simple lending, as long as the investing firm owns (or acquires) over 10 percent of the foreign firm.

MULTINATIONAL ENTERPRISES

A firm that owns and controls operations in more than one country is a **multinational enterprise (MNE).** The **parent firm** in the MNE is the headquarters or base firm, located in the **home country** of the MNE. The parent firm has one or more **foreign affiliates** (subsidiaries or branches) located in one or more **host countries.**

The multinational enterprise uses flows of foreign direct investment to establish or finance its foreign affiliates. However, in two different ways a multinational firm is *more* than just the flow of foreign direct investment. First, foreign affiliates usually receive only part, and often a rather small part, of their total financing from the direct investment flows. Second, the multinational enterprise transfers many other things to its foreign affiliates in addition to the direct investment financing. The multinational enterprise typically provides its affiliates with a variety of intangible assets for the affiliates to use. These intangible assets can include proprietary technology, brand names, marketing capabilities, trade secrets, and managerial practices. In this section we focus on the first issue, the financing of the affiliates.

---

[1]This 10 percent standard is used by the United States and many other countries, but not by all countries that report FDI data. In addition, another form of FDI recognized by the international standards involves a group of investors in a home country that establish control of a foreign affiliate, even if each investor individually owns less than 10 percent of the foreign firm.

A foreign affiliate can obtain financing either from its parent (or other parts of the MNE) or from outside lenders and investors (for instance, banks or the buyers of bonds that the affiliate issues). Only the former is foreign direct investment, and it is often a small part of the total financing of the affiliate. For all MNEs in the world in 2000, foreign affiliates had $21 trillion of financing in place, but only $6 trillion of that financing was provided by foreign direct investment by the multinational enterprises. Evidence for U.S.-based multinationals indicates that borrowing in the host countries provides more than half of the outside financing.

Why does FDI provide so little of the affiliates' total funding? An important reason is that a parent firm wants to reduce the risks to which its foreign activities are exposed. One risk is unexpected changes in exchange rates, which can alter the value of its direct investments. A good risk-reducing strategy for a parent company that has foreign-currency assets in its affiliates is to take on foreign-currency liabilities as well, by borrowing in foreign currencies that are used to finance the affiliate. (We will examine hedging of exchange rate risk in Chapter 17.)

Another risk is political risk, the possibility that the government of a host country will alter its policies in ways that harm the multinational enterprise. For instance, the possibility of expropriation or nationalization of an affiliate by the host-country government is a political risk. Since World War I and the Russian revolution, host countries have shown willingness to seize the assets of multinationals, sometimes without compensating the investors. Realizing the danger of expropriation, many multinationals reduced their exposure to this kind of risk by matching much of the value of their physical assets in a host country with borrowings in that country. If political change brings expropriation, the parents also can tell the host-country lenders to try to collect their repayments from their own (expropriating) government. The shedding of liabilities offsets part or all of their asset losses in the country. The parent firms' technology, marketing secrets, and managerial skills typically preclude expropriation.

FDI: HISTORY AND CURRENT PATTERNS

Although data on foreign direct investment tell us only about one aspect of the global operations of MNEs, these data have the advantage that they are available for most countries and for long periods of time. We use data on FDI as general indicators of the importance of MNEs across countries and over time. Data on FDI are available for two related but different measures:

- *Flows* of FDI measure new equity investments and loans within MNEs during a period of time. This is the measure of FDI we used in the section in which we defined FDI.

- *Stocks* of FDI measure the total amount of direct investments that exist at a point in time. These stocks are the sums of past flows of FDI.

Let's look first at information on flows of FDI.

Foreign direct investment has been rising and falling, mainly rising, throughout the 20th century and into the 21st. It had its fastest growth, and took its largest share of all international investment, in the period dating roughly from the end of Korean War (1953) to the first oil shock (1973–74). During that period, direct investments were dominated by investment outflows from the United States. U.S. firms have historically shown a greater preference for FDI and direct control than have firms from other investing countries. Britain, France, and the oil-rich nations have channeled a greater proportion of their foreign investments into portfolio lending.[2] Thus, the early postwar rise of U.S. FDI propelled U.S.-based multinationals into international prominence. In the 1970s and early 1980s, global FDI grew more slowly, being eclipsed by two waves of portfolio lending: the ill-fated surge of lending to developing countries in 1974–1982 (discussed in Chapter 20) and the surge of lending to the United States in the 1980s.

Since the mid-1980s, global FDI has again grown quickly, driven by increasing FDI by Japanese firms in the second half of the 1980s and by increasing FDI by U.S. firms, European firms, and firms based in South and East Asia in the 1990s. The value of cross-border mergers and acquisitions, mostly between firms in the industrialized countries, exploded in the late 1990s. The global flow of foreign direct investment peaked in 2000 at $1.3 trillion, before falling back in 2001 as much of the world slipped into slow growth or recession.

Foreign direct investment has also changed direction. First, in the 1970s and 1980s, it moved away from the developing countries, where it had met with resistance and expropriations climaxing in the 1970s. This trend reversed itself beginning in about 1990, as FDI flows into developing countries increased dramatically. Growing domestic markets, low production costs, and reforms of economic policies attracted direct investment, especially into a small number of developing countries in South and East Asia and Latin America. Included in these is the People's Republic of China, following its opening to foreign trade and investment in the late 1970s. Second, the United States attracted more FDI inflows than any other nation in the 1980s. The share of the United States then declined somewhat, but it continued to receive about one-fifth of new FDI flows in the late 1990s. Third, the deepening of integration in the European Union has encouraged FDI into and within the EU, and the formation of the North American Free Trade Area (along with Mexico's own policy reforms) has encouraged FDI into Mexico.

Let's turn now to information on the stocks of FDI. Recall that FDI stocks are the cumulation of the FDI flows that we have just been talking about. FDI stocks measure total amounts in existence as of the stated time. Figure 14.1 shows the geographic pattern of direct investment stocks by the nine largest home (or source) countries at the end of 1998. These nine countries are the source of about 77 percent of all existing direct investments, which totaled about $4.1 trillion in 1998. In

---

[2] Japan has occupied an intermediate position. Much of its outward investment in the 1970s took the form of FDI, but in the 1980s, it shifted relatively toward portfolio lending, especially lending to the U.S. government, although it also became a large direct investor.

FIGURE 14.1   Major Home Countries' Direct Investments, End of 1998 (Billions of U.S. Dollars)

Home Country	Total Outward FDI	NAFTA[a]	Host Region				
			European Union	Other Industrialized	Latin America	Developing Asia[b]	Other Developing[c]
United States	1,014	130	470	121	172	83	38
Canada	161	83	33	9	26	7	3
Japan	270	116	49	11	16	71	7
United Kingdom	492	213	164	39	21	24	31
Germany	348	98	173	25	17	13	22
Netherlands	231	60	114	21	15	9	12
France	229	54	119	13	11	7	25
Switzerland	182	49	85	7	2	13	6
Italy	159	17	99	13	4	*	26*

These nine largest home (or source) countries accounted for about three-quarters of the world's stock of existing FDI. FDI shows noticeable regional patterns, with substantial direct investments between the United States and Canada, from Japan into the developing countries of Asia, and between European countries.

[a]North American Free Trade Area: Canada, Mexico, and the United States.

[b]Includes South Korea, even though it is a member of the Organization for Economic Cooperation and Development.

[c]Includes the Czech Republic, Hungary, and Poland, even though they are members of the Organization for Economic Cooperation and Development. Includes FDI not allocated to specific host countries. The amount not allocated is rather large for France, so its large value for "Other Developing" should be interpreted cautiously.

*For Italy, value for "Developing Asia" is included in "Other Developing."

Source: Organization for Economic Cooperation and Development, *International Direct Investment Statistics Yearbook, 2001.*

fact, industrialized countries as a group are overwhelmingly the home countries of direct investments, accounting for about 90 percent of the world total.

The six columns toward the right in Figure 14.1 indicate different regions that host the direct investments. Reading across a row shows where the nine source countries invest. Close to half of U.S. direct investment is in Europe. The United States is also a major investor in Canada. (Most of the $130 billion of U.S. direct investment in the two other countries of NAFTA is in Canada.) Canada has placed about half of its direct investment in the United States. Japan has large direct investments in the developing countries of Asia, and it also built a large position in the United States in the 1980s. Germany, the Netherlands, France, Switzerland, and Italy have close to half of their direct investments in other European countries. Most of Britain's direct investments are in other European countries and in the United States.

Two-thirds of the stock of direct investment is in industrialized countries, and over nine-tenths of that is in West European countries, Canada, and the United States. To a large extent, FDI involves firms from industrialized countries investing in other industrialized countries. With one exception, the major home countries are also major host countries. The exception is Japan. One way in which Japan is truly different from other major industrialized countries is that it is host to little direct investment. In 1998, the stock of direct investment in Japan was only $27 billion, less than one-quarter of the FDI that the Netherlands, a much smaller country, had received.

In which industries does FDI occur? That has changed over time. In 1970, about one-quarter of the world's direct investment was in the primary sector, mainly mining and extraction activities. About half was in the manufacturing sector, and about a quarter was in the services sector. The share of mining and extraction has since declined, especially in the 1970s as developing countries nationalized many firms and exerted greater control over the extraction of their natural resources. The share of manufacturing has declined somewhat, and the importance of direct investment in services has risen. In manufacturing, firms that produce pharmaceuticals and other chemicals, electrical and electronic equipment, automobiles, machinery, and food tend to be active in direct investment, while firms in industries like textiles, clothing, and paper products tend to do rather little direct investment. Within the services sector substantial direct investment occurs in banking and other financial services, in business services such as consulting, accounting, and advertising, and in wholesaling and retailing.

WHY DO MULTINATIONAL ENTERPRISES EXIST?

This seems to be a silly question! The answer seems simple—because they are profitable. But the issue is more complicated than it sounds.

We should first dispose of one possible explanation, that multinationals are simply a way of shifting financial capital between countries based on national differences in returns and risks. Although return and risk must play a role in the decisions by firms about whether to make direct investments, this financial theory of direct investment is not adequate. It does not explain why these international investments would be large enough to establish managerial control over the foreign companies. If the challenge is to transfer capital from one country to another, international portfolio investment can accomplish this task better than direct investment by firms whose major preoccupation lies in production and marketing.

There is some agreement that five different pieces together provide a good explanation of why multinational firms exist (and why they are as large as they are). The five (easy?) pieces are:

1. Inherent disadvantages of being foreign.

2. Firm-specific advantages (to overcome the inherent disadvantages).

3. Location factors (that favor foreign production over exporting).

4. Internalization advantages (that favor direct investment over contracting with independent firms).

5. Oligopolistic rivalry (among multinational enterprises).

The combination of these pieces into a framework for understanding the multinational enterprise is often called the eclectic approach, with credit for the synthesis going to John Dunning.

Inherent Disadvantages

Our first step is to recognize that there are good reasons why multinational enterprises should not exist. An MNE has **inherent disadvantages** in trying to compete against foreign rivals on their own turf. The multinational is at a disadvantage in this foreign environment because it does not initially have the native understanding of local laws, customs, procedures, practices, and relationships. In addition, the firm has the extra costs of maintaining management control. It is expensive to operate at a distance, expensive in travel and communications, and especially expensive in misunderstanding. Furthermore, the MNE may lack useful connections with political leaders in the foreign country, or it could face actual or potential hostility from the foreign country's government.

Firm-Specific Advantages

What makes it possible for a multinational to overcome the inherent disadvantages of being foreign? To be successful, the multinational must have one or more **firm-specific advantages**—that is, one or more assets of the multinational enterprise that are not assets held by its local competitors in the host country (or, perhaps, by any other firm in the world). A firm's secret technology or its patents are a firm-specific advantage (examples: IBM, Hitachi). Or the advantage may inhere in the MNE's access to very large amounts of financial capital, amounts far larger than the ordinary national firm can command (example: General Motors). Or, as in the case of petroleum refining (Royal Dutch Shell) or metal processing (Alcoa), the firm may gain advantage by coordinating operations and capital investments at various stages in a vertical production process. Because of heavy inventory costs and its knowledge of the requirements at each stage, the firm may be able to economize through synchronizing operations. Or the firm may have marketing advantages based on skilled use of advertising and other promotional methods that establish product differentiation—for instance, through highly regarded brand names (examples: Nestlé, Procter & Gamble). Or it may have truly superior management techniques (example: General Electric). But some special advantage is necessary for the firm to overcome the disadvantages of operating at a distance in a foreign environment. It is costly for the firm to develop these assets (for instance, the cost of research and development to develop new technology, the marketing expenses to establish and maintain a strong brand name). The challenge to the firm is to maximize its returns on these assets.

We now have an enterprise that has firm-specific advantages such that it could operate profitably as a multinational. But should it? Even for the firm that has firm-specific advantages, it must also consider alternatives to foreign direct investment for earning profits from activities in a foreign market. It must be more profitable for a multinational enterprise to own and manage a foreign operation, rather than adopting some other way of earning profits. Let's focus on the situation in which a firm wants to earn profits by selling to local buyers in the foreign country. Here are two questions for the firm's managers:

1. Should the firm sell to foreign buyers by exporting from its home country, or should the firm set up local production in the foreign country to produce the products that are sold to the foreign buyers?

2. Should the firm license local firms in the foreign country to use its advantages in their own operations that serve the foreign buyers, or should the firm set up foreign operations that it owns and controls?

The answers to these questions bring location factors and internalization advantages into the explanation.

Location Factors

Location factors are all of the advantages and disadvantages of producing in one country (the home country) or in another country (the foreign country). We have already developed in the previous chapters in Parts One and Two many of the location factors that we need to answer the question "Export or FDI?" Here are four key location factors from our previous explorations:

- *Comparative advantage:* the effects of resource availability (labor, land and so forth) on the costs of producing in different countries.

- *Economies of scale:* Conditions that favor concentrating production in a few locations and serving other national markets by exporting.

- *Governmental barriers to importing into the foreign country:* tariffs and non-tariff barriers that make it difficult to export from the home country.

- *Trade bloc:* setup that favors FDI if the foreign country is a member of a free-trade area (or similar arrangement) but the home country is not a member, because production in the foreign country can also be used to serve buyers in the other member countries.

There are many other location factors that are important in some industries. High costs of transporting a product favor FDI to locate production units close to foreign buyers, rather than serving faraway buyers by exporting. Government taxes and subsidies affect the profitability of producing in different countries. The need to adapt products to the specific tastes of foreign buyers can favor FDI, because it is more effective to have close links between the local marketing group, the product redesign group, and the operations group that must produce the redesigned products at acceptable costs.

Location factors are key to answering the question "Export or FDI?" Note that the answer could go either way for a specific firm and product. In some cases it is more profitable to export from the home country, for instance, because the home country has a comparative advantage in the availability and low cost of the most important resource needed in producing the product. In other cases foreign production in an affiliate established by direct investment is more profitable, for instance, because the foreign country has high tariffs on imports of the product.

Internalization Advantages

Even if the firm rules out exporting as a way of serving the foreign market, it still has alternatives for earning profits from that foreign market. Instead of using foreign direct investment to set up an affiliate, the firm could sell or rent its firm-specific advantages to foreign firms for them to use in their own production. For instance, if the advantages are based on superior technology, a strong brand name, or better management practices, the firm could license one or more foreign firms to use these assets. A **license** is an agreement for one firm to use another firm's asset, with restrictions on how the asset can be used, and with payments for the right to use the asset.

In making the decision between FDI and licensing of foreign firms, the firm with the asset must weigh the advantages and disadvantages of each alternative. An important advantage of licensing foreign firms is that the firm avoids (most of) the inherent disadvantages of establishing and managing its own foreign operations, as we discussed above. On the other side there are advantages to keeping the use of the firm-specific advantages within (internal to) the enterprise. **Internalization advantages** are the advantages of using an asset within the firm rather than finding other firms that will buy, rent, or license the asset. Internalization advantages exist because there are drawbacks to using the market for many firm-specific advantages, particularly intangible assets like technology, brand names, marketing techniques, and management practices.

Internalization advantages arise from *avoiding the transaction costs and risks of licensing* an independent firm. Negotiating the license is often costly and difficult. The licensor wants a high payment, and the licensee wants a low payment. The licensee is likely to be skeptical of claims by the licensor that the intangible asset is valuable and should command a high price. The licensor also wants to put various restrictions on how the licensee can use the asset, but the licensee wants to have as few restrictions as possible. Then, even if the license agreement can be negotiated, the licensor still faces some important risks. The licensee may not be as careful with the asset as the licensor would be. For instance, the licensee may let secret technology leak out to other competitors, or the licensee may itself apply the technology to other activities not covered by the license. Or the licensee may fail to maintain product quality, leading to news reports ("brand-name cola causes widespread illness in Austria") that harm the global reputation and value of the brand.

Foreign direct investment keeps the use of the assets under the control of the enterprise itself. It avoids many of the drawbacks of using the market for these kinds of assets. The advantages of internalization are based on the ability of the MNE's management to set the terms for the use of the assets in its foreign affiliates. The returns to the use of the assets are part of the profits earned by the affiliate, and the enterprise can enforce policies to safeguard the ongoing value of its intangible assets. The multinational enterprise uses FDI to better appropriate the returns to its intangible assets.[3]

---

[3] Buckley and Casson (1976) stressed the importance of internalization advantages for our understanding of MNEs. Magee (1977) developed a similar approach that stresses the importance

The importance of internalized use of firm-specific intangible assets explains why foreign direct investment occurs to a greater extent in high-technology industries (electronic products or pharmaceuticals, for example) and marketing-intensive industries (food products or automobiles, for example), than it does in standard-technology industries (clothing, for example) or less-marketing-intensive industries (paper products, for example).

Oligopolistic Rivalry

Many multinational enterprises are not the tiny firms that populate perfectly competitive markets. Instead, they are large firms that often compete among themselves for market shares and profits. They have used their intangible assets (like new technologies and strong brand names) to obtain large market shares. These same intangible assets drive their FDI. These multinationals are involved in global oligopolistic rivalry of the sort that we discussed in Chapters 5 and 10.

Multinationals can use their decisions about foreign direct investment as part of their strategies for competing. For instance, multinationals compete for location. A multinational sometimes seems to set up an affiliate that looks only marginally profitable, yet it does so with the stated purpose of beating its main competitors to the same national market. Kodak may set up a foreign affiliate mainly because it fears that if it doesn't Fuji will. Ford and GM seem to have set up automaking firms in developing countries to try to shut each other out. With some regularity other multinational rivals then quickly respond by setting up their own affiliates in this country, to prevent the first mover from gaining any lasting advantage. Such follow-the-leader behavior results in a bunching of the timing of entries by rival multinationals into a host country. Most of the affiliates may have a tough time earning profits.

Multinationals can also use FDI to try to mute competition and enhance their market power.[4] First, a multinational may acquire foreign firms that are beginning to challenge their international market position. Second, a multinational may set up an affiliate in the home country of one its rivals, to establish a competitive threat to this rival. The message is "Don't compete too vigorously against me in other countries, or I will make life tough for you in your own home market."

TAXATION OF MULTINATIONAL ENTERPRISES' PROFITS

The profits of multinational enterprises come from the operations of the parent firms and their foreign affiliates. Governments impose taxes on business profits, and the taxation of the profits of multinational enterprises can become complicated

---

of approbriability—the ability of an MNE to earn the best returns on its investment in intangible assets. The analysis by Nobel Prize winner Ronald Coase is also relevant. The economics of whether to engage in FDI is an international extension of the decision about the boundaries of the firm (whether to make or buy, whether to own or rent, and so forth).

[4] Stephen Hymer (1976) stressed that a large multinational is a monopolist or, more often, an oligopolist in its product market. Hymer was concerned that multinationals would use their market power in ways that hurt the national interests of the host countries.

Case Study   CEMEX A Model Multinational from an Unusual Place

Our discussion in the text stresses that multinationals succeed by using their firm-specific advantages throughout their global operations. We have also noted that most foreign direct investments are made by firms based in the industrialized countries. This is the story of CEMEX, a firm that rapidly has become multinational since 1990. The reasons for its multinational success fit very well with the advantages stressed in the eclectic approach. What makes the firm unusual is that it is based in Mexico. CEMEX is an example of a small but growing group of multinationals based in developing countries.

CEMEX began business in 1906. For most of its life this cement company focused on selling in the Mexican market. Cement is a product that is expensive to ship, especially overland, so that cement plants ship mostly to customers within 300 miles of a plant. Shipment by water is moderately (but not prohibitively) expensive. Most cement producers in the 1980s were local producers with traditional business practices. New managers at CEMEX broke with tradition by introducing extensive use of automation, information technology, and a satellite-based communication network into CEMEX operations. They used the technology to improve quality control and to provide detailed information on production, sales, and distribution to top managers in real time. Delivery of ready-mix concrete is particularly challenging in cities. Traditionally, cement firms could assure delivery only within a time period of about three hours. CEMEX pioneered the use of computers and a global positioning system to guarantee delivery to construction sites within a 20-minute window. These innovations became the company's firm-specific advantages.

Also in the 1980s CEMEX began to export more aggressively to the United States using sea transport, and it was increasingly successful. However, competing U.S. cement producers complained to the U.S. government, and in 1990 CEMEX exports to the United States were hit by a 58 percent antidumping duty. With exporting to the United States limited by the antidumping order, CEMEX looked for other foreign opportunities.

In 1991, it began exporting to Spain, and in 1992 it made its first foreign direct investment by acquiring two Spanish cement producers. CEMEX minimized its inherent disadvantages by investing first in a foreign country that had the same language and a similar culture to the firm's home country. In addition, CEMEX used its expansion into Europe as competitive response to the previous move by the Swiss-based firm Holcim into the Mexican cement industry.

The management team sent by CEMEX to reorganize the acquired companies were amazed to find companies that kept handwritten records and used almost no personal computers. They upgraded the Spanish affiliates to CEMEX technology and management practices. The improvement in affiliate operations from this internal transfer of CEMEX's intangible assets was surprising—profit margins improved from 7 percent to 24 percent in two years.

Since then, CEMEX has made a series of foreign direct investments by acquiring cement producers in Latin America (including Venezuela, Panama, the Dominican Republic, Colombia, and Costa Rica), the United States, the Philippines, Indonesia, and Egypt. CEMEX used the same type of process that it used in Spain to bring its technology and management practices into its new foreign affiliates, and generally achieved similarly impressive improvements in performance.

By 2000, CEMEX was the third largest cement producer in the world, behind Lafarge of France and Holcim. More than 60 percent of its physical assets were in its foreign affiliates. It was also the largest exporter of cement in the world (a fact consistent with the proposition discussed in the text that FDI and trade are often complementary). CEMEX is considered one of the best networked companies globally by computer industry experts, well ahead of its rivals. It is also highly profitable, with a profit rate on sales that was 10 to 15 percentage points higher than its rivals in the late 1990s. Its investments in developing and enhancing its firm-specific advantages have been paying off globally.

and contentious. Let's look first at how the profits of these global firms are taxed, and then at two important issues that arise from this taxation.

Part of how a multinational enterprise's profits are taxed is conceptually straightforward (although the details can be vexing). The host-country governments tax the profits of the local affiliates of the multinational, and the home-country government taxes the parent company's "local" profits earned on its own activities. A key question is, then, whether the home-country government also imposes any taxes on the profits earned by the foreign affiliates of the parent company.

Because the profits of these foreign affiliates have been taxed already by the host government, the home government usually tries to avoid double taxation of the foreign affiliate profits. While the exact rules vary by country and can be complicated, the outcome is that the home-country government collects few or no extra taxes on the profits of foreign affiliates.[5] Thus, the tax rate on the profits of a foreign affiliate is largely that imposed by the host government. Because tax rates vary across host countries, and because global multinational enterprises try to minimize the total taxes that they pay (as long as lower tax payments increase global after-tax profits), two important issues arise.

First, a multinational enterprise can shop around among countries and locate its affiliates in the jurisdictions of governments offering lower tax rates. FDI allows a multinational enterprise to settle in countries with lower taxes. Whether this is good or bad from a world point of view depends on the uses to which tax revenues are put and whether the productivity of the investing firm is lower in the lower-tax country.

Second, multinational enterprises can use transfer pricing and other devices to report more of their profits in low-tax countries, even though the profits were actually earned in high-tax countries. **Transfer pricing** is the setting by the company of prices (or monetary values) for things that move between units of the company. Many things move between the parent and an affiliate or between affiliates of a multinational enterprise. These include materials and components, finished products, the rights to use technology and brand names, and financial capital. For accounting for each unit (the parent or an affiliate), each of these things must be assigned a price or value. Therefore, all multinationals must engage in setting these transfer prices.

The multinational can set transfer prices to achieve any of a number of enterprise objectives, and one of these is reducing the global taxes that the multinational pays. For instance, to lower its corporate income taxes, the MNE can have its unit in a high-tax country be overcharged (or underpaid) for goods and services that the unit buys from (sells to) an affiliate in a low-tax country. That way,

---

[5]For instance, Australia, Canada, France, Germany, the Netherlands, and Sweden impose no taxes on the profits of the foreign affiliates of firms based in their countries. Italy, Japan, the United Kingdom, and the United States impose taxes on the portion of foreign affiliate profits sent home to the parents, but they also allow tax credits for the taxes already paid to the host-country governments on these profits.

the unit in the high-tax country doesn't show its tax officials much profit, while the unit in the low-tax country shows high profits. Profits are shifted from the unit in the high-tax country to the unit in the low-tax country. The result: net tax reduction for the multinational enterprise in question.

Here is a numerical example to show how this could work. An MNE produces a component in Germany where the tax rate on corporate income is, say, 50 percent. The component costs $8 per unit to produce in Germany, and the MNE sells all units that it produces there to its affiliate in Singapore, where the tax rate on corporate income is, say, 20 percent. The affiliate in Singapore uses this component and $7 of labor to produce a finished product that it sells to outside buyers for $20 per unit. Thus, for each unit sold to a final buyer the multinational has $5 of *before-tax* global profit ($20 – $8 – $7). But the multinational is most interested in the profit that it gets to keep after it pays its corporate income taxes. Its *after-tax* global profit depends on what price it set for the sale of the component by its German affiliate to its Singapore affiliate. Here are three possibilities and the resulting after-tax global profit per unit:

	German Affiliate		Singapore Affiliate		Global MNE	
Component Price	Before-Tax Profit	After-Tax Profit	Before-Tax Profit	After-Tax Profit	Before-Tax Profit	After-Tax Profit
$13.00	$5.00	$2.50	$0.00	$0.00	$5.00	$2.50
10.00	2.00	1.00	3.00	2.40	5.00	3.40
8.00	0.00	0.00	5.00	4.00	5.00	4.00

Governments know that multinational enterprises can use transfer prices to shift their profits and lower their taxes. Many governments attempt to police transfer pricing to ensure that the transfer prices used between units within a multinational enterprise are similar to the market prices that independent firms would pay to each other for similar transactions. However, determining whether transfer prices differ from market prices is complex and costly, so multinational enterprises usually have some scope to use transfer pricing to alter the taxes the multinationals pay (and to which countries they pay those taxes).

MNES AND INTERNATIONAL TRADE

It is natural to think of foreign direct investment in a host country as a substitute for exports by the parent firm (or other home-country firms) to the host country, just as we concluded in Chapter 4 that trade and international movements of production factors are substitutes. Yet it turns out that multinational enterprises are actually heavily involved in international trade. About one-third of the world's international trade in goods occurs as **intrafirm trade** between units of the multinational enterprises located in different countries. Another third of the world's international trade involves a multinational enterprise as the seller (exporter) or buyer (importer), trading with some other firm.

Why are multinational enterprises so involved in world trade? Especially, why is intrafirm trade so important? When are trade and FDI substitutes? Can FDI complement trade? We will answer these questions, first for the easier case in which a parent and its affiliates are engaged in different stages of overall production, and then for the harder case in which the affiliate is largely doing the same types of production activities as the parent (or other affiliates).

As long as transport costs and trade barriers are low enough, FDI can be used to reduce total costs by locating different stages of overall production in different countries. Compared with the situation in which the firm would perform most of these activities in a single country, FDI leads to more trade as the firm's overall production is spread across units in different countries.

For instance, for electronics products like televisions, communications equipment, and computer hard drives, each stage of production can be located according to the country's comparative costs advantage (or, in the case of marketing and distribution, according to the need to locate close to the customers for the final products). Design and development of new products is located in countries (often the home country) abundant in engineers and other skilled labor; production of components in countries with capabilities to make high-quality, complex products; and assembly in countries abundant in less-skilled labor. In this case, FDI is pro-trade, with large amounts of intrafirm trade as components produced by units in one set of countries are shipped to units in other countries for assembly, and the assembled final products are shipped to units around the world for sale to final customers.

Trade among parents and affiliates engaged in different stages of production shows that FDI and trade can sometimes be *complements*. Yet most FDI is not used primarily to locate different stages of production in different countries. Rather, most affiliates largely duplicate the production activities of the parent firm or affiliates located in other countries.

In the case in which foreign affiliates undertake the same kind of production as that of the parent firm or other affiliates, FDI and trade could be substitutes or complements. To some extent they are *substitutes*. In many industries a firm must find a reasonable trade-off between (1) centralizing production in one or a few locations and exporting to many other countries, to achieve scale economies (recall the discussion of scale economies from Chapter 5), and (2) spreading production to many host countries where the buyers are, to reduce transport costs, to avoid actual or threatened barriers to importing into these countries, or to gain local marketing advantages. When scale economies are less important, or when transport costs and trade barriers are higher, for example, the trade-off would tilt toward FDI. Foreign production through direct investment then substitutes for international trade.

However, the effects of this kind of FDI on trade are actually more complex. To some extent this FDI is also likely to *promote or complement* trade, for two reasons. First, the affiliates' production of the final product requires components and materials as inputs into production. Often, it is most economic to acquire these components and materials from the parent firm, affiliates in other countries, or independent suppliers in other countries. Although trade in final products may decrease, trade in materials and components increases.

Second, this FDI can increase trade in final products because the affiliate improves the marketing of all of the firm's products in the host country. In many cases the affiliate produces only some of the firm's entire product line locally. Other parts of the product line must be imported from the parent or other affiliates. The affiliate *displaces* some trade for the specific products that it produces, but it *expands* trade through better local marketing of other products produced by the multinational in other countries.

We have just seen that there are good reasons to think that FDI and trade could be substitutes, and good reasons to think that they could be complements. While each instance of FDI has its own outcome, can we say anything about the overall relationship? Most studies conclude that FDI, on average, is somewhat complementary to international trade. For instance, studies of U.S., German, Japanese, and Swedish multinationals find that, controlling for other influences, FDI is associated with higher home exports of products in the same broad industry. The overall complementarity seems to reflect both higher home exports of components used in affiliate production and higher home exports of final goods (the latter applies to many but not all industries).

SHOULD THE HOME COUNTRY RESTRICT FDI OUTFLOWS?

To decide whether FDI should be restricted by the home (or source) country is a difficult task. Let's approach it using a framework similar to the approach we used to examine restrictions on international trade. We can then identify several key effects:

- The effect on workers and others who provide inputs into production in the home country.

- The effects on the owners of the multinational enterprises based in this home country.

- The effects on the government budget, especially the effects on government tax revenues.

- Any external benefits or costs associated with direct investments out of the country.

Notice that we are now dividing the producer side of the market into (1) workers and other providers of inputs and (2) the owners of the multinational enterprises. Our presumption is that the multinational enterprises are more mobile internationally than are the workers and some of the providers of other inputs.

A good starting point for policy judgments about FDI and multinationals is a static economic analysis of the effects of shifting some of the country's capital stock out of the country. If FDI shifts some of the home country's capital to other countries, then less is available to use in production at home. With less capital to use in production, workers may be harmed. Some workers will experience temporary unemployment as they adjust to the reduction in home production by the multinationals. If the demand for labor decreases in the home country, then the real wages of workers will decline broadly.

Representatives of organized (unionized) labor in the United States and Canada have fought hard for restrictions on the freedom of companies to set up affiliates producing overseas and in Mexico, arguing that their jobs are being exported. Basically, their protest is correct, even though there are indirect ways in which FDI creates some jobs in the United States and Canada. Organized labor may be especially affected, because firms faced with strong labor organizations in the home country often replace or threaten to replace home-country production and jobs with production and jobs in other countries.

Workers are not the only ones in the home country who lose from FDI. The home-country government in general loses. It receives few or no taxes from the part of the multinationals' profits that becomes the profits of their foreign affiliates, and spending on government services provided to the multinationals probably does not decline by as much as the tax revenues decline. Other home-country taxpayers then have the choice of paying more taxes or cutting back on government-funded public programs.

The key group that gains from the FDI are the owners of the multinationals. They receive increased returns to their equity investments as the returns to the multinational enterprises' assets increase. In fact, in the standard economic analysis, the gains to the owners can be greater than the losses to workers and the government. If the home country is made up of the workers, owners, and the government, there can be a net gain for the country as a whole. But it also possible that the gains to the owners are less than the losses to workers and to the home-country government. In addition, some of the owners of the multinationals can be foreign investors, so some of the owners' gains do not accrue to the home country.

There is one more effect of FDI outflows that can be important. FDI may carry external technological benefits out with it. For all the multinationals' attempts to appropriate all the fruits of their technology, many gains may accrue to others in the location of the firms' production, through training of workers and imitation by other local producers. If so, outward FDI takes those external benefits away from the home country.

When we put all the possible losses and gains from FDI outflows together, the economics of the situation do not provide clear guidance on whether the home country would gain or lose well-being by restricting FDI outflows. Both are possible.

What are the actual policies of home-country governments toward outward FDI? Industrialized countries, the source of most of the world's FDI, actually impose few restrictions on outbound FDI. If anything, their policies are somewhat supportive of outbound FDI, because they impose little or no extra tax on affiliates' profits.

A key reason for the neutral-to-supportive home policies is that the multinationals have used their resources and common interests to enhance their political influence through lobbying. In particular, multinationals have been successful in emphasizing the competition among firms from different countries for global market shares and profits. In this competition, using foreign affiliates is often the best way for the multinationals to compete (for instance, through the affiliates' better marketing in the host countries, as we discussed in the previous section). Home-country governments generally refrain from restricting outbound FDI so that firms from the country can compete better globally. Indeed, multinationals sometimes gain enough political power to bend the foreign policy of a home-country government to their own ends. Historically, the governments of the United States, Britain, and other investing nations have been involved in costly foreign conflicts in defense of MNE interests that do not align with the interests of other voters in the home country.

SHOULD THE HOST COUNTRY RESTRICT FDI INFLOWS?

The effects of FDI on the host country, and the pros and cons of host-country restrictions on it, are symmetrical in form to those facing the home country.

First, the standard static analysis of foreign direct investment finds that workers in the host country gain from increased demand for their services, as do other suppliers of inputs to the affiliates of foreign multinationals. The host country government gains from the taxes collected on affiliate profits, as long as these exceed the extra costs of any additional government services provided to the affiliates. Domestic firms that must compete with the affiliates lose. Overall there is a presumption that the host country gains welfare in this standard analysis. Workers and suppliers to the affiliates, along with the national taxing government, gain more than owners of competing domestic firms lose. One residual concern mirrors that of predatory dumping, that the foreign multinationals will exercise substantial market power to raise prices once they have thinned the ranks of the local competitors.

Second, as with the home country's perspective, the host country must weigh indirect economic effects when deciding what its policy toward incoming FDI should be. And again the main kind of effects to consider are positive externalities. Multinational enterprises bring technology, marketing capabilities, and managerial skills to the host country. While the multinational attempts to keep these intangible assets to itself, some of them do leak out to local firms. Workers in the affiliates receive training and insights into the practices of the multinational. Local firms can use the proximity to affiliates to learn about their technologies and practices.

The actual thrust of the policies of host-country governments toward MNEs has shifted dramatically in the past 40 years. From the 1950s to the 1970s, host-country policies, especially those of developing countries, were based more on ideology and politics than on economics. The ideology ascendant in many developing countries at that time stressed government intervention in the economy.

National goals emphasized political and economic independence, national identity and autonomy, and self-reliance. There was skepticism about the workings of markets and the benefits of international trade. One result of this way of thinking was the focus of development policies on industrialization by import protection and import substitution, which we discussed in Chapter 13.

Skepticism and suspicion led to the characterization of MNEs as the instruments of injustice. Although there was recognition of the economic benefits that MNEs could bring to host countries, much of the discussion focused on complaints about MNEs. Here are some of the allegations: Economic gains were tilted toward MNEs because of their economic size and monopolistic power, leaving little for the host countries. MNEs used capital-intensive production methods that were not suitable to developing countries, and they "denationalized" the host country's industries by displacing local firms. MNEs acted as an extension of the power of their home-country governments, and they enlisted the support of home-country governments to pressure the host country in a confrontation. They also bought host-country politicians and bankrolled plots against the government, as International Telephone and Telegraph did against the Allende government in Chile in 1972–1973.

In short, at that time multinationals were seen by many as threats to the sovereignty (power) of host-country governments and to the well-being of the host countries. To reassert sovereignty and to minimize the alleged adverse effects of the local activities of foreign MNEs, many host-country governments adopted controls and restrictions on the entry and operations of MNEs. For instance, the governments of countries like India and Mexico adopted policies that required that a majority of ownership of any foreign affiliate be in local hands.

As we saw in Chapter 13, the economic effects of these inward-oriented government policies (antitrade and anti-FDI) came to be see as quite negative. Instead, the countries that began to grow fastest were those that adopted outward-oriented policies. Heavy-handed government intervention sank in perceived value, and the strengths of using markets increasingly were accepted. Even developing countries that might have resisted this policy shift had to confront the problems of the high levels of international debt they had built up by borrowing from banks. With the debt crisis of the early 1980s, lending by foreign banks and financing from other foreign portfolio investors dried up.

Although concerns about the MNEs' political and economic power did not disappear, policy discussions began to stress the static economic gains from direct investment into the country plus the possibility of technological and other side benefits. MNEs were viewed more favorably as a source of inflows of foreign capital, and as a set of investors that did not rush to the exits at the first whiff of trouble. These advantages increasingly impressed developing-country governments that had previously restricted inward FDI. Since the mid-1970s, many governments have liberalized their previous restrictions on direct investments into their countries. They have also shifted to competing aggressively by offering special tax breaks and other subsidies as each government attempts to woo direct investors to locate affiliates in its country rather than some other country.

MIGRATION

We have now completed our look at the role of multinational enterprises as conduits for the international movement of such resources as technology, capabilities, and financial capital. For the rest of the chapter we will shift to examining the international movement of labor that accompanies emigration and immigration.

International migration is the movement of people from one country (the **sending country**) to another country (the **receiving country**) in which they plan to reside for some noticeable period of time. International migration has played an enormous role in the past expansion of receiving counties. Indeed, most of the populations of the Western Hemisphere and of Australia and New Zealand consist of descendants of those who immigrated in the past several centuries.

The basic modern history of immigration flows into North America and Europe is sketched in Figures 14.2 and 14.3. Figure 14.2 shows that the rising tide of immigration into North America since World War II has still not reached its levels before World War I, when both Canada and the United States opened their doors to immigrants and even advertised in Europe to attract them. After World War I, the door swung toward shut. The United States severely restricted immigration in 1924, using a system of quotas by national origin, in response to unprecedented public fear of strange cultures, revolutionary radicalism, and job competition. Canada also switched from actively recruiting immigrants to limiting them, especially when hard times hit in the 1930s.

After World War II, both countries relied on partial controls that favored immigrants arriving with training and experience. In 1965, the United States replaced the national-origin quotas with a system that gave preference to applicants with family relatives already in the United States, and subsequent changes opened the door to more refugees. In 1974, Canada also shifted to a liberal policy toward relatives. Family members and refugees began to arrive at a quickening rate in the 1980s. In the Immigration Reform and Control Act (IRCA) of 1986, the United States tried to solve two immigration policy problems at once: cutting the further inflow of "illegal" (undocumented) immigrants and giving amnesty (permanent residence rights) to those who came earlier. One result of IRCA was the temporary jump in legal immigration for 1989–1991, a jump that helped reawaken natives' concern about being burdened with a new wave of immigrants. Even without the post-IRCA bulge, more immigrants were moving to North America in the 1990s, especially people from Mexico and the former Soviet Union into the United States, and Asians into Canada.

The doors in the European Union (EU) have also swung open, then shut, and then temporarily more open again, in this case within the shorter period since the EU was formed in 1957. In the 1950s and 1960s, the EU countries welcomed and even recruited workers from Turkey and other nonmember countries to help with the postwar reconstruction boom. In the early 1970s, however, the mood changed, as suggested by Figure 14.3. One EU country after another tightened up its immigration policy, partly out of rising cultural frictions and partly to protect jobs after

FIGURE 14.2 Gross Immigration Rates into the United States, 1820–2000, and Canada, 1851–2000

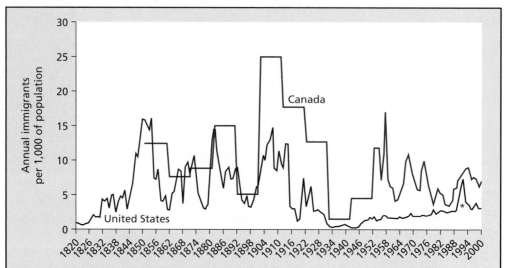

*The temporary jump in immigration, 1989–1991, reflected the amnesty granted to previously unrecorded immigrants and their families under the Immigration Reform and Control Act of 1986.

Source: U.S. annual rates, 1820–1970, from U.S. Bureau of the Census, *Historical Statistics of the United States, Colonial Times to 1970* (1976); and 1971–2000, from U.S. Bureau of Census, *Statistical Abstract of the United States,* various years; Canadian decennial averages, 1851–1951, and the 1951–1954 average from Statistics Canada, *Canada Yearbook 1994;* Canadian annual rates 1955–1993 from the *Canadian Economic Observer 1993/94,* and 1994–2000 from SOPEMI, *Trends in International Migration, Annual Report, 2001* (OECD, 2001).

FIGURE 14.3 Net Immigration Rates into the European Union, 1960–1999

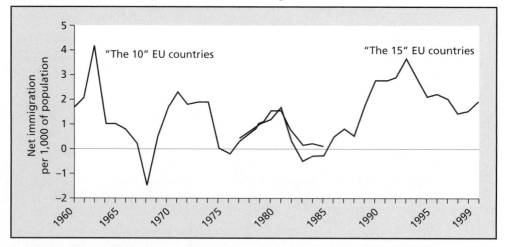

Net immigration = (Gross) immigration minus emigration.
"The 10" EU countries = The original six (Belgium, France, Germany, Italy, Luxembourg, and the Netherlands) plus the UK, Ireland, Denmark, and Greece.
"The 15" EU countries = "The 10" plus Portugal, Spain, Austria, Finland, and Sweden

Source: European Communities, Statistical Offices (Eurostat), *Bevolkerungsstatistik* (Demographic Statistics), Brussels, 1986; and Eurostat, *Eurostat Yearbook,* Brussels, various years.

the first oil crisis began to raise unemployment in 1974. Fewer immigrants were granted entry in the EU from 1974 to 1988. Then, however, the inflow began to rise again. The reason is not that EU immigration policy liberalized after 1988, but rather that a change in conditions outside the EU forced more immigrants through the same half-open doors. In particular, the rise of asylum seekers from Eastern Europe made greater demands on those countries whose laws allowed for compassion toward refugees. The strain was particularly great on Germany because of its prosperity, the reunification of West and East Germany, Germany's proximity to the transition countries of Eastern Europe, and the German constitution's provision that refugees must be given safe haven. In 1993, Germany repealed the constitutional safe-haven guarantees and began clamping down on immigration.

HOW MIGRATION AFFECTS LABOR MARKETS

To see some important economic effects of migration, let's squeeze as much as we can out of a thrice-squeezed orange, the familiar demand–supply framework already used extensively in Parts I and II. To simplify the analysis, we aggregate the whole world into two stylized countries: a low-income "South" and a high-income "North." Let's start with a situation in which no migration is allowed, as at the points *A* in the two sides of Figure 14.4. In this initial situation northern workers earn $6.00 an hour and southern workers of comparable skill earn $2.00 an hour. (Realistically, we presume that factor-price equalization, as discussed in Chapter 4, does not hold, perhaps because of governmental barriers to free trade or differences in technologies.)

If all official barriers to migration are removed, southern workers can go north and compete for northern jobs. If moving were costless and painless, they would do so in large numbers until they had bid the northern wage rate down and the southern wage rate up enough to equate the two.

Yet moving also brings costs to the migrants. Monetary costs include the transportation and other expenses of migration, as well as lost wages while relocating. In addition, migrants usually feel uprooted from friends and relatives. They feel uncertain about many dimensions of life in a strange country. They may have to learn new customs and a new language. They may have to endure hostility in their new country. All these things matter, so much so that we should imagine that wide wage gaps would persist even with complete legal freedom to move. Thus only a lesser number of persons, 20 million of them in Figure 14.4, find the wage gains from moving high enough to compensate them for the migration costs (*c*), here valued at $1.80 per hour of work in the North. The inflow of migrant labor thus bids the northern wage rate down only to $5.00, and the outflow of the same workers only raises southern wages up to $3.20. The new equilibrium, at points *B*, finds the number who have chosen to migrate just equal to the demand for extra labor in the North at $5.00 an hour.

Those who decide to migrate earn $5.00 an hour in the North, but it is worth only as much as $3.20 in the South because of the costs and drawbacks of working

FIGURE 14.4   Labor-Market Effects of Migration

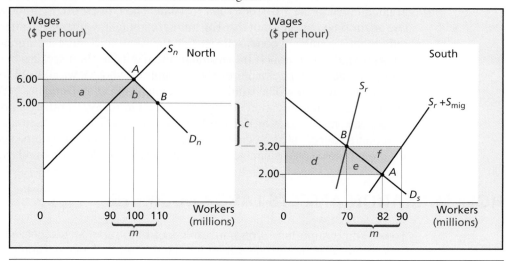

Group	Their Economic Gains or Losses	
Migrants	Gain area (*e* + *f*)	
Workers remaining in the South	Gain area *d*	} Lose area *e*
Southern employers	Lose area (*d* + *e*)	
Native northern workers	Lose area *a*	} Gain area *b*
Northern employers	Gain area (*a* + *b*)	
The world	Gains area (*b* + *f*)	

m = Number of migrants = 20 million

c = Annuitized cost of migrating, both economic and psychic (being uprooted, etc.), which offsets $1.80 per hour of extra pay

(By holding the labor demand curves fixed, we gloss over the small shifts in them that would result from the migrants' own spending.)

in the North. To measure their net gain, we take the area above the migrants' labor supply curve between the old and new wage rates ($2.00 and $3.20), or areas *e* and *f*.[6]

It is not hard to identify the other groups of net gainers and losers in the two regions. Workers remaining in the South, whose labor supply curve is S_r, gain because the reduction in competition for jobs raises their wage rates from $2.00 to $3.20. We can quantify their gains as sellers of their labor with a standard surplus measure, area *d*, in the same way used to quantify the gains to producers as sellers of their products in previous chapters. Their employers lose profits by

[6]The migrants' labor supply curve S_{mig} can be derived by subtracting the curve S_r from the combined curve $S_r + S_{mig}$. Note that their welfare gain does not equal the full product of ($3.20 − $2.00) times the 20 million unless their labor supply curve (S_{mig}) is perfectly vertical, in which case the amount of time they devote to work is independent of the wage rate. (Remember that their supply curve can be interpreted as a curve showing the marginal cost of their time.)

having to offer higher wage rates. The southern employers' loss of surplus is area $d + e$. (They lose surplus because they are buyers of now higher-priced labor, just as consumers as buyers of products lose surplus when the product price increases.) Employers in the North gain, of course, from the extra supply of labor. Having the northern wage rate bid down from $6.00 to $5.00 brings them area $a + b$ in extra surplus. Workers already in the North lose area a by having their wage rate bid down. So here, as in the analysis of product trade in Part I, some groups absolutely gain and others absolutely lose from the new international freedom.

The analysis in Figure 14.4 shows some clear and perhaps unexpected effects on the well-being of entire nations (excluding those who migrate, because it is debatable which country they belong to). Let's turn first to the effects on the North, here defined so as to exclude the migrants even after they have arrived. As a nation the North gains in standard economic terms—the gain to employers (and the general public buying their products) clearly outweighs the loss to "native" workers. Area b is the net gain. The case of restricting immigration cannot lie in any net national economic loss unless we can introduce substantial negative effects not shown in Figure 14.4.

The sending country, defined as those who remain in the South after the migrants' departure, clearly loses. Employers' losses of $d + e$ exceed workers' gain of d alone. So far it looks as though receiving countries and the migrants gain, while sending countries lose. The world as a whole gains, of course, because freedom to migrate sends people toward countries where they will make a greater net contribution to world production.

Does migration really work that way? Does it make wage rates more equal in different countries? Are competing workers harmed in receiving countries? Do immigrants catch up with them in pay? Does the world as a whole gain? Several studies have shown that the predictions of Figure 14.4 are borne out by the history of migration, both in the great integration of the world economy before 1914 and again in experience since the mid-1970s. Here are some of the main findings of the empirical studies:[7]

- Freer migration makes wage rates in the migrant-related occupations more equal between countries.

- Directly competing workers in the receiving countries do have their pay lowered, relative to less immigrant-threatened occupations and relative to such nonlabor incomes as land rents. However, these directly competing workers are now fewer in number than most people think because immigrants often take jobs that are increasingly unpopular with natives of the prosperous receiving

---

[7]For a recent sampling from this vast literature, see Borjas, Freeman, and Katz (1997, on the United States); Abowd and Freeman (1991, on North America and Australia); Pope and Withers (1993, on Australia); Bloom, Grenier, and Gunderson (1994, on Canada); O'Rourke, Taylor, and Williamson (1993 and 1994, on pre-1914); Friedberg and Hunt (1995); and Zimmerman (1995).

countries (taxi driving, long hours in small convenience stores, etc.). In the United States the major group of workers hurt by rising immigration since 1980 consists of the least-skilled American workers (e.g., high school dropouts).

- Immigrants' earnings catch up partly, but not completely, within their own lifetimes. Numerous studies have traced their convergence toward the better pay enjoyed by native-born workers, but the deficit is not erased in the first generation after migration. The pay deficit has grown more pronounced in Canada and the United States since the 1970s.

- World output is raised by allowing more migration.

SHOULD THE SENDING COUNTRY RESTRICT EMIGRATION?

Our analysis of the labor market shows that the sending country loses economic well-being because of emigration. Employers (and consumers of the products produced by these firms) lose more than the remaining workers gain. Before deciding that this means that the sending countries should try to restrict out-migration, it is important to look at several other important costs and benefits of emigration for the sending country.

First, let's look at the effects on the government budget. The sending-country government loses the future tax payments that the emigrants would have made (and perhaps also their military service). At the same time, those who emigrate no longer require government goods, services, and public assistance, so government spending also goes down. However, many public-expenditure items are true "public goods" in the economic sense that one person's enjoyment does not increase if there are fewer other users. That is, to provide the same level of benefits to the people who do not emigrate, the government has to continue spending the same amount of money. Examples of true public goods include national defense or flood-control levees.

Because some government spending is for true public goods, *the loss of future tax contributions is likely to be larger than the reduction in future government spending as people migrate from the sending country.* The likelihood of a net fiscal drain from emigration is raised by the life-cycle pattern of migration. People tend to migrate in early adulthood. This means that emigrants are concentrated in the age group that has just received some public schooling funded by the government, yet the migrants will not be around to pay taxes on their adult earnings. For this age group, the net loss to the sending country is likely to be largest for highly skilled emigrants—the *brain drain.* They have received substantial education at public expense, and they would pay substantial taxes on their above-average earnings if they stayed. For example, in some of the poorest countries in the world, nearly all the medical doctors emigrate to Europe and North America soon after they complete their training.

There is one monetary benefit to the sending country that is not captured in the examination of the labor market effects of migration. Those who emigrate often send voluntary remittances back to relatives and friends in their home country. The remittances are often large, as Italian and Mexican experiences have shown.

One estimate is that globally emigrants send home about $100 billion in remittances per year. *Sending countries that do not receive much in the way of remittances probably lose well-being, but those that receive substantial remittances probably gain well-being.*

What could the sending country do to try to restrict emigration or its negative effects? It could simply block departures. However, this would probably require severe restrictions on any foreign travel, with all of the losses that such travel restrictions would impose on the businesses and people of the country. A more defensible policy would be a tax on emigrants that is roughly equal to the net contributions the country has made to them through public schooling and the like. An alternative policy approach is to encourage return after the emigrant has been gone for a while, by appealing to national pride, offering good employment, and so forth. Taiwan and South Korea have encouraged the return of their scientists and engineers to work in their rapidly developing high-tech industries.

SHOULD THE RECEIVING COUNTRY RESTRICT IMMIGRATION?

Our analysis of the labor market shows that the receiving country gains economic well-being because of immigration, even if we ignore the gains to the migrants themselves. Employers (and consumers of the products produced by these firms) gain more than the native workers lose. Before deciding that this means that the receiving countries should not restrict in-migration, we should look at several other important costs and benefits of immigration for the receiving country.

Effects on the Government Budget

The effects here are symmetrical to those noted for the sending country. Immigrants pay taxes in their new country, and they use government goods and services. Some of the government goods and services are pure public goods, so we begin with a presumption that the tax payments are larger than the extra government spending required to serve the immigrants. However, there is a concern in many receiving countries that immigrants use government social services disproportionately. This suspicion was the basis for a 1996 U.S. law that made even legal immigrants ineligible for some forms of public assistance.

The true fiscal effects of immigrants are hard to measure, as discussed in the box "Are Immigrants a Fiscal Burden?" For immigration into the United States before 1980 or so, there is consensus that immigrants generally were major net taxpayers, not a fiscal drain. There is also consensus that the fiscal effects of an immigrant depend on the skill level of the immigrant. More educated, more skilled immigrants have higher earnings, pay larger taxes, and are less likely to use public assistance. For the United States since 1970, the fiscal balance is shifting toward immigrants being a fiscal burden, because the average skill level of immigrants is declining relative to that of natives. But there is no consensus that the mix has shifted enough to result in a net negative effect on the government budget from current immigration into the United States.

Case Study   Are Immigrants a Fiscal Burden?

It is widely suspected that immigrants are a fiscal burden, swelling the rolls of those receiving public assistance, using public schools, and raising police costs more than they pay back in taxes. This suspicion, applied to illegal immigrants, was the basis for California's voting that public services be denied to immigrants whose papers are not in order. It was also the basis for a U.S. law that made legal immigrants ineligible for some forms of public assistance.

Are immigrants a burden to native taxpayers? The answer to this question is more complicated than it sounds, for two reasons:

- While some effects are easy to quantify using government data, other effects must be estimated without much guidance from available data.

- The full fiscal effects of a new immigrant occur over a long time—the immigrant's remaining lifetime and the lives of his descendants.

Let's look first at the effects of the set of immigrants that are in a country at a particular time. This kind of analysis provides a snapshot of the fiscal effects of immigrants during a year. We can see clearly what we can and cannot quantify well, but we do not see effects over lifetimes.

George Borjas (1995a, Tables 9 and 10) has examined the fiscal effects of all immigrants in the United States in 1990. (Immigrants were 8 percent of the U.S. population in 1990.) Borjas calculates that immigrants in 1990 received about $24 billion in public assistance (often called welfare programs). They earned $285 billion of income and paid income taxes, sales taxes, and other kinds of taxes. The amount of taxes paid cannot be determined exactly. If a reasonable average tax rate is about 30 percent of gross income, then immigrants paid about $85 billion in taxes in 1990. That's the easy part, and if these were all the fiscal effects of the immigrants, they contributed far more in taxes than they took out in welfare payments, a net fiscal contribution of about $61 billion.

The remaining part is hard. Immigrants share in using all kinds of public services, including schools, hospitals, and the national defense. If the government expenditure on these services is held constant, are the services provided to the immigrants taking away from what natives get, or is it costless to share the services? The answer varies by type of public service. Immigrants probably do not harm the effectiveness of national defense expenditures. (Indeed, they might add effective soldiers.) Immigrants' use of hospitals and schools probably does detract from the natives' consumption of these public services. But Borjas concludes that there is no good way to estimate how large this adverse fiscal effect is. So, for 1990, the fiscal balance between immigrants and natives in the United States could have tipped in either direction.

Ekberg (1999) provides a similar study for immigrants in Sweden for 1991. (Immigrants were 12 percent of the Swedish population in 1991.) Ekberg determines that the immigrants received about $8 billion in public assistance and similar transfer payments and paid about $13 billion in taxes. He also estimates spending on public services that vary by age, including health and dental care, child care, education, labor retraining. If immigrants use these services at the same rates as natives, and if serving immigrants requires proportionate expansions of total services to keep the level of services provided to natives steady, then immigrants add another $5 billion of fiscal costs. Then Ekberg hits the same problem that Borjas had. What is the effect of the immigrants on the other kinds of government expenditures? Ekberg provides an estimate that immigrants probably add at least another $1.5 billion to fiscal costs through their effects on other government expenditures. If so, then immigrants in Sweden created a fiscal burden of at least $1.5 billion, equal to about 0.4 percent of Swedish GDP in 1991. The main reason for this burden is that immigrants were much more likely than natives to be unemployed in 1991.

Another way to look at the fiscal effects of immigrants is over their entire remaining lifetimes, and even to examine the fiscal effects of their descendants. For government programs that have costs for recipients of some ages but generate tax revenues from these same recipients at other ages, the lifetime approach is the more sensible way to calculate the fiscal effects of a small increase in immigration. One example is public schooling. Immigrants' children increase the cost of providing public schooling. But the schooling increases the children's future earnings, so the government collects more taxes. Another example is social security. While working, immigrants pay social security taxes, but in the future they will collect social security payments.

Analysis of the fiscal effects of immigrants over lifetimes is complicated and requires many assumptions, including assumptions about how much immigrants add to costs as they consume various public services. Smith and Edmonston (1997, Chapter 7) examine the lifetime fiscal effects of typical immigrants in the United States as of 1996. Over the lifetime of the average immigrant (not including descendants), the net fiscal effect is slightly negative, about $3,000 net cost to native taxpayers. However, the effect depends strongly on how educated the immigrant is. (Education is used as an indicator of earnings potential based on labor skill or human capital.)

- The average immigrant who did not complete high school imposes a lifetime net cost of $89,000.

- The average immigrant who is a high school graduate imposes a net fiscal cost of $31,000.

- The average immigrant who has at least one year of college provides a lifetime net fiscal *benefit* of $105,000.

These findings indicate that the fiscal effects of immigrants depend very much on the levels of labor skills of the immigrants. More educated, more skilled immigrants have higher earnings, resulting in larger payments of taxes. Immigrants with greater skills and higher earnings are also less likely to use public assistance.

In addition, Smith and Edmonston conclude that the descendants of the typical immigrant provide a net fiscal benefit of $83,000. Thus, the typical immigrant and her descendants provide a net fiscal benefit of $80,000 (= −$3,000 + $83,000). Interestingly, this net fiscal benefit is not spread evenly over government units. State and local governments bear a net fiscal cost of $25,000, while the U.S. federal government receives a net benefit of $105,000.[*] We can see a clear basis for tension between states and the federal government over immigration policies. Especially, we can see the basis for California's efforts to limit its outlays for immigrants, because California has by far the largest proportion of immigrants of any state.

---

[*]This differential is not unique to immigrants. The typical native-born child also imposes a net cost on state and local governments. They largely bear the costs of education, health care, and other transfers early in the child's life, while the federal government collects most of taxes paid after the child grows up.

External Costs and Benefits

Other possible effects of migration elude both labor-market analysis and fiscal accounting. Migration may generate external costs and benefits outside private and public-fiscal marketplaces. Three kinds of possible externalities merit mention:

1. *Knowledge benefits.* People carry knowledge with them, and much of that knowledge has economic value, be it tricks of the trade, food recipes, artistic talent, farming practices, or advanced technology. American examples include migrants Andrew Carnegie, Albert Einstein, and many virtuosi of classical music. Often only part of the economic benefits of this knowledge accrues to the migrant and those to whom he sells his services. Part often spills over to others, especially others in the same country. Migration may thus transfer external benefits of knowledge from the sending to the receiving country.

2. *Congestion costs.* Immigration, like any other source of population growth, may bring external costs associated with crowding: extra noise, conflict, and crime. If so, then this is a partial offset to the gains of the receiving country and the losses of the sending country.

3. *Social friction.* Immigrants are often greeted with bigotry and harassment—even from native groups that would benefit from the immigration. Long-lasting restrictions on the freedom to migrate, such as American discrimination against Asian immigrants at the turn of the century, the sweeping restrictions during the "red scare" of the early 1920s in the United States, and Britain's revocation of many Commonwealth passport privileges since the 1960s, have been motivated largely by simple dislike for the immigrating nationalities. Although the most appropriate form of social response to this kind of prejudice is to work on changing the prevailing attitudes themselves, policymakers must also weigh the frictions in the balance when judging how much immigration and what kind of immigration to allow.

There is at least indirect support for the idea that admitting immigrants gradually would go far to removing social frictions and congestion costs. The United States experienced its worst surge of anti-immigrant feeling in the early 1920s, when the immigration rate was increasing toward the peak rate it had reached just before World War I. The immigration rate was higher then, just before and after World War I, than it is today, even if we add reasonable estimates of the number of unrecorded illegal aliens. Even though some of the historic reasons for the anti-immigrant sentiment of that time (e.g., the Bolshevik Revolution) transcend economics, the high rate of immigration itself must have contributed to the fears and resentments of those Americans whose families migrated earlier.

What Policies to Select Immigrants?

The major industrialized countries have policies to limit the rate of immigration. If a country is going to limit immigration, on what basis should it select the immigrants that it accepts? Our economic analysis offers some insights. Two features of the analysis are prominent. First, the types of immigrant workers admitted will affect which groups within the native population win and which groups lose as a result of the immigration. For instance, if relatively less-educated and less-skilled immigrants are admitted, these immigrant workers will compete for jobs against less-skilled native workers, further reducing their already low earnings. Second, the types of immigrants admitted will affect the net fiscal benefit or burden of immigration. To gain greater fiscal benefits, the country should admit young adults who have some college education. In addition, admitting highly educated and skilled immigrants is likely to enhance the external knowledge benefits we just mentioned.

Australian policies toward immigration seem to draw from these economic lessons. Australia has used a point system to screen applicants, focusing on those whose age and skills are likely to be beneficial to the Australian economy. Canada also uses a point system to screen some of its applicants, but about three-fourths of immigrants into Canada enter based on family links or refugee status.[8] Immigration into the United States is even more heavily skewed toward family and refugees, with about one-tenth entering based on their worker skills. For both the United States and Canada, the results of these policies are that the average skill levels of their immigrants have been declining.

Economic analysis can make a strong case for a country like the United States or Canada to tilt its immigration policies toward encouraging and selecting more skilled immigrants while reducing the number of less skilled immigrants that it admits. Of course, economic objectives are not the only national goals. A shift toward pursuing national economic gain would come at a cost of achieving less toward other worthy goals, including promoting family reunification and providing humanitarian assistance to refugees. And the shift toward pursuing economic objectives would make the brain drain worse and leave more people in the rest of the world with very low income levels.

Summary

A **multinational enterprise (MNE)** is a firm that owns and controls operations in more than one country. Multinationals usually send a bundle of financial capital and intangible assets like technology, managerial capabilities, and marketing skills to their **foreign affiliates. Foreign direct investment (FDI)** is any flow of lending to, or purchase of ownership in, a foreign firm that is largely owned by residents of the investing, or home, country.

FDI grew rapidly for several decades after World War II, with the United States being the largest source country. FDI grew more slowly from the mid-1970s to the mid-1980s, but since the mid-1980s, FDI has grown rapidly. From the mid-1970s to the early 1990s, direct investment flows into developing countries slowed, but these flows have recently increased substantially. Nonetheless, most direct investment is from one industrialized country into another industrialized country. In the 1980s, the United States became an important host country, leaving Japan as the only major home country that is not also a major host to direct investment.

---

[8]To see how you score on the Canadian system, go to www.cic.gc.ca/english/immigr/guide-ce.html.

Explaining why multinational enterprises exist requires us to go beyond a simple competitive model. Multinationals can overcome the **inherent disadvantages** of being foreign by using their **firm-specific advantages.** Still, there are at least two alternatives to direct investment. The firm could export from its home country, but **location factors** often favor foreign production. The firms could rent or sell their advantages to foreign firms using licenses. Multinationals see **internalization advantages** to controlling the foreign use of their firm-specific advantages, especially their intangible assets like proprietary technology, marketing capabilities, brand names, and management practices. Negotiating **licenses** with independent foreign firms for them to use these assets would be costly and risky. Large multinationals are often involved in oligopolistic competition among themselves. For instance, one multinational attempts to gain an advantage by entering a foreign country first, and the others follow quickly to try to neutralize any advantage to the first firm.

The profits of foreign affiliates are taxed by the host-country government, but generally not taxed or taxed little by the home-country government. When multinationals shop around the globe for the lowest-cost sites, they favor low tax rates. Part of deciding of which country to invest in involves the desire to keep taxes down. In addition, firms can use **transfer pricing** to shift some reported profits to low-tax countries.

FDI could lead to less international trade in products (substitute for trade) or to more (complement to trade). FDI used to locate different stages of production in different countries increases trade. FDI used to establish affiliate production of final goods for local sales substitutes for imports. But better marketing by the affiliate can also expand imports of other final goods produced by the multinational enterprise in other countries. And affiliate production of final goods often requires use of imported components and materials. Studies of FDI and trade conclude that they are somewhat complementary, on average.

The home (or investing) country gains from the basic market effects of FDI as long as the investors themselves count. If they do not count as part of the home country, so that we exclude their investment incomes from measures of the national gain, then the home country can lose from FDI. The home country may also have other reasons to restrict outward-bound FDI: the possibility that it loses external benefits that accompany FDI, and the possibility of foreign-policy distortion from lobbying by multinationals. The actual policies of the industrialized countries (the major home countries) toward outward FDI are approximately neutral.

The host country has less reason to restrict FDI than does the home country. It gains from the basic market effects of FDI, and it gains from positive external technological and training benefits. In the past three decades many developing countries have shifted from restricting FDI inflows to encouraging them. Political dangers remain, however, in the relationship between host-country governments and major multinational enterprises.

Free **international migration** of people, like free trade in products, is the policy most likely to maximize world income. Yet perfect freedom to migrate is politically unlikely. The main beneficiaries of such a liberal policy, the migrants themselves, have little political voice in any country. More vocal are groups that resent the departure of emigrants or, more often, the arrival of immigrants.

The labor-market analysis of migration flows shows who wins and who loses from extra migration, and by how much. The main winners and losers from migration are the ones intuition would suggest: the migrants, their new employers, and workers who stay in the sending country all gain; competing workers in the new country and employers in the old country lose. Yet the net effects on nations, defined as excluding the migrants themselves, may clash with intuition.

The sending country as a whole loses, both in the labor markets and in the negative effect on the government budget. However, if the emigrants make large enough remittances back to the country, the sending country can gain from emigration. A case can be made for a brain-drain tax that compensates the sending country for its public investments in the emigrants.

The receiving country is a net gainer according to the labor-market analysis. In addition, it has often been true that immigrants pay more to their new country in taxes than they receive in public services. However, the declining relative quality of immigrants to the United States suggests that the government-budget effect is not so positive as it once was, and may now be negative. Immigrants also cause externalities, both positive (new knowledge) and negative (congestion, social friction).

The reason for the U.S. drift toward immigrants being a net fiscal burden is that the relative education and skill levels of immigrants has declined, as U.S. admission policy has given preference to family relatives and refugees since the mid-1960s. A country can improve the net economic effects of immigration by skewing its admissions toward selecting young, educated, and skilled adults and away from less skilled persons. While this policy would improve the economic side of the immigration accounts, it may clash with other objectives such as reuniting families and providing humanitarian aid to refugees.

Suggested Reading

Caves (1996) provides a good survey of the economics of multinationals. Markusen (1995) discusses how multinational enterprises can enrich the theories of international trade examined in Part I of this book. Brainard (1997) presents a careful analysis of the trade-off between FDI and trade. A good survey of research on the determinants of the patterns of FDI is found in United Nations Centre on Transnational Corporations (1992). The annual *World Investment Report,* published by the United Nations Conference on Trade and Development, presents a broad discussion of trends and issues involving FDI and multinational enterprises.

Graham and Krugman (1995) and Woodward and Nigh (1998) examine direct investments into the United States. Vernon (1998) explores some of the conflicts between multinationals and national governments. Moran (1998) discusses developing countries' policies toward FDI.

Smith and Edmonston (1997); Borjas, Freeman, and Katz (1997); Borjas and Hilton (1996); Borjas (1990, 1991, 1994, 1995a, 1995b); and Chiswick (1988) analyze U.S. immigration and immigration policy. Simon (1989) gives an optimistic view of the benefits of allowing immigration. See also the studies cited in footnote 7 of this chapter.

Questions and Problems

◆ 1. "Most FDI is made to gain access to low-wage labor." Do you agree or disagree? Why?

2. "Industrialized countries are the source of most FDI because they have large amounts of financial capital that they must invest somewhere." Do you agree or disagree? Why?

◆ 3. "Multinational enterprises often establish affiliates using little of their own financial capital because they want to reduce their exposure to risks." Do you agree or disagree? Why?

4. What might be the reasons that Japan is host to little direct investment?

◆ 5. Why does much FDI occur in such industries as pharmaceuticals and electronic products while little FDI occurs in such industries as clothing and paper products?

6. Which of the following is foreign direct investment?

   a. A U.S. investor buys 1,000 shares of stock of BMW AG, the German automobile company.

   b. Procter & Gamble lends $2 million to a firm in Japan that is half-owned by Procter & Gamble and half-owned by a Japanese chemical company.

   c. Mattel, a U.S.-based toy company, buys the 51 percent of its Mexican affiliate that it did not already own.

   d. Intel sets up an affiliate in Brazil using only two sources of financing for the affiliate: $100,000 of equity capital from Intel and a $1 million loan from a Brazilian bank to the new affiliate.

◆ 7. A firm has affiliates in both Japan, whose corporate income tax rate is 40 percent, and Ireland, whose corporate income tax rate is 15 percent. The major activity of the Irish affiliate is to produce a special component that it sells to the Japanese affiliate, initially at a price of $18 per unit. The cost of producing the component in Ireland has just risen from $12 per unit to $14 per unit. The controller of the MNE is considering three possible changes in the price of the component (for the sales between the Irish and Japanese affiliate):

   Ignore the cost increase, and leave the price at $18 (no price change).

   Increase the price to $20, to reflect exactly the increase in cost.

   Increase the price to $22, and, if necessary, explain the price increase by making general reference to unavoidable cost increases at the Irish affiliate.

   a. If the goal of the MNE is to maximize its global after-tax profit, which of these three should the controller choose? Why?

   b. What does each national government think of this use of transfer pricing?

8. Labor groups in the United States seek restrictions on the flow of direct investment out of the country. Why? Is their opposition to FDI defending only their special interest, or might it also be in the national interest? Explain.

◆ 9. A country currently prohibits any FDI into the country. Its government is considering liberalizing this policy. You have been hired as a consultant to a group of foreign firms that wants to see the policy loosened. They ask you to prepare a report on the major arguments for why the country should liberalize this policy. What will your report say?

10. What are two reasons that immigration into the United States was so low in the 1930s?

◆ 11. For each of the following observed changes in wage rates and migration flows from the low-wage South to the high-wage North, describe one shift in conditions that, by itself, could have caused the set of changes:

a. A rise in wage rates in both South and North, and additional migration from South to North.

b. A drop in wage rates in both South and North, and additional migration from South to North.

c. A drop in the northern wage rate, a rise in the southern wage rate, and additional migration from South to North.

12. Consider the labor-market effects of migration shown in Figure 14.4. What is the effect of a decrease in the annualized cost of migration (a decrease in c) on each group?

◆ 13. Review the areas of gain and loss to different groups in Figure 14.4. Why do the migrants gain only areas e and f? Why don't they each gain the full southern wage markup ($3.20 – $2.00)? Why don't they each gain ($5.00 – $2.00)?

14. "Sending countries should cheer for emigration because the migrants improve their economic well-being." Do you think this statement is true or false? Why?

◆ 15. Japan currently has a very low rate of immigration, because of very restrictive Japanese government policy. You are trying to convince your Japanese friend that Japan should change its laws to permit and encourage substantially more immigration. What are your three strongest arguments?

16. Continuing from question 15, your Japanese friend is skeptical. What are his three strongest arguments that Japan should continue its policy of permitting little immigration?

◆ 17. Which of the following kinds of immigrants probably contributed the greatest net taxes, after deducting public-assistance and similar payments, to the U.S. government? Which probably contributed the least?

a. Political refugees arriving around 2000.

b. Electrical engineers arriving around 1980.

c. Earlier immigrants' grandparents, arriving around 1990.

Part **Three**

Understanding Foreign Exchange

Chapter **Fifteen**

Payments among Nations

Throughout Parts I and II we focused on international trade in products. This focus is justified by the need to understand the basis for international trade and the effects of various government policies toward trade. In that discussion countries seemed to exchange exports of goods and services for imports of goods and services. Little attention was given to the monetary and financial aspects of international transactions.

In Parts III and IV we add money and international finance to our discussion. We will recognize (1) that many international transactions are trades in financial assets like bonds, loans, deposits, stocks, and other ownership rights and (2) that nearly all international transactions involve the exchange of money (or some other financial asset) for something else—for a good, service, or a different financial asset.

This chapter examines the framework used to summarize a country's international transactions. The bridge that links all the separate parts of international economics is the **balance of payments,** the set of accounts recording all flows of value between a nation's residents and the residents of the rest of the world during a period of time. Until one is familiar with the balance of payments, it is hard to see what the U.S. government's borrowing abroad has to do with an American's decision to buy a Panasonic DVD player in a department store, how repaying that foreign debt relates to U.S. exports of aircraft, or how trade events like the purchase of the DVD player or the sale of the aircraft could affect the nation's money supply and interest rates. Understanding the balance of payments is also key to understanding how people trade one country's money for that of another country. Even the international flow of humans shows up in the balance of payments, when the migrants make purchases or send money back home.

Fortunately, for all the diverse traffic over that bridge, its design is straightforward. We now cross it to widen our view from trade alone to all the exchanges of values between nations, with their many links to macroeconomic concerns like growth, inflation, and unemployment.

TWO SIDES TO ANY INTERNATIONAL EXCHANGE

An exchange between a country and the rest of the world involves two flows of value to be recorded in the balance-of-payments accounts. From that country's point of view, each exchange, each transaction, involves two opposite flows of equal value:

A **credit** (+) is a flow for which the country is paid. Exports are an example.

A **debit** (–) is a flow for which the country must pay. Imports are an example.

Any exchange automatically enters the balance-of-payments accounts twice: as a credit (+) and as a debit (–) of the same value. This is just an international application of the fundamental accounting principle of double-entry bookkeeping.

To build a set of accounts showing useful summary information, accountants distinguish between different categories of flows and put each of the two flows for a transaction into its category. The main kinds of flows in the balance-of-payments accounts are

Merchandise trade flows (flows of goods)

Service flows

Income flows

Unilateral transfers (gifts)

Private capital flows (nonofficial flows of financial assets)

Official reserve asset flows

To show how international transactions affect these six useful categories, let us imagine a set of five illustrative transactions between the United States and the rest of the world during a short time period.

First, suppose that the U.S. government sells $29 million worth of wheat to Russia from its surplus stockpiles, being paid with $29 million in gold by the Russian government. There is an outflow of $29 million worth of wheat, an export of merchandise, for which the United States must be paid. The offsetting inflow is the payment itself, in this case $29 million in gold to the U.S. government. The wheat-for-gold transaction creates these two bookkeeping entries (in millions of dollars):

	Credit (+) ($ million)	Debit (–) ($ million)
Merchandise exports (wheat)	$29	
Increase in official reserve assets (gold)		$29

Note that the payment of gold is a debit item, an inflow of value. It qualifies as a debit because it is something for which the United States must give up something else, namely, wheat.[1] Gold is viewed as an official reserve asset, but wheat is not, even though the wheat might have been held by government officials. **Official international reserve assets** are moneylike assets that are held by governments and that are recognized by governments as fully acceptable for payments between them.

Consider a second international transaction also involving merchandise trade. Northern Illinois Gas, a U.S. utility company, buys $34 million in natural gas from a Canadian firm. Suppose that it pays for the natural gas by writing a check on its deposits in a New York bank. Two accounting entries are made regarding the U.S. accounts:

	Credit (+) ($ million)	Debit (−) ($ million)
Merchandise imports (natural gas)		$34
Private capital inflow (bank's deposit liability to a foreign resident)	$34	

The debit entry probably seems easier and more natural than the credit entry in this case. It is clear that importing natural gas is an inflow of something valuable for which the United States must pay. But why should the payment be recorded as a "private capital inflow"? Because the writing of the check placed a bank liability (obligation to pay) into the hands of foreign residents. Before the purchase, the bank owed that bank deposit to Northern Illinois Gas, a resident of the United States. That was a purely domestic matter, not involving the balance of international payments. Once the gas is paid for, however, the New York bank owes an obligation—the right to redeem the checking deposit for cash—to a resident of Canada. This means that the New York bank is borrowing (incurring a new obligation to repay in the future) from Canada, which the bank used to cancel its obligation to somebody in the United States (Northern Illinois Gas). When you borrow, you gain the right to be paid now. In this key respect, borrowing is like an export of goods. It entitles you to be paid now. It is a credit item.

The rules regarding capital flows are:

Capital inflows are credits (+). They take the form of either an increase in a nation's financial liabilities to foreign residents or a decrease in financial assets previously obtained from other countries. Each of these is a flow for which the nation must be given payment right now, so each is a credit entry.

---

[1] In every case, the credit and debit entries have the opposite signs in the accounts of the other country. In Russia's balance of payments, this transaction entails a credit of $29 million for gold exports and a debit of $29 million for wheat imports.

Capital outflows are debits (–). They take the form of either an increase in a nation's financial assets obtained from other countries or a decrease in its financial liabilities to other countries. Each of these is a flow for which the nation must give up payment right now, so each is a debit entry.[2]

A capital outflow arises in the example to which we now turn.

Next, imagine that Brazilian soccer fans spend $6 million as tourists in the United States during a soccer tournament, paying for their hotels, meals, and transportation through New York bank deposits. The two flows are entered in the U.S. accounts as

	Credit (+) ($ million)	Debit (–) ($ million)
Service exports (travel)	$6	
Private capital outflow (reduction in bank's obligations to foreign residents)		$6

Again, one entry fits intuition more easily than the other. It is easy to see that the sales of tourist services to Brazilians are a U.S. export, for which the United States must be paid. And if that is clearly a credit item, it makes sense that the other entry must be a debit item. But why would it be labeled a "private capital outflow"? The answer is because reducing your liability to foreigners is like buying a claim on them, the usual sense of the phrase *capital outflow*. It is a use for which you must pay right now, just like any form of lending. Both repaying your liabilities and lending (buying somebody else's IOUs) are debits.

Our fourth transaction offers a further look at the financial side of the accounts. Suppose that the U.S. Treasury pays $25 million in interest on its past borrowing from Japanese investors, paying with checks on a New York bank. The two accounting entries are

	Credit (+) ($ million)	Debit (–) ($ million)
Income payment (interest paid)		$25
Private capital inflow (increase in bank's obligations to foreign residents)	$25	

The payment of interest to Japanese owners of U.S. government bonds is a payment of income to foreign residents, so this is a debit. The means of payment

---

[2] *Capital inflow* (or *capital import*) and *capital outflow* (or *capital export*) refer to the directions in which the funds (payments) are flowing (in or out of the country). Capital inflows can also be considered "asset exports" and capital outflows can also be considered "asset imports" if we focus instead on the direction of flows of the financial assets themselves.

is a credit. Why is this credit counted as a "private capital inflow"? The private New York bank on which the U.S. government wrote the checks now has a new liability to residents of Japan. It is borrowing anew from foreigners. The bank uses the borrowing from foreigners to cancel an equal checking-account obligation to the U.S. government, which has less claim on the private bank now that it has written checks.

So far, we can see that every transaction has two equal sides. If we add up all the credits as pluses and all the debits as minuses, the net result is zero. That is, the total credits must always equal the total debits. That is correct. To see just how correct it is, though, let us turn to a case that might look like a violation of this accounting balance.

Our fifth hypothetical transaction involves giving something away. Suppose that the U.S. government simply gives $8 million in foreign aid to the government of Egypt in the form of wheat from U.S. government stockpiles. This case differs from our earlier example of the sale of wheat to Russia because Egypt is not paying, with gold or checks or anything else. The correct way to record the credit and debit flows is as follows:

	Credit (+) ($ million)	Debit (–) ($ million)
Merchandise export (wheat)	$8	
Unilateral transfer to Egypt		$8

The $8 million credit is straightforward since this is just another merchandise export, for which the United States must be paid. The accountants get around the fact that the United States was *not* paid by Egypt by inventing a debit item for the unilateral transfer (gift) to Egypt. They invent the fiction that the United States received $8 million in goodwill—or gratitude—from Egypt for its gift of wheat. That goodwill is something received, a debit, for which the United States pays in wheat. In this way, even a one-way flow is transformed by accounting fiction into a two-way flow, preserving the all-in zero balance of double-entry bookkeeping.

PUTTING THE ACCOUNTS TOGETHER

To arrange the credit and debit flows from separate transactions into a useful summary set of accounts, group them according to the six types of flows. Figure 15.1 does this for our simplified set of five transactions. In this set of transactions, the United States was a slight net exporter of merchandise (exporting $37 million of wheat and importing $34 million of natural gas). It was a net exporter of services (its sales of travel services to the Brazilian soccer fans). For all goods and services together, the United States was a net exporter by $9 million, which is a surplus in the **goods and services balance** of $9 million. It made net payments of income to foreigners (its interest payments to Japan). For all goods,

FIGURE 15.1   A Simple Balance-of-Payments Account for the United States, Resulting From only Five Transactions ($ millions)

Flows and Balances	Credits (+)	Debits (–)	Credits Minus Debits = Net Surplus (+) or Deficit (–)
Merchandise trade flows	$(29 + 8 =) 37	$34	$ 3
Service flows	6		6
Income flows		25	–25
Unilateral transfers (gifts)		8	–8
Private capital flows	(34 + 25 =) 59	6	53
Official reserve asset flows		29	–29
Grand balance of credits minus debits			0
Six Key Balances			
Merchandise trade (goods) balance			3
Goods and services balance			9
Goods, services, and income balance			–16
Current account balance (goods, services, income, gifts)			–24
Net private capital flows			53
Overall balance (current account + private capital flows)			29

services, and income together, the United States had a deficit in its **goods, services, and income balance** of $16 million. In addition, the nation gave away $8 million in unilateral transfers to Egypt, so a total of $24 million had to be paid for (or financed) somehow.

The net value of the flows of goods, services, income, and gifts is the **current account balance.**

- If this is positive (a *surplus*), the nation earns that much in extra assets or reduced liabilities in its dealings with other countries.

- If it is negative (a *deficit*), the country must pay by giving up assets or increasing its liabilities.

In the simple case of Figure 15.1, the United States has a current account deficit of $24 million. It paid for this by incurring greater debts to foreigners. In this case, its extra debts took the form of extra private-bank deposit liabilities to foreigners, worth $53 million, minus a buildup of $29 million in official gold reserves acquired from Russia. The net new liabilities of $24 million covered the $24 million deficit for goods, services, income, and gifts.

The simple view of Figure 15.1 shows us a skeletal balance of payments with the main categories in clear view: goods flows, service flows, income payments, gifts, private capital flows, and official asset flows. Now that we understand the

FIGURE 15.2   U.S. Balance-of-Payments Account, 2001 ($ billions)

		Credit	Debit
1.	**Exports of goods and services and income received**	**$1,282**	
2.	Merchandise exports	719	
3.	Service exports (travel, business services, etc.)	279	
4.	Income receipts from foreigners	284	
5.	**Imports of goods and services and income paid**		**−1,626**
6.	Merchandise imports		−1,146
7.	Services imports (travel, business services, etc.)		−210
8.	Income payments to foreigners		−269
9.	**Unilateral transfers, net**		**−49**
10.	U.S. government transfers to foreigners		−17
11.	Private remittances and other transfers		−32
12.	**Changes in U.S. holdings of foreign assets (excluding official international reserves), net**		**−366**
13.	U.S. direct investments abroad		−128
14.	Other U.S. investments abroad		−238
15.	**Changes in foreign holdings of U.S. assets (excluding official international reserves), net**	**748**	
16.	Foreign direct investments in the U.S.	131	
17.	Other foreign investments in the U.S.	617	
18.	**Changes in holdings of official international reserves, net**	**0**	
19.	Foreign official holdings of U.S. assets	5	
20.	U.S. holdings of official reserve assets		−5
21.	**Statistical discrepancy**	**11**	
22.	Net balance of credits minus debits	0	
Six Key Balances			
23.	Merchandise trade balance (lines 2 and 6)		−427
24.	Goods and services balance (lines 2, 3, 6, and 7)		−358
25.	Goods, services, and income balance (lines 1 and 5)		−344
26.	Current account balance (lines 1, 5, and 9)		−393
27.	Net private capital flows and statistical discrepancy*	393	
28.	Overall balance (lines 26 and 27, or the negative of line 18)	0	

In the source, lines 12 and 20 are included in the category "U.S. assets abroad, net," and lines 15 and 19 are included in the category "Foreign assets in the United States, net."

*Lines 12, 15, and 21.
Source: U.S. Bureau of Economic Analysis, *Survey of Current Business,* July 2002, p. 51.

main categories, let us take a closer look at those categories in actual use. Figure 15.2 shows the actual balance-of-payments accounts of the United States for 2001.

At the top of the accounts, there is little detail to add. Merchandise exports and imports are easy to understand. The only wrinkle is that some of them go unrecorded, due to smuggling, negligence, or national secrecy (such as hiding some military sales and gifts from the U.S. balance of payments).

Services take a miscellany of forms. In the simple example above, we only considered travel services. In addition to travel or tourism services, nations trade transportation, insurance, education, financial, technical, telecommunications, and other business and professional services. Nations also pay each other royalties for use of technologies or brand names. The net balance of trade in goods and services (line 24) is often called the *trade balance,* although this somewhat imprecise term also sometimes refers to the merchandise trade balance (line 23).[3]

Income flows are mainly payments to holders of foreign financial assets. In addition to interest, these payments include dividends and other claims on profits by the owners of foreign businesses. Income flows also include payments to foreign workers who are only in the country for a short time, such as the honorarium paid to a U.S. professor for giving a talk at a Canadian university.

Unilateral (or unrequited) transfers also take a variety of forms. There are official government grants in aid to foreigners, as in the simple example of a U.S. grant of wheat to Egypt. Private individuals also make unilateral transfers. Historically, the largest kind of private transfer is international migrants' remittances of money and goods back to their families in the home country. Another kind of private aid is charitable giving, such as international famine relief.

The net flows of financial assets and similar claims (excluding official asset flows) is the private **capital account balance.** The IMF now uses the name *financial account* for this part of the balance payments, and the United States and many other countries have recently adopted this term.[4] Here we will continue to use the traditional term, *capital account.*

The values reported in the capital account are for the *principal amounts* only of assets traded—any flows of *earnings* on foreign assets are reported in the current account.[5] Some varieties of private capital flows call for special comment here. **Direct investments,** discussed in depth in Chapter 14, are defined as any flow of lending to, or purchases of ownership in, a foreign enterprise that is largely owned and controlled by the entity (usually a multinational firm) doing this lending or investing. Foreign investments that are not direct include international flows of securities, loans, and bank deposits. The securities are bonds and stocks. A foreign investment in a bond or a stock that is not a foreign direct investment is sometimes called an *international portfolio investment,* indicating

---

[3] The United States reports the goods and services balance monthly. This provides monthly information that is meaningful for many economic analyses. Nonetheless, there is considerable noise or variation in these data, so be careful when interpreting month-to-month changes. The United States reports its complete balance-of-payments accounts quarterly.

[4] Confusingly, the IMF also has a separate very small category that it calls the "capital account." The IMF's capital account is made up mostly of capital transfers that traditionally were included in unilateral transfers.

[5] Note that each asset or liability category is defined as an increase in that asset or liability. Decreases in one or the other will have the opposite sign. Thus, for example, Mexican repayment of principal on a U.S. bank loan would reduce the bank (asset) claims of the United States against foreigners, bringing a credit entry (a capital inflow) on line 14 in Figure 15.2. Another example: U.S. repayment of principal on a Treasury bond held by investors in Japan would bring a debit entry (a capital outflow) on line 17.

that the investor does not own a large share of the enterprise being invested in, but is just investing as part of a diversified portfolio.

The distinction between private capital flows and official capital flows is not quite the same as the distinction between private and government. The term *official* in Lines 18 through 20 refers to official reserve assets held by *monetary*-type officials, not all government. Other ("nonofficial") government assets are included in the private category. The purpose of that distinction is to focus on the monetary task of regulating currency values, to which we return in discussing the overall surplus or deficit.

Early in this century *gold* was the major official reserve asset. While gold is still held as a reserve asset, it is now little used in official reserve transactions. The majority of countries' official reserve assets are now *foreign exchange assets,* financial assets denominated in a foreign currency that is readily acceptable in international transactions. For the United States, these foreign exchange assets feature euro (formerly German mark) and Japanese yen assets. For other countries these foreign exchange assets are often U.S. dollar assets. Two other small categories of official reserve assets are certain claims that a country has on the International Monetary Fund (IMF), especially its reserve position in the fund, and the country's holdings of special drawing rights (SDRs), a reserve asset created by the fund.

At the bottom of the accounts comes the suspicious item, *statistical discrepancy.* If the flows on the two sides of every transaction are correctly recorded, there should not be any statistical discrepancy at all. Line 21 in Figure 15.2 should be zero. In fact, it is a credit of $11 billion, meaning that the credit items for the United States are less fully measured than its debit items. The accountants add the statistical discrepancy to make the accounts balance and to warn us that something was missed. In fact, the statistical discrepancy probably understates what was missed. It is the *net result of errors and omissions* on both the credit and debit sides. In truth, more than $11 billion of credits were missed, but some were offset by failure to measure all the debits.

How do the measurement errors arise? Which items appear to be most seriously undermeasured? It is hard to know just by looking at one nation's accounts. We get good clues, however, by adding up all the balance-of-payments accounts in the world. These should balance, but they do not. For the world as a whole, there is a tendency to underreport merchandise imports, income receipts (especially investment incomes), and capital exports. (See the box "Planet Earth's Balance of Payments.") The main difficulty is probably that many people succeed in hiding their imports, their foreign investment incomes, and their capital flight from their own government officials.

THE MACRO MEANING OF THE CURRENT ACCOUNT BALANCE

The current account balance (CA) has several meanings. The first meaning of the balance on goods, services, income, and gifts has already been introduced. When all these flows for current uses have been netted out, what is left is the increase in

Case Study   Planet Earth's Balance of Payments

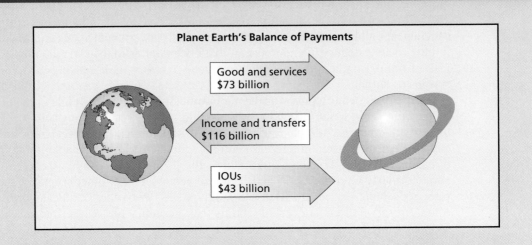

Planet Earth's Balance of Payments

Good and services $73 billion

Income and transfers $116 billion

IOUs $43 billion

Planet Earth has been trading heavily with the rest of the galaxy for years. Since the early 1980s and perhaps earlier, we have been exporting billions of dollars of goods and services into space, for which we are entitled to payment. But we have been sending even bigger amounts of income payments and transfers to space. To cover our current account deficit, we have been sending out IOUs (promises to repay somebody out there in space). On average during 1994–2000, we exported $73 billion in goods and services, made income and transfer payments of $116 billion, and sent out $43 billion in promises to repay. How long can this continue?

You may feel that something is wrong with the basic facts here. Yet these flows are consistent with all the world's official balance-of-payments statistics. If you add up the current account flows of every country for an average year during 1994–2000, you will find that $81 billion of merchandise imports, $8 billion of services exports, $81 billion of income receipts, and $35 billion of transfers received are unaccounted for. How could that happen? We cannot rule out the possibility that the missing flows went to the rest of the galaxy, as suggested. A more likely explanation, however, is that there are systematic patterns of misreporting international flows right here on Earth. The $81 billion of lost merchandise imports are probably

imports that went unreported because of smuggling or other incentives to underreport. (Drug traffic is probably not the reason, since drug trade is unreported on both the export and the import sides.) The $81 billion in lost income receipts is probably income on foreign investments, hidden to avoid taxes and regulation. A related problem arises in the world's capital account, in which the world appears to be a recipient of capital inflows from the rest of the galaxy. This most probably represents unreported "capital flight," the secret sending of wealth to foreign countries, away from the supervision of one's home government. Separate estimates suggest that unreported capital flight is particularly severe from developing nations, especially Latin America.

How serious are errors of this magnitude? Since the early 1980s, the total of the errors in the current account categories has usually been about 2 percent of the value of the world's exports of goods and services, international income payments, and unilateral transfers. By itself, that may be an acceptable rate of error. However, it is just a *net* error, the result of partly offsetting errors in both directions in each category.

Sources: IMF, *Balance of Payments Yearbook, 2001,* Parts 2 and 3.

all of the foreign financial assets minus all of the country's foreign financial liabilities. The reason is straightforward. The only (nonhuman) things being exchanged between nations are goods, services, income, gifts, and financial assets. If all credits must equal all debits, then the balance on goods, services, income, and gifts—that is, the current account surplus—must equal **net foreign investment** (I_f), the net accumulation of foreign assets minus foreign liabilities. That is, *a country's current account balance equals the country's net foreign investment.*

The current account balance is also linked to its national saving and domestic investment. A country can do two things with its national saving (S):

- Invest at home in domestic capital formation, which is domestic investment (I_d).

- Invest abroad in net foreign investment (I_f).

That is, national saving $S = I_d + I_f$. Looked at another way, the country's net foreign investment equals the difference between national saving and domestic investment ($I_f = S - I_d$) or, equivalently, *the country's current account balance equals national saving that is not invested at home* (CA = $S - I_d$).

The current account balance also is linked to domestic production, income, and expenditure. *A country's current account balance is the difference between its domestic production of goods and services and its total expenditures on goods and services.* Recall from basic macroeconomics that domestic production of goods and services (Y) equals the demand for the country's production,

$$Y = C + I_d + G + X - M$$

where

C = Domestic household consumption of goods and services

I_d = domestic real investment in buildings, equipment, and inventories

G = government spending on goods and services

X = foreign purchases of the country's exports of goods and services

M = the country's purchases of imports from other countries

C, I_d, and G all include purchases of both domestically produced and imported goods and services. Imports must be subtracted separately because imports are not demand for this country's products.

The country's total expenditures on goods and services (E, sometimes called absorption) simply equals consumption, domestic investment, and government spending:

$$E = C + I_d + G$$

Therefore, domestic product equals the country's total expenditures plus net exports, or $Y = E + (X - M)$. Again looked at another way, the country's current account balance (which is approximately equal to the country's net exports) is also (approximately) equal to difference between domestic product and national spending on goods and services:[6]

$$CA = X - M = Y - E$$

To summarize, the current account balance turns out to be equal to three other things:

Current account balance	CA
= Net foreign investment	$= I_f$
= The difference between national saving and domestic investment	$= S - I_d$
= The difference between domestic product and national expenditure	$= Y - E$

To see how we use these three identities, here is what they mean for a country that has a current account *surplus:*

- The country has positive net foreign investment (that is, the country is acting as a net lender to or investor in the rest of the world).

- The country is saving more than it is investing domestically.

- The country is producing more (and has more income from this production) than it is spending on goods and services.

The opposite is true for a country with a current account *deficit:* net foreign borrower, domestic saving less than domestic investment, and spending more than production (or income). Note that we are not saying that any of these is good or bad (at least not yet). Right now we just want to know that they are all ways of looking at the same situation.

These identities help us see what must be changed if the current account balance is to be changed. For instance, consider a country that seeks to reduce its current account deficit (that is, increase the value of its current account balance, making it less negative). An improvement in the country's current account balance *must* be accompanied by an increase in the value of domestic product (Y) relative to the value of national expenditure (E). If domestic production cannot expand much, then national spending must fall in order to decrease imports or to permit more local production to be exported.

The identities also help us to understand what forces might be causing changes in the current account balance. To see some uses for the current account, let's look at how it has behaved since the early 1960s for the four countries in Figure 15.3. Figure 15.3 shows both the country's current account balance and its net exports of goods and services—its goods and services balance—each as a share

---

[6] In equating $X - M$, exports minus imports of goods and services, with the current account balance, we are ignoring income flows and unilateral transfers. This is one of several simplifications generally used in macroeconomic analysis. (Another is equating domestic product with national income.)

FIGURE 15.3 Current Account Balances and Goods and Services Balances for the United States, Canada, Japan, and Mexico, 1963–2001

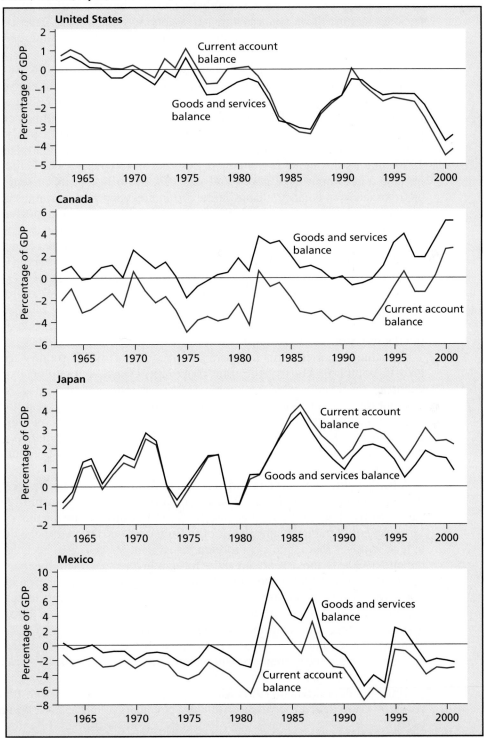

Source: International Monetary Fund, *International Financial Statistics Yearbook, 2001;* and International Monetary Fund, *International Financial Statistics,* August 2002.

of the country's gross domestic product. The two measures differ by the country's net income flows and transfers. (It is good to look at these latter two items here, especially income flows, although we usually ignore them in broad macroeconomic analysis.)

The first panel in Figure 15.3 shows that the United States has evolved from a net exporter and lender after World War II to a net importer and borrower. Up through the 1960s, the United States had a positive current account balance and a positive trade balance. The United States was a net exporter and lender largely because Europe and Japan, still recovering from World War II, badly needed American goods and loans (and foreign aid under the Marshall Plan). During the 1970s and up through 1981, a new pattern began to emerge. The United States became a net importer of goods and services, but still kept its current account approximately in balance, thanks largely to interest and profit earnings on previous foreign investments. After 1982, the United States shifted into dramatic trade and current account deficits, becoming the world's largest borrower. The underlying reason: Led by new federal government deficits, the United States cut its rate of national saving (S/Y) much faster than its domestic investment (I_d/Y) and therefore borrowed heavily from Japan and other countries (negative I_f/Y = negative CA/Y). The deficits declined in the late 1980s, but then began to grow again after 1991. (The current account deficit for 1991 was unusually low because of transfer payments from the allied countries to the United States related to Operation Desert Storm against Iraq.)

Canadian experience fits a classic pattern of a borrowing country with good growth potential. Most of the time Canada has borrowed capital from other countries (especially from the United States), as indicated by Canada's current account deficits for most years shown. Canada has used its typical goods and services surplus to pay foreign investors some of the earnings on their earlier investments. The payment of interest and profits on past borrowings is much of the gap between the goods and services balance and the current account balance in Figure 15.3.

Japan's goods and services balance and current account balance were nearly the same until the mid-1980s. These typically have been in surplus since the early 1960s. The surpluses became large and controversial in the 1980s, as Japanese goods gained major shares of foreign markets. Of course, the other way to look at this is that Japan's net foreign investment ($I_f = CA > 0$) became large in the mid-1980s. In those years Japanese foreign investment, including heavy lending to the United States, became the dominant force in international finance (although its role then diminished in the 1990s). Behind this shift to net foreign lending in the early and mid-1980s lay a widening gap between Japan's high national savings and its domestic capital formation. ($CA = I_f = S - I_d > 0$.) In addition, the income from Japan's holdings of foreign assets has created a positive gap between the current account balance and the goods and services balance since the mid-1980s.

Until the debt crisis of 1982, Mexico was a consistent borrower. Its current account was in deficit (negative I_f), and net payments of interest and dividends to foreign creditors showed up as a widening gap between the goods and services balance and the current account balance. Figure 15.3 shows part of the tremendous shock Mexico felt when its debt crisis hit in 1982. Its trade balance jumped to a surplus of more than 9 percent of GDP in 1983, not because exports grew (they did not) but because Mexico had to cut out two-thirds of its imports in the belt tightening necessary to meet most of its swollen interest and repay principal to foreign creditors. Between 1983 and 1987, Mexico was actually a net "investor," in that it reduced its net foreign liabilities by running current account surpluses. From 1988 to 1994, Mexico returned to being a net foreign borrower ($CA < 0$). The peso crisis of late 1994 again forced Mexico into a radical readjustment of its current account, with a shift to a goods and services surplus in 1995 and 1996 and little net foreign borrowing (CA almost equal to zero) during those years. Moderate deficits reappeared in 1998.

THE MACRO MEANING OF THE OVERALL BALANCE

The overall balance should indicate whether a country's balance of payments has achieved an overall pattern that is sustainable over time. Unfortunately, there is no one indicator that represents overall balance perfectly. The indicator often used is based on the division of net foreign investment (or borrowing), I_f, into two components: the balance on net private (or nonofficial) capital flows (KA) and flows of official reserve assets (OR). The **official settlements balance** (B) measures the sum of the current account balance plus the private capital account balance,[7]

$$B = CA + KA$$

Because all items in the balance of payments must sum to zero, any imbalance in the official settlements balance must be financed (or paid for) through official reserves flows:

$$B + OR = 0$$

If the overall balance B is in surplus, it equals an accumulation of official reserve assets by the country or a decrease in foreign official reserve holdings of the country's assets (that is, a debit in the official reserves account). If the overall balance is in deficit, it equals a decrease in the country's holdings of official reserve assets or an accumulation of foreign official reserve holdings of the country's assets (that is, a credit in the official reserves account). In some situations such changes in official reserve holdings can be specifically desired by the monetary authorities (for instance, gradually to increase the country's holdings of official reserve assets). In other situations these changes are not specifically desired and indicate an overall imbalance.

---

[7] The official settlements balance also includes the statistical discrepancy, because we assume that the discrepancy results from mismeasurement of private transactions.

The official settlements balance measures the net flows of all private transactions in goods, services, income, transfers, and (nonofficial) financial assets. However, it is the counterbalancing items—the changes in official reserve holdings—that show the macroeconomic meaning of the official settlements balance. Most of the transactions by countries' monetary authorities that result in changes in official reserve holdings are official intervention by these authorities in the foreign exchange markets. The monetary authorities enter the foreign exchange markets to buy and sell currencies, usually exchanging domestic currency and some foreign currency. For instance, the monetary authority of a country can buy domestic currency and sell foreign currency. The selling reduces the authority's holdings of foreign exchange assets that count as official international reserves. Or the authority can sell domestic currency and buy foreign currency. The buying adds to its official international reserves.

As reported in Figure 15.2, the official settlements balance for the United States was zero in 2001. This indicates that there was probably rather little official intervention in foreign exchange markets (at least on net) that involved the U.S. dollar during 2001. In contrast, in 1999, foreign central banks added $44 billion to their official reserve holdings of dollars, mostly by intervening in foreign exchange markets to buy dollars. Their willingness to acquire dollars and dollar assets provided most of the financing for the United States to run its official settlement balance deficit of $52 billion for that year.

As we will see in the chapters that follow in Parts III and IV, changes in official international reserves resulting from foreign exchange intervention can have impacts on many other economic variables. This activity can affect exchange rates, money supplies, interest rates, private international flows of financial capital, domestic capital formation, domestic product, and exports and imports of goods and services.

THE INTERNATIONAL INVESTMENT POSITION

Complementing the balance of payments accounts (which record flows of transactions) is a balance sheet called the **international investment position,** a statement of the stocks of a nation's international assets and foreign liabilities at a point in time, usually the end of a year. Flows change stocks, and so it is with the balance of payments and the international investment position. For instance, if the country has a current account surplus for the year, its net foreign investment (as a flow) is positive. The country is adding to its holding of foreign financial assets (or decreasing its foreign liabilities). The value of its international investment position at the end of that year will be more positive (or less negative) than it was at the beginning of the year.[8]

---

[8] Changes in the market values of assets previously acquired can also change the international investment position.

FIGURE 15.4   U.S. International Investment Position at the End of Selected Years, 1897–2001 ($ billions)

	1897	1914	1930	1946	1960	1982	2001
U.S. investments abroad	$1.3	$5.0	$21.5	$39.4	$85.6	$961.0	$6,862.9
Private	0.7	3.5	17.2	13.5	49.3	740.7	6,647.3
Direct investments*	0.6	2.6	8.0	7.2	31.9	226.6	2,289.9
Other	0.1	0.9	9.2	6.3	17.4	514.1	4,357.4
U.S. government (nonofficial)	0.0	—	—	5.2	16.9	76.9	85.7
U.S. official reserve assets†	0.6	1.5	4.3	20.7	19.4	143.4	130.0
Foreign investments in the United States	3.4	7.2	8.4	15.9	40.9	725.1	9,172.1
Direct investments*	—	1.3	1.4	2.5	6.9	130.4	2,526.7
Other	3.4	5.9	7.0	13.4	34.0	594.7	6,645.4
U.S. net international investment position	**−2.1**	**−2.2**	**13.1**	**23.5**	**44.7**	**235.9**	**−2,309.1**

*Direct investment refers to any international investment in a foreign enterprise owned in large part by the investor's home country. For 1982 and subsequent years, these investments are reported at estimated market values. For previous years, they are reported at historic cost.
†U.S. official reserve assets consist of gold and foreign exchange assets plus the reserve position at the IMF and Special Drawing Rights. For 1982 and subsequent years, reserve gold is reported at market values.

Sources: U.S..Bureau of the Census, *Historical Statistics of the United States: Colonial Times to 1970* (Washington, DC: U.S. Government Printing Office, 1976); and U.S. Bureau of Economic Analysis, *Survey of Current Business,* July 2002.

The link between the two kinds of accounts relates to a subtle but common semantic distinction. We say that a nation is a *lender* or a *borrower* depending on whether its current account is in surplus or deficit during a time period. We say that a nation is a *creditor* or *debtor* depending on whether its net stock of foreign assets is positive or negative. The first set of terms refers to flows over time, and the second set to stocks (or holdings) at a point in time.

Within the 20th century and into the 21st, the United States has come full circle in its international investment position. As shown in Figure 15.4, the nation was a net debtor before World War I. World War I abruptly transformed the United States into the world's leading creditor, a role the country played reluctantly for the next 20 years. Over several decades after 1945, the United States was increasingly a creditor in nominal dollar terms, though not as a share of GDP, reaching a peak nominal creditor position by the end of 1983. However, the large current account deficits that the United States experienced during the 1980s required financing through increased international borrowing. The creditor position built up over 60 years was erased and reversed in the next 6 years. By early 1989, the United States again became a net debtor, and the indebtedness kept rising into the 1990s. Figure 15.4 dramatizes the change with the stark contrast in the net positions at the end of 1982 and the end of 2001. Even for direct investment, long an American specialty, the net position has now reversed.

Summary

Basic definitions abound in this chapter. Terms introduced here appear constantly in the news media, and they will reappear throughout this book. Definitely review any of them that are not familiar at first sight.

A country's **balance of payments** is a systematic account of all the exchanges of value between residents of that country and the rest of the world during a given time period. Two flows occur in any exchange, or transaction, according to double-entry bookkeeping:

- A **credit** (+) is a flow for which the country is paid.
- A **debit** (–) is a flow for which the country must pay.

Flows from international transactions are grouped into six flow categories. Each category contains flows of more detailed types whose definitions also should be learned. The six flow categories, with some important subcategories, are

1. **Merchandise trade** flows (i.e., goods flows).
2. **Service flows,** including such services as travel, transportation, and insurance.
3. **Income flows,** especially earnings of interest, dividends, and profits.
4. **Unilateral transfers,** including government foreign aid grants and private gifts and remittances.
5. **Private capital flows,** including direct investments, portfolio investments in securities, changes in bank loans and deposits, and statistical discrepancy.
6. **Official reserve asset flows,** including changes in official gold and foreign exchange assets, changes in other official reserve assets related to the IMF, and changes in liabilities that foreign countries consider to be their official reserve assets.

Flow categories are summed into six net balances, each defined so that a surplus is positive and a deficit is negative:

1. The **merchandise trade balance** equals the net credits minus debits, on merchandise flows.
2. The **goods and services balance** equals the net exports of both goods and services. It is often called the *trade balance.*
3. The **goods, services, and income balance** adds net income flows to the goods and services balance.
4. The **current account balance** equals the net credits minus debits on the flows of goods, services, income, and unilateral transfers. It also equals the change in the nation's foreign assets minus foreign liabilities, also known as **net foreign investment.**
5. The net private **capital account balance** equals net credits minus debits involving changes in nonofficial foreign financial assets and liabilities.
6. The **overall balance** (or **official settlements balance**) equals the sum of the current account balance plus the private capital account balance. If it is in surplus, it is counterbalanced by an increase in the country's official reserve

holdings or a decrease in its official liabilities to other countries' monetary authorities (debit items at the bottom of the accounts). If it is in deficit, it is counterbalanced by a decrease in the country's official reserve assets or an increase in its official liabilities (credit items at the bottom of the accounts).

The current account balance (CA) has special macroeconomic meaning. Because the current account balance equals net foreign investment (I_f), it also equals the part of national saving (S) that is not used in domestic capital formation (I_d). A nation that is running a current account deficit, like the United States since 1982, is a nation that is saving less than its domestic capital formation. The current account deficit represents net foreign borrowing used to finance part of its relatively high level of domestic investment. The current account balance also equals the difference between domestic production of goods and services (Y) and national expenditures (E, expenditure on consumption, domestic capital formation, and government goods and services). Thus, yet another way of looking at the U.S. current account deficit is that the United States is buying more goods and services than it is producing (or spending more than its national income).

The overall balance is intended to indicate whether the overall pattern of the country's balance of payments has achieved a sustainable equilibrium. The official settlements balance does not quite match this concept, but it is still useful in macroeconomic analysis. It indicates the extent of official intervention in the foreign exchange markets—the buying and selling of currencies by the monetary authorities. As we will see in subsequent chapters, such intervention can have effects on exchange rates, money supplies, and many other macroeconomic variables.

A nation's **international investment position** shows its stocks of international assets and liabilities at a moment of time. These stocks are changed each year by the flows of private and official assets measured in the balance of payments. As a result of large current account deficits since the early 1980s, the United States switched from being the world's largest net creditor to being its largest net debtor.

Suggested Reading   Lane and Milesi-Ferretti (2001) develop and analyze estimates of the international investment positions of a large number of industrialized and developing countries. The balance-of-payments accounts of most nations are summarized in the IMF's *International Financial Statistics* and also in its *Balance of Payments Statistics Yearbook.* More detailed accounts for the United States appear regularly in the *Survey of Current Business,* and those for Canada are in the *Canada Yearbook.*

Questions and Problems

✦ 1. What is the current account balance of a nation with a government budget deficit of $128 billion, private saving of $806 billion, and domestic capital formation of $777 billion?

2. "A country is better off running a current account surplus rather than a current account deficit." Do you agree or disagree? Explain.

✦ 3. "National saving can be used domestically or internationally." Explain the basis for this statement, including the benefits to the nation of each use of its saving.

4. "Consider a country whose assets are not held by other countries as official international reserves. If this country has a surplus in its official settlements balance, then the monetary authority of the country is decreasing its holdings of official reserve assets." Do you agree or disagree? Explain.

✦ 5. Which of the following transactions would contribute to a U.S. current account surplus?

a. Boeing barters a $100 million plane to Mexico in exchange for $100 million worth of hotel services on the Mexican coast.

b. The United States borrows $100 million long term from Saudi Arabia to buy $100 million of Saudi oil this year.

c. The United States sells a $100 million jet to Turkey for $100 million in bank deposits.

d. The U.S. government makes a gift of $100 million to the government of Greece, in the form of New York bank deposits, to pay for injuries caused by Turkish jet attacks.

e. The British central bank buys $100 million in U.S.-dollar bank deposits from a New York bank, paying by providing pound bank deposits to the New York bank.

6. Which of the transactions in question 5 contribute to a U.S. deficit in the overall (official settlements) balance?

✦ 7. Using the line numbers in Figure 15.2, decide which lines should contain the credit and debit items for each of the following transactions from the point of view of the United States:

a. Pepsico signs an agreement with Russia bartering Pepsico's managerial services and trademarks in making Pepsi Cola in Russia for an equivalent dollar value of Stolichnaya vodka and Soviet merchant ships.

b. Citibank of New York lends the government of Brazil $184 million in a new loan so that Brazil simultaneously pays Citibank $184 million in interest on an old loan.

c. The city of Kyoto, Japan, pays Americans $3 billion in Kyoto city bonds (IOUs) to buy the Dallas Cowboys football franchise (i.e., Kyoto acquires all future paper title to profits from the Cowboys and their name).

d. U.S. tourists pay $280, with a check written on a Vermont bank, to stay in Toronto's SkyDome Hotel overlooking the Blue Jays baseball stadium.

8. You are given the following information about a country's international transactions during a year:

Merchandise exports	$330
Merchandise imports	198
Service exports	196
Service imports	204
Income flows, net	3
Unilateral transfers, net	−8
Increase in the country's holding of foreign assets, net (excluding official reserve assets)	202
Increase in foreign holdings of the country's assets, net (excluding official reserve assets)	102
Statistical discrepancy, net	4

   a. Calculate the values of the country's merchandise trade balance, goods and services balance, current account balance, and official settlements balance.

   b. What is the value of the change in official reserve assets (net)? Is the country increasing or decreasing its net holdings of official reserve assets?

◆ 9. What are the effects of each of the following on the U.S. international investment position?

   a. Foreign central banks increase their official holdings of U.S. government securities.

   b. U.S. residents increase their holdings of stocks issued by Japanese companies.

   c. A British pension fund sells some of its holdings of the stocks of U.S. companies in order to buy U.S. corporate bonds.

10. On December 31, a country has the following stocks of international assets and liabilities to foreigners.

   • The country's residents own $30 billion of bonds issued by foreign governments.

   • The country's central bank holds $20 billion of gold and $15 billion of foreign-currency assets as official reserve assets.

   • Foreign firms have invested in production facilities in the country, with the value of their investments currently $40 billion.

   • Residents of foreign countries own $25 billion of bonds issued by the country's companies.

   a. What is the value of the country's international investment position? Is the country an international creditor or debtor?

   b. If the country during the next year runs a surplus in its current account, what will the impact be on the value of the country's international investment position?

Chapter **Sixteen**

The Foreign Exchange Market

In foreign commerce, as in international dialogue, somebody has to translate. People in different countries use different currencies as well as different languages. The translator between different currencies is the exchange rate, the price of one country's money in units of another country's money. You can go only so far using just one currency. If an American wants to buy something from a foreign resident, the foreign resident will typically want to have the payment translated into her home currency.

What determines the exchange rate, or the pressures on it, is the subject of the rest of Part III. This chapter introduces the real-world institutions of currency trading. It also begins to build a theory of exchange rates, starting with the role of forces that show up in the balance-of-payments entries of Chapter 15.

Much of the study of exchange rates is like a trip to another planet. It is a strange land, far removed from the economics of an ordinary household. It is populated by strange creatures—hedgers, arbitrageurs, the Gnomes of Zurich, the Snake in the Tunnel, the crawling peg, and the dirty float. Yet the student of exchange rates is helped by the presence of two familiar forces: profit maximization and competition. The familiar assumption that individuals act as though they are out to maximize the real value of their net incomes (profits) appears to be at least as valid in international financial behavior as in other realms of economics. To be sure, people act as though they are maximizing a subtle concept of profit, one that takes account of a wide variety of economic and political risks. Yet the parties engaged in international finance do seem to react to changing conditions in the way that a profit-maximizer would.

It also happens that competition prevails in most international financial markets despite a folklore full of tales about how wealthy speculators manage to corner those markets. There is competition in the markets for foreign exchange and in the international lending markets. Thus, for these markets, we can use the familiar demand–supply analysis of competitive markets. It is important also to make one disclaimer: It is definitely not the case that all markets in the international arena are competitive. Monopoly and oligopoly are evident in much of the direct investment activity discussed in Chapter 14 as well as in the cartels discussed in Chapter 13. Ordinary demand and supply curves would not do justice to the facts in those areas. Yet in the financial markets that play a large role in the material of Parts III and IV, competitive conditions do hold, even more so than in most markets usually thought of as competitive.

THE BASICS OF CURRENCY TRADING

Foreign exchange is the act of trading different nations' moneys.[1] The moneys take the same forms as money within a country. The greater part of the money assets traded in foreign exchange markets are demand deposits in banks. A very small part consists of coins and currency of the ordinary pocket variety.

An **exchange rate** is the price of one nation's money in terms of another nation's money.[2] There are actually two basic types of exchange rate, depending on the timing of the actual exchange of moneys. The **spot exchange rate** is the price for "immediate" exchange. (For standard large trades in the market, immediate exchange for most currencies means exchange or delivery in two working days after the exchange is agreed, while it means one working day after the exchange is agreed for exchanges between U.S. dollars, Canadian dollars, and Mexican pesos.) The **forward exchange rate** is the price now for an exchange that will take place sometime in the future. Forward exchange rates are prices that are agreed today for exchanges of moneys that will occur at a specified time in the future, such as 30, 90, or 180 days from now. This chapter focuses on foreign exchange in general and spot exchange rates specifically. Chapter 17 examines forward foreign exchange and its uses.

In today's increasingly international world, many newspapers keep track of exchange rates with quotations like those shown in Figure 16.1. Notice that each price is stated in two ways: first as a U.S. dollar price of the other currency and next as the price of the U.S. dollar in units of the other currency. The pairs of prices are just reciprocals of each other. Saying that the British pound sterling equals 1.4486 U.S. dollars is the same as saying that the U.S. dollar is worth 0.6903 British pounds (1.4486 = 1/0.6903), and so forth. Each exchange rate can be stated in two ways. Each of the two ways sounds reasonable because both sides of the price are moneys. In contrast, for regular prices of goods and services, only one of the things being traded is money. So there is one natural way to quote the price (for instance, $1.60 per gallon of gasoline). It is good practice to

---

[1] The term *foreign exchange* also refers to holdings of foreign currencies.

[2] Exchange rates are one kind of price that a national money has. Another is its ability to buy goods and services immediately. The second kind of a price, the usual "value of the dollar," is just the reciprocal of the money cost of buying a bundle of goods and services. A third kind of price of money is the cost of renting it, and having access to it, for a given period of time. This is (roughly) the rate of interest that borrowers pay for the use of money, and it is analogous to other rental prices such as the price of renting an apartment or a rental car.

be careful to specify how an exchange rate value is quoted, by stating the units in both the numerator and the denominator. As with other prices, the item that is being priced or valued is in the denominator. For instance, $1.4486/£ is the price or value of the pound.[3]

The foreign exchange market is not a single gathering place where traders shout buy and sell orders at each other. Rather, banks and the traders who work at banks are at the center of the foreign exchange market. These banks and their traders use computers and telephones to conduct foreign exchange trades with their customers and also with each other. The trading done with customers is called the *retail part of the market*. Some of this is trading with individuals in small amounts. We see this part of the market, for instance, when we travel to a foreign country, but individuals' exchanges are a very small part of overall foreign exchange trading. Most of the retail part of the market involves nonfinancial companies, financial institutions, and other organizations that undertake large trades as the customers of the banks that actively deal in the market. The trading done between the banks active in the market is called the *interbank part of the market.*

The banks active in foreign exchange trading are located in countries around the world, so this is a 24-hour market. On working days, foreign exchange trading is always occurring somewhere in the world. Although banks throughout the world participate, nearly half of foreign exchange trading involves banks in two locations: London and New York.

The total volumes traded in the foreign exchange market are enormous. Foreign exchange trading in 2001 has been estimated at about $1.2 trillion *per day* versus a daily turnover of only about $280 billion for U.S. government securities and only about $42 billion on the New York Stock Exchange. Yet the number of people employed as traders in banks in this industry is several thousand for the world as a whole. (See the box "Foreign Exchange Trading.")

Most foreign exchange trading involves the exchange of U.S. dollars for another currency. Indeed, although some trades are made directly between currencies other than the U.S. dollar, many such trades are actually done in two steps. One foreign currency is exchanged for dollars, and these dollars are then exchanged for the other foreign currency. Because the dollar is often used in this way to accomplish trading between two other currencies, the dollar is called a *vehicle currency.*

---

[3] Traders in the market also have conventions for stating exchange rates. In the market, most rates referring to the U.S. dollar are quoted as units of other currency per U.S. dollar, but some (including the euro, British pound, Australian dollar, and Canadian dollar) are quoted as U.S. dollars per unit of this currency. In addition, traders who are willing to buy or sell foreign exchange quote two exchange rates: one for buying and the other for selling. The resulting *bid–ask* spread is a source of profits to the traders. Furthermore, the difference between buying and selling rates (or the *bid–ask* spread) varies by size (or type) of trade. It is larger for smaller trades, and largest for small transactions in actual currency and coins. The difference between buying and selling rates typically is relatively small for large trades in major currencies. We will ignore differences in buy and sell rates in most subsequent discussion, talking instead about the exchange rate as a single number.

FIGURE 16.1   Exchange Rate Quotations, April 24, 2002

The New York foreign exchange mid-range rates below apply to trading among banks in amounts of $1 million and more, as quoted at 4 p.m. Eastern time by Reuters and other sources. Retail transactions provide fewer units of foreign currency per dollar.

Country	U.S. $ Equivalent		Currency Per U.S. $		Country	U.S. $ Equivalent		Currency Per U.S. $	
	Wed.	Tue.	Wed.	Tue.		Wed.	Tue.	Wed.	Tue.
Argentina (Peso)-y	.3160	.3160	3.1650	3.1650	Malaysia (Ringgit)-b	.2632	.2632	3.8001	3.8001
Australia (Dollar)	.5429	.5380	1.8421	1.8586	Malta (Lira)	2.2262	2.2212	.4492	.4502
Bahrain (Dinar)	2.6525	2.6525	.3770	.3770	Mexico (Peso)				
Brazil (Real)	.4239	.4235	2.3590	2.3610	Floating Rate	.1077	.1080	9.2855	9.2555
Britain (Pound)	1.4486	1.4472	.6903	.6910	New Zealand (Dollar)	.4492	.4464	2.2262	2.2401
1-month forward	1.4458	1.4444	.6917	.6923	Norway (Krone)	.1171	.1169	8.5398	8.5556
3-months forward	1.4407	1.4393	.6941	.6948	Pakistan (Rupee)	.01667	.01666	59.975	60.025
6-months forward	1.4329	1.4317	.6979	.6985	Peru (new Sol)	.2911	.2912	3.4358	3.4336
Canada (Dollar)	.6378	.6354	1.5680	1.5737	Philippines (Peso)	.01964	.01962	50.925	50.975
1-month forward	.6375	.6352	1.5687	1.5743	Poland (Zloty)	.2475	.2478	4.0410	4.0347
3-months forward	.6368	.6345	1.5704	1.5760	Russia (Ruble)-a	.03207	.03208	31.185	31.175
6-months forward	.6356	.6334	1.5733	1.5788	Saudi Arabia (Riyal)	.2666	.2666	3.7505	3.7505
Chile (Peso)	.001529	.001529	653.95	653.95	Singapore (Dollar)	.5505	.5498	1.8165	1.8190
China (Renminbi)	.1208	.1208	8.2774	8.2773	Slovak Rep. (Koruna)	.02130	.02131	46.938	46.928
Colombia (Peso)	.0004408	.0004416	2268.50	2264.60	South Africa (Rand)	.0917	.0913	10.9000	10.9550
Czech. Rep. (Koruna)					South Korea (Won)	.0007681	.0007685	1302.00	1301.30
Commercial rate	.02946	.02952	33.945	33.874	Sweden (Krona)	.0970	.0967	10.3139	10.3448
Denmark (Krone)	.1200	.1196	8.3305	8.3635	Switzerland (Franc)	.6086	.6058	1.6431	1.6507
Ecuador (US Dollar)	1.0000	1.0000	1.0000	1.0000	1-month forward	.6088	.6060	1.6426	1.6502
Hong Kong (Dollar)	.1282	.1282	7.7997	7.7993	3-months forward	.6092	.6063	1.6416	1.6493
Hungary (Forint)	.003704	.003691	269.95	270.96	6-months forward	.6101	.6072	1.6391	1.6469
India (Rupee)	.02043	.02042	48.950	48.960	Taiwan (Dollar)	.02877	.02877	34.760	34.760
Indonesia (Rupiah)	.0001072	.0001060	9325	9430	Thailand (Baht)	.02312	.02309	43.260	43.305
Israel (Shekel)	.2057	.2072	4.8610	4.8270	Turkey (Lira)	.00000074	.00000076	1347500	1323000
Japan (Yen)	.007711	.007681	129.68	130.19	United Arab (Dirham)	.2723	.2723	3.6730	3.6730
1-month forward	.007724	.007694	129.47	129.98	Uruguay (Peso)				
3-months forward	.007747	.007717	129.08	129.58	Financial	.05958	.05970	16.785	16.750
6-months forward	.007793	.007762	128.33	128.83	Venezuela (Bolivar)	.001183	.001172	845.50	853.50
Jordan (Dinar)	1.4104	1.4104	.7090	.7090					
Kuwait (Dinar)	3.2648	3.2637	.3063	.3064	SDR	1.2601	1.2587	.7936	.7945
Lebanon (Pound)	.0006605	.0006605	1514.13	1514.00	Euro	.8924	.8886	1.1206	1.1254

Special Drawing Rights (SDR) are based on exchange rates for the U.S. dollar, the euro, the British pound, and the Japanese yen.
Source: International Monetary Fund.
a-Russian Central Bank rate. b-Government rate. y-Floating rate.

Source: *The Wall Street Journal,* April 25, 2002.

Using the Foreign Exchange Market

In the customer or retail part of the spot foreign exchange market, individuals, businesses, and other organizations can acquire foreign moneys to make payments, or they can sell foreign moneys that they have received in payments. The spot foreign exchange market thus provides clearing services that permit payments to flow between individuals, businesses, and other organizations that prefer to use different moneys. These payments are for all of the types of items included in the balance-of-payments accounts, including payments for exports and imports of goods and services and payments for purchases or sales of foreign financial assets.

One of the currencies shown in Figure 16.1 was not there a few years earlier, and several that had been listed in early 2002 were gone by April. On January 1, 1999, a major new currency, the euro (€), was born. The European Union (EU) created the euro, and 11 of the 15 EU countries began using it immediately, with Greece joining the club on January 1, 2001. For several years after its birth in 1999, both the euro and the national currencies of these countries coexisted. Then, during the first two months of 2002, the national currencies of these 12 countries were completely replaced by the euro. The conversion rates were that 1 euro replaced each of:

13.7603	Austrian schillings
40.3399	Belgium francs
5.94573	Finnish markka
6.55957	French francs
1.95583	German marks
0.787564	Irish punt
1,936.27	Italian lira
40.3399	Luxembourg francs
2.20371	Netherlands guilder
200.482	Portuguese escudos
166.386	Spanish pesetas
340.750	Greek drachma

Good-bye marks, good-bye francs, good-bye lira, good-bye guilder, and so forth.

As recently as the late 1980s, the idea of merging the EU national currencies seemed like science fiction. But, in 1991, the EU countries drafted the Maastricht Treaty, and it became effective in 1993 after all EU countries approved it, some by close national votes. The Maastricht Treaty set a process for establishing a monetary union and a single union-wide currency, including a timetable and criteria for a country to join. But the system that preceded the euro, the Exchange Rate Mechanism of the European Monetary System, came under severe pressure in 1992–1993 and nearly collapsed. Monetary union still looked far away. In early 1995, only one EU country (Luxembourg!) met the five criteria, covering the country's inflation rate, long-term interest rate, exchange-rate value of its currency, government budget deficit, and government debt.

The national governments persisted, and people began to believe. In early 1998, 11 EU countries were deemed to meet the criteria (after some fudging on government debt). Three countries—the United Kingdom, Denmark, and Sweden—could have met the criteria but chose not to join the euro at the beginning. Each had serious political concerns about the loss of national power and the loss of the national money as a symbol. The 15th EU country, Greece, did not meet the criteria at first but joined two years later.

In 1998, banks spent months revising and testing their computer systems and communications links to financial exchanges, clearinghouses, and interbank settlement systems. This culminated in "changeover weekend," the days from December 31, 1998, when the actual permanent conversion rates were announced, to January 4, 1999, when financial markets reopened after the New Year's holiday. Financial securities had to be redenominated in euros, and final tests made on systems. A goodly number of financial folks had no New Year's Eve parties and no holiday. The preparations and work paid off. Banks and financial markets performed with no major glitches on January 4, 1999.

The introduction of euro paper money and coins in early 2002 also went surprisingly smoothly. In preparation 15 billion pieces of paper money were produced, enough to stretch end-to-end to the moon *and* back two and a half times. And 50 billion coins were minted, in total weight about 250,000 tons.

Then in late 2001 the technical folks went to work big-time again. On January 1, 2002, the first day of full use of the euro, about 80 percent of the automated teller machines in the euro zone were able to dispense euros, and by January 3 this had risen to 97 percent. Half of all vending machines were converted by January 4 to accept euro coins. By January 10 people had replaced half of their holdings of national paper moneys with euros.

The euro is now one of the three major world currencies, along with the U.S. dollar and the Japanese yen. It is part of the growing integration within the EU, a process that also includes the "Europe 1992" drive for a single European market (discussed in Chapter 11). In Part IV we will examine the implications of the euro for macroeconomic performance of the EU countries.

Case Study   Foreign Exchange Trading

In 2001, foreign exchange trading was an astounding $1.2 trillion per day. It is difficult to comprehend how large this number is. One comparison offers some guidance. In less than nine *days* the amount of money traded in the foreign exchange market is a little larger than the value of U.S. production of goods and services for an *entire year.* (After rapidly growing for several decades, the amount of foreign exchange trading actually decreased from $1.5 trillion per day in 1998. The decrease from 1998 to 2001 seems to be the result of several forces, including the birth of the euro, which eliminated trading among its underlying national currencies, the rise of efficient electronic brokering, and some consolidation in the banking industry.)

What exactly is being traded in the huge global foreign exchange market? Where is the trading done? And who are the traders?

First, the what. In addition to spot and forward foreign exchange, there is one other traditional foreign exchange contract, the foreign exchange swap. The **foreign exchange swap** is a *package* trade that includes both a *spot exchange* of two currencies and an agreement to the reverse *forward exchange* of the two currencies (the future exchange back again). This type of package contract is useful when the parties to the trade have only a temporary need for the currency each is buying spot. In the global market, spot exchange is about 33 percent of trading, forward exchange about 11 percent, and foreign exchange swaps about 56 percent. For all of this foreign exchange trading in 2001, the U.S. dollar was involved in 90 percent of all trades, the euro in 38 percent, the Japanese yen in 23 percent, the British pound in 13 percent, and the Swiss franc in 6 percent.

Second, the where. The global business was distributed in 2001 as follows:

United Kingdom	31%
United States	16
Japan	9
Singapore	6
Germany	5
Hong Kong	4
Switzerland	4
Australia	3
Canada	3
France	3
Netherlands	2
Sweden	2
Other countries	12

Nearly half of global trading is done in the United Kingdom (mostly London) and the United States (mostly New York). Even though the British pound itself is not that important in foreign exchange contracts, London is clearly the center of global foreign exchange trading.

An example can show how this works. The example also demonstrates the role of demand deposits as the major form of money traded in the foreign exchange market. Consider a British firm that has purchased a small airplane (a corporate jet) from the U.S. producer of the plane and now is making the payment for it. If the British firm pays by writing a check in pounds sterling, the U.S. firm receiving the sterling check must be content to hold on to sterling bank deposits or sell the sterling for dollars. Alternatively, if the U.S. firm will accept payment only in dollars, then it is the British buyer who must sell sterling to get the dollars to pay the U.S. exporter.

Let's assume that the latter is the case. The British firm contacts its bank and requests a quotation of the exchange rate for selling pounds and acquiring dol-

© AP Photo/Chiaki Tsukumo

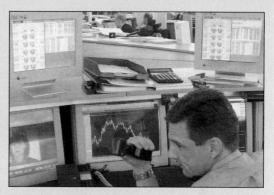

© AP Photo/Frank Augstein

Now, the who. Most foreign exchange trading is done by and through a network of several hundred banks worldwide, banks that actively "make a market" in foreign exchange by quoting rates and being willing to buy or sell currencies for their own account. According to *Euromoney* magazine, in 2001 three banks conducted about one-quarter of the global trading in foreign exchange: Citigroup, about 10 percent; Deutsche Bank, about 9 percent; and Goldman Sachs, about 7 percent.

Most trading is done by several thousand traders who are employed at these several hundred banks. This is a surprisingly small number of traders, relative to the huge volume of trading conducted. There are good reasons why there are so few foreign exchange traders. One is the capital intensity of this particular business. It takes a lot of money and substantial investments in computer and telecommunications hardware and software, but only a few decision makers. Another is the nature of the work itself.

Trading millions of dollars of foreign exchange per minute is a harrowing job; it's almost in the same category with being an air traffic controller or a bomb defuser. A trader should be somebody who loves pressures and can take losses. Many who try it soon develop a taste for other work. Once an economics student visiting a foreign exchange trading room in a major bank asked a trader, "How long do people last in this job?" The enthusiastic answer: "Yes, it is an excellent job for young people."

lars. If the rate is acceptable, the British firm instructs its bank to take the pounds from its demand deposit (checking) account, to convert these pounds into dollars, and to transfer the dollars to the U.S. producer. The British bank holds dollar demand deposits in the United States, at its correspondent bank in New York. The British bank instructs its correspondent bank in New York to take dollars from its demand deposit account and transfer the dollars to the U.S. producer, by transferring them to the U.S. producer's bank for deposit into the producer's demand deposit account.[4]

---

[4] The British bank could also use dollars available at its own U.S. branch to carry out this payment in the United States, if it has a branch there.

As with most payments that are purely domestic, demand deposits are used in this foreign exchange trade and in completing the international payment for the airplane. The British firm used the pounds in its demand deposit account to acquire the dollars needed. The U.S. producer used its demand deposit account to receive the dollar payment. The British bank used its dollar demand deposits in its correspondent bank in New York for two purposes: (1) as the dollars that it sold to its customer in the foreign transaction and (2) as the (same) dollars that were then transferred to the U.S. producer as payment.

Two systems involving modern computer and telecommunication technologies are likely to be used in this and similar foreign exchange and international payments activities. The first is the Society for Worldwide Interbank Financial Telecommunications (SWIFT), which is used to transmit instructions from one member bank to another (in our example, from the British bank to its correspondent bank in New York). SWIFT has over 2,000 member banks in nearly 200 countries. Over 4 million payments messages per day are sent through SWIFT instantly, error free, securely, and at low cost. The second is the Clearing House International Payments System (CHIPS). This system clears dollar transfers among its member banks, which include all large and internationally active banks. In our example CHIPS would be used if the New York correspondent bank and the bank of the U.S. producer were members. CHIPS handles several hundred thousands of payments totaling over $1 trillion each day, safely and at a low cost. Each bank's payments and receipts through CHIPS are totaled each day, and only the differences are settled up by actual flows of dollar funds among the banks. CHIPS reinforces the role of the U.S. dollar as a vehicle currency by ensuring that dollar transfers between its member banks can be done very efficiently.

Interbank Foreign Exchange Trading

Most foreign exchange trading, perhaps 60 percent or more, is trading among the banks themselves in the interbank part of the foreign exchange market. What's being traded is still the same—demand deposits denominated in different currencies. But each deal is between one foreign exchange trader and another trader, not an "outside" customer.

The interbank part of the market serves several functions. Participation in the interbank part of the market provides a bank with a continuous stream of information on conditions in the foreign exchange market through talking with traders at other banks and through observing the prices (exchange rates) being quoted. Interbank trading allows a bank to readjust its own position quickly and at low cost when it separately conducts a large trade with a customer. For instance, if Citibank buys a large amount of yen from Toyota (and sells dollars to Toyota), Citibank may be unwilling to continue holding the yen. Citibank then can sell the yen to another bank (and buy dollars) quickly and at low cost. Interbank trading also permits a bank to take on a position in a foreign currency quickly if the bank and its traders want to speculate on exchange rate movements in the near future. Such speculative positions are usually held only for a short time, typically being closed out by the end of the day.

Some interbank trading is conducted directly between the traders at different banks. In this case the traders know to whom they are quoting exchange rates for possible trades. Computer terminals show current exchange rate ranges on all major currencies for delivery at various dates. Major banks post the exchange rates at which each is probably willing to trade currencies with other banks. If a trader is shopping for the best rate directly, he consults the ranges quoted on the computer screens. Finding a likely prospect, the trader typically contacts the other bank directly by phone to get a firm price quote. Within about a minute, as a rule, any haggling is settled and a transaction is made by verbal agreement.

Other trades between banks are conducted through foreign exchange brokers. The use of brokers provides anonymity to the traders until an exchange rate is agreed on for a trade. The use of brokers can also allow the bank to economize on the costs of searching for the best available exchange rates, because the broker's business is to know the rates at which various banks are willing to trade. In the past decade brokering has shifted from being a telephone-based process to one that is mostly conducted electronically. Brokers earn commissions for their services.

Foreign exchange trading in this interbank part of the market is not for the little guy. Notice that the quoted interbank rates in Figure 16.1 are for amounts of $1 million or more. In fact, traders often save time by referring to each million dollars as a "dollar." With millions being exchanged each minute, extremely fine margins of profit or loss can loom large. For example, a trader who spends a minute shopping and secures 10 million pounds at $1.6354 per pound, instead of accepting a ready offer at $1.6355, has brought his bank an extra $1,000 within that minute. That's equivalent to a wage rate of $60,000 an hour. Correspondingly, anyone who reacts a bit too slowly or too excitedly to a given news release (e.g., announcement of rapid growth in the Canadian money supply, rumors of a coup in Libya, or a wildcat steel strike in Italy) can lose money at an even faster rate. On the average, these professionals make more than they lose, enough to justify their rates of pay. But foreign exchange trading is a lively and tense job. That department of a large bank is usually run as a tight ship with no room for "passengers" who do not make a good rate of return from quick dealings at fine margins.

DEMAND AND SUPPLY FOR FOREIGN EXCHANGE

To understand what makes the exchange rate value of a country's currency rise and fall, you should proceed through the same steps used to analyze any competitive market. First, portray the interaction of demand and supply as determinants of the equilibrium price and quantity, and then explore what forces lie behind the demand and supply curves.

Within the foreign exchange market, people want to trade moneys for various reasons. Some are engaged in trading goods and services and are making or receiving payments for these products. Some are engaged in international flows of financial assets. They are investing or borrowing internationally, and need to convert one nation's money to another money in the process of buying and selling financial assets, incurring and paying back debts, and so forth.

A nation's export of goods and services typically causes foreign moneys to be sold in order to buy that nation's money. For instance, the importer in a foreign country desires to pay using his currency, while the U.S. exporter desires to be paid in dollars. Somewhere in the payments process, foreign money is exchanged for dollars. We saw a specific example of this in the previous section on using the foreign exchange market. Thus, U.S. *exports of goods and services will create a supply of foreign currency* and a demand for U.S. dollars to the extent that foreign buyers have their own currencies to offer and U.S. exporters prefer to end up holding U.S. dollars and not some other currency. Only if U.S. exporters are happy to hold on to pounds (or the U.K. importers somehow have large holdings of dollars to spend) can U.S. exports to Britain keep from generating a supply of pounds and a demand for dollars.

Importing goods and services correspondingly tends to cause the home currency to be sold in order to buy foreign currency. For instance, if a U.S. importer desires to pay in dollars, and the British exporter desires to be paid in pounds because he wants to end up holding his home currency, then somewhere in the payments process dollars must be exchanged for pounds. Thus, U.S. *imports of goods and services will create a demand for foreign currency* and a supply of U.S. dollars to the extent that U.S. importers have dollars to offer and foreign exporters prefer to end up holding their own currencies. Only if foreign exporters are happy to hold on to dollars (or the U.S. importers somehow have large holdings of foreign currencies to spend) can U.S. imports keep from generating a supply of dollars and a demand for foreign currency.[5]

Similar reasoning applies to transactions in financial assets. Consider a U.S. insurance company that wants to replace some of its current holdings of U.S.-dollar-denominated bonds with British-pound-denominated bonds, perhaps because it expects a higher rate of return on the sterling investment. The company will need to sell dollars and buy pounds in the foreign exchange market, and then use these pounds to make payment in the process of buying the pound-denominated bonds. U.S. *capital outflows will create a demand for foreign currency* and a supply of U.S. dollars to the extent that the investors begin with dollars and a desire to invest in foreign financial assets that must be paid for in foreign currencies.

In another case, a British resident currently holding sterling demand deposits wishes to buy shares in Microsoft. The person will need to sell pounds and buy dollars in the foreign exchange market, and then use these dollars to make payment in the process of buying the stock. U.S. *capital inflows will create a supply of foreign currency* and a demand for dollars to the extent that investors begin

---

[5] International payments of income and unilateral transfers can also result in demand or supply of foreign currency. For instance, if a foreign company pays a dividend in its own currency, U.S. holders of its stock supply foreign currency if they want to take payment in dollars. As another example, some people in the United States and Canada demand foreign currency in order to be able to send remittances and cash gifts to relatives in Italy, Mexico, or some other country from which they emigrated.

with foreign currency and desire to invest in U.S. financial assets that must be paid for in dollars.

All of these transactions create supply and demand for foreign exchange. The supply and demand determine the exchange rate, within certain constraints imposed by the nature of the foreign exchange system or regime under which the country operates.

Floating Exchange Rates

The simplest system is the **floating exchange rate system** without intervention by governments or central bankers. The spot price of foreign currency is market-driven, determined by the interaction of private demand and supply for that currency. The market clears itself through the price mechanism. The two parts of Figure 16.2 show how such a system could yield equilibrium exchange rates for the pound sterling ($1.60/£) and the Swiss franc ($0.60/SFr) at the *E* points.

Let's digress for a little while, to examine the logic behind the slopes of the curves in Figure 16.2. We'll focus on the demand curve for foreign currency. What makes the demand curve slope downward? That is, why should a lower (higher) price of a currency generally mean that more (less) of it is demanded?

To see the likelihood of the downward slope, imagine that the exchange rate in Figure 16.2A has just shifted from $1.98 to $1.60. As the pound declines below $1.98, Americans will discover more uses for it. One use would be to buy wool

FIGURE 16.2   The Spot Exchange Market: Floating and Fixed Exchange Rates

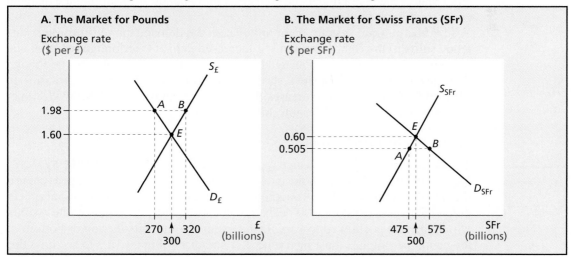

The demand and supply curves represent all demand and supply for that currency in the foreign exchange market, except for any official intervention by the official government monetary authorities (like central banks). With a *floating exchange rate,* the market reaches an equilibrium at points *E* in panels A and B. If the government wishes to *fix the exchange rate* at a different level, then it must intervene to buy or sell the currency to meet any difference between private (or nonofficial) quantity demanded and quantity supplied. In panel A, if the British government is committed not to let the pound fall below $1.98/£, the government must buy 50 billion pounds, equal to the gap *AB*. In panel B, if the Swiss government is committed not to let the franc rise above $0.505/SFr, the government must sell 100 billion Swiss francs, equal to the gap *AB*.

sweaters in Britain. Before the pound sinks, a sweater selling for £50 in London would cost American tourists $99 (= 50 × $1.98). If the pound suddenly sinks to $1.60, the same £50 wool sweater would cost American tourists only $80. They would start buying more. To pay for the extra sweaters, they would want more pounds sterling, to be paid to British merchants. As long as the level of business remains higher, there is more demand for pounds to conduct that business.

The case of British wool sweaters is just one illustration of the forces that would make the demand curve for a currency slope downward. There are usually many such responses of trade to a change in the exchange rate. A sinking pound means more cheese bought from British producers and less bought from cheese-makers in Wisconsin. There is more reason to buy British products and therefore more demand for pounds as a currency to facilitate such transactions. As long as a lower exchange rate raises the quantity demanded, the demand curve will slope downward.[6]

Now let's return to our market-driven floating exchange rate. What makes the floating exchange rate rise or fall over time? To answer we need to know the forces that shift the supply and demand curves. Again, let's focus on the demand curve. The demand curve is shifted by a variety of changes in the economy. Many of the demand-side forces relate to the balance-of-payments categories of Chapter 15. Shifts in demand away from U.S. products and toward U.K. products (caused by forces other than changes in the exchange rate) would result in extra attempts to sell dollars and buy pounds. This can be graphed as an upward (rightward) shift of the demand for pounds. Similarly, a rise in U.S. residents' willingness to lend money to U.K. borrowers or to invest in pound-denominated financial assets usually requires that extra dollars be converted into pounds, thus shifting the demand curve for pounds to the right.

In a floating-rate system, if for any reason the demand curve for foreign currency shifts to the right (representing increased demand for foreign money), and the supply curve remains unchanged, then the exchange rate value of the foreign currency rises. Such a shift is shown in Figure 16.3. The rightward shift in demand for pounds to D_2 increases the price of pounds from $1.60 to $1.80 per pound, as the market equilibrium shifts from E to E_2.

Fixed Exchange Rates

The other main foreign exchange regime is the **fixed exchange rate system.** Here, officials strive to keep the exchange rate virtually fixed (or pegged) even if the rate they choose differs from the current equilibrium rate. Their usual procedure under such a system is to declare a narrow "band" of exchange rates within which the rate is allowed to vary. If the exchange rate hits the top or bottom of the band, the officials must intervene. Let's return to Figure 16.2 to see how this could work.

---

[6] Similar logic can be applied to examine the slope of the supply curve for foreign exchange, but the actual slope of the supply curve is not so clear-cut. We presume for now that the supply curve has the usual upward slope.

FIGURE 16.3

A Shift in
Demand for
Pounds in the
Spot Exchange
Market

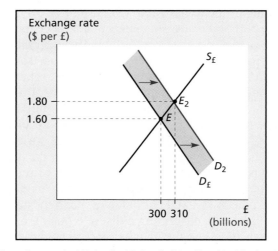

The demand curve for foreign exchange can be shifted to the right (or raised) by either of the following changes related to the balance of payments:

A shift of demand away from U.S. goods and services toward those of other countries.
A rise in U.S. willingness to lend money to or invest in other countries.

If the demand curve shifts to the right, then the market equilibrium exchange rate value of the pound rises. (Chapter 18 discusses in more depth the forces that shift the demand and supply curves and change the exchange rate.)

In Figure 16.2A, consider an officially declared "par value" of $2.00, at which the pound is substantially overvalued relative to its market-clearing rate of $1.60 per pound. British officials have announced that they will support the pound at 1 percent below par (about $1.98), and the dollar at 1 percent above par (about $2.02). In Figure 16.2A, they are forced to make good on this pledge by officially intervening in the foreign exchange market, buying £50 billion (and selling $99 billion, equal to £50 billion times $1.98 per pound). This intervention fills the gap *AB* between nonofficial supply and demand at the $1.98 exchange rate.[7] Only in this way can they bring the total demand for pounds, private plus official, up to the 320 billion of sterling money supplied. If their purchases of pounds with dollars fall short, total demand cannot meet the supply and the price will fall below the official support pound of $1.98. However, British officials wanting to defend the fixed exchange rate may not have sufficient reserves of dollars to keep the price fixed indefinitely, a point to which we will return several times in the rest of the book.

Another case of official intervention in defense of a fixed exchange rate is shown in Figure 16.2B. Swiss government officials have declared that the par

---

[7] Such official intervention could also be pictured as shifting the demand or supply curves. However, it seems more descriptive, when examining the defense of a fixed rate, to consider official exchange market intervention as filling the gap between quantity demanded and quantity supplied in the absence of the intervention.

value of the Swiss franc (SFr) shall be 50 cents in U.S. currency, and that the support points are 50.5 cents and 49.5 cents. As the demand and supply curves are drawn, the franc is substantially undervalued at this fixed rate, relative to the market-clearing rate of $0.60 per franc. To defend the fixed rate, government officials must intervene in the foreign exchange market and sell 100 billion SFr to meet the strong demand at 50.5 cents. If the Swiss government officials cannot tolerate buying enough dollars to plug the gap *AB* and keep the exchange rate down at 50.5 cents, they may give up and let the price rise.

Changes in exchange rates are given various names depending on the kind of exchange rate regime prevailing. Under the floating-rate system a fall in the market price (the exchange rate value) of a currency is called a **depreciation** of that currency; a rise is an **appreciation.** We refer to a discrete official reduction in the otherwise fixed par value of a currency as a **devaluation; revaluation** is the antonym describing a discrete raising of the official par. Devaluations and revaluations are the main ways of changing exchange rates in a nearly fixed-rate system, a system where the rate is usually, but not always, fixed.

Current Arrangements

Which countries have floating exchange rates for their currencies and which have fixed exchange rates? Here is an overview, without getting into everything now. First, most major currencies, including the U.S. dollar, the euro, the Japanese yen, the British pound, the Swiss franc, the Canadian dollar, the Australian dollar, and the Swedish krona, have floating exchange rates relative to each other. Second, the governments of a large number of other countries say they have floating exchange rates, though many use some amount of official exchange market intervention to "manage" the float. Third, some countries have fixed exchange rates between their currencies and the U.S. dollar. These countries include China, Egypt, Hong Kong, Malaysia, and Saudi Arabia. Fourth, some countries, including Denmark, Bulgaria, Estonia, and former French colonies in Africa, fix the exchange rate value of their currencies to the euro. We will examine these and other exchange rate policies in more depth in Chapter 19.

ARBITRAGE WITHIN THE SPOT EXCHANGE MARKET

We have pictured foreign exchange as a single market for trading between two currencies. Yet we have also noted that trading occurs in different locations around the world. For instance, for a period of time each day, trading is occurring in both New York and London as well as in other money centers in Europe. Will the rates in the different locations be essentially the same at a point in time, or can they diverge as local supply and demand conditions differ? Furthermore, exchange rates exist for many different currencies, both rates representing the dollar price of various foreign currencies and the *cross-rates* between foreign currencies. Are these exchange rates and cross-rates related in some way, or can they have independent levels?

Arbitrage, the process of buying and selling to make a (nearly) riskless pure profit, ensures that rates in different locations are essentially the same, and that rates and cross-rates are related and consistent among themselves. What would happen if pounds were being exchanged at $1.70 per pound in London, and $1.60 per pound at the same time in New York? If foreign exchange trading and money transfers can be done freely, then there is an opportunity to make a riskless profit by arbitraging between the two locations. Buy pounds where they are cheap (in New York) and simultaneously sell them where they are expensive (in London). For each pound bought and sold at the initial exchange rates, the arbitrage profit is 10 cents. Such arbitrage would occur on a large scale, increasing the demand for pounds in New York and increasing the supply of pounds in London. The dollar–pound exchange rate then would increase in New York and/or decrease in London, and the two rates would be driven to be essentially the same (that is, within the small range reflecting transactions costs that prevent any further profitable arbitrage).

What would happen if the exchange rate for the pound in terms of dollars is $1.60, the exchange rate for the Swiss franc in terms of dollars is $0.50, and the cross-rate between the franc and the pound is 3 francs per pound? Although it is more subtle, there is also an opportunity to make a riskless profit by arbitraging through the three rates—a process called **triangular arbitrage.** To see this, start with some number of dollars, say $150. Your $150 buys 300 francs (100/0.50). Use these francs to buy pounds at the cross-rate, and you have 100 pounds (300/3). Convert these pounds back into dollars and you end up with $160 (100 × 1.60). Your triangular arbitrage has made $10 profit for each $150 you start with. This profit occurs almost instantly and with essentially no risk if you establish all three spot trades at the same time.

As a large amount of this triangular arbitrage occurs, pressures are placed on the exchange rates to bring them into line with each other. The extra demand for francs tends to increase the dollar–franc exchange rate. The extra demand for pounds (paid for by francs) tends to increase the franc–pound cross-rate. The extra supply of pounds (to acquire dollars) tends to reduce the dollar–pound exchange rate. One or more of the exchange rates will change (due to demand and supply pressures) so that the cross-rate of francs per pound essentially equals the ratio of the dollar–pound exchange rate to the dollar–franc exchange rate. For instance, if only the cross-rate changes, then its value must shift to 3.2 francs per pound (1.60/0.50). At this cross-rate there is no further opportunity for profits from triangular arbitrage.

Just the threat of arbitrage of these types usually keeps the exchange rate between two currencies essentially the same in different locations, and keeps cross-rates in correct alignment with other exchange rates. Opportunities for actual arbitrage of these types are rare.

Summary

A **foreign exchange** transaction is a trade of one national money for another. The **exchange rate** is the price at which the moneys are traded. The **spot exchange rate** is the price for immediate exchange of the two currencies. The **forward exchange rate** is the price agreed now for a currency exchange that will occur sometime in the future. Banks and their traders are at the center of the foreign exchange market. They use computers and telephones to conduct foreign exchange trades with customers (the retail part of the market) and with each other (the interbank part of the market).

Spot foreign exchange serves a clearing function, permitting payments to be made between entities who want to hold or use different currencies. The exchange rate is determined by supply and demand, within any constraints imposed by the governmental choice of an exchange rate system or regime. Under a freely flexible or **floating exchange rate system,** market supply and demand set the equilibrium price (exchange rate) that clears the market. A floating exchange rate changes over time as supply and demand shift over time. Under a **fixed exchange rate system** (also called a pegged exchange rate system), monetary officials buy and sell a currency so as to keep its exchange rate within an officially stipulated band. When the currency's value lies at the bottom of its official band, officials must buy it by selling other currencies. When the currency's value presses against the top of its official price range, officials must sell it in exchange for other currencies.

Suggested Reading

Three good textbook views of the foreign exchange market are Levich (2001, Chapter 3); Eun and Resnick (2001, Chapter 4); and Eitman, Stonehill, and Moffet (2001, Chapter 4). Cheung and Wong (2000) and Cheung and Chinn (2001) report information obtained from their surveys of foreign exchange traders.

Questions and Problems

✦ 1. What are the major types of transactions or activities that result in demand for foreign currency in the spot foreign exchange market?

2. What are the major types of transactions or activities that result in supply of foreign currency in the spot foreign exchange market?

✦ 3. What has happened to the exchange rate value of the dollar in each case?
   a. The spot rate goes from $0.50/SFr to $0.51/SFr.
   b. The spot rate goes from SFr 2/$ to SFr 1.96/$.
   c. The spot rate goes from $0.010/yen to $0.009/yen.
   d. The spot rate goes from 100 yen/$ to 111 yen/$.

4. A U.S. firm must make a payment of 1 million yen to a Japanese firm that has sold the U.S. firm sets of Japanese baseball-player trading cards. The U.S. firm begins with a dollar checking account. Explain in detail how this payment would be made, including the use of the spot foreign exchange market and banks in both countries.

✦ 5. A British bank has acquired a large number of dollars in its dealings with its clients. How could this bank use the interbank foreign exchange market if it was unwilling to continue holding these dollars?

6. A trader at a U.S. bank believes that the euro will strengthen substantially in exchange rate value during the next hour. How would the trader use the interbank market to attempt to profit from her belief?

✦ 7. For each of the following, is it part of demand for yen or supply of yen in the foreign exchange market?

   a. A Japanese firm sells its U.S. government securities to obtain funds to buy real estate in Japan.

   b. A U.S. import company must pay for glassware purchased from a small Japanese producer.

   c. A U.S. farm cooperative receives payment from a Japanese importer of U.S. oranges.

   d. A U.S. pension fund uses some incoming contributions to buy equity shares of several Japanese companies through the Tokyo stock exchange.

8. You have access to the following three spot exchange rates:

   $0.01/yen
   $0.20/krone
   25 yen/krone

   You start with dollars and want to end up with dollars.

   a. How would you engage in arbitrage to profit from these three rates? What is the profit for each dollar used initially?

   b. As a result of this arbitrage, what is the pressure on the cross-rate between yen and krone? What must the value of the cross-rate be to eliminate the opportunity for triangular arbitrage?

✦ 9. The spot exchange rate between the dollar and the Swiss franc is a floating or flexible rate. What are the effects of each of the following on this exchange rate?

   a. There is a large increase in Swiss demand for U.S. exports as U.S. culture becomes more popular in Switzerland.

   b. There is a large increase in Swiss demand for investments in U.S. dollar-denominated financial assets because of a Swiss belief that the U.S. economy and political situation are improving markedly.

   c. Political uncertainties in Europe lead U.S. investors to shift their financial investments out of Switzerland, back to the United States.

   d. U.S. demand for products imported from Switzerland falls significantly as bad press reports lead Americans to question the quality of Swiss products.

10. Assume instead that the spot exchange rate between the dollar and Swiss franc is a fixed or pegged rate within a narrow band around a central rate. For each change shown in problem 9, assume that just before the change private (or nonofficial) supply and demand intersected at an equilibrium exchange rate within this narrow band. For each change shown in problem 9, what intervention is necessary by the monetary authorities to defend the fixed rate if the change shifts the intersection of private supply and demand outside the band?

Chapter **Seventeen**

Forward Exchange and International Financial Investment

Many international activities lead to money exchanges in the future. This is true of many international trade activities, whose payments are not due until sometime in the (usually near) future. It is also true of international financial activities, which are specifically designed to create future flows of moneys as returns are received, debts are repaid, or financial assets are sold to others. A major challenge in conducting all of these activities is that we do not know for sure the exchange rates that will be available in the future to translate one country's money into another country's money.

This chapter examines future exchanges of moneys and the exposure to the risks of uncertain future exchange rates. It discusses how forward foreign exchange contracts can be used to reduce the risk exposure or to speculate on future exchange rates. Much of the chapter focuses on the returns to and risks of investments in foreign financial assets.

EXCHANGE RATE RISK

Exchange rates change over time. In a floating-rate system, spot exchange rates change from minute to minute because supply and demand are constantly in flux. Indeed, as we have seen since the early 1970s, floating rates sometimes change quickly by large amounts as a result of large shifts in supply and demand. In a fixed-rate system, spot exchange rates also can change from minute to minute, but the range of the rate is typically limited to a small band around the par value as long as the fixed rate is defended successfully by the government authorities. Nonetheless, even in a fixed-rate system large changes can and do sometimes occur when the currency is devalued or revalued by the authorities. While some portion of the change in spot exchange rates in either system can be predicted by participants in the foreign exchange market, another part—often a large part—of exchange rate change cannot be predicted.

A person (or an organization like a firm) is exposed to **exchange rate risk** if the value of the person's income, wealth, or net worth changes when exchange rates change unpredictably in the future. This is a broad concept, but it has specific meanings in particular situations. If you take a vacation in Japan and bring U.S. dollars along with you to convert into yen as needed to pay for your expenses and purchases, you are exposed to exchange rate risk. The dollar value of the things that you buy and the number of things that you can afford to do will be affected by the dollar–yen exchange rates during your vacation. While you have some expectation of what those exchange rates will be, the actual rates will probably be different. From your point of view, the risk is that the yen could appreciate substantially so that it would take more dollars to obtain the same number of yen. The dollar prices of the things that you want to do and to buy will be higher; you will enjoy your vacation less. Of course, the yen might instead depreciate. In this case you will be pleasantly surprised by the increased buying power of your dollars. Still, as you begin your vacation you are exposed to exchange rate risk because you do not know what will happen to the yen during your vacation.

Another example of exposure to exchange rate risk is your first purchase of a financial asset denominated in a foreign currency—for instance, an investment in Mexican stocks. You may have heard that an investment in emerging markets is "where the action is." This may turn out to be too true. The dollar value of your investment depends not only on changes in the market prices of your Mexican stocks (valued in pesos) but also on changes in the dollar value of the peso. If the peso depreciates, the dollar value of your stock investment falls. Even if you expect some amount of peso depreciation, and incorporate that into the overall dollar return that you expect on your investment, the risk to you is that the peso could depreciate more than you are expecting.

The fact that exchange rates can change over time leads people to two types of responses. These appear contradictory, but actually just represent the responses of different people to different situations.

Some people do not want to gamble on what exchange rates will be in the future. They have acquired exposures to exchange rate risk in the course of their regular activities, but they seek to reduce or eliminate their risk exposure by hedging. **Hedging** a position exposed to rate risk, here exchange rate risk, is the act of reducing or eliminating a net asset or net liability position in the foreign currency.

Other people, thinking they have a good idea of what will happen to exchange rates, are quite willing to gamble on what exchange rates will be in the future. They are willing to take on or to hold positions that are exposed to exchange rate risk. They are willing to bet that the rates are going to move in their favor so that they make a profit. **Speculating** is the act of taking a net asset position ("long") or a net liability position ("short") in some asset class, here a foreign currency.

These two attitudes have been personified into the concepts of hedgers and speculators, as though individuals were always either one or the other. Actually, the same person can choose to behave like a hedger in some situations and like a speculator in others.

THE MARKET BASICS OF FORWARD FOREIGN EXCHANGE

There are a number of ways to hedge an exposure to exchange rate risk, or to take on additional exposure in order to speculate. For your vacation in Japan, you could buy yen (or yen-denominated traveler's checks) before you depart, thus having yen money to pay for your yen expenses and purchases.

For larger transactions involving international trade in goods and services, international financial investment, or pure speculation on future exchange rate movements, forward foreign exchange and forward exchange rates are often useful. As we mentioned in the previous chapter, a **forward foreign exchange contract** is an agreement to exchange one currency for another on some date in the future at a price set now (the **forward exchange rate**).

Banks acting as foreign exchange dealers generally are willing to meet the needs of their customers for the specific size of the forward exchange contract (the amount of foreign exchange) and the specific date in the future for the exchange. Common dates for future exchange are 30, 90, and 180 days forward (one, three, and six months).[1] For instance, to buy £100,000 of 90-day forward sterling at $1.4407/£, you sign an agreement today with your bank that 90 days from now you will deliver $144,070 in dollar bank deposits and receive £100,000 in pound bank deposits. The exchange of these amounts will take place to carry out the forward contract, regardless of what the actual spot exchange rate turns out to be in 90 days. In the opposite trade, somebody agreeing now to sell 90-day forward sterling must deliver pounds at the agreed price of $1.4407 in 90 days. That person need not own any sterling at all until then, but the rate at which he gives it up in 90 days is already set now. *Do not confuse the forward rate with the future spot rate,* the spot rate that ends up prevailing 90 days from now. The actual spot price of sterling that exists in 90 days could be above, below, or equal to the forward rate. In this respect, a forward exchange rate is like a commodity futures price or an advance hotel reservation.

The forward exchange market is particularly convenient for large customers, typically corporations, that are viewed by their banks as acceptable credit risks. These customers typically do not need to commit anything other than the written agreement until the exchange actually occurs in the future. Some customers must

---

[1] In the usual forward exchange contract, the actual exchange of currencies will occur two (or one) days after the stated time period, to match the two-day (or one-day) delay in settling standard spot contracts. The discussion in this chapter ignores the two- or one-day delay in actually exchanging the currencies.

pledge a margin that the bank can seize if the customer fails to fulfill the contract in the future, but this margin is only a fraction of the total size of the contract (because the bank only needs to recover any net loss on the other party's position).

Hedging Using Forward Foreign Exchange

Hedging involves acquiring an asset in a foreign currency to offset a net liability position already held in the foreign currency, or acquiring a liability in a foreign currency to offset a net asset position already held. Hedgers in international dealings are persons who have a home currency and seek a balance between their liabilities and assets in foreign currencies. In financial jargon, hedging means avoiding both kinds of "open" positions in a foreign currency—both "long" positions (holding net assets in the foreign currency) and "short" positions (owing more of the foreign currency than one holds). An American who has completely hedged a position in euros has ensured that the future of the exchange rate between dollars and euros will not affect her net worth. Hedging is a perfectly normal kind of behavior, especially for people whose main business is not international finance. Simply avoiding any net commitments in a foreign currency saves on the time and trouble of keeping abreast of fast-changing international currency conditions.

There are usually a number of ways to hedge a position that is exposed to exchange rate risk. For many types of exposure, a forward exchange contract is a direct way to hedge. Consider a U.S. company that has bought some merchandise and will have to pay £100,000 three months from now. Assuming that this represents an overall net liability position in pounds (perhaps because the company has no other assets or liabilities in pounds), the company is exposed to exchange rate risk. It does not know the dollar value of its liability because it does not know the spot exchange rate that will exist 90 days from now. One way to hedge its risk exposure is to enter into a forward contract to acquire (or buy) £100,000 in 90 days. If the current forward rate is $1.4407/£, then the company must deliver (or sell) $144,070 in 90 days. The company has an asset position in pounds through the forward contract (the company is owed pounds in the contract). This exactly matches its pound liability to pay for the merchandise, creating a "perfect hedge." The company now is assured that the merchandise will cost $144,070 regardless of what happens to the spot exchange rate in the next 90 days.[2]

---

[2] There are several other ways in which the U.S. company can acquire an asset in pounds that hedges its pound liability. It could sell merchandise to someone else and bill the buyer in pounds payable in 90 days. Or it could use dollars that it has now to buy pounds now at the current spot rate, and invest those pounds to earn interest for 90 days. The pound proceeds from the investment can then be used to pay the pound debt. Or it could enter into a long position (buying pounds) in a pound futures contract traded on an organized exchange. Or it could buy a currency option call contract that gives the company the right to buy pounds at a price set in the option contract (the exercise or strike price). Each of these establishes an asset in pounds that hedges its pound liability. The company's decision to hedge using a forward contract or one of the other methods depend on the cost of each method and how closely each method offsets its exposed position. In many cases the forward contract is a low-cost way of establishing the exact hedge desired by the company. Futures and options contracts are discussed further in the box "Futures, Options, and Swaps."

Forward exchange contracts can be used to hedge exposures to exchange rate risk in many other situations. A U.S. company that will receive a payment of £1 million in 60 days is unsure of the dollar value of this receivable, because the spot exchange rate in 60 days is uncertain. It can hedge by selling pounds (and buying dollars) in a 60-day forward exchange contract, using the forward exchange rate to lock in the number of dollars it will receive. A British firm needing to pay $200,000 in 30 days on its dollar-denominated debt can hedge its exchange rate risk exposure by buying dollars (and selling pounds) in a 30-day forward contract. A British individual inheriting $2 million that will be disbursed (in dollars) in 180 days can hedge by selling the dollars (and buying pounds) in a 180-day forward contract.

Speculating Using Forward Foreign Exchange

Speculating means committing oneself to an uncertain future value of one's net worth in terms of home currency. A rich imagery surrounds the term *speculator.* Speculators are usually portrayed as a class apart from the rest of humanity. These speculators are viewed as being excessively greedy—unlike us, of course. They are also viewed as exceptionally jittery and as adding an element of subversive chaos to the economic system. They come out in the middle of storms—we hear about them when the markets are veering out of control, and then it is their fault. Although speculation sometimes has played such a sinister role, it is an open empirical question whether it does so frequently.

More to the present point, we must recognize that the only concrete way of defining speculation is the broad way just offered. A speculator is anybody who is willing to take a net position in a foreign currency, whatever his motives or expectations about the future of the exchange rate. There is nothing necessarily sinister about this. Still, banks and other international financial players often claim that they invest while others speculate, implying that the latter action is more risky and foolhardy. Yet there is no clear difference here. Any investment that is exposed to exchange rate risk has a speculative element to it.

There are a number of ways deliberately to establish speculative foreign-currency positions. One direct way to speculate on the value of the future spot exchange rate is a forward foreign exchange contract. Forward foreign exchange provides the same bridge to future currency exchanges for speculators as for hedgers, and there are no credentials checks that can sort out the two groups in the marketplace. If a speculator thinks she has a fairly good idea of what will happen to the spot exchange rate in the future, it is easy to bet on the basis of that idea using the forward market. It is so easy, in fact, that the speculator can even bet with money she does not have in hand.

To illustrate this point, suppose that in April you are convinced that the pound sterling will take a dive from its current spot exchange rate value of about $1.45 and be worth only $1.20 in July. Perhaps you see a coming political and economic crisis in Britain that others do not see. You can make an enormous gain by using the forward market. Contact a foreign exchange trader at your bank and agree to sell £10 million at the current 90-day forward rate of $1.4407. If the bank believes in

Extension   Futures, Options, and Swaps

A forward foreign exchange contract is one type of agreement that can be reached now about an exchange of currencies that will occur in the future. This traditional form of future-oriented currency agreement has some relatives that have been introduced since the early 1970s. Someone wishing to hedge or speculate can now choose from among currency futures, currency options, and currency swaps in addition to traditional forward exchange.

Currency futures are contracts that are traded on organized exchanges, such as the Chicago Mercantile Exchange. By entering into a **currency futures** contract, you can effectively lock in the price at which you buy or sell a foreign currency at a set date in the future. This sounds very much like a forward foreign exchange contract, and it is. There are some differences, though. First, a futures contract is a *standard* contract (making it tradable on the organized exchange)—for instance, 12.5 million yen to be exchanged for dollars in March of next year. A forward contract can be *customized* by the bank to meet the needs of the customer. Second, if you enter into a futures contract, the exchange requires that you provide money as a *margin* to ensure that you will honor the contract. A margin might be required in a forward contract, but usually it is not. Third, the profits and losses on your futures contract accrue to you daily, as the contract is *"marked to market"* daily. Too many losses and you will receive a call to add to your margin account. The profit or loss on a forward contract usually is not taken until the *maturity* date. Fourth, and perhaps most important from your perspective, *almost anyone* able to put up a margin can enter into a futures contract, whereas banks usually are willing to enter into forward contracts only for large amounts (millions of dollars) with *highly creditworthy customers*. Futures contracts give ordinary people and small businesses access to a low-cost direct method for currency hedging or speculation.

For some purposes a major drawback to forward and futures contracts is that losses on your open positions can become very large. You must honor your agreements. If the spot rate has moved in a way that is against your position, you will have to buy high and sell low, resulting in what can be a large loss. Some hedgers and speculators may dislike this feature. There is another alternative— an option contract.

A **currency option** gives the buyer (or holder) of the option the right, but not the obligation, to buy foreign currency (a call option) or to sell foreign currency (a put option) at some time in the future at a price set today. The price set into the contract now for the foreign exchange transaction that the holder may make in the future is called the *exercise, or strike, price*. The option is a valuable right, and the buyer pays a *premium* (a fee) to the seller (or writer) of the option to acquire the option.

Let's say that you believe that the Swiss franc is going to appreciate substantially during the next month. The current spot price is $0.60 per franc and the current 30-day forward rate (or, for that matter, the current futures price for franc contracts maturing next month) is $0.61 per franc. You expect the spot value of the franc to be $0.64 in 30 days. If you speculate using a forward (or futures) contract, going long in francs, you will make a profit if the actual spot rate in 30 days is above $0.61 per franc. But if the actual spot rate in 30 days is below $0.61 per franc, you will make a loss, and the loss is larger the lower the spot rate is in 30 days. If the actual spot rate in 30 days is $0.57, you must buy francs at the forward price of $0.61 when the francs are worth only $0.57. You have a large actual loss.

You can instead speculate on the franc exchange rate using a currency option contract. The disadvantage of the option is that you must pay a premium to obtain it. (There is no comparable charge to obtain a forward contract.) The advantage of the option is that the size of any loss on the contract is limited to this premium—you cannot lose more. For instance, you can buy a 30-day currency call option that gives you the right to buy Swiss francs at an exercise price of $0.61 per franc. If the actual spot rate in 30 days is above $0.61 per franc, you exercise the option. Your overall profit here is somewhat lower than the comparable forward contract because you had to pay the premium to buy the option. Still, your profit can be large if the actual spot rate in 30 days has moved well above the $0.61 exercise price. (You buy francs low by exercising the option and sell the francs high at the higher spot rate.) If the actual spot rate in 30 days is below $0.61, you let the option expire unexercised. You have lost the premium, but you are not required to lose any more, even if the actual spot rate is substantially below the exercise price.

Another important future-oriented currency agreement is the currency swap. In a **currency swap** two parties agree to exchange flows of different currencies during a specified period of time. For instance, Microsoft might enter into a swap with its bank in which Microsoft agrees (1) to deliver a large number of euros in exchange for a comparable number of dollars now, (2) every three months to make dollar interest payments and to receive euro interest payments, and (3) at the end of the swap to return the large number of dollars and receive back the comparable number of euros. Because Microsoft has committed to exchanging dollars for euros, at various times now and in the future, you might think that this sounds something like spot and forward foreign exchange contracts, and you would be right. A swap is basically a set of spot and forward foreign exchanges packaged into one contract. The advantages of the swap over a package of separate foreign exchange contracts are two: lower transactions costs by using one contract and a subtle but important decrease in risk exposure. In a swap any failure by the other side to honor the contract cancels all future obligations, while in the package of separates the other side might try to default on some contracts but force you to honor others.

Why would Microsoft want to enter into such a swap? One reason could be that Microsoft discovers that it has an unusual opportunity to issue euro-denominated bonds at a low interest rate, perhaps because EU investors strongly desire to add some Microsoft bonds to their portfolios. But Microsoft actually needs dollars to finance the expansion of its business and wants to pay dollar interest on its debt. Microsoft can take advantage of the EU opportunity by issuing euro-denominated debt, and then swapping the euros into dollars. Microsoft must pay euro interest to its EU investors, but it is receiving euro interest in the swap. These euro flows approximately equal each other, so Microsoft mostly is left with the obligation to pay dollar interest into the swap. Microsoft accomplishes two things with the structured combination of euro bonds and swap. First, Microsoft can lower its overall cost of financing by taking advantage of the unusually low interest cost in the EU, even though it really does not want euro-denominated debt. Second, Microsoft effectively does not have euro-denominated debt—the cash flows (on net) are converted through the swap into the dollar cash flows that Microsoft prefers to have.

Currency futures, options, and swaps are relatively recent additions to the set of foreign exchange products. The first foreign-currency futures contract was offered in 1972. The first exchange-traded foreign-currency option was offered in 1982. Foreign-currency options are also offered directly by banks and other financial institutions in customized contracts with their customers. The first major currency swap was contracted in 1981 between the World Bank and IBM (dollars for German marks and Swiss francs).

Exchange-traded currency futures and options are of some importance, with the equivalent of $40 billion and $27 billion in existence at midyear 2001. Still, most foreign exchange is transacted directly among banks, other financial institutions, and their customers. The size of the "over-the-counter" products (spot exchange, forward exchange, directly written currency options, and currency swaps) is much larger than the size of the exchange-traded foreign-currency futures and options. Currency swaps have become a big product, with about $4.3 trillion of swap contracts in force at midyear 2001. And about $2.8 trillion of directly written currency options existed at midyear 2001.

your ability to honor your forward commitment in July, you do not even need to put up any money now in April. Just sign the forward contract. How will you be able to come up with £10 million in July? Given your knowledge of a coming crisis, there is nothing to worry about. Relax. Take a three-month vacation in Hawaii. From time to time, stroll off the beach long enough to glance at the newspaper and note that the pound is sinking, just as you knew it would. On the contract date in July, instruct your bank to settle the forward contract against the actual spot rate, which has sunk as you expected to $1.20. Effectively, in July you are buying £10 million in the spot market at $1.20 (total cost of $12 million) and selling the pounds at $1.4407 into the forward contract (total receipt of $14.407 million). You net a profit of $2.407 million for a few minutes' effort, a lot of foresight, and an understanding of "buy low, sell high." If you are smarter than the others in the marketplace, you can get rich using the convenient forward exchange market.

Your speculation may turn out differently, however. Suppose you are wrong. Suppose that Britain's prospects brighten greatly between April and July. Suppose that when July comes around, the spot value of the pound has risen to $1.80. Now in July you must come up with $18 million to get the £10 million you committed to sell in the forward contract for only $14.407 million. It does not take much arithmetic to see what this means for your personal wealth. It is time to reevaluate your lifestyle.

What happens if in April *many* people expect the spot exchange rate value of the pound to depreciate to $1.20 by July, and they are willing to speculate using the forward exchange market? They will sell pounds forward in large amounts. The increased supply of pounds forward will put downward pressure on the forward exchange rate value of the pound, driving it toward $1.20. Generally, all speculators will not have the exact same view as to the expected future spot exchange rate. Nonetheless, *we hypothesize that speculators' pressures on supply and demand should drive the forward exchange rate to equal the average expected value of the future spot exchange rate.* For instance, the 90-day forward rate may indicate what informed opinion thinks the pound should be worth spot in 90 days' time. It would be an average expectation of the future spot value, much as the point spread in football betting is the number of points by which the average bettor expects the stronger team to win.

INTERNATIONAL FINANCIAL INVESTMENT

International financial investment has grown rapidly in recent decades. Decisions about international investments are based on the returns and risks of the available investment alternatives. How do we calculate the overall returns on financial assets denominated in foreign currencies? What are the sources of risk that apply specifically or especially to foreign financial investments? Can the investor hedge exposure to exchange rate risk? The remainder of this chapter explores these questions about international financial investment. Although our discussion focuses on investing, most of the principles also apply to a borrower deciding whether to take out loans or issue securities denominated in foreign currencies.

Consider an investor who holds dollars now and plans to end up a year from now also holding dollars (or, at least, who calculates her wealth and returns in dollars). If she invests in a dollar-denominated financial asset like a U.S. government security or a dollar time deposit, then she will earn dollar returns and have dollar wealth a year from now. No currency translation is necessary. If she invests in a foreign-currency-denominated financial asset, like a British government security or a pound time deposit, her situation is not so simple. First, she must convert her dollars into pounds at the initial spot exchange rate. Then, she uses the pounds to buy the pound-denominated financial asset. She holds this asset, earning pound returns and having wealth in pounds a year from now. This can be converted back into dollars (either actually or simply to determine the dollar value of wealth) at some dollar–pound exchange rate that applies to foreign exchange transactions a year from now.

What exchange rate can be used to convert pounds back into dollars a year from now? There are two major alternatives, and these correspond to our concepts of hedging and speculation. First, she can contract now for the exchange of pounds back into dollars at the one-year *forward exchange rate* using a forward exchange contract. Her pound liability in the forward contract matches her pound asset position, so she has hedged her exposure to exchange rate risk. She has a hedged or **covered international investment.** Second, she can wait and convert back into dollars at the *future spot exchange rate,* the one that will exist a year from now. She does not know for sure what this future spot exchange rate will be so her investment is exposed to exchange rate risk. This unhedged investment has a speculative element to it, and it is called an **uncovered international investment.**

INTERNATIONAL INVESTMENT WITH COVER

We can compare domestic investment and covered international investment using Figure 17.1, which shows ways of investing (or borrowing) as paths around a "lake." People moving their assets from left to right are buying pounds and selling dollars, whereas those transferring from right to left are buying dollars with pounds. People moving upward in either country are investing or lending, whereas those moving downward from future to current positions are either selling off interest-earning assets or borrowing at interest. The corresponding expressions in terms of exchange rates (the current spot rate e and the current forward rate f) and current interest rates (i_{US} and i_{UK}) show how the value of one's assets get multiplied by each move. The exchange rates are quoted as dollars per pound. The interest rates are measured for the actual time period examined and are in decimal, not percent, form.[3]

Studying how one gets from any corner to any other for any purpose, you will find that the choice of the more profitable of the two possible routes always depends on the comparison of two expressions. Suppose we want to convert present dollars into future dollars. We could route our money through Britain,

---

[3] That is, the interest rates are not annual rates unless the time period is one year. If interest rates are quoted as annualized rates, they must be converted. For instance, the 90-day interest rate is approximately one-quarter the annualized interest rate.

FIGURE 17.1

Current and Future Asset Positions in Two Currencies: The "Lake" Diagram

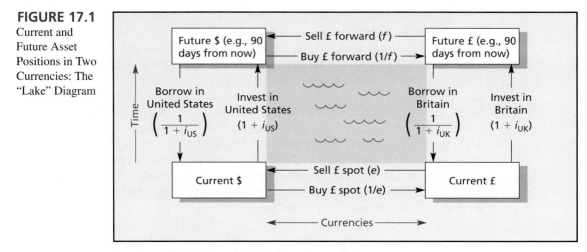

i_{US} = Current 90-day interest rate in the United States (not annualized)
i_{UK} = Current 90-day interest rate in Britain (not annualized)
e = Current spot price of the pound ($/£)
f = Current forward price of the pound, for exchange 90 days from now ($/£)

buying pounds in the spot market, obtaining $1/e$ pounds for each dollar. We would then invest these pounds at interest and have $(1 + i_{UK})/e$ pounds at maturity for each initial dollar. At the time of the investment we also sell the upcoming pounds in the forward market (at the rate of f) to get an assured number of dollars in the future. Overall, this yields $(1 + i_{UK}) \times f/e$ future dollars for every dollar invested now. Or we could simply invest our money at interest in America, getting $(1 + i_{US})$ future dollars for every present dollar. Which road we should take depends on the sign of the difference between the two returns. This difference is sometimes called the **covered interest differential** (CD):

$$CD = (1 + i_{UK}) \bullet f/e - (1 + i_{US})$$

If the covered interest differential is positive, one would be better off investing in Britain. If it is negative, one should avoid investments in Britain, investing in America instead. Why is it called *covered?* Because the investor is fully hedged or covered against exchange rate risk if she uses a foreign-currency investment to get from her own currency today to the same currency in the future.

There is an approximation that provides insight into what the covered differential is actually comparing. Before we see this handy formula, we first need to define the **forward premium** as the proportionate difference between the *current* forward exchange rate value of the pound and its *current* spot value:[4]

$$F = (f - e)/e$$

[4] This is often stated on an annualized percent basis:

$$F = \frac{(f - e)}{e} \times \frac{360}{n} \times 100$$

where n is the number of days forward and a year is taken to be 360 days for convenience.

The forward premium (converted into a percentage) shows the rate at which the pound gains value between a current spot transaction to buy pounds and future selling of pounds at the forward rate that we can lock in today. (If F is negative, the pound is at a forward *discount* because it loses value between buying it at the current spot rate and selling it at the current forward rate.)

The handy approximation is that the covered interest differential is approximately equal to the forward premium on the pound plus the interest rate differential:[5]

$$CD \;=\; F + (i_{UK} - i_{US})$$

The formula shows that the net incentive to go in one particular direction around the lake depends on how the forward premium on the pound compares with the difference between interest rates.

There is another way to interpret the approximation. The overall covered return (in dollars) to a U.S. investor from investing in Britain is approximately equal to the sum of two components: the gain (or loss) from the spot and forward currency exchanges (the forward premium F on the pound) plus the interest return on the pound investment itself (i_{UK}). The covered interest differential is then approximately equal to the difference between the overall covered return to investing in pound-denominated assets ($F + i_{UK}$) and the return to investing in dollar-denominated assets (i_{US}).[6]

Covered Interest Arbitrage

The covered differential is such a handy guide to the profitable exchange between currencies that traders use it to make arbitrage profits on any differential. **Covered interest arbitrage** is buying a country's currency spot and selling that country's currency forward, to make a net profit from the *combination* of the difference in interest rates between countries and the forward premium on that country's currency. Covered interest arbitrage is essentially riskless, although it does tie up some assets for a while. One way of engaging in this arbitrage is in fact the ultimate in hedging: We can start with dollars today and end up with a guaranteed greater amount of dollars today by going all the way around the lake.

---

[5] To see the approximation involved, first complete the multiplication of terms in the first equation for CD:

$$CD = f/e + i_{UK} \bullet f/e - 1 - i_{US}$$

Next, add and subtract i_{UK}:

$$CD = f/e + i_{UK} \bullet f/e - i_{UK} - 1 + i_{UK} - i_{US}$$

Now group terms, using the fact that the forward premium $F = f/e - 1$:

$$CD = F + i_{UK} - i_{US} + i_{UK} \bullet F$$

If the British interest rate (i_{UK}) and forward premium on the pound (F) are small (in decimal form), then the last term (the product of two small numbers) is very small, and it is ignored in the approximation.

[6] The approximation is also useful because all rates can be stated on an annualized basis and in percent terms—the way we usually say them. In this case, F is the annualized percent forward premium (as defined in footnote 4) and the interest rates are annualized percent rates, regardless of the number of days forward being considered.

To see how this arbitrage works, let's suppose that British and U.S. interest rates are $i_{UK} = .04$ (4 percent) and $i_{US} = .03$ (3 percent), respectively, for 90 days, and that both the spot and forward exchange rates are \$2.00/£, so that there is neither a premium nor a discount on forward sterling ($F = 0$). Seeing that this means CD = .01 (1 percent), a New York arbitrageur uses the telephone and sets up a counterclockwise journey around the lake. He contracts to sell, say, \$20 million in the spot market, buying £10 million. He informs his London correspondent bank or branch bank of the purchase and instructs that bank to place the proceeds in British Treasury bills that will mature in 90 days. This means that after 90 days he will have £10 million $\times$ 1.04 to dispose of. He covers himself against exchange rate risk by contracting to sell the £10.4 million in the forward market, receiving \$20.8 million deliverable after 90 days. He could leave the matter there, knowing that his phone trip in and out of Britain will give \$20.8 million in 90 days' time, instead of the \$20.6 million he would have received by investing his original \$20 million within the United States. Or if he has excellent credit standing, he can celebrate his winnings by borrowing against the \$20.8 million in the United States at 3 percent, giving himself \$20,194,175 = \$20.8 million/(1.03) right now, or about 1 percent more than he had before he used the telephone. So that's \$194,175 in arbitrage gains minus the cost of the telephone calls, any transactions fees, the use of part of a credit line in the United States, and a few minutes' time. Not a bad wage. The operation is also riskless as long as nobody defaults on a contract. (The reader can confirm that if forward sterling instead were at a 2 percent discount [$F = -.02$ because $f = \$1.96$] the New York arbitrageur would invest in the United States, buy forward sterling, borrow or sell bills in Britain, and sell pounds spot, making a net profit of about 1 percent.)

Interest arbitrage looks like the perfect money machine. It is especially attractive today, now that telecommunications and computers have reduced transactions costs almost to zero. If traders failed to take advantage of such opportunities, we should wonder about their business acumen.

In fact, though, arbitrage is such a sure thing that it is an endangered species. Banks can program their computers to tell their traders instantly of any discrepancy in rates that would seem to allow profitable arbitrage. Such opportunities can persist only as long as other banks deal at rates that pass up arbitrage profits for themselves, or until market pressures from supply and demand alter the rates. Soon enough the rates change, removing the chance for instant moneymaking. Traders still make money on pure arbitrage, such as covered interest arbitrage, but they have to be fast. A profitable covered differential is usually gone within a minute or two.

Covered Interest Parity

John Maynard Keynes, himself an interest arbitrageur, argued that the opportunities to make arbitrage profits would be self-eliminating because the forward exchange rate would adjust so that the covered interest differential returned to zero. Since Keynes we have referred to the condition CD = 0 as **covered interest parity.** Here are two equivalent ways to think of covered interest parity:

- A currency is at a forward premium (discount) by as much as its interest rate is lower (higher) than the interest rate in the other country (that is, $F = i_{US} - i_{UK}$ in our example).

- The overall covered return on a foreign-currency investment equals the return on a comparable domestic-currency investment ($F + i_{UK} = i_{US}$).

In the numerical example on page 428, covered interest parity would exist if the forward rate is \$1.98/£ (rather than \$2.00/£). Then the forward discount on the pound of 1 percent (equal to the proportionate difference between the \$1.98 forward rate and the \$2.00 spot rate) offsets the amount by which the British interest rate (4 percent) is higher than the U.S. interest rate (3 percent). U.S. investors would earn only 3 percent on their covered investments in pound-denominated assets—the 4 percent interest minus the 1 percent lost in the currency exchanges. This 3 percent is equal to the rate that they receive on investments in dollar-denominated assets, so there is no incentive for arbitrage.

Covered interest parity provides an explanation for differences between current spot and current forward exchange rates. A country with an interest rate that is lower than the corresponding rate in the United States will have a forward premium on its currency, with the percentage point difference in the interest rates equal to the percent forward premium. Referring back to the exchange rate quotations in Figure 16.1, the currencies of Japan and Switzerland have 90-day forward rates (dollars per this currency) above their current spot rates. These currencies are at a forward premium, and we could confirm that their 90-day interest rates were less at that time than the interest rates on comparable assets denominated in dollars. The currencies of Britain and Canada have forward rates below their current spot rate, showing a forward discount that is related to relatively high interest rates in these countries.

Covered interest parity links together four rates: the current forward exchange rate, the current spot exchange rate, and the current interest rates in the two countries. If one of these rates changes, then at least one of the other rates also must change to maintain (reestablish) covered interest parity. For instance, if the spot exchange rate increases and the interest differential is unchanged, then the forward exchange rate also must rise to keep the forward premium steady. In this case, whatever moves the spot rate up (or down) will do the same to the forward rate. In fact, short-term interest differentials have not varied much over the past several decades for the major world currencies, so spot and forward rates between any two of these currencies have tended to go up or down together over time. That is, the current spot and current forward rates are highly positively correlated over time.[7]

---

[7] Covered interest parity also has implications for our earlier discussion of hedging a future pound liability. The goal is to get from current dollars to future pounds (needed to pay for the merchandise). If covered interest parity holds, then the cost of hedging using a forward contract (going up the lake and then across at the top toward the right) will essentially equal the cost of hedging by buying pounds spot now and investing these pounds for 90 days (going across the lake to the right at the bottom and then going up).

INTERNATIONAL INVESTMENT WITHOUT COVER

Uncovered international financial investment involves investing in a financial asset denominated in a foreign currency without hedging or covering the future proceeds of the investment back into one's own currency. In the simplest case, the foreign currency proceeds will be translated back into domestic currency using whatever spot exchange rate exists at the future date (either actually, or to calculate wealth and overall returns in one's own currency). The future spot rate is not known for sure at the time of the initial investment, so the investment is exposed to exchange rate risk (assuming that the investor has no other offsetting liability in this currency).

At the time of the initial investment, the investor presumably has some idea of what the future spot rate is likely to be. The investor's expected future spot rate (e^{ex}) can be used to determine an expected overall return on the uncovered international investment. (This expected future spot rate is the same type of rate used in deciding whether to speculate using a forward contract.)

A kind of "lake" diagram similar to that used in Figure 17.1 applies here, but the top side of the lake refers to currency exchanges in the future at the future spot exchange rate. At the time of the foreign investment ("ex ante"), we only have a notion or an expectation of what the future spot rate will be. Of course, once we get to the future date (the end or maturity of the foreign investment— "ex post"), we will know what the future spot rate actually is, and then we can determine the actual overall return on the uncovered foreign investment.

To see how this works, again consider that we want to convert present dollars into future dollars. We again could route our money through Britain, but in this case we decide not to cover against exchange rate risk. We first buy pounds in the spot market, obtaining $1/e$ pounds for each dollar. We then invest these pounds, and we will have $(1 + i_{UK})/e$ pounds at maturity for each initial dollar. We have an expectation that we can convert these pounds back into dollars the rate of e^{ex} to obtain $(1 + i_{UK}) \times e^{ex}/e$ future dollars expected for each dollar invested now. This can be compared to the future dollars $(1 + i_{US})$ that we could obtain simply by investing each present dollar in a dollar-denominated asset. The comparison is the **expected uncovered interest differential (EUD):**

$$\text{EUD} = (1 + i_{UK}) \cdot e^{ex}/e - (1 + i_{US})$$

If this is positive, then the expected overall return favors uncovered investing in a pound-denominated asset. If it's negative, then the expected overall return favors staying at home.[8]

The expression for the expected uncovered interest differential is almost the same as the expression for the covered interest differential. The only difference is

---

[8] From the perspective of a U.K. investor considering an uncovered dollar investment, the expected uncovered interest differential is $(1 + i_{US}) \cdot e^{ex}/e - (1 + i_{UK})$, where the exchange rates are now measured as pounds per dollar.

that the expected future spot rate e^{ex} replaces the forward rate f. This is not surprising—the difference between the two is specifically the decision not to cover or hedge the exposure to exchange rate risk by using a forward contract.

We can also show that the expected uncovered interest differential has a handy approximation. It approximately equals the expected rate of appreciation (depreciation, if negative) of the foreign currency plus the regular interest rate differential:[9]

$$\text{EUD} = \text{Expected appreciation} + (i_{UK} - i_{US})$$

For a different view of this, note that the expected overall uncovered return (in dollars) to a U.S. investor from investing in Britain is approximately equal to the sum of the expected gain (or loss) from the currency exchanges (current spot and future spot) as the pound appreciates (or depreciates) during the time of the investment, plus the interest return on the pound investment itself. This expected overall return on the pound investment (Currency appreciation + i_{UK}) is compared to the return on investing in dollar-denominated assets (i_{US}) to approximate the expected uncovered interest differential.

Let's consider a numerical example similar to the one used in the section on covered investment. The current spot exchange rate e is \$2.00/£, and the current interest rates on 90-day investments are $i_{UK} = 0.04$ (4 percent) and $i_{US} = 0.03$ (3 percent). If a U.S.-based investor expects the spot rate (e^{ex}) to remain at \$2.00/£ in 90 days, what is the expected uncovered interest differential? Because he expects no change in the pound's exchange rate value, the expected differential is 1 percent (equal to the interest rate differential, $4 - 3$) in favor of the pound investment. The investor expects a higher return to investing uncovered in pound assets, but he is not certain of the extra return. The actual spot exchange rate in 90 days could be quite different from what he is expecting.

If an uncovered foreign financial investment is exposed to exchange rate risk, why would anyone want to invest uncovered? The answer has two components: one related to return and one to risk. First, the expected overall return on the uncovered investment may be higher than the return that can be obtained at home (EUD is positive), as in the numerical example just completed. Presumably, the investor would undertake such an uncovered investment if she expects to be adequately compensated for the risks that she is taking on, especially the exchange rate risk that the actual future spot rate could be much lower than she is expecting.

However, the issue of risk exposure is really more subtle. It is not the risk of this individual investment that matters, but rather the contribution of this uncovered investment to the riskiness of the investor's full investment portfolio. While we will not develop this fully, analysis of portfolios indicates that the addition of an uncovered foreign investment can sometimes increase overall riskiness, but in

---

[9] For the actual time period involved, the expected rate of appreciation equals $(e^{ex} - e)/e$. This is often stated on a percent annualized basis,

$$\frac{e^{ex} - e}{e} \times \frac{360}{n} \times 100$$

where n is the number of days in the future for the expected future spot rate.

Case Study   The World's Greatest Investor

George Soros was born Dzjchdzhe Shorask (pronounced "Shorosh") in Budapest in 1930. The son of a lawyer, he became a global investment superstar, with a net worth in 2002 estimated at $6.9 billion. In the 32 years since its founding in 1969, his investment fund earned an incredible average return of 35 percent per year.

As a Jewish boy, he and his family struggled to evade the Nazis, and they managed to survive. In 1947 he went to England, expecting to continue his engineering studies. Instead, he enrolled in the London School of Economics and graduated in 1952. He began working at a small London brokerage, but he was frustrated by the lack of responsibilities.

In 1956, Soros moved to New York City, where he worked at two securities firms before joining the firm Arnold & Bleichroeder in 1963. In 1967, he became head of investment research, and he was successful at finding good investment opportunities in undervalued European stocks. In 1969, he founded an offshore hedge fund, using $250,000 of his own money and about $6 million from non-American investors whom he knew. (A hedge fund is an investment partnership that is not restricted by regulations of government agencies like the U.S. Securities and Exchange Commission. Each hedge fund can establish its own investment style and strategy, and these vary. While some hedge funds do use investment strategies that involve different kinds of hedging, others do not. The manager of a fund usually gets fees and a percentage of the profits, as well as having a substantial amount of his or her own money invested in the fund.)

Soon Soros left Arnold & Bleichroeder, taking his Soros Fund with him. While the 1970s were poor years for the U.S. stock market generally, the Soros Fund prospered. As the manager, Soros focused on finding undervalued sectors in the United States and other countries. He bought unpopular low-priced stocks and

Courtesy of Open Society Institute

sold short popular high-priced stocks. He expected oil demand to outstrip oil supply, so he bought stocks of companies in oil-field services and oil drilling before the first oil shock in 1973. In the mid-1970s, he invested heavily in Japanese stocks. In 1979, he changed the name of the fund to Quantum Fund, in honor of Heisenberg's uncertainty principle in quantum mechanics. In 1980, the fund return was 103 percent. It had grown to $380 million.

In 1981, *Institutional Investor* magazine named him "the world's greatest investor." But 1981 was a difficult year. The fund lost 23 percent, and one-third of his investors withdrew their investments. This was their mistake. Spectacular returns were still to come.

In early September 1985, Soros became convinced that the U.S. dollar was overvalued relative to the Japanese yen and the German mark, and that a correction was coming soon. He decided to establish speculative investment positions to try to profit from the changes he expected. For instance, he borrowed dollars, used the dollars to buy yen and marks, and bought Japanese and German government bonds. In total, he established an $800 million position, a position larger than the entire capital of the fund. In late September the major governments announced the Plaza Agreement, in which they vowed to take coordinated actions (like intervention in the foreign exchange markets) to raise the values of other major currencies relative to the dollar. Within a month, as the dollar depreciated, Soros had profits of $150 million. The fund's total return for 1985 was 122 percent, as he had also invested in foreign stocks and long-term U.S. Treasury bonds. Of course, not all of his positions turned out so well. For instance, in 1987, the Quantum Fund lost up to $840 million when the U.S. and other stock markets crashed in October. But the fund still earned a return of 14 percent for the entire year.

In September 1992, Soros placed his most famous bet. Following German reunification in 1989, German interest rates increased, and the mark tended to appreciate. But most EU currencies were pegged to each other in the Exchange Rate Mechanism (ERM) of the European Monetary System. So the other countries had to raise their interest rates to maintain the pegged exchange rates. Soros predicted that the British government could not sustain this policy because the British economy was already weak and unemployment was high. He expected that Britain would either devalue the pound within the ERM or pull out of the ERM. In either case, the exchange rate value of the pound would decline. He established his speculative investment positions short in pounds and long in marks, using pound borrowings and mark investments, as well as futures and options. And the positions were big—$10 billion. As Soros and other speculative investors established their positions, they sold pounds, putting downward pressure on the exchange rate value of the pound. The central banks tried to defend the pegged rate, but soon the British government gave up and pulled out of the ERM. The pound depreciated against the mark. Within a month the Quantum Fund made a profit of about $1 billion on its pound positions, and a profit of up to $1 billion on other European currency positions. The *Economist* magazine called Soros "the man who broke the Bank of England."

After 1992, Soros turned over most trading decisions in the Quantum Fund to his chosen successor, Stanley Druckenmiller. The Quantum Fund continued to have some large successes and some large losses. In early 1997, Soros and Druckenmiller foresaw weakness in the Thai baht, and Quantum established short baht positions in January and February. The crisis hit in July, the Thai baht depreciated, and Quantum made money. But when the Thai baht and other Asian currencies continued to depreciate, they thought that the market had taken the rates too far. For instance, when the Indonesian rupiah fell from 2,400 per dollar to 4,000 per dollar, they established long positions in rupiah, and then lost money as the rupiah continued to fall beyond 10,000 per dollar.

In 1998, the Quantum Fund lost $2 billion on investments in Russia when Russian financial markets and the ruble collapsed. But the fund still earned more than 12 percent for the entire year. In 1999 the fund was down 20 percent in the first half of the year. It then shifted to investing in tech stocks and ended up 35 percent for the year. The tech investments and long positions in the euro took revenge in early 2000. For the first four months the fund was down 22 percent. Weary of the battles, Druckenmiller resigned in April. Soros announced that the fund was shifting to investing with less risk and lower returns. The fund shrank from over $20 billion in 1998 to $11 billion in 2001.

As he reduced his role in fund management, Soros turned to writing articles and books and to philanthropy. His writing is curious. He is deeply critical of excessive capitalism and individualism—what he calls "market fundamentalism." He believes that unregulated global financial markets are inherently unstable, and he calls for greater national regulation and the establishment of new global institutions like an international credit-insurance organization to guarantee loans to developing countries.

Although Soros is not active much in investment decisions anymore, he remains the quintessential international speculative investor. His name is synonymous with hedge funds, especially those that take large speculative positions. He has been denounced by government officials, like Prime Minister Mahathir Mohamad of Malaysia in 1997, as the source of immense and unjustified speculative pressures on their countries' currencies and financial markets. Soros continues to defend his own investment activities, stating that he merely perceived changes that were going to happen in any case. But, as his writings indicate, at a broader level he has mixed feelings about the current global financial system.

other cases it can instead lower it because of the benefits of diversification of investments. If it lowers overall riskiness, then the investor would look favorably on an uncovered foreign investment even if the expected uncovered interest differential is somewhat negative.

To see the importance of uncovered foreign investments and the expected uncovered interest differential, let's examine what is likely to be true if risk considerations are small. Risk considerations can be small if investors do not care much about risk exposures (they are *risk neutral*) or if the benefits of diversification indicate that additional uncovered investments add little or nothing to the overall riskiness of the investor's portfolio. In this case each investor is willing to undertake uncovered foreign investments if the uncovered interest differential is positive. As investors make shifts in their portfolios, they place supply and demand pressures on the current spot exchange rate, by buying or selling pounds for dollars to shift into or out of pound-denominated investments. (They may also place pressures on the interest rates as they buy and sell the financial assets themselves.)

Generally, the pressures on the rates will subside only when there is no further incentive for large shifts in investments. When the expected uncovered differential equals zero (EUD = 0), at least for the average investor, we have a condition called **uncovered interest parity.** (This parity is also called the "international Fisher effect," named for Irving Fisher, the economist who first proposed it.) Here are two ways to say it:

- A currency is expected to appreciate (depreciate) by as much as its interest rate is lower (higher) than the interest rate in the other country (for instance, expected appreciation of the pound = $i_{US} - i_{UK}$).

- The expected overall uncovered return on the foreign-currency investment equals the return on the domestic currency investment (expected appreciation + $i_{UK} = i_{US}$).

Consider the rates used in our previous numerical example: a current spot rate of \$2.00/£ and British and U.S. interest rates of 4 and 3 percent. For these rates uncovered interest parity holds if investors generally expect the future spot rate in 90 days to be \$1.98/£. Then the expected depreciation of the pound of 1 percent (from the current spot rate of \$2.00 to a future spot rate of \$1.98) equals the 1 percent by which British interest rates exceed U.S. interest rates (4 − 3).

If uncovered interest parity holds, then it links together four rates: the current spot exchange rate, the spot exchange rate that is currently expected to exist (on average) in the future, and the current interest rates in the two countries. As with covered interest parity, if one of these four rates changes, then at least one of the other rates must change to maintain or reestablish uncovered interest parity. Consider several possible changes that can lead to quick appreciation of the pound. If the interest rate in the United Kingdom increases, this can increase the current spot exchange-rate value of the pound, thus reducing the expected rate of further pound appreciation (or increasing the expected rate of pound depreciation) into the future (assuming that the value of the expected future spot rate is unchanged). If, instead, the value of the expected future spot rate increases and there is no change in interest rates, then the value of the current spot exchange rate must increase to maintain the same rate of further pound appreciation (or depreciation) expected into the future. We will look at these relationships more deeply in the next chapter, when we search for the determinants of spot exchange rates.

DOES INTEREST PARITY REALLY HOLD? EMPIRICAL EVIDENCE

The relationships among exchange rates and interest rates that we have discussed in this chapter are powerful concepts. Do these rate relationships hold for actual exchange rates and interest rates? Let's look at the evidence.

Evidence on Covered Interest Parity

Covered interest parity states that the forward premium should be (approximately) equal to the difference in interest rates. All of these rates can be seen in the foreign exchange markets and the short-term financial markets, so a test of covered interest parity is straightforward. The only further requirement is to identify comparable financial assets denominated in different currencies. Generally, we want to use financial assets with little or no risk of default so that any subtle differences in default risk do not muddy the empirical test.

A basic test is to examine financial assets offered by the same institution but differing in their currencies. A good choice is the set of Eurocurrency deposits offered by large banks to their international customers. A bank active in the Eurocurrency market is willing to accept interest-paying time deposits denominated in any of a number of currencies, not just the currency of the country in which the bank is located. (The box "Eurocurrencies—Not [Just] Euros and Not Regulated" says more about this market.) Various tests have shown that covered interest parity applies almost perfectly to Eurocurrency deposits. That is, the difference in interest rates between Eurodollar deposits and Eurosterling deposits, for instance, equals the forward premium on the pound (within the limits of the small amount of transactions costs incurred in making the various exchanges). This is full support for covered interest parity, but it is perhaps not surprising. The same banks are quoting all four rates (forward and spot exchange rates and the Euro-interest rates), and they base their quotes of the forward exchange rates on the interest rate differential.

A more stringent test of covered interest parity involves closely comparable assets issued by different institutions in separate national financial markets. Figure 17.2 shows the results from one careful study that examined the covered interest differentials between short-term financial assets in the United States and those in Germany, Japan, and France. For Germany and Japan, the covered interest differential is consistently very close to zero (and thus within the small range created by modest transactions costs) beginning in about 1985. For France this is true beginning in about 1987. Since about the mid-1980s, covered interest parity has held for comparable short-term assets for these four currencies (and for a number of others not shown as well).

Case Study   Eurocurrencies: Not (Just) Euros and Not Regulated

The Eurocurrency market is a worldwide wholesale money market of enormous scope, one beyond the easy control of any government. In this market any large business or government can borrow or lend at interest any weekday, day or night. This large, complex, and sometimes mysterious market has sprung up since the late 1950s.

The traditional definition of a **Eurocurrency deposit** is a bank deposit denominated in a currency different from the currency of the country where the bank is located. However, this definition is no longer completely accurate. Since 1981, the equivalent of Eurodollar deposits can be booked in New York in the International Banking Facility of a U.S. bank. The better definition of a Eurocurrency deposit is a *bank deposit that is not subject to the usual government regulations* imposed by the country of the currency in which the deposit is denominated. Eurodollar deposits are dollar deposits that are not subject to the same regulations imposed by the U.S. banking authorities on regular dollar deposits. In fact, the prefix *Euro* has now come to be used in international finance to refer not to geographic location but rather to financial instruments or activities that are subject to little or no government regulation. Eurobonds are bonds that are issued outside of the usual regulations imposed by the country in whose currency the bond is denominated.

Eurocurrency deposits are large time deposits. In 2001, banks in various areas of the world, including Europe, North America, Asia, and the Caribbean, had

Eurocurrency deposits totaling about $11 billion. A little less than half of these deposits are Eurodollar deposits. About one-quarter are euro Eurodeposits! (Yes, we have some confusing terminology—the *euro* as a currency is different from *Euro* as a prefix.) Eurosterling and Euroyen deposits are sizable too.

Eurocurrency deposits seem to have begun in Europe in the late 1950s. Several reasons explain the development and rapid growth of Eurocurrencies. First, European firms active in international trade began to hold dollars temporarily because the dollar had become the currency used for many trade transactions. These firms found it convenient to deal with their local banks that were willing to accept dollar deposits. Second, the Soviet Union was acquiring dollars in its foreign transactions. With the Cold War in full force, the Soviets feared that the U.S. government might block any deposits that they made in U.S. banks, so they began to deposit dollars in European banks. In the 1970s, Arab countries earning dollars on oil exports also feared possible restrictions if they placed their dollars on deposit in the United States, and turned to Eurodollar deposits. Third, and most important to the long-run development of the market, banks involved in taking these deposits (and making loans with the funds) found that they could avoid various regulations otherwise imposed on their banking activities.

One type of regulation that can be avoided is any restriction of international flows of moneys. Thus, in

The divergences in the earlier period appear to reflect actual or threatened government **capital controls,** which are restrictions on the ability of financial investors to transfer moneys in or out of the country. Germany and Japan largely eliminated these capital controls in the early 1980s. With freer flows of moneys, covered interest arbitrage became possible, and covered interest parity has held between the United States and these two countries since the mid-1980s.

With the election of Mitterrand, a socialist, as president of France in 1981, foreign investors began to fear the imposition of more severe capital controls. This added a risk to covered investments into France, the *political risk* that investors would not be able to remove their moneys from France when they wanted to.

the late 1950s, the British government restricted the ability of British banks to lend pounds to foreigners, but permitted them to lend dollars to foreigners. In the 1960s, the U.S. government attempted to restrict capital outflows. Borrowers turned to the Eurodollar market to obtain dollars that they could no longer borrow from the United States.

Other regulations that can be avoided in the Eurocurrency market are the standard regulations imposed on domestic banking activities. Countries that wish to attract Eurocurrency deposit activity generally do not impose reserve requirements on these deposits, or deposit insurance premiums, and they lighten or eliminate other regulations as well. Freedom from the burdens and extra costs of various regulations permits banks to offer somewhat higher interest rates on Eurocurrency deposits than are available on regular domestic bank deposits and perhaps also to charge somewhat lower interest rates on loans funded by these deposits. The lack of regulation implies that Eurocurrency deposit claims are somewhat riskier for depositors. They face somewhat more uncertainty about whether their claims will be honored if the bank should fail.

Some effects of Eurocurrency markets are straightforward, while others are controversial. Eurocurrency deposits and loans are generally credited with enhancing the efficiency of international financial markets. Eurocurrencies offer large corporations, financial institutions, and governments another alternative as to where they can invest their funds to earn interest or where they can borrow to obtain low-cost financing. Some of the efficiencies here come from the lack of burdens and costs imposed by government regulations, while others come from additional and fierce competition among banks from many countries for the same business.

The possible effects of Eurocurrencies on money supplies and inflation pressures are more controversial. Eurocurrency deposits are time deposits. They are not part of the narrowly defined money supply (currency, coin, and demand deposits—M1 in the United States). But they would be part of the more broadly defined money supply that includes "near moneys" such as time deposits (M2 or M3 in the United States). Various studies have concluded that the rise of Eurocurrencies:

- Generally has not reduced the ability of monetary authorities to control national money supplies and influence national inflation rates, and
- Has had little impact on average world inflation.

Nonetheless, the large amount of near-money existing in Eurocurrency deposits, and the ability of the market to grow quickly, could still influence inflation pressures in the future. In subsequent chapters we will examine the relationships between money and inflation in different countries, and how these in turn influence exchange rates and the international performance of different countries.

Because of this additional risk, major deviations from covered interest parity arose in 1981, at times reaching an annualized covered interest differential of 10 percentage points. Foreign investors' fears were correct. France tightened its restrictions in 1981 and did not substantially liberalize these controls until 1986. Once the restrictions were removed, and the risk that they might be reimposed subsided, covered interest parity began to hold in 1987.

Thus, covered interest parity is an important and empirically useful concept. It applies almost perfectly in the Eurocurrency market, and it applies to a growing number of countries that have liberalized or eliminated their restrictions on international movements of financial capital.

FIGURE 17.2   Covered Interest Differentials: The United States against Germany, Japan, and France, 1978–1993

The (annualized) covered interest differential is measured in favor of the United States, $CD = F + i_{US} - i_F$, where F is the forward premium on the dollar, and i_F is the interest rate for the other country (Germany, Japan, or France). The forward rate and the interest rates are 90-day rates. The interest rates are for commercial paper in the United States and for interbank borrowing in the other three countries.

Source: Pigott (1993–1994).

Evidence on Uncovered Interest Parity

Uncovered interest parity states that the expected rate of appreciation of the spot exchange rate value of a currency should (approximately) equal the difference in interest rates. Testing uncovered interest parity is much more difficult than testing covered interest parity. We have no direct information on people's actual expectations of exchange rate changes.

One approach is to survey knowledgeable market participants about their exchange rate expectations (and hope that they answer truthfully). The average expected future spot rate can then be used to calculate the expected appreciation and the expected uncovered interest differential. Figure 17.3 shows the results of one study using this approach. The two panels show the uncovered interest differential for the United States relative to Germany and to Japan. In both panels it appears that market participants often expected large uncovered interest differentials. This suggests that uncovered interest parity does not hold nearly as closely as does covered interest parity.

A second approach is to examine actual returns on uncovered international investments to draw out inferences about expected returns and exchange rate expectations. Looking at the *actual* overall return (including both the foreign interest return and the actual gain or loss on the currency exchanges) on any *one* uncovered foreign investment does not tell us much. The actual uncovered return may not equal the return on a comparable domestic investment simply because the actual future spot exchange rate turned out to be somewhat different from the future spot exchange rate that was expected at the time of the investment.

FIGURE 17.3   Uncovered Interest Differentials: The United States against Germany and Japan, 1991–1993

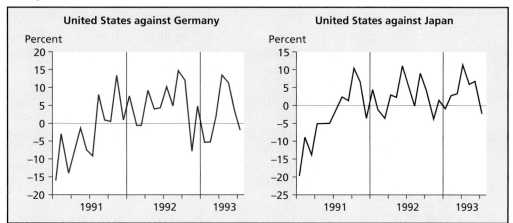

The (annualized) expected uncovered interest differential is measured in favor of the United States. EUD = expected appreciation of the dollar + $i_{US} - i_F$. The expected 90-day appreciation of the dollar is based on forecasts of currency movements from *Consensus Forecasts*. Interest rates are those on 90-day Eurocurrency deposits.

Source: Pigott (1993–1994).

Nonetheless, if expected uncovered returns are typically at parity, then over a *large number* of investments the actual uncovered differentials should be random and on average approximately equal to zero. Various studies have shown that the actual uncovered differentials are not completely random and for some time periods are not on average equal to zero. Uncovered interest parity applies roughly, but there also appear to be deviations of some importance.

Why does uncovered interest parity not hold perfectly? One possible explanation is simple— exchange rate risk matters. Investors will not enter into risky uncovered foreign investments unless they expect to be compensated adequately for the risk that this adds to their portfolios. Divergences from uncovered interest parity then reflect the risk premium necessary to compensate for exchange rate risk. However, some studies conclude that the uncovered interest differential is often larger than the risk premium necessary to compensate for this risk.

To the extent that the differential is larger than that necessary to compensate for risk, it appears that the expectations of market participants about future spot exchange rates are biased. For some periods of time the market participants are consistently expecting an exchange rate change that is different from what will actually occur. Current research is attempting to determine the nature of the biases that appear to exist in market expectations of future spot exchange rates. One possible explanation is troubling. If the biases are simply consistent errors, the foreign exchange market is an inefficient market. Other possible explanations are more subtle and probably less troubling. One is that market participants learn slowly about exchange rate behavior, but their forecasts are biased while they are learning. Another is that market participants (correctly) expect a large, rather sudden shift in an exchange rate at some point in the future. During the time before the large shift occurs, forecasts appear to be biased because they give some probability to the much different exchange rate that has not yet arrived. For instance, if the market expects a large devaluation of a now fixed-rate currency, the expected value of the spot exchange rate 90 days from now is an average of the current spot rate (if the devaluation does not occur within the next 90 days) and a much lower rate (if the devaluation does occur within the next 90 days). During the time before the devaluation actually occurs, the expected exchange rate appears to be biased— it is consistently lower than the actual (fixed) rate that continues to hold.

The conclusions that we reach are cautious. Uncovered interest parity is useful at least as a rough approximation empirically, but it also appears to apply imperfectly to actual rates.

Evidence on Forward Exchange Rates and Expected Future Spot Exchange Rates

If there is substantial speculation using the forward exchange market, then the forward rate should equal the average market expectation of the future spot exchange rate. Although this seems quite different from the interest parity relationships, it is actually closely related to them. If covered interest parity applies to actual rates, then testing whether the forward rate is a predictor of the future spot exchange rate is the same as testing uncovered interest parity. The only difference between covered and uncovered interest parity is the replacement of the current forward exchange rate with the currently expected future spot exchange rate.

For currencies for which covered interest parity holds, conclusions about the forward rate are then the same as those about uncovered interest parity. The forward exchange rate is roughly useful as an indicator of the market's expected future spot rate or as a predictor of this future spot rate, but there are also indications of biases in the predictions. Some part of the biases probably reflects risk premiums, but another part appears to reflect biases in the forecasts themselves. In addition, the forward rate is not a particularly accurate predictor of the future spot exchange rate. The errors in forecasting are often large. Indeed, as we will see in Chapter 18, no method of forecasting exchange rates into the near future is particularly accurate!

Summary

A person holding a net asset position (a *long* position) or a net liability position (a *short* position) in a foreign currency is exposed to **exchange rate risk.** The value of the person's income or net worth will change if the exchange rate changes in a way that the person does not expect. **Hedging** is the act of balancing your assets and liabilities in a foreign currency to become immune to risk resulting from future changes in the value of foreign currency. **Speculating** means taking a long or a short position in a foreign currency, thereby gambling on its future exchange value. There are a number of ways to hedge or speculate in foreign currency.

A **forward exchange contract** is an agreement to buy or sell a foreign currency for future delivery at a price (the **forward exchange rate**) set now. Forward foreign exchange contracts are useful because they provide a straightforward way to hedge an exposure to exchange rate risk or to speculate in an attempt to profit from future spot exchange rate values. An interesting hypothesis that emerges from the use of the forward market for speculation is that the forward exchange rate should equal the average expected value of the future spot rate.

International financial investment has grown rapidly in recent years. It is more complicated than domestic investment because of the need for currency exchanges, both to acquire foreign currency now and to translate the foreign currency back in the future. If the rate at which the future sale of foreign currency will occur is locked in now through a forward exchange contract, we have a hedged or **covered international investment.** If the future sale of foreign currency will occur at the future spot rate, we have an **uncovered international investment,** one that is exposed to exchange rate risk and therefore speculative.

As a result of **covered interest arbitrage** to exploit any **covered interest differential** between the returns on domestic and covered international investments, we expect that **covered interest parity** will exist (as long as there are no actual or threatened government restrictions on international money flows). Covered interest parity states that the percentage by which the forward exchange value of a currency exceeds its spot value equals the percentage point amount by which its interest rate is lower than the other country's interest rate. For countries with no **capital controls** and for comparable short-term financial assets, covered interest parity holds almost perfectly when actual rates are examined empirically.

At the time of the investment, the expected overall return on an uncovered international investment can be calculated using the investor's expected future spot exchange rate. The overall expected return on the uncovered international investment can be compared to the return available at home. The **expected uncovered interest differential** is one factor in deciding whether to make the uncovered international investment. Exposure to exchange rate risk must also be considered in the decision. If this risk is of little or no importance, then we hypothesize that **uncovered interest parity** will exist. The expected rate of appreciation of a currency should equal the percentage point amount by which its interest rate is lower than the other country's interest rate. Uncovered interest parity is not easy to test or examine empirically using actual rates, because we do not directly know the expected future spot rate or the expected rate of appreciation. It appears that uncovered interest parity is useful as a rough approximation, but it does not apply almost perfectly. Rather, exchange rate risk appears to be of some importance, and investors' expectations or forecasts of future spot exchange rates appear to be somewhat biased. (A similar conclusion is that, empirically, the forward exchange rate is a rough but somewhat biased predictor of the future spot exchange rate.)

Suggested Reading

Good presentations of theory and evidence on the parity relationships among forward exchange rates, spot exchange rates, and interest rates include Pigott (1993–94), Koedijk and Ott (1987), Taylor (1989), and Marston (1995). Froot and Thaler (1990) and Levich (1989) discuss evidence about the efficiency or inefficiency of the foreign exchange market. A good textbook view of foreign exchange futures, options, and swaps is found in Levich (2001, Chapters 11, 12, and 13). On Eurocurrencies, a readable guide is Goodfriend (1986). For more depth, see Dufey and Giddy (1994). Bartram and Dufey (2001) provide an overview of portfolio aspects of international investment.

Questions and Problems

✦ 1. "For an investment in a foreign-currency-denominated financial asset, part of the return comes from the asset itself and part from the foreign currency." Do you agree or disagree? Explain.

2. You have been asked to determine whether covered interest parity holds for one-year government bonds issued by the U.S. and British governments. What data will you need? How will you test?

✦ 3. Explain the nature of the exchange rate risk for each of the following, from the perspective of the U.S. firm or person. In your answer, include whether each is a long or short position in foreign currency.

   a. A small U.S. firm sold experimental computer components to a Japanese firm, and it will receive payment of 1 million yen in 60 days.

   b. An American college student receives as a birthday gift Japanese government bonds worth 10 million yen, and the bonds mature in 60 days.

   c. A U.S. firm must repay a yen loan, principal plus interest totaling 100 million yen, coming due in 60 days.

4. The current spot exchange rate is $0.010/yen. The current 60-day forward exchange rate is $0.009/yen. How would the U.S. firms and people described in question 3 each use a forward foreign exchange contract to hedge their risk exposure? What are the amounts in each forward contract?

✦ 5. The current spot exchange rate is $0.50/SFr. The current 180-day forward exchange rate is $0.52/SFr. You expect the spot rate to be $0.51/SFr in 180 days. How would you speculate using a forward contract?

6. The current spot exchange rate is $1.20/euro. The current 90-day forward exchange rate is $1.18/euro. You expect the spot rate to be $1.22/euro in 90 days. How would you speculate using a forward contract? If many people speculate in this way, what pressure is placed on the value of the current forward exchange rate?

✦ 7. You have access to the following rates:

   Current spot exchange rate: $0.0100/yen
   Current 180-day forward exchange rate: $0.0105/yen
   180-day U.S. interest rate (on dollar denominated assets): 6.05%
   180-day Japanese interest rate (on yen denominated assets): 1.00%

The interest rates are true 180-day rates (not annualized). You can borrow or invest at these rates. Calculate the actual amounts involved for the two ways around the lake (Figure 17.1) to get between each of the following.

a. Start with $1 now and end with dollars in 180 days.

b. Start with $1 now and end with yen in 180 days.

c. Start with 100 yen now and end with yen in 180 days.

8. The following rates are available in the markets:

Current spot exchange rate: $0.500/SFr

Current 30-day forward exchange rate: $0.505/SFr

Annualized interest rate on 30-day dollar-denominated bonds: 12% (1.0% for 30 days)

Annualized interest rate on 30-day Swiss franc-denominated bonds: 6% (0.5% for 30 days)

a. Is the Swiss franc at a forward premium or discount?

b. Should a U.S.-based investor make a covered investment in Swiss franc-denominated 30-day bonds, rather than investing in 30-day dollar-denominated bonds? Explain.

c. Because of covered interest arbitrage, what pressures are placed on the various rates? If the only rate that actually changes is the forward exchange rate, to what value will it be driven?

✦ 9. The following rates exist:

Current spot exchange rate: $1.80/£

Annualized interest rate on 90-day dollar-denominated bonds: 8% (2% for 90 days)

Annualized interest rate on 90-day pound-denominated bonds: 12% (3% for 90 days)

Financial investors expect the spot exchange rate to be $1.77/£ in 90 days.

a. If he bases his decisions solely on the difference in the expected rate of return, should a U.S.-based investor make an uncovered investment in pound-denominated bonds rather than investing in dollar-denominated bonds?

b. If she bases her decision solely on the difference in the expected rate of return, should a U.K.-based investor make an uncovered investment in dollar-denominated bonds rather than investing in pound-denominated bonds?

c. If there is substantial uncovered investment seeking higher expected returns, what pressure is placed on the current spot exchange rate?

10. Why is testing whether uncovered interest parity holds for actual rates more difficult than testing whether covered interest parity holds?

Chapter **Eighteen**

What Determines Exchange Rates?

Thinking in terms of supply and demand is a necessary first step toward understanding exchange rates. The next step is the one that has to be taken in any market analysis: finding out what underlying forces cause supply and demand to change.

We need to know what forces have caused the changes in exchange rates observed since the start of widespread "floating" back in the early 1970s. Figure 18.1 reminds us just how variable exchange rates have been. Between 1971 and the end of 1973, most currencies of other industrialized countries rose in value relative to the dollar, the average rise being about 20 percent. After 1973, when the modern era of floating exchange rates clearly took hold, we can see three types of variability for these exchange rates.

First, there are *long-term trends*. As shown in Figure 18.1A, over the entire period the Japanese yen, Swiss franc, and German mark (DM) have tended to appreciate, with the yen and the Swiss franc almost tripling in value, and the DM (fixed to the euro in 1999 and then retired in 2002) increasing more than 50 percent. As shown in Figure 18.1B, over the entire period the Italian lira, British pound, and Canadian dollar have tended to depreciate. The lira (also fixed to and then replaced by the euro) has lost over two-thirds of its exchange rate value against the dollar, the pound has lost more than a third, and the Canadian dollar has lost about a third. Still other currencies, such as the Israeli shekel or Argentine peso, dropped so far in value that the vertical axis would need to be extended down (close) to zero if we wanted to add them to Figure 18.1B.

Second, there are *medium-term trends* (over periods of several years), and these medium-term trends are sometimes counter to the longer trends. For instance, the Swiss franc, DM, and to a lesser extent the yen depreciated during the period 1980–1985. Another trend is the appreciation of the pound and the lira from 1985 to 1988. Furthermore, the French franc has experienced a series of medium-term swings, but its value in 1998 was not much different from its value back in the early 1970s. The decline in the dollar value of the euro since its introduction in 1999 is seen in any of three currencies shown (DM, French franc, lira) that it has replaced.

FIGURE 18.1   Selected Exchange Rates, 1970–2002 (Monthly)

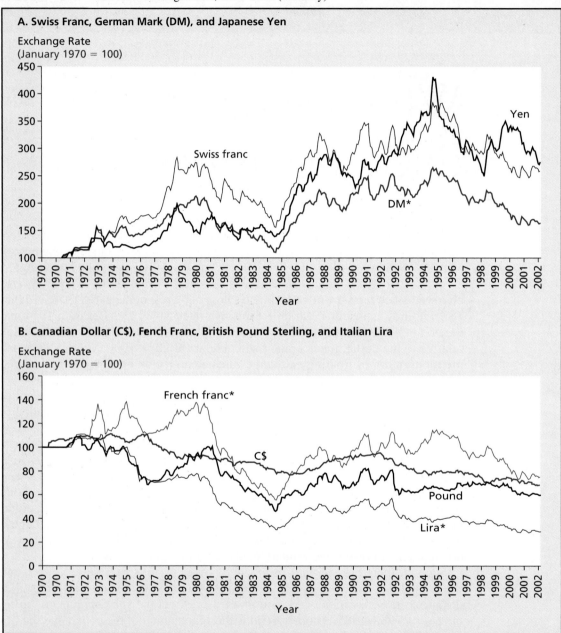

A. Swiss Franc, German Mark (DM), and Japanese Yen

Exchange Rate
(January 1970 = 100)

B. Canadian Dollar (C$), Fench Franc, British Pound Sterling, and Italian Lira

Exchange Rate
(January 1970 = 100)

*Beginning January 1999, these three currencies are fixed to the euro, so each of these rates is tracking the U.S.$/euro exchange rate movement from that date.

   For each currency, the dollar price of that currency (e.g., $/£) is shown, with units adjusted so that its January 1970 value is 100. For any currency, an increase in the value shown from one time to another indicates that the currency has increased in exchange rate value (appreciated) relative to the U.S. dollar during that time period; a decrease in the value shown indicates that the currency has depreciated relative to the U.S. dollar. For the currencies shown, the Japanese yen, Swiss franc, and German mark have appreciated over the entire 32-year period, while the Italian lira, British pound sterling, and Canadian dollar have depreciated. The French franc has fluctuated, and its 1998 value was similar to its 1970 value. At the beginning of 1999, the German mark, French franc, and Italian lira were fixed to the euro, and in 2002 the euro replaced these three currencies.

Source: International Monetary Fund, *International Financial Statistics.*

Third, there is substantial *short-term variability* in these exchange rates from month to month (and indeed, from day to day, hour to hour, and even minute to minute).

We can look at the movements in the exchange rate value of the dollar as the reverse of those for each foreign currency, or we can calculate the average movement against a set of other currencies. On average against the currencies of other industrialized countries, after losing about 20 percent in exchange rate value during 1971–1973, the dollar gained back almost 10 percent, but then lost about 13 percent from 1977 to 1979. After it changed little during the next two years, nearly all observers were stunned as the dollar rallied. By the time the dollar peaked in early 1985, it had gained over 50 percent in value since 1980 and was about 20 percent above its value in 1970. From early 1985 to early 1988, the dollar then fell (even more quickly) by a little more than it had risen in the previous five years. From early 1988 to 1995, the dollar fluctuated somewhat in average value against the currencies of the other industrialized countries, but it did not show any pronounced overall trend. Then, from a low point in 1995 to 2002, the dollar gained about 40 percent.

Why do we see large changes in the values of floating exchange rates? How does short-run variability turn into long-run trends? Why are medium-run trends sometimes opposite to these longer trends? This chapter presents what economists believe, what they think they know, and what they admit they do not know about this challenging puzzle.

A ROAD MAP

This chapter focuses on what we know about the determinants of exchange rates.[1] The first part of the chapter focuses on short-run movements in exchange rates. To understand exchange rates in the short run, we must focus on the perceptions and actions of international financial investors. We believe that rather little of the more than $1 trillion of foreign exchange trading that occurs each day is related to international trade in goods and services. Instead, most of it is related to the positioning or repositioning of the currency composition of the portfolios of international financial investors.

The **asset market approach to exchange rates** emphasizes the role of portfolio repositioning by international financial investors. As demand for and supply of financial assets denominated in different currencies shift around, these shifts place pressures on the exchange rates among the currencies. Fortunately, we have a head start on this analysis because we can use the concept of uncovered

---

[1] The forces examined here are central not only to understanding what causes floating rates to change but also to understanding the pressures on a system of fixed rates. Whatever would make a floating currency sink or rise would also make a fixed exchange rate harder to defend. The material has more uses than simply the search for determinants of floating exchange rates. It also applies to the analysis of the balance of payments under a fixed-rate system or a managed floating rate.

interest parity from Chapter 17. Major conclusions of our analysis are that the exchange rate value of a foreign currency (*e*) is raised *in the short run* by the following changes:

- A rise in the foreign interest rate relative to our interest rate ($i_f - i$).

- A rise in the expected future spot exchange rate (e^{ex}).

The second part of the chapter turns to long-term trends. Why do some currencies tend to appreciate over the long run, while others tend to depreciate? A key economic "fundamental" that appears to explain these long trends is the difference in national rates of inflation of the prices of goods and services. The concept of **purchasing power parity (PPP)** contains our core understanding of the relationship between product prices and exchange rates in the long run.

The third part of the chapter examines the role of money as a determinant of national product price levels and inflation rates. Through the link of money to price levels and inflation rates, the **monetary approach to exchange rates** emphasizes the importance of money supplies and demands as key to understanding the determinants of exchange rates. A major conclusion of the monetary approach is that the spot exchange rate *e,* the price of foreign currency in units of our currency, is raised *in the long run* by the following changes:

- A rise in our money supply relative to the foreign money supply (M^s/M^s_f).

- A rise in foreign real domestic product relative to our real domestic product (Y_f/Y).

The fourth part of the chapter shows one way in which the short term flows into the medium term and then into the long term. We examine the tendency for exchange rates to "overshoot," to change more than seems necessary in reaction to changes in government policies or to other important economic or political news. After the overshooting in the short run, the exchange rate moves in the medium run toward its long-run fundamental value.

The final part of the chapter looks at how useful these concepts and relationships really are. How well can we forecast future exchange rates?

EXCHANGE RATES IN THE SHORT RUN

Economists believe that pressures on exchange rates in the short run can best be understood in terms of the demands and supplies of assets denominated in different currencies. In principle the asset market approach to exchange rates incorporates all financial assets. Fortunately, we can grasp its key elements by focusing on investments in debt securities, such as government bonds, denominated in different currencies. In the analysis here we build on the discussion of uncovered international financial investment and uncovered interest parity from Chapter 17. Recall that investors determine the expected overall return on an uncovered investment in a bond denominated in a foreign currency by using

- The basic return on the bond itself (the interest rate or yield), and

- The expected gain or loss on currency exchanges (the expected appreciation or depreciation of the foreign currency).

While we may not believe that uncovered interest parity holds exactly, we still expect that there will be a noticeable relationship between the return on home-currency bonds and the expected overall return on foreign-currency bonds. These two returns will tend to be equal (or at least not too different). Emerging differences in these two returns will cause international financial investors to reposition their portfolios, and this repositioning creates the pressures that move the two returns toward equality.[2]

Uncovered interest parity (whether exact or approximate) links together four variables: the domestic interest rate, the foreign interest rate, the current spot exchange rate, and the expected future spot exchange rate. (The two exchange rates together imply the expected appreciation or depreciation.) Change in any one of these four variables implies that adjustments will occur in one or more of the other three. We will here focus on implications for the current spot exchange rate of changes in each of the other three variables. Figure 18.2 provides a road map by summarizing the effects.

The Role of Interest Rates

Foreign exchange markets do seem sensitive to movements in interest rates. Jumps of exchange rates often follow changes in interest rates. The response often looks prompt, so much so that press coverage of day-to-day rises or drops in an exchange rate typically point first to interest rates as a cause.

If our interest rate (i) increases, while the foreign interest rate (i_f) and the spot exchange rate expected at some appropriate time in the future (e^{ex}) remain constant, the return comparison shifts in favor of investments in bonds denominated in our currency. If international financial investors want to shift toward domestic-currency assets, they first need to buy domestic currency before they can buy the domestic-currency bonds. This increase in demand for domestic currency increases the current spot exchange rate value of domestic currency (so e decreases). Given the speed with which financial investors can initiate shifts in their portfolios, the effect on the spot exchange rate can happen very quickly (instantaneously or within a few minutes).

---

[2] This broad asset market approach built on the uncovered interest parity is a kind of portfolio balance approach because it emphasizes the role of portfolio repositioning in the determination of exchange rates. However, the portfolio balance approach can go further than this. One further conclusion of the portfolio balance approach is that a change in the supplies of assets denominated in different currencies affects the deviation from uncovered interest parity (in the form of a risk premium) that is necessary to induce investors to hold (demand) all of these assets. This conclusion results because assets denominated in different currencies actually are not perfect substitutes for each other in investors' portfolios.

FIGURE 18.2   Determinants of the Exchange Rate in the Short Run

Change in Variable	Direction of International Financial Repositioning	Implications for the Current Spot Exchange Rate (e = Domestic currency/Foreign currency)
Domestic Interest Rate (i)		
Increases	Toward domestic-currency assets	e decreases (domestic currency appreciates)
Decreases	Toward foreign-currency assets	e increases (domestic currency depreciates)
Foreign Interest Rate (i_f)		
Increases	Toward foreign-currency assets	e increases (domestic currency depreciates)
Decreases	Toward domestic-currency assets	e decreases (domestic currency appreciates)
Expected Future Spot Exchange Rate (e^{ex})		
Increases	Toward foreign-currency assets	e increases (domestic currency depreciates)
Decreases	Toward domestic-currency assets	e decreases (domestic currency appreciates)

The analysis for each change in one of the variables assumes that the other two variables are unchanged.

Let's consider an example involving the United States, Switzerland, and 90-day bonds. Initially, the U.S. interest rate is 9 percent per year, the Swiss interest rate is 5 percent per year, the current spot rate is $.50 per Swiss franc (SFr), and the spot rate expected in 90 days is about $.505 per SFr, implying that the franc is expected to appreciate at an annual rate of about 4 percent. (Uncovered interest parity holds at these rates, as the expected annualized overall return on the SFr-denominated bonds is about 9 percent, equal to 5 percent interest plus about 4 percent expected currency appreciation.) What happens if the U.S. interest rate increases to 11 percent? Given the other initial rates, the return differential shifts in favor of U.S.-dollar-denominated bonds. International financial investors have an incentive to shift toward dollar-denominated bonds, and this increases the demand for dollars in the foreign exchange market. The dollar tends to appreciate immediately. Furthermore, we can determine that the dollar should appreciate to about $.4975 per SFr, assuming that the interest rates and the expected future exchange rate do not change. Once this new current spot exchange rate is posted in the market, the SFr then is expected to appreciate during the next 90 days at a faster rate, equal to about 6 percent. This reestablishes uncovered interest parity (5 percent interest plus about 6 percent expected appreciation matches the 11 percent U.S. interest) and eliminates any further desire by international investors to reposition their portfolios.

If our interest rate instead decreases, with foreign interest rates and the expected future spot rate unchanged, the spot exchange rate value of our currency is predicted to decrease (e increases).

If the foreign interest rate (i_f) increases, the story is similar. Assuming that the domestic interest rate and the expected future spot exchange rate are constant, the return comparison shifts in favor of investments in bonds denominated in foreign currency. A shift by international financial investors toward foreign-currency bonds would require them first to buy foreign currency in the foreign exchange market. This increase in demand for the foreign currency increases the current spot exchange rate *e* (the domestic currency depreciates).

Consider a variation on our previous example. If the U.S. interest rate is 9 percent, the spot exchange rate is $.50 per SFr, and the expected future spot rate is about $.505 per SFr, what is the effect of an increase in the Swiss interest rate from 5 to 7 percent? The return differential shifts in favor of Swiss bonds. The increased demand for francs in the foreign exchange market results in a quick appreciation of the franc (and depreciation of the dollar). The current spot exchange rate must jump immediately to about $.5025 per SFr to reestablish uncovered interest parity.

If instead the foreign interest rate decreases, the spot rate *e* decreases. (The domestic currency appreciates.)

What happens if both interest rates change at the same time? The answer is straightforward. What matters is the interest rate differential $i - i_f$. If the interest rate differential increases, the return differential shifts in favor of domestic-currency bonds, and *e* tends to decrease. (The domestic currency appreciates.) If it decreases, *e* tends to increase.

The Role of the Expected Future Spot Exchange Rate

Expectations of future exchange rates can also have a powerful impact on international financial positioning, and through this on the value of the current exchange rate. Consider what happens when financial investors decide that they now expect the future spot exchange rate to be higher than they previously expected. Relative to the current spot rate, this means that they expect the foreign currency to appreciate more, or to depreciate less, or to appreciate rather than depreciate. Assuming that the interest rate differential is unchanged, the increase in the expected future spot rate alters the return differential in favor of foreign-currency-denominated bonds. The story from here is familiar. If international financial investors want to shift toward foreign-currency assets, they first need to buy foreign currency in the foreign exchange market before they can buy the foreign-currency bonds. This increase in demand for foreign currency increases the current spot exchange rate *e*. (The foreign currency appreciates; the domestic currency depreciates.) If instead the expected future spot exchange rate decreases, with the interest rate differential unchanged, the return differential changes in favor of domestic-currency investments, and the current spot exchange rate value of our currency increases (*e* decreases).

Consider another variation on our previous example. With the U.S. interest rate at 9 percent, the Swiss interest rate at 5 percent, and the current spot exchange rate at $.50 per SFr, what happens if the spot exchange rate expected in 90 days increases from about $.505 to about $.515 per SFr (perhaps because international investors believe that the political situation in Switzerland will improve rapidly)? Relative to the initial current spot rate, investors now expect the franc to appreciate more in the next 90 days, at about a 12 percent annual rate (rather than the previously expected 4 percent). This shifts the return differential in favor of Swiss-currency bonds. Because investors desire to reposition their portfolios toward Swiss assets, demand for the franc increases in the foreign exchange market. The current spot exchange rate increases (the franc appreciates and the dollar depreciates). In fact, the spot exchange rate moves to about $.51 per SFr. At this new spot rate, the franc then is expected to appreciate further by only about 4 percent (annual rate). Uncovered interest parity is reestablished, and there is no further incentive for international investors to reposition their portfolios.

As with a change in interest rates, the effect of a change in the expected future spot rate on the current spot exchange rate can happen very quickly (instantaneously or within a few minutes). This can be like a rapid-fire self-confirming expectation. In the Swiss franc example, the expectation that the franc would appreciate more than was previously expected resulted in a rapid and large appreciation of the franc. For another example, consider what happens if international financial investors shift from expecting no change in spot exchange rates (e^{ex} equals the initial e) to expecting a depreciation of the foreign currency (e^{ex} decreases so that it is then below the initial current spot rate e). The willingness of international investors to reposition their international portfolios away from foreign-currency bonds results in a depreciation of the foreign currency (e decreases)—exactly what they were expecting.

Given the powerful effects that exchange-rate expectations can have on actual exchange rates, we would like to know what determines these expectations. Many different things can influence the value of the expected future exchange rate.

Some investors, especially for expectations regarding the near-term future (the next minutes, hours, days, or weeks), may expect that the recent trend in the exchange rate will continue. They extrapolate the recent trend into the future. This is a **bandwagon.** For instance, currencies that have been appreciating are expected to continue to do so. The recent actual increase in the exchange rate value of a country's currency leads some investors to expect further increases in the near future. If they act on this belief, the currency will tend to appreciate further. This bandwagon effect is the basis for fears that speculation can sometimes be *destabilizing* in that the actions of international investors can move the exchange rate away from a long-run equilibrium value consistent with fundamental economic influences. Expectations can be destabilizing if they are formed without regard to these economic fundamentals, which is quite possible if recent exchange rate trends are simply extrapolated into the future.

Expectations can also be based on the belief that exchange rates eventually return to values consistent with basic economic conditions (for instance, purchasing power parity, which we will discuss in the next section). Expectations of this sort are considered *stabilizing* in the sense that they lead to stabilizing speculation, which tends to move the exchange rate toward a value consistent with some economic fundamentals such as relative national product price levels.

Changes in expectations can be based on various kinds of new information. The important part of the "news" is any unexpected information about government policies, about national and international economic data or performance, and about political leaders and situations (both domestic politics and international political issues and tensions). An example is that foreign exchange markets often react to news of official figures about a country's trade or current account balances, measures that largely reflect the balance or imbalance between a country's exports and imports of goods and services. There is logic to the market's reactions to such news. For instance, an unexpected increase in a country's trade deficit or (especially) its current account deficit indicates that the country requires an increasing amount of foreign financing of the deficit. If the increased foreign financing is not assured to be forthcoming, then the country's currency will tend to fall in the foreign exchange market. The increasing demand for foreign currency as part of the process of paying for the excess of imports over exports tends to appreciate the foreign currency and depreciate the domestic currency. If this logic is built into the changed expectations of international investors, then the exchange rate change can occur quickly, rather than gradually as the trade imbalance would slowly add to market pressures.

THE LONG RUN: PURCHASING POWER PARITY (PPP)

In the short run, floating exchange rates are often highly variable, and there are times when it is not easy to understand why the rates are changing as they are. In the long run, economic fundamentals become dominant, providing an "anchor" for the long-term trends. Our understanding of exchange rates in the long run is based on the proposition that there is a predictable relationship between product price levels and exchange rates. The relationship relies on the fact that people choose to buy goods and services from one country or another according to the prices they must pay. We can present three versions of this relationship, depending on whether we are examining one product or a set of products, and whether we are looking at a snapshot of the product price–exchange rate relationship or how product prices and exchange rates are changing over time.

The Law of One Price

The **law of one price** posits that a product that is easily and freely traded in a perfectly competitive global market should have the same price everywhere, once the prices at different places are expressed in the same currency. In Part I we called this the equilibrium international, or world, price, although we did not specifically bring exchange rates into the picture. Now we can. The law of one price proposes that the price (P) of the product measured in domestic currency will be equated to the price (P_f) of the product measured in the foreign currency through the current spot exchange rate (e, Domestic currency/Foreign currency):

$$P = e \cdot P_f$$

The law of one price works well for heavily traded commodities, either at a point in time or for changes over time, as long as governments permit free trade in the commodity. Such heavily traded commodities include gold, other metals, crude oil, and various agricultural commodities.

Consider, for example, No. 2 soft red Chicago wheat, and suppose that it costs $4.80 a bushel in Chicago. Its dollar price in London should not be much greater, given the cheapness of transporting wheat from Chicago to London. To simplify the example, let us say that it costs nothing to transport the wheat. It seems reasonable, then, that the pound price of wheat will be £3.00 if the exchange rate is $1.60 per pound. The dollar price of the wheat in London then is $4.80 per bushel (= 3.00 × 1.60). If it is not, it would pay someone to trade wheat between Chicago and London to profit from the price gap. For example, if an unexpected increase in British demand for wheat temporarily forces the price of wheat in London up to £3.75 per bushel, and the exchange rate is still $1.60 per pound, the dollar price in London is $6.00. As long as free trade is possible, we expect that the two prices would soon be bid back into equality, presumably somewhere between $4.80 and $6.00 per bushel for both countries. In the case of wheat (a standardized commodity with a well-established world market), we expect that arbitrage will bring the two prices into line within a week.

However, the law of one price does not hold closely for most products that are traded internationally, including nearly all manufactured products. It is not hard to find the culprits that explain the discrepancy. International transport costs are not negligible. Governments do not practice free trade. And many markets are imperfectly competitive. Firms with market power sometimes use price discrimination to increase profits by charging different prices in different national markets (as we discussed in Chapter 10). One recent study concluded that the effect of the national border between the United States and Canada on product price differences is like adding thousands of miles of distance between Canadian and U.S. cities. *For many products the law of one price does not hold closely.*

Absolute Purchasing Power Parity

Absolute purchasing power parity posits that a basket or bundle of tradable products will have the same cost in different countries if the cost is stated in the same currency. Essentially, the average price of these products, often called the product-price level, or just price level, stated in different currencies is the same when converted to a common currency:

$$P = e \cdot P_f$$

Here P and P_f refer to the average product price or price level in the domestic and foreign country. The equation can be rearranged to provide an estimate of the spot exchange rate that is consistent with absolute PPP:

$$e = P/P_f$$

Absolute PPP is clearly closely related to the law of one price. The equations are the same, except that the price variables refer either to only one product (law of one price) or to a bundle of products (absolute PPP). If the law of one price holds for all the products, then absolute PPP will also hold (as long as the product bundle is the same in both countries). Even if the law of one price does not hold exactly, absolute PPP could still be a useful guide, if the discrepancies tend to average out over the different products in the bundle.

Based on the evidence, however, absolute PPP does not fare much better than the law of one price in the real world. Divergences from absolute PPP can be large at any given time. (The divergences are even larger if nontraded products are included in the bundles. See the box "Price Gaps and International Income Comparisons.") In addition, we can get into technical difficulties of comparing index numbers if the information sources, like national governments, do not use the same bundles of products for the different countries. Nonetheless, there is evidence that large divergences from absolute PPP do tend to shrink over time for traded products.

Relative Purchasing Power Parity

Both the law of one price and absolute purchasing power parity are posited to hold at a point in time. Another version of PPP looks specifically at how things are changing over time. **Relative purchasing power parity** posits that the difference between changes over time in product-price levels in two countries will be offset by the change in the exchange rate over this time. The exact formula for relative PPP is:

$$\left(\frac{e_t}{e_0} \right) = \frac{\left(P_t / P_0 \right)}{\left(P_{f,t} / P_{f,0} \right)}$$

where the subscripts indicate the values for the initial year 0 and some later year *t,* for each variable. Each ratio in parentheses shows the increase from the initial year to the later year for each variable. If you compare this equation to the second one for absolute PPP, you will see that relative PPP holds if absolute PPP holds for both the initial year and the later year. In addition, relative PPP may be useful as a guide to why exchange rates change over time, even if absolute PPP does not hold closely at specific times.

Relative PPP is often defined using an approximation. The ratio of the two exchange rates can be approximated by the percentage rate of appreciation (depreciation if negative) of the foreign currency over time. The ratio of the country's product price levels can be approximated by the percentage increase in the price level over time, which is the inflation rate. Relative PPP can then be stated approximately as:

$$\text{Rate of appreciation of the foreign currency} = \pi - \pi_f$$

where π and π_f are the (product-price) inflation rates for the domestic country and the foreign country.

Relative PPP provides some strong predictions about exchange rate trends, especially in the long term. It implies that countries with relatively low inflation rates have currencies whose values tend to appreciate in the foreign exchange market. Looked at the other way, countries with relatively high inflation rates have currencies whose values tend to depreciate in the foreign exchange market. In fact, a strict application of PPP implies that each percentage point more of a country's inflation per year tends to be related to a 1 percent faster rate of depreciation of the country's currency (or slower rate of currency appreciation) per year. PPP

There is tremendous social importance to international comparisons of average income or production levels. To judge which nations are most in need of United Nations aid, World Bank loans, and other help, officials compare their incomes per capita. To judge whether Japan has overtaken the United States in supply capability, we compare Japanese and U.S. gross domestic product per capita. All such comparisons are dangerous as well as unavoidable. The comparisons are likely to contain a host of large errors.

One of the worst pitfalls comes in converting from one national currency to another. It turns out that the market exchange rate is a poor way to convert, because the purchasing power parity (PPP) hypothesis is not reliable when applied to all the goods and services that make up national expenditure or domestic production. Many of the products in such a broad bundle are not traded internationally. There is no direct reason (like arbitrage) to think that the prices of nontraded products should equalize internationally when stated in a common currency using market exchange rates, and they usually do not.

If the market exchange rate is unreliable, what should we use for comparing values of income per capita between countries? The principle is clear: We want to take the national income per capita measured using whatever prices exist in each country and convert these into values of national incomes per capita using a set of common international prices like those that would exist if PPP applied. That way, we are comparing how many units of a consistently priced bundle of goods and services the average resident of each nation could buy. But it is difficult to get data on the prices of a wide-ranging bundle of goods and services for every country.

That is where the United Nations International Comparisons Project (ICP) came in. A team of economists at the University of Pennsylvania, led by Alan Heston, Irving Kravis, and Robert Summers, did the hard work of measuring the prices of items in separate countries, with financial backing by the United Nations, the World Bank, and the U.S. National Science Foundation. The ICP group has assembled useful annual data on the price structures and income levels of over 130 countries since the 1950s. What they have found, in effect, are the true levels of P and P_f for deflating the current-price national income figures. They confirm what was widely feared: On average for all goods and services, the market exchange rate e is often far from the ratio P/P_f that absolute PPP says it should equal.

The accompanying table shows the typical pattern in departures from absolute PPP and the importance of replacing exchange rate conversions of income per capita with the better comparisons based on common price levels.

If purchasing power parity really held, then every number in the right-hand column would be 100. The departures from that PPP norm are great enough to reshuffle some of the international rankings, making the better (PPP-based) measurements of the center column differ from the exchange-rate-based measures on the left. Two patterns are apparent in the figures. One is that the price-difference ratio in the right-hand column is above unity for Japan and most West European nations. Their PPP-measured real average income is not as high relative to that of the United States as the exchange rate figures imply.

Another pattern is that the usual comparisons—the ones using exchange rates—overstate the real income gaps between rich and poor nations, because the price-difference ratio is below unity for the lower-income countries in the bottom half of the list. For some of the poorest countries the price disparity can be as large as 1:5, a substantial deviation from absolute PPP.

Why should lower-income countries have prices so much lower than U.S. prices? Almost all of the departures come from the wide international gaps in the prices of nontraded products like housing, haircuts, and other local services. The prices of nontraded products differ radically between lower-income and higher-income countries. The gaps in the prices of these products seem to be widened by two forces. One is the tendency for the price of land in towns and cities to be highly sensitive to the income of the country's residents. So a country with twice as high an income would have more than twice as high a cost for business and residential space, making space-intensive nontraded products cost much more. A second explanation is that as a country develops, its productivity in making traded goods rises much

National Income per Capita, 2000, Relative to the United States = 100

Country	Using the Exchange Rate	Using Common Prices	Domestic Price Level (This Country/U.S.) as a Percentage of the Level Predicted by PPP
United States	100	100	100%
Switzerland	111	89	126
Norway	98	87	113
Canada	61	80	77
Denmark	93	79	118
Japan	100	77	129
Netherlands	73	76	96
Australia	60	74	81
Germany	73	73	100
Singapore	72	73	99
France	69	71	97
Sweden	78	69	113
United Kingdom	72	69	104
Italy	58	68	86
Israel	48	56	84
Korea	26	51	51
Czech Republic	14	40	36
South Africa	9	27	33
Chile	13	27	50
Poland	12	26	47
Mexico	15	26	58
Russia	5	23	21
Brazil	10	21	49
Turkey	9	21	44
Thailand	6	18	32
Philippines	3	12	25
China	2	12	21
Egypt	4	11	40
Indonesia	2	8	20
India	1	7	19
Ghana	1	6	18
Nigeria	1	2	33

Source: World Bank, *World Development Report 2002.*

faster than its productivity in making nontraded goods and services. The higher productivity in making traded goods tends to increase wage rates in more developed countries. Firms making nontraded goods and services must also pay these higher wage rates. With less productivity advantage, this results in costs and prices of nontraded products that are higher in more developed countries.

thus has an important message to offer countries such as Switzerland, which are seeking to keep domestic prices stable when the rest of the world is inflating. If prices elsewhere are rising 10 percent a year, in the long run a country can keep its domestic prices stable only by accepting a rise of about 10 percent a year in the exchange value of its currency in terms of inflating-country currencies.

Relative PPP: Recent Experience

We just suggested that PPP holds reasonably well in the long run, but poorly in the short run. We can examine specific evidence about PPP for recent years. Figure 18.3 provides evidence on the long run during the current period of floating exchange rates. For each country included in samples of industrialized and developing countries, the average annual rate of change of its currency's exchange rate against the U.S. dollar is compared to the difference between the average U.S. inflation rate and the country's inflation rate.[3] Relative PPP predicts that when the inflation differential is positive (the United States has a higher inflation rate, or the country has a lower one), the country's currency should appreciate. When the inflation differential is negative, the country's currency should depreciate. Looking across the countries in each sample, we can see that this relationship is clear. In fact, the relationships are very close to the one-to-one relationship implied by a strict version of relative PPP.[4]

We can also examine recent performance of PPP for both short and long periods using data on the exchange rates of individual countries over time. Figure 18.4 shows the actual exchange rates against the U.S. dollar and the exchange rates that would be consistent with PPP (relative to the base year 1975), month-by-month, for the German mark (DM) and Japanese yen. The exchange rate consistent with PPP is the rate that equals the ratio of the national price levels P/P_f (relative to the value of this ratio in the base year). If relative PPP always held, the actual exchange rate would equal the exchange rate implied by PPP. As we can see easily in the figure, the deviations of the actual exchange rate from its PPP value can be large and can persist for a number of years. The DM was substantially undervalued relative to the implied PPP value from 1981 through 1986,

---

[3] The period is 1975–2000. The beginning year 1975 is somewhat arbitrary; it was chosen to be close to the beginning of the current floating-rate period, but also to allow several years of adjustment following the end of the previous fixed-rate period. Inflation rates are measured using the wholesale price index or a similar price index that includes only (or mostly) traded products.

[4] A standard statistical test of the relationship is to fit the best straight line to the data points using a simple regression. For the industrialized countries, the slope of the line (0.959) is not significantly different from 1 (and the intercept is not significantly different from zero), strongly supporting the one-to-one relationship. For the developing countries, the slope coefficient (0.975) is also not statistically significantly different from 1, but the intercept (–0.863) is statistically significantly different from zero. These results for developing countries indicate a mild divergence from the one-to-one relationship predicted by PPP. The currencies of developing countries tend to depreciate by about 1 percent per year, in addition to changing by the difference in inflation rates. In both cases the straight lines fit the data very well. Over 94 percent of the variation in the rates of exchange rate change across the countries is "explained" by the inflation rate differences.

FIGURE 18.3 Relative Purchasing Power Parity: Inflation Rate Differences and Exchange Rate Changes, 1975–2000

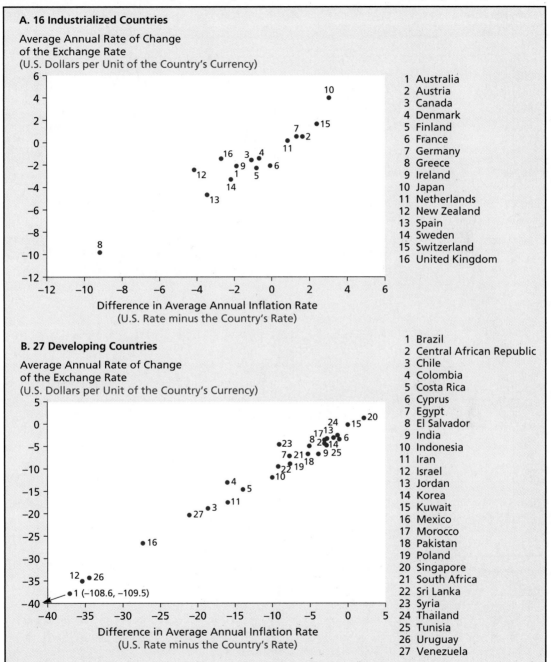

On average from 1975 to 2000, strong support is found for PPP. If the U.S. inflation rate is higher than the other country's inflation rate, the country's currency tends to appreciate; if the U.S. inflation rate is lower, the currency tends to depreciate.

Inflation rates are measured using wholesale (or similar producer-oriented) price indexes. Annual rates of change are calculated using the differences in natural logarithms.

FIGURE 18.4   Actual Exchange Rates and Exchange Rates Consistent with Relative PPP, Monthly, 1975–2002

*Beginning January 1999, the German mark is fixed to the euro, so its rate is tracking the U.S. $/euro exchange rate movement from that date.

The exchange rate implied by PPP equals the ratio of national price levels P/P_f. The actual exchange rate can differ substantially from this PPP rate, and the divergences can persist for several years. Nonetheless, there is a tendency for the actual exchange rate to follow the PPP rate in the long run.

National price levels are measured by wholesale (or producer) price indexes.

Case Study   PPP from Time to Time

Something like the purchasing power parity (PPP) theory has existed throughout the modern history of international economics. The theory keeps resurfacing whenever exchange rates have become more variable as a result of wars or other events. Sometimes the hypothesis is used as a way of describing how a nation's general price level must change to reestablish some desired exchange rate, given the level and trend in foreign prices. At other times it is used to guess at what the equilibrium exchange rate will be, given recent trends in prices within and outside the country. Both of these interpretations crept into the British "bullionist–antibullionist" debate during and after the Napoleonic Wars, when the issue was why Britain had been driven by the wars to dislodge the pound sterling from its fixed exchange rates and gold backing, and what could be done about it.

The PPP hypothesis came into its own in the 1920s, when Gustav Cassel and others directed it at the issue of how much European countries would have to change their official exchange rates or their domestic price levels, given that World War I had driven the exchange rates off their prewar par values and had brought varying percentages of price inflation to different countries. For instance, PPP was a rough guide to the mistake made by Britain in returning to the prewar gold parity for the pound sterling in 1925 despite greater price inflation in Britain than in Britain's trading partners.

With the restoration of fixed exchange rates following World War II, the PPP hypothesis again faded from prominence, ostensibly because its defects had been demonstrated, but mainly because the issue it raised seemed less compelling as long as exchange rates were expected to stay fixed. After the resumption of widespread floating of exchange rates in the early 1970s, the hypothesis has been revived once again.

and then was somewhat overvalued for much of the first half of the 1990s. The yen tracked its PPP value reasonably well from 1976 through 1986, but then became overvalued. In 1998 and again in 2001 the yen came closer to its PPP value. In the long run there is a tendency for the actual exchange rates to move in a manner consistent with PPP. According to PPP, both the DM and the yen should have appreciated over this entire period, and they did.

If we examine evidence for other countries, we would generally reach similar conclusions: noticeable deviations from PPP in the short run, but a tendency for PPP to hold in the long run. Based on a survey of rigorous studies, Froot and Rogoff (1995) conclude that it takes about four years on average for a deviation from PPP to be reduced by half, for the exchange rates of major industrialized countries.

THE LONG RUN: THE MONETARY APPROACH

Purchasing power parity indicates that, at least in the long run, exchange rates are closely related to the levels of prices for products in different countries. But this also suggests the next question: What determines the average national price level or the rate at which it changes, the inflation rate? Economists believe that the money supply (or its growth rate) determines the price level (or the inflation rate), in the long run. This suggests that money supplies in different countries, through their links to national price levels and inflation rates, are closely linked to exchange rates in the long run. Indeed, this is not surprising. An exchange rate is the price of one money in terms of another. Trying to analyze exchange rates or international payments without looking at national money supplies and demands is like presenting *Hamlet* without the Prince of Denmark.

Relative money supplies affect exchange rates. On the international front as on the domestic front, a currency is less valuable the more of it there is to circulate. Extreme cases of hyperinflation dramatize this fundamental point. The trillion-fold increase in the German money supply in 1922–1923 was the key proximate cause of the trillionfold increase in the price of foreign exchange and of everything else in Germany at that time. Hyperinflation of the money supplies is also the key to understanding why the currencies of Israel and several Latin American countries lost almost all their value in recent times.

Money, Price Levels, and Inflation

The relationship between money and the national price level (or inflation rate) follows from the relationship between money supply and money demand. Why do we "demand," or hold, money? The key reason is that money is used as a medium of exchange. People and businesses want to hold a certain amount of money to cover an uncertain value of transactions that require the exchange of money for other items. This transaction demand varies with the annual turnover of transactions requiring money, a turnover that is fairly well proxied by the money value of gross domestic product.

The link between domestic product and the demand for a nation's money is central to the quantity theory of demand for money. The **quantity theory equation** says that in any country the money supply is equated with the demand for money, which is directly proportional to the money value of gross domestic product. In separate equations for the home country and the rest of the world, the quantity theory equation becomes a pair:

$$M^s = k \times P \times Y$$

and

$$M_f^s = k_f \times P_f \times Y_f$$

where M^s and M_f^s are the home and foreign money supplies (measured in dollars and foreign currency, respectively), P and P_f are the home and foreign price levels, and Y and Y_f are the real (constant-price) domestic products. For each country, the nominal or money value of GDP equals the price level times the real GDP ($P \times Y$ and $P_f \times Y_f$). The k and k_f indicate the proportional relationships between money holdings and the nominal value of GDP. They represent people's behavior. If the value of GDP and thus the value of transactions increase, k indicates the amount of extra money that people want to hold to facilitate this higher level of economic activity. Sometimes quantity theorists assume that the ks are constant numbers, sometimes not. (The facts say that any k varies.) For the present long-run analysis, we follow the common presumption that each money supply (M^s and M_f^s) is controlled by each government's monetary policy alone, and that each country's real production (Y and Y_f) is governed by such supply-side forces as factor supplies, technology, and productivity.

By taking the ratio of these two equations and rearranging the terms, we can use the quantity theory equations to determine the ratio of prices between countries:

$$(P/P_f) = (M^s/M_f^s) \bullet (k_f/k) \bullet (Y_f/Y)$$

Money and PPP Combined

Combining the absolute purchasing power parity equation with the quantity theory equations for the home country and the rest of the world yields a prediction of exchange rates based on money supplies and national products:

$$e = P/P_f = (M^s/M_f^s) \bullet (k_f/k) \bullet (Y_f/Y)$$

The exchange rate e between one foreign currency (say, the British pound) and other currencies (here represented by the dollar, the home currency in our example) can now be related to just the M^ss, the ks, and the Ys. The price ratio (P/P_f) can be set aside as an intermediate variable determined, in the long run, by the M^ss, ks, and Ys.

The equation predicts that a foreign nation will have an appreciating currency (e up) if it has some combination of slower money supply growth (M^S/M_f^s up), faster growth in real output (Y_f/Y up), or a rise in the ratio k_f/k. Conversely, a nation with fast money growth and a stagnant real economy is likely to have a depreciating currency.

Going one step further, we can use the same equation to quantify the percent effects of changes in money supplies or domestic products on the exchange rate. The equation implies that some key elasticities are equal to 1. That is, if the ratio (k_f/k) stays the same, then e rises by 1 percent for

- Each 1 percent rise in the domestic money supply (M^s), or

- Each 1 percent drop in the foreign money supply (M_f^s), or

- Each 1 percent drop in domestic real GDP (Y), or

- Each 1 percent rise in foreign GDP (Y_f).

The exchange rate elasticities imply something else that seems reasonable too: An exchange rate will be unaffected by balanced growth. If money supplies grow at the same rate in all countries, leaving M^S/M_f^S unchanged, and if domestic products grow at the same rate, leaving Y_f/Y unchanged, there should be no change in the exchange rate.

Changes in the ks would have comparable effects on the exchange rate in the long run, but we choose not to examine these here. Instead, let's look a little more closely at the effects of money supply and real income.

The Effect of Money Supplies on an Exchange Rate

Let's look at an example in which Britain is the foreign country and the United States is the domestic country. If, for instance, the supply of pounds is cut by 10 percent, each pound would become more scarce and more valuable. The cut would be achieved by a tighter British monetary policy. This contractionary policy would restrict the reserves of the British banking system, forcing British banks to tighten credit and the outstanding stock of sterling bank deposits, which represent most of the British money supply. The tighter credit would make it harder to borrow and spend, cutting back on aggregate demand, output, jobs, and product prices in Britain. With the passage of time, the fall in output and jobs should reverse, and the reduction in prices should reach 10 percent. Over time, relative PPP predicts that the pound should rise in value. The 10 percent cut in Britain's money supply should eventually lead to a 10 percent higher exchange rate value of the pound.

The same shift should result from a 10 percent rise in the dollar money supply. If the U.S. central bank lets the dollar money supply rise 10 percent, the extra dollar money available should end up inflating dollar prices by 10 percent. For a time, the higher dollar prices might cause international demands for goods and services to shift in favor of buying the sterling-priced goods, which are temporarily cheaper. Eventually, relative purchasing power parity should be restored by a 10 percent rise in the exchange rate *e*. One other result predicted above follows as a corollary: If the preceding equations are correct, a balanced 10 percent rise in all money supplies, both pounds and dollars, should have no effect on the exchange rate.

The Effect of Real Incomes on an Exchange Rate

The same kind of reasoning can be used to explore how long-run changes in real income and production should affect an exchange rate. Let us first follow this reasoning on its own terms and then add a word of caution.

Suppose that Britain's real income shifts up to a growth path 10 percent above the path Britain would otherwise have followed. This might happen, for instance, as the result of a spurt in British productivity. The extra transactions associated with the higher British production and income would call forth a new demand for holding pounds. If the extra productivity results in a 10 percent rise in real British national income, the quantity theory predicts a 10 percent higher transactions demand for the pound. But this extra demand cannot be met, assuming that Britain's money stock has not increased. Instead, the price level must decline in Britain by 10 percent so that the overall money value of British national income is unchanged. Essentially, in this case the increase in productivity is passed forward to buyers in the form of lower product prices. Then, according to relative PPP, the decline in British prices leads to a rise in the value of the pound. The rise again equals 10 percent. Again, we have two corollaries that can be seen from the equations: A 10 percent decline in U.S. real income should also raise *e* by 10 percent, and a balanced 10 percent rise in incomes in both Britain and the United States should leave the exchange rate the same.

A caution must be added to this tidy result, however. You can be misled by memorizing a single "effect of income" on the exchange rate. Income is not an independent force that can simply move by itself. What causes it to change has a great effect on an exchange rate. In the British productivity example above, real income was being raised for a *supply-side* reason—Britain's ability to produce more with its limited resources. It is easy to believe that this would strengthen the pound by using the quantity theory equation (or by thinking about the extra British exports, made possible by its rising productivity, as something other countries would need pounds to pay for). But suppose that Britain's real income is raised by the Keynesian effects of extra government spending or some other aggregate-*demand* shift in Britain. This real-income increase might or might not strengthen the pound. If its main effect is to add inflation in Britain (or to make Britons buy more imports), then there would be reason to believe that the extra aggregate demand would actually lower the value of the pound.

Since the effects of aggregate demand shifts tend to dominate in the short run, while supply shifts dominate in the long run, the quantity theory yields the long-run result, the case in which higher production or income means a higher value of the country's currency.

To conclude this section, let's briefly return to the major-currency experience shown in Figure 18.1. Can we use the monetary approach to understand the long-term trends in some of the exchange rates shown in this figure? Over the whole long sweep of the flexible-exchange-rate era since the early 1970s, we know part of the reason why the Japanese yen rose: Japan's stronger real economic growth (growth in *Y*), combined with the fact that its money supply did not grow much faster that the average, kept inflation down in Japan and raised the international value of the yen. The Swiss franc rose because Switzerland kept tight control over its money supply. The lira sank because Italy's money supply rose faster than average.

EXCHANGE RATE OVERSHOOTING

Our view of exchange rates as being determined in the long run by purchasing power parity, with its emphasis on average rates of inflation over many years, seems quite removed from the view that exchange rates in the short run are buffeted by rapid shifts in investors' portfolio decisions, as we discussed earlier in the chapter. Yet the two must be related. The short run eventually flows into the long run. We have already mentioned one basis for this flow. International investors form their expectations of future exchange rates partly on the belief that exchange rates will move toward their PPP values, because eventually the economic fundamentals of money supply, GDP, and inflation rates become the key determinants of exchange rates.

It is useful to consider this relationship in more depth, to explore the phenomenon of **overshooting.** We will see that international investors can react *rationally* to news by driving the exchange rate *past* what they know to be its ultimate

Extension   Tracking the Exchange Rate Value of a Currency

We are often interested in "the" exchange rate value of a currency like the U.S. dollar, but this measurement is not as simple as it sounds. For each currency there are several hundred exchange rates with other currencies. These "regular" exchange rates are the ones quoted in the foreign exchange markets and are technically termed **nominal bilateral exchange rates.** For many purposes we are interested in only one or a few of these regular market exchange rates with specific other currencies.

For other purposes, including those related to macroeconomic analysis, we are interested in knowing how the exchange rate value of a country's currency is doing overall or on average. Furthermore, we probably do not want a simple average because some foreign countries are more important than others. Rather, we want a weighted average exchange rate value, with the weights showing the importance of the other countries. For instance, an analysis of the effect of exchange rates on the country's exports and imports suggests using weights based on the country's amounts of international trade with the other countries. The weighted-average exchange rate value of a country's currency is called the **nominal effective exchange rate.** We have already used this idea in the introduction to this chapter, when we discussed the average value of the U.S. dollar against the currencies of other industrialized countries. In principle, the units used to measure the nominal effective exchange rate are "average foreign currency units per unit of this country's currency." Because we don't really have a measure of "average foreign currency units," the nominal effective exchange rate is usually measured as an index with some base year equal to 100.

Another issue in exchange rate analysis is the extent to which the actual exchange rate deviates from PPP. We showed this in Figure 18.4 by comparing the actual nominal bilateral exchange rates (for the DM and yen) to the values that the nominal exchange rates would be if they followed relative PPP

(as P/P_f changed over time). The deviation from PPP can also be measured using the *real exchange rate (RER).* By convention, we usually measure the real exchange rate value of the *domestic* currency:

$$RER = \frac{(P/P_0) \bullet (e/e_0)}{P_f/P_{f,0}} \times 100$$

In this formula e is measured as *foreign currency units per unit of domestic currency.* (More generally, the formula shows the real exchange rate value of the currency that is being priced in the nominal exchange rate [e], and the product prices [P/P_0] in the numerator are those of the country whose currency is being priced.)

The subscript 0 indicates the values for P, e, and P_f in the base year. If PPP holds continuously, then the value of the real exchange rate will always be 100. If PPP holds in the long run, then RER will tend to return to (or fluctuate around) the 100 value (assuming that the base year is chosen judiciously). If the nominal exchange rate value of the currency being priced is above its implied PPP value, then the RER is above 100. In this case we sometimes say the currency is *overvalued relative to the PPP standard.* If the nominal exchange rate value is below its implied PPP value, then the RER is below 100. Then we sometimes say the currency is *undervalued relative to PPP.* In addition, increases in the RER values over time are called *real appreciations;* decreases are called *real depreciations.* We can calculate a **real bilateral exchange rate** (relative to one other specific country), and we can calculate a **real effective exchange rate** (as a weighted average relative to a number of other countries).

In summary, we have four ways to track the exchange rate value of a country's currency: nominal bilateral, nominal effective, real bilateral, and real effective. Each has its uses. For instance, in Part IV we will link the real effective exchange rate to the international price competitiveness of a country's products.

Nominal and Real Effective Exchange Rate Values for the U.S. Dollar, January 1975–April 2002 (Monthly)

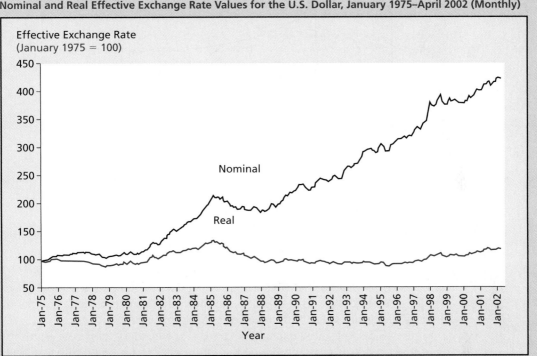

Source: Federal Reserve Board of Governors.

The accompanying figure shows the nominal effective exchange rate value of the U.S. dollar and its real effective exchange rate value, monthly from 1975 through 2002, for a broad sample including 36 other countries (17 industrialized and 19 developing countries). We can see that the dollar has tended to appreciate on average on a nominal basis (especially because the dollar has tended to appreciate nominally against the currencies of many developing countries like Mexico). The real effective exchange rate also fluctuates over time, but it stays closer to the 100 value.

The tendency to return to the 100 value indicates that relative PPP tends to hold in the long run. Still, the divergences can be rather large at times, although the scale used in the graph does not show this so clearly. In particular, the dollar went through a large real appreciation (of nearly 50 percent) during 1981–1985. It then experienced a large real depreciation during the next three years that left the real exchange value of the dollar back close to its 100 value. Starting in 1995 the dollar again experienced a pronounced real appreciation, this time about 33 percent as of 2002.

FIGURE 18.5

A Case of
Exchange Rate
Overshooting

An unexpected 10 percent increase in the domestic money supply causes the spot exchange rate value of the country's currency to decline quickly by more than 10 percent, "overshooting" its eventual long-run value. Then the country's currency appreciates slowly until its exchange-rate value is 10 percent lower than what it was before the unexpected money-supply increase.

long-run equilibrium value. The actual exchange rate then moves slowly back to that long-run rate later on. That is, in the short run the actual exchange rate overshoots its long-run value and then reverts back toward it.

Figure 18.5 shows how exchange rates could overshoot their new equilibrium, even if all investors correctly judge the future equilibrium rate. Suppose that the domestic money supply unexpectedly jumps 10 percent at time t_0 and then resumes the rate of growth investors had already been expecting. Investors understand that this permanent increase of 10 percent more money stock should eventually raise the price of foreign exchange by 10 percent, if they believe that purchasing power parity and the monetary approach hold eventually. In the long run, both the domestic price level (P) and the price of foreign exchange (the exchange rate e) should be 10 percent higher.

Two realistic side effects of the increase in the domestic money supply intervene and make the exchange rate take a strange path to its ultimate 10 percent increase:

- Product prices are somewhat sticky in the short run, so considerable time must pass for domestic inflation to raise domestic prices P by 10 percent (relative to foreign prices P_f).

- Because prices are sticky at first, the increase in the money supply drives down the domestic interest rate, both real and nominal.

With the domestic interest rate (i) lower, the return differential shifts to favor foreign-currency assets. In addition, the expected future spot exchange rate should increase, with investors expecting that eventually the future spot rate will be 10 percent higher (as PPP is established in the long run). Relative to the initial spot exchange rate before the money increase, this implies that the foreign currency is expected to appreciate. Therefore, at the initial spot exchange rate, the overall return differential actually favors foreign-currency assets for two reasons:

- The domestic interest rate has decreased, and

- The foreign currency is expected to appreciate.

The desire by investors to reposition their portfolios toward foreign-currency assets increases the demand for foreign currency and results in a quick appreciation of the foreign currency.

By how much will the foreign currency appreciate immediately? If the domestic interest rate i has just dropped and the foreign interest rate i_f remains unchanged, then the current spot exchange rate must rise immediately by *more than* 10 percent. After this rapid adjustment, the much higher spot rate will then slowly decline back toward its expected future value. That is, the new current spot rate e immediately rises above the new e^{ex} so that the foreign currency is then expected to depreciate slowly back toward the new expected rate. This is necessary to reestablish uncovered interest parity once the current spot rate adjusts. The domestic return is lower because of the lower domestic interest rate i. After the current spot rate overshoots, the overall return on foreign investments then also becomes lower. Even though the foreign interest rate i_f is unchanged, the overall expected foreign return is lower because the foreign currency is expected to depreciate from its now high value. Investors must have the prospect of seeing the foreign currency depreciate later in order to stem their outflow encouraged by higher foreign interest rates.

So, once the news of the extra 10 percent money supply is out, investors will quickly bid up the spot price of foreign exchange by more than 10 percent (Dornbusch, 1976). One test by Jeffrey Frankel (1979) suggested that perhaps the announcement of a surprise 10 percent increase in the domestic money supply would trigger a jump of the spot rate by 12.3 percent, before it begins retreating back to just a 10 percent increase.

Viewed another way, the overshooting is even larger. The exchange rate overshoots by even more in the short run if we compare the actual exchange rate to the path implied by PPP for each time period. Because the domestic price level rises only slowly toward its ultimate 10 percent increase, PPP alone implies that the exchange rate should rise only gradually toward its 10 percent increase. Thus, in the year or so after the money supply increase, little of the large increase in the actual spot exchange rate appears to be consistent with the limited amount of additional domestic inflation that occurs during that first year.

This case shows how exchange rates can be highly variable in the short run (driven by the reactions of international financial investors to policy surprises and other news), while at the same time exchange rates eventually change in the long run in ways consistent with PPP. The case also shows that it can be difficult

Case Study   Forecasting Using a Modified Monetary Model

A simple application of the monetary approach (or any other approach) fails to predict exchange rate changes in the short run. Yet purchasing power parity and the monetary approach do provide insights into movements in exchange rates in the long run. How quickly does the predictive power of the monetary approach assert itself?

To examine this predictive power, we need to develop a modified version of the monetary approach. The modified version admits that the actual exchange rate is often different from the exchange rate predicted by the basic monetary approach. Still, the exchange rate predicted by the basic monetary approach does represent a long-run equilibrium value. When the actual exchange rate is different from this long-run equilibrium value, the actual rate will then tend to move toward it. If the actual rate is below the long-run value, the actual rate is predicted to increase in the future, and, if above, to decrease. This modified version attempts to use the long-run validity of the monetary approach to make predictions for shorter periods. Its basic propositions are essentially those of the overshooting model (although it does not attempt to explain why the overshooting occurs in the first place).

Mark (1995) sets up a test of this modified version of the monetary approach in three stages, following an approach used by Meese and Rogoff (1983) and other similar studies. First, Mark formulates a "structural" model that captures the essence of the modified monetary approach in two equations. The first equation is drawn from the basic monetary approach. The long-run equilibrium exchange rate e^* is determined by relative money supplies and relative real incomes:

$$e^* = (M^s/M_f^s) \bullet (Y_f/Y)$$

The second equation shows that the exchange rate predicted for a time in the future (e^p) is based on both the actual current exchange rate e and how the long-run equilibrium value of the exchange rate e^* compares to the current rate:

$$e^p = e \times (e^*/e)^b$$

The coefficient b shows adjustment—how much of the deviation between the long-run equilibrium and the actual exchange rate is predicted to be eliminated over the time period of the prediction. A larger b indicates that more of the deviation will disappear. Consider, for instance, benchmark values for b. If b is zero, then none of the deviation is predicted to disappear because e^* is irrelevant. (Anything raised to the zero power is simply 1.) If b is 1, then all of the deviation is predicted to disappear, and the actual future exchange rate is predicted to equal its long-run equilibrium value.

The second step toward a direct test is to fit this model statistically to some data. Mark substitutes the first equation into the second, and then uses a logarithmic form of the combined equation. He fits this equation to quarterly data beginning with the second quarter of 1973, for exchange rates between the U.S. dollar and, separately, the Canadian dollar, German mark (DM), yen, and Swiss franc. The initial statistical effort is to estimate, using regression, the values for the adjustment coefficients b, using actual future spot exchange values in place of the predicted values (e^p). Mark's estimates of b are shown in the accompanying table. The estimates of b for the different exchange rates and time horizons into the future are all positive and of reasonable value, although the estimates for the Canadian dollar exchange rate are somewhat smaller than those for the other three exchange rates. The estimates of b that are nearly 1 for the three-year horizon for the other three exchange rates indicate that close to all of the deviation of the current spot rate from its long-run equilibrium value tends to be eliminated over the next three years.

Now comes the tough part. The third step taken by Mark is one that any predictive model should have to pass: How well does it predict beyond the time for which is has been fitted statistically? Does it predict better than some crude and simpler forecasting device? Mark lets the model show its stuff by forecasting exchange rates for the period 1981–1991. The results (the second column of numbers in the table) show a statistical measure of the average percent error in the forecasts.

Forecast Errors, Modified Monetary Approach, and a "Naive" Approach, 1981–1991

Predicted Exchange Rate	Predicted How Far Ahead?	Estimate of the b Coefficient	Forecast Errors Made By	
			Modified Monetary Approach	Just the Current Spot Rate
U.S.$/Canadian $	1 quarter	0.040	2.1%	2.1%
	1 year	0.155	5.0	4.5
	3 years	0.438	15.7	10.9
U.S.$/DM	1 quarter	0.035	6.7	6.6
	1 year	0.205	15.3	14.8
	3 years	0.966	23.4	29.4
U.S.$/yen	1 quarter	0.047	6.8	6.8
	1 year	0.263	13.9	15.0
	3 years	0.945	24.0	33.8
U.S.$/Swiss franc	1 quarter	0.074	7.0	7.0
	1 year	0.285	15.7	16.0
	3 years	0.837	21.6	29.3

The forecast errors are approximate percent root-mean-square errors.

Source: Mark (1995).

The structural model based on the modified monetary approach has the virtue of making explicit what forces economists think the exchange rate depends on. Yet its predictive power is certainly far from perfect, given the substantial size of the percent forecast errors indicated by the values in this middle column of numbers.

Are these errors large or small? It depends on what you might compare them to. They are large errors relative to perfect foresight. If you made the Faustian bargain to sell your soul for a lifetime of perfect foreign exchange foresight, and managed to keep your information secret from others, you could make huge profits at the expense of other speculators who lacked perfect foresight. Clearly, there is financial value in information that the market does not now have. But perfect foresight is an unrealistic norm.

Another possible norm is a naive model predicting that the future spot exchange rate will simply equal the current spot exchange rate—the random walk. The percent errors that result from using this naive model (the current spot rate) to forecast the future spot rate are shown in the final column of the table.

When we compare the forecast errors from the modified monetary model with the forecast errors from the naive random walk model, we see several patterns. First, the errors in forecasting the Canadian dollar exchange rate using the modified monetary approach are equal to or larger than the errors using the naive model, for all forecast horizons. The structural model provides no ability to forecast this exchange rate. Second, for the other three exchange rates, the errors in forecasting spot exchange rates one quarter ahead using the modified monetary approach are about as large as those using the naive model. The structural model also provides no ability to forecast these exchange rates at short forecast horizons like one quarter into the future. Third, the structural model performs better for longer forecast horizons. The errors using the modified monetary approach are a little smaller than those using the naive model for forecasts of the Japanese yen and Swiss franc exchange rates one year into the future, and the errors are substantially smaller for forecasts of the mark, yen, and Swiss franc exchange rates three years into the future.

to identify clearly cases of "destabilizing speculation." Exchange rate movements that appear to be extreme and inconsistent with the economic fundamentals in the short run can be part of a process that is understandable, reasonable, and stabilizing in the long run.

HOW WELL CAN WE PREDICT EXCHANGE RATES?

We would like to be able to forecast exchange rates. One purpose of having theories is to predict tendencies in the real world. International experience since the switch to floating exchange rates in the early 1970s provides a rich data set against which to test the value of our theories.

How accurate would we want our theories to be in predicting changes in exchange rates? Clearly we should not expect perfect forecasts. But presumably we would expect a useful economic model at least to be able to outpredict a naive model that says the future exchange rate is predicted simply to be the same as the current spot exchange rate. This is a minimal standard. The naive model is equivalent to saying that the spot exchange rate follows a *random walk,* so we have no ability to predict whether it will go up or down. The predictions of any useful economic structural model presumably ought to be able to do better than this naive model.

Somewhat to our consternation, there is now general agreement that economic structural models are of little use in predicting exchange rates in the short run (for future periods up to about one year). Frankel and Rose (1995) survey many studies that use various models based on many different economic fundamentals, including money supplies and real incomes, interest rates, expected inflation rates, and the trade and current account balances. They conclude that structural economic models cannot reliably outpredict the naive alternative of a random walk for short forecast horizons.[5] At the same time, the economic fundamentals stressed by purchasing power parity and the monetary approach are of noticeable value in forecasting exchange rates for a year or more in the future. The box "Forecasting Using a Modified Monetary Model" presents an example of one recent study examining our ability to predict exchange rates.

Why is it so difficult to predict exchange rates in the short run using economic models? There appear to be two parts to the answer.

First, and probably more important, the exchange rate reacts strongly and immediately to new information. Exactly because news is unexpected, it cannot be incorporated into any predictions. The reaction to such news often involves

---

[5] Some recent studies (e.g., Wu and Chen, 2001; Mark and Sul, 2001; MacDonald, 1999; MacDonald and Marsh, 1997; MacDonald and Taylor, 1994) suggest that it may be possible to beat the random walk with a structural model for forecasts of as little as three months in the future. It is not yet clear how reliable these approaches are. In any case, the studies generally do not beat the random walk for forecast periods of less than three months.

large movements in the exchange rate. Actual exchange rate movements appear to overshoot movements in smoothly adjusting long-run equilibrium rates like those from PPP or the monetary approach. Studies have documented the immediate effects of a variety of different types of news on exchange rates, although some of these types seem to have power during some time periods but not others. For instance, the U.S. dollar tends to appreciate when there are unexpected contractions in the U.S. money supply, unexpected increases in U.S. interest rates (relative to foreign interest rates), unexpected growth in U.S. real GDP, unexpected decreases in the U.S. inflation rate, unexpected improvements in the U.S. trade or current account balance, and unexpected increases in the U.S. government budget deficit. In addition, casual observation indicates that the exchange rate reacts to new information concerning both actual events and changes in probabilities about what will happen, not only for economic variables such as those just mentioned but also for political variables such as elections, appointments, international tensions, and wars.

The second reason is that exchange rate expectations can be formed without much reference to economic fundamentals. Surveys indicate that many foreign exchange market participants just extrapolate the latest trends up to one month ahead. Because the actions taken by investors can make their expectations self-confirming, recent trends in exchange rates can be reinforced and persist for a while. If the resulting movement in the exchange rate appears to be simply inconsistent with any form of economic fundamentals, it is called a *bubble* (or *speculative bubble*). While it is difficult to identify such bubbles with complete certainty, the final stage of the appreciation of the dollar against many other currencies in 1984 and early 1985 appears to have been such a bubble. The strong possibility that bubbles occur in the foreign exchange market from time to time suggests that there is some economic inefficiency in foreign exchange markets. You may recall that we reached a similar conclusion at the end of Chapter 17, when we discussed why estimated deviations from uncovered interest parity appear to be too large to be explained completely by risk premiums.

Summary

This chapter has surveyed what we know (and don't know) about the determinants of exchange rates. The **asset market approach** explains exchange rates as being part of the equilibrium for the markets for financial assets denominated in different currencies. We gain insights into short-run movements in exchange rates by using a variant of the asset market approach that focuses on portfolio repositioning by international investors, especially decisions regarding investments in bonds denominated in different currencies. If uncovered interest parity tends to hold (at least approximately), then any changes in domestic or foreign interest rates (i and i_f) or the expected future spot exchange rate (e^{ex}) create an uncovered interest differential and also create pressures for a return toward uncovered interest parity. Focusing on the pressures on the current spot exchange rate e, the price of foreign currency, it tends to be raised by:

- An increase in the interest rate differential $(i_f - i)$.
- An increase in the expected future spot exchange rate (e^{ex}).

Changes in the expected future spot exchange rate tend to be self-confirming expectations in that the current spot rate tends to change quickly in the direction expected. Furthermore, there appear to be several types of influences on the expected future spot exchange rate, including recent trends in the actual spot rate, beliefs that the exchange rate eventually moves toward its PPP value, and unexpected new information ("news") about economic performance or about political situations. The rapid large reaction of the current exchange rate to such news as a change in monetary policy is called **overshooting.** The current exchange rate changes by much more than would be consistent with long-run equilibrium.

Our understanding of the long-run trends in exchange rates begins with **purchasing power parity (PPP). Absolute PPP** posits that international competition tends to equalize the home and foreign prices of traded goods and services so that $P = e \cdot P_f$ overall, where the Ps are price levels in the countries and e is the exchange rate price of foreign currency. **Relative PPP** focuses on the product-price inflation rates in two countries and the change in the exchange rate that offsets the inflation-rate difference. Relative PPP works tolerably well for longer periods of time, say, a decade or more. Over the long run, a country with a relatively high inflation rate tends to have a depreciating currency, and a country with a relatively low inflation rate tends to have an appreciating currency.

The **monetary approach** seeks to explain exchange rates by focusing on demands and supplies for national moneys since the foreign exchange market is where one money is traded for another. The transactions demand for a national money can be expressed as $k \cdot P \cdot Y$, a behavioral coefficient (k) times the price level (P) times the level of real domestic product (Y). The equilibrium $M^s = k \cdot P \cdot Y$ matches this demand against the national money supply (M^s), which is controlled by the central bank's monetary policy. A similar equilibrium holds in any foreign country: $M_f^s = k_f \cdot P_f \cdot Y_f$.

Combining the basic monetary equilibriums with PPP yields an equation for predicting the exchange rate value of the currency of a foreign country; $e = (M^s/M_f^s) \cdot (Y_f/Y) \cdot (k_f/k)$. Ignoring any changes in the ks, we can use this equation to predict that the price of foreign currency (e) is raised by:

- An increase in the relative size of the money supply (M^s/M_f^s).
- An increase in the relative size of foreign production (Y_f/Y).

Furthermore, the elasticities of the impact of (M^s/M_f^s) and (Y_f/Y) on e should approximately equal 1.

We would like to be able to use economic models to predict exchange rates in the future, but our ability to do so is limited. Economic models provide almost no ability to predict exchange rates for short periods into the future, say, about a year or less. This inability is based largely on the importance of unpredictable news as an influence on short-term exchange rate movements, but it may also reflect the role of expectations that extrapolate recent trends in the exchange rate, leading to **bandwagon** effects and (speculative) **bubbles.** We have some success in predicting exchange rate movements in the long run. Over long periods, exchange rates tend to move toward values consistent with such economic fundamentals as relative money supplies and real incomes (the monetary approach) or, similarly, relative price levels (PPP).

We also presented four ways of measuring the exchange-rate value of a currency. The **nominal bilateral exchange rate** is the regular market rate between two currencies. The **nominal effective exchange rate** is a weighted average of the market rates across a number of foreign currencies. The **real bilateral exchange rate** incorporates both the market exchange rate and the product price levels for two countries. The **real effective exchange rate** is a weighted average of real bilateral exchange rates across a number of foreign countries. A *real exchange rate* can be used as an indicator of deviations from PPP or as an indicator of a country's international price competitiveness.

Suggested Reading

Surveys of research on the determinants of exchange rates, including work based on the asset market approach and the monetary approach, are found in Frankel and Rose (1995) and MacDonald and Taylor (1992). Lyons (2001) provides an overview of a different approach to understanding exchange rates, one that focuses on actual trading activity.

Purchasing power parity (PPP) has been subjected to a wide range of tests. Froot and Rogoff (1995) survey many of these studies. Hakkio (1992) provides an accessible summary of the theory of PPP and its empirical validity. The survey by Sarno and Taylor (2002) is more technical.

Questions and Problems

◆ 1. "Short-run pressures on market exchange rates result mainly from gradual changes in flows of international trade in goods and services." Do you agree or disagree? Why?

2. The following rates currently exist:

   Spot exchange rate: $1.000/euro.
   Annual interest rate on 180-day euro-denominated bonds: 3%.
   Annual interest rate on 180-day U.S. dollar-denominated bonds: 4%.
   Investors currently expect the spot exchange rate to be about $1.005/euro in 180 days.

   a. Show that uncovered interest parity holds (approximately) at these rates.

   b. What is likely to be the effect on the spot exchange rate if the interest rate on 180-day dollar-denominated bonds declines to 3 percent? If the euro interest rate and the expected future spot rate are unchanged, and if uncovered interest parity is reestablished, what will the new current spot exchange rate be? Has the dollar appreciated or depreciated?

◆ 3. The current rates are

Spot exchange rate: $2.00/£.
Annual interest rate on 60-day U.S.-dollar-denominated bonds: 5%
Annual interest rate on 60-day pound-denominated bonds: 11%
Investors currently expect the spot exchange rate to be $1.98/pound in 60 days.

a. Show that uncovered interest parity holds (approximately) at these rates.
b. What is likely to be the effect on the spot exchange rate if the interest rate on 60-day pound-denominated bonds declines to 8 percent? If the dollar interest rate and the expected future spot rate are unchanged, and if uncovered interest parity is reestablished, what will the new current spot exchange rate be? Has the pound appreciated or depreciated?

4. You observe the following current rates:

Spot exchange rate: $0.01/yen.
Annual interest rate on 90-day U.S.-dollar-denominated bonds: 4%.
Annual interest rate on 90-day yen-denominated bonds: 4%.

a. If uncovered interest parity holds, what spot exchange rate do investors expect to exist in 90 days?
b. A close U.S. presidential election has just been decided. The candidate whom international investors view as the stronger and more probusiness person won. Because of this, investors expect the exchange rate to be $0.0095/yen in 90 days. What will happen in the foreign exchange market?

◆ 5. As a foreign exchange trader, how would you react to each of the following news items as it flashes on your computer screen?

a. Mexico's oil reserves prove to be much smaller than touted earlier.
b. The Social Credit Party wins the national elections in Canada and promises generous expansion of the supply of money and credit.
c. In a surprise vote the Swiss government passes a law that will result in a large increase in the taxation of interest payments from Switzerland to foreigners.

6. Will the law of one price apply better to gold or to Big Macs? Why?

◆ 7. For your next foreign vacation, would it be better to go to a country whose currency is overvalued relative to PPP or one whose currency is undervalued relative to PPP (other attractions being equal)?

8. According to PPP and the monetary approach, why did the nominal exchange rate value of the DM (relative to the dollar) rise between the early 1970s and the late 1990s? Why did the nominal exchange rate value of the pound decline?

◆ 9. Mexico currently has an annual domestic inflation rate of about 20 percent. Suppose that Mexico wants to stabilize the floating market exchange rate value of its currency (dollars/peso) in a world in which dollar prices are generally rising at 3 percent per year. What must the rate of inflation of domestic peso prices come down to? If the quantity theory of money holds with a constant k, and if Mexican real output is growing 6 per year, what rate of money growth should the Mexican government try to achieve?

10. To aid in its efforts to get reelected, the current government of a country decides to increase the growth rate of the domestic money supply by two percentage points. The increased growth rate becomes "permanent" because once started it is difficult to reverse.

    a. According to the monetary approach, how will this affect the long-run trend for the exchange rate value of the country's currency?

    b. Explain why the nominal exchange rate trend is affected, referring to PPP.

♦ 11. In 1975, the price level for the United States was 100, the price level for Pugelovia was also 100, and in the foreign exchange market one Pugelovian pnut was equal to $1. In 2002, the U.S. price level had risen to 260, and the Pugelovian price level had risen to 390.

    a. According to PPP, what should the dollar-pnut exchange rate be in 2002?

    b. If the *actual* dollar-pnut exchange rate is $1/pnut in 2002, is the pnut overvalued or undervalued relative to PPP?

12. Here is further information on the U.S. and Pugelovian economies.

	1975			2002		
	M^s	Y	P	M^s	Y	P
United States	20,000	800	100	65,000	1,000	260
Pugelovia	10,000	200	100	58,500	300	390

    a. What is the value of k for the United States in 1975? For Pugelovia?

    b. Show that the change in price level from 1975 to 2002 for each country is consistent with the quantity theory of money with a constant k.

♦ 13. Consider our example of overshooting shown in Figure 18.5, in which the domestic money supply increased by 10 percent. Assume that the path of slow adjustment of prices is that the price level rises by about 2 percent per year for five years. What would the path of the nominal exchange rate be if PPP held for each year? Given the actual path for the exchange rate shown in Figure 18.5, does PPP hold in the short run? Does it hold in the long run?

14. A country has had a steady value for its floating exchange rate (stated inversely as the domestic currency price of foreign currency) for a number of years. The country now tightens up on (reduces) its money supply dramatically. The country's product price level is not immediately affected, but the price level gradually becomes lower (relative to what it otherwise would have been) during the next several years.

    a. Why might the market exchange rate change a lot as this monetary tightening is announced and implemented?

    b. What is the path of the market exchange rate likely to be over the next several years? Why?

Chapter Nineteen

Government Policies toward the Foreign Exchange Market

Chapters 15 through 18 presented the basic analysis of how currencies are exchanged and what seems to determine the exchange rate if the determination is left mainly to market forces. For better or worse, many governments do not usually just let the private market set the exchange rate. Rather, governments have policies toward the foreign exchange market in the form of policies toward exchange rates themselves, policies toward who is allowed to use the market, or both.

Our previous discussion suggests one reason why governments adopt such policies. Exchange rates, if left to private market forces, sometimes fluctuate a lot. They are prone to overshoot, and may occasionally also be influenced by bandwagons among investors or speculators. Exchange rates are very important prices—they can affect the entire range of a country's international transactions. One objective for government policy then can be to reduce variability in exchange rates.

Governments often have other reasons for adopting policies toward the foreign exchange market. A government may want to keep the exchange rate value of its currency low, preventing appreciation or promoting depreciation. This benefits certain activities or groups in the country, including the country's exporters and import-competing businesses. Or, in a different setting, a government may want to do the opposite: keep the exchange rate value of its currency high, preventing depreciation or promoting appreciation. This can benefit other activities or groups—for instance, buyers of imports. It can also be used as part of an effort to reduce domestic inflation by using the competitive pressure of low import prices. In addition, the government policy may reflect other, relatively noneconomic goals. The government may believe that it is defending national honor or encouraging national pride by maintaining a steady exchange rate or a strong currency internationally. Devaluation or depreciation may be feared as a confirmation of the ineptitude of the government in selecting policies.

This chapter has three objectives. First, it provides a framework for understanding the range of possible government policies toward the foreign exchange market. Second, it begins the analysis of these policies, focusing on the economics of official buying and selling of currencies in the market and the economics of restrictions on who can use the market. Third, it explores some lessons of history by surveying exchange rate systems that have existed during the past 130 years, concluding with a description of the current system. In Chapter 20 we continue to explore history by discussing the causes of recent financial crises and proposals for how make them less frequent. Part IV of this book then examines in depth the broader macroeconomic implications of the foreign exchange policies chosen by governments.

TWO ASPECTS: RATE FLEXIBILITY AND RESTRICTIONS ON USE

Government policies toward the foreign exchange market are of two types:

- Those policies that are directly applied to the exchange rate itself.

- Those policies that directly state who may use the foreign exchange market and for what purposes.

The first type of policies acts directly on price (the exchange rate), while the second type acts directly on quantity (by limiting some people's ability to use the foreign exchange market). We saw this distinction before when we examined tariffs and quotas as two forms of government policies toward imports. As in the case of imports, we expect that any one policy has impacts on both price and quantity in the market, even though the policy directly acts on only one of these. A policy toward the exchange rate affects the quantity of foreign exchange traded in the market (the turnover), and a policy restricting use has an impact on the exchange rate.

Government policies toward the exchange rate itself are usually categorized according to the flexibility of the exchange rate—the amount of movement in the exchange rate that the policy permits. In the simplest terms, governments choose between floating and fixed exchange rates, although, as we will see, the reality is often richer than this.

Government policies can also restrict access to the foreign exchange market. One type of policy is no restriction—everyone is free to use the foreign exchange market. The country's currency is *fully convertible* into foreign currency for all uses, for both trade in goods and services (current account transactions) and international financial activities (capital account transactions). The other type of policy is **exchange control**—the country's government places some restrictions on use of the foreign exchange market. In the most extreme form of exchange control, all foreign exchange proceeds (for instance, proceeds resulting from foreign payments for the country's exports) must be turned over to the country's monetary authority. Anyone wanting to obtain foreign exchange must request it from the authority, which then determines whether to approve the request. Less extreme forms of control limit access for some types of transactions, while permitting free access for other types of transactions. For instance, the government may:

- Permit use of the foreign exchange market for all payments for exports and imports of goods and services (that is, the currency is *convertible for current account transactions*).

- Impose some form of **capital controls,** by placing limits or requiring approvals for payments related to some (or all) international financial activities.

Another example of a less extreme form of restriction is limits on the use of the foreign exchange market for transactions related to broad types of imports, such as consumer luxury goods.

FLOATING EXCHANGE RATE

If government policy lets the market determine the exchange rate, the rate is free to go wherever the market equilibrium is at that time. This policy choice results in a **clean float.** Market supply and demand are solely private (nonofficial) activities. As private market supply and demand shift around, the value of the floating exchange rate changes. A clean float is the polar case of complete flexibility.

Even when the country's exchange rate policy is to permit flexibility by floating the rate, the government often is not willing to simply let the rate go wherever private supply and demand drive it. Rather, the government often tries to have a direct impact on the rate through **official intervention.** That is, the monetary authority enters the foreign exchange market to buy or sell foreign currency (in exchange for domestic currency). Through this intervention, the government hopes to alter the configuration of supply and demand, and thus influence the equilibrium value of the exchange rate—the rate that clears the market. This policy approach—an exchange rate that is generally floating (or flexible) but with the government willing to intervene to attempt to influence the market rate—is called a **managed float** (if you are an optimist about the capabilities of the government) or a **dirty float** (if you are a pessimist). Often the government is attempting to lean against the wind to moderate movements in the floating rate. For instance, if the exchange rate value of the country's currency is rising (and that of foreign currency falling), then the authorities intervene to buy foreign currency (and sell domestic currency). They hope that the intervention and the extra supply of domestic currency can slow or stop their own currency's rise in value (or, correspondingly, that the extra demand for foreign currency can slow or stop its decline). The actual effectiveness of intervention is controversial, and we will examine this issue further in Chapter 23. Nonetheless, most governments that choose a floating exchange rate policy also do manage, or "dirty," the float to some extent.

FIXED EXCHANGE RATE

If the government chooses the policy of a fixed exchange rate, then the government sets the exchange rate that it wants. Often, some flexibility is permitted within a range, called a *band,* around this chosen fixed rate, called the *par value* or *central value.* Nonetheless, the flexibility is generally more limited than would occur if the government instead permitted a floating rate.

In implementing its choice of a fixed exchange rate, the government actually faces three specific major questions: To what does the government fix the value of its currency? When or how often does the country change the value of its fixed rate? How does the government defend the fixed value against any market pressures pushing toward some other exchange rate value?

What to Fix To?

A fixed rate means that the value of the country's currency is fixed to something else, but what is this something else? As we will see later in this chapter, the answer about a century ago was to fix to gold. If several countries all fix the values of their currencies to specific amounts of gold, then arbitrage ensures that the exchange rates among the currencies will also be fixed at the rates implied by their gold values. That is, currencies tied to the same thing (such as gold) are all tied to each other. In principle, any other commodity or group of commodities could serve the same purpose—the gold standard is one example of the broader idea of a commodity standard.

The country could choose to fix the value of its currency to some other currency, rather than to a commodity. Since the end of World War II many countries have often fixed the value of their currency to the U.S. dollar. Any other single currency can serve the same purpose.

Or the country could choose to fix the value of its currency not to one other currency but to the average value of a number of other currencies. Why would a country choose to fix to such a "basket" of other currencies? The logic is the same as that of diversifying a portfolio (or not putting all your eggs in one basket). If the country fixes to one single other currency, then it will ride along with this other currency if the other currency's value experiences extreme changes against any third-country currencies. Fixing to a basket of currencies moderates this effect, in that the average value is kept steady.

What basket of currencies might the country fix to? There is one ready-made basket—the **special drawing right (SDR)**, a basket of the four major currencies in the world.[1] Or a country can create its own basket. For instance, the country might be interested in maintaining a steady exchange rate value to facilitate its international trade activities. In this case the basket would include the curren-

---

[1] As we mentioned in Chapter 15, the SDR is a reserve asset created by the International Monetary Fund (IMF). The IMF periodically adjusts the specific composition of the SDR. As of 2002, one SDR equaled the collection of U.S. $0.577 plus 0.426 euros plus 21 Japanese yen plus British £0.0984. Market exchange rates can then be used to compute the SDR's value in terms of any specific single currency.

cies of its major trading partners, and the importance of these other countries in the basket would be based on their importance in the country's trade. In designing its basket in this way, the country is using the same logic as that used to calculate an effective exchange rate.

No country today fixes its currency to gold or any other commodity. Although we examine the gold standard later in this chapter, the rest of our fixed-rate discussion presumes that a country fixes the exchange rate value of its currency to one or more other currencies.

When to Change the Fixed Rate?

Once the country has chosen what to fix to, it establishes a specific value for its currency in terms of the item chosen. As the government attempts to maintain this fixed value over time, it faces the question of when to change the fixed rate.

The government may insist that it will never change the fixed rate. A permanently fixed exchange rate is useful as a polar case—the opposite of a clean float. However, it is not clear that the government's commitment is credible. The commitment is not truly binding—the government has the capability to alter its policy. Most probably, nothing is fixed forever. On this basis, we often use the term **pegged exchange rate** in place of *fixed exchange rate,* in recognition that the government has some ability to move the peg value.

Although the fixed rate may not be fixed forever, the government may try to keep the value fixed for long periods of time. Nonetheless, in the face of a substantial or "fundamental" disequilibrium in the country's international position, the government may change the pegged-rate value. This approach is called an **adjustable peg.**

In other situations, the government may recognize that a specific pegged-rate value cannot be maintained for long. For instance, if the country has a relatively high inflation rate, then an attempt to maintain a pegged rate against the currency of a low-inflation country will quickly lead to large violations of purchasing power parity and declining international price competitiveness. Nonetheless, the country may prefer to maintain some form of pegged exchange rate, perhaps because it believes that a floating exchange rate would be too volatile. The solution chosen by some countries in this position is a **crawling peg.** With a crawling peg the peg value is changed often (for instance, monthly) according to a set of indicators or according to the judgment of the government monetary authority. If indicators are used, the discussion of Chapter 18 suggests one reasonable choice—the difference between the country's inflation rate and the inflation rate of the country whose currency it pegs to. If the inflation difference is used, the nominal pegged rate will track purchasing power parity over time, and this bilateral real exchange rate will be stabilized. Other indicators that might be used include the country's holdings of official international reserve assets (indicating pressure from the country's balance of payments), the growth of the country's money supply (indicating underlying inflation pressure), or the current actual market exchange rate relative to the central par value of the pegged rate (indicating, within the allowable band, the foreign exchange market pressure away from the par value).

In fact, the choice of the width of the allowable band is closely related to the issue of when to change the pegged rate. If the band is larger, then the actual exchange rate has more room to move around the par value. Market pressures can result in wider variations in the actual exchange rate, without necessarily forcing the government to face the decision of whether to change the pegged-rate value.

At this point, it is useful to summarize the main points of our survey. For government policies toward the exchange rate itself, we often frame the decision facing the government as choosing between a floating or a fixed exchange rate. A floating exchange rate seems to permit substantial flexibility or variability in the actual rate, while a fixed rate seems to impose strict limits on this variability or flexibility. While this proposition is true to a large extent, the reality is also more complicated. In a clean float, the rate is purely market-driven, but in a managed float the government takes actions such as exchange market intervention to influence the floating rate. In a heavily managed float, the exchange rate may show little flexibility—it is almost pegged, even though this is not the way that the government describes its choice. Even with a fixed rate, much variability or flexibility may still exist for several reasons. The band around the central pegged rate can be wide, permitting substantial variability within the band. The exchange rate value of the country's currency can also vary substantially with respect to other currencies that are not involved in the same type of peg. Furthermore, the government can change the pegged rate, sometimes frequently, as in a crawling peg. The *polar cases of a clean float and a permanently fixed exchange rate* are useful in order to contrast the implications of a country's choice of exchange rate policy. At the same time we must remember that in reality there is more of a *continuum in which the country permits more or less flexibility in the movements of the exchange rate* value of the country's currency. A full analysis of a specific country requires examination of the true nature of government policy toward the exchange rate.

Defending a Fixed Exchange Rate

The third major question confronting a country that has chosen a fixed exchange rate is how to defend its fixed rate. The pressures of private (or nonofficial) supply and demand in the foreign exchange market may sometimes drive the exchange rate toward values that are not within the permissible band around the par value. The government then must use some means to defend the pegged rate—to keep the actual exchange rate within the band.

How does the government defend the fixed rate that it has announced? There are four basic ways:

1. The government can intervene in the foreign exchange market, buying or selling foreign currency in exchange for domestic currency, to maintain or influence the actual exchange rate in the market.

2. The government can impose some form of exchange control to maintain or influence the exchange rate by constricting demand or supply in the market. (A closely related approach would use trade controls such as tariffs or quotas to attempt to accomplish this result.)

3. The government can alter domestic interest rates to influence short-term capital flows, thus maintaining or influencing the exchange rate by shifting the supply–demand position in the market.

4. The government can adjust the country's whole macroeconomic position to make it "fit" the chosen fixed exchange rate value. Macroeconomic adjustments driven by changes in fiscal or monetary policy can alter the supply–demand position in the foreign exchange market, for instance, by adjusting export capabilities, the demand for imports, or international capital flows.

We should also remember that there is a fifth option for the country—to surrender rather than defend:

5. The country can alter its fixed rate (devaluing or revaluing its currency) or switch to a floating exchange rate (in which case the currency will immediately depreciate or appreciate).

The four ways of defending a fixed rate are not mutually exclusive—a country can use several methods at the same time. Indeed, they are often closely interrelated. For instance, changing interest rates to influence short-term capital flows relates to overall macroeconomic management. In the next two sections of this chapter, we turn to a closer examination of the first two options: intervention and exchange control. Part IV is devoted to examining the broader implications of the country's foreign exchange policies for the whole national economy.

DEFENSE THROUGH OFFICIAL INTERVENTION

In defending a fixed exchange rate, the country's first line of defense is usually official intervention in the foreign exchange market. This is the defense that we introduced in Chapter 16, and we can now examine it in more depth. For much of our discussion in the first parts of this section, we will examine a country that has chosen to peg its currency to the U.S. dollar. We state the spot exchange rate value *e* as units of this country's currency per dollar. (The exchange rate stated this way is directly pricing the U.S. dollar.)

Defending against Depreciation

Consider first the case in which the pressure from private (or nonofficial) supply and demand in the foreign exchange market is attempting to drive the exchange rate above the top of its allowable band—the country's currency is tending toward depreciation. For instance, say that this is a Latin American country that is attempting to maintain a fixed rate of 25 pesos per dollar, with a band of plus or minus 4 percent (plus or minus one peso). As shown in Figure 19.1, nonofficial supply and demand are attempting to push the exchange rate to 28 pesos per dollar, the intersection where the market would clear on its own. If the country's monetary authority is committed to defending the fixed rate within its band using intervention, then the authority must enter into the foreign exchange market in its

FIGURE 19.1

Intervention
to Defend a
Fixed Rate:
Preventing
Depreciation of
the Country's
Currency

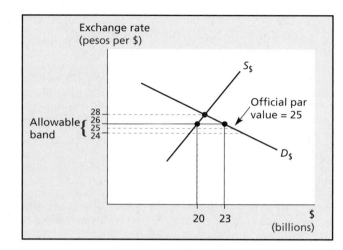

To prevent the market exchange rate from piercing through the top of the allowable band, the country's central bank must sell 3 billion dollars at the exchange rate of 26 pesos per dollar.

official role. It must sell dollars and buy domestic currency. To keep the currency in the allowable band, it must sell 3 billion dollars into the foreign exchange market at the rate of 26 pesos per dollar (the top of the band), so it is buying 78 billion pesos from the foreign exchange market. We can also see how this intervention is reflected in the country's balance of payments. The relatively strong demand for dollars is generally related to strong demand by the country for purchases of foreign goods, services, and (nonofficial) financial assets (relative to the demand by foreigners for this country's goods, services, and nonofficial financial assets). This results in an official settlements balance deficit if the country's monetary authority intervenes to defend the fixed rate. The intervention provides the foreign exchange for the country to buy more (in total value) from foreigners than it is selling to them (for goods, services, and nonofficial financial assets). *Through intervention the monetary authority is financing the country's deficit in its official settlement balance.*

Where does the country's monetary authority get the dollars to sell into the foreign exchange market? This Latin American country cannot just create U.S. dollars. Rather, the authority either *uses its own official international reserve assets* (or some other similar government assets) to obtain dollars from some foreign source, most likely the U.S. monetary authority (the Federal Reserve), or it *borrows the dollars.* Let's examine each of these.

As we noted in Chapter 15, there are four major components to a country's official reserve assets: the country's holdings of foreign exchange assets denominated in the major currencies of the world, the country's reserve position with the International Monetary Fund, the country's holdings of special drawing rights, and the country's holdings of gold. To indicate the magnitudes, Figure 19.2 provides information on world holdings of official reserve assets.

FIGURE 19.2
Official
Holdings of
Reserve Assets,
End of Year,
1970–2000
(Billions of
U.S. Dollars)

	1970	1980	1990	2000
Foreign exchange assets	45	381	806	1,941
U.S. dollar	34	263	463	1,324
German mark	1	59	150	—
Other currencies now in the euro	1	12	28	—
Euro	—	—	—	247
Japanese yen	0	17	71	103
British pound	6	12	27	76
Other and unspecified currencies	3	18	66	192
Special drawing rights	3	15	28	24
Reserve position in the IMF	8	22	32	63
Gold	40	573	345	264
(millions of ounces)	(1,057)	(953)	(940)	(951)
Total reserve assets	96	991	1,211	2,292

Most official reserves are held as foreign exchange assets. Most of these are in dollar-denominated assets. The two reserve assets provided by the IMF are relatively minor. The value of official holdings of gold has fluctuated as the dollar price of gold has varied, while the amount (ounces) of gold held as official reserves has changed little since 1980.

The dollar value of gold reserves is shown at the market price. For 1980 and 1990, the European currency unit is not treated as a separate reserve asset. At the beginning of 1999, as the euro came into existence, all official reserves previously denominated in German marks and the other member currencies became euro-denominated official reserve assets.

Source: International Monetary Fund, *Annual Report,* various years.

Most official reserve assets are in the form of foreign exchange assets, typically invested in safe, highly liquid interest-earning debt securities such as government bonds. Our Latin American country can use this type of asset to obtain dollars by selling it. If the asset is denominated in dollars (as most are, according to Figure 19.2), it obtains dollars that can then be used in its intervention. If the asset is denominated in some other major currency (such as euros or yen), the currency must be exchanged for dollars, and this can easily be accomplished if the other currency is readily traded.

If our country has a reserve position in the IMF, then it can obtain dollars from the IMF on request. If the country is holding SDRs, then it can use these SDRs to obtain dollars from the U.S. monetary authority or from the IMF. The SDRs actually act as a line of credit permitting the country to borrow dollars, but SDRs are counted as reserves because the country can automatically draw on this line. If the country has gold, then it can sell gold to obtain dollars, but officials today almost never use gold sales to obtain foreign currency.

In addition to using its reserve assets to obtain dollars, the country's monetary authority can borrow dollars. It may be able to borrow dollars (or other major currencies) from the monetary authorities of other countries. Some countries maintain arrangements called *swap lines* with each other to facilitate this type of official borrowing. The monetary authority also may be able to borrow dollars from private—that is, nonofficial—sources. Sometimes these borrowings are disguised to keep them secret from other participants in the foreign exchange market.

These borrowings usually are considered to be different from normal transactions in official international reserves, because the country may not have "automatic" access to dollars through borrowings—the lender must be willing to make the loan. There is, however, a special case, the case of a country (like the United States) whose currency is readily held by the monetary authorities of other countries. If the country's currency is a **reserve currency,** then the country can effectively borrow through official channels by issuing assets that will be held as reserves by the central banks of other countries. Specifically, this has allowed the United States to run what French economist Jacques Rueff called *deficits without tears.* The United States, especially in the 1950s and 1960s, was given extraordinary leeway to finance its deficits. Needless to say, this option is probably not available to the Latin American country that was the focus of our previous example.

What is the implication of the other part of the intervention, that the country's monetary authority is buying domestic currency from the foreign exchange market? In buying domestic currency, the country's monetary authority is removing domestic currency from the economy. This will tend to reduce the domestic money supply unless the authority separately takes another action (called **sterilization**) to restore the domestic money back into the economy. If the authority does take action to prevent the domestic money supply from changing, then the authority is relying only on intervention to defend the fixed rate. This is called **sterilized intervention.** If the monetary authority instead allows the intervention to reduce the money supply, then we have a clear interrelationship with two of the other defense methods. The change in the domestic money supply is likely to alter domestic interest rates, and these changes are likely to influence the entire macroeconomy of the country (including the country's price level).[2] We will examine these broader issues in depth in Part IV.

Defending against Appreciation

Consider now the case in which the pressure from private (or nonofficial) supply and demand in the foreign exchange market is attempting to drive the exchange rate, the price of foreign currency, below the bottom of its allowable band—the country's currency is tending toward appreciation. For instance, say that this is an Asian country attempting to maintain a fixed rate of 100 "locals" per dollar, with a band of plus or minus 5 percent (plus or minus five locals). As shown in Figure 19.3, nonofficial supply and demand are attempting to push the exchange rate to 85 locals per dollar, the intersection where the market would clear on its own. If the country's monetary authority is committed to defending the fixed rate within its band using intervention, then the authority must enter into the foreign exchange market in its official role. It must buy dollars and sell domestic currency. To keep

---

[2] The intervention may also change the foreign country's money supply as the monetary authority sells foreign currency, but we usually do not focus much on this effect.

FIGURE 19.3

Intervention
to Defend a
Fixed Rate:
Preventing
Appreciation of
the Country's
Currency

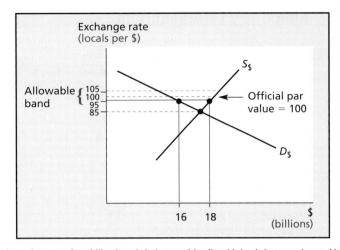

To prevent the market exchange rate from falling through the bottom of the allowable band, the country's central bank must buy 2 billion dollars at the exchange rate of 95 locals per dollar.

the currency in the band, it must buy 2 billion dollars from the foreign exchange market at the rate of 95 locals per dollar (the bottom of the band), so it is selling 190 billion locals into the foreign exchange market.

The relatively strong demand for locals is generally related to relatively strong demand by foreigners for the country's goods, services, and (nonofficial) financial assets. This results in an *official settlements balance surplus* if the country's monetary authority intervenes to defend the fixed rate. The intervention provides the local currency for the foreigners to buy more from the country than they are selling to the country (for goods, services, and nonofficial financial assets).

What does the country's monetary authority do with the dollars that it obtains from the foreign exchange market? It adds these dollars to its official international reserve holdings (or, if appropriate, repays prior official borrowings of dollars). Most likely, the authority will use the dollars to obtain U.S.-dollar-denominated foreign exchange assets, probably U.S. government bonds. The country's *holdings of official reserve assets increase.* Note that this case is closely related to the idea of a U.S. "deficit without tears." A U.S. deficit is a surplus for some other countries. If the other countries want to prevent an appreciation of their currencies, they may intervene to buy dollars. In the process, the United States finances its own official settlements deficit by issuing financial assets that other countries hold as their reserves.

What is the implication of the other part of the intervention, that the country's monetary authority is selling domestic currency into the foreign exchange market? This will expand the domestic money supply unless the authority separately takes another action to remove the additional domestic money from the economy. If the domestic money supply does increase, then domestic interest rates and the entire macroeconomy of the country are likely to be affected.

Temporary Disequilibrium

A major issue for the use of intervention to defend a fixed exchange rate is the length of time for which the intervention must continue. How long will the gap between nonofficial supply and demand at the edge of the band persist? That is, how long will the imbalance in the official settlements balance persist at this exchange rate?

If imbalances are clearly temporary, then defending the fixed exchange rate purely through intervention can work and makes sense. In this case the monetary authorities can finance a succession of deficits and surpluses indefinitely. In fact, we can make a case that financing temporary deficits and surpluses is better than letting the exchange rate float around.

Consider, for example, a situation in which Canada maintains a fixed exchange rate with its major trading partner, Britain. (The exchange rate *e* is in Canadian dollars per pound, the price of foreign currency if our home country is Canada.) Figure 19.4 gives an example of a successful and socially desirable financing of temporary surpluses and deficits with a fixed exchange rate. We have imagined that the temporary fluctuations in the balance of payments and the foreign exchange market arise from something predictable, such as a seasonal pattern in foreign exchange receipts, with Canada exporting more and earning more foreign exchange (£) during the autumn–winter harvest season than during the nonharvest spring–summer season. To help the example along, let us assume that it is costly for producers of the export crop to refrain from selling it during the harvest season and that something also prevents private investors or speculators from stepping in and performing the equilibrating function being assigned to government officials here. If the officials did not finance the temporary imbalances, the exchange rate would drop to $1.40 at point *B* in the harvest season, when the nation had a lot of exports to sell, and it would rise to $1.80 in the off-season. In this instance there is some economic loss since it would be better if the people who wanted foreign exchange to keep up imports during the off-season did not have to pay $1.80 for foreign exchange that is readily available for only $1.40 during the harvest season. The officials can avoid this economic loss by stabilizing the price at $1.60. Their stabilization is made possible because they have somehow picked the correct price, $1.60, the one at which they can sell exactly as much foreign exchange during one season as they buy during the other, exactly breaking even while stabilizing the price.

The official financing of spring–summer deficits with autumn–winter foreign exchange reserves brings a net social gain to the world. This gain arises from the fact that the monetary authority gave a net supply of foreign exchange at $1.60 to people who would have been willing to pay up to $1.80 a pound during the spring–summer season, while also buying at $1.60 the same amount of foreign exchange from people who would have been willing to sell it for as little as $1.40. The net social gain is measured as the sum of areas *ACD* and *BDE* (or about $1 billion a year). In this case, official intervention was successful and superior to letting the exchange rate find its own equilibrium in each season.

FIGURE 19.4

A Successful
Financing of
Temporary
Deficits and
Surpluses at a
Fixed Exchange
Rate

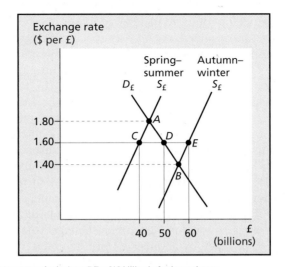

Autumn and winter: The monetary authority buys $DE = £10$ billion in foreign exchange.
Spring and summer: The monetary authority sells $CD = £10$ billion in foreign exchange.

For intervention to finance temporary disequilibriums to be the correct policy option, some stringent conditions must be met. First, it must be the case that private speculators do not see, or cannot take advantage of, the opportunity to buy foreign exchange in the fall and winter, invest it for a few months, and then sell it in the spring and summer. If private parties could do this, their own actions would bring the exchange rate close to $1.60 throughout the year, and there would be no need for official intervention.

It is also crucial that the officials correctly predict the future demand and supply for foreign exchange and that they predict what would be an equilibrium path for the exchange rate in the absence of their intervention. If they do not forecast correctly, their attempt to finance a deficit or a surplus at a fixed exchange rate can be costly because their accumulation of official reserves at some times will not balance against their loss of reserves at other times.

Disequilibrium That Is Not Temporary

What happens if the disequilibrium that results in an imbalance in the country's official settlements balance is not temporary? Rather, what if the disequilibrium is ongoing or *fundamental?* If the country defends its fixed rate using intervention, then the country's monetary authority is continually losing reserves (or borrowing foreign exchange) if the imbalance is a deficit, or it is continually accumulating reserves if the imbalance is a surplus.

If the domestic currency is facing pressure toward depreciation because of an ongoing deficit, the authority must continually intervene to sell foreign currency. Eventually its official reserves will run low, as will its ability to borrow foreign currencies. Furthermore, its problems can become worse if private investors and speculators observe its reserve losses and begin to bet heavily that the currency must be devalued. A one-way speculative gamble exists. As investors and speculators sell domestic currency and buy foreign currency, the gap that must be filled by official intervention widens, hastening the loss of reserves. As the country loses reserves, it also loses the ability to defend the fixed rate by intervention alone. It must shift to one of the other three defenses or surrender (devalue).

To see some of the economic costs of intervening to finance a "temporary" disequilibrium that turns out to be a fundamental disequilibrium, consider a stunning example of a failed defense of a currency—the depreciation of the Mexican peso in late 1994. The Mexican monetary authority was using a heavily managed "float" to effectively peg the Mexican currency at about 3.5 pesos per dollar. They were intervening to defend this value, and their holdings of official reserves declined from nearly $30 billion to about $6 billion during 1994. With their reserves so low, on December 20, 1994, they were forced to surrender, and the peso declined by about one-third, to about 5 pesos per dollar by year-end. They lost billions of dollars of taxpayers' money. Having bought pesos at about $0.29 per peso, they subsequently had to sell pesos at a much lower dollar value to buy dollars in order to rebuild their official reserves. Buying high and selling low is a formula for large losses.

If, in the opposite case, the domestic currency is facing pressure toward appreciation because of an ongoing surplus, the authority must continually intervene to buy foreign currency. The country eventually accumulates large international reserves. These eventually may be viewed as too large by the country itself for several reasons. First, the basic rate of return on this particular form of national wealth tends to be low, given the types of low-interest investments that are usually chosen for international reserve assets. Second, the value of foreign-exchange assets will decline if the country eventually must "retreat" by revaluing its own currency (which devalues foreign currency). Furthermore, these reserves may be viewed as too large by other countries, because some other countries are running deficits if this country is running a surplus and building its reserve holdings.

An example of this surplus case is Japan in the early 1970s. The Japanese government did not want the dollar value of the yen to rise in August 1971, even though President Richard Nixon had openly invited speculation in favor of the yen by calling for its revaluation (rise in dollar value). Hoping to ride out a temporary surplus situation in order to keep Japan's export and import-competing goods competitive (to the advantage of powerful trading groups but to the disadvantage of Japanese consuming groups), Japanese officials bought up billions of dollars during a few months as a way of financing the "temporary" surplus. Dollars threatened to become the sole asset of the Bank of Japan if the trend continued. Japanese officials soon gave up and let the dollar value of the yen jump. This involved the Japanese officials in the same kind of currency losses as the Mexican officials sustained in 1994. The difference was that the Japanese officials were stuck holding *foreign* currency that was worth less than they had paid for it (the depreciating dollars), whereas the Mexican officials ended up holding less-valuable domestic currency.

These experiences do not prove that it is futile to try to keep exchange rates fixed. They do prove that when the existing official exchange rate is becoming a disequilibrium exchange rate for the long run, trying to ride out the storm with intervention alone is costly. Something more must be added. *Fundamental disequilibrium calls for adjustment, not merely financing.* However, it is not easy for officials to judge what constitutes fundamental disequilibrium. We are left with the knowledge that a fundamental disequilibrium is one that is too great and/or too enduring to be financed, but we have no clear way of identifying one until after it has happened.

EXCHANGE CONTROL

Among the options for defending a fixed exchange rate, one—exchange control—can be indicated as socially inferior to the others. Oddly enough, exchange controls are widely used. According to compilations of official policies done by the International Monetary Fund, in 2001, 78 countries, all developing countries, had fairly comprehensive exchange control policies in place, controls that included requirements to surrender export proceeds and restrictions on international portfolio investments. A large number of other countries had some more limited form of exchange control in place. For instance, about 40 other countries, including a few industrialized countries, had substantial controls on capital transactions. A number of these countries are responding to persistent deficits in their external payments by defending a fixed exchange rate with elaborate government controls restricting the ability of their residents to buy foreign goods or services, to travel abroad, or to invest abroad.

Exchange controls are closely analogous to quantitative restrictions (quotas) on imports, already analyzed in Chapter 8. In fact, the analogy with import quotas fits very well, so well that the basic economics of exchange controls is simply the economics of import quotas expanded to cover imports of IOUs (investing abroad) and tourist services as well as imports of ordinary products. In Chapter 8, we demonstrated that an import quota is at least as bad as an import tariff using a one-dollar, one-vote analysis of changes in well-being. So it is with exchange controls as well: They are at least as damaging as a uniform tax on all foreign transactions, and probably they are worse.

To show the economic case against exchange controls, it is useful to start with an oversimplified view of exchange controls that is almost certain to underestimate the social losses coming from real-world controls. Figure 19.5 sketches the effects of a system of binding comprehensive exchange control that is about as well managed and benign as we can imagine. Figure 19.5 imagines that the U.S. government has become committed to maintaining a fixed exchange rate that officially values foreign currencies less, and the dollar more, than would a free-market equilibrium rate. This official rate is $1.00 for the pound sterling, with similar subequilibrium rates for other foreign currencies. The exchange control laws require exporters to turn over all their revenues from foreign buyers to the

FIGURE 19.5

The Best of the
Worst: Welfare
Losses from
Well-Managed
Exchange
Controls

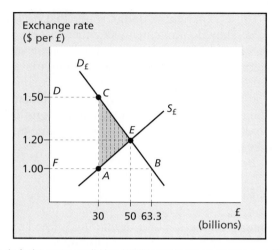

The exchange control limits the foreign currency available to 30 billion pounds, the amount that is earned by the country's exporters at the exchange rate of $1.00 per pound. Even if only those who value the foreign currency most highly (at $1.50 or more per pound) get it, the country suffers a loss of well-being of area *CEA*.

U.S. government. The U.S. government, in turn, gives them $1.00 in domestic bank deposits for each pound sterling they have earned by selling abroad. At this exchange rate, exporters are earning, and releasing to authorities, only £30 billion per month. This figure is well below the £63.3 billion per month that residents of the United States want to buy at this exchange rate to purchase foreign goods, services, and assets. If the U.S. government is committed to the $1.00 rate, yet is not willing to intervene or to contract the whole U.S. economy enough to make the demand and supply for foreign exchange match at $1.00, then it must ration the right to buy foreign exchange.

Let us imagine that the U.S. officials ration foreign exchange in a sound but seldom-tried way. Every month they announce that it is time for another public auction-by-mail. On January 21, they announce that anyone wanting sterling (or any other foreign currency) for March must send in bids by February 15. A family that plans to be in England in March might send in a form pledging its willingness to pay up to $3 per pound for 700 pounds to spend in England and its willingness to pay $2.50 per pound for 1,000 pounds. An importer of automobiles would also submit a schedule of amounts of foreign currencies he wishes to buy at each exchange rate in order to buy cars abroad. Receiving all these bids, the government's computers would rank them by the prices willingly pledged, and the totals pledged would be added up at each price, thus revealing the demand curve $D_£$ in Figure 19.5. The government would announce on February 20 that the price of $1.50 per pound was the price that made demand match the available £30 billion. The family who wants to be in England for March would thus get £1,000 by taking a check for $1,500 = £1,000 × $1.50 to the local post office, along with the officially signed pledge form it had submitted before February 15. Thus, all who were willing to pay $1.50 or more for each pound would receive the pounds they applied for, at the price of only $1.50 a pound, even if they had agreed to pay more. Anyone who did not submit bids with prices as high as $1.50 would be denied the right to buy pounds during March.

This system would give the government a large amount of revenues earned from the exchange control auctions. Collecting $1.50/£ × £30 billion = $45 billion while paying exporters only $1.00/£ × £30 billion = $30 billion, the government would make a net profit of $15 billion, minus its administrative costs. This government profit could be returned to the general public either as a cut in other kinds of taxes or as extra government spending. Area *DCAF* in Figure 19.5 represents these auction profits taken from importers but returned to the rest of society, and it does not constitute a net gain or loss for society as a whole.

The exchange control just described does impose a *loss of well-being* on society as a whole, however. This loss is measured by the area *CEA*. To see why, remember the interpretation of demand and supply curves as marginal benefit and cost curves. When the exchange controls are in effect and only £30 billion is available, some mutually profitable trades are being prohibited. At point *C*, the demand curve is telling us that some American is willing to pay $1.50 for an extra pound. At point *A*, the supply curve is telling us that somebody else, either a U.S. exporter or her customers, would be willing to provide an extra pound per year for $1.00. Yet the exchange controls prevent these two groups from getting together to split the $0.50 of net gain in a marketplace for pounds. Thus the vertical distance *AC* = $0.50 shows the social loss from not being able to trade freely another pound. Similarly, each extra vertical gap between the demand curve and the supply curve out to point *E* also adds to the measure of something lost because the exchange controls hamper private transactions. All these net losses add up to area *CEA* (£5 billion).

Actual exchange control regimes are likely to have several other effects and costs. First, in practice, governments usually do not hold public foreign currency auctions. Instead, they allocate the right to buy foreign currency at the low official rate according to more complicated rules. To get the right to buy foreign currency, we must go through involved application procedures to show that the purpose of the foreign purchase qualifies it for a favored-treatment category. Importing inputs for factories that would otherwise have to remain idle and underutilized is one purpose that often qualifies for priority access to foreign exchange, over less crucial inputs, or imports of luxury consumer goods, or acquisition of private foreign bank deposits. One difference between actual exchange controls and our hypothetical one is that the actual controls often incur greater *administrative costs* to enforce the controls, as well as greater *private resource costs* in dealing with them. Another difference is that some *lower-valued uses may be approved in place of higher-valued uses.* The government is not necessarily serving the demanders toward the top of the demand curve. For both of these reasons the net loss is larger than area *CEA*.

Second, another effect of exchange controls—efforts to evade them—is predictable. People are frustrated when they are not allowed to buy foreign exchange, even though they are willing to pay more than the recipients of foreign exchange will get from the government when these holders sell their foreign currency. The frustrated demanders will then look for other ways to obtain foreign exchange. One way is to *bribe the government functionaries* in charge of determining the official approvals. Another is to offer more to the recipients of foreign exchange than the government is offering, thus making it worthwhile for the recipients to "sell direct," in violation of the exchange controls. In this way a second foreign exchange market—a **parallel market** or black market—develops as a way for private demanders and sellers of foreign exchange to evade the exchange controls. Parallel markets exist in most countries that have exchange controls. The degree to which users of these illegal markets are punished varies widely. Some countries ignore violations of the exchange control, while others impose death penalties. If you visit a country that has exchange controls, be sure that you know the penalties before you use the parallel market. Your effort to take advantage of free-market economics might make you decidedly unfree.[3]

The costs of actual exchange controls are generally great enough to raise the question of what good purpose they are intended to serve. Because controls can be used to defend a fixed rate, we might imagine that they reduce economic uncertainty by holding fixed the external value of the national currency. Yet they are unlikely to help reduce uncertainty if they leave individual firms and households in doubt as to whether they will be allowed to obtain foreign exchange at the official price. Controls are likely to appeal mainly to government officials as a device for increasing their discretionary power over the allocation of resources. Controls undeniably have this effect. A charitable interpretation is that the extra power makes it easier for government officials to achieve social goals through comprehensive planning. A less charitable interpretation, consistent with the facts, is that officials see in exchange controls an opportunity for personal power and its lucrative exercise. In addition, the emergence of parallel markets or other methods to evade the controls calls into question their true effectiveness.

INTERNATIONAL CURRENCY EXPERIENCE

The first part of this chapter has laid out a framework for describing government policies toward the foreign exchange market, and has examined some of the economics of official intervention and exchange control. The rest of the chapter surveys the historical experience of actual government policies since the establish-

---

[3] In a number of countries the government itself creates two or more foreign exchange markets and rates—a dual- or multiple-exchange-rate system. Each rate applies to transactions of a specific type. For instance, a dual-rate system might have one rate for current transactions and another rate for capital transactions. In 2001, 19 developing countries had some form of dual- or multiple-exchange-rate system. As part of this type of policy, some form of exchange control is needed to direct each transaction to its appropriate rate. Again, the system creates incentives for evasion. For instance, transactions may be disguised to qualify for a more favorable rate.

ment of a nearly worldwide gold standard over a century ago. It reports some lessons learned from that experience. The history leads into a description of the current system (or perhaps "nonsystem") in the final section of the chapter.

The Gold Standard Era, 1870–1914 (One Version of Fixed Rates)

Read

Ever since 1914, the prewar gold standard has been the object of considerable nostalgia. In the decades after World War I, government officials in many countries believed that the experience of the gold standard proved the desirability of a fixed-exchange-rate system. Among scholars too, the "success" of the gold standard has been widely accepted and research has focused on *why,* not whether, it worked so well.

The international **gold standard** emerged by 1870 with the help of historical accidents centering on Britain. Britain tied the pound sterling ever more closely to gold than to silver from the late 17th century on, in part because Britain's official gold–silver value ratio was more favorable to gold than were the ratios of other countries, causing arbitrageurs to ship gold *to* Britain and silver *from* Britain. The link between the pound sterling and gold proved crucial. Britain's rise to primacy in industrialization and world trade in the 19th century enhanced the prestige of the metal tied to the currency of this leading country. Also, Britain had the advantage of not being invaded in wars, which further strengthened its image as the model of financial security and prudence. The prestige of gold was raised further by another lucky accident. The waves of gold discoveries both in the middle of the 19th century (California, Australia) and at the end of the century (South Africa, the Klondike) were small enough not to make gold suddenly too abundant to be a standard for international value. The silver-mining expansion of the 1870s and 1880s, by contrast, yielded too much silver, causing its value to plummet. Through such accidents, the gold standard, in which each national currency was fixed in gold content, remained intact from about 1870 until World War I.

Under the gold standard each country's government fixed its currency to a specified quantity of gold. The government also freely permitted individuals to exchange domestic currency for gold and to export and import gold. Through gold arbitrage the exchange rates between currencies then remained within a band (whose width reflected the transactions costs of gold movements between countries). Furthermore, changes in the government's gold holdings were linked to changes in the country's money supply—and thus to the country's average price level, its inflation rate, and other aspects of its macroeconomic performance.

The actual functioning of the gold standard was not this simple. Indeed, the process of actual payments adjustment under the prevailing fixed exchange rates puzzled Frank Taussig and his Harvard students after World War I. They found that international gold flows seemed to eliminate themselves very quickly, too quickly for their possible effects on national money supplies to change incomes, prices, and the balance of payments. The puzzle was heightened by the postwar finding of Arthur I. Bloomfield that central banks had done little to adjust their national economies to their exchange rates before 1914. Far from speeding up the economy's adjustment to payment surpluses or deficits, prewar central banks, similar to their successors in the interwar period, offset (sterilized) external reserve flows in the majority of cases, so that their national money supplies did not change much. What, then, actually kept the prewar balance of payments in line?

First, it must be noted that most countries were able to run payments surpluses before 1914, raising their holdings of gold and foreign exchange. This removed the cost of adjustment to fixed exchange rates because surplus countries were under little pressure to adjust. Widespread surpluses were made possible by, aside from the slow accumulation of newly mined gold in official vaults, the willingness and ability of Britain—and Germany to a lesser extent—to let the rest of the world hold growing amounts of its monetary liabilities. Between 1900 and 1913, for example, Britain ran payments deficits that were at least as large in relation to official (Bank of England) gold reserves as the deficits that caused so much hand-wringing in the United States in the 1960s. In fact, it would have been impossible for Britain to honor even one-third of its liquid liabilities to foreigners in 1913 by paying out official gold reserves. The gold standard was thus helped along considerably by the ability of the key-currency country to give the rest of the world liquid IOUs whose buildup nobody minded—or even measured.

There were times, of course, when Britain was called on to halt outflows of gold reserves which were more conspicuous than the unknown rise in its liquid liabilities. The Bank of England showed an impressive ability to halt gold outflows within a few months, faster than it could have if it had needed to contract the whole British economy to improve the balance of payments. It appears that higher British interest rates, resulting from monetary tightening by the Bank of England, were capable of calling in large volumes of short-term capital from abroad, even when central banks in other countries raised their interest rates by the same percentage. This command over short-term capital seems to have been linked to London's being the financial center for the world's money markets. As the main short-term international lender (as well as borrower), London could contract the whole world's money supply in the short run if and when the Bank of England ordered private banks in London to do so. In this way, the prewar gold standard combined overall surplus for most countries with short-run defensive strength on the part of the main deficit country.

In retrospect, it is clear that the success of the gold standard is explained partly by the tranquillity of the prewar era. The world economy was not subjected to shocks as severe as World Wars I and II, the Great Depression of the 1930s, and the OPEC oil price shocks of 1973–1974 and 1979–1980. *The gold standard looked successful, in part, because it was not put to a severe worldwide test.*

The prewar gold standard seemed to succeed for one other reason: *"success" was leniently defined* in those days. Central banks were responsible only for fixing the gold or exchange rate value of the currency. Public opinion did not hold central bankers (or government officials) responsible for fighting unemployment or stabilizing prices as much as after World War I. This easy assignment shielded

FIGURE 19.6

Selected
Exchange Rates,
1860–1913

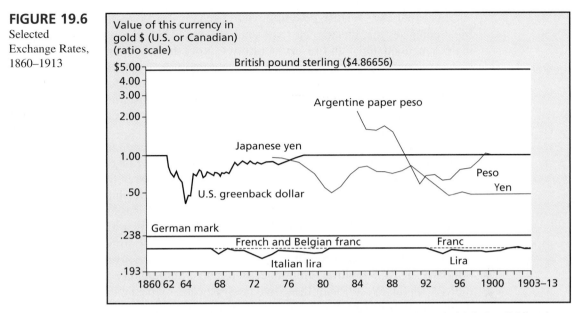

Sources: The data are annual averages of market exchange rates, except for the rates on the greenback dollar from 1862 through 1872, which are monthly averages for every third month. The Argentine paper peso rates are the John H. Williams gold premiums cited in Alec G. Ford, *The Gold Standard, 1880–1914: Great Britain and Argentina* (Oxford: Clarendon, 1962), p. 139. The Italian series is from Istituto Centrale di Statistica, *Sommario di Statistiche Storiche Italiane, 1861–1955* (Rome, 1958), p. 166. The gold value of the paper Japanese yen was calculated using the midrange New York dollar value of the metal-backed yen (Bank of Japan, Statistics Department, *Hundred Year Statistics of the Japanese Economy* [Tokyo, 1966], p. 318) and the average price of silver in paper yen for the period 1877–1886 (Henry Rosovsky, "Japan's Transition to Modern Economic Growth, 1868–1885," in *Industrialization in Two Systems*, ed. Henry Rosovsky [New York: Wiley, 1966], pp. 129 and 136). The U.S. greenback dollar series is the W. C. Mitchell series cited in Don C. Barrett, *The Greenback and Resumption of Specie Payments, 1862–1879* (Cambridge, Mass.: Harvard University Press, 1931, pp. 96–98). The virtually fixed rates are available in the *Economist* for prewar years.

officials from the policy dilemmas between defending a fixed exchange rate and stabilizing the domestic economy that will be discussed in Chapter 22.

The pre-1914 tranquillity also allowed some countries to have *favorable experiences with flexible exchange rates.* Several countries abandoned fixed exchange rates and gold convertibility in short-run crises. Britain itself did so during the Napoleonic Wars. Faced with heavy wartime financial needs, Britain suspended convertibility of the pound sterling into gold and let the pound drop by as much as 30 percent in value by 1813, restoring official gold convertibility after the wars. Other countries repeated the experience, as shown for selected countries in Figure 19.6. During the American Civil War, the North found itself unable to maintain the gold value of the paper dollar, given the tremendous need to print dollars to finance the war effort. The newly issued greenback dollars had dropped in value by more than 60 percent as of 1864, before beginning a long, slow climb back to gold parity in 1879. Heavy short-run financial needs also drove other countries off gold parity. War was the proximate culprit in the cases of Russia, Austria–Hungary, and Italy.

This experience with fixed and flexible exchange rates reveals some patterns. Most countries that abandoned fixed exchange rates did so in a context of growing payments deficits and reserve outflows. Note that in Figure 19.6 the end of fixed exchange rates was accompanied by a drop in the value of the national currency. This drop shows indirectly that *the fixed-rate gold standard imposed strain mostly on countries that were in payments deficit situations, not on countries in surplus.* Indeed, countries in surplus found it easy to continue accumulating reserves with a fixed exchange rate.

In general, the pre-1914 experiences with flexible exchange rates did not reveal any tendency toward destabilizing speculation. For the most part, the exchange rate fluctuations did not represent wide departures from the exchange rate we would have predicted, given the movements in price indexes. Two possible exceptions relate to the U.S. greenback dollar and the Russian ruble. In 1864, the greenback dollar fell in value 49 percent between April and July, even though the wholesale price index rose less than 15 percent, suggesting that speculation greatly accelerated the drop in the greenback, which then promptly rebounded. Similarly, in 1888, political rumors caused a dive in the thinly marketed Russian ruble. With the exception of these two possible cases of destabilizing speculation, it appears that flexible rates were quite stable in the prewar setting, given the political events that forced governments to try them out.

Interwar Instability

If the gold standard era before 1914 has been viewed as the classic example of international monetary soundness, the interwar period has played the part of a nightmare that officials have been determined to avoid repeating. Payments balances and exchange rates gyrated chaotically in response to two great shocks: World War I and the Great Depression. Figure 19.7 plots the exchange rate history of the interwar period. The chaos was concentrated into two periods: the first few years after World War I (1919–1923) and the currency crisis in the depths of the Great Depression (1931–1934).

After World War I the European countries had to struggle with a legacy of inflation and political instability. Their currencies had become inconvertible during the war because their rates of inflation were much higher than that experienced in the United States, the new financial leader. In this setting, Britain made the fateful decision to return to its prewar gold parity, achieving this rate by April 1925. Although the decision has been defended as a moral obligation and as a sound attempt to restore international confidence as well as Britain's role at the center of a reviving world economy, the hindsight consensus is that bringing the pound back up to $4.86656 was a serious mistake. It appears to have caused considerable unemployment and stagnation in traded-goods industries, as theory would predict, because the high real exchange rate value of the pound corresponded to a loss of international price competitiveness.

France, Italy, and some other European countries chose a more inflationary route for complicated political reasons. A succession of French revolving-door

FIGURE 19.7

Selected
Exchange
Rates, 1913,
1919–1938

Source: Monthly
averages from U.S.
Federal Reserve
Board, Board of
Governors, *Banking
and Monetary
Statistics* (Washington,
D.C., 1943).

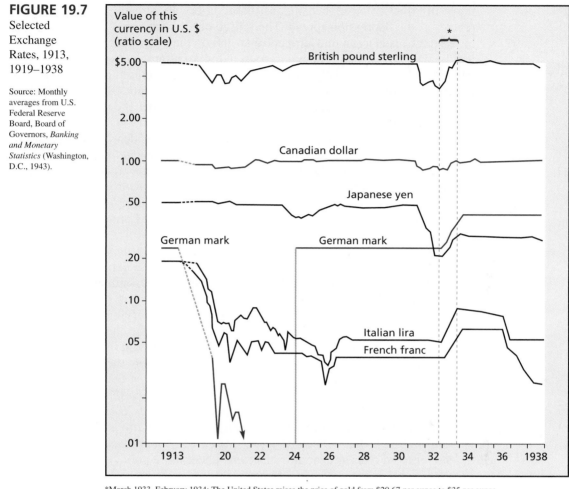

*March 1933–February 1934: The United States raises the price of gold from $20.67 per ounce to $35 per ounce.

governments was unable to cut government spending or raise taxes to shut off large budgetary deficits that had to be financed largely by printing new money. Something similar happened in Italy, both before and immediately after the 1922 coup d'état that brought Mussolini to power. The ultimate in inflation, however, was experienced by Germany, where the money supply, prices, and cost of foreign exchange all rose more than a trillionfold in 1922–1923. Money became totally worthless, and by late 1923 not even a wheelbarrowful of paper money could buy a week's groceries. The mark had to be reissued in a new series equal to the prewar dollar value, with old marks forever unredeemable.

The early 1930s brought another breakdown of international currency relations. The financial community, already stunned by the early postwar chaos and the Wall Street collapse, became justifiably jittery about bank deposits and currencies as the depression spread. The failure of the reputable Creditanstalt bank in Austria caused a run on German banks and on the mark because Germany had lent heavily to Austria. The panic soon led to an attack on the pound sterling, which had been perennially weak and was now compromised by Britain's making heavy loans to the collapsing Germans. On September 19, 1931, Britain abandoned the gold standard it had championed, letting the pound sink to its equilibrium market value. Between early 1933 and early 1934, the United States followed suit and let the dollar drop in gold value as President Franklin D. Roosevelt and his advisers manipulated the price of gold in an attempt to create jobs. Other countries also used devaluations, tariffs, and other trade restrictions to boost domestic employment. Such *beggar-thy-neighbor policies* (intended to benefit a country's economy at the expense of other countries) were widespread and probably added to worldwide depression (beggared almost everyone) as international trade shrank rapidly in the early 1930s.

What lessons does the interwar experience hold for policymakers? During World War II, expert opinion seemed to be that the interwar experience called for a compromise between fixed and flexible exchange rates, with emphasis on the former. Ragnar Nurkse, in his book *International Currency Experience,* written for the League of Nations in 1944, argued, with some qualifying disclaimers, that the interwar experience showed the instability of flexible exchange rates. Figure 19.7 adds some evidence to his premise: Exchange rates did indeed move more sharply during the interwar era than at any other time before the 1970s.

Yet subsequent studies have shown that a closer look at the interwar experience reveals the opposite lesson: *The interwar experience shows the futility of trying to keep exchange rates fixed in the face of severe shocks and the necessity of turning to flexible rates to cushion some of the international shocks.* Studies also have shown that it became more difficult for central banks to maintain defense of fixed rates as central banks came under more political pressure to pursue other goals such as reducing domestic unemployment.

At the same time, these studies have shown that even during the unstable interwar era, speculation tended to be stabilizing—it was domestic monetary and fiscal policy that was destabilizing. This revisionist conclusion began to emerge from studies of Britain's fluctuating rates between 1919 and 1925. Both Leland Yeager and S. C. Tsiang found that the pound sterling fluctuated in ways that are easily explained by the effects of differential inflation on the trade balance. Relative to the exchange rate movements that would be predicted by the purchasing power parity theory of the equilibrium exchange rate (see Chapter 18), the actual movements stayed close to the long-run trend. The cases in which Figure 19.7 shows rapid drops in currency values were cases in which the runaway expansion of the national money supply made this inevitable under any exchange rate regime. This was true of France up until 1926; it was even more true, of course, of the German hyperinflation.

Closer looks at the currency instability of the early 1930s suggest the same conclusion. The pound sterling, the yen, and other currencies dropped rapidly in

1931–1932 due to the gaping disequilibrium built into the fixed-exchange-rate system by the depression (and, for Japan, by the invasion of Manchuria). Once fixed rates were abandoned, flexible rates merely reflected, rather than worsened, the varying health of national economies.

The Bretton Woods Era, 1944–1971 (Adjustable Pegged Rates)

Meeting at the Bretton Woods resort in New Hampshire in 1944, the monetary leaders of the Allied powers had an opportunity to design a better system. Everyone agreed that the system needed reform. The United States dominated the Bretton Woods conference, just as it dominated the world economy and the world's gold reserves at the time. America wanted something like fixed exchange rates. Indeed, all leaders sought to get close to the virtuous fixed-exchange-rate case sketched in Figure 19.4. If only there were enough reserves to tide countries over temporary disequilibria, and if only countries followed policies that made all disequilibria temporary, then we could capture those welfare gains from successful stabilization.

Two expert economists, John Maynard Keynes of Britain and Harry Dexter White of the United States, came up with workable plans to give the world a new central bank that would allow deficit countries enough reserves to ride out their temporary deficits. White's plan also called for international pressure on national governments to change their macroeconomic policies to serve the goal of balanced international payments. The grand design, in other words, was fully fixed exchange rates defended by government intervention, with international reserves sufficient to permit defense by deficit countries.

In the end, however, the United States, Britain, and other governments had difficulty accepting the grand design. The Americans balked at putting billions of dollars at the disposal of other governments and at having to inflate the American economy just because it had a balance-of-payments surplus (as was then expected). Seeing the limits to what the Americans were prepared to give raised the fears of Britain and others about how they could adjust to their likely balance-of-payments deficits. In exchange, they insisted on the right to resort to devaluations and exchange controls when deficits threatened to persist.

The resulting compromise was what we have come to call the **Bretton Woods system.** Its central feature was the **adjustable peg,** which called for a fixed exchange rate and temporary financing out of international reserves until a country's balance of payments was seen to be in "fundamental disequilibrium." A country in that condition might then change its "fixed" exchange rate to a new official par value that looked sustainable. The international reserves were augmented by the **International Monetary Fund (IMF).** The IMF was set up with contributions of gold and foreign exchange from member governments. It grants all member countries the right to borrow reserves to finance temporary deficits. The IMF, in other words, is something like the global central bank that Keynes and White tried to design. Its resources and prerogatives, however, were more limited than Keynes and White envisioned. Also limited was the international community's ability to bend nations' macroeconomic policies to keep their international payments in line.

After the immediate postwar exchange rate adjustments, which were completed by about 1950, the Bretton Woods system looked remarkably successful for almost two decades. Countries grew rapidly and unemployment stayed low. Most exchange rates stayed fixed for long time periods, as shown in Figure 19.8.

The strong economic growth probably contributed more to the look of success for monetary institutions than they contributed to the strong growth. The good growth climate was consistent with flexible exchange rates, too, to judge from the Canadian experience of floating during 1950–1962. As shown in Figure 19.8, the annual average exchange rates between Canada and the United States showed little movement. By itself this does not prove that the Canadian experience was one in which flexible rates worked well. However, detailed studies of Canada's floating rate have borne out this inference. Statistical analysis suggests that if the exchange rate on the Canadian dollar had any effect on capital movements, this effect was in the stabilizing direction; that is, a lower value of the Canadian dollar tended to cause greater net capital inflows into Canada, as though investors expected the Canadian dollar to rise more when it was at low levels. Other studies have confirmed that fluctuations in the exchange value of the Canadian dollar were no greater than we would have predicted by following movements in the relative U.S. and Canadian prices of traded goods. In this stable economic environment, the floating rate of the Canadian dollar was well behaved and almost as stable as the fixed rates of other currencies.

The One-Way Speculative Gamble

The postwar experience with adjustable pegged rates recorded only rare changes in exchange rates among major currencies up to 1971, as Figure 19.8 suggests. Yet the adjustable-peg system revealed a new pattern in private speculation, one that caused a great deal of official consternation. As the world economy grew, so did the volume of internationally mobile private funds. The new system of pegged but adjustable exchange rates spurred private speculators to attack currencies that were "in trouble." The adjustable-peg system then gave private speculators a **one-way speculative gamble.** It was always clear from the context whether a currency was in danger of being devalued or revalued. In the case of a devaluation-suspect currency, such as the pound sterling in the mid-1960s, the astute private speculator knew that the currency could not rise significantly in value. She thus had little to lose by selling the currency in the spot (or forward) market. If the currency did not drop in value, she had lost nothing but a slight gap between the domestic interest rate and the foreign interest rate (or between the forward rate and the spot rate), but if she was right and the currency was devalued, it might be devalued by a large percentage over a single weekend, bringing her a handsome return. In this situation, private speculators would gang up on a currency that was moving into a crisis phase. As one foreign exchange specialist in a leading U.S. bank put it, "In those days we could make money just by following the crowd."

FIGURE 19.8
Selected
Exchange Rates,
1950–1981

Source: Year-end
figures, 1950–1969,
and end-of-month
figures, 1970–March
1981, from
International
Monetary Fund,
*International
Financial Statistics,*
various issues.

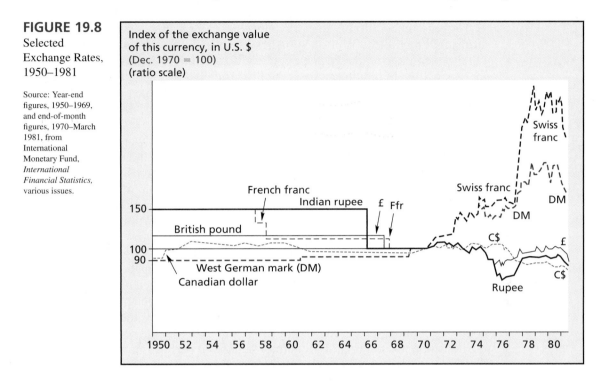

This pattern of speculation under the adjustable-peg system meant serious difficulties for any government or central bank that was trying to cure a payments disequilibrium without adjusting the peg. A classic illustration of these difficulties was the attempt of Harold Wilson's Labor government to keep the pound worth $2.80 between 1964 and November 1967. When Wilson took office, he found that Britain's trade and payments balances were even worse than previous official figures had admitted. His government used numerous devices to make the pound worth $2.80: tighter exchange controls; soaring interest rates; selective tax hikes; promises to cut government spending; and massive loans from the IMF, the United States, and other governments. Speculators who, in increasing number, doubted Britain's ability to shore up the pound were castigated by the chancellor of the Exchequer as "gnomes of Zurich." Yet, in the end, all of the belt-tightening and all of the support loans worked no better than had the attempt to make the pound worth $4.86656 from 1925 to 1931. On November 18, 1967, Britain devalued the pound by 14.3 percent, to $2.40. The gnomes had won handsomely. Those who had, for instance, been selling sterling forward at prices like $2.67 just before the devaluation were able to buy the same sterling at about $2.40, pocketing the 27 cents difference. The British government and its taxpayers lost a similar difference, by paying close to $2.80 to buy sterling that they had to concede was worth only $2.40 after November 18.

The existence of the one-way speculative gamble seems to make the adjustable peg of the Bretton Woods system look less sustainable than either purely fixed rates or purely flexible rates. If speculators believe that the government is willing to turn the entire economy inside out to defend the exchange rate, then they will not attack the exchange rate. Britain could have made speculators believe in $2.80 in the mid-1960s if it had shown its determination to slash the money supply and contract British incomes and jobs until $2.80 was truly an equilibrium rate. But as the speculators realized, few postwar governments are prepared to pay such national costs in the name of truly fixed exchange rates. Alternatively, the speculators might have been more cautious in betting against sterling if the exchange rate had been a floating equilibrium rate. With the float, speculators face a two-way gamble. Because the current spot exchange rate is an equilibrium rate and not an artificial official disequilibrium rate, the actual exchange rate in the future could turn out to be higher or lower than the current spot rate or the rate that speculators expect in the future.

Although the speculative attacks on an adjustable-pegged rate are certainly unsettling to officials, it is not clear that they should be called *destabilizing*. If the official defense of a currency is primarily just a way to postpone an inevitable devaluation and not a way to raise the equilibrium value of the currency, then it could be said that the speculative attack is stabilizing in the sense that it hastens the transition to a new equilibrium rate. Whether it performs this stabilizing function is uncertain, however. Officials may be induced to overreact to the speculative attack and to overdevalue the pegged rate.

The Dollar Crisis

The postwar growth of the international economy led to a crisis involving the key currency of the system, the U.S. dollar. Under the Bretton Woods system, other countries effectively pegged their currencies to the U.S. dollar. The dollar became the major reserve currency, and the U.S. government was committed to exchanging the dollars held as reserves by other countries' monetary authorities for gold at an official price of $35 per ounce. (The system is sometimes described as a *gold-exchange standard*.)

As the European and Japanese economies recovered from the war, and as their firms gained in competitive ability relative to that of U.S. firms, the U.S. payments position shifted into large official settlements balance deficits. In part, those deficits represented the fact that the monetary authorities of other countries wanted to run surpluses to increase their international reserves as international transactions generally grew rapidly. After a time, however, the deficits became a source of official concern in Europe and Japan. More and more dollars ended up in official hands. Something like this had happened in 1914, when other countries accumulated growing official reserves of sterling. In the postwar setting, however, few governments felt that they could be as relaxed about the gold backing of the U.S. dollar as the rest of the world had felt about the link between gold and Britain's pound before 1914. U.S. gold reserves dwindled as France led the march to Fort Knox (actually, the basement of the New York Federal Reserve

Bank), demanding gold for dollar claims. It became questionable whether the U.S. dollar was worth as much gold as the official gold price implied.

In this situation, the United States had the option of shrinking the U.S. economy until foreign central banks were constrained to supply gold to the United States to pay for U.S. exports. Other alternatives were tight exchange controls and devaluing the dollar in terms of gold. Exchange controls were tried to a limited extent (in the form of the Interest Equalization Tax on lending abroad, the "Voluntary" Foreign Credit Restraint Program, and the like), but these controls ran counter to the official U.S. stance of encouraging free mobility of capital between countries. Devaluation of the dollar in terms of gold would have marked up the dollar value of U.S. gold reserves but would have brought politically distasteful windfall gains to the Soviet Union and South Africa (the two major gold producers).

Faced with these choices under the existing international rules, the United States opted for changing the rules. On March 17, 1968, a seven-country meeting hastily called by the United States announced the "two-tier" gold price system. The private price of gold in London, Zurich, and other markets was now free to fluctuate in response to supply and demand. The official price for transactions among the seven agreeing governments would still be $35 an ounce. Nonetheless, the U.S. overall payments deficits continued and had to be financed by increasing sales of U.S. foreign exchange reserves. Eventually, the United States would have to adjust, either by restraining its economy or by imposing exchange controls or by changing the international monetary rules. Again, the United States chose to change the rules.

In August 1971, President Nixon suspended convertibility of dollars into gold, effectively severing the official gold–dollar price link. He also imposed a 10 percent temporary additional tariff on all imports coming into the United States, to remain in place until other countries agreed to revalue their currencies against the dollar (so that the dollar was similarly devalued). Most major currencies then floated against the dollar until December 1971, when the Smithsonian Agreement attempted to patch the system back together. Under this agreement the DM was revalued by about 17 percent, the yen by about 13 percent, and other currencies by smaller percentages, overall creating an effective devaluation of the dollar of close to 10 percent, and the United States removed its import surcharge. The official dollar price of gold also was raised to $38 per ounce, but this was symbolic because the suspension continued. The agreement failed to save the system. By March 1973, most major currencies shifted to floating against the dollar. After effectively ending in 1971, the pegged exchange rate regime known as the Bretton Woods system was officially abandoned in 1973.

The Current System: Limited Anarchy

The current system is sometimes described as a *managed floating regime.* Since the early 1970s, a growing number of countries, including many major industrialized countries, have floating or relatively flexible exchange rates, but government authorities often attempt to have an impact through intervention or some other form of management of the floating or flexible exchange rates.

A noteworthy feature of the experience since 1973 is the extent of official resistance to floating. Some of this resistance is seen in the management of the float. For instance, at various times since 1973, the government of Japan has tried to hold down the dollar value of the yen, apparently to prevent a loss in the international price competitiveness of Japanese products. In the process, the Japanese central bank has bought huge numbers of dollars (that subsequently declined in yen value anyway, as the yen did appreciate against the dollar). Another part of the resistance is seen in the substantial number of countries that continue to peg their currencies to the dollar or to other currencies.

The European Union has been a center of resistance to floating exchange rates, at least for the cross-rates among the EU currencies. The governments of the European Economic Community (the forerunner of the European Union) strove to prevent movements in exchange rates among their currencies, first setting up the "snake" within the "tunnel" in December 1971. They agreed on maximum ranges of movement of the most appreciated versus the most depreciated member currency (the tunnel) and on maximum bands within which pairwise exchange rates could oscillate (the snake). This scheme was short-lived. Britain, Italy, and France soon allowed their currencies to drop well below the tunnel, leaving only a fixed set of exchange rates between the West German mark and the currencies of the Benelux countries. The governments of the European Community then developed a successor scheme, the Exchange Rate Mechanism (ERM) of the European Monetary System, in 1979. In the early 1990s, the governments of the European Union established a process for moving toward permanently fixed exchange rates and a single currency. As we discussed in Chapter 16, at the beginning of 1999, the new common currency, the euro, came into existence, and in 2002 it replaced the national currencies of 12 of the 15 EU countries.

The official desire for fixed or managed exchange rates has remained strong, but fixed or steady rates have been hard to maintain. Once the Bretton Woods system broke down, the U.S. government switched to advocacy of floating rates. It often (e.g., in the early 1970s, 1980–1984, and 1995–2002) has followed a policy of "benign neglect" toward the exchange rate value of the dollar, with almost no official exchange-market intervention by U.S. monetary authorities during these long periods of time. At other times, especially in the late 1980s, the U.S. government has been active in managing the dollar float. After the dollar soared in value during 1981–1985, the U.S. government participated in two major international accords to manage exchange rates through coordinated intervention. The first accord, the Plaza Agreement of September 1985, was intended to promote a decline in the exchange rate value of the dollar, and the dollar did fall. The second accord, the Louvre Agreement of February 1987, was intended to stabilize the exchange rate value of the dollar against other major currencies. Formal coordination faded by the early 1990s, and as we have seen, exchange rates between the dollar and other major currencies still oscillate widely at times.

The series of exchange rate crises in the 1990s and early 2000s shows how difficult it is to defend pegged rates or heavily managed floating rates in the face of large flows of private funds. When speculators believe they have spotted attempts by officials to maintain unrealistic exchange rates, they have a one-way speculative gamble that can overwhelm the defenses of the monetary authorities.

The first major crisis of the 1990s centered on the European Union. In the early 1990s, all EU countries but Greece had joined the ERM system of pegged rates among these currencies. (In addition, several European countries, including Sweden and Finland, also pegged to this system, although they were not formally part of it.) Following the shock of German reunification and the subsequent tight monetary policy followed by Germany, a major speculative attack hit the ERM in 1992 and 1993. Governments mounted defenses that included massive intervention, high short-term interest rates, and tightening of capital controls. Nonetheless, Britain and Italy surrendered and dropped out of the ERM in 1992, and Sweden and Finland also ceased their peg to it. Several other currencies that remained in the system were devalued in 1992 and 1993. In addition, the bands for most currencies that remained in the system were widened in 1993 to 15 percent on each side of the central rate (from 2.25 percent) to deter speculation by permitting more room for the pegged rate to fluctuate.

Since 1994, a series of exchange crises has hit developing countries, resulting in dramatic devaluations of pegged exchange rates or depreciations following abandonment of pegged or heavily managed rates. Here we provide a summary. We examine these crises in depth in Chapter 20.

As discussed earlier in this chapter, after using a large part of its official reserve holdings to defend the peso exchange rate, the Mexican government had to abandon its heavily managed rate in late 1994. The CFA franc, a currency used by 13 African countries, was devalued by 50 percent in 1994, after it had been pegged at the same rate to the French franc for 45 years. In 1996, the Venezuelan government abandoned its pegged rate, and the bolivar declined by 42 percent in one day. In May 1997, the Czech government, after spending about 30 percent of its international reserves to defend the pegged rate it had maintained for 6 years, shifted to a floating exchange rate, and the koruna declined by about 10 percent during the first few days of the float.

In 1997, the Asian crisis hit. In July the Thai government gave up its pegged exchange rate for the Thai baht. By the end of the year the baht's value had fallen by 45 percent against the U.S. dollar. Then the Malaysian government floated its currency, and the ringgit fell by 35 percent. Soon Indonesia switched to a float, and the rupiah fell by 47 percent. In November the Korean government gave up its defense of the won, whose value then fell by 48 percent.

In 1998, the Russian government shifted to a floating rate and the ruble declined by 60 percent in value against the dollar in about a month and a half. From April 1998 to January 1999, the Brazilian government used about half of its official reserves defending the pegged value of the real. Capital outflows and other speculative pressures increased, and Brazil shifted to a floating rate in January 1999. In two and a half weeks the real declined by 39 percent. In early 2001 the Turkish government abandoned the pegged exchange rate for the lira, and its value fell by almost half during the year. As we discussed in Chapter 1, in early 2002 the Argentinean government shifted to a floating exchange rate for its peso. The value of the peso plummeted, and Argentina's economy imploded.

After all of these schemes and crises, what is the current international monetary system? Perhaps it is best to describe it as a nonsystem—countries can choose almost any exchange rate policies they want and change them whenever they want. The policies of various countries at the beginning of 2002 are shown in Figure 19.9.

Column 1 in Figure 19.9 shows that eight countries use some other country's currency as their own. (We examine this "dollarization" as an extreme form of a fixed exchange rate in Chapter 24.) Columns 2 and 3 show the 12 EU countries that use the euro as their currency, and the 23 countries whose currencies are pegged to the euro. Among these 23 countries are Denmark, which maintains a tight band of 2.25 percent around the euro in a continuation of the Exchange Rate Mechanism, and the 14 African countries that use the CFA franc. Column 4 shows that 33 countries peg their currencies to the U.S. dollar. (We also know that in early 2002, shortly after the snapshot of policies shown in Figure 19.9, Argentina abandoned its peg to the dollar, and Lithuania shifted to pegging its currency to the euro.)

Column 5 shows that 6 countries peg to some other single currency, usually the currency of a larger neighboring country. Column 6 shows the 11 countries that peg to a basket of currencies. The 10 countries shown in Column 7 use a crawling pegged exchange rate in which the pegged value is changed frequently, often according to specific indicators.

Moving to the other end of the spectrum, column 9 shows the 39 countries that say their exchange rates are floating and mainly determined by market supply and demand, although the floats are managed to a greater or lesser extent by each of these countries. Included here are a number of industrialized countries. Column 8 shows that 42 countries have floating rates that their governments say are rather heavily managed. The monetary authorities of these countries influence the exchange rates through active intervention without committing to announced exchange rate targets. The number of countries with floating exchange rates has grown during the past decade. In 1991, only 36 countries indicated that they had floating exchange rates. By 2001 this number rose to 81 countries (combining Columns 8 and 9).

In summary, under the current system each country chooses its own exchange rate policy. Two major blocs of currencies exist: currencies pegged to the U.S. dollar and currencies pegged to the euro. The exchange rates among the U.S. dollar, the euro, and such other major currencies as the Japanese yen, British pound, Swiss franc, and Canadian dollar are floating rates, with some (usually small) amount of official management. Economists are still debating the merits and demerits of this "nonsystem," as well as the strengths and weaknesses of the policy choices made by individual countries. Critics of floating rates start at the obvious point: Floating exchange rates have fluctuated "a lot," "more than anyone expected." But pegged exchange rates have sometimes been difficult to maintain, so they are prone to currency crises. We will return to these issues in Chapter 24.

FIGURE 19.9 Exchange Rate Arrangements, January 1, 2002

| (1) Use foreign currency (no separate local currency)[2] | (2) Euro Area (use euro as currency) | Currency Pegged To[1] | | | | (7) Crawling Peg | (8) Heavily Managed Float | (9) Market-Driven Float |
		(3) Euro	(4) U.S. Dollar	(5) Other Currency	(6) Currency Basket			
Ecuador	Austria	Denmark (ERM)	Antigua & Barbuda	Bhutan (Indian rupee)	Botswana	Belarus	Algeria	Albania
El Salvador	Belgium	CFA Franc Zone	Aruba	Brunei Darussalam (Singapore dollar)	Fiji	Bolivia	Angola	Armenia
Kiribati	Finland	Benin	Argentina	Lesotho (S. African rand)	Kuwait	Costa Rica	Azerbaijan	Australia
Marshall Islands	France	Burkina Faso	Bahamas	Libya	Latvia	Honduras	Burundi	Brazil
Micronesia	Germany	Cameroon	Bahrain	Malta	Libya	Israel	Cambodia	Canada
Palau	Greece	Central African Rep.	Bangladesh	Namibia (S. African rand)	Morocco	Nicaragua	Croatia	Chile
Panama	Ireland	Chad	Barbados	Nepal (Indian rupee)	Samoa	Romania	Dominican Republic	Colombia
San Marino	Italy	Congo, Rep. of	Belize	Swaziland (S. African rand)	Seychelles	Solomon Islands	Eritrea	Congo, Dem. Rep. of
	Luxembourg	Cote d'Ivoire	China		Tonga	Uruguay	Ethiopia	Czech Republic
	Netherlands	Equatorial Guinea	Djibouti		Vanuatu	Venezuela	Ghana	Gambia
	Portugal	Gabon	Dominica				Guatemala	Georgia
	Spain	Guinea-Bissau	Egypt				Guinea	Haiti
		Mali	Grenada				Guyana	Iceland
		Niger	Hong Kong				India	Japan
		Senegal	Iran				Indonesia	Korea, South
		Togo	Jordan				Iraq	Liberia
		Other	Lebanon				Jamaica	Madagascar
		Bosnia and Herzegovina	Lithuania				Kazakhstan	Malawi
		Bulgaria	Malaysia				Kenya	Mexico
		Cape Verde	Maldives				Kyrgyz Republic	Moldova
		Comoros	Netherlands Antilles				Lao PDR	Mongolia
		Cyprus	Oman				Mauritania	Mozambique
		Estonia	Qatar				Mauritius	New Zealand
		Hungary	St. Kitts & Nevis				Myanmar	Norway
		Macedonia	St. Lucia				Nigeria	Papua New Guinea
			St. Vincent & the Grenadines				Pakistan	Peru
			Saudi Arabia				Paraguay	Philippines
			Sudan				Russia	Poland
			Suriname				Rwanda	Sierra Leone
			Syrian Arab Republic				Sao Tome & Principe	South Africa
			Turkmenistan				Singapore	Sweden
			United Arab Emirates				Slovak Republic	Switzerland
			Zimbabwe				Slovenia	Tajikistan
							Sri Lanka	Tanzania
							Thailand	Turkey
							Trinidad & Tobago	Uganda
							Tunisia	United Kingdom
							Ukraine	United States
							Uzbekistan	Yemen
							Vietnam	
							Yugoslavia	
							Zambia	

[1]The countries shown as having currencies pegged to the U.S. dollar include nine that state an official policy of a floating exchange rate but informally maintain a peg to the U.S. dollar, and three that have an official peg to the SDR but informally maintain a peg to the dollar. In addition, one country shown as having its currency pegged to the euro has an official policy of floating but informally maintain a peg to the euro.

[2]These countries are often called *dollarized*. All but Kiribati (Australian dollar) and San Marino (euro) use the U.S. dollar as their currency.

Source: *International Financial Statistics*, August 2002.

Summary

The two major aspects of government policy toward the foreign exchange market are the degree of exchange rate flexibility and restrictions (if any) on use of the market. Foreign exchange restrictions are called **exchange controls.**

Policies toward the exchange rate itself cover a spectrum. The polar case of complete flexibility is a **clean float,** with the exchange rate determined solely by nonofficial (or private) supply and demand. Governments often do not allow a clean float, but rather take actions (such as **official intervention**) to **manage** (or **dirty**) the float.

The other kind of exchange-rate policy is a **fixed,** or **pegged, exchange rate.** The government must decide what to fix to. The alternatives include a commodity like gold, a single other currency, or a basket of other currencies. The government also must decide the width of a band around the central fixed rate. The exchange rate has some flexibility around this par value, but the flexibility is limited by the size of the band. Although a permanently fixed rate is a polar case, it is nearly impossible for a government to commit never to change the fixed rate. If the exchange rate is not permanently fixed, then the government must also decide when to change the fixed rate. If the answer is seldom, the approach is called an **adjustable peg;** if often, it is called a **crawling peg.**

If the government chooses a fixed exchange rate, it must also decide how to defend the rate if private supply and demand pressures tend to push the actual rate outside of the allowable band. One or more of four ways can be used to defend the fixed rate:

1. Use official intervention in the foreign exchange market, in which the monetary authority buys and sells currencies to alter the supply and demand situation.

2. Impose exchange controls to restrict or control some or all aspects of supply and demand.

3. Alter domestic interest rates to influence short-term capital flows.

4. Adjust the macroeconomy to alter nonofficial supply and demand.

The government may also exercise a fifth option—to surrender by changing the fixed rate (revaluation or devaluation) or by shifting to a floating exchange rate.

Government intervention in the foreign exchange market is closely related to official reserves transactions and the official settlements balance of the country's balance of payments. If the government attempts to prevent the value of its currency from declining, it must buy domestic currency and sell foreign currency in the foreign exchange market. The government can use its official reserve holdings as a source of foreign currency to sell in the intervention or it can borrow. This provides the financing for the country to run an official settlements balance deficit. If instead the government attempts to prevent the value of its currency from rising, it must sell domestic currency and buy foreign currency. The government can use the foreign currency that it buys to increase its official reserve holdings (or to repay past borrowings). The country's official settlements balance is in surplus.

Defense of the fixed rate using only intervention can work and make economic sense if the imbalances in the official settlements balance are temporary and self-reversing. This approach assumes that private speculators cannot perform the same stabilizing function and that officials correctly foresee the sustainable long-run value for the exchange rate. If these assumptions do not hold, the case for financing deficits and surpluses with a fixed exchange rate is weakened.

Defense using exchange control creates deadweight loss similar to that of an import quota, and also probably has high administrative costs. Efforts to evade exchange controls, including bribery of government officials and the development of an illegal **parallel market,** reduce the actual effectiveness of the controls.

The success or failure of different exchange rate regimes has depended historically on the severity of the shocks with which those systems have had to cope. The fixed-rate **gold standard** seemed successful before 1914, largely because the world economy itself was more stable than in the period that followed. Many countries were able to keep their exchange rates fixed because they were lucky enough to be running surpluses at established exchange rates without having to generate those surpluses with any contractionary macroeconomic policies. The main deficit-running country, Britain, could control international reserve flows in the short run by controlling credit in London, but it was never called upon to defend sterling against sustained attack. During the stable prewar era, even floating-exchange-rate regimes showed stability (with two brief possible exceptions).

The interwar economy was chaotic enough to put any currency regime to a severe test. Fixed rates broke down, and governments that believed in fixed rates were forced into flexible exchange rates. Studies of the interwar period showed that in cases of relative macroeconomic stability, flexible rates showed signs of stabilizing speculation. Those signs were less evident in economies whose money supplies had "run away" or whose previous fixed exchange rates were far from equilibrium.

Postwar experience showed some difficulties with the **Bretton Woods system** of adjustable pegged exchange rates set up in 1944. Under this system, private speculators were given a strong incentive to attack reserve-losing currencies and force large devaluations. The role of the dollar as a reserve currency also became increasingly strained in the Bretton Woods era. Under Bretton Woods, foreign central banks acquired large holdings of dollars through official intervention, when the United States shifted to running official settlements balance deficits. At first, these were welcomed as additions to official reserve holdings in these foreign countries, but the dollars became unwanted as the reserves grew too large. Foreign central banks' conversions of dollars into gold decreased U.S. official gold holdings, further reducing foreign officials' confidence in the dollar. The United States had to adjust its balance-of-payments position or change the rules. The United States opted for new rules, divorcing the private gold market from the official gold price in 1968, suspending gold convertibility and forcing a devaluation of the dollar in 1971, and shifting to general floating in 1973.

The current exchange rate system permits each country to choose its own exchange rate policy. Two major blocs exist, one of currencies pegged to the U.S. dollar and the other of the euro and currencies pegged to it. The euro is the successor to previous schemes, including the Exchange Rate Mechanism of the European Monetary System, as the countries that are members of the EU seek a zone of exchange rate stability for transactions within the union.

The dollar bloc and the euro bloc float against each other, and the currencies of a number of industrialized countries—Australia, Canada, Japan, New Zealand, Sweden, Switzerland, and the United Kingdom—float independently. For countries with flexible exchange rates, governments generally are skeptical of purely market-driven exchange rates, and they practice some degree of management of the floating rate.

Most developing countries have a pegged exchange rate of some sort, but the trend is toward greater flexibility and floating. A series of exchange rate crises in the 1990s and early 2000s, including the Mexican peso in 1994, the Asian crisis (Thai baht, Malaysian ringgit, Indonesian rupiah, and South Korea won) in 1997, the Russian ruble in 1998, the Brazilian real in 1999, the Turkish lira in 2001, and the Argentinean peso in 2002, shows the difficulty of defending a pegged rate against speculative flows of short-term capital when the speculators have a **one-way speculative gamble** against a currency that they believe is misvalued.

Suggested Reading

Information on each country's policies toward the foreign exchange market can be found in the IMF's *Annual Report on Exchange Arrangements and Exchange Restrictions.* On exchange control, see Bhagwati (1978), Collins (1988), and Dooley (1996). On the issue of stabilizing and destabilizing speculation, see Friedman's classic argument (1953) and Stern (1973, Chapter 3).

For broad surveys of international currency experience during the past century, see McKinnon (1993 and 1996) and Giovannini (1989). The prewar gold standard is analyzed in more depth in Bloomfield (1959), Lindert (1969), and Bordo and Schwartz (1984).

A masterly survey of the interwar experience is Eichengreen (1992). Two pioneering studies of the stability of fluctuating exchange rates in the interwar period are Tsiang (1959) and Aliber (1962).

For more detail on the Bretton Woods era, see Solomon (1977) and Bordo and Eichengreen (1992). The dollar crisis under the Bretton Woods system was predicted and diagnosed in Robert Triffin's classic work (1960) and by Jacques Rueff (translation, 1972). Reinhart and Rogoff (2002) reassess exchange rate policies since 1949.

Organization for Economic Cooperation and Development (1999), Pitchford and Cox (1998), Eichengreen (1997), and Obstfeld (1997) analyze the European Monetary System, monetary union in Europe, and the euro.

Questions and Problems

✦ 1. What is the difference between a clean float and a managed float?

2. What is the difference between an adjustable peg and a crawling peg?

✦ 3. For a country that is attempting to maintain a fixed exchange rate, what is the difference between a temporary disequilibrium and a fundamental disequilibrium? Contrast the implications of each type of disequilibrium for official intervention in the foreign exchange market to defend the fixed exchange rate.

4. "The emergence of expectations that a country in the near future will impose exchange controls will probably result in upward pressure on the exchange rate value of the country's currency." Do you agree or disagree? Why?

✦ 5. A government has just imposed a total set of exchange controls to prevent the exchange rate value of its currency from declining. What effects and further developments do you predict?

6. The Pugelovian government is attempting to peg the exchange rate value of its currency (the pnut, pronounced "p'noot") at a rate of three pnuts per U.S. dollar (plus or minus 2 percent). Unfortunately, private market supply and demand is putting downward pressure on the pnut's exchange rate value. In fact, it appears that under current market conditions, the exchange rate would be about 3.5 pnuts per dollar if the government did not defend the pegged rate.

   a. How could the Pugelovian government use official intervention in the foreign exchange market to defend the pegged exchange rate?

   b. How could the Pugelovian government use exchange controls to defend the pegged exchange rate?

   c. How could the Pugelovian government use domestic interest rates to defend the pegged exchange rate?

✦ 7. Under the gold standard the fixed price of gold was $20.67 per ounce in the United States. The fixed price of gold was £4.2474 per ounce in Britain.

   a. What is the "fixed" exchange rate (dollars per pound) implied by these fixed gold prices?

   b. How would you arbitrage if the exchange rate quoted in the foreign exchange market was $4.00 per pound? (Under the gold standard, you could buy or sell gold with each central bank at the fixed price of gold in each country.)

   c. What pressure is placed on the exchange rate by this arbitrage?

8. Consider the international currency experience for the period of the gold standard before 1914.

   a. What type of exchange rate system was the gold standard and how did it operate?

   b. What country was central to the system? What was the role of this country in the success of the currency system?

   c. What was the nature of economic shocks during this period?

   d. What is the evidence on speculation and speculative pressures on exchange rates during this period?

◆ 9. What are the key features of the international currency experience in the period between the two world wars? What lessons did policymakers learn from this experience? Why are these lessons now questioned and debated?

10. Consider the international currency experience for the Bretton Woods era from 1944 to the early 1970s.

   a. What type of exchange rate system was the Bretton Woods system? How did it operate?

   b. What country was central to the system? What was the role of this country in the success of the currency system?

   c. What is the evidence on speculation and speculative pressures on exchange rates during this period?

◆ 11. Why did the Bretton Woods system of fixed exchange rates collapse?

12. The current exchange rate regime is sometimes described as a system of managed floating exchange rates, but with some blocs of currencies that are tied together.

   a. What are the two major blocs of currencies that are tied together?

   b. What are the major currencies that float against each other?

   c. Given the discussion in this chapter and the previous chapters of Part III, how would you characterize the movements of exchange rates between the U.S. dollar and the other major currencies since the shift to managed floating in the early 1970s?

Chapter Twenty

International Lending and Financial Crises

International financial capital flows have grown rapidly in the past several decades. The lenders (or investors) give the borrowers money to be used now in exchange for IOUs or ownership shares entitling them to interest and dividends later. International flows of financial claims are conventionally divided into different categories by type of lender or investor (private versus official), by maturity (long term versus short term), by existence of management control (direct versus portfolio), and by type of borrower (private or government). For the first three distinctions, here are the key categories:

A. Private lending and investing

   1. Long term

      a. Direct investment (lending to, or purchasing shares in, a foreign enterprise largely owned and controlled by the investor)
      b. Loans (to a foreign borrower, maturity more than one year, mostly by banks)
      c. Portfolio investment (purchasing stock or bonds with maturity of more than one year, issued by a government or a foreign enterprise not controlled by the investor)

   2. Short term (lending to a foreign borrower, or purchasing bonds issued by a government or a foreign enterprise not controlled by the investor, maturing in a year or less)

B. Official lending and investing (by a government or a multilateral institution like the International Monetary Fund or the World Bank, mostly lending, both long term and short term)

In this chapter we take a close look at the causes and effects of bank lending and portfolio investment. (Foreign direct investment and the role of management control received their own separate analysis in Chapter 14.)

International lending and investing have been revolutionized. From before World War II to the early 1980s, the main lender was the United States, joined in the 1970s by the newly rich oil exporters. Since the early 1980s, the United States has been the world's largest net borrower, and the oil exporters have also become borrowers. The dominant lender since then has been Japan. The major type of lending has been private loans and portfolio investments, a shift from the official loans from governments and direct foreign investment that were dominant from the late 1940s to the early 1970s.

International lending can bring major benefits of two types. First, it represents intertemporal trade, in which the lender gives up resources today in order to get more in the future, and the borrower gets resources today but must be willing to pay back more in the future. Second, it allows lenders and investors to diversify their investments more broadly. The ability to add foreign financial assets to investment portfolios can lower the riskiness of the entire portfolio of investments through greater diversification. The chapter begins with an analysis of some of the benefits of international lending and borrowing. We focus on the benefits of intertemporal trade that takes advantage of different rates of return in different countries.

International lending is not always well-behaved. International lending to developing countries swings between surges of lending and crises of confidence. During the financial crises, lending shrinks and lenders scramble to get repaid. The rest of the chapter discusses why these financial crises occur, how we try to resolve them, and what we might be able to do to make them less frequent.

GAINS AND LOSSES FROM WELL-BEHAVED INTERNATIONAL LENDING

If the world is stable and predictable, and if borrowers fully honor their commitments to repay, then international lending can be efficient from a world point of view, bringing gains to some that outweigh losses to others. In such a world, the welfare effects of international lending are exactly parallel to the welfare effects of opening trade (Chapter 2) or those of allowing free labor migration (Chapter 14).

Figure 20.1 shows the normal effects of allowing free international lending and borrowing. We divide the world into two large countries: "Japan," having abundant financial wealth and less attractive domestic investment opportunities; and an "America" in the image of Argentina, Brazil, Canada, and the United States, having less wealth relative to its abundant opportunities for profitable investment (for instance, in its new technologies or its open areas rich in natural resources). The length of the horizontal axis in Figure 20.1 shows total world wealth, equal to Japan's wealth W_J plus America's wealth W_A. This wealth is used to finance capital investments. The vertical axes indicate rates of return earned on capital investments. (We often refer to an equilibrium rate of the return as the interest rate, although it may also incorporate the return to equity investment.) Capital investment opportunities in Japan are shown as the marginal-product-of-capital curve

FIGURE 20.1

Gains and Losses from Well-Behaved International Lending

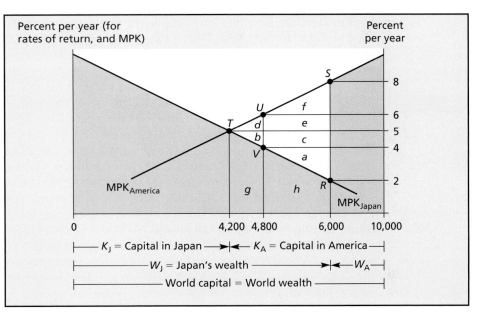

From no international lending (*RS*) to free lending (*T*):

Japan	gains ($a + b + c$)	= 27
America	gains ($d + e + f$)	= 27
World	gains (*a* through *f*)	= 54

If Japan imposes a 2 percent per year tax on lending abroad (from *T* to *UV*):

Japan	gains ($e - b$)	= 9
America	loses ($d + e$)	= 15
World	loses ($b + d$)	= 6

If America imposes a 2 percent per year tax on borrowing abroad (from *T* to *UV*):

Japan	loses ($b + c$)	= 15
America	gains ($c - d$)	= 9
World	loses ($b + d$)	= 6

MPK$_{Japan}$, which begins at the left vertical axis, and ranks possible investments in Japan according to the returns the investments produce. Investment opportunities in America are shown as the marginal-product-of-capital curve MPK$_{America}$, which begins at the right vertical axis and ranks investments in the opposite direction, from right to left.

We begin with a situation in which international financial transactions are prohibited. In this situation each country must use its financial wealth to finance its own stock of real capital. If all Japanese wealth W_J is used domestically, Japan's lenders must accept a low rate of return, because the return on domestic capital investments follows the declining MPK$_{Japan}$ curve. Competition thus forces lenders in Japan to accept the low rate of return of 2 percent per year at point *R*. Meanwhile, in America, the scarcity of funds prevents any capital formation to the left of point *S* since W_A is all the wealth that America has. Competition for borrowing the W_A of national wealth bids the American rate of interest on lending up to 8 percent at point *S*. We can also use this figure to show the value of total production in each country and in the world, assuming that some capital is used in all production. If we add up the product of each unit of capital (the MPK), we get the total production by all capital, equal to the area under the MPK curve. With no international financial flows, the world's product equals the shaded area in Figure 20.1. Japan's product is the shaded area to the left of the vertical line through point R, and America's is the shaded area to the right.

Now imagine that there are no barriers to international finance. Wealthholders in Japan and borrowers in America have a strong incentive to get together. Why should one group lend at only 2 percent and the other borrow at 8 percent if, as we assume here, the riskiness or creditworthiness of the different borrowings is the same? Lenders in Japan should do part of their lending in America. Over time, their lending to America will allow more capital formation in America, with less capital formation in Japan. The international lending leads to a different equilibrium, one in which the worldwide rate of return is somewhere between 2 percent and 8 percent. Let's say that it ends up at 5 percent, at point T. In this situation the wealth of Japan exceeds its stock of domestic real assets by the same amount $(W_J - K_J)$ that America has to borrow to finance its extra real assets $(K_A - W_A)$.

With international financial freedom, world product is maximized. It equals everything under either marginal product curve or all the shaded area plus area RST. This is a clear gain of area RST (or areas a through f) over the situation in which international lending was prohibited. The reason for this gain is that freedom allows individual wealthholders the chance to seek the highest return anywhere in the world.

The world's gains from international lending are split between the two countries. Japan's national income comes from two places:

- Its domestic production, which equals the area under its MPK$_{Japan}$ curve down to point T (the product of the 4,200 of its wealth that it invests at home),

- *Plus* foreign source income on its investments in America, which equals area $a + b + c + g + h$ (the 5 percent return on the 1,800 that Japan has invested in America).

Japan gains area $a + b + c$ in national income through its foreign investment. America's national income is the difference between two flows:

- Its domestic production, which equals the area under its MPK$_{America}$ curve down to point T (the product of the total 6,800 that is invested in America),

- *Minus* what it has to pay Japan for what it has borrowed from Japan, a payment equal to area $a + b + c + g + h$ (5 percent on the 1,800 that America has borrowed from Japan).

America also gains from its international borrowing, a gain of area $d + e + f$.

Within each country there are gainers and losers from the new freedom. Japanese lenders gain from lending at 5 percent instead of at 2 percent. That harms

Japanese borrowers, though, because competition from foreign borrowers forces them to pay the same higher rate on their borrowings. In America borrowers have gained from being able to borrow at 5 percent instead of 8 percent. Yet American lenders will be nostalgic for the old days of financial isolation, when borrowers still had to pay them 8 percent. In addition, the smaller capital stock in Japan lowers the productivity and earnings of other resources (like labor and land) in Japan, whereas the larger capital stock in America raises the productivity and earnings of other resources in America.

TAXES ON INTERNATIONAL LENDING

We have compared free international lending with no international lending and have found the orthodox result: Freedom raises world product and national incomes. Another standard result also carries over from trade analysis: the **nationally optimal tax.** *If* a country looms large enough to have power over the world market rate of return, it can exploit this market power to its own advantage, at the expense of other countries and the world as a whole.

In Figure 20.1, Japan can be said to have market power. By restricting its foreign lending, it could force America's borrowers to pay higher interest rates (moving northeast from point T toward point S). Let us say that Japan exploits this power by imposing a tax of 2 percent per year on the value of assets held abroad by residents of Japan. This will bid up the rate that America's borrowers have to pay and bid down the rate that domestic lenders can get after taxes. Equilibrium will be restored when the gap between the foreign and domestic rates is just the 2 percent tax. This is shown by the gap UV in Figure 20.1. Japan's government collects total tax revenues (area $e + c$) equal to the tax rate times the 1,200 of international assets that Japan continues to have after the adjustment to the tax. Japan has made a net gain on its taxation of foreign lending. It has forced America to pay 6 percent instead of 5 percent on all continuing debt. With a 2 percent tax, the markup, area e, is large enough to outweigh Japan's loss of some previously profitable lending abroad (triangle b). Setting such a tax at just the right level (which might or might not be the one shown here) gives Japan a nationally optimal tax on foreign lending.

Two can play at that game. Figure 20.1 shows that America also has market power, since by restricting its borrowing it could force Japan's lenders to accept lower rates of return (moving southeast from point T toward point R). What if it is America (instead of Japan) that imposes the 2 percent tax on the same international assets? Then all the results would work out the same as for the tax by Japan—except that the American government pockets the tax revenue (area $c + e$). America, in this case, gains income (area c minus area d) at the expense of Japan and the world as a whole. (If both countries impose taxes on the same international lending, the amount of international lending shrinks. At most, one country can gain compared to its position with free lending, and it is rather likely that both countries lose.)

INTERNATIONAL LENDING TO DEVELOPING COUNTRIES

International lending and borrowing between industrialized countries generally is well-behaved and provides the sort of mutual benefits that we have discussed. Financial capital flows from industrialized countries like Japan and Germany, where it is relatively abundant, to countries like the United States that offer rich investment opportunities. Both lender and borrower benefit from the gains from intertemporal trade, as countries with net savings get higher returns and countries that are net borrowers pay lower costs. Additional gains arise as international financial investments are used to lower risk through portfolio diversification. Conflicts sometimes arise over tax policies, but these are manageable.

International lending by industrialized countries to developing countries is another story. It should create these same gains from intertemporal trade and risk diversification, and to large extent it does. But there are also periodic international crises—lending from industrialized countries to developing countries is sometimes not well-behaved. In a financial crisis the borrowing country experiences difficulties in servicing its debts, and it often *defaults*—that is, fails to make payments as specified in the debt agreements. Lenders cut back or stop new lending, as the borrower is viewed as too risky. This section presents a brief history of capital flows to developing countries and the nature of the financial crises. Subsequent sections look at why crises occur, how they are resolved, and suggestions for ways to reduce the frequency of crises.

The Surge in International Lending, 1974–1982

Before World War I there was a large amount of international lending, with Britain as the main creditor and the growing newly settled countries (the United States, Canada, Argentina, Australia) as the main borrowers. To a large extent this international lending fit the well-behaved model of Figure 20.1, as lending sought out high returns (although defaults were also common).[1] During the 1920s, a large number of foreign governments issued foreign bonds, especially in New York, as the United States became a major creditor country. But in the 1930s, the depression led to massive defaults by developing countries, which frightened away lenders through the 1960s. Lending to developing countries remained very low for four decades.

The oil shocks of the 1970s led to a surge in private international lending to developing countries. Between 1970 and 1980, developing country debt outstanding increased sevenfold, with debt rising from 9.8 percent of the countries' national product in 1970 to 18.2 percent in 1980.

The oil shocks quadrupled and then tripled the world price of oil, and these shocks caused recessions and high inflation in the industrialized countries. How

---

[1] The United States was the borrower in one of the default episodes. Britain lent substantial amounts to finance canals and cotton growing in the United States during 1826–1837. A depression began in 1837, and eight states had defaulted on their debts by 1843.

did the shocks also revive the lending? Four forces combined to create the surge. First, the rich oil-exporting nations had a high short-run propensity to save out of their extra income. While their savings were piling up, they tended to invest them in liquid form, especially in bonds and bank deposits in the United States and other established financial centers. The major international private banks thereby gained large amounts of new funds to be lent to other borrowers. The banks had the problem of "recycling" or reinvesting the "petrodollars." But where to lend?

Second, there was widespread pessimism about the profitability of capital formation in industrialized countries. Real interest rates in many countries were unusually low. One promising area was investment in energy-saving equipment, but the development of these projects took time. For a time the banks' expanded ability to lend was not absorbed by borrowers in the industrial countries, which encouraged banks to look elsewhere. Attention began to shift to developing countries, which had long been forced to offer higher rates of interest and dividends to attract even small amounts of private capital.

Third, in developing countries, the 1970s was an era of peak resistance to foreign direct investment (FDI), in which the foreign investor, usually a multinational firm based in an industrialized country, keeps controlling ownership of foreign affiliated enterprises. Banks might have lent to multinational firms for additional FDI, but developing countries were generally hostile to FDI. Populist ideological currents and valid fears about political intrigues by multinational firms brought FDI down from 25 percent of net financial flows to developing countries in 1960 to less than 10 percent by 1980. To gain access to the higher returns offered in developing countries, banks had to lend outright to governments and companies in these countries.

Fourth, "herding" behavior meant that the lending to developing countries acquired a momentum of its own once it began to increase. Major banks aggressively sought lending opportunities, each showing eagerness to lend before competing banks did. Much of the lending went to poorly planned projects in mismanaged economies. But everyone was doing it.

The Debt Crisis of 1982

In August 1982, Mexico declared that it was unable to service its large foreign debt. Dozens of other developing countries followed with announcements that they also could not repay their previous loans. Several factors explain why the crunch came in 1982. Interest rates increased sharply in the United States, as the U.S. Federal Reserve shifted to a much tighter monetary policy to reduce U.S. inflation. The United States and other industrialized countries sank into a severe recession. Developing countries' exports declined and commodity prices plummeted, while real interest rates remained high. The debtors' ability to repay fell dramatically.

At first the responses of the bank creditors depended on how much each bank had lent. Smaller banks (those holding small shares of all loans) headed for the exits and eliminated their exposure by selling off their loans or getting repaid. The larger banks could not extricate themselves without triggering a larger crisis, and they hoped that the problems were temporary. They rescheduled loan payments to establish repayment obligations in the future, and they loaned smaller amounts of new money to assist the debtors to grow so that repayment would be possible. Figure 20.2 provides information on long-term financial flows to developing countries. Bank loans, which were most of the private lending to developing countries in the early 1980s, declined somewhat in 1983 and 1984. As shown in Figure 20.3, the long-term debt of developing countries doubled between 1980 and 1985, the ratio of debt to national product rose from 18 percent in 1980 to 35 percent in 1985, and the share of export revenues that was committed to service the debt nearly doubled, to almost 25 percent. As large banks reassessed the prospects for developing country debtors, they concluded that it was imprudent to lend more. The net flows of bank loans to developing countries became small in 1985 and remained low until 1995.

As the debt crisis wore on through the 1980s, it became clear that the debtor countries were suffering low economic growth and lack of access to international finance, but that this cost was not leading to repayments that would end the crisis. In response, U.S. Treasury officials crafted the Brady Plan (named after U.S. Treasury Secretary Nicholas Brady). Beginning in 1989, each debtor country could reach a deal in which its bank debt would be partially reduced, with most of the remaining loans repackaged as "Brady bonds." By 1994, most of the bank debt had been reduced and converted into bonds. The debt crisis that began in 1982 was effectively over.

The Resurgence of Capital Flows in the 1990s

Beginning in about 1990, lending to and investing in developing countries began to increase again. Four forces converged to drive this new lending. First, the size and scope of the Brady Plan led investors to believe that the previous crisis was being resolved. As each debtor country agreed to a Brady deal, it was usually able to receive new private lending almost immediately. Second, low U.S. interest rates again led lenders to seek out higher returns through foreign investments. Third, the developing countries were becoming more attractive places to lend as governments reformed their policies. Governments were opening up opportunities for financing profitable new investments as they deregulated industries, privatized state-owned firms, and encouraged production for export with outward-oriented trade policies (as discussed in Chapter 13). Fourth, individual investors, as well as the rapidly growing mutual funds and pension funds, were looking for new forms of portfolio investments that could raise returns and add risk diversification. Developing countries became the emerging markets for this portfolio investment.

Figure 20.2 shows the rapidly growing flows of long-term investments into developing countries, as total net financial inflows increased every year from 1989 to 1997. The majority of this money went to a small number of developing countries viewed as the major emerging markets—Mexico, Brazil, and Argentina in Latin America and China, Indonesia, Malaysia, South Korea, and Thailand in Asia. The types of investments were different from those that drove the lending

FIGURE 20.2 Net Long-Term Financial Flows to Developing Countries, 1981–2001 (Billions of U.S. Dollars)

Source and Type	1981	1982	1983	1984	1985	1986	1987	1988	1989
Official	34	35	35	34	41	45	45	42	42
Loans	22	24	24	21	25	28	27	23	23
Grants	11	11	10	13	16	17	18	19	20
Private debt	53	45	31	27	22	10	10	15	14
Bank loans	44	33	23	23	9	2	2	9	6
Bonds	1	4	2	0	6	2	1	4	5
Other loans	8	8	6	5	8	6	7	3	4
Portfolio equity (stock)	0	0	0	0	0	0	0	0	4
Foreign direct investment	13	11	9	9	11	10	14	20	23
Total	100	91	74	72	73	65	68	76	83

Source and Type	1990	1991	1992	1993	1994	1995	1996	1997	1998	1999	2000	2001
Official	55	62	54	53	46	54	30	41	53	47	35	37
Loans	27	27	23	25	13	21	2	15	26	18	5	8
Grants	28	35	31	28	33	33	28	26	27	29	30	29
Private debt	16	19	38	50	51	63	97	98	89	6	8	−27
Bank loans	3	5	16	4	9	31	32	46	52	−23	−6	−32
Bonds	1	11	11	37	38	31	62	50	41	30	17	10
Other loans	11	3	11	9	4	2	2	3	−3	−1	−3	−4
Portfolio equity (stock)	4	8	14	51	35	36	49	30	16	35	51	19
Foreign direct investment	24	36	47	67	90	107	131	173	178	184	167	168
Total	99	124	154	221	222	260	307	341	337	272	261	196

Note: Net inflows of short-term finance have been variable: $17 billion in 1990, rising to $61 billion in 1995, then declining to $4 billion in 2000.

Source: 1990–2001: World Bank, *Global Development Finance, 2002;* 1985–1989: World Bank, *World Debt Tables, 1992–93;* 1981–1984: Rachel McCulloch and Peter A. Petri, "Equity Financing of East Asian Development," in Kahler (1998).

surge in the late 1970s. Foreign portfolio investors' net purchases of stocks and bonds rose from almost nothing in 1990 to one-third of total net financial flows in 1996. Bank lending was less important, but even bank lending increased substantially from 1993 to 1997. Figure 20.3 shows that developing country debt outstanding rose as a percentage of national product from 30.9 percent in 1990 to 38.2 percent in 1995, but that lower interest rates actually lowered the share of exports of goods and services that had to be devoted to debt service.

The Mexican Crisis, 1994–1995

A series of crises punctured the generally strong flows of international lending to developing countries since 1990. The first of these struck Mexico in late 1994.

Mexico received large capital inflows in the early 1990s, as investors sought high returns and were impressed with Mexico's economic reforms and its entry into the North American Free Trade Area. But strains also arose. The real exchange rate value of the peso increased, because the government permitted

FIGURE 20.3
Developing
Countries' Debt
Outstanding,
1970–2000
(Billions of U.S.
Dollars, Unless
Otherwise
Indicated)

Source: World Bank,
*Global Development
Finance, 1999;* World
Bank, *Global
Development Finance,
2002;* and World
Bank, *World Debt
Tables, 1992–93.*

Type of Debt	1970	1980	1985	1990	1995	2000
Long-term debt	63	436	899	1,180	1,674	2,061
Public and publicly guaranteed	47	365	797	1,115	1,454	1,527
Private nonguaranteed	15	71	102	66	220	534
Loans from the IMF	1	12	41	35	61	64
Short-term debt	10	139	184	245	427	402
Total debt	73	587	1,123	1,460	2,163	2,528
Debt/GNP ratio (percentage)	9.8	18.2	35.4	30.9	38.2	40.5
Debt service–exports of goods and services ratio (percentage)	NA	12.8	24.7	18.1	16.0	17.0

NA = Not available

only a slow nominal peso depreciation, while the Mexican inflation rate was higher than that of the United States, its main trading partner. The current account deficit increased to 8 percent of Mexico's GDP in 1994, although this was readily financed by the capital inflows. Mexico's banking system was rather weak, with inadequate bank supervision and regulation by the government. With the capital inflows adding funds to the Mexican banking system, bank lending grew rapidly, as did defaults on these loans. The year 1994 was an election year with some turmoil, including an uprising in the Chiapas region and two political assassinations. The peso came under some downward pressure. The government used sterilized intervention to defend its exchange rate value, so its holdings of official international reserves fell.

Mexico's fiscal policy was reasonable, with a modest government budget deficit. Still, the fiscal authorities made the change that became the center of the crisis, by altering the form of the government debt. Beginning in early 1994, the government replaced peso-denominated government debt with short-term dollar-indexed government debt called *tesobonos.* By the end of 1994, there were about $28 billion of *tesobonos* outstanding, most maturing in the first half of 1995.

The crisis was touched off by a large flight of capital, mostly by Mexican residents who feared a currency devaluation and converted out of pesos. In December the currency was allowed to depreciate, but Mexican holdings of official reserves had declined to about $6 billion. The financial crisis arose as investors refused to purchase new *tesobonos* to pay off those coming due, because it appeared that the government did not have the ability to make good on its dollar obligations. Each investor wanted to be paid off in dollars—a rush to the exit—but what was rational for each investor individually was not necessarily rational for all of them collectively. The Mexican government might not be able to repay all of them within a short time period. As investors reassessed their investments in emerging markets, they pulled back on investments not only in Mexico but also in many other developing countries (the "tequila effect").

The U.S. government became worried about the political and economic effects of financial crisis in Mexico, and it arranged a large rescue package that permitted the Mexican government to borrow up to $50 billion, mostly from the U.S. government and the International Monetary Fund (IMF).[2] The Mexican government did borrow about $25 billion, using the money to pay off the *tesobonos* as they matured and to replenish its official reserve holdings. The currency depreciation and the financial turmoil caused rapid and painful adjustments in Mexico. The Mexican economy went into a severe recession, and the current account deficit disappeared as imports decreased and exports increased.

As the rescue took hold, the pure contagion that led investors to retreat from nearly all lending to developing countries calmed after the first quarter of 1995. The adverse tequila effect lingered for a smaller number of countries, as investors continued to pull out of Argentina, Brazil, and to lesser extents, Venezuela and the Philippines. Still, much of the Mexican financial crisis of 1994–1995 was resolved quickly. As shown in Figure 20.2, overall capital flows to developing countries continued to increase in 1995 and 1996.

The Asian Crisis, 1997

In the early and mid-1990s, foreign investors looked favorably on the rapidly growing developing countries of Southeast and East Asia. In these countries macroeconomic policies were solid. The governments had fiscal budgets with surpluses or small deficits; steady monetary policies kept inflation low, and trade policies were outward-oriented. Most of the foreign debt was owed by private firms, not by the governments.

A closer look showed a few problems. In Thailand and South Korea, much of the foreign borrowing was by banks and other financial institutions. Government regulation and supervision were weak. The banks took on significant exchange rate risk by borrowing dollars and yen and lending in local currencies. And the lending boom led to loans to riskier local borrowers and rising defaults on loans. In Indonesia, much of the foreign borrowing was by private nonfinancial firms, which took on the exchange rate risk directly.

The external balance of the countries also showed some problems. The real exchange rate values of these countries' currencies seemed to be somewhat overvalued, and the growth of exports slowed beginning in 1996. With the exception of Thailand, the current account deficits were not large. Thailand's current account deficit rose to 8 percent of GDP in 1996. Still, the strong capital inflows provided financing for the deficits.

Crisis struck first in Thailand. Beginning in 1996, the expectation of declining exports led to large declines in Thai stock prices and real estate prices. The exchange rate value of the Thai baht came under downward pressure. By mid-1997, the pressures had become intense. Banks and other local firms that had borrowed dollars and yen without hedging rushed to sell baht to acquire foreign currency assets. The Thai government could not maintain its defense, and the baht was allowed to depreciate beginning in July 1997.

---

[2] For information on what the IMF is and how it makes loans to countries with balance of payments problems, see the box "Short of Reseves? Call 1-800-IMF-LOAN."

Case Study   Short of Reserves? Call 1-800-IMF-LOAN

The International Monetary Fund (IMF) was designed as part of the 1944 Bretton Woods agreement that also set up the postwar fixed-rate system. The IMF began operation in 1946 and by 2002 had 184 member countries. On joining the IMF, each member contributes resources, called the country's *quota*. One quarter of these contributed resources are assets generally recognized as official international reserves and the other three-quarters are its own currency. The size of the quota is roughly related to the country's economic size, and the size determines the country's voting rights on the board of directors. For instance, the United States has about 17 percent of the voting rights. Periodically, the sizes of the countries' quotas are increased to expand the IMF's financial resources. The IMF also borrows from some of its members and receives voluntary contributions from some.

The IMF has several major purposes. It promotes the expansion of international trade and international monetary cooperation among countries. It seeks to maintain orderly foreign exchange arrangements through surveillance of the exchange rate policies of its member countries. Especially, countries should not manipulate their exchange rate to gain unfair competitive advantages. The IMF seeks to establish unrestricted convertibility of currencies for current account payments. It created the special drawing right (SDR) as a new official reserve asset and occasionally makes new allocations to its members (the most recent during 1979–1981). The IMF collects and publishes national economic and financial data. And, most important to our purpose here, the IMF lends to its members when appropriate to give them time to correct payment imbalances. In the early years, most such loans were to industrialized countries recovering from wartime destruction and disruptions. In recent decades nearly all IMF loans have been to developing countries.

Most IMF lending is to countries with large payments deficits, countries whose official reserves are declining to low levels. The loans provide additional official reserve assets to the country. The country can use these additional reserves to buy time for the country to make orderly macroeconomic adjustments to reduce the deficit, without resorting to exchange controls or trade restrictions. Ideally, the adjustment can occur without excessive costs or disruptions to the country or to other countries. The IMF makes loans under a number of different programs. Standard loans are made from the country's *credit tranches* linked to the country's quota contributions. The IMF can also make longer (extended fund) or larger (supplemental reserve) loans. In addition, several other programs target specific purposes, including loans to cover temporary shortfalls in export earnings due to declines in world commodity prices and loans with very low interest rates to very poor countries. Most IMF loans are to be repaid in 5 years; some are to be repaid in 10 years. Maximum amounts of loans from various programs are in proportion to a country's quota.

Throughout the rest of 1997 the crisis spread to a number of other Asian countries, especially to Indonesia and South Korea, but also to Malaysia and the Philippines, as foreign investors lost confidence in local bank borrowers and the local stock markets, and as local borrowers scrambled to sell local currency to establish hedges against exchange rate risk. Figure 20.4 shows the declines of about 50 percent in the exchange rate values of the currencies of Thailand, Indonesia, Korea, Malaysia, and the Philippines during the second half of 1997. (The figure also shows that the value of the Singapore dollar was affected much less, and the value of the Hong Kong dollar, fixed to the U.S. dollar through its currency board, not at all.)

The IMF only makes loans that it expects to be repaid. The IMF requires a borrowing country to agree to how it intends to correct its payments imbalance. That is, the IMF imposes **conditionality**—the IMF makes a loan only if the borrowing country commits to and enacts changes in its policies with quantified performance criteria. The policies should promise to achieve external balance within a reasonable time. The IMF disburses some loans in pieces over time. It withholds pieces if the performance criteria are not met. The policy changes that are usually included in an IMF adjustment program are not surprising. They include fiscal and monetary restraint, liberalization of restrictions on domestic markets and on international trade, and deregulation.

What is the record for these IMF loans? Do they work? One answer is repayment. Prior to the mid-1980s, nearly all loans had been repaid on time. However, from 1985 to 1992, rising amounts, reaching over 10 percent of IMF loans outstanding, had not been repaid on time. These overdue payments then declined to about 5 percent of loans outstanding in 2001.

Do the loans assist payments adjustment? Evaluation of the effects of the loans and the conditions attached to them is difficult—what would have happened without them? Nonetheless, the programs accompanying IMF loans typically appear to result in increases in a country's exports, decreases in imports, and reduction in the payments deficits, but these changes are often temporary. Many countries appear to be chronically dependent on IMF loans. Sixty countries have borrowed in almost every year since their first borrowing from the IMF.

The conditions that a government is required to meet for a loan are often not popular domestically. The policy changes are usually contractionary, for instance, reductions in the rate of new lending by banks in the country. The policy changes often reduce the country's rate of real investment and economic growth. Indeed, the conditions are often resisted, and half or more of the lending programs break down because the conditions are not met by the country's government, as happened in Russia in 1998 and Argentina in 2001.

In the programs for the Asian crisis countries, the use of conditions seemed to get out of hand. The agreement with Indonesia had 140 conditions, and the agreement with the Philippines over 100. Some of these conditions required changes in basic economic structures and institutions, including changes in labor rules and business governance. Critics saw these structural conditions as unnecessary to address the external imbalances. In 2001 the IMF committed to focusing its conditionality on measures crucial to the needed macroeconomic adjustment, with fewer conditions that are easier to monitor for compliance. The fund hopes that this change will elicit more support for its requirements from the governments (and the people) of the borrowing countries.

In response, the IMF organized large rescue packages, with commitments to lend up to $17 billion to Thailand ($13 billion actually borrowed), up to $42 billion to Indonesia ($9 billion borrowed), and up to $58 billion to South Korea ($27 billion borrowed). As in Mexico, these large rescue packages and policy changes did contain the crises, though not without costs. The currency depreciations and the recessions did lead to improvements in the current account balance, largely through decreases in imports. However, these countries also went into severe multiyear recessions.

FIGURE 20.4   Exchange Rates, Asian Countries, 1994–2001

Source: International Monetary Fund, *International Financial Statistics.*

The Russian Crisis, 1998

Russia weathered the Asian crisis in 1997 very well, but its underlying fundamental position was remarkably weak. It had a large fiscal budget deficit, and government borrowing led to rapid increases in government debt to both domestic and foreign lenders. In mid-1998, lenders balked at buying still more Russian government debt. In July 1998, the IMF organized a lending package under which the Russian government could borrow up to $23 billion, and the IMF made the first loan of $5 billion. However, the Russian government failed to enact policy changes included as conditions for the loan. The exchange rate value of the ruble came under severe pressure as capital flight by wealthy Russians led to large sales of rubles for foreign currencies. With substantial debt service due on government debt during the second half of 1998, investor confidence declined, with selling pressure driving down Russian stock and bond prices.

In August 1998, the Russian government announced drastic measures. The government unilaterally "restructured" its ruble-denominated debt, effectively wiping out most of the creditors' value. It placed a 90-day moratorium on payments of many foreign currency obligations of banks and other private firms, a move designed to protect Russian banks. And it allowed the ruble to depreciate by shifting to a floating exchange rate. Russia requested the next installment of its loan from the IMF, but the IMF refused, because the government had not met the conditions for fiscal reforms.

Foreign lenders were in shock. They had expected that Russia was too important to fail and that the IMF rescue package would provide Russia with the funds to repay them. They reassessed the risk of investments in all emerging markets and rapidly sought to reduce their investments. The selloff caused stock and bond prices to plummet, with a general flight to high-quality investments like U.S. government bonds. The reversal of international bank lending and stock and bond investing in 1998 led to the first decline in net long-term financial flows to developing countries since the mid-1980s (see Figure 20.2).

The Brazilian Crisis, 1999

Brazil was among the countries hit hard by the fallout from the Russian crisis. In November 1998, the IMF organized a package that allowed the Brazilian government to borrow up to $41 billion, in an effort to allow Brazil to fight pressures pushing toward a crisis. Brazil had a large current account deficit, and the government was defending its crawling exchange rate with intervention and high domestic interest rates. However, the government failed to enact the fiscal reforms called for in the IMF loan, and capital outflows increased.

In January 1999, the Brazilian government ended its pegged exchange rate, and the real depreciated. However, this situation did not escalate into a full crisis because the problems did not spread to the Brazilian banking system, which was sound and well regulated. By April 1999, Brazil and other developing countries were able to issue new bonds to foreign investors. More generally, the market prices of emerging market financial assets began to increase, although the net capital flows to developing countries remained lower than they had been in 1997.

The Turkish Crisis, 2001

Turkey's economy and its government policies had been problematic for decades, and it had borrowed from the IMF continually since 1958. In January 2000 Turkey entered into another borrowing program of $8 billion from the IMF and the World Bank, and committed to reduce its inflation rate (which had been close to 100 percent for a number of years), improve its regulation of the banking system and close failing banks, privatize state-owned businesses, end various subsidies, and reduce its fiscal deficit. As part of the inflation fight, Turkey adopted a crawling exchange rate (pegged to a basket of the euro and the U.S. dollar).

The announcement of the new program brought large capital inflows. Turkish banks were able to borrow foreign currencies at low interest rates to invest the funds in high-interest Turkish government bonds. The country grew quickly, and inflation was lowered below 50 percent, but the fiscal deficit remained high, and the current account deficit widened to about 5 percent of GDP. November brought the first signs of new trouble, and foreign lenders began to pull back. The Turkish government used a large amount of its official reserves to defend the pegged exchange rate. December brought new pressures as several prominent bankers were arrested. Overnight interest rates rose to an annual rate of nearly 2,000 percent, to stem the capital outflows. A new IMF program promised additional loans of up to $7.5 billion during the next year.

After calming for a while, conditions deteriorated again in February 2001, because of legislative delays and political fighting between the president and prime minister about reforms. Overnight, interest rates again went into quadruple digits, and the government again used up a large amount of its official reserves defending the pegged exchange rate. Then the government gave up, and the lira lost a third of its value in two days. Turkey's banks incurred large losses. Turkey entered into yet another IMF program in May 2001.

Argentina's Crisis, 2001–2002

As we described in Chapter 1, for much of the 1990s Argentina was viewed as a major success story. It tamed a hyperinflation, fixed its peso to the U.S. dollar using a currency board, and grew rapidly up to 1998. It also strengthened its banking system and established sound regulation and supervision.

But beginning in 1997 the peso experienced a real appreciation, first because the dollar strengthened against other currencies, and then because Brazil's currency depreciated by a large amount in 1999. Argentina's trade prospects dimmed. Its fiscal situation had been one of its weak points all along, and this situation deteriorated further as the economy went through years of recession beginning in 1998. Most of the government debt was denominated in foreign currency and owed to foreign lenders and bondholders.

In late 2000 Argentina reached agreement for a package of loans of up to $40 billion, with $14 billion coming from the IMF. However, things did not improve, and the Argentinean government did not meet its obligations under the conditions of the IMF program to reduce its fiscal deficit. In September the IMF made an unusually large disbursement of $6 billion, but it was to be the last. In response to depositor runs on banks, the banks were closed in November, and when they reopened withdrawals were severely limited.

In early 2002 the government surrendered the fixed exchange rate, and the peso lost 75 percent of its value in the first six months of the year. The government also defaulted on its debt. In addition, the peso depreciation caused huge losses in the banks because of the mismatch of dollar liabilities and dollar assets, and because of the terms under which the government mandated the conversion of dollar assets and liabilities into pesos. A number of banks closed up. The public lost confidence in banks and in the government. In mid-2002 Argentina was in a severe recession.

At first it appeared that Argentina's collapse would have few effects on other developing countries, since it had been widely expected. But after a few months Argentina's problems did spread to its neighbors. Uruguay relied on Argentina for tourism and banking business. The tourism dried up, and Argentinean withdrawals from their Uruguayan accounts increased. After its holdings of official reserves plummeted defending Uruguay's crawling pegged exchange rate, the Uruguay government floated its currency in June; within two weeks, the currency had fallen by half. In August an emergency loan from the United States allowed Uruguay to reopen its banks, which had been closed for four days to stop a run by nervous depositors.

Brazil was also hit by fallout from Argentina's crisis. In July foreign investors pulled out of their Brazilian investments, and the exchange rate value of the real fell by almost 20 percent. In August the IMF announced a new lending program of $30 billion, and the real stabilized.

FINANCIAL CRISES: WHAT CAN AND DOES GO WRONG

International lending to developing countries brings benefits, but, as we just saw in the history of the past several decades, it also brings recurrent financial crises. How can we understand the frequency and scope of these crises? We gain major insights by focusing on five major forces that can, and do, lead to financial crises:

1. Waves of overlending and overborrowing.

2. Exogenous international shocks.

3. Exchange rate risk.

4. Fickle international short-term lending.

5. Global contagion.

Waves of Overlending and Overborrowing

Our model of well-behaved lending, shown in Figure 20.1, assumes that lenders only lend (and that borrowers only borrow) for investment projects that generate the returns in the future that can be used to service the debt. This is not always true. In the late 1970s and again in the mid-1990s, lenders seemed to lend excessive amounts to some countries.

The classic explanation of overlending/overborrowing is that it results from excessively expansionary government policies in the borrowing country. These policies lead to government borrowing to finance growing budget deficits, and the government may also guarantee loans to private borrowers in order to finance the growing current account deficits. Lending to national governments, like the Mexican government in the late 1970s and early 1980s or the Argentinean government in the 1990s, seems to be low risk, but it's not. When the government realizes that it has borrowed too much, it has an incentive to default, and a financial crisis arises. (The box "The Special Case of Sovereign Debt," examines government defaults in more depth.)

The Asian crisis (and to a lesser extent the Mexican crisis of 1994–1995) presented a new form of overlending and overborrowing: too much lending to private borrowers rather than to national governments. In the 1990s, lending to banks in Asian countries seemed to be low risk, because the countries' governments provided a guarantee that creditors would be repaid. Large capital inflows lead to easy domestic credit. In a domestic lending boom, some of the lending is for cur-

Extension   The Special Case of Sovereign Debt

Most debt of developing countries is *sovereign debt*—debt of the government of the country or debt of private borrowers that is guaranteed by the country's government. According to the information in Figure 20.3, sovereign debt was 94 percent of total long-term debt in 1990, and this was still 74 percent in 2000, notwithstanding the rising importance of investments in the securities of private companies.

Sovereign borrowers are different. They cannot be legally forced to repay if they do not wish to do so. Creditors cannot sue them in court or seize their assets. Granted, there have been times in the past when creditors could force repayments: Britain and France were able to take over Egyptian tax collections in the latter half of the 19th century after Egypt failed to repay English and French creditors, and creditors were backed by gunboats when they demanded repayment from Venezuela at the beginning of the 20th century. But the gunboat days are over. If Malaysia defaults on its debts, the United States and other lending countries cannot send gunboats to Malaysia. Nor can they send thugs to beat up the Malaysian finance minister.

If sovereign debtors cannot be forced to repay, why should they ever repay? The usual answer—that the debtor will repay on time to protect its own future creditworthiness—surprisingly turns out to be false, at least by itself. If fresh loans keep growing fast enough, the debtor country can afford to repay an ever-growing debt service. But this is no solution if the debtor never actually repays the full amount. If lenders tire of "repaying themselves" and cut their new lending, the debtor then defaults.

The correct answer to why sovereign debtors repay requires that they have something more to lose than just access to future loans. In domestic lending, collateral works well as the something more to lose. National laws allow the creditor to take over assets of the nonrepaying debtor, but only in amounts tied to the value defaulted.

Aside from creditworthiness, what might the sovereign debtor lose when it defaults? There are ways to create seizable international collateral, even though they are not perfect counterparts to the collateral recognized by domestic law. If a debtor country has actual gross investments in the banks and enterprises of the creditor country, it should worry that these could be seized in retaliation, as when the United States froze Iranian assets in response to the Teheran hostage crisis in 1979–1981 and several countries froze Iraqi assets after Iraq invaded Kuwait in 1990. In practice, however, the international collateral mechanism is not finely tuned. The value of such assets is not necessarily close to the size of the possible default by the debtor country, and it may be legally difficult for the creditors to seize them.

There are two other sources of loss to the debtor country from default. First, the country can experience macroeconomic costs. We have seen that defaults linked to financial crises disrupt the domestic financial system and the domestic economy. The economy usually goes into a severe recession, exacting a large cost on the country. In addition, the debtor country may lose some ability to export and import if it loses access to trade financing or if new barriers are erected to its trade by the creditor countries. Second, the country can experience a general loss of reputation that results in a loss of other benefits. For instance, multinational firms may see the default as a sign of increased country risk. If multinationals fail to invest or they pull out of the country, it loses the spillover benefits from the technology, management practices, worker training, and marketing skills that the multinational firms bring to the country.

These extra losses create a true benefit–cost problem for the sovereign debtor considering default. And the answer to this benefit–cost problem indicates the limits to prudent lending to the sovereign borrower. The key forces are summarized in the accompanying graph. To simplify, let's examine the case in which the sovereign borrower owes full payment of all debt and interest at the end of the period, equal to the stock of debt (D) plus the interest due on this debt (iD). The debtor is considering full default, so that the straight line $(1 + i)D$ shows the benefits of not repaying. The debtor's cost (C) of not repaying also depends on the stock of debt, but only to some extent. There is a fixed cost (C_0) to any nonrepayment, regardless of the amount of debt. The fixed cost could be in the form of reduced creditworthiness, macroeconomic costs, or

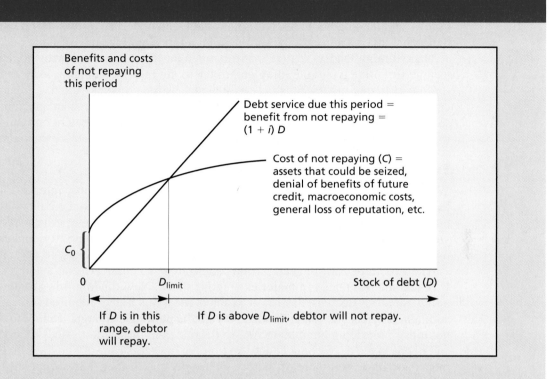

Benefits and costs of not repaying this period

Debt service due this period = benefit from not repaying = $(1 + i)\, D$

Cost of not repaying (C) = assets that could be seized, denial of benefits of future credit, macroeconomic costs, general loss of reputation, etc.

C_0

0   D_{limit} Stock of debt (D)

If D is in this range, debtor will repay.

If D is above D_{limit}, debtor will not repay.

some loss of general reputation. Beyond C_0, the cost of not repaying probably rises with the amount of debt not honored, but not as fast as the stock of debt itself. Loss of access to future loans, asset seizures, macroeconomic costs, and more serious loss of general reputation are probably larger if the default is larger, but these losses are limited. A bigger default does not bring a much bigger penalty.

The fact that the cost of not repaying rises more slowly with extra debt than does the benefit of default means that the sovereign debtor repays debt faithfully as long as the debt is not too large. However, beyond some threshold amount of debt (D_{limit}), the willingness to repay disappears. Well-behaved lending occurs to the left of the limit, because the cost of nonrepayment exceeds the amount of debt service that could be avoided.

Actual default can occur for any of several reasons. First, the borrower may amass debt larger than D_{limit}. This is overlending and overborrowing discussed in the text. We gain a subtle insight from the analysis here. Sovereign debtors may decide that it is not wise to repay even if they are *able* to repay. Second, a rise in the real rate of interest raises the benefit of not repaying. This is an upward rotation of the benefit line $(1 + i)D$ in the graph. If the sovereign debt just equaled D_{limit} before the increase in the interest rate, then it is now above the new D_{limit} for the higher interest rate. The country has the incentive to default. This is an example of how exogenous shocks discussed in the text apply to the special case of sovereign debt.

Should lenders make new loans if the sovereign debtor announces that it "cannot" repay without new loans to cover its current debt service? The graph suggests a negative answer. The debtor's announcement suggests that the stock of debt is already over the safe limit $(D > D_{\text{limit}})$. Extending more loans to cover current interest payments moves us farther to the right $(D$ rises$)$. The gap between the debtor's benefits and the costs of not repaying grows wider. Unless something else changes, default will occur.

rent consumption, so that it is not invested to generate future returns.[3] Other lending goes to investments that are of low quality—projects that offer low returns or are too risky (too likely to fail to produce returns). More generally, the capital inflows and lending boom tend to inflate stock and real estate prices. For a while the capital inflows appear to be earning high returns, until the price bubble bursts.

Once foreign lenders realize that too much has been lent and borrowed, each has the incentive to stop lending and to try to get repaid as quickly as possible (before available money runs out). All cannot be repaid quickly, and a financial crisis erupts. The excessive lending/borrowing that can lead to a financial crisis is sometimes called a **debt overhang**—the amount by which the debt obligations exceed the present value of the payments that will be made to service the debt.

Exogenous International Shocks

When exogenous international shocks hit a country's economy, international lenders and the borrower must reassess the borrower's ability to meet its obligations to service its debt. For instance, a decline in export earnings, perhaps due to a decline in the world price of the country's key export commodity, makes it more difficult for the country to service its debt and thus more likely to default.

The experiences of the early 1980s and mid-1990s indicate that a change in U.S. real interest rates is a major exogenous shock. New funding flows to developing countries decrease, as fewer projects meet this higher required return. In addition, projects previously funded may not be profitable enough, leading to difficulties in servicing bank loans and to decreases in the market prices of stocks and bonds in the developing countries. Foreign investors can sour on their investments and try to sell them off before values decline further. The abrupt shift in flows can result in a crisis if the borrowers cannot adjust quickly enough.

Exchange Rate Risk

Sometimes the form of the debts can help us understand financial crises. In the Mexican, Asian, and Turkish crises, private borrowers took on large liabilities denominated in foreign currency while acquiring assets valued in local currency. The borrowers took on these positions exposed to exchange rate risk because they expected (hoped?) that the government would continue to defend the fixed or heavily managed exchange rate value of the foreign currency. A major part of this uncovered foreign borrowing was the "carry trade," in which financial institutions borrow dollars or yen at a low interest rate, exchange the money to local currency, and lend in the borrowing country at a higher interest rate. This is very profitable as long as the exchange value of the local currency is steady (so that local currency can be exchanged back to dollars or yen at the same rate in the future, to repay the foreign borrowing).

---

[3] Borrowing for current consumption can be sensible, if it is part of a strategy to smooth the country's consumption over time. It makes sense if the country's income will be higher in the future, so that part of the higher future income can be used to repay the loan. But borrowing for current consumption also is risky, because it is not adding to future income potential.

When the likelihood of devaluation or depreciation becomes noticeable, the borrowers attempt to hedge their exposed positions by selling local currency, but this puts additional pressure on the government defense of the fixed exchange rate. If the government gives up the fixed rate, borrowers suffer losses to the extent that their positions are still unhedged. The losses make it more difficult for them to service their foreign debts. Foreign lenders then may reduce new lending and try to be repaid more quickly, leading to a financial crisis.

Fickle International Short-Term Lending

Another form of debt can help us understand financial crises. Short-term debt—debt that is due to be paid off soon—can cause a major problem because foreign lenders can refuse to refinance it. The inability of the Mexican government to refinance the large amount of short-term *tesobonos* that were coming due was a major contributor to the Mexican crisis of 1994–1995. In the Asian crisis, the large amount of short-term borrowing by banks that was coming due created a policy dilemma for the countries' governments. The governments could raise interest rates to attract continued foreign financing, but this would weaken local borrowers and hurt the banks' loan returns. Instead, the governments could guarantee or take over the banks' foreign borrowings, based on the need to prevent the local banks from failing. But the governments themselves did not have sufficient foreign exchange to pay off the debts, so they risked setting off a financial crisis on their own if foreign lenders demanded repayment.

Short-term debt is risky to the borrowing country because international lenders can readily shift from one equilibrium to another, based on their opinion of the country's prospects. In one equilibrium, the lenders refinance or roll over the short-term debt, and this can continue into the future. But a rapid shift to another equilibrium in which lenders demand repayment is also possible. If the borrowing country cannot come up with the payoff quickly, a financial crisis occurs.

Global Contagion

The four forces already discussed—overlending/overborrowing, exogenous shocks, exchange rate risk, and short-term borrowing—provide major insights into why a financial crisis could hit a country. But the financial crises since 1980 were more than this. When a crisis hits one country, it usually spreads and affects many other countries. It appears that some kind of **global contagion** is at work. Some contagion is the result of close trade links between the affected countries; thus, a crisis downturn in one country, like Argentina, has spillover effects in another country, like Uruguay.

Contagion can be an overreaction by foreign lenders as they engage in a scramble for the exits. Herding behavior can occur. Borrowers often do not provide full information to lenders. The high costs of obtaining accurate information on their own can lead some lenders to imitate other lenders who may have better information about the borrowers, or to fear that other borrowing countries are likely to have similar problems to those of the crisis country, even if there is no evidence that this is true.

Contagion can also be based on new recognition of real problems in other countries that are similar to those in the country with the initial crisis. The financial crisis in one country can serve as a "wake-up call" that other countries really do have similar problems. The crisis in Mexico led to a more severe tequila effect in countries that had problems similar to those of Mexico—currencies that had experienced real appreciations, weak banking systems and domestic lending booms, and relatively low holdings of official international reserves. In Asia the crisis in Thailand led to a recognition that Indonesia and South Korea had similar problems, including a weak banking sector, declining quality of domestic capital formation, a slowdown in export growth, and fixed exchange rates that may not be defensible for very long.

Analysis suggests that different forms of contagion are probably important and occur together in many crises. The initial reaction to a crisis in one country is often pure contagion, as international lenders pull back from nearly all investments in developing countries. Lenders then examine the other countries more closely. International lenders resume lending to those countries that do not seem to have problems. But the financial crisis spreads to those countries that seem to have similar problems. Although the spread of the crisis has a basis in the recognition of actual problems, it is still a kind of contagion effect. Without the crisis in the first country, the other countries probably would have avoided their own crises.

RESOLVING FINANCIAL CRISES

A financial crisis has serious negative consequences for the borrowing country and its economy. As new lending to the country dries up, the economy goes into recession. Also, a financial crisis in one country can threaten the economies of other countries and the broader global financial system, through contagion effects that reduce capital flows to other borrowers and can send some into their own crises. In the crises of the past several decades, the two major types of international efforts to resolve financial crises have been rescue packages and debt restructuring. Let's look at each of these, how they work, and the questions that arise about their efforts.

Rescue Packages

When a financial crisis hits a country, that country's government usually seeks a **rescue package** of loan commitments to assist it in getting through the crisis. As indicated in the discussion of the history of lending to developing countries, the sizes of these rescue packages have been large since the mid-1990s, for example, $17 billion for Thailand and $58 billion for South Korea. The lenders generally included the IMF, the World Bank, and some national governments.

A rescue package can have several purposes. First, the loans in the rescue package compensate for the lack of private lending during the crisis. The money allows the country to meet its needs for foreign exchange, to provide some financing for new domestic investments, and to cushion the decline in aggregate demand and domestic production. Second, the package can restore investor confidence by replenishing official reserve holdings and by signaling official international support for the country and its government. This can stem the capital outflow, even if it does not immediately restart new private foreign lending to the country. Third, the IMF and the other official lenders in the rescue package hope that the package will limit contagion effects that could spread the crisis to other countries. As the leader in most of these efforts, the IMF is organizing an international safety net, in a way similar to national efforts (like deposit insurance and discount lending) to prevent problems at one bank from spreading to other banks in the national financial system. Fourth, the IMF imposes conditions as part of its lending, to require the government of the crisis country to make policy changes that should speed the end of the financial crisis. These policy reforms usually include tighter monetary policy and tighter fiscal policy, and they may include other structural reforms like liberalizing restrictions on international trade or improving regulation of the banking system (an issue that we will take up in the final section of this chapter).

One major question about these rescue packages is how effective they actually are. The rescue package for Mexico in 1995 seemed to be very successful in helping Mexico to resolve its financial crisis. The packages for the Asian countries in 1997 were at best moderately successful. The economies went into surprisingly deep and long recessions, and the exchange rate values of the countries' currencies declined greatly before stabilizing. Russia was a nontest—Russia did not abide by the IMF conditions, so the package never took hold. The package for Brazil did not prevent a currency fall, probably largely because the Brazilian government did not enact the fiscal reforms that it promised. But the package appeared to be helpful in heading off a full financial crisis. The package for Turkey again seemed successful mainly in preventing much contagion. The package for Argentina did not succeed in heading off a crisis, but it also was withdrawn before the crisis because the Argentinean government did not meet the IMF's conditions.

The other major question about the rescue packages is whether they actually increase the likelihood of financial crises because they encourage overlending and overborrowing. A large rescue package provides a bailout for lenders and borrowers when a crisis hits. But if lenders and borrowers expect to be bailed out, then they should worry less about the risk of a financial crisis. This leads them to lend and borrow more than is prudent—an example of **moral hazard,** in which insurance leads the insured to be less careful because the insurance offers compensation if bad things happen. Given the costs that the borrowers incur when a crisis hits, it seems that the moral hazard for them is probably not too large. Borrowers still lose a lot even with a rescue package.

The rescue package can create moral hazard for lenders. In the Mexican crisis of 1994–1995, the rescue package was used to pay off foreign investors, including full payment to the holders of the *tesobonos.* The lack of large losses to rescued creditors in the Mexican crisis probably encouraged too much international lending during 1996–1997 because the lenders worried too little about the risks of the lending.

In the Asian crisis, lenders to banks in the crisis countries were generally repaid in full, using money from the rescue packages. Still, the scope for moral hazard had its limits. Foreign investors in private bonds and stocks suffered large losses as the market price of these securities declined, and foreign banks suffered large losses on loans to private nonfinancial borrowers.

The failure of the rescue package for Russia led to large losses for all foreign creditors. Many of these lenders were specifically relying on a rescue to limit their downside risk (moral hazard in action), so they received quite a surprise. Some of the caution in lending to developing countries after the Russian crisis is probably the result of a reappraisal of the risks of this lending. This message was reinforced when Argentina defaulted in 2002 without any bailout appearing. Moral hazard has declined because lenders realize that rescue packages may not provide a bailout.

Debt Restructuring

Debt restructuring refers to two types of changes in the terms of debt:

- *Debt rescheduling* changes *when* payments are due, by pushing the repayments schedule further into the future. The amount of debt is effectively the same, but the borrower has a longer time to pay it off.

- *Debt reduction* lowers the *amount* of debt.

When a financial crisis hits a country because the country has more debt than it is willing or able to service, resolution of the crisis often requires debt restructuring. By stretching out payments or reducing debt, the borrowing country gains a better chance of meeting a more manageable stream of current and future payments for debt service. A key issue is the process of reaching a restructuring agreement among creditors and borrowers. There is a free-rider problem here. Each individual creditor has the incentive to hold out, hoping that others restructure their lending agreements, but not altering its own. Then the free rider can be repaid faster or fully, while other creditors that agreed to restructuring must wait longer or get less. But if free riding prevents a restructuring deal, then all creditors will probably lose, as the crisis is not resolved.

The debt crisis of 1982 dragged on through the 1980s partly because there was no framework for overcoming the coordination problem among the hundreds of banks that had lent to the crisis countries. In addition to the free-rider problem, legal clauses in many syndicated loan agreements limited debt restructuring. As we saw earlier, the Brady Plan of 1989 finally established a process for debt restructuring. It offered a menu of choices to the creditor banks, as well as coercion when necessary, to overcome the free-rider problem. In a typical Brady deal, each creditor bank was offered a choice between partial debt reduction and continuance of its loan agreements along with required new lending to the crisis country. The debt reduction occurred when the bank exchanged its bank loans for a smaller amount of new bonds that were backed by collateral (usually U.S. government bonds). The borrowing country was able to establish the collateral by borrowing part of the value from the IMF and World Bank. (As usual, the IMF also imposed conditions for policy changes by the country along with its loan). Brady deals succeeded in reducing the debt of 18 crisis countries by $65 billion, about one-third of their total debt. As the Brady deals resolved the lingering crisis, international lending to these countries resumed.

During the crises of the 1990s, restructuring of bank debt went smoother. The limited number of debtors and creditors eased the negotiations. The key issue that arose in the 1990s was the great difficulty of restructuring bonds. There are often hundreds or thousands of bondholders. The legal terms of the typical international bond require that all bondholders agree to the terms of a restructuring. And a small number of bondholders can sue to force immediate full repayment if the issuer defaults on any payment. Since the late 1990s there have been bond restructurings in a few countries, including Pakistan, Ukraine, and Ecuador. In 1999, Ecuador defaulted on its Brady bonds. Although the bondholders resisted, they eventually accepted new bonds that were worth less than the face value of the old bonds but more than the then-current market value of the old bonds.

Given the growing importance of bonds in financial flows to developing countries, there are a number of suggestions to revise the terms of the bonds, to mandate majority voting on restructuring, to share equally any partial payments, and to limit the ability of small numbers of bondholders to force immediate full repayment or take other legal actions concerning the bond. But these suggestions have not yet been adopted, so bond restructuring remains very difficult.

REDUCING THE FREQUENCY OF FINANCIAL CRISES

Financial crises create large losses for international lenders though defaults, debt rescheduling, debt reduction, and declines in the market prices of bonds, stocks, and loans that are traded on secondary markets. Financial crises also impose large costs on borrowing countries through sudden declines in access to lending and the macroeconomic costs of recessions and slow economic growth that usually accompany the crises. While we have ways for trying to resolve crises once they occur, it would also be great to find ways to prevent financial crises from occurring, or at least to reduce their frequency.

There is no scarcity of proposals for improving the "international financial architecture." Four proposed reforms enjoy widespread support. First, developing countries should pursue sound macroeconomic policies, to avoid creating conditions in which overborrowing or a loss of confidence in the government's capability could lead to a crisis. Second, countries should improve the data that they report publicly, to provide sufficient details on total debt and its components, as well as on holdings of international reserves, and they should report these data promptly. The belief is that with better data lenders would make more informed decisions on lending and investing, making overlending less likely and also reducing the risk of pure contagion against emerging markets debt. While the call for more information is not controversial, it also has its limits.

Developing country governments have the incentive to provide misleading or incomplete data at exactly the times when lenders most need accurate information. Third, developing country governments should avoid short-term borrowing denominated in foreign currencies, to avoid crises that begin when foreign lenders abruptly demand repayment. In the next part of this section we look more closely at a fourth proposal that enjoys widespread support—better regulation and supervision of banks in developing countries.

Other proposals for reform are more controversial, and in some cases serious competing proposals suggest moving in opposite directions. One proposal is that developing countries should end efforts to fix or heavily manage the exchange rate values of their currencies. Among other possible benefits, the shift to more flexible exchange rates makes the existence of exchange rate risk palpable, and so private borrowers are less likely to build up large unhedged liabilities in foreign currencies. But a competing proposal is that developing countries should move to nearly permanently fixed exchange rates, with greater use of currency boards and dollarization. Such arrangements may discipline government macroeconomic policies to be more sound. In another set of competing proposals, one is that the IMF should receive more resources so that it can establish large lines of credit to developing countries with sound economic policies. These countries then can use this backing to fight off any financial attacks. The other is that the IMF should be abolished, or at least that its rescue activities be severely limited, because it creates substantial moral hazard with its lending. By encouraging overlending, it makes crises more likely.[4]

After we discuss proposals for better bank regulation, which is *not* controversial, we conclude the chapter with a look at a proposal that is controversial: expanding the use capital controls to limit borrowing.

Bank Regulation and Supervision

Banks are considered to have a special role in an economy. They are at the center of the payments system that facilitates transactions in the economy. They acquire deposits from customers based on trust that the banks can pay back the deposits in the future, but if this trust is broken, depositors create a run on the bank as they all try to get their money out quickly.

In developing countries banks are often especially important, because bank lending is also the major source of financing for local businesses. Stock and bond markets are often underdeveloped. But government regulation and supervision of banks in developing countries is often weak. With weak regulation, banks engage in more risky activities. Banks make loans based on relationships—"crony capitalism" loans to bank directors, managers, friends of directors and managers, politically important people, and their businesses. Banks take on large exposures to exchange rate risk by borrowing foreign currencies to fund local-currency

---

[4] This is an example of Jeffrey Frankel's theorem: For every critique of the IMF, there exists an equal and opposite critique coming from the other direction. For a summary of the views of Joseph Stigliz, an outspoken critic of the IMF, see the box "Mighty Joe Meets the Incredible Monetary Force."

loans (the carry trade). Banks operate with little equity capital, so they are more likely to take risks and require government rescues. In addition, the government often exerts direct influence on lending decisions, to favor some borrowers based on the government's strategy for economic development.

Thus, with weak supervision and an explicit or implicit guarantee that the government will rescue banks in trouble, banks have incentives to borrow too much internationally (and lenders are comfortable lending so much), and banks are more willing to take the risk of unhedged foreign-currency liabilities. A financial crisis becomes more likely.

There is a clear need for better government regulation and supervision of local banks in the borrowing countries. Regulators should require banks to use better accounting and disclose more information publicly, to use risk assessment and risk management to reduce risk exposures, to recognize bad loans and make provision for them, and to have more equity capital. The regulators should be willing to identify weak banks, to insist on changes in practices and management at these banks, and to close them if they are insolvent. In addition, the government probably should permit more foreign banks to operate locally because these foreign banks bring better management and better techniques for controlling risks. Furthermore, a country's government should get the sequencing of its reforms right. To reduce the risk of a crisis, the country should solidify its regulation of banks and other financial institutions *before* it liberalizes its capital account and provides them with easy access to foreign-currency exposures.

In the abstract, the proposal for better bank regulation and supervision in developing countries is not controversial. The challenge is in the implementation. There is likely to be political resistance—from the banks, from the borrowers favored by crony capitalism, and from the government officials who lose some power to direct bank lending. Even if such political resistance can be overcome, there is also a shortage of people with the expertise to regulate banks effectively. Bank regulation and supervision meet world standards in some countries like Brazil, and it will continue to improve in developing countries more generally, but the improvement is likely to be a slow process.

Capital Controls

A controversial proposal for reducing the frequency of financial crises is to increase developing countries' use of controls or impediments to capital inflows.[5] Such controls could take any of several forms, including an outright limit or

---

[5] Another possible use of capital controls is to limit capital outflows during a financial crisis. Malaysia adopted such controls as a temporary measure in 1998. The goal is to prevent continued capital flight and remove the pressures that it places on local financial institutions, local capital markets, and the exchange rate value of the country's currency. Government fiscal and monetary policy can then be directed to addressing the internal imbalance of recession, with less fear that the shift to expansionary policies will worsen the financial crisis. Such controls are probably only effective for a short time, as pressures build and investors find ways around the controls. The major cost of such controls is that they are likely to scare off new capital inflows in the future, even after the controls are removed, so that the country loses the gains from international borrowing.

Case Study   Mighty Joe Meets the Incredible Monetary Force

Nobel Prize winner Joseph Stiglitz had a front-row seat for observing the IMF during its rescue and crisis-resolution efforts during the 1990s. He served first as the chairperson of President Bill Clinton's Council of Economic Advisors and then as chief economist for the World Bank, the development-promoting organization also set up by the Bretton Woods agreement. He was not happy with what he saw. He jumped into the ring with speeches, articles, and a book, *Globalization and Its Discontents* (2002).

MIGHTY JOE

Stiglitz begins from Keynes's view of what the IMF should be (recall the mention of Keynes and White at Bretton Woods in Chapter 19). Stiglitz sees the purpose of IMF lending as the financing of temporary deficits without forcing a country to adopt excessively contractionary policies. This objective is important because the global system puts most of its pressure on deficit countries to adjust their balance of payments. The tendency to solve problems by causing recessions must be resisted. From his vantage, Stiglitz gives the IMF a low grade for its policies in Asia during 1997 and 1998: "[O]nce a country was in crisis, IMF funds and programs not only failed to stabilize the situation but in many cases actually made matters worse, especially for the poor" (p.15).

Stiglitz says that the IMF used the same macroeconomic prescriptions and solutions for all crises, without regard to the actual conditions of the crisis countries. It required the borrowing countries to tighten monetary and fiscal policies. High interest rates had to be used to stop the declines of the exchange rate values of the currencies. With the countries already headed into recessions because of the adverse effects of the crisis itself, the tight policies made the recessions deeper and longer. Bankruptcies of small and medium-sized businesses rose alarmingly.

Stiglitz says that it would have been much better to let the exchange rates fall to whatever levels they would. The rates would eventually stabilize and then presumably bounce back after the overshooting. He questions whether the IMF loans focused too much on repayments to foreign creditors, and not enough on the economic performance of the borrower countries and their people.

He notes that Malaysia refused to seek an IMF program and eventually enacted policies opposite to what the IMF was prescribing. Malaysia imposed capital controls to limit investors from taking their funds out of the country, reestablished the fixed rate between the ringgit and the dollar, and kept interest rates low. Malaysia's recession was shorter and shallower.

prohibition, a tax that must be paid to the government equal to some portion of the borrowing, or a requirement that some portion of the borrowing be placed in a deposit with the country's central bank. (If this deposit does not earn interest, then it is effectively a tax on the borrowing.) There are three ways in which such controls can reduce the risk of financial crisis. First, the controls can prevent large inflows that could result in overlending and overborrowing. Second, the controls can be used to discourage short-term borrowing. Third, the controls can reduce the country's exposure to contagion by limiting the amount that foreign lenders could pull out of the country.

Chile is usually offered as the example of a country that used controls on capital inflows successfully during the 1990s. The Chilean government required that a percentage of the value of new lending and investments into the country be

He also questions the structural conditions included in the loan agreements. They seem to be unnecessary for addressing the crisis and to undermine the country's sovereignty. For instance, what was the necessity of requiring South Korea to change its government structure to one that has an independent central bank with price stability as its goal? Or of requiring it to speed up some trade liberalizations?

In short, he found the IMF used the wrong economic theories and was technically incompetent: "How could an organization with such talented (and highly paid) government bureaucrats make so many mistakes?" (p. 230).

THE IMF REPLIES

In July 2002, Kenneth Rogoff, the IMF's economic counsellor and director of the research department, responded with an open letter to Professor Stiglitz, published in the *IMF Survey* (July 8, 2002). Rogoff notes that countries that come to the IMF have very difficult problems: "[Y]ou condemn the IMF because everywhere it seems to be, countries are in trouble. Isn't this a little like observing that where there are epidemics, one tends to find more doctors?" (p. 210). If the problems were easy to solve, a country's government would not call in the IMF. Instead, the government is in an unsustainable position, and the government asks the IMF for battlefield medicine.

He argues that Stiglitz is simply unrealistic. In the Asian crisis setting, the government could not have increased government spending or cut taxes without printing money to do so, because there was no one who was willing to buy the government's debt or lend to it. If the government printed money, the country would end up with the problem of uncontrollable inflation. Instead, the policy of temporarily raising interest rates was necessary to stabilize exchange rates before any other useful policies could be adopted. The IMF also quickly admitted that it had made a mistake on fiscal policy, and it agreed to let the fiscal deficit increase somewhat, to let the automatic stabilizers work.

Rogoff states that Stiglitz is too fast to see market failures that require government policies to mend them. Rogoff believes that government failure is a far bigger problem than market failure for most developing countries. He concludes: "Joe, as an academic you are a towering genius. Like your fellow Nobel Prize winner John Nash, you have a 'beautiful mind.' As a policymaker, however, you are just a bit less impressive."

placed in an interest-free deposit with the central bank for one year. And the government required that foreign investors keep their investments in Chile for at least one year. These requirements seem to have had their major effect by altering the mix of borrowing—less short-term debt. The Chilean government also changed the percentage that must be deposited to tune it to changing market conditions over time. It began at 20 percent, was raised to 30 percent, then lowered to 10 percent and to zero in 1998, as capital inflows fell off following the Russian crisis. In 2000, Chile also removed the one-year rule.

What are the overall benefits and costs of controls on capital inflows? A major cost of the controls is the loss of the gains from international borrowing, to the extent that they discourage capital inflows. While they can provide benefits by reducing the risk of a financial crisis, they are a second-best policy. It would be better if the government of the borrowing country could identify the specific problems that might lead to a crisis and address these directly (recall the specificity rule from Chapter 9). For instance, if overborrowing or too much short-term foreign-currency borrowing occurs because of the excessive risks taken by local banks, the direct policy response is to improve bank regulation and supervision. If bank regulation cannot be improved immediately, then capital controls can be a second-best policy response. However, the capital controls are likely to lose their effectiveness over time, as investors and borrowers find ways to circumvent them. They probably only buy time for the government to adopt the direct policy improvement like better bank regulation. Furthermore, governments can also make mistakes with controls on capital inflows. For instance, South Korea removed controls on short-term bank borrowing while continuing to restrict longer term capital inflows like foreign purchases of stocks and direct foreign investments. Korean banks then borrowed on a massive scale, and this became a key part of the Korean crisis of late 1997.

In conclusion, we have a variety of proposals for reducing the frequency of financial crises, ranging from the unrealistic to the controversial to the useful and feasible, and some reforms are being implemented. International lending brings major benefits to both the lending and the borrowing countries. But international lending is prone to financial crises from time to time. We can hope to reduce the frequency of crises while resolving those crises that do occur and trying to minimize contagion.

Summary

Well-behaved international lending (or international capital flows) yields the same kinds of welfare results as international trade in products. International lending increases total world product and brings net gains to both the lending and borrowing countries, although there are some groups who lose well-being in each country. The lending-country government or the borrowing-country government can impose taxes on international lending. If either country has market power (that is, if it is able to affect the world interest rate), it can try to improve its well-being by imposing a **nationally optimal tax** on international lending. But if the other country retaliates with its own tax, both countries can end up worse off.

The history of international lending to developing countries shows surges of lending and recurrent financial crises. The dramatic increase of lending in the 1970s as banks recycled petrodollars led to the debt crisis beginning in 1982. This crisis stretched throughout the 1980s, with low capital flows to developing countries. The Brady Plan of 1989 led to the resolution of the crisis through debt reductions and the conversion of much bank debt to Brady bonds. Capital flows to developing countries increased dramatically during the 1990s, with more in the form of portfolio investments in bonds and stocks. However, we also saw a series of financial crises: Mexico in 1994–1995, several Asian countries in 1997, Russia in 1998, Turkey in 2001, and Argentina in 2001–2002, as well as a brief exchange rate crisis in Brazil in 1999.

We can identify five major forces that can lead to or deepen financial crises. First, overlending and overborrowing can occur, as a result of government borrowing to finance expansionary government policies, excessive borrowing by banks, or the herding behavior of lenders seeking what seem to be high returns. For sovereign debt owed by borrowing governments, lending can turn out to be excessive even if the government has the ability to repay, because the benefits of default exceed the costs. Second, exogenous shocks like increases in foreign (especially U.S.) interest rates can shift flows away from developing country borrowers and make repaying their debts more difficult. Third, borrowers, especially banks, can take on too many unhedged foreign currency liabilities, which then become very expensive to pay off if the local currency depreciates unexpectedly. Fourth, the borrowing country can borrow too much using short-term loans and bonds. The borrower can experience difficulties if foreign investors refuse to refinance or roll over the debt. And finally, **contagion** can spread the crisis from the initial crisis country to other countries. These other countries may be vulnerable because of problems with their policies or economic performance, but it is the contagion from the initial crisis country that leads foreign lenders to fear a crisis and pull back from lending to these other countries. Financial crises have elements of self-fulfilling panics, in which investors fear defaults, so they stop lending and demand quick repayment. If many lenders try to do this at once, the borrower cannot repay, and default and crisis occur.

The two major types of international efforts to resolve financial crises are rescue packages and debt restructuring. A **rescue package** provides temporary financial assistance, can help to restore foreign investor confidence, and can try to limit contagion. In the past decade, these packages have been large. A key question is whether the packages create substantial **moral hazard,** in which lenders believe that they can lend with little risk because a rescue will bail them out. **Debt restructuring** attempts to make debt service more manageable for the borrowing country. Debt rescheduling stretches out the repayments further into the future, and debt reduction lowers the amount of debt. Restructuring can be difficult because each individual creditor has the incentive to free-ride, hoping others will restructure while the free rider receives full repayment on time. The Brady Plan set up a process of successful restructuring of bank debt from the 1980s' crisis. Because of legal clauses in international bonds, they are very difficult to restructure.

There are a range of proposals for reforms of the "international financial architecture" to reduce the frequency of financial crises. Some are radical and unlikely, and others are controversial. Several are widely supported: Developing country governments should have sound macroeconomic policies, they should provide better data for lenders and investors to use in their decision making, they should minimize short-term debt, and they should improve their regulation and supervision of their banks. One controversial proposal is that developing country governments should make greater use of controls on capital inflows. While this could limit overborrowing, short-term borrowing, and exposure to contagion, it would also reduce the benefits to be gained from international borrowing.

Suggested Reading

Obstfeld and Taylor (2002) and Kahler (1998) provide broad discussions of international capital movements. Rogoff (1999), Eichengreen (1999), and Goldstein (1998) discuss recent financial crises and proposals for reform. Kindleberger (1998) offers a readable look of several centuries of crises. Edwards (1995) and Eichengreen and Lindert (1989) examine the debt crisis of the 1980s. Beim and Calomiris (2001) and Malkiel and Mei (1998) discuss financial crises and other aspects of investing in emerging markets.

Fieleke (1994) discusses the purposes and activities of the International Monetary Fund. Bird (2001) reviews evidence on the macroeconomic effects of IMF loan programs. Aylward and Thorne (1998) present statistical analysis of countries that are overdue in repaying loans from the IMF.

Questions and Problems

✦ 1. "It is best for a country never to borrow from foreign lenders." Do you agree or disagree? Why?

2. "Because a national government cannot go bankrupt, it is safe to lend to a foreign government." Do you agree or disagree? Why?

✦ 3. Why was there so much private lending to developing countries from 1974 to 1982, although there had been so little from 1930 to 1974?

4. What triggered the debt crisis in 1982?

✦ 5. Consider Figure 20.1. What is the size of each of the following? (Each answer should be a number.)

a. World product without international lending.

b. World product with free international lending.

c. World product with Japan's tax of 2 percent on its foreign lending.

What does the difference between your answers to parts *a* and *b* tell us? What does the difference between your answers to parts *b* and *c* tell us?

6. Consider Figure 20.1. In comparison with free international lending, what happens if each country imposes a 2 percent tax on the international lending (so that there is a total of 4 percent of tax)? What is the net gain, or loss, for each country?

✦ 7. How could each of the following cause or contribute to a financial crisis in a developing country?

a. A large amount of short-term debt denominated in dollars.

b. A financial crisis in another developing country in the region.

8. Consider the graph in the box "The Special Case of Sovereign Debt."

a. Show graphically the effect of an increase in the interest rate *i*. If the country's government would not default before this change, could this change lead to default?

b. Show graphically the effect of an increase in the cost of defaulting. If the country's government would not default before this change, could this change lead to default?

◆ 9. How could each of the following reforms reduce the frequency of financial crises?

   a. Quick release of detailed, accurate information on the debt and official reserves of most developing countries.

   b. Use by more developing countries of controls to limit capital inflows.

10. The "Optimal Deadbeat" Problem: The World Bank is considering a stream of loans to the Puglian government to help it develop its nationalized oil fields and refineries. This is the only set of loans that the World Bank would ever give Puglia. If Puglia defaults, it receives no further funds from this set of loans from the World Bank. Whether the Puglian government repays the loan or defaults has no other impact on Puglia. If the World Bank's stream of loans would have the effects shown in the accompanying table, would it ever be in Puglia's interest to default on the loans? If not, why not? If so, why and when?

	Loan Effects ($ millions)			
Year	Inflow of Funds from World Bank	Stock of Accumulated Borrowings at End of Year	Interest Paid on Borrowings (at 8 percent)	Profits on Extra Oil Export Sales
1	$200 (loan)	$200	0	0
2	100 (loan)	300	16	30
3	50 (loan)	350	24	30
4	0	350	28	30
5	−50 (repayment)	300	28	30
6	−50 (repayment)	250	24	30
7	−50 (repayment)	200	20	30
8	−50 (repayment)	150	16	30
9	−50 (repayment)	100	12	30
10	−50 (repayment)	50	8	30
11	−50 (repayment)	0	4	30

Part **Four**

Macro Policies
for Open Economies

Chapter Twenty-One

How Does the Open Macroeconomy Work?

The analysis of Part III brought us part of the way toward a judgment of what kinds of policies toward foreign exchange would best serve a nation's needs. Chapters 18 and 19 in particular spelled out some of the implications of different policies for the performance of the foreign exchange market, in terms of the efficiency—or inefficiency—of the market itself.

In Part IV, our focus shifts to the other kind of performance issue previewed when the basic policy choices were laid out at the start of Chapter 19. This and the next two chapters address the problem of *macroeconomic* performance—the behavior of a country's output, jobs, and prices in the face of changing world conditions. There are many ways in which the national economy and the world economy interact. Yet some valuable conclusions about policy can be established. Once these conclusions have been laid out in Chapters 21 through 23, Chapter 24 can provide a series of lessons about where the international macroeconomic system is headed and how well different exchange rate institutions work.

This chapter develops a general framework for analyzing the performance of a national economy that is open to international transactions. It provides a picture of how the open macroeconomy works. This framework will then be used in Chapters 22 and 23 to examine macroeconomic performance in settings of fixed exchange rates and floating exchange rates.

THE PERFORMANCE OF A NATIONAL ECONOMY

Each of us is comfortable judging our own performance in various activities. Did I perform in a sport up to the level at which I am capable? How did I perform on an examination relative to my own capabilities in the subject and relative to how others in the class performed? Judgments about performance also drive most macroeconomic analysis. How well is a country's economy performing? Is it performing up to its potential—for instance, its capabilities for producing goods and services? How close is it to achieving broad objectives that most people would agree are desirable, such as stability in average product prices (no inflation), low unemployment, and the maintenance of a reasonable balance of payments with the rest of the world?

We judge a country's macroeconomic performance against a number of broad objectives or goals. We can usefully divide these broad goals into two categories. The first category involves two objectives oriented to the domestic economy. One objective is keeping actual domestic production up to the economy's capabilities so that (1) the country achieves *full employment* of its labor and other resources and (2) the economy's production grows over time. Another domestic objective is achieving *price stability* (or, at least, a low or acceptable rate of product price inflation). These two domestically oriented goals taken together define the goal of achieving **internal balance.**

The other category involves objectives related to the country's international economic activities. This is the problem of **external balance,** which is usually defined as the achievement of a reasonable and sustainable balance of payments with the rest of the world. Specifying a precise goal here is not so simple. Most broadly, the goal may be to achieve balance in the country's overall balance of payments. For instance, the goal may be to achieve a balance of approximately zero in the country's official settlements balance, at least over a number of years, so that the country is not losing official reserves or building up unwanted official reserves. This implies that the sum of the current account and the capital account (excluding official reserves transactions) should be approximately zero. If it is substantially different from zero for a long enough time, then we have the disequilibrium in the country's balance of payments (and exchange rate) that we discussed in Chapter 19. If the disequilibrium in the country's balance of payments becomes severe enough, it can lead to the kind of crises that we examined in Chapter 20.

For some purposes we focus on a somewhat narrower reading of external balance, one that focuses on the country's current account (or balance on goods and services trade). The goal here need not be a zero balance. Rather, it is a position that is sustainable in that the value for the current account balance can readily be financed by international capital flows (or official reserves transactions). Some rich industrialized countries probably achieve external balance by running a current account surplus because this allows the country to use some of its national saving to act as a net investor in the rest of the world (capital outflows or capital account deficit). Other countries that are in the process of developing their economies can achieve external balance while running a current account deficit. The deficit may include imports of machinery that directly are part of the development effort. The deficit can be financed by borrowing from the rest of the world (capital inflows or capital account surplus). As long as the surpluses and deficits on current account are not too large, then the positions are sustainable over time. Each can become too large, however, and can become an external imbalance.

A FRAMEWORK FOR MACROECONOMIC ANALYSIS

To analyze the performance of an economy, we need a picture of how the economy functions. Such a picture is not without controversy—macroeconomists do not fully agree on the correct way to analyze the macroeconomy. One of the main difficulties has been to form a satisfactory framework for predicting both changes in domestic production and changes in the price level. We will use a synthesis that attempts to combine the strongest features from several different schools of thought. Our analysis of the behavior of the economy in the short run (say, a time period of one year or less) is relatively Keynesian in that the price level is not immediately responsive to aggregate demand and supply conditions in the economy. The price level is sticky or sluggish in the short run. Our view of the economy in the longer run is more classical. As we move beyond the short run, the price level does respond to demand and supply conditions. Furthermore, the amount of price inflation that the economy experiences eventually depends mainly on the growth rate of the country's money supply. In addition, the economy tends toward full employment in the long run. We have already developed some of the key features and implications of this long-run analysis in the discussion of the monetary approach in Chapter 18. Here and in the next two chapters we focus more on the economy in the shorter run. We want to develop a picture of how the economy works in the short run that is pragmatic and useful, even if it is not perfect.

The next three major sections of this chapter focus on the determinants of real GDP (representing both domestic product and national income) and the relationships between international trade and national income. Then the next major section adds the market for money and the country's overall balance of payments, resulting in a broad and flexible model of the open economy in the short run. The final two sections of the chapter take up issues related to product prices in order to enhance the framework. These final sections explore the determinants of changes in the country's product price level (or its inflation rate) over time and the effects of international price competitiveness on a country's international trade.

DOMESTIC PRODUCTION DEPENDS ON AGGREGATE DEMAND

A major performance goal of an economy is to achieve production of goods and services that is close to the economy's potential. The economy's potential for producing is determined by the supply-side capabilities of the economy. Supply-side capabilities include both the factor resources (labor, capital, land, and natural resources) that the economy has available—the factor endowments from Parts I and II—and intangible influences such as technology, resource quality, climate, and motivation. The intangibles determine the productivity of the resources.

The value of production of goods and services is the economy's real GDP (Y). Because production activity creates income (in the form of wages, profits and other returns to capital, and rents to landowners), real GDP is nearly the same thing as real national income.

In the short run (and within the economy's supply-side capabilities), domestic production is determined by aggregate demand (AD) for the country's products. Essentially, if someone demands a product, some business (or other organization) will try to produce it. Aggregate demand can be split into four components that represent different sources of demand: household consumption of goods and services (C); domestic investment (I_d) in new real assets like machinery, buildings, housing, and inventories; government spending on goods and services (G); and net exports of goods and services ($X - M$). Net exports capture two aspects of aggregate demand:

- Foreign demand for our exports (X) is an additional source of demand for our products.

- Our demand for imports (M) must be subtracted because these imports are already included in the other kinds of spending but actually represent demand for the products of other countries.

Equilibrium occurs when domestic production (Y, our GDP) equals desired demand for domestically produced goods and services:

$$Y = \text{AD} = C + I_d + G + (X - M) \tag{21.1}$$

The level of actual domestic production (relative to the economy's potential for producing) tends to be closely related to the economy's labor unemployment rate. Increases of actual GDP (relative to potential) tend to decrease the unemployment rate, while decreases tend to increase the unemployment rate.

In order to focus on international trade issues, we can add up the national spending components into national expenditures (E) on goods and services:

$$E = C + I_d + G \tag{21.2}$$

From basic macroeconomic analysis, we know something about the determinants of each of these components.

Household consumption expenditures are positively related to disposable income, and disposable income is (approximately) the difference between total income (Y) and taxes (T) paid to the government. Many taxes are based directly on income or are related indirectly to income because they are based on spending (for instance, sales or value added taxes). Rather than carry around all of this detail, we will summarize the major determinant of consumption as income:

$$C = C(Y) \tag{21.3}$$

remembering that the relationship incorporates taxes that have to paid out of income before consumer spending is done. There are other influences on consumption, including interest rates that set the cost of borrowing to finance the purchase of items like automobiles, as well as household wealth and consumer sentiment about the future. To keep the analysis simple, we do not formally build these other influences into the framework. Instead, we can treat major changes in these other influences as shocks that occasionally disturb the economy.

Real domestic investment spending is negatively related to the level of interest rates (i) in the economy:

$$I_d = I_d(i) \tag{21.4}$$

Higher interest rates increase the cost of financing the capital assets, thus reducing the amount of real investment undertaken. There are a number of other influences on real investment spending, including business sentiment about the future, current capacity utilization, and the emergence of new technologies that require capital investments in order to bring the technologies into use. Again, we can picture these other influences as a source of shocks to the economy.

We treat government spending on goods and services as a political decision. Decisions about government spending are a major part of a country's **fiscal policy;** the other part of fiscal policy is decisions about taxation.

TRADE DEPENDS ON INCOME

According to a host of empirical estimates for many countries, the volume of a nation's imports depends positively on the level of real national income or production:

$$M = M(Y) \tag{21.5}$$

This positive relationship seems to have two explanations. One is that imports are often used as inputs into the production of the goods and services that constitute domestic product. The other explanation is that imports respond to the total real expenditure or "absorption" (E) in our economy. The more we spend on all goods and services, the more we tend to spend on the part of them that we buy from abroad. Although a nation's expenditures on goods and services are not the same thing as its national income from producing goods and services, the close statistical correlation between income and expenditure allows us to gloss over this distinction. We can estimate the amount by which our imports increase when our income goes up by one dollar. This amount is called the **marginal propensity to import** (m).

It is also possible that the volume of our *exports* depends on *our* national income. If domestic national income is raised by a surge in domestic aggregate demand, there is a good chance that the increase in national income will be accompanied by a drop in export volumes, as domestic buyers bid away resources that otherwise would have been used to produce exports. Although such a negative dependence of export volumes on national-income-as-determined-by-domestic-demand is plausible, the evidence for it is somewhat sparse. We will assume that export volumes are independent of this country's national income.[1]

---

[1] Another way that export volumes can vary with our national income is through the supply side. A supply-side expansion of the economy permits production to increase, and some of this extra production may be available to increase exports.

Exports nonetheless do depend on income—the *income of foreign countries.* If foreign income is higher, then foreigners tend to buy more of all kinds of things, including more of our exports. The amount by which their imports (our exports) increase if foreign income increases is the foreign marginal propensity to import.

EQUILIBRIUM GDP AND SPENDING MULTIPLIERS

With these pieces of the framework we can gain some major insights into macroeconomic performance in an open economy. To gain these insights we make a few assumptions that are useful now (but will be relaxed in later analysis). We assume that all price and pricelike variables are constant. In relation to our discussion so far, this means that the interest rate (in addition to the average product price level) is constant.

Equilibrium GDP

The condition for equilibrium real GDP is that it must equal desired aggregate demand, which in turn equals desired national expenditure plus net exports. Holding interest rates constant, our desired national expenditure depends on national income, as does our volume of imports. These relationships indicate that the value of aggregate demand itself depends on national income. The equilibrium condition is

$$Y = \text{AD}(Y) = E(Y) + X - M(Y) \qquad (21.6)$$

Although our exports depend on foreign income, we initially ignore this (or assume that foreign income is constant).

Figure 21.1A illustrates the equilibrium level of domestic production and income, showing the matching between domestic product and aggregate demand at point *A.* At levels of domestic production below 100, the aggregate demand would exceed the level of production, as shown by the fact that the AD line is above the 45-degree line to the left of *A.* At any such lower levels of production, the combination of home and foreign demand for what this nation is producing would be so great as to deplete the inventories of goods held by firms, and the firms would respond by raising production and creating more jobs and incomes, moving the economy up toward *A.* Similarly, levels of production above 100 would yield insufficient demand, accumulating inventories, and cutbacks in production and jobs until the economy returned to equilibrium at point *A.*

Figure 21.1A does not demonstrate how the nation's foreign trade and investment relate to the process of achieving the equilibrium domestic production. To underline the role of the foreign sector, it is convenient to convert the equilibrium condition into a different form. National saving (*S*) equals the difference between national income (*Y*) and national expenditures on noninvestment items (*C* and *G*). Subtracting (*C* + *G*) from both sides of Equation 21.6, the condition becomes an equilibrium between saving, domestic investment, and net exports:

FIGURE 21.1

Equilibrium
Domestic
Production
in an Open
Economy
Shown in Two
Equivalent
Ways

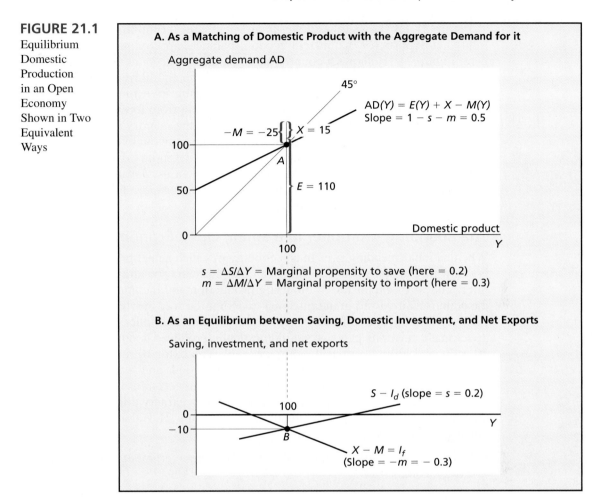

A. As a Matching of Domestic Product with the Aggregate Demand for it

Aggregate demand AD

45°

$AD(Y) = E(Y) + X - M(Y)$
Slope $= 1 - s - m = 0.5$

$-M = -25 \{ \} X = 15$

100

A

$E = 110$

50

0

Domestic product

Y

100

$s = \Delta S/\Delta Y =$ Marginal propensity to save (here $= 0.2$)
$m = \Delta M/\Delta Y =$ Marginal propensity to import (here $= 0.3$)

B. As an Equilibrium between Saving, Domestic Investment, and Net Exports

Saving, investment, and net exports

$S - I_d$ (slope $= s = 0.2$)

0

100

Y

-10

B

$X - M = I_f$
(Slope $= -m = -0.3$)

$$Y = E + X - M$$

$$(Y - C - G) = (E - C - G) + (X - M)$$

or

$$S = I_d + (X - M) \tag{21.7}$$

Recall from Chapter 15 that net exports are (approximately) equal to the country's current account balance, which in turn equals its net foreign investment (I_f). If we replace $(X - M)$ with I_f, we see that this equilibrium condition is the same as saying that a country's desired national saving must match its desired domestic investment in new real assets plus its desired net foreign investment.

Figure 21.1B shows this saving–investment equilibrium in a way that high-lights net exports (or the current account balance, approximately). As drawn here, Figure 21.1B shows a country having a current account deficit with more imports than exports of goods and services. For the equilibrium at point *B,* the country's domestic saving is less than its domestic investment, so the extra domestic investment must be financed by borrowing from foreigners (or selling off previously acquired foreign assets, including the country's official reserve assets). This could serve as a schematic view of the situation of the United States since 1982 because the United States has had a deficit in its current account bal-ance financed by net capital inflows since then. In contrast, Japan has usually had its version of point *B* lying above the horizontal axis, representing a net export surplus and positive net foreign investment.

The Spending Multiplier in a Small, Open Economy

When national spending rises in an economy in which actual production initially is below the economy's supply-side potential, this extra spending sets off a multi-plier process of expansion of domestic production and income, whether or not the country is involved in international trade. Yet the way in which the country is involved in trade does affect the size of the spending multiplier. Suppose that the government raises its purchases of domestically produced goods and services by 10 units and holds them at this higher level. The extra 10 means an extra 10 income for whoever produces and sells the extra goods and services to the gov-ernment. The extent to which this initial income gain gets transmitted into further domestic income gains depends on how the first gainers allocate their extra income. Let us assume, as we already have in Figure 21.1, that with each extra dollar of income, people within this nation

- Save 20 cents (part of which is "saved" by the government as taxes on their extra income),
- Spend 30 cents on imports of foreign goods and services, and
- Spend 50 cents on domestically produced goods and services.

In other words, the marginal propensity to save (*s,* including the marginal tax rate) is 0.2; the marginal propensity to import (*m*) is 0.3; and the marginal propensity to consume domestic product $(1 - s - m)$ is 0.5.

The first round of generating extra income produces an extra 2 units in saving, an extra 3 in imports, and an extra 5 in spending on domestic goods and services. Of these, only the 5 in domestic spending will be returned to the national econ-omy as a further demand stimulus. Both the 2 saved and the 3 spent on imports represent "leakages" from the domestic expenditure stream. Whatever their indi-rect effects, they do not directly create new demand or income in the national economy. (Here, we specifically rule out one indirect effect by assuming that this country is small and thus has no impact on production or income in the rest of the world. If the country is small, then there is no indirect effect on foreign demand for our exports.) In the second round of income and expenditures, only 5 will be passed on and divided up into further domestic spending (2.5), saving (1), and imports (1.5). And for each succeeding round, as for these first two, the share of extra income that becomes further domestic expenditures is $(1 - s - m)$, or $(1 - 0.2 - 0.3) = 0.5$.

The overall effects of this process are summarized in the spending multiplier. The **spending multiplier for a small open economy** is:[2]

$$\frac{\Delta Y}{\Delta G} = \frac{1}{(s + m)} \tag{21.8}$$

In our example, the rise in government spending by 10 billion ultimately leads to twice as great an expansion of domestic production (an increase of 20) since the spending multiplier equals $1/(0.2 + 0.3) = 2$. The value of this multiplier is the same, of course, whether the initial extra spending is made by the government or results from a surge in consumption, a rise in private investment spending, or a rise in exports. Note also that the value of the multiplier is smaller in a small open economy than the multiplier in a closed economy. Had m been zero, the multiplier would have been $1/s = 5$.

We can also see the spending multiplier at work using either panel of Figure 21.1. In panel A, the increase in government spending of 10 shifts the AD line straight up by 10. Because of the slope of the AD line, the new intersection with the 45-degree line shows that domestic product increases to 120. In panel B, the increase in government spending of 10 is a *decrease of government saving* (the difference between tax revenue and government spending) by 10. The $S - I_d$ line shifts straight down by 10. Again, because of the slopes of the lines, the intersection of the new $S - I_d$ line with the (unchanged) $X - M$ line indicates that domestic product increases to 120.

The spending multiplier of 2 works its effects not only on the rise in production but also on the rise in imports. Imports rose by 3 in the first round of expenditures, and they rise by twice as much, $6 (= 0.3 \times 20)$ over all rounds of new expenditures. With exports constant for this small country, the country's trade balance thus deteriorates by 6.

Foreign-Income Repercussions

In describing the marginal propensity to import as a leakage, we have argued as though whatever is spent on imports is permanently lost as a component of aggregate demand for our domestic product. This assumption works well enough for a small country whose trade is negligible as an average or marginal share of

---

[2] The multiplier formula can be derived from the fact that the change in production and income equals the initial rise in government spending plus the extra demand for the country's product stimulated by the rise in income itself:

$$\Delta Y = \Delta G + (1 - s - m) \bullet \Delta Y$$

so that

$$\Delta Y \bullet (1 - 1 + s + m) = \Delta G$$

world income. However, when a nation looms larger in the economies of its trading partners, this assumption underestimates the multiplier. When a large nation's extra spending leads to extra imports, these imports noticeably raise foreign incomes and create foreign jobs. The expansion of foreign incomes encourages foreign purchases of the first country's exports in amounts dictated by the foreign marginal propensities to import from that country. The extra demand for exports raises the country's income further, thus raising the value of the multiplier response to the initial domestic spending. Thus, *the more our country's imports affect foreign incomes, and the more the foreign countries have a propensity to import from our country, the more our true spending multiplier exceeds the simple formula $1/(s + m)$.*

Figure 21.2 illustrates the process of foreign repercussions. An initial rise in our government purchases of goods and services, on the left, creates extra income in our national economy. Some fraction (s) of the extra income will be saved, some will be spent on domestic product, and some will be spent on imports. The fraction (m) spent on imports will create an equal amount of demand for foreign production, as well as income for foreign sellers. They, in turn, will save a fraction of this additional income (s_f), spend some in their own countries, and import a fraction (m_f) from us. We then divide that extra export income into saving, domestic purchases, and imports, and the cycle continues. Each round passes along a smaller stimulus until the multiplier process comes to rest with a finite overall expansion.

The existence of such foreign-income repercussions helps account for the parallelism in business cycles that has been observed among the major industrial economies. Since early in the 20th century, when America has sneezed, Canada, Europe, Japan, and many other countries have caught cold. Such a tendency was already evident in the business cycles in Europe and the United States in the mid-19th century, though the correlation between the European cycles and the U.S. cycles was far from perfect. The Great Depression of the 1930s also reverberated back and forth among countries, as each country's slump caused a cut in imports (helped by beggar-thy-neighbor import barriers that were partly a response to the

FIGURE 21.2
Foreign Trade and Income Repercussions Starting from a Rise in Our Spending

slump itself) and thereby cut foreign exports and incomes. Correspondingly, the outbreak of the Korean War brought economic boom to West Germany, Italy, and Japan, as surging U.S. war spending raised their exports and incomes, leading to a further partial increase in their purchases from the United States.

The same interdependence of incomes persists today. The "locomotive theory" represents a recent application of repercussions analysis. The theory is based on the fact that the three largest economies in the world are the United States, Japan, and Germany. During times when world real growth is sluggish, such as the late 1970s, early 1990s, and early 2000s, increasing growth in two or three of these countries may be sufficient to raise world growth overall. Growth in the largest economies raises their imports, tending to pull the rest of the world along, with repercussions reinforcing the higher growth of all countries.

Economists have estimated the spending multipliers in major industrial countries that are subject to foreign-income repercussions. They came up with plausible patterns like those in Figure 21.3. The multipliers tell the tales we would expect of such international multipliers even though they are expressed in elasticity form (*percent* change/*percent* change), instead of the usual multiplier form (absolute change/absolute change). To follow the numbers down the first column, Figure 21.3 says that U.S. production and income would be raised 1.1 percent if aggregate demand rose by 1 percent in the United States alone, or by 0.1 percent if demand rose 1 percent in Japan alone, or by 0.1 percent if demand rose by 1 percent in euro land (the 12 EU countries that now use the euro as their currency). Or following the numbers across the Japan row, the estimates say that a 1 percent rise in Japanese spending would raise U.S. production and income by 0.1 percent, Japanese production and income by 1.7 percent, euro area production and income by 0.1 percent, and so forth.

A basic pattern emerging from the estimates in Figure 21.3 is the role of *national size*. The bigger the country, the more its spending tends to affect other countries. The effect of U.S. spending in any other country is usually greater than the effect of any other foreign country's spending. For example, the euro area is more affected by spending shifts in the United States (0.4 percent) than it is by those in Japan (0.1). The importance of *close trading ties* is also evident in the large effect that the United States has on Canada.

FIGURE 21.3

Spending Multipliers with Foreign-Income Repercussions

Source: Dalsgaard, André, and Richardson (2001), Tables A1, A2, and A3.

The Effect of a 1 Percent Rise of Spending in	On Real Domestic Product in				
	United States	**Japan**	**Euro Area**	**United Kingdom**	**Canada**
United States	1.1	0.5	0.4	0.2	1.0
Japan	0.1	1.7	0.1	0.1	0.1
Euro area	0.1	0.2	1.2	0.2	0.2

Each number gives the *percent* rise in the domestic product of the country whose column is named along the top that is caused by a 1 percent rise in the spending of the country whose row is named on the left of the table. In the analysis interest rates and exchange rates are held constant. The multipliers shown here are the results for the first year after the initial increase in spending.

A MORE COMPLETE FRAMEWORK: THREE MARKETS

The discussion of spending multipliers provides insights into macroeconomic performance, but it is too limited to be useful as a full framework for our analysis. We need to be able to picture three major components of the macroeconomy at the same time, adding the supply and demand for money and the country's overall balance of payments. In the process of developing this more complete framework, we can also drop the assumption that interest rates are constant. In fact, we will focus on the level of interest rates in the country as a second variable of major interest in addition to the country's real GDP.

Figure 21.4 sketches the basic approach, which is often called the Mundell-Fleming model, after its developers, Nobel Prize winner Robert Mundell and Marcus Fleming of the International Monetary Fund. The three markets that give us a broader picture of the country's economy are shown in the center. The first two, the goods and services market and the market for money, directly determine two key variables of interest (Y and i). At the same time, these two variables have a major impact on the country's balance of payments and thus on the foreign exchange market. All three of the markets can be affected by different kinds of outside (exogenous) forces, shown on the left side of the figure. These outside forces represent shocks or disturbances that create pressures for macroeconomic changes.[3]

The Domestic Product Market

The aggregate demand for what our country produces depends not only on income (Y). It also depends on the interest rate (i) since a higher real interest rate discourages spending. We can picture these relationships in a graph as an IS curve. (IS stands for investment–saving.) The **IS curve** shows all combinations

---

[3] This model of the open macroeconomy is not perfect, but it does allow us to examine the interrelationships among a large number of important macrovariables, and to examine the dynamics of national adjustments to achieve external balance. Here are some of the things that it does not do well. First, changes in the price level or the inflation rate are not modeled explicitly. Instead we infer that there are upward pressures on the price level or inflation rate when aggregate demand tries to push the economy beyond its supply-side potential. Second, the supply-side of the economy is not modeled, so the approach cannot easily analyze supply-side shocks or long-run economic growth. Third, international capital flows are modeled as responsive to the difference in interest rates. However, a large effect cannot be sustained beyond the short run, once international investors have adjusted their portfolios. Fourth, expectations are not modeled explicitly, but instead they are brought in as exogenous forces.

Appendix F presents an approach that can address some of the issues raised in the first two points. This approach examines aggregate demand, aggregate supply, and price adjustment over time. We also briefly discuss, later in this chapter, how to add analysis of inflation to the Mundell-Fleming model. In addition, at several places in the analysis of this chapter and the next two, we will remind ourselves of how the third point about international capital flows should affect our interpretation of some of the results obtained using the Mundell-Fleming model.

FIGURE 21.4

An Overview of
the Macromodel
of an Open
Economy

In addition to the linkages shown here, pressure in the foreign exchange market (or imbalance in the country's balance of payments) can feed back into and affect the country through the domestic product market or the money market. The ways in which this occurs depend on whether the country has a fixed or a floating exchange rate. These issues are taken up in the next two chapters.

of domestic product levels and interest rates for which the domestic product market is in equilibrium. As in the previous section of this chapter, we can think of this equilibrium as following from the condition $Y = C + I_d + G + (X - M)$, or we can think of it as following from the condition that national saving equals the sum of domestic investment and net exports. If we use the latter, the domestic product market is in equilibrium when

$$S(\overset{+}{Y}) = I_d(\overset{-}{i}) + X - M(\overset{+}{Y}) \tag{21.9}$$

Here the signs above the equation indicate the direction of each influence in parentheses on the value of the variable it affects.[4]

To see why the IS curve slopes downward, let's start with one equilibrium point on it and then ask where other equilibria could lie. Let us start at point A in Figure 21.5, where domestic product equals 100 and the interest rate is 0.07 (7 percent a year). We somehow know that this combination brings an equilibrium in the domestic product market. That is, given other basic economic conditions, having $Y = 100$ and $i = 0.07$ makes domestic investment plus net exports $I_d + (X - M)$ match national saving S. How could equilibrium in the product market be maintained if the interest rate is lower, say, only 0.05? The lower interest rate would induce the nation to invest in more domestic real capital. The

---

[4] Additional influences of Y and i are possible. S may be a positive function of i, for instance, if higher interest rates reduce borrowing (that is, reduce negative saving) by households. I_d may be a positive function of Y, for instance, if high current production levels make the need for new investment to expand capacity more urgent. These additions would somewhat change the slope of the IS curve, but the picture would not be different in its essentials.

FIGURE 21.5

The IS Curve:
Equilibria in
the Domestic
Product Market

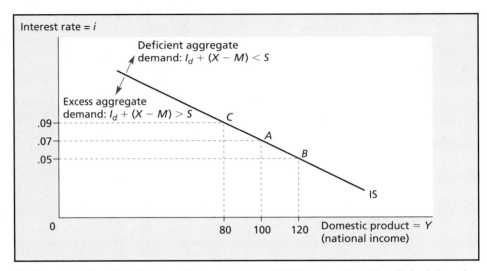

The IS curve shows all possible combinations of the interest rate *i* and real GDP *Y* that are consistent with equilibrium in the goods and services sector of the national economy, given the state of other fundamental influences. If any of these other fundamental influences changes, then the entire IS curve shifts. Here are some changes in fundamental influences (usually called exogenous shocks) that shift the IS curve to the right (or up):

- Expansionary fiscal policy (an increase in government spending or a tax cut).
- An exogenous increase in household consumption (for instance, due to improved consumer expectations about the future of the economy or an increase in wealth).
- An exogenous increase in domestic real investment (for instance, due to improved business expectations about the future of the economy).
- An exogenous increase in exports (for instance, due to rising foreign income, a shift in the tastes of foreign consumers toward the country's products, or an improvement in the international price competitiveness of the country's products).
- An exogenous decrease in imports (for instance, due to a shift in the tastes of local consumers away from imported products or an improvement in the international price competitiveness of the country's products).

To see what exogenous shocks can cause the IS curve to shift to the left (or down), reverse all of these.

higher level of aggregate demand (because I_d is larger) results in a higher level of domestic product. (In fact, because of the spending multiplier, the increase in domestic product is larger than the increase in real domestic investment resulting directly from the lower interest rate.) According to the IS curve, the higher level of domestic product matching aggregate demand for that low interest rate is $Y = 120$, as represented at point *B*. Similarly, if point *A* is one equilibrium, then others with higher interest rates must lie at lower production levels, as at point *C*. So the IS curve slopes downward. The higher the interest rate, the lower the level of domestic product that is consistent with it. Points that are not on the IS curve find the domestic product market out of equilibrium.

Changes in any influence other than interest rates that can directly affect aggregate demand cause a shift in the IS curve. These are the exogenous forces or shocks noted in Figure 21.4. For instance, an increase in government spending, or an improvement in consumer sentiment that leads people to increase their consumption spending, increases aggregate demand and shifts the IS curve to the right.

The Money Market

The next market in which macroeconomic forces interact is that for the money of each nation. As usual, there is a balancing of supply and demand.

The supply side of the market for units of a nation's money is, roughly, the conventional "money supply." **Monetary policy,** the set of central-bank policies, institutions, and bank behavioral patterns governing the availability of bank checking deposits and currency in circulation, is the top influence on the money supply.

Our view of the demand for money is an extension of the money demand discussed in Chapter 18. There we posited that the (nominal) demand for money depends on the value of (nominal) GDP, which equals the price level P times Y (real GDP). Money is held to carry out transactions, and the value of transactions should be correlated with the value of income or production. The larger domestic product is during a time period such as a year, the greater the amount of money balances that firms and households will want to keep on hand to cover uncertain amounts of spending needs.

In addition to the benefits of money in facilitating transactions, there is an opportunity cost to holding money. The opportunity cost is the interest that the holder of money could earn if her wealth were instead invested in other financial assets such as bonds. Some forms of money (currency and coin, traveler's checks, zero-interest checking accounts) earn no interest. Others (interest-paying checking accounts) earn some interest, but the interest rate earned is generally relatively low. Interest forgone is an opportunity cost of holding money. This cost leads us to attempt to economize on our money holdings, and we attempt to economize more as the interest rate available on other financial assets rises. A higher interest rate tempts people to hold interest-earning bonds rather than money. That is, it lowers the demand for money.

The demand for (nominal) money L is positively related to nominal GDP and negatively related to the level of interest rates available on other financial assets:

$$L = L(\overset{+}{P}\overset{-}{Y,}\ i) \tag{21.10}$$

The equilibrium between money supply M^s and money demand is then

$$M^s = L(\overset{+}{P}\overset{-}{Y,}\ i) \tag{21.11}$$

where the plus and minus signs again serve to remind us of the direction of influence of PY and i.

The money market equilibrium can be pictured as the "LM curve" of Figure 21.6. The **LM curve** shows all combinations of production levels and interest rates for which the money market is in equilibrium, given the money supply (set by policy), the price level P, and the money demand function (representing how people decide their money holdings). LM stands for liquidity–money, where money demand is viewed as demand for the most highly liquid financial assets in the economy.

To see why the LM curve slopes upward, begin with the equilibrium at point A and think of where the other equilibria could lie. If the interest rate were higher,

FIGURE 21.6

The LM Curve:
Equilibria in the
Money Market

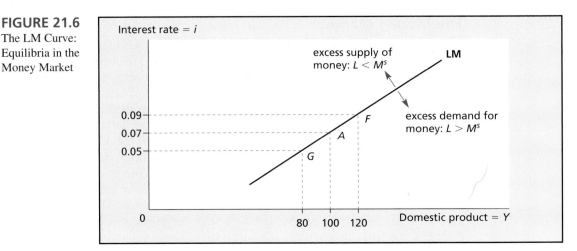

The LM curve shows all possible combinations of the interest rate *i* and real GDP *Y* that are consistent with equilibrium in the money sector of the national economy, given the state of other fundamental influences. If any of these other fundamental influences changes, then the entire LM curve shifts. Here are some changes in fundamental influences (exogenous shocks) that shift the LM curve down (or to the right):

- Expansionary monetary policy (increase in the money supply).
- Decrease in the country's average price level (for instance, due to a sudden decline in oil prices).
- Exogenous decrease in money demand (for instance, due to the introduction of credit cards that allow people to buy things without using money directly).

To see what exogenous shocks can cause the LM curve to shift up (or to the left), reverse all of these.

say, at 0.09, people would hold less money in order to earn the higher interest rate by holding bonds instead. To have the money market in equilibrium at that higher interest rate, people would have to have some other reason to hold the same amount of money supply as at point *A*. They would be willing to hold the extra money only if the level of domestic product and income were higher, raising their transactions demand for holding money. That happens to just the right extent at point *F*, another equilibrium. In contrast, going in the other direction, we can ask how people would be content to hold the same money supply as at point *A* if the interest they gave up by holding money were suddenly lower than at point *A*. By itself, the lower interest rate on bonds would mean a greater demand for cash because cash is convenient. People would be willing to refrain from holding extra cash only if some other change reduced the demand. One such change is lower domestic product, meaning lower transactions demand for cash. Point *G* is a point at which the lower interest rate and lower production leave the demand for money the same as at point *A*.

Changes in any of the influences on money supply and money demand other than the interest rate and domestic product represent exogenous forces that shift the entire LM curve. Consider an increase in the nominal money supply M^s by the central bank. If the price level *P* is sticky in the short run (so there is no immediate effect on the country's price level or inflation rate), then the increase in the money supply tends to reduce interest rates (or, equivalently, the increased money supply can support a higher level of domestic product and transactions). The LM curve shifts down (or to the right).

So far, we have two markets whose equilibria depend on how domestic product (Y) and interest rates (i) interact in each market. For any given set of basic economic conditions (fiscal policy, the business mood, consumer sentiment, foreign demand for the country's exports, monetary policy, and so forth), these two markets simultaneously determine the level of domestic product and the level of the interest rate in the economy. The intersection of the IS and LM curves shows the levels of Y and i that represent equilibrium in both the market for goods and services and the market for money. For instance, if the IS curve from Figure 21.5 is added to Figure 21.6, the intersection is at point A. The short-run equilibrium level of real GDP (Y) is 100, and the equilibrium interest rate is 0.07 (7 percent).

The Foreign Exchange Market (or Balance of Payments)

The third market is the one where the availability of foreign currency is balanced against the demand for it. This market can be called either the *foreign exchange market,* if we want to keep the exchange rate in mind, or *the balance of payments,* if we are using the country's official settlements balance (B) to reflect the net private or nonofficial trading between our currency and foreign currency. In order to picture this third market, it is easier to think through the balance-of-payments approach.

The country's official settlements balance is the sum of the country's current account balance (CA) and its capital account balance (KA, which does not include official reserves transactions). The influences on B can be divided into trade flow effects and financial flow effects. How do our key variables—real product or income (Y) and the country's interest rate (i)—affect the country's balance of payments? Previous discussion has shown two major effects. First, the balance on goods and services trade (or the current account) depends negatively on our domestic product, through the demand for imports. Second, international capital flows depend on interest rates (both at home and abroad). A higher interest rate in our country will attract a capital inflow, provided that the higher domestic interest rate is not immediately offset by higher foreign interest rates.

The easy intuition that a higher interest rate in our economy will attract investment from abroad and give us a capital inflow is valid, but only in the short run (say, for a year or less after the interest rate rises). Over the longer run, this effect stops and is even reversed for at least two reasons:

1. A higher interest rate attracts a lot of capital inflow from abroad at first, as investors adjust the shares of their stock of wealth held in assets from our country. Soon, though, the inflow will dwindle because portfolios have already been adjusted.

2. If a higher interest rate in our country succeeds in attracting funds from abroad and raising B in the short run, it may have the opposite effect later on for the simple reason that bonds mature and loans must be repaid. If a higher interest

rate gives us borrowed funds now, we must repay with interest later. We cannot talk of using higher interest rates to attract capital (lending) to this country without reflecting on the fact that those higher interest rates will have to be paid out in the future, along with the borrowed principal.[5]

For these reasons, the notion that a higher interest rate in our country can "improve" the balance of payments is valid only in the short run. We can use the short-run reasoning if the issue before us is the effect on *B* now. We will often use this short-run focus, but only with the warning that in the long run a higher interest rate has an ambiguous effect on the overall balance of payments.

We can reexpress the dependence of the balance of payments (or the foreign exchange market) on production and interest rates in two other ways. One is with an equation. The official settlements balance *B* equals the current account balance CA (which is approximately equal to net exports, *X − M*) plus the capital account balance KA:

$$B = CA(\overset{-}{Y}) + KA(\overset{+}{i}) \tag{21.12}$$

Raising our domestic product lowers the current account surplus (or raises the deficit) because it gives us more demand for imports of foreign goods and services. Raising our interest rate, on the other hand, attracts an inflow of capital from abroad, raising our capital account surplus (or reducing the deficit).

To link the balance of payments with *i* and *Y*, we can also use the FE curve of Figure 21.7. For a given set of other basic economic conditions that can influence the country's balance of payments, the **FE curve** shows the set of all interest-and-production combinations in our country that result in a zero value for the country's official settlements balance.

The FE curve, like the LM curve, slopes upward. To see why, begin again with an equilibrium at point *A*. Let's say that this is the same point *A* as in the previous two figures, although it need not be. If point *A* finds our international payments in overall balance, how could they still be in balance if the interest rate is higher,

---

[5] The balance-of-payments cost of attracting the extra capital from abroad could be even greater than the interest rate alone might suggest. To see how, let us suppose that the home country (*a*) is a net debtor country and (*b*) is large enough to be able to raise its own interest rate even though it is part of a larger world capital market. Let us imagine Canada is in this position.

Suppose that a rise in Canada's interest rate from 9 percent to 12 percent succeeds in raising foreign investments into Canada from $500 billion to $600 billion. What interest will Canada pay out each year on the extra $100 billion of borrowing (a temporarily higher *B*)? The annual interest bill on the new $100 billion itself comes to $12 billion a year. But, in addition, to continue to hold the original investments of $500 billion within the country—that is, to "roll over" these bonds and loans as they come up for renewal or repayment—Canadian borrowers have to pay an extra $15 billion [= $500 billion × (.12 − .09)]. The total extra interest outflow each year is thus the $12 billion plus the extra $15 billion, or payments of $27 billion just to hold on to an extra $100 billion in borrowings. That's an incremental interest cost of 27 percent, not just 12 percent. This is an expensive way to attract international "hot money."

FIGURE 21.7

The FE Curve:
Balance-of-
Payment
Equilibria

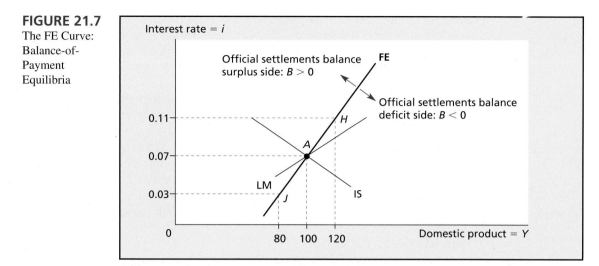

The FE curve shows all possible combinations of the interest rate *i* and real GDP *Y* that are consistent with an official settlements balance of zero for the country, given the state of other fundamental influences. If any of these other fundamental influences changes, then the entire FE curve shifts. Here are some changes in fundamental influences (exogenous shocks) that shift the FE curve to the right (or down):

- An exogenous increase in exports (for instance, due to rising foreign income, a shift in the tastes of foreign consumers toward the country's products, or an improvement in the international price competitiveness of the country's products).
- An exogenous decrease in imports (for instance, due to a shift in the tastes of local consumers away from imported products or an improvement in the international price competitiveness of the country's products).
- Exogenous changes that result in an increase in capital inflows or a decrease in capital outflows (for instance, a decrease in the foreign interest rate, an increase in the expected rate of appreciation of the country's currency, or a decrease in the perceived riskiness of investing in this country's financial assets).

To see what exogenous shocks can cause the FE curve to shift to the left (or up), reverse all of these.

say, at 11 percent? That higher interest rate attracts a greater inflow of capital, bringing an official-settlements-balance surplus unless something else also changes. With the higher interest rate, *B* could still be zero (no surplus, no deficit) if domestic product and income are higher. Higher product and income induce us to spend more on everything, including imports. The extra imports shift the balance of payments toward a deficit. In just the right amounts, extra production and a higher interest rate could cancel each other's effect on the balance of payments, leaving *B* = 0. That happens at point *H*. Correspondingly, some combinations of lower interest rates and lower production levels could also keep our payments in overall balance, as at point *J*.

How does the slope of the FE curve compare to the slope of the LM curve? As drawn in Figure 21.7, the FE curve is steeper. This is not the only possibility, though. It depends on how responsive money demand and the balance of payments are to changes in the interest rate and domestic product. If, for instance, capital flows are very sensitive to interest rates, then the FE curve is relatively flat, flatter than the LM curve. The FE curve is relatively flat because only a small increase in the interest rate is needed to draw in capital and offset the decline in the current account if domestic product is higher. (Point H would be lower, with an interest rate that is not much above 0.07.) If capital flows are extremely sensitive to interest rates, then we have the case of **perfect capital mobility,** and the FE curve is essentially completely flat (a horizontal line).

What happens when some other condition or variable that affects the country's balance of payments changes? These are the exogenous forces of Figure 21.4. When one of these changes occurs, it shifts the FE curve (just as a change in an exogenous condition relevant to the IS curve or the LM curve causes a shift in that curve). For instance, an increase in foreign income increases demand for our exports, improving our balance of payments and shifting the FE curve to the right. Or, an increase in foreign interest rates causes a capital outflow from our country, deteriorating our balance of payments, and shifting the FE curve to the left.

Three Markets Together

Bringing the three markets together, we get a determination of the level of domestic product (Y), the interest rate (i), and the overall balance of payments (B). The economy will gravitate toward a simultaneous equilibrium in the domestic product market (on the IS curve) and the money market (on the LM curve). With Y and i thus determined, we also know the state of the balance of payments (B).

- The official settlements balance is in surplus if the IS–LM intersection is to the left of the FE curve.

- The official settlements balance is zero if the IS–LM intersection is on the FE curve (for example, point A in Figure 21.7).

- The official settlements balance is in deficit if the IS–LM intersection is to the right of the FE curve.

This section has given the same reasoning about three markets in three alternative forms: the causal-arrow sketch of Figure 21.4; the listing of Equations 21.9, 21.11, and 21.12; and the use of IS–LM–FE diagrams (Figures 21.5 through 21.7). The way that we use this framework—especially the way that we use the FE curve—depends on the type of exchange rate policy that the country has adopted. As we will examine in the next chapter, if a country adopts a fixed exchange rate, then any divergence between the IS–LM intersection and the FE curve shows that official intervention is needed to defend the fixed rate. The official settlements balance is not zero—official intervention to defend the fixed rate results in official reserves transactions. As we will examine in Chapter 23, if the country adopts a clean float, then the official settlements balance must be zero, and somehow a triple intersection between the IS, LM, and FE curves must occur. In different ways, to be explored in each chapter, these situations create pressures for adjustments that affect the country's macroeconomic performance.

THE PRICE LEVEL DOES CHANGE

In developing the framework so far, we have generally ignored the product price level (P). We assumed that the price level is a constant for the short run, given by previous history. While this may be reasonable for most short-run analysis, it is clearly not appropriate generally. The price level does change over time for three basic reasons.[6]

First, most countries have some amount of ongoing inflation. This amount can be anticipated and built into inflation expectations. Generally, ongoing positive inflation requires sufficient ongoing growth of the country's nominal money supply. The role of ongoing inflation was prominent in Chapter 18, especially in discussing the monetary approach.

Second, strong or weak aggregate demand can put pressure on the country's price level. If the price level is somewhat sluggish, then this effect will not be felt in the immediate short run, but it will have an impact as the economy moves beyond the initial short run. The strength of aggregate demand must be evaluated against the economy's supply-side capabilities for producing goods and services. If aggregate demand is very strong, then actual production strains against the economy's supply capabilities. The economy will "overheat" and there will be upward pressure on the price level. (In a setting in which there is ongoing inflation, this really means that the price level will rise more than it otherwise would have anyway. The inflation rate will increase.) If aggregate demand is weak, then product markets will be weak, creating downward pressure on the price level because of the "discipline" effect of weak demand. (Again, in a setting of ongoing inflation, this really means that the inflation rate will be lower than it otherwise would have been—the price level may still be rising, but it will rise more slowly.)

Third, shocks occasionally can cause large changes in the price level even in the short run. One dramatic example was the pair of oil price shocks in the 1970s. Another source of a price shock is a large abrupt change in the exchange rate value of a country's currency. As we will discuss in the next chapter, a large devaluation or depreciation is likely to cause a large increase in the domestic-currency price of imported products. The general price level tends to increase quickly because of both the direct effects of higher import prices and the indirect effects on costs and other prices in the country.

For subsequent analysis using our framework, the effect of strong or weak aggregate demand on the price level is of major interest. As we move beyond the initial short run, we do expect adjustment in the country's product price level. This can have an impact on the country's international price competitiveness, as discussed in the next section. If international price competitiveness is affected, then the country's current account balance changes. In addition, although we will not focus on this

---

[6] Appendix F presents a formal framework for analyzing the adjustment of the price level over time.

effect in subsequent analysis, a change in the price level changes money demand (through the *PY* term). If the nation's money supply is not changing in line with the change in money demand, then the LM curve will shift over time.[7]

TRADE ALSO DEPENDS ON PRICE COMPETITIVENESS

As previously discussed, a country's exports, imports, and net exports depend on production and incomes in both this country and the rest of the world. Standard microeconomics indicates that demand for exports and imports each should also be affected by the prices of these products. Quantity demanded depends on both income and relative prices.

Our demand for imports depends not only on our income, but also on the price of imports relative to the price (*P*) of domestic products that are substitutes for these imports. What is this relative price? Consider that an imported product (say, a bottle of French wine) is initially priced in foreign currency (say, 10 euros). Once imported into the United States, its price is converted into dollars using the going exchange rate (say, $1.10 per euro). The domestic-currency price of the import is then equal to $P_f \cdot e$ ($11.00 for the bottle), where the exchange rate *e* is stated in units of domestic currency per unit of foreign currency. Our decision about whether to buy this import depends partly on its dollar price relative to the price of a comparable domestic product (say, a bottle of California wine). The price ratio is $(P_f \cdot e)/P$. This ratio may look familiar—it is essentially the real exchange rate introduced in Chapter 18.

Thus, by expanding our previous Equation 21.5, we see that the demand for imports has two major determinants:

$$M = M(\overset{+}{Y}, \overset{-}{P_f \cdot e/P}) \tag{21.13}$$

The volume of imports tends to be higher if our production and income are higher, but lower if imports are relatively expensive (meaning $P_f \cdot e/P$ is high).

Foreign demand for our exports depends not only on foreign income, but also on the price of our products exported into the foreign market relative to the prices of their comparable local products (P_f). Our export product (say, a personal computer) is initially priced in our currency (say, $1,500). This can be converted into a foreign currency (say, yen) at the going exchange rate (say, $e = \$0.01$ per yen).

---

[7] If the aggregate demand pressure continues for a sufficient period of time, it can also affect the ongoing rate of inflation. For instance, the United States went into the 1990–1991 recession with an ongoing inflation rate of about 4.5 percent. The weak aggregate demand that caused the recession (and slowed the subsequent recovery) reduced the actual inflation rate to less than 3 percent. In addition, the ongoing inflation rate expected to continue into the future (even when the economy had fully recovered from the recession) was reduced to about 3 percent, according to most estimates. (The expected ongoing inflation rate fell to 2–2.5 percent by the late 1990s, largely because technical changes lowered the measured inflation rate.)

The foreign-currency price of our export is then equal to P/e. (Here $1,500/.01 = 150,000$ yen.) The foreign decision about whether to buy their domestic product (say, an NEC computer) or our exported product is based partly on the relative price, which equals $P_f/(P/e)$ or $(P_f \cdot e)/P$. The higher is this ratio, the less attractive is their domestic product, and the more attractive is our exported product.

Thus, the demand for our exports has two major determinants:

$$X = X(\overset{+}{Y_f}, \overset{+}{P_f \cdot e/P}) \tag{21.14}$$

The volume of our exports tends to be higher if foreign production and income are higher or if foreign substitute products are relatively expensive.

Thus, in addition to the income effects, net exports $(X - M)$ tend to be higher if the price competitiveness of our products is higher, both because the volume of exports tends to be larger and because the volume of imports tends to be smaller. Our general indicator of international price competitiveness is the ratio $(P_f \cdot e)/P$ (the real exchange rate).[8] Our international price competitiveness improves if the foreign-currency price of foreign substitute products (P_f) is higher, if the domestic-currency price of our products (P) is lower, or if the nominal exchange rate value of our currency is lower (e is higher). Over time, our price competitiveness improves if the foreign inflation rate is higher, our inflation rate is lower, or our currency appreciates less (or depreciates more).

Changes in international price competitiveness can be incorporated into our IS–LM–FE framework. They are one of the other economic conditions (or exogenous forces) that can cause shifts in the curves. A change in international price competitiveness shifts two curves: the FE curve and the IS curve. To see this, consider an improvement in a country's international price competitiveness, perhaps because the country has had low product price inflation or because the country's currency has depreciated or devalued. The improved price competitiveness increases exports and decreases imports. The increase in net exports increases aggregate demand, so the IS curve shifts to the right. The current account improves, so the FE curve also shifts to the right.

---

[8] While the real exchange rate provides a useful broad indicator of a country's international price competitiveness, it is not perfect. For any particular product, the relative price is affected by several influences not usually captured in the ratio. First, transport costs and government barriers to imports can alter the price ratio by increasing the price of the imported product. Second, exporters may use strategic pricing so that the local-currency price of the imported product is not just the domestic-currency price in the home market converted at the going exchange rate. This reflects international price discrimination. It is particularly interesting here because exporters may resist passing through the full effect of any exchange rate change into foreign-currency prices for their products. This is called *incomplete pass-through* or *pricing to market*. When the yen appreciated sharply from 1985 to 1987, Japanese firms did raise the dollar prices of the products that they exported to the United States, but by far less than the amount of the exchange rate change. They did this, presumably, to minimize their loss of export sales. From the point of view of the U.S. economy, this means that the volume of imports did not fall as much as might have been expected following the large dollar depreciation.

Summary

The performance of a country's macroeconomy has both internal and external dimensions. We evaluate the country's internal balance against goals oriented toward the domestic economy. **Internal balance** focuses on achieving domestic production that matches the country's supply capabilities so that resources are fully employed, while also achieving price-level stability or an acceptably low rate of inflation. We evaluate external balance against goals related to the country's international transactions. **External balance** focuses on achieving an overall balance of payments that is sustainable over time.

A key aspect of how an open macroeconomy works is the relationship between domestic production and international trade in goods and services. International trade in goods and services is one component of total aggregate demand, which determines domestic product and income in the short run. In addition, domestic production and income have an impact on international trade, especially through the demand for imports.

These relationships influence how shifts in aggregate demand affect our domestic production. Holding interest rates (as well as the product price level and exchange rates) constant, we generally expect that an increase in some component of aggregate demand (like government spending) has a larger effect on domestic production—a phenomenon summarized in the spending multiplier. In a closed economy, the size of the multiplier is $1/s$, where s is the marginal propensity to save (including any government saving "forced" through the marginal tax rate). For the open macroeconomy, a rise in domestic product and income increases imports. The size of the **spending multiplier for a small open economy** is $1/(s + m)$, where m is the **marginal propensity to import.** The larger is the country's propensity to import, the smaller is the spending multiplier. The leakage into imports, like the leakage into saving, dampens the effects of the initial extra spending on the ultimate change in domestic product and income.

If the country is not small, then changes in its demand for imports have noticeable effects on other countries, with several specific implications. First, any boom or slump in one country's aggregate demand can spread to other countries. Second, the changes in production and income in the other countries can then feed back into the first country—**foreign-income repercussions.** These foreign-income repercussions make the true spending multiplier larger than the simple formula $1/(s + m)$. Swings in the business cycle (recession or expansion) are not only internationally contagious but also self-reinforcing, a conjecture easily supported by the experience of the 1930s. More recently, the "locomotive theory" posits that growth in the United States, Japan, and Germany (the three largest economies in the world) can spur growth in the entire world.

A more complete framework for analyzing a country's macroeconomy in the short run requires that we are able to picture not only domestic product, income, and aggregate demand but also supply and demand for money and the country's overall balance of payments. The IS–LM–FE approach, also called the Mundell-Fleming model, provides this framework.

The **IS curve** shows all combinations of interest rate and domestic product that are equilibriums in the national market for goods and services. Because lower interest rates encourage borrowing and spending, the IS curve slopes downward. The **LM curve** shows all combinations of interest rate and domestic product that are equilibria between money supply and money demand. For money demand to remain equal to a given, unchanged money supply, the increase in money demand that accompanies a higher domestic product must be offset by a higher interest rate that reduces money demand, so that the LM curve slopes upward.

The **FE curve** shows all combinations of interest rate and domestic product that result in a zero balance in the country's overall international payments (its official settlements balance). The FE curve also generally slopes upward. An increase in domestic product and income increases demand for imports so that the country's current account and overall payments balance deteriorate. This can be offset (at least in the short run) by a higher interest rate that draws in foreign financial capital (or reduces capital outflows) so that the capital account (excluding official reserves transactions) improves.

The intersection of the IS and LM curves indicates the short-run equilibrium values for domestic product *Y* and the interest rate *i* for the country. The position of this IS–LM intersection relative to the FE curve indicates whether the official settlements balance is positive, zero, or negative.

Although we often assume that the country's product price level is constant in the short run, over time the price level changes. Most countries have some amount of ongoing inflation that is expected to continue. The monetary approach presented in Chapter 18 emphasizes that ongoing inflation is related to continuing growth of the money supply. In addition, the strength of aggregate demand relative to the economy's supply capabilities can affect the price level or inflation rate. If aggregate demand is too strong, the economy overheats and the price level or inflation rate rises. If aggregate demand is weak, the discipline effect of weak market demand tends to lower the price level or inflation rate. Furthermore, price shocks can cause large changes in the price level or inflation rate even in the short run.

International price competitiveness is another key determinant of a country's international trade in goods and services, in addition to the effects of national income on the country's imports and foreign income on the country's exports. If the price of foreign products relative to the price of our country's products is higher, our demand for imports tends to be lower, and foreign demand for our exports tends to be higher. The real exchange rate (introduced in Chapter 18) is a useful general indicator of this relative price and thus of the country's international price competitiveness. A change in international price competitiveness shifts both the IS curve and the FE curve because the current account balance changes. For instance, if competitiveness improves, then exports increase and imports decline. The increase in aggregate demand shifts the IS curve to the right, and the improvement in the country's payments position shifts the FE curve to the right.

Suggested Reading

Algebraic treatments of foreign-trade repercussions are given in Vanek (1962, Chapters 6–9) and Stern (1973, Chapter 7). Bosworth (1993, Chapter 2) discusses the concepts of internal and external balance and develops the IS–LM–FE model. Dalsgaard, André, and Richardson (2001) and Bryant et al. (1988) present empirical estimates of the domestic and foreign effects of policy changes using dynamic macroeconomic models that incorporate trade and other linkages among countries. Helliwell and Padmore (1984) summarize earlier empirical work using dynamic linkage models.

Questions and Problems

✦ 1. According to Figure 21.3, on which country other than Canada does the United States have the largest multiplier impact? Why do you think that this is so?

2. "A recession in the United States is likely to raise the growth of real GDP in Europe." Do you agree or disagree? Why?

✦ 3. An economy has a marginal propensity to save of 0.2 and a marginal propensity to import of 0.1. An increase of $1 billion in government spending now occurs. (Assume that the economy is initially producing at a level that is below its supply-side capabilities.)

    a. According to the spending multiplier for a small open economy, by how much will domestic product and income increase?

    b. If instead this is a closed economy with a marginal propensity to save of 0.2, by how much would domestic product and income increase if government spending increases by $1 billion? Explain the economics of why this answer is different from the answer to part *a.*

4. A country has a marginal propensity to save of 0.15 and a marginal propensity to import of 0.4. Real domestic spending now decreases by $2 billion.

    a. According to the spending multiplier (for a small open economy), by how much will domestic product and income change?

    b. What is the change in the country's imports?

    c. If this country is large, what effect will this have on foreign product and income? Explain.

    d. Will the change in foreign product and income tend to counteract or reinforce the change in the first country's domestic product and income? Explain.

✦ 5. How does the intersection of the IS and LM curves relate to the concept of internal balance?

6. How does the FE curve relate to the concept of external balance?

✦ 7. Explain the effect of each of the following on the LM curve:

    a. The country's central bank decreases the money supply.

    b. The country's interest rate increases.

8. Explain the effect of each of the following on the IS curve:
   a. Government spending decreases.
   b. Foreign demand for the country's exports increases.
   c. The country's interest rate increases.

◆ 9. Explain the effect of each of the following on the FE curve:
   a. Foreign demand for the country's exports increases.
   b. The foreign interest rate increases.
   c. The country's interest rate increases.

10. Explain the impact of each of the following on our country's exports and imports:
   a. Our domestic product and income increase.
   b. Foreign domestic product and income decrease.
   c. Our price level increases by 5 percent, with no change in the (nominal) exchange rate value of our currency and no change in the foreign price level.
   d. Our price level increases by 5 percent, the foreign price level increases by 10 percent, and there is no change in the (nominal) exchange rate value of our currency.

Chapter Twenty-Two

Internal and External Balance with Fixed Exchange Rates

Fixed exchange rates can reduce the variability of currency values if governments are willing and able to defend the rates. This chapter examines the macroeconomics of a country whose government has chosen a fixed exchange rate.

Many major countries of the world have instead chosen floating rates (albeit with modest amounts of government management). Why study fixed rates? There are three major reasons. First, within the current system a substantial number of countries do fix their exchange rates. As shown in Chapter 19, there are two major blocs of currencies with fixed exchange rates. A large number of developing countries that fix their currencies to the U.S. dollar form the dollar bloc. The euro bloc includes the 12 European Union countries that use the euro; one other EU country that fixes its currency to the euro through the Exchange Rate Mechanism, and a number of countries outside the EU that fix their currencies to the euro. In addition, a number of other countries fix their moneys to currencies other than the dollar or the euro. Second, in the current system a number of countries have floating rates in name, but the rates are so heavily managed by the governments that they are closer to being fixed rates in many respects. Third, there are continuing discussions about returning to a system of fixed rates among the world's major currencies. Proposals range from target zones that would be a kind of crawling peg with wide bands, to a return to the gold standard. Before we can assess the desirability or feasibility of such proposals, we need to understand how a fixed exchange rate affects both the behavior of a country's economy and the use of government policies to affect the economy's performance.

The analysis of the chapter shows that defense of a fixed exchange rate through official intervention in the foreign exchange market dramatically affects the country's monetary policy. The intervention can change the country's money supply, setting off effects that tend to reduce the payments imbalance. But this process also limits the country's ability to pursue an independent monetary policy. Defending the fixed rate also has an impact on fiscal policy, which actually becomes more powerful if international financial capital is highly mobile. In addition, intervention to defend the fixed rate affects how the country's economy responds to shocks, both shocks that come from within the country and shocks that are international in origin.

Fixed rates challenge government policymakers who are attempting to guide the country to both external balance (balance in the country's overall international payments) and internal balance (actual production equal to the economy's supply potential, or a high level of employment—"full employment"—without upward pressure on the country's inflation rate). Internal and external balance are often hard to reconcile in the short and medium runs. A government that pursues external balance alone, tidying up its balance of payments while letting inflation or unemployment get out of hand at home, may be thrown out of office. On the other hand, controlling domestic production alone, with fiscal or monetary policies, may widen a deficit or surplus in the balance of payments, jeopardizing the promise to keep the exchange rate fixed.

One possible solution is a subtle mixture of policies, with monetary policy assigned to reducing international payments imbalances, and fiscal policy assigned to stabilizing domestic production (GDP). Another possible "solution" is surrender—to change the fixed rate by devaluing, revaluing, or shifting to a floating rate. The chapter looks at both ideas, and concludes by considering the conditions that influence whether a change in the fixed rate will be successful in improving the country's internal and external macroeconomic performance.

FROM THE BALANCE OF PAYMENTS TO THE MONEY SUPPLY

Once a country's government has decided to have a fixed exchange rate, the government must defend that rate. As discussed in Chapter 19, the first line of defense is official intervention—the monetary authority (central bank) buys or sells foreign currency in the foreign exchange market as necessary to steady the rate within the allowable band around the central value chosen for the fixed rate. Chapter 19 showed that several implications follow from official intervention. First, the holdings of official reserves change as the central bank buys or sells foreign currency. Second, the country's money supply may change as the central bank sells or buys domestic currency as the other half of its official intervention.

Our goal in this and the next three sections of the chapter is to show how these effects occur and what implications they have for the country's macroeconomy. Let's begin with the assets and liabilities of the central bank that will be key to our story. Here is a simplified balance sheet that shows these key items:

Central Bank	
Selected Assets	**Selected Liabilities**
Domestic assets (D)	*Monetary base (MB)*
Debt securities	Currency
Loans to banks	Deposits from banks
International reserve assets (R)	
Foreign-currency assets	

Figure 22.1 shows that magnitude of these key items for the Federal Reserve; the U.S. central bank; and the European Central Bank (ECB), the central bank for the euro area.

The two key types of assets are **domestic assets** (*D*) and **international reserve assets** (*R*), especially the central bank's holdings of foreign currency and foreign-currency-denominated securities. The domestic assets are not international reserves because they are denominated in domestic currency. Two major types of domestic assets held by the central bank are (1) bonds and similar debt securities and (2) loans that the central bank has made to (regular) domestic banks or other domestic financial institutions.

FIGURE 22.1

Key Balance-Sheet Items, the Fed and the ECB, December 31, 2001 (Millions of U.S. Dollars)

	Federal Reserve (Consolidated System)	European Central Bank (Consolidated System)
Key Assets		
Securities (denominated in local currency)	601,935	85,122
Loans to banks (domestic currency)	34	179,431
Foreign-currency-denominated assets	14,559	233,514
Key Liabilities		
Currency (paper notes and coins)	611,757	237,560
Deposits from banks (domestic currency)	17,478	163,244

The differences in the holding of the key *domestic assets* reflects the difference in operating procedures. The Fed conducts its domestic monetary policy using *open-market operations,* in which the Fed buys and sells U.S. government securities, so it holds a lot of these assets. The ECB conducts its domestic monetary policy mostly by *making loans (in euros) to banks and other financial institutions.* These are two alternative ways of regulating the two key liability items, which together form the monetary base.

The difference in holdings of *foreign-currency assets* mainly reflects history. The U.S. government seldom intervenes in the foreign exchange market, so the Fed has little need to hold international reserve assets. The ECB inherited its official reserve assets from the 12 national central banks of the euro zone. Historically, these national banks actively intervened, so they needed to hold substantial international reserves.

Source: Federal Reserve Board of Governors, annual report, 2001; European Central Bank, annual report, 2001.

On the other side of the balance sheet, the liabilities of interest to our story are (1) the domestic currency (paper money and coins) issued by the central bank and (2) the deposits that the country's (regular) domestic banks (or other domestic financial institutions) have placed with the central bank. The deposits from regular banks may be required by regulations of the central bank. In addition, the central bank often uses the deposits from banks in the process of settling payments between domestic banks (for instance, in the process of clearing checks drawn on one bank but payable to another). The total of these two central-bank liabilities, currency and deposits from banks, is called the **monetary base.**

The country's **money supply** consists (mainly) of currency held by the public and various types of deposits (like checking accounts) that the public has at regular banks. The country's central bank has the ability to influence the total amount of these bank deposits from the public because banks are required to hold, or wish to hold, certain assets as bank reserves to "back up" these deposit liabilities. We presume that the types of assets that count as bank reserves are a bank's holdings of currency "in its vault" and the bank's holdings of deposits at the central bank. The amount of reserves that a bank is required to hold is typically some fraction of the deposits that the bank owes to its customers—a system called **fractional reserve banking.**[1]

In this setting the central bank controls the country's money supply by controlling its own balance sheet and by setting the reserve requirements that (regular) banks must meet. To see this, consider what happens if the central bank allows its liabilities (the monetary base) to increase. This will expand the money supply. If the increase is in the form of an increase in currency that is held by the public, then the money supply increases directly. If the increase is in the form of central bank liabilities that count as bank reserves (either currency in bank vaults or deposits from banks), then banks can increase the value of their deposit liabilities, and they can increase deposits by a multiple amount of the value of the increase in bank reserves. With fractional reserve banking, each dollar of extra bank reserves can back up several dollars of deposits (where *several* is the reciprocal of the

---

[1] As you can see, the standard terminology seems intended to confuse us. *Bank* shows up in two ways. The country's *central bank* is the official monetary authority that controls monetary policy and also (usually) is the authority that undertakes official intervention in the foreign exchange market. Regular banks, often just called *banks,* conduct regular banking business (making loans, taking deposits, transacting in foreign exchange) with regular customers (for instance, individuals, businesses, and government units) and among themselves (for instance, interbank loans and interbank foreign exchange trading). *Reserves* is an even more dangerous term. A central bank (or the country's relevant monetary authority if it is not exactly a central bank) holds *official reserve* assets. Regular banks hold *bank reserves* as assets, usually in proportion to their deposit liabilities. Part of these bank reserves is usually in the form of deposits that these regular banks have at the central bank. (Just to add to the soup, there is another type of reserve in bank accounting—liability items such as reserves for bad loans—but these are not part of our main story.)

reserve requirement fraction). The multiple expansion of the money supply with fractional reserve banking is called the **money multiplier process.**[2]

With this background on the country's central bank and its control of the country's money supply, let's return to the effects of official intervention used to defend the fixed exchange rate. If the country has an *official settlements balance surplus, so that the exchange rate value of the country's currency is experiencing upward pressure,* the central bank must *intervene to buy foreign currency and sell domestic currency.* On its balance sheet this is:

- An increase in official international reserve holdings ($R\uparrow$), and
- An increase in its liabilities ($MB\uparrow$ as the domestic currency is added to the economy).

The increase in liabilities could be in the form of an increase in actual currency outstanding (if the central bank delivers the domestic currency as currency itself). More likely, and more efficiently in terms of the process, the central bank delivers the domestic "currency" to a regular bank (the bank with whom it is transacting in the foreign exchange market) by increasing the deposits that the bank has at the central bank. In either case, the country's *money supply will increase.* If, as is likely, the reserves held by banks increase (because their deposits at the central bank increase or their holdings of vault cash increase), then the money supply can increase by a multiple of the size of the central bank intervention in the foreign exchange market.

If instead the *country's official settlements balance is in deficit and the exchange rate value of the country's currency is under downward pressure,* the central bank must *intervene to sell foreign currency and buy domestic currency.* On its balance sheet this is

- A decrease in official international reserve holdings ($R\downarrow$) and
- A decrease in its liabilities ($MB\downarrow$ as the domestic currency is removed from the economy).

The central bank probably collects the domestic "currency" by decreasing the deposits that the regular bank involved in the foreign exchange transaction has at the central bank. Then the reserves held by banks decline (because their deposits at the central bank decrease), and the *money supply must decrease* by a multiple of the size of the central bank intervention in the foreign exchange market (the money multiplier in reverse).

The conclusion here is that official intervention alters the central bank's assets and liabilities in ways that change not only the country's holdings of official international reserve assets but also the country's money supply, unless the central bank does something else to attempt to resist the change in the money supply. Indeed, under fractional reserve banking, the change in the money supply will be a multiple of the size of the intervention.

---

[2] This description of the central bank and the way in which it controls the country's money supply is appropriate for the United States (the Federal Reserve or "Fed") and for many other countries. Still, some countries use different procedures (for instance, implementing monetary policy through limits on the expansion of loans by banks to their customers). Analysis of such countries would need to be modified somewhat to match their procedures, but the major conclusions to be reached in the sections below generally still apply.

FROM THE MONEY SUPPLY BACK TO THE BALANCE OF PAYMENTS

If official intervention changes the country's money supply, what are the implications for the country's balance of payments and for the country's macroeconomic performance in general? The change in the money supply sets off several effects that tend to reduce the payments imbalance.

Consider first the case in which the country begins with a surplus in its overall balance of payments. The surplus requires official intervention in which the central bank buys foreign currency and sells domestic currency. The domestic money supply increases "automatically" as the central bank increases its liabilities when it sells domestic currency. Figure 22.2 summarizes the effects of the increase in the money supply on the balance of payments.

As the central bank increases bank reserves, banks are more liquid and want to expand their business. They seek to make more loans. In the process, their competition to lend more is likely to bid down interest rates.

The lowering of interest rates in the economy, at least in the short run, has several effects on the balance of payments. One is through the country's capital account. The decline in interest rates causes some holders of financial assets denominated in the domestic currency to seek higher returns abroad. The international capital outflow causes the capital account to "deteriorate" (become less positive or more negative).[3] This effect on the capital account can occur quickly, but it may not last long. Once portfolios are adjusted, any ongoing capital flows are likely to be smaller. In fact, the outflows could reverse when bonds mature or loans come due. (In addition, the extra foreign investment is likely to set up a stream of income payments that the country receives in the future.)

Another effect is on the current account because of changes in real income, in the price level, or in both. The decrease in domestic interest rates encourages interest-sensitive spending—for instance, through more borrowing to support additional new real investment projects. The expansion in spending results in an increase in real domestic product and income (assuming that there is some availability of resources to expand production in the economy). The rise in income increases imports of goods and services and "worsens" the current account balance. (A smaller surplus or a larger deficit results.) In addition, the extra spending can put upward pressure on the price level in the economy, especially if the expansion of aggregate demand pushes against the supply capabilities of the economy. If prices and costs in the economy rise, then the country's international price competitiveness deteriorates, and the country's current account worsens. Which of

---

[3] We are assuming that the change in the domestic interest rate lowers the interest differential because foreign interest rates have not changed or have not changed as much. In addition, we are assuming that expectations of future spot exchange rates have not changed. For instance, international investors believe that the fixed rate will be maintained, so the expected future spot rate remains about equal to the current spot rate.

FIGURE 22.2   Expanding the Money Supply Worsens the Balance of Payments With Fixed Rates

For a decrease in the money supply, reverse the direction of all changes.

these two effects actually occurs depends on the starting point for the economy and the time frame involved. If the economy begins with unemployed resources, then the effect through real income is likely to be larger. If the economy starts close to full employment, then the effect through the price level is likely to be more important, at least beyond the short-run period when prices are sticky.

Thus, official intervention by a country that initially has a balance-of-payments surplus can increase the money supply, and this increase in the money supply sets off adjustments in the economy that tend to reduce the size of the surplus. Key features of the adjustment can be pictured using an IS–LM–FE diagram. Suppose that the economy is initially at point A in Figure 22.3, the intersection of the initial IS and LM_0 curves. This point is to the left of the FE curve, showing that the country has a surplus in its official settlements balance. Official intervention to defend the fixed rate increases the money supply, shifting the LM curve down or to the right. As the LM curve shifts down, the equilibrium interest rate decreases and domestic product and income increase. The intersection of the IS curve and the new LM curve is moving closer to the FE curve. If the price level does not change, then full adjustment has occurred (probably over several years) when the LM curve has shifted down to the triple intersection at point E. The equilibrium interest rate has fallen from 7 percent to 6 percent, domestic product has risen from 100 to 110, and the official settlements balance is zero (because the economy is on the FE curve).[4]

---

[4] If the price level also increases, then both the FE and IS curves will shift to the left as the country loses international price competitiveness. The LM curve will shift by less, and the triple intersection will occur with a somewhat lower real domestic product.

FIGURE 22.3

Payments
Adjustments
for a Surplus
Country with
Fixed Rates

If the country begins at point *A* with a payment surplus, intervention to defend the fixed exchange rate results in an increase in the money supply. The LM curve shifts down or to the right, and the surplus falls toward zero as the IS–LM intersection shifts toward point *E*.

If the country instead begins with a deficit in its official settlements balance and downward pressure on the exchange rate value of its currency, then all of these effects work in the reverse direction. The domestic money supply decreases, and domestic interest rates increase, at least in the short run. The rise in interest rates draws a capital inflow, improving the capital account. The rise in interest rates also lowers aggregate demand and real domestic product, reducing imports and improving the current account. The weak aggregate demand also puts downward pressure on the economy's price level, at least beyond the short-run period in which prices are sticky. This increases the country's international price competitiveness and improves its current account. The overall balance of payments improves—the deficit declines toward zero. The country's IS–LM intersection is initially to the right of the FE curve. The LM curve then shifts up or to the left, and eventually a triple intersection is achieved.

The thrust of the analysis is clear. If an external imbalance exists, intervention to defend the fixed rate changes the domestic money supply. The money supply change causes adjustments that move the country back toward external balance. So what is the problem? Possible problems are of two types.

First, the process is based on changes in the country's holdings of international reserve assets. For a country that begins with a payments surplus, the monetary authority will acquire official international reserve assets. For a deficit, the author-ity will lose official reserves. Officials may view either change as undesirable. However, this may not really be a problem if the authority *accepts that the money supply must change* (and the LM curve must shift). The central bank can simply use its *domestic* operations to speed up the adjustment. For instance, the country can use open market operations in which it buys or sells government securities.

In the surplus situation, the country could expand the money supply more quickly, and lower interest rates more quickly, by buying domestic government securities. This open market operation adds to both the domestic assets ($D\uparrow$) and the liabilities ($MB\uparrow$) of the central bank. By changing monetary conditions more quickly, external balance is achieved more quickly. Official reserve assets (R) increase by less because some of the increase in the domestic money supply is the result of the increase in domestic assets (D) held by the central bank.

In the deficit situation, the country could contract the money supply by selling domestic government bonds in an open market operation. Bank reserves decrease, the money supply contracts, and interest rates rise more quickly. The payments deficit shrinks more quickly, and external balance is achieved more quickly. Official international reserves do not decrease as much; instead, part of the money supply decrease is the result of a decrease in domestic assets held by the central bank.

A second possible problem with the adjustment toward external balance is that it may not be consistent with internal balance. In the surplus situation, the increase in the money supply can put upward pressure on the country's price level, and this pressure toward a positive (or higher) rate of inflation may be viewed as undesirable—a shift toward internal imbalance. In the deficit situation, the decrease in the money supply can result in a recession (declining real production), with rising unemployment.

STERILIZATION

Rather than allowing automatic adjustments to proceed (or speeding them up), the monetary authority instead may want to *resist* the change in the country's money supply. One reason for resistance is that the money supply change would tend to create an internal imbalance, as just described. Another is that the authority may believe that the international imbalance is temporary and will soon reverse. This is the case of temporary disequilibrium discussed in Chapter 19.

The central bank can keep the external surplus or deficit from having an impact on the domestic money supply by taking an *offsetting* domestic action. **Sterilization** is taking an action to reverse the effect of official intervention on the domestic money supply. If the central bank is intervening to defend the fixed rate in a situation of payments surplus by selling its national currency in exchange for foreign currency, the money supply would tend to increase ($R\uparrow$ and $MB\uparrow$). This can be sterilized if the central bank, for instance, undertakes an open market operation in which the central bank sells domestic government bonds. While the intervention in currency markets tends to expand the money supply, the open market operation tends to reduce it by reducing both the domestic assets held by the central bank and the central bank liabilities that serve as the base for the domestic money supply. ($D\downarrow$ and $MB\downarrow$). The effects on the monetary base and the money supply of the combination of intervention and sterilization tend to cancel out ($MB\uparrow = MB\downarrow$). The net effects of the sterilized intervention are to alter the composition of the central bank's assets (in this case, $R\uparrow$ and $D\downarrow$).

In the case of a deficit, the central bank can sterilize the official intervention (buying the nation's currency) by buying domestic government bonds with that same currency in an open market operation. In this case, the intervention reduces official reserve holdings ($R\downarrow$) and the central bank's liabilities (MB$\downarrow$). The sterilization increases the central bank's holding of domestic securities ($D\uparrow$) and increases its liabilities (MB$\uparrow$). The effects on the monetary base and the money supply tend to cancel out, and the net effects are on the central bank's assets ($R\downarrow$ and $D\uparrow$).

Because a sterilized intervention does not change the money supply, the LM curve does not change. In Figure 22.3 the economy's equilibrium remains at point A. There is no adjustment toward external balance. Often this is a wait-and-see or a wait-and-hope strategy. Perhaps something else will shift the FE curve toward point A, or some other source of change will shift the IS–LM intersection toward the FE curve. If nothing else moves the economy toward external balance, there are limits to the ability of the monetary authority to use sterilized intervention to continue to run a payments imbalance.

In the case of the payments surplus, the limit may be (1) the unwillingness of the central bank to continue to increase its holdings of official reserve assets or (2) the complaints by other countries about the country's ongoing surplus. Taiwan found itself in this situation in the 1980s, when its interventions resulted in official reserve holdings that grew rapidly to a value equal to about three-quarters of the value of its annual national income. Pressure by the U.S. government then induced Taiwan to allow its currency to appreciate quickly during 1986–1987. Or, more concretely, the limit may come when the central bank has decreased its holdings of domestic assets to zero and thus has no domestic assets left to sell in open market operations.

In the case of a payments deficit, the limit is the inability of the central bank to obtain foreign currency to sell in the official intervention. The country's official reserve assets may dwindle toward zero (and it also cannot borrow more foreign currencies because of its precarious international position). This limit can be dramatic—if international investors and speculators believe that the central bank is low in its holdings of official reserves, a currency crisis based on the one-way speculative gamble discussed in Chapters 19 and 20 can develop.

MONETARY POLICY WITH FIXED EXCHANGE RATES

The discussion of the preceding two sections has a major implication—*fixed exchange rates greatly constrain a country's ability to pursue an independent monetary policy.* To a large degree the country's monetary policy must be consistent with maintaining the value of the fixed rate. Payments imbalances place pressure for changes in the money supply driven by the intervention to defend the fixed rate. Sterilization can be used to resist these money supply changes, but there are limits to how long the country's central bank can use sterilization, especially if the central bank's holdings of official reserves are declining because of a payments deficit.

Even if the country begins with a payments balance, its ability to pursue an independent monetary policy is greatly constrained. To see this, consider a country that initially has an official settlements balance of zero. While the country has achieved external balance, the country may believe that it has not achieved internal balance. Specifically, it has a high unemployment rate and wants to expand its domestic product. To pursue this goal with monetary policy, it attempts to implement an expansionary monetary policy.

For a time this policy may increase real product. But the country's official settlements balance will go into deficit through the process shown in Figure 22.2. Both the current account and capital account will deteriorate. The country then must intervene to defend its fixed rate, selling foreign currency and buying domestic currency. This reduces the domestic money supply, effectively forcing the country to abandon its expansionary policy. Even if the central bank resists this for a while using sterilization, it cannot continue to sterilize indefinitely. Eventually, the country must allow its money supply to shrink (or pursue some other adjustment like an exchange rate change).

This process can be seen in Figure 22.4, where the country is initially at point *E*, a triple intersection. The increase in the money supply shifts the LM curve down or to the right. The IS–LM intersection at point *H* indicates that real domestic product has increased, but the new intersection is to the right of the FE curve, indicating a payments deficit. As the country intervenes to defend the fixed exchange rate, the money supply shrinks and the LM curve shifts back. If nothing else changes, the LM curve shifts back to the original triple intersection.

In this example, in contrast to the analysis in the earlier sections, we are starting from payments balance and conducting the analysis as "from the money supply to the balance of payments" and then "from the balance of payments back to

FIGURE 22.4

Expansionary
Monetary
Policy with
Fixed Rates

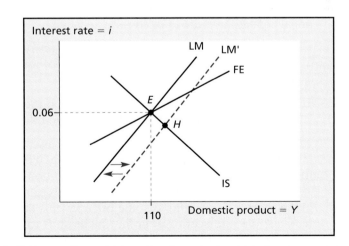

Starting from point *E* with an overall payments balance of zero, the country attempts to implement an expansionary policy. The LM curve shifts down or to the right, but at point *H* the payment balance is in deficit. Intervention to defend the fixed exchange rate decreases the money supply, and the LM curve shifts back up, eventually returning the country to point *E*.

the money supply." In the process we conclude that the ability to change the money supply is limited, and eventually stops, because of the feedback from the balance of payments and the need to defend the fixed rate.

FISCAL POLICY WITH FIXED EXCHANGE RATES

Fiscal policy is implemented by changing government spending and taxes. A change in fiscal policy affects the balance of payments through both the current account and the capital account. Let's examine the case of an expansionary fiscal policy, say a rise in government purchases of goods and services. This case is summarized in Figure 22.5. (Contractionary fiscal policy is analyzed in the same way, with all of the changes occurring in the opposite direction.)

The extra government spending means a bigger government budget deficit (or a reduced budget surplus). We'll tell the story using a budget deficit. To finance the larger budget deficit, the government is borrowing more and driving up interest rates. The higher interest rates should attract a capital inflow, "improving" the country's capital account.

The extra government spending also increases aggregate demand and increases real domestic product (assuming that some resources are available to expand production).[5] The extra spending spills over into extra import demand, "worsening" our current account balance. In addition, the extra aggregate demand may put upward pressure on the price level once we pass beyond the short-run period in which the price level is sticky. If the price level increases, then the country loses international price competitiveness, another reason that the current account deteriorates.

The effect on the country's overall balance of payments depends on the magnitudes of these changes. Given the worsening of the current account, we can examine the effect on overall balance as a question of how responsive international capital flows are to interest rate changes.

- If international capital flows are very responsive to interest rate changes, then the capital inflows will be large, and the official settlements balance will go into surplus.

- If the capital flows are unresponsive, then the capital account will improve only a little, and the overall balance will go into deficit.

The effect on the overall balance is probably also affected by timing—the capital inflows may be large at first, but they probably will dwindle as international portfolios are adjusted to the new economic conditions.

Figure 22.6 shows the effects of a fiscal expansion with fixed exchange rates in the short run assuming that the price level is steady. For both cases we begin with a triple intersection at point *E*. The shift to an expansionary fiscal policy

---

[5] In the short run real GDP increases even if there is partial crowding out, as interest-sensitive domestic spending decreases somewhat when interest rates increase.

FIGURE 22.5

How
Expansionary
Fiscal Policy
Affects the
Balance of
Payments with
Fixed Rates

For contractionary fiscal policy, reverse the direction of all changes.

shifts the IS curve to the right, to IS'. The new intersection with the LM curve is at point K, with a higher interest rate and a higher level of real domestic product.[6]

The two cases shown in Figure 22.6 differ in how responsive international capital flows are to changes in the interest rate. The left graph shows the case of relatively responsive capital flows so that the FE curve is relatively flat. The right graph shows the case of unresponsive capital flows so that the FE curve is relatively steep. If capital flows are responsive, as in Figure 22.6A, then the new intersection point K lies to the left of the FE curve, and the overall payments balance goes into surplus. If they are unresponsive (Figure 22.6B), then point K lies to the right of FE, and the overall balance goes into deficit.[7]

The discussion so far has offered conclusions about the effects of a fiscal policy change on the domestic economy and on external balance. It might seem that we can stop here, but we should not. If the official settlements balance shifts into surplus or deficit, then official intervention is needed to defend the fixed exchange rate, and the country's money supply will change (although this effect might be postponed if the intervention is sterilized). If the intervention is not sterilized, then interest rates and domestic product will be affected further as the money supply changes. The direction of this effect depends on whether the overall balance shifts into surplus or deficit.

[6] Another way to see the pressure for a higher interest rate is to use the direct logic of the IS–LM analysis. The increase in real income and spending increases the transaction demand for money, but there is no increase in the money supply (assuming, at least initially, that the central bank does not permit any increase because of an unwillingness to shift its monetary policy). The extra money demand must be choked off by an increase in interest rates. (All of this represents a movement along the LM curve from E to K.)

[7] The slope of the FE curve does not matter much in analyzing monetary policy, because there is no ambiguity in the direction of effects on the overall balance for an attempted shift in monetary policy such as that analyzed in Figure 22.4.

FIGURE 22.6   Expansionary Fiscal Policy with Fixed Exchange Rates

Expansionary fiscal policy shifts the IS curve to the right and the IS–LM intersection shifts from *E* to *K*. The effects of fiscal policy depend on how strongly international capital flows respond to the interest rate increase. In panel A, the overall payments balance goes into surplus. (*K* is to the left of FE.) In panel B, the overall payments balance goes into deficit. (*K* is to the right of FE.) In either case the payments imbalance leads to a change in the money supply (assuming that the central bank does not or cannot "sterilize" it). In panel A, intervention to defend the fixed rate increases the money supply, shifting the LM curve down, and the economy shifts toward a new full equilibrium at point *E′*. In panel B, intervention to defend the fixed rate decreases the money supply, shifting the LM curve up, and the economy shifts toward a new full equilibrium at point *E″*.

If capital flows are very responsive to interest rates, then overall payments go into surplus, and the central bank must intervene by selling domestic currency and buying foreign currency. With no sterilization, the domestic money supply expands, reducing interest rates and supporting a further expansion in domestic product. In Figure 22.6A, the increase in the money supply shifts the LM curve down or to the right. It will eventually shift to the dashed LM′, where a new triple intersection is achieved at point *E′*. In this case, fiscal policy becomes more powerful in increasing real GDP because the monetary authority expands the money supply as it intervenes to defend the fixed exchange rate.[8]

If capital flows instead are not that responsive, then the overall payments deficit requires official intervention in which domestic currency is purchased and foreign currency is sold. If the intervention is not sterilized, then the domestic money supply decreases, raising interest rates and reversing some of the increase in real domestic product. In Figure 22.6B the decrease in the money supply shifts the LM curve up or to the left, eventually to the dashed LM″. In this case, expansionary fiscal policy loses some of its power to increase real GDP.

[8] If the price level also increases, the FE curve shifts to the left, and the IS curve shifts back somewhat to the left. Real domestic product does not increase by as much in this case and in the one discussed in the next paragraph.

PERFECT CAPITAL MOBILITY

The case of perfect capital mobility is an extreme case of how international movements can alter the effectiveness of monetary and fiscal policies under fixed rates. **Perfect capital mobility** means that a practically unlimited amount of international capital flows in response to the slightest change in one country's interest rates.

Perfect capital mobility may be a good basis to analyze countries whose capital markets are open to international activity and whose political and economic situation is considered stable (so that no perceptions of political and economic risks limit capital inflows). Indeed, the success of a system of fixed exchange rates makes perfect capital mobility more likely. If investors are convinced that exchange rates will remain fixed, they will be more willing to move back and forth between currencies in response to small differences in interest rates.

For a small country (one that is too small to influence global financial markets by itself), perfect capital mobility implies that the country's interest rate must be equal to the interest rate in the larger global capital market. When exchange rates were fixed, this gave substance to the Canadian complaint that "Canadian interest rates are made in Washington." There is evidence that interest rate correlations between countries grew stronger during prolonged periods of fixed rates (the gold standard and Bretton Woods periods).

If international capital flows are highly sensitive to slight temporary interest rate changes, then they practically dictate the country's money supply, even in the short run. Why? Consider what happens if an incipient reduction of the money supply begins to increase the country's interest rates. The slightly higher interest rates draw a large capital inflow. Intervention to defend the fixed exchange rate requires selling domestic currency, thus expanding the money supply. Furthermore, sterilization is nearly impossible under such circumstances because of how large the capital inflows could be. Conversely, a nearly unlimited outflow of capital could occur if the country expanded its money supply and lowered interest rates slightly. The capital outflow forces the money supply back down to its original level to eliminate the slight drop in interest rates. The balance of payments rules the money supply. *Perfect capital mobility with fixed exchange rates robs monetary policy of its ability to influence interest rates or the domestic economy.*

For fiscal policy, perfect capital mobility actually means enhanced impacts on the domestic economy in the short run. Expansionary fiscal policies do not raise interest rates because the extra government borrowing is met by a large influx of lending from abroad. Thus, the government borrowing does not crowd out private domestic borrowers with higher interest rates, allowing fiscal policy its full spending multiplier effects on the economy. In other words, with perfect capital mobility and interest rates set outside the country, fiscal expansion cannot be guilty of crowding out private real investment from lending markets. This extra potency of fiscal policy under fixed exchange rates and perfect capital mobility

FIGURE 22.7
With Perfect
Capital
Mobility,
Monetary
Policy Is
Impotent but
Fiscal Policy
Is Strong

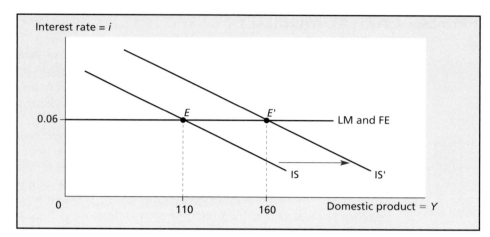

may be a poor substitute for the loss of monetary control since government handling of spending and taxes is often crude and subject to the vagaries of politics. Yet this is apparently a fact of life for small countries under truly fixed exchange rates.[9]

Figure 22.7 shows the effect of perfect capital mobility on the IS–LM–FE picture. The FE curve is flat because the tiniest change in interest rates would trigger a potentially infinite international flow of capital. If the global interest rate is 6 percent, then any point above the flat FE, corresponding to a domestic interest rate greater than 6 percent, results in a massive capital inflow and payments surplus. Any point below results in a massive capital outflow and payments deficit.

With perfect capital mobility the LM curve is also effectively flat and the same as FE. Any flood of international capital swamps any other influence on the nation's money supply. The money supply must be whatever is necessary to keep the domestic interest rate at 6 percent. Only the interest rate of 6 percent, dictated by financial conditions in the world as a whole, is consistent with equilibrium in the country's market for money. Under the conditions shown in Figure 22.7, the country has no independent monetary policy. The monetary authorities cannot change the domestic interest rate or control the money supply.

By contrast, fiscal policy takes on its greatest power under these conditions. Raising government spending or cutting tax rates causes the usual rightward shift of the IS curve to IS'. As soon as the extra government deficit raises the home country's interest rate even slightly, there is a rush of capital inflow, as international investors seek the slightly higher interest rate in this country. The inflow raises the money supply until the interest rate is bid back down to 6 percent. So a

---

[9] With perfect capital mobility, as with the other cases discussed in this chapter, we must remember that any attracted capital must be paid for later with reflows of interest and principal back to the foreign creditors.

rightward shift of the IS curve has a large effect on domestic product and no effect on the interest rate.[10]

The case of perfect capital mobility shows clearly that monetary policy is subordinated to the defense of the fixed exchange rate, and that fiscal policy can be powerful with fixed exchange rates. For the rest of this chapter we now return to the case of moderate capital mobility and an upward-sloping FE curve. Perfect capital mobility can be considered the limiting case (flat) of the general case (upward-sloping) that we examine.

SHOCKS TO THE ECONOMY

From time to time a country's economy is hit by major shocks—both shocks that represent changes in basic conditions in the domestic economy and those that arise externally in the international economy. What are the effects of these exogenous forces on an economy that has a fixed exchange rate? To provide a simple base for our analysis, we will usually examine cases in which the country has achieved external balance (a triple intersection in the IS–LM–FE graph) just before the shock hits the economy.

Internal Shocks

One type of internal shock arises in the market for money. A **domestic monetary shock** alters the equilibrium relationship between money supply and money demand because (1) the money supply changes or (2) the way in which people decide on their money holdings changes. The latter can arise, for instance, from financial innovations like money market mutual funds, the spread of credit cards, or automated teller machines (ATMs). A domestic monetary shock causes a shift in the LM curve. Its effect on domestic interest rates and domestic product is quite limited with fixed rates. As we saw in our analysis of the attempt to run an independent monetary policy, a shift in the LM curve tends to reverse itself as the central bank must intervene to defend the fixed rate. A major effect of a monetary shock instead can be on the country's holdings of official reserve assets, if intervention is the basis for the money supply change that shifts the LM curve back toward its initial position.

Another type of domestic shock arises from exogenous changes in domestic spending on goods and services. A **domestic spending shock** alters domestic real expenditure (E) through an exogenous force that alters one of its components (consumption, real domestic investment, or government spending). A change in fiscal policy is one such shock. Another would be a change in the business mood

---

[10] In fact, fiscal policy's impact on domestic product fits the spending multiplier formula of Chapter 21. For example, suppose that the country in Figure 22.7 had a marginal propensity to save of 0.2 and a marginal propensity to import of 0.3. This would make the multiplier equal to 2, according to Chapter 21. In this case, the rightward shift of $\Delta Y = 50$ from point E to point E' in Figure 22.7 could be achieved by $\Delta G = 25$.

or consumer sentiment, resulting in a change in real investment or consumption spending. The discussion of fiscal policy provides an example of the analysis of this type of shock. In addition, it is important to remember that effects on foreign countries will be transmitted through changes in our imports, and that this can have repercussions back to our economy if the induced changes in the foreign economies alter their imports from us (as discussed in Chapter 21).

International Capital-Flow Shocks

One type of external shock arises from unexpected changes in the country's capital account. An **international capital-flow shock** is the unpredictable shifting of internationally mobile funds in response to such events as rumors about political changes or new restrictions (capital controls) on international asset holdings. Let's examine an international capital-flow shock in the form of a shift by international investors and speculators to a belief that the country's government is likely to devalue its currency in the near future. Although this is not necessary to the analysis, we begin with a country that has an external balance. (In this case the shift in belief is not related to a payments imbalance today—rather, it may be related to doubts about the political leadership of the country, or to a belief that the country may try to use devaluation to boost international price competitiveness in order to increase net exports and lower domestic unemployment.)

The shift in belief leads to a capital outflow as international investors attempt to reposition their portfolios away from assets denominated in this country's currency *before* the devaluation occurs. This type of capital outflow is a form of "capital flight," in which investors flee a country because of doubts about government policies. If the country begins with an external balance, then the overall balance shifts into deficit as the capital account deteriorates. There is downward pressure on the exchange rate value of the country's currency, and the central bank must intervene to defend the fixed rate. The central bank buys domestic currency and sells foreign currency. If the intervention is not sterilized, then the domestic money supply shrinks. Interest rates increase, and real domestic product decreases.

The increase in interest rates here becomes part of the defense of the fixed exchange rate. If the interest differential shifts in favor of this country, then international investors are more willing to keep investments in this country's financial assets (or are less interested in fleeing) even if there is some risk of devaluation. (Recall our discussions of uncovered financial investments in Part III.) In fact, countries faced with a capital-outflow shock often immediately shift policy to raise short-term interest rates dramatically, for instance, from annual rates of less than 10 percent to annual rates of over 100 percent. This is an example of using monetary policy *actively* to reestablish external balance, rather than waiting for the slower effects of intervention on the domestic money supply to move the country toward external balance.

The effects of this shock are pictured in Figure 22.8. The economy begins at point *E*. The international capital-flow shock causes the FE curve to shift up or to

FIGURE 22.8

An Adverse
International
Capital-Flow
Shock

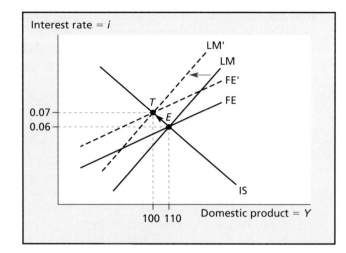

A shift of international capital flows away from the country causes the FE curve to shift up or to the left, and the overall payments balance goes into deficit. Intervention to defend the fixed rate shifts the LM curve up or to the left. The economy shifts toward a new full equilibrium at point *T*.

the left. Once the FE curve has shifted, the official settlements balance is in deficit at point *E*. The central bank must intervene to defend the fixed rate. The central bank may attempt to keep the economy at point *E* by sterilizing the intervention. The central bank may hope that the disequilibrium in the overall balance is temporary, perhaps because the fears of the international investors will subside and the FE curve will shift back to the right in the near future. If the monetary authority cannot or does not sterilize the intervention, then the LM curve will begin to shift up or to the left. If the new FE curve remains where it is, the LM curve must shift to LM', with a new triple intersection at point *T*. External balance has been reestablished at point *T*. However, real domestic product has declined. The country now has an internal imbalance, in the form of low aggregate demand and higher unemployment, assuming that the country did not begin with the opposite imbalance of excessively strong aggregate demand. *Under fixed exchange rates, external capital flow shocks can have powerful impacts on internal balance through the changes in the money supply driven by official intervention to defend the fixed rate.*

International Trade Shocks

A second type of external shock arises from exogenous changes in the country's current account. An **international trade shock** is a shift in a country's exports or imports that arises from causes other than changes in the real income of the country. For instance, demand for a country's exports can change for many reasons. Export shocks seem to be largest for countries specializing in exporting a narrow range of products, especially primary commodities for which demand is sensitive to the business cycle in importing countries. Instability has strongly affected exporters of metals, such as Chile (copper), Malaysia (tin), and, to a lesser extent, Canada. Import shocks can occur if our consumers unexpectedly alter their purchases between import products and domestically produced substitutes, for instance, because of changing perceptions of the relative quality of the products. Trade shocks can also occur because of shifts in the prices or availability of domestic and foreign products. An important example of this type of shock is a shock to the supply of a major import, such as oil for most industrialized countries.[11]

An international trade shock alters the country's current account. Thus, it directly affects both the country's overall balance of payments and aggregate demand for the country's domestic production. For instance, a shift of foreign demand away from our exports, or a shift of our demand toward imports (and away from our own products), leads to a worsening of the current account and the overall balance (assuming that there is little effect on international capital flows). It also reduces aggregate demand, lowering real domestic product.[12] In addition, the country's central bank must intervene to defend the fixed rate by buying domestic currency and selling foreign currency. If the intervention is not sterilized, then the domestic money supply contracts, leading to a further decline in aggregate demand. External balance can be reestablished through these changes, but the internal imbalance of low aggregate demand and high unemployment will be increased.

Figure 22.9 shows the effects of this shock. Beginning at point E, the adverse international trade shock shifts the FE curve to the left and the IS curve to the left as well. At the new IS–LM intersection (point V), real domestic product declines (as does the domestic interest rate). With point V to the right of the new FE' curve, the country's overall payments are in deficit. Intervention to defend the fixed rate reduces the domestic money supply (assuming that it is not sterilized). The LM curve begins to shift up or to the left. External balance is reestablished at point W when the LM curve shifts to the dashed LM'. However, real domestic product has declined even more.[13]

---

[11] The analysis of a decline in the supply of a major import is a bit complicated. Examples of such supply shocks for crucial imports are the oil shocks of 1973–1974 and 1979–1980, and the smaller one of 1990. The shock is likely to lower the quantity of imports of this product while raising its price. The analysis is similar to that about to be discussed in the text if the cutback in foreign supply initially raises the total value of imports and lowers national purchasing power (with the higher price acting like a "tax" on the economy imposed by the exporters). These conditions hold if imports of the product take a large share of our national spending and our demand for the product is very price-inelastic (at least in the short run). An additional twist is that the oil price shocks quickly increased the price level P so that the LM curve also shifted up or to the left as a result of the shock.
[12] We are assuming that the current account actually does deteriorate even though the reduction in our real income will offset some of the initial decline by lowering the country's demand for imports through the domestic-income effect on imports. In Figure 22.9 this assumption ensures that point V is to the right of the new FE curve even if the FE curve is steeper than the LM curve.
[13] As shown, the interest rate returns to 0.06. This is not the only possibility—the interest rate could be higher or lower, depending on the magnitudes of the curve shifts and the slopes of the curves.

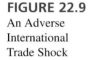

FIGURE 22.9

An Adverse
International
Trade Shock

A shift of international trade away from the country's products causes the FE and IS curves to shift to the left, and the overall payments balance goes into deficit. Intervention to defend the fixed rate shifts the LM curve up or to the left. The economy shifts toward a new full equilibrium at point W.

Thus, as with international capital-flow shocks, *international trade shocks can have a powerful effect on the internal balance of a country with a fixed exchange rate.* The intervention needed to defend the fixed rate tends to magnify the effect of the shock on domestic production.

IMBALANCES AND POLICY RESPONSES

A country wants to achieve both internal balance and external balance. Yet its actual performance is often short of these goals. In many situations it has imbalances in both its internal and external situations as a result of shocks that hit the economy, or previous government policies that resulted in poor economic performance.

Internal and External Imbalances

Figure 22.10 catalogs the four possible cases in which the country has both internal and external imbalances. With fixed exchange rates a country's policymakers could get lucky and face the straightforward problems represented by the upper-left and lower-right cells.

The government of a country experiencing high unemployment and a payments surplus can use expansionary policies to address both problems. Most obviously, an expansion of the domestic money supply can increase aggregate demand and lower unemployment, while also reducing the payments surplus (as summarized previously in Figure 22.2). This shift occurs automatically if the country intervenes to defend the fixed exchange rate and does not sterilize, but the country can also speed it up by using active monetary policy to expand the money supply more quickly.

FIGURE 22.10

Policies for Internal and External Balance

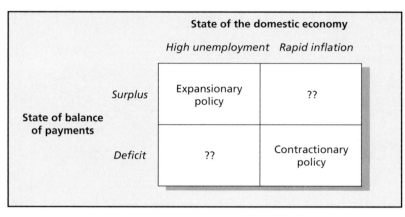

In some situations a policy to change aggregate demand can serve both internal and external goals, but in some cases (marked "??" here) it cannot. To deal with high unemployment and a payments surplus, policy-makers should expand aggregate demand (upper-left case). To deal with inflation and a payment deficit, they should cut aggregate demand (lower-right case). But with the other two combinations of imbalances, there is no clear prescription for aggregate-demand policy.

The government of a country experiencing an inflation rate that is viewed as being too high and a payments deficit can use contractionary policies to address both. Again, an obvious choice is a contraction of the money supply (or perhaps more realistically, a reduction of the growth rate of the money supply).

Even in these cases the exact policy solution may be tricky because balance in one dimension may be achieved while part of the other imbalance remains. Nonetheless, the initial direction of the desirable policy change that reduces (if not eliminates) both imbalances is clear.

What about the other two cells in Figure 22.10? In broad terms the correct policy response is not clear. The dilemma of having to choose which goal to pursue has been felt most acutely by countries in the lower-left cell, where low aggregate demand has resulted in high unemployment, but the balance of payments is in deficit. This was the near tragedy of Britain after it rejoined the gold standard in 1925 at its prewar gold parity, with the high value for the pound making British products uncompetitive in international trade. This was the problem facing the United States in the early 1960s. France faced a similar problem in the early 1990s, as discussed in the box "A Tale of Three Countries."

In these cases, reducing unemployment called for raising aggregate demand with expansionary policies. However, this would worsen the trade balance and tend to worsen the overall balance. The dilemma was not well solved in any of the cases. Britain was driven off the gold standard in 1931. The United States reduced its unemployment rate with a series of fiscal policy changes (the tax cut of 1964, domestic "Great Society" spending programs, and Vietnam War spending) but the payments imbalance led toward the breakup of the Bretton Woods fixed-rate system. Through the mid-1990s, France continued to suffer from high unemployment.

In 1992, unemployment in France was high and rising. Inflation was almost nothing. The French government seemed to respond by tightening up on money and raising interest rates.

Madness? Not really, but an example of the policy dilemma that can arise with fixed exchange rates. France was a member of the Exchange Rate Mechanism (ERM) of the European Monetary System (EMS). Membership committed the French government to keep the exchange rates between the French franc and the currencies of the other member countries within small bands around the central rates chosen for the fix.

To understand France we actually need to start with Germany, the largest member of the ERM. The Berlin Wall fell in 1989, and German unification proceeded rapidly over the next year, politically, financially, and economically. German government policy toward unification included support for the eastern part in the form of transfers, subsidies, and other government expenditures on such things as public infrastructure investments. This expansionary fiscal policy increased aggregate demand. Domestic production expanded rapidly in 1990 and 1991, and unemployment fell, but the economy began to overheat as demand exceeded production capabilities, so that the inflation rate increased. German policymakers, especially those at the Bundesbank (Germany's central bank), loathe inflation. History matters—the hyperinflation of the 1920s in Germany is considered to be the economic disaster of the past century for Germany.

In response to the rise in inflation, the German monetary authorities tightened up on monetary policy, after a spurt in money growth in 1990–1991 resulting from monetary unification. Interest rates rose. This monetary tightening slowed the economy during 1992–1993.

We can capture the main elements of the German story in an IS–LM picture. Germany began at point A. The fiscal expansion shifted IS_1 to IS_2, and the increased growth rate of the money supply shifted LM_1 to LM_2. At the new equilibrium point B, real domestic product was higher, but the economy was trying to push past its supply capabilities. In response to the internal imbalance of rising inflation,

the Bundesbank reduced money growth, shifting LM_2 to LM_3. Interest rates rose (on a nominal basis, although less so on a real basis), and domestic product declined as the economy moved toward point C.

In this way the German government adopted policies that focused almost completely on internal political and economic problems. (In fact, although we could add the FE curve to Germany's picture, we have instead omitted it to emphasize this internal focus of German policy.) Meanwhile, back in France . . .

In 1990, the French economy was already weak and weakening. The unemployment rate was 9 percent and rising. For internal reasons the French government probably wanted to shift to an expansionary policy. But it had an external problem. Rising interest rates in Germany could set off a capital outflow that would threaten the fixed exchange rate between the franc and the DM. France had to respond to this incipient external imbalance by tightening up on money and raising French interest rates. (Given France's low inflation rate, the higher nominal interest rates also were higher real interest rates.) Unfortunately, for political reasons, fiscal policy could not turn expansionary. The assignment rule could not be used. Instead, the higher interest rates made the French economy worse. The growth rate of real French GDP declined from 1989 through 1993, and real GDP actually fell in 1993. The French unemployment rate rose from 1990 through 1994.

In France's picture, France began at point F, with aggregate demand already weak and unemployment high. The rise in Germany's interest rate shifted France's FE curve up or to the left (FE_1 to FE_2). To avoid capital outflows and a payments deficit, the French monetary authorities responded by tightening money, shifting LM_1 to LM_2. As the economy moved toward point H, demand and production weakened and the unemployment rate rose.

However, this was not always enough. International investors and speculators doubted the resolve of the French (and most other non-German members of the ERM) to stick to fixed exchange rates. Major speculative attacks occurred in September 1992, November 1992, and July 1993. In these the FE curve for France shifted sharply up or to the left.

—Continued on next page

The French government responded with massive official intervention, buying francs and selling DM, and with high short-term interest rates to discourage the speculative outflows. Total intervention by all ERM members in September 1992 was over $100 billion, with capital losses of about $5 billion to the central banks that bought currencies of the countries (Britain, Italy, Spain, and Portugal) that then devalued or depreciated anyway. Total intervention in July 1993 was also more than $100 billion, with the French central bank alone selling more than $50 billion of DM in defense of the franc. Official reserve holdings of the French central bank declined close to zero, but the French government was "successful." The franc was not devalued.

The third largest economy in the European Union is Britain. Britain's journey through these years was different. Britain was not a member of the ERM until joining in 1990, when it committed to a pound–DM rate of about 0.35. The next two years were not good for Britain. To defend the fixed rate, the growth rate of the British money supply had to be kept low (although at the same time British interest rates could decline, starting from a high level). A severe recession with two years of decline in real GDP hit, and the unemployment rate rose to about 10 percent. Broadly, this picture is similar to that of France, but the recession was worse.

In 1992, Britain's story diverges. As a result of the speculative attack on non-DM currencies in September 1992, Britain left the ERM. The British government spent close to half of its official reserves defending the pound before surrendering. Britain shifted to a floating exchange rate, and the pound depreciated by over 10 percent against the DM. This improved British price competitiveness. In addition, the British government could allow its money supply to grow more quickly. Interest rates fell sharply in 1993, and real GDP began to grow. Britain's unemployment rate plateaued in 1993 and declined in 1994 (while the unemployment rate was still rising in both France and Germany). After declining in 1993, the inflation rate increased a little in Britain in 1994, but not even close to enough to reverse the gain in price competitiveness from currency depreciation. Britain's depreciation of 1992 seems to have been successful.

Let's pick up Britain's picture as Britain left the ERM in 1992. (Its picture for 1990–1992 is similar to that of France.) The initial situation, just before the departure, was at point J. With the depreciation of the pound, the improvement in price competitiveness shifts FE_1 right to FE_2 and moves IS_1 right to IS_2. The money expansion shifts LM_1 right as well to LM_2. The British economy shifts toward point K, with higher real domestic production and a lower interest rate.

Tales have lessons. The lesson of this tale is that countries must choose between fixed exchange rates and control over their internal balance. When large countries choose internal balance, the choice gets tougher for smaller countries. Germany, the largest economy in the EU, ran its policies mainly to satisfy internal objectives (like the United States in the 1960s). This created problems for other ERM members—conflicts for them between internal and external balance. Both France and Britain faced a dilemma: high unemployment and a tendency toward payments deficits. For a while, both responded with tight money that tried to achieve external balance but made the internal imbalance (high unemployment) worse.

All of this did not completely convince international investors and speculators. With the speculative attack of September 1992, the paths diverged. France defended the fixed rate, at further cost to internal balance.

Britain surrendered, withdrawing from the ERM. This allowed Britain to address its internal imbalance. Expansionary policy and the competitiveness gained from the pound's depreciation rekindled economic growth. The unemployment rate declined.

The speculative attack in July 1993 led to a semi-surrender even by France and other ERM members. They widened the allowable bands around the central rates from plus or minus 2.25 percent to plus or minus 15 percent. This widening of the band forestalled any further speculative attacks. But, during the next years, the franc–DM rate seldom was more than 3 percent from its central value. France continued to direct its policies to keeping the franc exchange rate steady against the DM, and France's unemployment rate remained high.

	1988	1989	1990	1991	1992	1993	1994
Growth Rate of Real GDP (%)							
Germany	3.7	4.2	5.5	4.3	1.8	−1.2	2.7
France	4.2	3.9	2.4	0.6	1.2	−1.3	2.8
Britain	4.5	2.2	0.6	−2.1	−0.5	2.1	4.3
Unemployment Rate (%)							
Germany	8.7	8.9	7.2	5.5	5.8	7.3	8.2
France	10.0	9.4	9.0	9.4	10.3	11.7	12.3
Britain	8.4	6.3	5.8	8.0	9.8	10.3	9.4
Inflation Rate (%)							
Germany	1.3	2.8	2.7	3.5	4.0	4.2	3.0
France	2.7	3.5	3.4	3.2	2.4	2.1	1.7
Britain	4.9	7.8	9.5	5.9	3.7	1.6	2.4
Short-Term Interest Rate (%)							
Germany	4.0	6.6	7.9	8.8	9.4	7.5	5.3
France	7.5	9.1	9.9	9.5	10.4	8.8	5.7
Britain	9.7	13.6	14.6	11.8	9.4	5.5	4.8
Money Supply Growth Rate (%)							
Germany	7.5	4.6	8.4	9.4	6.7	8.1	7.8
France	4.1	8.1	3.8	−4.7	−0.2	1.4	2.8
Britain	7.6	5.7	2.6	3.0	2.5	5.6	7.3
Exchange Rate							
Franc/DM	3.4	3.4	3.4	3.4	3.4	3.4	3.4
Pound/DM	0.32	0.32	0.35	0.34	0.36	0.40	0.40

Source: Growth rate of real GDP, unemployment rate, (CPI) inflation rate, and money supply growth rate (M1 for France, M3 for Germany, and M0 for Britain) from Economic Intelligence Unit, *Country Report,* various issues for these three countries. Short-term (money market) interest rates and exchange rates from International Monetary Fund, *International Financial Statistics Yearbook,* 1998.

The opposite dilemma faces governments worried about a rising or high inflation rate while the country is running a payments surplus (the upper-right cell of Figure 22.10). This was the sort of position frequently faced by Germany and Switzerland during the Bretton Woods fixed-rate years. The unacceptably high inflation rate calls for restraint on aggregate demand, but the surpluses are likely to increase as the demand restraint improves the current account balance.

The government of a country in one of the two dilemma cells has three basic choices:

1. It can abandon the goal of external balance, which eventually means that the country will abandon its fixed exchange rate.

2. It can abandon the goal of internal balance, at least in the short run, and set its policies (especially its monetary policy and money supply) to achieve external balance. This is sometimes called the "rules of the game" in a fixed-rate system such as the gold standard. Defending the fixed rate is the highest goal.

3. The government can try to find more policy tools or more creative ways to use the tools that it already has.

Giving up is unpopular, and the natural tendency is to search for more tools and creative solutions.

A candidate for addressing the dilemma of high unemployment and payments deficit is enhancement of the economy's supply capabilities. Why not come up with policies that create more national income by improving our productivity? Productivity improvements would enhance our ability to compete in international trade, thereby shifting demand to our products, expanding production and employment, and improving our current account balance. It sounds too good to be true. And it probably is. Policymakers usually have no fast, low-cost way of improving the economy's supply capabilities. That comes through sources of growth, such as the advance of human skills and technology, that respond sluggishly, if at all, to government manipulation.

A Short-Run Solution: Monetary–Fiscal Mix

There is a way to buy time and serve both internal and external goals using conventional demand-side policies while staying on fixed exchange rates. Looking more closely at the basic policy dilemma, Robert Mundell and J. Marcus Fleming noticed that monetary and fiscal policies have different relative impacts on internal and external balance. This difference can be the basis for a creative solution.

The key difference between the impacts of fiscal and monetary policies is that easier monetary policy tends to lower interest rates and easier fiscal policy tends to raise them, as noted in Figures 22.2 and 22.5. An expansion of aggregate demand and domestic product can be achieved with different mixes of fiscal policy and monetary policy, and the mix matters for the resulting level of the interest rate, at least in the short run. Expansion of domestic product can result in a low interest rate if it is driven mainly by expansionary monetary policy. Expansion can result in a high interest rate if it is driven mainly by expansionary fiscal policy. Because interest rates affect the country's payments balance, the interest rate is important. If the interest rate is lower, the payments balance deteriorates. If, instead, the interest rate is pushed high enough (for instance, by using very expansionary fiscal policy coupled with somewhat contractionary monetary policy), the payments balance improves (as long as capital flows are responsive to interest rate changes).

More generally, *monetary and fiscal policies can be mixed so as to achieve any combination of domestic product and overall payments balance in the short run.* Figure 22.11 illustrates the opportunities for solving one of the four policy challenges posed in Figure 22.10, namely, the case of excessive unemployment and payments deficits, starting at point Z. The goal is to raise the economy to full employment, which can be achieved at the level of domestic product Y_{full}. Shifting only one policy would not work, as we have seen, but shifting both can work. In this case, it is best to shift to tighter (contractionary) monetary policy to attract foreign capital with higher interest rates, and to easier (expansionary) fiscal policy in pursuit of full employment. In the right amounts, the monetary tightening and fiscal easing can bring us exactly to full employment and payments balance. In Figure 22.11, this is achieved by shifting IS to IS' and LM to LM'.

A similar recipe can be used to get from any starting point to internal balance and payments balance. The principle is clear: As long as there are as many different policies as target variables, as in the present case of two policies and two targets, there is a solution.

Furthermore, the pattern of policy prescriptions reveals a useful guideline for assigning policy tasks to fiscal and monetary policy. This is Robert Mundell's **assignment rule:** Assign to fiscal policy the task of stabilizing the domestic

FIGURE 22.11

How Monetary and Fiscal Policy Could Combine to Cure Both Unemployment and a Balance-of-Payments Deficit

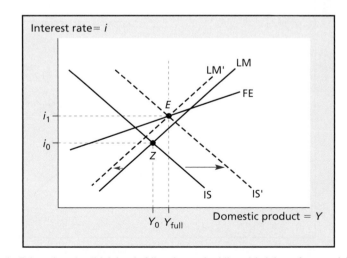

At the starting point Z, domestic product Y_0 is below the full employment level Y_{full} and the balance of payments is in deficit. To reach full employment and payments balance at point E, combine the right amounts of tight monetary policy and easy fiscal policy.

economy only, and assign to monetary policy the task of stabilizing the balance of payments only. We can see from Figure 22.12 that such marching orders would guide the two arms of policy toward internal balance and payments balance. Studying the different cases in Figure 22.12, you will find that the assignment rule generally steers each policy in the right direction. There are exceptions, as Figure 22.12 notes, but even in these cases it is likely that following the assignment rule does nothing worse than make the economy follow a less direct route to the goal of internal and external balance.

The assignment rule is handy. It allows each arm of policy to concentrate on a single task, relieving the need for perfect coordination between fiscal and monetary officials. It also directs each arm to work on the target it tends to care about more, since the balance of payments (and exchange rate stability) have traditionally been of more concern to central bankers than to politicians who make fiscal decisions.

The rule might or might not work in practice. We have already mentioned problems with the interest rate effect on capital flows that is supposed to guarantee the existence of a solution. Furthermore, if either branch of policy lags in getting signals from the economy and responding to them, the result could be

FIGURE 22.12

Monetary–Fiscal Recipes for Internal and External Balance

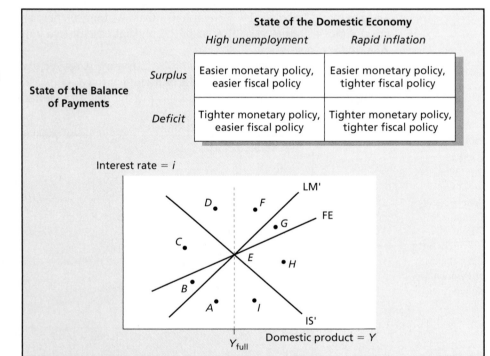

These recipes conform to the assignment rule: Assign monetary policy the task of balancing the country's international payments, and assign fiscal policy the task of bringing the domestic economy to full employment without excessive inflation. There are exceptional cases, however, when the assignment rule fails to follow the most direct route to the goal. In the diagram the assignment rule is wrong for monetary policy at points like *B* and *G,* and it is wrong for fiscal policy at points like *D* and *I.*

unstable oscillations that are even worse than having no policy at all. Or monetary policy may be run largely to accommodate the country's fiscal policy (and the need of the government to fund its deficit spending), in which case independent policies are not really possible. In addition, the mix influences both the composition of domestic spending and the level of foreign debt. A policy of high interest rates, such as that used in Figure 22.11, reduces domestic real investment. This can harm the growth of the economy's supply capabilities by reducing the growth of the capital stock. It also builds up foreign debt, which must be serviced in the future, reducing the amount of national income that the country keeps for itself.[14]

SURRENDER: CHANGING THE EXCHANGE RATE

If an imbalance in a country's overall balance of payments is large enough or lasts for long enough (a "fundamental disequilibrium"), the country's government may be unwilling to change domestic policies by enough to eliminate the imbalance. The country's government instead may conclude that surrendering the fixed rate is the best choice available. If the payments balance is in deficit, a devaluation may be used; if it's in surplus, revaluation may occur.

The government may hope that the exchange rate change can adjust the external imbalance without excessive disruption to the domestic economy. Nonetheless, the exchange rate change will affect aggregate demand, domestic production, unemployment, and inflation. In some situations these domestic changes represent a departure from internal balance. The internal effects of the exchange rate change may then need to be offset by other policy changes, creating a rationale for a policy mix that includes the exchange rate change and one or both of a fiscal policy change and a monetary policy change.

In other situations the internal effects of an exchange rate change can themselves be desirable. Interestingly, these are precisely the dilemma cases of Figure 22.10. Consider a country that has a fixed exchange rate, a payments deficit, and also a rather high unemployment rate (the lower-left cell in Figure 22.10). This country's government is not willing to allow an "automatic" adjustment to external balance through a decline in the money supply, because this would raise interest rates, lower demand and production, and increase unemployment further. Instead, the government has been sterilizing its intervention. It is also not capable of following the assignment rule, perhaps because domestic politics precludes adopting the right policy mix.

---

[14] Another possible problem might seem to be the case of perfect capital mobility because the country has no control of its money supply. This is not a problem. In fact, the case of perfect capital mobility effectively forces the government to follow the assignment rule. Monetary policy must allow the money supply to be whatever is necessary to achieve external balance on the FE curve. Fiscal policy can then be directed toward achieving internal balance, addressing any problems of domestic unemployment or inflation pressures.

What happens if this country devalues (or shifts to a floating exchange rate and allows its currency to depreciate)? What effects does this exchange rate surrender have on external and internal balance?

The devaluation should improve international price competitiveness (as long as any changes in the domestic price level or the foreign price level do not offset the exchange rate change).

- Exports tend to increase as firms from this country can lower the foreign-currency prices of their products (and as higher profits draw resources into producing for export).

- Imports tend to decrease as the domestic-currency price of imported products rises (and as higher profits in producing domestic products that can now compete more successfully with imports draws resources into producing these import substitutes).

Thus, the current account tends to improve. The effects on the capital account are less clear-cut. The capital account may also improve. If some capital was fleeing the country in fear of the impending devaluation, then this flight could stop or even reverse once the devaluation is done. Overall, we expect an improvement in the payments balance (a decrease in the deficit).

If exports increase and imports decrease, then these changes increase aggregate demand and domestic production, reducing domestic unemployment. However, import prices in local currency increase, and this increase puts some upward pressure on the average price level or inflation rate in the country. The extra demand could also put upward pressure on the price level, but this effect may be small if the economy begins with high unemployment.

Figure 22.13 shows these effects in the IS–LM–FE diagram, assuming that the domestic price level is steady. The country begins at point *B* with a payments deficit. The (low) level of domestic production at *B* results in rather high unemployment. The devaluation improves the current account (and may also improve the capital account), shifting the FE curve down or to the right. The increase in net exports as a result of the change in price competitiveness shifts the IS curve to the right. The figure shows that a devaluation (of the correct size) can shift the economy to a triple intersection (external balance) with a higher domestic product (and lower unemployment). The new equilibrium at point *E* may not exactly be internal balance (full employment), but it is a move in the correct direction.[15]

This sounds good—another possible answer to the dilemma of deficit and unemployment. In some cases it seems to work well. (See the discussion of Britain in the box "A Tale of Three Countries.") The comparable analysis, with all the signs reversed, indicates that a revaluation (or appreciation after the gov-

---

[15] If the price level also rises as a result of the devaluation, the FE and IS curves do not shift as much, and the LM curve shifts up or to the left. This reduces the effect on the payments balance and on domestic product. In fact, if the price level rises by enough, there is no gain in competitiveness, and the benefits of devaluation on external and internal balance are lost.

FIGURE 22.13

Devaluation of the Country's Currency

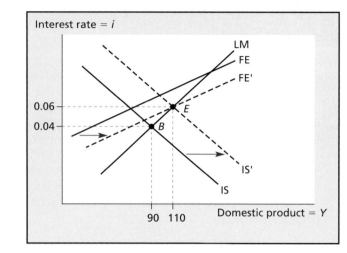

In response to the payments deficit at point *B*, the country's government devalues its currency. The devaluation improves its international price competitiveness, so it shifts the FE and IS curves to the right. If the devaluation is of the correct size, it can shift the economy toward a new full equilibrium at point *E*.

ernment allows the country's currency to float) can be an appropriate policy response to surplus and inflation (the upper-right cell in Figure 22.10) because it can lower a surplus while reducing inflation pressure in the economy by decreasing demand and lowering the local-currency price of imports.

However, there are also times that a devaluation fails to reduce the external imbalance. One possible reason for failure is taken up in the next section—the value of the current account may not actually increase because of low responsiveness of export and import volumes to the exchange rate change. Another possible reason for failure is that the government pursues fiscal or monetary policies that themselves are driving to expand the payments deficit, and these are so strong that they overwhelm the benefits of the devaluation. For instance, expansionary monetary policy can expand income and import demand, and also increase the price level through extra inflation so that the improved price competitiveness is lost. A third possible reason is that capital flows react in the "wrong" direction. For instance, a devaluation could lead to fears among international investors that the devaluation will not be successful in reducing the deficit (perhaps for one of the first two reasons). They then expect that another devaluation will be needed soon. Rising capital outflows (capital flight) could deteriorate the capital account and make the payments deficit bigger.

A key to much of this is how other government policies are used with the devaluation. If other government policies (especially monetary policy) can limit any increase in the country's price level or inflation rate, then the devaluation probably will improve the current account balance. International investors, seeing this, are less likely to fear that another devaluation will be needed. If the current account improves and the capital account does not deteriorate, then the devaluation will be successful in reducing the payments deficit.

HOW WELL DOES THE TRADE BALANCE RESPOND TO CHANGES IN THE EXCHANGE RATE?

According to the discussion in the preceding section, a change in the nominal exchange rate should alter net exports, at least as long as it alters international price competitiveness. The conclusion is straightforward for effects on the *volumes* (or quantities) of exports and imports, although we can still wonder about the speed or magnitude of the changes. However, the effect on the *value* of the trade balance is not so obvious because both prices and volumes are changing. Yet, the effect on the value of net exports or current account is what matters for the country's balance of payments and for its FE curve.

The value of the country's current account, measured in foreign currency (here pounds) is:

$$\text{CA (our current account balance, measured in £/year)} \quad = \quad P_x^£ \quad \bullet \quad X \quad - \quad P_m^£ \quad \bullet \quad M$$

where $P_x^£$ and $P_m^£$ are the pound prices of the country's exports and imports, and X and M are the quantities. Now consider the likely direction of changes in the trade prices and quantities when the country's currency (here the dollar) drops in value:

	£ Price of Exports	*Quantity of Exports*	*£ Price of Imports*	*Quantity of Imports*
Effects of a devaluation of the dollar	= No change or *down*	• No change or *up*	− No change or *down*	• No change or *down*

A dollar devaluation is likely to lower the pound price of exports (if it has any net effect on this price). This is because U.S. exporters are to some extent willing to lower pound prices while still receiving the same (or even higher) dollar prices because pounds are now worth more. If there is any effect of this price change on export quantities, the change is upward, as foreign buyers take advantage of any lower pound prices of U.S. exports to buy more from the United States. It is already clear that the net effect of devaluation on export value is of uncertain sign since pound prices probably drop and quantities exported probably rise. On the import side, any changes in either pound price or quantity are likely to be downward. The devaluation is likely to make *dollar* prices of imports look higher, causing a drop in import quantities as buyers shift toward U.S. substitutes for imports. If this drop in demand has any effect on the *pound* price of imports, that effect is likely to be negative. The sterling value of imports thus clearly drops, but if this value is to be subtracted from an export value that could rise or fall, it is still not clear whether the value of the net trade balance rises or falls. We need to know more about the underlying price elasticities of demand and supply in both the export and import markets.

How the Response Could Be Unstable

A drop in the value of the dollar actually could worsen the trade balance. It would clearly do so in the case of *perfectly inelastic demand* curves for exports and imports. Suppose that buyers' habits are rigidly fixed so that they will not change the quantities they buy from any nation's suppliers despite changes in price. Examples might be the dependence of a non-tobacco-producing country on tobacco imports, or a similar addiction to tea or coffee, or to petroleum for fuels. In such cases of perfectly inelastic demand, devaluation of the country's currency backfires completely. Given the perfect inelasticity of import demand, no signals are sent to foreign suppliers by devaluing the dollar. Buyers go on buying the same amount of imports at the same pound price, paying a higher dollar price without cutting back their imports. No change in the foreign exchange value of imports results. On the export side, the devaluation leads suppliers to end up with the same competitive dollar price as before, but this price equals fewer pounds. U.S. exporters get fewer pounds for each bushel of wheat they export, yet foreigners do not respond to the lower price by buying any more wheat than they would otherwise.

In the case of perfectly inelastic demand curves for exports and imports, the changes in the current account are as follows:

$$CA^£ = P_x^£ \cdot X - P_m^£ \cdot M$$

$$Down = (Down \cdot No\ change) - (No\ change \cdot No\ change)$$

A numerical illustration of this case is given in Figure 22.14A. There, devaluing the dollar merely lowers the value of foreign exchange the United States earns on exports, from 80 (= 1.00 × 80) to 60 (= 0.75 × 80), worsening the trade balance.

It might seem that this perverse, or unstable, result hinges on something special about the export market. This is not the case, however. It only looks as though the change is confined to the export side because we are looking at the equation expressed in sterling. If we had looked at the CA equation in dollar prices, the deterioration would still appear:

$$CA^\$ = P_x^\$ \cdot X - P_m^\$ \cdot M$$

$$Down = (No\ change \cdot No\ change) - (Up \cdot No\ change)$$

Why the Response Is Probably Stable

In all likelihood, however, a drop in the value of the home currency improves the current account balance, especially in the long run. The reason, basically, is that export and import demand elasticities end up being sufficiently high, and, as Appendix G proves, this is enough to ensure the stable response.

One quick way to see why the case of perfectly inelastic demand does not prevail is to note its strange implications. It implies, first, that we make it harder for ourselves to buy foreign goods with each unit of exports (i.e., $P_x^£/P_m^£$ drops), yet this impoverishing effect fails to get us to cut our spending on imports. The result looks even stranger upside down. It implies that a country could succeed in cutting its trade deficit and at the same time buy imports more cheaply (in terms of

FIGURE 22.14
Devaluation Affects the Trade Balance

A. How Devaluation Could Worsen the Trade Balance

Exchange Rate	$P_x^£$	•	X	−	$P_m^£$	•	M	=	$CA^£$
Before dollar devaluation: $1.60/£	1.00	•	80	−	1.00	•	120	=	−40
After dollar devaluation: $2.00/£	0.75	•	80	−	1.00	•	120	=	−60

The key to this case: Demand curves are inelastic, so the volumes of exports and imports do not change. Devaluing our currency just lowers the value of foreign exchange we earn on exports, worsening the trade deficit.

B. The Small-Country Case

Exchange Rate	$P_x^£$	•	X	−	$P_m^£$	•	M	=	$CA^£$
Before dollar devaluation: $1.60/£	1.00	•	80	−	1.00	•	120	=	−40
After dollar devaluation: $2.00/£	1.00	•	105	−	1.00	•	100	=	+ 5

The small-country case illustrates the ability of high demand elasticities to guarantee that devaluation improves the trade balance. The essence of the small-country case is that foreign curves are infinitely elastic so the world (£) prices are not affected by our country's actions. On the export side, the infinite elasticity of foreign demand means that our own supply elasticity dictates what happens to the volume of exports (X). We probably export more, raising our earnings of foreign exchange. On the import side, the infinite elasticity of foreign supply means that our demand elasticity dictates what happens to volume (M). We probably import less, cutting our demand for foreign exchange.

Appendix G generalizes from such special cases, showing how larger demand elasticities raise the ability of devaluation to improve the trade balance.

the export good) by cleverly *revaluing* its currency (for example, raising the value of the dollar from $1.60/£ to $1.00/£). If that were a common occurrence, governments would have discovered it long ago, and they would have solved their trade deficits by happily raising the values of their currencies.

Over the long run, price elasticities tend to be higher, and each nation tends to face elastic curves from the outside world, both the foreign demand curve for its exports and the foreign supply curve for its imports. In the extreme *small-country case,* the home country faces infinitely elastic foreign curves. Foreign-currency (£) prices are fixed, and the current account balance is affected by a drop in our currency as follows:

$$CA^£ = \quad (P_x^£ \quad • \quad X) - \quad (P_m^£ \quad • \quad M)$$
$$Up = (No\ change\ • \ Up) - (No\ change\ • \ Down)$$

We know that if the real volume of exports (X) changes, it will rise, because the same pound price of exports means more dollars per unit for sellers. They will respond to the new incentive with extra production and export sales. Similarly, we know that any change in the real volume of imports (M) will be a drop because the same pound price for imports leaves the dollar-country consumers with a higher dollar price. In the small-country case, both sides of the current account move in the right direction: Export revenues rise and import payments decline. Figure 22.14B provides a numerical illustration that underlines the contrast with the pessimistic case of Figure 22.14A. The crucial role of elasticities, illustrated in the two halves of Figure 22.14, also emerges from the technical formulas of Appendix G.

Timing: The J Curve

The fact that the elasticities of response to a given change (here, the devaluation or depreciation of the dollar) usually rise over time brings a second key result: *Devaluation is more likely to improve the trade balance, the longer the span of elapsed time.* The current account balance may dip for several months after a devaluation or depreciation of the home currency. The changes in prices are likely to occur faster than any changes in trade quantities. The changes in trade quantities at first are small because it takes time for buyers to respond to the price changes by altering their behavior. Contracts previously concluded must expire or be renegotiated, and alternative sources of products must be identified and evaluated. Eventually the quantity responses become larger, as buyers do switch to lower-priced products. As quantity effects become larger, the current account balance improves.

Figure 22.15 gives a schematic diagram of what economists think is a typical response of the current account balance to a drop in the the exchange rate value of a country's currency. The typical pattern is called a **J curve** because of its shape over the first couple of years of response to devaluation. The value of the country's current account at first deteriorates, but then begins to improve. After a moderate time period, perhaps about 18 months, the value of the current account returns to where it started, and thereafter it moves above its initial value. This analysis indicates that it may take some time for a large devaluation or depreciation of the country's currency to have a positive impact on the country's current account. The shift in the FE curve is more complicated than in the previous section. In the short run the FE curve could (perversely) shift to the left unless a capital inflow (perhaps based on the anticipation of the eventual beneficial effects of the devaluation) stabilizes the curve. Eventually the FE curve should shift to the right, but perhaps not until a year or more after the devaluation.

FIGURE 22.15

The J Curve: How the Trade Balance Probably Responds to a Drop in the Value of a Country's Currency

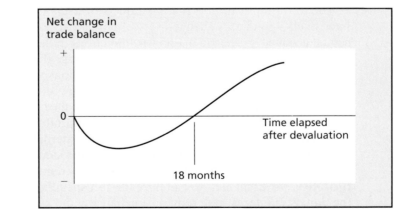

Summary

If a country has a fixed exchange rate, it must defend the fixed rate chosen. The first part of this chapter examined four major implications of having a fixed exchange rate and defending it using official intervention.

The first implication is that intervention to defend the fixed rate alters monetary conditions in the country. Faced with an external imbalance in the country's overall international payments, the central bank defends the fixed rate by buying or selling domestic currency in the foreign exchange market. The intervention changes the central bank's liabilities that serve as the **monetary base** for the domestic **money supply.** The change in the domestic money supply then results in macroeconomic adjustments that tend to reduce the external imbalance. The domestic interest rate changes, altering international capital flows, at least in the short run. The change in real domestic product and income alters demand for imports. In addition, a change in the domestic price level can alter both exports and imports by changing the country's international price competitiveness.

The central bank can attempt to resist this monetary process through **sterilization,** which prevents the domestic money supply from changing. But there are limits to how long the central bank can use sterilized intervention to defend the fixed exchange rate. If the external imbalance continues, then the country's holdings of official reserves continue to change because the central bank is also selling or buying foreign currency as the other half of the intervention. Eventually the change in official reserve holdings forces the central bank to make some adjustment. For instance, if the central bank is selling foreign currency in its intervention, then eventually the central bank runs low on its holdings of official reserves.

The second implication is that a fixed exchange rate and its defense constrain a country's ability to pursue an independent monetary policy. If the country begins with an external deficit, the defense of the fixed rate eventually forces the country to contract its money supply. If the country begins with an external surplus, the defense of the fixed rate eventually forces the country to expand its money supply. If the country begins with an external balance, then any change in monetary policy and the money supply would create an external imbalance, and the intervention to defend the fixed rate would tend to reverse the monetary change.

The third implication is that the effects of fiscal policy are also altered by a fixed exchange rate. A change in fiscal policy causes the country's current and capital accounts to change in opposite directions in the short run, so the effect on the overall payments balance depends on how large the two changes are. If international financial capital flows are not that responsive to interest rate changes, then the resulting external imbalance following a fiscal policy change leads to intervention that changes monetary conditions in the other direction, reducing the effect of the fiscal policy change on domestic product. If international capital flows are sufficiently responsive, the resulting external imbalance leads to intervention that changes monetary conditions in the same direction, enhancing the effect of fiscal policy on real product. In the extreme case of **perfect capital mobility,** the fiscal change can have the full spending multiplier effect because the domestic interest rate remains unchanged and equal to the foreign interest rate. (However, with perfect capital mobility and a fixed exchange rate the country has *no* independent monetary policy.)

The fourth implication is that defending a fixed exchange rate without sterilization alters how different exogenous shocks affect the country's macroeconomy in the short run. The effects of **domestic monetary shocks** are greatly reduced. The effects of **domestic spending shocks** on domestic product depend on how responsive international financial capital flows are to changes in the interest rate. If international capital is more responsive, a domestic spending shock has more effect.

International capital-flow shocks can have major effects on the domestic economy because they require intervention to defend the fixed rate as the shock hits. For instance, a shift to capital outflow leads to intervention that results in a lower domestic money supply. Domestic interest rates tend to increase, and domestic product and income tend to decline.

International trade shocks affect the economy directly by changing aggregate demand. In addition, the resulting intervention to defend the fixed exchange rate causes a monetary change that generally reinforces the change in demand, resulting in a larger change in domestic product and income.

The second part of the chapter examined broad policy issues for countries that have fixed exchange rates. A country wants to achieve both internal and external balance. Yet, stabilizing an open macroeconomy with a fixed exchange rate is not easy. If a country has only one policy for influencing aggregate demand (for instance, monetary policy that changes the money supply), it would have to be very lucky for the level of aggregate demand that is best for the domestic economy to turn out to be the one that keeps external payments in balance.

There is a way out of the dilemma if the country can use two policies (monetary and fiscal policies). Expansionary monetary and fiscal policies have opposite effects on domestic interest rates. The difference can be used to influence international capital flows in the short run. Monetary policy has a comparative advantage in affecting the external balance, whereas fiscal policy has a comparative advantage in affecting the domestic economy. We can thus devise a monetary–fiscal mix to deal with any pairing of imbalances in the external accounts and the domestic economy.

In fact, policymakers can follow a simple **assignment rule** with fair chances of at least approaching the desired combination of internal and external balance. When policies are adjusted smoothly and take quick effect, internal and external balance can be reached by assigning the internal task to fiscal policy and the external task to monetary policy.

Faced with a large or continuing external imbalance, a country's government may decide to react by surrendering—by changing the exchange rate: devaluing, revaluing, or shifting to a floating exchange rate that immediately depreciates or appreciates. A change in the exchange rate can reduce the external imbalance by altering the country's international price competitiveness. Changes in exports and imports alter the current account balance. The exchange rate change also has an impact on internal balance. The export and import changes alter aggregate demand, and the change in the domestic prices of imported goods can alter the country's general price level or inflation rate.

However, it is not certain that the exchange rate change actually does reduce the external imbalance. The effect on the *value* of the current account balance depends on changes in both the volumes (quantities) and prices of exports and imports. Consider a devaluation. Measured in foreign currency, the price of exportable products tends to decrease, the quantity of exports tends to increase, and the price and quantity of imports tend to decrease. The value of exports could increase or decrease. If the value of exports decreases, the current account balance only improves if the decline in the value of imports is larger. A general condition that ensures that the current account balance improves is that the price elasticities of demand for exports and imports be sufficiently high so that the changes in the volumes of exports and imports are large enough. In practice, the price effects, especially the decrease in the foreign-currency price of exports, often occurs quickly, while the volume effects occur more slowly but eventually become sufficiently large. The current account balance thus deteriorates at first, but after a period of months it tends to improve, tracing out a pattern called the **J curve.**

Suggested Reading

A technical treatment of the economics of fixed exchange rates is presented in Rivera-Batiz and Rivera-Batiz (1994, Chapter 14). Some of Robert Mundell's pioneering articles on internal and external balance and the implications of international capital mobility are reprinted in Mundell (1968, Chapters 16 and 18). The same path-breaking analysis was simultaneously developed by Fleming (1962). Kamin (1988) reviews the effects of nearly 100 instances of currency devaluations since the early 1950s.

Questions and Problems

◆ 1. "A country with a deficit in its overall international payments runs the risk of increasing inflation if it defends its fixed exchange rate by (unsterilized) official intervention in the foreign exchange market." Do you agree or disagree? Why?

2. A country with a fixed exchange rate has achieved external balance. Government spending then increases in an effort to reduce unemployment. What is the effect of this policy change on the country's official settlements balance? If the central bank uses unsterilized intervention to defend the fixed rate, will intervention tend to reduce the expansionary effect of the fiscal policy?

◆ 3. What does perfect capital mobility mean for the effectiveness of monetary and fiscal policies under fixed exchange rates?

4. What is the assignment rule? What are its possible advantages and drawbacks?

◆ 5. "According to the logic of the J-curve analysis, a country that revalues its currency should have an improvement in the value of its current account balance in the months immediately after the revaluation." Do you agree or disagree? Why?

6. The Pugelovian central bank intervenes in the foreign exchange market by selling U.S. $10 billion to prevent the Pugelovian currency (the pnut) from depreciating.

   a. What impact does this have on the Pugelovian holdings of official international reserves?

   b. What effect will this have on the Pugelovian money supply if the central bank does not sterilize? Explain.

   c. What effect will this have on the Pugelovian money supply if the central bank does sterilize (using an open market operation in Pugelovian government bonds)? Explain.

✦7. A country initially has achieved both external balance and internal balance. International financial capital is reasonably mobile, so the country's FE curve is upward sloping (and flatter than the LM curve). The country has a fixed exchange rate and defends it using official intervention. The country does not sterilize. As a result of the election of a new government, foreign investors become bullish on the country. International financial capital inflows increase dramatically and remain higher for a number of years.

   a. What shift occurs in the FE curve because of the increased capital inflows?

   b. What intervention is necessary to defend the fixed exchange rate?

   c. As a result of the intervention, how does the country adjust back to external balance? Illustrate this using an IS–LM–FE graph. What is the effect of all of this on the country's internal balance?

8. A country initially has achieved both external balance and internal balance. The country prohibits international financial capital inflows and outflows, so its capital account (excluding official reserves transactions) is always zero because of these capital controls. The country has a fixed exchange rate and defends it using official intervention. The country does not sterilize. An exogenous shock now occurs—foreign demand for the country's exports increases.

   a. What is the slope of the country's FE curve?

   b. What shifts occur in the IS, LM, or FE curves because of the increase in foreign demand for the country's exports?

   c. What intervention is necessary to defend the fixed exchange rate?

   d. As a result of the intervention, how does the country adjust back to external balance? Illustrate this using an IS–LM–FE graph. What is the effect of all of this on the country's internal balance?

✦9. What is the mixture of monetary and fiscal policies that can cure each of the following imbalances?

   a. Rising inflation and overall payments deficit (e.g., point *H* in Figure 22.12).

   b. Rising inflation and overall payments surplus (e.g., point *F* in Figure 22.12).

   c. Insufficient aggregate demand and overall payments surplus (e.g., point *C* in Figure 22.12).

10. The Pugelovian government has just devalued the Pugelovian currency by 10 percent. For each of the following, will this devaluation improve the Pugelovian current account deficit? Explain each.

   a. People are very fixed in their habits. Both Pugelovian importers and foreign buyers of Pugelovian exports buy the same physical volumes no matter what.

   b. Pugelovian firms keep the Pugelovian pnut prices of Pugelovian exports constant, and foreign firms keep the foreign-currency prices of exports to Pugelovia constant.

Chapter **Twenty-Three**

Floating Exchange Rates and Internal Balance

One way to reconcile the goals of external balance and internal balance is to let the exchange rate take care of external balance and to direct macroeconomic policy toward the problem of internal balance. If the exchange rate is allowed to float cleanly, without government intervention, then the exchange rate changes to achieve external balance. If there are no transactions in official reserves, then the official settlements balance must be zero, and the exchange rate must change to whatever value is needed to achieve this external balance. Changes in the exchange rate are the "automatic" mechanism for adjusting to achieve external balance.

Even if a floating exchange rate is used to achieve external balance, this still leaves the problem of achieving internal balance. How does use of floating exchange rates affect the behavior of the economy and the effectiveness of monetary and fiscal policies that might be directed to achieving internal balance? The purpose of this chapter is to examine the macroeconomics of floating exchange rates. It first examines how monetary policy and fiscal policy work in an economy that has a floating exchange rate. Then it explores the impacts of various shocks on such an economy. The shocks are the same types that we examined in Chapter 22, so we can see how the choice of fixed or flexible exchange rates alters how the economy responds to different shocks.

In our analysis of floating exchange rates, we use the same basic model of the open macroeconomy that we developed in Chapter 21 and applied to fixed rates in Chapter 22. The key difference from the previous chapter is that the exchange rate is now a variable determined endogenously by the macroeconomic system rather than a rate set (and defended) by the government. With a floating rate, the exchange rate brings the foreign exchange market (or the overall balance of payments) into equilibrium by affecting people's choices about whether to buy goods and services abroad or at home and whether to invest in this country's financial assets or another country's financial assets. The impact on demand for goods and services then has a feedback effect on the country's domestic product.

The analysis of how a country with a floating exchange rate responds to a policy change or another type of economic shock can usefully proceed through three steps:

1. At the initial value of the exchange rate, what are the effects of the shock on the country's economy? In particular, does the shock push the official settlements balance away from a zero value?

2. If there is a tendency away from zero for the official settlements balance, what change in the exchange rate value of the country's currency (appreciation or depreciation) is needed to move back to a zero balance?

3. What are the additional effects on the country's macroeconomy of this change in the exchange rate?

The additional effects indicate the "special" ways in which floating rates alter the behavior of the economy (just as the additional effects resulting from intervention to defend the fixed rate indicated the "special" ways in which fixed rates alter the behavior of the economy). The additional effects show how floating rates alter the effectiveness of government policies. They also suggest how floating rates alter the country's ability to keep internal balance in a changing world.

MONETARY POLICY WITH FLOATING EXCHANGE RATES

With floating or flexible exchange rates, monetary policy exerts a strong influence over domestic product and income. To see how, let us consider the case of a deliberate expansion of the domestic money supply. Such a change is implemented by using a domestic tool of monetary policy. For instance, the country's monetary authority might use open market operations to buy domestic securities. As the monetary authority pays for its securities purchase, it issues new liabilities that expand the country's monetary base and money supply.

An expansion of the money supply increases banks' willingness to lend, and interest rates decrease. Borrowing and spending rise. As we saw in Chapter 22, the drop in interest rates tends to worsen the overall balance of payments in the short run. The capital account tends to worsen as capital flows out of the country, and the current account worsens as imports rise. The demand for foreign currency is now greater than the supply. In the fixed-rate analysis of Chapter 22, the government had to intervene to defend the fixed rate against the pressure resulting from this payments deficit. With floating exchange rates, the pressure results in a depreciation of the exchange rate value of the country's currency, as summarized in Figure 23.1.

Depreciation of our currency increases the international price competitiveness of the products produced by our country's firms (assuming that the nominal depreciation is larger than any increase in domestic prices and costs in the short

FIGURE 23.1   Effects of Expanding the Money Supply with Floating Exchange Rates

For a decrease in the money supply, reverse the direction of all changes.

run—a form of overshooting like that discussed in Chapter 18). The improvement in our firms' ability to compete with foreign firms is likely to improve our current account balance, as export volumes increase and import volumes decline. (Improvement in the current account balance occurs only after the initial stage of the J-curve has played itself out. This assumes that the stability conditions of Chapter 22 and Appendix G eventually hold. In this chapter we focus on situations in which the response is stable.)

The improvement in the current account balance lowers the overall payments deficit, reducing and eventually eliminating pressure for further depreciation of the exchange rate value of our currency. External balance is restored through the exchange rate change.

The new competitive edge for the country's firms raises aggregate demand for what the country produces. Such extra demand due to the depreciation augments the direct domestic effects of the increase in the money supply. Due to the extra demand, real domestic product and income may rise even more. However, the depreciation may also enhance the effects of monetary policy on the price level and inflation rate as well. The depreciation results in higher domestic prices for imported products, and the extra demand can create general upward pressure on prices.

Thus, under floating exchange rates, monetary policy is powerful in its effects on internal balance. The induced change in the exchange rate reinforces the standard domestic effects of monetary policy. Monetary policy gains power under floating exchange rates, whereas, as we saw in the previous chapter, it loses power under fixed exchange rates.

This general conclusion holds whatever the degree of capital mobility. Whatever the degree, expanding the money supply causes a depreciation, and this further expands aggregate demand. Consider, for instance, perfect capital mobility.

Capital flows respond to both interest rates and the expected change in the exchange rate into the future. Perfect capital mobility implies that uncovered interest parity always holds, because nearly unlimited flows of international financial capital occur if there is any deviation from this parity.[1] The overshooting discussed in Chapter 18 is a form of perfect capital mobility. There we saw that if a monetary expansion reduced the domestic interest rate, the exchange rate value of the country's currency would depreciate immediately by a large amount. The overshooting results in a large improvement in the country's international price competitiveness in the short and medium runs.

How large are the follow-on effects from the currency depreciation? Simulations using a computer model of the global economy developed by the Organization for Economic Cooperation and Development (OECD) provide some answers.[2] Consider a monetary expansion in a country that reduces interest rates by 1 percentage point (e.g., from 6 percent to 5 percent), with monetary policy unchanged in the rest of the world. Here is what the OECD model shows for each of the three largest countries/currencies:

	Change in the Country's Real GDP After Two Years	
	Holding the Exchange Rate Steady	**Allowing the Floating Exchange Rate to Depreciate**
United States	0.5%	0.8%
Japan	0.7	0.9
Euro area	0.6	0.9

Thus the induced depreciation of the country's currency increases the effect of the monetary expansion by about 50 percent on average.

We can see the effects of monetary policy in the IS–LM–FE picture used in the previous two chapters. Consider a country that begins with external balance—a triple intersection shown as point E_0 in Figure 23.2. The country's central bank now uses a domestic change (such as an open market purchase of domestic securities) to expand the domestic money supply, and the LM curve shifts down to LM'. Even if the exchange rate value of the domestic currency were unchanged, the direct domestic effects of this policy change reduce the domestic interest rate from 6 percent to 5 percent and increase real domestic product from 110 to 120. In addition, the country's balance of payments tends to go into deficit. (The intersection of LM' and the original IS curve at point T_1 is to the right of the initial FE curve.) The country's currency depreciates in the

---

[1] For the fixed-rate analysis of Chapter 22, perfect capital mobility also implied uncovered interest parity, but the expected change in the exchange rate was assumed to be approximately zero if investors expected the fixed rate to hold into the future. With no change expected in the fixed rate, uncovered interest parity means that the domestic interest rate is equal to the foreign interest rate.

[2] Dalsgaard, André, and Richardson (2001).

FIGURE 23.2

Expansionary
Monetary
Policy with
Floating
Exchange Rates

Starting from point E_0 with an overall payments balance of zero, the country implements an expansionary policy. The LM curve shifts down or to the right, but at point T_1 the payments balance tends toward deficit. The country's currency depreciates, and the FE and IS curves shift to the right, reestablishing external balance at E_1.

foreign exchange market. As the country's price competitiveness improves, exports increase and imports decrease. The current account balance improves, so the FE curve shifts to the right and the IS curve shifts to the right. If the floating exchange rate adjusts to maintain external balance (a zero balance in the country's official settlements balance), then the economy will be at a triple intersection of all three curves after the exchange rate has adjusted. The new triple intersection is point E_1. Because of the depreciation, real GDP increases even more, to 125. *Monetary policy is powerful in affecting real GDP in the short run under floating exchange rates.*[3]

FISCAL POLICY WITH FLOATING EXCHANGE RATES

How fiscal policy works with floating exchange rates is a little more complicated. Fiscal policy can affect exchange rates in either direction, as shown in Figure 23.3. The left side of the figure shows the same effects of expansionary policy as we saw in Chapter 22. The fiscal expansion bids up domestic interest rates as the government borrows more. Higher domestic interest rates tend to attract capital

---

[3] The monetary expansion and the induced depreciation are also likely to increase the domestic price level through inflation, especially beyond the short run. If the domestic price level increases, then the LM curve shifts back up (or does not shift down by as much in the first place). The higher domestic price level reverses some of the gain in international price competitiveness, so the FE and IS curves also shift back (or do not shift by as much in the first place). The increase in real GDP is not as large. Indeed, in the long run, the currency depreciation will be exactly offset by the higher price level if money is neutral in the long run and purchasing power parity holds.

FIGURE 23.3   Effects of Expansionary Fiscal Policy with Floating Exchange Rates

For contractionary fiscal policy, reverse the direction of all changes.

from abroad, at least temporarily. Meanwhile, aggregate spending, product, and income are raised by higher government spending and/or lower tax rates. This raises imports and worsens the current account balance. So there are two opposing tendencies for the country's overall balance of payments and thus for the exchange rate value of the country's currency. The interest rate rise tends to draw a capital inflow that strengthens the country's currency, but the rise in aggregate demand and imports weakens it. Which tendency will prevail? There is no firm answer. If capital is mobile internationally, then the capital inflow effect at first is probably large enough to appreciate the country's currency. Eventually the aggregate-demand effect is probably stronger and longer lasting, so eventually the currency depreciates.[4]

The "feedback" effects on the domestic economy depend on which way the exchange rate changes. If the country's currency at first appreciates, then the country loses price competitiveness. The country's exports decline and its imports increase. The decline in the country's current account reduces the expansionary effects of the fiscal change on the country's domestic product. That is, the expansionary effect is reduced by "international crowding out"—the appreciation of the country's currency and the resulting decline in the current account. If the country's currency instead (or eventually) depreciates, the enhanced price competitiveness and resulting increase in the current account give a further trade-based stimulus to domestic production.

---

[4] The extreme case of perfect capital mobility is also consistent with this pattern. The initial interest rate increase leads to an immediate appreciation of the domestic currency. The exchange rate overshoots so that the currency is expected subsequently to depreciate slowly. Uncovered interest rate parity is reestablished because the interest differential in favor of the country is offset by the expected depreciation.

FIGURE 23.4   Expansionary Fiscal Policy with Floating Exchange Rates

Expansionary fiscal policy shifts the IS curve to the right, and the IS–LM intersection shifts from E_0 to T_2 or T_3 initially. The effects of fiscal policy depend on how strongly international capital flows respond to the interest rate increase. In panel A, the overall payments balance tends toward surplus. (T_2 is to the left of FE.) In panel B, the overall payments balance tends toward deficit. (T_3 is to the right of FE.) In either case the payments imbalance leads to a change in the exchange rate. In panel A, the country's currency appreciates, and the FE and IS curves shift to the left, reestablishing external balance at E_2. In panel B, the country's currency depreciates, and the FE and IS curves shift to the right, reestablishing external balance at E_3. Here we assume that the LM curve does not move, because the central bank can keep the money supply steady if it doesn't need to defend a fixed exchange rate.

The effects of fiscal expansion can be pictured using an IS–LM–FE graph. Figure 23.4 shows the two cases possible. In both cases the economy begins at the triple intersection E_0. The fiscal expansion directly shifts the IS curve to IS', increasing the domestic interest rate from 6 percent to 8 percent and boosting domestic product from 110 to 130.

The two cases differ by whether the country's overall payments balance tends to go into surplus or deficit. The left graph in Figure 23.4 shows the case of a tendency to surplus because the capital inflow effect is larger. In this graph the incipient payments surplus is shown by the IS'–LM intersection to the left of the initial FE curve. The country's currency appreciates, the current account balance worsens, and the FE and IS curves shift to the left. The new triple intersection is at point E_2. Because of the currency appreciation, domestic product declines somewhat from 130 to 125 (or does not rise as much from its initial value of 110). International crowding out reduces the expansionary thrust of the fiscal change.[5]

The right graph in Figure 23.4 shows the case of a tendency to deficit, because the aggregate-demand effect is larger—the IS'–LM intersection is to the right of

[5] If the fiscal expansion causes the price level to increase, then the LM curve also shifts up, and both the FE and IS curves shift to the left somewhat (or do not shift as much to the right) as a result of some loss of international price competitiveness due to the higher domestic prices. For either of the two cases discussed here in the text, these additional shifts reduce the amount by which real domestic product increases from its initial value of 110.

the initial FE curve. The country's currency depreciates, the current account balance improves, and the FE and IS curves shift to the right. The new triple intersection is at point E_3. Because of the currency depreciation, domestic product rises to 140 rather than 130.

The large U.S. fiscal expansion implemented in the early 1980s illustrates the nature and timing of the effects of a change in fiscal policy under floating exchange rates. The box "Why Are U.S. Trade Deficits So Big?" discusses the U.S. experience.

SHOCKS TO THE ECONOMY

Major shocks occasionally strike a country's economy. What are the effects of these exogenous changes on a country that has a floating exchange rate? We will look at the same shocks that we examined in Chapter 22 for a country with a fixed exchange rate so that we can contrast the results.

Internal Shocks

Domestic monetary shocks affect the equilibrium relationship between money supply and money demand, causing a shift in the LM curve. A change in the country's monetary policy is an example of such a shock. As we saw in the analysis of expansionary monetary policy, domestic monetary shocks have powerful effects on an economy with a floating exchange rate. If the monetary shock tends to expand the economy, then the exchange rate value of the country's currency tends to depreciate, further increasing domestic product (or putting additional upward pressure on the country's price level or inflation rate). If the monetary shock tends to contract the economy, then the country's currency tends to appreciate, decreasing domestic product.

Domestic spending shocks alter domestic expenditure, causing a shift in the IS curve. A change in fiscal policy is an example. As we saw for fiscal policy, the effect of this kind of shock on the exchange rate depends on which changes more: international capital flows or the country's current account.

International Capital-Flow Shocks

Shocks to international capital flows occur because of changes in investors' perceptions of economic and political conditions in various countries. For instance, an adverse international capital-flow shock, leading to a capital outflow from our country, can occur because foreign interest rates increase, because investors shift to expecting more depreciation of our currency in the future, or because investors fear negative changes in our country's politics or policies.

The shift leads to a capital outflow. The outflow puts downward pressure on the exchange rate value of the country's currency, and the currency depreciates. The depreciation improves the international price competitiveness of the country's products. Our exports increase, and our imports decrease, improving the country's current account. The extra demand tends to increase our domestic product.

The effects of this shock are pictured in Figure 23.5. The economy begins at point E_0, a triple intersection. The adverse international capital-flow shock causes the FE curve to shift to the left to FE'. The country's overall payments balance tends to go into deficit, as the intersection of the (initially unchanged) IS–LM curves at E_0 is below FE'. The country's currency depreciates, shifting the FE and IS curves to the right. A new triple intersection occurs at point E_4, with domestic product and the interest rate higher.

Thus, under floating exchange rates external capital-flow shocks can have effects on internal balance, by altering the exchange rate and the country's international price competitiveness. Interestingly, an adverse shock tends to expand the domestic economy by depreciating the country's currency. We probably should add several cautions about this result. First, the reason for the capital-flow shift is important. If capital is flowing out because of political or economic problems in the country, then these problems may cause the economy to contract even though the exchange rate depreciation is pushing in the other direction. Second, the capital outflow may disrupt domestic financial markets in ways that go beyond our basic analysis. Any disruptions in domestic financial markets may harm the broader domestic economy, also tending to contract it. We saw in Chapter 20 that a country often has domestic problems, large capital outflows, a depreciating currency, financial disruption, and a severe recession during a financial crisis. Thus, it is risky to conclude, on the basis of the simpler IS–LM–FE analysis, that an adverse capital-flow shock is simply good for the country's economy.

FIGURE 23.5
An Adverse
International
Capital-Flow
Shock

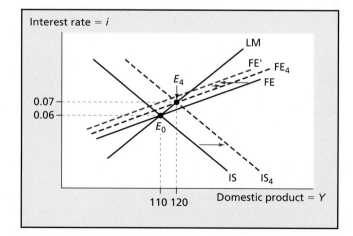

A shift of international capital flows away from the country causes the FE curve to shift up or to the left, and the overall payments balance tends toward deficit. The country's currency depreciates, and the FE and IS curves shift to the right, reestablishing external balance at E_4. Here again we assume that the LM curve does not shift, because the central bank can keep the money supply steady.

The United States has had a trade deficit every year since 1980, and at times the annual trade deficit has been large (over $100 billion). Why does the United States have this trade deficit? Why did it become very large in the mid-1980s and late 1990s–early 2000s?

The United States has a floating exchange rate, so one place to look for an explanation is in changes in the real exchange rate value of the U.S. dollar (recall our discussion of the real exchange rate in Chapter 18). The top graph in the accompanying figure shows the value of the real effective exchange rate value of the dollar, as an indicator of the international price-competitiveness of U.S. products, and the value of the U.S. trade balance (measured as a percentage of U.S. GDP, to make the size more comparable over time). It is clear that we may have a pretty good explanation here, if we allow for the lag of one to two years (recall the J curve from Chapter 22). That is, the dollar begins a large real appreciation in 1980, and the trade balance begins to deteriorate in 1982. The value of the dollar peaks in 1985, and it begins a real depreciation that returns the real value in 1988 back to what it was in 1980. The trade balance begins to improve in 1987. The next big swing begins when the dollar starts another real appreciation in 1995. The trade balance deteriorates beginning in 1997.

So an explanation of the large U.S. trade deficits is the change in international price competitiveness caused by exchange rate swings. When the dollar experiences a real appreciation, the loss of price competitiveness hurts U.S. exports and encourages U.S. imports, so the trade balance deteriorates. The problem with this explanation is that it is not very deep. With a floating rate, the exchange rate value of the U.S. dollar is an endogenous variable. We should probe further to find out what is behind the broad swings in the exchange rate and the trade balance.

One place to look is in the relationships between national saving and investment that we introduced in Chapter 15 and used again in Chapter 21. The bottom graph in the accompanying figure shows two aspects of national saving, private saving by households and businesses, and government saving, which is the government budget surplus or deficit (if it is negative). If the government runs a surplus, then it is collecting more in tax revenues than it is spending, so

the difference is a form of saving. If the government runs a deficit, then it is dissaving. The graph also shows domestic private investment and the trade balance again.

In the 1980s the closest relationship is between the government budget and the trade balance. In 1981 the Reagan administration sought and obtained a major change in U.S. fiscal policy. The government reduced taxes while government expenditures continued to grow. The government budget deficit increased to about 6.5 percent of GDP in early 1983 and remained at about 5 percent of GDP until 1987. In the graph the increase in the government budget deficit is shown as a decline in government saving in the early 1980s, with the line then remaining at about –5 percent for several years. Essentially, both the government budget deficit and the trade deficit increased in the first half of the 1980s and declined in the late 1980s. They came to be called the twin deficits.

Our model provides some insights into this relationship. Expansionary fiscal policy shifted the IS curve to the right, increasing both U.S. interest rates and U.S. national income. The rise in income alone tended to increase the trade deficit. The relatively high U.S. interest rates also drew large capital inflows, and the real exchange rate value of the dollar increased (as we saw in the top graph). In 1985 the capital inflows declined, so the large trade deficit became an important driver of the exchange rate value of the dollar. The dollar began to depreciate in early 1985. (In September, the governments of the major countries announced an agreement to reinforce this depreciation by intervening if necessary to ensure the decline in the value of the dollar.)

The explanation for the rise of the trade deficit in the second half of the 1990s is different. The government budget is not the explanation, because the deficit began to decline in 1993, and the government (combined federal, state, and local) had positive saving (budget surpluses) during 1998–2000. Instead, the explanation of the rising U.S. trade deficit in the later 1990s is the boom in real domestic investment. In the 1980s both private saving and private investment declined as shares of GDP. In the 1990s private saving continued to decline, but private domestic investment rose strongly, from 13 per-

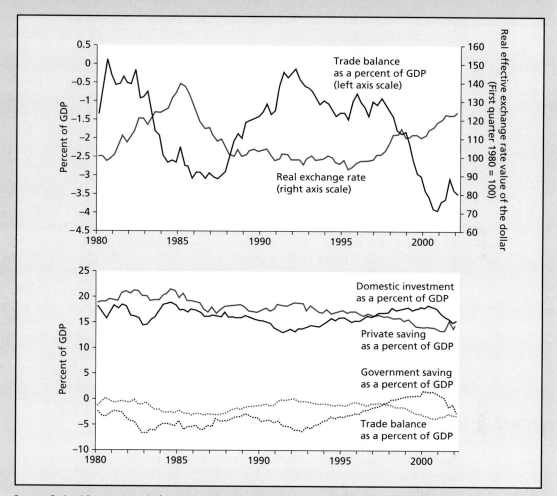

Source: Federal Reserve Board of Governors for the real effective exchange rate; U.S. government national income and product accounts for the other variables.

cent of GDP to about 18 percent. Businesses perceived major opportunities for profitable capital investments in the United States. So did financial investors, with a booming stock market drawing in large amounts of foreign capital. In terms of our macromodel, the story is much the same, though the driver is different (real domestic investment in the 1990s, fiscal policy in the 1980s). The increase in real domestic investment shifts the IS curve to the right.

The trade balance deteriorates because of strong growth in U.S. GDP. The capital inflows appreciate the dollar, so the trade balance also deteriorates because of declining price competitiveness.

As of early 2002, we knew that the business investment boom and the stock market boom were both over. We were still waiting to see what would happen to the exchange rate value of the dollar and the U.S. trade deficit.

International Trade Shocks

Shocks to international trade flows cause the value of the country's current account balance to change. For instance, an adverse international trade shock might occur because of a decline in foreign demand for our exports, an increase in our taste for imported products, or a decline in the supply of an important import such as oil.

An adverse international trade shock reduces both the current account and the country's domestic product and income.[6] As the current account worsens, the overall payments balance tends to go into deficit, and the country's currency depreciates. The improvement in price competitiveness leads to an increase in the country's exports and a decline in imports. The current account improves and domestic product and income rise. If all of this happens with no change in international capital flows, then the currency must depreciate enough to completely reverse the deterioration in the current account, putting the overall payments balance back to zero.

Figure 23.6 shows the effects of this adverse international trade shock. The shock causes the FE and IS curves to shift to the left. The intersection of IS' with LM at T_5 is below the new FE'. The country's currency depreciates, resulting in shifts back to the right in the FE and IS curves. If nothing else changes (such as international capital flows or the domestic price level), then the curves shift back to their original positions, and the new triple intersection is back to E_0.[7]

With floating exchange rates, the *effects of international trade shocks on internal balance are mitigated by the effects of the resulting change in the exchange rate*. An adverse trade shock tends to depreciate the country's currency, and this reverses some of the effects of the shock. By reversing all of the directions of change, we would also conclude that a positive trade shock appreciates the country's currency, reversing both the improvement in the country's current account balance and the increase in demand for the country's domestic product.

INTERNAL IMBALANCE AND POLICY RESPONSES

Shocks to the economy alter both the international performance of the country's economy and its domestic performance. With floating exchange rates a change in the exchange rate takes care of achieving external balance following a shock. If

---

[6] We presume that the current account does actually decline. The shock itself worsens the current account. The decline in national income lowers demand for imports, but we assume that this is not enough to reverse the deterioration of the current account. In Figure 23.6, this assumption ensures that the new IS'–LM intersection at T_5 is to the left of the new FE', even if the FE curve is steeper than the LM curve.

[7] The depreciation of the currency may put some upward pressure on the country's price level by increasing the domestic-currency price of imported products. If the overall domestic price level increases, then the LM curve shifts up somewhat, and the new triple intersection will still result in some decline in domestic product. Nonetheless, the decline is less than what would occur without the currency depreciation.

FIGURE 23.6

An Adverse
International
Trade Shock

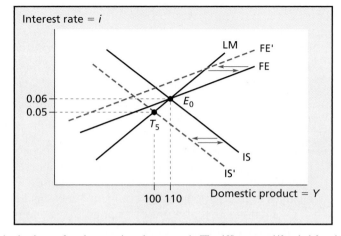

A shift of international trade away from the country's products causes the FE and IS curves to shift to the left, and the overall payments balance tends toward deficit. The country's currency depreciates, and the FE and IS curves shift back to the right. Here, to simplify the diagram, we imagine the case in which external balance is reestablished at E_0.

the country's overall payments tend to go into deficit, then the country's currency depreciates, reversing the tendency toward deficit. If the country's overall payments tend to surplus, then appreciation reverses the tendency to surplus.

A floating exchange rate does not ensure that the country achieves internal balance, but changes in the floating rate do affect the country's internal balance. A depreciation tends to expand the country's economy. If the country begins with excessive unemployment before the exchange rate change, then the expansionary thrust of the depreciation is welcome, as it reduces the internal imbalance. If the country instead begins with internal balance or with an inflation rate that is rising or too high, then the expansionary thrust of the depreciation will create or add to the internal inflationary imbalance.

An appreciation tends to contract the country's economy. If the economy begins with inflationary pressure, then this may be welcome. But if the economy is already in or tending toward a recession with excessive unemployment, then the exchange rate change adds to the internal imbalance.

Government monetary or fiscal policy can be used to address any internal imbalances that do arise. If excessive unemployment is the internal imbalance, then expansionary monetary or fiscal policy can be used. The size of the change in policy needed to address the imbalance depends on the change in the exchange rate that will occur. Monetary policy is powerful with floating exchange rates, so a relatively small change may be enough to reestablish internal balance. The power of fiscal policy is more variable and may be difficult to predict if it is difficult to predict the appreciation or depreciation of the exchange rate following the fiscal change.

INTERNATIONAL MACROECONOMIC POLICY COORDINATION

The dollar may be our currency but it's your problem.

U.S. Treasury Secretary John Connally, speaking to a group of Europeans (as quoted in Paul A. Volcker and Toyoo Gyohten, Changing Fortunes: The World's Money and the Threat to American Leadership, *New York: Times Books, 1992, p. 81)*

The policies adopted by one country have effects on other countries. With floating exchange rates these spillover effects happen in several ways, including foreign income repercussions as changes in incomes alter demands for imports, and changes in international price competitiveness as floating exchange rates change.

One danger is that a policy change that benefits the country making it can harm other countries. For instance, a shift to expansionary monetary policy causes the currencies of other countries to appreciate. This can appear to be a beggar-thy-neighbor policy in that the first country benefits from increased growth, but the exchange rate appreciation can harm the price competitiveness and trade of other countries.

Another danger is that each country acting individually may fail to make a policy change whose benefits mostly go to other countries. If a number of countries could coordinate so that they all make this policy change, all would reap substantial benefits. For example, following the nearly global stock market crash of October 1987, the global financial system needed additional liquidity to counteract the

Financial Times, April 21, 1995. Picture: Reuters.

decline in banking and financial activity. If any one central bank added liquidity, the rest of the global system would benefit, probably more than the individual country would. Each individual central bank might be slow to act, or reluctant to add liquidity aggressively, on its own. Fortunately, several central banks coordinated their actions to inject liquidity, and the financial markets stabilized.

Given these spillover effects and interdependencies, it seems that it should be possible to improve global macroeconomic performance through international cooperation and international coordination. International policy cooperation refers to such activities as sharing of information about each country's performance, problems, and policies. Sharing of information occurs in many places, including high-level meetings of national finance ministers and heads of state as well as international organizations such as the International Monetary Fund and the Bank for International Settlements. International cooperation of this sort is not controversial.

International macroeconomic policy coordination is more than this. It is the joint determination of several countries' macroeconomic policies to improve joint performance. It implies the ability of one country to influence the policies of other countries and the willingness of a country to alter its policies to benefit other countries. In some situations coordination could be easy. For instance, in a deep global recession with no inflation, the advantages of mutual expansionary policies are clear. All countries can benefit if each country finds an alternative to beggar-thy-neighbor policies that harm other countries. In other situations coordination is more controversial.

We have several examples of major coordination efforts in the past quarter-century. At the Bonn Summit of 1978, the United States agreed to implement policies to reduce U.S. inflation while also agreeing to reduce oil imports by decontrolling domestic oil prices. Germany agreed to increase its government spending to stimulate its economy. Japan also agreed to continue its expansionary policies, while taking steps to slow its growth of exports. In the Plaza Agreement of 1985, the major countries agreed to intervene in the foreign exchange markets to lower the exchange rate value of the U.S. dollar (but there was no other substantial coordination of policies). In the Louvre Accord of 1987, the United States committed to reduce its fiscal deficit, while Germany and Japan committed to expansionary policies. All committed to stabilize the exchange rate value of the dollar, if necessary through higher U.S. interest rates and lower interest rates in Germany and Japan, as well as through official intervention.[8]

We can see possible benefits of coordination by examining the Louvre Accord. Tightening of U.S. policies (both fiscal and monetary) would tend to slow down the U.S. economy, and slow down the economies of other countries by reducing U.S. demand for imports. Expansionary policies in Germany and Japan could offset the contractionary effects of the U.S. policy shift, not only in these two

---

[8] The box "Can Governments Manage the Float?" discussed the use of intervention to influence floating exchange rates.

Floating exchange rates allow a country to achieve external balance while maintaining control over its money supply and monetary policy. But floating exchange rates are also highly variable, more variable than we expected when many countries shifted to floating rates in 1973.

Governments that have chosen floating exchange rates worry about the large amount of variability, and nearly all manage the float to some extent. Some governments manage their floating rates closely. If the floating exchange rate is heavily managed, then it behaves more like a fixed exchange rate, and the analysis of the previous chapter is relevant. Other governments, including the governments of most major countries that have chosen floating rates, use management selectively. Occasionally the government intervenes in the foreign exchange market.

Is selective or occasional intervention effective in influencing exchange rates? Twenty years ago the conventional wisdom was clear. If the intervention is not sterilized, then it can be effective. However, it is effective not because it is intervention but rather because it changes the money supply. Unsterilized intervention is simply another way to implement a change in the domestic money supply and monetary policy. By changing the money supply, it can have a substantial effect on the exchange rate. If the intervention is sterilized, the conventional wisdom was that it would not be effective in changing the exchange rate, at least not much or for long. Yet interventions by the U.S., Japanese, and British monetary authorities are fully sterilized.

The conventional wisdom was based on a number of studies that showed little effect of sterilized intervention. It was also based on the relatively small sizes of interventions. In a market where total daily trading is hundreds of billions of dollars, interventions that typically were less than $1 billion seemed too small to have much impact.

More recent studies have challenged this conventional wisdom. How might sterilized intervention be effective, even though it does not change the domestic money supply and is relatively small? The most likely way is by changing the exchange rate expectations of international financial investors and speculators. Intervention can act as a signal from the monetary authorities that they are not happy with the current level or trend of the exchange rate. The authorities show that they are willing to do some-

thing (intervention) now and they signal that they may be willing to do something more in the future. For instance, the authorities may be willing to change monetary policy and interest rates in the future if the path for the exchange rate remains unacceptable. Sterilized interventions then can be a type of news that influences expectations. If international investors take the signal seriously, they adjust their exchange rate expectations. Changed expectations alter international capital flows, changing the exchange rate in the direction desired by the authorities. For instance, in 1985 the major governments announced in the Plaza Agreement that they were committed to reducing the exchange rate value of the dollar. They intervened to sell dollars. International investors shifted to expecting the dollar to depreciate by more than they had previously thought, and the exchange rate value of the dollar declined rapidly.

Recent studies indicate that sterilized intervention can be effective. One indirect measure of effectiveness is whether the monetary authority makes a profit or a loss on its interventions over time. If the authority buys a currency and succeeds in driving its value up (and sells to drive the value down), the authority makes a profit (buy low, sell high). An early study found that central banks generally incurred losses on their intervention in the 1970s. However, a study of U.S. intervention during the 1980s found that the U.S. monetary authority made a profit of over $12 billion on its dollar–DM intervention activities, with large profits earned during 1980, 1985–1986, and 1988–1989. It made a profit of over $4 billion on its dollar–yen interventions during this period, with especially large profits earned during 1985–1988. Another study concluded that interventions during the mid- and late 1980s significantly affected exchange rate expectations in the direction intended.

Recently, a number of monetary authorities began releasing data on their daily intervention activities, information that had previously been kept secret. With this data the quality of statistical studies has improved dramatically. The typical findings are as follows:

- Intervention is usually effective in the short period of two weeks or less, in reversing the direction of the trend of the exchange rate, or at least in reducing the speed of the trend (when the authority is leaning against the wind).

- Larger interventions are more successful.

- Coordinated intervention, in which two more monetary authorities intervene jointly to try to influence an exchange rate, is much more powerful than an intervention by one country of the same total size.

- The effectiveness of the intervention often diminishes after this two-week period, and often there is no discernible effect one month later.

Here is one recent example. Between the introduction of the euro in 1999 and mid-2002, the European Central Bank (ECB) intervened to influence the exchange rate value of the euro on only four days, in the fall of 2000 (even though for much of the time period the euro's value was low or declining). On September 22 a coordinated intervention by the ECB and the monetary authorities of the United States, Japan, and Britain bought several billions of euros. The initial impact was to increase the euro's value by over 4 percent, though about half of the effect was lost during the remainder of the day. The intervention was successful in reversing the direction of the trend for about 5 days, and after 15 days the euro's decline was less than what it would have been if the previous trend had simply continued. Still, the euro's decline continued, and the ECB intervened again on November 3, 6, and 9. The same effects of reversing the trend for about 5 days and smoothing the decline for about 15 days occurred. These interventions may have had some lasting impact, because at about this time the value of the euro stopped its downward trend and began to vary around a trend that was essentially flat.

Of the major countries, Japan has been by far the most active in intervention. The Japanese government has been quite concerned by the variability of the yen's value. From early 1991 to 1995, the yen appreciated from 140 per dollar to 80. Then the yen depreciated to 146 in 1998, appreciated to about 100 in 2000, and then depreciated to about 125 by April 2001. Japan's monetary authority bought dollars (and sold yen) on 168 days during this time period, for total purchases of over $200 billion. It sold dollars (and bought yen) on 33 days, a total of $37 billion.

Ito (2002) reckons that these interventions were highly profitable for the Japanese government. It bought dollars at an average price of 104 and sold dollars at an average price of 130. It realized capital gains of $8 billion, earned an interest differential on its holdings of the dollars it bought of about $31 billion, and had an unrealized capital gain at the end of the period of $29 billion. In fact, we can observe that the Japanese government seems to have an unstated target exchange rate of about 125 per dollar. Sales of dollars were at rates above 125, and purchases below.

By combining days of intervention that are close together, Fatum and Hutchison (2002a) identify 43 separate instances of intervention, 29 of buying dollars during 1993–1996 and 1999–2000, and 14 of selling dollars during 1991–1992 and 1997–1998. In 34 of these, Japan's monetary authority was clearly leaning against the wind—intervening against the trend during the previous two days. Of these, 24 reversed the trend for the two days after the intervention, and in another 5 the trend rate of exchange rate change was lowered. The major failures occurred in the first half of 1995, when continual interventions could not prevent the yen from appreciating from 100 to the amazing level of 80 yen per dollar. However, even when the Japanese authorities succeeded during this short two-day window, there was generally little effect on the exchange rate a month after the intervention.

Coordinated interventions with the U.S. monetary authority (which occurred on 22 days during the decade) were *much* more powerful than interventions only by Japan. Ito estimates that for 1996–2001, independent intervention of $2 billion by the Japanese authority moves the yen value by 0.2 percent on average. Coordinated intervention of $1 billion by each of the two authorities moves the yen value by about 5.0 percent.

Our beliefs about the effectiveness of sterilized intervention by the major countries is now cautious and nuanced. If the time frame is a few days, intervention seems often to be successful. If the time frame is one month or more, it usually seems to be unsuccessful. Still, there are times, such as late 2000 for the euro, when the monetary authorities believe that the market has pushed an exchange rate far from its fundamental value. As Michael Mussa, then chief economist for the International Monetary Fund, said a few days before the September 2000 euro intervention, "Circumstances for intervention are very rare, but they do arise. One has to ask, if not now, when?"

countries, but also in other countries (including the United States) by expanding German and Japanese demands for imports. If this is done on a coordinated basis, the result can be a reduction of the U.S. current account deficit, reductions in the German and Japanese current account surpluses, and a stabilization of the exchange rate value of the dollar, without a global recession caused by the tightening of U.S. policies.

If the benefits of international policy coordination seem clear, why do we actually see rather little of it? There seem to be several reasons. First, the goals of different countries may not be compatible. For instance, the United States may want to maintain growth while stabilizing the exchange rate value of the dollar. Policymakers at the European Central Bank are mandated to focus solely on preventing inflation, so they may be unwilling to expand the money supply, lower interest rates, and expand the EU economy. It is simply difficult for a government to adopt policies that do not suit the economic and political conditions of the country, even if these policies would benefit other countries. Indeed, governments may disagree about how the domestic and global macroeconomy works. For instance, they may disagree about how much expansion is possible before inflation begins to increase noticeably.

Second, the benefits of international policy coordination may actually be small in many situations. Often the appropriate "coordinated" policies actually appear to be close to the appropriate policies that would be chosen by the countries individually (as long as blatant beggar-thy-neighbor policies such as new trade barriers are avoided). For instance, in 1987, the United States on its own probably should have shifted to somewhat contractionary policies and reduced its government budget deficit. In turn, both Germany and Japan, for their own benefit, probably should have shifted to more expansionary policies. Even in this situation, a coordination agreement could have some benefit, not because governments do something different from what each wants to do, but rather because each government can use the commitment to international coordination to firm up domestic support for the policy changes that are in the best interests of the individual countries.

Major instances of international macroeconomic policy coordination are rare. Coordination is more likely when countries clearly see and agree to goals and the means to achieve these goals. In practice this means that the countries commit to doing what they largely should have done on their own. Even in these cases, governments often have difficulty delivering on their commitments. For instance, during the 1980s, international commitments by the U.S. government to reduce its government budget deficit seem to have had little impact.

Summary

With a cleanly floating exchange rate, the exchange rate changes to maintain external balance. If a country is tending toward a surplus in its overall international payments, the exchange rate value of the country's currency will appreciate enough to reverse the tendency. If the country is tending toward a deficit, the currency will depreciate. The contrast with fixed exchange rates is clear. With a clean float external balance is not an issue, but the exchange rate can be quite variable or volatile.

Monetary policy is more powerful with floating exchange rates. After a shift in monetary policy, the exchange rate is likely to change in the direction that reinforces or magnifies the effect of the policy shift on aggregate demand, domestic product, national income, and the price level. In contrast, as we saw in Chapter 22, with fixed exchange rates monetary policy loses power because the need to defend the fixed rate tends to reverse the policy thrust (assuming that the intervention is not or cannot be sterilized).

The effects of floating exchange rates on fiscal policy are not clear. Consider a fiscal expansion. If the resulting inflow of international financial capital is the dominant effect on external balance, then the country's currency appreciates. The loss of international price competitiveness leads to international crowding out, as the current account balance deteriorates. This reduces the effectiveness of fiscal policy in altering domestic product and income. If, instead, the initial deterioration in the current account balance is the dominant effect on external balance, then the country's currency depreciates. The gain in international price competitiveness improves the current account, and this enhances the effectiveness of fiscal policy. We also saw an ambiguity in how fixed exchange rates affect fiscal policy. But the conclusions are the opposite. With fixed exchange rates, fiscal policy is more effective in altering domestic product and income if capital is highly mobile internationally; it is less effective if capital is less mobile.

The ways in which different kinds of shocks affect the country's economy also differ according to whether the country has a fixed or floating exchange rate. Figure 23.7 summarizes the conclusions of the analysis of this chapter and Chapter 22. This figure indicates whether a particular shock would change domestic product and income more (be more disruptive or less stable) with fixed or with floating

FIGURE 23.7
Ranking of Exchange Rate Systems by Unit Impacts of Various Exogenous Shocks on Domestic Product and Income

	More Disruptive– Less Stable	Less Disruptive– More Stable
Internal Shocks		
Domestic monetary shock	Floating	Fixed
Domestic spending shock	Floating*	Fixed*
External Shocks		
International trade shock	Fixed	Floating
International capital-flow shock	Fixed†	Floating†

Comparison is between (1) a fixed exchange rate defended by intervention with no sterilization, so adjustment is through money supply changes, and (2) a floating exchange rate with adjustment through exchange rate changes. If sterilized intervention is used to defend the fixed exchange rate, this raises the disruptiveness of internal shocks, and it lowers the disruptiveness of external shocks, each relative to fixed rates with unsterilized intervention.

*This is the result if international capital flows are unresponsive to interest rate differences, or if the current account change eventually is the dominant pressure on the exchange rate. The opposite result applies if the capital account change is the dominant pressure.
†The effect of the shock on national income is in the opposite direction for the two cases. The sense in which the shock is less disruptive under a floating exchange rate is that the induced exchange rate change with floating exchange rates shifts the FE curve back toward its original position.

exchange rates. We can reach several general conclusions. First, internal shocks, especially domestic monetary shocks, are more disruptive to an economy with a floating exchange rate, and are less disruptive with a fixed exchange rate. Second, external shocks, especially international trade shocks, are more disruptive to an economy with a fixed exchange rate, and are less disruptive with a floating exchange rate. Floating exchange rates provide some insulation from foreign trade shocks.

While cleanly floating exchange rates can ensure that the country achieves external balance, they do not ensure internal balance. In several situations the exchange rate change that reestablishes external balance can make an internal imbalance worse. If a country has rising inflation and a tendency toward external deficit, the depreciation of the currency can exacerbate the inflation pressures in the country. If the country has excessive unemployment and a tendency toward surplus, the appreciation of the currency can make the unemployment problem worse. To achieve internal balance, the country's government may need to implement domestic policy changes (contractionary to fight inflation, expansionary to fight unemployment).

In theory, **international macroeconomic policy coordination** can improve global macroeconomic performance. International policy coordination means that countries set their policies jointly. The benefits of coordination include the opportunity to consider spillover effects on other countries that arise from interdependence and the opportunity to avoid beggar-thy-neighbor policies that benefit one country at the expense of others. In practice, major instances of international policy coordination are infrequent.

Suggested Reading

See Bergsten (1991) for a discussion of the experience with external adjustment under floating exchange rates during the late 1980s and early 1990s. Genberg and Swoboda (1989) present a technical analysis of the effects of government policies on current account balances under floating exchange rates. Fieleke (1996) provides estimates of how often external shocks hit industrialized countries. International macroeconomic policy coordination is discussed in Feldstein (1988, Parts One and Two), Espinosa and Yip (1993), Bryant (1995), Bergsten and Henning (1996), and Meyer et al. (2002).

Sarno and Taylor (2001) survey the theory of and evidence on the use of sterilized intervention to manage floating exchange rates. Ito (2002) and Fatum and Hutchison (2002a) examine Japan's intervention during the 1990s, and Fatum and Hutchison (2002b) look at the ECB intervention in 2000.

Humpage (1994) explains how the United States undertakes official intervention. Neely (2001) presents the results of a survey of central banks about their intervention practices.

Questions and Problems

✦1. "Overshooting is the basis for the enhanced effectiveness of monetary policy under floating exchange rates." Do you agree or disagree? Why?

2. A country has a floating exchange rate. Government spending now increases in an effort to reduce unemployment. What is the effect of this policy change on the exchange rate value of the country's currency? Under what circumstances does the exchange rate change reduce the expansionary effect of the fiscal change?

✦3. "A drop in the foreign demand for our exports has a larger effect on our domestic product and income under floating exchange rates than it would under fixed exchange rates." Do you agree or disagree? Why?

4. Describe the effects of a sudden decrease in the domestic demand for holding money (a shift from wanting to hold domestic money to wanting to hold domestic bonds) on our domestic product and income under floating exchange rates. Is the change in domestic product and income greater or less than it would be under fixed exchange rates? (*Hint:* A decrease in the demand for money is like an increase in the supply of money.)

✦5. A country has a rising inflation rate and a tendency for its overall payments to go into deficit. Will the resulting exchange rate change move the country closer to or further from internal balance?

6. Britain has instituted a contractionary monetary policy to fight inflation. The pound is floating.

   a. If the exchange rate value of the pound remained steady, what are the effects of tighter money on British domestic product and income? What is the effect on the British inflation rate? Explain.

   b. Following the shift to tighter money, what is the pressure on the exchange rate value of the pound? Explain.

   c. What are the implications of the change in the exchange rate value of the pound for domestic product and inflation in Britain? Does the exchange rate change tend to reinforce or counteract the contractionary thrust of British monetary policy? Explain.

✦7. In the late 1980s, the United States had a large government budget deficit and a large current account deficit. The dollar was floating. One approach suggested to reduce both of these deficits was a large increase in taxes.

   a. If the exchange rate value of the dollar remained steady, how would this change affect U.S. domestic product and income? How would it affect the U.S. current account balance and the U.S. capital account balance? Explain.

   b. What are the possible pressures on the exchange rate value of the dollar as a result of this change in fiscal policy? Explain.

   c. If the dollar actually depreciates, what are the implications for further changes in U.S. domestic product and the U.S. current account balance? Explain.

8. What are the effects of a sudden surge in foreign money supplies on our domestic product and income under floating exchange rates? (*Hint:* The increase in the foreign money supplies will have an impact on demand for our exports and on international capital flows as well as on exchange rates.)

◆ 9. A country initially has achieved both external balance and internal balance. International financial capital is reasonably mobile, so the country's FE curve is upward sloping (and flatter than the LM curve). The country has a floating exchange rate. As a result of the election of a new government, foreign investors become bullish on the country. International financial capital inflows increase dramatically and remain higher for a number of years.

   a. What shift occurs in the FE curve because of the increased capital inflows?
   b. What change in the exchange rate occurs to reestablish external balance?
   c. As a result of the exchange rate change, how does the country adjust back to external balance? Illustrate this using an IS–LM–FE graph. What is the effect of all of this on the country's internal balance?

10. A country initially has achieved both external balance and internal balance. The country prohibits international financial capital inflows and outflows, so its capital account (excluding official reserves transactions) is always zero because of these capital controls. The country has a floating exchange rate. An exogenous shock now occurs—foreign demand for the country's exports increases.

   a. What shifts would occur in the IS, LM, and FE curves because of the increase in foreign demand for the country's exports if the exchange rate value of the country's currency were to remain unchanged?
   b. What change in the exchange rate value of the country's currency actually occurs? Why?
   c. As a result of the exchange rate change, how does the country adjust back to external balance? Illustrate this using an IS–LM–FE graph. How does all of this affect the country's internal balance?

Chapter Twenty-Four

National and Global Choices: Floating Rates and the Alternatives

Parts III and IV examined many aspects of international economic and financial performance. This chapter provides a capstone for the construct by exploring the issues that surround countries' choices of policies toward the exchange rate.

What exchange rate policy should a country use? Should it use a clean float in which private supply and demand determine the exchange rate? Should it commit to a fixed rate that it defends and attempts never to change? Should it generally use a floating, market-driven exchange rate but manage that rate to try to modify the market outcome some of the time? Should it use a fixed rate but be willing from time to time, or perhaps even quite frequently, to change the pegged-rate value?

Each country must choose its policy. The analysis of Parts III and IV provides a broad range of insights into the economics of this choice. This chapter pulls these insights together by exploring the key issues to consider. We will see that the issues suggest that each policy has both strengths and weaknesses, so different countries might wisely choose different policies.

The composite of all countries' choices results in the global exchange rate system. As we noted in Chapter 19, at times in the past century countries have created a coherent global regime around a single policy—fixing to gold during the gold standard, and the adjustable pegged system based on the U.S. dollar that we call the Bretton Woods system. At other times countries have made more varied choices, so characterizing the system during those times is not so easy. For instance, the period between the two world wars did not have a dominant policy, especially after the attempt to return to the gold standard broke down in the early 1930s.

In the current period different countries use different exchange rate policies. Our analysis provides insights into their choices and into the general trend toward floating exchange rates. After discussing this trend, the chapter takes a look at three paths in the opposite direction, toward fixed exchange rates that are (nearly) permanent. The members of the European Union are on the most far-reaching of these paths, to a monetary union with a single European currency.

KEY ISSUES IN THE CHOICE OF EXCHANGE RATE POLICY

A country must choose its exchange rate policy from a menu of many alternatives. The aspect of the policy that we examine is the extent of flexibility that is permitted by the policy. On the one side is a policy that permits substantial flexibility, with a rate that is floating and largely (if not completely) market-driven. The polar case here is a cleanly floating exchange rate, but a lightly managed floating rate also fits the type. On the other side is a policy that fixes or pegs the exchange rate value of the country's currency to a major foreign currency or a basket of foreign currencies.[1] A permanently fixed exchange rate is the polar case, but we should keep in mind that it is impossible for a country to commit never to change its policy.

Our previous analysis suggests that five major issues can influence the country's choice: the effects of macroeconomic shocks; the effectiveness of government policies; differences in macroeconomic goals, priorities, and policies; controlling inflation; and the real effects of exchange rate variability. Let's look at each major issue and what it says about the advantages and disadvantages of floating or fixing. Figure 24.1 provides a road map that you can use as you read through this section of the chapter.

Effects of Macroeconomic Shocks

The analysis of Chapters 22 and 23 has shown that the effects of various macroeconomic shocks depend on the exchange rate policy adopted by the country.[2] A country would look favorably on an exchange rate policy that reduced the domestic effects of macroeconomic shocks. The performance of the country's economy is better if shocks are less disruptive because the economy is more stable. Our analysis indicates that the effects of various macroeconomic shocks depend not only on the exchange rate policy but also on the type of shock.

Internal shocks generally cause less trouble with a fixed rate than with a float.

---

[1] The country could also choose to fix the value of its currency to a commodity like gold. The box "What Role for Gold?" explores this possibility.

[2] Most of our discussion here continues to make the assumptions that product prices are rather sticky in the short run, but that they do adjust to spending and monetary pressures in the long run. The discussion of the effects of shocks focuses on the short and medium runs, when shocks can cause cyclical movements in spending, production, and unemployment. In addition, our discussion of macroeconomic effects under fixed exchange rates focuses on the case in which the government does not or cannot sterilize, so the intervention does affect the domestic money supply.

FIGURE 24.1   Advantages of Floating Exchange Rates and Fixed Exchange Rates in Terms of Various Issues

Issue	Advantage of Floating Exchange Rates	Advantage of Fixed Exchange Rates
Effects of macroeconomic shocks	With floating rates external shocks, especially foreign trade shocks, are less disruptive.	With fixed rates internal shocks, especially domestic monetary shocks, are less disruptive.
Effectiveness of government policies	With floating rates monetary policy is more effective in influencing aggregate demand.	—
	With floating rates fiscal policy is more effective if capital flows are not very responsive to interest rates.	With fixed rates fiscal policy is more effective if capital flows are sufficiently responsive to interest rates.
Differences in macroeconomic goals and policies	Floating rates allow goals and policies to differ across countries	Fixed rates require coordination or consistency of goals and policies across countries.
Controlling inflation	Floating rates allow each country to choose its own acceptable inflation rate.	With fixed rates countries should have about the same inflation rates. This creates a discipline effect on high-inflation countries (but low-inflation countries may "import" higher inflation).
Real effects of exchange rate variability	Variability of floating rates is desirable. It shows that the market is working well as supply and demand shift. The rates reflect unstable economic and political environments. Real effects on international trade are not that large because much exchange rate risk can be hedged.	Variability of floating rates, especially between the major currencies, is excessive. The rates may be driven at times by bandwagons and speculative bubbles. The variability causes undesirable real effects. Exchange rate risk lowers trade volumes. Overshooting causes excessive resource shifts into and out of trade-oriented industries.
	A fixed rate is simply a form of price control. The fixed rate value is often inefficiently low or high, causing inefficient resource allocations.	The relative stability of fixed rates may promote higher levels of international transactions, especially trade.

Case Study   What Role for Gold?

Gold was at the center of the international monetary system during the gold standard. As we discussed in Chapter 19, individuals had the right to obtain or sell gold (in exchange for national currency) with the country's central bank at the fixed official gold price. Gold was also an important part of the Bretton Woods system of fixed exchange rates. The U.S. government was expected to buy or sell gold to foreign central banks (but not to individuals) at the official U.S. dollar price of gold.

What is the role for gold now? Gold remains an official reserve asset, but currently central banks make almost no official use of gold. Gold is also held by private individuals as part of their investments. Let's look at both the official role and private role for gold more closely.

OFFICIAL ROLE: THE ONCE AND FUTURE KING?

You shall not crucify mankind upon a cross of gold.

William Jennings Bryan, U.S. presidential candidate, 1896

Most observers of the current system are comfortable with the lack of a role for gold in official international activity. Indeed, some believe that central banks and the International Monetary Fund should sell off their current official holdings of gold. One reason to sell is that gold plays no active role and earns no interest. The part of national wealth (or IMF assets) held in gold could be invested more productively. Another reason is that the proceeds of gold sales could be used for assistance to the poorer countries of the world. Central banks and the IMF have made some gold sales into the private market in recent decades (a process called *demonetization of gold*), and they plan to continue gold sales.

A small group of people are strong advocates of a return to a real gold standard in which countries tie their currencies to gold. These proponents believe that a return to a gold standard would greatly reduce national and average global rates of inflation by creating a strong discipline effect on countries' abilities to expand their money supplies. They also believe that a return to a gold standard would eliminate the variability of exchange rates by establishing full confidence in the system and by enforcing monetary adjustments to achieve external balance. By creating stability and confidence in national moneys and exchange rates, they believe that the return to a gold standard would stabilize and lower both nominal and real interest rates.

Most international economists oppose a return to the gold standard. To most, a gold standard is not nearly as stabilizing as its proponents claim, except perhaps in the very long run. The supply of new gold to the world is governed not by some master regulator, but rather by mining activities. A major discovery of new minable gold deposits leads to a rapid expansion of the world gold supply. As central banks buy gold to defend the fixed gold prices, national money supplies would expand rapidly and inflation rates would increase. On the other hand, if there are no new discoveries, and if current mines slow output as mines are exhausted (or if major strikes or similar disruptions slow output), national central banks would have to sell gold to defend its price (assuming that private demand continues to grow). National money supplies would shrink, and countries would enter into painful deflations (with weak economic conditions forcing price levels lower).

Looking at the other side of the market for gold, decreases in private demand for gold would require central banks to buy gold to defend its price, expanding money supplies. Increases in private demand would force central banks to sell gold, shrinking national money supplies.

Supply swings were evident even during the classical gold standard. Between 1873 and 1896, the British price level fell by about one-third, and it then inflated back up from 1896 to 1913. These shifts were closely related to changes in the growth rates of world stocks of monetary gold, and these were closely related to cycles in mining driven by gold discoveries.

Between 1850 and 1873, the world gold stock grew by 2.9 percent per year, with discoveries leading to mining booms in California and Australia. This permitted money supplies to keep up with the growing real demand for money, so that price levels remained about steady. Between 1873 and 1896, the world gold stock grew by only 1.7 percent per year. This was not enough to keep up with continued growth in real money demand, and the price level was forced down. Then from 1896 to 1913, new discoveries of gold led to mining booms in the Klondike (Canada) and the Transvaal (South Africa). The world gold stock rose 3.2 percent per year, faster than real money demand was growing, so the price level increased. With such fluctuations in the growth of monetary gold, it is difficult to claim that the gold standard ensured steady expansion of the world money base (although the gold standard did limit money growth and inflation in the long run).

Because a gold standard probably would not be nearly as stable as its proponents claim, most international economists oppose a return to a gold standard. Bolstering their belief are the more typical arguments about the advantages of flexible or floating exchange rates, including independence in choosing priorities and using policies. In addition, the resource costs of

expanding official gold reserves is itself high. New gold must be mined. This seems to be an inefficient use of resources, to produce something that will largely sit in the vaults of central banks.

PRIVATE ROLE: A SOUND INVESTMENT?

The official link between gold and currencies effectively ended in 1968, and it seems unlikely to be revived. Even though its official role has largely ended, should gold play a role in the investments of private individuals? Holding gold pays no interest, so the return to gold comes from increases in its price. (The return earned is actually lower than the price increase suggests, because of the costs of buying and selling as well as the costs of storing and safekeeping.)

The accompanying graph shows the monthly dollar price of gold since 1970. There are three lessons from this graph. First, anyone who bought gold in the early 1970s earned a high rate of return through 1980, as the dollar price increased from under $100 per ounce to over $600 per ounce. This increase far exceeded general price inflation or the rates of return available on most financial assets.

Source: International Monetary Fund, *International Financial Statistics.*

—Continued on next page

Second, anyone who bought gold since 1980 would generally be disappointed. The typical price of gold stayed below $400 between 1982 and 1997, and it fell below $300 in 1998. The gold price has not kept up with broad price inflation, and it has underperformed compared to the returns available on many financial assets like stocks and bonds.

Third, far from being stable, or tracking general price inflation as an "inflation hedge," the gold price has fluctuated a lot. It soared during 1979–1980, falling back during 1980–1982, rose strongly during 1982, and so forth.

Why has the price of gold jumped around so much during the past several decades? Shifts in supply have some impact, and the depressed gold price since early 1998 seems to reflect the expectation that central banks and the IMF will continue their sales of gold into the private market. Still, pressure often comes from shifts in demand. To a large extent gold is what frightened people invest in. Suppose you are wealthy and live in an unstable region of the world. Clandestine gold ownership can protect you from having your assets seized or heavily taxed. Or suppose you fear an explosion of inflation. Holding real assets like gold provides at least some protection against the loss of purchasing power that will afflict most paper assets. These demands increase and decrease as fears and tensions rise and subside.

Thus, private investments in gold are bets about the future course of gold prices. Over the long term the price of gold has roughly kept up with the rise of general prices (though past performance is no indicator of future performance). But for any short- or medium-term period of time, gold's value is anybody's guess. For a commodity that symbolizes stability, unpredictable shifts in demand and supply can and do cause large swings in gold's real price.

A *domestic monetary shock* is less disruptive with a fixed exchange rate because the intervention to defend the fixed rate tends to reverse the shock and its effects. With a floating exchange rate the resulting change in the exchange rate would actually magnify the domestic effects of the monetary shock. For example, consider what happens if the demand for holding money increases unexpectedly, perhaps because people become wary of using credit cards and begin to pay more often with cash. The extra money demand increases domestic interest rates and reduces domestic product by discouraging interest-sensitive spending. The country's overall balance of payments tends toward surplus, as the capital account improves because of increased capital inflows and the current account improves because of lower domestic spending and demand for imports.

1. With a fixed exchange rate, the country's central bank must intervene to prevent the country's currency from appreciating. As the central bank sells domestic currency, the intervention increases the domestic money supply. (Recall the analysis of Chapter 22.) The extra money demand is now met by an increased money supply, and interest rates can fall back toward their original level. The fall in interest rates spurs a recovery of interest-sensitive spending and domestic product.

2. With a floating exchange rate, the tendency toward surplus causes the domestic currency to appreciate, reducing the country's international price com-

petitiveness. (Recall the analysis of Chapter 23.) As exports decline and imports rise in response to the shift in price competitiveness, the effect of the shock on the domestic economy is magnified. Domestic product tends to decline more.

The effects of a *domestic spending shock,* such as an unexpected change in real domestic investment spending or in consumption spending, or a sudden shift in fiscal policy, depend on how responsive international flows of financial capital are to interest rate changes. If capital is not responsive, then domestic spending shocks are also less disruptive with fixed rates than with floating rates. For instance, a decline in domestic spending tends to improve the country's current account balance as the demand for imports declines. If this is the dominant effect, the country's overall international payments also tend toward surplus. As in the monetary example, the payments surplus results in intervention that expands the domestic money supply if the country has a fixed exchange rate, and this tends to expand domestic spending, stabilizing the economy to some extent. With a floating exchange rate, the appreciation of the currency tends to lower demand and production further. Of course, if capital is highly responsive, then the reverse is true—domestic spending shocks are more disruptive with fixed rates.

For *external shocks,* we reach opposite conclusions about stability and disruption. We can see this most clearly for *international trade shocks.* Suppose that foreign demand for our exports declines (or, for that matter, that our country's demand shifts toward imported foreign products and away from the comparable domestic products). The decrease in demand for our products tends to put the economy into a recession. In addition, the country's current account balance tends to deteriorate, and this tends to worsen the country's overall payments balance. With a fixed exchange rate, the central bank must intervene to defend the fixed rate by buying domestic currency. The resulting contraction of the domestic money supply reinforces the initial contraction of demand for our products, adding to the recession. With a floating exchange rate, the tendency to deficit depreciates the value of our currency. The improvement in price competitiveness boosts demand for our products, countering the recession tendency.

The effects of foreign trade shocks are important because changes in foreign trade are a major way in which business cycles are transmitted from one country to another. With fixed exchange rates business cycles are transmitted through foreign trade and foreign repercussions, and the intervention to defend the fixed rate can magnify the transmission. With floating exchange rates the transmission is muted because exchange rate changes tend to insulate the economy from foreign trade shocks.

International trade shocks are particularly important for small developing countries, which are frequently affected by changes in the world prices (stated in foreign currency) of their exportable products. Christian Broda (2002) examines the effects of a 10 percent decrease in the price a developing country's exports. He confirms that a floating exchange rate buffers the effects on the country. For a typical developing country that has a fixed exchange rate, the decline in the country's terms of trade causes a sharp decline of real GDP of about 2 percent in two years. For a typical developing country with a floating exchange rate, the two-year decrease in real GDP is only 0.2 percent. With a floating exchange rate, a quick nominal depreciation of the country's currency results in a 5 percent decrease in the real exchange rate value of the country's currency. The country's enhanced price competitiveness increases exports and decreases imports, so the tendency toward declining GDP is offset.

International capital-flow shocks have domestic effects under both fixed and floating exchange rates, but there is a sense in which they are less disruptive under floating exchange rates. With a fixed exchange rate, an adverse capital-flow shift, which results in a capital outflow, requires intervention to defend the fixed rate by buying domestic currency. The reduction in the domestic money supply (if the intervention is not sterilized) has an adverse effect on the economy by raising interest rates and reducing spending. Under floating exchange rates, the currency depreciates. Any adverse effect that the capital outflow itself might have on the country's production is countered by the improvement in trade that results from better international price competitiveness.

The differences in the effects of shocks on the economy can have an impact on a country's choice of exchange rate policy. If the country believes that it is buffeted mainly by internal shocks, the country would favor a fixed exchange rate. If it believes that most shocks are external, then it would favor a floating exchange rate.

However, we also must add a caution to this conclusion. While its conceptual basis is clear, its practical importance is actually debatable for several reasons. The most important reason is that the effects of shocks under fixed exchange rates depend on whether interventions are sterilized. The previous discussion has assumed that intervention is not sterilized. If, instead, the intervention is sterilized, the domestic money supply does not change. This reduces the stabilizing properties of fixed rates when internal shocks hit the economy, and it also reduces the disruptive effects when external shocks hit. (Of course, continued sterilization may not be feasible if the payments imbalance persists, but the short-run behavior is still altered.)

The Effectiveness of Government Policies

Chapters 22 and 23 showed that government policies' influence on aggregate demand and domestic product is altered by the type of exchange rate policy chosen by the country. Monetary policy loses its control over the money supply if the country has a fixed exchange rate because monetary policy is constrained by the need to defend the fixed exchange rate. If the country tries to implement an expansionary monetary policy, the payments balance tends to go into deficit, and intervention to defend the fixed rate reduces the domestic money supply and reverses the monetary expansion. Indeed, if the country has a payments deficit for any reason, the intervention reduces the domestic money supply. If instead the country tries to implement a contractionary monetary policy, the payments balance tends to go into surplus, and the intervention to defend the fixed rate increases the domestic money supply and reverses the monetary contraction. In fact, a payments surplus for any reason expands the domestic money supply.

The country's monetary authority can attempt to regain some control over domestic monetary policy by sterilizing to reverse the effect of the intervention on the money supply, but there is a limit to how long it can continue to sterilize. Indeed, if international capital is highly or perfectly mobile, sterilized intervention cannot work. With perfect capital mobility, a country that is committed to defending a fixed exchange rate loses it power to have an independent monetary policy (because its monetary policy, such as it is, must be directed to defending the fixed exchange rate). The impossibility for a country to maintain a fixed exchange rate, to permit free capital flows, and to have a monetary policy directed toward domestic objectives is often called the *inconsistent trinity*.

Monetary policy gains effectiveness under floating exchange rates. The resulting change in the exchange rate reinforces the thrust of the policy change. A shift to expansionary monetary policy results in a depreciation of the country's currency. The improvement in price competitiveness further expands demand for the country's products. A shift to contractionary policy appreciates the country's currency, resulting in a further reduction in demand for the country's products.

The effectiveness of fiscal policy depends on how responsive international capital flows are to interest rates. If capital is highly mobile, then fiscal policy gains effectiveness under fixed rates. The intervention to defend the fixed rate reduces the change in domestic interest rates, so that there is less domestic crowding out. With floating exchange rates and highly mobile capital, fiscal policy loses effectiveness. The resulting exchange rate change leads to international crowding out. If capital is not that mobile, or if capital flows decline beyond a short-run period, the reverse is true. Fiscal policy then loses effectiveness with a fixed exchange rate and gains effectiveness with a floating rate.

The country's choice of exchange rate policy can be influenced by its impact on the effectiveness of fiscal policy. A country whose capital markets are closely linked to the rest of the world, so that capital is highly mobile, will view a fixed exchange rate more favorably if it wants fiscal policy to be highly effective in the short run. A country whose capital flows are less responsive, or one that is worried about the effectiveness of fiscal policy beyond the short-run period when capital flows are responding, will look more favorably on floating rates.

While the impact of fiscal policy effectiveness on the choice of exchange rate policy is conditional, the impact of monetary policy effectiveness is straightforward. *If a country desires to use monetary policy to address domestic objectives, then the country will favor a floating exchange rate.* A floating rate frees monetary policy from the need to defend the exchange rate.

Differences in Macroeconomic Goals, Priorities, and Policies

Government policymakers in each country must decide on the goals and objectives of macroeconomic policy. Even if countries generally pursue the same set of macroeconomic performance goals—including real economic growth, low unemployment, low inflation, and external balance—the priorities that governments place on the goals can differ, as can the specific policies adopted to achieve the goals.

For fixed exchange rates between the currencies of two or more countries to be successful, a kind of consistency or coordination between the countries involved is necessary. A country choosing a fixed exchange rate must follow policies that permit successful defense of the rate, given the policies and performance of the other countries linked by the fixed rates. If the policies diverge noticeably, large payments imbalances are likely to develop, making the defense of the fixed rates difficult or impossible.

One example is that countries should be willing to refrain from policy changes that lead to large international capital flows, or coordinate such changes in policies across countries. For instance, a big reduction in the taxes that one country imposes on financial investments can lead to large international capital flows into the country. If the other countries must intervene to defend the fixed rates as capital flows out of their countries, their international reserve holdings decline, threatening their ability to continue to defend the fixed rates. To maintain fixed rates, the first country may need to temper policy changes such as this. Or the other countries may need to adopt their own policy changes to mute the incentives for capital flows. For instance, the other countries could also lower their taxes on financial investments, or they could raise their interest rates. These changes would create a kind of consistency or coordination that reduces the threat to the viability of the fixed-rate system.

Another example is the priority that each country places on controlling inflation, or the trade-off that each country is willing to make between inflation and unemployment. For instance, during the years of the Bretton Woods system, Germany and Switzerland placed the highest priority on maintaining a very low inflation rate. The United States was less concerned with inflation and more concerned with growth and employment. Even if there is no long-run trade-off between inflation and unemployment, such differences in priorities can still influence policy in the short run. The United States was willing to risk somewhat higher inflation to reduce unemployment in the short run, while Germany and Switzerland were not. The United States ended up with a higher inflation rate than Germany or Switzerland, and neither side was willing to compromise to achieve consistency. The fixed rates could not be maintained. We examine the relationship of inflation rates and exchange rate policy in more depth in the next subsection.

Floating exchange rates are tolerant of diversity in countries' goals, priorities, and policies. As long as the country is willing to let the exchange rate change according to market pressures, external balance in the country's overall payments is maintained whatever the country's policies. International policy coordination is still possible across countries, as we discussed in the previous chapter, but it is not necessary. There is no doubt that floating exchange rates permit a country to be more independent in its choices of policies, but we should also be a little cautious with this proposition. Policymakers in a country often are concerned about movements in the exchange rate value of the country's currency, so their policy choices are somewhat constrained even with floating rates. For instance, in the early 1980s unemployment rates were high in a number of the major European countries.

However, they did not shift to expansionary policies because their currencies were already weak against the dollar. In fact, they tightened up and raised their interest rates to prevent their currencies from weakening further.

Controlling Inflation

The relationship between the choice of exchange rate policy and a country's inflation rate is an important issue for the country. In addition, this issue has broad meaning for global macroeconomic performance, especially for the average rate of global inflation.

Countries that choose to fix the exchange rates among their currencies are committing to have similar inflation rates over the long run. This is the prediction of purchasing power parity—a nominal exchange rate can be steady only if the difference in inflation rates between the countries is about zero. The logic is based on the need to maintain reasonable price competitiveness for the products of each country. If inflation rates are consistently different over a substantial period of time, and exchange rates are fixed, a low-inflation country would steadily gain international price competitiveness, leading to current account surpluses. A high-inflation country would steadily lose price competitiveness, leading to deficits. These continuing and growing surpluses and deficits are not sustainable, and something would need to adjust. The inflation rate in the low-inflation country could increase, the inflation rate in the high-inflation country could decrease, or the exchange rate could change. If inflation rates change, then the fixed rate can be maintained, but the inflation difference instead could result in surrender of the fixed rate.

A number of implications follow from the conclusion that countries that fix their exchange rates should have similar inflation rates. First, proponents of fixed rates argue that fixed rates create a discipline effect on national tendencies to run high inflation rates. *For the fixed rate to be sustained, a country cannot have an inflation rate that is much above the inflation rate(s) of its partner(s).*[3] In fact, a country embarking on a serious effort to reduce its high inflation rate may deliberately choose to fix its currency to the currency of another country that has a lower inflation rate. The high-inflation country is using the discipline effect as part of its anti-inflation program. The high-inflation country hopes that the peg to the other country's currency can establish the credibility of its anti-inflation program. If it can gain credibility, it has a greater chance of success because people will lower their estimate of how much inflation will occur in the future. If inflation expectations are lowered, then it is easier to lower actual inflation and keep it low. Argentina used this strategy successfully in the early 1990s. In 1989, prices in Argentina rose by about 3,000 percent; in 1990, they climbed by about 2,300 percent. Argentina began an anti-inflation program and, in 1991, fixed the value

---

[3] There is a limit to this discipline effect. Rather than reducing its inflation rate, the country instead can change its exchange rate, devaluing or switching to a floating exchange rate.

of peso to the U.S. dollar. The discipline of this peg helped to reduce the growth rate of the money supply and the inflation rate in Argentina. By 1994, Argentinean inflation was about 4 percent, nearly the same as that in the United States, and it remained close to zero through the rest of the 1990s.

Second, a fixed-rate system in which most countries participate may also impose **price discipline** to lower the average global rate of price inflation. The fixed-rate system puts more pressure on governments whose countries have international deficits than on governments that have surpluses:

- Deficit countries face an obvious limit on their ability to sustain deficits; they soon run out of reserves and creditworthiness. Even if they attempt to sterilize their interventions, they must tighten up on their money supplies fairly quickly if they are to maintain the fixed rate. This forces them to contract, which lowers their money growth and inflation rate.

- Surplus countries, in contrast, face only more distant and manageable inconveniences from perennial surpluses. As long as they are willing to accumulate additional official reserves, they should be able to use sterilized intervention for an extended period.

Thus, the deficit countries tend to lower their money growth, while the surplus countries tend not to raise theirs. Overall *there is less money growth in the world and a lower average inflation rate.*

With the price discipline of fixed exchange rates, there is a greater chance that countries have similar inflation and that the average inflation rate may be somewhat lower than the average that each country would choose on its own. If the system has a leading country, such as the United States in Bretton Woods, then countries tend to have to match the inflation rate of this lead country. For countries that would have had a higher inflation rate, the system is imposing a discipline effect. But other countries might prefer an even lower inflation rate.

This observation leads to the third implication. With fixed exchange rates, a country that prefers to have a lower inflation rate than that of other countries, especially the lead country in the system, will have difficulty maintaining this low inflation rate. It will tend to "import inflation" from the other countries. Germany complained of this pressure in the 1960s as the inflation rate in the United States rose.

In contrast to all of this, *floating exchange rates simply permit countries to have different inflation rates.* According to purchasing power parity, high-inflation countries tend to have depreciating currencies, and low-inflation countries tend to have appreciating currencies. The nominal exchange rate changes maintain reasonable price competitiveness for both types of countries in the long run. Proponents of floating rates generally view this as a virtue. Different countries' policymakers may have different beliefs as to what an acceptable inflation rate is. These beliefs may be the result of historic events, such as the hyperinflation of the 1920s in Germany that has resulted in a strong German preference for very low inflation. Or they may be the result of a series of decisions about acceptable trade-offs of a little more inflation in order to reduce unemployment. This was the situation of the United States in the 1970s, and it resulted in rather high inflation. Or the government may choose to "finance" its large budget deficit by printing money (rather than by borrowing through the issue of government bonds). The rapid money growth leads to high rates of inflation. This has been the case in some developing countries.

Opponents of floating exchange rates suggest that the ability of each country to choose its own policies toward inflation results in more inflation worldwide. The exchange rate does not impose any discipline on money growth and inflation. Instead, with floating exchange rates a country can be caught in a vicious circle in which (1) high inflation leads to currency depreciation and (2) the depreciation increases the domestic currency prices of imports so the high inflation rate is reinforced. Continuing high inflation requires further depreciation and so forth. Domestic money growth simply accommodates this dynamic.

The world experience in the first decade after the shift to general floating in 1973 seemed to be consistent with the concerns of these opponents of floating rates. Average world inflation in the 1970s was substantially higher than it had been in the 1950s or 1960s. The seeds for some of this higher inflation had been sown, especially in the United States, beginning in the fixed-rate 1960s. In addition, the two oil shocks of the 1970s presumably would have resulted in higher average inflation even if exchange rates had remained fixed. Nonetheless, some of the higher inflation was probably the result of the removal of the discipline of fixed rates.

The world experience since the early 1980s indicates that the tendency toward higher inflation with floating rates actually may not be a serious problem. The inflation rates in many of the major countries whose currencies have generally been floating—including Japan, the United States, and Britain—fell noticeably and remain low. Since the early 1990s, inflation rates in most developing countries have also been low. The experience since the early 1980s indicates that *what really matters in controlling national inflation rates is the discipline and resolve of the national monetary authorities.*

Real Effects of Exchange Rate Variability

A major concern about floating exchange rates is that they are highly variable. Some variability presumably is not controversial, including exchange rate movements that offset inflation rate differentials and exchange rate movements that promote an orderly adjustment to shocks. However, the substantial variability of exchange rates within fairly short time periods like months or a few years is more controversial. What are the possible effects of exchange rate variability that might concern us?

If the variability simply creates unexpected gains and losses for short-term financial investors who deliberately take positions exposed to exchange rate risk, we probably would not be much concerned. However, we would be concerned if heightened exchange rate risk discourages such international activities as trade in goods and services or foreign direct investment. Exchange rate variability then would have *real effects,* by altering activities in the part of the economy that produces goods and services.

Consider international trade in goods and services. Does exchange rate variability create risk that leads to lower volumes of trade? First, simple short-run variability may have little direct impact on trade activities. Anyone engaged in international trade has a range of foreign exchange contracts, including forward foreign exchange, currency futures, and currency options, that can be used to hedge exposures to exchange rate risk in the short run, at least for the major currencies in the world. These contracts can be obtained with low transactions costs. Second, exchange rate variability beyond the short run can affect the real investments that must be made to support export-oriented production. If exchange rate variability raises the riskiness of these real investments, they tend to be lower if firms are risk-averse. This form of exchange rate risk is more difficult to hedge because (1) longer maturities of many contracts do not exist or are rather expensive to buy and (2) the specific amounts of payments that might need to be hedged several years in the future are themselves often highly uncertain.

Economists have studied the overall effect of increased exchange rate risk on the volumes of international trade activities. Early studies typically found almost no effect of exchange rate variability on trade volumes. Some more recent studies have found negative effects, although the effects generally are estimated to be rather small.

Overshooting raises another concern about the real effects of the variability of floating exchange rates. When exchange rates overshoot (as discussed in Chapters 18 and 23), they send signals about changes in international price competitiveness that seem to some observers to be far too strong. Big swings in price competitiveness create incentives for large shifts in real resources. If overshooting leads to a large appreciation of the country's currency (for instance, the U.S. dollar in the early 1980s), this creates the incentive for labor to move out of export-oriented and import-competing industries, as the country loses a large amount of price competitiveness. New capital investment in these industries is strongly discouraged, and some existing facilities are shut down. However, as the overshooting then reverses itself, these resource movements appear to have been excessive. Resources then must move back into these industries.

Relative price adjustments are an important and necessary part of the market system. They signal the need for resource reallocations. The concern here is not with relative price changes in general. The concern is with the possibility that the dynamics of floating exchange rates sometimes send false price signals or signals that are too strong, resulting in excessive resource reallocations.

This discussion of exchange rate variability and the real effects of this variability leads into a broader debate. Proponents and defenders of floating exchange rates agree that variability has been high, and that some real effects occur. But they believe that this is what markets should do. Exchange rates as prices send signals about the relative values of currencies. These signals represent the summary of information about the currencies that is available at that time. As economic and political conditions change, the prices and signals should change. The variability of exchange rates represents the ongoing market-based quest for economic efficiency.

The proponents of floating rates believe that the supporters of fixed rates delude themselves by claiming that the lack of variability of fixed rates is a virtue. A fixed exchange rate is simply a form of *price control.* Price controls are generally inefficient because the price is often too high or too low. That is, with a fixed rate the country's currency is often overvalued or undervalued by government fiat.

In addition, a fixed rate is sometimes changed, often suddenly and by a large amount, when the peg is adjusted through a devaluation or a revaluation. This *sudden change* can be highly disruptive, and it often occurs in a crisis atmosphere brought on by large capital flows as speculators believe that they have a one-way speculative gamble on the direction of the exchange rate change. In addition, as we saw in Chapter 20, with the comfort of a fixed exchange rate, financial institutions and others in the country that borrow foreign currencies can ignore or underestimate their exposure to exchange rate risk. They do not hedge their currency risk exposure. When a devaluation occurs, their losses can contribute to a deep financial crisis for the country.

Detractors and opponents of floating exchange rates believe that floating exchange rates are *excessively variable,* and that this variability has real effects that are inefficient. Some of these detractors view the variability of floating rates as excessive because the exchange rates themselves are sometimes inefficient, as they are affected by speculative bandwagons and bubbles that do not reflect the underlying economic fundamentals. Other detractors, while conceding that floating exchange rates are reasonably efficient prices from the point of view of their function within the international *financial* system, believe that exchange rates set in this way do not serve the *broader economy* well. Variability and overshooting may have a logic in international finance, but they nonetheless cause undesirable real effects like discouragement of international trade and excessive resource shifts.

To these opponents, with floating exchange rates the market often undervalues or overvalues a country's currency, at least in relation to the signals that should be sent to the goods-and-services part of the economy. Exchange rates should make transactions between countries as smooth and easy as possible. To the opponents of floating rates, exchange rates, like money, serve their transactions functions best when their values are *stable.*

NATIONAL CHOICES

We have just examined five major issues that can affect a country's choice of its exchange rate policy. Each country must make its own decision, and that decision depends on the balancing of a number of factors, including the economic issues explored here as well as political concerns. While each country will have its own important issues because of its own economic and political situation, we can nonetheless discern in our set of five issues several factors that are likely to be of major importance for most countries.

There are several strong arguments in favor of a country adopting a floating exchange rate. First, a floating exchange rate provides more effective use of two important tools for adjusting toward internal and external balances. Exchange rate changes can promote adjustment to external balance, and monetary policy can be directed toward achieving internal balance because it does not need to be directed toward defending the exchange rate. Second, a floating exchange rate permits a country to pursue goals, priorities, and policies that meet its own domestic preferences and needs, with less concern about how these will put pressure on the exchange rate. Third, the country does not need to defend a fixed rate against speculative attacks, a task that is increasingly difficult as large amounts of internationally mobile capital can be shifted quickly from country to country.

The strongest argument against a country adopting a floating exchange rate is that floating rates have been disturbingly variable since 1973. This variability increases exchange rate risk, and this risk does seem to have some effect in discouraging international activities such as trade in goods and services. In addition, overshooting of floating exchange rates may have promoted too much adjustment into or out of trade-oriented production from time to time. A major advantage of fixed rates is the substantial reduction in variability and exchange rate risk if the fixed rate can be defended and the peg is not adjusted too often.

In Chapter 19 we presented countries' current choices of exchange rate policy. We saw that a growing number of countries use some form of floating-rate policy. The world has been shifting toward floating exchange rates. The advantages of independence in crafting and using policies to attain domestic objectives make the choice of a floating exchange rate increasingly attractive. Put the other way, an increasing number of governments are unwilling to subordinate money supply, interest rates, and other policies to defending a fixed exchange rate.

The governments of these countries generally do not adopt the polar case of a clean float. Rather, they use some form of management of the float. While they like the advantages of adopting a floating exchange rate, they are also worried about the variability of floating rates. Through management of the float, the government attempts to moderate wide swings without becoming chained to a fixed rate that would give speculators a clear one-way bet at times.

There are still questions about the management of the float. A government can make mistakes, or act out of political motives, so that the government is attempting to resist exchange rate trends that are justified by the economic fundamentals. There are also questions about how effective the management can be, at least for the exchange rate values of the major currencies. Intervention often seems to have little impact on the floating rate, and even with management the floating rates are still substantially variable. For many countries, a managed floating exchange rate seems to be a reasonable compromise choice. It gains much of the policy independence while offering governments some ability to reduce exchange rate variability.

While the global trend is toward floating, a number of countries continue to maintain fixed exchange rates. For most of these countries, the compelling argument is that floating exchange rates are too variable. A number of these countries are smaller countries that fix to the currency of a major trading partner (or to a basket of currencies of major trading partners). For these countries reducing exchange rate risk to promote smooth trade and avoiding overshooting that would disrupt their trade-oriented industries seem to be the major objectives in choosing an exchange rate policy. These countries are willing to sacrifice some economic policy autonomy to obtain exchange rate stability.

However, a fixed exchange rate that is adjustable—a *soft peg* that provides substantial leeway for the country's monetary authority to change or abandon the fixed value—sometimes invites attack through a one-way speculative gamble if the country is reasonably open to international capital flows. Such a speculative attack can all but force the monetary authority to surrender, as in Mexico in late 1994, in Thailand, Indonesia, and South Korea in 1997, in Brazil in early 1999, and in Turkey in 2001. In response, some countries have adopted or are considering arrangements that create more permanent fixes (often called *hard pegs*).

EXTREME FIXES

The general trend in national exchange rate policies is toward greater flexibility. But some countries have moved in the opposite direction—to exchange rates that are not only fixed but also rather difficult or nearly impossible to change. In this section we examine currency boards and "dollarization," two "extreme" forms of fixed rates that can be adopted by a single country. In the final section of the chapter we examine what may be the ultimate form of fixed rates—a monetary union among several countries that agree to a single unionwide currency.

Currency Board

A **currency board** attempts to establish a fixed exchange rate that is long-lived by mandating that the board, acting as the country's monetary authority, should focus almost exclusively on maintaining the fixed rate. A currency board holds only foreign-currency assets (official reserve assets). The board issues domestic currency liabilities only in exchange for foreign currency assets that it acquires. Because the board owns no domestic-currency assets, it has no ability to sterilize. This arrangement increases the credibility of a country's commitment to maintaining the fixed exchange rate by automatically linking the domestic money supply to the defense of the fixed rate. For instance, if increased private selling is putting downward pressure on the exchange-rate value of the country's currency, the currency board defends the fixed rate by buying domestic currency and selling foreign currency. As the board buys domestic currency, the domestic money supply decreases. This money supply decrease sets in motion the adjustments discussed at length in Chapter 22, and the currency board has no power to resist. With no domestic assets, the currency board cannot sterilize the intervention— the domestic money supply must decrease.

Several very small countries have had currency boards since before 1970, and Hong Kong established one in 1983 to defend the value of its dollar. During the

1990s, four transition countries—Estonia, Lithuania, Bulgaria, and Bosnia/Herzegovina—established currency boards. Argentina set up a currency board in 1991, and abandoned the board amid the turmoil of its 2002 financial crisis.

The experience of Argentina shows the advantages and disadvantages of a currency board. Argentina's government established a currency board to signal its commitment to stop the country's hyperinflation, by imposing strict discipline to limit the growth of Argentina's money supply. As we saw earlier in the chapter, this effort was successful in its early years. With inflation quickly reduced, interest rates decreased, and economic growth increased. After almost no growth of its real GDP during the 1980s, Argentina's real growth averaged nearly 4 percent during 1992–1998.

However, the Argentinean economy was vulnerable to adverse external shocks. The fallout from the Mexican peso crisis caused a recession during 1995. In this period of foreign financial turmoil, international investors pulled back from investments in Argentina, its money supply shrank, and its interest rates increased. In addition, concerns about whether Argentina would maintain its fixed rate led to speculative outflows that further decreased Argentina's money supply. In the mid-1990s Argentina did stick with its currency board and the fixed dollar–peso exchange rate, but probably at the cost of a deeper recession.

Argentina experienced the same pressures in the late 1990s because of the series of crises in Asia, Russia, and Brazil. As we saw in Chapter 20, this time the outcome was bad. A deep recession began in 1998 and persisted. Other shortcomings of its government policies, including a lack of fiscal discipline, overregulation, and corruption, interacted with the recession. After rather desperate attempts to shore up the currency board arrangement by preventing people from using their bank accounts, the government gave up and shifted to a floating exchange rate. Argentina by then was in the middle of a severe financial and economic crisis.

The currency board arrangement worked well in Argentina for a number of years, and it has worked well for the other countries that have currency boards. But a currency board does not force a country to follow sensible fiscal and regulatory policies, and it leaves the country more exposed to adverse foreign shocks. In addition, Argentina's experience shows another potential drawback of a currency board, the difficulty of finding an *exit strategy* that does not add disruption to the country's economy.

"Dollarization"

So much of barbarism, however, still remains in the transactions of most civilized nations, that almost all independent countries choose to assert their nationality by having, to their own inconvenience and that of their neighbors, a peculiar currency of their own.

John Stuart Mill, 1870

A currency board establishes a strongly fixed exchange rate, but it is still at risk of a speculative attack. It is a hard peg, but perhaps still not hard enough, because the country's government could decide to shift to some other exchange-rate policy for its currency.

A more extreme form of fixed exchange rate is for the country's government to abolish its own currency and use the currency of some other country. Because the other currency is often the U.S. dollar, this arrangement is called **dollarization.** This is a harder peg, but even this is not permanent. The government still cannot credibly commit *never* to change the exchange rate. That is, the government can still "de-dollarize" and reintroduce local currency, as Liberia did in the early 1980s. Panama, Micronesia, and the Marshall Islands use the U.S. dollar as their official local currency, and several other very small countries use the currency of a large neighboring country as their own currency. In 1999 the president of Argentina expressed support for adopting the dollar as the local currency, but Argentina did not make this change. In September 2000 Ecuador dollarized in an effort to turn around its struggling economy. At the beginning of 2001 El Salvador dollarized in a smooth transition from the fixed rate between the colón and the dollar that it had maintained for many years.

In comparison with a well-maintained fixed exchange rate with the dollar, what are the advantages and disadvantages of full dollarization? The major advantage for a country like El Salvador is *removing the exchange rate risk* that its government might devalue or depreciate the local currency in the future. This eliminates the risk of a speculative attack on the currency.[4] It also eliminates the risk premium (to compensate lenders for this exchange rate risk) that is built into local-currency interest rates. For El Salvador, interest rates fell by about five percentage points as the country dollarized. Another advantage is the *elimination of the transaction costs of currency exchanges* between the local currency and the dollar. The major disadvantage of full dollarization is the *loss of interest income on the country's holdings of international reserve assets* that are used in the process of full dollarization. The government must replace all local currency with dollars. To do this the government uses its official holdings of U.S. government bonds to obtain dollars. In El Salvador's case, the loss of interest income is equal to about 0.6 percent of its GDP. That is, with dollarization the *seigniorage profit* from issuing currency in El Salvador goes to the U.S. government (the issuer of dollar bills) rather than to El Salvador's government (the issuer of colones).[5]

With full dollarization, El Salvador completely cedes its monetary policy to the United States. The U.S. Fed will make its monetary policy decisions based on

[4] An international crisis is still possible, as the experience of Panama shows. Foreign investors can run for the exits if they fear either default on government debt that is rising quickly because of large fiscal deficits or losses because of weaknesses in the local financial system.

[5] El Salvador's government could attempt to negotiate an agreement with the U.S. government to gain a share of the forgone interest, but the U.S. government has not appeared to be receptive to encouraging dollarization by sharing seigniorage profits with other countries.

economic conditions in the United States, with almost no concern for economic conditions in El Salvador. This sounds like a major drawback, but El Salvador was already fully committed to defending the fixed exchange rate, so it had already almost completely given up its own monetary policy anyway.

The dollarization of Ecuador is a more aggressive use of this policy, because Ecuador shifted from a flexible exchange rate value for the sucre. In the two years prior to dollarization, Ecuador had defaulted on its foreign debt, and its currency had lost 73 percent of its dollar value. Dollarization was shock treatment for an economy that had serious problems. In the first year and half, this treatment was surprisingly successful. Inflation fell from 96 percent in 2000 to 14 percent in the first half of 2002. Real GDP grew by 5.4 percent in 2001. Still, international trade was one problem in the transition. With an inflation higher than that of the United States, Ecuador lost international price competitiveness. Its non-oil exports were hurt, and its imports increased.

THE INTERNATIONAL FIX—MONETARY UNION

Since the breakup of the Bretton Woods fixed-rate system, the countries of the European Union have attempted to establish and maintain fixed exchange rates among their currencies. In 1979, they established the European Monetary System, and a subset of the countries established fixed exchange rates among their currencies through the **Exchange Rate Mechanism (ERM).** The Maastricht Treaty, approved in 1993, committed the countries to a monetary union and a single currency, the euro. In a **monetary union,** exchange rates are permanently fixed and a single monetary authority conducts a single unionwide monetary policy. Eleven EU countries established the monetary union in 1999, with one more joining in 2001. This final section of the chapter examines the economics of monetary union as the ultimate fixed exchange rate arrangement, by looking at the experience of the EU during the past several decades.

Exchange Rate Mechanism

In 1979, Germany, France, Italy, the Netherlands, Belgium, Denmark, Ireland, and Luxembourg began to fix the exchange rates among their currencies as participants in the Exchange Rate Mechanism. Until 1993, most countries in the ERM committed to maintaining their actual exchange rates within a band of plus or minus 2.25 percent around the central rate. Spain joined the ERM in 1989, Britain in 1990, and Portugal in 1992.

The ERM was an adjustable-peg system. There were 11 realignments during the first nine years, 1979–1987. Then from 1987 through 1992, there were no realignments. In fact, the discipline effect on national inflation rates seemed to work quite well. Germany was generally regarded as the lead country in the system due to its economic size and the prestige of its central bank. Germany maintained a low inflation rate, and the other ERM countries were disciplined by the fixed exchange rates to lower their inflation rates toward the German level. In

1979, the range of inflation rates was about 10 percentage points. In the early 1990s, the average inflation rate was lower and the range was halved.

Figure 24.2 shows the exchange rates of EU countries' currencies relative to the German mark (pictured as the DM value of the other currency). Of the original ERM members shown in the top half, the DM value of the Netherlands guilder was the steadiest—it changed little from 1979 to 1998. The general tendency for the Belgian franc, Danish kroner, French franc, and Italian lira to devalue in the realignments is seen clearly from 1979 into 1987. The figure also shows that the exchange rate values (relative to the DM) of all of these ERM members were less variable than that of the British pound up to 1990. Britain was the EU country that deliberately did not join the ERM in 1979.

By mid-1992, the ERM seemed to be working very well. At that time all EU countries but Greece were in the ERM. No realignments had occurred since 1987. As part of "Europe 1992," the general effort to dismantle barriers to permit free movements of goods, services, and capital within the EU, most countries had removed capital controls by 1990. The EU countries had completed the drafting of the Maastricht Treaty, which contained the plans for monetary union, and they were in the process of approving it.

As we discussed in Chapters 19 and 22, the ERM exchange rates came under serious pressure beginning in September 1992. Several things contributed to the severity of the pressure. International investors became worried that the exchange rate values of several currencies in the ERM were not appropriate. For instance, the lira appeared to be overvalued, given that the Italian inflation rate had remained above that of the other ERM members. In addition, international investors became worried by policy tensions among the ERM members. German policymakers were placing full emphasis on reducing and controlling German inflation, while policymakers in several other countries, including France and Britain, probably preferred to shift the emphasis to reducing unemployment. Furthermore, in a general vote in 1992, Denmark rejected the Maastricht Treaty, and the upcoming French vote was expected to be close. These votes raised doubts about eventual monetary union, and they also raised doubts about the countries' current commitments to fixed exchange rates. Finally, the removal of capital controls meant that international investors and speculators could move large amounts of financial capital quickly from one country and currency to another. Official defense of the fixed rates was difficult in the face of these large speculative flows.

As international investors and speculators shifted to expecting devaluations against the DM by a number of ERM countries, large amounts of capital flowed, and the central banks mounted massive defenses. Italy and Britain surrendered and left the system. Figure 24.2 shows the quick depreciation of the pound and lira as they switched to floating. Over the next year speculative attacks continued. The Spanish peseta was devalued three times, the Portuguese escudo twice, and the Irish punt once.

Another large speculative attack occurred during July 1993. As a result, the ERM changed the allowable band to plus or minus 15 percent (though the

FIGURE 24.2 Exchange Rates for the Currencies of the European Union Countries, 1979–1998 (Monthly)

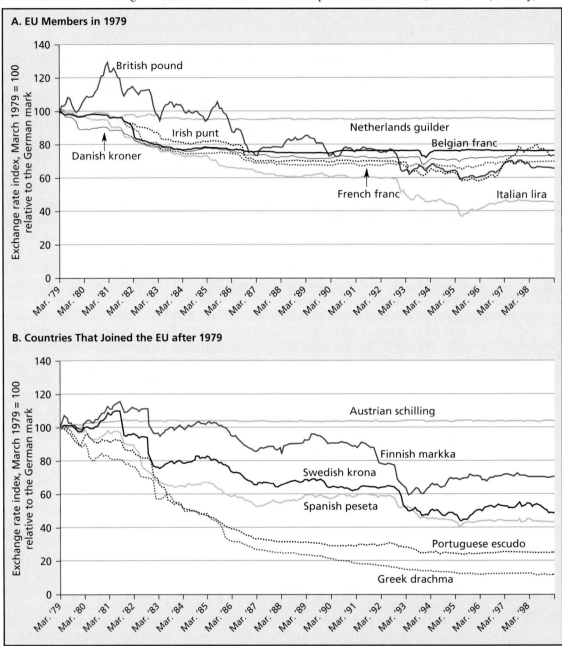

The figure shows the nominal exchange rate values of EU currencies as German marks per other currency, shown as an index with a value of 100 in March 1979, the date that the Exchange Rate Mechanism began. The original members of the ERM were Germany, the Netherlands, Belgium, Ireland, France, Italy, and Luxembourg. (The Luxembourg franc is the same as the Belgian franc, so it is not shown separately.) The Belgian franc, Danish kroner, French franc, Italian lira, and Irish punt were devalued during realignments from 1979 to 1987. Spain joined the ERM in 1989, Britain in 1990, and Portugal in 1992. Britain and Italy withdrew from the ERM in 1992, and their currencies quickly depreciated. Austria, whose currency had been effectively pegged to the German mark for many years, joined the ERM in 1994, Finland in 1996, and Greece in 1998. Italy rejoined in 1996. With the exception of the Irish punt, the DM values of other ERM member currencies were generally steady from late 1993 to the end of 1998.

Source: International Monetary Fund, *International Financial Statistics*.

DM–guilder rate remained fixed within a 2.25 percent band). Though the bands were widened, there was no realignment. Exchange rates among the ERM currencies then were generally calm during the next years, mostly staying within or close to the old 2.25 percent bands. However, in March 1995, the peseta and escudo were devalued again. Also, at the end of 1994, Austria joined the ERM as it joined the EU. The entry of the Austrian schilling was easy. It had been effectively pegged closely to the DM for many years, as the bottom half of Figure 24.2 shows. Finland joined the ERM in 1996, Italy rejoined in 1996, and Greece joined in 1998.

As this brief history indicates, the ERM illustrates many of the points made in the first half of the chapter about the strengths and weaknesses of fixed exchange rates. The ERM exchange rates were generally steadier than floating rates were during this period, although occasional realignments disturbed the stability. The fixed rates applied pressure on other ERM countries to reduce their inflation rates toward the German level. Differences in goals between Germany and several other ERM countries in the early 1990s led to strains in the system, and these other countries could not use monetary policy to address their internal imbalances. The removal of capital controls made the defense of the fixed rates through official intervention more difficult in 1992 and 1993. In fact, several countries temporarily reimposed or tightened their capital controls as part of their defense efforts. These controls helped in the defense of the fixed exchange rates, but they ran counter to the broad efforts to create a single EU market.

European Monetary Union

In 1991, the EU countries completed the draft of the **Maastricht Treaty** (named for the Dutch town where it was negotiated). The Maastricht Treaty amended the Treaty of Rome, the founding charter of the European Union, to set a process for establishing a monetary union and a single unionwide currency. After several close national votes, including a defeat in Denmark that was later reversed, all EU countries approved the treaty, and it became effective in November 1993.

The Maastricht Treaty set a specific process for the establishment of the **European Monetary Union.** To participate in the monetary union, a country had to meet five criteria:

- The country's inflation rate must be no higher than 1.5 percentage points above the average inflation rate of the three EU countries with the lowest inflation rates.

- Its exchange rates must be maintained within the ERM bands with no realignments during the preceding two years.

- Its long-term interest rate on government bonds must be no higher than 2 percentage points above the average of the comparable interest rates in the three lowest-inflation countries.

- The country's government budget deficit must be no larger than 3 percent of the value of its GDP.

- The gross government debt must be no larger than 60 percent of its GDP (or the country must show satisfactory progress to achieving these two fiscal criteria in the near future).

These criteria were intended to measure whether the country's performance had converged toward that of the best-performing EU countries so that the country was ready to enter the monetary union.

In May 1998, a summit of EU leaders decided which countries met the five criteria and would be members of the new euro area. With some liberal use of the "satisfactory progress" exception for the government debt criterion, 11 countries were deemed to meet the criteria and chose to join the monetary union. EU countries not joining at the beginning can join later if they meet the criteria. Greece did not then qualify but was able to join two years later. Britain, Denmark, and Sweden could have qualified but chose not to join the union at its inception.

The monetary union began in 1999, and the euro replaced the national currencies in early 2002. The **European Central Bank (ECB)** was established in 1998 as the center of the European System of Central Banks, a federal structure that also includes the national central banks as operating arms. On January 1, 1999, the ECB assumed responsibility for unionwide monetary policy in the euro area.

What can the EU countries achieve with monetary union and what did they give up or risk? European Monetary Union provides examples of almost all of the issues that we discussed in the first half of the chapter.[6]

The gains from monetary union are based on the elimination of all exchange rate concerns. The shift to a common currency is a permanent fix and more. It will end exchange rate variability and risk. It will end one-way speculation about changes in pegged exchange rates. It will end all foreign exchange transactions costs. By reducing costs and risks, larger volumes of trade will occur. In this sense monetary union is part of the broad drive to European integration and single European markets.

There are two major sources of risks and possible losses from European Monetary Union. The first risk is about how effective the new European Central Bank (ECB) will be in its conduct of unionwide monetary policy. The second risk is about how each member country's economy will perform when economic shocks affect different countries in different ways.

Before monetary union, monetary policy within the ERM was effectively set by the German central bank. This arrangement was very successful in reducing EU inflation to almost nothing, but the Bundesbank set its policy mainly to achieve good German economic performance. Other EU countries, especially France, supported monetary union as a way of gaining more say over unionwide monetary policy, by establishing the ECB as a unionwide institution. However, the Germans would only support monetary union if the ECB was modeled closely after the Bundesbank.

---

[6] This discussion is also largely an application of the analysis of an *optimum currency area*—the size of the geographic area that shows the best economic performance with fixed exchange rates (or one currency) within the area and floating exchange rates with currencies outside the area.

The ECB is designed to be independent from direct political influence and mandated to conduct unionwide monetary policy to achieve price stability. Its monetary policy decisions are made by a majority vote of the governing council, composed of the heads of the member national central banks and the six members of the executive committee. While not overtly political, there is room for national economic needs to sway unionwide policy decisions.

Some concern over the ECB's effectiveness remains. It announced a target of 0–2 percent inflation, but in 2000, 2001, and the first half of 2002, the actual unionwide inflation rate was somewhat above this target. In addition, as shown in Figure 24.3, the exchange rate value of the euro declined from its introduction in 1999 to late in 2000. While there are many reasons for variability in exchange rates, as we have seen throughout Parts III and IV, at times statements by ECB officials seemed to adversely affect market sentiment toward the euro.

The second risk is to the national economic performance of each member country. The economies of the member countries are different. It is likely that shocks will affect the countries differently, so that economic conditions sometimes will vary across the countries. Especially, weak demand will cause recessions in some countries, for example Germany during 2000–2002. Demand in other countries will grow too quickly, causing inflation pressures; Ireland during 2000–2002, for example, experienced rapidly rising wages and a housing price bubble. With monetary union, each country has given up both the ability to run an independent monetary policy that could respond to domestic imbalances and the ability to use exchange rate changes as an adjustment tool.

Each country, then, must rely on other mechanisms to reduce national imbalances. Fiscal policy remains available, but there are two concerns about how effective it can be. First, there is little fiscal policy that includes the entire euro

FIGURE 24.3

Nominal Exchange Rate Value of the Euro, 1999–2002

Source: International Monetary Fund, *International Financial Statistics*.

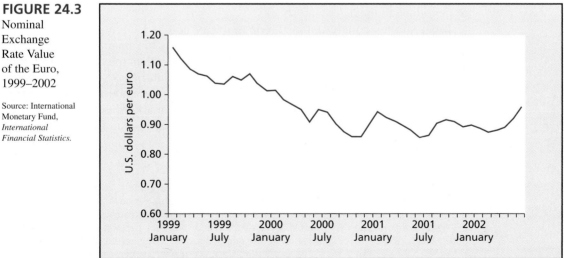

area. With almost no unionwide fiscal policy, there are almost no "automatic stabilizers" across countries. That is, higher tax revenues from the growing countries are not "automatically" shifted to the recession countries through lower taxes and larger expenditures in the recession countries. And there is no active unionwide fiscal policy to help the recession countries.

This leads to the second concern, whether each country will be able to use its national fiscal policy effectively to improve its domestic performance. A major constraint on the effective use of national fiscal policy is political. Fiscal policy can be changed only with lags created by the political process of enacting changes and the bureaucratic process of implementing them. In addition, as part of the process of moving toward monetary union, the German government insisted on the "Stability and Growth Pact," which establishes the ongoing rule that national government budget deficits should be no more than 3 percent of GDP, with temporary exceptions for unusual external shocks or severe national recessions. Countries that have a budget deficit above 3 percent of GDP are subject to monetary penalties, unless an exception is granted.

If this agreement is taken seriously, it will limit the use of national fiscal policy, and it could at times turn national fiscal policy into a destabilizer. For instance, if the government budget deficit begins close to 3 percent, and a mild national recession hits, the government may be compelled to raise taxes or cut government expenditures to prevent the deficit from rising above 3 percent. These fiscal changes would make the recession worse. Germany faced this problem in 2002, with a budget deficit of nearly 3 percent and a weak economy that would be hurt more by a cut in government spending or an increase in taxes.[7]

Another method of adjustment to national imbalances is for resources to move from areas of weak demand to areas of strong demand. If labor mobility is high, adjustments to internal imbalances can be speeded by people moving from places where unemployment is high to places where demand for labor is strong. Regional migration is the main way in which different regions in the United States adjust to local demand shocks.

Most studies conclude that labor mobility across EU countries (and even within these countries) is relatively low and is likely to remain low. Only about 1.5 percent of EU citizens live in an EU country other than the one in which they were born. Even mobility between regions within countries is small. Adjustment could occur with capital moving to seek out and employ underutilized resources like unemployed labor. But, given rigidities in labor markets and labor practices, capital may not move in this way—in fact, capital may instead flee from problem areas to those that are booming.

---

[7] Portugal had a government budget deficit of 4.1 percent of GDP in 2001. Its new government blamed the unexpected deficit on creative accounting that the previous government had used during the run-up to the election in 2001. The EU started sanction proceedings, with fines of up to 0.5 percent of Portugal's GDP possible. It will take a year or two for a decision, and the fine is not automatic. For instance, Portugal can avoid the fine by showing that it has taken steps to reduce the deficit.

Our discussion indicates that a major risk facing each member nation of the euro area is the inability to address national recession (or some other internal imbalance) quickly, especially if the thrust of unionwide monetary policy is not helping. There is essentially no unionwide fiscal policy, and national fiscal policy may be limited and clumsy. Labor mobility is generally low, and capital movements may not be enough.

In conclusion, the European Monetary Union is an unprecedented effort by a group of countries that had separate monetary policies and separate central banks to establish a common central bank, a common monetary policy, and a common currency. While there are risks, there are also major benefits, as well as strong political commitments in the member countries to deepen the economic and political union. If the European Monetary Union and the euro continue to work well, other countries that favor fixed exchange rates are likely to consider forming monetary unions (or replacing their national currencies with the dollar or the euro). One global trend is toward floating exchange rates, but another trend may be developing as well—toward more permanent regional fixes and fewer currencies.

Summary

A major decision for a country's government is its choice of exchange rate policy. This chapter has examined the extent of rate flexibility that a country's policy allows. We discussed what five major issues say about the advantages and disadvantages of choosing a floating rate or a fixed rate. You may want to review Figure 24.1 for a summary of this discussion.

For each issue there are usually ways in which the issue favors a floating rate and other ways in which the issue favors a fixed rate. Because countries differ in their economic situations, policymaking institutions, economic histories, and political interests, different countries can view the balance of advantages and disadvantages differently, leading to different policy choices. Indeed, as economic and political conditions change over time, the policy chosen by a country can change.

In a country's choice between a more flexible rate and a more fixed-rate policy, several points are typically prominent. Strong arguments in favor of a floating exchange rate include the country's ability to use independent monetary policy and exchange rate changes to adjust internal and external imbalances; the country's ability, more generally, to pursue goals and policies that meet its own domestic needs; and the difficulty of defending fixed rates against speculative attacks, given the large and growing amounts of financial capital that can move quickly between countries. The strongest argument in favor of a fixed exchange rate is that floating rates have been too variable, and this excessive variability disrupts and discourages international trade and other international transactions.

In recent decades, countries have shifted toward choosing more flexible exchange rates. Countries generally attempt to manage the float in order to moderate the variability of the floating rate, although the effectiveness of this management, at least for the major currencies, is questionable.

Still, a number of countries continue to have fixed exchange rates. However, soft pegs (fixed rates that are easily adjustable) are difficult to sustain because they seem at times to encourage speculative attacks. Some countries use forms of hard pegs (fixed rates that are more nearly permanent). A **currency board** is a monetary authority that holds only international reserve assets, so sterilization is not possible. With a currency board, the country's money supply is automatically linked to the intervention to defend the fixed exchange rate. **Dollarization** involves completely replacing the local currency with a foreign currency (for instance, the U.S. dollar). Monetary conditions in the country are almost completely controlled by the foreign central bank (for instance, the U.S. Federal Reserve).

The most ambitious fixed-rate effort is occurring in the European Union, where 12 EU countries are members of the **European Monetary Union,** established in 1999 and based on the **Maastricht Treaty** of 1993. In a **monetary union,** exchange rates are permanently fixed, and a single monetary authority conducts a unionwide monetary policy. For European Monetary Union, the 12 countries use a single currency, the euro, and the **European Central Bank (ECB)** conducts unionwide monetary policy.

The European Monetary Union is the successor to the fixed exchange rates of the **Exchange Rate Mechanism (ERM)** of the European Monetary System, established in 1979. Under the ERM, the fixed exchange rates were generally less variable than comparable floating exchange rates, although the fixed ERM rates were occasionally adjusted in realignments. Inflation rates in other ERM countries declined toward the low German inflation rate. However, following the removal of capital controls by some ERM countries, differences in macroeconomic goals between Germany and some other ERM countries led to speculative attacks in 1992 and 1993. Britain and Italy left the ERM, and the allowable bands were widened for all rates but the mark–guilder rate. After 1993, the ERM exchange rates were generally steady.

The European Monetary Union can be used to indicate the major advantages and disadvantages of a monetary union. First, the gains flow largely from reduced transactions costs and reduced exchange rate risk. For the European Monetary Union, with its shift to a single currency, these gains are probably substantial.

Second, the establishment of the unionwide monetary authority can bring uncertainty, at least at first, about what its priorities and decision-making procedures will be. The ECB was established to be largely free from direct political influence, but the euro area inflation rate was somewhat above the ECB's target during 2000–2002.

Third, economic shocks can affect member countries differently, with some countries in recession and others growing quickly. When this occurs, the countries will need ways to adjust their internal imbalances, but each nation no longer has national monetary policy or national exchange rate policy. Fiscal policy at the union level could be useful, by providing automatic stabilizers as well as active fiscal policy changes. If unionwide fiscal policy is not sufficient, each nation may need to use national fiscal policy actively. In addition, labor mobility can assist in adjusting imbalances, as people move from areas of high unemployment to areas of low unemployment. European Monetary Union faces its major challenges in this third broad area of shocks, national imbalances, and policy and adjustment responses. The member countries are different and experience different internal imbalances, there is almost no fiscal policy at the union level, national fiscal policies are limited, and labor mobility is low.

Suggested Reading

The classic article favoring floating exchange rates is Friedman (1953). Obstfeld and Rogoff (1995) discuss why fixed rates have been so hard to defend. Fischer (2001) explores the unsustainability of soft pegs. McKinnon (1988) and Williamson (1985) propose reforms to the current system that incorporate shifts back toward relatively fixed (or less flexible) exchange rates. Goldstein (2002) presents the case in favor of managed floating.

Enoch and Gulde (1998) look at currency boards. Mundell (1961), McKinnon (1963), and Tower and Willett (1976) examine fixed rates within optimum currency areas. Wyplosz (1997) and Feldstein (1997) review and critique European Monetary Union. Clausen and Donges (2001) examine the ECB's monetary policy. Murray (2000) explores whether Canada should dollarize.

Questions and Problems

◆ 1. "Countries whose currencies are linked to each other through fixed exchange rates usually should pursue very different monetary and fiscal policies." Do you agree or disagree? Why?

2. "If most countries adhered to a system of fixed exchange rates, global inflation would be lower." Do you agree or disagree? Why?

◆ 3. A country is worried that business cycles in other countries tend to disrupt its own economy. It would like some "insulation" from foreign business cycles. Why would this country favor having a floating exchange rate?

4. "If a country's government decides to have a flexible exchange rate, then it should have a clean float." Do you agree or disagree? Why?

◆ 5. A country now has a floating exchange rate. Its government would like to fix the exchange rate value of its currency to another currency. You have been hired as an advisor to the country's government. Suggest three major criteria for deciding what other country's currency to fix to. Why is each important?

6. The variability of floating exchange rates since 1973 has been higher than most economists expected.

   a. Why are some economists not concerned about this?

   b. Why are other economists quite worried about this?

◆ 7. A new government has been elected in a country that now has a high inflation rate and a floating exchange rate. The new government is committed to reducing the country's inflation rate.

   a. If the government continues to use a floating exchange rate, what will the government need to do to reduce the high inflation rate?

   b. As part of its effort to reduce the country's inflation rate, why might the country's government consider a change to using a currency board and a fixed exchange rate with one of the major currencies of the world?

8. According to the Maastricht Treaty, what are the five convergence criteria for an EU country to be allowed to join the European Monetary Union. What logic do you see for having each as a requirement? Which of the five criteria seem to be more or less important as a basis for excluding a country from the monetary union?

◆ 9. The time is 2006. The European Monetary Union and the euro have worked reasonably well. Britain has remained outside. You are attempting to convince a British friend that Britain should join the monetary union as soon as possible. What are your two strongest arguments?

10. Consider the same scenario in question 9. Your British friend is trying to convince you that Britain should stay out of the monetary union. What are her two strongest arguments?

Appendix **A**

The Web and the Library: International Numbers and Other Information

The World Wide Web has fundamentally changed how we do international research. If you want to explore international trade competition, a recent financial crisis, a trade dispute between the United States and the European Union, the policy of the Korean government toward exchange rates, or almost any other topic in international economics, useful information is available. You can find a lot of it by putting the topic name into a good search engine. You usually will get links to several useful websites. (You will probably also get links to a number of less useful sites, and sometimes even links to sites whose information is not reliable. One aspect of good Web research is identifying the best sites and validating the information you obtain.) Of course, some sources of information are available only in hard copy, so access to a good library is also important for many research projects.

This appendix presents some of the best sources of international data and information. Figure A.1 shows a number of useful Web sites, ranging from those maintained by official international organizations to those maintained by individual experts. The rest of the appendix presents information sources that can be found in hard copies in libraries. Some of this information can also be found through the Web.

FIGURE A.1
Useful Websites

Creator/Description	Address
Official International Organizations	
World Trade Organization	www.wto.org
International Monetary Fund	www.imf.org
World Bank	www.worldbank.org
Organization for Economic Cooperation and Development	www.oecd.org
Bank for International Settlements: Information on foreign exchange markets, international banking, and national central banks, including links to many central bank sites	www.bis.org
United Nations: Collections of national statistics	unstats.un.org/unsd
United Nations Conference on Trade and Development: Collections of national statistics, including extensive data on foreign direct investment	www.unctad.org/en/enhome.htm (click on Publications)
International Trade	
International Trade Centre: Data on trade by product (3-digit Standard International Trade Classification) and country	www.intracen.org/tradstat
U. S. Trade Representative: Information on foreign barriers to U.S. exports and other trade policy issues	www.ustr.gov
International Trade Administration, U.S. Department of Commerce: Information on U.S. dumping and subsidy cases	www.ita.doc.gov (click on Import Administration)
U.S. International Trade Commission: Information on dumping and subsidy cases, and on other trade policy issues	www.usitc.gov
U.S. Commercial Service: Information on foreign markets for U.S. exports	www.usatrade.gov
Canadian International Trade Tribunal: Information on dumping and subsidy actions by the Canadian government	www.citt.gc.ca/menu_e.htm
Canadian Trade Commissioner Service: Information on foreign markets for Canadian exports	www.infoexport.gc.ca
DG Trade, European Commission: Information on EU trade policy and foreign barriers to EU exports	europa.eu.int/comm/trade
Global Trade Watch: Alternative views on trade policy and globalization issues, presented by Ralph Nader's group Public Citizen	www.citizen.org/trade

FIGURE A.1
continued

Creator/Description	Address
Exchange Rates, International Finance, and Macroeconomics	
OANDA, the Internet arm of Olsen & Associates, Company: Exchange rate data and news	www.oanda.com
Pacific Exchange Rate Service (University of British Columbia): Exchange rate data and information	pacific.commerce.ubc.ca/xr
Yahoo! Finance: Information on countries, country risk, and much more	biz.yahoo.com/ifc
Barclays Bank: Commentary on foreign exchange markets and macroeconomic developments in the United Kingdom and the European Union	www.business.barclays.co.uk (click Information Centre, then click Publications)
Professor Nouriel Roubini: Links to many other sites with information on the international financial system, including international financial crises	www.stern.nyu.edu/globalmacro
National, Regional, and International Data	
U.S. federal government: Access to a wide range of data and information	www.fedstats.gov
White House Briefing Room: Data on the U.S. economy	www.whitehouse.gov/fsbr/esbr.html
St. Louis Federal Reserve Bank: Data on United States and other countries	research.stlouisfed.org/fred/exchange.html
U.S. Bureau of Economic Analysis: U.S. balance of payments data	www.bea.doc.gov
European Union	www.europa.eu.int
Social Science Information Gateway: Links to many sources of information about the European Union and European countries	www.sosig.ac.uk/eurostudies
Central Banks	
U.S. Federal Reserve System	www.federalreserve.gov
European Central Bank	www.ecb.int
Bank of Japan	www.boj.or.jp/en
Environmental Data and Analysis	
World Resources Institute: Environmental data and information	earthtrends.wri.org
United Nations Environment Programme: Periodic report on the global environment	grid2.cr.usgs.gov/geo/geo3

continued on next page

FIGURE A.1
continued

Creator/Description	Address
Other Useful Sites	
Resources for Economists on the Internet: Links to a broad range of sites with economics information	www.rfe.org
Michigan State University: Links to many useful sites and a glossary	globaledge.msu.edu/ibrd
University of Kansas: Links to many sites with information on international trade and business	www.ibrc.bschool.ukans.edu
Institute for International Economics: Information on its publications, including some available online	www.iie.com
Abyz News Links: Links to the websites of newspapers from around the world	www.abyznewslinks.com

For many research projects, you want to take a close look at the international economic dealings of a single country, perhaps your own. One useful source is usually that country's statistical yearbook, which is likely to be found somewhere in the HA_ range if your library shelves books according to the Library of Congress system. Here are some examples, with the first parts of their typical Library of Congress call numbers in parentheses:

- U.S. Bureau of the Census, *Statistical Abstract of the United States* (HA37.U4).

- Statistics Canada, *Canada Year Book* (HA744.581).

- Great Britain, Central Statistical Office, *Annual Abstract of Statistics* (HA1122.A33).

- Japan, Statistical Bureau, *Japan Statistical Yearbook* (HA1832.J36).

- Australian Bureau of Statistics, *Year Book Australia* (HA3001.B5).

If you want to compare countries in the same region, you can get numbers for all the countries in the region from such compilations as

- United Nations, Economic Commission for Latin America and the Caribbean, *Statistical Yearbook for Latin America and the Caribbean* (HA751.U49).

- United Nations, *African Statistical Yearbook* (HD1955.U5).

- European Bank for Reconstruction and Development, *Transition Report* (HC331.E2).

For really global coverage of the most often cited national averages and aggregates, see the World Bank's annual *World Development Report* (HC59.7.W659) or its *World Development Indicators* (HC59.15.W656). For most of the main economic aggregates, you can also see the International Monetary Fund's monthly or annual *International Financial Statistics* (HG3881.I626), which covers more than just international finance. The United Nations Development Project produces its annual *Human Development Report* (HD72.H85), which focuses on measures of living conditions, education, and male–female differences in achievements.

Some global volumes cover specific aspects of international economics that are evident from their titles:

- United Nations, *International Trade Statistics Yearbook* (HF91.U5).

- United Nations, *National Accounts Statistics* (HC75.I5.N388).

- International Monetary Fund, *Balance of Payments Yearbook* (HF1014.I512).

- United Nations Conference on Trade and Development, *World Investment Report* (HG4538.W67).

- Organisation for Economic Cooperation and Development, *International Direct Investment Statistics Yearbook* (HG4583.I58).

- International Monetary Fund, *Direction of Trade Statistics Yearbook* (HA13.U4).

- International Monetary Fund, *Annual Report on Exchange Arrangements and Exchange Restrictions* (HG3834.I61A3).

- World Bank, *Global Development Finance* (HJ8899.W672).

Multilateral organizations produce other useful periodic reports, including the World Trade Organization, *Annual Report* (HF1371.A56), the International Monetary Fund, *World Economic Outlook* (HC59.W654), and the Bank for International Settlements, *Annual Report* (HG1997.I6A3).

There are also good global data annuals on topics that are more comparative than international in the sense of dealings between nations, yet still relate to international economics. For environmental data involving issues like those in Chapter 12, see World Resources Institute, *World Resources* (GF1.W667).

Appendix B

Deriving Production-Possibility Curves

The shape of the production-possibility curve used so much in the theory of international trade depends on the factor supplies of the country and on the technology for combining these factors to produce outputs. The usual device for portraying the state of technology is the **production function,** which expresses the output of any one commodity as a function of its inputs.

Geometrically, the production function for each commodity can be shown in two dimensions by plotting the various combinations of two factors needed to produce given amounts of the commodity in question. Figure B.1 shows several **production isoquants,** each showing the different combinations of land and labor that could yield a given level of output. The smooth isoquants of Figure B.1A portray a case in which land and labor are partial substitutes for one another in cloth. Starting from a point like W, it would be possible to keep the same cloth output per year (i.e., stay on the isoquant T—T) with less labor if we used enough more land, as at V. By contrast, in Figure B.1B, the production function has a special form (sometimes called the Leontief production function) in which land and labor are not substitutes at all. Thus, starting from point W, we cannot give up any labor inputs without falling to a lower output isoquant, regardless of how much extra land is added. Thus the isoquant moves vertically up from point W to points like R demanding the same labor inputs. Some industries are thought to resemble this special case, though the factors of production are usually partial substitutes for one another, as in Figure B.1A.

What combination of resources should be used to produce a specific amount of output of a product? If the factors are partial substitutes, then the lowest-cost combination of resources to use depends on the factors' prices. The relative prices of the two factors are summarized in factor-price slopes like that of **isocost lines** S—S and S'—S' in Figure B.1A, which are parallel. This slope shows the ratio of the wage rate for labor to the rental rate for land—the number of acres of land use that can be traded for each hour of labor in the marketplace. For given factor prices, isocost lines farther from the origin indicate higher total costs.

FIGURE B.1

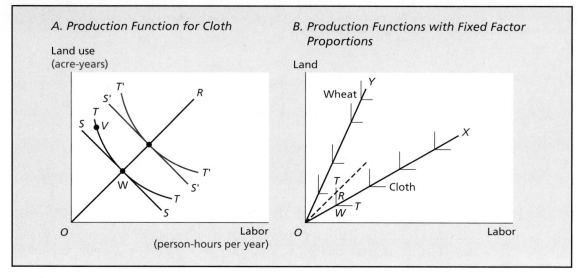

To minimize the cost of producing a specific level of output, a firm would seek the lowest isocost line, the one that is just tangent to the isoquant for that output level. For instance, if factor prices are shown by the slope of line *S—S,* then the least-cost way of producing the output level for isoquant *T—T* is to use the combination of labor hours and land acres shown by point *W.* If land then becomes cheaper relative to labor, the factor-price slope would be steeper than *S—S.* Firms should substitute the lower-priced land for labor, and production would shift to a point like *V.*

How would the use of labor and land increase if the industry wanted to expand output, assuming that factor prices are constant? In Figure B.1A, we have shown the often-imagined case in which any expansion of output would be achieved along the *expansion path R,* a straight line from the origin as long as the factor-price ratio is still the slope *S—S.* In Figure B.1B the factor proportions would always be fixed, on the more labor-intensive expansion path *X* for cloth and the more land-intensive expansion path *Y* for wheat, regardless of the relative prices of land and labor.

To know the most efficient combinations a nation can produce, we must now combine the technological possibilities represented by the production-function isoquants with the nation's total supplies of land and labor. A handy device for doing this is the so-called **Edgeworth–Bowley box diagram,** in which the dimensions of the box represent the amounts of land and labor in a country, which we call Britain. These factor supplies are assumed to be homogeneous in character and fixed in amount.

Figure B.2 shows an Edgeworth–Bowley box for production functions with fixed factor proportions and constant returns to scale (so that a proportionate increase in all inputs used to produce a product results in an increase in the product's output by the same proportion). The production function for cloth is drawn with its origin in the lower-left corner of the box at O, and with its isoquants, T—T, T'—T', and so on, moving out and up to the right. Its expansion path is OX. If all the labor in Britain (OR) were used to make cloth, only RX of land would be required, and $O'X$ of land would be left unemployed. At X, the marginal physical product of land would be zero.

The production function for wheat is drawn reversed and upside down, with its origin at O' and extending downward and to the left. Its expansion path is OY. At Y, all the land and YR of labor would be employed, but OY of labor would be unemployed. OX and $O'Y$ intersect at W, which is the only production point in the box diagram where there can be full employment and positive prices for both factors. At any other point on either expansion path, say, F on OX, land and labor will be able to produce at J on the expansion path for wheat; OG of labor will be engaged in cloth, and HR in wheat. RK of land will be employed in cloth, and $O'K$ in wheat. But GH of labor will be unemployed.

The curve OWO', as in Figure B.2, is in effect a production-possibility curve, showing the various combinations of wheat and cloth that can be produced in Britain, given the factor endowments of the country. The only point providing full employment of the two factors and positive factor prices is W. OWO' does not look like a production-possibility curve because it is given in terms of physical units of land and labor, rather than physical units of production. If we remap the OWO' curve in Figure B.2 from factor space into commodity space in terms of units of wheat and cloth and turn it right side up, it is a production-possibility curve, kinked at W, as in Figure B.3.

FIGURE B.2

Edgeworth–
Bowley Box
Diagram with
Fixed Factor
Proportions

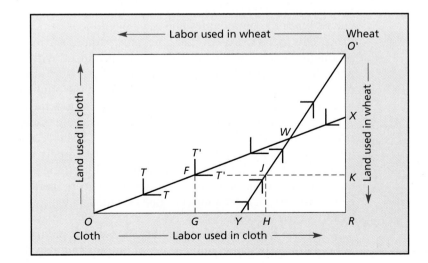

FIGURE B.3
Production-
Possibility
Curve Derived
from
Edgeworth–
Bowley Box
Diagram with
Fixed Factor
Proportions

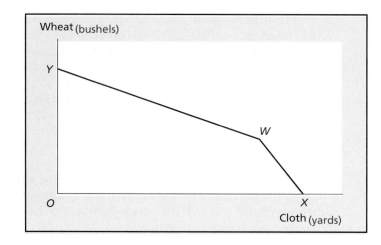

If cloth and wheat were produced with fixed factor coefficients, and these were identical, the two expansion paths would coincide, as in Figure B.4A. In this case, if production also involves constant returns to scale for both products, then the production-possibility curve becomes a straight line, as in Figure B.4B. Because land and labor are always used in the same combination, they might well be regarded as a single factor. This is equivalent to Ricardo's labor theory of value and its resultant straight-line production-possibility curve. A similar straight-line production- possibility curve would be produced for any economy in which the production functions are constant returns to scale and identical factor-intensity for the two commodities.

When there is the possibility of substitution between factors in the production of a commodity, there is no unique expansion path. Instead, a separate expansion path can be drawn for any given set of factor prices. Or we can draw in the iso-quants for both commodities and trace out a locus of points of tangency between them. This locus represents the efficiency path, or the maximum combinations of production of the two goods that can be produced with the existing factor sup-plies. It is shown in Figure B.5A. To see why it is an efficient path, suppose that production were to take place at *W,* away from the efficiency locus. *W* is on cloth isoquant 7 and on wheat isoquant 5. But there is a point *T,* also on cloth isoquant 7, that is on a higher isoquant (6) of wheat. It would therefore be possible to pro-duce more wheat without giving up any cloth. There is also point *T'* on wheat iso-quant 5 that is on cloth isoquant 8. It would be equally possible to produce more cloth and the same amount of wheat. Any point off the locus of tangencies of iso-quants of the two production functions is therefore inefficient, insofar as it would be possible to get more output of one commodity without losing any of the other, by moving to the locus.

When the Edgeworth–Bowley box is used for picturing production, it shows not only the efficient combinations of outputs but also factor combinations and

FIGURE B.4

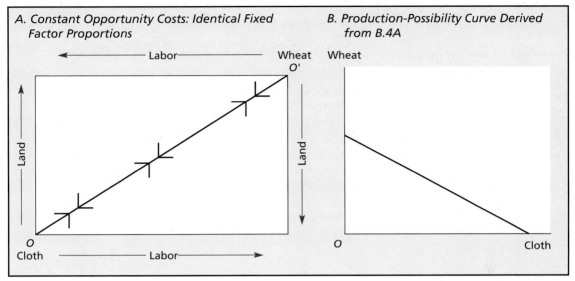

A. *Constant Opportunity Costs: Identical Fixed Factor Proportions*

B. *Production-Possibility Curve Derived from B.4A*

FIGURE B.5

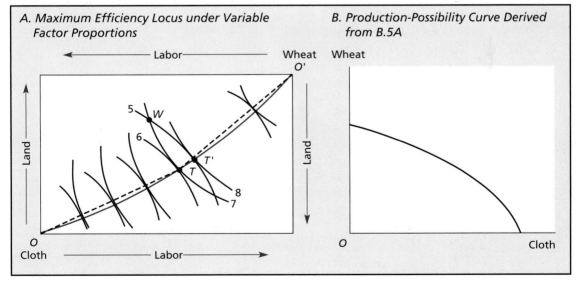

A. *Maximum Efficiency Locus under Variable Factor Proportions*

B. *Production-Possibility Curve Derived from B.5A*

factor prices. If production is at *T*, the factor proportions in cloth are represented by the slope of the dashed line *OT*, and the factor proportions in wheat by the dashed line *O′T*. The relative price of land and labor with these outputs is represented by the slope of the tangency to the isoquants at *T*.

If the production function for each product shown in Figure B.5A is constant returns to scale, then the bowed shape of the efficiency locus translates into the bowed-out production-possibility curve in Figure B.5B. One way to see the basis for this is first to recognize that production along the diagonal of this Edgeworth–Bowley box would result in a straight-line "production-capability" curve. (The logic is essentially the same as that sketched for the case of identical constant-returns-to-scale production functions.) Because moving off the diagonal to produce instead on the efficiency locus increases output for all points except the corners of the box, the actual production-possibility curve lies outside of this straight line connecting the end points (where the country is completely specialized in producing only one product, corresponding to the corners of the Edgeworth–Bowley box). The resulting production-possibility curve is bowed out.

Appendix C

Offer Curves

The supply and demand curves used in Chapters 2 and 3 have several advantages. They are familiar, and they offer the easiest way of seeing how to quantify the effects of trade on the well-being of producer and consumer groups in each country. They are also easily extended to the task of analyzing trade effects in many different goods, each taken one at a time. Another geometric device that gives some of the same information is the *offer curve,* which shows how the export and import quantities a nation chooses will vary with the international price ratio. This appendix gives the geometric derivation of the offer curve. Appendix D shows how it can be used in discussing optimal tariff policy.

A region or nation's offer curve is equivalent to both its supply curve for exports and its demand curve for imports. (For examples of the latter two curves, see the center panel of Figure 2.3.) It graphs trade offers as a function of the international price ratio. And it can be derived from the same production-possibility curves and community indifference curves used extensively in Chapter 3.

Figure C.1 shows the derivation, starting from the usual production and consumption trade-offs. For each international price ratio, the behavior of the United States produces a quantity of exports willingly offered in exchange for imports at that price ratio. At 2 bushels per yard, the United States does not want to trade at all, as shown at S_0. At 1 bushel per yard, the United States would find cloth cheaper, and wheat more valuable, than without trade. It would be willing to export 40 billion bushels and import 40 billion yards, by efficiently producing at S_1 and consuming at C_1. A price of 1/2 bushel per yard would again induce the United States to offer 40 billion of wheat exports, but this time in exchange for 80 billion yards of cloth. Each offer of exports for imports is pictured as a trade triangle with corners at the production and consumption points for the price ratio.

Each of these offers is plotted on the lower half of Figure C.1 (as points O, O_1, and O_2), where the axes are the exports and imports to be exchanged, and the slope of any ray from the origin is a price ratio. The resulting curve O_{US} is the U.S. offer curve. A similar derivation produces the rest of the world's offer curve, O_{RW}. Only at the equilibrium price of 1 bushel per yard, at point O_1, will the United States and the rest of the world be able to agree on how much to trade.

FIGURE C.1

Deriving the
Offer Curve

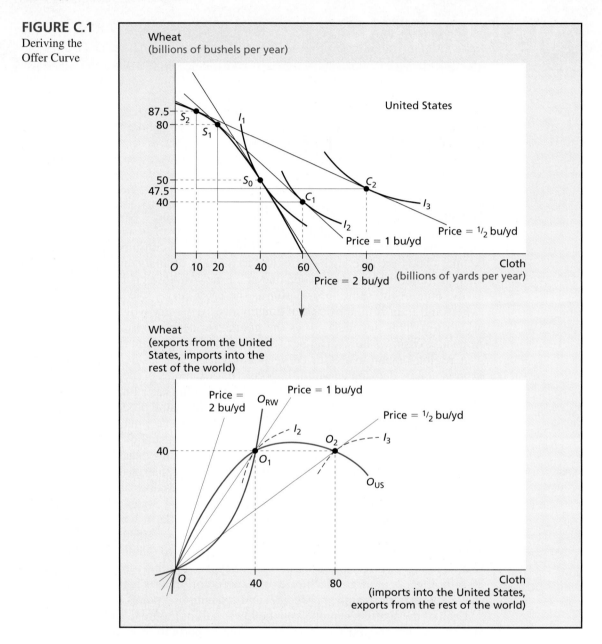

There is another way to derive the same offer curve for a country. We can use *trade indifference curves,* which show the level of well-being attained by a country for different amounts of imports received and exports paid. Imports add to national well-being by expanding consumption while exports detract from well-being because they are not available for local consumption. A trade indifference curve pictures the trade-off that the country would be willing to make while remaining at the same level of overall well-being. The bottom half of Figure C.1 shows two U.S. trade indifference curves: I_2 and I_3.[1] These two trade indifference curves correspond to the levels of U.S. well-being shown by community indifference curves I_2 and I_3 in the top half of the figure. The trade indifference curves have the upward slope and rather peculiar shape for the United States (and I_3 is better than I_2) because more cloth imports are the desirable item, while more exports are undesirable.

We can find a point on the U.S. offer curve by determining the highest trade indifference curve that can be reached if the price ratio is 1 bushel per yard. The highest trade indifference curve, and therefore the highest level of welfare that the United States can reach at this price ratio, is the tangency with trade indifference curve I_2 at point O_1. Thus, O_1 is a point on the U.S. offer curve. For the price ratio of 1/2 bushel per yard, the tangency is with I_3, so O_2 is another point on the U.S. offer curve.

Offer curves can be used to analyze what happens when one of the offer curves shifts. For instance, the implications for the United States of a shift in the offer curve of the rest of the world are straightforward. If it shifts out, the two offer curves' intersection shifts from point O_1 to a point like O_2. The extra supply of cloth exports from the rest of the world decreases the relative price of cloth. (The price line becomes flatter.) This represents an improvement in the U.S. terms of trade, and the United States is better off, reaching an indifference curve like I_3 instead of I_2.

Growth of production capabilities in the United States usually shifts the U.S. offer curve. We can use offer curves to show how the international price ratio is affected by this growth. For instance, if the growth increases the willingness to trade (as discussed in Chapter 6), then the U.S. offer curve shifts out (or up), and the relative price of cloth increases in moving to the new equilibrium intersection. The U.S. terms of trade decline.[2]

Holding the country's production capabilities steady, and assuming that the foreign offer curve is also steady, is there anything that a country can do to improve its well-being by moving its own offer curve? Not if the nation consists

---

[1] The trade indifference curves for the country can be derived from its production-possibility curve and community indifference curves.

[2] We cannot use the original trade indifference curves to analyze the effects of this growth on U.S. well-being because the growth in the U.S. production capabilities means that the United States has a new set of trade indifference curves. Chapter 6 shows how changes in well-being can be examined using production-possibilities curves and community indifference curves once the change in the equilibrium price ratio is determined.

of large numbers of private individuals competing against each other in production and consumption with no government intervention. Such private competition merely puts us on the offer curve in the first place, and does not shift the curve. Yet if the nation acted as a single decision-making unit, there is the glimmering of a chance to squeeze more advantage out of trade in Figure C.1. Starting at the free-trade equilibrium O_1, the United States might be able to come up with a way to move a short distance to the southwest along the foreign offer curve O_{RW}, reaching somewhat higher indifference curves than at O_1. How could this be done? Through an optimal tariff of the sort discussed in Appendix D, where the offer curves reappear.

Appendix D

The Nationally Optimal Tariff

DERIVING THE OPTIMAL TARIFF

In the latter part of Chapter 7 we presented the nationally optimal tariff for a country that can affect the foreign-supply price of its imports without fear of retaliation. This appendix derives the formula for the nationally optimal tariff using both the demand–supply framework of Part II and the offer-curve framework of Appendix C. An analogous formula is derived for the optimal export duty, both for a nation and for an international cartel.

We saw in the demand–supply framework in Chapter 7 that a small increase in an import tariff brings an area of gain and an area of loss to the nation. Figure D.1 compares these two areas for a tiny increase in the tariff above its initial amount per unit, which is the fraction t times the initial price P paid to foreign exporters. The extra gains come from being able to lower the foreign price on continuing imports, gaining the level of imports M times the foreign price drop dP/dt. The extra losses come from losing the extra imports (dM/dt) that were worth tP more per unit to consumers than the price (P) at which foreigners were willing to sell them to us.

The optimal tariff rate is that which just makes the extra losses and extra gains from changing the tariff equal each other. That is, the optimal tariff rate t^* as a share of initial price is the one for which

$$\text{Extra gains} - \text{extra losses} = M\frac{dP}{dt} - t^* P\frac{dM}{dP} = 0$$

so that

$$t^* = \frac{dP/dt}{dM/dt}\frac{M}{P}$$

FIGURE D.1

The Gains and
Losses from a
Slight Increase
in the Tariff,
in a Demand–
Supply
Framework

Since the foreign supply elasticity is defined as

$$s_m = \frac{dM/dt}{dP/dt} \cdot \frac{P}{M}$$

along the foreign supply curve, the formula for the optimal tariff is simply $t^* = 1/s_m$, as stated in Chapter 7. If the world price is fixed beyond our control, so that $s_m = \infty$, then the optimal tariff rate is zero. The more inelastic the foreign supply, the higher the optimal tariff rate.[1]

---

[1] Figure D.1 makes it easy to show that the nationally optimal tariff is lower than the tariff rate that would maximize the government's tariff revenue, even when the foreign supply curve slopes upward. The optimal tariff in Figure D.1 is one that equates the "extra gains" area with the "extra losses" area. But at this tariff rate a slight increase in the tariff still brings a net increase in government tariff revenue. By raising the tariff rate slightly, the government collects more duty on the remaining imports, M, while losing the "extra losses" area on the discouraged imports. However, its gain in revenue on M is not just the "extra gains" area already introduced, but this plus the thin unlabeled rectangle above the tP gap, which takes the form of a higher price to consumers importing M. A slight increase in the tariff would still raise revenue even when it brings no further net welfare gains to the nation. It follows that the revenue-maximizing tariff rate is higher than the optimal tariff rate. Thus a country would be charging too high a rate if it tried to find its nationally optimal tariff rate by finding out what rate seemed to maximize tariff revenues.

OPTIMAL EXPORT TAXES

We can derive the optimal rate of *export* duty in the same way. Just replace all terms referring to imports with terms referring to exports, and redraw Figure D.1 so that the extra gain at the expense of foreign buyers of our exports comes at the top of the tariff gap instead of at the bottom. It turns out, symmetrically, that the optimal export duty equals the absolute value of $1/d_x$, or the reciprocal of the foreign demand elasticity for our exports.

The formula for the optimal export duty can also be used as the optimal rate of markup of an international cartel. Since both the international cartel maximizing joint profits from exports and the single nation optimally taxing its exports are monopolistic profit maximizers, it stands to reason that the formula linking optimal markup to foreign demand elasticity should hold in both cases. So the optimal markup for an international exporting cartel is $t^* = |1/d_c|$, or the absolute value of the reciprocal of the world demand elasticity for the cartel's exports.

We can extend the formula to show how the optimal export markup for cartel members depends on the other elasticities and the market share discussed in Chapter 13's treatment of cartels like OPEC. We can link the elasticity of demand for the cartel's exports to world demand for the product, the supply of perfect substitutes from other countries, and the cartel's share of the world market by beginning with a simple identity:

$$\text{Cartel exports} = \text{World exports} - \text{Other countries' exports}$$

or

$$X_c = X - X_0$$

Differentiating with respect to the cartel price yields

$$\frac{dX_c}{dP} = \frac{dX}{dP} - \frac{dX_0}{dP}$$

This can be reexpressed in ways that arrive at an identity involving elasticities:

$$\frac{dX_c/dP}{X} = \frac{dX/dP}{X} - \frac{dX_0/dP}{X}$$

$$\frac{dX_c}{dP}\frac{P}{X_c}\frac{X_c}{X} = \frac{dX}{dP}\frac{P}{X} - \frac{dX_0}{dP}\frac{P}{X_0}\frac{X_0}{X}$$

The cartel's share of the world market is defined as $c = X_c/X = 1 - (X_0/X)$. The elasticity of demand for the cartel's exports is defined as $d_c = (dX_c/dP)(P/X_c)$; the elasticity of world export demand for the product is $d = (dX/dP)(P/X)$; and the elasticity of noncartel countries' competing export supply of the product is $s_0 = (dX_0/dP)(P/X_0)$. Substituting these definitions into the equation above yields

$$d_c \cdot c = d - s_0(1 - c)$$

so that

$$d_c = \frac{d - s_0(1-c)}{c}$$

Now since the optimal markup rate is $t^* = |1/d_c|$, this optimal cartel markup rate is

$$t^* = \frac{c}{|d - s_0(1-c)|}$$

The optimal markup as a share of the (markup-including) price paid by buying countries is greater, the greater the cartel's market share (c), or the lower the absolute value of the world demand elasticity for exports of the product (d), or the lower the elasticity of noncartel countries' export supply (s_0).

THE OPTIMAL TARIFF AGAIN WITH OFFER CURVES

The nationally optimal tariff on imports (or exports) can also be portrayed using the offer-curve framework of Appendix C, though this framework is less convenient for showing the *formula* for the optimal tariff. A trade-taxing country can use the tariff to move its own offer curve until it reaches the point on the foreign offer curve that maximizes the country's well-being. Figure D.2 shows this optimal tariff for a wheat-exporting country. Our country, the wheat exporter, has pushed its offer curve to the right by making the price of imported cloth in units of wheat higher within the country than the price received by our foreign cloth suppliers. At point T domestic consumers must pay for cloth at the domestic price ratio *SR/RT*, giving up *SR* in wheat for *RT* in cloth. The foreign suppliers receive only *OR* in wheat for their *RT* of cloth. The government has intervened to collect tariff revenue at the tariff rate *SO/OR*.

Figure D.2 shows that this particular tariff rate happens to be optimal, since at point T the foreign offer curve is tangent to I_0, the best indifference curve we can reach through trade. The optimal tariff is positive because the foreign offer curve is not infinitely elastic. If it were infinitely elastic, in the form of a fixed world price line coming out of the origin, our optimal tariff would be zero since no other tariff can put us on as high an indifference curve as we can reach on our free-trade, no-tariff offer curve. The same principle emerges here as in the demand–supply framework: The more elastic the foreign trading curve, the lower is our optimal tariff.

Deriving the formula for the optimal tariff rate is a little more complicated with offer curves than with demand and supply curves. The elasticity of the foreign offer curve is conventionally defined differently from a foreign supply curve, and defined in a way that is hard to identify in the offer-curve diagram itself. Any country's offer-curve elasticity is conventionally defined as the ratio of the percent response of its import demand to a percent change in the relative price of its imports:

FIGURE D.2

An Optimal
Tariff, Portrayed
with Offer
Curves

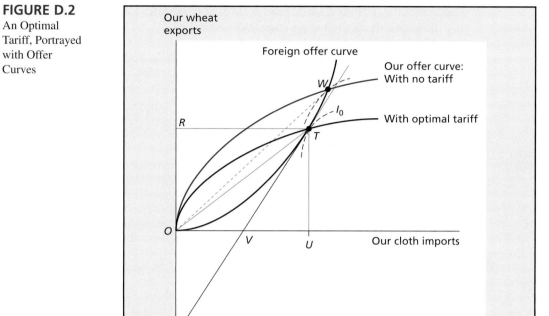

At point *T*, foreign sellers are paid only *OR* of our wheat for *OU* of their cloth. But domestic buyers have to pay the *OR* plus the tariff revenue of *OS* in extra wheat to get that *OU* of cloth. While that is bad for our cloth consumers in their role as cloth consumers, our nation gets to the better trade indifference curve I_O, helped by the fact that foreign suppliers pay some of the tariff, in effect, when they are forced to accept a lower world price (the slope of *OT*) than the price reflected by the slope *OW*, which they would receive for cloth with no tariffs.

$$\text{Offer-curve elasticity } (E_{OC}) = \frac{-(\% \text{ change in } M)}{[\% \text{ change in } (X/M)]}$$

Since the change in the price ratio X/M is not easy to spot on an offer-curve diagram like Figure D.2, let's convert this definition into a more usable equivalent:

$$E_{OC} = \frac{-(\% \text{ change in } M)}{(\% \text{ change in } X) - (\% \text{ change in } M)}$$

$$= \frac{-1}{\dfrac{(\% \text{ change in } X)}{(\% \text{ change in } M)} - 1} = \frac{1}{1 - \left(\text{slope} \dfrac{\partial X}{\partial M}\right)(M/X)}$$

This last expression can be translated into a relationship among line segments in Figure D.2. We now take the foreigners' point of view since it is their offer curve we are trying to interpret. The foreigners export cloth and import wheat. Thus the slope showing how a change in cloth exports relates to a change in their wheat imports at point *T* is the ratio *RT/RS*, and the ratio (*M/X*) is *OR/RT*. Therefore the elasticity of their offer curve becomes

$$E_{OC} = \frac{1}{1 - \dfrac{RT}{SR}\dfrac{OR}{RT}} = \frac{1}{1 - \dfrac{OR}{SR}} = \frac{SR}{SR - OR} = \frac{SR}{SO}$$

(Some authors derive an equivalent ratio on the cloth axis: $E_{OC} = UO/VO$.)

We can now see the close link between the optimal tariff rate at point *T* and the elasticity of the foreign offer curve:

$$t^* = SO / OR = \frac{SO}{SR - SO} = \frac{1}{\dfrac{SR}{SO} - 1}$$

or

$$t^* = \frac{1}{E_{OC} - 1}$$

This expression seems to differ slightly from the formula relating to the foreign supply elasticity for our imports, derived above. But the difference is only definitional. The elasticity of the foreign offer curve is defined as the elasticity of the foreigners' wheat imports with respect to the world price of wheat, not the elasticity of their cloth exports (supply of our cloth imports) with respect to the world price of cloth. Since the ratio of the foreigners' cloth exports to their wheat imports is just the world price of wheat, the foreign offer-curve elasticity [(Percent change in wheat)/(Percent change in cloth/wheat)] is equal to one plus their elasticity of supply of our import, cloth. So the above expression is equivalent to the reciprocal of the foreigners' supply elasticity of our import good, as in the demand–supply framework.[2]

---

[2] One word of caution in interpreting the optimal tariff formula relating to the foreign offer curve: The tariff rate can equal the formula $1/(E_{OC} - 1)$ for *any* tariff rate, not just the optimal one. To know that the rate is optimal, as at point *T*, you must also know that the foreign offer curve is tangent to our indifference curve.

Appendix **E**

Many Parities at Once

In Chapter 17 we introduced two parity conditions relating interest rates in different countries and exchange rates. In Chapter 18 we introduced another parity condition, purchasing power parity, that linked the prices of goods in different countries through exchange rates. These parity conditions are all based on people's ability to arbitrage between countries. As long as there are different ways of starting with one asset or product and ending up with another asset or product, the prices at which the assets or products can be exchanged will be closely related.

These parity conditions reveal relationships between foreign exchange markets and such macroeconomic phenomena as inflation and real interest rates. To see the relationships, let's think about the fact that investors can move between currencies and products. To simplify here, let us think about uniform products that can be bought or sold in either country. In addition to holding currencies today or in the future, you can hold products today or in the future. Investors must always worry about price trends for products as well as price trends for currencies. Suppose, for example, you fear more inflation in the prices of products in Britain than in America over the next 90 days. How should your decision about where to hold your wealth relate to this fear and to the interest rates and trends in exchange rates? If others share your fear, what will happen to currency and commodity markets?

There are a number of links here, portrayed by Figure E.1. The central rectangle is just the lake diagram of Figure 17.1, revisited. Now, however, there also are ways to buy and sell products with currencies. You can trade either currency for products today at the dollar price $P_\$$ or the sterling price $P_£$. If you start with today's dollars, your way of buying products depends on the relative prices shown at the bottom of Figure E.1. You might just take, say, \$10,000 and buy $10,000/P_\$$ in current products with it. Or you could take a more roundabout route, using the \$10,000 to buy £10,000/e worth of sterling and then using it to buy $10,000/(eP_£)$ in products today. Do whichever is cheaper. That is, you have an incentive to travel the cheaper of the two routes between today's dollars and today's products. The availability of this choice means that the two prices will tend to be bid into line: $P_\$ = eP_£$. This is the purchasing power parity (PPP) condition discussed in Chapter 18. As argued in that chapter, it is a general tendency that works quite well over decades, but only more roughly over shorter periods,

FIGURE E.1

Spot and
Forward
Positions
in Currencies
and Products

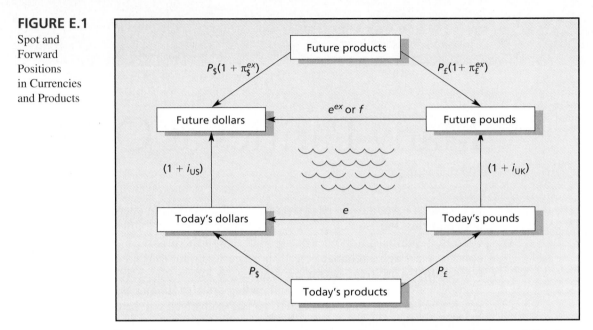

Moving with the arrow, multiply the value of your goods or investment by the expression. Moving against the arrow, divide by it.
Symbols: $P_\$$, $P_£$ = today's price level for goods (wheat, DVD movies, etc.) in terms of \$, £; $\pi_\$^{ex}$, $\pi_£^{ex}$, = the expected rate of inflation in the dollar and sterling goods price levels; e, f = the spot and forward prices of the £ (in \$/£); e^{ex} = the expected future level of the spot price of the £ (not to be confused with the present forward price of it); i_{US}, i_{UK} = the interest rates on widely marked assets (e.g., treasury bills) in America and Britain. (Ignore transactions fees and ignore futures markets in goods such as grain futures.)

because of trade barriers, the costs of transactions and transportation, and the underlying differences in the goods whose prices are being compared.

A version of purchasing power parity should also hold for the future. If it doesn't, there may be unexploited chances for profitable arbitrage. Buying goods with dollars in the future should look equally cheap whether we expect to buy directly at the future dollar price or at the future pound price of goods times the dollar price of getting each pound. These different prices will depend on how much price inflation people expect between now and the future (say, 90 days from now). If people expect dollar prices to go up by the fraction $\pi_\$^{ex}$ and pound prices to go up by the fraction $\pi_£^{ex}$, then these average expectations should be tied to what future exchange rate people expect (e^{ex}). Their expectations should equate the direct and indirect dollar prices of goods shown at the top of Figure E.1, or $P_\$(1 + \pi_\$^{ex}) = e^{ex} P_£(1 + \pi_£^{ex})$. This condition can be called **expected future PPP.** It is only a rough tendency, like today's PPP, when actual changes in prices are used as measures of the expected changes $\pi_\$^{ex}$ and $\pi_£^{ex}$.

The tendencies toward purchasing power parity today and in our expectations about the future provide links between expected price inflation, interest rates, and exchange rates. Recall from Chapter 17 that the forward price of the pound, f, should equal e^{ex}, the average expectation about the future value of the spot rate. Combining the equality $e^{ex} = f$ with the interest parity conditions of Chapter 17 gives further results shown in Figure E.2's summary of key parity conditions.

One result that emerges from all these arbitrage equilibria is that real interest rates should tend to be the same across countries. This is only a rough long-run tendency. In fact, expected real interest rates, as best (such) expectations can be measured, can differ noticeably between countries for years at a stretch. There is nonetheless a tendency toward equality.

Figure E.2 shows some of the intricacy we must expect from increasingly international financial and product markets. To illustrate, let us return to a question posed above: What would happen if more inflation in Britain were expected in the near future? If you alone have this new perception of higher British inflation, you can act on it by moving away from sterling into dollars or products over any of the routes shown in Figure E.1. As long as your fear is confirmed, you will gain from the eventual general exodus from sterling. If everyone eventually agrees with your quick interpretation of the latest news, then prices and rates must change. The nominal interest rate must rise in Britain and the forward premium on the pound must decline, as the parity conditions in Figure E.2 show.

The moral of Figure E.1 and Figure E.2 is that interest rates, exchange rates, and expected inflation rates are tied together. Whatever affects international differences in one is likely to affect international differences in the other two. It should be stressed, though, that one parity is much more reliable than the others. That one is the covered interest parity condition.

FIGURE E.2

International Parities

1. **Purchasing power parity (PPP) today:** $e\, P_£ = P_\$$, roughly (see Chapter 18).
2. **Expected future PPP:** $e^{ex}\, P_£(1 + \pi_£^{ex}) = P_\$(1 + \pi_\$^{ex})$, roughly, so that $e^{ex}/e = (1 + \pi_\$^{ex})/(1 + \pi_£^{ex})$, or, approximately, Expected appreciation of £ = Expected \$ inflation – Expected £ inflation.
3. **Covered interest parity:** $(f/e) = (1 + i_{US})/(1 + i_{UK})$ definitely.
4. **Speculators' forward equilibrium:** Forward rate measures average expected future spot rate, or $e^{ex} = f$, we think.
5. **Uncovered interest parity:** $(e^{ex}/e) = (1 + i_{US})/(1 + i_{UK})$, we think. Combining parities 2, 3, and 5, we see that

$$e^{ex}/e = f/e = (1 + i_{US})/(1 + i_{UK}) = (1 + \pi_\$^{ex})/(1 + \pi_£^{ex}),$$

or, approximately,

Expected appreciation of £ = Premium on forward £
= Difference between \$ and £ interest rates
= Expected difference between \$ and £ inflation rates

So we expect real interest rates to be roughly equal internationally:
6. **Real interest rate equilibrium:** $(1 + i_{US})/(1 + \pi_\$^{ex}) = (1 + i_{UK})/(1 + \pi_£^{ex})$ or, approximately, $(i_{US} - \pi_\$^{ex}) = (i_{UK} - \pi_£^{ex})$.

Appendix F

Aggregate Demand and Aggregate Supply in the Open Economy

In Chapter 21 we noted that a difference between the actual level of real GDP and its full-employment level will put pressure on the country's product price level or inflation rate. The formal IS-LM-FE model that we used in Chapters 21, 22, and 23 does have not an explicit role for the adjustment of the country's level of prices. This appendix develops a model of a country's macroeconomy that focuses on price adjustment over time. The standard way to analyze price adjustment is to picture the economy as a combination of aggregate demand and aggregate supply.

THE AGGREGATE DEMAND CURVE

A country's **aggregate demand curve** shows the level of real GDP that represent a short-run equilibrium for each possible price level, given fundamental conditions in the economy. We presume that this short-run equilibrium incorporates all adjustments to a triple intersection in the IS-LM-FE picture for the country. That is, for a country with a fixed exchange rate, the aggregate demand curve includes induced intervention to defend the fixed exchange rate (as discussed in Chapter 22). If the country instead has a floating exchange rate, the aggregate demand curve includes the induced adjustment of the exchange rate value (as discussed in Chapter 23).

Figure F.1A shows an aggregate demand curve. To see how it is derived, consider that we start at point A, where we know that aggregate demand level Y_1 corresponds to price level P_1. What is the effect on the level of aggregate demand if the price level changes to P_2? At this higher price level, the level of aggregate demand changes for two reasons:

- First, the nominal demand for money increases (see equation 21.10 in Chapter 21). The LM curve shifts to the left, and the level of aggregate demand tends to decrease.

- Second, the increase in the country's price level decreases the country's international price competitiveness. The IS curve shifts to the left, and the level of aggregate demand tends to decrease.

For both of these reasons, the level of aggregate demand falls to Y_2 at point B if the price level increases to P_2.[1] The aggregate demand curve AD is downward-sloping.

The AD curve shifts if there is a change in anything fundamental (other than the price level) that affects the level of aggregate demand in the economy. Examples include exogenous changes in consumption and domestic real investment, changes in fiscal policy, and a devaluation by a country using a fixed exchange rate.

AGGREGATE SUPPLY

Figure F.1B shows two types of aggregate supply curves. The **long-run aggregate supply curve** (AS_{LR}) is vertical and corresponds to the full-employment level of real GDP. This level of real GDP, also called potential real GDP, is the output the country can produce using the factor resources available in the country and the technologies in use in the country. (It corresponds to production being on the country's production possibility curve we used in Part One.) We presume that markets in the country work well enough that the economy tends toward full employment in the long run. That is, in the long-run prices fully adjust so the economy achieves full employment of its resources. The AS_{LR} curve shifts if there are changes in factor resource availability or changes in technologies used in production.

The **short-run aggregate supply curve** (AS_{SR}) is upward sloping, because some prices in the economy do not adjust quickly. That is, some prices are sticky in the short run. For instance, a dry cleaner does not continuously adjust its prices as it sees what business arrives. Instead, the dry cleaner has a price list that it sticks to, and it typically changes the price list infrequently. Similarly, tuition at most universities is adjusted at most once per year. Essentially, the short-run supply curve is anchored by a set of prices that are given for the short-run time period.

---

[1] The decrease in international price competitiveness also shifts the FE curve to the left. In addition, the new IS-LM intersection is not necessarily on the new FE curve. If not, then with a fixed exchange rate there will be intervention to defend the fixed rate. Or, with a floating exchange rate the exchange rate will change. The adjustments to external balance will alter the specific slope of the AD curve, but it will still be downward-sloping. There is no general rule that says that the aggregate demand curve is necessarily steeper or flatter with a fixed or floating exchange rate, and we will ignore any differences in the slope in the remainder of this appendix.

FIGURE F.1

Aggregate Demand and Aggregate Supply

To see the slope of the short-run aggregate supply curve consider first an extreme case. If no prices can change in the short-run, then the short-run aggregate supply curve would be a horizontal line (up to some high level of real GDP). If instead some prices change in the short-run but others do not, then the aggregate supply curve is upward-sloping. That is, it is "in-between" the horizontal aggregate supply curve where no prices change and the long-run aggregate supply curve where all prices are completely flexible. We also presume that the economy in the short run can operate beyond its long-run full-employment level of production, so part of the short-run aggregate supply curve is to the right of the long-run aggregate supply curve. Essentially, it is possible for people to work more hours than they normally want to, and for firms to run their machines more than they normally do, but this high level of factor use cannot be sustained for long periods of time.

The short-run aggregate supply curve shifts because the level of the sticky prices that anchors the curve changes over time. In fact, this is the essence of the slow price adjustment that characterizes the macroeconomics of many countries. The short-run aggregate supply curve also shifts if there is a shock to the country's price level, or if there is a shift in the long-run aggregate supply curve.

THE PRICE ADJUSTMENT PROCESS: AN EXAMPLE

Before we analyze various kinds of shocks that can hit an open macroeconomy, let's first look at the nature of price adjustment as the economy moves beyond a short-run period of time. Consider Figure F.2, in which the country's economy is at a short-run equilibrium at point A_1. Because A_1 is to the left of the AS_{LR}, the

FIGURE F.2
The Price
Adjustment
Process

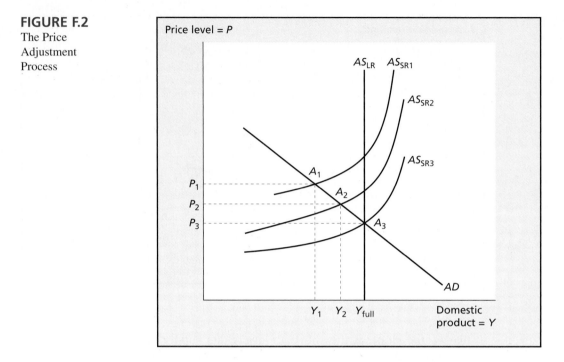

actual level of production Y_1 is below the full-employment level Y_{full}. The level of aggregate demand is low, relative to the economy's potential for producing goods and services.

With weak product markets and high levels of unemployment of labor and other resources, there is downward pressure on product and factor prices. As the economy moves beyond the short-run, the price level falls as the short-run aggregate supply curve falls from AS_{SR1} to AS_{SR2}. The decline in the price level from P_1 to P_2 moves the economy down its aggregate demand curve from A_1 to A_2. This occurs because interest rates fall as the nominal demand for money decreases, and the country gains international price competitiveness as its price level declines. Interest sensitive spending increases and net exports increase, so real GDP increases, from Y_1 to Y_2.

The process continues until the short-run aggregate supply curve has shifted down to AS_{SR3}, and the price level has declined to P_3. At this triple intersection the economy is now in a long-run equilibrium operating at potential real GDP Y_{full}. However, the process of getting to this long-run equilibrium may be slow and painful, if there is resistance to reductions in product prices, wages, and other resource prices. There may be a case for speeding up the process of achieving full employment by using expansionary government policy to shift the AD curve to the right, rather than waiting for the price adjustment.

SHOCKS AND PRICE ADJUSTMENT

The aggregate demand-aggregate supply model can be used to gain additional insights into the effects of shocks in the open macroeconomy. We are building on what we have already learned in Chapters 22 and 23 using the IS-LM-FE analysis. We will first examine the same four types of shocks that we examined in those chapters, for both a fixed exchange rate and a floating exchange rate. We will then turn to look at two types of shocks to aggregate supply.

Internal Shocks

As we saw in Chapter 22, a *domestic monetary shock* has no effect with a fixed exchange rate, assuming that the country's monetary authority cannot or does not sterilize. The monetary shock is neutralized by the induced adjustments in the domestic money supply as the country's monetary authority intervenes to defend the fixed rate. So there is nothing for the AD-AS analysis to show.

A domestic monetary shock does have an effect with a floating exchange rate. Figure F.3 shows the effect of a shift to an expansionary monetary policy, which shifts the AD curve to the right, from AD_1 to AD_2. If the economy starts from a position of long-run equilibrium at point C_1 (P_1 and Y_{full}), the economy shifts to point C_2, with a higher price level P_2 and a higher real GDP Y_2. Excessively strong aggregate demand is driving the price level up, and inflation is rising. As

FIGURE F.3
Domestic
Monetary
Shock, Floating
Exchange Rate

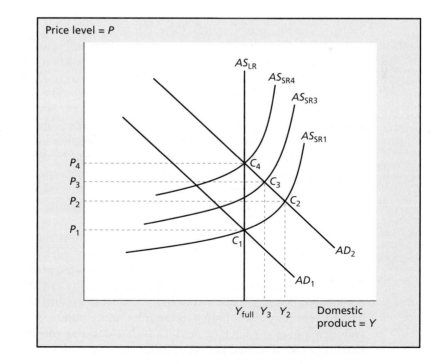

the economy moves beyond the short-run, even the sticky prices begin to increase, and the short-run aggregate supply curve shifts up from AS_{SR1} to AS_{SR3}. The price level rises to P_3. The higher price level takes some of the strength out of the level of aggregate demand, because the interest rate is increasing back up as the nominal demand for money increases, and because the country is losing international price competitiveness as the price level rises. This process continues until the aggregate supply curve has shifted up to AS_{SR4}, and the economy is back to production Y_{full} with a higher price level P_4. In the long run, expansionary monetary policy causes inflation and a higher price level, the relationship that we focused on in Chapter 18 when we discussed the monetary approach to exchange rate determination. In the short- and medium-runs, the slow price adjustment is a key part of exchange rate overshooting that was also discussed in Chapter 18.

A *domestic spending shock* causes a shift in the aggregate demand curve. The magnitude of the shift may differ depending on whether the country has a fixed or floating exchange rate, but the general direction is the same. For instance, a shift to an expansionary fiscal policy causes a shift to the left in the AD curve. If the economy begins at full employment, then the price-adjustment story is similar to the one that we just looked at for monetary policy with a floating exchange rate. Actual real GDP is temporarily above its long-run potential, the inflation rate and the price level increase, and production falls back to Y_{full}.

International Capital Flow Shock

An international capital-flow shock shifts the aggregate demand curve, because of the induced effect on the money supply (fixed exchange rate) or on the exchange rate (if it is floating). Consider an adverse shock in which investors are pulling their financial capital out of the country. In Figure F.4 the country begins at point E_1, and then the shock hits. If the country has a *fixed exchange rate,* the intervention to defend the fixed rate requires that the country's monetary authority sell foreign currency and buy domestic currency. The country's money supply shrinks, and *the aggregate demand curve shifts to the left,* from AD_1 to AD_2. The country goes into a recession, and production falls from Y_{full} to Y_2. Downward price adjustment could eventually return the economy to full employment as the economy will move down the AD_2 curve to point E_3. But this could be a slow process. Expansionary fiscal policy could be used to speed the process, by shifting the aggregate demand curve back to the right.

Consider now that the country instead has a *floating exchange rate,* again starting from point E_1 in Figure F.4. The capital outflow results in a depreciation of the country's currency. The depreciation improves the country's international price competitiveness, and *the aggregate demand curve shifts to the right* from AD_1 to AD_4. The strong aggregate demand causes the price level to increase, and the price adjustment process is moving the economy toward point E_5. If the economy is overheating, there is a case for a shift to contractionary monetary policy or contractionary fiscal policy. If contractionary policy is used to shift the aggregate demand curve back to the left, it can stabilize the economy at production level Y_{full} and avoid the period of inflation.

FIGURE F.4

An International
Capital Flow
Shock: Fixed
Exchange Rate
or Floating
Exchange Rate

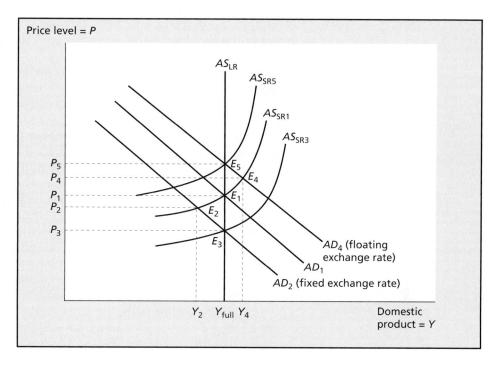

International Trade Shock

With a floating exchange rate, an international trade shock has no lasting effect
on the economy, once we include the induced change in the exchange rate. As we
saw in Chapter 23, an adverse international trade shock leads to a depreciation of
the country's currency, and the currency depreciation reverses the negative effect
on real GDP. There is nothing for the AD-AS analysis to show.

With a fixed exchange rate, an adverse international trade shock reduces the
net exports and the intervention to defend the fixed exchange rate leads to a
reduction in the domestic money supply. Both of these changes result in a reduction in aggregate demand. The economy goes into a recession. Downward adjustment in the country's price level will return the economy to full employment over
time, but the country instead could use a shift to expansionary fiscal policy to
shift the AD curve back to the right and speed the adjustment.

Shocks to Aggregate Supply

Shocks to aggregate supply can affect one or both of the short-run and long-run
aggregate supply curves. A shock to the short-run aggregate supply curve, sometimes called a price shock, occurs when some economic change causes a quick
and substantial change in the price level. A shock to the long-run aggregate supply
curve occurs when some economic change alters the full-employment level of real
production, perhaps because of a change in the amount of resources available, or a

change in the technology used in production. Let's examine two types of aggregate supply shocks, an oil price shock in an oil-importing country, and a large improvement in technology.

Oil price shock. In the 1970s two major oil-price shocks hit the world economy, and smaller shocks occurred in 1990 and the early 2000s. When an oil-price shock hits, it has several effects on the economy of an oil-importing country. First, it causes a sudden jump upward in the country's price level, because oil and the products produced from oil are important to and used throughout the economy, and because the short-run demand for oil is price inelastic. Second, the higher oil prices can have long-lasting effects on the country's supply capabilities. For instance, some capital equipment that can be used profitably when oil prices (or energy prices more generally) are low, is uneconomic to use when oil (energy) costs are higher. Third, the jump in oil prices tends to increase the value of imports, so the country's trade balance deteriorates. That is, the oil price shock also causes an international trade shock. Here we focus more on the first two effects.

Figure F.5 shows an oil-importing country, initially in long-run equilibrium at point F_1. An oil-price shock now hits—a sudden large increase in world oil prices. The price shock causes an upward shift in the short-run aggregate supply curve from AS_{SR1} to AS_{SR2}. The decline in the useful capital stock causes a shift to the left in the long-run aggregate supply curve from AS_{LR} to AS'_{LR}. (We presume, as seems realistic, that the shift in the short-run curve is large relative to the shift in the long-run curve.) The economy shifts in the short run to point F_2,

FIGURE F.5

Oil Price Shock

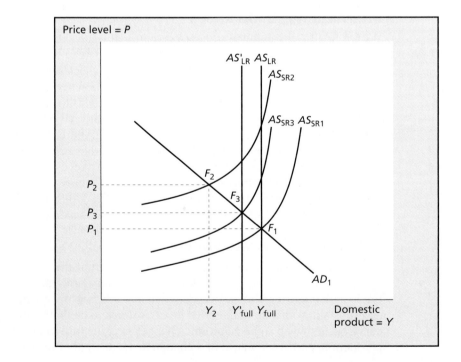

the intersection of the new short-run aggregate supply curve with the aggregate demand curve.[2] The country is experiencing two macroeconomic problems at the same time:

- The unemployment rate is increasing because the economy goes into recession as real GDP declines.

- The inflation rate is rising because of the oil price shock.

This combination of rising unemployment and rising inflation is sometimes called stagflation.

   If there is no response by government policies, then the economy will adjust back toward long-run equilibrium as the economy moves beyond the short run. At the high price level the weak level of aggregate demand puts downward pressure on prices and wages. Once again, a process of downward price adjustment can shift the short-run aggregate supply curve down and move the economy back toward full employment at point F_3. Because of the adverse effect of the oil price shock on the economy's production capabilities, the new level of potential real GDP is lower, only Y'_{full}.[3]

   How should government policies respond to the oil price shock? The policy decision-makers face a dilemma. If they respond by loosening policy to fight the recession, the aggregate demand curve shifts to the right. The recovery from recession is faster, but the country experiences additional price inflation. If the policymakers instead tighten policy to fight the rising inflation, the aggregate demand curve shifts to the left, and the recession is deeper and longer. There are no easy decisions for policymakers in responding to an oil price shock.

   Technology improvement. Another kind of shock to aggregate supply is a period of rapid improvements in production technology in the economy. We can use Figure F.6 to illustrate this case. Again the economy begins in a long-run equilibrium at point G_1. The improvement in technology then shifts both the long-run and short-run aggregate supply curves to the right, as the economy's production capabilities expand. In the short-run, the economy moves to an equilibrium at point G_2, with an increase in real GDP and a somewhat lower price level as some of the technology improvement is passed forward to consumers in the form of lower prices. However, the economy is still short of its new potential GDP Y'_{full}. If there is no change in government policy, the price level will continue to fall as the economy moves beyond the short run. The full adjustment to the new technology is the triple intersection at point G_3 as the short-run aggregate supply falls to AS_{SR3}. Government policymakers could speed the adjustment to the new potential real GDP by using expansionary policy to shift the aggregate demand curve to the right.

---

[2] If the country has a fixed exchange rate, the adverse international trade shock also causes the aggregate demand curve to shift to the left.
[3] If, instead, there is no change in the long-run aggregate supply curve, then the downward price adjustment must return the economy all the way back to point F_1.

DEVALUATION OF A FIXED EXCHANGE RATE

Our final example of using AD-AS analysis is the devaluation of a fixed exchange rate, from its initial fixed value to a new lower fixed value for the country's currency. Figure F.7 shows the effects of a currency devaluation.

If the country begins at point H_1, the currency devaluation results in an increase in aggregate demand as the country gains international price competitiveness, so the aggregate demand curve shifts from AD_1 to AD_2. Assuming that the short-run aggregate supply curve is unaffected, real GDP increases from Y_{full} to Y_2. There is some upward pressure on the price level, which rises from P_1 to P_2. As the economy moves beyond the short run, the strong aggregate demand causes further upward pressure on the price level, and the short-run aggregate supply shifts up. The economy is headed for a new long-run equilibrium at point H_3, with a higher price level of P_3 and production returned to Y_{full}.

The AD-AS analysis of devaluation brings out two important points. First, the devaluation has little effect in the long run. The gain in price competitiveness from the decline in the nominal exchange-rate value of the country's currency is offset by the rise in domestic prices. This is the reversion to purchasing power parity in the long run that we examined in Chapter 18. Second, there is a risk that the devaluation could have little effect even in the short run. The devaluation results in an increase in the domestic currency price of imports. If people in the country also quickly raise domestic prices and wages when they see or anticipate that import prices are rising, the short-run aggregate supply curve shifts up quickly. The country quickly moves to point H_3. There is little effect of the devaluation, because the higher inflation has quickly offset the devaluation.

FIGURE F.6
Technology
Improvement
Increases
Potential GDP

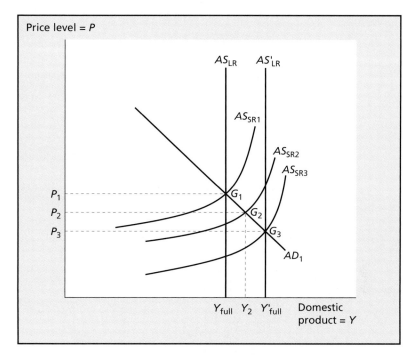

FIGURE F.6
Technology
Improvement
Increases
Potential GDP

FIGURE F.7
Devaluation
of a Fixed
Exchange Rate

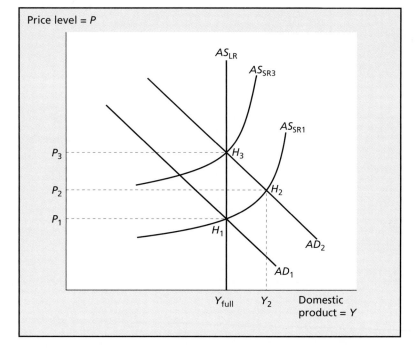

FIGURE F.7
Devaluation
of a Fixed
Exchange Rate

Appendix G

Devaluation and the Current Account Balance

This appendix extends Chapter 22's explorations of the possible effects of a drop in the value of the home currency on the trade balance or the net balance on current account.[1] It derives a general formula for such effects and applies it to some special cases that establish the range of possible results.

CURRENT ACCOUNT ELASTICITIES

The current account (or trade) balance defined in foreign currency (here, pounds, the foreign currency) is[2]

$$CA_{\pounds} = V_x - V_m = P_x^{\pounds} X - P_m^{\pounds} M \tag{G.1}$$

where V_x is the value of exports, and V_m is the value of imports. To derive the elasticity of the current account balance with respect to the exchange rate, begin by differentiating the balance:

$$dCA_{\pounds} = dV_x - dV_m \tag{G.2}$$

or

$$dCA_{\pounds}/V_m = dV_x/V_m - dV_m/V_m \tag{G.3}$$

---

[1] There are other determinants of the current account balance besides the exchange rate, of course. We focus on the role of exchange rate changes.
[2] The derivation follows that given in Jaroslav Vanek (1962).

Let us define

$$E_{ca} = \frac{dCA_{£}/V_m}{de/e} = \text{The elasticity of the current account balance with respect to } e, \text{ the exchange rate (measured as the price of the foreign currency, \$/£)}$$

$$E_x = \frac{dV_x/V_x}{de/e} = \text{The elasticity of the value of exports with respect to the exchange rate } e$$

$$E_m = \frac{dV_m/V_m}{de/e} = \text{The elasticity of the value of imports with respect to the exchange rate } e$$

Then if we divide both sides of (G.3) by the proportion of change in the exchange rate (de/e), we get

$$E_{ca} = \frac{V_x}{V_m} E_x - E_m \qquad (G.4)$$

Deriving the formula for the effect of the exchange rate on the current account balance amounts to deriving a formula relating E_{ca} to the underlying elasticities of demand and supply for exports and imports.

EXPORT AND IMPORT ELASTICITIES

The export (or import) value is defined as the product of a trade price and a traded quantity. We therefore need to derive expressions giving the elasticities of these trade prices and quantities with respect to the exchange rate. Let's do so on the export side. There the supply, which depends on a dollar price ($P_x^{\$} = P_x^{£} \cdot e$), must be equated with demand, which depends on a pound price. We start with the equilibrium condition in the export market, differentiate it, and keep rearranging terms until the equation takes a form relating elasticities to the change in export prices:

$$X = S_x(P_x^{£}e) = D_x(P_x^{£}) \qquad (G.5)$$

$$dX = \frac{\partial S_x}{\partial P_x^{\$}}(edP_x^{£} + P_x^{£}de) = \frac{\partial D_x}{\partial P_x^{£}}dP_x^{£} \qquad (G.6)$$

$$dX / X = \frac{\partial S_x}{\partial P_x^{\$}}\frac{1}{S_x}(edP_x^{£} + P_x^{£}de) = \frac{\partial D_x}{\partial P_x^{£}}\frac{1}{D_x}dP_x^{£} \qquad (G.7)$$

Multiplying within both sides by $P_x^{\$}/e = P_x^{£}$ and dividing by de/e yields

$$\frac{dX/X}{de/e} = \left[\frac{\partial S_x}{\partial P_x^{\$}}\frac{P_x^{\$}}{S_x}\right]\left(\frac{dP_x^{£}/P_x^{£}}{de/e} + 1\right) = \left[\frac{\partial D_x}{\partial P_x^{£}}\frac{P_x^{£}}{D_x}\right]\frac{dP_x^{£}/P_x^{£}}{de/e} \qquad (G.8)$$

The expressions in brackets on the left and right are the elasticities of export supply (s_x) and demand (d_x), respectively, so that

$$\frac{dX/X}{de/e} = s_x\left(\frac{dP_x^£/P_x^£}{de/e}+1\right) = d_x\frac{dP_x^£/P_x^£}{de/e} \tag{G.9}$$

and the percent response of the pound price of exports to the exchange rate is

$$\frac{dP_x^£/P_x^£}{de/e} = \frac{s_x}{d_x - s_x} \tag{G.10}$$

This has to be negative or zero, since d_x is negative or zero and s_x is positive or zero. (The response of the dollar price of exports to the exchange rate equals this same expression plus one.)

Recalling that the value of exports equals the price times the quantity of exports, we can use the fact that any percent change in this export value equals the percent price change plus the percent quantity change:

$$E_x = \frac{dX/X}{de/e} + \frac{dP_x^£/P_x^£}{de/e} \tag{G.11}$$

From (G.9) and (G.10), we get the relationship between the elasticity of the value of exports and the elasticities of demand and supply of exports:

$$E_x = \frac{d_x s_x}{d_x - s_x} + \frac{s_x}{d_x - s_x} = \frac{d_x + 1}{(d_x/s_x) - 1} \tag{G.12}$$

which can be of any sign.

Going through all the same steps on the imports side yields expressions for the responses of the pound price of imports, the quantity of imports, and the value of imports with respect to the exchange rate:

$$\frac{dP_m^£/P_m^£}{de/e} = \frac{d_m}{s_m - d_m}(\leq 0) \tag{G.13}$$

$$\frac{dM/M}{de/e} = \frac{s_m d_m}{s_m - d_m}(\leq 0) \tag{G.14}$$

and

$$E_m = \frac{s_m + 1}{(s_m/d_m) - 1}(\leq 0) \tag{G.15}$$

THE GENERAL TRADE BALANCE FORMULA AND THE MARSHALL–LERNER CONDITION

We have now gathered all the materials we need to give the general formula for the elasticity of response of the current account (or trade) balance to the exchange rate. From (G.4), (G.12), and (G.15), the formula is

The elasticity of the trade balance with respect to the exchange rate =

$$E_{ca} = \frac{V_x}{V_m}\left(\frac{d_x+1}{(d_x/s_x)-1}\right) - \frac{s_m+1}{(s_m/d_m)-1} \tag{G.16}$$

By studying this general formula and some of its special cases, we can determine what elasticities are crucial in making the trade balance response stable (i.e., in making E_{ca} positive). It turns out that

> The more elastic are import demand and export demand, the more "stable" (positive) will be the response of the current account balance.

Demand elasticities are crucial, but supply elasticities have no clear general effect on the trade balance response.

These results can be appreciated more easily after we have considered four important special cases listed in Figure G.1. The perverse result of a trade balance that worsens after the domestic currency has been devalued is the *inelastic-demand case,* discussed in Chapter 22. As shown in Figure G.1, this Case 1, in which $d_m = d_x = 0$, yields clear perversity regardless of the initial state of the trade balance. The "J curve" of Chapter 22 is based on the suspicion that this case may sometimes obtain in the short run, before demand elasticities have had a chance to rise.

FIGURE G.1
Devaluation and the Trade Balance: Applying the General Formula to Special Cases

	Assumed Elasticities	Effect of Devaluation on the Trade Balance
Case 1: Inelastic demands	$d_m = d_x = 0$	Trade balance worsens: $E_{ca} = -\dfrac{V_x}{V_m} < 0$
Case 2: Small country	$s_m = -d_x = \infty$	Trade balance improves: $E_{ca} = \dfrac{V_x}{V_m}s_x - d_m > 0$
Case 3: Prices fixed in buyer's currencies	$d_m = d_x = -\infty$	Trade balance improves: $E_{ca} = \dfrac{V_x}{V_m}s_x + s_m + 1 > 0$
Case 4: Prices fixed in sellers' currencies	$s_x = s_m = \infty$	It depends: $E_{ca} = \dfrac{V_x}{V_m}(-d_x - 1) - d_m \gtrless 0$

In Case 4, if trade was not initially in surplus, the Marshall–Lerner condition is sufficient for improvement: $|d_x + d_m| > 1$.

A second special case, also discussed in Chapter 22, is the *small-country case,* in which both export prices and import prices are fixed in terms of foreign currencies in large outside-world markets. This Case 2 is represented in Figure G.1 by infinite foreign elasticities: $s_m = -d_x = \infty$. In the small-country case, devaluation or depreciation of the home currency definitely improves the current account balance.

Consistent with the emphasis on the importance of demand elasticities is the extreme result for Case 3. With *prices fixed in buyers' currencies,* for example, by infinitely elastic demands for imports both at home and abroad ($d_m = d_x = -\infty$), the general formula yields the most improvement.

The fourth special case considered here is one in which *prices are kept fixed in sellers' currencies.* This fits the Keynesian family of macromodels, in which supplies are infinitely elastic and prices are fixed within countries. In Case 4, the net effect of devaluation on the current account balance depends on a famous condition, the **Marshall–Lerner condition,** which says that the absolute values of the two demand elasticities must exceed unity: $|d_x + d_m| > 1$. This is sufficient for a stable result if the current account balance is not initially in surplus (i.e., if $V_x \leq V_m$, as is typical of devaluations). While the Marshall–Lerner condition strictly holds only in a narrow range of models, it is a rougher guide to the likelihood of the stable result, since it reminds us of the overall pattern that higher demand elasticities give more stable results.

Suggested Answers—
Questions and Problems

Chapter 2

1. Consumer surplus is the net gain to consumers from being able to buy a product through a market. It is the difference between the highest price someone is willing to pay for each unit of the product and the actual market price that is paid, summed over all units that are demanded and consumed. The highest price that someone is willing to pay for the unit indicates the value that the buyer attaches to that unit. To measure consumer surplus for a product using real-world data, three major pieces of information are needed: (1) the market price, (2) the quantity demanded, and (3) the slope (or shape) of the demand curve in terms of how quantity demanded would change if the market price increased. Consumer surplus could then be measured as the area below the demand curve and above the market-price line.

3. The country's supply of exports is the amount by which the country's domestic quantity supplied exceeds the country's domestic quantity demanded. The supply-of-exports curve is derived by finding the difference between domestic quantity supplied and domestic quantity demanded for each possible market price for which quantity supplied exceeds quantity demanded. The supply-of-exports curve shows the quantity that the country would want to export for each possible international market price.

5. There is no domestic market for winter coats in this tropical country, but there is a domestic supply curve. If the world price for coats is above the minimum price at which the country would supply any coats (the price at which the supply curve hits the price axis), then in free trade the country would produce and export coats. The country gains from this trade because it creates producer surplus—the area above the supply curve and below the international price line, up to the intersection (which indicates the quantity that the country will produce and export).

7. It is true that opening trade bids prices into equality between countries. With a competitive market this also means that marginal costs are equal between countries. But ongoing trade is necessary to maintain this equilibrium. If trade were to stop, the world would return to the no-trade equilibrium. Then prices would differ, and there would be an incentive for arbitrage. The ongoing trade in the free-trade equilibrium is why prices are equalized—trade is not self-eliminating.

9. The demand curve D_{US} shifts to the right. The U.S. demand-for-imports curve D_m shifts to the right. The equilibrium international price rises above 1,000. It is shown by the intersection of the new U.S. D_m curve and the original S_x curve.

11. a. With no international trade, equilibrium requires that domestic quantity demanded (Q_D) equals domestic quantity supplied (Q_S). Setting the two equations equal to each other, we can find the equilibrium price with no trade:

$$350 - (P/2) = -200 + 5P$$

The equilibrium no-trade price is $P = 100$. Using one of the equations, we find that the no-trade quantity is 300.

b. At a price of 120, Belgium's quantity demanded is 290, and its quantity supplied is 400. In free trade Belgium exports 110 units.

c. Belgian consumer surplus declines. With no trade it is a larger triangle below the demand curve and above the 100 price line. With free trade it is a smaller triangle below the demand curve and above the 120 price line. Belgian producer surplus increases. With no trade it is a smaller triangle above the supply curve and below the 100 price line. With free trade it is a larger triangle above the supply curve and below the 120 price line. The net national gain from trade is the difference between the gain of producer surplus and the loss of consumer surplus. This gain is a triangle whose base is the quantity traded (110) and whose height is the change in price ($120 - 100 = 20$) so the total gain is 1,100.

Chapter 3

1. Disagree. This statement describes absolute advantage. It would imply that a country that has a higher labor productivity in all goods would export all goods and import nothing. Ricardo instead showed that mutually beneficial trade is based on comparative advantage— trading according to maximum relative advantage. The country will export those goods whose *relative* labor productivity (relative to the other country *and* relative to other goods) is high, and import those other goods whose relative labor productivity is low.

3. Pugelovia has 20 percent of the world's labor [$20/(20 + 80)$], whereas it has 30 percent [$3/(3 + 7)$] of the world's land. Pugelovia is land-abundant and labor-scarce relative to the rest of the world. H–O theory predicts that Pugelovia will export the land-intensive good (wheat) and import the labor-intensive good (cloth).

5. To derive the country's cloth demand curve, we need to find the price line for each price ratio, and then find the tangency with a community indifference curve. The tangency indicates the quantity demanded at that price ratio. The price line has the slope indicated by the price ratio, and it is tangent to the country's production-possibilities curve. (This tangency indicates the country's production at this price ratio.) As each price ratio is lower, the tangency with the production-possibilities curve shifts to the northwest, as shown in the graph on the next page. As the price line shifts and becomes flatter, the tangency with a community indifference curve shifts to the right. Representative numbers are shown, with each decrease of price by 0.5 increasing quantity demanded by 10.

7. a. Lindertania has an absolute disadvantage in both goods. Its labor input per unit of output is higher for both goods, so its labor productivity (output per unit of input) is lower for both goods.

b. Lindertania has a comparative advantage in producing rice. Its relative disadvantage is lower ($75/50 < 100/50$).

c. With no trade, the relative price of rice would be $75/100 = 0.75$ yards of cloth per bushel of rice.

d. With free trade the equilibrium international price ratio will be greater than or equal to 0.75 yard per bushel, and less than or equal to 1.0 yard per bushel (the no-trade price ratio in the rest of the world). Lindertania will export rice and import cloth.

9. a. With no trade, the real wages in the United States are $1/2 = 0.5$ bushel per hour and $1/4 = 0.25$ yard per hour. The real wages in the rest of the world are $1/1.5 = .67$ bushel per hour and $1/1 = 1.0$ yard per hour. The absolute advantages (higher labor productivities) in the rest of the world translate into higher real wages in the rest of the world.

b. With free trade the United States completely specializes in producing wheat. The U.S. real wage with respect to wheat remains

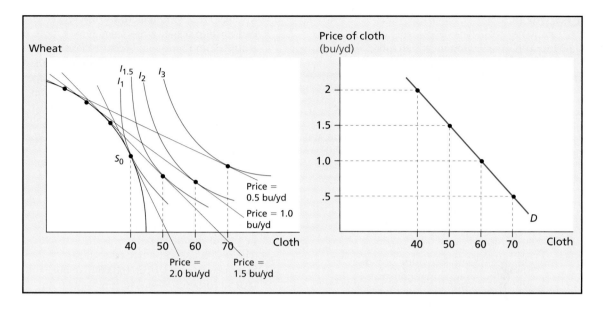

0.5 bushel per hour. Cloth is obtained by trade at a price ratio of one, so the U.S. real wage with respect to cloth is 0.5 yard per hour. The gains from trade for the United States are shown by the higher real wage with respect to cloth (0.5 > 0.25). As long as U.S. labor wants to buy some cloth, the United States gains from trade by gaining greater purchasing power over cloth. With free trade the rest of the world completely specializes in producing cloth. Its real wage with respect to cloth is unchanged at 1.0 yard per hour. Its real wage with respect to wheat rises to 1.0 bushel per hour, because it can trade for wheat at the price ratio of one. The rest of the world gains from greater purchasing power over wheat.

  c. The rest of the world still has the higher real wage. Absolute advantage matters— higher labor productivity translates into higher real wages.

11. a. They could make 7 wheat, with no cloth production.

  b. They could make 6 cloth, with no wheat production.

  c. The ppc is not a straight line between (6 cloth, 0 wheat) and (0 cloth, 7 wheat).

Rather it has four parts with different slopes. Here is a tour of the ppc, starting down on the cloth axis (x axis). They could produce anything from (6 cloth, 0 wheat) up to (5, 2) by having A shift between cloth and wheat while the others make only cloth. Then they could make anything from (5, 2) up to (3, 5) by keeping A busy growing wheat and B and C busy at cloth, while D switches between the two tasks. Then they could make anything from (3, 5) up to (2, 6) by choosing how to divide C's time, keeping B in wheat making and A and D in cloth. Finally, they could make anything between (2, 6) and (0, 7) by varying B's tasks while the others make cloth.

  Study this result to see how the right assignments relate to people's comparative advantages. Note that with four different kinds of comparative advantage, there is a convex curve with four slopes. In general, the greater the number of different kinds of individuals, the smoother and more convex the curve. Therefore, we get an increasing-cost ppc for the nation, even if every individual is a Ricardian constant-cost type.

Chapter 4

1. Mexico is abundant in unskilled labor and scarce in skilled labor relative to the United States or Canada. With freer trade Mexico will export a greater volume of unskilled-labor–intensive products and import a greater volume of skilled-labor-intensive products. According to the Stolper–Samuelson theorem, a shift toward freer trade then will increase the real wage of unskilled labor in Mexico, reduce the real wage of unskilled labor in the United States or Canada, decrease the real wage of skilled labor in Mexico, and increase the real wage of skilled labor in the United States or Canada.

3. Disagree. Opening up free trade does hurt people in import-competing industries in the short run—essentially due to the loss of producer surplus. The long-run effects are different because people and resources can move between industries, but everyone will not gain in the long run. If trade develops according to the Heckscher–Ohlin theory, then the owners of the factors of production that are relatively scarce in the country lose real income. Because the country imports products that are intensive in these factors, trade effectively makes these factors "less scarce" and reduces their returns.

5. Leontief conducted his research shortly after World War II, when it seemed clear that the United States was abundant in capital and scarce in labor, relative to the rest of the world. According to the Heckscher–Ohlin theory, the United States then should export capital-intensive products and import labor-intensive products. But in his empirical work using data on production in the United States and U.S. trade flows, Leontief found that the United States exported relatively labor-intensive products and imported relatively capital-intensive products.

7. a. With prices of 100, the two equations are

$$100 = 60w + 40r$$
$$100 = 75w + 25r$$

Solving these simultaneously, the equilibrium wage rate is 1 and the equilibrium rental rate is also 1. The labor cost per unit of wheat output is 60 (60 units of labor at a cost of 1 per unit of labor). The labor cost per unit of cloth is 75. The rental cost per unit of wheat is 40. The rental cost per unit of cloth is 25.

b. With the new price of cloth, the two equations are

$$100 = 60w + 40r$$
$$120 = 75w + 25r$$

Solving these simultaneously, the new equilibrium wage rate is about 1.53 and the new equilibrium rental rate is 0.2.

c. The real wage with respect to wheat increases from 0.01 (or 1/100) to about 0.0153 (or 1.53/100). The real wage with respect to cloth increases from 0.01 (or 1/100) to about 0.01275 (or 1.53/120). On average the real wage is higher—labor benefits from the increase in the price of cloth. The real rental rate with respect to wheat decreases from 0.01 (or 1/100) to 0.002 (or 0.2/100). With respect to cloth it decreases from 0.01 (or 1/100) to about 0.0017 (or 0.2/120). On average the real rental rate is lower—landowners lose real income as a result of this increase in the price of cloth.

d. These results are an example of the Stolper–Samuelson theorem. Wheat is relatively intensive in land, and cloth is relatively intensive in labor. The increase in the price of cloth raises the real income of labor (its intensive factor) and lowers the real income of the other factor (land).

9. The total input share of labor in each dollar of cloth output is the sum of the direct use of labor plus the labor that is used to produce the material inputs into cloth production:

$$0.5 + 0.1 \times 0.3 + 0.2 \times 0.6 = 0.65$$

The total input share of capital is calculated in the same way:

$$0.2 + 0.1 \times 0.7 + 0.2 \times 0.4 = 0.35$$

Cloth is labor-intensive relative to the country's import substitutes (0.65 > 0.55). Thus the country's trade pattern is consistent with the Heckscher–Ohlin theory. This labor-abundant country exports the labor-intensive product.

Chapter 5

1. Disagree. The Heckscher–Ohlin theory indicates that countries should export some products (products that are intensive in the country's abundant factors) and import other products (products that are intensive in the country's scarce factors). Heckscher–Ohlin theory predicts the pattern of interindustry trade. It does not predict that countries would engage in a lot of intra-industry trade, which involves both exporting and importing products that are the same (or very similar).

3. There are two major reasons. First, product differentiation can result in intra-industry trade. Imports do not lead to lower domestic output of the product, because exports provide demand for much of the output that previously was sold at home. Output levels do not change much between industries, so there is (1) little shift between industries in factor demand and (2) little pressure on factor prices. There are likely to be fewer losers from Stolper–Samuelson effects. Second, there is a gain from trade that is shared by everyone—the gain from having access to greater product variety through trade. Some groups that otherwise might believe that they are losers because of trade could instead believe that they are winners if they place enough value on this access to greater product variety.

5. a. External economies of scale mean that the average costs of production decline as the size of an industry in a specific geographic area increases. With free trade and external economies, production will tend to concentrate in one geographic area to achieve these external economies. Whichever area is able to increase its production can lower its average costs. Lower costs permit firms in this area to lower their prices so that they gain more sales, grow bigger, and achieve lower costs. Eventually production occurs in only one country (or geographic area) that produces with low costs.

   b. Both countries gain from trade in products with external economies. The major effect is that the average cost of production declines as production is concentrated in one geographic area. If the industry is competitive, then the product price declines as costs decline. In the importing country, consumers' gains from lower prices more than offset the loss of producer surplus as the local industry ceases to produce the product. In the exporting country, producer surplus may increase as production expands, although this effect is countered by the decrease in the price that producers charge for their products. In the exporting country, consumer surplus increases as the product price declines. Thus the exporting country can gain for two reasons: an increase in producer surplus and an increase in consumer surplus.

7. a. Consumers in Pugelovia are likely to experience two types of effects from the opening of trade. First, consumers gain access to the varieties of products produced by foreign firms, as these varieties can now be imported. Consumers gain from greater product variety. Second, the additional competition from imports can lower the prices of the domestically produced varieties, creating an additional gain for domestic consumers.

   b. Producers in Pugelovia also are likely to experience two types of effects from the opening of trade. First, imports add extra competition for domestic sales. As we noted in the answer to part *a,* this is likely to force domestic producers to lower their prices, and some sales will be lost to imports. Second, domestic producers gain access to a new market, the foreign market. They are likely to be able to make additional sales as exports to consumers in the foreign market who prefer these producers' varieties over the ones produced locally there.

9. a.

Product Category	Intra-industry Trade Share	Net Trade as a Percentage of Total Trade
Food, beverages, and tobacco	92.2%	7.8%
Petroleum and other fuels	28.4	71.6
Chemicals	45.9	54.1
Machinery and transport equipment	83.0	17.0
Clothing	25.9	74.1

b. The product categories with the highest intra-industry trade shares are (1) food, beverages, and tobacco and (2) machinery and transport equipment. Some of this intra-industry trade could result from two-way trade in goods that are very similar but differentiated in the eyes of consumers. This could be true, for instance, for beverages or transport equipment. However, much of the apparent intra-industry trade may simply be the result of adding up different types of products into these broad categories. For instance, industrialized countries' food exports tend to be products that grow in temperate climates, while their food imports are different products that grow in tropical climates.

c. The categories that show substantial net trade are petroleum and other fuels, clothing, and chemicals. Explanations of net trade between industrialized countries and the rest of the world usually are based on the Heckscher–Ohlin theory. The industrialized countries are substantial importers of oil because they are not blessed with substantial endowments of oil in the ground. They are substantial importers of clothing because production of these products is intensive in unskilled labor, which is relatively scarce in industrialized countries. They are substantial net exporters of chemicals because production of chemicals is intensive in capital and more skilled labor, factors that are relatively abundant in the industrialized countries.

Chapter 6

1. By expanding its export industries, Pugelovia wants to sell more exports to the rest of the world. This increase in export supply tends to lower the international prices of its export products, so the Pugelovian terms of trade (price of exports relative to the price of imports) tend to decline.

3. The drought itself reduces production in these Latin American countries and tends to lower their well-being. (Their production-possibilities curves shrink inward.) But the lower export supply of coffee tends to raise the international price of coffee so the terms of trade of these Latin American countries tend to improve. The improved terms of trade tend to raise well-being. (The purchasing power of their exports rises.) If their terms of trade improve enough, the countries' well-being improves. The greater purchasing power of the remaining exports is a larger effect than the loss of export (and production) volumes. The gain in well-being is more likely (1) if these Latin American countries represent a large part of world coffee supply so that their supply reduction can have a noticeable impact on the world price, (2) if foreign demand for coffee is price-inelastic (as it probably is) so that the coffee price rises by a lot when supply declines, and (3) if exports of coffee are a major part of the countries' economies so that the improvement in the terms of trade can have a noticeable benefit to the countries. (This answer is an example of immiserizing growth "in reverse.")

5. R&D is a production activity that is intensive in the use of highly skilled labor (scientists and engineers) and perhaps also in the use of capital that is willing to take large risks (e.g., venture capital). The industrialized countries are relatively abundant in highly skilled labor and

in risk-taking capital. According to Heckscher–Ohlin theory, a production activity tends to locate where the factors that it uses intensively are abundant.

7. a. This is balanced growth through increases in factor endowments. The production-possibilities curve shifts out proportionately so that its relative shape is the same.

   b. This is balanced growth through technology improvements of similar magnitude in both industries. The production-possibilities curve shifts out proportionately so that its relative shape is the same.

   c. The intercept of the production-possibilities curve with the cloth axis does not change. (If there is no wheat production, then the improved wheat technology does not add to the country's production.) The rest of the production-possibilities curve shifts out. This is growth biased toward wheat production.

9. a. The entire U.S. production-possibilities curve shifts out, with the outward shift relatively larger for the good that is intensive in capital. If the U.S. trade pattern follows the Heckscher–Ohlin theory, then this good is machinery. Growth is biased toward machinery production.

   b. According to the Rybczynski theorem, the quantity produced of machinery increases and the quantity produced of clothing decreases if the product price ratio is unchanged. The extra capital is employed in producing more machinery, and the machinery industry must also employ some extra labor to use with the extra capital. The extra labor is drawn from the clothing industry, so clothing production declines.

   c. The U.S. willingness to trade increases. With growth of production and income, the United States wants to consume more of both goods. Demand for imports of clothing increases because domestic consumption increases while domestic production decreases. (Supply of exports also increases because the increase in domestic production of machinery is larger than the increase in domestic consumption.)

   d. The increase in demand for imports tends to increase the international equilibrium relative price of clothing. (The increase in supply of exports tends to lower the international equilibrium relative price of machinery.)

   e. The change in the international equilibrium price ratio is a decline in the U.S. terms of trade. U.S. well-being could decline—immiserizing growth is possible. If the decline in the terms of trade is large enough, then this negative effect can be larger than the positive effect of growth in production capabilities.

11. a. The U.S. production-possibilities curve shifts out for all points except its intercept with the food axis. This is growth biased toward clothing production.

   b. The U.S. willingness to trade probably decreases because the United States is now capable of producing its import good at a lower cost. Although the extra production and income lead to an increase in U.S. demand for clothing, the expansion of the supply of clothing that results from the improved technology is likely to be larger, so U.S. demand for clothing imports probably decreases.

   c. The decrease in U.S. demand for imports reduces the equilibrium international relative price of clothing. The U.S. terms of trade improve.

Chapter 7

1. You could calculate it if you know only the size of the tariff and the amount by which it would reduce imports. (See Figure 7.4.)

3. The production effect of a tariff is the deadweight loss to the nation that occurs because the tariff encourages some high-cost domestic production (production that is inefficient by the world standard of the international price). Producing the extra domestic output that occurs when the tariff is imposed has a domestic resource cost that is higher than the international price that the

country would have to pay to the foreign exporters to acquire these units as imports with free trade. The domestic resource cost of each unit produced is shown by the height of the domestic supply curve. Thus, the production effect is the triangle above the free-trade world price line and below the domestic supply curve, for the units between domestic production quantity with free trade and domestic production quantity with the tariff. It can be calculated as one-half of the product of the change in domestic price caused by the tariff and the change in production quantity caused by the tariff.

5. (a) Consumers gain $420 million per year. (b) Producers lose $140 million per year. (c) The government loses $240 million per year. (d) The country as a whole gains $40 million a year.

7. (a) Consumers gain $5,125,000. (b) Producers lose $1,875,000. (c) The government loses $6,000,000 in tariff revenue. (d) The country as a whole loses $2,750,000 each year from removing the tariff. The national loss stems from the fact that the tariff removal raises the world price paid on imported motorcycles. In question 5, it was assumed that removing the duty had no effect on the world price (of sugar).

9. The $1.25 is made up of 60 cents of value added, 35 cents of cotton payments, and 30 cents of payments for other fibers. The effective rate is (60¢ – 40¢)/ 40¢ = 50%.

Chapter 8

1. Import quotas are government-decreed quantitative limits on the total quantity of a product that can be imported into the country during a given period of time. Here are three reasons why a government might want to use a quota rather than a tariff: (1) Quotas ensure that imports will not exceed the amount set by the quota. This could be useful if the government wants to assure domestic producers that imports are actually limited. (2) A quota gives government officials greater power and discretion over who gets the valuable right to import. (3) The government may accede to the desires of domestic producers who could have monopoly pricing power if import competition is removed at the margin. For instance, a quota would be preferred by a domestic monopoly, because the monopoly could raise its price with no fear of growing imports as long as a quota limits the quantity imported.

A quota does not bring a greater national gain. From the point of view of the national interest, a quota is no better than an equivalent tariff, and it may be worse.

3. This would happen if the domestic product market is perfectly competitive, and the import quota rights are auctioned off competitively.

5. The tariff would be less damaging to the United States, because it gives the United States the tariff revenue that instead would be a price markup pocketed by foreign film makers with a VER. Both would bring the same overall loss in world welfare.

7. a. The change in producer surplus is a gain of $0.02 per pound for the 120 million pounds that is produced with free trade *plus* the producer surplus on the increased production of 40 million pounds. The latter is $1/2 \times \$0.02$ per pound $\times 40$ million pounds (assuming a straight-line domestic supply curve). The gain in producer surplus totals $2.8 million.

   b. The change in consumer surplus is a loss of $0.02 per pound for the 400 million pounds that the consumers continue to purchase after the quota is imposed *plus* the loss of consumer surplus on the 20 million pounds that consumers no longer purchase because of the quota. The latter is $1/2 \times \$0.02 \times 20$ million (assuming a straight-line domestic demand curve). The loss in consumer surplus totals $8.2 million.

   c. The right to import is a right to buy sugar at the world price of $0.10, import it, and sell it domestically at the price of $0.12. If the bidding for the rights is competitive, then the buyers of the rights bid $0.02 per pound. The government collects $4.8 million (= $0.02 per pound $\times$ 240 million pounds).

d. The net loss to the country is $0.6 million. By limiting imports, the quota causes two kinds of economic inefficiency. First, the increased domestic production is high-cost by world standards. The country uses some of its resources inefficiently producing this extra sugar rather than producing other products. Second, the consumers squeezed out of the market by the higher price lose the consumer surplus that they would have received if they were allowed to import freely.

9. Before the demand increase, the tariff and the quota are essentially equivalent (domestic price P_1, domestic production quantity S_1, domestic consumption quantity D_1, import quantity $D_1 - S_1$, domestic producer surplus VAP_1, domestic consumer surplus UBP_1, deadweight losses AEC and BGJ, and government tariff revenue or quota import profits $ABGE$). With the increase in demand to D_d', the unchanged tariff and the unchanged quota are no longer equivalent:

	Tariff	Quota
Domestic price	P_1	P_2
Production quantity	S_1	S_2
Consumption quantity	D_3	D_2
Producer surplus	VAP_1	VLP_2
Consumer surplus	TRP_1	TNP_2
Deadweight losses		
Production	AEC	LFC
Consumption	RIK	NHK
Tariff revenue or quota import profits	$ARIE$	$LNHF$

After domestic demand increases, with the quota domestic price is higher, domestic quantity produced is higher, domestic quantity consumed is lower, the quantity imported is lower, domestic producer surplus is larger, domestic consumer surplus is smaller, and the deadweight losses are larger.

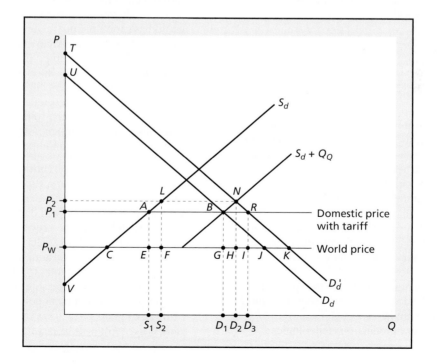

11. a. Relative to free trade, the tariff gives the United States a terms-of-trade gain of $180 million and an efficiency loss of $100 million for a net gain of $80 million. In terms of Figure 8.3, this is area *e* minus area (*b* + *d*). The VER costs the United States $300 million (area *c*) plus $100 million (*b* + *d* again) for a loss of $400 million. For the United States, then, the tariff is best and the VER is worst.

   b. If the United States imposes the $80 tariff, Canada loses $180 million (area *e*) and $60 million (area *f*) for a total loss of $240 million. By contrast, if the United States and Canada (Bauer) negotiate a VER arrangement, Canada gains $300 million on price markups (area *c*) and loses $60 million (area *f*) for a net *gain* of $240 million. For Canada, the U.S. tariff is the most harmful, whereas the VER actually brings a net gain.

   c. For the world as a whole (United States plus Canada here), either the tariff or the VER brings a net loss of $160 million (areas *b* + *d* and *f*). Free trade is still best for the world as a whole.

Chapter 9

1. a. Yes, there are external benefits—a positive spillover effect. The benefits to the entire country are larger than the benefits to the single firm innovating the new technology. Other firms that do not pay anything to this firm receive benefits by learning about and using the new production technology.

   b. The economist would say that the production subsidy is preferable to the tariff. Both can be used to increase domestic production, but the tariff distorts domestic consumption, leading to an unnecessary deadweight loss (the consumption effect).

   c. The economist would use the specificity rule. The actual problem is that innovating firms do not have enough incentives to pursue new production technologies

(because other firms get benefits without paying). The economist would recommend some form of subsidy to new production technology as better than a production subsidy or tariff. The technology subsidy could be a subsidy to undertake research and development, or monetary awards or prizes for new technology once it is developed.

3. One such set of conditions described in this chapter is the developing government argument. If the government is so underdeveloped that the gains from starting or expanding public programs exceed the costs of taxing imports, then the import tariff brings net national gains by providing the revenue so badly needed for those programs. Another answer could be: Tax imports if our consumption of the product brings external costs. For example, a country that does not grow tobacco could tax tobacco imports for health reasons.

5. Yes, even though no such case was explicitly introduced in this chapter. Think about incentive distortions, and ask how a nation could have too little private incentive to buy imports. The most likely case is one in which buying and using foreign products could bring new knowledge benefits throughout the importing country, benefits that are not captured by the importers alone. To give them an incentive matching the spillover gains to residents other than the importers, the national government could use an import subsidy.

7. Policy A, the production subsidy, would be the lowest cost to the country. By comparison, the tariff (Policy B) would raise the domestic price of aircraft, which will distort buyer decisions and thwart the growth of the domestic airline industry. The tariff adds a deadweight loss (the consumption effect). Policy C, the import quota, would be the most costly to the country. The sole Australian producer would gain monopoly power, and it will raise the domestic price even higher. The deadweight loss will be larger.

9. In favor: Adjustment assistance is designed to gain the benefits of increased imports by encouraging workers to make a smooth transition out of domestic production of the import-competing good. A key problem is that workers pushed out of import-competing production suffer large declines in earnings when forced to switch to some other industry or occupation. Adjustment assistance can overcome this problem by offering workers retraining, help with relocation, and temporary income support during retraining and relocation. Adjustment assistance represents an application of the specificity rule. It is better than using a tariff or nontariff barrier to limit imports and resist shrinking the domestic industry. And politically, it can reduce the pressure to enact these import barriers.

Opposed: Workers are faced with the need to relocate and develop new skills for a variety of reasons—not only increased imports but also changing consumer demand and changing technologies. There is nothing special about increasing imports, and workers affected by increasing imports deserve no special treatment. In fact, offering adjustment assistance could encourage workers to take jobs in import-competing industries that are shrinking, because they have the social insurance offered by adjustment assistance. In addition, adjustment assistance is not that effective. It does offer temporary income assistance to those who qualify, but it is much less successful at effective retraining and smooth relocation.

11. None. The loss in consumer surplus from imposing a tariff is larger than the gain in producer surplus. (The consumer loss is also larger than the combined gains of producer surplus and government tariff revenue, if the latter has "votes.")

13. Imposing the quota will create one clear winner—domestic baseball bat producers. It will create one clear loser—domestic consumers of baseball bats. And it will create one group that may have mixed feelings—the three import distributors—because they will have a smaller volume of business, but the profit margin on the limited business that they conduct will be very profitable. Baseball bat producers probably will be an effective lobbying group because there are a small number of firms that need to organize to lobby (and they may already have a trade association). Baseball bat consumers are unlikely to be an effective lobbying group because each has a small stake and it would be difficult to organize them into a political group. The three import distributors should be an effective lobbying group if they can agree among themselves whether to favor or oppose the quota.

Chapter 10

1. One definition of dumping is selling an export at a price lower than the price charged to domestic buyers of the product within the exporting country. This definition emphasizes international price discrimination. The second definition is selling an export at a price that is lower than the full average cost of the product (including overhead) plus a reasonable profit margin. This definition emphasizes pricing below cost (counting some profit as a cost of capital).

3. Tipper Laurie, because its at-brewery price is lower for exports to the United States than for domestic sales. Bigg Redd, because its at-brewery export price is below average cost.

5. The $5 export subsidy would lower the price charged to Canadian buyers, but the $5 countervailing duty would raise the price back up. If Canadian buyers are paying the same price (inclusive of the export subsidy and the countervailing duty) that they would pay with free trade (no export subsidy and no duty), then they are importing the same quantity that they would import with free trade. World well-being is the same in both cases, because all of the quantities are the same.

The United States would lose. The U.S. government pays a subsidy of $5 for each pair of blue jeans to Canada. The export price is lower, but the quantity exported is the same as with free trade. Canada would gain the $5 on each pair. The gain would be collected as government revenue from the countervailing duty. Otherwise, the domestic price in Canada and all quantities are the same as with free trade. Because Canada's gain equals the U.S. loss, this is another way to see that the well-being of the world as a whole is the same as it would be with free trade.

7. a. In this case, Airbus would gain by producing even without government intervention. Airbus would gain 5 if Boeing did produce, and 100 if Boeing did not produce. There would be no reason for European governments to subsidize Airbus.

   b. In this case, Boeing is sure to produce since Boeing gains whether or not Airbus produces. The EU should recognize this. With Boeing producing, the net gain for Airbus without government help is zero. If none of Airbus's customers were in Europe, there would be no reason to encourage Airbus to produce. Notice, however, that consumers might be better off if Airbus did produce. You can see this either by noticing that production by Airbus would deprive Boeing of 100 in profits taken from consumers (presumably by charging higher prices), or by reasoning that more competition is always a good thing for consumers. Either way, the EU would have reason to subsidize Airbus if its consumers could reap gains from the competition.

9. One way to build the case is to claim that the industry is a global oligopoly, with substantial scale economies and high profit rates (like the Boeing–Airbus example in this chapter). The nation can gain if the country's firm(s) can establish export capabilities and earn high profits on the exports. Another way to build the case is to claim that this industry is an infant industry (discussed in Chapter 9). If the industry could get some assistance, it can grow up and generate new producer surplus when it is strong enough to export.

Chapter 11

1. Members of a customs union have the same tariff on each category of imported good or service, regardless of which member country receives the imports. In this case, there is no need to scrutinize goods that move between countries in the customs union, even if the product might have been imported from outside the union.

   In a free-trade area, by contrast, each member country can have a different tariff rate on the import of a product. Therefore the free-trade area needs to scrutinize goods that move between countries in the free-trade area to make sure that they were not imported from outside the area into a low-tariff country and then shipped on to a high-tariff country in an effort to avoid the high tariff.

3. Trade creation is the increase in total imports resulting from the formation of a trade bloc. Trade creation occurs because importing from the partner country lowers the price in the importing country, so that some high-cost domestic production is replaced by lower-priced imports from the partner, and because the lower price increases the total quantity demanded in the importing country. Trade diversion is the replacement of imports from lower-cost suppliers outside the customs union with higher-cost imports from the partner. It occurs because the outsider suppliers remain hindered by tariffs, while there is no tariff on imports from the partner. Trade creation creates a gain for the importing country and the world. Trade diversion creates a loss for the importing country and the world. The importing country and the world gain from the trade bloc if trade creation gains exceed trade diversion losses.

5. (a) 10 million radios times ($110 – $100) = $100 million. (b) To offset this $100 million loss, with linear demand and supply curves, the change in imports, ΔM, would have to be such that the trade-creation gains (area b in Figure 11.2) had an area equal to $100 million. So $1/2 \times ($130 – $110) \times \Delta M = $100 million

requires ΔM = 10 million, or a doubling of Homeland's radio imports.

7. This case resembles that shown in Figure 11.2A, assuming the United States is a price-taking country.

   U.S. consumers would gain, as the domestic price drops from $30 to $25. We cannot quantify the dollar value of their consumer-surplus gain without knowing the level of domestic consumption or production.

   U.S. producers would lose from the same price drop, though again we cannot say how much they lose. (We do know, however, that the consumer gain would exceed this producer loss plus the government revenue loss by the triangular area $(1/2) \times \$5 \times 0.2$ million = $0.5 million.)

   The U.S. government would lose the $10 million it had collected in tariff revenue on the imports from China.

   The world as a whole would gain the triangular area $(1/2) \times \$5 \times 0.2$ million = $0.5 million, but lose the rectangular area $(\$25 - 20) \times 1$ million = $5 million because of the diversion of 1.0 million pairs from the lower-cost producer (China) to the higher-cost producer (Mexico). So overall, the world loses $4.5 million.

9. The "most certain" is (a), a countervailing duty, which brings net gains for the world as a whole if it just offsets the foreign export subsidy that provoked it. Whether the world as a whole gains from a customs union depends on whether it brings more trade creation than trade diversion. Whether the world gains from an antidumping duty also depends on the specifics of the case, as explained in Chapter 10.

Chapter 12

1. There are two effects. First, rising production and consumption bring rising pollution if the techniques used to produce and consume are unchanged. Second, rising income brings increased demand for pollution control, because a cleaner environment is a normal good (and one with a fairly high income elasticity). As Figure 12.1 shows, there are three basic patterns that arise for different types of pollution and related issues like sanitation. For some types of pollution, the first effect is larger, and pollution rises with rising income and production per person. For other types, the second effect is generally larger, so pollution declines with rising income and production per person. For yet other types, there is a turning point, so pollution at first rises and then falls as income and production per person increase.

3. Both (b) and (d). For item (b), the WTO is unwilling to let a country use trade limits to punish a foreign country for having environmental standards for production in the foreign country that are different from those of the importing country. For (d), the WTO would consider the pollution issue to be a pretext for unacceptable protectionist import barriers, because the imported products are not the only source of the pollution.

5. While there is some room for interpretation here, the specificity rule definitely prefers (c), followed by (d), then (a), then (b).

   The defeatism of (e) is misplaced. Oil spills are the result of shippers' negligence to a large extent, and not just uncontrollable acts of God.

   One drawback to (a) and (b) is that they force each nation's importers or consumers to pay insurance against shippers' carelessness. The more direct approach is to target the shippers themselves. In addition, many oil spills ruin the coastlines of nations that are not purchasers of the oil being shipped, making it inappropriate to charge them.

   It might seem that the most direct approach, (c), is unrealistic because it is hard to get full damages from the oil-shipping companies in court. Yet it is not difficult to make them pay for most or all of the damages. A key point is that the most damaging spills occur within the 200-mile limit, meaning that they occur in the national waters of the country suffering the damage. Full legal jurisdiction applies. The victimized country can legally seize oil shippers' assets, apply jail sentences, and even demand that a shipping company post bonds in advance of spills in exchange for the right to pass through national waters.

As for (d), intercepting and taxing all tankers in national waters is a reasonable choice. Its workability depends, however, on the cost of such coast-guard vigilance. If all tankers entering national water must put into port, they could be taxed in port. That is unlikely, however, and it might be costly to pursue them all along the whole 200-mile coast. Furthermore, such a tax, like many insurance schemes, makes the more careful clients (shippers) pay to insure the more reckless.

7. Item (c). This tax would lead to substantial reductions in the use of fossil fuels, the major source of manmade greenhouse gases. The other items would have small effects over the next 20 years.

9. No trade barriers are called for by the information given here. If the wood is in fact grown on plantation land that would have been used for lower-value crops anyway, there is no clear externality, no basis for government intervention. Only if the plantations would have been rain forest and only if there is serious environmental damage (e.g., extinction of species or soil erosion) from the clearing of that rain forest land for plantations would there be a case for Indonesia's restricting the cultivation of jelutong. As for the greenhouse-gas effects of cutting more tropical rain forest, they could easily be outweighed by the longer growing life of cedar trees in the temperate zone.

Chapter 13

1. The four arguments in favor of ISI are the infant-industry argument, the developing-government argument, the chance to improve the terms of trade for a large importing country, and economizing on market information by focusing on selling in the local market rather than in more uncertain foreign markets. The drawbacks to ISI are the deadweight losses from the inefficiencies of import protection, the danger that government officials directing the policy will try to enrich themselves rather than

the country, and the lack of competitive pressure on local firms to "grow up" by reducing costs, improving technology, and raising product quality. The arguments in favor of a policy of promoting manufactured exports are that it encourages use of the country's abundant resources (comparative advantage), that export sales can help to achieve scale economies, and that the drive to succeed in foreign markets creates competitive pressure. A major drawback is that the importing countries may erect trade barriers that limit the exporter's ability to expand its exports of manufactures.

3. The available data do indicate that the relative prices of primary products have declined since 1900, perhaps by as much as 0.7 percent per year. But there are biases in the data. Some of the decline could reflect declining transport costs, and some could be offset by the rising quality of manufactured products that is not reflected in the price comparison. The true trend decline is probably less than 0.7 percent per year, and it may even be no decline.

5. For its first few years, TAR has the ability to be successful as an international cartel, if its member countries can agree on and abide by its policies. TAR will have several advantages during its first few years. It has a fairly large share of world production, so its actions can have a substantial impact on the world price. The price elasticity of demand is rather low, so it can raise the world price without too much of a falloff in world sales. It will not face much pressure from outside suppliers, because they cannot enter or increase their production quickly. The biggest challenges facing TAR in its first few years are establishing its policies and having its members comply with them. The five countries may have different views on how much to increase the price in the first few years, they may disagree on how much each of them should reduce their own production to limit global supply, and so forth. Even if they can reach agreement on the cartel's policies, each of them has an incentive to cheat on the agreement. Given how different the five countries are, agreeing to and abiding by the cartel policies are major challenges.

In the longer run, the cartel is unlikely to remain successful, even if it achieves success in its first few years. If it succeeds in raising the world price in its first years, two forces come into play that erode its effectiveness over time. First, the price elasticity of demand becomes larger, so world sales of tobacco decline if the price is kept high. Second, new outside suppliers can enter into production, and existing outside suppliers can expand their production. The cartel members are squeezed from both sides. The price that maximizes the cartel's total profit declines. More important, it becomes more difficult, and eventually impossible, to reach agreement on which cartel members should continue to reduce their own production to keep the world price above its competitive level by limiting total global supply.

7. a. The demand that remains for the cartel's oil falls by 10 million barrels per day, for any price above $5.00 per barrel. In the graph below, this is a shift of the demand curve for cartel oil to the left, from D to D'. The new demand curve for the cartel's oil is parallel to the original demand curve and lower by 10 million barrels. Its intercept with the price axis is below $80.00. (Using the equation for the market demand curve, P = 80 − (37.50/30) · Q_D, the intercept for the new demand curve is $67.50.) The marginal revenue curve for the cartel also shifts down and to the left, from MR to MR'. The intersection of the new marginal revenue curve and the (unchanged) marginal cost curve for cartel production occurs when oil exports are X', less than 30 million barrels, and the new profit-maximizing price for the cartel is P', less than $42.50 per barrel.

   b. The quantity demanded for the cartel's oil is unchanged if the market price is $5.00 per barrel, but each $1.00 increase in the market price takes away another 1 million barrels from the demand remaining for the cartel's oil. The new demand curve for the cartel's oil is shown as the colored line D" in the graph on the next page. With the new outside supply the quantity demanded of the cartel's oil falls to zero at a price less than $42.50. (The price intercept of the new demand curve for the cartel's oil is about $38.33.) Because both the old and the new straight-line demand curves show the same quantity demanded at a price of $5.00, the new marginal revenue

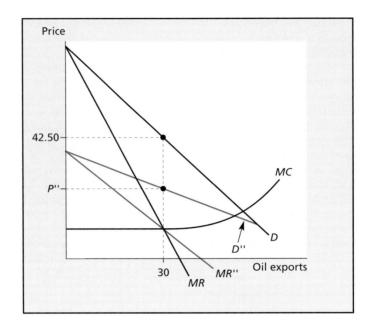

curve MR" intersects the original marginal revenue curve MR at the price $5.00. This point is also the intersection with the cartel's marginal cost curve, so the cartel continues to produce 30 million barrels. Because of the new and elastic outside supply of oil, the cartel's new profit-maximizing price P" is much less than $42.50.

9. The alternative is strong, rapid reforms of policies ("cold turkey" or "big bang"). There are several arguments in favor of fast reform. First, a quick shift to free trade means that international prices quickly become the signals that guide business and consumer decisions. Efficiency gains from resource reallocations can be large. Second, this quick shift also quickly creates competitive pressure on businesses to improve their productivity and product quality. Third, fast reforms can be accomplished before those interested in maintaining the status quo can marshal their political opposition. Fourth, fast reforms can quickly remove government officials from interfering in business decisions. Finally, the policy of rapid reform appears to be more successful, if we compare the performance of the various transition countries of central and eastern Europe and the former Soviet Union.

Chapter 14

1. Disagree. Most FDI goes to industrialized countries, especially the United States and Europe. Wages are not low in these countries. This FDI instead is used to gain access to large markets and to gain the insights and marketing advantages of producing locally in these markets.

3. Agree. One exposure is to exchange rate risk. The home-currency value of the assets of foreign affiliates will vary as exchange rates vary. If foreign-currency borrowings and other liabilities are used to finance the affiliates' assets, they provide a hedge against exchange rate risk by more closely balancing foreign-currency assets and liabilities. Another exposure is to the risk of expropriation. The host government sometimes exercises its power to seize the affiliates of multinational firms. If most of the affiliates' assets are financed by local borrowings and other local liabilities, then the parent firms lose less because they can refuse to honor the liabilities once the assets are seized.

5. There are inherent disadvantages of FDI arising from lack of knowledge about local customs,

practices, laws, and policies, and from the costs of managing across borders. Therefore, firms that undertake FDI successfully generally have some firm-specific advantages that allow them to compete successfully with local firms in the host country. Major types of firm-specific advantages include better technology, managerial and organizational skills, and marketing capabilities. These types of firm-specific advantages are important in industries such as pharmaceuticals and electronic products. The firms that have the advantages can undertake FDI successfully. These types of firm-specific advantages are less important in industries such as clothing and paper products. Fewer firms posses these types of advantages, and there is less FDI in these industries.

7. a. To maximize global after-tax profit, the controller should try to show as much profit as possible in Ireland, and as little profit as possible in Japan, because Ireland's tax rate of 15 percent is lower than Japan's tax rate of 40 percent. If possible, the controller should choose the third alternative, to raise the price of the component to $22. For each unit of the component exported from Ireland to Japan, this shifts $2 of profit from Japan to Ireland in comparison with the second alternative (price of $20) and it shifts $4 of profit compared to the first alternative (keep the price at $18). For each unit of the component exported, tax paid in Japan is reduced by $0.80 (or $1.60), and the extra tax paid in Ireland is only $0.30 (or $0.60). For each unit exported, the increase in global after-tax profit is $0.50 compared to the second alternative, and $1.00 compared to the first alternative.

  b. Ireland's government may be pleased with this change in transfer price. More profits are shown in the country, so its tax revenues are higher than they would be if the transfer price were lower. Japan's government is likely to be displeased. Its tax revenues are lower. It can try to police transfer pricing to ensure that the "correct" prices are used to show the "correct" amount of profit in the affiliates in its country.

9. Key points that should be included in the report:

  (1) FDI brings new technologies into the country.
  (2) FDI brings new managerial practices into the country.
  (3) FDI brings marketing capabilities into the country. These can be used to better meet the needs of the local market. They may be particularly important in expanding the country's exports by improving the international marketing of products produced by the multinational firms that begin production in the country.
  (4) FDI brings financial capital into the country, and expands the country's ability to invest in domestic production capabilities.
  (5) The local affiliates of the multinationals raise labor skills by training local workers.
  (6) Technological (and similar) side benefits accrue to the country as it hosts FDI, because some of the multinationals' technology, managerial practices, and marketing capabilities spread to local firms as they learn about and imitate the multinational's intangible assets. Taken together, these first six items serve to increase the country's supply-side capabilities for producing (and selling) goods and services.
  (7) In addition, the country's government can gain tax revenues by taxing (in a reasonable way!) the profits of the local affiliates established by the foreign multinationals.

11. a. A rise in labor demand in the North.
  b. Any "push" factor in the South, such as population pressure or political upheaval.
  c. A drop in the cost or difficulty of migration.

13. The migrants don't gain the full Southern wage markup from $2.00 to $3.20 because some of their extra labor was supplied only at a marginal cost of their own time that rose from $2.00 to $3.20. That's shown in Figure 14.4 by the fact that the curve $S_r + S_{mig}$ leans further out to the right than does the curve S_r.

As for the full international wage gain from $2.00 up to $5.00, it is true that the migrants do get paid that full extra $3. However, $1.80 of it is not a real gain in their well-being. It's just compensation for the economic and psychic costs of migrating.

15. Here are several arguments. First, standard economic analysis shows that there are net economic gains to the Japanese economy, even if the gains to the immigrants are not counted. Japanese employers gain from access to a larger pool of workers, and these gains are larger than any losses to Japanese workers who must compete with the new immigrants (see Figure 14.4). Second, some of the immigrants will take on work that most Japanese shun, such as janitorial work. These immigrants view this work as an opportunity and better than what they had back in their home countries. Third, if immigrants are selectively admitted, the Japanese government can assure that they are net contributors to public finance—that they will pay more in taxes than they add to the costs of running government programs. The Japanese government should favor young adult immigrants, including many with skills that will be valued in the workplace. This effect on public finance is especially important for Japan, because it has a rapidly aging native population, so the costs of providing social security payments to retirees is going to rise quickly in the next decades. Fourth, immigrants bring with them a range of knowledge that can create spillover benefits for Japan. The immigrants bring food recipes, artistic talent, know-how about science and technology, and different ways of doing things. Japan wants to increase the creativity of its people and firms to be more successful in high-tech and information-intensive industries. Immigrants can be a source of creative sparks.

17. The greatest net contributors were probably (*b*) electrical engineers arriving around 1970, whose high average salaries made them pay a lot of U.S. taxes and draw few government benefits. As for who contributed least, one could make a case for either (*a*) the political refugees or (*c*) the grandparents. The political refugees, as people who had not been preparing themselves for life in a new economy until displaced by political events, are generally less well equipped to earn and pay taxes in the economy when they arrive. The grandparents are also likely to pay little taxes and may make some claims on government aid networks, though their qualification for social security is limited.

Chapter 15

1. National saving S equals private saving plus government saving (or dissaving if the government budget is in deficit). For this country, national saving equals $678 billion (or $806 – $128). The current account balance equals the difference between national saving and domestic real investment (I_d). For this country, the current account balance is a deficit of $99 billion (or $678 – $777).

3. Saving can be used to make investments. The country can use its national saving to make domestic real investments in new production capital (buildings and machinery), in new housing, and in additions to inventories, or it can use its national saving to invest in foreign financial assets. If it uses its national saving to make domestic real investments, benefits to the nation include the increases in production capacity and capabilities that result from new production capital and the housing services that flow from a larger stock of housing. If it uses its national saving to make foreign investments, benefits to the nation include the dividends, interest payments, and capital gains that it earns on its foreign investments, which add to the national income of the country in the future.

5. Transaction c contributes to a surplus in the current account because it is an export of merchandise that is paid for through an item in the capital account. (Transaction a leaves the current account unchanged because it is both

an export and an import. Transaction *b* contributes to a deficit in the current account because it is an import. Transaction *d* also contributes to a current account deficit because of the outflow as a unilateral transfer. Transaction *e* affects no items in the current account.)

7. a. Credit item in line 3, exports of services. Debit item in line 6, merchandise imports.
    b. Credit item in line 4, income receipts from foreigners (investment income). Debit item in line 14, U.S. investments abroad, in this case a loan.
    c. Credit item in line 16, foreign direct investments in the United States, as the Japanese resident buys a U.S. business (in this case, a football team). Debit item in line 14, U.S. investment abroad (in this case bonds issued by a Japanese city).
    d. Credit item in line 7, services import. Debit item in line 17, foreign investments in the United States, in this case a foreign claim on a U.S. bank.

9. a. The U.S. international investment position declines—an increase in foreign investments in the United States (an increase in what the United States owes to foreigners.)
    b. The U.S. international investment position rises—an increase in private U.S. investment abroad (an increase in U.S. claims on foreigners).
    c. The U.S. international investment position is unchanged. The composition of foreign investments in the United States changes, but the total amount does not change.

Chapter 16

1. *Imports of merchandise and services* result in demand for foreign currency in the foreign exchange market. Domestic buyers often want to pay using domestic currency, while the foreign sellers want to receive payment in their currency. In the process of paying for these imports, domestic currency is exchanged for foreign currency, creating demand for foreign currency. *International capital outflows* result in a demand for foreign currency in the foreign exchange market. In making investments in foreign financial assets, domestic investors often start with domestic currency and must exchange it for foreign currency before they can buy the foreign assets. The exchange creates demand for foreign currency. Foreign sales of this country's financial assets that the foreigners had previously acquired, and foreign borrowing from this country are other forms of capital outflow that can create demand for foreign currency.

3. a. The value of the dollar decreases. (The SFr increases.)
    b. The value of the dollar decreases. (This is the same change as in part *a*.)
    c. The value of the dollar increases. (The yen decreases.)
    d. The value of the dollar increases. (This is the same change as in part *c*.)

5. The British bank could use the interbank market to find another bank that was willing to buy dollars and sell pounds. The British bank could search directly with other banks for a good exchange rate for the transaction, or it could use a foreign exchange broker to identify a good rate from another bank. The British bank should be able to sell its dollars to another bank quickly and with very low transactions costs.

7. a. Demand for yen. The Japanese firm will sell its dollars to obtain yen.
    b. Demand for yen. The U.S. import company probably begins with dollars, and the Japanese producer probably wants to receive payments in yen. Dollars must be sold to obtain yen.
    c. Supply of yen. The Japanese importer probably begins with yen, and the U.S. cooperative probably wants to receive payment in dollars. Yen must be sold to obtain dollars.
    d. Demand for yen. The U.S. pension fund must sell its dollars to obtain yen, using these yen to buy the Japanese shares.

9. a. Increase in supply of Swiss francs reduces the exchange rate value ($/SFr) of the franc. The dollar appreciates.
   b. Increase in supply of francs reduces the exchange rate value ($/SFr) of the franc. The dollar appreciates.
   c. Increase in supply of francs reduces the exchange rate value ($/SFr) of the franc. The dollar appreciates.
   d. Decrease in demand for francs reduces the exchange rate value ($/SFr) of the franc. The dollar appreciates.

Chapter 17

1. Agree. As an investor, I think of my wealth and returns from investments in terms of my own currency. When I invest in a foreign-currency–denominated financial asset, I am (actually or effectively) buying both the foreign currency and the asset. Part of my overall return comes from the return of the asset itself—for instance, the yield or rate of interest that it pays. The other part of my return comes from changes in the exchange rate value of the foreign currency. If the foreign currency increases in value (relative to my own currency) while I am holding the foreign asset, the value of my investment (in terms of my own currency) increases, and I have made an additional return on my investment. (Of course, if the exchange rate value of the foreign currency goes down, I make a loss on the currency value, which reduces my overall return.)

3. a. The U.S. firm has an asset position in yen—it has a long position in yen. The risk is that the dollar exchange rate value of the yen in 60 days is uncertain. If the yen depreciates, then the firm will receive fewer dollars.
   b. The student has an asset position in yen—a long position in yen. The risk is that the dollar exchange rate value of the yen in 60 days is uncertain. If the yen depreciates, then the student will receive fewer dollars.
   c. The U.S. firm has a liability position in yen—a short position in yen. The risk is that the dollar exchange rate value of the yen in 60 days is uncertain. If the yen appreciates, then the firm must deliver more dollars to buy the yen to pay off its loan.

5. For forward speculation the relevant comparison is between the current forward exchange rate and the expected future spot exchange rate. Comparing these two rates, we hope to make a profit by buying low and selling high. You expect the Swiss franc to be relatively cheap at the future spot rate ($0.51) compared with the current forward rate ($0.52). To speculate you should therefore enter into a forward contract today that requires that you sell (or deliver) SFr and buy (or receive) dollars. If the spot rate in 180 days is actually $0.51/SFr, then you can buy SFr at this low spot rate, deliver them into your previously agreed forward contract at the higher forward rate, and pocket the price difference, $0.01, for each franc that you agreed to sell in the forward contract.

7. a. Invest in dollar-denominated asset:
   $\$1 \times (1 + 0.0605) = \$1.0605$.
   Invest in yen-denominated asset:
   $\$1 \times (1/0.0100) \times (1 + 0.01) \times (0.0105)$
   $= \$1.0605$.
   b. Invest in dollar-denominated asset:
   $\$1 \times (1 + 0.0605) \times (1/0.0105) = 101$ yen.
   Invest in yen-denominated asset:
   $\$1 \times (1/0.0100) \times (1 + 0.01) = 101$ yen.
   c. Invest in dollar-denominated asset:
   100 yen $\times (0.01) \times (1 + 0.0605) \times (1/0.0105)$
   $= 101$ yen.
   Invest in yen-denominated asset: 100 yen $\times (1 + 0.01) = 101$ yen.

9. a. From the point of view of the U.S.-based investor, the expected uncovered interest differential is $[(1 + 0.03) \times 1.77/1.80] - (1 + 0.02) = -0.0072$. Because the differential is negative, the U.S.-based investor should stay at home, investing in dollar-denominated bonds, if he bases his decision on the difference in expected returns. (The approximate formula could also be used to reach this conclusion.)

b. From the point of view of the U.K.-based investor, the expected uncovered differential is $[(1 + 0.02) \times (1/1.77) \times 1.8] - (1 + 0.03) = 0.0073$. (Note that the position of the interest rates is reversed, and that the exchange rates are inverted so that they are pricing the dollar, which is now the foreign currency. Note also that this differential is approximately equal to the negative of the differential in the other direction, calculated in part *a.*) Because the differential is positive, the U.K.-based investor should undertake an uncovered investment in dollar-denominated bonds, if she bases her decision on the difference in expected returns. (Again, the approximate formula could be used to reach this conclusion.)

c. If there is substantial uncovered investment flowing from Britain to the United States, this increases the supply of pounds in the spot exchange market. There is downward pressure on the spot exchange rate to drop below $1.80/pound. The pound tends to depreciate. (The dollar tends to appreciate.)

Chapter 18

1. Disagree. First, exchange rates can be quite variable in the short run. This much variability does not seem to be consistent with the gradual changes in supply and demand for foreign currency that would occur as trade flows changed gradually. Second, the volume of trading in the foreign exchange market is much larger than the volume of international trade in goods and services. Only a small part of total activity in foreign exchange markets is related to payments for exports and imports. Most is related to international financial flows. International financial positioning and repositioning are likely to be quite changeable over short periods of time, explaining the variability of exchange rates in the short run.

3. a. If we use the approximation formula, uncovered interest parity holds (approximately) when the foreign interest rate plus the expected rate of appreciation of the foreign currency equals the domestic interest rate. Using the pound as the foreign currency, it is expected to change (depreciate) at an annual rate of –6% (or $(1.98 - 2.00)/2.00 \times 360/60 \times 100$). The uncovered annualized return on a pound-denominated bond is expected to be approximately $11\% - 6\% = 5\%$, which equals the annual return of 5% on a dollar-denominated bond. Uncovered interest parity holds approximately. (We could also use the full formula from Chapter 17 to show that the uncovered expected interest differential is approximately zero.)

   b. This shifts the uncovered differential in favor of investing in dollar-denominated bonds. The additional demand for dollars in the foreign exchange market results in an appreciation of the dollar. To reestablish uncovered interest parity with the other rates unchanged, the expected annual rate of change (depreciation) of the pound must be 3 percent so the spot rate now must change to about $1.99/pound. The pound depreciates.

5. a. Sell pesos. Weaker Mexican exports of oil in the future are likely to lower the peso's exchange rate value.

   b. Sell Canadian dollars. The expansion of money and credit is likely to lower the exchange rate value of the Canadian dollar because Canadian interest rates will decline (in the short run) and Canadian inflation rates are likely to be higher (in the long run).

   c. Sell Swiss francs. Foreign investors are likely to pull some investments out of Swiss assets (and to invest less in the future), reducing the exchange rate value of the franc.

7. As a tourist, you will be importing services from the country you visit. You would like the currency of this foreign country to be relatively cheap, so you would like it to be undervalued relative to PPP. If it is undervalued, then the current spot exchange rate allows you to buy a lot of this country's currency, relative to the local-currency prices that you must pay for products in the country.

9. According to purchasing power parity, attaining a stable exchange rate between the peso and the dollar requires that the Mexican inflation rate fall so that it is about equal to the 3 percent inflation in the United States. If k is constant, then the rate of growth of the Mexican money supply must fall to about 9 percent (or 6 percent real growth in $Y + 3$ percent inflation in Mexican prices P).

11. a. Using 1975 as a base year, the nominal exchange rate of $1/pnut corresponded to a ratio of U.S. prices to Pugelovian prices of 100/100. According to PPP, this relationship should be maintained over time. If the price level ratio changes to 260/390 in 2002, then the nominal exchange rate should change to $0.67/pnut. The pnut should depreciate during this time period because of the higher Pugelovian inflation rate (the reason why Pugelovia's price level increased by more than the U.S. price level increased).

    b. If the actual exchange rate is $1/pnut in 2000, then the pnut is overvalued. Its exchange rate value is higher than the rate that would be consistent with PPP (using 1975 as a base year).

13. If PPP held, the exchange rate e should rise steadily by 2 percent per year for five years, ending up 10 percent higher after five years. This matches the path of changes in the domestic price level (relative to the foreign price level) during these five years. PPP does not hold in the short run because the actual exchange rate jumps immediately by more than 10 percent (rather than rising gradually by about 2 percent per year). In the medium run, the actual rate remains above its PPP value, but the two are moving closer together, as the actual rate declines and the PPP rate rises over time. In the long run, PPP holds. According to PPP, the exchange rate eventually should be 10 percent higher, and it actually is 10 percent higher.

Chapter 19

1. In a clean float, the government allows the exchange rate value of its currency to be determined solely by private (or nonofficial) supply and demand in the foreign exchange market. The government takes no direct actions to influence exchange rates. In a managed float, the government is willing and sometimes does take direct actions to attempt to influence the exchange rate value of its currency. For instance, the monetary authorities of the country may sometimes intervene in the market, buying or selling foreign currency (in exchange for domestic currency) in an effort to influence the level or trend of the floating exchange rate.

3. The disequilibrium is the difference between private demand for foreign currency and private supply of foreign currency at the fixed level of the exchange rate. Official intervention by the central bank can be used to defend the fixed exchange rate, selling foreign currency if there is an excess private demand, or buying foreign currency if there is an excess private supply. Another way to see the disequilibrium is that the country's overall payments balance (its official settlements balance) is not zero.

   A temporary disequilibrium is one that will disappear within a short period of time, without any need for the country to make any macroeconomic adjustments. If the disequilibrium is temporary, official intervention can usually be used successfully to defend the fixed exchange rate. The country usually will have sufficient official reserve holdings to defend the fixed rate if there is a temporary private excess demand for foreign currency (or a temporary overall payments deficit); the country usually is willing and able to accumulate some additional official reserves if there is a temporary private excess supply of foreign currency (or a temporary overall payments surplus). Indeed, for temporary disequilibriums the well-being of the country can be higher if the government stabilizes the currency by defending the fixed exchange rate through official intervention, as Figure 19.4 shows.

If the disequilibrium is fundamental, then it tends to continue into the future. The country cannot simply use official intervention to defend the fixed exchange rate. The country will run out of official reserves (if its defense involves selling foreign currency), or it will accumulate unacceptably large official reserves (if the defense involves buying foreign currency). Thus, a major adjustment is necessary if the disequilibrium is fundamental. The government may surrender the fixed rate, changing its value or shifting to a floating exchange rate. Or, the government may adjust its macroeconomy to alter private demand and supply for foreign currency.

5. The exchange controls are intended to restrain the excess private demand for foreign currency (the source of the downward pressure on the exchange rate value of the country's currency). Thus, some people who want to obtain foreign currency, and who would be willing to pay more than the current exchange rate, do not get to buy the foreign currency. This creates a loss of well-being for the country as a whole because some net marginal benefits are being lost. Furthermore, these frustrated demanders are likely to turn to other means to obtain foreign currency. They may bribe government officials to obtain the scarce foreign currency. Or they may evade the exchange controls by using an illegal parallel market to obtain foreign currency (typically at a much higher price than the official rate).

7. a. The implied fixed exchange rate is about $4.87/pound (or 20.67/4.2474).
   b. You would engage in triangular arbitrage. If you start with dollars, you buy pounds using the foreign exchange market (because as quoted the pound is cheap). You then use gold to convert these pounds back into dollars. If you start with $4, you can buy one pound. You turn in this one pound at the British central bank, receiving about 0.2354 (or 1/4.2474) ounces of gold. Ship this gold to the United States, and exchange it at the U.S. central bank for about $4.87 (or 0.2354 × 20.67). Your arbitrage gets you (before expenses) about 87 cents for each $4 that you commit.

   c. Buying pounds in the foreign exchange market tends to increase the pound's exchange rate value so the exchange rate tends to rise above $4.00/pound (and toward $4.87/pound).

9. Key features of the interwar currency experience were that exchange rates were highly variable, especially during the first years after World War I and during the early 1930s. Speculation seemed to add to the instability, and governments sometimes appeared to manipulate the exchange rate values of their currencies to gain competitive advantage. One lesson that policymakers learned from this experience was that fixed exchange rates were desirable to constrain speculation and variability in exchange rates, as well as to constrain governments from manipulating exchange rates. These lessons are now debated because subsequent studies have shown that the experience can be explained or understood in other ways. Exchange rate changes in the years after World War I tended to move in ways consistent with purchasing power parity, which suggests that the fundamental problems were government policies that led to high inflation rates in some countries. The currency instability of the early 1930s seems to be reflecting the large shocks caused by the global depression. Indeed, the research suggests that it may not be possible to keep exchange rates fixed when large shocks hit the system.

11. The Bretton Woods system of fixed exchange rates collapsed largely because of problems with the key currency of the system, the U.S. dollar. The dollar's problems arose partly as a result of the design of the system, and partly as a result of U.S. government policies. As the system evolved, it became a gold-exchange standard in which other countries fixed their currencies to the U.S. dollar, largely held U.S. dollars as their official reserve assets, and intervened to defend the fixed exchange rates using dollars. The United States was obligated to exchange dollars for gold with other central banks at the official gold price. This caused two problems for the system. First, other

central banks accumulated dollar official reserves when the United States ran a deficit in its official settlements balance. In the early years of Bretton Woods this was desirable, as other central banks wanted to increase their holdings of official reserves. But in the 1960s, this became undesirable as the U.S. deficits became too large. Expansionary U.S. fiscal and monetary policies led to the large U.S. deficits and also to rising inflation in the United States. Second, other central banks saw their rising dollar holdings and a declining U.S. gold stock, and they began to question whether the United States could continue to honor the official gold price.

The U.S. government probably could have maintained the system, as least for longer than it actually lasted, if it had been willing to change its domestic policies, tightening up on government spending to contract the economy and cool off its inflation. The United States instead reacted by changing the rules of Bretton Woods, severing the link between the private gold market and the official gold price in 1968, and suspending gold convertibility and forcing other countries to revalue their currencies in 1971. An agreement in late 1971 reestablished fixed exchange rates after a short period in which some currencies floated, but most major currencies shifted to floating in 1973.

Another contributor to the collapse of the system was the ability of investors to take one-way speculative gambles against currencies that were perceived to be candidates for devaluation. The adjustable-peg system gave speculators a bet in which they could gain a lot if the currency was devalued but would lose little if it was not. Most governments did not have large enough holdings of official reserves to defend the fixed exchange rate against a determined speculative attack.

Chapter 20

1. Disagree. Borrowing from foreign lenders provides a net gain to the borrowing country, as long as the money is used wisely. For instance, as long as the money is used to finance new capital investments whose returns

are at least as large as the cost of servicing the foreign debt, then the borrowing country gains well-being. This is the gain of area $(d + e + f)$ in Figure 20.1.

3. The surge in bank lending to developing countries during 1974–1982 had these main causes: (1) a rise in bank funds from the "petrodollar" deposits by newly wealthy oil-exporting governments, (2) bank and investor concerns that investments in industrialized countries would not be profitable, because the oil shocks had created uncertainty about the strength of these economies, (3) developing countries' resistance to foreign direct investment, which led these countries to prefer loans as the way to borrow internationally, and (4) some amount of herding behavior by bank lenders, which built on the momentum of factors (1) through (3) and led to overlending.

5. a. World product without international lending is the shaded area. We first need to calculate the intercepts for the two MPK lines. The negative of the slope of MPK_{Japan} is 1 percent per 600, so the intercept for Japan is 12 percent. The "negative" of the slope of $MPK_{America}$ is also 1 percent per 600, so the intercept for America is about 14.7 percent. Japan's product is the rectangle of income from lending its wealth at 2 percent (120) plus the triangle above it (300), which is income for everyone else in Japan. America's product is the rectangle of income from lending its wealth at 8 percent (320) plus the triangle above it (about 134), which is income to everyone else in America. Adding up these four components, total world product is 874.

  b. Free international lending adds area RST (54), so total world product rises to 928.

  c. The 2 percent tax results in a loss of area TUV (6), so total world product falls to 922.

7. a. A large amount of short-term debt can cause a financial crisis, because lenders can refuse to roll over the debt or refinance it and instead demand immediate repayment. If the borrowing country cannot meet its obligations to repay, default becomes more likely.

b. Lenders can become concerned that other countries in the region are also likely to be hit with financial crises. This contagion can then become a self-fulfilling panic. If lenders refuse to make new loans and sell off investments, the country may not be able to meet its obligations to repay, so default becomes more likely. And the prices of the country's stocks and bonds can plummet as investors flee.

9. a. If lenders had detailed, accurate, and timely information on the debt and official reserves of a developing country, they should be able to make better lending and investing decisions, to avoid overlending or too much short-term lending. Better information should also reduce pure contagion, which is often based on vague concerns that other developing countries might be like the initial crisis country. In addition, developing countries that must report such detailed information are more likely to have prudent macroeconomic policies so that they do not have to report poor performance.

b. Controls on capital inflows can (1) limit total borrowing by the country to reduce the risk of overlending and overborrowing, (2) reduce short-term borrowing if the controls are skewed against this kind of borrowing, and (3) reduce exposure to contagion by reducing the amount of loans and investments that panicked foreign lenders can pull out when a crisis hits some other country.

Chapter 21

1. Japan. After Canada, Japan is the second largest trading partner of the United States. Japan has closer trading ties with the United States than do the euro area or the United Kingdom. Therefore, more of the change in U.S. spending is transmitted as a change in demand for Japanese production. In addition, Japan is also a large economy, so its change in income after its exports to the United States change then results in a large change in its imports from the United States, setting off a strong set of foreign income repercussions that affect both the United States and Japan.

3. a. The spending multiplier is $1/(0.2 + 0.1) = 3.3$, so domestic product will increase by $3.3 billion.

b. For a closed economy, the spending multiplier is $1/0.2 = 5$, so domestic product will increase by $5 billion. This spending multiplier is larger for a closed economy than for a small open economy because there is no import "leakage" for the closed economy. For both economies, as production and income rise following the initial increase in spending, some of the extra income goes into saving (and to pay taxes) so that the next rounds of increases in production and income are smaller. For the open economy, as production and income rise, there is an additional leakage out of the domestic demand stream as some of the country's spending goes to additional imports. Spending on imports does not create extra demand for this country's production. The next rounds of increases in the country's production and income become smaller more quickly, resulting in a smaller multiplier.

5. The intersection of the *IS* and *LM* curves indicates a short-run equilibrium in the country's market for goods and services (the *IS* curve) and a short-run equilibrium in the country's market for money (the *LM* curve). The intersection indicates the equilibrium level of the country's real domestic product and income (its real GDP) and the equilibrium level of its interest rate. We evaluate internal balance by comparing the actual level of domestic product to the level that we estimate the economy is able to produce when it is fully using its supply-side production capabilities. If the short-run equilibrium level of domestic product is too low—less than this "full-employment" level—the country has an internal imbalance that results in high unemployment. If the short-run equilibrium level of domestic product is pushing to be too high—more than its "full-employment" level—the country has an internal imbalance that results in rising inflation (driven by excessive demand).

7. a. A decrease in the money supply tends to raise interest rates (and lower domestic product). Thus, the *LM* curve shifts up (or to the left).
   b. An increase in the interest rate does not shift the *LM* curve. Rather, it results in a movement along the *LM* curve.

9. a. An increase in foreign demand for the country's exports tends to drive the country's overall international payments into surplus. To reestablish payments balance, the country's domestic product and income could be higher (so imports increase), or the country's interest rates could be lower (to create a capital outflow and reduce the country's capital account balance). Thus, the *FE* curve shifts to the right or down.
   b. An increase in the foreign interest rate tends to drive the country's overall international payments into deficit because of capital outflows seeking the higher foreign returns. To reestablish payments balance, the country's domestic product could be lower (to reduce imports), or its interest rates could be higher (to reverse the capital outflow). Thus, the *FE* curve shifts to the left or up.
   c. An increase in the country's interest rate does not shift the *FE* curve. Rather, it results in a movement along the *FE* curve.

Chapter 22

1. Disagree. The risk is rising unemployment, not rising inflation. The deficit in its overall international payments puts downward pressure on the exchange rate value of the country's currency. The central bank must intervene to defend the fixed exchange rate by buying domestic currency and selling foreign currency in the foreign exchange market. As the central bank buys domestic currency, it reduces the monetary base and the country's money supply falls. The tightening of the domestic money supply puts upward pressure on the country's interest rates. Rising interest rates reduce interest-sensitive spending, lowering aggregate demand, domestic product, and national income. The risk is falling real GDP and rising unemployment.

3. Perfect capital mobility essentially eliminates the country's ability to run an independent monetary policy. The country must direct its monetary policy to keeping its interest rate in line with foreign interest rates. If it tried to tighten monetary policy, its interest rates would start to increase, but this would draw a massive inflow of capital. To defend the fixed exchange rate, the central bank would need to sell domestic currency into the foreign exchange market. This would increase the domestic money supply, forcing the central bank to reverse its tightening. If it tried to loosen monetary policy, interest rates would begin to decline, but the massive capital outflow would require the central bank to defend the fixed rate by buying domestic currency. The decrease in the domestic money supply forces the central bank to reverse its loosening.

   Perfect capital mobility makes fiscal policy powerful in affecting domestic product and income in the short run. For instance, expansionary fiscal policy tends to increase domestic product, but the increase in domestic product could be constrained by the crowding out of interest-sensitive spending as interest rates increase. With perfect capital mobility the domestic interest rate cannot rise if foreign interest rates are steady, so there is no crowding out. Domestic product and income increase by the full value of the spending multiplier.

5. Agree. Consider the value of the country's current account measured in foreign currency (superscript *F*):

$$CA^F = (P_x^F \cdot X) - (P_m^F \cdot M)$$

According to the logic of the J-curve analysis, the price changes resulting from the exchange rate change occur first, and the effects on export and import volumes occur more slowly. The revaluation quickly increases the foreign currency price of the country's exports (because it now takes more foreign currency to yield the same home-currency price). Therefore, the current account improves in the months immediately after the revaluation. (Eventually the revaluation leads to a decrease in export volume, an increase in import volume, and perhaps also an increase in the foreign-currency price of imports, so eventually the current account value is likely to decrease.)

7. a. The FE curve shifts to the right or down.
    b. The capital inflows drive the country's overall international payments into surplus. They put upward pressure on the exchange rate value of the country's currency. The central bank must intervene to defend the fixed exchange rate by selling domestic currency in the foreign exchange market.
    c. As the central bank intervenes by selling domestic currency in the foreign exchange market, the country's monetary base and its money supply increase. The increase in the money supply lowers domestic interest rates. The lower interest rates encourage interest-sensitive spending, raising aggregate demand, domestic product, and income. External balance is reestablished through two adjustments. First, domestic product and income are higher so imports increase. Second, the country's interest rates are lower so the capital inflows are discouraged and capital outflows are encouraged.

    The increase in the country's domestic product and income alter its internal balance. If the country began with high unemployment, then this would be welcome as a move toward internal balance. If, instead, the country does not have the resources to produce the extra output, the country would develop the internal imbalance of rising inflation as the economy tries to expand and overheats.

    In the accompanying IS–LM–FE graph, the increased capital inflows shift the FE curve to the right to FE'. The country's international payments are then in surplus as the intersection of the original IS and LM curves at E_0 is to the left of FE'. The intervention to defend the fixed rate shifts the LM curve down (or to the right). External balance is reestablished at the new triple intersection E_1.

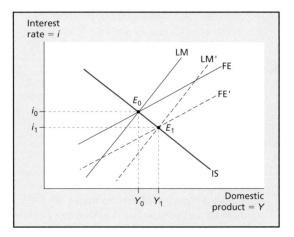

9. a. Tighten fiscal policy to address the internal imbalance of rising inflation, and tighten monetary policy to address the external imbalance of the deficit.
    b. Tighten fiscal policy to address the internal imbalance of rising inflation, and loosen monetary policy to address the external imbalance of the surplus.
    c. Loosen fiscal policy to address the internal imbalance of low demand, and loosen monetary policy to address the external imbalance of the surplus.

Chapter 23

1. Agree. The change in the exchange rate that occurs when there is a change in monetary policy is the basis for the enhanced effectiveness of monetary policy under floating exchange rates. For instance, when monetary policy shifts to be more expansionary, the decrease in the country's interest rate results in a depreciation of the country's currency. This is essentially overshooting (although overshooting also emphasizes that this depreciation is very large). It is overshooting relative to the path of the exchange rate implied by PPP so that the depreciation improves the country's international price competitiveness. The improvement in price competitiveness enhances the effectiveness of the policy. The country

exports more and shifts some of its spending from imports to domestic products, further increasing aggregate demand, domestic product, and income.

3. Disagree. Under floating exchange rates the decrease in our exports reduces demand for our currency in the foreign exchange market so our currency depreciates. The depreciation improves our international price competitiveness so exports tend to rebound somewhat, and some spending is shifted from imports to domestic products. This increase in aggregate demand counters the initial drop in demand for our exports, so the adverse effect on our domestic product and income is lessened. This exchange rate adjustment is not possible if the exchange rate is fixed. In addition, with a fixed exchange rate our overall international payments go into deficit when our exports decline. The central bank then intervenes to defend the fixed rate by buying domestic currency. The reduction in the domestic money supply raises our interest rate and makes the decline in our domestic product larger.

5. The tendency for the overall international payments to go into deficit puts downward pressure on the exchange rate value of the country's currency, and it depreciates. This moves the country further from internal balance. The depreciation of the currency tends to increase aggregate demand by making the country's products more price-competitive internationally. The extra demand adds up to the inflationary pressure. In addition, the depreciation raises the domestic-currency price of imports, adding to the inflation pressure.

7. a. The increase in taxes reduces disposable income and reduces aggregate demand. U.S. domestic product and income will fall (or be lower than they otherwise would be). If national income is lower, spending on imports will be lower, so the U.S. current account will improve. The increase in taxes reduces the government budget deficit. The government borrows less, and U.S. interest rates are lower. If international capital flows are mainly responsive to changes in interest

differentials, then the lower U.S. interest rates lead to capital outflows (or less capital inflows). The U.S. capital account declines.

b. The pressures on the exchange rate value of the dollar depend on which change is larger: the improvement in the current account or the deterioration in the capital account. If the effect on capital flows is larger, then demand for dollars will decrease (relative to the supply of dollars) in the foreign exchange market so the dollar will depreciate. If the current account change is larger, then the supply of dollars (relative to demand) will decrease, so the dollar will appreciate.

c. If the dollar depreciates, then the United States gains international price competitiveness. U.S. exports increase and imports decrease. The current account improves further. The increase in exports and shift of domestic spending from imports to domestic products add some aggregate demand, so domestic product and income rebound somewhat (or do not decline by as much).

9. a. The FE curve shifts to the right or down.

b. The country's international payments tend toward surplus. The extra demand for the country's currency leads to its appreciation.

c. The appreciation reduces the country's international price competitiveness so the country's exports decrease and its imports increase. The current account worsens, reducing the overall surplus. In addition, the decrease in aggregate demand as the current account worsens reduces domestic product and income. Money demand declines and the country's interest rate declines. The decline in the interest rate discourages some capital inflow or encourages some capital outflow. The capital account worsens, so the overall surplus also falls for this reason. The combined effects on the current and capital accounts reestablish external balance. The declines in aggregate demand and domestic product affect the county's internal balance. If rising inflation was initially a problem, then this change is desirable. However, the decrease in aggregate demand could instead create or add to an internal imbalance of high unemployment.

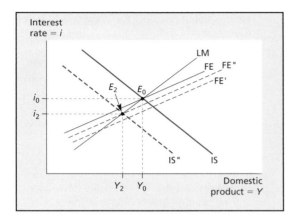

In the accompanying IS–LM–FE graph, the increased capital inflows shift the FE curve to the right or down to FE'. The country's currency appreciates so the FE curve shifts back to the left somewhat to FE'', and the IS curve shifts to the left to IS'' as the country loses international price-competitiveness. The new triple intersection is at point E_2. External balance is reestablished, the interest rate is lower, and domestic product is lower, relative to the initial equilibrium at point E_0.

Chapter 24

1. Disagree. Countries must follow policies that are not too different if they are to be able to maintain the fixed exchange rates. The policies need not be exactly the same, but the policies must lead to private demand and supply in the foreign exchange market that permits the countries to defend the fixed rates successfully. The most obvious need for consistency is in policies toward inflation rates. For fixed rates to be sustained, inflation rates must be the same or very similar for the countries involved. If inflation rates are the same, then fixed rates are consistent with purchasing power parity over time. If, instead, the inflation rates are different, then with fixed exchange rates the high-inflation countries will lose price-competitiveness over time. Their international payments will tend toward deficits, and the fixed rates will not be sustainable in the face of the "fundamental disequilibrium." Another need for consistency is in policies that can have a major influence on international capital flows. If policies lead to large capital flows, especially outflows, they may overwhelm the government's ability to defend the fixed exchange rate.

3. A floating exchange rate provides some insulation from foreign business cycles because the rate tends to change in a way that counters the spread of the business cycle through international trade. For instance, when one country goes into recession, its demand for imports declines. This lowers the other country's exports, reducing its aggregate demand, and it also tends to go into recession. With floating exchange rates, the country's international payments tend to go into deficit when the country's exports decline, and the country's currency depreciates. The depreciation improves the country's international price-competitiveness. Its exports rebound somewhat, and it shifts some spending away from imports and toward domestic products. Therefore, aggregate demand rises back up. The tendency toward recession is not so strong, so floating exchange rates provide some insulation from foreign business cycles.

5. Possible criteria include the following. First, if the country wants to shift to a fixed exchange rate to promote international trade by reducing exchange rate risk, then it should consider fixing its exchange rate to the currency of one of its major trading partners. Second, the country should look for a country whose priorities and policies are compatible with its own. For instance, if the country wants to have and maintain a low inflation rate, then it should consider fixing its rate to the currency of a country that has and is likely to maintain policies that result in a low inflation rate. Third, the country should look for a country that is seldom subject to large domestic shocks. With a fixed exchange rate, any economic shocks in the other country will be transmitted to this country. (From this country's point of view, these are external shocks.) The country will lose the ability of floating exchange rates to buffer the

disruptiveness of these external shocks, so it should consider fixing its rate to a country that has a relatively stable domestic economy.

7. a. In the short run the country must implement policies to reduce aggregate demand. The reduction in aggregate demand will create the discipline of weak demand in putting downward pressure on the inflation rate. Tightening up on monetary policy is one way to do this in the short run, and it is crucial to reducing the inflation rate in the long run. In the long run the growth of the money supply is the major policy-controlled determinant of the country's inflation rate. The floating exchange rate can be affected by these policy changes, but the key to reducing the inflation rate is getting domestic policies pointed in the right direction.

   b. The major countries of the world generally have low inflation rates. Adopting a currency board and a fixed exchange rate with one of these currencies may help the country reduce its inflation rate for several reasons. First, the country is accepting the discipline effect of fixed exchange rates. If the country's demand expands too rapidly or its inflation rate is too high, its international payments tend to go into deficit. By intervening to defend the fixed exchange rate, the country's currency board will buy domestic currency. This tends to force a tighter monetary policy on the country. Second, the shift to the currency board and fixed exchange rate can enhance the credibility of the government's policy, signaling that the government is truly

serious about reducing the country's inflation rate. Actually reducing the inflation rate is easier if people expect that it is going to decrease. Third, with a fixed exchange rate the local-currency prices of imported goods tend to be steady. The steady prices of imports not only reduce the country's measured inflation rate directly but also put competitive pressure on the prices of domestic products, so these prices do not rise as much.

9. There are several strong arguments. Here are four. First, joining the monetary union and adopting the euro will eliminate the transactions costs of exchanging pounds for euros. Resources used for this purpose can be shifted to other uses. The lower costs will encourage more British trade and investment with the member countries of the euro-zone. Second, joining the monetary union will eliminate exchange rate risk between the pound and the euro. Again, trade and investment with the euro-zone are encouraged. Third, the risk of rising British inflation is reduced, to the extent that the European Central Bank, with its mandate to keep inflation in the euro area to two percent or below, is likely to be better at controlling inflation than the British central bank would be. And finally, the shift to the euro can enhance the role of London as a center of international finance. As long as Britain stays out of the monetary union, European financial activities are likely to drift away from London to other centers (Frankfurt, Paris) where the euro is local currency.

References*

Abowd, John M., and Richard B. Freeman, eds. *Immigration, Trade, and the Labor Market.* Chicago: University of Chicago Press for the National Bureau of Economic Research, 1991.

Aliber, Robert Z. "Speculation in the Foreign Exchanges: The European Experience, 1919–1926." *Yale Economic Essays* 2 (1962), pp. 171–245.

Anderson, Kym, and Richard Blackhurst, eds. *The Greening of World Trade Issues.* New York: Harvester Wheatsheaf, 1992.

Anderson, Michael A., and Stephen L. S. Smith. "Canadian Trade and Wages: Lessons from the Past, Prospects for the Future." *World Economy* 23, no. 8 (August 2000), pp. 1005–1029.

Aylward, Lynn, and Rupert Thorne. "Countries' Repayment Performance Vis-à-Vis the IMF." *IMF Staff Papers* 45, no. 4 (December 1998), pp. 595–618.

Balassa, Bela. *The Structure of Protection in Developing Countries.* Baltimore: Johns Hopkins University Press, 1971.

—————. *European Economic Integration.* Amsterdam: North-Holland, 1975.

Baldwin, Richard E., and Anthony J. Venables. "Regional Economic Integration." In Grossman and Rogoff (1995).

Baldwin, Robert E. "The Case Against Infant-Industry Protection." *JPE* 77 (1969), pp. 295–305.

—————. "Trade Policies in Developed Countries." In Jones and Kenen, eds., *Handbook,* vol. I (1984).

Bartram, Söhnke M., and Gunter Dufey. "International Portfolio Investment: Theory, Evidence and Institutional Framework." *Financial Markets, Institutions & Instruments* 10, no. 3 (August 2001), pp. 85–155.

Bayard, Thomas O., and Kimberly Ann Elliott. *Reciprocity and Retaliation in U.S. Trade Policy.* Washington, DC: Institute for International Economics, 1994.

Beim, David O., and Charles W. Calomiris. *Emerging Financial Markets.* New York: Irwin McGraw-Hill, 2001.

Bergsten, C. Fred, ed. *International Adjustment and Financing: The Lessons of 1985–1991.* Washington, DC: Institute for International Economics, 1991.

—————, and C. Randall Henning. *Global Economic Leadership and the Group of Seven.* Washington, DC: Institute for International Economics, 1996.

Berry, Steven, James Levinsohn, and Ariel Pakes. "Voluntary Export Restraints on Automobiles: Evaluating a Trade Policy." *AER* 89, no. 3 (June 1999), pp. 400–430.

Bhagwati, Jagdish N. "Immiserizing Growth: A Geometrical Note." *Review of Economics Studies* 25, no. 3 (June 1958), pp. 201–205.

—————. *Trade, Tariffs and Growth.* Cambridge, MA: MIT Press, 1969.

—————. *Anatomy and Consequences of Exchange Control Regimes.* Cambridge, MA: Ballinger, 1978.

*Often-cited journals:
AER = American Economic Review
JEL = Journal of Economic Literature
JEP = Journal of Economic Perspectives
JIE = Journal of International Economics
JPE = Journal of Political Economy

————, and Robert E. Hudec, eds. *Fair Trade and Harmonization: Prerequisites for Free Trade? Vol. 1, Economic Analysis.* Cambridge, MA: MIT Press, 1996.

————, and Anne Krueger. A series of volumes on *Foreign Trade Regimes and Economic Development.* New York: Columbia University Press for the National Bureau of Economic Research, 1973–1976.

Bird, Graham. "IMF Programs: Do They Work? Can They Be Made to Work Better?" *World Development* 29, no. 11 (November 2001), pp. 1849–1865.

Bloom, David E., Gilles Grenier, and Morley Gunderson. "The Changing Labor Market Position of Canadian Immigrants." Working Paper no. 4672. National Bureau of Economic Research, March 1994.

Bloomfield, Arthur I. *Monetary Policy Under the International Gold Standard, 1880–1914.* New York: Federal Reserve Bank of New York, 1959.

Bonner, Raymond. *At the Hand of Man: Peril and Hope for Africa's Wildlife.* New York: Knopf, 1993.

Bordo, Michael D., and Barry Eichengreen, eds. *Retrospective on the Bretton Woods International Monetary System.* Chicago: University of Chicago Press, 1992.

Bordo, Michael D., and Anna J. Schwartz, eds. *A Retrospect on the Classical Gold Standard, 1821–1931.* Chicago: University of Chicago Press, 1984.

Boreman, Stephen M. "Dolphin-Safe Tuna: What's in a Label? The Killing of Dolphins in the Eastern Tropical Pacific and the Case for an International Legal Solution." *Natural Resources Journal* 32, no. 3 (Summer 1992), pp. 425–447.

Borjas, George J. *Friends or Strangers: The Impacts of Immigrants on the U.S. Economy.* New York: Basic Books, 1990.

————. "Immigration and Self-Selection." In Abowd and Freeman (1991), pp. 29–76.

————. "The Economics of Immigration." *JEL* 32, no. 4 (December 1994), pp. 1667–1717.

————. "Immigration and Welfare, 1970–1990." In *Research in Labor Economics,* vol. 14, ed. Solomon W. Polachek. Greenwich, CT: JAI Press, 1995a.

————. "The Economic Benefit from Immigration." *JEP* 9, no. 2 (Spring 1995b), pp. 3–22.

————, Richard B. Freeman, and Laurence F. Katz. "How Much Do Immigration and Trade Affect Labor Market Outcomes?" *Brookings Papers on Economic Activity,* no. 1 (1997), pp. 1–90.

————, and Lynette Hilton. "Immigration and the Welfare State: Immigrant Participation in Means-Tested Entitlement Programs." *Quarterly Journal of Economics* 111, no. 2 (May 1996), pp. 575–604.

Bosworth, Barry P. *Saving and Investment in a Global Economy.* Washington, DC: Brookings Institution, 1993.

Bowen, Harry P., Edward E. Leamer, and Leo Sveikauskas. "Multicountry, Multifactor Tests of the Factor Abundance Theory." *AER* 77, no. 5 (December 1987).

Brainard, S. Lael. "An Empirical Assessment of the Proximity-Concentration Trade-Off Between Multinational Sales and Trade." *AER* 87, no. 4 (September 1997), pp. 520–544.

Brander, James A. "Strategic Trade Policy." In Grossman and Rogoff (1995).

Brecher, Richard A., and Ehsan U. Choudri. "The Leontief Paradox, Continued." *JPE* 90, no. 4 (August 1982), pp. 820–823.

Breton, Albert. *The Economic Theory of Representative Government.* Chicago: Aldine, 1974.

Broda, Christian. "Terms of Trade and Exchange Rate Regimes in Developing Countries." Federal Reserve Bank of New York, Staff Report no. 148, January 2002.

Brown, Drusilla K., Alan V. Deardorff, and Robert M. Stern. "A North American Free Trade Agreement: Analytical Issues and a Computational Assessment." *World Economy* 15 (January 1992), pp. 11–30.

Bruton, Henry J. "A Reconsideration of Import Substitution." *JEL* 36, no. 2 (June 1998), pp. 903–936.

Bryant, Ralph C. *International Coordination of National Stabilization Policies.* Washington, DC: Brookings Institution, 1995.

Bryant, Ralph, Dale W. Henderson, Gerald Holtman, Peter Hooper, and Steven A. Symansky, eds. *Empirical Macroeconomics for Interdependent Economies.* Washington, DC: Brookings Institution, 1988.

Buckley, Peter, and Mark Casson. *Future of Multinational Enterprise.* New York: Macmillan, 1976.

Burfish, Mary E., Sherman Robinson, and Karen Thierfelder. "The Impact of NAFTA on the United States." *JEP* 15, no. 1 (Winter 2001), pp. 125–144.

Bütler, Monika, and Heinz Hauser. "The WTO Dispute Settlement System: A First Assessment from an Economic Perspective." *Journal of Law, Economics, and Organization* 16, no. 2 (October 2000), pp. 503–533.

Caves, Richard E. *Multinational Enterprise and Economic Analysis,* 2d ed. New York: Cambridge University Press, 1996.

Cecchini, Paolo. *The European Challenge, 1992: The Benefits of a Single Market.* Aldershot, Hants.: Wildwood House, 1988.

Cheung, Yin-Wong, and Clement Yuk-Pang Wong. "A Survey of Market Practitioners' Views on Exchange Rate Dynamics." *JIE* 51, no. 2 (August 2000), pp. 401–419.

———, and Menzie David Chinn. "Currency Traders and Exchange Rate Dynamics: A Survey of the US Market." *Journal of International Money and Finance* 20, no. 4 (August 2001), pp. 439–471.

Chiswick, Barry R. "Illegal Immigration and Immigration Control." *JEP* 2, no. 3 (Summer 1988), pp. 101–116.

Choksi, A., et al. *Trade Liberalization Episodes.* Oxford, England: Basil Blackwell, 1991.

Clausen, Jens, and Juergen B. Donges. "European Monetary Union: The Ongoing Debate on Conceptual Issues." *World Economy* 24, no. 10 (November 2001), pp. 1309–1326.

Cline, William R. *Exports of Manufactures from Developing Countries.* Washington, DC: Brookings Institution, 1984.

———. *The Economics of Global Warming.* Washington, DC: Institute for International Economics, 1992.

———. *Trade and Income Distribution.* Washington, DC: Institute for International Economics, 1997.

Collins, Susan. "Multiple Exchange Rates, Capital Controls, and Commercial Policy." In *Open Economy: Tools for Policy Makers in Developing Countries,* ed. Rudiger Dornbusch. New York: Oxford University Press, 1988.

Dalsgaard, Thomas, Christophe André, and Pete Richardson. "Standard Shocks in the OECD Interlink Model." Organization for Economic Cooperation and Development, Economics Department Working Paper no. 306, September 6, 2001.

Deardorff, Alan V. "Testing Trade Theories and Predicting Trade Flows." In Jones and Kenen, eds., *Handbook,* vol. I, 1984.

———, and Robert M. Stern. *Measurement of Nontariff Barriers.* Ann Arbor: University of Michigan Press, 1998.

Destler, I. M. *American Trade Politics,* 3d ed. Washington, DC: Institute for International Economics, 1995.

Dixit, Avinash. "Tax Policy in Open Economies." In *Handbook of Public Economics,* eds. Alan Auerbach and Martin Feldstein. New York: North-Holland, 1985.

Dooley, Michael P. "A Survey of Literature on Controls over International Capital Transactions." *IMF Staff Papers* 43, no. 4 (December 1996), pp. 639–687.

Dornbusch, Rudiger. "Expectations and Exchange Rate Dynamics." *JPE* 84, no. 6 (December 1976), pp. 1161–1176.

Downs, Anthony. *An Economic Theory of Democracy.* New York: Harper & Row, 1957.

Dufey, Gunter, and Ian H. Giddy. *International Money Market,* 2d ed. Englewood Cliffs, NJ: Prentice Hall, 1994.

Edwards, Sebastian. *Crisis and Reform in Latin America.* New York: Oxford University Press, 1995.

Eichengreen, Barry. *Gold Fetters: The Gold Standard and the Great Depression, 1919–1939.* New York: Oxford University Press, 1992.

———. *European Monetary Union: Theory, Practice, and Analysis.* Cambridge, MA: MIT Press, 1997.

———. *Toward a New International Financial Architecture: A Practical Post-Asia Agenda.* Washington, DC: Institute for International Economics, 1999.

———, and Peter H. Lindert, eds. *The International Debt Crisis in Historical Perspective.* Cambridge, MA: MIT Press, 1989.

Eiteman, David K., Arthur I. Stonehill, and Michael H. Moffet. *Multinational Business Finance,* 9th ed. New York: Addison-Wesley, 2001.

Ekberg, Jan. "Immigration and the Public Sector: Income Effects for the Native Population of Sweden." *Journal of Population Economics* 12, no. 3 (1999), pp. 411–430.

Ekins, Paul, and Terry Barker. "Carbon Taxes and Carbon Emissions Trading." *Journal of Economic Surveys* 15, no. 3 (July 2001), pp. 325–376.

Elliott, Kimberly Ann, and J. David Richardson. "Determinants and Effectiveness of 'Aggressively Unilateral' U.S. Trade Actions." In Feenstra (1997).

Enders, Alice, and Amelia Porges. "Successful Conventions and Conventional Success: Saving the Ozone Layer." In Anderson and Blackhurst (1992), pp. 130–144.

Enoch, Charles, and Ann-Marie Gulde. "Are Currency Boards a Cure for All Monetary Problems?" *Finance and Development* 35, no. 4 (December 1998), pp. 40–43.

Espinosa, Marco, and Chong K. Yip. "International Policy Coordination: Can We Have Our Cake and Eat It Too?" *Federal Reserve Bank of Atlanta Economic Review* 78, no. 3 (May/June 1993), pp. 1–12.

Esty, Daniel C. "Bridging the Trade-Environment Divide." *JEP* 15, no. 3 (Summer 2001), pp. 113–130.

———. *Greening the GATT: Trade, Environment, and the Future.* Washington, DC: Institute for International Economics, 1994.

Ethier, Wilfred J. "Dumping." *JPE* 90, no. 3 (June 1982), pp. 487–506.

Eun, Cheol S., and Bruce G. Resnick. *International Financial Management,* 2d ed. Burr Ridge, IL: Irwin/McGraw-Hill, 2001.

Fatum, Rasmus, and Michael M. Hutchison. "Is Foreign Exchange Market Intervention an Alternative to Monetary Policy? Evidence from Japan." Santa Cruz Center for International Economics, Working Paper no. 02-5, March 28, 2002a.

———. "ECB Foreign Exchange Intervention and the Euro: Institutional Framework, News and Intervention." Santa Cruz Center for International Economics, Working Paper no. 02-3, February 22, 2002b.

Feenstra, Robert C. "Estimating the Effects of Trade Policy." In Grossman and Rogoff (1995).

———. "How Costly Is Protectionism?" *JEP* 6, no. 3 (Summer 1992), pp. 159–178.

———, ed. *Effects of U.S. Trade Protection and Promotion Policies.* Chicago: University of Chicago Press, 1997.

Feldstein, Martin, ed. *International Economic Cooperation.* Chicago: University of Chicago Press, 1988.

———. "The Political Economy of the European Economic and Monetary Union: Political Sources of an Economic Liability." *JEP* 11, no. 4 (Fall 1997), pp. 23–42.

Fieleke, Norman S. "The International Monetary Fund 50 Years After Bretton Woods." *New England Economic Review,* September/October 1994, pp. 17–30.

———. "International Capital Movements: How Shocking Are They?" *New England Economic Review* (March/April 1996), pp. 41–60.

Findlay, Christopher, and Tony Warren, eds. *Impediments to Trade in Services: Measurement and Policy Implications.* New York: Routledge, 2000.

Findlay, Ronald, and Harry Grubert. "Factor Intensities, Technological Progress, and the Terms of Trade." *Oxford Economic Papers* 11, no. 1 (February 1959), pp. 111–121.

Finger, J. Michael, ed. *Antidumping: How It Works and Who Gets Hurt.* Ann Arbor: University of Michigan Press, 1993.

Fischer, Stanley. "Distinguished Lecture on Economics in Government—Exchange Rate Regimes: Is the Bipolar View Correct?" *JEP* 15, no. 2 (Spring 2001), pp. 3–24.

Flam, Harry. "Product Markets and 1992: Full Integration, Large Gains?" *JEP* 6, no. 4 (Fall 1992), pp. 7–30.

Fleming, J. Marcus. "Domestic Financial Policies Under Fixed and Floating Exchange Rates." *IMF Staff Papers* 9 (March 1962), pp. 369–377.

Flores, Jr., Renato G. "The Gains from MERCOSUR: A General Equilibrium, Imperfect Competition Evaluation." *Journal of Policy Modeling* 19, no. 1 (February 1997), pp. 1–18.

Footer, Mary E., and Christoph Beat Graber. "Trade Liberalization and Cultural Policy." *Journal of International Economic Law* 3, no. 1 (March 2000), pp. 115–144.

Frankel, Jeffrey A. "On the Mark: A Theory of Floating Exchange Rates Based on Real Interest Differentials." *AER* 69, no. 4 (September 1979), pp. 610–622.

———, and Andrew K. Rose. "An Empirical Characterization of Nominal Exchange Rates." In Grossman and Rogoff (1995).

Friedberg, Rachel M., and Jennifer Hunt. "The Impact of Immigrants on Host Country Wages, Employment, and Growth." *JEP* 9, no. 2 (Spring 1995), pp. 23–44.

Friedman, Milton. "The Case for Flexible Exchange Rates." In his *Essays in Positive Economics.* Chicago: University of Chicago Press, 1953.

Froot, Kenneth A., and Kenneth Rogoff. "Perspectives on PPP and the Long-Run Real Exchange Rate." In Grossman and Rogoff (1995).

Froot, Kenneth A., and Richard H. Thaler. "Anomalies: Foreign Exchange." *JEP* 4, no. 3 (Summer 1990), pp. 179–192.

Galloway, Michael P., Bruce A. Blonigen, and Joseph E. Flynn. "Welfare Costs of the U.S. Antidumping and Countervailing Duty Laws." *JIE* 49, no. 2 (December 1999), 211–244.

Gardner, Bruce L. *The Economics of Agricultural Policies.* New York: Macmillan, 1988.

Genberg, Hans, and Alexander K. Swoboda. "Policy and Current Account Determination Under Floating Exchange Rates." *IMF Staff Papers* 36, no. 1 (March 1989), pp. 1–30.

Gilbert, Christopher L. "International Commodity Agreements: An Obituary Notice." *World Development* 24, no. 1 (January 1996), pp. 1–19.

Giovannini, Alberto. "How Do Fixed Exchange-Rate Regimes Work: The Evidence from the Gold Standard, Bretton Woods and the EMS." In *Blueprints for Exchange Rate Management,* eds. Marvin Miller, Barry Eichengreen, and Richard Portes. London: Center for Economic Policy Research, 1989.

Goldstein, Morris. *Asian Financial Crisis: Causes, Cures, and Systemic Implications.* Washington, DC: Institute for International Economics, 1998.

Goldstein, Morris. *Managed Floating Plus.* Washington, DC: Institute for International Economics, 2002.

Golub, Stephen S. *Labor Costs and International Trade.* Washington, DC: AEI Press, 1999.

Goodfriend, Marvin. "Eurodollars." In *Instruments of the Money Market,* eds. Timothy Q. Cook and Timothy D. Rowe. Richmond, VA: Federal Reserve Bank of Richmond, 1986.

Graham, Edward M., and Paul R. Krugman. *Foreign Direct Investment in the United States,* 3d ed. Washington, DC: Institute for International Economics, 1995.

Greenaway, David, and Chris Milner. *The Economics of Intra-Industry Trade.* Oxford, England: Basil Blackwell, 1986.

Grilli, Enzo R., and Maw Cheng Yang. "Primary Commodity Prices, Manufactured Goods Prices, and the Terms of Trade of Developing Countries: What the Long Run Shows." *World Bank Economic Review* 2, no. 1 (January 1988), pp. 1–47.

Grossman, Gene M., and Elhanan Helpman. "Protection for Sale." *AER* 84, no. 4 (September 1994), pp. 833–850.

Grossman, Gene M., and Elhanan Helpman. "Technology and Trade." In Grossman and Rogoff (1995).

———, and Kenneth Rogoff. *Handbook of International Economics,* vol. III. New York: North-Holland, 1995.

Grubel, Herbert G., and P. J. Lloyd. *Intra-Industry Trade: The Theory and Measurement of Trade in Differentiated Products.* New York: John Wiley & Sons, 1975.

Hakkio, Craig S. "Is Purchasing Power Parity a Useful Guide to the Dollar?" *Federal Reserve Bank of Kansas City Economic Review* 77, no. 3 (Third Quarter 1992), pp. 37–51.

Hare, Paul. "Trade Policy During Transition: Lessons from the 1990s." *World Economy* 24, No. 4 (April 2001), pp. 483–511.

Hathaway, Dale E., and Merlinda D. Ingco. "Agricultural Liberalization and the Uruguay Round." In *Uruguay Round and the Developing Countries,* eds. Will Martin and L. Alan Winters. New York: Cambridge University Press, 1996.

Hayes, J. P. *Economic Effects of Sanctions on Southern Africa.* Thames Essay no. 53. Aldershot, Hants.: Gower, 1987.

Heckscher, Eli. "The Effects of Foreign Trade on the Distribution of Income," originally published in 1919. In *Readings in the Theory of International Trade,* eds. Howard S. Ellis and Lloyd M. Metzler. Philadelphia: Blakiston, 1949.

Heliwell, John F., and Tim Padmore. "Empirical Studies of Macroeconomic Interdependence." In Jones and Kenen, eds., *Handbook,* vol. 2, (1984), pp. 1107–1151.

Helpman, Elhanan. "Monopolistic Competition in Trade Theory." *Special Papers in International Finance,* no. 16. Princeton, NJ: Princeton University, June 1990.

———. "The Structure of Foreign Trade." *JEP* 13, no. 2 (Spring 1999), pp. 121–144.

———, and Paul R. Krugman. *Market Structure and Foreign Trade.* Cambridge, MA: MIT Press, 1985.

Hindley, Brian, and Patrick A. Messerlin. *Antidumping Industrial Policy: Legalized Protectionism in the WTO and What to Do About It.* Washington, DC: AEI Press, 1996.

Hoekman, Bernard. "The Next Round of Services Negotiations: Identifying Priorities and Options." *Federal Reserve Bank of St. Louis Review* 82, no. 4 (July/August 2000), pp. 31–47.

———, and Michel Kostecki. *Political Economy of the World Trading System: The WTO and Beyond,* 2d ed. New York: Oxford University Press, 2001.

Hufbauer, Gary Clyde. "Surveying the Costs of Protection." In *World Trading System: Challenges Ahead,* ed. Jeffrey J. Schott. Washington, DC: Institute for International Economics, 1996.

———, and Kimberly Ann Elliott. *Measuring the Costs of Protection in the United States.* Washington, DC: Institute for International Economics, 1994.

Hufbauer, Gary Clyde, Daniel C. Esty, Diana Orejas, Luis Rubio, and Jeffrey J. Schott. *NAFTA and the Environment: Seven Years Later.* Washington, DC: Institute for International Economics, 2000.

———, and Jeffrey J. Schott. *Economic Sanctions Reconsidered,* 3d ed. Washington, DC: Institute for International Economics, 2002.

———. *NAFTA: An Assessment,* rev. ed. Washington, DC: Institute for International Economics, 1993.

Humpage, Owen F. "Institutional Aspects of U.S. Intervention." *Federal Reserve Bank of Cleveland Economic Review* 30, no. 1 (Quarter 1, 1994), pp. 2–19.

Hymer, Stephen H. *The International Operation of National Firms: A Study of Direct Foreign Investment.* Cambridge, MA: MIT Press, 1976.

Irwin, Douglas A. *Against the Tide: An Intellectual History of Free Trade.* Princeton, NJ: Princeton University Press, 1996.

———. *Free Trade Under Fire.* Princeton: Princeton University Press, 2002.

Ito, Takatoshi. "Is Foreign Exchange Intervention Effective? The Japanese Experiences in the 1990s." National Bureau of Economic Research, Working Paper no. W8914, April 2002.

Johnson, Harry G. *Money, Trade and Economic Growth.* Cambridge, MA: Harvard University Press, 1962.

———. "Optimal Trade Policy in the Presence of Domestic Distortions." In *Trade, Growth and the Balance of Payments,* ed. Robert E. Baldwin. Chicago: Rand McNally, 1965.

Jones, Kent A. *Export Restraint and the New Protectionism: The Political Economy of Discriminatory Trade Restrictions.* Ann Arbor: University of Michigan Press, 1994.

Jones, Ronald W., and Peter B. Kenen, eds. *Handbook of International Economics.* Two volumes. New York: North-Holland, 1984.

Kahler, Miles, ed. *Capital Flows and Financial Crises.* Ithaca, NY: Cornell University Press, 1998.

Kamin, Steven B. "Devaluation, External Balance, and Macroeconomic Performance: A Look at the Numbers." *Princeton Studies in International Finance,* no. 62. Princeton, NJ: Princeton University, August 1988.

Kherellah, Mylene, and John Beghin. "U.S. Trade Threats: Rhetoric or War." *American Journal of Agricultural Economics* 80, no. 1 (February 1998), pp. 15–29.

Kindleberger, Charles P. *Manias, Panics, and Crashes,* 3d ed. New York: John Wiley & Sons, 1998.

Kletzer, Lori G. *Job Loss from Imports: Measuring the Costs.* Washington, DC: Institute for International Economics, 2001.

Koedijk, Kees G., and Mack Ott. "Risk Aversion, Efficient Markets, and the Forward Exchange Rate." *Federal Reserve Bank of St. Louis Review* 69, no. 6 (December 1987), pp. 5–13.

Krueger, Anne O. "Trade Policies in Developing Countries." In Jones and Kenen, eds., *Handbook,* vol. I (1984).

———. *Economic Policy at Cross Purposes.* Washington, DC: Brookings Institution, 1993.

———. Maurice Schiff, and Alberto Valdés, eds. *The Political Economy of Agricultural Price Policies.* Oxford, England: Oxford University Press, 1992.

Krugman, Paul R. "Increasing Returns, Monopolistic Competition, and International Trade." *JIE* 9 (1979), pp. 469–479.

———. "New Theories of Trade Among Industrial Countries." *AER* 73, no. 2 (May 1983), pp. 343–347.

Lane, Philip R., and Gian Maria Milesi-Ferretti. "The External Wealth of Nations: Measures of Foreign Assets and Liabilities for Industrial and Developing Countries." *JIE* 55, no. 2 (December 2001), pp. 263–294.

Lawrence, Robert Z. *Single World, Divided Nations? International Trade and OECD Labor Markets.* Washington, DC: Brookings Institution Press, 1996.

———, ed. *Brookings Trade Forum 1998.* Washington, DC: Brookings Institution Press, 1998.

Leamer, Edward E. "The Leontief Paradox, Reconsidered." *JPE* 88, no. 3 (June 1980), pp. 495–503.

———. *Sources of International Comparative Advantage: Theory and Evidence.* Cambridge, MA: MIT Press, 1984.

———, and James Levinson. "International Trade Theory: The Evidence." In Grossman and Rogoff (1995).

Leontief, Wassily. "Factor Proportions and the Structure of American Trade: Further Theoretical and Empirical Analysis." *Review of Economics and Statistics* 38, no. 4 (November 1956), pp. 386–407.

———. "Domestic Production and Foreign Trade: The American Capital Position Reexamined." *Economia Internazionale* 7 (February 1954), pp. 3–32.

Levich, Richard M. "Is the Foreign Exchange Market Efficient?" *Oxford Review of Economic Policy* 5, no. 3 (October 1989), pp. 40–60.

———. *International Financial Markets: Prices and Policies,* 2d ed. Burr Ridge, IL: Irwin/McGraw-Hill, 2001.

Lindert, Peter H. *Key Currencies and Gold, 1900–1913.* Princeton, NJ: Princeton University Press, 1969.

———. "Foreign Trade and Trade Policy in the Twentieth Century." In *Cambridge Economic History of the United States,* vol. III, eds. Stanley Engerman and Robert Gallman. New York: Cambridge University Press, 2000.

Low, Patrick. *Trading Free: The GATT and U.S. Trade Policy.* New York: Twentieth Century Fund, 1993.

Lustig, Nora. *Mexico: The Remaking of an Economy.* Washington, DC: Brookings Institution, 1992.

———, Barry P. Bosworth, and Robert Z. Lawrence, eds. *North American Free Trade: Assessing the Impact.* Washington, DC: Brookings Institution, 1992.

Lyons, Richard K. *Microstructure Approach to Exchange Rates.* Cambridge, MA: MIT Press, 2001.

MacDonald, Ronald. "Exchange Rate Behavior: Are Fundamentals Important?" *Economic Journal* 109, no. 459 (November 1999), pp. F673–F691.

———, and Ian W. Marsh. "On Fundamentals and Exchange Rates: A Casselian Approach." *Review of Economics and Statistics* 79, no. 4 (November 1997), pp. 655–664.

———, and Mark P. Taylor. "Exchange Rate Economics: A Survey." *IMF Staff Papers* 39, no. 1 (March 1992), pp. 1–57.

———. "The Monetary Model of the Exchange Rate: Long-Run Relationships, Short-Run Dynamics and How to Beat a Random Walk." *Journal of International Money and Finance* 13, no. 3 (June 1994), pp. 276–290.

Magee, Stephen P. "Information and Multinational Corporations: An Appropriability Theory of Direct Foreign Investment." In *New International Economic Order,* ed. Jagdish N. Bhagwati. Cambridge, MA: MIT Press, 1977, pp. 317–340.

———. "Twenty Paradoxes in International Trade Theory." In *International Trade and Agriculture: Theory and Policy,* eds. Jimmye Hillman and Andrew Schmitz. Boulder, CO: Westview, 1979, pp. 91–116.

Malkiel, Burton, and J. P. Mei. *Global Bargain Hunting: The Investor's Guide to Profits in Emerging Markets.* New York, Touchstone, 1998.

Mark, Nelson C. "Exchange Rates and Fundamentals: Evidence on Long-Horizon Predictability." *AER* 85, no. 1 (March 1995), pp. 201–218.

———, and Donggyu Sul. "Nominal Exchange Rates and Monetary Fundamentals: Evidence from a Small Post-Bretton Woods Panel." *JIE* 53, no. 1 (February 2001), pp. 29–52.

Markusen, James R. "The Boundaries of Multinational Enterprises and the Theory of International Trade." *JEP* 9, no. 2 (Spring 1995), pp. 169–189.

Marston, Richard C. *International Financial Integration: A Study of Interest Differentials Between the Major Industrial Economies.* New York: Cambridge University Press, 1995.

Maskus, Keith E. "A Test of the Heckscher–Ohlin–Vanek Theorem: The Leontief Commonplace." *JIE* 19, nos. 3/4 (November 1985), pp. 201–212.

McKinnon, Ronald. "Optimum Currency Areas." *AER* 53, no. 1 (March 1963), pp. 717–725.

———. "Monetary and Exchange Rate Policies for International Financial Stability: A Proposal." *JEP* 2, no. 1 (Winter 1988), pp. 83–103.

———. "International Money in Historical Perspective." *JEL* 31, no. 1 (March 1993), pp. 1–44.

———. *Rules of the Game.* Cambridge, MA: MIT Press, 1996.

Meade, James. *Trade and Welfare.* Oxford, England: Oxford University Press, 1955.

Meese, Richard, and Kenneth Rogoff. "Empirical Exchange Rate Models of the Seventies: How Well Do They Fit Out of Sample?" *JIE* 14 (February 1983), pp. 3–24.

Messerlin, Patrick A. *Measuring the Costs of Protection in Europe: European Commercial Policy in the 2000s.* Washington, DC: International Institute for Economics, 2001.

Meyer, Laurence H., Brian M. Doyle, Joseph E. Gagnon, and Dale W. Henderson. "International Coordination of Macroeconomic Policies: Still Alive in the New Millennium?" Board of Governors of the Federal Reserve System, International Finance Discussion Paper no. 723, April 2002.

Milner, Chris, ed. *Export Promotion Strategies: Theory and Evidence from Developing Countries.* New York: New York University Press, 1990.

Moran, Theodore H. *Foreign Direct Investment and Development.* Washington, DC: Institute for International Economics, 1998.

Morici, Peter. *Making Free Trade Work: The Canada–U.S. Agreement.* New York: Council on Foreign Relations, 1991.

Mundell, Robert. *International Economics.* New York: Macmillan, 1968.

———. "A Theory of Optimum Currency Areas." *AER* 51, no. 4 (September 1961), pp. 657–665.

Murray, John. "Why Canada Needs a Flexible Exchange Rate." *North American Journal of Economics and Finance* 11, no. 1 (August 2000), pp. 41–60.

Mussa, Michael. "Tariffs and the Distribution of Income." *JPE* 82, no. 6 (December 1974), pp. 1191–1204.

Mutti, John. *NAFTA: The Economic Consequences for Mexico and the United States.* Washington, DC: Economic Strategy Institute, 2001.

Neal, Larry, and Daniel Barbezat. *Economics of the European Union and the Economies of Europe.* New York: Oxford University Press, 1998.

Neeley, Christopher J. "The Practice of Central Bank Intervention: Looking Under the Hood." *Federal Reserve Bank of St. Louis Review* 83, no. 3 (May/June 2001), pp. 1–10.

Neumayer, Eric. "Trade and the Environment: A Critical Assessment and Some Suggestions for Reconciliation." *Journal of Environment and Development* 9, no. 2 (June 2000), pp. 138–159.

Niels, Gunnar. "What Is Antidumping Policy Really About?" *Journal of Economic Surveys* 14, no. 4 (September 2000), pp. 467–492.

Nurkse, Ragnar. *International Currency Experience: Lessons of the Interwar Period.* Geneva, Switzerland: League of Nations, 1944.

Obstfeld, Maurice. "Europe's Gamble." *Brookings Papers on Economic Activity,* no. 2 (1997), pp. 241–300.

———, and Kenneth Rogoff. "The Mirage of Fixed Exchange Rates." *JEP* 9, no. 4 (Fall 1995), pp. 73–96.

Obstfeld, Maurice, and Alan M. Taylor. "Globalization and Capital Markets." National Bureau of Economic Research, Working Paper no. W8846, March 2002.

Ohlin, Bertil. *International and Interregional Trade.* Cambridge, MA: Harvard University Press, 1933.

Olson, Mancur. *The Logic of Collective Action.* Cambridge, MA: Harvard University Press, 1965.

Organization for Economic Cooperation and Development (OECD). *EMU: Facts, Challenges, and Policies.* Washington, DC: OECD, 1999.

———. *European Union's Trade Policies and Their Economic Effects.* Paris: OECD, 2000.

O'Rourke, Kevin, Alan M. Taylor, and Jeffrey G. Williamson. "Land, Labor, and the Wage-Rental Ratio: Factor-Price Convergence in the Late Nineteenth Century." Discussion Paper no. 1629. Cambridge, MA: Harvard Institute of Economic Research, March 1993.

O'Rourke, Kevin, and Jeffrey G. Williamson. "Were Heckscher and Ohlin Right? Factor-Price Convergence in Economic History." *Journal of Economic History* 54, no. 4 (December 1994).

Ottaviano, Gianmarco I. P., and Diego Puga. "Agglomeration in the Global Economy: A Survey of the 'New Economic Geography.'" *World Economy* 21, no. 6 (August 1998), pp. 707–731.

Pigott, Charles A. "International Interest Rate Convergence: A Survey of the Issues and Evidence." *Federal Reserve Bank of New York Quarterly Review* 18, no. 4 (Winter 1993–1994), pp. 24–37.

Pitchford, Ruth, and Adam Cox, eds. *EMU Explained: Markets and Monetary Union,* 2d ed. London: Kegan Paul, 1998.

Pomfret, Richard. *Economics of Regional Trading Arrangements.* Oxford: Clarendon Press, 1997.

Pope, David, and Glenn Withers. "Do Migrants Rob Jobs? Lessons of Australian History, 1861–1991," *Journal of Economic History* 53, no. 4 (December 1993), pp. 719–742.

Porter, Michael E. *The Competitive Advantage of Nations.* New York: Free Press, 1990.

Postner, Harry. *The Factor Content of Canada's Foreign Trade.* Ottawa: Economic Council of Canada, 1975.

Prusa, Thomas J. "The Trade Effects of U.S. Antidumping Actions." In Feenstra (1997).

Reagan, Ronald. *An American Life.* New York: Simon & Schuster, 1990.

Reinhart, Carmen M., and Kenneth S. Rogoff. "Modern History of Exchange Rate Arrangements: A Reinterpretation," National Bureau of Economic Research, Working Paper no. W8963, May 2002.

Ricardo, David. *On the Principles of Political Economy and Taxation.* London: John Murray, 1817.

Rivera-Batiz, Francisco L., and Luis A. Rivera-Batiz. *International Finance and Open Economy Macroeconomics,* 2d ed. New York: Macmillan, 1994.

Rivera-Batiz, Luis A., and Paul M. Romer. "Economic Integration and Endogenous Growth." *Quarterly Journal of Economics* 106, no. 2 (May 1991), pp. 531–556.

Robertson, Raymond. "Trade Liberalization and Wage Inequality: Lessons from the Mexican Experience." *World Economy* 23, no. 6 (June 2000), pp. 827–849.

Rogoff, Kenneth. "International Institutions for Reducing Global Financial Instability." *JEP* 13, no. 4 (Fall 1999), pp. 21–42.

———. "Rogoff's Discontent with Stiglitz: An Open Letter." *IMF Survey* 31, no. 13 (July 8, 2002), pp. 209–211.

Romer, Paul. "New Goods, Old Theory, and the Welfare Cost of Trade Restrictions." *Journal of Development Economics* 43, no. 1 (February 1994), pp. 5–38.

Rueff, Jacques. Translated by Roger Glemet. *The Monetary Sin of the West.* New York: Macmillan, 1972.

Ruffin, Roy J. "The Missing Link: The Ricardian Approach to the Factor Endowments Theory of Trade." *AER* 78, no. 4 (September 1988), pp. 759–772.

Rybczynski, T. M. "Factor Endowments and Relative Commodity Prices." *Economica* 22, no. 84 (November 1955), pp. 336–341.

Sachs, Jeffrey D., and Andrew M. Warner. "Economic Reform and the Process of Global Integration." *Brookings Papers on Economic Activity,* no. 1 (1995), pp. 1–95.

Sampson, Gary P. "The World Trade Organization After Seattle." *World Economy* 23, no. 9 (September 2000), pp. 1097–1117.

Samuelson, Paul A. "International Factor-Price Equalization Once Again." *Economic Journal* 59, no. 234 (June 1949), pp. 181–197.

Sarno, Lucio, and Mark P. Taylor. "Official Intervention in the Foreign Exchange Market: Is It Effective and, If So, How Does It Work?" *JEL* 39, no. 3 (September 2001), pp. 839–868.

———. "Purchasing Power Parity and the Real Exchange Rate." *IMF Staff Papers* 49, no. 1 (2002), pp. 65–105.

Scandizzo, Pasquale L., and Dimitris Diakosawas. *Instability in the Terms of Trade of Primary Commodities, 1900–1982.* Rome: UN, FAO 1987.

Schott, Jeffrey J. *Prospects for Free Trade in the Americas.* Washington, DC: Institute for International Economics, 2001.

———. *The Uruguay Round: An Assessment.* Washington, DC: Institute for International Economics, 1994.

Simon, Julian L. *The Economic Consequences of Immigration.* Oxford, England: Basil Blackwell, 1989.

Slaughter, Matthew J. "Globalization and Wages: A Tale of Two Perspectives." *World Economy* 22, no. 5 (July 1999), pp. 609–629.

———. "What Are the Results of Product-Price Studies and What Can We Learn from Their Differences?" In *Impact of International Trade on Wages,* ed. Robert C. Feenstra. Chicago: University of Chicago Press, 2000, pp. 129–170.

Smith, Adam. *Wealth of Nations.* Originally published 1776. New York: Random House (Modern Library edition), 1937.

Smith, James P., and Barry Edmonston, eds. *New Americans: Economic, Demographic, and Fiscal Effects of Immigration.* Washington, DC: National Academy Press, 1997.

Solomon, Robert. *The International Monetary System, 1945–1976.* New York: Harper & Row, 1977.

Stern, Robert M. *The Balance of Payments.* Chicago: Aldine, 1973.

———, and Keith E. Maskus. "Determinants of the Structure of U.S. Foreign Trade, 1958–76." *JIE* 11, no. 2 (May 1981), pp. 207–224.

Stiglitz, Joseph E. "Dumping on Free Trade: The U.S. Import Trade Laws." *Southern Economic Journal* 64, no. 2 (October 1997), pp. 402–424.

———. *Globalization and Its Discontents.* New York: W. W. Norton & Company, 2002.

Stolper, Wolfgang F., and Paul A. Samuelson. "Protection and Real Wages." *Review of Economic Studies* 9 (November 1941), pp. 58–73.

Summers, Robert, and Alan Heston. "A New Set of International Comparisons of Real Product and Price Levels: Estimates for 130 Countries, 1950–1985." *Review of Income and Wealth,* series 34, no. 1 (March 1988), pp. 1–25.

Suranovic, Steven M. "A Positive Analysis of Fairness with Applications to International Trade." *World Economy* 23, no. 3 (March 2000), pp. 283–307.

Taylor, Mark P. "Covered Interest Arbitrage and Market Turbulence." *Economic Journal* 99, no. 396 (June 1989), pp. 376–391.

Tower, Edward, and Thomas D. Willett. "The Theory of Optimum Currency Areas and Exchange Rate Flexibility." *Special Papers in International Economics* no. 11. Princeton, NJ: Princeton University, May 1976.

Trefler, Daniel. "International Factor Price Differences: Leontief Was Right!" *JPE* 101, no. 6 (December 1993), pp. 961–987.

———. "The Case of the Missing Trade and Other Mysteries." *AER* 85, no. 5 (December 1995), pp. 1029–1046.

Triffin, Robert. *Gold and the Dollar Crisis.* New Haven, CT: Yale University Press, 1960.

Trionfetti, Federico. "Discriminatory Public Procurement and International Trade." *World Economy,* 23, no. 1 (January 2000), pp. 1–23.

Tsiang, S. C. "Fluctuating Exchange Rates in Countries with Relatively Stable Economies: Some European Experiences After World War I." *IMF Staff Papers* 7 (October 1959), pp. 244–273.

Tyson, Laura D'Andrea. *Who's Bashing Whom? Trade Conflict in High-Technology Industries.* Washington, DC: Institute for International Economics, 1992.

Uimonen, Peter, and John Whalley. *Environmental Issues in the New World Trading System.* New York: St. Martin's Press, 1997.

United Nations Centre on Transnational Corporations. *Determinants of Foreign Direct Investment: A Survey of the Evidence.* New York: United Nations, 1992.

Vanek, Jaroslav. *International Trade: Theory and Economic Policy.* Homewood, IL: Richard D. Irwin, 1962.

Vernon, Raymond G. "International Investment and International Trade in the Product Cycle." *Quarterly Journal of Economics* 80, no. 2 (May 1966), pp. 190–207.

———. *In the Hurricane's Eye: The Troubled Prospects of Multinational Enterprise.* Cambridge, MA: Harvard University Press, 1998.

———. "The Product Cycle Hypotheses in a New International Environment." *Oxford Bulletin of Economics and Statistics* 41 (November 1979), pp. 255–267.

Vona, Stefano. "Intra-Industry Trade: A Statistical Artifact or a Real Phenomenon?" *Banca Nazionale del Lavorno Quarterly Review* 175 (December 1990), pp. 383–412.

———. "On the Measurement of Intra-Industry Trade: Some Further Thoughts." *Weltwirtschaftliches Archiv.* 127, no. 4 (1991), pp. 678–700.

Whalley, John, and Colleen Hamilton. *Trading System After the Uruguay Round.* Washington, DC: Institute for International Economics, 1996.

Williamson, John. *Exchange Rate System,* rev. ed. Washington, DC: Institute for International Economics, 1985.

Wonnacott, Paul, and Ronald J. Wonnacott. "Free Trade Between the United States and Canada: Fifteen Years Later." *Canadian Public Policy,* October 1982, supplement.

Wonnacott, Ronald J., and Paul Wonnacott. *Free Trade Between the United States and Canada: The Potential Economic Effects.* Cambridge, MA: Harvard University Press, 1967.

Woodward, Douglas, and Douglas Nigh, eds. *Foreign Ownership and the Consequences of Direct Investment in the United States: Beyond Us and Them.* Westport, CT: Quorum Books, 1998.

World Bank. *Trade Blocs.* New York: Oxford University Press, 2000.

World Bank. *Globalization, Growth, and Poverty: Building an Inclusive World Economy.* Washington, DC: World Bank, 2002a.

World Bank. *Transition the First Ten Years: Analysis and Lessons for Eastern Europe and the Former Soviet Union.* Washington, DC: World Bank, 2002b.

World Trade Organization. *Trade and the Environment,* Special Studies no. 4. Geneva: World Trade Organization, 1999.

Wu, Jyh-Lin, and Show-Lin Chen. "Nominal Exchange-Rate Prediction: Evidence from a Nonlinear Approach." *Journal of International Money and Finance* 20, no. 4 (August 2001), pp. 521–532.

Wyplosz, Charles. "EMU: Why and How It Might Happen." *JEP* 11, no. 4 (Fall 1997), pp. 3–21.

Yeager, Leland B. "A Rehabilitation of Purchasing-Power-Parity." *JPE* 66, no. 6 (December 1958), pp. 516–530.

———. *International Monetary Relations.* New York: Harper & Row, 1976.

Zimmerman, Klaus F. "Tackling the European Migration Problem." *JEP* 9, no. 2 (Spring 1995), pp. 45–61.

Index